CLASSICAL SCHOLARSHIP

An Annotated Bibliography

CLASSICAL SCHOLARSHIP

An Annotated Bibliography

Thomas P. Halton
Stella O'Leary

KRAUS INTERNATIONAL PUBLICATIONS
Division of Kraus-Thomson Organization Limited
White Plains, New York

First printing 1986

Printed in the United States of America

Library of Congress Cataloging-in-Publication Data

Halton, Thomas P. (Thomas Patrick)
   Classical scholarship.

   Includes indexes.
   1. Civilization, Classical—Bibliography.
2. Classical antiquities—Bibliography.   3. Classical
philology—Bibliography.   I. O'Leary, Stella.
II. Title.
Z6207.C65H34 1986 [DE59]   016.938   82-48984
ISBN 0-527-37436-9 (cloth)
        0-527-37437-7 (paper)

Contents

Introduction

Background

Classical Scholarship: An Annotated Bibliography was initiated as an updated edition of Martin R. P. McGuire, *Introduction to Classical Scholarship: A Syllabus and Bibliographic Guide*. The McGuire volume had become an immensely useful tool for all levels of study on the classics; originally published in 1955, McGuire's work was so popular that a second printing was needed only three years later and a revised edition was produced in 1961. The vast amount of work published in the classics in recent years, however, has necessitated a completely different approach to the material.

Fifteen years after the new edition of McGuire appeared, the editors set about to accumulate sources for the preparation of the present work. They received a generous grant from the National Endowment for the Humanities to produce a bibliographical guide to classical scholarship with all materials organized in a comprehensive subject scheme. Under the terms of the grant, the text would be keyed into a computer system for manipulation into subject order and for keyboarding. The computer storage would also allow for periodic updates as needed.

Once all the materials were collected for annotation, it became clear that the present Bibliography would be much larger than the McGuire work on which it was modelled. The editors decided to include materials published through 1980, with a few exceptions for more recent, significant works. All entries were annotated and then assigned subject codes.

Organization

This Bibliography is divided into fifteen major subject chapters. Within these chapters, materials are organized into topical sections; these sections are assigned a double-letter code (e.g., the letters AE refer to the section on "Encyclopedias and Dictionaries" in the "Bibliography" chapter). In each of these sections the entries are arranged alphabetically by author or anonymous title. An entry is assigned a unique number, consisting of the two-letter code for the section in which it appears and a sequence number. These entry numbers are cited in the Author Index and Subject Index. Most entries appear once only; due to inevitable overlaps in some of the classifications, certain entries appear in more than one section.

A typical entry is as follows:

RENEHAN, Robert. Greek textual criticism; A reader. Cambridge, Mass., Harvard University Press, 1969. viii, 152p.   **DE33**

Loeb classical monographs.

CPh LXVI 1971 202–205 Hunt · AJPh XCII 1971 503–506 Young · Gnomon XLIV 1972 712–714 Alexanderson

Intended as a workbook, not a handbook, this collection of passages, classical, postclassical and patristic, illustrates the problems confronting an editor in selecting the right reading. The length of the sections varies from a few lines to ten pages. When we have variants or conjectures or both, we must apply all available tests to establish the text. It is the choice between possible readings, "one of the most exacting offices of criticism," that is Renehan's main concern. See also Renehan, "Studies in Greek texts," *Hypomnemata* XLIII (1975), for critical observations on textual problems in Homer, Plato, Euripides, Aristophanes and other Greek authors.

The author's name appears in boldface; if this entry was listed by title, the title itself would have been in bold. Following the author and title is a listing of full bibliographic information, including place of publication, name of publisher, date of publication, and the number of volumes and/or pages, illustrations, and/or plates. Below this, at the right margin, is the entry number.

Below the main entry are several types of information. There may be series data if the entry was published as part of a large project. There may also be information on reprints or other editions of the work. Following this is a listing of reviews done on the work cited; this information is taken from *l'Année Philologique* (a full list of abbreviations for journal titles will be found starting on p. xi of this Bibliography).

Following the reviews is a short abstract or annotation concerning the entry. The contents of the work are discussed, together with its significance to the field of classical scholarship. In order to provide critical annotations, the opinions of some of the reviews have been incorporated here.

At the end of the volume are two indexes. The Author Index cites all authors of works appearing in the bibliography, both in the main entries and in the annotations. The Subject Index provides an alternative means of access to the entries, since it cites the entries through a more detailed subject classification system. In both indexes, all materials are cited by entry number.

Acknowledgments

The editors are indebted to the Director and staff of the Catholic University of America library, and especially to Mrs. B. L. Gutekunst, for assistance in locating the reference material that formed the basis of this book. We are also grateful to the National Endowment for the Humanities for the grant that helped to make the work possible.

List of
Title Abbreviations

AA	Archäologischer Anzeiger. Berlin, de Gruyter.
A&A	Antike und Abendland. Beiträge zum Verständnis der Griechen und Römer und ihres Nachlebens. Berlin, de Gruyter.
AAAH	Acta ad archaeologiam et artium historiam pertinentia. Institutum Romanum Norvegiae et Roma, Giorgio Bretschneider.
AAHG	Anzeiger für die Altertumswissenschaft, hrsg. von der Österreichischen Humanistischen Gesellschaft. Innsbruck, Wagner.
AArchHung	Acta Archaeologica Academiae Scientiarum Hungaricae. Budapest, Akadémiai Kiado.
AASO	The Annual of the American Schools of Oriental Research. Cambridge, Mass.
AAWW	Anzeiger der Österreichischen Akademie der Wissenschaften in Wien, Philos.-Hist. Klasse. Vienna.
ABAW	Abhandlungen der Bayerischen Akademie der Wissenschaften, Philos.-Hist. Klasse. Munich, Beck.
ABG	Archiv fur Begriffsgeschichte. Bausteine zu emem historischen Worterbuch der Philosophie. Bonn, Bouvier.
ABSA	Annual of the British School at Athens. London.
ABull	The Art Bulletin. A Quarterly published by the College Art Association of America. New York.
AC	L'Antiquité Classique. Louvain-la-Neuve.
Acme	Acme. Annali della Facolta di Filosoflia e Lettere dell'Università statale di Milano. Milan, Università degli Studi.
ACR	American Classical Review. City University of New York.
AEA	Archivo Español de Arqueologia. Madrid, Inst. Rodrigo Caro.
Aegyptus	Aegyptus. Rivista italiana di Egittologia e di Papirologia. Milan, Soc. ed. Vita & Pensiero.
AErt	Archaeologiai Ertesitö. Budapest, Akadémiai Kiado.
Aevum	Aevum. Rassegna di Scienze storiche, linguistiche e filologiche. Milan, Soc. Ed. Vita & Pensiero.
AGPh	Archiv für Geschichte der Philosophie. Berlin, de Gruyter.
AGR	Akten der Gesellschaft für griechische und römische Rechtsgeschichte. Cologne, Böhlau.
AHAArch	Annales d'Histoire de l'art et d'archéologie. Bruxelles, Univ. libre.
AHAM	Anales de Historia antigua y medieval. Buenos Aires, Inst. de Estud. clásicos.
AHR	American Historical Review. Washington, D.C., American Historical Association.
AIHS	Archives Internationales d'histoire des Sciences (devient Archeion).
AJ	The Archaeological Journal. London, Archaeological Institute of Great Britain and Ireland.

AJA	American Journal of Archaeology. New York, Archaeol. Inst. of America.
AJAH	American Journal of ancient History. Cambridge, Mass., Robinson Hall, Harvard University.
AJPh	American Journal of Philology. Baltimore, Johns Hopkins Press.
AKG	Archiv für Kulturgeschichte. Cologne, Böhlau.
ALing	Archivum Linguisticum. A Review of comparative Philology and general Linguistics. Menston, The Scolar Pr.
ALMA	Archivum Latinitatis Medii Aevi (Bulletin Du Cange). Leiden, Brill.
American Scholar	American Scholar. Washington, D.C., United Chapters of Phi Beta Kappa.
AMW	Archiv für Musikwissenschaft. Wiesbaden, Steiner.
AncW	The ancient world. Chicago, Ares Publ.
ANRW	Aufstieg und Niedergang der römischen Welt. Geschichte und Kultur Roms im Spiegel der neueren Forschung. Berlin, de Gruyter.
Anthropos	Anthropos. Revue internationale d'ethnologie et de linguistique. Fribourg, Impr. Saint-Paul.
Antiquity	Antiquity. A quarterly Review of Archaeology. Newbury, The Wharf.
AntJ	The Antiquaries Journal, being the Journal of the Society of Antiquaries of London. Oxford University Press.
AntR	Antioch Review. Yellow Springs, Ohio, The Antioch Press.
ANum	Acta Numismatica. Barcelona, Sección num. del Circulo filatélico y numismatico.
APF	Archiv für Papyrusforschung und verwandte Gebiete. Leipzig, Teubner.
APh	L'Année Philologique. Paris, Les Belles Lettres.
A&R	Atene e Roma. Rassegna trimestrale dell'Associazione Italiana di Cultura classica. Florence, Le Monnier.
Archaeologia	Archaeologia or Miscellaneous Tracts relating to Antiquity. London, Soc. of Antiquaries.
Archaeology	Archaeology. A magazine dealing with the Antiquity of the World. New York.
ArchClass	Archeologia Classica. Rivista della Scuola naz. di Archeologia, pubbl. a cura degli Ist. di Archeologia e Storia dell'arte greca e romana e di Etruscologia e antichità italiche dell'Univ. di Roma. Rome, L'Erma.
Archeologia	Archeologia. Rocznik Instytutu Historii Kultury materialnej Polskiej Akademii Nauk. Warszawa, Zakl. Narod. Im. Ossolińskich.
Arch Philos	Archiv für Philosophie, Stuttgart, Kohlhammer.
ArchN	Archaeological News, Tallahassee, Fla., Dept. of Classics, Florida State University.
ArchPhilos	Archives de Philosophie. Recherches et documentation. Paris, Beauchesne.
Arctos	Arctos. Acta philologica Fennica. Helsinki, Klass.-Filol. Yhdistys.
ASAE	Annales du Service des Antiquités d'Egypte. Le Caire, Impr. de l'Inst. Français d'Archéol. Orientale.
ASNP	Annali della Scuola Normale Superiore di Pisa, Cl. di Lettere e Filosofia. Pisa, Piazza dei Cavalieri.
ASPap	American Studies in Papyrology. Toronto, Hakkert.
AST	Analecta Sacra Tarraconensia. Barcelona, Bibl. Balmes.
ASTI	Annual of the Swedish Theological Institute. Leiden, Brill.
Athenaeum	Athenaeum. Studi periodici di Letteratura e Storia dell'Antichita. Pavia, Università.
AU	Der altsprachliche Unterricht. Arbeitshefte zu seiner wissenschaftlichen Begründung und praktischen Gestalt. Stuttgart, Klett.
AugStud	Augustinian Studies. Villanova, Pa., Villanova University Press.
Augustinus	Augustinus. Revista publicada por los Padres agustinos recoleros. Madrid, General Dávila 5B.
AVM	Accademia Virgiliana di Mantova. Atti e Memorie. Mantova.
AW	Antike Welt. Zürich, Raggi-Verlag.

BAB	Bulletin de la Classe des Lettres de l'Académie Royale de Belgique. Bruxelles, Lamertin.
BAGB	Bulletin de l'Association G. Budé. Paris, Les Belles Lettres.
BASP	Bulletin of the American Society of Papyrologists. New York, Columbia University.
BBF	Bulletin des Bibliothèques de France. Paris, Secrétariat d'Etat aux Universités, Service des Bibliothèques.
BCH	Bulletin de Correspondance Hellénique. Paris, de Boccard.
BCTH	Bulletin Archéologique du Comité des Travaux Historiques. Paris, Impr. Nationale.
BECh	Bibliothèque de l'École des Chartes. Geneva, Droz.
BIAL	Bulletin of the Institute of Archaeology of the Univ. of London. London.
BiblH&R	Bibliothèque d'Humanisme et Renaissance. Geneva, Droz.
Biblica	Biblica. Commentarii editi cura Pontificii Instituti Biblici. Rome.
BIBR	Bulletin de l'Institut historique belge de Rome. Rome, Accademia Belgica.
BICS	Bulletin of the Institute of Classical Studies of the University of London. London.
BIFG	Bollettino dell'Istituto di Filologia greca dell'Università di Padova. Rome, L'Erma.
BJ	Bonner Jahrbücher des Rheinischen Landesmuseums in Bonn und des Vereins von Altertumsfreunden im Rheinlande. Kevelaer, Butzon & Bercker.
BLE	Bulletin de Littérature Ecclésiastique. Toulouse, Institut Catholique.
BLR	The Bodleian Library Record. Oxford, Bodleian Library.
BMM	Bulletin of the Metropolitan Museum of Art. New York.
BMNE	Bulletin of the Museum of Mediterranean and Near Eastern Antiquities. Stockholm, Medelhavsmuseet.
BMusB	Bulletin of the Museum of Fine Arts in Boston. Boston.
BO	Bibliotheca Orientalis, uitg. van het Hederlandsch Instituut voor het Nabije Oosten. Leiden.
BollClass	Bollettino del classici, a cura del Comitato per la preparazione dell'Edlzione nazionale dei Classici greci e latini. Rome, Accad. dei Lincei.
BPhM	Bulletin de la Société internationale pour l'étude de la Philosophie médiévale. Louvain la Neuve, Chemin d'Aristote 1.
BRGK	Bericht der Römisch-Germanischen Kommission des Deutschen Archäologischen Instituts. Berlin, de Gruyter.
BritAA	British Archaeology Abstracts. London, Council for British Archaeology.
BRL	Bulletin of the John Rylands Library. Manchester University Press.
BSAF	Bulletin de la Société nationale des Antiquaires de France. Paris, Klincksieck.
BSEAA	Boletin del Seminario de Estudios de Arte y Arqueologia. Valladolid, Inst. Diego Velázquez.
BSFN	Bulletin de la Société française de Numismatique. Paris, Cabinet des Médailles.
BSL	Bulletin de la Société de Linguistique de Paris. Paris, Klincksieck.
BSPh	Bulletin de la Société française de Philosophie. Paris, Colin.
BStudLat	Bollettino di Studi latini. Periodico quadrimestrale d'informazione bibliografica. Naples, Soc. ed. Napoletana.
BTh	Bulletin de Théologie ancienne et médiévale. (Supplement to RecTh.)
Bulletin papyrologique	Bulletin papyrologique. Paris.
B&W	Bibliothek und Wissenschaft. Wiesbaden, Harrassowitz.
Byzantion	Byzantion. Revue internationale des Études byzantines. Bruxelles, 4, Boul. de l'Empereur.
ByzF	Byzantinische Forschungen. Internationale Zeitschrift für Byzantinistik. Amsterdam, Hakkert.
ByzZ	Byzantinische Zeitschrift. Munich, Beck.

Caesarodunum	Caesarodunum. Tours, Inst. d'Études latines de l'Universite, Centre de Recherches A. Piganiol.
CahNum	Cahiers de Numismatique. Bulletin de la Société d'études numismatiques et archéologiques. Boulogne.
Cambridge Review	Cambridge Review. Cambridge, England.
CArch	Cahiers Archéologiques. Fin del'antiquité et Moyen age. Paris, Klincksieck.
CB	The Classical Bulletin. Saint Louis, Mo., Department of Classical Languages at Saint Louis University.
CE	Chronique d'Egypte. Bruxelles, Fondation Egyptologique Reine Elisabeth.
CF	Classical Folia. Studies in the christian perpetuation of the Classics. Catholic Classics Association of Greater New York.
CH	Cahiers d'Histoire publ. par les Universités de Clermont-Lyon-Grenoble. Lyons, Faculté des Lettres.
Chiron	Chiron. Mitteilungen der Kommission für alte Geschichte und Epigraphik des Deutschen Archäologischen Instituts. Munich, Beck.
CHR	Catholic Historical Review. Washington, D.C., Cath. Univ. of America Press.
CJ	The Classical Journal. Athens, University of Georgia.
ClAnt	Classical antiquity. Berkeley, University of California Press.
C&M	Classica et Mediaevalia. Revue danoise d'Histoire et de Philologie publiée par la Société danoise pour les Études anciennes et médiévales. Copenhagen, Gyldendal.
CO	The Classical Outlook. Journal of the American Classical League. Oxford, Ohio, Miami University.
CodMan	Codices manuscripti. Zeitschrift für Handschriftenkunde. Vienna, Hollinek.
CompLit	Comparative Literature. Eugene, University of Oregon.
CPh	Classical Philology. Chicago, University of Chicago Press.
CQ	Classical Quarterly. Oxford University Press.
CR	Classical Review. Oxford University Press.
CRAI	Comptes rendus de l'Académie des Inscriptions et Belles-Lettres. Paris, Klincksieck.
CRIPEL	Cahiers de Recherches de l'Institut de Papyrologie et d'Egyptologie de Lille. Lille, Université.
CSCA	California Studies in Classical Antiquity. Berkeley, Univ. of California Press.
CSSH	Comparative Studies in Society and History. Cambridge University Press.
CW	The Classical World. Pittsburgh, Pa., Duquesne University.
Dacia	Dacia. Revue d'Archéologie et d'Histoire ancienne. Bucharest, Ed. de l'Académie de la République populaire roumaine.
DB	Dictionary of the Bible. New York, Scribner.
Dionysius	Dionysius. Halifax, Nova Scotia, Dept. of Classics, Dalhousie University.
DLZ	Deutsche Literaturzeitung für Kritik der internationalen Wissenschaft. Berlin, Akademie-Verlag.
DOP	Dumbarton Oaks Papers. New York, Augustin.
EEAth	Ἐπιστημονικὴ Ἐπετηρὶς τῆς φιλοσοφιχῆς Σχολῆς τοῦ Πανεπιστημιου Ἀθηνῶν. Athens, Typ. Myrtidou.
EHBS	Ἐπετηρὶς Ἐταιρείας Βυζαντινῶν Σπουδῶν. Athens, Typ. Myrtidou.
EHR	English Historical Review. London, Longmans Green.
Eirene	Eirene. Studia Graeca et Latina. Prague, Ceskoslovenská Akad. Vèd.
Emerita	Emerita. Revista de Lingüistica y Filologia clásica. Madrid, Instituto Antonio de Nebrija.
Enc Catt	Encyclopedia cattolica. Vatican City.
Encyc Brit	Encyclopaedia Britannica. Chicago.
EPh	Études philosophiques. Paris, Presses Universitaires.

Epigraphica	Epigraphica. Rivista italiana di Epigrafia. Faenza, Lega.
Eranos	Eranos. Acta Philologica Suecana. Uppsala, Eranos' Förlag.
Erasmus	Erasmus. Speculum Scientiarum. Bulletin international de la Science contemporaine. Wiesbaden, Steiner.
EThR	Études Théologiques et Religieuses. Montpellier, 26 bd. Berthelot.
Euphrosyne	Euphrosyne. Revista de Filologia clássica. Lisbon, Centro de Estudos clássicos.
FBSM	Forschungen und Berichte, hrsg. von den Staatlichen Museen. Berlin, Akademie-Verlag.
FR	Felix Ravenna. Faenza, Lega.
GBA	Gazette des Beaux-Arts. Paris, 140, Faubourg-Saint-Honoré.
GCFI	Giornale critico della Filosofia italiana. Firenze, Sansoni.
Germania	Germania. Anzeiger der Röm.-Germ. Kommission des Deutschen Archäol. Instituts. Berlin, de Gruyter.
GGA	Göttingische Gelehrte Anzeigen. Göttingen, Vandenhoeck & Ruprecht.
GIF	Giornale Italiano di Filologia. Rivista trimestrale di Cultura. Rome, Cadmo ed.
GJ	The Geographical Journal. London, Geographic Society.
GLO	Graecolatina et Orientalia. Zbornik Filoz. Fak. Univerz. Komenského. Bratislava, Slov. Pedag. Naklad.
Glotta	Glotta. Zeitschrift für griechische und lateinische Sprache. Göttingen, Vandenhoeck & Ruprecht.
Gnomon	Gnomon. Kritische Zeitschrift für die gesamte klassische Altertumswissenschaft. Munich, Beck.
GNS	Gazette Numismatique Suisse. Bàle, Blochmonterstr. 19.
Gott Gel Anz Jahrg	Gottingische Gelehrte Anzeigan. Göttingen, Vandenhoeck & Ruprecht.
G&R	Greece and Rome. Oxford, Clarendon Press.
GRBS	Greek, Roman and Byzantine Studies. Durham, N.C., Duke University.
Gregorianum	Gregorianum. Commentarii de re theologica et philosophica. Rome, Pont. Univ. Gregoriana.
Gymnasium	Gymnasium. Zeitschrift für Kultur der Antike und humanistische Bildung. Heidelberg, Winter.
HA	Helvetia archaeologica. Basel, Schwabe.
HBN	Hamburger Beiträge zur Numismatik. Hamburg, Museum für Hamburg. Gesch., Abt. Münzkabinett.
Helios	Helios. Journal of the Classical Association of the Southwestern United States. Lubbock, Texas Tech Univ.
Hellenica	Ἑλληνιχά. Φιλολ., ἱστορ. χαὶ λαογρ. Περιοδιχὸν Σύγγραμμα τῆς Ἑταιρείας Μαχεδονιχῶν Σπουδῶν. Thessalonique, Bas. Sophias 2.
Helmantica	Helmantica. Revista de Filologia clásica y hebrea. Salamanca, Pontificia Universidad.
Hermathena	Hermathena. A Series of Papers by Members of Trinity College, Dublin. Dublin, Hodges & Figgis.
Hermes	Hermes. Zeitschrift für klassische Philologie. Wiesbaden, Steiner.
Hesperia	Hesperia. Journal of the American School of Classical Studies at Athens.
Historia	Historia. Revue d'histoire ancienne. Wiesbaden, Steiner.
History	History. The Quarterly Journal of the Historical Association. London, Macmillan.
HR	History of Religions. Chicago, University of Chicago Press.
HSPh	Harvard Studies in Classical Philology. Cambridge, Mass., Harvard University Press.
HT	History To-day. A monthly magazine. London, Bracken House.
Humanitas	Humanitas. Revista do Instituto de Estudos clássicos. Coimbra, Faculdade de Letras.
HZ	Historische Zeitschrift. Munich, Oldenbourg.

ICS	Illinois Classical Studies. Urbana, Champaign & Chicago, University of Illinois Press.
IPQ	International Philosophical Quarterly. Bronx, N.Y., Fordham University Press.
Isis	Isis. International Review devoted to the History of Science and its cultural influences. Washington, Smithsonian Institution.
Janus	Janus. Revue internationale de l'histoire des sciences, de la médecine, de la pharmacie et de la technique. Amsterdam, Joh. Verhuststr. 185.
JAOS	Journal of the American Oriental Society. Baltimore.
JARCE	Journal of the American Research Center in Egypt. Boston, 479 Huntington Avenue.
JArchSc	Journal of Archaeological Science. London & New York, Academic Press.
JBAA	The Journal of the British Archaeological Association. London, 20 Portman Square.
JCS	Journal of Classical Studies. The Journal of the Class. Soc. of Japan. Kyoto, Kyoto Univ. Dept. of Literature & Tokyo, Iwanami-shoten.
JDAI	Jahrbuch des Deutschen Archäologischen Instituts. Berlin, de Gruyter.
JEA	Journal of Egyptian Archaeology. London, The Egypt Exploration Society.
JEH	Journal of Ecclesiastical History. Cambridge University Press.
JFA	Journal of Field Archaeology. Boston Univ. Press.
JHistStud	Journal of Historical Studies. Princeton, University Press.
JHPh	Journal of the History of Philosophy. Berkeley, Univ. of California Press.
JHS	Journal of Hellenic Studies. London.
JMagH	Journal of Magic History. Toledo, Ohio, Department of Philosophy, University of Toledo.
J Lib Hist	Journal of Library History. Austin, University of Texas Press.
JNES	Journal of Near Eastern Studies. Chicago, University of Chicago Press.
JPh	Journal of Philosophy. New York.
JRH	Journal of Religious History. Univ. of Sydney, Dept. of History.
JRS	Journal of Roman Studies. London.
JS	Journal des Savants. Paris, Klincksieck.
JSAH	Journal of the Society of Architectural Historians. Philadelphia.
JThS	Journal of Theological Studies. Oxford, Clarendon Press.
JWG	Jahrbuch für Wirtschaftsgeschichte. Berlin, Akademie-Verlag.
JWI	Journal of the Warburg and Courtauld Institute. London, Warburg Institute.
Karthago	Karthago. Revue d'archéologie africaine. Paris, Klincksieck.
Klio	Klio. Beiträge zur alten Geschichte. Berlin, Akademie-Verlag.
Kratylos	Kratylos. Kritisches Berichts- und Rezensionsorgan für indogermanische und allgemeine Sprachwissenschaft. Wiesbaden, Reichert.
Labeo	Labeo. Rassegna di Diritto romano. Naples, Jovene.
Lampas	Lampas. Tijdschrift voor Nederlandse classici. Muiderberg, Dick Coutinho.
Language	Language. Journal of the Linguistic Society of America. Baltimore, Waverly Press.
Latinitas	Latinitas. Commentarii linguae Latinae excolendae. Vatican City, Libr. Ed. Vaticana.
Latomus	Latomus. Revue d'études latines. Bruxelles, Société d'Études latines.
LEC	Les Études Classiques. Namur, Facultés N.D.-de-la-Paix.
LF	Listy Filologicke. Praha, Naklad. Cs. Akad. Véd, Lazarská 8.
Lingua	Lingua. Revue internationale de linguistique générale. Amsterdam, Noord-Holl. Uitg. Maats.
L&S	Lingua e Stile. Milano, Soc. ed. Il Mulino.
LThPh	Laval Théologique et Philosophique. Québec, Ed. de l'Université Laval.

Lustrum	Lustrum. Internationale Forschungsberichte aus dem Bereich des klassischen Altertums. Göttingen, Vandenhoeck & Ruprecht.
MA	Le Moyen Age. Revue trimestrielle d'histoire et de philologie. Bruxelles, Renaissance du Livre.
MAAR	Memoirs of the American Academy in Rome.
MAev	Medium Aevum. Oxford, Blackwell.
MAI	Mémoires de l'Académie des Inscriptions et Belles Lettres. Paris, Klincksieck.
Maia	Maia. Rivista di letterature classiche. Bologna, Cappelli.
Manuscripta	Manuscripta, publ. by St. Louis University Library. Saint Louis, Mo.
MCSN	Materiali e contributi per la storia della narrativa greco-latina. Perugia, Ist. di Filologia latina; & Rome, Cadmo ed.
MEFR	Mélanges d'Archéologie et d'Histoire de l'École Française de Rome. Paris, de Boccard.
MGR	Miscellanea greca e romana. Studi pubblicati dall'Ist. ital. per la storia antica. Rome, Arti grafiche.
MH, MusHelv	Museum Helveticum. Revue suisse pour l'Étude de l'Antiquité classique. Bàle, Schwabe.
Mind	Mind. A Quarterly Review of Psychology and Philosophy. London, Macmillan.
Minos	Minos. Revista de Filologia egea. Salamanca, Universidad, Secretariado de Publicaciones, Apart. 20.
MIŒG	Mitteilungen des Instituts für Österreichische Geschichtsforschung. Vienna, Böhlau.
MLatJb	Mittellateinisches Jahrbuch. Cologne, Mittellat. Abt. des Inst. für Altertumskunde der Universität; Stuttgart, Hiersemann.
MLR	Modern Language Review. Cambridge, England.
Mnemosyne	Mnemosyne. Bibliotheca Classica Batava. Leiden, Brill.
MonStud	Monastic Studies. Pine City, N.Y., Mount Saviour Monastery.
MPhL	Museum Philologum Londiniense. Amsterdam, Hakkert.
MS	Mediaeval Studies. Toronto, Pontif. Inst. of Mediaeval Studies.
MSR	Mélanges de Science Religieuse. Lille, Facultés Catholiques.
MSS	Münchener Studien zur Sprachwissenschaft. Munich, Kitzinger.
Muséon	Muséon. Revue d'Études Orientales. Louvain, Impr. Orientaliste, B.P. 41.
NAWG	Nachrichten der Akademie der Wissenschaften in Göttingen, Philol.-Hist. Klasse. Göttingen, Vandenhoeck & Ruprecht.
NC	Numismatic Chronicle. London, Numismatic Society.
NCE	New Catholic encyclopedia. New York, McGraw-Hill.
NCirc	Numismatic Circular. London, Spink.
Nestor	Nestor. Mycenaean bibliography. Madison, Inst. for Research in the Humanities, University of Wisconsin.
NL	Numismatic Literature. New York, American Numismatic Society.
NNB	Numismatisches Nachrichtenblatt. Organ des Verbandes der Dt. Münzvereine, Speyer.
NRS	Nuova Rivista Storica. Rome, Soc. Ed. Dante Alighieri.
NRTh	Nouvelle Revue Théologique. Tournai, Casterman.
NT	Novum Testamentum. An international Quarterly for New Testament and related Studies. Leiden, Brill.
NTS	New Testament Studies. An international Journal publ. quarterly under the auspices of Studiorum Novi Testamenti Societas. Cambridge University Press.
Numen	Numen. International Review for the History of Religions. Leiden, Brill.
NYRB	New York Review of Books. Milford, Conn., Whitney Ellsworth.
NZ	Numismatische Zeitschrift. Vienna, Num. Gesellschaft.

OCD	Oxford Classical Dictionary. Oxford University Press.
OLZ	Orientalistische Literaturzeitung. Berlin, Akademie-Verlag.
Orbis	Orbis. Bulletin International de Documentation linguistique. Louvain, Centre Internat. de Dialectologie générale.
Orient	Orient. Bulletin of the Society of Near Eastern studies in Japan. Tokyo, Nippon Orient Gakkai.
Paideia	Paideia. Rivista letteraria di Informazione bibliografica. Genoa, via San Luca 15.
Pallas	Pallas, fasc. 3 des Annales de l'Université de Toulouse-Le Mirail. Toulouse, 4, rue Albert-Lautman.
Pan	Pan. Studi dell'Istituto di Filologia latina dell'Università di Palermo.
Pantheon	Pantheon; internationale Zeitschrift für Kunst. Munich.
PBA	Proceedings of the British Academy. Oxford University Press.
PCA	Proceedings of the Classical Association. London, Murray.
Philologus	Philologus, Zeitschrift für klassische Philologie. Berlin, Akademie-Verlag.
Philosophia	Φιλοσοφία. Ἐπετηρὶς τοῦ Κέντρου ἐρεύνης τῆς ἑλληνιχῆς φιλοσοφίας. Athens.
Philosophy	Philosophy. The Journal of the British Institute of Philosophy. London, Macmillan.
PhilosQ	The Philosophical Quarterly. Univ. of St. Andrews, Scots Philos. Club.
PhJ	Philosophisches Jahrbuch. Freiburg, Alber.
Phoenix	The Phoenix. The Journal of the Classical Association of Canada. Toronto, University of Toronto Press.
PhQ	Philological Quarterly. Iowa University Press.
PhR	Philosophical Review. New York, Longmans Green.
Ph&Rh	Philosophy and Rhetoric. University Park, Pa., Pennsylvania State University Press.
Phronesis	Phronesis. A Journal for ancient Philosophy. Assen, van Gorcum.
Platon	Πλάτων. Δελτίον τῆς Ἐταιρείας Ἑλλήνων Φιλολόγων. Athens.
Poetica	Poetica. Zeitschrift für Sprach- und Literaturwissenschaft. Amsterdam, Grüner.
PP	La Parola del Passato. Rivista di Studi antichi. Naples, Macchiaroli.
PRIA	Proceedings of the Royal Irish Academy, Section C. Dublin.
Prometheus	Prometheus. Rivista quadrimestrale di studi classici. Florence, Tipolitografia STAF.
Prudentia	Prudentia. A journal devoted to the intellectual history of the Hellenistic and Roman periods. Auckland, University of Auckland Press.
PVS	Proceedings of the Virgil Society. London, King's College.
Pyrenae	Pyrenae. Crónica arqueológica. Barcelona, Inst. de Arqueologia y Prehistoria.
QJS	Quarterly Journal of Speech. New York, Speech Association of America.
RA	Revue Archéologique. Paris, Presses Universitaires.
RAE	Revue archéologique de l'Est et du Centre-Est. Dijon, 36 rue Chabot-Charny.
Ramus	Ramus. Critical studies in Greek and Latin Literature. Clayton, Victoria (Australia), Monash University.
RBea	Revue Bénédictine. Abbaye de Maredsous, Belgique.
RBN	Revue Belge de Numismatique et de Sigillographie. Bruxelles, 5 rue du Musée.
RBPh	Revue Belge de Philologie et d'Histoire. Mechelen, Van Passel.
RCCM	Rivista di Cultura classica e medioevale. Rome, Ed. dell'Ateneo.
RD	Revue Historique de Droit français et étranger. Paris, Sirey.
RdA	Rivista di Archeologia. Rome, Giorgio Bretschneider.

RE	Paulys Real-Encyclopädie der classischen Altertumswissenschaft. Stuttgart, Druckenmüller.
REA	Revue des Études Anciennes. 33405 Talence, Domaine Univ., Sect. d'histoire.
REByz	Revue des Études byzantines. Paris, Inst. Français d'Études byzantines.
REC	Revista de Estudios Clásicos. Mendoza, Inst. de Leng. y Lit. clásicas.
RecSR	Recherches de Science Religieuse. Paris, 15, rue Monsieur.
RecTh	Recherches de Théologie ancienne et médiévale. Gembloux, Duculot.
REG	Revue des Études Grecques. Paris, Les Belles Lettres.
REL	Revue des Études Latines. Paris, Les Belles Lettres.
RELO	Revue de l'Organisation internationale pour l'étude des langues anciennes par ordinateur. Liège.
RelStud	Religious Studies, Cambridge University Press.
REPh	Revue de l'Enseignement philosophique. Aurillac, Impr. du Cantal.
RF	Rivista di Filosofia. Torino, Einaudi.
RFIC	Rivista di Filologia e di Istruzione Classica. Torino, Loescher.
RH	Revue Historique. Paris, Presses Universitaires.
RHE	Revue d'Histoire Ecclésiastique. Louvain, Université Catholique.
RHES	Revue d'histoire économique et sociale. Paris, Rivière.
Rhetorik	Rhetorik. Ein internationales Jahrbuch. Stuttgart, Frommann-Holzboog.
RHR	Revue de l'Histoire des Religions. Paris, Presses Universitaires.
RHS	Revue d'Histoire des Sciences et de leurs applications. Paris, Presses Universitaires.
RHT	Revue d'Histoire des Textes. Paris, Centre national de la Recherche scientifique.
RIFD	Rivista Internazionale di Filosofia del Diritto. Milan, Bocca.
RIL	Rendiconti dell'Istituto Lombardo, Classe di Lettere, Scienze morali e storiche. Milan.
RLAC	Reallexikon für Antike und Christentum. Stuttgart, Hiersemann.
RMAL	Revue du moyen âge latin. Strasbourg, Palais de l'Université.
RMeta	Review of Metaphysics. Washington, D.C., Catholic University of America.
RMM	Revue de Métaphysique et de Morale. Paris, Colin.
RN	Revue Numismatique. Paris, Les Belles Lettres.
RPAA	Rendiconti della Pontificia Accademia di Archeologia. Rome, Tip. Poliglotta Vaticana.
RPh	Revue de Philologie. Paris, Klincksieck.
RPhilos	Revue Philosophique de la France et de l'étranger. Paris, Presses Universitaires.
RPhL	Revue Philosophique de Louvain. Louvain, Inst. Sup. de Philosophie.
RQS	Revue des Questions scientifiques. Namur, Courtay et Paris, Masson.
RSA	Rivista storica dell'Antichità. Bologna, Pàtron.
RSAA	Revue Suisse d'Art et d'Archéologie. Zurich, Berichthaus.
RSCI	Rivista di Storia della Chiesa in Italia. Rome, Herder.
RSHum	Revue des Sciences Humaines. Lille, Faculté des Lettres.
RSI	Rivista Storica Italiana. Naples, Ed. Scientifiche Italiane.
RThL	Revue théologique de Louvain. Louvain-la-Neuve, Collège Albert-Descamps.
RThPh	Revue de Théologie et de Philosophie. Lausanne, Ancienne Académie.
SA	Sovietskaja Archeologija. Moscow, Nauka.
San	Journal of the Society of ancient Numismatics. Santa Monica, Calif.
S&C	Scrittura e Civiltà. Ist. di Paleografia dell' Univ. di Roma. Torino, Bottega d'Erasmo.
Scriptorium	Scriptorium. Revue internationale des Études relatives aux manuscrits. Anvers, Standaard-Boekhandel.
ScrPhil	Scripta Philologa. Milan, Ist. ed. Cisalpino-La Goliardica.
SDHI	Studia e Documenta Historiae et Iuris. Rome, Pontif. Univ. Lateranensis.

SE	Studi Etruschi. Florence, Olschki.
SicGymn	Siculorum Gymnasium. Rassegna semestrale della Facoltá di Lettere e Filosofia dell'Università di Catania. Catania, Bibl. della Facoltà.
SIF	Studi internazionali di Filosofia. Torino, "Filosofia."
SL	Studia Linguistica. Revue de linguistique générale et comparée. Lund, Gleerup; Copenhagen, Munksgaard.
SMSR	Studi e materiali di storia delle religioni (reprend l'ancien titre et continue SSR).
SNR	Schweizerische Numismatische Rundschau. Bern, Schweizer. Num. Gesellschaft.
Speculum	Speculum. Journal of Medieval Studies. Cambridge, Mass., Medieval Academy of America.
StudClas	Studii Clasice. Bucureşti, Soc. de Studii clasice din RSR.
StudLang	Studies in Language. International Journal sponsored by the Foundations of Language. Amsterdam, Benjamins.
StudMed	Studi medievali. Spoleto, Centro italiano di Studi sull'alto medioevo.
StudMon	Studia Monastica. Abadia de Montserrat.
StudPap	Studia Papyrologica. Revista española de Papirologia. Barcelona, Univ. central; Rome, Pontif. Ist. Bibl.
StudRom	Studi Romani. Rivista bimestrale dell'Istituto di Studi Romani. Rome, 2 Piazza Cavalieri di Malta.
ThLZ	Theologische Literaturzeitung. Berlin, Evangelischer Verlagsanstalt.
ThS	Theological Studies. Baltimore, Theol. Faculties of the Society of Jesus in the U.S.
ThZ	Theologische Zeitschrift. Basel, Reinhardt.
TLS	The Times Literary Supplement. London, Times Printing House Square.
T&MByz	Travaux et Mémoires. Centre de recherche d'histoire et de civilisation byzantines. Paris, de Boccard.
TPhS	Transactions of the Philological Society. Oxford, Blackwell.
Traditio	Traditio. Studies in ancient and medieval History, Thought and Religion. New York, Fordham University Press.
TZ	Trierer Zeitschrift. Trier, Rheinisches Landesmuseum.
VChr	Vigiliae Christianae. A Review of early christian Life and Language. Amsterdam, Noord-Holl. Uitg. Maatschappij.
Vergilius	Vergilius. The Vergilian Society of America. Vancouver, University of British Columbia.
VetChr	Vetera Christianorum. Bari, Ist. di Letteratura cristiana antica.
WJA	Würzburger Jahrbücher für die Altertumswissenschaft. Würzburg, Schöningh.
Word	Word. Journal of the Linguistic Circle of New York. New York.
WS	Wiener Studien. Zeitschrift für klassische Philologie und Patristik. Vienna, Verl. der Österr. Akademie.
YClS	Yale Classical Studies. New Haven, Yale University Press.
YUS	Yale University Studies. New Haven, Yale University Press.
Zephyrus	Zephyrus. Crónica del Seminario de Arqueologia y de la Sección arqueológica del Centro de Estudios Salmantinos. Salamanca, Fac. de Filosofia y Letras.
ZKG	Zeitschrift für Kirchengeschichte. Stuttgart, Kohlhammer.
ZKTh	Zeitschrift für Katholische Theologie. Vienna, Herder.
ZPE	Zeitschrift für Papyrologie und Epigraphik. Bonn, Habelt.
ZWG	Sudhoffs Archiv. Zeitschrift für Wissenschaftsgeschichte. Wiesbaden, Steiner.

CLASSICAL SCHOLARSHIP

An Annotated Bibliography

Bibliography

AA   GENERAL BIBLIOGRAPHY

Bibliographical Guides

DISSERTATION abstracts international. Microfilm abstracts. 1938–50. Dissertation abstracts. 1951–June 1969. [Ann Arbor, Mich.], University Microfilms, v. 1– , 1938– . **AA1**

Issued July 1966– in 2 sections: A. The Humanities and Social Sciences; B. The Sciences and Engineering.

The new title of *Dissertation abstracts*, beginning with v. III, no. 1, p.1A–436A (1969) reflects the projected enlargement of University Microfilms dissertation publication program by the addition of dissertations from European universities. *DAI* is divided into two sections: Humanities (A) and Sciences (B), beginning with v. XXVII, no. 1. Classics are located in section A Literature, Classical.

MALCLÈS, Louise Noelle. Les sources du travail bibliographique. Genève, Droz, 1950–1958. 3 v. **AA2**

REL XXX 1952 374 Ernst
A textbook and guide to bibliographical manuals.

SHEEHY, Eugene Paul, comp. Guide to reference books. With the assistance of Rita G. Keckeissen and Eileen McIlvaine. 9th ed. Chicago, American Library Association, 1976. xviii, 1015p. **AA3**

Rev., expanded, and updated version of the 8th ed. by Constance M. Winchell.

Most sections are now about a third longer than in the 8th edition. A general guide to basic reference books in all fields and various language materials, including Greek and Latin. Works are arranged according to subject groupings; most items are annotated. There are five main sections: A. General Reference, B. Humanities, C. Social Sciences, D. History and Area Studies, E. Pure and Applied Sciences. There are important omissions in areas such as history, literature and education. Considering the quality and quantity of bibliographical resources available today this new edition of Winchell is not adequate. Most annotations are brief; they are descriptive but seldom critical. For incunables see p.20–22, for classical languages, p.367–371.

ULRICH'S international periodicals directory; Classified guide to current periodicals, foreign and domestic. 23rd ed., 1984. New York, R. R. Bowker Company, 1984. xliii, 2289p. **AA4**

Classical studies periodicals are listed on p.378–379; other relevant periodicals will be found listed under Archaeology, History, Linguistics, Literature, Museums and Galleries.

ULRICH'S quarterly; A supplement to Ulrich's international periodicals directory and Irregular serials and annuals. v. 1– , 1977– . New York, R. R. Bowker Company, 1977– . **AA5**

VAN HOESEN, Henry Bartlett. Bibliography: practical, enumerative, historical; An introductory manual. With the collaboration of Frank Keller Walter. New York, B. Franklin, 1971. xiii, 519p. **AA6**

Burt Franklin bibliography and reference series; 235. Reprint of the 1928 ed.

A comprehensive survey dealing with methods of research, subject bibliographies, library science, general reference books, special, national and universal bibliographies, the history of writing and printing, book decoration, bookselling and publishing. Bibliographical items are identified by number in the surveys and given in full in the Bibliographical Appendix.

For the classicist the section Auxiliary Sciences is of interest in c.4 Subject Bibliography. Historical and Social Sciences deals with archives, diplomatics, paleography, chronology, numismatics, and epigraphy. See also the section on classics in c.5, and c.12–13 on the History of Writing and Printing.

WALFORD, Albert John, ed. Guide to reference material. 3rd ed. London, Library Association, 1973. 3 v. **AA7**

Volume contents: 1. Science & Technology; 2. Social and historical sciences, philosophy and religion; 3. Generalia, language and literature, the arts.

This *Guide* intends to provide a signpost to reference books and bibliographies published mainly in recent years. The volumes are international in scope but with emphasis on items published in Britain. Volume 1 provides about 5,000 reference works, with critical or descriptive annotations. The arrangement is by Universal Decimal Classification, which could be confusing for the reader unfamiliar with the subject divisions. Generally annotations are longer in Walford than in Sheehy. Section 87 Classical Literature in v. 3 covers bibliographies, encyclopedias and dictionaries. For Latin literature there are sections on Bibliographies, Manuals, History, Latin Poetry, Horace, Lucretius, Ovid, Virgil, Latin Drama, Latin Prose, Translations, Medieval Latin Literature. Greek literature is similarly divided. Useful for recent lexica and concordances. See also section 09 Manuscripts, Rare books, Incunabula.

Bibliography of Bibliographies

BESTERMAN, Theodore. A world bibliography of bibliographies and of bibliographical catalogues, calendars, abstracts, digests, indices, and the like. 4th edition., rev. and greatly enl. throughout. Genève, Societas Bibliographica, 1965–1966. 5 v. **AA8**

In 1686 there appeared the first bibliography of bibliographies, Antoine Teissier's *Catalogus autorum qui librorum catalogos, indices, bibliothecas, vivorum litteratorum elogia, irtas, aut ovationes funebres, scriptis consignarunt.* This 4th and final edition of Besterman records and separately collates over 117,000 volumes, arranged under about 16,000 headings and subheadings.

A bibliography is defined by Besterman as a list of books arranged according to some permanent principle. Along with bibliographies of books are included bibliographies of catalogs, abstracts, digests, periodicals, and the more substantial types of manuscript material. The bibliography is international, excluding only lists in Oriental languages. It is arranged by subject with an author index: Classical literature p.1370–1379, classical studies p.1380–1389, Greek literature p.2732–2751, illustrated books p.2994–3011, p.3014–3018, Latin language p.3415–3416, Latin literature p.3417–3430. Some of the entries will have an antiquarian rather than a practical interest for the classicist. *See also:* Toomey, Alice F. *A world bibliography of bibliographies 1964–1974,* a decennial supplement to Theodore Besterman. Totowa, N.J., Rowman and Littlefield, 1977.

BIBLIOGRAPHIC index; A cumulative bibliography of bibliographies. (v.5 1956–1959– .) New York, H. W. Wilson, 1961– . v. 1, 1931. **AA9**

Editor 1956–1959: Marga Franck.

An alphabetical subject list of separately-published bibliographies and bibliographies that have been published in books and magazine articles. Beginning in 1970 it is published in April and August with annual cumulations in December. In 1976 the Bibliographic Index examined about 2,200 periodicals for bibliographic material, making it a useful complement to Besterman.

BIBLIOGRAPHISCHE Berichte; Bibliographical bulletin. Frankfurt am Main, Klostermann, 1.– Jahrg., 1959– . **AA10**

Volumes 1–5, 1959–1963, 1 v.; v. 6–10, 1964–1968, 1 v.

Frequency has changed: quarterly, 1959–1962; semiannual, 1963–1969; annual, 1970– . The title is also in English: *Bibliographical bulletin.*

A classified listing of recent bibliographies. Coverage is international with a high percentage of German titles. For classics see section II Language and Literature under II.3; Classical Languages and Literatures, Byzantinology, and Medieval Latin.

TOTOK, Wilhelm, WEIMANN, Karl-Heinz and WEITZEL, Rolf. Handbuch der bibliographischen Nachschlagewerke. 4., erw., völlig neu bearb. Aufl. Frankfurt am Main, Klostermann, [c1972]. xxxiv, 367p. **AA11**

Table of contents and Bibliographische Terminologie in English, French and German.

A comprehensive work on reference books in all scholarly areas. Part I covers General Bibliographies: Bibliographies of Bibliographies, International General Bibliographies, Literary Catalogs. The National Bibliographies section is particularly good for Germany but includes over 20 countries. There are excellent sections on bibliography of periodicals and catalogs of doctoral dissertation topics. For bibliography on incunabula see p.107–113, classical philology, p.195–197, paleography, p.167. A useful complement to Malclès *Les sources.*

Library Catalogues

BRITISH MUSEUM. Dept. of Printed Books. General catalogue of printed books. Photolithographic ed. to 1955. London, Trustees of the British Museum, 1959–1966 [v. 1, 1965]. 263 v. **AA12**

"The new edition was started with v. 52 at the point where the previous edition had been abandoned; it will conclude with the publication of volumes 1–51."

British Museum. Dept. of Printed Books. General catalogue of printed books. Ten-year supplement, 1956–1965. London, Trustees of the British Museum, 1968. 50 v. "The first in a projected series of ten-yearly supplements to the General catalogue of printed books, photolithographic edition, 1959–66."

British Museum. Dept. of Printed Books. General catalogue of printed books: five-year supplement, 1966–1970. Compact edition. New York: Readex Microprint, 1974, c1971. 3 v. "Approximately ten volumes of the original edition are contained in each volume of this edition."

The 263 volumes of the catalogue to 1955 contain more than 4 million entries for books, pamphlets and periodicals in Western languages in the British Museum from the 15th century. Includes many titles not found in the Library of Congress catalog. This photolithographic edition is kept up to date with first a ten-year, then a five-year supplement. The General Catalogue is primarily an author catalogue. A subject index of works from 1881–1900 was published in 1901 and supplemented by volumes received in each succeeding period of five years. The British Library is now producing the author and subject catalogues by computer.

THE NATIONAL union catalog, pre-1956 imprints; A cumulative author list representing Library of Congress printed cards and titles reported by other American libraries. Compiled and edited with the cooperation of the Library of Congress and the National Union Catalog Subcommittee of the Resources Committee of Resources and Technical Services Division, American Library Association. London, Mansell, 1968– . **AA13**

The National union catalog, pre-1956 imprints lists the holdings of the Library of Congress and of major libraries of the United States and Canada in the form of photographic reproduction of the actual library cards. This catalog will eventually fill 610 volumes and include books, pamphlets, maps, atlases and periodicals in all languages written in Cyrillic, Gaelic, Greek, Hebraic or Roman alphabets. The Library of Congress also issues *The National union catalog: a cumulative author list for books published since 1956* and the *Library of Congress Catalog. Books, Subjects* (after 1950). Both these works are issued serially and cumulated at five-year intervals.

PARIS. BIBLIOTHÈQUE NATIONALE. Département des imprimés. Catalogue générale des livres imprimés de la Bibliothèque nationale. Auteurs. Paris, Imprimerie Nationale, 1897–19– . **AA14**

Paris. Bibliothèque Nationale. Catalogue générale des livres imprimés: auteurs, collectivités-auteurs. 1960–1964. Paris, 1965– Vol. "Cette nouvelle tranche du Catalogue général des livres imprimés de la Bibliothèque nationale comprend les livres entrés et catalogue du ler janvier 1960 au 31 décembre 1964."

Since the Bibliothèque Nationale traces its origin to the private library of John II, 14th century king of France, its catalog is rich in early works, particularly strong for French history and literature. Each individual volume includes titles acquired up to its date of publication, e.g., v. I represents the collection of 1897. Beginning with v. 189 recent acquisitions are listed in the new series "Catalogue générale des livres imprimés; auteurs, collectivités-auteurs, anonymes."

WIDENER LIBRARY, Harvard University. Classical studies: classification schedules, classified listing by call number, chronological listing, author and title listing, Harvard University Library. Cambridge, Mass., Harvard University Press, 1979. 215p. **AA14a**

Festschriften

LEISTNER, Otto. Internationale Bibliographie der Festschriften; mit Sachreg. International bibliography of Festschriften; with subject-index. Osnabrück, Biblio-Verlag, 1976. 895p. **AA15**

Contains a list of Festschriften (without annotations or table of contents) arranged by names of the personality or institution honored (p.1–754), a subject index (p.757–868), a list of frequently employed terms in foreign languages in German and English translations (p.871–890), and general abbreviations (p.893–895). Easily consulted for classical antiquity through the subject index s.v. Antike, Klassische Archäologie, Klassische Literaturgeschichte, Klassische Philologie, Klassische Altertums. Under one or other of these headings there are references to both ancient and modern authors and to literary genres.

ROUNDS, Dorothy. Articles on antiquity in Festschriften, an index; The ancient Near East, the Old Testament, Greece, Rome, Roman Law, Byzantium. Cambridge, Mass., Harvard University Press, 1962. 560p. **AA16**

CW LVI 1963 216 Smith • Gnomon XXXV 1963 824–827 Seyffert

The index lists all Festschriften articles dealing with the period from the Neolithic to the rise of Islam and with all the area (except India) deeply affected by Mesopotamian, Egyptian and Greco-Roman culture. It lists all Festschriften articles to 1453 but omits those on Western Europe in the Middle Ages covered by H. T. Williams, *An index of medieval studies.* The index stops with 1954. The cross-indexing is very full: not only are articles indexed under author and subjects, but there are general headings Archaeology, Art and so on, under which the relevant articles are again listed. A concluding essay urges the abolition of the Festschrift.

See also Rounds, D. and Dow, Sterling, "Festschriften," *Harv. Univ. Bull.* VIII (1954), 283–298.

AB INCUNABULA CATALOGUES

ABBOTT, T. K. Catalog of fifteenth-century books in the Library of Trinity College, Dublin, and in Marsh's Library, Dublin. New York, Franklin, 1970. Reprint of the 1905 ed. vi, 255p.
AB1

BERKOWITZ, David S. Bibliotheca bibliographica incunabula; A manual of bibliographical guides to inventories of printing, of holdings, and of reference aids. With an appendix of useful information on place-names and dating, collected and classified for the use of researchers in incunabulistics. Waltham, Mass., 1967. vi, 336p.
AB2

An attempt to fill the need for a guide to bibliographies of incunabula. A general section on guides to sources of information on the topic is followed by chapters on registers or catalogs of incunabula.

BRITISH MUSEUM. Dept. of Printed Books. Catalogue of books printed in the XVth century now in the British Museum. London, Trustees of the British Museum, 1908– .   **AB3**

Parts 1–4 edited by A. W. Pollard; parts 5–8 by V. Scholderer; parts 9– by G. D. Painter.

Gives full bibliographical descriptions; each volume includes excellent reproduced facsimiles of a sampling of the characteristic types in use [Proctor's Index to the early printed books in the British Museum provides the basis for this much fuller catalog.] Part 3 has an introduction to the whole of the German section (parts 1–3), with a typographical map and indices to Hain's and Proctor's numbers; part 7 has an introduction to the whole of the Italian section (parts 4–7), with similar indices. Part 9 brings the total number of entries past the 10,000 mark. Arranged in "Proctor order," i.e., by countries, towns and presses chronologically, according to date of printing.

BURGER, Konrad. Supplement zu Hain und Panzer; Beiträge zur Inkunabelbibliographie. Num
mernconcordanz von Panzers lateinischen und deutschen Annalen und Ludwig Hains Repertorium bibliographicum. (Reprografischer Nachdruck der Ausg. Leipzig 1908.) Hildesheim, G. Olms, 1966. vii, 440p.   **AB4**

On cover: Beiträge zur Inkunabelbibliographie. Hain, Ludwig Friedrich Theodor, 1781–1836. Repertorium bibliographicum.

COPINGER, Walter Arthur. Supplement to Hain's *Repertorium bibliographicum;* or, Collections toward a new edition of that work. In 2 parts. Milano, Ghorlich, [1950].   **AB5**

Copinger's *Supplement* added about 6,000 new entries to Hain. Part 1 contains nearly 7,000 corrections of and additions to the collation of works described in Hain. Part 2 is a list of nearly 6,000 works printed in the 15th century and not in Hain (p.319–670): "The printers and publishers of the XVth century with lists of their works" by Konrad Burger.

FLODR, Miroslav. Incunabula classicorum; Wiegendrucke der griechischen und römischen Literatur. Amsterdam, A. M. Hakkert, 1973. xv, 530p.
AB6

BBF XIX 1974 450–451 Labarre

An easy-to-consult, alphabetically arranged register of Greek and Latin authors from Anius to Zenobius. Homerus has 25 entries, Horatius 86, Vergilius 185, and Donatus Aelius 457. There are detailed numerical concordances with *Gesamtkatalog der Wiegendrucke* and Hain.

GESAMTKATALOG der Wiegendrucke; Herausgegeben von der Kommission für den Gesamtkatalog der Wiegendrucke. Leipzig, Hiersemann, 1925– .   **AB7**

Publications suspended from 1940–1971. Resumed with revised Bd. VIII, fasz. 1, ed. by the Deutsche Staatsbibliothek zu Berlin, published by Anton Hiersemann, Stuttgart and Akademie-Verlag, Berlin.

As far as published, the most comprehensive record of incunabula in existence, with much more bibliographical detail than in Hain, dealing with types, capitals and illustrations, transcripts of title, colophon, and other extracts. The volumes issued record nearly half again as many editions (estimated to be at least 40,000 volumes) as does Hain. Band I includes lengthy entries on Aelianus Tacticus and Aesopus, Vita et Fabulae.

GOFF, Frederick R. Incunabula in American libraries; A third census of fifteenth-century books recorded in North American collections. Reproduced from the annotated copy maintained by Frederick R. Goff, compiler and editor. Millwood, N. Y., Kraus Reprint Co., 1973 [c1964]. lxiii, 798p.   **AB8**

Reprint of the ed. published by the Bibliographical Society of America, New York; annotated and corrected, with new introd. and list of dealers.

Between 1964 and 1972 an astonishing number of incunabula were added to libraries and collections in the United States. The Third Census of 1964 recorded 47,188 incunabula in the United States, whereas the reprint with annotations records more than 51,000. A new feature in the reprint edition is a list of dealers and auction houses whose names appear within the text. The new census follows the pattern of the 1940 edition by Stillwell. The author entries remain essentially as they appeared in 1940. Hain's entries serve as the basis, and changes in his basic order were made only when both the British Museum Catalogue and the Gesamtkatalog der Wiegendrucke agreed on a new entry differing from Hain.

HAEBLER, Konrad. The study of incunabula. Trans. by Lucy Eugenia Osborne, with a foreword by Alfred W. Pollard. New York, The Grolier Club, 1933. New York, Kraus Reprint Co., 1967. 241p. **AB9**

"Translated from the German *Handbuch der Inkunabelkunde,* 1925, but embodies also certain revisions of the text made by the author in 1932." (Translator's note.)

A practical description, unencumbered by footnotes or bibliography, dealing with all aspects of the production and form of the early book.

HAIN, Ludwig Friedrich T. Repertorium bibliographicum; In quo libri omnes ab arte typographica inventa usque ad annum MD. typis expressi, ordine alphabetico vel simpliciter enumerantur vel adcuratius recensentur. Opera Ludovici Hain. Stuttgartiae, J. G. Cotta; 1826–1838. 2 v. **AB10**

"Index urbium et typographorum": v. 2, part 2.

Describes over 16,000 editions of incunabula in alphabetical order and numbered serially. A successor to Wolfgang Panzer, *Annales typographici ab artis inventae origine ad annum MD* (Nürnberg, 1793–1797), which recorded 15,000 entries. It falls short of recording the total number of incunabula, now put at over 35,000. Incunabula (Latin, swaddling clothes, hence cradle) refer to books produced in the first stages of the art of printing and especially those printed before 1500, of which a very large proportion were religious. The earliest known book printed with movable type is the Mazarin Bible. The first known book with a date and the printer's name is the *Mainz psalter* of 1457. The first printers working in Germany devoted much labor to reproducing the classics of medieval learning in large volumes, most of them ending up in monastic libraries. In Italy the demand for Latin classics was over-estimated and after four years of intense activity the market was overstocked for a time, but there was a gradual recovery. The Latin presses were responsible for more than 200 of some 340 recorded editions of Cicero, the favorite of the humanists. Besides authors Hain's *Repertorium* includes useful information under such headings as Biblia Latina, Breviarium, Missale, Psalterium.

LEGRAND, Émile Louis Jean. Bibliographie hellénique; ou, Description raisonnée des ouvrages publiés en grec par des Grecs aux XVe et XVIe siècles. Paris [E. Leroux] 1885–1906. Bruxelles, Culture et Civilisation, 1963. 4 v., illus., ports. **AB11**

"Reimpression anastatique."

Begins with the year 1601 and arranges works published by Greeks chronologically. There are no annotations. Each volume has an alphabetical index and a chronological table. Useful for patristic and Byzantine works. Legrand's work was completed posthumously by Mgr. Louis Petit and Hubert Pernot.

PALMER, Henrietta Raymer. List of English editions and translations of Greek and Latin classics printed before 1641. With an introduction by Victor Scholderer. Norwood, Pa., Norwood Editions, 1976. xxxii, 119p. **AB12**

Reprint of the 1911 ed., issued in series by the Bibliographical Society, London: Publications.

An alphabetical list of works by author in the British Library, Bodleian and Cambridge University libraries and elsewhere. Translations are given in chronological order of publication. Detailed bibliographical data.

PEDDIE, Robert Alexander. Fifteenth-century books; A guide to their identification. With a list of Latin names of towns and an extensive bibliography of the subject. New York, B. Franklin, [1969]. 89p. **AB13**

Burt Franklin bibliography and reference series; 294. "Originally published: 1913."

This short work aims at cataloging and describing all the important works dealing with books printed before 1501, giving information on the author, the printer or the place of publication of a book, as also works dealing with types, illustrations, watermarks and all the other minutiae which go to make up the study of the 15th-century book. The preface points out that the collection of incunabula is almost impossible for anyone but the millionaire, but the study of the subject, thanks to the great libraries, is open to all.

Chapter headings include Catalogues of Libraries, National Catalogues, Bibliographies of Special Subjects, Types, Facsimiles, Greek Printing, Woodcuts and Engraving, Block Books, Single Prints, Book Illustration, Colour Printing, Maps, Initials, Printers' Marks, Colophons, Little Pages, Signatures, Water Marks. Appendix A (43f.) provides an alphabetical index of the Latin names of towns in which printing was established during the 15th century, with their vernacular equivalents.

PROCTOR, Robert G. C. An index to the early printed books in the British Museum. London, Holland Press, 1960– . **AB14**

Because of his extraordinary eye for a variety of types and his ability to classify printers in their various centers of work, Proctor revolutionized the study of incunabula and laid the basis for its scientific study. Part 1, to 1500: v. 1. Germany; v. 2. Italy; v. 3. Switzerland to Montenegro, including France, the Netherlands, Austria-Hungary, Spain, England, Scandinavia, Portugal; v. 4. Register, 1898–1899. It is arranged as a chronological list under each country by names of presses.

(There is a list of books mentioned by Hain.) Part 2, 1501–1520: section 1. Germany, 1903; section 2. Italy; section 3. Switzerland and Eastern Europe, by Frank Isaac, London.

REICHLING, Dietrich. Appendices ad Hainii-Copingeri Repertorivm bibliographicvm; Additiones et emendationes. Milano, Görlic Editore, [1953]. 8 v. in 2. **AB15**

Parts 1–6 consist of two sections each: I. Additiones; II. Emendationes. Part [7]: Indices fascicvlorvm I.–VI. Svpplementvm (maximam partem e bibliothecis Helvetiae collectvm) cvm indice vrbivm et typographorvm. Accedit index avctorum generalis totivs operis. Reprint of 1905–1914 edition.

STILLWELL, Margaret B. Incunabula in American libraries; A second census of fifteenth-century books owned in the United States, Mexico and Canada. New York, Bibliographical Society of America, 1940. xiv, 619p. **AB16**

This project was begun by the Bibliographical Society of America in 1924 as a successor to Winship's *Census of fifteenth century books owned in America* which was published five years before. Authors are listed alphabetically; titles also are alphabetical. Editions are entered chronologically, with those without date-assignment appearing at the end. As in Hain, Latin editions appear first. Hain is used as the basis for the format. If unknown to Hain, usage in the other bibliographies of incunabula has been followed.

AC BIBLIOGRAPHY, GREEK AND LATIN

AMERICAN Bibliographical Service International guide to classical studies. Darien, Conn., American Bibliographic Service, v. 1– , June 1961– . **AC1**

ABS International guides is a series of quarterly subject indices to current periodical literature. Major articles and minor contributions appearing in journals throughout the world in English, French, German and other European languages are indexed numerically and alphabetically by author. Uninformative titles are amplified by explicatory notes. The detailed Subject Index in every quarterly issue provides a direct guide to the contents (topics, personalities, texts, manuscripts, inscriptions, etc.) of each paper.

AMERICAN Bibliographical Service international guide to medieval studies. Darien, Conn., American Bibliographic Service, v. 1– , June 1961– . **AC2**

Each issue lists articles alphabetically by author, followed by cumulative author and subject indices. Also includes a book review index.

L'ANNÉE philologique; Bibliographie critique et analytique de l'antiquité gréco-latine. 1. année; 1924/26– . Paris, Société d'édition "Les Belles lettres," 1928– . **AC3**

Collection de bibliographie classique publiée sous le patronage de l'Association Guillaume Budé, Editor: 1924/26– Jules Marouzeau.
The standard bibliography for classical studies since 1924. It consists of two main parts, the first an alphabetical listing of Auteurs et Textes, the second covering Métiers et Disciplines. Part II has ten sub-divisions: Histoire Littéraire, Linguistique et Philologie, Histoire des Textes, Antiquités, Histoire, Droit, Philosophie, Sciences, Techniques et Métiers, Les Études Classiques,

Mélanges et Recueils. Each section has sub-divisions, e.g., Histoire des Textes: Paléographie, Papyrologie, Critique des Textes. Issued annually, there are no cumulative editions and no value judgments. Generally the year of publication is two years later than the year of coverage. Books continue to be listed for five years if reviews are forthcoming, and occasionally for longer, in the event of later reviews of considerable length or importance. Unchanged reprints are generally not recorded. Beginning with Tome XLVII (1976) each item has an identifying number.

ARCHÄOLOGISCHE Bibliographie. Berlin, De Gruyter, 1973– . **AC4**

Issued 1973– by Deutsches Archäologisches Institut. Continues *Archäologische Bibliographie* which was issued until 1972 as a supplement to *Deutsches Archäologisches Institut. Jahrbuch.* One of the most important reference tools for the study of ancient art. See also the *Deutsches Archäeologisches Institut.* Autoren-und Periodica Kataloge (Boston Hall, 1969), which consists of the author and classified catalogs, in all over 200,000 photolithographically produced cards.

ARTHUR, Marilyn. Classics and psychology. Urbana, American Philological Assoc., 1978. **AC5**

BIBLIOGRAFÍA de los estudios clásicos en España, 1939–1955; Redactada por un grupo de estudiosos y publicada con motivo del primer Congreso Español de Estudios Clásicos. Madrid, Congreso Español de Estudios Clásicos, 1956. xvi, 453p. **AC6**

Athenaeum XXXIV 1956 229 Malcovati • BAGB 1957 297–298 Rochefort • Latomus XVI 1957 210 Préaux • RPh XXXI 1957 336 Ernout

This work was composed and published on the occasion of the first Spanish congress on classical languages held in Salamanca, April 1956. It is systematically divided into 20 sections: texts and translations, dictionaries, hermeneutics, linguistics, metrics, literature, history, geography, law, history of science, archaeology, epigraphy and paleography, humanistics, scholarly works, methodology of ancient classics, history of classical scholarship, the classical heritage, and bibliography. The work as a whole, over 6,000 references, testifies to the vitality and diversity of classical studies in Spain for the period covered. There are accurate indices. It is especially useful for pre-Roman and Visigothic Spain.

BIBLIOGRAPHIE internationale de l'Humanisme et de la Renaissance. Genève, Librairie Droz, 1965– .   **AC7**

Prepared under the patronage of the Fédérato internationale des sociétés et instituts pour l'étude de la Renaissance.
MLR LXVII 1972 607–609
In v. VI there were 6,751 entries, an increase of almost 600 over v. V, with more periodicals and more volumes of miscellanies sifted than previously. Coverage seems to be best for literature and less extensive for history and art. An index of proper names and subjects runs to about 100 pages. Initial volumes were criticized as a very amateur effort and far from complete.
See also: Id. XIV: Travaux parus en 1978: Genève, Droz, 1983. clxii, 922p.
Also: Id. XV: Travaux parus en 1979: Genève, Droz, 1983. cxxviii, 731p.

BIBLIOTHECA classica orientalis. Berlin, [Akademie der Wissenschaftern. Institut für griechisch-romische Altertumskunde], 1956–1969. Volumes 1–14.   **AC8**

Ceased publication. A quarterly survey of classical scholarship in the USSR and other Slavic countries, especially in Byzantine studies. It surveys books and scholarly articles in 18 sections: General; Texts and Authors; Scholarly Aids to Philology; Scholarly Aids to Ancient History; Ethnography, Geography, Topography; Political, Social and Economic History; Linguistics; Literary History; Archaeology and History of Art; Religion and Mythology; State and Law; Philosophy and Pedagogy; Ancient Science; Medieval and Neo-Latin; Nachleben den Antike; Altertum und Schule. No more than one or two items are reviewed (all in German) in some sections; mostly Russian or German titles.

ENGLEMANN, Wilhelm. Bibliotheca scriptorum classicorum; 8. Aufl. umfassend die Literatur von 1700 bis 1878, neu bearb. von dr. E. Preuss. Hildesheim, George Olms, 1959. 2 v.   **AC9**

1. Abt. Scriptores graeci. 2. Abt. Scriptores latini. Reprint of 1880 ed. published by W. Englemann.
Continues classical scholarship to 1878. Volume 1.

Scriptores Graeci: Section A covers Collectiones (Anecdota graeca, Oratores, Poetae, Rhetores, Scriptores, e.g., biographici, erotici, geographici). Section B (p.76–799) covers the individual Scriptores Graeci alphabetically from Abantis fragmenta to Zosimus Panopolitanus. Volume 2. Scriptores Latini follows the same twofold division and (p.37–738) covers writers from Ablavias to Vulcacius. There is a brief Nachträge und Berichtigungen at the end of v. I and a more extensive one for both volumes, at the end of v. II.

FABRICIUS, Johann Albert. Bibliotheca graeca. Hildesheim, G. Olms, 1966–1970. 12 v.   **AC10**

Facsimile reprint of Hamburg ed., 1790–1809.

FABRICIUS, Johann Albert. Bibliotheca latina mediae et infimae aetatis. Florentiae, typ. T. Barracchi et f., 1858–1859. [Graz, Akademische Druck-u. Verlagsanstalt Graz, 1962]. 6 v. in 3; 2 port. (incl. front.).   **AC11**

Fabricius completed the *Bibliotheca latina* in 1697. He then began his far more extensive *Bibliotheca graeca,* a work that in the course of 14 quarto volumes (1705–1728) traverses the whole range of Greek literature down to the fall of Constantinople. It is founded, as much as possible, on a first-hand knowledge of every edition quoted, and it has supplied the basis for all subsequent histories of Greek literature. The 350 quarto pages assigned to Homer alone include indices to all the authors cited in the scholia and in Eustathius. The work on Latin literature was subsequently continued in five volumes of the *Bibliotheca latina mediae et infimae aetatis* (1734).

FABRICIUS, Johann Albert. Jo. Alberti Fabricii Bibliotheca latina; Sive Notitia auctorum veterum latinorum, quorumque scripta ad nos pervanerunt, distributa in libros IV. Supplementis., quae antea sejunctim excusa maximo lectorum incommodo legebantur, suis quibusque locis nunc primum insertis. Venetiis, apud Sebastium Coleti, 1728. 2 v.   **AC12**

GOODWATER, L. Women in antiquity; An annotated bibliography. Metuchen, N. J., 1975. iv, 171p.   **AC13**

CJ LXXIII 1978 264 Snyder • CW LXX 1977 413 Pomeroy
This is one librarian's attempt to provide a bibliographic introduction to "historical women of antiquity . . . for college undergraduates in either women's studies or ancient history classes, or as a starting point for more advanced research by graduate students and professors." The principal rubrics are Women Authors (ancient); Male Authors (ancient); General Works on Women (Greece and Rome); Women in Greece; Etruscan Women; and Women in Rome and its Provinces. There are two indices: Women in Antiquity, and Authors, Editors and Translators.

GWINUP, Thomas and DICKINSON, Fidelia. Greek and Roman authors; A checklist of criticism. Metuchen, N. J., Scarecrow Press, 1973. x, 194p. **AC14**

G&R XXI 1974 100–101 Walcot
Aims to provide a comprehensive list of recent criticism (in English only) of about 70 authors of belles-lettres of ancient Greece and Rome. Primarily literary bibliography, in general it excludes items of a character abstractly philosophical, narrowly philological or clearly doctrinal. There is a definite emphasis on more recent items. The work has been designed primarily for the use of students in the increasingly popular courses in comparative and world literature, as well as other courses in the humanities.

HERESCU, Niculae I. Bibliographie de la littérature latine. Paris, Société d'édition "Les Belles lettres," 1943. xviii, 426p. **AC15**

Collection de bibliographie classique, pub. sous la direction de J. Marouzeau.
AJPh LXIX 1948 341–344 McDermott
The aim is to provide within a compact volume and arranged alphabetically a critical bibliography useful for students and teachers. The work appeared in 1943 but only covers down to 1939. Each period of Latin literature gets a single chapter: archaic, pre-Ciceronian, Ciceronian, Augustan, early Empire, Christian to the 5th century. Authors are generally treated under such headings as bibliography, manuscripts, scholiasts, complete editions, partial editions, indices and dictionaries, translations, studies. The work was undertaken under the influence of Marouzeau and is a worthy supplement to *L'Année philologique* for the period before World War II. There is an alphabetical index to Latin authors, but none for secondary authors.

HOFFMANN, Samuel Friedrich W. Lexicon bibliographicum; Sive Index editionum et interpretationum scriptorum graecorum tum sacrorum tum profanorum. Lipsiae, Sumptibus J.A.G. Weigel, 1832–1836. 3 v. **AC16**

Second edition published 1838–1845 under title: *Bibliographisches Lexikon der gesammten Litteratur der Griechen.*

HÜBNER, Ernst Willibald Emil. Bibliographie der klassischen Altertumswissenschaft; Grundriss zu Vorlesungen über d. Geschichte u. Encyklopädie d. klass. Philologie. Nachdr. d. 2., verm. Aufl. Berlin 1889. Hildesheim, New York, Olms, 1973. xiii, 434p. **AC17**

First ed. published in 1876 under title: *Grundriss zu Vorlesungen über die Geschichte und Encyklopädie der classischen Philologie.*
An introductory chapter gives bibliography on the place of classical scholarship in university studies, and on the definition of classical scholarship. Part I covers the history of classical scholarship from the Sophists to the grammarians of the 5th and 6th centuries, through the Middle Ages and the Renaissance, with separate sections on Italy, France, the Netherlands, England and Germany. The present is surveyed with its varied university activities and scholarly journals. Part II encompasses Die Encyclopedie der Klassischen Philologie: Languages, Grammar, Metrics, Rhetoric, Palaeography, Criticism and Hermeneutics, History of Literature, Religions, Political History, Geography, Individual countries, Chronology, Art and Architecture, Metrology and Numismatics, Epigraphy, Domestic Life. There are subject and author indices. Sandys, *History of classical scholarship,* pays deserved tribute to Hübner's "many works especially the *History of classical philology* including an excellent bibliography which has been of service in the preparation of the present work."

JAHRESBERICHT über die fortschritte der Klassischen Altertumswissenschaft. Berlin and Leipzig, S. Calvary and Company, O. R. Reisland, 1873–1956. 285 v. **AC18**

The years 1873 and 1874/75 are in 2 v. each; v. 1 of 1874/75 is entitled Die Fortschritte der philologie; v. 2 Die Fortschritte der Altertumswissenschaft. Beginning with 1876 each year consists of 3 v., Griechische Klassiker (later, Griechische autoren), Lateinische Klassiker (later, Lateinische autoren) and Altertumswissenschaft, with the addition of the supplements Bibliotheca philologica classica and Biographisches Jahrbuch für Altertumskunde (called from 1907 to 1924 Bibliographisches Jahrbuch für die Altertumswissenschaft). Jahresbericht and Bibliographisches Jahrbuch each combine the years 1916/18; Bibliotheca philologica classica has a separate volume for each year.
The *Jahresbericht* is frequently referred to as Bursian's Jahresbericht. It was superseded by *Lustrum.* For a classical list of articles to 1923 see McFayden, D., "Fifty years of Bursian's Jahresberichte," Washington, D.C., University Studies XII Humanistic series (1924), 111–114.

KLUSSMANN, Rudolf. Bibliotheca scriptorum classicorum et graecorum et latinorum. Die Literatur von 1878 bis 1896 einschliesslich umfassend. Hildesheim, Georg Olms, 1961, 1976. Reprint of the 1909–1913 edition. 4 parts in 2 v. ii, 115p. **AC19**

Each volume issued in 2 parts, each part with special title page and separate paging. "Erscheint auch als . . . [bd.] 146, [151, 156, 165] des Jahresberichtes über die Forschritte der klassischen Altertumswissenschaft."
Continues Englemann from 1878 to 1896. Originally published in Bursian's *Jahresbericht.*

KRISTELLER, Paul Oscar and CRANZ, F. Edward. Catalogus Translationum et Commentariorum; Medieval and Renaissance Latin translations and commentaries. Annotated lists and guides. Washington, D.C., The Catholic University of America Press, v. 1, 1960– . **AC20**

At head of title: Union académique internationale. RPhL LXXII 1974 201 Pattin • Gnomon XLV 1973 185–195 Krautter • Gnomon L 1978 545–549 Krautter • Gnomon LV 1983 456–459 Krautter

Among the Greek authors that have already appeared in this excellent series (v. IV, 1980) are Aeschylus, ps.-Longinus, Strabo, and Theophrastus, while Latin authors include Caesar, Livy, Juvenal, Persius and Petronius.

LAMBRINO, Scarlat. Bibliographie de l'antiquité classique, 1896–1914. Paris, Société d'édition "Les Belles Lettres," 1951– . **AC21**

Collection de bibliographie classique; 1. Continued by Jules Marouzeau's *Dix années de bibliographie classique.*

REA LIV 1952 119–120 Boyancé • Paideia IX 1954 45–47 Herescu

The works of Englemann-Preuss and Klussmann with the common title *Bibliotheca scriptorum classicorum* brought coverage of classical scholarship down to 1878 and 1896, i.e., to the beginning of the most productive period in the domain of classical antiquity. The present work fills the lacuna between 1896 and 1914 where Marouzeau begins his *Dix années,* and was undertaken by Lambrino at the suggestion of Marouzeau. The work was planned for two volumes: I. Auteurs et Textes, which appeared in 1951, and II. Matières et Disciplines, which was for long announced as in preparation, but now: il n'est pas envisagé de publier la 2 partie. Part 1 extends from Abercii Vita to Zosimus Panopolitanus, and includes notices of reviews. There are about 30,000 entries.

LEEMAN, Anton Daniël. Bibliographia latina selecta; Composita ab A. D. Leeman; operam praebentibus G. Bouma, H. Pinkster. Amsterdam, A. M. Hakkert, 1966. 173p. **AC22**

BBF XII 1967 158–160 Ernst

Has two parts: I–Artes, II–Auctores. Part I is divided into sections: Bibliographica, Encyclopaedia, Ars grammatica, Ars Metrica, Historia, Litteraria, Ius Romanum, Palaeographia, Ars critica, Historia philologiae, Antiquitas superstes, Collectanea et fragmenta. Part II deals with the archaic literature to Pacuvius and Atticus and then the individual authors and works from Plautus to Pervigilium Veneris chronologically. Useful for identifying the chief editions, translations and commentaries down to 1966, and the availability of indices or concordances for individual authors. Alternate pages are left blank for insertion of addenda by the reader.

MAROUZEAU, Jules. Dix années de bibliographie classique; bibliographie critique et analytique de l'antiquité gréco-latine pour la période 1914–1924. Paris, Société d'édition "Les Belles lettres," 1969. 2 v. **AC23**

Collection de bibliographie publiée sous le patronage de l'Association Guillaume Budé.

These two volumes cover the period 1914–1924 and are similar in coverage to Lambrino. Volume 1 covers Auteurs et Textes; v. 2, Matières et Disciplines. The order is substantially the same as in *L'Année philologique.*

MASQUERAY, Paul. Bibliographie pratique de la littérature grecque; des origines à la fin de la période romaine. Paris, C. Klincksieck, 1914. 334p. **AC24**

AJPh XXXV 1914 109–110 • CR 1914 285 Appleton • REA 1914 109–110 Navarre

The book's stated aim is "indiquer sur chaque auteur le livre capital, l'article important, l'édition dont il faut se servir, le manuscrit . . . auquel il est nécessaire de remonter; puis—dire pour chaque auteur, pour chaque ouvrage, ce qu'on sait, ce qu'on ne sait pas, ce qu'on cherche, les principales questions qu'on tâche de resondre." The introduction gives a bibliography of works on literature, grammar, dialects, metrics, lexicography and history. There are good remarks on how to construct a bibliography. The main body of the work is divided into two books—before and after Aristotle—and classifies the authors as historians, orators, etc. The bibliography is very personal, as is the presentation; the primacy of Germany in philology is rightly insisted upon.

MENÉNDEZ Y PELAYO, Marcelino. Biblioteca de traductores españoles; Edición preparada por Enrique Sánchez Reyes. Santander, Aldus, 1952–1953. 4 v. **AC25**

His *Edición nacional de las obras completas;* 54–57.

RBPh XXXI 1953 556–557 Bakelants • LEC XIX 1951 274–275 Van Ooteghem

A bibliography listing Spanish editions of Latin classics including manuscripts, editions, commentaries, translations, critical works, imitations and works showing the influence of Latin classics on Spanish literature. This bibliography is more a collection of notes than a repertory of titles, and the notes will have more interest for the humanist than the philologist, but they testify to immense erudition in all domains and all authors of Latin antiquity.

NAIRN, John A. J. A. Nairn's classical hand-list. Edited by B. H. Blackwell Ltd. 3d ed., rev. and enl. Oxford, Blackwell, 1953. viii, 164p. **AC26**

First ed. published in 1931 under title: *A hand-list of books relating to the classics and classical antiquity.*

This bibliography is a classified list without annotations, giving the author, brief title and publisher. It covers general reference works under the headings: collections and individual texts, histories of Greek and Latin literature, philology, paleography, papyrology, epigraphy, history, religion and mythology, philosophy, music, science, mathematics and medicine, geography, archeology, art, numismatics and periodicals.

OOTEGHEM, Jules van. Bibliotheca graeca et latina à l'usage des professeurs des humanités gréco-latines. 2. éd. rev. et augm. Namur, Les Études classiques, [1946]. 386p. **AC27**

"La première édition . . . parut dans la revue les Études classiques, la Bibliotheca latina . . . avril 1936, la Bibliotheca graeca a partir d'octobre 1936."

Latomus 1947 281–283 Delvaux • AJPh LXIX 1948 341–344 McDermott

The work is divided into three parts: Part I. Indications préliminaires, general works, bibliography, geography, Greek history, Roman history, history of Greek and Latin literature, Greek grammar, Greek and Latin metre, Latin grammar, Greek lexicography, Latin lexicography. Parts II and III deal chronologically with the main Greek and Latin authors. In his preface van Ooteghem states that his aims are limited: it is planned, not as a complete bibliography, but particularly as an aid for teachers in secondary schools. The organization is simpler than in the case of Herescu's, *Bibliographie de la littérature latine*. For the majority of the items a very brief comment is included at the end in parenthesis.

PÖSCHL, Viktor et al. Bibliographie zur antiken Bildersprache. Unter Leitung von Viktor Pöschl bearb. von Helga Gärtner und Waltraut Heyke. Heidelberg, C. Winter, 1964. xvi, 674p.   **AC28**

Bibliothek der klassischen Altertumswissenschaften; n. F. 1, Reihe.

This extremely useful bibliography on imagery in antiquity surveys general works under the following headings: Linguistik; Literaturgeschichte; Literaturwissenschaft; Mythologie; Philosophie; Religion.

Greek and Latin authors are treated alphabetically, including Greek and Latin Fathers, Hermetica, Testamentum Novum et Vetus, Oracula Sibyllina. The images are listed alphabetically with cross-references to the previous sections and there are three Anhänge. An index of modern scholars, with cross-references and a list of abbreviations complete the work.

QUARTERLY CHECK-LIST of classical studies. Darien, Conn. [etc.], American Bibliographic Service, v. 1, October 1958– .   **AC29**

Published as ABS quarterly checklists.
See *International guide to classical studies.*

QUARTERLY CHECK-LIST of medievalia. Darien, Conn. [etc.], American Bibliographic Service, v. 1, January 1958.   **AC30**

An international index of current books, monographs and brochures.

SCHNEEMELCHER, W. Bibliographia patristica; Internationale patristische bibliographie. Berlin, Walter de Gruyter & Co., 1959– .   **AC31**

After a somewhat slow start because of technical problems, this extremely well organized tool is now at XXII–XXIII, Die Erscheinungen der Jahre 1977 und 1978, published in 1982. The list of abbreviations

(IX–XL) shows the range of coverage. Generalia has 11 subsections, including series editionum et versionum; collectanea et miscellanea. There is a special section on Novum Testamentum atque Apocrypha. The most frequently consulted section, doubtless, will be Auctores (p.44–128) which is arranged alphabetically and includes in the sub-section Hagiographica such unlikely figures as Martha and Pontius Pilate. There are excellent sections on Liturgica, Iuridica, symbola, doctrina auctorum et historia dogmatum, Gnostica, Patrum exegesis Veteris et Novi Testamenti, and the final section Recensiones collects references to reviews of entries in previous years, alphabetically. This omits titles, is by author only and presumes access to previous volumes of *Bibliographia patristica*. A register of modern scholars completes a most valuable bibliographical tool.

SCHWEIGER, Franz Ludwig A. Handbuch der classischen Bibliographie. Leipzig, F. Fleischer, 1830–1834. 2 v. in 3.   **AC32**

1. th. Griechische Schriftsteller. 2. th., 1. abt. Lateinische Schriftsteller. A–L. 2. th., 2. abt. Lateinische Schriftsteller. M–V. Sammlungen mehrerer lateinischer Schrifsteller. Berichtigungen und Zusätze.
Continues the work of Fabricius to 1820.

THOMPSON, Lawrence Sidney. A bibliography of American doctoral dissertations in classical studies and related fields. [Hamden, Conn.], Shoe String Press, 1968. xii, 250p.   **AC33**

According to the preface, "all aspects of the culture of Greece and Rome, from the prehistory of Greece and Italy through the arbitrary terminal date of 500 A.D. are included . . . literature, history, art, architecture, archaeology, folklore, religion, law, linguistics, science, philosophy, politics and government, manners and customs, social and economic conditions, indeed, cultural history in general." Author listing with detailed subject and title index.

THOMPSON, Lawrence Sidney. A bibliography of dissertations in classical studies: American, 1964–1972; British, 1950–1972; with a cumulative index, 1869–1972. Hamden, Conn., Shoe String Press, 1976. viii, 296p.   **AC34**

This volume is a continuation of the compiler's "A bibliography of American doctoral dissertations in classical studies and related fields." (1968). It includes British dissertations, both for the doctorate and for other degrees which were listed in the "Index to theses accepted for higher degrees in the universities of Great Britain and Ireland" for the years 1950–1951 through 1971. The index is cumulative for authors, subjects, titles and places.

TOBEY, J. L. The history of ideas; a bibliographical introduction. 1. Classical Antiquity. Santa Barbara, Cal., Clio Books, 1975– .   **AC35**

AD CRITICAL BIBLIOGRAPHICAL SURVEYS

ANZEIGER für die Altertumswissenschaft. Wien, A. Sexl., 1948– . **AD1**

4 no. a year. "Hrsg. von der Österreichischen Humanistischen Gesellschaft."

Contains annotated bibliographical surveys on individual authors (especially Homer) and literary genres (especially Greek tragedy) as well as individual reviews of new books.

BÜCHNER, Karl and HOFMANN, J. B. Lateinische Literatur und Sprache in der Forschung seit 1937. Bern, A. Francke, 1951. 299p. **AD2**

Wissenschaftliche Forschungsberichte. Geisteswissenschaftliche Reihe; Bd. 6.

A & R II 1952 172–174 Prato • AC XXI 1952 477 Lambrechts • Latomus XII 1953 99 Leroy

Büchner's section (p.4–240, p.285–293) is especially valuable on Latin literature down to Boethius. Hofmann's contribution on Latin language is less well organized and less comprehensive. Büchner's indebtedness to Fuchs's earlier masterly survey of the development of Latin studies (*Mus. Helv.* IV 1946, 147–198) is acknowledged, but the present work is more helpful, with detailed critical reviews of important works and valuable directions on what remains to be done. Hofmann's part only covers the period 1931–1937, reprinted from Bursian's *Jahresberichte* CCLXX (1940), 3–122, with some additions.

BYZANTINISCHE Zeitschrift. München, C. H. Beck'sche Verlagsbuchhandlung [etc.], v. 1– , 1892– . **AD3**

Contains very complete annual surveys on all aspects of Byzantine studies. See *Dumbarton Oaks biblioga-phies.*

CLASSICAL ASSOCIATION. The year's work in classical studies. Bristol, J. W. Arrowsmith, 34 v. [1st]–34th year, 1906–1947. **AD4**

In 1907 published in London by J. Murray. Classical Association.

AAHG III 1950 235 Muth • CPh 1949 280 Larsen • JHS LXX 1950 78 Jones • REL 1949 406 Marouzeau

Suspended publication after 34 numbers in 1945–1947, since it was felt that *L'Année philologique* (which did not exist in 1906 when *The year's work* started) met specialists' needs better, and *Greece and Rome* and *Classical review* kept the schoolmaster and the amateur informed.

The format remained pretty constant during the life of this useful annual: extended survey articles on Greek literature, Latin literature, history, ancient philosophy, comparative philology, Latin paleography, papyrology, etc., each by a well-known scholar generally surveying the outstanding work in monographs and periodicals of the previous year, but sometimes covering a longer period. Bibliographical references, in abbreviated form, are given at the end of each survey.

DAREMBERG, Charles V. and SAGLIO, Edm. Dictionnaire des antiquités grecques et romains; [Photomechanischer Nachdruck der 1962–1963 ed.]. Graz, Akademische Druck-u. Verlagsanstalt, 1969. 6 v. in 10, illus., facsims., maps, plans. **AD5**

REA 1917 301 Radet • REG XXXI 1918 103 Peuch

This greatly respected dictionary of Greek and Roman antiquities is based on the texts and the monuments. It is a collaborative work of signed entries with over 7,000 black and white figures. As its subtitle indicates it contains an explanation of terms which refer to mores, institutions, religion and in general to public and private life in antiquity. Its entries, some of which understandably are badly out-of-date, are always methodical and clear. A valuable guide to the material culture of antiquity, covering such topics as commerce, furniture, military affairs, money, weights and measures.

DEE, James E. "A survey of recent bibliographies of classical literature." CW LXXIII (1979–1980): 275–290. **AD6**

A useful checklist for the major individual authors.

DONLAN, Walter, ed. The Classical World Bibliography of Greek drama and poetry. New York, Garland Publishing, 1977. **AD7**

"Reprints of the Classical World bibliographical surveys, published from 1953 to 1976."

Includes bibliographies already published in *CW* on Homer, Greek lyric poetry, Aeschylus, Sophocles, Euripides, Aristophanes and Menander.

See also Donlan, Walter, ed., *The Classical World bibliography of Greek and Roman history* (1977); *The Classical World bibliography of philosophy, religion, and rhetoric* (1977); *The Classical World bibliography of Roman drama and poetry and ancient fiction* (1977), *The Classical World bibliography of Vergil* (1978).

ENCICLOPEDIA italiana di scienze, lettere ed arti. Roma, Istituto della Enciclopedia, 1952. 35 v. **AD8**

Contains excellent long articles, many bibliographies and a wealth of illustrations of all types, good maps and colored plates. All articles are signed. See, for example, Latina, Lingua, v. 20 (p.581–592), by Pier Ga-

briele Goidanich; Orazio, v. 25 (p.440–444), by Ferdinando Neri.

ERANOS; Acta philologica suecana. Upsaliae
[etc.], Eranos' Förlag [etc.], v. 1–, 1896– .
                                                    AD9

Volumes 1–50, 1896–1952, in v. 50.
See the irregular feature Bibliografisk Översikt for
critical bibliographical surveys, e.g., v. 71 (1973), 121–
192.

FIFTY years (and twelve) of classical scholarship.
2d ed., having been only *Fifty years of . . .* , rev.
with appendices. Oxford, Blackwell, 1968. xv,
523p.   **AD10**

1st ed. published in 1954 as *Fifty years of classical
scholarship,* ed. by Maurice Platnauer.
CPh LXIV 1969 64 Bruère • CW XLIX 1956 113–
128, 145–160 Dow et al • Hermathena LXXXVI 1955
45–49 Stanford • Hermathena CVIII 1969 58–59 Rodgers
To commemorate the jubilee of the Classical Association some Oxford scholars combined under the editorship of the vice-principal of Brasenose College, M. Platnauer, to produce this survey of classical research
since 1904. The product is less a synoptical account
of the whole field than a series of chapters on the
traditional genres: epic, tragedy, comedy, etc. The
opening chapter on Homer by Dodds is extremely partial to the analysts and unfair to such Unitarians as
J. A. Scott.
The first edition covered 50 years up to 1954. Each
chapter has discussion of trends and influences in research, and extensive bibliography. The second edition
adds an appendix to most chapters to bring work current to 1966. Some appendices include discussion, as
in original chapters, others just bibliographies. Of 523
pages in the second edition, 83 are concerned with
Homer, 109 with Greek genre and 131 with Roman
genre. The work is especially useful in providing a rapid
orientation in the present state of scholarship in the
selected literary genres, indicating main trends of opinion and what still remains to be done. The volume,
unfortunately, still lacks an index.

FOCK, Gustav, booksellers, Leipzig. Catalogus dis-
sertationum philologicarum classicarum. Zusammengestellt von der Zentralstelle für Disserta-
tionen und Programme der Buchhandlung
Gustav Fock. Editio 2. et 3. Leipzig, 1910–[1937].
New York, Johnson Reprint Corp., [1963].
                                                    AD11

The facsimile reproduction includes the 2d ed., with
subtitle Verzeichnis von etwa 27400 Abhandlungen aus
dem Gesamtgebiete der Klassischen Philologie und Altertumskunde, and the 3d ed. with subtitle Erläuter-
unsschriften zu den griechischen und lateinischen und
eine Auswahl früher erschienener Schriften.

FUCHS, Harald. "Rückschau und Ausblick im
Arbeitsbereich der lateinischen Philologie." Museum Helveticum IV (1947): 147–198.   **AD12**

An excellent overview, in the tradition of Richard
Heinze, "Die gegenwartigen Aufgaben der Römischen
Literaturgeschichte," *NJbb* 19 (1907), 161f.

GNOMON: Kritische Zeitschrift für die gesamte
klassische Altertumswissenschaft. München
[etc.], C. H. Beck'sche [etc.], 1925– .   **AD13**

Eight nos. a year. Publication suspended after v. 20,
no. 3, 1944. Resumed with v. 21, 1949. Cf. Union list
of serials. Volumes accompanied by separately paged
supplement: "Bibliographische Beilage."
Consists almost entirely of book reviews, mostly in
German, "für die gesamte klassische Altertumswissenschaft." Divided into 2 sections: Inhalt, for longer reviews; Vorlagen und Náchrichten, for briefer notices.

GREECE and Rome; New surveys in the classics.
Oxford, Clarendon Press, 1967– .   **AD14**

Published for the Classical Association.
Bibliographical surveys published, to date, in this
series are *Virgil,* R. D. Williams, 1967; *Cicero,* A. E.
Douglas, 1968; *Homer,* J. B. Hainsworth, 1969;
Tacitus, F. R. D. Goodyear, 1970; *Greek Tragedy,*
T. B. L. Webster, 1971; *Horace,* Gordon Williams, 1972;
Thucydides, K. G. Dover, 1973; *Livy,* P. J. Walsh,
1974; *Menander, Plautus, Terence,* W. G. Arnott, 1975;
Plato, J. B. Skemp, 1976, *Lucretius,* E. J. Kenney,
1977, *Ovid,* John Barnsby, 1978.

HARVEY, Paul, Sir. The Oxford companion to
classical literature. Oxford, Clarendon Press,
[1974]. xiv, 468p., illus., maps, plans.   **AD15**

"First published October 1937, reprinted with corrections."
This is a reprint with corrections of the 1937 edition.
The aim of the book, as designed by the publishers,
is to present in convenient form information which
the ordinary reader, not only of the literature of Greece
and Rome but also of that large proportion of modern
European literature which teems with classical allusions, may find useful. It endeavors to do two things:
in the first place to bring together what one may wish
to know about the evolution of classical literature, the
principal authors and their chief works; in the second
place to define as much of the historical political, social
and religious background as may help to make the
classics understood.

LEXIKON der alten Welt. [Herausgeber: Carl
Andresen u.a. Redaktion: Klaus Bartels und
Ludwig Huber. Zeichnungen: Walter Oberhol-
zer] Zurich, Artemis Verlag, [1965]. xv, 3524 columns, illus., maps (part col.).   **AD16**

DLZ LXXXVII 1966 1068–1073 Irmscher • Latomus XXV 1966 1005–1006 Bibauw • CW LX 1966
164 Calder • JJP XVI–XVII 1971 240–251 Wolf
This is the heftier German equivalent to *OCD.* The
work is meant to replace and update the 7th edition
of Lubker, *Reallexikon des klassischen Altertums* published by Teubner before World War I. It is a collaboration of 237 contributions (five American), addressing

itself to students, university professors and specialists in other disciplines. It provides entries on all aspects of culture and history, including Ancient Middle East and Early Christianity. Quality runs from excellent and useful (e.g., the masterly technological articles of Werner Krenkel) to provincial (Homer) and simply incompetent (Calder). The inclusion of copious maps, some in color, drawings, plans, genealogical and chronological tables provides a great improvement over *OCD*. There are six well-chosen appendices, including nomenclature of Greek and Roman mss., collections of papyrus, a chronological list of the most important excavations in the Graeco-Roman world. The articles are generally short but give the essential state of the questions and, generally, the most recent bibliography.

LEXIKON der Antike. (HRSQ. V. Johannes Irmscher in Zsarb. mit Helga Reusch et al.) Leipzig, Bibliographisches Institut, 1971. 607p.   **AD17**

CW LXVIII 1974 145–147 Schnur • BBF XVII 1972 354–355 Ernst
Published under the auspices of the East German Academy of Sciences this Marxist-oriented lexicon has many merits, not least the help it gives in understanding the Marxist interpretation of ancient history, philosophy and civilization. There are many entries for the history of classical scholarship. Forty pages of art paper illustrations give an adequate idea of art, architecture and numismatics covering all periods from Minoan-Mycenaen to Hellenistic.

LUSTRUM; Internationale Forschungsberichte aus dem Bereich des klassischen Altertums. Göttingen, Vandenhoeck & Ruprecht, Bd.1– 1956– , Bd. 27, 1985.   **AD18**

Editors: 1956– , H. J. Mette, A. Thierfelder.
Began as an annual, but irregular in appearance. Follows the mode of presentation of Bursian's *Jahresbericht*. It presents the state of the question on selected Greek and Roman authors, e.g., Jackson, D. F. and Rowe, G. O., "Demosthenes, 1915–1965," *Lustrum*

XIV (1969), and on selected subjects, e.g., Greek metre, Roman tragedy, 1 modi del Verbo Greco e Latino, 1903–1966.

McGUIRE, Martin Rawson P. and DRESSLER, Hermigild. Introduction to Medieval Latin studies; a syllabus and bibliographical guide. 2d ed. Washington, D.C., Catholic University of America Press, 1977. xiii, 406p.   **AD19**

Hermigild Dressler's 1977 revised edition of Martin McGuire's *Introduction* adds a great number of new bibliographical items and makes some improvements in the order of presentation. An excellent orientation into all aspects of medieval studies.
See also: McGuire, Martin Rawson P. *Introduction to classical scholarship; a syllabus and bibliographical guide.* New and rev. ed. Washington, D.C., Catholic University of America Press, 1961. 257p. (See entry NA21.)

TEMPORINI, Hildegard, ed. Aufstieg und Niedergang der römischen Welt; Geschichte und Kultur Roms im Spiegel der neueren Forschung. Berlin and New York, W. de Gruyter, 1972– .   **AD20**

Text in English, French, German, Italian or Spanish. Bd. I/1. Von den Anfängen Roms bis zum Ausgang der Republik.
AC XLI 1972 742–746 Raepsaer-Charlier • Latomus XXXIII 1974 717–730 Préaux • AC XLII 1973 633–637 Raepsaet-Charlier
A monumental work of international collaboration to celebrate the 75th birthday of Professor Vogt, it is divided into: I. The Kings and the Republic, II. The Principate, III. Late Antiquity and Nachleben. Volume I, part 1 appeared in 1972, containing 31 contributions on political history in almost 1,000 pages. Volume I, part 2 covered law, religion, languages, and literature. Volume I Dritter Band is virtually a treatise on the history of Latin Republican literature in some 1400 pages. This includes very complete bibliographies on Caesar, 1945–1970, p.457–487.

AE   ENCYCLOPEDIAS AND DICTIONARIES

ANDRESEN, Carl, et al. DTV-Lexicon der Antike. München, Deutscher Taschenbuch-Verl.   **AE1**

"Zusammengestellt aus dem Lexicon der Alten Welt des Artemis Verlags." 1. Philosophie, Literatur, Wissenschaft. 4 v.

AVERY, Catherine B. The new century classical handbook. New York, Appleton-Century-Crofts, [1962]. 1162p.   **AE2**

Archaeology XVI 1963 298 Vermeule • CPh LVII 1962 252–256 Bruère • CW 1962 298 Schoenheim
The purpose of this book is to provide convenient and detailed information on the Classical Age in a form that is readily accessible to the general reader and to the student. Included are the figures of myth and legend, gods and heroes, persons and places. There are biographies of dramatists, poets, sculptors, painters and potters; philosophers, generals, statesmen and politicians. The aim of the book is to present the material as it appeared to the ancients rather than to apply

modern interpretations. The period of time covered runs from prehistory to the last of the Julian emperors of Rome (68 A.D.). There are over 6,000 entries in this completely restyled version of a one-volume encyclopaedia. There are fairly detailed synopses of the Homeric epics, the plays of Aeschylus, Sophocles, Euripides and Aristophanes. The main defect is that there are no bibliographies nor any citations of ancient or modern authors. Users must be on guard against the many errata in the Handbook.

AVI-YONAH, Michael and SHATZMAN, Israel. Illustrated encyclopaedia of the classical world. Jerusalem, Sampson Low, 1976. 509p., illus.   **AE3**

Designed by Ofra Kamar.
Over 2,300 entries, 250 photographs, 32 pages in full color covering the mythology, literature and history of the classical world and its many contributions to our own age in art, language, philosophy, politics, religion and science. With bibliographies, chronological and genealogical tables, and index.

BUCHWALD, Wolfgang, HOHLWEG, Armin, and PRINZ, Otto. eds. Tusculum-Lexikon griechischer und lateinischer Autoren des Altertums und des Mittelalters. Ungekürzte Ausg. Reinbek bei Hamburg, Rowohlt, 1974, 1963. xvi, 544p.   **AE4**

First edition published in 1948 under title: *Tusculum Lexikon der griechisch und lateinischen Literatur vom Altertum bis zur Neuenzeit.*
Gnomon XXI 1949 176 Marg • WJA 1948 416 Pfister
This work first appeared in 1948 replacing Edward Stemplinger's, *Griechisch lateinischen Literaturführer.* Entries range from Abaelard (Petrus A.) to Zwolftafelgesetz. A one- or two-line bibliography with most items; lists recent standard texts and/or translations. Of the same range and interest as Otto Hiltbrunner's *Kleines Lexicon der Antike.*

DEVAMBEZ, Pierre et al. A dictionary of ancient Greek civilisation. London, Methuen, 1967. 491p., illus., plans, col. maps on endpapers.
AE5

Trans. of *Dictionnaire de la civilisation grecque.*
An English translation of the French *Dictionnaire,* edited by Devambez et al. Appeared in America as *Praeger encyclopedia of ancient Greek civilization* (New York, Praeger, 1967). Brief signed articles; about 750 entries, with emphasis on daily life aspects of civilization.

ENCICLOPEDIA classica. [Direzione: G. Battista Pighi, Carlo del Grande, Paolo E. Arias.] Torino, Società editrice internazionale, [1957]–   .   **AE6**

Contents: Vol. Sezione 1 Storia e antichità. Vol. Sezione 2. Lingua e letteratura. Vol. Sezione 3. Archeologia e storia dell'arte.
Stud. Class XV 1973 267–269 Piatkowski • Gnomon XXXVIII 1966 488–498 Riemann • REL XLII 1964

141–145 Chevallier • JRS LXVIII 1973 290–291 Barton

GRANT, Michael. Greek and Latin authors 800 B.C.–A.D. 1000. A volume in the Wilson Authors series. New York, Wilson, 1980. xiv, 490p.
AE7

Sketches of 376 authors from Homer to the Middle Ages, with lists of best editions of works, available translations and critical commentary.

HAMMOND, N. G. L. and SCULLARD, H. H., eds. The Oxford classical dictionary. 2d ed. Oxford, Clarendon Press, 1970. xxii, 1176p.
AE8

JRS LXI 1971 269–271 W. den Boer • TLS LXIX 1970 1203 • BO XXVIII 88–89 Heubeck
The *OCD* has fulfilled an important function since its original publication in 1949, especially for undergraduates who can turn to the relevant entries in making their first acquaintance with any subject. The first edition used the eighth edition of Lubker's *Reallexicon* as a general model. The *OCD* devotes more space to biography and literature and less to geography and to bibliographical information. In planning the new edition every article of the original 1949 edition was submitted to revision or replaced. Thus all articles and the bibliographies have been brought up to date, that is up to within the years 1967–1968, and there are more than 500 new entries. The new material consists mainly, to quote from the preface, of "places, peoples and persons, and more coverage has been given to the later Roman Empire and to Christian writers. New discoveries and new outlooks are taken into account." Professor Paul Maas contributed the short bibliographical article at the end of the book.

HILTBRUNNER, Otto. Kleines Lexicon der Antike; Umfassend die griechisch-römische Welt von ihren Anfängen bis zum Beginn des Mittelalters (6. Jh. n. Chr.). 5. neubearbeite und erweiterte Aufl. Bern, A. Francke, [1974]. 611p.
AE9

Sammlung Dalp; Bd. 14.
Gnomon XXI 1949 176 Marg • REL 1950 460 Marouzeau
Articles range in length from 2 or 3 lines to about a page and deal with names of people and places and also a wide variety of topics, e.g., Apotheose, Basilica, Geschichtsschreibung, Paraklausithryon, Skolia, Stichomythie, Tyche, Zeitrechnung. Entries on authors include notices of best available texts and recent critical studies. The work first appeared in 1946.

KROH, Paul. Lexikon der antiken Autoren. Stuttgart, A. Kröner, [1972]. xvi, 675p.   **AE10**

Kröners Taschenausgabe; Bd. 366.
BBF XVIII 1973 492–493 Ernst • DLZ XCV 1974 579–581 Hofmann • Gymnasium LXXX 1973 541–544 Buchwald

Contains about 2400 biographical articles, with up-to-date bibliography at the end of each on editions.

KROH, Paul. Wörterbuch der Antike; Mit Berücks. ihres Fortwirkens in Verbindung mit E. Bux u. W. Schöne begr. von Hans Lamer; fortgef. von Paul Kroh. 8., verb. u. erg. Aufl. Stuttgart, Kröner, 1976. 832p. **AE11**

Kröners Taschenausgabe; Bd. 96.
Helpful for identifying such common expressions as *ab ovo, parturiunt montes, post festum.* Brief but up-to-date bibliographical details at the end of many articles.

NEW CATHOLIC encyclopedia. Prepared by an editorial staff at the Catholic University of America. Washington, D.C., and New York, Publishers Guild, Inc., in association with McGraw-Hill, 1967, 1981. Illus. **AE12**

The *New Catholic encyclopedia* describes itself as "an international work of reference on the teachings, history, organizations and activities of the Catholic Church, and on all institutions, religions, philosophies and scientific and cultural developments affecting the Catholic Church from its beginnings to the present." It is a monumental work of 17,000 separate, signed articles by some 4,900 scholars and it includes more than 7,500 illustrations, 300 maps and numerous tables and diagrams. In Biblical Texts, B4, the section on textual criticism is necessarily short but there follows an impressively long historical survey of exegesis. The bibliographies at the end of articles on literature, usually include ten or twelve books. Coverage of literature in the *NCE* compares well with literature coverage in Encyclopaedia Britannica and Encyclopaedia Americana. There are excellent short treatments of many classical, patristic and medieval authors, generally prepared by specialists.

THE NEW Encyclopaedia Britannica. 15th ed. Chicago, Encyclopaedia Britannica, Inc., 1977. 30 v., illus. **AE13**

[1] Propaedia: outline of knowledge, guide to the Britannica. [2] Micropaedia: ready reference and index. 10 v. [3] Macropaedia: knowledge in depth. 19 v.
The new edition is referred to as Britannica 3: a 1-volume Propaedia, a 10-volume Micropaedia, and a 19-volume long Macropaedia. The purpose of the Propaedia is to present the encyclopaedia's contents in logical arrangement, demonstrating something of the structure of knowledge and its interrelationship. It is keyed with volume and page references to the 19-volume Macropaedia for which it forms a kind of table of contents. The Micropaedia provides quick, brief answers to simple reference questions and indicates where long articles are available in the Macropaedia. Articles in the Macropaedia contain bibliographies.

PAULY, August Friedrich von. Der kleine Pauly: Lexikon der Antike; Auf der Grundlage von Pauly's Realencyclopädie der klassischen Alter-

tumswissenschaft unter Mitwirkung zahlreicher Fachgelehrter/bearb. und hrsg. von Konrat Ziegler, Walther Sontheimer, und Hans Gaertner. Stuttgart, A. Druckenmüller, 1964–1975. 5 v. **AE14**

An abridgement of Pauly-Wissowa, containing a high percentage of its articles in concise form. Articles are initialled. Bibliographic references have been updated. Reference to the longer material in the parent work is often given, which is time-saving.

PAULY, August Friedrich von. Real-Encyclopädie der klassischen Altertumswissenschaft; Neue bearbeitung unter mitwirkung zahlreicher fachgenossen, herausgegeben von Georg Wissowa. Stuttgart, Metzler, 1893–1970. 80 v. **AE15**

The standard scholarly work for classical literature, history, antiquities, biography. Long, signed articles by specialists with extensive bibliographies.
Contents: Bd. 1–24 A–Quosenus; 2 Reihe (R–Z), Bd. 1–10A, R–Zythos; Supplementband I–XIV, 1903–1974.
Many volumes include Nachträge und Berichtigungen; v. 23 includes a listing of the articles in the Nachträge of v. 1–23, 2 Reihe v. 1–8A, and the volumes of the Supplement. Some of the Supplement articles are available as Sonderausgaben, e.g., Homeros.
Index to the Supplements and Suppl. Volumes of Pauly-Wissowa's R. E. Index to the Nachträge and Berichtigungen in vols. I–XXIV of the first series, vols. I–X of the second series, and supplementary vols. I–XIV Pauly-Wissowa's Realencyclopädie, comp. by Murphy, J. P., 2nd ed. Chicago, Ares Publ., 1980. 144p.

SEYFFERT, Oskar. A dictionary of classical antiquities; mythology, religion, literature & art; From the German of Dr. Oskar Seyffert. Rev. and ed., with additions, by Henry Nettleship . . . [and] J. E. Sandys . . . with more than 450 illustrations. London, Glaisher, [1895]. vi, 716p., illus. **AE16**

First published in 1891.
This 1957 edition is a reprint of the third edition (1894) of the English translation. Founded on Seyffert's *Lexicon der classichen Altertumskunde* (1882). A standard small-scale work, compact yet readable. Adequate cross-references; some references to sources; general index.

SMITH, William, Sir. A dictionary of Greek and Roman antiquities. 3rd American ed. New York, American Book Co., [1900, 1843]. ix, 9–1124p. **AE17**

WARRINGTON, John. Everyman's classical dictionary; 800 B.C.–A.D. 337. London, Dent (New York, Dutton), [1969, 1961]. xxxvii, 537p., illus. **AE18**

Everyman's reference library.
Destined to replace Sir William Smith's smaller *Classical dictionary*. It is a useful source of rapid information for beginning graduate students. The bibliographic references are limited to works in English. Articles vary

in length from about eight words to two pages (e.g., on Herakles). For writers the articles cite the "best" editions and translations. Less well planned and less reliable than the *Oxford companion to classical literature*.

AF   HANDBOOKS, MANUALS, AND GUIDES

BIGNONE, Ettore. Introduzione alla filologia classica. Milano, Marzorati, 1951. ix, 944p.
AF1

AAHG VI 1953 19–22 Muth • Latomus XII 1953 85 Préaux • Paideia VI 1951 316–321 Pisani
This copious introduction belongs in the collection Problemi e Orientamenti Critica di lingua e di letteratura classica directed by Ettore Bignone. The table of contents reveals the richness and diversity of this collaboration of ten Italian scholars: 1. C. Giarratano, La storia della filologia classica (p.1–72). 2. *Id.,* La critica del testo (p.73–132). 3. A. Calderini, La papirologia e l'epigrafia (p.133–216). 4. R. Pariberti, Archeologia. Storia dell'arte antica. Numismatica (p.217–250). 5. A. R. Natale, Il codice e la scrittura. Nozioni elementari de paleografia greca (p.251–262). 6. *Id.,* Il codice e la scrittura. Avviamento allo studio della paleografia latina (p.263–342). 7. G. Ghedini, Bibliografia generale (p.343–368). 8. G. Bolognesi, Profilo storico-critico degli studi linguistici greci e latini (p.369–452). 9. G. Semerano, Bibliografia degli autori greci e latini (p.453–656). 10. B. Riposati, Problemi di retorica antica (p.657–788). 11. M. Lenchantin de Gubernatis, Problemi ed orientamenti di metrica greco-latina (p.789–880). 12. G. Devoto, Problemi ed orientamenti di grammatica e di storia delle lingue classiche (p.881–944).

CHEVALLIER, R. Les études supérieures de Latin; Initiation à la recherche. Pref. de Marcel Durry. Paris, Soc. d'éd. d'enseign. sup., 1960. 160p.
AF2

RPh XXXVI 1962 182 André • REL XXXVII 1959 452 Marouzeau.
A concise well-written work addressed to the needs of students for the French *licence*. It gives what is essential in the *instruments de travail* and bibliography (not always up-to-date) concerning the language, literature, history and civilization of Rome, but it hardly deserves its subtitle.

CORTE, Francesco della. Avviamento allo studio delle lettere latine. Genova, M. Rozzi, 1968. xv, 233p.
AF3

AC XLIII 1974 417–418 van Looy
There is an introduction (hardly still valid) on Latin requirements in Italian schools. The opening chapter deals with the principal bibliographical tools—encyclopaedias, reviews, collections of texts. There is a chapter on the transmission of texts with explanations of stemmata, *codex unicus,* emendation, but it is short on bibli-

ography. Other chapters deal with the history of classical scholarship, tendencies in modern scholarship, and the auxiliary disciplines (in which is included a glossary of linguistic terminology). There is a similar glossary in the chapter on metrics. Individual authors from Ennius to Apuleius are dealt with in Orientamento Critico sagli Scrittori Latini (p.165–214), with some final space also devoted to the Vulgate, Christian writers, and "Poeti Umanistici" who hardly belong.

CORTE, Francesco della. Introduzione allo studio della cultura classica. Milano, Marzorati, 1972– . xvi, 701p.; xi, 739p.; xi, 841p.   **AF4**

Contents: v. 1. Letteratura; v. 2. Linguistica e filologia; v. 3. Scienze sussidiare.
AC XLII 1973 587–589 van Looy • Athenaeum LIV 1976 214–216 Frassinetti
This work, in three volumes, is intended to replace the two volumes of E. Bignone, ed., *Problemi e orientamenti critica di lingua e letteratura classica.* The first volume is entirely devoted to Greek and Latin literature. Instead of the traditional chronological treatment the approach here is by genre. M. Bonaria provides a general bibliography (p.15–56), which devotes four pages to Marouzeau's *Dix Années* and eight pages to Müller's *Handbuch* (p.32–39), but omits such works as the *Oxford classical dictionary, Lexikon der Alten Welt,* and Hunger's *Lexikon der griechischen und römischen Mythologie.* Archaic Lyric Poetry is remarkably well-treated by Gentili (p.57–105), as is Greek Theatre by A. Garzia (p.211–258). Ettore Paratore on the Latin Theatre (p.259–291) devotes most of his space to Plautus and the problem of the origin of cantica. Latin satire is provided with an excellent bibliography by B. Cicchetti (p.313–329).
In v. 2 nothing appears which is not already to be found in Bignone. Chapters repeated almost word for word include those on the history of classical philology (p.596–672) and on textual criticism (p.673–739). The first of nine new chapters is devoted to the history of philosophy (p.1–39).
The chief failure in the encyclopaedia is the lack of equilibrium between the treatment of various topics—78 pages devoted to the literature of law, 40 pages to ancient philosophy, none to Homer or Hesiod, until v. 3 incorporated (p.597–642) a translation of Hainsworth's *Homer* (Greece and Rome surveys, 1969).

DEFRADAS, Jean. Guide de l'étudiant helléniste. Paris, Presses Universitaires de France, 1968. viii, 159p.   **AF5**

AC XXXVIII 1969 218–219 Lasserre • REG LXXXII 1969 177 Bruneau • RPh XLIII 1969 286 Dobias-Lalou

Beginning students in classical scholarship will find here useful counsel on methodology and an indication of the principal *instruments de travail*. Even advanced students will find the bibliography well organized and judiciously selected with a useful collection of reviews, bibliographical collections and encyclopedias. After introductory sections on the place of Greek in higher studies and the pedagogical exercises *la Version, le Thème and Traduction commentée* so favored in France, Defradas deals successively with collections of annotated texts, especially Budé, Teubner, Oxford, Loeb, Migné and with general works on Greek literature: Christ-Schmid-Staehlin, Lesky. Greek Language deals with lexicography, etymology, history of the language and dialects. There are very short sections on Stylistics and Metrics. This is followed by sections on History and Civilization, Religion and Art, Encyclopedic works (Pauly-Wissowa, etc.) and the great Répetoires Bibliographiques (Fabricius, Engelmann, Klussmann) are briefly noted. Chapter IV contains a *bibliographie sommaire des principaux auteurs,* and will doubtless prove most useful. In the second part of the work, Defradas deals with four auxiliary disciplines: paleography and the establishment of texts, papyrology, epigraphy and archaeology, with helpful hints on methodology and bibliography. This is an eminently practical guide for beginning classicists, in spite of certain deficiencies, e.g., in philosophy and the sciences, and of failure to mention some of the largest enterprises in editing to which young scholars could make a useful contribution. The work is a valuable updating of the author's earlier *Les études supérieures de grec; Initiation á la recherche* (Paris, 1955).

FEDER, Lillian. Crowell's handbook of classical literature. Crowell, [1964]. 448p.   **AF6**

CJ LXI 1965 78–80 Avery • CPh LX 1965 204–207 Bruère • CW LVIII 1965 160–161 Dick.

One of the best works of its kind available in English, providing reliable biographical and critical data on the major classical authors, and the major figures of mythology. Its 950 entries provide "a guide to the drama, poetry and prose of Greece and Rome" for students and general readers. The bibliographies recommend good translations. There are a number of misprints and inaccuracies in detail.

GARDNER, Richard K. and GRUMM, Phyllis, eds. Choice; a classified cumulation, March 1964–February 1974. With the assistance of Julia Johnson. Totowa, N. J., Rowman and Littlefield, 1976. 9 v.   **AF7**

This is a classified cumulation from the monthly journal *Choice: Books for college libraries.* The reference and bibliography section of v. 1 is divided into General Reference Works and Reference Works and Bibliographies of specific subjects. In the second see Classical Literatures for good critical annotated entries. Volume 2, Language and Literature, is especially useful for the classicist in its first two main sections, Compara-

tive Literature and Classical Literature. In v. 2 the section on Classical Languages is short but includes useful articles on the techniques of language teaching. The annotations, generally about 250 words, are unsigned but reliable. The section on Classical Literatures includes only works written in English, but provides a useful checklist for college teachers of the best works of criticism especially on the major authors, and the best translations to appear in the last ten years.

GERCKE, Alfred and NORDEN, Eduard, eds. Einleitung in die Altertumswissenschaft. 3. Aufl. Leipzig and Berlin, B. G. Teubner, 1922– .   **AF8**

Informative introduction by various scholars to the separate fields of classical antiquity and scholarship.

GRIMAL, Pierre. Guide de l'étudiant latiniste. Paris, Presses Universitaires de France, 1971. 319p.   **AF9**

AC XLI 1972 370–371 Raepsaet-Charlier • G&R XVIII 1971 226 Sewter • RPh XLVI 1972 140–141 André

In his preface—entitled Pourquoi le Latin?—Grimal gives a remarkably clear justification of the place of classical studies in modern culture. Part I analyzes the methods of approach to the study of Latin and defines clearly and concisely the organic and auxiliary disciplines. Part II Instruments is a bibliography of 170 pages, for the most part very sketchy, in which editions are listed uncritically, with Budé texts occupying chief place. Indices are also incomplete. Especially useful for French students.

JÄGER, Gerhard. Einführung in die klassische Philologie. München, Beck, 1975. 234p.   **AF10**

Beck'sche Elementarbücher.

Gnomon XLVIII 1976 529–534 Schwinge • IF LXXXI 1976 334–338 Fauth • Gymnasium LXXXIII 1976 501–505 Rösler

Consists of six chapters: I. Klassische Philologie. Begriff, Geschichte, Situation; II. Wortlaut des Textes; III. Die Sprache der Texte; IV. Die Texte als Literatur V. Das Studium der Klassischen Philologie; VI. Hinweise zur wissenschaftlichen Literatur. This useful introduction for students of classical philology grew out of a proseminar of Professor Hermann Bengtson. Bibliographical materials, almost entirely in German, are kept to the final section (p.185–217) and are meant primarily for wider orientation.

LAURAND, Louis and LAURAS, A. Manuel des études grecques et latines 14. édition entièrement refondue par A. Lauras. Paris, A. et J. Picard, 1970– . 2 v.   **AF11**

REL XXXIII 1955 543–544 Marouzeau • RPh XXXIII 1959 283 Chantraine • CR VIII 1958 180–181 Tate

The 12th edition of this work was "entièrement refondue" by A. Lauras, 1955. Described by Van Hoesen as "an encyclopaedic syllabus." The treatment of some topics is largely bibliographical, but the bibliographies are careful and up-to-date, thanks to revisions. In the 1955 revision the work was reduced to six fascicles and confined to two volumes (in place of an original three). In Tome I, the first fascicle Geographie, histoire et institutions grecs, a dozen pages on the geography of Greece lead to a resumé of Greek history from Minoan times to 146 B.C. Institutions occupy about 100 pages and include housing, education, religion and the theatre. The second fascicle covers the history of Greek literature from Homer to Plotinus with a chapter on Christian literature down to St. John Chrysostom. Fascicle 3 contains a concise historical grammar of Greek (phonetics, morphology, syntax) and a section on Greek and Latin metrics, more detailed for Latin than Greek. Tome II: Rome (614p.) follows the same plan as Tome I, fascicle 4, Géographie, histoire, institutions romaines (p.1–169) with index and maps; fascicle 4. 5 Litterature latine (p.170–400), and fascicle 6 Grammaire historique latine (p. 401–614).

MÜLLER, Iwan von, ed. Handbuch der klassischen Altertumswissenschaft. Fortgeführt von Robert von Pöhlmann. München, C. H. Beck, 1893–1948. 52 v.   **AF12**

A collected work often called after its founder I. von Müller with whom the most eminent scholars in Germany collaborated. It treats in 12 main sections, each containing many volumes, the whole of Antiquity through Byzantium. Each volume is a summary of knowledge on the subject, giving the state of the question and rich bibliographies. Each volume will be listed in the subject area to which it belongs.

THE PENGUIN companion to literature. Harmondsworth, Penguin, 1969– .   **AF13**

Penguin reference books; R35.
Volume 4 in this companion is devoted to classical and Byzantine, edited by D. R. Dudley, and Oriental and African, edited by D. M. Lang.

RADICE, Betty. Who's who in the ancient world; A handbook to the survivors of the Greek and Roman classics. Selected with an introd. by Betty Radice. Rev. ed. Harmondsworth and Baltimore, Penguin Books, 1973. 335p., 56 plates.   **AF14**

First published 1971.
BBF XX 1975 164 Ernst • G&R XVIII, ser. 2, 1971 234 Sewter
Designed to remedy the deficiencies of modern education, where a knowledge of Greek and Latin can no longer be presumed yet reminiscences of the Greco-Roman world in literature, art, architecture, music and sculpture on radio and television were never so frequent. The lengthy and finely illustrated introduction deserves to be widely consulted and there is an extensive and extremely helpful index (p.165–225). Includes treatment of mythological persons, historical characters and places.

SANDYS, John Edwin, Sir, ed. A companion to Latin studies. 3rd ed. New York, Hafner Publishing Co., 1963. 891p.   **AF15**

First published in 1910, this companion, despite its age, is still useful. Chapters are by specialists, covering such subjects as the geography and ethnology of Italy, fauna and flora, history, religion and mythology, private and public antiquities, art, literature, epigraphy, paleography. Includes bibliographies.

SEMI, Francesco. Manuale di filologia classica; Con repertorio di termini linguistici e filologici a cura di Paolo Zonelli. Padova, Liviana, 1969 [i.e., 1970]. viii, 372p., illus.   **AF16**

ASNP III 1973 1141–1147 Manfredini
This manual is divided into four sections: La Filologia (p.3–115); Studi Linguistici Greci e Latini (p.119–193); Storia della Filologia Classica (p.197–205); La Storia Letteraria (p.209–344). La Filologia includes a section on fundamental bibliography (mostly a detailed account of Müller's *Handbuch,* and Pighi's *Encyclopedia*), and rudimentary material on manuscripts, epigraphical texts and interpretation of texts. Studi linguistici covers grammar, vocabulary, Greek and Italic dialects, metrics, rhetoric and poetics.

SOUTHAN, Joyce E. A survey of classical periodicals; Union catalogue of periodicals relevant to classical studies in certain British libraries. [London], University of London, Institute of Classical Studies, 1962. xii, 181p.   **AF17**

University of London. Institute of Classical Studies: Bulletin supplement; 13.
A union list of 632 periodicals (including annuals) in 51 British libraries, of latest titles with references from earlier titles. Since papers on classical subjects appear in a wide range of journals other than those exclusively devoted to classical subjects an attempt has been made to include as many titles as possible, especially those in which important classical material is regularly published. The libraries holding the periodical are indicated in each entry.

UNITED STATES. Library of Congress. General Reference and Bibliography Division. Union lists of serials; A bibliography. Compiled by Ruth S. Freitag. Boston, Gregg Press, 1972. xiii, 150p.   **AF18**

Reprint of the 1964 ed. published by Library of Congress, General Reference and Bibliography Division, Washington, D.C.
See also *New serial titles: Subject index to new serial titles, 1950–70,* 2 v. (New York, Bowker, 1975).

WHIBLEY, Leonard, ed. A companion to Greek studies. 4th ed., rev. New York, Hafner Publishing Co., 1963. 790p.   **AF19**

First edition, 1905, 3rd in 1916. Prepared on the same plan as Sandys' *Companion* similarly arranged. A series of signed articles by specialists on such topics as geography, ethnology, flora, science, chronology, coins, ships, buildings. Articles have useful bibliographies and the work has four indices: I. Persons, Deities, Races; II. Places, Rivers and Mountains; III. Scholars and Modern Writers; IV. Greek Words and Phrases.

History and Criticism of Greek and Latin Literature

BA INDIVIDUAL AUTHORS

Aeschylus

AESCHYLUS. Persae. Edited with introd., critical notes and commentary by H. D. Broadhead. Cambridge, Cambridge University Press, 1960. lxxii, 349p.   **BA1**

JHS LXXXIV 1964 164–165 Fitton Brown • Mnemosyne XVII 1964 309–310 Verdenius • CR XII 1962 122–125 Winnington-Ingram • Hermathena XCV 1961 94–96 Stanford

An excellent edition, revealing acute critical judgment. The introduction covers the *Persae's* tragic qualities, dramatic techniques, original production and textual history. The commentary is full and penetrating, but could do with pruning. There are useful appendices on metre, necromancy, "Kommos-threnos amoibaion," Persian names and the battle of Salamis.

BECK, Robert. Aeschylus: Playwright, educator. The Hague, Nijhoff, 1975. xviii, 204p.   **BA2**

REG XC 1977 152 Roy-Saïd

Addressed alike to philologists and to those interested in the history of education or of the theater, this work offers a complete treatment of Aeschylus' moral philosophy as revealed in his plays.

EARP, Frank Russell. The style of Aeschylus. New York, Russell & Russell, [1970]. 175p.   **BA3**

Reprint of the 1948 ed.

JHS LXVII 1949 139 Forster • CW XLIII 1950 90–91 Solmsen • Paideia V 1950 127–131 Buzio

Similar to the author's *The style of Sophocles* in its lists of words and phrases to illustrate certain features of style. The lists contain compound words, rare and epic words, epithets, metaphors, similes, and stylistic development and maturity are shown from varying usages. The evolution of Aeschylus' own outstanding characteristics, vividness, naturalness, and humanity is documented from his vocabulary. Interest is increased by comparisons with Sophocles, Euripides and other non-Greek writers.

GAGARIN, Michael. Aeschylean drama. Berkeley, University of California Press, 1976. xi, 239p.   **BA4**

RPh LII 1978 362–364 Jouan • AC XLVII 1978 242–243 Mund-Dopchie • CW LXXI, 3 1977 193–194 McCall • REG XC 1977 497–498 Saïd

Both more and less than the title promises. An introductory chapter, The Early Greek World View, ranges from Homeric values to Aristotelian *hamartia*. There is one chapter on *Persae* (p.29–56) and two on the *Oresteia* (p.57–118), but *Septem, Supplices* and *Prometheus* are all in one short chapter (p.119–138). There are two appendices, *Páthei máthos* and *Eteocles* and the chorus in *Septem,* a bibliography, index locorum and general index. A learned work which contains much good exegesis on individual passages and combines a lively imagination with sound scholarship.

GARVIE, A. F. Aeschylus' *Supplices;* Play and trilogy. Cambridge, Cambridge University Press, 1969. viii, 279p.   **BA5**

AJPh XCI 1970 352–357 McCall • CPh LXVI 1971 54–61 Burnett • Phoenix XXV 1971 377–380 Podlecki • CJ LXVII 1971 85–87 Peradotto

A thorough and excellent study of the *status quaestionis* of the dating of *Supplices,* based on over 400 items listed in the bibliography. The starting point is the evidence of POxy 2256 fr. 3, which is carefully and lucidly discussed, leading to the conclusion that it certainly indicates a production date of 466 B.C. or later, quite probably 463, for the Danaid tetralogy. The next three chapters deal thoroughly with the style, structure and historical-social background of the *Supplices* and show that none of these phenomena conflicts with that date, *pace* those many writers who have used the same data to argue for an earlier date. The final chapter analyzes in detail the many attempts that have been made to reconstruct and interpret the entire trilogy. The going is often heavy and the argument is more successful at undermining the positions of others than in presenting any strikingly original or positive position.

GRIFFITH, Mark. The authenticity of *Prometheus bound.* Cambridge, Cambridge University Press, 1977. x, 420p.   **BA6**

AC XLVII 1978 607–608 van Looy • CR XXIX 1979 5–7 Davies • JHS XCIX 1979 172–173 Garvie • LEC XLVII 1979 64 Diez

Must surely rank as the most thorough and reasoned investigation of a Greek tragedy's authenticity ever made. An introductory chapter gives an historical survey of the problem and lists the criteria to be used in the authenticity test. External evidence and metrical practice in Aeschylus are next examined, followed by an examination of structure, dramatic technique, staging, vocabulary, style and syntax. A most stimulating, careful and disturbing work of scholarship, with exemplary methodology.

The sobering conclusion: "We do not know who wrote *Prometheus bound*—that is almost all that we can truly say" (p.254). But the weight of evidence is now clearly strongly against Aeschylean authorship.

HERINGTON, C. J. The author of the *Prometheus bound.* Austin, University of Texas Press, [1970]. 135p.   **BA7**

The original version of this work was composed for a seminar on ancient tragedy held during the American Philological Association's meeting in Toronto in December 1968.

ACR I 1971 169–170 McKay • CPh LXVIII 1973 305–306 Tracy • Phoenix XXVIII 1974 258–264 Stinton • AJPh XCIV 1973 305–307 Podlecki

A careful re-examination, after the down-dating of *Supplices,* of the evidence for the date and authenticity of *PV.* The cumulative effect of the arguments is that if the play is by Aeschylus it is his latest play (a product of his final sojourn in Sicily, 458–455 B.C.) and that the existing evidence does not point to authorship by anyone other than Aeschylus. The most telling part of the work is c. II on metre and language. Chapter III, Second Criterion: Cosmic View and Trilogic Composition is too brief to be cogent. If Herington has not established Aeschylean authorship he has at least firmly established a date later than the *Oresteia* and rebutted Smid's *Untersuchungen zum Gefesselten Prometheus,* 1929.

HOMMEL, Hildebrecht. Wege zu Aischylos. Darmstadt, Wissenschaftliche Buchgesellschaft, 1974. xii, 475p.; vii, 393p.   **BA8**

Wege der Forschung; Bd. 87, 465. I. Zugang, Aspekte der Forschung. Nachleben; II. Die einzelnen Dramen. Bibliography: v. 2, p.[381]–393.

WS N.F. XI 1977 227–229 Schwabl • CR XXVII 1977 164–166 Taplin • Gnomon XLIX 1977 743–747 Kraus • AC XLIV 1975 699–702 Schamp

A valuable and enterprising collection. In both volumes over half the papers have been translated into German from other languages, mostly English: Lloyd-Jones, Winnington-Ingram, Herington, Jackson, Pack, Rose, Dawe.

LEBECK, Anne. The Oresteia; A study in language and structure. Washington, D.C., Center for Hellenic Studies, 1971. x, 222p.   **BA9**

CW LXVI 1972 167–168 Peradotto • JHS XCII 1972 193–195 Lloyd-Jones • AJPh XCV 1974 288–292 McCall • CR XXIV 1974 16–17 Whittle

An intensive study of imagery, especially of recurrent imagery, in the trilogy in which the formula "proleptic introduction and gradual development" is successfully applied to a number of images, especially the well-known hunting-net, the robe, and the carpet. First she examines the plays individually and then the trilogy as a whole where "the images are interwoven by associative repetition." An exciting and powerful book, written with great sensitivity and critical expertise, and shedding much new light on the ambiguity, ambivalence and plurality of meanings in the diction of Aeschylus.

PAGE, Denys, ed. Aeschyli septem quae supersunt tragoediae. Oxonii, E Typographeo Clarendoniano, [1975, 1972]. xii, 335p.   **BA10**

Scriptorum classicorum bibliotheca oxoniensis.

Gnomon XLVIII 1976 321–336 Friis Johansen • Gymnasium LXXXI 1974 239–242 Korzeniewski • CW LXVIII 1974 121–122 Kirkwood • Hermathena CXVII 1974 86–88 Stanford • JHS XCV 1975 196–197 Garvie

An entirely new OCT Aeschylus, unlike the 1955 revision of Murray's 1937 text, which incorporates the recent work of Turyn and Dawe and is based on a collation of thirty codices and six papyri, as against Murray's ten. Page is conservative about conjecture but his scholarship and editorial skill, already so well established in lyric and epigram, are everywhere apparent. The plays are arranged chronologically, with PV (etiam de auctore Aeschylo dubitatur, 288) in last place.

PETROUNIAS, Evangelos. Funktion und Thematik der Bilder bei Aischylos. Göttingen, Vandenhoeck und Ruprecht, 1976. xx, 439p.

    BA11

Hypomnemata, Untersuchungen zur Antike und zu ihrem Nachleben; Heft 48. Originally presented as the author's thesis, Tübingen, 1967.

AC XLVII 1978 243–244 van Looy • CR XXIX 1979 8–10 Garvie

After clearly demarcating the principal themes of the imagery in Aeschylus, the author of this *magnum opus* turns to a study of their function. There is a systematic and exhaustive study of the seven surviving tragedies in chronological order. Using Earp's *The style of Aeschylus* as his basis for classification, the author seeks to determine for each tragedy the principal motifs which constitute at the same time the connecting thread of the action. This methodology is more successfully employed on the *Oresteia* and *Prometheus* than on the *Suppliants,* but in sum Petrounias has been more successful than his predecessors in the study of imagery as a key to the technique of Aeschylus. An important book, likely to become the standard work on the subject. The introduction contains a very fair critical survey of earlier literature, and documentation and bibliography are excellent throughout.

PODLECKI, Anthony J. The political background of Aeschylean tragedy. Ann Arbor, University of Michigan Press, [1966]. xii, 188p.

BA12

Gnomon XXXIX 1967 641–646 Winnington-Ingram • JHS LXXXVIII 1968 156–157 Whittle • CR XVIII 1968 28–30 Fitton Brown • AJPh LXXXIX 1968 498–500 Boegehold

A sensible, well-balanced study which does not seek political allegory in the plays but merely examines them against the 5th century political background as it might have affected Aeschylus and his audience. Podlecki interprets *Persae* as a manifestation of political support for Themistocles at a time when he was facing ostracism. The *Supplices* is seen as providing a mythological paradigm for the reception of Themistocles by Argos after his ostracism. The long chapter on the *Oresteia* is mostly occupied by a careful analysis of the theme of δίκη. The statement against tyranny in *PV* is derived ultimately from Aeschylus' admiration of Themistocles. This short but carefully and courteously reasoned book provides a consistent account of the political attitudes of the poet and nowhere suggests that contemporary political overtones are anything more than that.

SANSONE, David. Aeschylean metaphors for intellectual activity. Wiesbaden, Steiner, 1975. xii, 100p.

BA13

Hermes, Zeitschrift für klassische Philologie: Einzelschriften Heft 35.

CR XXIX 1979 8–10 Garvie • AC XLVI 1977 614–615 Mund-Dopchie • Gnomon XLIX 1977 512–514 Mette

A University of Wisconsin dissertation, 1972, which examines all the metaphors for intellectual activity, which is divided into the (sometimes overlapping) categories of cognition, noesis, prescience, memory, etc. The methodology allows for a systematic account of parallels between metaphors in different plays. There is an excellent index locorum.

STANFORD, William. Aeschylus in his style; A study in language and personality. Dublin, University Press, 1942. 147p.

BA14

CR LVII 1943 71–72 Pickard-Cambridge • JHS LXII 1942 95 Webster • CJ XLI 1945 138–139 Grene

A detailed analysis of stylistic elements and an attempt to explain them as illustrative of the poet's temperament. Ancient criticisms of Aeschylus are first dealt with, then the poet's borrowings from literary and colloquial sources. Chapters include The Choice of Words, Imagery and Imagination, Characterization by Stylistic Means, Sources of Obscurity, and Conclusions. The treatment of Aeschylus' use of metaphor is excellent, as is that of the dominant images in the *Oresteia.* The subtitle suggests that the style is the man, which may be trying to prove too much.

TAPLIN, Oliver P. The stagecraft of Aeschylus; The dramatic use of exits and entrances in Greek tragedy. Oxford and New York, Clarendon Press, 1977. vi, 508p.

BA15

Originally presented as the author's thesis, Oxford.

AC XLVII 1978 605–607 van Looy • TLS LXXVII 1978 1123 Knox • AJPh C 1979 570–574 Sider

A major contribution to the "grammar" of the dramatic technique of Aeschylus, this work provides a scene-by-scene analysis of the plays, constantly asking such questions as who? how? why? where?

THOMSON, George. Aeschylus and Athens; A study in the social origins of drama. New York, Haskell House Publishers, 1972. xii, 478p., illus.

BA16

Hermathena LVIII 1941 176–179 Stanford • CR LVI 1942 21–26 Pickard-Cambridge • CPh XXXVII 1942 437–441 Norwood

A reprint of a 1941 work (which cost a guinea then). Under a misleading title (the two A's get hardly a third of the book), Professor Thomson indulges in an exercise in Marxist philosophy calculated to make ancient Athens relevant to modern Birmingham. He uses social anthropology to good effect when he is seeking to illuminate texts and not turning them into weapons against bourgeois contemporary society.

WARTELLE, André. Bibliographie historique et critique d'Eschyle et de la tragédie grecque 1518–1974. Paris, Société d'édition "Les belles lettres," 1978. xvi, 685p.

BA17

Collection d'Études anciennes.

Gnomon XLVII 1975 641–645 Dawe • AC XLVIII 1979 236 van Looy • AJPh XCV 1974 286–288 Herrington

This book is a great repository of learning, covering Sophocles and Euripides in antiquity almost as thoroughly as Aeschylus. Almost 9,000 items.

WILAMOWITZ-MOELLENDORFF, Ulrich von. Aischylos; Interpretationen. 2. unveränderte Aufl. Dublin and Zürich, Weidmann, 1966. 260p.

BA18

"Die zweite Aufl. ist ein unveränderter Nachdruck der ersten Aufl. von 1914."

RF 1916 158–171 Romagnoli • WKPh 1916 603 Sitzler

WINNINGTON-INGRAM, R. P. Studies in Aeschylus. New York, Cambridge University Press, 1983. xii, 225p.   **BA18a**

CW LXXIX 1985 53 McCall

Ammianus Marcellinus

AMMIANUS MARCELLINUS. Römische Geschichte, hrsg, Wolfgang Seyfarth. Rerum gestarum libri. 4. unveränderte Aufl. Darmstadt, Wissenschaftliche Buchgesellschaaft, 1978. 4 v.   **BA19**

Schriften und Quellen der Alten Welt; Bd. 21.
CW LXIV 1971 205 Oost • Gnomon XLVII 1975 272–278 Demandt
An excellent edition, with German translation, of Ammianus Marcellinus, better than Rolf's Loeb edition or Clark's. Conservatively sticks to MSS., especially V, and rejects much 19th century emendation. A useful contribution to the study of Late Latin.

BLOCKLEY, R. C. Ammianus Marcellinus; A study of his historiography and political thought. Bruxelles, Latomus, 1975. 210p.   **BA20**

Collection Latomus; v. 141.
BStudLat V 1975 354–356 Viparelli Santangelo • MH XXXIV 1977 260 Paschoud • REL LIV 1976 462–464 Sabbah
Less ambitious than the title might lead one to suppose, this revised thesis consists of ten relatively brief and autonomous chapters on certain aspects of the historiography and political thought of Ammianus Marcellinus. Each chapter focuses on a theme, an episode or a particular problem.

CRUMP, Gary A. Ammianus Marcellinus as a military historian. Wiesbaden, Steiner, 1975. viii, 140p.   **BA21**

Historia, Zeitschrift für alte Geschichte: Einzelschriften; Heft 27.
REL LIII 1975 508–510 Fontaine • CR XXVIII 1978 159–160 Alonso-Núñez • AC XLVI 1977 652–653 De Decker
A very good study of the strategic and tactical aspects of the *Res Gestae*. Seven chapters deal with the soldier and the Greek, the historian at work, the historian's use of geography, strategy, operations in the field, sieges and the frontiers. The last four chapters are more detailed and substantial, especially the last.

DREXLER, Hans. Ammianstudien. Hildesheim and New York, G. Olms, 1974. 208p.   **BA22**

Spudasmata; Bd. 31.
AAHG XXX 1977 15–17 Eisenhut • Gnomon L 1978 607–609 Demandt • REL LII 1974 518–519 Fontaine

A strange work by a late convert to Ammianus studies constituting a sort of dialog with recent commentators on the text and with the text itself.

JONGE, Pieter de. Philological and historical commentary on Ammianus Marcellinus; XVII. Trans. by P. de Waard-Dekking. Groningen, Bouma, 1977. xi, 404p.   **BA23**

REL LV 1977 515–517 Sabbah • Phoenix XXXII 1978 365–367 Simpson • Gnomon LII 1980 33–36 Seyfarth
De Jonge's careful commentary on Ammianus has been ongoing since 1935 and the style and format of his work are by now well-known, as is his rigor in considering the textual tradition. He is particularly good on prose rhythm and clausulae. As an historical commentary the work is less satisfactory. There are deficiencies in the content of the bibliography (viii–xi), which is also marked by typographical errors.

Anacreon

ANACREON. Anacreon; Edidit Bruno Gentili. Romae, In aedibus Athenaei, 1958. xliii, 218p.   **BA24**

Lyricorum Graecorum quae exstant; II, 3.
AC XXVIII 1959 341–344 Lasserre • CR IX 1959 234–237 Page • Mnemosyne XII 1959 345–348 Koster
A complete edition of the fragments, with the *testimonia* and a good *index verborum*. There is a short but sensitive and suggestive introduction.

Anthologia Graeca

ANTHOLOGIA graeca; The Greek anthology: Hellenistic epigrams. Edited by A. S. F. Gow and D. L. Page. Cambridge, Cambridge University Press, 1965. 2 v.   **BA25**

JHS LXXXVI 1966 199–200 Webster • CW LIX 1966 199 Rosenmeyer • Gnomon XXXVIII 1966 20–25 Ludwig
"A superb text and commentary on the Hellenistic epigrams of the Greek Anthology. No praise can be too high for the industry, care, taste, and sound judgment which have gone into it" (Webster). There are 65 named poets and circa 850 epigrams, plus 60 anonymous ones. The poets are arranged alphabetically, with Meleager kept for the end. There are excellent Greek and English indices, but no attempt is made to marshal the secondary literature, and there is no translation.

Apollonius

LEVIN, Donald Norman. Apollonius' *Argonautica* re-examined. Leiden, Brill, 1971. viii, 268p.   **BA26**

Mnemosyne. Bibliotheca classica Batava: Supplementum; v. 13. V. 1: The neglected first and second books.
Gnomon XLVI 1974 346–353 Vian • JHS XCII 1972

203–205 Griffiths • AC XLII 1973 246 Schwartz • CR XXIV 1974 36–38 Giangrande • CPh LXX 1975 150–151 Garson

Even admirers of the *Argonautica* tend to begin with Book III. The thesis here is that Books I and II have been unjustly neglected and the tone is decidedly panegyrical. Seven chapters are devoted to each book, much of it wordy and unfortified by bibliography later than 1967, and unlikely to reverse the alleged neglect. A second volume, devoted to Books III and IV, is promised.

Apuleius

SCHLAM, C. C. "The scholarship on Apuleius since 1938." CW LXIV (1971): 285–309.

BA27

Schlam chooses 1938 as the starting point because a good pre-1938 bibliography is available in Molt, M., Ad Apulei Madaurensis Metamorphoseon librum primum commentarius exegeticus. Diss., Gröningen, 1938.

Archilochus

ARCHILOCHUS. Fragmenta Edidit, veterum testimonia collegit Iohannes Tarditi. Romae, In aedibus Athenaei, 1968. viii, 35, 298p.

BA28

Lyricorum Graecorum quae exstant; v. 2.
Gnomon XLIII 1971 304–305 Dover • Mnemosyne XXIV 1971 410–414 Radt • REA LXXI 1969 139–141 Pouilloux

Contains a substantial introduction, very full bibliography, 184 testimonia, text, apparatus criticus, translation, phraseological parallels, indices and concordance of numeration with the editions of Diehl, Bergk and Bonnard-Lasserre. There is a conspectus of classified linguistic and metrical data. The translation is separate from the text at the end (p.259–295).

POUILLOUX, J., et al. Archiloque; Sept exposés et discussions. Genève, Fondation Hardt, 1964. 307p., illus.

BA29

Entretiens sur l'antiquité classique; t. 10.
Contents: Archiloque et Thasos: histoire et poésie, par J. Pouilloux. Archilochos und Paros, von N. M. Kontoleon. Die Sprache des Archilochos, von A. Scherer. Archilochus and the oral tradition, by D. Page. The Poetry of Archilochus, by K. J. Dover. Archilochus und Kallimachos, von W. Bühler. Archilochus and Horace, by E. Wistrand.

CW LVIII 1965 283–284 Combellack • CJ LX 1965 325–326 Wassermann • CR XV 1965 263–267 Lloyd-Jones • Phoenix XIX 1965 248–249 Davison

A work of great interest from a distinguished group: Pouilloux and Kontoleon on the recently discovered archaeological background in Thasos and Paros, Scherer on language, Page on the possible affinities with oral poetry, Dover on the origin and nature of elegiac verse, Bühler on the Nachleben of Archilochus

in Kallimachos, Wistrand on Archilochus and Horace, with Snell, Reverdin and Treu acting as interlocutors in the discussions. The various indices facilitate rapid consultation on individual fragments.

RANKIN, H. D. Archilochus of Paros. Park Ridge, N.J., Noyes Press, 1977. ix, 142p.

BA30

Noyes classical studies.
CJ LXXIV 1978 68–72 Podlecki • CR XXIX 1979 137 West • G&R XXVI 1979 88 Ireland • Helios VIII 1979–1980 75–82 Donlan

This is the first book in English about Archilochus, now enjoying enormous popularity since the Cologne epode publication. [See Merkelbach, R. and West, M. L., "Ein Archilochos-Papyrus," *ZPE* XIV (1974), 97–113.] It is not well designed as an introduction, as the order of chapter headings will show: His Reputation in Antiquity, His Life and Chronology, Epic and Heroic, The Fate of the Lycambids, Beauty and Obscenity, Politics and Thought, and A View of the Fragments. The Strasbourg epodes are included, with only the vaguest hint that there is any question about their authorship. There are some slipshod translations and scholarly details. Also it is highly questionable to use evidence provided by poems themselves as the basis for so much analysis of the poet's life and work.

TREU, Max. "Archilochos." RE Suppl.-Bd. XI (1968): 136–156.

BA31

The most complete recent introduction, with full bibliographies.

Aristophanes

ARISTOPHANES. Clouds. Edited with introd. and commentary by Kenneth James Dover. Oxford, Clarendon Press, [1970, 1968]. 285p.

BA32

AJPh XCII 1971 100–103 Segal • Phoenix XXV 1971 168–171 O'Brien • AC XXXVIII 1969 223–225 Lasserre

An excellent edition, thorough, lucid and erudite. The introduction of over 100 pages gives ample coverage to linguistic usage, metre, orthography, philosophy, religion, economics and law. Empirical evidence is frequently invoked and the textual evidence (41 of the 136 MSS have been fully collated) often spills over from the simplified apparatus into the notes which are sensible on problems of staging and frank in matters of translation.

ARISTOPHANES. Ecclesiazusae. Edited with introd. and commentary by R. G. Ussher. Oxford, Clarendon Press, 1973. xlviii, 259p. **BA33**

AC XLII 1973 608–609 van Looy • AJPh XCVI 1975 308–309 Schreiber • JHS XCIV 1974 184–185 MacDowell

Neglected by English editors, apart from Rogers (1902), the *Ecclesiazusae* is here edited with a most useful and up-to-date commentary on all linguistic and textual, archaeological, historical, social and theatrical matters. All seven MSS have been collated for the text. The apparatus criticus is a model of its kind, and Ussher is reasonably cautious in emendation. A heartening edition of a government-by-women play from, of all places in 1973, the new University of Ulster.

ARISTOPHANES. The Frogs. Edited with introd., rev. text, commentary and index by W. B. Stanford. 2d ed. Basingstoke, Macmillan, [1971, 1958]. lx, 211p.   **BA34**

CR IX 1959 242–244 Jones • Mnemosyne XIII 1960 169–172 de Vries • Gnomon XXXII 1960 750–754 Newiger • CPh LVI 1961 190–191 Arnott
The first English edition of *The Frogs* in over 50 years (Rogers, 1902, Merry, 1905, Tucker, 1906). Addressed to English-speaking students in schools and universities it is generally very helpful pedagogically but at times fails both student and scholar. The author sensibly treats *Frogs* primarily as a play to be acted and so there are interspersed action notes and introductory chapters on staging and performance. There is no *apparatus criticus* to the text and the Notes (p. 69–201) treat of textual matters only fitfully.

ARISTOPHANES. Peace. Edited with introd. and commentary by Maurice Platnauer. Oxford, Clarendon Press, 1964. xxvi, 174p.   **BA35**

CR n.s. XV 1965 271–273 Morrison • Erasmus XVIII 1966 160–163 Bader • Mnemosyne XIX 1966 415–416 Pieters
This new edition and commentary, the first in a series, is a model of concision and good sense.

ARISTOPHANES. Wasps. Edited with introd. and commentary by Douglas M. MacDowell. Oxford, Clarendon Press, 1971. x, 346p.   **BA36**

Greek text; English introd. and commentary.
CR XXIII 1973 133–135 Austin • ACR I 1971 246 Vaio • Hermathena CXIV 1972 96–97 Stanford • Mnemosyne ser. IV XXX 1977 309–312 Pieters
Approaching the play "not as a work of literature but as the script of a performance" the editor, unlike Starkie, pays welcome attention to problems of staging in an extensive commentary (210p.) which is witty and intelligent, lucid and concise. His established competence in legal antiquities proves useful for the technicalities of the law courts, and he is very helpful on prosopography. He also has an unerring ear for puns, euphony, cacophany, etc., and he is in the livelier modern set when translation is called for. Lexicographical, grammatical, historical and metrical matters are well covered. A worthy edition of "one of the world's best comedies."

DEARDEN C. W. The stage of Aristophanes. London, University of London; Athlone Press ([Atlantic Highlands], N.J., [distributed by] Humanities Press), 1976. xiii, 203p., illus.   **BA37**

REG XC 1977 499–500 Ghiron-Bistagne • JHS XCVII 1977 177–178 Dover • AC XLV 1976 667–669 van Looy

Does not take into account scholarly work since 1971, and is not always reliable in reporting on scholarly work previous to that, apart from work in English. Nine chapters deal with religious feasts, the theater, scenery, the ekkyklema, the mechane, the actors, the chorus, costume and masks.

DOVER, Kenneth J. Aristophanic comedy. London, Batsford, 1972. xv, 253, [7] p., illus., facsims.   **BA38**

JHS XCIV 1974 186–187 Dunbar • AC XLII 1973 227–228 Schamp • Arion n.s. I 1973–1974 530–537 Henderson • Phoenix XXVIII 1974 364–369 Sifakis • CR n.s. XXIV 1974 27–29 MacDowell
Begun as a series of conferences at Berkeley in 1967 to an audience in which scientists pure and social intermingled with classicists, this work is aimed primarily at readers who do not know Greek but are interested in Greek culture or in the history of comedy as an art form. The resulting work is a masterpiece of balance between statement of the general and attention to detail. Chapters 1 and 2 survey the text transmission and the theatrical conditions in the Athens of Aristophanes. Three very entertaining chapters describe and interpret the distinctive features of Old Comedy, followed by eleven chapters dealing individually with the surviving plays. The translations of passages are witty and forthright. Concluding chapters are Contemporaries and Predecessors and Posterity. An excellent general introduction is clear, concise and unfailingly lively. This work challenges Gilbert Murray, *Aristophanes,* 1933, as the best introduction in English to its subject.

DUNBAR, Henry. A complete concordance to the comedies and fragments of Aristophanes. Hildesheim and New York, G. Olms, 1973. ix, 362p.   **BA39**

New ed. completely rev. and enl. by Benedetto Marzullo. Reprint of the 1883 ed., Clarendon Press, Oxford.

EHRENBERG, Victor. The people of Aristophanes; A sociology of old Attic comedy. London, Methuen (New York, Barnes & Noble), 1974. xii, 384p., [10] leaves of plates, illus.
                                                          BA40

Reprint of the 1951 ed., with minor revisions.
JHS LXXIII 1953 154 Hopper • LEC XIX 1951 441 Domont • RPh XXVI 1952 224–227 Aymard
The author draws upon Old Attic comedy and the corpus of Aristophanes to recreate the life of contemporary Athens, its social structure, the place of family and religion and the political relationships within the state.

GELZER, Thomas. Aristophanes der Komiker. Stuttgart, Alfred Druckmüller, 1971. p.1391–1570.   **BA41**

Sonderausgaben der Paulyschen Realencyclopädie der klassischen Altertumswissenschaft.
Gymnasium LXXXIII 1976 124–127 Werner

This is a separate edition of Gelzer's magisterial Pauly-Wissowa article: *RE Supplbd.* XII (1971), 1391–1569.

See also Dover K. J., "Aristophanes 1938–1955," *Lustrum* II (1957), 52–112, and Murphy, C. T., *CW* XLIX (1956), 201–211, LXV (1972), 261–273.

LITTLEFIELD, David J., comp. Twentieth century interpretations of *The Frogs;* A collection of critical essays. Englewood Cliffs, N.J., Prentice-Hall, [1968]. viii, 118p.   **BA42**

CR XX 1970 262 Wilson

NEWIGER, Hans. Aristophanes und die alte Komödie. Darmstadt, Wissenschaftliche Buchgesellschaft, 1975. xiv, 528p.   **BA43**

Wege der Forschung; Bd. 265.
Athenaeum L 1978 204–205 Lanza • JHS XCVII 1977 178 Arnott • AC XLV 1976 236–238 van Looy • DLZ XCVII 1976 412–415 Luppe
Twenty-seven articles, nine in English and eighteen in German, original or translated. Only two are new. There are six essays on general topics of Aristophanic comedy; the rest are on individual plays. The editor adds a most valuable bibliography. The choice of topics—technique, style, political overtones, ideology—is commendably broad. Contributors range from Wilamowitz to Segal, Reinhardt to Cantarella, Süss to Russo, with varying approaches, methodologies and cultural perspectives.

TAILLARDAT, Jean. Les images d'Aristophane; Études de langue et de style. Paris, Société d'édition Les Belles Lettres, 1965. 553p.   **BA44**

Annales de l'Université de Lyon. 3. sér. Lettres; fasc. 36.
REG LXXIX 1966 533–536 Roux • AJPh LXXXIX 1968 241–243 Murphy • Gnomon XL 1968 133–138 Herington • JHS LXXXIX 1969 129–131 Dunbar
This attractively produced work (which began as a doctoral thesis in 1956) provides an elaborate catalog of all words and expressions used by Aristophanes in simile or metaphor (p.39–493). It then attempts to determine whether each image is the original creation of the poet. It also provides detailed analysis of text and interpretation of many Aristophanic passages. This is at times excessively rambling and detailed and should be studied through the indices rather than at a sitting. The introduction (p.5–29) and conclusion (p.495–506) can be read as a unity. The bibliography (p.507–515) is longer and more linguistically varied than the use to which it is put in the body of the work; it effectively stops at 1959. Especially useful as a quarry for metaphor hunters or lexicographers.

WHITMAN, Cedric Hubbell. Aristophanes and the Comic Hero. Cambridge, Mass., published for Oberlin College by Harvard University Press, 1964. ix, 333p.   **BA45**

Martin Classical Lectures, v. 19.

Gnomon XXXVII 1965 618–620 Austin • Phoenix XIX 1965 314–323 Herington • CR XVI 1966 159–161 Dover • Arion V 1966 99–119 Stewart
Whitman completes a trilogy following his earlier studies of heroism in Homer and Sophocles. He first explores the inadequacies of previous literary criticism of Aristophanes and then, armed with the tools of New Criticism, sets out to remedy the situation. His main "new" discovery is that fantasy, not satire, is the heart of Aristophanic comedy. The controlling and directing element in the fantasy structure is the Comic Hero. The unifying element in the plots, *pace* the whole race of earlier critics who have been calling them episodic or worse, is the imagery. There is much anachronism in the overall social and literary analysis, and much imprecision, exaggeration and error in matters of detail and translation. The book was received with excessive frigidity by British critics and excessive elation by fellow Americans.

Aristotle

BARNES, Jonathan, SCHOFIELD, Malcolm and SORABJI, Richard, eds. Articles on Aristotle. London, Duckworth, 1975– .   **BA46**

v. 1. Science. v. 2. Ethics and politics. v. 3. Metaphysics. v. 4. Psychology and Aesthetics.
LEC XLIV 1976 79 R.E. • TLS LXXIV 1975 1482 Lloyd • CR XXIX 1979 164–165 Longrigg • CR XXXII 1982 99–100 Rees
These four volumes seek to cover the whole of Aristotle's thought. Volume 1, Science, consists of 12 articles, most of which were translated from German or French. Most deal with Aristotle and Demonstration, others with mechanics, physics and biology. The first two articles in v. 1 (by Ross and Owen) criticize Jaeger's views on the development of Aristotle's thought.

COPE, Edward Meredith. An introduction to Aristotle's *Rhetoric;* With analysis, notes and appendices. Hildesheim and New York, G. Olms, 1970. xvi, 464p.   **BA47**

Reprint of the ed. published in London in 1867.

DÜRING, Ingemar. Aristoteles. Stuttgart, A. Druckenmüller, 1968. p.162–335.   **BA48**

Sonderausgaben der Paulyschen Realencyclopädie der Klassischen Altertumswissenschaft.
The first contribution on Aristotle to Pauly-Wissowa was by A. Gercke, *RE* 2. 1012–1054, published in 1895. The present article appeared in *RE Supplbd*, XI (1968), 159–336 and is the standard introduction.

DÜRING, Ingemar. Aristoteles; Darstellung und Interpretation seines Denkens. Heidelberg, Winter, 1966. xv, 670p.   **BA49**

Bibliothek der klassischen Altertumswissenschaften; n. F. 1. Reihe.
Gnomon XXXIX 1967 657–672 Solmsen • JHS LXXXVIII 1968 163–166 Lloyd • Phoenix XXI 1967 226–229 Philip • REG LXXX 1967 633–637 Weil

A comprehensive interpretation of Aristotle's life and thought, constituting a landmark in modern Aristotelian scholarship. Provides a wealth of factual information, with a great deal of interpretation, hypothesis, reconstruction and conjecture. The weakest treatment is of the *Rhetoric,* the best, the biological writings. The author has chosen to discuss Aristotle's thought not as presented in the treatises but in the chronological order of its development, and his chronology is radically different from Jaeger's. There is an Italian translation by P. Donini (1976).

ERICKSON, Keith V. Aristotle; The classical heritage of rhetoric. Metuchen, N. J., The Scarecrow Press, 1974. viii, 315p.   **BA50**

QJS LXI 1975 479–481 Corbett • REG LXXXIX 1976 637–638 Bompaire
A collection of 17 important articles in English on the *Rhetoric* with a good introduction by Erickson, emphasizing Aristotle's originality. There is a good bibliography on Anglo-Saxon work on the *Rhetoric* for the past half-century.
See also Erickson, K. V. *Aristotle's Rhetoric. Five centuries of philological research.* Metuchen, N.J., Scarecrow Press, 1974. viii, 315p.

FERGUSON, John. Aristotle. New York, Twayne Publishers, [1972]. 195p.   **BA51**

Twayne's world authors series; TWAS 211, Greece.
CR XXV 1975 21–22 Kirwan • CW LXVIII 1974 122–123 Stough • REA LXXV 1973 368 Moreau
A modern counterpart to Ross's *Aristotle* (1923), following Ross's chapter division on the Dialogues, Logic, Philosophy of Nature, Biology, Psychology, Metaphysics, Ethics and Politics, Rhetoric and Poetics. Updates Ross on the bibliographical side but does not replace it. Dependable for its précis of the teachings of Aristotle and for detailed summaries of his individual works.

FORTENBAUGH, W. W. Aristotle on emotion; A contribution to philosophical psychology, rhetoric, poetics, politics, and ethics. New York, Barnes & Noble Books, 1975. 99p.   **BA52**

MH XXXIII 1976 257 Wehrli • CR XXVIII 1978 283–284 Woods • JHS XCVII 1977 183 Rowe • Philosophy LI 1976 236–239 Robins • Philos Q XXVI 1976 102–103 Dybikowski
An attempt to sketch the developed theory of the emotions of the *Rhetoric* and *Ethics,* and to trace out the implications for Aristotle's mature philosophy in general, especially for political theory and ethics.

GAUTHIER, René Antoine. La morale d'Aristote. [3. éd, revue et corr.]. Paris, Presses universitaires de France, 1973 [1958]. 142p.   **BA53**

Collection SUP. Le Philosophe; 34.
AC XXVIII 1959 368–369 Moraux • JPh LVI 1959 736–742 • REG LXXII 1959 429–431 Aubenque
This work, by the joint editor of an erudite commentary on the *Nicomachean ethics,* is a good exposé of earlier inadequate views on morality in Aristotle, and a new and more satisfactory treatment of the subject, bringing it into line with the other parts of Aristotle's philosophy, especially his psychology, and showing its development within the evolution of his thought. An excellent short treatment.

GRAYEFF, Felix. Aristotle and his school; An inquiry into the history of the Peripatos with a commentary on Metaphysics Z, H, Λ and Θ. [London], Duckworth, [1974]. 230p.   **BA54**

CR XXVI 1976 212–213 Kerferd • JHS XCVI 1976 185–186 Evans • REA LXXVI 1974 364–366 Moreau
A sketch of Aristotle's life, with special stress on the political and Macedonian factors, leads to the conclusion that his peripatetic tendencies precluded the extended leisure which would be necessary for sole authorship of his esoteric works. The anomalies in the four books of the *Metaphysics* analyzed are explained by supposing an editor at work, endeavoring to compose a representative volume. An unconvincing case is made for direct post-Aristotelian references to Stoic, Sceptic and Epicurean doctrines, and it remains unproven that these books are more the work of his school than of the master.

GRIMALDI, William M. A. Studies in the philosophy of Aristotle's *Rhetoric.* Wiesbaden, F. Steiner, 1972. 151p.   **BA55**

Hermes: Zeitschrift für klassische Philologie. Einzelschriften; Heft 25.
CPh LXXI 1976 174–178 Solmsen • CW LXXI 1977 79–80 Coulter • Gnomon XLVIII 1976 13–18 Lossau
Not an easy book to read, leaving one at times uncertain whether the confusion and inherent contradictions with which the author valiantly wrestles are in the original material or in the subsequent exposition. The author finds the enthymeme the key to understanding Books 1 and 2.

HAGER, Fritz-Peter. Ethik und Politik des Aristoteles. Darmstadt, Wissenschaftliche Buchgesellschaft, 1972. xxxiii, 442p.   **BA56**

Wege der Forschung; Bd. 208.
CW LXVII 1974 395 Nix • Gymnasium LXXXI 1974 244–247 Schwarz • REA LXXV 1973 366 Moreau
This work can be divided into two sections, the first containing philological discussion concerning the chronology of the writings on ethics and politics in which von Arnim and Jaeger figure prominently. The second contains studies of various main themes in the *Ethics* and *Politics.*

HAGER, Fritz-Peter. Metaphysik und Theologie des Aristoteles. Darmstadt, Wissenschaftliche Buchgesellschaft, 1969. xvii, 467p.   **BA57**

Wege der Forschung; Bd. 206.

HAGER, Fritz-Peter, ed. Logik und Erkenntnislehre des Aristoteles. Darmstadt, Wissen-

schaftliche Buchgesellschaft, 1972. xxvii, 346p.
BA58

Wege der Forschung; Bd. 226.
CR XXVI 1976 133 Huby • CW LXVIII 1975 323–324 Hathaway • REA LXXV 1973 367–368 Moreau
A collection of 12 important articles in German (original or translation), published over a period of 50 years.

HAPP, Heinz. Hyle; Studien z. aristotel. Materie-Begriff. Berlin and New York, de Gruyter, 1971. xv, 953p. **BA59**

A revision of the author's Habilitationsschrift, Tübingen, 1966.
AC XLI 1972 667–668 Byl • CR XXIV 1974 44–46 Huby • CW LXVI 1973 358–359 Ambrose
An exhaustive study of one of the most fundamental concepts of Aristotelian philosophy. Begins with a survey of scholarship on matter in Aristotle from Georg von Hertling (1871) to Ingemar Düring (1966), and a survey of the concept in Plato, Speusippus and Xenocrates.

HARDIE, William Francis Ross. Aristotle's ethical theory. Oxford, Clarendon Press, 1968. ix, 370p. 2nd ed., 1980, x, 448p. **BA60**

CR XX 1970 162–164 Hamlyn • Mind LXXIX 1970 445–453 Kirwan • Phoenix XXIV 1970 84–86 Sparshott
A comprehensive examination of Aristotle's ethical doctrine in the form of essays on successive portions of the *Nicomachean ethics,* omitting only III, 6–IV, 9. The bulk of the book is devoted to detailed discussion of "crucial passages." Will be of greater general use to the student than the running commentaries of Grant, Stewart, Burnet, Joachim or Gautier-Jolif.

HINTIKKA, Kaarlo J. J. Time & necessity; Studies in Aristotle's theory of modality. Oxford, Clarendon Press, 1973. viii, 225p. **BA61**

Philos Q XXIV 1974 369–370 Kneale • JHS XCVII 1977 183–186 Barnes • R Meta XXIX 1975 343–344 Sweeney
Most of this book's chapters have been published earlier as separate papers. The main subjects discussed are Aristotle's theory of modal notions (necessity and possibility), and those Aristotelian doctrines and assumptions it is necessary to understand to appreciate his ways with modal notions. Chapters IV–IX, taken together, present Aristotle as a forerunner of Diodorus Chronus, an incipient tense-logician and a determinist.

JAEGER, Werner Wilhelm. Aristotle; Fundamentals of the history of his development. Trans., with author's corrections and additions, by Richard Robinson. 2d ed. London, Oxford University Press, 1962. 475p. **BA62**

CR XXXVIII 1924 193 Dodd • PhW 1924 516–521 Hoffmann • JHS XLIII 1923 201–203 J.L.S.
First published in German in 1923, this early but influential work of Professor Jaeger first tries to reconstruct from fragments the argument of three of the early lost writings and then to use the results in analyzing the most important works in Aristotle's *Corpus,* to show that there is a development within them that continues an earlier development. The two turning points in Aristotle's development are the death of Plato and the foundation of the Lyceum, and the tripartite development hinging around them constitute Platonism, Reform-Platonism, and Aristotelianism. The middle period for Jaeger (p.347–342) was one of intense literary activity in Asia Minor at Assos and Mytilene. A work, in many respects tentative and in most controversial, which can now be seen as a landmark in Aristotelian studies.

LE BLOND, Jean Marie. Logique et méthode chez Aristote; Étude sur la recherche des principes dans la physique aristotélicienne. 3. ed. Paris, Librarie Philosophique J. Vrin, 1973. xxxvi, 454p. **BA63**

Bibliothèque d'histoire de la philosophie.
Études CCXXXIX 1939 231–235 Bremond • RMM 1940 343–344 • NRTh LXVII 1945 970 de Munter
First published in 1939, in conjunction with the author's *Eulogos et l'argument de convenance chez Aristote* (cf. AJPh 1940 504 Greene).

LEFÈVRE, Charles. Sur l'évolution d'Aristote en psychologie. Préface de Suzanne Mansion. Louvain, Éditions de l'Institut supérieur de philosophie (de l'Université catholique de Louvain). 1972. ix, 344p. **BA64**

Aristote. Traductions et études.
AC XLVI 1977 249–252 Byl • MSR XXXI 1974 47–48 Spanneut • NRTh XCV 1973 563 Jacobs
A useful corrective to Nuyens' celebrated *L'évolution de la psychologie d'Aristote,* Louvain, 1948. The work is based on an excellent knowledge of Aristotle's writings and witnesses to a sound philological and critical sense.

LESZL, Walter. Aristotle's conception of ontology. Padova, Università di Padova, Editrice Antenore, 1975. 558p. **BA65**

AC XLVI 1977 246–249 Couloubaritis • Gnomon LI 1979 310–315 Bärthlein • JHPh XV 1977 331–334 Owens • REG XCI 1978 244–245 Goldschmidt
One of the major difficulties of the *Metaphysics,* perhaps even for Aristotle himself, is to know what exactly is the object of this science.

LESZL, Walter. Logic and metaphysics in Aristotle; Aristotle's treatment of types of equivocity and its relevance to his metaphysical theories. Padova, Antenore, 1970. xii, 601p. **BA66**

Studia Aristotelica; v. 5.
Gnomon XLVII 1975 340–349 Frede • JHPh XII 1974 103–105 Edel • CR XXIII 1973 212–214 Hamlyn
An overextended examination of "focal meaning"

and analogy in Aristotle, differing from most commentators, and rambling and repetitious in the process.

LLOYD, Geoffrey E. R. Aristotle; The growth and structure of his thought. Cambridge, Cambridge University Press, 1968. xiii, 324p.   **BA67**

AC XXXVIII 1969 231–232 Moraux • CPh LXIV 1969 268–269 Sprague

LOUIS, Pierre. La découverte de la vie; Aristote. Paris, Hermann, 1975. 209, [4]p.   **BA68**

Collection Savoir.
AC XLV 1976 608–617 Byl
An historical study of Aristotle's contribution to biology by an editor of his biological works. Louis says at the outset that he will be content with description and statement and for the most part abstain from judging but fortunately he does not abide completely by this rule. His work is a satisfactory introduction for the non-specialist.

LYNCH, John P. Aristotle's school; A study of a Greek educational institution. Berkeley, University of California Press, 1972. xiv, 247p.   **BA69**

AC XLIII 1974 451 Moraux • CW LXVIII 1974 194–195 Sparshott • Gnomon XLVIII 1976 128–134 Wehrli
A revised Yale dissertation which investigates the institutional, as distinct from the doctrinal, aspects of the Athenian schools of philosophy, particularly the Peripatos.

McKEON, Richard. Introduction to Aristotle. 2d ed., rev. and enl. Chicago, University of Chicago Press, 1973. lii, 759p.   **BA70**

CW LXIX 1976 396–397 Tracy
Based on the conviction that Aristotle is the best introduction to what Aristotle thought and meant, this is essentially a very useful collection of texts, divided into seven sections with a special introduction and table of contents before each. The General Introduction is expanded in the second edition.

MILO, Ronald D. Aristotle on practical knowledge and weakness of will. The Hague, Mouton, 1966. 113, [1]p.   **BA71**

Studies in philosophy; 6.
CW LXII 1968 137 Urdahl
A critical exposition and examination of Aristotle's analysis of "practical knowledge" and "weakness of will," largely based on the Nicomachean ethics.

MONAN, J. Donald. Moral knowledge and its methodology in Aristotle. Oxford, Clarendon Press, 1968. xv, 163p.   **BA72**

CR XX 1970 164–167 Taylor • CW LXIII 1969 19 Fortenbaugh • RIFD XLVI 1969 538–540

This work examines Aristotle's treatment of moral knowledge in the Protrepticus, the Eudemian and Nicomachean ethics, criticizing various modern views and offering the author's own analysis.

MORAUX, Paul et al. Aristoteles graecus; Die griechischen Manuskripte des Aristoteles. Berlin and New York, W. de Gruyter, 1976.   **BA73**

1. Bd. Alexandrien-London.
AC XLVI 1977 625 Byl • Byz Z LXX 1977 357–359 Hunger • CR XXVIII 1978 335–336 Wilson
This is the first fruits of a team project undertaken in 1965 by an Institute at the Free University in West Berlin. It is the first volume of a series of four (the last to be an index), which will give full descriptions of all Greek manuscripts containing works by Aristotle. The cataloguers have visited the libraries concerned with autopsy and have built up a splendid collection of microfilm in Berlin. The present work, of high quality and accuracy, augurs well for the series.

MORAVCSIK, J. M. E., ed. Aristotle; A collection of critical essays. 1st ed. Garden City, N. Y., Anchor Books, 1967. 341p.   **BA74**

JHPh VI 1968 309–310 Louch • PhR LXXVIII 1969 402–405 Taylor
Mostly contemporary authors, but also Cook, Wilson and Prichard (1935). Most of the essays have been published already, but there is a previously unpublished one by J. L. Austin (in response to Prichard) and new ones by Woods and Urmson. All deal with one of four topics: Logic, the Categories, the Metaphysics, the Ethics. The aim of the volume is to display the range of Aristotle's thought and its relevance to contemporary problems. The work succeeds better in realizing the first objective than the second.

OATES, Whitney Jennings. Aristotle and the problem of value. Princeton, Princeton University Press, 1963. x, 387p.   **BA75**

AC XXXIII 1964 170–171 Joly • CW LVII 1964 356 Long • Hermathena XCIX 1964 114 Charlton
The first large scale work on the subject, this is a careful investigation of texts in Plato and Aristotle with an analysis of their "latent" axiologies. Beginning with the theory of ideas in its relation to Plato's axiology, the author takes up the relevant Aristotelian passages and concludes that in rejecting the Ideas, Aristotle lost the chance of even developing a unified system of values. Thomas Aquinas had to supplement Aristotle with Augustine to delineate a coherent Christian system of values. There is little in the way of bibliography beyond Ross and some English scholars.

OWENS, Joseph. The doctrine of being in the Aristotelian metaphysics; A study in the Greek background of mediaeval thought. 3rd ed., rev. Toronto, Pontifical Institute of Mediaeval Studies, 1978. xxxi, 539p.   **BA76**

CR III 1953 22–24 Rees • Gnomon XL 1968 139–147 Kuhn • RPhL L 1952 471–478 Verbeke • Speculum XXVII 1952 567–578, LIV 1979 412–413 Bourke

A 1951 Toronto dissertation, which appeared in a 2d revised edition in 1963 and now in a 1978 3rd revised edition, represents a high point in the scholarship of the Pontifical Institute of Mediaeval Studies at Toronto. The successive editions have incorporated ongoing discussions with the main writers on Aristotle's ontology—Aubenque, Hope, Merlan, De Vogel, Mansion, Muskens, Foá, Moraux, and Chung-Hwan Chen. The present edition adds p.35–67, reviewing the literature of the last quarter-century. They restate the basic theses of Owen's original position. The exhaustive bibliography has been updated.

PATZIG, Günther. Aristotle's theory of the syllogism; A logicophilological study of book A of the Prior analytics. Trans. by Jonathan Barnes. Dordrecht, D. Reidel, [1969]. xvii, 219p. **BA77**

Trans. of *Die Aristotelische Syllogistik.*

CW LXIV 1970 121 McCall • RPh XLIV 1970 128–129 Louis • QJS LVI 1970 337–338 Griffin • Gnomon XXXIX 1967 454–464 Scheibe

Barnes translates the second (1963) German edition of a work which was greeted with enthusiasm on its appearance. An intricate work, making uninhibited use of modern formal mathematical logic but presented so clearly and cogently that it will give the reader a heightened respect for Aristotle's logical genius.

ROSS, David William, Sir. Aristotle. 5th ed., rev. London, Methuen & Co. Ltd., 1966. xi, 300p. **BA78**

CR XXXVIII 1924 195 Dodd

A clear and detailed account of the relatively complete works of Aristotle. Comparisons with modern philosophers are used suggestively.

SAFFREY, H. D. Le "Peri philosophias" d'Aristote et la théorie platonicienne des idées nombres. Leiden, E. J. Brill, 1971. xii, 74p. **BA79**

Deuxieme édition revue et accompagnée du compte-rendu critique par Harold Cherniss. 1st ed., 1955.

RFil XVII 1958 514–515 Herrero • RPh XXXI 1957 119 Louis • Gnomon XXXI 1959 36–51 Cherniss

An elegant short volume devoted to an interpretation of *De anima* 1.2 404b19. The previous interpretations of the passage are reviewed and Saffrey proposes that the citation is from the lost *Peri philosophias,* a work of Aristotle's youth. Cherniss' largely negative review of the original is included.

SOLMSEN, Friedrich. Aristotle's system of the physical world; A comparison with his predecessors. Ithaca, Cornell University Press, 1970, 1960. xiv, 468p. **BA80**

Cornell studies in classical philology; v. 33.

AJPh LXXXIII 1962 202–204 Merlan • CW LIV 1961 227 Minar

A sequel to the author's *Plato's theology* (1942),

where he saw Plato introducing the concept of an intelligent world-soul to bridge the gap between Ideas and sensibles.

SYMPOSIUM ARISTOTELICUM, Louvain, 1960. Aristote et les problèmes de méthode. Communications présentées au Symposium Aristotelicum tenu à Louvain du 24 août au 1er septembre 1960. Louvain, Publications universitaires, 1961. vii, 362p. **BA81**

Aristote; traductions et études.

JHS LXXXV 1965 256 Furley • Mind LXXIV 1965 144 Kneale • REG LXXVII 1964 613–616 Defradas

An important collection of 16 papers in the language in which they were delivered at the 1960 Louvain Symposium. There are papers on general problems of method (Aubenque, Moreau, Mansion, Owen) and on specific problems: Method in Metaphysics (Verbeke, De Vogel, Gigon), Method in Natural Philosophy (Moraux, Balme, Düring, Dörrie) and Method in Ethics (Monan, Rabinowiz, Allan). A concluding piece by Wehrli relates Aristotelian dialogs to Socratic and later Peripatetic literature.

Caesar

ADCOCK, Frank Ezra, Sir. Caesar as man of letters. Hamden, Conn., Archon Books, 1969. ix, 114p. **BA82**

Reprint of the 1956 ed.

AJPh LXXVII 1956 447–448 Daly • REA LVIII 1956 406–407 Bardon • Gnomon XXVIII 1956 634–635 Collins

A surprisingly pedestrian summary from a foremost authority, mainly addressed to British undergraduates. Chapter 1 on literary form seeks to place the Commentaries in the development of the genre. The chapter on style is disappointing and the work as a whole does not live up to its title.

COLLINS, J. H. "A selective survey of Caesar scholarship since 1935." CW LVII (1963): 45–51, 81–88. **BA83**

GELZER, Matthias. Caesar; Politician and statesman. Oxford, Basil Blackwell, 1969. viii, 359p., 3 plates (1 fold.), illus. **BA84**

Trans. of *Caesar; der Politiker und Staatsmann.*

CR XII 1962 99 Stavely • Latomus XXVII 1968 944–947 Stuveras • G&R XV 1968 204 Sewter

First published in 1921, reissued in considerably revised form in 1940. A second revision was published in French in 1960, with some re-assessment in minor details and notes added for the first time. The English translation is of the sixth edition.

GESCHE, Helga. Caesar. Darmstadt, Wissenschaftliche Buchgesellschaft [Abt. Verl.], 1976. xxi, 357p. **BA85**

Erträge der Forschung; Bd. 51.

CR XXVIII 1978 48–49 Ogilvie • Gnomon LI 1979 68–69 Balsdon

An invaluable instrument of research for the whole of Caesar's career, in two parts: an objective summary of the *status quaestionis* of all major matters of controversy, and an analytic bibliography of work over the last half-century (over 1900 items), extending through p.212–325.

KROYMANN, Jürgen. "Caesar und das Corpus Caesarianum in der neueren Forschung; Gesamtbibliographie 1945–1970." ANRW 1.3 (1973): 457–487.   **BA86**

MEUSEL, Heinrich. Lexicon Caesarianum. Berolini, Weidmann, 1958. 2 v. in 3.   **BA87**

Vol. 1 A–Humilitas. Vol. 2. pt. 1 Iaceo–Pulso. pt. 2. Pulso–Uxor. Tabula Coniecturarum.

MUTSCHLER, Fritz-Heiner. Erzählstil und Propaganda in Caesars Kommentarien. Heidelberg, Winter, 1975. 251p.   **BA88**

A revision of the author's thesis, Heidelberg, 1973, presented under title: "Beobachtungen zur literarischen Forum des Curioabschnittes in Caesars Bellum Civile.
AC XLV 1976 682–683 Liénard • CR XXVII 1977 185–187 Ogilvie • Latomus XXXVI 1977 815–817 Hellegouarc'h • REL LV 1977 54–60 Rambaud
Mutschler's study begins with the special attention which Caesar gives to Curio's debacle in Africa (bell.civ.11.32). The analysis here is sensitive, and the writing displays great clarity and sensibility to the text. More questionable is the author's classification of six stylistic features which he believes to be foreign to the style of a commentary and his choice of illustrations of these features. All told, a useful and instructive study.

RAMBAUD, Michel. L'Art de la déformation historique dans les "Commentaires" de César. 2d édition. Paris, Les Belles lettres, 1966. 451p.
                                                                 BA89

Collection d'études anciennes.
REA LVII 1955 389–394 Carcopino • Gnomon XXVI 1954 527–533 Collins
A new and fundamental work—"the strongest, most sustained, and best-armed attack that has yet been mounted on the general historical reputation of the conqueror of Gaul and of Rome" (Collins). The tendentious phraseology of the *Commentaries* is mercilessly exposed, revealing an inhuman, hypocritical and hateful Caesar beneath the apparent simplicity. There is a good bibliography (p.375–395) as well as Études césariennes (p.397–436).

RASMUSSEN, Detlef. Caesar. 2., verb. Aufl. Darmstadt, Wissenschaftliche Buchgesellschaft, Abt. Verl., 1976. xi, 522p., 14 leaves of plates, illus.   **BA90**

Wege der Forschung; Bd. 43.

CR XVIII 1968 311–313 Walsh • Gnomon XL 1968 310–312 Mensching • AAHG XXII 1969 175–177 Vretska

An extensive collection of papers, divided into five parts: historical background, personality of Caesar, Caesar's *Commentarii* (the largest section); Caesar's military prowess, and Caesar-scholarship (one survey of the present state of Caesar studies by Oppermann, and one of Caesar-scholarship in Italy in the 20th century).

Callimachus

CAPOVILLA, Giovanni. Callimaco. Roma, L'Erma di Bretschneider, 1967. 2 v.   **BA91**

Studia philologica; v. 10.
CR XIX 1969 159–161 Giangrande • JHS LXXIX 1969 134–135 Griffiths • Gnomon XXXIX 1968 505–506, XLI 1969 205 Lloyd-Jones
A portentous work, full of masses of prehistoric material (prehistory is the author's specialization), very full but badly arranged bibliographical data, and rapid generalizations that contribute little new light on the literary or stylistic techniques of Callimachus.

KALLIMACHOS. Hrsg. Aristoxenos D. Skiadas. Darmstadt, Wissenschaftliche Buchgesellschaft, 1975. xi, 418p.   **BA92**

Wege der Forschung; Bd. 296.
JHS XCVI 1976 186–187 Griffiths
Twenty-one articles which appeared between 1925 and 1971, all in German here though eight were originally in French, English or Italian. The editor provides a bibliography (p.401–418).

McKAY, Kenneth J. The poet at play; Kallimachos: The bath of Pallas. Leyden, E. J. Brill, 1962. 139p.   **BA93**

Mnemosyne. Bibliotheca classica Batava: Supplement; v. 6, Callimachus.
Gnomon XXXV 1963 566–568 Bühler • CJ LIX 1963 139 Rutledge • CR XIII 1963 151–153 Griffin • AJPh LXXXV 1964 423–426 Otis
Written with learning, diligence and enthusiasm, but the question remains: Is this a virtuoso display about a virtuoso display? Text and translation are supplied and the notes and commentary are in the best Alexandrine library tradition.
See also McKay, K. J. *Erysichton. A Callimachean Comedy.* Leiden, E. J. Brill, 1962. x, 202p.

Catullus

BARDON, Henry. Propositions sur Catulle. Bruxelles, Latomus, 1970. 159p.   **BA94**

Collection Latomus; v. 118.
AJPh XCV 1974 171–174 Grimm • Phoenix XXVI 1972 312–314 Quinn
A companion to Bardon's edition, *Catulli Carmina coll. Latomus* 112, Bruxelles, 1970. In the *Propositions,*

Bardon uses the poetry to construct an internal biography of the poet's own unconsciously revealed motivations. The treatment is generally impressionistic, a series of gestures to the new socio-anthropological approach to literature. There are fairly detailed opening chapters on Catullus' vocabulary, figures of speech, syntax and imagery. The whole is remarkably brilliant and entertaining, but ultimately unconvincing.

See also Bardon, H., "Philologie et nouvelle critique," *RBPh* XLVIII (1970), 5–15, and "Catulliana," *Latomus* XXXIII (1974), 640–641, *contra* Kenney's review, *CR* XXIII (1973), 165–167.

CATULLUS; A Commentary by C. J. Fordyce. Oxford, Clarendon Press, 1978. xxviii, 422p. **BA95**

Reprinted with corrections, 1978.
AJPh LXXXIV 1963 422–432 Putnam • Gnomon XXXIV 1962 253–263 Fraenkel
A bowdlerized Catullus, omitting 32 poems comprising a total of over 325 lines. Editorial comments are lucid and competent, although occasionally prosaic and overly studious. Many errors, typographical and otherwise, mar the work. Translations are plentiful, fresh and exact. With these caveats, an excellent school text.

CATULLUS, C. Valerius. C. Valerii Catulli Carmina; Recognovit brevique adnotatione critica instruxit R. A. B. Mynors. Oxonii, E Typographeo Clarendoniano, 1972, 1958. xvi, 113p. **BA96**

Scriptorum classicorum bibliotheca Oxoniensis.
AJPh LXXX 1959 415–424 Levine • Phoenix XII 1958 93–116 Goold • CPh LIV 1959 51–53 Oliver
A model text by an eminent paleographer and editor. The apparatus admirably combines compact simplicity with fullness of essential information. In the constitution of the text the editor combines reasonable conservatism with solid independence of judgment. There is an interesting reconstruction of the arrangement of the poems and titles in the archetypes. Occasionally a specious emendation is accepted.
See also *Catulli Veronensis Liber,* edited by W. Eisenhut. Leipzig, Teubner, 1983. xviii, 120p.

CATULLUS, C. Valerius. Catullus: The poems. Edited with introd., revised text and commentary by Kenneth Quinn. London, Macmillan; (New York, St. Martin's Press), 1970. xli, 456p. **BA97**

REL XLIX 1971 405–410 Granarolo • Phoenix XXVI 1972 109–110 Crowther • JRS LXII 1972 212–214 Rudd • CJ LXIX 1973–74 184–185 Putnam
The latest commentary in English on the complete poems had been that of E. T. Merrill, 1893. Quinn here has absorbed the best of earlier philological work and has employed skillfully the latest critical techniques to give us an up-to-date literary and historical commentary. There is much useful information in the introduction on style, morphology, vocabulary, syntax, imagery, metre. The body of the commentary raises and answers most of the usual questions, both textual and interpreta-

tive. A selected bibliography of worthwhile recent criticism follows both introduction and commentary on individual poems. There are some inaccuracies in translation and unnecessary hesitations in commentary. Mynors' OCT text is used with minor changes, but no apparatus criticus. Not as good as Fordyce for introducing students to Catullus, and equally prissy about how much to tell them about sex.

GRANAROLO, Jean. "Catulle, 1948–1973." Lustrum XVII (1973–1974): 27–70. **BA98**

GRANAROLO, Jean. L'oeuvre de Catulle; Aspects religieux, éthiques et stylistiques. Paris, Les Belles lettres, 1967. 408p. **BA99**

Collection d'études anciennes.
REA LXX 1968 486–489 Boyancé • Latomus XXVII 1968 916–918 Bardon • RPh XLII 1968 372 Ernout
The *brevis lux/nox est perpetua* antithesis suggests a study of the religious aspects of Catullus' *oeuvre* (Granarolo is a doctoral student of Boyancé), which occupies the first third of the work. *Aspects éthiques* (p.168–249) investigates the serious and philosophical Catullus behind all the badinage, and *Aspects stylistiques* (p.253–372) examines the resources of imagery and the modes of interrogation employed by the poet.

HARRAUER, Hermann. A bibliography to Catullus. Hildesheim, Gerstenberg, 1979. xii, 206p. **BA100**

Bibliography to the Augustan poetry; v. 3.

HEINE, Rolf. Catull. Darmstadt, Wissenschaftliche Buchgesellschaft, 1975. vii, 481p. **BA101**

Wege der Forschung; Bd. 308.
AAHG XXX 1977 18–21 Vretska • RBPh LIV 1976 892 Liénard • REL LV 1977 48–53 Granarolo • REA LXXVIII–LXXIX 1976–1977 282–283 Bardon
An exclusively German and Anglo-Saxon selection of authors, apart from L. Alfonsi, betraying a certain editorial provincialism.

LEON, H. J. "A quarter century of Catullan scholarship, 1934–1959." CW LIII (1959–1960): 104–113, 141–148, 173–180, 281–282. **BA102**

LIEBERG, Godo. Puella divina; Die Gestalt der göttlichen Geliebten bei Catull im Zusammenhang der antiken Dichtung. Amsterdam, P. Schippers, 1962. 343p. **BA103**

A&R VII 1962 227–231 Zicari • CW LVII 1963 67 Anderson • Gnomon XXXV 1963 575–577 Copley • RBPh XLI 1963 859–862 Grimal
The beloved girl regarded as a goddess is studied here in a wide context to determine Catullus' special treatment of the topos. Lieberg believes that Catullus meant the name Lesbia to suggest Sappho, the tenth

muse (AP 9.506). Four preliminary chapters sketch the way lovers deified the beloved in Greek and pre-Catullan Latin. The study of Catullus concentrates especially on c.2, 51, and 68, the last receiving over 100 pages of careful commentary. The continuation of the theme in Dante, Goethe, Baudelaire and Rilke among others, is studied in the concluding chapter. An interesting thesis, if somewhat overstated.

LOOMIS, Julia Wolfe. Studies in Catullan verse; An analysis of word types and patterns in the polymetra. Leiden, E. J. Brill, 1972. xii, 160p.   **BA104**

Mnemosyne. Bibliotheca Classica Batava: Supplementum; v. 24.
CR XXV 1975 209–211 Kenney • Gnomon XLVIII 1976 453–458 Korzeniewski • CW LXX 1976 207–208 Elder
This work attempts to apply to the study of the Catullan polymetra the methodology of H. N. Porter, "The early Greek hexamter," Y.C.S. XII (1951), 3–63. Porter should be read first, for his analysis in terms of semantic colometry. The advantage claimed for the new approach is that it facilitates the recognition of words as the fundamental unit of said verse.

McCARREN, V. P. A critical concordance to Catullus. Edited with the computer assistance of William Tajibnapis. Leiden, Brill, 1977. 210p.   **BA105**

CW LXXIV 1980 Gaisser • JRS LXVIII 1978 230–231 McKie
A ridiculously expensive luxury, unnecessary for those who have Wetmore, *Index verborum Catullianus,* 1912 (1961).

QUINN, Kenneth. Approaches to Catullus. New York, Barnes and Noble, 1972. xii, 297p.   **BA106**

Views and controversies about classical antiquity.
CW LXVII 1974 307–308 Ross • CR XXV 1975 149 Kenney • CF XXVI 1972 323–328 Brannan
Seventeen essays by various hands exemplifying the different ways Catullus may be read by experienced readers: Copley and Putnam on c.4, Rudd and Quinn on c.17, Elder and Copley on the Lesbia poems in general. Levens's survey from *Fifty Years of Classical Scholarship* is rightly included, as well as Clausen's "Callimachus and Latin Poetry" from GRBS, 1964, and three contributions from E. Fraenkel. Quinn tries to set some ground rules for literary criticism in "The Commentator's Task."

QUINN, Kenneth. The Catullan revolution. [1st ed. 1959] revised impression. Cambridge, Heffer, 1969. [xi], 119p.   **BA107**

CR XI 1961 42–43 Kenney • RBPh XLIX 1971 182 Bardon • REL XXXVII 1959 285 Bardon
Shows how Catullus employed the traditions of the *poetae novae* to express his private sensibilities. His

revolutionary contribution is to abandon the service of the community for a more esoteric, more purely poetic kind of poetry. There is much that is fresh and illuminating in this work, but the writing style is often slovenly.

QUINN, Kenneth. Catullus; An interpretation. London, B. T. Batsford, 1972. xi, 305p.   **BA108**

CW LXVIII 1974–1975 263 Elder • Latomus XXXII 1973 885–886 Bardon • Phoenix XXVII 1973 300–305 MacKay
Based on the assumption that the collection of poems was organized in three parts by Catullus himself, this interpretation of the poetry of Catullus tries to set it in the social and intellectual context to which it belonged. Chapter I deals chattily with the composition of the collection, c.II with the Lesbia Poems (p.53–130), and c.III attempts a reconstruction of The Affair (p.131–203). In c.IV Quinn turns from the Lesbia poems—25 to 30, out of the total 113—to the Poetry of Social Comment (p.204–282) which includes the homosexual poems, the long poems, and the poetry of political invective, all crowded together. "Sketching in the hypothesis each (poem) seems to invite" (p.130) is Quinn's own job description; it is an occupation more full of hazards than rewards.

QUINN, Kenneth. "Trends in Catullan criticism." ANRW I, 3: 369–389.   **BA109**

ROSS, David O. Style and tradition in Catullus. Cambridge, Mass., Harvard University Press, 1969. viii, 188p.   **BA110**

Loeb classical monographs.
JRS LXII 1972 214–215 Mills • Gnomon XLVIII 1976 559–566 Coppel • Phoenix XXV 1971 82–85 Quinn • REA LXXII 1970 196–197 Bardon
Argues convincingly from word studies that the epigrams proper (Poems 69–116) represent a Roman, pre-neoteric tradition which goes back to Ennius, and the neoteric poems consist only of the polymetrics (1–61) and the hexameter and elegiac poems (62–68).

THOMSON, D. F. S. "Recent Scholarship on Catullus (1960–1969)." CW LXV (1971): 116–126.   **BA111**

WHEELER, Arthur Leslie. Catullus and the traditions of ancient poetry. Berkeley, University of California Press, 291p.   **BA112**

Sather classical lectures; v. 9.
AJPh 1935 180–183 Harrington • Latomus XXV 1966 641 Préaux • REG 1935, 458–459 Bayet
Wheeler's Sather lectures of 1928 were published posthumously in 1934 and brought out in paperback in 1964. Wheeler's work marks a turning point in Catullan exegesis, especially his treatment of the Wedding Poems.

WISEMAN, Timothy Peter. Catullan questions. Leicester, Leicester University Press, 1969. [x], 70p.   **BA113**

"Distributed in North America by Humanities Press, Inc., New York."

CW LXIV 1970 26 Elder • LXIV 1971 270 Wohlberg • CPh LXV 1970 200–201 Putnam • Gnomon XLII 1970 835–836 Schäfer • CR XXI 1971 43–45 Kenney • CJ LXVII 1971 90–91 Ross

Two questions are examined: arrangement and chronology. The tripartite arrangement, it is claimed, was Catullus' own. All the datable poems are moved down to between 56 and 54. The traditional identification of Lesbia with Clodia Metelli is rejected and a new candidate tentatively proposed: Clodia, wife of A. Ofilius. Searching questions are proposed here with the right blend of scepticism, scholarship and hesitancy about new solutions.

Cicero

ALLEN, W., Jr. "A survey of selected Ciceronian bibliography 1939–1953." CW XLVII (1953–1954): 129–139. **BA114**

BOYANCÉ, Pierre. Études sur l'humanisme cicéronien. Bruxelles, Latomus, 1970. 352p. **BA115**

Collection Latomus; v. 121.
AC XL 1971 738–740 van den Bruwaene • RPh XLV 1971 361 Ernout • LEC XXXIX 1971 382 Wankenne

Eighteen articles of unequal length and importance are here reissued spanning thirty years. They include a bibliographical survey (1938–1958) and reviews of important works, including the celebrated disclaimer of Carcopino's Les sécrets de la correspondence de Cicéron, 1947. Cicero's place in the history of culture and of ideas is more important to Boyancé than his place in the history of eloquence or in the political history of Rome.

BÜCHNER, Karl. Das neue Cicerobild. Darmstadt, Wissenschaftliche Buchgesellschaft, 1971. xxv, 520p. **BA116**

Wege der Forschung; Bd. 27.
REL L 1972 334 Richard • RIFD LI 1974 181–182 d'Agostino • GLO VI 1974 207–211 Kuklika

This volume aims at rehabilitating Cicero as a philosopher. There is an introduction by Büchner and six essays, mostly post-World War II. Particularly good are the contributions of Gigon, Villey, Kumaniecki, Büchner and Boyancé. There are three useful indices.

CICERONIANA; Hommages à Kazimierz Kumaniecki publiés par Alain Michel et Raoul Verdière. Leiden, Brill, 1975. x, 236p. **BA117**

Roma aeterna; 9.
CR XXVII 1977 282 Winterbottom • JRS LXVII 1977 253–254 Douglas

A handsome volume of 17 contributions to honor the Polish scholar's 70th birthday. Contributors include Grimal, André, Kroymann, La Penna, Borszák, Leeman, Michel, Büchner and Pöschl. The 184 items of

the bibliography are an astonishing testimony to Kumaniecki's width of interests.

DOUGLAS, Alan Edward. Cicero. Oxford, Clarendon Press, 1968. [2], 41p. **BA118**

Greece & Rome. New surveys in the classics; v. 2.
A balanced critical survey of major trends in Ciceronian scholarship, in six chapters: 1. Cicero and Roman politics, 2. The Speeches—Matter and Manner, 3. The Letters, 4. An Aspect of Cicero's Personality (his conceit), 5. The Philosophical Writings, 6. The Rhetorical Writings.

GELZER, Matthias. Cicero; Ein biographischer Versuch. Wiesbaden, F. Steiner, 1969. x, 426p. **BA119**

Based on the author's article "M. Tullius Cicero als Politiker" published in 1939 in Pauly's Real-Encyclopädie der Klassischen Altertumswissenschaft.
Latomus XXXI 1972 222–224 van den Brauwaene • JRS LXII 1972 228–229 Douglas • HZ CCXI 1970 645–646 Volkmann

An expansion of Gelzer's classic Pauly-Wissowa article, Tullius 29, RE VII, A, 1, 1939, 827–1274.

GOAR, R. J. Cicero and the state religion. Amsterdam, A. M. Hakkert, 1972. 141p. **BA120**

Gnomon XLVII 1975 86–88 Boyancé • CW LXVII 1973 45 Weaver

The study is limited to Cicero's attitude toward the state religion, leaving the more subjective question of his 'personal' religion to be treated in an appendix. The opening chapter is a somewhat superfluous general survey of Roman religion. The works searched for statements on the state religion include the Catilinarius, De domo sua, De haruspicum Responso, De legibus and De divinatione II, which are seen to be increasingly dependable and sincere on the question. There are many misprints and bibliographical deficiencies.

GÖRLER, Woldemar. Untersuchungen zu Ciceros Philosophie. Heidelberg, C. Winter, 1974. 224p. **BA121**

Bibliothek der klassischen Altertumswissenschaften: n.F. Reihe 2; Bd. 50.
LEC XLIII 1975 217 A.W.

A useful reflective study on the apparent contradictions in the eclecticism of Cicero's philosophical views.

GOTOFF, H. C. Cicero's elegant style; An analysis of the Pro Archia. Urbana, University of Illinois Press, 1979. xiii, 255p. **BA122**

KUMANIECKI, Kazimierz Feliks. Cicerone e la crisi della repubblica romana. [Traduzione di Lionello Constantini]. Roma, Centro di studi ciceroniani editore, 1972. 561p. **BA123**

Collana di studi ciceroniani; 5.
Latomus XXXIV 1975 510–511 Brost
The great Polish master of humanism here appears

in Italian translation. The 19th and 20th century detractors of Cicero are passed in review: Drumann, Mommsen, Carcopino.

KYTZLER, Bernhard. Ciceros literarische Leistung. Darmstadt, Wissenschaftliche Buchgesellschaft, 1973. xii, 544p.   **BA124**

Wege der Forschung; Bd. 240.
REL LII 1974 484–486 Poncelet • Latomus XXXIV 1975 835 Briot
Particularly concerned with the rhetorical writings and works of Cicero, and excluding the letters and the philosophical works (for which cf. Büchner, *Das neue Cicerobild*). The first section includes the celebrated and unjust verdict of Mommsen (1904) and three refutations thereof (Gundolf, 1926, Boyancé, 1958, and Schmid, 1960/1971). This section is followed by twelve excerpts on the oratorical style and art of Cicero. The third section contains eight studies, each of which focuses attention on a single work of Cicero. The last contribution is from the editor and is a reprint of his introduction to *Cicero, Brutus,* München, Heimeran, 1970. An excellent volume of synthesis, masterfully evoking the lasting greatness of Cicero.

MERGUET, Hugo. Lexikon zu den philosophischen schriften Cicero's; Mit angabe sämtlicher stellen. Hildesheim, G. Olms, 1961. 3 v.
BA125

Unveränderter Nachdruck der Ausgabe, Jean, 1887–1894.

ROWLAND, R. J. "A survey of selected Ciceronian bibliography (1965–1974)." CW LXXI (1978): 289–327.   **BA126**

See also (for 1953–1965) Rowland, *CW* LX (1966), 51–65, 101–115.

SCHMIDT, Peter L. "Cicero, De re Publica; Die Forschung der letzten fünf Dezennien." ANRW I, 4 (1973): 262–333.   **BA127**

Useful for its listing of texts, commentaries and studies in text tradition and source studies of the philosophical works of Cicero.

SHACKLETON BAILEY, David Roy. Cicero. London, Duckworth, 1971. xii, 290p.
BA128

Classical life and letters.
ACR III 1973 14 Mix • JRS LXII 1972 216–218 Rawson • CR XXIV 1974 68–70 Stockton
A *parergon* of Shackleton Bailey's monumental edition of the *Epistula ad Atticum* (cf. Gnomon XXXVIII 1966 364–371 Goodyear), and to a large extent Cicero is allowed here to speak for himself, in Shackleton Bailey's very fine translations (with Greek quotations done in French). Shackleton Bailey's own comments are learned and lively. Over-concentration on the letters results in a portrait of Cicero *dimidiatus,* with not enough about Cicero the orator, political thinker, philosopher and historian.

SMETHURST, S. E. "Cicero's rhetorical and philosophical works; A bibliographical survey (1939–1956)." CW LI (1957–1958): 1–4, 24, 32–41.   **BA129**

Continued in (for 1957–1963) *CW* LVIII (1964), 36–45, and (for 1964–1967) *CW* LXI (1967), 125–133.

STOCKTON, David. Cicero; A political biography. London, Oxford University Press, 1978, 1971. ix, 359p., Leaf of plates: maps, ports.
BA130

CR XXIV 1974 66–68 Lintott • Mnemosyne XXVIII 1975 106–108 Jonkers
A largely accurate and forcefully written account of Cicero's political career.

STRAUME-ZIMMERMANN, L. Ciceros Hortensius. Bern, Lang, 1976. 283p.   **BA131**

Europ. Hockschulschriften Reihe 15 Klass. Philol. & Lit. IX.
VChr XXXIII 1979 412–414 den Boeft

SUMNER, G. V. The orators in Cicero's *Brutus;* Prosopography and chronology. Toronto, University of Toronto Press, 1973. 197p.
BA132

Phoenix Suppl. XI.
AJPh XCVI 1975 332–334 Shackleton Bailey • CR XXVII 1977 285 Douglas • LEC XLII 1974 327 Stenuit • Phoenix XXX 1976 88–91 Broughton
A major contribution to Republican prosopography, presenting a chronological analysis of the 221 orators in *Brutus* and investigating the chronological and prosopographical reliability of Cicero. At times the commentary is tediously speculative.

THOMAS, Klaus Bernd. Textkritische Untersuchungen zu Ciceros Schrift De officiis. Münster and Westfalen, Aschendorff, 1971. 124p.

BA133

Orbis antiquus; Heft 26.
ACR II 1972 230–231 Mix • Gymnasium LXXXII 1975 476–478 Ehlers • Mnemosyne XXVII 1974 320–321 Kleywegt
One thoroughly familiar with the plethora of MSS and the major lines of criticism deals here in an eclectic fashion with such problems as repetitions, variations, lacunae and interpolations. In general the approach is more conservative than conjectural.

Corpus Hermeticum

DELATTE, Louis, GOVAERTS, S. and DE-NOOZ, J., eds. Index du Corpus hermeticum. Roma, Edizioni dell' Ateneo & Bizzarri, 1977. xxi, 359p.   **BA134**

Lessico intellettuale europeo; 13.
Maia XXXI 1979 79–80 della Corte

Demosthenes

ELLIS, J. R. and MILNS, R. D. The spectre of Philip; Demosthenenes' first Philippic, Olynthiacs and speech, On the peace; A study in historical evidence. [Sydney], Sydney University Press, [1970]. xiii, 122p.**BA135**

Sources in ancient history.
Phoenix XXVI 1972 202–203 Cole • CW LXVI 1973 303 Koonce
A help from Australia for the Ancient History Survey course in a Greekless student world. Five speeches are presented as an introduction to an evaluation of Demosthenes' works as a source for Philip. There are useful tables and a select bibliography.

Empedocles

BEN, N. van der. The proem of Empedocles' Peri physios; Towards a new edition of all fragments; thirty-one fragments. Amsterdam, Grünter, 1975. 230p. Thesis, University of Amsterdam.**BA136**

AC XLV 1976 238 Byl • CR XXVIII 1978 167–168 Kerferd
Thirty of the thirty-one fragments edited here are detached from their attribution by Diels, *Vorsokratiker* to the *Katharmoi* and combined with fragment 30 Diels-Kranz to form a unity, the proem of Peri Pyseos. The case for this new disposition is well if not convincingly argued, and the promised edition of all the fragments will be awaited with interest.

BOLLACK, Jean. Empédocle. Paris, Les Éditions de Minuit, 1965. 1. Introduction à l'ancienne physique. 2. Les origines: éd. critique. 3. Les origines: commentaire. 2 vols.**BA137**

Gnomon XLI 1969 439–447 Kahn • AGPh VIII 1973 76–79 Long • CR XVII 1967 147–149, XXII 1972 325–327 Kerferd • REG LXXXVI 1973 212–223 Defradas • AC XXXIX 1970 579–581 Joly
By far the most extended text and commentary so far published. Attempts to study Empedocles *de novo*, going behind the work of Diels and 19th century scholarship on the doxographic tradition. Contains a great mass of new interpretations or reinterpretations. A very difficult work, not easy to consult, but displaying great literary sensitivity combined with complete mastery of traditional scholarship. The commentary—philological, linguistic, literary, historical—is remarkably full.

O'BRIEN, Denis. Empedocles' cosmic cycle; A reconstruction from the fragments and secondary sources. Cambridge, Cambridge University Press, 1969. x, 459p., 1 illus.**BA138**

Cambridge classical studies.
JHS XC 1970 238–239 Long • Thought XLV 1970 308–310 Llanszon • RPh XLIV 1970 125–126 Mugler
Particularly valuable for its 60-page (p.337–398) critical bibliography of all works exclusively devoted to Empedocles from 1805 to 1965. Most of this work was completed before 1965 when a trio of challenges was issued to the traditional interpretation (a cycle of four periods) by Bollack, Hölsher and Solmsen. O'Brien is largely traditional, but he has many original observations and close exegesis of many of the fragments and doxographical evidence.
See also O'Brien, D., *Pour interpréter Empédocle*. College d'Études anciennes. Paris, Les Belles Lettres, 1981.
Philos antiqua XXXVIII. Leiden, Brill. ix, 138p.

WRIGHT, M. R., ed. Empedocles: The extant fragments. New Haven, Yale University Press, 1981. vii, 364p.**BA138a**

TLS LXXX 1981 1437 Schofield

Ennius

ENNIUS, Quintus. Ennianae poesis reliquiae. Iteratis curis. Recensuit Johannes Vahlen. Amsterdam, A. M. Hakkert, 1967. ccxxiv, 312p.**BA139**

Reprint of Leipzig ed. 1928.

ENNIUS, Quintus. The tragedies of Ennius; The fragments. Edited with an introd. and commentary by H. D. Jocelyn. Cambridge, Cambridge University Press, 1969. viii, 473p.**BA140**

Cambridge classical texts and commentaries; v. 10. First published 1967, reprinted with corrections 1969.
AC XXXVII 1968 693–695 van Looy • JRS LVIII 1968 301–302 Morel • REL XLVI 1968 459–461 Heurgon
The detailed introduction to this welcome new edition of the fragments of the 20 tragedies has chapters on Athenian drama and the Roman festivals, the Hellenizing of the Roman stage, Athenian drama and the Roman poets, and the form of Roman tragedy, as well as sections on Ennius, the text tradition of his tragedies and their titles. The commentary is a work of prodigious learning, diligence and accuracy. There is a concordance of the present numbering of the fragments with that in the well-known earlier editions of Ribbeck and Vählen.

MÜLLER, Lucian. Quintus Ennius; Eine Einleitung in das Studium der römischen Poesie. St. Petersburg, C. Ricker, 1884. ix, 313p.**BA141**

SKUTSCH, Otto. Ennius. Sept exposés suivis de discussions par Otto Skutsch [et al.]. Entretiens préparés et présidés par Otto Skutsch. Vandouvres-Genève, 23–29 août 1971. [Genève], Fondation Hardt, 1972. 376p.**BA142**

Entretiens sur l'antiquité classique; t. 17.
JRS LXVI 1976 262–265 Mariotti • CJ LXX, 4 1975 77–78 Wassermann • CR XXV 1975 203–206 Goodyear

Seven contributors differing in their approach and interests.

SKUTSCH, Otto. Studia Enniana. London, Athlone, 1968. x, 204p.   **BA143**

AJPh XCI 1970 255–256 Rowell • CR XIX 1969 378 Williams
Contains two new and fourteen revised papers.

TIMPANARO, S. J. "Ennius." AAHG V (1952): 195–212.   **BA144**

Epicurus

EPICURUS. Epicurus, the extant remains; With short critical apparatus, trans. and notes by Cyril Bailey. Wesport, Conn., Hyperion Press, [1979].   **BA145**

Reprint of the 1926 ed., Clarendon Press, Oxford.
JHS XLVII 1927 279–280 V.S. • REG 1929 233 Robin
Bailey's lifelong interest in Lucretius led him to make his own text, translation and commentary of Epicurus. The commentary occupies three-fifths of the volume and the translation is the first English rendering of all the extant documents.

LEMKE, Dietrich. Die Theologie Epikurs; Versuch einer Rekonstruktion. München, Beck, 1973. 118p.   **BA146**

Zetemata; Monographien zur klassischen Altertumswissenschaft; 5. A revision of the author's thesis, Tübingen, 1971.
Athenaeum LIV 1976 193–198 Arrighetti • WS LXXXVII 1974 210 Schwabl
A Tübingen dissertation analyzes anew the intractable materials for a theology of Epicurus, esp. Cic. n.d. 1.49.

RIST, John M. Epicurus; An introduction. Cambridge, Cambridge University Press, 1977, c1972. xiv, 185p.   **BA147**

"First paperback edition."
CW LXVII 1973–1974 118–119 Jope • Gnomon XLVI 1974 752–756 Boyancé • CR XXVIII 1978 90–92 Skemp
Aims at providing up-to-date, unbiased introduction to Epicurus and generally succeeds. Most approaches of recent research are touched upon, but some points in Epicurus' philosophy are treated too summarily.

Euripides

BARLOW, Shirley A. The imagery of Euripides; A study in the dramatic use of pictorial language. London, Methuen (New York, distributed by Harper & Row), 1974. xii, 169p.   **BA148**

University paperback based on the author's thesis, University of London, 1963.

RPh XLVII 1973 132–133 Ronnet • CR XXIV 1974 21–23 Whittle • CJ LXIX 1974 255–257 Beye
"Imagery" is used by Barlow both for language clearly metaphorical or comparative and (surely questionably) for descriptive language which is sensuous but not metaphorical. In fact study of the latter constitutes five of the six chapters, simile and metaphor receiving minimal treatment (p.96–119). "Imagery" covers Euripides' use of language to enable his audience to imagine scenes, situations and emotional states. The work steers clear of excessive subjectivism and presents a fruitful fusion of classical philology and literary criticism. The attempt to link contemporary Greek art with the artistry of Euripides is less successful. The classification of images according to their dramatic interest casts considerable new light on the poetic achievement of Euripides, as does the study of his varied technique and effects in choral passages, monodies and dialog. There is a good index locorum.

BASTA Donzelli, G. Studio sull'Elettra di Euripide. Catania, Universita di Catania, 1978. xxiii, 383p.   **BA149**

Univ. di Catania Pubbl. Fac. di Lett. e Filos. XXXII.

BENEDETTO, Vincenzo di. Euripide; Teatro e società. Torino, Einaudi, 1971. xv, 337p.   **BA150**

Saggi; 484.
Gnomon XLIX 1977 249–252 Matthieson • CW LXVI 1973 465–466 Hamilton • CR XXV 1975 12–13 Whittle • AC XLII 1973 602–604 van Looy • LEC XLI 1973 350–351 Delaunois
Despite its discursiveness, this is a major contribution to Euripidean criticism, stressing the actuality of the art of Euripides and its relevance to a modern audience. The point of departure is *Hippolytus* (ll.377–383), the confrontation with Socratic ideas. The first of three main sections is devoted to rationalism and tragic sentiment in the theatre of Euripides. Part 2 examines political and social influences on the plays and part 3 deals with the last plays in which pathos becomes a dominant element. Apart from its central thesis the work abounds in astute and fresh critical judgments and is based on an unrivalled knowledge of the dramatist and his times. The almost complete bibliographical coverage makes it a useful work of reference.

BLAIKLOCK, E. M. The male characters of Euripides; A study in realism. Wellington, New Zealand University Press, 1952. xvi, 267p.   **BA151**

JHS LXXIV 1954 198 Griffith
Blaiklock's justification for this competent but somewhat pedestrian study is that with the exception of *IT*, Euripides' main interest was in character not in plot. Eleven major characters are studied in as many chapters. The Introduction and Appendix are straightforward and unpretentious.

BURNETT, Anne P. Catastrophe survived; Euripides' plays of mixed reversal. Oxford, Clarendon Press, 1971. ix, 234p.   **BA152**

Arion n.s. 111 1976 101–108 Burian • Phoenix XXVII 1973 204–205 Wilson • CJ LXX, 4 1975 67–69 Golden • CR n.s. XXIV 1974 23–25 Baldry

Seven plays of Euripides, with rescue as their common symbolic action, are studied in this stimulating work. These plays—*Alcestis, IT, Helen, Ion, Andromache, Heracles, Orestes*—seem to violate the normal tragic mode by happy or apparently happy endings. Their complexities of plot and characterization are studied with sensitivity, but too much seems to be made of an intervening benign divine pity. The study provokes fresh thought even where it may not command belief.

CONACHER, D. J. Euripidean drama; Myth, theme and structure. [Toronto], University of Toronto Press, [1967]. xiii, 354p.   **BA153**

Gnomon XLI 1969 16–29 Seeck • CJ LXIV 1968 80–82 Wilson • CW LXII 1968 30 Petroff • CPh LXIV 1969 129–130 Dearden • AJPh XCI 1970 87–91 Peradotto

In an interesting thematic, non-chronological approach Conacher divides the plays into seven groups for discussion: mythological tragedy, political tragedy, war and its aftermath, realistic tragedy, tragédie manqué, romantic tragedy and Satyric tragedy. Within this framework the plays are discussed separately and comprehensively, highlighting the problems and the solutions for each, and offering a personal interpretation. One weakness in his approach to Euripides is the search for the hero, and there are important subjects not touched. "Structure" in the title promises more than it delivers, and the totality is more a series of articles than a book with a unifying theme.

GREENWOOD, Leonard H. Aspects of Euripidean tragedy. New York, Russell & Russell, [1972]. vii, 143p.   **BA154**

Reprint of the 1953 ed.
JHS LXXIV 1954 198–199 Griffith
Verrall *redivivus*. Three of the five chapters in this slender volume—The Fantasy Theory, The Symbolist Theory, The Rationalist Theory—have a unified theme in proposing and defending a new solution to an old problem: "Whereas the poet's representation of the nature and actions of the gods . . . conflicts sharply with what appear to be his own religious beliefs, nevertheless these gods and their activities are presented as an integral and irremovable element." Chapter IV is a reconsideration of the *Suppliants* and c.V widens into Realism and Greek Tragedy.

GRUBE, George M. The drama of Euripides. London, Methuen (New York, Barnes & Noble), [1973]. viii, 456p.   **BA155**

First published in 1941; reprinted with minor corrections in 1961.
CR LVII 1943 16–17 Kitto
A comprehensive and valuable study, sensible and judicious in its discussion of the separate plays. Unfortunately there is little cross-reference to Aeschylus and

Sophocles, which leaves Euripides in a sort of vacuum. There are good chapters entitled Prologues and Epilogues, The Chorus, and The Problem of Relevance which exonerate much of the so-called episodic scenes, detached odes and philosophical passages from the charge of irrelevance. The greater part of the book deals with discussions of individual plays, where *Bacchae, Heracles* and the war-plays fare best.

McDONALD, M. A semilemmatized concordance to Euripides' *Alcestis*. Costa Mesa, Cal., TLG Publ., 1977. 133p.   **BA155a**

See also *A semilemmatized concordance to Euripides' Andromache.* Ibid, 1978. 143p.
See also *A semilemmatized concordance to Euripides' Cyclops.* Ibid, 1977. 94p.

MELCHINGER, Siegfried. Euripides. Trans. by Samuel R. Rosenbaum. New York, Ungar, [1973]. vi, 218p., illus.   **BA156**

CR XXVI 1976 120 Whittle
Analyzes all 18 extant plays of Euripides, attempting to convey a sense of Greek drama as total theatre by attention to details of choreography, aria recitative, stage machinery, masks, setting, dramatic verse, etc.

MILLER, H. W. "A survey of recent Euripidean scholarship, 1940–1954." CW XLIX (1955–1956): 81–92.   **BA157**

Survey is continued in "Euripidean drama, 1955–1965" *CW* LX (1966–1967), 177–187, 218–220.

RITCHIE, William. The authenticity of the *Rhesus* of Euripides. Cambridge, Cambridge University Press, 1964. viii, 384p.   **BA158**

"Revised and enlarged version of a doctoral dissertation . . . University of Cambridge in 1957."
Gnomon XXXVII 1965 228–241 Fraenkel • CR n.s. XV 1965 268–271 Stevens • Athenaeum XLV 1967 422–425 Barigazzi
An attempt to give the *Rhesus* back to Euripides, contrary to majority opinion. Divided into two parts—external and internal evidence—it shows a complete mastery of the immense literature on the question from Scaliger and Valekenajer onwards. A most careful survey of the evidence derived from dramatic technique, plot construction, vocabulary, style and metre convinces the author that this is genuine early Euripides. Divergences from the Euripidean manner are outweighed by similarities. An important contribution to Euripidean scholarship regardless of whether the case is proven. Many will still be sufficiently disturbed by the episodic nature of the plot to feel that the hand is the hand of Euripides, but not the voice.

RIVIER, André. Essai sur le tragique d'Euripide. 2. éd. entièrement revue. Paris, Diffusion De Boccard, 1975. xiv, 218p.   **BA159**

AC XLIV 1975 709 van Looy
Rivier had left a 1964 dated manuscript of an almost

complete 2d edition of his well-known work. After his heart attack in 1973, Lassere and Sulliger published this welcome work, with minor editorial *toilette.* There is a new introduction (ix–xiv). As much a reaction against the exaggerations of structural analysts as those of the "Rationalists." The work wears remarkably well after 30 years and gives an excellent overview of critical activity on Euripides in the period 1890–1940.

SALE, William. Existentialism and Euripides; Sickness, tragedy and divinity in the *Medea,* the *Hippolytus* and the *Bacchae.* Berwick, Australia, Aureal, 1977. iii, 142p.   **BA160**

Ramus monographs.
CW LXXII, 2 1978 118–119 Grimaldi • G&R XXV, 2 1978 196 Ireland • RPh LII 1978 368–370 Ronnet
An effort to look at three plays in terms of six fundamental concepts of existential psychoanalysis.

SEGAL, Erich W., comp. Euripides; A collection of critical essays. Englewood Cliffs, N. J., Prentice-Hall, [1968]. xi, 177p.   **BA161**

Twentieth century views.
A good introduction by Segal is followed by Arrowsmith on Euripides' theater of Ideas; a chapter on Euripides and the Gods from Grube's 1941 book; Anne Pippin Burnett on The Virtues of Admetus (from *CPh* LX, 1965); Eilhard Schlesinger on Euripides' *Medea* (from *Hermes* XCIV, 1966); Bernard Knox, The Hippotytus of Euripides (from *YClS* XIII, 1952); Eric Havelock, to whom the work is dedicated, on Watching *The Trojan women* (written especially for this collection but without benefit of the movie featuring Katherine Hepburn and Vanessa Redgrave, *Why the Trojan women?*); Jean Paul Sartre's introduction to his *Les Troyennes* adaptation; *Orestes* by Christian Wolff; A Tragedy and Religion: The "Bacchae," by Thomas G. Rosenmeyer. There is a Chronology of Important Dates and a bibliography which features several names that one might have expected in the body of the work.

STEVENS, Philip. Colloquial expressions in Euripides. 1. Aufl. Wiesbaden, Steiner, 1976. 72p.   **BA162**

Hermes, Zeitschrift für klassische Philologie: Einzelschriften, Heft 38.
AC XLVI 1977 617–618 van Looy • CW LXXI 1977 196–197 Tarkow • CR XXVIII 1978 224–226 Collard
A welcome contribution to our knowledge of Greek colloquialisms in general, and the Euripidean evidence in particular. Stevens, long an expert in colloquialisms (CQ XXI 1937 182–191, XXXIX 1945 95–105), is admirably cautious. He defines "colloquialism" as an expression natural to ordinary conversation but foreign to distinctively poetic writing or to formal prose. The study has nearly 120 expressions under nine headings: Exaggeration, Pleonasm, Understatement, Brevity, Interjections, Particles, Metaphors, Miscellaneous and Forms and Syntax.

VELLACOTT, Philip. Ironic drama; A study of Euripides' method and meaning. London and New York, Cambridge University Press, 1975. x, 266p.   **BA163**

TLS LXXIV 1975 919 Taplin • AJPh XCVII 1976 183–185 Schmiel • Phoenix XXXI 1977 70–74 Cropp
For Vellacott "ironic" drama allows some of the audience to take the script at its face value, while the more favored can delve for deeper meaning. These deeper meanings have generally to do with two moral issues: the place of women in machismo society and man's behaviour in war. Unsupported hypotheses, improbable assumptions and facile generalizations take the place of detailed argument. Vellacott invokes Verrall in claiming that the ironic method was forced on Euripides because revolutionaries were unacceptable in the theatre. The work combines some sound insights with a good deal of idiosyncrasy.

WEBSTER, Thomas B. L. The tragedies of Euripides. London, Methuen, 1967. [vii], 316p.   **BA164**

JHS LXXXIX 1969 128–129 Borthwick • REG LXXXII 1969 22–23 Duchemin • Mnemosyne XXI 1968 424–425 Kamerbeek
A Euripidean *summa,* for the 19 extant plays and especially for the fragments. The latter are fleshed out from whatever small hints are contained in the papyri and pottery representations. An outline of the probable structure of the lost ones is also attempted. (Webster has attempted similar reconstruction for Menander and has been proven wrong by subsequent discoveries.) A plausible chronological pattern of Euripidean productions emerges, helped in large part by careful study of changes in metrical practices. The study provides the best perspective of the poet's evolution in its entire repertoire of 66 tragedies.

WHITMAN, Cedric. Euripides and the full circle of myth. Cambridge, Mass., Harvard University Press, 1974. vii, 152p.   **BA165**

Loeb classical monographs.
Arion n. s. III 1976 108–113 Burian • TLS LXXIV 1975 919 Taplin • CW LXIX 1976 464–465 Schein
Four essays, three on *IT, Helen* and *Ion,* and a general one entitled The Scope of Myth. The choice of the three plays is dictated by a Northrop Frye distinction between the order, harmony and totality of literary works in the mythic mode and the chaos, discord and particularity of works in the ironic mode. The three plays are considered to belong to the mythic mode. The chapter called The Scope of Myth forms one-third of the book and is the most intellectually provocative. Its value is independent of the somewhat subjective, inconclusive, far-fetched and disjointed treatment of the three selected plays.

WILSON, John R., comp. Twentieth-century interpretations of Euripides' *Alcestis;* A collection of critical essays. Englewood Cliffs, N. J., Prentice-Hall, [1968]. 122p.   **BA166**

A Spectrum book.
CPh LXV 1970 268–270 Henry • CR XX 1970 300–302 Fitton Brown

WINNINGTON-INGRAM, Reginald. Euripides and Dionysus; An interpretation of the *Bacchae*. Cambridge, Cambridge University Press, 1948. viii, 190p.   **BA167**

Photocopy. Ann Arbor, Mich.: University Microfilms, 1976.

AJPh 1949 317–320 Norwood • JHS LXVII 1947 139 Davison • CR 1949 96–98 Morrison

A work meant to be complementary to Dodd's edition despite differences on individual points. The first chapters provide a detailed analysis of the play. The last two chapters try to answer questions posed in the two preliminary ones, especially on the part played by Dionysus. The work is a reflection of the earlier "rationalism" of Verrall and Norwood. It is based on the conviction that Euripides recognized Dionysus but hated him.

ZUNTZ, Günther. The political plays of Euripides. [Corr. reprint]. [Manchester], Manchester University Press, [1963]. xi, 157p.   **BA168**

CPh LII 1957 213 Blaiklock • CR n.s. VI 1956 109–111 Stevens • CJ LII 1957 233 Wassermann

The first part discusses the interpretation of the *Supplices* and *Heraclidae*. It tries to show that so-called political allusions in these plays are dramatically organic and that the plays are better than they are generally rated. Part 2 contains a discussion of the scene of the *Heraclidae*, notes on selected passages, and a chapter on the nature and transmission of the Tragic Hypothesis.

Gellius, Aulus

BALDWIN, Barry. Studies in Aulus Gellius. Lawrence, Kans., Coronado Press, 1975. 130p.
                    BA169

Spine title: *Aulus Gellius*.

CPh LXXIV 1979 173–174 Marshall • CW LXXI 1977 87–88 Sandy

Essentially a catalogue raisonée which seeks to evaluate Gellius and his work within the intellectual, political and social conventions of the Antonine period.

MARACHE, R. "Fronton et A. Gellius (1938–1964)." Lustrum X (1965): 213–245.   **BA170**

Heraclitus

ROUSSOS, Euangelos N. Heraklit-Bibliographie. Darmstadt, Wissenschaftliche Buchges., 1971. xx, 164p.   **BA171**

Erasmus XXIV 1972 880–881 Lasserre • WS LXXXVI 1973 266 Schwabl

A useful bibliographical tool, with a good introduction and alphabetical and chronological (1499–1970) indices.

Herodotus

BERNADETE, Seth. Herodotean enquiries. The Hague, Nijhoff, 1969. 213p.   **BA172**

BAGB 1971 131–133 Lachenand • CJ LXIX 1973 165–166 Anderson • Gnomon XLIII 1971 439–449 von Fritz • Phoenix XXV 1971 291 Grant • RPhL LXXIII 1975 109–117 Brague

At times brilliant and fascinating, but often far-fetched, fantastical and bewildering. The continuing problem here is to know where Herodotus ends and strictly Bernadetean enquiries begin. The structural analysis of the first four books in particular is over-clever.

COBET, Justus. Herodots Exkurse und die Frage der Einheit seines Werkes. Wiesbaden, F. Steiner, 1971. ix, 207p.   **BA173**

Historia. Einzelschriften, Heft 17. A revision of the author's thesis, Frankfurt am Main, 1968.

AC XLI 1972 650 Piérart • Athenaeum LIV 1976 198–201 Ambaglio • Gymnasium LXXXI 1974 103–104 Kinzl • Gnomon XLVII 1975 329–334 Drews

In this careful analysis of *prosthekai* and *parenthekai* (excursus and digressions), the author, an avowed "unitarian" who assumes that the *Histories* constitute a literary unity, investigates their thematic unity. He finds that the digressive elements are not meant to render the historical action more intelligible, but rather to demonstrate the diversity of human response to the universal limitations of the human condition. The overall purpose of Herodotus in the *Histories* is seen as an articulated response to the dictum, "Know Thyself."

FEHLING, Detlev. Die Quellenangaben bei Herodot. Studien zur Erzählkunst Herodots. Berlin, de Gruyter, 1971. xii, 198p.   **BA174**

Gnomon LXVI 1974 737–746 Cobet • REA LXXIV 1972 261–263 Orsini • RPh XLIX 1975 119–121 Will

The problem of Herodotus' historical method and his attitude toward sources was the subject of two studies in 1971, the present work and that of H. Verdin in Dutch (cf. H. Verdin, "Hérodote Historien? Quelques interprétations récentes," *AC* XLIV 1975 668–685). For Fehling, Herodotus is above all a master of literary narrative and even a master illusionist. Bent above all on telling captivating stories all the sources he cites should be treated as belonging to the domain of fiction and should be interpreted as instruments of literary technique. All this revives the older interpretations of Sayce (1883), Panofsky (1885) and Howald (1923). Fehling extends the suspicion of fiction beyond the sources to large areas of the narrative.

FORNARA, Charles W. Herodotus; An interpretative essay. Oxford, Clarendon Press, 1971. [x], 98p.   **BA175**

ACR II 1972 78 Sheffield • AJPh XCV 1974 164–165 Bruce • CR XXIV 1974 39–41 Hammond • Hermathena CXIV 1972 99 Parke

In keeping with the subtitle, Fornara analyzes only two aspects of Herodotus' work and that selectively: the composition of the History and Herodotus' attitude to contemporary questions. The treatment is light and lively, with subjective judgments that will by turns amuse and amaze. In treating of the composition he tries to fuse the seemingly conflicting views of those who see unity and those who see only "an aggregation of *disiecta membra.*" He would see Book II as a sort of travel diary and Book I as a later, more mature reflection on the travel notes, this *pace* Bauer, How, and Wells who would see Book II as the later part of the work. There are good sections on Herodotus and Athens, Herodotus and Persia.

HOHTI, Paavo. The interrelation of speech and action in the Histories of Herodotus. Helsinki, Societas Scientiarum Fennica, 1976. 151p.

BA176

AC XLVII 1978 233–235 Verdin • JHS XCVIII 1978 173–174 Usher

The speeches in Herodotus hitherto have not received as much attention as those in Thucydides. The present study is confined to a close examination of the relationship between the speeches and the historical narrative. The first part of the work, The Speeches in their Context: A Commentary (p.11–79) distinguishes three types of speech: monolog, dialog, oratory, and classifies all the speeches accordingly. Part II Forms of Speech Sections (p.80–129) analyzes different types of speeches in the light of the function assigned them by Herodotus and studies the structure of the part of the work which contains different types of speech. There is a short third section, The Speech as an Element of the Account (p.130–138) and Conclusions (p.139–142).

POHLENZ, Max. Herodot; Der erste Geschichtschreiber des Abendlandes. 3., unveränderte Aufl. Stuttgart, B. G. Teubner, 1973. 221, [2]p.

BA177

CPh XXXIII 1938 415–417 Pearson • Klio 1938 109–112 Lesky • RPh XII 1938 283 Hatzfeld

The expressed aim of the work is to establish the essential unity of the History and to vindicate for Herodotus the title "Father of History." Pohlenz's interest is in the literary motives and ideals of his subject rather than in his veracity or accuracy. His affinities to epic poetry, *Odyssey* at least as much as *Iliad,* are well outlined, as also to Aeschylus and the concept of divine envy. The λόγοι are taken to be composed for public recital.

POWELL, John Enoch. The history of Herodotus. Amsterdam, A. H. Hakkert, 1967. viii, 96p.

BA178

Reprint of the 1939 ed.
Cambridge classical studies.
AJPh LXII 1941 509–511 Heidel • CR LIII 1939 123–125 Harrison • CW XXXIII 1939 32–33 Gudeman

The author's purpose is to determine the order and chronology of Herodotus' history. It is the first really scientific attempt to apply the study of cross-references in Herodotus to the problem of the composition. The problem had been finely articulated by Kirchoff 70 years previously in a fundamental essay, *Über die Abfassungszeit des herodotischen Geschichtswerkes,* 1868, 1878.

An interesting exercise in distinguishing between the certain, the probable and the barely possible in which the reasoning is ingenious and intricate but not very well stated, and the proposed solutions remain unproven.

POWELL, John Enoch. A lexicon to Herodotus. 2d ed. Hildesheim, Georg Olms, 1977. x, 391p.

BA179

Reprint of the Cambridge ed., 1938.
AC VII 1938 387 Severyns • CR LII 1938 178–179 Lorimer • JHS LVIII 1938 284 Myres

Compiled from a complete collection of word-slips to Herodotus, made in 1912–1914 by L. Kalpers and F. Nawaok, which tries successfully to combine the best elements of a lexicon and an index, noting every occurrence of every word or name used in Herodotus except καί. A model (for its day) of specialized lexica. It is based on Hude's text (Oxford, 1926), but important MS variants are noted.

WATERS, Kenneth H. Herodotus on tyrants and despots; A study in objectivity. Wiesbaden, F. Steiner, 1971. 100p.   **BA180**

Historia. Einzelschriften, Heft 15.
REA LXXV 1973 360–361 Mossé • RFIC CI 1973 356–358 Virgilio

More a refutation of previous views than a new contribution to the problem of the origin of historiography in Greece. The work is in three parts: Herodotus' treatment of tyrants and despots, his treatment of the Persian Kings, and a reflection on Herodotus and tragedy. His objectivity is proved by showing that he had no political or moral axe to grind when dealing with tyranny. Rejecting the view of many who would read concepts like *hybris* and *phthonos theōn* into it, Waters claims in the third part that the History as a whole is too vast and heterogeneous to have had any kind of tragic scheme imposed upon it.

Hesiod

EDWARDS, G. Patrick. The language of Hesiod in its traditional context. Oxford, Published for the Philological Society by B. Blackwell, 1971. vi, 248p.   **BA181**

Revision of the author's thesis, "Un-Homeric features in the language of Hesiod," Cambridge, 1965.
AJPh XCIV 1973 384–386 Sale • RPh XLVIII 1974 118–120 Casevitz • Scriptorium XXVII 1973 145 Masai

Attempts to answer such questions as these: Was Hesiod an oral poet? (Yes.) Which works were his? (*Theogony, Works and Days.*) What were his dialects? (Post-Homeric Ionic with un-Homeric intrusions.) When did he live? (Long enough after Homer to know Homer as we do.) The work is flawed by a basic confusion about what constitutes a formula; it has useful contributions to our knowledge of the non-Homeric elements in Hesiod.

von FRITZ, Kurt et al. Hésiode et son influence; Six exposés et discussions. Vandoeuvres-Genève,

5–10 septembre 1960. Genève, [Fondation Hardt, 1962]. 311p. **BA182**

Entretiens sur l'antiquité classique; t. 7.

Mnemosyne XVII 1964 172–175 Vos • Latomus XXIII 1964 617–618 Préaux

Contains three papers about the poems (von Fritz, Kirk, Verdenius), and three about their influence (on Plato, Solmsen; on Virgil, La Penna; on Tibullus, Grimal). Kirk in his Structure and Aim of the Theogony, following Jacoby, rejects large sections of the poem on the basis of "rhapsodic interpolations" between composition and first publication. A good introduction to the state of research on Hesiod.

HESIODUS. Theogony. With prolegomena and commentary by M. L. West. Oxford, Clarendon Press, 1966. xiii, 459p. **BA183**

Greek text, English prolegomena and commentary.
CW LX 1967 376 Calder • CR XVII 1967 265–267 Walcot • AC XXXVI 1967 259–261 Hofinger

A doctoral dissertation of enormous proportions, providing the first English commentary since Paley (1883), a greatly improved text (West collated 66 MSS, Paley 14), taking cognizance of 29 papyri, and a commentary that situates the material in its wider Near Eastern context. The *Theogony* is dated to 730–700 B.C. There are over 100 pages of prolegomena and of introductions to the separate sections of the poem.

HEITSCH, Ernst. Hesiod. Darmstadt, Wissenschaftliche Buchgesellschaft, 1966. x, 725p. **BA184**

Wege der Forschung; Bd. 44.
AAHG XXIII 1970 22–27 Erbse • Gnomon XL 1968 714–715 Schwartz • Maia XXI 1969 286–289 Arrigheti

Contains 26 articles, in date ranging from 1842 to the near present, dealing with the personality of the poet and the literary, religious and philosophical problems posed by his two major works. Contributions are all in German, translated where necessary, e.g., Rosenmeyer and Robert. Abundant materials for an adequate cross-view of present positions and remaining problems.

HOFINGER, M. et al. Lexicon Hesiodeum; Cum indice inverso. Leiden, Brill, 1978. 4 v. in 1. [ix, 745] p. **BA185**

Introd. in French; lexicon in Greek.
AC XLII 1973 592–593, XLIV 1975 692–693 van Looy • RPh LI 1977 111 Weil • CR XXVII 1977 268 West

An excellent, indispensable reference tool, which will satisfy the most exacting demands.

NICOLAI, Walter. Hesiod's *Erga;* Beobachtungen zum Aufbau. Heidelberg, C. Winter, 1964. 213p. **BA186**

Bibliothek der klassischen Altertumswissenschaften, Neue Folge; v.
CJ LXI 1965 88 Wassermann • CR XV 1965 159–

161 Walcot • CW LVIII 1964–1965 52 Williams • Gnomon XXXVII 1965 330–334 van Groningen

The structure of the *Erga* has recently been submitted to several examinations. The present study divides it into 17 large units or Blöcke, and these in turn are split into 70 smaller groups, or Zellen, all of which are carefully analyzed. There is perhaps too much ingenuity and cleverness in this structural analysis which sees the literary work as a counterpart to geometric style/pottery, but the verse-by-verse commentary is often very acute and helpful.

PEABODY, Berkeley. The winged word; A study in the technique of ancient Greek oral composition as seen principally through Hesiodus' *Works and days.* Albany, State University of New York, 1975. xvi, 562p. **BA187**

Arion n.s. 3/3 1976 365–377 Nagler • CR XXVIII 1978 207–208 Hainsworth • Gnomon L 1978 524–526 Prier

A highly original and important work which deserves the publisher's blurb: a landmark not only in Hesiodic scholarship but also in Homeric research and in the study of oral traditional literature in general. Major contributions of the work include detailed proof (quite independent of Nagy's *Comparative studies*) that the dactylic hexameter is an inherited Indo-European meter, and liberation of the study of Greek epic as oral poetry from the "Yugoslav analogy." A convincing case is made for the orality of the genuine Hesiodic works, and a preference is expressed for a higher date and more archaic temper for Hesiod than for Homer. Shows a wide mastery in important allied fields: oral poetics, linguistics, behavioral psychology as a necessary background to writing this poetical grammar of Hesiod's work.

TEBBEN, J. R. Hesiod-Konkordanz. A computer concordance to Hesiod. Hildesheim, Olms, 1977. viii, 326p. **BA187a**

Alpha–Omega R.A. Lexica, indices, Konkordanzen zur klass. Philol XXXI.
Phoenix XXXI 1977 361–364 McLeod

WALCOT, Peter. Hesiod and the Near East. Cardiff, University of Wales Press, 1966. xiii, 154p. **BA188**

CPh LXIII 1968 216–217 Combellack • CR XVII 1967 268–269 West • Gnomon XL 1968 225–230 Lesky • JHS LXXXVIII 1968 150–152 Barnett • RPh XLII 1968 131–132 Chantraine

A pioneering study of possible points of contact between Hesiod's poetry and the surviving remains of Egyptian, Mesopotamian, Phoenician and Hittite literatures, 9th to 7th centuries. Walcot studies Hesiod c.750 B.C. around the time of the origin of the Greek alphabet at, possibly, al Mina, a crossroads of mercantile (and literary?) activity. The comparison with the Babylonian poem *Enuma Elish* is particularly fruitful, as is the examination of gnomic literature from Egypt.

WEST, M. L. Hesiod Works & Days. Oxford, Clarendon Press, 1978. xiv, 339p. **BA189**

G&R XXVI 1979 87 Ireland • JHS XCIX 1979 169–171 Richardson

Similar in form to the editor's *Theogony* and of the same high standard, this work is the fruit of 18 years of study of the poem. At the outset there is a rapid but wide-ranging survey of wisdom literature with special emphasis on the ancient Near East. There is a careful and perceptive analysis of Hesiod's method of composition, an exemplary discussion of the transmission of the text, and the apparatus and commentary are very complete and thorough.

Historia Augusta

BARNES, T. D. The sources of the Historia Augusta. Bruxelles, 60 Rue Colonel Chaltin, 1978. 135p. **BA190**

Coll. Latomus CLV.
LEC XLVI 1978 385 van Esbroeck • JRS LXIX 1979 225–228 Green

CHASTAGNOL, André. Recherches sur l'histoire Auguste; Avec un rapport sur les progrès de la Historia Augusta-Forschung depuis 1963. Bonn, R. Habelt, 1970. vii, 112p. **BA191**

Antiquitas. Reihe 4: Beiträge zur Historia-Augusta-Forschung; Bd. 6.
JRS LXI 1971 309–310 Birley • CR XXIII 1973 58–60 Cameron • LF XCV 1972 111–112 Burian • AJPh XCV 1974 91–92 Benario
A slender volume containing three learned papers on parallels and sources of the *Historia Augusta*. Chastagnol continues to date the *HA* to the period 394–398, seeing it as the work of one author. The first paper is a clearly arranged Forschungsbericht for the years 1963 to 1969. Vast erudition is here marshalled in the search for parallels in this greatest of Latin literary frauds.

STRAUB, Johannes A. Heidnische Geschichtesapologetik in der christlichen Spätantike; Untersuchungen über Zeit und Tendenz der Historia Augusta. Bonn, R. Habelt, 1963. xxix, 216p. **BA191a**

Antiquitas. Reihe Beiträge zur Historia-Augusta-Forschung; Bd. 1.
JRS LV 1965 240–250 Cameron • Latomus XXII 1963 878–882 Chastagnol
Already in 1953 Professor Straub published *Studien zur Historia Augusta* in which he proposed one author or forger writing around 420 A.D. for *HA*. Meantime he has been a pivotal figure in the annual HA Colloquia at Bonn. See: Straub, J., ed. *Bonner Historia-Augusta-Colloquium 1975–1976*. Bonn, Habelt, 1978. 244p. (Antiquitas R. 4 Beitr. zur Historia-Augusta-Forsch. XIII).
Here he examines the relationship of *HA* to Ammianus Marcellinus and to St. Jerome. For Straub *HA* is a *historia adversus Christianos*, not so much an attack on Christianity as a pagan apology, a pagan reply to works like that of Orosius.

SYME, Ronald, Sir. Ammianus and the *Historia Augusta*. Oxford, Clarendon Press, 1968. viii, 238p. **BA192**

HZ CCXI 1970 660–662 Straub • JThS n.s. XX 1969 320–321 Jones • JRS LXI 1971 255–267 Cameron
Syme characterizes the author of *HA* as a *Rogue grammaticus* interested in oddities but unequipped for historical thought. His thesis is that the author of the *HA* shows familiarity with the history of Ammianus and so wrote not earlier than the 390's, but that he champions Suetonian biography against Ammianus' return to the standards and aims of history proper. Nonetheless the *HA* has no consistent purpose beyond imposture and deception for its own sake, with lavish citation of forged documents, countless inventions and distortions of names, a work of historical romance.

SYME, Ronald, Sir. Emperors and biography; Studies in the "Historia Augusta." Oxford, Clarendon Press, 1971. ix, 306p. **BA193**

AJPh XCIV 1973 392–395 Frank • REA LXXIV 1972 317–321 Demougeot • REL XLIX 1971 451–453 Fontaine
Reviewing *HA* on the emperors from Decius to Diocletian, Syme's blanket condemnation is "all bogus"; for the first nine imperial biographies (down to Caracalla) there is a good biographical source ("Ignotus"). See also R. Syme, "The composition of the *Historia Augusta;* Some recent theories," *JRS* LXII (1972), 123–133.

Homer

ARCHAEOLOGIA Homerica: Die Denkmäler und das frühgriechische Epos. Im Auftrage des Deutschen Archäologischen Instituts hrsg. von Friedrich Matz und Hans-Günter Buchholz. Göttingen, Vandenhoeck u. Ruprecht, 1967– . Illus. **BA194**

AJA LXXIX 1975 95–96 Lang, LXXX 1976 205–206 Alexiou, LXVI 1971 50–51, 40–41 • Gnomon XLI 1969 389–394 Snodgrass, XLIX 1977 499–505 Hiller • AAHG XXV 1972 169–182 Dönt
Densely packed tracts of information, well illustrated on all aspects of "Homeric" archaeology, both words interpreted widely. The series when completed will consist of three volumes and 23 fascicles. The editors hope thereby to present a full picture of the material and spiritual background of Homer as it appears to the present generation, with emphasis on those fields for which monumental evidence is most apposite. The early contributions by Marinatos show great daring and do not hesitate to question old assumptions.

AUSTIN, Norman. Archery at the Dark of the Moon; Poetic problems in Homer's *Odyssey*. Berkeley, University of California Press, 1975. xiii, 297p. **BA195**

CW LXXII, 2 1978 177–178 Buttrey • XXVIII 1978 144 Willcock • Arion n.s. 1/2 1973–1974 219–274

A long-overdue confrontation with some of the inconsistencies in Homeric criticism engendered by Parry and Snell. In particular, Austin clearly establishes, at least for the *Odyssey*, that stock epithets are not just line-fillers but are artistically related to their context. Snell's depiction (in the *Discovery of mind*) of Homer's thought as primitive and pre-scientific is also successfully challenged. The dark of the moon, *lykabas* (Od. 14. 161, 19.306), is the period between the old moon and the new. A remarkable and rewarding book.

AUTENRIETH, Georg Gottlieb Philipp. A Homeric dictionary; For use in schools and colleges. Trans., with additions and corrections, by Robert P. Keep. New York, St. Martin's Press, 1967. xiv, 337p., illus. **BA196**

Reprint of the 4th ed., with preface dated 1886.

BECHTEL, Friedrich. Lexicologus zu Homer. [Hildesheim], G. Olms, 1964. vii, 341p. **BA197**

BOWRA, Cecil Maurice, Sir. Homer. New York, Scribner, [1972]. viii, 191p., illus. **BA198**

Classical life and letters.
CR XXV 1975 4–5 Willcock • ACR III 1973 76–77 Combellack • REG LXXXVII 1974 411 Germain • WS LXXXVI 1973 265 Lesky
Unfinished at the author's death, 4 July 1971, this work was edited with as little interference as possible by Hugh Lloyd-Jones. It is directed toward making the Homeric world and Homeric scholarship understandable for the general reader. A fitting conclusion to a prolific publishing career that began with *Tradition and design in the Iliad*, 1933.

CLARKE, Howard W. The art of the *Odyssey*. Englewood Cliffs, N. J., Prentice-Hall, [1967]. 120p. **BA199**

A Spectrum book; S-155.
G&R XV 1968 96 • CJ LXIV 1968 85–88 Beye
A pleasant, readable introduction, mainly for Greekless readers.

CODINO, Fausto. Einführung in Homer. [Vom Verfasser autorisierte Übersetzung von Ragna Enking. Mit einem Geleitwort von Bruno Snell]. Berlin, De Gruyter, 1970. xi, 242p. **BA200**

ACR III 1973 80 Romano • Gnomon XLV 1973 1–7 Lesky • RPh XLVII 1973 121 Dobias-Labou
A translation of Codino, *Introduzione a Omero*, Turin, Einaudi, 1965 212p. [see *CR* XXVI (1966), 283–284, Davison]. A good, unpretentious general introduction aimed at the Greekless reader. Covers important textual and archaeological discoveries that shed light on the poems. Most attention is paid to the Homeric world, personalities in Homer, and religion and mythology.

CUNLIFFE, Richard John. A lexicon of the Homeric dialect. [New ed.]. Norman, University of Oklahoma Press, [1963]. ix, 445p. **BA201**

DEICHGRÄBER, Karl. Der letzte Gesang der Ilias. Mainz, Verlag der Akademie der Wissenschaften und der Literatur; Wiesbaden, In Kommission bei F. Steiner, 1972. 128p. **BA202**

Akademie der Wissenschaften und der Literatur. Abhandlungen der Geistes und Sozialwissenschaftlichen Klasse. Jahr. 1972; n. F. 5.
AJPh XCVI 1975 76–77 Dimock • Gnomon XLVII 1975 117–121 Erbse • DLZ XCIV 1973 895–898 Ebener • CR XXVI 1976 115 Hainsworth
Seeks to demonstrate that *Iliad* XXIV is the proper ending of the poem and that we have it just as it was composed. Division into books is less important for Deichgräber than division into recital units, each unit having its own theme and development. There are good central chapters of exegesis of individual points in Book XXIV. Still of interest is J. L. Myres, "The last book of the *Iliad*," *JHS* LII 1932 264–296.

DIHLE, Albrecht. Homer-Probleme. Opladen, Westdeutscher Verlag, 1970. 180p. **BA203**

Wissenschaftliche Abhandlungen der Arbeitsgemeinschaft für Forschung des Landes Nordrhein-Westfalen; Bd. 41.
Gnomon XLIX 1977 529–543 Kullmann • CW LXV 1971 131–132 Nagler • REG LXXXV 1972 237–238 Germain • CR XXII 1972 316–318 Hainsworth
The first full-length German study devoted to an assessment of the Milman Parry school, taking discussion beyond the old divisions of unitarians, analysts and neo-analysts to the complexities of oral poetry and oral composition. This is an excellent work, testifying to the up-to-date knowledge and good critical sense of the author.

EBELING, Heinrich, ed. Lexicon homericum. Composuerunt F. Albracht . . . et al. Hildesheim, G. Olms Verlagsbuchhandlung, 1963. 2 v. **BA204**

Reprint of the edition published in Leipzig, 1880–1885.

EISENBERGER, Herbert. Studien zur Odyssee. Wiesbaden, F. Steiner, 1973. x, 352p. **BA205**

Palingenesia; Bd. 7.
JHS XCVII 1977 170 Hainsworth • AC XLIV 1975 242 Bodson • Gnomon XLVIII 1976 534–539 Krehmer
A first-rate reference work, covering recent scholarship with great thoroughness and fairness, ranging over the Higher Criticism of the whole *Odyssey*. The focus is on the traditional problems of analytical and unitarian scholarship, and there is little coverage of the newer approaches which rely on comparative literature, myth, and modern literary criticism.

FINLEY, John H. Homer's *Odyssey*. Cambridge, Mass., Harvard University Press, 1978. vi, 244p. **BA206**

CO LVI 1979 63 Rexine • CW LXXIII 1979 51–52 Austin

This book is the product of a lifetime of reflection and teaching about the *Odyssey* which will be used by comparist, classicist and generalist alike. The analysis carries the reader in nine chapters through Odysseus' three stages as famous man, lone man, and man at home. Odysseus' lone self is the bond between the two parts of the poem, the travels and the homecoming.

There are two highly technical appendices on the Second Nekyia and the Reunion at the Farm. There is a good bibliography (p.235–238), an index of Greek passages and a subject index. A deft and sensitive treatment of the poem as a unity.

FINLEY, Moses I. The world of Odysseus. Rev. ed. 1st ed., 1954. New York, Viking Press, 1978. 192p., map.   **BA207**

REA LVIII 1956 371–372 Defradas • CJ LI 1956 405–406 Abrahamson • CR n.s. VII 1957 199–201 Stanford, XXIX 1979 135 Hainsworth • G&R XXV, 2 1978 197 Ireland

This work first appeared in 1954. The second edition replaces one appendix with two: The World of Odysseus Revisited (see *PCA* LXXI 1974 13–31), a revision of a 1974 presidential address to the Classical Association, and Schliemann's Troy—One Hundred Years Later, a 1974 lecture which should be read in conjunction with the Trojan debate (in *JHS* LXXXIV 1964). In the new 1977 edition a revised bibliographical essay discusses recent developments.

HAINSWORTH, J. B. The flexibility of the Homeric formula. Oxford, Clarendon Press, 1968. ix, 147p.   **BA207a**

Hermathena CVIII 1969 51–53 Stanford

HANSEN, William Freeman. The consultation sequence; Patterned narration and narrative inconsistency in the *Odyssey*. 1970. Reprint, *The conference sequence*, 1972. v, 140p.   **BA208**

The subtitle is the better description of the work's design. More or less symmetrical conferences between pairs of characters are studied comparatively, the most probative of which is Tiresias and Odysseus / Proteus and Menelaus. The accidents that occur in oral composition are thereby illustrated and explained in terms of rudimentary narrative.

HAYMES, Edward R. A bibliography of studies relating to Parry's and Lord's Oral Theory. Cambridge, Mass., Harvard University Press, 1973. vii, 45p.   **BA209**

CW LXVIII 1974–1975 385–386 Holoka

This remarkably thorough bibliography contains complete listings of the main investigators of oral composition, covering other literature besides Homer, especially Anglo-Saxon. More than 500 items by 280 authors.

HOLOKA, James P. "Homeric Studies, 1971–1977." CW LXXXIII 1979: 65–150.   **BA209a**

A fine survey in eight divisions: I. Preliminary Declarations; II. Editions, Commentaries, Translations; III. Homer; IV. The Iliad; V. The Odyssey; VI. Ancient Scholarship, Scholia, Papyri, Palaeography; VII. History, Archaeology; VIII. Homer and Aftertimes.

See also CW LXVI 1973 257–293, and Packard, D. W. and Meyers, T., *A Bibliography of Homeric Scholarship, Preliminary edition, 1930–1970.* 1974, vi, 183p., based on *L'Année philologique.*

KAKRIDEES, Ioeoannees T. Homer revisited. Lund, Gleerup, 1971. 175p.   **BA210**

Publications of the New Society of Letters at Lund; 64.

REG LXXXV 1972 238–239 Germain • G&R XIX 1972 212 Rees

Revised version of nine previously published papers containing much anti-analyst criticism from a self-styled neo-analyst. He is critical of those who fail to distinguish poetic from natural reality. These studies are concerned with the female characters, especially Helen and Nausicaa.

KIRK, Geoffrey Stephen. Homer and the epic. Cambridge, Cambridge University Press, 1965. 242p.   **BA211**

REA LXVIII 1966 133 Germain • LEC XXXIV 1966 182 Desmet • CB XLII 1966 94 Rexine

A shortened form of *The songs of Homer*, aimed at making it accessible to a wider public. Nothing essential is eliminated. Plates have been reduced in number by half.

KIRK, Geoffrey Stephen. Homer and the oral tradition. Cambridge and New York, Cambridge University Press, 1976. viii, 222p.   **BA212**

CR XXVIII 1978 1–2 Richardson • AC XLVI 1977 605–607 Bodson • AJPh XCIX 1977 124–127 Athanassakis

The latest of Kirk's books on Homer, comprising nine studies, most of which (c.2, 3, 5, 8) have already appeared elsewhere between 1961 and 1973. Chapters 1, 4 and 9 are new, derived from the J. H. Gray lectures at Cambridge in 1974. But there are more *vetera* than *nova* in the entire work, which is unnecessary reading for those who have digested *The songs of Homer.*

KIRK, Geoffrey Stephen. The songs of Homer. Cambridge, Cambridge University Press, 1962. iv, 423p., 8 plates.   **BA213**

RPh XXXVII 1963 286–290 Chantraine • JHS LXXXIII 1963 157–158 Webster • CPh LVIII 1963 241–245 Combellack • CR XIII 1963 265–267 Gray • AJPh LXXXV 1964 81–85 Lord

A closely argued, well-written survey of the whole Homeric question which separates *Iliad* (mid-8th century) from *Odyssey* (late 8th century) by more than date. Part I deals with the historical background of the Homeric poems, part II with oral poetry, which is splendidly judicious in analyzing both the usefulness and the limitations of the Parry/Lord contribution.

KIRK, Geoffrey Stephen, ed. The language and background of Homer; Some recent studies and controversies, selected and introduced by G. S. Kirk. Cambridge, W. Heffer; (New York, Barnes & Noble), [1967, 1964]. xvi, 159p. **BA214**

Views and controversies about classical antiquity. CR XVI 1966 276–278 Willcock • REA LXVIII 1966 131–132 Germain • REG LXXIX 1966 524–525 Humbert
A collection of 13 articles dating from 1947 to 1961, reprinted photographically from the books or periodicals of origin. Begins with Dodds' useful survey from *Fifty years of classical scholarship*. A preponderance of British contributions with only one foreign language item: E. Risch, Die Gliederung der griechischen Dialekte in neuer Sicht. The language studies by Chadwick and Shipp explore possible Mycenaean prototypes. Dow's magisterial survey of the Greek Bronze Age is particularly welcome.

KNIGHT, William F. J. Many-minded Homer; An introduction. New York, Barnes & Noble, [1968, i.e. 1969]. 224p. **BA215**

CR XX 1970 13–15 Hainsworth • CPh LXVI 1971 51–53 Combellack • CW LXIV 1970 58 Williams
A posthumous production of essays of uneven merit on matters of Greek epic, background, myth and legend, sources, unity, and Homeric scholarship.

LEE, D. J. N. The similes of the *Iliad* and the *Odyssey* compared. [Parkville], Melbourne University Press, [1964]. v, 80p. **BA216**

JHS LXXXVI 1966 170–171 Coffey • CPh LXI 1966 125–127 Combellack • Mnemosyne XIX 1966 404–406 Ruijgh
This is a sort of supplement to Shipp's *Studies in the language of Homer*, with which it agrees on the "lateness" of the *Iliad's* similes. It compares the number, nature and style of the similes in the two poems and endeavours to show that many of the *Iliad's* similes are interpolations put into older materials. His two overall assumptions—longer is later, earlier is better—have not stood up well to subsequent research. (Cf. Scott, W. C., *The oral nature of the Homeric simile*, 1974; Moulton, C. *Similes in the Homeric poems*, 1977). The "lateness" of the similes in the *Iliad* is accounted for by post-Homeric activity reacting to audience boredom at the unrelieved battle narratives.

LESKY, Albin. Homeros. Stuttgart, Druckenmüller, 1967. 160 columns. **BA217**

"Sonderausgaben der Paulyschen Realencyclopädie der klassischen Altertumswissenschaft." Supplbd. XI, 687–846.
A very detailed outline on all aspects of Homeric scholarship: Life, Date, Oral Poetry, Oral and Written Composition, Style, Religion and Culture. There are separate treatments of the *Iliad* and *Odyssey*, the question of Unity, Transmission and Nachleben. The bibliography is very extensive, down to 1965. This can be supplemented from the Bericht on Homer by Lesky

in *AAHG;* by Doetn, "Homer 6 Forsetzung II Teil," *AAHG* XXV (1972), 257–267; and by Panagl und Hiller, *AAHG* XXIX 1976 1–70. See also Mette, H. J. "Homer 1971–1977," *Lustrum* XV (1970), 99–122; "Homer 1971–1977," *Lustrum* XIX (1976), 5–64.

LOHMANN, Dieter. Die Komposition der Reden in der *Ilias*. Berlin, De Gruyter, 1970. x, 309p. **BA218**

JHS XCII 1972 187–188 Hainsworth • CW LXV 1971 63–64 Levin • ACR I 1971 171–172 Russo
An interesting if somewhat ponderous study of various types of ring composition and parallel composition in the speeches of the *Iliad*.

LUCE, John V. Homer and the heroic age. 1st U.S. ed. New York, Harper & Row, 1975. 200p., 15 plates, illus. **BA219**

CW LXX 1976 271–272 Lang • JHS XCVII 1977 172–173 Lazenby • Hermathena CXX 1976 75–76 Huxley
A splendid book, beautifully illustrated. The best introduction to Homeric archaeology in English. For Luce, Homer reflects a Mycenaean age which is at least as good a possibility as the Finley/Kirk Dark Age background. However, we are further asked to believe in an historical Ulysses, an Achaean chieftain of the late Bronze Age who is not just a poetic creation.

PAGE, Denys Lionel, Sir. The Homeric Odyssey. Westport, Conn., Greenwood Press, 1976. vi, 186p. **BA220**

Reprint of the 1955 ed. published by Clarendon Press, Oxford.
JHS LXXVI 1956 109 Gray • Gnomon XXVIII 1956 411–419 Combellack
For Page, the *Odyssey* was composed between 900 and 700 B.C., probably towards the middle of that period, a little later than the *Iliad*, in a different city of the eastern Aegean, and by a poet who did not know the *Iliad*. The last chapter, in particular, represents the best case to date for the Separatist viewpoint. The Polyphemus episode is shown to have multiplicity not of authors but of stories.

PARRY, M. The making of Homeric verse. The collected papers of Milman Parry, ed. by A. Parry. Oxford, Clarendon Press, 1971. lxii, 483p., illus. **BA220a**

CW LXV 1971 60 Willcock • G&R XVIII 1971 226 Sewter • AUMLA No. 36 1971 218–219 Rankin

PATZER, Harald. Dichterische Kunst und poetisches Handwerk im homerischen Epos. Wiesbaden, Steiner, 1972. 49p. **BA221**

Sitzungsberichte der Wissenschaftlichen Gesellschaft an der Johann Wolfgang Goethe-Universität Frankfurt/Main, Jahrg. 1971, Bd. 10, Nr. 1.
Gnomon XLVI 1974 529–534 Heubeck • Gymnasium LXXXI 1974 552–554 Gruler • CW LXVIII 1974

187–188 Nagler • CPh LXXI 1976 278–279 Combellack

"A milestone in Homeric scholarship and the best available brief introduction to the essentials of Homer's oral artistry" (Nagler). The neglect of Parry in German scholarship is dealt with first, and the arming of Patroclus (II.16. 130–154) is chosen to demonstrate that the implements of craftsmanship represented in the formulary language and the oral techniques can be used, in the hands of a great artist, to produce a great work of art. The arming scene is analyzed to consider another aspect of the craftsmanship of Greek oral epic: the typical scene.

PRENDERGAST, Guy L. A complete concordance to the *Iliad* of Homer. New ed., completely rev. and enl. by Benedetto Marzullo. Hildesheim, G. Olms, 1971. vii, 427p.   **BA222**

Reprint of an 1875 London ed. "This concordance . . . has been compiled from Priestley's edition of Heyne's Homer, published in 1834 (Preface).
AJPh LXXXV 1964 4455-
These volumes originally appeared in 1875 (*Iliad*) and 1880 (*Odyssey*), before Ebeling's *Lexicon,* Gehring's *Index* or Schmidt's *Parallel-Homer.* The two authors were compulsive and amateur concordicizers, one of them a physician. Their results are incomplete and inaccurate, based on outmoded editions. The reissue at this time, however, is welcome because so much Homeric research is formulaic-based.
See also Dunbar, Henry, comp. *A complete concordance to the Odyssey of Homer.* Oxford, 1880. New ed. rev. and enl. by Benedetto Marzullo. Hildesheim, G. Olms, 1962. x, 398p.

WENDER, Dorothea. The last scene of the *Odyssey.* The Netherlands, Brill, 1978. 83p.
        BA223

Mnemosyne bibliotheca classica batava; Supp. 52.
CW LXXII 1979 373 Rose • JHS C 1980 214–215 Hainsworth
A useful and eminently readable summary of the arguments in favor of the authenticity of Od. XXIV. The four final scenes are discussed in separate chapters, the second Nekyia receiving two chapters. A poetic creation.

Horace

BO, Domenico. Lexicon Horatianum: A–K. Hildesheim, G. Olms, 1965. xiii, 276p.   **BA224**

Alpha-Omega; I, 1.

BRINK, Charles Oscar. Horace on poetry. I. Prolegomena to the literary Epistles. Cambridge, Cambridge University Press, 1963. 2 v.
        BA225

JRS LIV 1964 186–196 Williams, LXII 1972 158–163 Dilke • Athenaeum LXI 1963 449–454 La Penna • CW LXV 1971 135–136 Pöschl • Gnomon XLV 1973 653–663 Russell, XXXVI 1964 265–272 Otis

A major work, planned in three volumes, to cover in detail Horace's literary criticism of Greek and Latin poetry in the *Ars poetica* and *Epistles.* The Prolegomena of v. 1 greatly clarify many disputed questions and represent an advance on the work of Norden, Jensen and Rostagni.

BÜCHNER, Karl. Horaz. Darmstadt, Wissenschaftliche Buchgesellschaft, 1974. 179p.
        BA226

"Unveränderter reprografischer nachdruck aus: Jahresbericht über die Fortschritte der Klassischen Altertumswissenschaft . . . Supplementband, Band 267 (1939)."
This is Büchner's bibliographical report on Horace, 1929–1936, divided into three main sections: Person, Work, and Varia. The subsection on Interpretation and Meaning is particularly detailed.

CAMPBELL, Archibald Young. Horace; A new interpretation. New York, Haskell House, 1973.
        BA227

Reprint of the 1924 ed.
CR XXXIX 1925 33 Godley • JRS XIII 1923 211–213 • CPh XX 1925 73 Haight
An extremely (for the time) provocative exercise in literary criticism which unduly stresses the moral and didactic purpose in Horace seen as *Musarum sacerdos.* While many will disagree with the author's concept of Horace's role, his analyses of individual poems are generally illuminating and full of excellent observations.

CARRUBBA, Robert W. The epodes of Horace; A study in poetic arrangement. The Hague, Mouton, 1969. 114p.   **BA228**

Studies in classical literature; 9.
REA LXXIII 1971 245 Laugier • Gnomon XLIV 1972 260–266 Schetter • CW LXIV 1970 91–92 Suits • Latomus XXXII 1973 401–402 Salat
An acute structural analysis of the *Epodes,* the first in English to be devoted exclusively to them. The first chapter enunciates five possible principles of arrangement: (1) the influence of Archilochus, (2) an absence of an internal principle of arrangement, (3) chronology, (4) metre, (5) a thematic principle. The second and third are rejected, and while metre and archilochian seem to be important, thematic arrangement is shown to be paramount. There are nearly 200 bibliographic citations.

CODY, John Vincent. Horace and Callimachean aesthetics. Bruxelles, Latomus, 1976. 130p.
        BA229

Collection Latomus; v. 147.
AC XLVII 1978 278–279 Knecht • Gnomon LI 1979 60–62 Brink
The introduction provides an aperçu on the literary and aesthetic principles of Callimachus. Chapter 1 is devoted to Horace, *od.* 1.38, and seeks to portray him as a Socratic Callimachean. Other chapters offer inter-

pretations of *od.* 1.1, 1.3, *sat.* 2.6 and 1.2. The term "Callimachean" is overworked throughout as are the ethical/esthetical, Socratic/Callimachean distinctions, and many of the interpretations are more ingenious than persuasive.

CODY, John Vincent. Horace's imitation and transformation of Callimachean aesthetics. Princeton, N.J., 1971. vi, 464p. **BA230**

Thesis, Princeton University. Photocopy: Ann Arbor, Mich., University Microfilms, 1973.

COLLINGE, N. E. The structure of Horace's Odes. London and New York, Oxford University Press, 1962, 1961. ix, 158p. **BA231**

University of Durham publications.
Gnomon XXXV 1963 171–177 Ludwig • Phoenix XVII 1963 70–72 Rudd • CPh LVIII 1963 57–59 Cunningham
An attempt to analyze and classify all the types of lyric structure in the Odes, e.g., responsive and non-responsive, static and progressive. For Collinge "structure" means some kind of correlation between metrical units and units of thought. Not all readers will agree with all his correlations but his enthusiasm for Horace and New Criticism is infectious.

COMMAGER, Henry Steele. The Odes of Horace; A critical study. Bloomington, Indiana University Press, 1967, 1962. xiv, 365p. **BA232**

A Midland Book; MB-101
CR XIII 1963 293–294 Clarke • CJ LVIII 1963 370–373 Hornsby • CPh LVIII 1963 180–183 Collinge • Athenaeum XLI 1963 442–445 La Penna
After a preliminary treatment of literary conventions and stylistic criticism in the Augustan age there are illuminating chapters entitled Structural Characteristics, Qualities of Imagination, The Political Odes, The World of Nature, and the World of Art. Horace's other works are used as supporting evidence for the discussion of the *Odes*. The studies of the Cleopatra and Soracte odes are especially well done. The tension in Horace's art is emphasized to good effect; as *cliens Bacchi* he achieves in his odes a Dionysiac equilibrium of vitality and calm, turbulence and order, youth and age. Sometimes the study of verbal niceties becomes over-ingenious, but the Horace that emerges from this perceptive critical study is credible and more deeply intelligible. Texts are included of the poems studied, with rather wooden translations.

COSTA, Charles, ed. Horace. London, Routledge and Kegan Paul, 1974. ix, 166p. **BA233**

CJ LXX, 2 1974 79–82 Putnam • CW LXIX 1975 278–279 Reckford • JRS LXIV 1974 277–278 Woodman • CR XXVI 1976 30–31 Wilkinson
Six essays: Hubbard, The Odes; West, Horace's Poetic Technique in the Odes; McGann, The Three Worlds of Horace's Satires; Dilke, Horace and the Verse Letter; Russell, Ars Poetica; Edden, The Best of Lyrik Poets, the last dealing with Horace's reputation in England up to the 17th century, and the many English translations which he inspired. The essays contain useful background information and some respectable criticism but as a whole the volume is not very exciting.

FRAENKEL, Eduard. Horace. London, Oxford University Press, 1957, 1970. xiv, 463p. **BA234**

JRS XLVIII 1958 170–178 Klingner • CR IX 1959 32–37 Wilkinson • REL XXXV 1957 592–612 Becker
Published in the author's seventieth year, in 1957, this monumental work is the fruit of decades of teaching and study and of publications where the lines of his present interpretation have been sketched. The work is not too well organized and consists of a series of interpretations of selected or preferred poems rather than a complete chronological or thematic study. There is a brief exegesis of the *Vita Horati* of Suetonius, followed by treatments of the Epodes (especially X and XVI) and the Satires (all of Book I and two from Book II). Odes Books I–III are confined to one almost book-length (p.154–307) chapter; Book IV receives its own chapter and an interpretation of each ode, as do Epistles, Book I, Carmen Saeculare and the Letter to Augustus (Ep. II,I). What Fraenkel says of the letter to Tibullus (Ep. i.4) can be said of his own work: "It is graceful, warm-hearted, and rich in stylistic shades . . . full of mellow, unobtrusive wisdom" (p.323). But it has strangely little to say about some of the most hauntingly beautiful odes of the first three books.
There is a German translation: Horaz, Übersetz von Bayer, *G&E*, 2 durchges. Auflage, Darmstadt, Wiss Buchgess. (1970–1971), xv, 540p.

HIERCHE, Henri. Les Épodes d'Horace; Art et signification. Bruxelles, Latomus, 1974. 209p. **BA235**

Collection Latomus; v. 136.
Athenaeum 1977 495–498 Tempesti • REA LXXVII 1975 300 Lathière • REL LII 1974 493–496 Grimal
A somewhat immature *oeuvre d'ensemble* on the *Epodes* dealing at the outset with three structures: formal, intellectual and metrical, then with the language and style of the *Epodes* and finally with the poems themselves.

HUNT, Noel A. B. Horace the minstrel; A practical and aesthetic study of his Aeolic verse. Kineton, Roundabout Press, 1969. xvii, 268p. **BA236**

CR LXX 1956 56, XX 1970 401–402 Platnauer • Euphrosyne IV 1970 327–331 Vara
A considerable expansion over the first edition of this book. Almost all the metres of Horace are examined, chiefly as a guide for modern imitators, and many deft modern examples are given, some of the best by the author himself.

McGANN, M. J. Studies in Horace's first book of Epistles. Bruxelles, Latomus, 1969. 119p. **BA237**

Collection Latomus; v. 100.
CR XXI 1971 55–57 Rudd • REL XLVIII 1970
577–578 Perret • Gnomon XLIII 1971 213–215 Maurach
A careful study in three chapters of *Ep.*, with particular attention to its philosophical background well documented from Middle Stoicism. *Ep.* I is seen as a unity.

OKSALA, Teivas. Religion und Mythologie bei Horaz; Eine literarhistorische Untersuchung. Helsinki-Helsingfors, Societas Scientiarum Fennica, 1973. 233p.   **BA238**

REL LII 1974 497–98 Béranger • Gnomon XLVII 1975 757–761 Syndikus • JRS LXV 1975 230 McGann
As the subtitle indicates this is a literary-historical study of the religious-mythological motifs in Horace's work. The main part (p.16–197) is an extremely thorough examination of "Gods," "The Trojan cycle," "Rome as myth," "The immortal benefactors of mankind," "Orpheus and the Underworld," and "Heroines." A useful reference on religious-mythological topics in Horace.

OPPERMANN, Hans. Wege zu Horaz. Darmstadt, Wissenschaftliche Buchgesellschaft, 1972. vi, 392p.   **BA239**

Wege der Forschung; Bd. 99.
AC XLII 1973 650 Verdiere • REL LI 1973 412 Perret
Contains 19 essays, all in German (original or translated), the earliest going back to 1917, Fray Boll, the latest, Ernst Zinn (1971), Erlebnis und Dichtung bei Horaz. Included are well-known essays by well-known names: Marouzeau, Büchner, Amundsen, Solmsen, Duff Cooper; there are two contributions by the editor.

PÖSCHL, Viktor. Horazische Lyrik; Interpretationen. Heidelberg, C. Winter, 1970. 276p.   **BA240**

Bücherei Winter.
CJ LXXIX 1974 257–258 Wassermann • LEC XXXIX 1971 385 Wankenne • CR XXII 1972 272–273 Williams
Ten interpretative essays on various odes from the first 3 books, all but two previously published in journals. Much reliance on structural analysis, with a great familiarity with Pasquali, Kiessling-Heinze, Klingner, Wilkinson, Commager and Fraenkel, and modern literary criticism, but above all a remarkably erudite control of parallels in Hellenistic and Roman Literature.

RUDD, Niall. The 'Satires' of Horace; A study. Cambridge, Cambridge University Press, 1966. xi, 318p.   **BA241**

REL XLVI 1968 489–491 Grimal • CW LX 1966 125 Reckford • CR XVII 1967 291–293 Coffey
A systematic study of all the Satires, incorporating (sometimes with second thoughts) much of the author's previous journal publications. Urbane in argument and free from polemic. Professor Rudd is an excellent teacher and his fine blend of historical scholarship and

literary criticism is imparted with a lightness of touch befitting an expositor of Horace. *Ridentem dicere vera quid vetat?*

SYNDIKUS, Hans P. Die Lyrik des Horaz; Eine interpretation der Oden. Darmstadt, Wissenschaftliche Buchgesellschaft, 1972–1973. 2 v.   **BA242**

Impulse der Forschung; Bd. 6–7.
REL LII 1974 496–497 Perret • CR XXV 1975 212–214 Nisbet • Gymnasium LXXXII 1975 105–108 van Albrecht
Essays of from four to twenty pages on each of the Odes in Horace's first and second books. Sensitive, careful and erudite on style, structure, sources and interconnections. Less strong on chronology and prosopography. His freshness and independence help to make this work a notable achievement, establishing its author among the leading contemporary interpreters of Roman poetry.

Juvenal

GÉRARD, J. Juvénal et la réalité contemporaine. Paris, Belles Lettres, 1976. x, 536p.   **BA243**

Collection d'études anciennes.
Latomus XXXVI, 4 1977 996–1002, 1062 Bardon • AC XLVII 1978 287–290 Joly
A 1972 Sorbonne thesis which assembles an impressive dossier of documentation, very penetrating commentary and an excellent bibliography. Contains new precisions on the dating of the Satires. The main body of the work is in two parts: Juvénal et la société de son temps (p.117–279), and Politique et Religion dans les satires de Juvénal (p.281–447). A valuable examination of the religious and political realities c.100 A.D., as mirrored in Juvenal, and the different social classes.

HIGHET, Gilbert. Juvenal the satirist; A study. Oxford, Oxford University Press, 1962. xviii, 373p.   **BA244**

Oxford paperbacks.
REL XXXII 1954 375–377 Grimal • JRS XLV 1955 234–235 Nisbet • CPh L 1955 146–148 Anderson
A study in three parts: the reconstructed biography of Juvenal, an appraisal of the poems, and Juvenal's posthumous influence on European literature. In the last third of the work (p.233–373) there are extensive and useful notes, a good select bibliography and full indices. The posthumous influence is the most satisfactory section, as might be expected from the author of *The Classical Tradition.*

Livius Andronicus

BROCCIA, Giuseppe. Ricerche su Livio Andronico epico. Padova, Antenore, 1974. 133p.   **BA245**

Pubblicazioni della Facoltà di lettere e filosofia, Università di Macerata; 3.

RFIC CV 1977 338–349 Parroni • AC XLIV 1975 733–734 Liénard • Erasmus XXVII 1975 491–493 Lasserre

These three studies, based on university lectures, examine Homer as the exemplar of Livius in four fragments, the alleged utilization of the scholia in fragments 11, 22 and 30, and formulaic diction as utilized by Livius. The study lays to rest the earlier suggestion that Livius "Romanized" Homer. Adaptation was never an end in itself but a means to better translation.

Livy

BRISCOE, John. A commentary on Livy, books XXXI–XXXIII. Oxford, Clarendon Press, 1973. xviii, 370p. **BA246**

CW LXVIII 1975 456–457 Ward • AJPh XCVI 1975 317–322 Sumner • Gnomon XLVII 1975 252–262 Burck • CR XXVI 1976 44–46 Wellesley

Following on Jal's commentary on Books XLI–XLIII and Ogilvie's on Books I–V (1965), this formidable commentary covers Books XXXI–XXXIII (The Second Macedonian War). Believing that one of the purposes of a commentary is to serve as a repository of references to modern literature, the author goes beyond historical matters to questions of language, style, sources, methods of composition and textual criticism, and the coverage of modern literature is so thorough and exhaustive that at times it crowds out the editor's own exegesis, which is particularly weak on topography.

LUCE, Torrey J. Livy; The composition of his history. Princeton, N.J., Princeton University Press, 1977. xxvii, 322p. **BA247**

Phoenix XXXII 1978 171–174 Walsh • JRS LXVIII 1978 227–228 Briscoe • CR XXIX 1979 58–60 Ogilvie

A judicious assessment of Livy's virtues and weaknesses, rehabilitating him *qua* historian rather than *qua* superb rhetorician or skillful narrator of dramatic episodes as he is elsewhere depicted. Luce's chief concern in the first half of his book is with structure, especially that of Books 31–45. He believes the pentad was the basic structural unit, but that pentads could be flexibly combined twice or three times, and in this way 1–15 are seen as dealing with early Rome; 16–30, the Punic Wars, 31–45, the conquest of the East. This is close to Wille's position. Luce is less convincing in his detailed analysis of 31–45 in which he rather arbitrarily posits beginnings, middles and ends, and expansions and compressions of his sources to suit predetermined structures. A study refreshingly independent of received theory, thoughtful, provocative and highly important.

WALSH, P. G. Livy; His historical aims and methods. Cambridge, Cambridge University Press, 1961. 300p. **BA248**

Gnomon XXXV 1963 780–785 Burck • CR XII 1962 58–61 Baldson • JRS LII 1962 277–278 Henderson

A balanced and useful assessment of the advances

in Livian scholarship in the 20th century. There are good preliminary chapters: Patavium and Augustan Rome, The Tradition of Ancient Historiography and Religious, Philosophical and Moral Preconceptions. Livy's historical authorities occupy c. V, his methods c. VI–VII, and the literary analysis of narrative, speeches and Latinity, c. VIII–X. A very fair assessment of the strengths and weaknesses of Livy as historian and writer, done with Livian "ἐνάργεια, συντομία, σαφήνεια, καὶ πιθανότης."

WILLE, Günther. Der Aufbau des Livianischen Geschichtswerks. Amsterdam, Grüner, 1973. 132p. **BA249**

Heuremata; Bd. 1.

Gnomon XLIX 1977 516–517 Ogilvie • Gymnasium LXXXII 1975 485–487 Schmidt • JRS LXV 1975 224–225 Briscoe

For Wille the main structural feature is the unit of 15 books: 1–15 The early history of Rome until the First Punic War, 16–30 First and Second Punic Wars, 31–45 The War in the East with Antiochus and Macedonia. This pattern is extended to the less charted last books; thus: 46–60 Age of the Younger Scipio, 61–75 Age of Marius, 76–90 Age of Sulla, 91–105 Age of Pompey, 106–120 Age of Caesar, 121–135 Pax Augusta, 136–150 planned but incomplete: Augustus.

See also: Wille, Günther. *Der Aufbau Werke des Tacitus.* Amsterdam, Grüner, 1983. viii, 673p.

Lucan

LUCANUS, Marcus Annaeus. M. Annaei Lvcani Belli civilis libri decem. Editorvm in vsvm edidit A. E. Hovsman. Oxonii, apvd Basilivm Blackwell, 1926. xxxv, 343p. **BA250**

Gnomon II 1926 493–502 Fraenkel • CR XLI 1927 26–33 Anderson • JRS XV 1925 291 Souter

Housman's editions of Lucan (1926), Manilius (1937) and Juvenal (1938) were widely acclaimed, but reviewers did not fail to react to his *saeva indignatio.* For example, Anderson's: "There are many comments in his best vein on the textual problem and a few in his worst vein on recent editors," and he goes on to say of the work: "as a contribution at once learned and penetrating to the criticism of a Latin poet it is in the great tradition, in the line of Scaliger and Bentley, Lachmann and Munro." In contrast, Mr. Housman, writing in the same journal (*CR* XLI, 1927, p.189–191) of Bourgery's *Lucan* says, "In short, Mr. Bourgery is not fully equipped for his task; and in consequence his numerous decisions and pronouncements . . . carry no authority and are of little importance."

RUTZ, Werner, comp. Lucan. Darmstadt, Wissenschaftliche Buchgesellschaft, 1970. vii, 552p. **BA251**

Wege der Forschung; Bd. 235.

REL XLIX 1971 444 Richard • Latomus XXXI 1972 620–622 Jal

A welcome sign of the present-day revival of interest

in Lucan, this fine collection of 32 essays is divided into four sections of interest: I. Grundfragen neutigen Lucanverständnisses, II. Komposition und geplanter Endpunkt des Epos, III. Prooemium und Nero-Elogium, IV. Einzelfragen hinsichtlich Gehalt und Gestalt im Epos Lucans. The titles and original places of publication are listed in the *Latomus* review.

RUTZ, W. "Lucan 1943–1963." Lustrum IX (1964): 243–334; Lustrum X (1965): 246–256; Lustrum XXVI (1984): 105–203.   **BA252**

Lucian

BALDWIN, Barry. Studies in Lucian. Toronto, Hakkert, 1973. xv, 123p.   **BA253**

JHS XCVII 1977 189–190 Hall • Phoenix XXIX 1975 401–405 Bosworth • REG LXXXVIII 1975 226–229 Bompaire
A lively reaction, perhaps an overreaction, to some recent Lucian scholarship, especially that of Bompaire and Schwartz. For bibliographical survey cf. Fumarola, V., "La più recente critica su Luciano," *A&R* IX (1964), 97–107.
The first two chapters deal with the career of Lucian, and his friends and enemies, followed by c.3 The War of Words, c.4 The Loud Speakers (i.e., public orators), c.5 Clio Dethroned, and c.6 Men and Gods, which treats the actuality of the religious satire and the Lucian corpus. Despite erroneous or questionable details the work provides a good series of studies against the background of the literary world of the 2d century, A.D.

Lucilius

CHRISTES, Johannes. Der frühe Lucilius; Rekonstruktion und Interpretation des XXVI. Buches sowie von Teilen des XXX. Buches. Heidelberg, C. Winter, 1971. 212p.   **BA254**

Bibliothek der klassischen Altertumswissenschaft, n. F. 2. Reihe Bd. 39.
CJ LXIX 1974 247–249 Anderson
An excellent monograph on the important Books 26 and 30, making advances on the scholarly work on Lucilius already begun by Friedrich Marx and added to by Werner Krenkel (1970). Books 26 through 30 are the earliest Lucilius and more fragments survive from this segment of the work than from any other. Book 26 is Christes' main concern in this work which grew out of his 1968 Freiburg dissertation.
See also Christes, J., *ANRW* 1.2 (1972), 1182–1239 for bibliographical survey.

Lucretius

BOLLACK, Mayotte. La raison de Lucrèce; Constitution d'une poétique philosophique avec un essai d'interprétation de la critique lucrétienne. Paris, Les Éditions de Minuit, 1978. xliii, 630p.   **BA255**

CR XXIX 1979 32–33 Fowler
An overlong, repetitive book which takes to task a multitude of earlier Lucretian scholars, discusses a number of textual problems and gives an extended discussion of Book VI. The description of the plague at the end of VI is seen as "Le miroir du poème." A highly personal, provocative but sophisticated treatment of Lucretius, with an extensive bibliography (p.599–624).

BOYANCÉ, Pierre. Lucrèce et l'épicurisme. Paris, Presses universitaires de France, 1963. 347p.   **BA256**

RPh XXXVII 1963 343 Ernout • BAGB 1963 366–368 Granarolo • REL XLI 1963 91–100 Grimal
Based on long and deep reflection and frequent journal contributions since 1945, this very erudite work is a sort of commentary on all previous commentaries. Divided into eleven chapters, three of which are introductory (L. and Roman Epicureanism, L. and his master, L. and his poem), and two conclusive (the poetry of L., the glory of L.), the six central chapters each deal with one book of *De rerum natura* with translation and commentary, often verse by verse, touching on all major questions. There is an ample bibliography (p.329–347). An important *livre d'ensemble*, the first to appear in France since that of Martha, 1867, and a worthy contribution to the series, Les grandes penseurs.

BÜCHNER, Karl. Lukrez und Vorklassik. Wiesbaden, F. Steiner, [1964]. 211p.   **BA257**

Studien zur römischen Literatur; Bd. 1.
CR XV 1965 49–51 Goodyear • Erasmus XX 1968 110–116 Lasserre • Gnomon XXXIX 1967 472–478 Schmid
A dogmatic, prolix, and often obscure work, much of which should not have been republished but some of which is of interest and a little of importance.

DALZELL, Alexander. "A Bibliography of work on Lucretius 1945–1972." CW LXVI (1972–1973): 389–427, LXVII (1973): 65–112.   **BA258**

DUDLEY, Donald Reynolds et al. Lucretius. London, Routledge & K. Paul, [1967, 1965]. ix, 166p.   **BA259**

Studies in Latin literature and its influence.
JRS LVI 1966 275–276 West
This composite work starts with a brief introduction in which the editor sees Lucretius, the greatest poet of the Republic, suffering the neglect of Honesty in Juvenal (probitas laudatur et alget), a neglect which he hopes to help redress. The seven contributors are O. E. Lowenstein, The Pre-Socratics, Lucretius and Modern Science; B. Farrington, Form and Purpose in the *De rerum natura;* D. E. W. Wormell, The Personal World of Lucretius; W. S. Maguiness, The Language of Lucretius; S. Townend, Imagery in Lucretius; D. R. Dudley, The Satiric Element in Lucretius; T. J.

B. Spencer, Lucretius and the Scientific Poem in English.

GORDON, Cosmo A. A bibliography of Lucretius. London, Hart-Davis, 1962. 318p. **BA260**

The Soho bibliographies; 12.
Latomus XXII 1963 926 Boyancé
A misleading title in that all that is found here is a list of the editions and translations of Lucretius, with two appendices, one a simplified account of manuscripts, the other on the imitators of Lucretius.
See BA258.

KENNEY, E. J. Lucretius. Oxford and New York, Oxford University Press, 1977. 48p. **BA261**

Greece & Rome: New surveys in the classics; v. 11.
Four brief chapters: The Poet and his Times; The Poem: Text, Sources, Scope, Structure; The Poetry; and The Message and the Mission. List of Works Cited (p.45–48).

MINADEO, Richard. The lyre of science; Form and meaning in Lucretius: *De rerum natura.* Detroit, Wayne State University Press, 1969. 174p. **BA262**

CPh LXVII 1972 301–303 Henry • Comp Lit XXV 1973 94 Kelly
A self-proclaimed first in literary criticism of Lucretius in which the whole race of previous commentators are castigated for over-concern with the philosophy to the neglect of the poetry.

ROBERTS, Louis. A concordance of Lucretius. 2d ed. New York, Garland Publishers, 1977. **BA263**

"The text of Lucretius used throughout is the three volume edition of Cyril Bailey, *Titi Lucreti Cari De rerum natura,* Oxford, 1963."
CPh LXV 1970 58–61 Bassett • CR XX 1970 188–189 Brown
A concordance produced in "less than seventy minutes of IBM 7094 time," after the actual programming. The context provided is invariably the complete hexameter line.

WEST, David. The imagery and poetry of Lucretius. Edinburgh, Edinburgh University Press, 1969. viii, 142p. **BA264**

AJPh XCII 1971 380–381 Owens • REA LXXII 1970 193–195 Bollack • CPh LXXI 1976 178–181 Elder
A perceptive analysis of the imagery of selected passages which does not aim at completeness. This brings new light on a neglected aspect, and the Lucretian outbursts of indignation at this neglect on the part of translators and commentators make for enjoyable reading. The passages studied are thematically related (e.g., Theater, Games, Architecture, Light and Fires), though West stops short of structuring recurrent images into thematic or symbolic systems. The overall impression

will be dazzling for many, while conservative philologists will at least be intrigued.

Martial

CITRONI, Mario. M. Valerii Martialis; Epigrammaton liber 1. Firenze, La Nuova Italia, 1975. xcii, 390p. **BA265**

AC XLV 1976 699–701 Knecht • Gnomon XLIX 1977 729–731 Krenkel • LEC XLIV 1976 279 Stenuit • AJPh C 1979 325 Harrison
A worthy successor to the last substantial commentary on Martial, by Friedlander (Leipzig, 1886; reprint Amsterdam, 1967), filling many of the linguistic and literary lacunae in the latter. Each epigram in Book 1 is given a detailed commentary, situating it in its sociocultural and historical context.
There is an ample 93-page introduction, an excellent bibliography, and three indices. The citation of Greek parallels is particularly good.

HARRISON, G. W. M. "Martialis, 1901–1970." Lustrum XVIII (1975): 300–337, 352–355. **BA266**

See also Carratello, U., "Settant' anni di studi italiani su Valerio Marziale," *Emérita* 40 (1972), 177–204.

MICHIE, James, ed. Martialis, Marcus Valerius. The Epigrams of Martial. London, Hart-Davis, MacGibbon Ltd., 1973. 215p. **BA267**

Parallel Latin text and English translation by the editor; English introd. and notes.
G&R XXI 1974 91–92 Verity • TLS LXXII, 3713 1973 491
Translates about one-tenth of material with great skill and felicity. There is an index of first lines.

SIEDSCHLAG, E. von. Martial-Konkordanz. Hildesheim, Olms, 1979. iii, 965, 81p. **BA268**

Menander

ARNOTT, W. Geoffrey. Menander, Plautus, Terence. Oxford, Clarendon Press, 1975. 62p. **BA269**

Greece & Rome: New surveys in the classics; v. 9.
A useful brief summary by Arnott who has recently edited Menander for the Loeb Classical library series.

GOMME, A. W. and SANDBACH, F. H. Menander; A commentary. Oxford, Oxford University Press, 1973. xiii, 760p. **BA270**

AC XLIII 1974 452–455 van Looy • CPh LXXI 1976 182–185 Webster • G&R XXI 1974 87–88 Taplin • RFIC CII 1974 459–473 Barigazzi • Mnemosyne XXVIII 1975 209–215 Pieters
An extremely detailed and useful commentary, meant to be used with Sandbach's *Oxford classical text,* 1972. The work was begun by Gomme whose draft

covered the Cairo plays—*Heros, Epitrepontes, Perikeiromene, Samia*—but death prevented his taking into account the *Dyskolos* and later discoveries. The revision and completion are magisterially accomplished by Sandbach.

Each of the 18 plays gets an introduction and a detailed line-by-line commentary. There is a good general introduction on Menander's life and times, metre, manuscripts, and papyri.

HANDLEY, Eric Walter et al. Ménandre. Sept exposés suivis de discussions par E. W. Handley ... [e.a.] Entretiens préparés et présides par Eric G. Turner. Vandoeuvres-Genève, 26–31 août 1969. [Vandoeuvres-Genève], Fondation Hardt, [1970]. viii, 267p., 2 plates. **BA271**

Entretiens sur l'antiquité classique; t. 16.
AJPh XCIV 1973 206–207 Webster • CR XXIII 1973 23–24 Lowe • Gnomon XLVI 1974 10–16 Arnott • REG LXXXVI 1973 468–471 Blanchard
Begins with E. W. Handley's excellent paper The Conventions on the Comic Stage and their Exploitation by Menander. W. Ludwig's Die *Cistellaria* und das Verhältnis von Gott und Handlung bei Menander gives a summary of the action of *Synaristosae*, reconstructed from the incompletely preserved *Cistellaria*, and suggests that Selenium (449f.) is a Plautine addition. The religious aspect in other Menander plays is examined. F. Sandbach brilliantly discusses Menander's Manipulation of Language for Dramatic Purposes. F. Wehrli, in Menander und die Philosophie, is cautious about Peripatetic influence. C. Dedoussi concentrates on the *Samia,* prefers a late date and has many sensitive observations. C. Questa, in Alcuni strutture sceniche di Plauto e Menandro, discusses the light shed on Plautus by the new Menander, with the originality of Plautus in handling Menander more clearly emerging. In conclusion L. Kahil gives a fascinating account of the Menander mosaics from Mytilene.

HOLZBERG, Niklas. Menander, Untersuchungen zur dramatischen Technik. Nürnberg, Hans Carl, 1974. viii, 196p. **BA272**

Erlanger Beiträge zur Sprach- und Kunstwissenschaft; Bd. 50.
Gnomon L 1978 433–436 Blume • REG LXXXIX 1976 643–644 Blanchard
This Erlangen-Nuremberg dissertation consists of an introduction, two long chapters and a conclusion. Deals with the technique of exposition and the fifth act, and the symmetrical tendencies inherent in the division into five acts. The work constantly situates Menander within the whole context of Attic drama, tragedy and comedy, and illustrates his genius for renewing traditional elements. A valuable contribution on the division into acts with special focus on the first and last.

MENANDER, of Athens. Dyscolus. Introd., text, textual commentary and interpretative translation by Warren E. Blake. [New York], American Philological Association (available through the secretary of the association, Hunter College in the Bronx), 1966. 225p. **BA273**

Philological monographs; v. 24.
Gnomon XL 1968 342–346 Kraus • Mnemosyne XXI 1968 432–434 Koster • RPh XLIII 1969 314–316 Kambitsis
Contains a facsimile (21p.) of the original papyrus, now in the Bibliotheca Bodmeriana, Cologny, Switzerland.

MENANDER, of Athens. The Dyskolos of Menander. Edited by Eric Walter Handley. London, Methuen, 1965. x, 323p. **BA274**

AC XXXV 1966 282–284 Lasserre • JHS LXXXVI 1966 195–197 Sandbach
Began from a seminar whose results appeared in *BICS* VI (1959). Contents: a lengthy Introduction (p.1–73), Text (p.75–118) and Commentary (p.119–306), with two indices, Selected Topics and Selected Greek Words and Phrases.

MENANDER, of Athens. The girl from Samos; or, The in-laws. Trans. into English blank verse by Eric G. Turner. London, Athlone Press (Distributed in U.S.A. by Humanities Press, New York), 1972. 48p. **BA275**

AC XLII 1973 632 Lasserre • CW LXVIII 1974 213–214 Matzke • G&R XX 1973 200 Rees
The purpose of this blank verse translation of *Samia* is to provide a work suitable for stage production, so Turner fills the blanks in the manuscript tradition. The additions blend well both in content and form, and the translation is probably the most effective in English.

MENANDER, of Athens. Menandri Aspis. Milano, Istituto editoriale cisalpino La goliardica, 1972. 103p. **BA276**

Edited by Alberto Borgogno.
CW LXVIII 1974–1975 272 MacCary • Gnomon XLVIII 1976 74–76 Bader
A fine edition of a fine play, based on scholarship prior to Sandbach's Oxford text and commentary. Borgogno provides no introduction or commentary, but there is an instructive apparatus criticus and an appendix expanding upon it.

MENANDER, of Athens. The plays of Menander. Edited and trans. by Lionel Casson. New York, New York University Press, 1971. xx, 154p. **BA277**

CR XXIV 1974 128–129 Brown
An excellent prose translation of Dyskolos, Samia, Aspis, Epitrepontes and Perikeiromene. The translation is accurate, readable and lively, if occasionally slangy. The text is supplemented by perceptive stage directions. The translation is based on the texts of Handley, Austin and Körte, with Casson often showing fine independent judgment.

METTE, Hans J. "Der heutige Menander (insbesondere für die Jahre 1955–1965)." Lustrum X (1965): 5–211. **BA278**

See also Nachtrag, *Lustrum* XI (1966), 139–143; Zweite, Nachtrage, *Lustrum* XIII (1968): 535–568, *Lustrum* XVI (1971–1972): 5–80.

METTE, Hans J. "Menandros." RE Supplbd. XII (1970): 854–864.   **BA279**

Supplements Körte's excellent early "Menandros," *RE* XV, 1 (1931), 707–761.

WEBSTER, Thomas Bertram Londsdale. An introduction to Menander. Manchester, Manchester University Press, 1974. viii, 211p.   **BA280**

CR XXIX 1979 141 Lowe • CW LXXI, 3 1978 198–200 Grant • G&R XXIII 1976 84 Bulloch
This posthumously published work (Webster died in 1974) used the greatly increased material to make the earlier *Studies in Menander* a more systematic survey. Much of the reconstructions, chronology, etc., is still to be treated as no better than educated guesswork.

WEBSTER, Thomas Bertram Londsdale. Studies in Menander. [2d ed.]. Manchester, Manchester University Press, [1960]. 252p.   **BA281**

Gnomon XXV 1953 40–45 Harsh
Webster's primary purpose is to make our knowledge of Menander's plots more precise by imaginative reconstructions, based on existing fragments or Roman derivatives. There are also interesting chapters on Menander and earlier Greek drama and philosophy. Much of the admittedly ingenious reconstruction is based on a number of unproven assumptions, e.g., that Menander's plays were divided into five acts.

Ovid

BARSBY, John A. Ovid. Oxford, Clarendon Press, 1978. 49p.   **BA282**

Greece & Rome; new surveys in the classics; v. 12.
Like its predecessors this survey is a personal synthesis with bibliographical pointers, using Wilkinson's *Ovid Recalled* (1955) as a starting point. The Appendix of Principal References (p.48–49) is a useful bibliography, and there are separate chapters on *Amores, Heroides, Ars Amatoria* and *Remedia Amoris, Fasti, Metamorphoses, Tristia* and *Ex Ponto*.

BINNS, J. W., ed. Ovid. London and Boston, Routledge & K. Paul, 1973. viii, 250p.   **BA283**

Greek and Latin studies; classical literature and its influence.
CJ LXXII 1977 317–320 Clarke • CR XXV 1975 216–217 Wilkinson • JRS LXV 1975 231–232 McGann
Five essays on various aspects of Ovid's work (by Du Quesnay, Anderson, Hollis, Kenney, Dickinson) and two on his *Nachleben* by Robathan and Jameson. The two last may have the most surprises. A useful and attractive book.

BÖMER, Franz. P. Ovidius Naso. Metamorphosen. Buch I–III. Heidelberg, Carl Winter, 1976. Vol. 1, 625p.   **BA284**

CR XXII 1972 38 Kenney • CW LXXI 1977 278–279, LXXIII 1979 42–43 Anderson • JRS LXVII 1977 255–256 Griffin
A massive and magnificent commentary on Ovid's greatest poem, extending over two books per volume to a projected total of seven volumes and approximately 3,500 pages. Displays vast erudition and utter thoroughness throughout; particularly good on grammatical problems and parallel passages.
See now idem, Buch 10–11, 1980.

DUE, O. S. Changing forms; Studies in the *Metamorphoses* of Ovid. Copenhagen, Gyldendal, 1974. 210p.   **BA285**

Classica et mediaevalia, dissertationes; 10.
AJPh XCVI 1975 412–415 Anderson • CR XXVII 1977 112 Reeve • Latomus XXXIV 1975 794–795 Frécaut • Phoenix XXX 1976 297–303 Tarrant
Several thematic chapters (p.11–89) are followed by critical descriptions of three sections of the poem: Book 1 (p.94–122), Book 4 (p.123–133), and Book 12.1–13.622 (p.134–157). The book is discursive but pleasantly so, and has certainly succeeded in its stated priority (p.133): "The important thing to find out is how [the poem] works."

FRÉCAUT, Jean Marc. L'esprit et l'humour chez Ovide. Grenoble, Presses universitaires de Grenoble, 1972. 404p.   **BA286**

JRS LXV 1975 234 Griffin • REL L 1972 59–67 Saint-Denis
An excellent choice of subject matter for a book on the *poetarum ingeniosissimus*. Ovid emerges as a poet of great intellectual prowess who is complete master of his material. There are excellent chapters on use of vocabulary, stylistic devices, and imagery in this fine thesis on a fine subject.

GALINSKY, Gotthard Karl. Ovid's Metamorphoses; An introduction to the basic aspects. Oxford, Blackwell, 1975. xi, 285p., plate, 1 illus.   **BA287**

AJPh XCVII 1976 181–183 Cunningham • Phoenix XXX 1976 297–303 Tarrant • REL LIII 1975 497–499 Viarre • Athenaeum L 1978 212–214 Perutelli
Five large chapters deal with the Basic Aspects: Inspiration, Tone and Theme; Unity and Coherence; Ovid's Humanity; Death and Suffering; Humor and Seriousness; and Ovid, Virgil and Augustus. The book is less an introduction than a contribution to the continuing debate on disputed questions.

GARIEPY, R. J., Jr. "Recent Scholarship on Ovid (1958–1968)." CW LXIV (1970): 37–56.   **BA288**

A renewed interest in Ovid, who had been comparatively neglected in the first half of the century, was helped by the International Congress of Ovidian Studies held at Ovid's birthplace, Sulmona on May 20–24, 1958, the bimillenary of his birth. (See E. Paratore, *Bibliografia ovidiana,* Sulmona, 1958.) The present survey covers the next ten years (1958–1968), arranging 440 items by subject.

See also Kraus, W., "Ovid," *AAHG* XXV (1972), 55–76, 267–290, XXVI (1973), 129–150.

JACOBSON, Howard. Ovid's Heroides. Princeton, N.J., Princeton University Press, 1974. xiv, 437p.   **BA289**

Hermathena CXIX 1975 83–85 Courtney • Phoenix XXX 1976 94–97 Anderson

Careful analyses of all 15 single *Heroides* followed by chapters on the vexed questions of dating, the generic categorization of the *Heroides,* and an assessment of the achievements.

MORGAN, Kathleen. Ovid's art of imitation. Propertius in the Amores. Ludguni Batavorum, Brill, 1977. 116p.   **BA290**

Mnemosyne, bibliotheca classica Batava: Supplementum; v. 47.

CR XXVIII 1978 McKeown • CW LXXII, 2 1978 181 Allen • Phoenix XXXIII 1979 92–93 Tarrant

A successful re-examination of Propertian influence on the *Amores,* which is more a critical evaluation than a mere catalog of parallels. The criteria used for establishing parallels are exclusively philological. The author may be presuming too much when she assumes that Ovid in echoing Propertius expects the reader not merely to recognize the original but to check it.

SABOT, A. Ovide, poète de l'amour dans ses oeuvres de jeunesse; Amores, Héroidés, Ars amatoria, Remedia amoris, De medicamine faciei femineae. Ophrys, 1976. 634p.   **BA291**

G&R XXV, 2 1978 198 Verity • REL LV 1977 499 Viarre

A not very original examination of love as the dominant force in Ovid in which the poetry is generally allowed to speak for itself.

SEGAL, Charles Paul. Landscape in Ovid's *Metamorphoses;* A study in the transformations of a literary symbol. Wiesbaden, F. Steiner Verlag, 1969. x, 109p.   **BA292**

Hermes; Zeitschrift für klassische philologie. Einzelschriften; Heft 23.

AJPh XCII 1971 685–692 Anderson • Gnomon XLII 1970 418–419 Kenney • REA LXXII 1970 202–204 Marache

A fascinating examination of the way in which scenic descriptions are employed to assist in conveying the poem's message, which is defined as a mixture of urbanity and violence. Landscape is not mere décor: it plays a symbolic part in the narrative.

SYME, Ronald, Sir. History in Ovid. Oxford and New York, Clarendon Press, 1979. iv, 240p.
                                                    BA293

REL LVII 1979 484–486 Grimal • JRS LXX 1980 244–255 Levick

Parmenides

SCHWABL, H. "Parmenides 1957–1971." AAHG XXV (1972): 15–43.   **BA294**

Petronius

SCHMELING, Gareth L. and STUCKEY, Johanna H. A bibliography of Petronius. Lugduni Batavorum, Brill, 1977. x, 239p., 2 leaves of plates, facsims.   **BA295**

Mnemosyne, bibliotheca classica Batava: Supplementum; 39.

CR XXIX 1979 153–154 Smith • G&R XXV, 1 1978 85 Verity • CW LXXII, 1 1978 55–57 Schreiber

Stephen Gaselee's "Bibliography," *Transactions and Proceedings of the Bibliographical Society* 10 (1910), 141–233, is still standard for the period from 1482 down to Gaselee, and the present two collaborators attempt unsuccessfully to bring Gaselee up-to-date. Accuracy and consistency are everywhere violated and misprints abound. A treacherous guide. This is the first of three books, to be followed by a Petronian allusion book and a study of his influence in England and America.

See also Schnur, H., "Recent Petronian scholarship," *CW* L (1957), 133–136, 141–143; Schmeling, G., "Petronian scholarship since 1957," *CW* LXII (1969), 157–164, 352–353.

SULLIVAN, John Patrick. The *Satyricon* of Petronius; A literary study. London, Faber, 1968. 3–302p.   **BA296**

AJPh XCII 1971 92–100 Rowell • CR XIX 1969 300–302 Browning • Gnomon XLII 1970 31–36 Delz

The first general study of Petronius in English, addressed to beginning students in Petronius and students of literature in general, concentrates on the *Satyricon* as a work of literature. The perennial questions of chronology and authorship are disposed of in the first chapter. Chapter 2 addresses itself to A Reconstruction of the Text (p.34–80) in which the hypothetical reconstructions of the mutilated text are plausible enough. There are interrelated chapters: Choice of Form (emphasizing the traditional nature of some of the elements), and Satire in the Satyricon (which sees Encolpius as satirizing and satirized). The longest chapter is devoted to Criticism and Parody in the Satyricon (p.158–213). The final chapters deal with The Humor of Petronius and Sexual Themes of the Satyricon, the latter overly Freudian. Nine pages of bibliography and three indexes conclude the work.

Philo Judaeus

FELDMAN, Louis H. Studies in Judaica: Scholarship on Philo and Josephus, 1937–1962. New York, Yeshiva University, [1963]. vi, 62p.
                                                    BA297

JHS LXXXVI 1966 201–202 Stern • AC XXXIV 1965 595 Préaux • CR XV 1965 227 Smallwood

This is a useful bridge between *L'Anneé Philologique,* which is less complete on theological and Judaistic than on classical periodicals, and the biographical lists of *Biblica.* The work is conveniently divided into paragraphs according to subject matter: editions and translations, manuscript studies and textual criticism, book-length studies, shorter treatments, etc. The work is in fact larger than its title and may be regarded as a general bibliographical survey of Jewish history during the Hellenistic and Roman period.

See also Feldman, L. H., in *CW* LIV (1961), 281–291, LV (1961–1962), 36–49, 236–244, 252–255, 278–292, 299–301.

NAZZARO, A. V. Recenti studi filoniani (1963–1970). Napoli, Loffredo, 1973. 109p.   **BA297a**

Photius

HÄGG, Tomas. Photios als Vermittler antiker Literatur; Untersuchungen zur Technik de Referiens und Exzerpierens in der Bibliotheke. Stockholm, Almqvist & Wiksell International (distr.), 1975. 218p.   **BA298**

Studia Graeca Upsaliensia; v. 8.
AC XLV 1976 706–707 Henry • CW LXXII 1978 46–47 Marcovich
Photius' *Bibliotheca* is a vast repository of summaries and/or excerpts from some 270 Greek prose works belonging to 168 different authors. Of these 270 works 160 are no longer extant, hence the importance of knowing how reliable Photius was as transmitter. Hääg's pioneering work is exemplary in thoroughness and scholarship.

Pindar

BOWRA, C. M. Pindar. Oxford, Oxford University Press, 1964. xvii, 446p.   **BA299**

CW LIX 1965 51–52 Kirkwood • Phoenix XXI 1967 56–63 Woodbury

BUNDY, Elroy L. Studia Pindarica, I–II. Berkeley, University of California Press, 1962.   **BA299a**

1. The eleventh Olympian ode. 2. The first Isthmian ode.
AC XXXII 1963 226 Davison • CR XIII 1963 144–145 Burton • Gnomon XXXV 1963 130–133 Kirkwood
For Bundy, study of Pindar must become a study of genre, an analysis of the poet's choice of formulae, motives, themes, topics and set sequences. A strange choice, at first blush, of two odes, one of which has no mythic element, the other, little or none, but the resulting study is a brilliant and epoch-making contribution.

BURTON, Reginald W. Pindar's Pythian odes; Essays in interpretation. [Oxford], Oxford University Press, 1962. 202p.   **BA300**

CW LVI 1962 8 Kirkwood • RPh XXXVII 1963 124–126 Vian • LEC XXX 1962 445 Delande • Gnomon XXXV 1963 763–765 Irigoin
Based on a course of lectures given at Oxford over a period of several years, this book examines the structure and content of each of the Pythian odes as a finished work. It presumes access to a text and a commentary and aims at a deeper understanding and appreciation of the poetry. The Pythian odes, spanning almost the whole of Pindar's life (P10, 498 B.C., P8, 446 B.C.), are examined chronologically.

CALDER, William Musgrave and STERN, Jacob. Pindaros und Bakchylides. Darmstadt, Wissenschaftliche Buchgesellschaft, 1970. viii, 431p.   **BA301**

Wege der Forschung; Bd. 134.
BO XXX 1973 279–280 Jonkers • CR XXIII 1973 131–132 Willcock
For the first time in the *Wege der Forschung* series, articles in French and English are left in their original tongue. There are ten articles on Pindar and eight on Bacchylides. David Young's "Pindaric criticism" is reprinted with corrections from *The Minnesota Review,* occupying nearly one-fourth of the whole volume (p.1–95). Jacob Stern provides a similar survey of criticism of Bacchylides; older scholars like Wilamowitz, Blass, Comparetti, and Croiset are well represented. A collection of the greatest value.

FOGELMARK, Staffan. Studies in Pindar with particular reference to Paean VI and Nemean VII. Lund, Gleerup, 1972. 156p.   **BA302**

AJPh XCVI 1975 407–409 Hamilton • CR XXV 1975 6–9 Willcock • CW LXVII 1973 114–115 Stern • RFIC CIII 1975 71–73 Gianotti
This work argues painstakingly that Nemean VII and Paean VI are to be dated late and are interconnected. Recent scholarship is carefully and fearlessly considered, and color-words are cogently invoked in the chronology discussion. A good methodology at work, but the division of Pindar's poems into before and after 476 is not sufficiently discussed or demonstrated and may be an oversimplification. See also Lloyd-Jones, H., "Modern interpretation of Pindar; The second Pythian and seventh Nemean odes," *JHS* XCIII (1973), 127–137.

GERBER, Douglas E. A bibliography of Pindar, 1513–1966. [Cleveland], Published for the American Philological Association by the Case Western Reserve University Press, 1969. xv, 160p.   **BA303**

Philological monographs; 28.
CR XXI 1971 16–17 Willcock • Mnemosyne XXVI 1973 301 Verdenius • Phoenix XXIII 1969 410 Slater • REG LXXXIII 1970 234 Defradas
A solid, comprehensive work which will save Pindar scholars a lot of time and goes back to the first printed edition of Pindar in 1513. The material is divided into 30 sections. Four preliminary sections are Texts, Text

and Commentary, Text, Translation and Commentary, Translations (p.1–8). Individual odes and fragments, and the scholia receive separate treatment, each ode being further divided into general and specific verses. There are no value judgments and no indices, but cross-references are ample.

See also Gerber, D. E. *CW* LXI (1968), 373–385 and Gerber, D. E. *Pindar's Olympian One: A Commentary*. Toronto, University of Toronto Press, 1982. xx, 202p.

PINDARUS. The odes of Pindar. Trans., with an introd., by C. M. Bowra. Baltimore, Penguin Books, [1969]. 256p.   **BA304**

Penguin classics; L209.
CJ LXVI 1971 375–376 Ruck • CW LXIII 1970 303 Robertson
An attractive, if not overpowering, version. The translation is brisk, vivid and always clear, in lines of irregular rhythm and varying length. The odes are arranged chronologically and are provided with notes.

PINDARUS. Pindari Carmina, cum fragmentis. Edidit Alexander Turyn. Oxonii, Blackwell, 1952. xiii, 402p.   **BA305**

"Liber primum editus anno MCMXLVIII sumptibus Academiae Polonae Litterarum & Scientiarum . . . iterum impressus anno MCMLII.
LEC XXI 1953 257–258 Ruelle • RPh XXV 1951 236–243 Irigoin • JHS LXXI 1951 267–268 Lloyd-Jones • LXIV 1944 121 Forster
Based on a collation of all the manuscripts either either in the originals or in facsimiles, this work was completed in Poland on the eve of World War Two and published in the United States. A great deal of precise and up-to-date information is given between the text and the apparatus criticus.

PINDARUS. Pindari Carmina, Cvm fragmentis, recognovit brevique adnotatione critica instrvxit C. M. Bowra. Editio altera. Oxonii, Typographeo Clarendoniano, [1947]. xii, [288]p.   **BA306**

Scriptorum classicorum bibliotheca oxoniensis.
CJ XXXIV 1939 244–245 Duncan • Gnomon XII 1936 360–367 Turyn • CPh XXXII 1937 280–283 Robinson
Worthy to stand with Puech's Budé text and Schroeder's Teubner, this text is based on the seven best codices of the 13th and 14th centuries, though there is not agreement between Turyn and Bowra on what is best.

PINDARUS. The works of Pindar. Trans. with literary and critical commentaries by Lewis Richard Farnell. London, Macmillan and Co., 1930–1932. 3 v., plates.   **BA307**

v. 1. Translation in rhythmical prose with literary comments. v. 2. Critical commentary. v. 3. The text.
CR XLVI 1932 205–208 Robertson • JHS LII 1932 321–323 Rose • REG XLVI 1933 360 Puech

Includes the epinicia (odes) and "only those fragments which are appreciable and intelligible." Depends on Schroeder for an account of the text tradition. The text has no *apparatus criticus*, but merely spasmodic signposts on conjectures and corruptions. Up to its date of publication it provided the only English commentary on the whole of Pindar. The translation is in rhythmical and somewhat archaic prose. The scholarship noted is neither comprehensive nor very recent.

RICO, María. Ensayo de bibliografía pindárica. Madrid, Instituto Antonio de Nebrija, 1969. xii, 354p.   **BA308**

REG LXXXIII 1970 233–234 Defradas • RBPh XLIX 1971 165–167 Irigoin • CR XXII 1972 101–102 Willcock
Appeared almost at the same time as Gerber—a regrettable duplication of effort—and while it has more titles than Gerber it also has more mistakes.

RUCK, C. A. P. and MATHESON, W. H. Pindar, selected odes; With interpretive essays. Ann Arbor, University of Michigan Press, 1968. x, 269p.   **BA309**

CR XXI 1971 13–15 Willcock • CPh LXV 1970 136–138 Burnett
A lively translation of 21 of the 45 epinician odes, born out of scorn for past translators and good intentions to do justice to the poetry of Pindar. A long interpretive essay is prefixed to each ode. The only order in the choice seems to be the order in which the translations were made. The essays are probably more successful than the translations.

SLATER, William J. Lexicon to Pindar. Berlin, De Gruyter, 1969. xiv, 563p.   **BA310**

ACR 1 1971 85 Calder • CJ LXVIII 1972 79 Segal • BAGB 1971 280–281 Irigoin • Phoenix XXIV 1970 275–276 Gerber
A model of completeness, accuracy and sound exegesis, facilitated by listing of variant readings, significant emendations and marking the quantities of vowels. Beautifully printed and carefully organized.

VERDENIUS, Willem Jacob. Pindar's Seventh Olympian Ode; A commentary. Amsterdam, North-Holland Publishing Co., 1972. 33p.
                BA311

CR XXV 1975 5–6 Willcock
Represents a backlash of the older criticism against the new criticism's fondness for finding patterns of imagery to "explain" the unity of the odes. Verdenius believes that the hyper-interpretation of the new criticism needs to be pruned away. The targets are doubtless Young and Smith (in *Class et Med* XXVIII, 1967), and translators Lattimore, Ruck and Matheson; Bowra also comes in for attention. See also Verdenius,

W. J., "Supplementary comments," *Mnemosyne* XXIX (1976), 243–253.

Plato

DIÈS, Auguste. Autour de Platon; Essais de critique et d'histoire. New York, Arno Press, 1976. xvi, 615p. **BA312**

Reprint of the 1927 ed. published by G. Beauschesne, Paris, in series: Bibliothèque des Archives de philosophie.

JHS XLVIII 1928 260 J.H.S. • CPh XXII 1927 330 Shorey • CR XLI 1927 132 Taylor

A collection of articles and reviews which appeared throughout the first quarter of the century. Volume 1 is devoted to science, philosophy and religion before Socrates, and also to Socrates; v. 2 is devoted to Plato. Useful for covering again the old battles on the real Socrates and the chronology of the Platonic dialogs with an author who is invariably temperate and courteous. The fourth part of the book contains good chapters on Plato's conception of science, Plato's God, and Plato's religion.

HAVELOCK, Eric A. Preface to Plato. New York, Grosset & Dunlap, 1967, 1963. xiv, 328p. **BA313**

A History of the Greek mind. The Universal Library.

CW LVI 1963 257 Grimaldi • CPh LIX 1964 70–74 Hoerber • Phoenix XVIII 1964 163–164 Sparshott

The starting point here is Plato's attack on Homer and poetry in the *Republic*, which is rightly seen as a treatise on education, not politics or metaphysics. Before the end of the 5th century B.C., Havelock feels, the written word held little sway in education but instead memorization and recital of Homer formed the basis of pedagogy, and Homer was cultivated not as poetry but as a sort of encyclopedia of politics, ethics, history and technology. Plato, he argues, tries to move knowledge into a more objective epistemology. The result is a disappointing book, loosely argued and written.

HERMANN, Alfred. Untersuchungen zu Platons Auffassung von der Hedoné; Ein Beitrag zum Verständnis des platonischen Tugendbegriffes. Göttingen, Vandenhoeck & Ruprecht, 1972. 80p. **BA314**

Hypomnemata; Untersuchungen zur Antike und zu ihrem Nachleben; a revision of the author's thesis, Tübingen, 1968.

AC XLII 1973 621–623 De Ley • Gnomon XLVIII 1976 606–609 Voigtländer • CW LXVIII 1975 319–320 Robinson

The *Protagoras* excursus on hedonism (p.351–359) is a key text in the ethics of paganism and the prehistory of "puritan" psychology. Hermann's exegesis of this and other important passages in the *Gorgias, Laches, Phaedo* requires preliminary discussion on the chronology of certain dialogs. The conclusion on the *Protagoras* excursus is not very satisfactory.

PIÉRART, Marcel. Platon et la cité grecque; Théorie et réalité dans la constituton des Lois. Bruxelles, Académie royale de Belgique, 1974. xv, 536p. **BA315**

Mémoires de la Classe des lettres; Académie royale de Belgique Collection in-8; 2. sér.; t.62, fasc.3.

AC XLV 1976 243–244 Hannick • JHS XCVI 1976 184–185 Saunders

An important but difficult subject is here addressed, an examination of the institutional models which inspired Plato in his drafting of a constitution for Magnesia. Indispensable for an understanding of the Laws, this careful study is based on a sound methodology and extends beyond the title to many matters of importance in the Laws and in Greek constitutional history. Not all his solutions will meet with acceptance, but his survey of the historical material is persuasively presented, topic by topic, with copious reference to the primary and secondary sources. The main contribution of this intelligent and learned work is in its thoroughness in collecting, presenting and sifting evidence. It complements, but by no means replaces, Morrow's *Plato's Cretan City,* Princeton, 1960.

ROBINSON, T. M. Plato's psychology. Toronto, University of Toronto Press, 1970. ix, 202p. **BA316**

CPh LXVII 1972 63–64 Sprague • JHPh X 1972 217–221 Anagnostopoulos • REA LXXII 1970 424–425 Moreau • Gnomon XLIII 1971 342–346 Graeser

A work of exceptional value for both the specialist and the generalist. The chronology of the Dialogs proposed by L. Campbell and W. Iutoslawski is in general adopted, while that of G. E. L. Owen for the *Timaeus* (cf. CQ n.s. III 1953 74–95), is followed. Based on this, the word "ψυχη" is studied in the whole *corpus* and the fluidity of Plato's view of the individual soul throughout his life is demonstrated, using as he did particular models for particular contexts. Signs of alteration in Plato's thought on the cosmic soul are noted.

RYLE, Gilbert. Plato's progress. Cambridge, Cambridge University Press, 1966. viii, 311p. **BA317**

JHS LXXXVIII 1968 195–196 Hicken • PhR LXXXVIII 1969 362–373 Crombie • Cambridge Review LXXXIX 1967 279–281 O'Brien

A far-ranging and at times exasperating attempt to justify by historical argument and speculation a new chronology for the *Dialogues.* Easy to read, attractively written and presented, this work contains many novel, true and important propositions, and some false ones. For Ryle, Plato came to philosophy fairly late, and his early dialogs were less philosophical tracts on particular doctrines of his than literary entries in eristic contests in which a question/answer format was prescribed. During this early period Plato is seen as a teacher of argumentation, not a teacher of philosophy.

SAUNDERS, Trevor J. Bibliography on Plato's

Laws, 1920–1970; With additional citations through May, 1975. New York, Arno Press, 1976, 1975. 60 p.   **BA318**

CR XXVIII 1978 360–361 Ackrill • JHPh XV 1977 463 Tejera

Already well-known for his translation of the *Laws* for Penguin classics (1970) and for *Notes on the Laws of Plato* (London, Univ. of London Institute of Classical Studies, 1972), Saunders in his bibliography has an extraordinarily wide range of reference, listing books and articles under 13 headings. A final section refers to discussions of individual passages listed by Stephanus.

See also Cherniss, "Plato 1950–1957," *Lustrum* IV (1959), 5–308; V (1960), 321–648; L. Brisson, XX (1977), 5–304; XXV (1983), 31–320.

SKEMP, Joseph B. The theory of motion in Plato's later dialogues. Cambridge, Cambridge University Press, 1942. xv, 123p.   **BA319**

Photocopy: Ann Arbor, Mich.: Xerox University MicroFilms, 1976.

AJPh LXV 1944 298–301 Post • CW XXXVI 1943 202–203 Winspear • PhR LII 1943 412–413 Solmsen

In the dialogs later than the *Republic* Plato devotes increasing attention to the various aspects of "change." "Kinehsis" or "movement" is the Greek term which covers the whole field of changes and processes. For Skemp the source of movements is the Soul, which is as real and as eternal as the Forms. Each of the later dialogs, especially *Timaeus* and Book X of the *Laws* contributes much new material to Plato's teaching on movements, and represents Platonic reflection on, and assimilation of, certain aspects of Presocratic thought.

WEINGARTNER, Rudolph Herbert. The unity of the Platonic dialogue; The Cratylus, the Protagoras, the Parmenides. New York, Bobbs-Merrill Co., 1973. x, 205p.   **BA320**

RevMetaph XXVII 1973 626–627 Rudolf • JHPh XIII 1975 247–250 King and Dye • CPh LXXI 1976 365–366 Mejer

An impressive statement of the importance of treating each dialog as a dialog, complete in itself and deserving separate consideration in its form, presentation and theme. A useful antidote to those collections of essays that show a one-sided approach that is largely analytical or linguistic.

WHITE, Nicholas P. Plato on knowledge and reality. Indianapolis, Hackett Publishing Co., 1976. xvii, 254p.   **BA321**

Phoenix XXXI 1977 183–185 de Sousa • CW LXXI 1977 218–219 Anton

An excellent book for specialist and general philosophical reader alike, providing a long overdue complete and unified account of Plato's epistemology. The work succeeds in finding a continuous argument running through Plato's various attacks on epistemological problems.

Plautus

ARNOTT, W. Geoffrey. Menander, Plautus, Terence. Oxford, Clarendon Press, 1975. 62p.   **BA322**

Greece & Rome, new surveys in classics; 9.

Deals with Plautus and Terence together in one chapter (p.28–62).

BRAUN, Ludwig. Die Cantica des Plautus. Göttingen, Vandenhoeck u. Ruprecht, 1970. 210p.   **BA323**

Issued also as thesis, Frankfurt am Main, 1968

Latomus XXXI 1972 242–245 Soubiran • ACR 1 1971 165–166 Gillingham • CPh LXXIX 1974 140–145 Tarrant

The Plautine *Cantica* or intricate lyric sections (e.g., *Curculio* 96f., Bacchides 925f.) are new elements in comedy. For Braun the central problem in *Cantica* is structural and metrical analysis. There are detailed and penetrating discussions of colometry and structure, and the work marks a clear advance on that of Gregor Maurach and Cesare Questa. Still many uncertainties and unresolved matters remain.

FOGAZZA, Donatella. "Plauto, 1935–1975." Lustrum XIX (1976): 79–296.   **BA324**

FRAENKEL, Edward. Elementi plautini in Plauto. (Plautinische im Plautus) [Traduzione di Franco Munari]. Firenze, "La Nuova Italia," 1960. x, 463p.   **BA325**

JRS LIII 1963 244 Williams

A 1960 Italian translation of the 1922 German original, with 45 pages of addenda by the author.

HANSON, J. A. "Scholarship on Plautus since 1950." CW LIX (1965–1966): 103–107, 126–128, 141–148.   **BA326**

HUGHES, J. David. A bibliography of scholarship on Plautus. Amsterdam, Hakkert, 1975. ix, 154p.   **BA326a**

Augustinus XXI 1976 436 Orosio

SEGAL, Erich W. Roman laughter; The comedy of Plautus. New York, Harper and Row, 1971. 229p.   **BA327**

Harvard studies in comparative literature; v. 29; Harper Torchbooks; TB 1584.

CR XX 1970 333–335 Gratwick

Remarkably, this is the first English book exclusively devoted to Plautus. It is aimed at setting the playwright in relation to contemporary Roman culture and to the comic tradition. It is a bright introduction to Plautus for those who have read little or none of him, and all Plautine quotations are translated for those in need.

Plinius Maior

HANSLIK, Rudolf. "Plinius der Ältere 1928–1938." JAW CCLXXIII: 1–44.   **BA328**

This is continued in *AAHG* VIII (1955), 193–218.

RÖMER, F. "Plinius der Ältere." AAHG XXXI (1978): 129–206. **BA329**

Continues Hanslik's two reports, *AAHG* VIII (1955), 193–218, XVII (1964), 65–80.

SALLMANN, K. I. "Plinius der Ältere 1938–1970." Lustrum XVIII (1975): 5–209. **BA330**

Plinius Minor

BÜTLER, Hans-Peter. Die geistige Welt des jüngeren Plinius; Studien zur Thematik seiner Briefe. Heidelberg, C. Winter, 1970. 159p. **BA331**

Bibliothek der klassischen Altertumswissenschaften; n.F. Reihe 2, Bd. 38.
CR XXV 1975 316–317 Sherwin-White • REL L 1972 344 Durry
A source book of Pliny's views, under 24 headings, on such associated pairs as life and death, public and private occupations, and such concepts as *auctoritas, liberalitas, frugalitas*. Much useful information, but not a complete record.

COVA, P. V. "Sette anni di studi su Plinio il Giovane (1966–1973)." BStudLat IV (1974): 274–291. **BA332**

HANSLIK, R. "Plinius der Jungere, 1942–1954." AAHG VIII (1955): 1–18. **BA333**

Continued in *AAHG* XVII (1964), 1–16, XXVIII (1975), 153–200.

JACQUES, Xavier and VAN OOTEGHEM, J. Index de Pline le jeune. Bruxelles, Palais des académies, 1965. xx, 981p. **BA334**

LEC XXXIV 1966 191–192 Leroy • REL XLIV 1966 437 Durry
Based on the Schuster-Hanslik 1958 Teubner text this is a highly scientific work that will be of immense service. Greek words are included, and the letters of Trajan are separately identified, as are variants and dubia.

SHERWIN-WHITE, Adrian. The letters of Pliny; A historical and social commentary. Oxford, Clarendon Press, 1966. xv, 808p. **BA335**

AJPh XC 1969 342–347 McDermott • CR XVII 1967 311–314 Crook • JRS LVIII 1968 218–224 Miller • Latomus XXXVI 1967 723–751 Veyne
A remarkable book, the most useful and important ever published on Pliny the Younger, displaying profound erudition on all aspects of the subject: Roman law, prosopography, property, architecture, the early Church, etc. The starting point for all future work on Pliny, and one of the essential bases of future study of the empire.

Plotinus

CHARRUE, Jean Michel. Plotin, lecteur de Platon. Paris, Belles lettres, 1978. 279p. **BA336**

JHS C 1980 233 Blumenthal • REG XCIII 1980 590 Canévet

DODDS, E. R. et al. Les Sources de Plotin. Dix exposés et discussions. Genève, Fondation Hardt, 1960. xiii, 463p. **BA337**

Entretiens sur l'antiquité classique; t. 5.
Gnomon XXXIV 1962 204–207 Merlan
Important contributions by such well-known scholars as Dodds, Theiler, Hadot, Puech, Dörrie, Cilento, Harder, Schwyzer, Henry and Armstrong.

ELSAS, Christoph. Neuplatonische und gnostische Weltablehnung in der Schule Plotins. Berlin and New York, de Gruyter, 1975. xv, 356 p. **BA338**

LEC XLIV 1976 168–169 van Esbroeck • MH XXXIII 1976 259 Schwyzer
The author seeks to distinguish those in the school of Plotinus who favored rejecting the world from those Neoplatonists who did not believe with the Gnostics in its intrinsic evil. The work owes much to Hans Jonas and his structural phenomenological analysis of Gnosticism, and the work of many previous researchers is scrupulously analyzed.

Plutarch

FLACELIÈRE, R. "État présent des études sur Plutarque." Association G. Budé, Actes du VIIIe Congrès, Avril, 1968 (1969): 483–505. **BA339**

HAMILTON, J. R. Plutarch: *Alexander;* A commentary. Oxford, Clarendon Press, 1969. [1], lxix, 231p., geneal. table, 2 maps. **BA340**

CW LXIII 1969 18 Fredricksmeyer • Gnomon XLIII 1971 404–407 Breebart • REG LXXXII 1969 238–241 Babut
This first-rate commentary on Plutarch's *Alexander* focuses on those incidents which attracted the interest of Plutarch the biographer. There is a long and systematic introduction, including good sections on sources, style and methods. The commentary is a most helpful treasure-house of information, and an up-to-date guide through the mazes of specialist-research.

JONES, C. P. Plutarch and Rome. Oxford, Clarendon Press, 1971. xiii, 158p. **BA341**

CR XXIV 1974 202–204 Briscoe • JRS LXII 1972 226–227 Russell • Phoenix XXVI 1972 404–408 Murray • REG LXXXVIII 1975 206–211 Babut
A short work in two parts: the first reviews the evidence for Plutarch's life and society; the second considers those of his writings that reveal his attitude toward

Rome. While Rome provides the organizing principle, the primary subject is Plutarch. There are many corrections of recent opinions on Plutarch in part I. Concentrating on Plutarch's public life prosopographical skills are here combined with literary analysis (and with disciplined conjecture in the absence of hard information along the way) to give a convincing portrait of Plutarch in his Greco-Roman cultural milieu.

See also Scardigli, B., *Die Römerbiographien Plutarchs, in Forschungsbericht,* 1979, xi, 230p.

RUSSELL, Donald Andrew. Plutarch. New York, 183p. **BA342**

Appendix (p. [164]–178): 1. List of works in the "Moralia."–2. List of the "Lives."–3. Editions and translations.–4. General bibliography.

CR XXVI 1976 174–175 Gossage • Gnomon XLVIII 1976 546–551 Ingenkam • JRS LXIV 1974 279–280 Jones • Mnemosyne XXIX 1976 198–199 de Vries

A judicious choice of topics joined to lucid exposition results in an admirable introduction to Plutarch, which conveys the essence of his personality and shows how and why he has been so influential. Particularly good chapters on Plutarch's family and social background, language, style and form (with good translation of illustrations of the various styles employed by Plutarch); also The Scholar and His Books, Plutarch's philosophical and religious works, The Moralist and His Fellow-Men, and *The Lives*. There are two concluding chapters on Plutarch's *Nachleben*.

STADTER, Philip A. Plutarch's historical methods; An analysis of the *Mulierum virtutes*. Cambridge, Harvard University Press, 1965. 159p. **BA343**

CR XVI 1966 408–409 Walsh • CW LIX 1966 199 O'Neil • JHS LXXXVI 1966 205–206 Carney

Polybius

FOUCAULT, Jules Albert de. Recherches sur la langue et le style de Polybe. Paris, Belles lettres, 1972. x, 396p. **BA344**

Collection d'études anciennes.

AC XLII 1973 247 Schwartz • AJPh XCVI 1975 309–311 Cooper • Emerita XLII 1974 192–193 Díaz Tejero

De Foucault (with Pédech) is the editor of the Budé *Polybe* which lists in its Bibliographie (p.viii–x) some 56 *Études générales et particulières*. The present work is basically a copious and systematic resumé of these source-monographs arranged under general headings of Vocabulary, Morphology, Syntax, Style.

See also Musti, D., "Polibio negli studi dell' ultimo ventennio (1950–1970)," *ANRW* 1.2. (1972), 1114–1181.

FRITZ, Kurt von. The theory of the mixed constitution; A critical analysis of Polybius' political ideas. New York, Columbia University Press, 1954. Reprinted 1975. 490p. **BA345**

AHR LX 1954–1955 865–867 McDonald • JRS XLV 1955 150–155 Walbank • REG LXVIII 1955 385–388 Pédech

Polybius, Book VI has long been a problem on two scores: What does it say about the Roman constitution and how credible is it?

In this long book of 11 chapters, von Fritz maintains that the idea of biological growth was applied by Polybius to the mixed constitution only, and therefore the Roman constitution was always a mixed one. The second part (c. VI–X) is a veritable constitutional history of the Roman Republic. A ready reference for political philosopher and ancient historian alike.

GABBA, Emilio. Polybe; neuf exposés suivis de discussions par F. W. Walbank [and others]. Avec la participation de Raymond Weil et Denis van Berchem. Entretiens préparés et présidés par Emilio Gabba. Genève, Vandoeuvres, 1973. 397p. **BA346**

Entretiens sur l'antiquité classique; 20.

CW LXIX 1976 346–347 Wassermann • Erasmus XXVII 1975 303–306 Calame • Gnomon XLVIII 1975 785–790 Deininger

Nine papers, beginning with F. W. Walbank, Polybius between Greece and Rome (p.3–31), and including P. Pédech, La culture de Polybe et la science de son temps (p.41–60), covering psychology, chronology and geography; H. H. Schmitt, Polybius und das Gleichgewicht der Mächte (p.67–73); D. Musti, Polybio e la Storiografia Romana Arcaica (p.105–139); G. A. Lehmann, Polybios und die ältere und zeitgenössische griechische Geschichtsschreibung; einige Bemerkungen (p.147–200); C. Nicolet, Polybe et les institutions romaines (p.209–258); E. W. Marsden, Polybius as a military historian (p. 269–295); F. Paschoud, Influences et échos des conceptions historiographiques de Polybe dans l'antiquité tardive (p. 305–337); and A. Momigliano, Polybius' Reappearance in Western Europe (p. 347–372).

Propertius

BOUCHER, Jean Paul. Études sur Properce; Problèmes d'inspiration et d'art. Paris, E. de Boccard, 1965. 519p. **BA347**

Bibliothèque des Écoles françaises d'Athènes et de Rome; fasc. 204.

RPh XL 1966 277–279 Ernout • CR XVI 1966 327–329 Townend • REA LXVIII 1966 486–491 Boyancé

The subtitle defines the scope of this fine work and places out of limits such questions as textual criticism, stylistics, syntax, prosody and metre. The principal themes of inspiration are identified and treated with great sensitivity. The influence of Callimachus and Philetas is clearly assessed and likewise the relation between the poet's biography and his work. More comparisons with Catullus and Propertius' contemporaries would have been welcome. The bibliography (p.481–499) is helpful.

COMMAGER, Henry Steele. A prolegomenon to Propertius. 1st ed. Cincinnati, University of Cincinnati, 1974. 77p. **BA348**

Lectures in memory of Louise Taft Semple; 3rd series.
AJPh XCVI 1975 316–317 Nethercut
A brief but effective introduction, useful for the newcomer to Propertius and stimulating on a number of points for the specialist.

EISENHUT, Werner. Properz. Darmstadt, Wissenschaftliche Buchgesellschaft, 1975. xviii, 314p. **BA349**

Wege der Forschung; Bd. 237.
DLZ XCVI 1975 934–936 Hering • AC XLV 1976 679–680 Tordeur • JRS LXVII 1977 242–243 Henderson
This reprint of 17 articles, which appeared between 1887 and 1970, helps to show both what has been accomplished and what remains to be done in Propertian studies. Much could have been left unresurrected.

HARRAUER, Hermann. A bibliography to Propertius. Hildesheim, Gerstenberg, 1973. xviii, 219p. **BA350**

Bibliography to the Augustan poetry; v. 2.
CW LXIX 1975–1976 471 Hallet • REL LI 1973 406–407 Tupet
An extremely useful and easy-to-consult bibliography listing 1833 entries, which aims at completeness, especially for post-1900 scholarship. Works are catalogued under 16 general headings and listed chronologically within each category. Reviews in periodicals are noted where warranted. There are three comprehensive indices: locorum, rerum et nominum, auctorum. There are, however, numerous errors, misspellings, etc., especially in English entries.

HUBBARD, Margaret. Propertius. New York, Scribner, 1975. viii, 182p., 1 leaf of plates, illus. **BA351**

CPh LXXIII 1978 171–175 Ross • JRS LXVII 1977 242 Henderson • Phoenix XXIX 1975 398–401 Warden • CW LXXI 1977 150 Schechter
A major contribution, superseding all previous introductions. Each of four chapters deals with a book of poems as an individual *oeuvre* with its own aims, methods and standards. Propertius is seen as an experimenter who extends the range of elegiac subject matters. "A poet of finish, grace and charm" (p.3) expertly reevaluated by a critic with the same endowments.

NETHERCUT, William R. "Twelve years of propertian scholarship; 1960–1972." CW LXIX (1975–1976): 1–33, 225–257, 289–309. **BA352**

Nethercut chooses 1960 as the *terminus a quo,* since P. J. Enk's edition of the *Monobiblos* (Leiden 1946), p.78–124 and of Book II (Leiden 1962), p.47–68 covered editions between the *editio princeps* in 1472 and

the Teubner text (Schuster-Dornstieff) of 1958, and articles written into the year 1960. This is a model survey, divided into nine main sections, with sub-divisions.

SCHMEISSER, Brigitte. A concordance to the elegies of Propertius. Hildesheim, H. A. Gerstenberg, 1972. 950p. **BA353**

Originally presented as the author's thesis, Vienna.
Latomus XXXIII 1974 437 Boucher
The state of the text of Propertius makes work on a concordance especially difficult, and Schmeisser tries to do justice to Hanslik, Schuster, Barber, Camps, Luck, Enk and Fedeli.

SULLIVAN, John Patrick. Propertius; A critical introduction. Cambridge and New York, Cambridge University Press, 1976. xii, 174p. **BA354**

CPh LXXIII 1978 361–364 Udris • CW LXXI 1977 149–150 Schechter • Gnomon L 1978 540–545 Pasoli
For Sullivan, Propertius was a maverick who disingenuously opposed and undermined Augustan political ideals and literary ideals of Maecenas, Horace and Virgil. But with Book IV he reached a superficial reconciliation between his individualistic poetic and the Augustan ideology. A Freudian syndrome (Dirnenliebe) is invoked by him to explain Propertius' dalliance with the unreliable Cynthia, which if true for Propertius was true for all the elegists. Many fresh and provocative insights, but so much special pleading that the book scarcely attains its stated objective: "a standard introduction in English to which one may with confidence refer the neophyte classicist" (p.ix).

Sallust

BENNETT, Alva. Index verborum Sallustianus. Hildesheim and New York, G. Olms, 1970. xi, 280p. **BA355**

Alpha-Omega; 12.

BÜCHNER, Karl. Sallust. [Heidelberg], C. Winter, 1960. 463p. **BA356**

Gnomon XXXIII 1961 567–577 Drexler • JRS LII 1962 276–277 Earl
A well-balanced study of Sallust as a politician but above all as an historian, this work is in three parts: Der Politiker, Der Historiker and Leistung. The first section is the weakest. The discussion of Sallust as historian is carried out under the headings of Prologues, Digressions, Speeches and Presentation. Leistung is discussed under the headings of Geschichtsanschauung, Geschichtsbild, Vorgänger and Wirkung.

LA PENNA, Antonio. Sallustio e la "rivoluzione" romana. 3. ed. Milano, Feltrinelli, 1973. 501p. **BA357**

I Fatti e le idèa: Saggi e biografie; 181.
AJPh XCII 1971 103–107 Badian • Athenaeum

XLVII 1969 360–362 Frassinetti • CW LXIV 1970 63 Smethurst

Most of these essays have appeared before (the first three in 1959). Their author is widely recognized as one of the most important and stimulating writers on Sallust. He deals with Sallust's concept of historiography, the fear of revolution in Rome, the sense of responsibility in the Roman governing classes, and the republican crisis as seen in Sallust's prefaces. In La Penna's analysis of the Roman revolution (of which he sees Sallust as the best interpreter) he is closer to Soviet historians than to Syme.

PAANANEN, Unto. Sallust's politico-social terminology; Its use and biographical significance. Helsinki, Suomalainen Tiedeakatemia, 1972. 127p.   **BA358**

ACR III 1973 92–93 Yavetz • AHR LXXX 1975 1305–1306 Downey • Gnomon XLVII 1975 248–252 Pasoli

The purpose of this monograph is to show the semantic content and historical context of certain politico-social terminology in Sallust. The study is limited to the following concepts: *populus, plebs, nobilis, nobilitas, pauci, factio, factiosus, partes, boni (bonus, optimus), homo novus.* Within these self-imposed limits it is a useful contribution, with a good overview of earlier work.

SYME, Ronald, Sir. Sallust. Berkeley, University of California Press, 1964. 381p.   **BA359**

Sather classical lectures; v. 33.

CPh LXI 1966 273–275 Chambers • CR XVI 1966 337–340 McDonald • Gnomon XXXIX 1967 57–61 Leeman • JRS LV 1965 232–240 Earl

On a smaller scale than, but a similar plan to, his *Tacitus,* Syme gives us an examination of the life, times and works of Sallust, with some reconstruction of political history, analysis of style and demonstration of meaning and reliability. Vigorous in challenging conventional assumptions, Syme succeeds better than any other writer in presenting Sallust as a man of his own time.

There is a German translation by Scholz, Darmstadt, 1975. vii, 368p.

TIFFOU, Étienne. Essai sur la pensée morale de Salluste à la lumière de ses prologues. [Paris], Klincksieck, 1973. 612p.   **BA360**

Études et commentaires; 83.

Gnomon XLIX 1977 74–76 Vretska • Phoenix XXIX 1975 298–303 Hellegouarc'h • REL LIII 1975 484–486 Doignon

Believing that such moral themes as *gloria, virtus* and *otium* dominate Sallust's historical narrative, Tiffou submits the concepts to a rigorous analysis both in the prologues and in the rest of the works. He reestablishes the importance of the prologues in understanding Sallust's philosophical, political and moral thought.

WISTRAND, Erik Karl H. Sallust on judicial murders in Rome; A philological and historical study. Göteborg, Universitet; Stockholm, Almqvist & Wiksell, 1968. 88p.   **BA360a**

Studia Graeca et Latina Gothoburgensia; v 24.

AC XXXVIII 1969 250 Cebeillac • JRS LIX 1969 310–311 Seager • Phoenix XXVI 1972 199–201 Paul

Wistrand defends the Sallustian authorship of the *Epistulae ad Caesarem Senem,* with special attention to the passage *Ep.* 2.3.3ff. The discussions on many points are wide-ranging and can be read with profit, irrespective of belief in Sallust's authorship of the *Epistulae.*

Semonides

LLOYD-JONES, Hugh. Females of the species; Semonides on women. With photos by Don Honeyman of sculptures by Marcelle Quinton. Park Ridge, N.J., Noyes Press, [1975]. 109p., illus.   **BA361**

"Contains an essay on the poem Τὰ γένεα τῶν γυναικῶν a text and English translation, and a commentary."

REG LXXXIX 1976 631 Bennett

Semonides on women, a sort of female bestiary, has always been an embarrassment for its apparent misogyny. The present elaborate edition, with diverting sculptures by Marcelle Quinton, may encourage reading it in a less serious and more forgiving light.

Seneca

BUSA, R. et al. Concordantiae Senecanae; Curaverunt R. Busa [et] A. Zampolli auspicio auctoritate Societatis linguae Latinae historice investigandae ab Italico Consilio studiis provehendis (C.N.R.) constitutae. Hildesheim and New York, G. Olms, 1975. 2 v. 822, 826p. (1473, 59, 58p.)   **BA362**

Alpha-Omega: Reihe A: Lexika, Indizes, Konkordanzen zur klassische Philologie; v. 21. "Accedunt Index inversus. Indices frequentiae."

COSTA, Charles Desmond N. Seneca. London and Boston, Routledge & K. Paul, 1974. viii, 246p.   **BA362a**

Greek and Latin studies: classical literature and its influence.

CR XXVI 1976 196–197 Winterbottom • CW LXIX 1975–1976 413 Motto & Clark • REL LII 1974 500–505 Grimal

Seven chapters by different hands—all working in Great Britain—deal with the life and political career of Seneca. The authors' names are a guarantee of diverse interests and a certain quality: M. T. Griffin, J. R. C. Wright, D. A. Russell, C. D. N. Costa, G. M. Ross, G. K. Hunter, J. W. Binns. One more contribution to the rehabilitation of Seneca, but still somewhat lame and too much on the defensive.

GRIFFIN, Miriam T. Seneca; A philosopher in politics. Oxford, Clarendon Press, 1976. xii, 504p.   **BA363**

CPh LXXIII 1978 247–250 Bradley • CR XXVIII 1978 269–271 Wright • JRS LXVII 1977 243–246 Warmington

An excellent political biography, probing the dilemma of the political careerist and moral philosopher. Part 1 gives an account of Seneca's career, using only outside sources, with a full discussion of the politically oriented *Apocolocyntosis* and *de Clementia*. Part II studies Seneca's own treatment of subjects of political and ethical significance, e.g., slavery, wealth, suicide. The tragedies are not utilized. A substantial contribution to the study not only of Seneca but of the whole Julio-Claudian period.

GRIMAL, Pierre. Sénèque; ou, La conscience de l'Empire. Paris, Belles Lettres, 1978. 503p.
BA363a

Collection d'études anciennes.
G&R XXVI 1979 90 Woodman
Another 504-page study of Seneca like that of Miriam Griffin's 1976 work. Completed c.1972, this is the culmination of a 30-year interest of the author in Seneca. The work is in two parts: Sénèque et son temps and un philosophe hors de l'école. There is a full bibliography as well as helpful indices.

LEFÈVRE, Eckard, ed. Senecas Tragödien. Darmstadt, Wissenschaftliche Buchgesellschaft, 1972. vii, 592p.
BA364

Wege der Forschung, Bd. 310.
CW LXVIII 1975 331–332 Motto & Clark • Latomus XXXIV 1975 547 Hermann
A good collection of essays, nine general on Senecan theatre, the rest on individual plays, generally two per play. Most pieces are reprints but several previously unpublished (by Opelt, Zintzen) are included. There is a useful ten-page selected bibliography.
See also Coffey, M., "Seneca, Tragedies 1922–1955," *Lustrum* II (1957), 113–186.

MAURACH, Gregor. Seneca als Philosoph. Darmstadt, Wissenschaftliche Buchgesellschaft [Abt, Verl.], 1975. vi, 377p.
BA365

Wege der Forschung; Bd. 414.
JRS LXVII 1977 246 Warmington • Gymnasium LXXXIII 1976 559–562 Hartung
Contains 15 papers in German, some translated from English (Currie, Clark) or French (Boyancé). While the emphasis is on philosophy three items deal with the *Quaestiones naturales.*

MOTTO, Anna Lydia. Seneca. New York, Twayne Publishers, [1973]. 173p.
BA366

Twayne's world authors series; TWAS 268, Latin literature.
AC XLIV 1975 279 Verdière • Latomus XXXIII 1974 437–438 Herrmann • REA LXXVI 1974 169 Grimal
An excellent brief treatment, clear and concise; especially good on Stoic texts and on the spirit, style and art of composition in the prose of Seneca. The *Fortleben*

of Seneca down through Camus, Sartre, and Tillich makes exciting reading. See also Motto's "Seneca's prose writings; A decade of scholarship," *CW* LXIV (1971), 141–158, 177–191, and previously *CW* LIV (1960–1961): 13–18, 37–48, 111–112.

SENECA, Lucius Annaeus. Agamemnon. Edited with a commentary by R. J. Tarrant. Cambridge and New York, Cambridge University Press, 1976. viii, 409p.
BA367

Cambridge classical texts and commentaries; 18.
CO LVI 1978 15–16 Motto • Phoenix XXXII 1978 270–275 Herington
A well-documented, annotated edition of *Agamemnon* containing a new critical text composed directly from the 60-odd extant MSS, with a 93-page introduction. A welcome addition to the Cambridge Classical Texts and Commentaries series. A special feature is the accumulation of parallels from elsewhere in ancient literature, not merely to the diction, style and syntax of the *Agamemnon* text but to the *loci communes,* the rhetorical colors, the mythological elaborations and the dramatic techniques.

SENECA, Lucius Annaeus. Sénèque: Lettres à Lucilius; Index verborum. Relevés statistiques par L. Delatte [et al.]. La Haye, Mouton, 1975. 2 v., 893p.
BA367a

Université de Liège. Faculté de philosophie et lettres. Travaux publiés par le Laboratoire d'analyse statistique des langues anciennes, fasc. 10, t. 1–2.

TRAINA, Alfonso. Lo stile drammatico del filosofo Seneca. Bologna, Pàtron, 1974. 186p.
BA368

Testi e manuali per l'insegnamento universitario del latino; 11.
AC XLIV 1975 282 Liénard • BStud Lat V 1975 348–349 Cupaiuolo • REL LII 1974 505–508 Grimal
A stylistic and linguistic study which often digresses into an examination of the philosophic thought of Seneca. Based on an earlier work of the author (*Belfagor,* 1964, p.625–643), the present work is divided into two main chapters on the language of interiority and the language of *predicazione,* followed by a lengthy third section (p.43–130) on documentation, with up-to-date bibliography.

Sophocles

ADAMS, Sinclair M. Sophocles the playwright. Toronto, Toronto University Press, 1957. x, 182p.
BA369

Phoenix Suppl.; 3.
AJPh LXXX 1959 100–102 Lattimore • CPh LIV 1959 69–72 Calder • CW LII 1958 58 Musurillo
A rather traditional but full and generally fair discussion of all seven plays, prefaced by a chapter on Heritage and Achievement. There is careful attention to Sophocles' artistry and to textual problems. *Philoctetes*

and *Antigone* are particularly well served. Seems at times to be working from, not toward, conclusions about the serenity of Sophocles and the goodness of his gods.

BOWRA, C. Maurice, Sir. Sophoclean tragedy. Oxford, Clarendon Press, 1944. 384p
BA369a

CR LX 1946 20–23 Kitto • CPh XLI 1946 49–55 Norwood • JHS 1943 135 Webster

An exercise in historical criticism on Sophocles' ideas, with little attention to his style or dramatic effects. The main idea treated is the Gods' treatment of mankind, leaving us with a one-sided study, at times inaccurate since Sophocles was less "theological" than he is made out to be.

DILLER, H. Sophokles. Darmstadt, Wiss. Buchges., 1967. vi, 546p. **BA370**

Wege der Forschung; XCV.

CR XIX 1969 30–34 Lloyd-Jones • Gnomon XLII 1970 723–725 Imhof • RBPh XLVI 1968 947 Traversa

This collection of essays begins with the first chapter from Whitman's *Sophocles* (1951) and contains a chapter from Kitto's *Sophocles; Dramatist and philosopher* (1958). Contains a good Literatur-Übersicht, p.537–546) by the editor.

See also Johansen, H. F., "Sophocles 1939–1959," *Lustrum* VII (1962), 94–288, and Kirkwood, G. M., "A review of recent Sophoclean studies (1945–1956)," *CW* L (1957), 157–172.

EARP, Frank Russell. The style of Sophocles. New York, Russell & Russell, [1972]. 177p.
BA371

Reprint of the 1944 ed.

CW XXXVIII 1944–1945 126–127 Shaffer

A careful study of certain aspects of the style of Sophocles—the choice and use of words, the use of figures of speech (e.g., antithesis, anaphora, metaphor, simile), the use of amplification (doublets, periphrasis, epithets). A concluding chapter summarizes the nature of the development of style which the evidence has suggested.

GELLIE, G. H. Sophocles; A reading. Melbourne, University Press, 1972. viii, 307p. **BA371a**

CR XXVI 1976 119–120 Taplin • JHS XCVI 1976 178 Mason • CJ LXX 1974 76–79 Segal • CPh LXXII 1977 70–75 Conacher

The main part (p.1–183) of this work consists of a full survey of each surviving play. A second part (p.185–279) is made up of essays on plot, character, chorus, gods and poetry. A safe introduction in a rather old-fashioned way, especially aimed at Greekless undergraduates, but serious students of Sophocles will find it sound, logical, terse and lucid.

GOHEEN, R. F. The imagery of Sophocles' *Antigone;* A study of poetic language and structure.

Princeton, N.J., Princeton University Press, 1951. 180p. **BA372**

CW XLVI 1952 22 Post • JHS LXXIV 1954 196 Burton • Traditio VIII 1952 435–441 Callahan

A penetrating study of six dominant image-groups: money sequence, military sequence, animals and animal taming, marriage motif, disease and cure, and the ship of state metaphor. There is perhaps too much critical jargon in the presentation but the argument is careful and thorough. There is an exhaustive bibliography of about 150 books and articles.

KIRKWOOD, Gordon MacDonald. A study of sophoclean drama. Ithaca, N.Y., Cornell University Press, 1958. xiv, 304p. **BA373**

Hermathena XCIII 1959 88–90 Stanford • Gnomon XXXI 1959 336–340 Kamerbeek

A well-balanced study of dramatic method. There are valuable chapters on Construction, Character Portrayal, and the Role of the Chorus. The final chapter on Irony is the most comprehensive and the most important. A monument to the author's sound learning, judgment and taste. See also Kirkwood, G. M., "A Review of Recent Sophoclean Studies, (1945–1956)," *CW* L(1957), 157–172.

KNOX, Bernard M. W. The heroic temper. Studies in sophoclean tragedy. Berkeley, University of California Press, 1964. x, 210p. **BA374**

Sather Classical Lectures; XXXV.

Phoenix XX 1966 247–250 Kirkwood • Gnomon XXXVIII 1966 329–333 Alt

The author's competence was already well established in his *Oedipus at Thebes,* New Haven, 1957. Here he studies three plays: *Antigone, Philoctetes,* and *Oedipus at Colonus,* as exemplifying the concept of the tragic hero which, in two introductory chapters, is defined for Sophocles. This definition is carefully supported by lists of words and phrases exemplifying the hero's characteristics. Not everything said in the two chapters on *Antigone* will meet with universal approval but the treatment of the other two plays, though relatively brief, better illustrates the method outlined in the preliminary chapters. One of the book's many merits is that it rehabilitates the tragic hero in Sophocles, for long under critical siege.

LONG, A. A. Language and thought in Sophocles. A study of abstract nouns and poetic technique. London, Athlone Press, 1968. xiv, 186p.
BA374a

RPh XLIII 1969 298–300 Weil • CR XIX 1969 34–35 Lloyd-Jones

A clear and elegantly written study of Sophocles' use of abstract nouns in *-sis, -ma, -ia,* and *-eia.* The purpose is to illustrate the relation between language and thought in Sophocles, and there are comparative studies of such usages in other authors. Their frequency, originality and variation in Sophoclean usage clearly emerge, especially their employment in character portrayal and description of emotions and emotional activity.

MUSURILLO, Herbert A. The Light and the darkness. Studies in the dramatic poetry of Sophocles. Leiden, Brill, 1967. vi, 165p.   **BA375**

AC XXXVII 1968 673 des Places • CR XIX 1969 153–155 Diggle

For Musurillo 'the heart of poetry is the image' (p.1) and here images are presented as clues to the meaning of the seven plays and the *Ichneutai*. Though he sets himself on guard against any temptation to twist the interpretation of a piece in an eccentric direction, he does not always avoid such temptations. Clusters of images tend to replace characters and problems of dramatic technique and structure tend to be ignored or treated inadequately. There are many inaccuracies in points of interpretation and even translation. There are concluding chapters on the chronology of the surviving works and on the philosophy of Sophocles.

O'BRIEN, M. J., ed. Twentieth-century interpretations of Oedipus Rex. A collection of critical essays. Englewood Cliffs, N.J., Prentice-Hall, 1968. iv, 119p.   **BA376**

AAHG XXIV 1971 149 Strohm • CPh LXV 1970 268–270 Henry

This volume includes nine fairly long articles, or extracts from books, and seventeen 'View-Points.' The editor's Preface provides a good outline of the modern controversies surrounding the play, and his own general view. Dodds' famous article, "On Misunderstanding the O.T.," *G&R* XIII (1966), is included.

VELACOTT, Philip. Sophocles and Oedipus. A study of Oedipus Tyrannus, with a new translation. Ann Arbor, University of Michigan Press, 1971. xiv, 261p.   **BA376a**

Mnemosyne XXVIII 1975 206–208 Bremer • Athenaeum LI 1973 441–443 Tarditi • CR XXIV 1974 196–198 Whittle

This ingenious work offers two translations: one literal, the other blank verse, of *O.T.* on facing pages, with brief footnotes. There follows in seven essays a new thesis of a hidden 'play within the play,' subtly signposted for very astute members of the audience and/or subsequent readers of the text. The hypothesis of the hidden play is that Oedipus knows of his parricide and incest from the beginning of his reign but has dissimulated about it until the advent of the plague. The bulk of the audience and reading public would, however, only get the traditional lines of the plot.

WALDOCK, A. J. A. Sophocles the Dramatist. Cambridge, University Press, 1951, 1966. viii, 230p.   **BA377**

Gnomon XXV 1953 350–351 Winnington-Ingram • Phoenix IX 1955 133–134 Adams • REG LXXX 1967 599–600 Ronnet

Written from a background in the theater, this volume places welcome emphasis on Sophocles as a man of the theater. The author has little sympathy with the approach of historical criticism, or with those who are too much influenced by preconceived theories on the nature of tragedy, or too intent on making the plays square with what Aristotle said later in the *Poetics.*

WEBSTER, T. B. L. An introduction to Sophocles. London, Methuen, 1969, 1936. x, 230p.   **BA377a**

CR XX 1970 299–300 Lloyd-Jones • Emerita XLI 1973 257–258 de Hoz • CJ LXX 1975 83–85 Aichele

The 1969 re-issue of a 1936 work has some few *addenda* and *corrigenda,* with a new appendix on the early plays of Sophocles and Euripides. The 'Appendix' is a not very successful attempt to introduce further evidence to favor the author's 1938 chronology. The Introduction does not study Sophocles play by play, but deals in eight chapters with Life, Thought, Characters, Character Drawing, Plot-Construction, Song, Style, and Conclusion.

WHITMAN, Cedric. Sophocles: A study of heroic humanism. Cambridge, Mass., Harvard University Press, 1951. 292p.   **BA378**

JHS LXXIII 1953 150–151 Hartley • AJPh LXXIV 1953 168–174 Norwood • Gnomon XXIV 1952 109–110 Lucas

An expansion of a Harvard dissertation which was entitled The Religious Humanism of Sophocles, but the present subtitle is a more accurate reflection of the contents. The work is vigorous and stimulating but is an unsuccessful challenge to more traditional interpretations, vitiated by misstatements, misrepresentations of the Greek, self-contradictions, and various quirks and oddities. It nonetheless has many brilliant observations and there is a useful short survey of earlier Sophoclean scholarship.

Statius

VESSEY, David. Statius and the Thebaid. Cambridge, Cambridge University Press, 1973. viii, 357p.   **BA379**

AC XLIV 1975 284 Verdière • AJPh XCVI 1975 80–81 Schmeling • CW LXIX 1975 83–84 Neuman • Latomus XXXIII 1974 438–440 Delarue

This work consists of extended passages of exegesis of essential passages in the poem, grouped around certain large themes. The author's larger intention is to fix Statius in the history of epic writing and of Latin literature. The influence of Statius is perhaps overstated.

See also Frassinetti, P., "Stazio epico e la critica recente," *RIL* CVII (1973), 243–258.

Tacitus

BENARIO, Herbert W. An introduction to Tacitus. Athens, University of Georgia Press, [1975]. ix, 177p.   **BA380**

G&R XXIII 1976 87 Verity • Gnomon L 1978 606–607 Nicols

An excellent, well-organized introduction for undergraduate students. Deals with the Historical Background, The Man and His Milieu, The Minor Works, The Major Works, Sources and Antecedents, Language and Style, Characterization, and Political Thought, Historical Integrity, Survival and Popularity.

See also Benario's bibliographical surveys, *CW* LVIII (1964), 69–83; *CW* LXIII (1970), 253–267; and *CW* LXXI (1977), 1–32.

See also R. Hanslick, *AAHG* XIII (1960) 65–102, XX (1967) 1–31, XXVII (1974) 129–166; F. Römer, XXXVII (1984) 153–208.

DOREY, T. A. et al. Tacitus. New York, Basic Books, [1969]. xii, 180p.   **BA381**

Studies in Latin literature and its influence.
JRS LX 1970 258–259 Walker • Gnomon XLII 1970 419–420 Voss
Contains some good papers, especially Wellesley, K., Tacitus as a Military Historian; Martin, R. H., Tacitus and His Predecessors; and Miller, N. P., Style and Content in Tacitus. The editor provides a straightforward account of *Agricola* and *Germania*.

DUDLEY, Donald Reynolds. The world of Tacitus. [1st American ed.]. [Boston], Little, Brown and Company, [1969, 1968]. 271p.   **BA382**

CJ LXVI 1970 87–88 Baldwin • CR XX 1970 44–46 Miller • Phoenix XXIII 1969 411–412 Woloch
A sound presentation of Tacitus' world and his history, often by summary or translations (the author's), aimed at the general reader. There is a German translation, *Tacitus und die Welt der Römer,* übertr. von Eggert, H., Wiesbaden, Brockhaus (1969), 286p.

FLACH, Dieter. Tacitus in der Tradition der antiken Geschichtsschreibung. Göttingen, Vandenhoeck und Ruprecht, 1973. 245p.   **BA383**

Hypomnemata; Untersuchungen zur Antike und zu ihrem Nachleben; revision of the author's Habilitationsschrift, Marburg, 1970.
CW LXIX 1975 145–146 Benario • JRS LXV 1975 225–226 Martin • Latomus XXXIV 1975 512–514 Borzsak
Tacitus is here demoted from the unique role in which Klingner among others cast him and returned to the common ranks of Graeco-Roman historiographers. The merits of Flach's scholarship, methodology and industry are considerable. His survey of Tacitus' antecedents is very thorough and if his view that Tacitus conforms pretty much to that tradition is not currently popular it may be nonetheless true.

GOODYEAR, Francis R. Tacitus. Oxford, Clarendon Press, 1970. 44p.   **BA384**

Greece and Rome: new surveys in the classics; v. 4.
AAHG XXVII 1974 132 Hanslik
The introduction calls attention to such recent bibliographical surveys as those in Borzsak, S., "P. Cornelius Tacitus," *RE Supplbd* XI 373–512 (available as a *Sonderausgabe*); Koestermann's editions of the minor

works and *Annals* (Leipzig, 1962, 1960); R. Syme's *Tacitus* (Oxford, 1958); and A. H. McDonald on the Roman historians in *Fifty Years* (*and Twelve*). There are succinct chapters: I. Agricola, Germania, Dialogus; II Histories and Annals; III. Tacitus and the Writing of History; and IV. Language and Style, and Conclusion.

LUCAS, Joseph. Les obsessions de Tacite. Leiden, E. J. Brill, 1974. xii, 254p.   **BA385**

Roma aeterna; 8.
Gnomon XLIX 1977 579–591 Richter • Mnemosyne ser. 4 XXX 1977 331–333 Den Boer • REA LXXVII 1975 305–308 Engel
If psychology is to become an auxiliary science of classics, Tacitus is certainly a prime candidate for attention, and Lucas here gives an excellent bibliography to justify the collaboration. His own effort, however, is not very successful, largely because of his dilettante use of psychiatry.

MENDELL, Clarence W. Tacitus, the man and his work. [Hamden, Conn.], Archon Books, 1970 [1957]. vii, 397p.   **BA386**

AJPh LXXX 1959 92–95 Rogers • CW LII 1959 128 Hammond • JRS XLVIII 1958 191–192 Wellesley • Phoenix XIII 1959 38–39 Crook
A work in two parts: I. Tacitus as writer and historian, with chapters on his religious and philosophical positions, political theory, literary style, technique of composition, character delineation, sources, credibility; II. The fortunes of the text of Tacitus from publication to discovery in the 14th century, MSS of the major and minor works, and the MSS affiliations, history of the printed text. The work is unevenly written and has more than its share of infelicities and misprints. Some discussion, either more or less, on most points of interest in Tacitean studies, but in general a disappointing production.

SCOTT, Russell T. Religion and philosophy in the histories of Tacitus. Rome, American Academy, 1968. xiv, 139p.   **BA387**

Papers and monographs of the American Academy in Rome; v. 22.
CR XIX 1969 181–183 Henry & Walker • Gnomon XLI 1969 824–826 Gugel • JRS LIX 1969 312–313 Liebeschuetz
A valuable contribution to Tacitean scholarship, dealing with the Roman religious and ethical tradition as it relates to the structure and presentation of the *Histories.* Particular passages are examined to show where religious preoccupations have informed the structure and embody the significance of the narrative. Such analysis is useful but the author presses too far the case for the intervention of the gods in the Tacitean view of history.

SYME, Ronald, Sir. Tacitus. Oxford, Clarendon Press, 1958. 2 v. xi, 856p.   **BA388**

AJPh LXXX 1959 321–324 Mendell • Gnomon XXXIII 1961 55–58 Momigliano • JRS XLIX 1959

140–146 Sherwin-White • Mnemosyne XII 1959 369–375 Thiel

Covers everything concerning Tacitus and his work which must, or might, interest the student of history. An untidy but fascinating torrent of old and new information in 45 chapters, spilling over into 95 appendices. The abrupt, varied, condensed style is suitably Tacitean. What he says (p.541) of Tacitus could be said of himself: "an acute sense for words is paired with an unerring memory . . . echo and allusion everywhere. . . the play of wit and malice . . . the unfailing resources of wide reading . . . the habit of documentary inquiry . . . ferociously accurate in small details." A most triumphant march across the too often separated fields of literature, philology and history. There is an excellent bibliography, v. 2 p.809–823.

SYME, Ronald, Sir. Ten studies in Tacitus. Oxford, Clarendon Press, 1970. [xii], 152p. **BA389**

CR XXII 1972 221–222 Crook • Latomus XXXI 1972 285–286 Jal • Phoenix XXVI 1972 108–109 Swan

The ten studies date from 1949 to 1964, all but one previously published elsewhere. Here the arrangement is logical, not chronological. A handy supplement to the 2-volume monumental *Tacitus*. Five important pages of addenda bring slightly dated details in the essays up to date. There is a characteristic predilection for prosopographical detail and the writing is the by now characteristic combination of deduction and divination. The first three studies, and the last, are lectures of general interest, whereas chapters 4–9 are refinements on problems already treated or initiated in *Tacitus*.

WALKER, Bessie. The Annals of Tacitus; A study in the writing of history. [2d ed.]. [Manchester], Manchester University Press, [1952], 1960. viii, 284p. **BA390**

CPh XLVIII 1953 114–117 Bruère • Gnomon XXV 1953 512–518 Koestermann • JRS XLIII 1953 224–225 Browning

A detailed and stimulating study of the *Annals* with respect to Tacitus' method of composition, the variations in his style and reasons why he interpreted the events of the 1st century as he did. Within the annalistic framework, his treatment of events is shown to be very episodic. Other techniques of presentation besides this episodic treatment examined here include emphasis on certain themes throughout an entire reign, imputation of motives for actions which the factual narrative does not warrant, and dramatic arrangement of facts to elicit an emotional reaction from the reader. Tacitus' peculiar cast of mind and the political experience of his generation and class are seen as the reasons for the adoption of this curious method of writing history.

Terence

ARNOTT, W. Geoffrey. Menander, Plautus, Terence. Oxford, Clarendon Press, 1975. 62p. **BA391**

Greece & Rome: New surveys in the classics; v. 9.

A useful brief summary by Arnott.

MARTI, H. "Terenz, 1909–1959." Lustrum VI (1961): 114–238. **BA392**

This is continued in *Lustrum* VIII (1963), 5–101, 244–264. See also Prete, S., "Terence," *CW* LIV (1961), 112–121; Perelli, L. "Rassegna di studi terenziani (1968–1978), *BStudLat* IX (1979): 281–315.

Valerius Flaccus

EHLERS, W. W. "Valerius Flaccus, 1940–1971." Lustrum XVI (1971–1972): 105–142. **BA393**

SCHULTE, William Henry. Index verborum Valerianus. Hildesheim, G. Olms, 1965. 180p. **BA394**

Iowa studies in classical philology; v. 3. Reprint of the 1935 ed.

Varro

DALLMANN, H. "Varroniana, 1: Bericht." ANRW 1.3 (1973): 3–18. **BA395**

See also Riposati, B. and Marastoni, A., *Biblografia varroniana*, Milano, Celuc, 1974, 255p.

SKYDSGAARD, Jens Erik. Varro the scholar; Studies in the first book of Varro's De re rustica. Hafniae, Munksgaard, 1968. 133p. **BA396**

Analecta Romana Instituti Danici; 4 Supplementum. CR XX 1970 36–38 Gratwick • Gnomon XLVII 1975 548–552 Cardauns

TAYLOR, Daniel J. Declinatio; A study of the linguistic theory of Marcus Terentius Varro. Amsterdam, John Benjamins, 1974, cover 1975. xv. 131p. **BA397**

Amsterdam studies in the theory and history of linguistic science: series 3, Studies in the history of linguistics; v. 2. CR XXVII 1977 184–185 Sommerstein • REL LIII 1975 483 Collart

This book sets out to describe "what Varro had to say about the nature of language and language science." Its most valuable contribution is in showing how Varro's theory of language determined his methods of grammatical inquiry. For Varro, words if they are not Urwörter (*principia verborum*) owe their existence to one of three processes: *impositio, declinatio voluntaria, declinatio naturalis.*

Velleius

VELLEIUS Paterculus, C. Historiae Romanae libri; The Tiberian narrative, 2:94–131. Cambridge and New York, Cambridge University Press, 1977. xix, 292p. **BA398**

Cambridge classical texts and commentaries; 19.

JRS LXVIII 1978 229–230 Seager • REL LV 1977 503–504 Jal • CPh LXXIV 1979 64–68 Sumner
An admirable edition of the core of Velleius' work, with good introductions on the question of text, the literary nature of the work and linguistic matters.

Virgil

ANDERSON, William Scovil. The art of the Aeneid. Englewood Cliffs, N.J., Prentice-Hall, [1969]. v, 121p.   **BA399**

AJPh XCII 1971 343–345 Duckworth
An introduction for the general reader. Organized into six chapters, each devoted to two books of the Aeneid. Good on the major characters and on Virgil's relationship to his Homeric models and to Greek tragedy.

AUSTIN, Roland Gregory. A bibliography of Virgil. Rev. ed. London, Joint Association of Classical Teachers, 1968. 8p.   **BA400**

JACT paper; 1.

BARDON, Henry and VERDIÈRE, Raoul. Vergiliana. Recherches sur Virgile. Publiées par Henry Bardon et Raoul Verdière. Leiden, Brill, 1971. vi, 435p.   **BA401**

AC XLII 1973 272 Viarre • REL L 1972 336–338 Lesueur

BASSON, W. Pivotal catalogues in the Aeneid. Amsterdam, A. M. Hakkert, 1975. xii, 208p.
                                                   BA402

Gnomon XLIX 1977 309–311 Gasner • Latomus XXXVI, 1 1977 188–189 Lesueur
A study of the catalogues in Books VII, X, I and VI.

BERG, William. Early Virgil. London, Athlone Press (New York, distributed by Humanities Press), 1974. x, 222p.   **BA403**

Includes the text of Virgil's Bucolics in English and Latin.
REL LII 1974 489–493 Soubiran • JRS LXV 1975 227–228 Kahn • CW LXIX 1975 144–145 Segal
A disciple of Duckworth studies the Eclogues thematically. The mythic pattern of love, death and rebirth studied in the first chapter is one of the most engaging chapters. The work is addressed to students of ancient and modern poetry, poets and the educated public which, ironically, may account for the fact that about one-third of the book is occupied with a printed Latin text and an undistinguished translation (p.26–93). The work shows wide reading in the mythical, religious and literary background of the Eclogues and is a well-written appreciation of the union of Muse and Poet.

CAMPS, William Anthony. An introduction to Virgil's Aeneid. London, Oxford University Press, 1969. ix, 164p.   **BA404**

CR XXI 1971 47 Clarke • Mnemosyne XXV 1972 205–206 Westendorp Boerma • AJPh XCII 1971 124–126 Duckworth

CARCOPINO, Jérôme. Virgile et les origines d'Ostie. 2e éditions. Paris, Presses universitaires de France, 1968. xvi, 703p., illus., plates.
                                                   BA405

Collection Hier.

COMMAGER, Henry Steele. Virgil. Englewood Cliffs, N.J., Prentice-Hall, [1966]. 186p. **BA406**

Contains essays or excerpts from books by such well-known scholars as Snell, Perret, Bowra, Haecker, Clausen, Otis, and Pöschl. There is a brief bibliography (p.185–186).

CRUTTWELL, Robert Wilson. Virgil's mind at work; An analysis of the symbolism of the Aeneid. Westport, Conn., Greenwood Press, [1971]. ix, 182p., front.   **BA407**

Reprint of the 1947 ed.
JRS XXXVIII 1948 171 Tilly • LEC 1948 58–59 d'Hérouville
An ambitious theme inadequately documented and often based on unsafe assumptions in the spheres of archaeology and topography.

DI CESARE, Mario A. The altar and the city; A reading of Vergil's Aeneid. New York, Columbia University Press, 1974. xii, 278p. **BA408**

CW LXX 1977 346–348 Fantazzi

DONLAN, Walter. The classical world bibliography of Vergil; With a new introduction by Walter Donlan. New York, Garland Publishing, 1978. 176p.   **BA409**

Includes surveys by G. E. Duckworth, (1940–1956): CW LI, 1957–1958; (1957–1963): CW LVII, 1964, and A. G. MacKay (1964–1973): CW LXVIII, 1974. 1–92.

DUCKWORTH, George Eckel. Structural patterns and proportions in Vergil's Aeneid; A study in mathematical composition. Ann Arbor, University of Michigan Press, [1962]. x, 268p.
                                                   BA410

AJPh LXXXV 1964 71–77 Lloyd • Gnomon XXXVI 1964 56–60 Wimmel • CJ LVIII 1962–1963 272–273 Riddehough
Professor Duckworth proposes that the mathematical studies to which, according to Donatus and Suetonius, Virgil was much given, exercised a strong influence on the structure of his poetry. Duckworth finds in the Golden Mean one key to Virgilian structure; specifically, he painstakingly lists and charts in the 27 appendices 1,044 ratios in the complete works. He comes to several interesting conclusions: The essential soundness of the received text, the authenticity of the

Culex, Ciris, Aetna and to a lesser extent the *Moretum* and *Dirae,* the authenticity of the four lines *ille ego—horrentia Martis* prefix. Hailed here as the most exciting discovery in the history of Virgilian Criticism.

DUDLEY, D. R., ed. Vergil. London, Routledge and K. Paul, 1969. xi, 219p.   **BA411**

Vergilius XVI 1970 40–41 Quinn • CR XX 1970 335–337 Clarke • Gnomon XLII 1970 731–732 von Albrecht
A good collection of essays, containing two preliminary chapters on Virgil's originality—in the Eclogues, by Wormell; in the *Aeneid,* by Otis. Six essays on subsequent influence: Gossage, Vergil and the Flavian Epic; Whitfield, Virgil into Dante; R. D. Williams, Changing Attitudes to Virgil; A. G. McKay, Virgilian Landscape into Art; Jackson Knight, Virgil's Elysium; Ayrton, The Path to Daedalus. A further volume on the Georgics is promised.

GEORGE, Edward Vincent. *Aeneid* VIII and the *Aitia* of Callimachus. Leiden, Brill, 1974. 142p.   **BA412**

Mnemosyne; supplementum 27.
JRS LXV 1975 228–229 Horsfall • CR XXVI 1976 183–184 Gransden • REL LIII 1975 491 Perret
George's thesis is that it is likely that Virgil referred to Callimachus in composing VIII 1–369, and that he deliberately chose the *aition* form for this part of the *Aeneid* as a means of linking the heroic past and the Roman present. The work is curiously indecisive in method and conclusion and fails to take fully into account much excellent work published since 1966. Perhaps too much attention is focused on Callimachus at the expense of other possible Greek and Roman influences.

HEINZE, Richard. Virgils epische Technik. 6., unveränderte Aufl. Stuttgart, B. G. Teubner, 1976. xii, 502p.   **BA413**

Reprint of the 1915 ed. published in Leipzig and Berlin.
Ph Woch XXXV 1915 1621–1625 Helm

HIGHET, Gilbert. The speeches in Vergil's *Aeneid.* Princeton, N.J., Princeton University Press, [1972]. vii, 380p.   **BA414**

CJ LXX, 4 1975 78–79 Hornsby • JRS LXIV 1974 276–277 Kenney • CR XXV 1975 211–212 Koster • CPh LXXI 1976 290–291 Sullivan
Almost 50 percent of the poem is direct speech, cataloged here in seven appendices (333 speeches and 90 speakers): i) in sequence by books; ii) in 16 classifications according to purpose; iii) in categories; iv) by names of characters and as uttered; v) by disguised characters; vi) within speeches; vii) in oratio obliqua. There are four main chapters: The speeches and their speakers, formal speeches, informal speeches, the speeches and their models. Formal is distinguished from informal by use of rhetorical schemata, though informal can sometimes be the more effective. The

chapter on models owes much to Knauer. The concluding Vergilius Orator an Poeta fortunately finds for the latter.

HORNSBY, Roger A. Patterns of action in the *Aeneid;* An interpretation of Vergil's epic similes. Iowa City, University of Iowa Press, [1970]. ix, 156p.   **BA415**

CPh LXVII 1972 209–213 Sullivan • CR XXII 1972 276–277 Williams • Latomus XXXI 1972 889–892 Miniconi • ACR I 1971 80 Mench
A study of interconnecting similes in the *Aeneid* that leaves Virgil's intentions in the matter unexamined. Similes on the same general themes, e.g., storms, animals, are seen as all connected with one another and cumulative. In excessive eagerness to see interwoven patterns in his accumulated data, Professor Hornsby sometimes moves from exegesis to eisegesis, reading into the similes more than, and less than, is there. His title forces him to coerce all the similes into patterns which is more than they all can sustain. While one may disagree with the overall thesis one can still admire and profit from individual observations on the 85 similes from natural phenomena studied in chapter I, the animal similes in chapter II, vegetable world similes in chapter III, etc. Despite tendencies to oversubtlety the work is perceptive and readable.

HUNT, John William. Forms of glory; Structure and sense in Virgil's *Aeneid.* Carbondale, Southern Illinois University Press, [1973]. xiii, 123p.   **BA416**

CR XXVI 1976 181–183 Foster • CW LXVIII 1975 458 Lieberman
A study which softpedals *arma* and concentrates on *virumque,* providing us with a sensitive analysis of the inner development of Aeneas in his moments of reflection and painful decisions, and in his physical and psychic wanderings. The work, apparently aimed at students of Comparative Literature, offers an "intrinsic" approach, signalizing echoes, key phrases and such elements of poetic design.

JEANNERET, René. Recherches sur l'hymne et la prière chez Virgile; Essai d'application de la méthode d'analyse tagmémique à des textes littéraires de l'antiquité. Bruxelles, AIMAV, 1973. 247p.   **BA417**

Thèse; Université de Nauchâtel.
REL LIII 1975 490–491 Fontaine • Latomus XXXVI, 1 1977 186–187 Evrard-Gillis • AC XLIV 1975 318–319 Liénard
The special interest of this study is its methodology, the application of an instrument of modern linguistics (Tagmeme) to ancient texts.

JOHNSON, Walter Ralph. Darkness visible; A study of Vergil's *Aeneid.* Berkeley, University of California Press, 1976. xi, 179p.   **BA418**

Arion n.s. 3/4 1976 493–506 Porter • CPh LXXV 1980 162–164 Williams • JRS LXIX 1979 231–234 Horsfall

An attractive and sympathetic book, written with elegance, which surveys conflicting interpretations in the recent past and presents an extremely personal and often subjective study of the poetry, with excellent interpretations of selected passages.

KLINGNER, Friedrich. Virgil. *Bucolica, Georgica, Aeneis.* Zurich, Stuttgart, Artemis Verlag, [1967]. 607p.   **BA419**

Gnomon XXXVI 1964 670–679, XLI 1969 554–574 Otis

Includes Klingner's recently published book on the Georgics, and a wholly new section (p.367–597) on the *Aeneid.* This massive book presents not a synthesis but the results of the author's lifetime preoccupation with Virgil's works. Most of the section on the Eclogues is also new. Particularly good on *Aeneid* IX. The author remains unrivalled in his analysis of the movement and flow of Virgilian verse.

KNAUER, Georg Nicolaus. Die *Aeneis* und Homer; Studien zur poetischen Technik Vergils, mit Listen der Homerzitate in der Aeneis. Göttingen, Vandenhoeck & Ruprecht, [1964]. 549p.   **BA420**

Hypomnemata: Untersuchungen zur Antike und zu ihrem Nachleben; Heft 7.
CJ LXI 1966 276–278 Reinke • Gnomon XXXVII 1965 687–690 Clarke

LEACH, Eleanor Winsor. Vergil's Eclogues; Landscapes of experience. Ithaca, Cornell University Press, [1974]. 281p.   **BA421**

CPh LXXIII 1978 57–60 Betensky • Latomus XXXIV 1975 1160–1162 Soubiran • Phoenix XXIX 1975 409–410 Smith
Equally important as a general analysis of the pastoral tradition, this work owes much to the tools of modern literary criticism. Leach's key to Roman pastoral is in the imagery of the poetic landscape. The farm scene, the rustic countryside, the wilderness, the *locus amoenus* are studied as four modes of landscape in the Eclogues which have associations with patterns of conduct and thought. An overly intellectualized interpretation, but with many new and acceptable insights well collated with landscape painting.

McKAY, Alexander G. "Recent work on Vergil (1964–1973)." CW LXVIII (1974): 1–92.   **BA422**

A sequel to "Recent work on Vergil (1940–1956)" and "Recent work on Vergil (1957–1963)" by George E. Duckworth, this exemplary survey is divided into 16 main sections. There are good Preliminary Remarks which include a survey of bibliographical tools. The sections on the Eclogues, Georgics and the *Aeneid* are broken down for the individual books. The section on Vergil and his Milieu is subdivided into Life and Works, Religion and Philosophy, Rome and Augustus, Vergil and other Augustan Poets, and Varia. There are indi-

vidual sections on Style, Language, Meter; Interpretation and Text Criticism; and Computer Studies, and a concluding section on Vergil and Later Ages.
See also McKay, A. G., "Vergilian bibliography (1978–1979)," *Vergilius* XXV (1979), 46–50.

McKAY, Alexander Gordon. Vergil's Italy. Greenwich, Conn., New York Graphic Society, [1970]. 356p. illus., maps.   **BA423**

JRS LXII 1972 220–221 Wellesley • CR XXIII 1973 41–42 Ogilvie • ACR I 1971 246–247 Galinsky
A generally reliable and pleasantly written *vade mecum* through the various regions that figure in Virgil's writings as well as a literary critique of the landscape artistry of Virgil himself. McKay seems equally at home in Italian topography and Virgilian scholarship but with so many things on the mind of the guide—archaeology, aesthetics, literary content, historical background, art, religion, geography—there are many slips and oversights, and in some places it is the near blind leading the putative blind.

OTIS, Brooks. Virgil; A study in civilized poetry. Oxford, Clarendon Press, 1963. ix, 436p.   **BA424**

CPh LX 1965 30–33 Williams • AJPh LXXXVI 1965 409–420 Duckworth • CR XV 1965 182–185 Wilkinson • Arion IV, 1 1965 126–149 Segal • REL XLII 1964 576–580 Perret
A richly rewarding study, the first major work on Virgil in English in 20 years. Written with great literary sensitivity and historical acumen, the work seeks to answer the question: Why did Virgil resort to the obsolete genre of epic in the more subjective Augustan age? The Eclogues and Georgics are considered as stages on the way to the production of the masterpiece. Pages 1–214 are introductory; p.215–394, a running commentary on the *Aeneid,* with nine appendices mainly bibliographical. The long chapter VI, The Odyssean Aeneid (p.215–312) is in many ways the most important. For Otis, Virgil's greatness consists precisely in his ability to make civilization poetical (p.394). This book, with its careful structural analyses used as a key to Virgil's use of symbolism, will shed great light on this new kind of poetry. "Voici un des meilleurs livres qu' on puisse lire présentement sur l'Énéide" (Perret).

OTT, Wilhelm. Rückläufiger Wortindex zu Vergil; Bucolica, Georgica, Aeneis. Tübingen, Niemeyer, 1974. vi, 295p.   **BA425**

Materialien zu Metrik und Stilistick.
LEC XLIII 1975 309 Derouau • REL LIII 1975 431 Hellegouarc'h • RPh XLIX 1975 332 Soubiran
This is volume 8 in Ott's collection, Materialen zu Metrik und Stilistik, and is based on Mynor's edition, 1969–1972.

PEETERS, Félix. A bibliography of Vergil. Philadelphia, R. West, 1975. 92p.   **BA426**

AC XLV 1976 688–689 Deroux • CPh 1934 170–171

Useful for its survey of pre-1930 work on Virgil, with special attention to Belgian and American contributions.

PERRET, Jacques. Virgile. Nouv. ed., rev. et augm. Paris, Hatier, 1965. 191p., illus.

BA427

JRS XLIII 1953 221–223 Hardie • REA LXVII 1965 537–538 Bardon • CR n.s. XVI 1966 117–118 Williams • LXVIII 1954 34–35
The original (1952) subtitle L'Homme et l'oeuvre has disappeared, eight plates have been added, the new format is more attractive and there have been some additions, subtractions and modifications. The criticism remains very sensitive and personal, and the coverage of problems and scholarly views is a masterpiece of compression.

PÖSCHL, Viktor. The art of Vergil; Image and symbol in the *Aeneid*. Ann Arbor, University of Michigan Press, 1970, 1962. 216p.

BA428

Ann Arbor Paperbacks; AA170.
REL XXIX 1951 396–398 • REL LV 1977 495–496 Perret

PÖSCHL, Viktor. Die Hirtendichtung Virgils. Heidelberg, Winter, 1964. 154p. **BA429**

REL XLII 1964 575–576 Perret • CR XV 1965 180–182 Clarke
Contains a detailed study of Eclogues 1 and 7, seen as containing the essence of Virgilian bucolic or even Virgilian poetry. Art and architecture are interestingly invoked in the structural analysis of Ec. 1, and Ec. 7 is interpreted as a bucolic *ars poetica,* the contest being set up to provide Virgil with paradigms of how to, and how not to, write. Pöschl displays almost magical powers of divination in these interpretations, written with great delicacy and sensibility.
See also Pöschl, V., "Virgil 4. Fortsetzung, 1. Teil: Eklogen," *AAHG* XXXII (1979), 1–20.

PUTNAM, Michael C. J. The poetry of the *Aeneid;* Four studies in imaginative unity and design. Cambridge, Mass., Harvard University Press, 1966. xv, 238p. **BA430**

CPh LXI 1966 143–148 Henry • REL XLIII 1965 602–604 Fontaine • CW LIX 1965 18 Lund • Latomus XXIV 1965 671–672 Perret • Gnomon XXXVIII 1966 564–568 von Albrecht
Four sensitively reasoned and written chapters on Books 2, 5, 8 and 12 of the *Aeneid,* shedding considerable light on the symbolic unity of the work as a whole.

PUTNAM, Michael C. J. Virgil's pastoral art; Studies in the Eclogues. Princeton, N.J., Princeton University Press, 1970. xi, 398p. **BA431**

Latomus XXXI 1972 542–546 Veremans • CR XXII 1972 274–275 Williams • AJPh XCIV 1973 96–98 Witke • Mnemosyne XXVI 1973 435–437 Waszink

The author's purpose is to present a structural analysis of each of the ten Eclogues. His principal guide in working with the symbolic value of words has been the poet's total vocabulary. The single-eyed pursuit of linking words and association of ideas leaves a lot of other questions—historical background, Hellenistic antecedents, etc.—virtually ignored. The method leaves itself open to charges of subjectivism and sentimentality.

PUTNAM, Michael C. J. Virgil's poem of the earth; Studies in the Georgics. Princeton, N. J., Princeton University Press, 1979. xiii, 336p.

BA432

LEC XLVII 1979 384 Wankenne

QUINN, Kenneth. Virgil's *Aeneid;* A critical description. 2d printing with corrections. Ann Arbor, University of Michigan Press, 1968. xii, 448p. **BA433**

Gnomon XLII 1970 94–95 von Albrecht • CJ LXIV 1969 371–374 Otis • AJPh XCI 1970 363–367 Lloyd • REL XLVI 1968 494–496 Perret • CR XVIII 1968 306–308 Clarke
Particularly good on structure, form, style and narrative technique, the work is weakened by the implicit equation of Aeneas with Augustus and a subsequent attempt to read contemporary anti-war sentiment into the poem. Chapter IV contains an excellent book by book, episode by episode, analysis of the *Aeneid.*

THORNTON, Agathe. The living universe; Gods and men in Virgil's *Aeneid*. Leiden, Brill, 1976. xiii, 223p. **BA434**

Mnemosyne, Suppl., XLVI.
CR XXIX 1979 35–37 Townend • G&R XXV I 1978 85 Verity • CW LXXIII 1979 40–41 Brown
Aims to show that the *Aeneid* is, in fact, Virgil's cosmic poem describing a coherent universe, determined by the gods and believed in by the educated Roman of the 1st century. A limited view of Virgil's purpose and achievement which may bring comfort to the idealists but will leave the realists unconvinced.

WARWICK, Henrietta Holm. A Vergil concordance. With the technical assistance of Richard L. Hotchkiss. Minneapolis, University of Minnesota Press, 1975. viii 962p. **BA435**

"Based on the 1969 Oxford classical texts edition, *P. Vergili Opera* edited by R. A. B. Mynors."
CHum X 1976 125 Greenberg
A computer-produced, keyword-in-context concordance based on the OCT edition by Sir Roger Mynors. The 82,520 words of the Eclogues, Georgics and *Aeneid* are concorded together.

WETMORE, Monroe Nichols. Index verborum Vergilianus. 4., unveränderte Aufl. Hildesheim, Olms, 1979. x, 554p. **BA436**

Reprint of the 1930 ed. (New Haven, Yale University Press).

WIGODSKY, Michael. Vergil and Early Latin poetry. Wiesbaden, F. Steiner, 1972. x, 168p.
BA437

Hermes-Einzelschriften; Heft 24.
AJPh XCVI 1975 314–316 Galinsky • Gymnasium LXXXII 1975 100–104 Buchheit • CW LXVIII 1974 127–128 Newman • JRS LXIV 1974 272–273 Jocelyn
A worked-over 1964 dissertation about the *Aeneid's* putative and real borrowings from Livius Andronicus to Cicero, done systematically author by author. The 710 footnotes on 139 text pages preserve the dissertation type format, but this is a valuable work of collecting and classifying which provides a comprehensive, if not complete, overview of the subject.

WILKINSON, L. P. The Georgics of Virgil; A critical survey. 1st paperback ed. Cambridge, Cambridge University Press, 1978. xii, 364p.
BA438

AJPh XCIII 1972 491–492 Lloyd • Phoenix XXVI 1972 40–62 Otis • CPh LXV 1970 258–259 Putnam
The first full-scale study in English by a scholar who is noted for careful scholarship, great readability, shrewdness in verbal and stylistic analysis, and sober common sense. Deals in turn with the early life of Virgil, the conception of the Georgics, its composition and structure (where the four books are examined sequentially), and the Aristaeus Epyllion. Particularly

good chapters on Philosophical, Moral and Religious Ideas, Political and Social Ideas, and Poetic Approach. Art, Agricultural Lore and The Georgics in After Times, are the concluding chapters; there are seven appendices.

WILLIAMS, R. D. Virgil. Oxford, Clarendon Press, 1967. 45p.
BA439

G&R New Surveys; 1.
AC XXXVII 1968 703 Drecht • LEC XXVI 1968 283–284 Delanois • Latomus XXVII 1968 675–676 Brisson
Three separate bibliographically-oriented essays on the Eclogues (p.6–13), the Georgics (p.14–22), and the *Aeneid* (p.23–44). A useful state of the question survey, especially for non-specialists, but with notable gaps in the bibliography and in the questions raised. Otis, Putnam and Quinn are hailed as the new and acceptable critics in this general survey, whose object is to give in modern terms a general idea of the nature and importance of Virgil's poetry. There is a brief supplement in *Proceedings of the Virgil Society for 1976–1977*.

Appendix Virgiliana

CONTI, C. "Rassegna di studi sull' Appendix Vergiliana dal 1955 al 1971–1972." BStudLat 3 (1973): 351–392, 4 (1974): 229–263.   **BA440**

BB   LITERARY HISTORY AND CRITICISM

Generalia

ALSINA, José. Literatura griega; Contenido, problemas, y métodos. Con la colaboracion de Carlos Miralles. Barcelona, Ediciones Ariel, [1967]. 454p.
BB1

Colección Convivium; 6.
REL XII 1968 155–157 de Barbón • REA LXXI 1969 152–155 Ballotto
An unusual work which touches on a number of aspects of Greek literature usually given inadequate or no treatment in the standard manuals—the relations of literature to society, art, religion and myth, the connections between tradition and the personal contribution of the authors.

BALDRY, H. C. Ancient Greek literature in its living context. New York, McGraw-Hill, 1974. 144p., illus.
BB2

Reprint of the 1968 edition published by Thames and Hudson, Ltd.
CW LXII 1969 327 Best • History LIV 1969 247–248 Forrest
Fifty-six vase paintings are chosen to illustrate scenes from Greek literature. In addition, there are views of

Greek theatres, the Acropolis, statues, coins, pictures of writing on clay tablets and papyrus—all meant to serve as visual aids to teaching literature. The question remains: how do illustrations which postdate what they illustrate (sometimes by centuries) provide a living context?

BAYET, Jean. Littérature latine. Avec la collaboration de Louis Nougaret. Paris, Armand Colin, 1965. 542p.
BB3

RPh XL 1966 159 Ernout • Gymnasium LXXIII 1966 549–552 Burke • RBPh XLIV 1966 195–196 Stégen • REA LXXI 1969 177 Langier
The first edition was in 1934. Nougaret's additions are largely bibliographical at the end of each of the eleven chapters. There are many quotations from the Latin writers covered, making this work almost an anthology. With commentaries, especially suitable for beginners. An admirably written handbook.

BEYE, Charles R. Ancient Greek literature and society. Garden City, N. Y., Anchor Books, 1975. 469p.
BB4

CW LXX 1976 199–200 Sutton • Ph & Rh X 1977 128–130 Arnold.

The author's object is to give an exposition, analysis and discussion of the major pieces of Greek literature, excepting Plato, the orators and most fragments. Discussion is organized around some central themes. The result is selective, discursive and intermittently illuminating.

BIELER, Ludwig. History of Roman literature; condensed and adapted from the German. London, Melbourne, Macmillan; New York, St. Martin's Press, 1966. 209p., plates. **BB5**

CW LX 1967 551 Anderson • CR XXV 1975 63–64 Vienney • CJ LIX 1963 87–89, LXIV 1968 35–36 Halporn

Provides a great deal of mostly reliable information in a very compact form, but many of the literary judgments are rather stereotyped. This is an English adaptation of the original German. The condensation is aimed at a wider public than the German original, so all references to learned controversy as well as the bibliographical notes had to be sacrificed. Neither scholar nor general reader will be satisfied with the sacrificial remains.

BIGNONE, Ettore. Storia della letteratura latine. Firenze, G. C. Sansoni, [1945–51]. 3 v. **BB6**

Col. 1:2, ed. rev. [1946].
REL XXIV 1946 331–333 Marouzeau • RPh XXI 1947 92–93 Ernout • AC XVI 1947 170–171 Renard
Bignone combined a fine literary sensibility with a great love of ancient poetry, especially Aeschylus and Sophocles, and a deep knowledge of Greek philosophy. He regarded this as the crowning work of his scholarly career, and it is less a work of reference than a highly personal series of mostly laudatory appreciations, with abundant bibliographies at chapter ends. There are many translations of passages unaccompanied by the originals.

BINNS, J. W., ed. Latin literature of the fourth century. London, Routledge & K. Paul, 1974. x, 189p. **BB7**

Greek and Latin studies; classical literature and its influences.
CW LXIX 1976 475–476 Levy • CR XXIV 1976 200–201 Hudson-Williams • CPh LXXIII 1978 84 Cunningham
Introduced by an essay on Paganism, Christianity and the Latin classics by R. A. Markus [p.1–21] this work has chapters by specialists on five authors: Ausonius, Symmachus, Claudian, Prudentius, and Paulinus, the weakest of which is that on Ausonius, and the best on Claudian.

BOWRA, Cecil. Ancient Greek literature. 1st ed. reissued [with revisions]. London, New York, [etc.], Oxford University Press, 1967. xii, 137p. **BB8**

Oxford paperbacks university series, Opus 28.
REG LXXXII 1969 203–207 Weil • Gymnasium LXXVI 1969 473–474 Schwartz
First published in 1933 and reprinted five times, this

paperback fails to take account of many intervening developments, e.g. the decipherment of Linear B and the growth in finds in Menander. There is a brief final chapter on Alexandria and After [p.110–123], and the brief bibliography has been somewhat updated.

THE CAMBRIDGE history of classical literature. II: Latin literature. Ed. by E. J. Kenney and W. V. Clausen, Cambridge, Cambridge University Press, 1982. xviii, 974p. **BB9**

LCM VII 1982 102–108 Woodman • TLS LXXXI 1982 966 Sullivan

COPLEY, Frank. Latin Literature; From the beginnings to the close of the second century A.D. Ann Arbor, University of Michigan Press, 1969. vii, 372p. **BB10**

AJPh XCII 1971 479–484 Savage • CJ LXVII 1972 285–286 Curran • CPh LXVI 1971 276–278 Sullivan
An unsuccessful attempt to combine a comprehensive survey of Latin literature and a selective critical study of those authors or genres which the author in his long and wide experience has found most congenial. Style and language do not receive sufficient attention, bibliographies are slim even for the general reader who is no doubt the target, and Latin texts are rarely quoted.

D'ALTON, John. Roman literary theory and criticism, a study in tendencies. New York, Russell & Russell, 1962. 1st ed., 1932. 608p. **BB11**

Gnomon X 1934 615–616 Kroll • CR XLVI 1932 130–131 Duff • CW XXVI 1933 109–111 Duff • REL XI 1933 501–503 Guillemin
An old but absorbing treatment of the shaping of Roman critical thought under the influence of Hellenic and Hellenistic principles. This does not claim to be a systematic history of Roman literary theory, and it stops short of an adequate treatment of the two Senecas, Petronius and Quintilian, but it has excellent preliminary chapters on the Awakening of the Critical Spirit and Aspects of the Problem of Style. Cicero is dealt with at length in two chapters; Cicero as Critic, and Cicero and the Atticists. There is a fascinating treatment of Ancients versus Moderns, and concluding chapters on Horace and The Classical Creed, the Supremacy of Rhetoric and A Retrospect. There are ample footnotes and bibliography.

DIHLE, Albrecht. Griechische Literaturgeschichte. Stuttgart, Kröner, [1967]. xii, 442p. **BB12**

Gnomon XL 1968 411–413 Lesky • REG LXXXII 1969 203–207 Weil • CW LXII 1968 52 Combellack
An erudite work in twenty-five well-distributed chapters—five on archaic literature, five on the fifth century, five on the fourth, and ten on the Hellenistic period. A very detailed personal introduction, showing great originality and penetration, based on the sensible assumption that a book such as this is an aid to the reading of Greek literature, not a substitute for it. Inevi-

tably forced to be selective in such a compass, the author settles for a close analysis of one or two of the plays of the dramatists, or one or two works of, say, Aristotle than on an exhaustive study.

DOVER, K. J., BOWIE, E. L., GRIFFIN, J. and WEST, M. L. Ancient Greek Literature. Oxford, Oxford University Press, 1980. 186p., maps. **BB13**

G&R XXVIII 1981 214 Arnott • CR XXXI 1981 214–216 Styler

DUDLEY, D. R. and DOREY, T. A. Silver Latin. Boston, Routledge & Kegan Paul, [1972–1975]. 2 v. **BB14**

Greek and Latin studies.
V. 1. Neronians and Flavians, ed. by D. R. Dudley.— v. 2. Empire and aftermath, ed. by T. A. Dorey.
CR XXV 1975 105–106 Winterbottom • CW LXVIII 1974 131–132 Marti
In the first volume four Neronian and two Flavian authors are critically considered, Lucan and Seneca rate two essays each. 'Seneca the Man' is a cursory treatment by John Ferguson, 'Seneca the Philosopher' by H. MacL. Currie is more a general introduction to Roman stoicism. Professor Kilke provides the two Lucan essays, the one on 'Lucan and English literature' being the more illuminating. Sarah Grimes on Persius is somewhat pedantic and precious. J. P. Sullivan is at home in examining problems of translation in Petronius. A. J. Gossage surveys the works and life of the Flavian poet, Statius, and A. G. Carrington is disappointingly superficial on Martial.
The second volume includes chapters on Velleius Paterculus and Valerius Maximus, two essays on Quintilian [Quintilian and Rhetoric, M. Winterbottom, Quintilian and Education, M. L. Clarke], Pliny's Natural History and the Middle Ages, The Letters of Pliny, and Latin Prose Panegyrics.

DUFF, John Wight. A literary history of Rome. Edited by A. M. Duff. 3rd ed. New York, Barnes & Noble, 1963, 1960. 2 v. **BB15**

University Paperbacks; UP-41. Contents: v. 1. From the origins to the close of the golden age; v. 2. In the silver age from Tiberius to Hadrian.
REL XXXI 1953 407–408 Marouzeau • CPh XLIX 1954 281–282 Bruère • Phoenix IX 1955 194–195 Getty • Latomus XXIII 1964 396 Préaux
First published in 1909, Duff's son has added a rather incomplete supplementary bibliography which brings it up to about 1951. This is hardly a satisfactory substitute for the revision which 40 years of recent scholarship would seem to demand. It still remains the most literate of Latin literary histories in English, showing immense familiarity with Latin (and other) literatures and good critical sense. The early chapters have aged much more than the rest of the book.

FANTHAM, Elaine. Comparative studies in Republican Latin imagery. [Toronto], University of Toronto Press, [1972]. x, 222p. **BB16**

Phoenix supplementary volume, 10.
G&R XXI 1974 89 Verity • Phoenix XXIX 1975 389–392 Brown • CR XXV 1975 227–228 Winterbottom • ACR III 1973 81–82 Hornsby
Deals with the *sermo* of educated Romans as represented by the dialogues of Terence and the less formal letters of Cicero, and with variations from this norm as displayed by the fantastic exuberence of Plautus and the heightened prose of Cicero's speeches and of his *De oratore*. A modest and moderate book, lucid and well presented. The chapters on Terence are illuminated by a wealth of comparative material from Greek Middle and New Comedy.

FLACELIÈRE, Robert. A literary history of Greece. Trans. by Douglas Garman. New York, New American Library, 1968. 419p. **BB17**

CJ LXII 1966 76–77 Crossett • CR XVI 1966 196–198 Hudson-Williams
Meant as a supplement to the author's *Daily Life in the Athens of Pericles,* and written within the wider perspectives of the history, art, architecture, philosophy and science of the various periods. The approach is based on a close knowledge of the ancient authors but with a great antipathy to modern scholarship, e.g., Millman, Parry and Lord get no mention in the opening chapter on Homer, nor the Parthenion papyrus in the treatment of Aleman. Much of the broad humanity and vigor of the original is lost in the very unreliable English translation.

FRÄNKEL, Hermann F. Early Greek poetry and philosophy; A history of Greek epic, lyric, and prose to the middle of the fifth century. Trans. by Moses Hadas and James Willis. Oxford, B. Blackwell, [1975]. xii, 555p. **BB18**

Translation of Dichtung und Philosophie des frühen Griechentums.
Phoenix VII 1953 45–46 Davison
Fränkel's *magnum opus* at last (1975) in an English translation. An inspiring and indispensable guide to the literature and thought of Homeric and archaic Greece.

FUHRMANN, Manfred. Römische Literatur; in Verbindung von Hubert Cancik [et el.]. Frankfurt am Main, Akademische Verlagsgesellschaft, 1974. vii, 331p. **BB19**

Neues Handbuch der Literaturwissenschaft; Bd. 3.
W.S. n.f. IX 1975 239–240 Hanslik • Gnomon XLIX 1977 141–164 Bieler
Fuhrmann, in collaboration with eight others, surveys Roman literature, i.e. literature in Latin between c. 250 B.C. and 250 A.D. Treatment is by literary genre. Roman comedy (*palliata*) and its antecedents in New Comedy is dealt with by Lefèvre, Epic by W. Schetter, Historiography by A. D. Leeman, Cicero and Republican Kunstprosa, by P. L. Schmidt. Fuhrmann himself deals with Roman writings on Technology and D. Liebs with Roman jurisprudence. Kenneth Quinn deals with personal poetry from 60 B.C. to the death of Ovid,

H. Cancik with Seneca and Roman tragedy, and in the last chapter B. Kytzler deals with Die Nachklassische Prosa Roms. The book is well illustrated.

GARZYA, A. Storia della letteratura greca. Torino, Paravia, 1972. 408p. **BB20**

AC XLIV 1975 241 Van Looy

A solid and complete manual for students, conservatively following the historical approach with no concessions to contemporary literary theories or methodology. Hellenistic literature gets an unusually generous treatment [pp.238–368]. The author's knowledge of antiquity is encyclopedic and his knowledge of modern scholarship equally impressive. Synchronistic tables at the end [history literature—plastic arts] are a useful addition to what is probably the best of the Italian manuals on Greek literature.

GRONINGEN, Bernhard Abraham van. La composition littéraire archaïque grecque; Procédés et réalisations. Amsterdam, Noord-Hollandsche Utig. Mij., 1960. 349p. **BB21**

CW LIII 1959 86 Calder • Rlh XXXIV 1960 117–119 Irigoin • Gnomon XXXII 1960 414–421 Kirkwood

A splendid discussion of those procedures of archaic composition that are concerned with establishing literary unity. This is the first extended application of structural analysis to archaic literature, though ring-composition had already been seen at work in individual writings. The work is divided into two parts: I. the description and exemplification of nine procedures of composition; and II. literary unity in various genres and major examples in epic, elegy, melic monody, choral lyric, the philosophers and rhetoricians. Homer and Herodotus are not included.

GRUBE, George Maximilian Anthony. The Greek and Roman critics. Toronto, University of Toronto Press, [1968]. 372p. **BB22**

Canadian University paperbooks, 72.

CR XVI 1966 202–204 Clarke • Phoenix XX 1966 262–264 Russell • Latomus XXIX 1970 559 Bardon • REA LXXI 1969 529–530

First published in 1965, this paperback edition provides a competent survey of literary criticism from Homer to the 3rd century A.D. Texts are in English and there is no Greek or Latin except in the notes. An elegant resumé of a thousand years of criticism.

HADAS, Moses. A history of Greek literature. New York, Columbia University Press, 1950. vi, 327p. **BB23**

AJPh LXXII 1951 78–79 De Witt • CW XLIV 1951 154 Greene • JHS LXXIII 1953 147–148 Pollard

A compact yet comprehensive survey of Greek literature, written with great charm, freshness and independence of judgment, and with twenty pages of excellent bibliographical notes. A remarkable and stimulating *tour de force*.

HIGGINBOTHAM, John. Greek and Latin literature: A comparative study. London, Methuen, 1969. xi, 399p. **BB24**

"Distributed in the U.S.A. by Barnes & Noble, Inc."

Hermathena CX 1970 94–95 Stanford • REA LXXIV 1972 356–359 Meillier

The aim of this book of essays by various hands is to show the developments of genres in Greek and Latin, to help students of modern literature understand classical origins better, and to break down the barriers between classical and modern studies. Noteworthy are the contributions of David Gaunt on epic poetry, Robert Coleman on pastoral, and Christopher Turner on history.

KLINGNER, Friedrich. Studien zur griechischen und römischen Literatur. [Hrsg. von Klaus Bartels mit einem Nachwort von Ernst Zinn]. Zürich, Artemis Verlag, [1964]. 766p. **BB25**

Bibliography of the author's works; p.[739–745].

CPh LXI 1966 220 O'Neil • JRS LVI 1966 270–271 Browning • CB XLIII 1967 80 Costelloe

A representative selection of Klingner's articles and reviews published to mark the 70th birthday of this truly great classicist. Dates of original publication run from 1927 to 1956, authors dealt with range from Homer to Boethius, though classical Latin poetry gets the lion's share. A more erudite counterpart to his *Römische Geisteswelt*.

KROLL, Wilhelm. Studien zum Verständnis der römischen Literatur. New York, Garland Pub., 1978. 390p. **BB26**

Reprint of the 1924 ed. published by J. B. Metzler, Stuttgart.

AJPh XLVI 1925 378–380 Pease • CR XL 1926 128–129 Sonnenschein • PhW XLV 1925 986–995 Helm

Wide-ranging contributions to the study of Latin literature, containing much detailed scholarship on the Greek antecedents of Latin works in various genres.

LEO, Friedrich. Geschichte der römischen Literatur. (Unveränderter reprografischer Nachdruck der Ausg. Berlin 1913–.) Darmstadt, Wissenschaftliche Buchgesellschaft, 1967–. **BB27**

1. Bd. Die archäische Literatur. Im Anhang: Die römische Poesie in der sullanischen Zeit.

Latomus XXVII 1968 668–669 Bardon

A reprint of a work which first appeared in 1913 and which at that time revealed the author's methodological rigor. Changes in scholarship in the meantime are not adequately reflected by the updated bibliographies.

LESKY, Albin. A History of Greek literature. Trans. from the 2nd German ed. by James Willis and Cornelis de Heer. London, Methuen, 1966. xix, 921p. **BB28**

The standard history of Greek literature. See also Lesky, Albin. *Geschichte der griechischen Literatur.* 3. neu bearb. und erw. Aufl. Bern, Francke, [1971]. 1023p.

NORTH, Helen. Sophrosyne; Self-knowledge and self-restraint in Greek literature. Ithaca, Cornell University Press, 1966. 391p. **BB29**

Cornell studies in classical philology; v. 35.

Gnomon XL 1968 712–713 Adkins • CPh LXIII 1968 70–71 Sprague • CR XVIII 1968 192–194 Baldry • AJPh XC 1969 360–365 Else

A long and erudite survey of *sophrosyne* from Homer to Augustine in nine chapters: the Heroic and Archaic periods; Tragedy; the Age of the Sophists; Xenophon, the minor Socratic schools and the Attic orators of the fourth century; Plato; Philosophy after Plato; literary and popular usage after Plato; Sophrosyne in Rome; Sophrosyne in Patristic literature. Plato is the focal point since he canonized *sophrosyne* at the heart of the cardinal virtues. Somewhat arbitrarily, in the absence or scarcity of the word *sophrosyne* in early literature, Professor North extends her investigation to synonyms of her choice for the concept. A fascinating study of the evolution of the quintessential Greek virtue and its metamorphosis in early Christianity.

PALADINI, V. and CASTORINI, E. Storia della letteratura latina. I. Disegno storico. II. Problemi critici. Bologna, Patron, 1970. vii, 536; vi, 539p.
BB30

RPh XLV 1971 360–361 Andre • RCCM XII 1970 85–91 Paratore • CR XXII 1972 149–150 Kenney

Covers the essentials for university students, with a selection of critical discussions on a wide range of literary-historical problems, but with very narrow bibliographical guidance. Easy to utilize and dependable, at least in v. I.

PARATORE, Ettore. Storia della letteratura latina. [2 ed. Firenze], G. C. Sansoni, [1962]. 1023p.
BB31

CR n.s. 1 1951 171–173 Browning • Maia VI 1953 232–235 della Corte • Gnomon XXVII 1955 331 Büchner

This 2nd edition was first printed in 1950, and belongs in the Italian tradition of literary history (Bignone, Rostagni, Amatucci) rather than in the German (Schanz-Hosius-Kruger). Difficult to use as a work of reference—no index, no recurring titles, no paragraph headings—it is rather a highly subjective synthesis of Latin literature set against its historical background and aimed at readers unfamiliar with Latin. As such, it is often stimulating but not infrequently misleading.

PARATORE, Ettore. La letteratura latina dell'età imperiale. Nuova edizione aggiornata. Firenze, Sansoni; Milano, Accademia, 1970. 586p.
BB32

Bibliography: p.[339]–574.

RPh XLIV 1970 344–345 Ernout

A history in four parts: the age of the Julio-Claudian dynasty, the Flavian and Trajan era, the Antonine age, and the Age of the late Empire down to Boethius.

QUINN, Kenneth. Latin explorations; Critical studies in Roman literature. London, Routledge and K. Paul, [1969]. 282p.
BB33

"Second impression, with corrections, 1969."

CR XIV 1964 57–60 Wilkinson • Latomus XXIII 1964 846 Luck • CW LVIII 1964 18 Elder

A heterogeneous collection of eight critical essays on poems of his choice: Horace's Spring odes, the Propempticon as practised by Propertius, Horace and Ovid, Virgil's tragic queen, and, oddly, one essay on Tacitus' narrative technique.

RIPOSATI, Benedetto. Storia della Letteratura latina. Milan, Societa Editrice Dante Alighieri, 1965. xx, 819p.
BB34

Latinitas XIII 1965 304–306 Parisella • PPh XL 1966 159–161 Ernout • RSC XIII 1965 358–359 d'Agostino

A useful addition to the many Italian manuals on Latin literature. The work includes surveys of the early Christian writers. Riposati's treatment is animated by keen awareness of the role enjoyed by Latin literature in modern Western culture. The work, unlike that of Bayet, is rarely illustrated by translations. Controversial questions are presented with prudence and objectivity, e.g. the priority of dating problem of Tertullian's *Apologeticum* and Minutius Felix. Each chapter has a short, judiciously selected bibliography, and there is a general bibliography at the end.

RONCONI, Alessandro. La letteratura romana. Saggio di Sintesi Storica. Firenze, F. Le Monnier, 1968. 210p.
BB35

REL XLVI 1968 482 Richard

A brief but substantial essay of synthesis. In twenty-one chapters the principal problems are surveyed, with no major *quaestio vexata* passed over in silence. An original work, providing balanced aperçus to long-debated literary problems.

ROSE, Herbert Jennings. A handbook of Latin literature: From the earliest times to the death of St. Augustine. 3rd ed. reprinted; with a supplementary bibliography by E. Courtney. London, Methuen; New York, Dutton, [1966]. ix, 582p.
BB36

Bibliography: p.534–561.

Hermathena CIV 1967 95–96 Rodgers • CR n.s. XVII 1967 224–225 Clarke, LII 1938 127–128 Henry • JRS XXVIII 1938 260–262 Fletcher

Rose's *Handbook* first published in 1936 and reprinted several times has a supplementary bibliography by E. Courtney, covering work since 1939 with exemplary thoroughness. The strengths and weaknesses of Rose's general and factual survey are well known to generations of students. As a Handbook rather than a History, it does not discuss the development of the various literary forms in their historical setting. As a collection of facts which makes no claim to originality of matter or treatment, it is in general useful and reliable. Its main virtue is its pithy and succinct summaries.

ROSTAGNI, Augusto. Storia della letteratura latina. 3. ed. [Torino], Unione tipografico-editrice torinese, [1964]. 3 v., illus.
BB37

CR n.s. IV 1954 31–34 Browning • REL XLIV 1966 493–494 Fontaine • Latomus XXIV 1965 960–962 Préaux

The first edition appeared in two volumes in 1949–1952. Rostagni had revised and expanded practically the whole of the first half when he died in 1961. With admirable *pietas* Italo Lana has completed the revision. The work is well written and contains a great deal of information with well chosen illustrative excerpts from the authors discussed. Rostagni's humanism is revealed also in the wealth of illustrations in the book—frescoes, inscriptions, manuscripts, etc. Rostagni's energy, enthusiasm and discretion begin to flag when he passes beyond the 2nd century, A.D., but throughout the work the proportion of pages assigned to individual authors is too governed by the author's personal preferences. The introductory chapters to each section on the main social and cultural currents of the period are particularly well done.

RUDD, Niall, comp. Essays on classical literature; Selected from "Arion" with an introduction by Niall Rudd. Cambridge, Heffer; New York, Barnes and Noble, 1972. xx, 275p. **BB38**

Views and controversies about classical antiquity.
G&R XX 1973 97–98 Walcot • CR XXIV 1974 317 Williams

Consists of four articles each on Greek literature, Latin literature, and the Classical Tradition, with a lucid introduction on the present state of criticism by Rudd, displaying the mixture of discontent and new hope that was the *raison d'être* of *Arion*. Familiar names are here linked with favorite authors: Herington, Aeschylus; Quinn, Horace; Arrowsmith and Sullivan, Petronius; and there is a highly readable broadside on the Parry formulaic oral poetry theory by Douglas Young, 'Never blotted a line? Formula and premeditation in Homer and Hesiod.' A mixed bag, but lively, entertaining and scholarly.

THEILER, Willy. Untersuchungen zur antiken Literatur. Berlin, de Gruyter, 1970. 579p. **BB39**

LEC XXXIII 1970 372 Wankenne • CR XXI 1971 405–407 Lloyd-Jones • RBPh L 1972 177 Devijver

An assemblage of studies spanning the years 1934–1968. There are five chapters on Homer, three on Aristotle and predictably many on Neoplatonism, but the wide range of Theiler's interests and his learning, acuteness and originality are abundantly demonstrated. Most of his important papers on religion and philosophy, as distinct from literature, will be found in a complementary volume, *Forschungen zum Neoplatonismus,* 1966.

VIANSINO, Giovanni. Introduzione critica alla letteratura latina. Salerno, Societa editrice salernitana, [1975]. 700p. **BB40**

Published in 1970 under title: Introduzione allo studio critico della letteratura latina.
CR XXII 1972 420 Kenney • AJPh XCV 1974 165–

166 Silk • REA LXXIV 1972 283–285 Granarolo • CPh LXVII 1972 315 Sullivan

Not intended as a substitute for the standard handbooks, this book consists of twenty-eight short chapters, the first of which is a select bibliography and the rest compressed treatments of selected topics relating to twenty-seven Latin authors. Much information is presented with excessive economy of style in an attempt to provide students with orientation in the scholarly literature of the past twenty years. There is no obvious principle governing the order followed.

WILKINSON, L. P. Golden Latin artistry. Cambridge, Cambridge University Press, 1963. **BB41**

CR XIV 1964 60–62 Clarke • REA LXX 1968 195–196 Le Bonniec • Mnemosyne XX 1967 86–88 Leeman

Deals with euphony, rhythm and metre, especially prose rhythm. Highly personal in its choice of examples, in presentation, and in taking sides on hotly debated issues. The 'Golden' authors are Cicero, Sallust, Virgil and Horace. The study of literature here is largely a matter of form rather than content. The first two parts of the work deal with sounds and rhythms, the third, entitled Structures, is devoted to a study of the period in historians and orators, and to the architecture of verse. An important contribution in English to a neglected area: the sound and movement and architectonics of the Latin language.

WILLIAMS, Gordon. Change and decline: Roman literature in the early empire. Berkeley, University of California Press, 1978. viii, 344p. **BB42**

Sather classical lectures; v. 45.
CW LXXII 1979 314 Sullivan • Phoenix XXXIII 1979 72–77 Kenney

A well-argued and more trenchant successor to the author's *Tradition and Originality* on his by now familiar theme: after the Augustan age Roman literary gold turned to silver, and then to sand in the archaising age of Fronto. Factors in the decline such as imperial autocracy, censorship, patronage are carefully analysed. The author emphasizes the fusion of the Greek and Latin cultures in the period from the end of the Republic to the early Christian period, with the resultant stifling effects of Greek literary superiority. Seneca and Ovid get less than fair assessments, and there are many infelicities in the writing.

Poetry

ALBRECHT, Michael von. Römische Poesie: Texte und Interpretationen. 1. Aufl. Heidelberg, Stiehm, 1977. 371p. **BB43**

CW LXXII(2) 1978 111–112 Copley

A meticulous study of individual texts ranging from Ennius to Petrarch, each representative of its genre. Each poem receives a German translation, detailed interpretation and structural analysis. Most interesting is his analysis of poetic architecture, particularly his establishment of the *Ringform* as a significant element in poetic structure and also an influence on meaning.

BOWRA, Cecil Maurice, Sir. Greek lyric poetry from Alcman to Simonides. 2d ed. rev. [and corr.]. 1st ed., 1936. Oxford, Clarendon Press, 1967, 1961. xii, 444p.   **BB44**

CW LV 1961 10 Kirkwood • AC XXX 1961 544 Severyns • CR XIII 1963 140–144 Bond
An almost completely re-written revision of the 1936 work, but retaining its methodology: a summary of biographical information, a general survey with brief reference to numerous fragments, and an extraordinarily skillful analysis of the poetic diction and structure of most of the major lyrics. New papyri discoveries provide significant additions to five of the seven major poets discussed. Earlier judgments are frequently modified, with full account taken of intervening scholarship. A work of great erudition, written with grace and infectious enthusiasm.

BOYLE, A. J., ed. Ancient pastoral: Ramus essays on Greek and Roman pastoral. Berwick, Vic., Aureal Publications, 1975. 148p.   **BB45**

CR XXVIII 1978 63–66 Jenkinson • RFIC CV 1977 194–201 Van Sickle
Ramus is a new Australian journal devoted to literary interpretation of the classics with A. J. Boyle as its founder-editor. The seven contributors here are mostly well-known Americans, pursuing well-known personal interpretations, e.g. Charles Segal, Gilbert Lawall, Michael Putnam. The concluding essay by E. W. Leach, "Neronian Pastoral and the World of Power," is perhaps the most interesting.

CAIRNS, Francis. Generic composition in Greek and Roman poetry. Edinburgh, Edinburgh University Press, 1972. viii, 331p.   **BB46**

AAHG XXVII 1974 180–181 Pötscher • Phoenix XXVII 1973 403–407 Quinn • REL L 1972 346–349 Fontaine
A systematic, authoritative treatment of the thesis that the whole of classical poetry is written in accordance with ancient sets of rules of the various genres. These rules are embedded in the literature itself and became canonized in the ancient rhetorical handbooks. Four of the nine chapters deal with the theory of genres and the basic types. Chapters 5–9 deal with "Constructive Principles": Inversion, Reaction, Inclusion, Speaker-Variation, Addressee-Variation. The examination is mostly confined to lyric, pastoral and elegiac, and many detailed exegeses of individual poems are included. The author feels that these generic considerations are equally applicable to ancient prose.

THE GREEK Bucolic Poets, trans, with brief notes by A. S. F. Gow. Cambridge, Cambridge University Press, 1953. xxvii, 156p.   **BB47**

Prose translations of poetry selected from Theocritus, Moschus, and Bion.

FRANKEL, Hermann Ferdinand. Early Greek poetry and philosophy: A history of Greek epic, lyric, and prose to the middle of the fifth century. Trans. by Moses Hadas and James Willis. Oxford, B. Blackwell, [1975]. xii, 555p.   **BB48**

Translation of *Dichtung und Philosophie des frühen Griechentums.*
CR XIV 1964 209 Lloyd-Jones • Mnemosyne XVII 1964 176–177 Verdenius • CW LXXI 1977 74–75 Kirkwood
A translation of *Dichtung und Philosophie des frühen Griechentums* New York, 1951, 1969, 1976, pp.XIV, 637 [See CR LXVII 1953, 146–148, Tate]. *Geistesgeschichte* of the best kind, allied to common sense, independence, and close acquaintance with the texts, high technical proficiency, great clarity of presentation and real imaginative sympathy. Corrections suggested by earlier reviews have been incorporated. The quality of the translation in general is admirable, though the difference in style between Hadas and Willis is obvious.

FRIEDLÄNDER, Paul. Studien zur antiken Literatur und Kunst. Berlin, de Gruyter, 1969. ix, 701p.   **BB49**

Bibliography of the author's works: [683]–688.
Hellenica XXV 1972 209–213 Kakridis • CR n.s. XXI 1971 409–411 Lloyd-Jones • AAHG XXVI 1973 220 Herter
A collection of Friedländer's shorter pieces edited just before his death in 1968, many of them grouped around the topics of his chief larger works (e.g., Plato) and showing equal competence in literature and art.

FUHRMANN, Manfred. Einführung in die antike Dichtungstheorie. Darmstadt, Wissenschaftliche Buchgesellschaft, 1973. xv, 325p.   **BB50**

AC XLIII 1974 518 Tordeur • CPh LXX 1975 303–304 Golden • REL LII 1974 519–524 Grimal • Gnomon XLIX 1977 411–413 Flashar • CR XXVIII 1978 68–69 Silk
A serviceable introduction to the doctrines of ancient literary theory as expressed in Aristotle's *Poetics,* Horace's *Ars Poetica* and Longinus' *On the Sublime.* Detailed summaries, paraphrases and restatements of the arguments of these works are followed by discussions of the meaning of selected major ideas in the works or of the relationship of these works to contemporary criticism. A useful book for beginners, but with important deficiencies in recent bibliography. The second part of the work provides a very limited discussion of the influence of Aristotle's *Poetics,* stopping in the 18th century and excluding England.

GALINSKY, G. Karl, ed. Perspectives of Roman poetry; A classics symposium. Essays by Georg Luck [and others]. Austin, University of Texas Press, [1974]. 160p.   **BB51**

Symposia in the arts and the humanities, no. 1.
CW LXX 1976 212 Elder • CR XXVI 1976 199–200 Townend

A symposium seeking to present fresh critical interpretations. Georg Luck opens with 'The Woman's Role in Latin Love Poetry.' His thesis is that the woman's role as courtesan explains to a large extent the unique character of the love poetry from Catullus to Ovid.

William S. Anderson writes on Autobiography and Art in Horace, and sees Horace's father replaced by personal myths on divine forms like Apollo. Kenneth Heckford writes sensitively on some trees in Virgil and Tolkien. Eric Segal on The Business of Roman Comedy deals with the wealth of financial imagery in Plautus. Last, and perhaps best, the editor deals with Ovid's Metamorphosis of Myth, with a detailed analysis of the stories of Erysichthon and Narcissus. There is a panel discussion on The Originality of Roman Poetry.

HUXLEY, George Leonard. Greek epic poetry from Eumelos to Panyassis. Cambridge, Harvard University Press, 1969. 213p. **BB52**

CR n.s. XXI 1971 67–69 West • CPh LXVII 1972 205–206
A detailed study of particular epics, mainly lost ones, rather than a study of the literary genre. Much learning and ingenuity, but surprising mishandlings of source texts and unimaginative speculations make it disappointing.

KIRKWOOD, Gordon MacDonald. Early Greek monody; The history of a poetic type. Ithaca, [N.Y.], Cornell University Press, [1974]. xviii, 299p. **BB53**

Cornell studies in classical philology, v. 37.
AAHG XXX 1977 13–15 Eisenhut • Phoenix XXVIII 1974 361–363 Campbell • LEC XLIII 1975 208–209 Wankenne • AC XLIV 1975 243–244 Mund-Dopchie • CJ LXXI 1975–76 177–180 Kopff
The genre of monody is studied, with text and (usually) verse translation from its beginnings in Archilochus to its maturity in Alcaeus and Sappho. Anacreon, Telesilla, Praxilla, Timocreon, Myrtis, Charixena, Cydias and Corinna are also studied, with comprehensive documentation, providing an excellent aperçu of the work and temperament of these poets. The concluding chapter, Monody and Epigram, suggests a metamorphosis that proved the deathknell of the genre. Mimnermus and Theognis are excluded for what some might feel to be arbitrary reasons. An admirable supplement to Bowra's *Greek Lyric Poetry* (2nd ed.), but not a replacement for it. Particularly good for its full discussion on the textual and bibliographical side.

KITTO, Humphrey. Poiesis. Berkeley, University of California Press, 1966. 407p. **BB54**

Sather classical lectures, v. 36.
CR XVIII 1968 187–190 Baldry • AJPh LXXXI X 1968 483–487 Herington
An enlarged version of the Sather lectures given in 1960 which poses, in the first chapter "Criticism and Chaos," the urgent question: what criterion (if any) still remains by which the meaning of an ancient literary work may be determined? The chaotic state of profes-

sional criticism in the previous dozen years is amply demonstrated, and Kitto tries to restore order by the touchstone of *poiesis*—the poet's selection, juxtaposition and organization of his material. But his application of this criterion to Homer, the Greek dramatists, Thucydides, and Plato does not prove very workable in practice. The repeated emphasis on the structure of the whole work of art and on the importance of religious and ethical dimensions is a refreshing corrective to much critical misunderstanding.

LEFKOWITZ, Mary R. The Victory ode: An introduction. Park Ridge, N.J., Noyes Press, 1976. 186p. **BB55**

Translation of selections from Pindar and Bacchylides.
G&R XXIV, no. 2 1977 199 Ireland • Phoenix XXXI,2 1977 181–183 Gerber
The aim of this book is to guide stanza by stanza the non-specialist through six odes written for Hieron. The odes are Pyth. 2, Bacchyl. 5, Ol. 1, Pyth. 1, Bacchyl. 3 and Pyth. 3. The methodology is perhaps the book's main weakness, never allowing us to see the victory ode as a whole. Translations, not always reliable, are fragmented in the commentary. An over-zealous pursuit of verbal and imagistic associations vitiates a work that has much sound scholarship on structure and themes.

LIVERPOOL Latin Seminar, 1979, ed. Francis Cairns. Papers of the Liverpool Latin Seminar, 2d v., 1979; Vergil and Roman elegy: Medieval Latin poetry and prose; Greek lyric and drama. Liverpool, Francis Cairns, 1979. 360p. **BB56**

The Liverpool Latin Seminar has been steadily gaining attention and the name of Francis Cairns guarantees a type of literary criticism that is refreshing and responsible.

LUCK, Georg. The Latin love elegy. 2d ed. London, Methuen, 1969. 192p. **BB57**

Distributed in the U.S.A. by Barnes & Noble.
CR n.s. X 1960 224–226 Kenney • Phoenix XV 1961 55–57 McKay • Latomus XX 1961 163 LeBonniec • Arion II, 3 1963 150–154 Salerno
A second edition of a 1959 work with some revision and an augmented bibliography. A new preface and an epilog on the love poem after Ovid enhance the work, which is an excellent historical and critical study of the love poems of Tibullus, Propertius and Ovid, with careful attention to origins and Hellenistic influences. The analysis of selected poems or passages is always shrewd and sensitive.

MENDELL, Clarence. Latin poetry. The new poets and the Augustans. New Haven, Yale University Press, 1965. 258p. **BB58**

CPh LXI 1966 275–276 Williams • CJ XLI 1966 370–372 Rutledge • Arion V 1966 89–98 Sullivan
A very traditional survey of the works of Lucretius, Catullus, Virgil, Horace and the three Roman elegists.

The book is addressed to nostalgic readers whose knowledge of Latin is rusty. The work is competent in its erudition, brisk in narrative and straightforward in its translations of Latin poetry, but represents no advance on Sellar or Duff.

NEWMAN, J. Augustus and the new poetry. Bruxelles, Berchem, 1967. 458p.   **BB59**

Collection Latomus; v. 88.

REL XLV 1967 562–563 Perret • CW LXII 1968 54–55 Esler • Gnomon XLI 1969 156–159 Wilkinson

The Augustan poets (Augustus in the title is misleading) were 'new' not because they reacted against the Alexandrianism of their immediate predecessors but because they created a novel concept of the poet's role, that of *vates*—seer, castigator and civilizer of society and its leaders. The second half of Newman's thesis is easier to sustain than the first, for along with undoubted Alexandrianisms continuing in their work (fully exploited here), there is an obvious return to the Ancients with their more national and Roman preoccupations. A provocative, sometimes exasperating book, not well organized but nonetheless wide-ranging, erudite and stimulating. The section on *vates* is more fully developed in a separate monograph: *The Concept of Vates in Augustan Poetry* (Coll. Latomus, LXXXIX), Bruxelles, 1967.

PAGE, Denys Lionel. Sappho and Alcaeus; An introduction to the study of ancient Lesbian poetry. Oxford, Clarendon Press, [1975]. viii, 340p.   **BB60**

Reprint of the 1955 edition.

CW XLIX 1955 61 Musurillo • AC XXIV 1955 467–471 Lasserre • CPh LI 1956 140–141 Calder III • CJ LII 1956 90 Kirkwood

A charming and scholarly commentary on the Lesbian poets, complementing the critical edition by Lobel and Page, *Poetarum Lesbiorum Fragmenta*. For Sappho (p.3–146) extensive commentary is devoted to twelve major fragments and over thirty others; for Alcaeus (p.149–317) over sixty-five of his fragments get some commentary. The exegesis is textual, grammatical, historical and literary. Texts and translations are provided, and the essays are full of erudition, wit (often at the expense of his predecessors), and common sense, but sometimes lacking in literary insight, with little attention to imagery and symbolism.

ROSS, David O. Backgrounds to Augustan poetry: Gallus, elegy, and Rome. Cambridge; New York, Cambridge University Press, 1975. vii, 176p.   **BB61**

TLS LXXIV 1975 1326 McLeod • AJPh XCVII 1976 412–413 Nethercut • G&R XXII 1976 198 Verity • Phoenix XXX 1976 293–297 Quinn

Really a book about the poetry of Cornelius Gallus.

RUDD, Niall. Lines of enquiry: Studies in Latin poetry. Cambridge; New York, Cambridge University Press, 1976. xi, 215p.   **BB62**

CR XXVIII 1978 76–78 West • G&R XXIII 1976 197–198 Verity

The author describes a variety of critical methods and approaches to Latin poetry—historical background, language or structure, place in a literary tradition—in seven highly readable essays.

SILK, M. S. Interaction in poetic imagery: With special reference to Greek poetry. London; New York, Cambridge University Press, 1974. xiv, 263p.   **BB63**

G&R XXII 1975 193 Taplin • CPh LXXII 1977 146–159 Mueller • AC XLIV 1975 704–705 van Looy • LEC XLIII 1975 302 Delaunois

An uncompromisingly difficult and technical work, aiming at classifying and clarifying the relationships between a metaphor (or vehicle) and its surrounding literal context (or tenor). The work makes valuable contributions to lexicography down to Pindar and Aeschylus. Interaction is a new critical concept that may not win wide acceptance, and many will be put off by the grandiose prolegomena, but all will benefit from this overly-conscious new study of the imagery of Aeschylus and Pindar.

SULLIVAN, John Patrick. Critical essays on Roman literature; Elegy and lyric. London, Routledge & K. Paul, 1962. 225p.   **BB64**

CR XIII 1963 297–299 Kenney • JRS LIII 1963 243 Browning • CPh LIX 1964 298–300 O'Neil

An introduction by Sullivan explains that each contributor is working in isolation: Cherniss on the biographical approach to literary criticism, Quinn on Catullus, Elder on Tibullus, Allen on Propertius, Lee on Ovid, and Nisbet on Horace. It is all too clear that the other critics are not following the lines marked out by Sullivan and Cherniss (the latter is particularly stimulating), but the very diversity may be a stimulation to students to make their own choices between critical approaches. A good introduction to the application of modern critical evaluation to ancient texts. There is a companion volume on Roman satire.

TREU, Max. Von Homer zur Lyrik. Wandlungen des griechischen Weltbildes im Spiegel der Sprache. 2., durchgesehene Aufl. München, Beck, 1968. xiv, 335p.   **BB65**

Zetemata; Monographien zur klassischen Altertumswissenschaft, v. Heft 12.

AJPh LXXIX 1958 74–79 Kirkwood • AC XXV 1956 478–480, XXXVIII 1969 222 Lasserre • CR VIII 1958 23–26 Davison • REA LIX 1957 142–144 Defradas • Gnomon XXVIII 1956 574–578 Wehrli

The book is in two main sections: Das homerische Weltbild, p.1–135 and das Weltbild der Lyrik, p.136–306, followed by a short summary and three indexes. The work is a word-study, owing much to Snell's *Discovery of the Mind,* studying words not for themselves but for the mentality they portray. Part 1 studies the Homeric perceptions of man, landscape and time, and the contrasting outlook and the new perceptions of lyric on the same subjects are studied in Part II.

The book is more important for the information it collects on word usage than for its generalizations and conclusions, some of which are larger than the evidence can support.

The second edition contains only three pages of Addenda to the first.

TUPET, Anne M. La Magie dans la poésie latine. [Lille], Service de reproduction de thèses, Université de Lille III, 1976– . **BB66**

1. Des origines à la fin du règne d'Auguste.
CR XXVIII 1978 358 Macleod • AC XLVII 1978 275 Poucet
A rambling and long-winded study of the poetic meaning of magic as a theme in the Latin poets down to Ovid, with an introductory survey of magic in Greek literature down through the Alexandrians. Some of the commentary on selected passages is very illuminating, notably on Dido's recourse to magic in *Aeneid* IV, but in general the work is too limited on the side of magic and too superficial on the side of Latin poetry.

WEBSTER, Thomas. Hellenistic poetry and art. [New York], Barnes & Noble, [1965]. 321p. **BB67**

AC XXXVI 1967 280 van Looy • CPh LXII 1967 127–128 Havelock • JHS LXXXVII 1967 151–152 Sparkes
The last of four volumes in which Webster seeks to relate the verbal and visual arts of Greece, thus creating a parallel history of Greek literature and art from Homer to the Roman period. The choice of illustrative material is judicious, and the visual character of so much Hellenistic poetry is thereby emphasized.

WEST, Martin. Studies in Greek elegy and iambus. Berlin; New York, de Gruyter, 1974. viii, 198p. **BB68**

Untersuchungen zur antiken Literatur und Geschichte; Bd. 14.
LEC XLIII 1975 208 Stenuit • AC XLIV 1975 693–695 Lasserre • Mnemosyne XXIX 1976 189–191 Verdenius • CW LXIX 1976 393–395 Romano
Should serve as an introduction and partial commentary to the author's *Iambi et Elegi Graeci*, 1972. The treatment of Theognidea is particularly illuminating and new, and the long commentary on chosen pages in Chapter VII shows the author's manifold talents at work to best effect.

WILLIAMS, Gordon W. Tradition and originality in Roman poetry. Oxford, Clarendon Press, 1968. ix, 810p. **BB69**

CJ LXVI 1970–1971 164–169 Segal • JRS LX 1970 255–257 Wilkinson • REL XLVIII 1970 544–546 Le Bonniec
This enormous and widely ranging work discusses (with printed texts and plain translations) nearly all the major Latin poetry of the late Republic and Augustan age. The *terminus ad quem* is the death of Horace 8 B.C., and the first two hundred pages or so really constitute a book on Horace. Catullus, Virgil and Propertius are also treated generously, and Ennius, Plautus and Terence are constantly looked back to. The work is well organized, though it sometimes drags, and shows to good effect the author's skill at discerning underlying similarities of technique or intention between apparently disparate poems or passages.

WITKE, Charles. Numen litterarum; The old and the new in Latin poetry from Constantine to Gregory the Great. Leiden, Brill, 1971. 249p. **BB70**

Mittellateinische Studien und Texte, Bd. 5.
CPh LXIX 1974 296–297 Cunningham • CR XXIV 1974 221–223 Walsh
This work deals with Ausonius, Paulinus of Nola, Prudentius and lesser known poets from Juvencus to Arator. Discussion is organized around the concept of 'poetic persona'—how does the poet conceive of himself, his role and his poetry. An attempt to establish the continuity of the Latin poetic tradition is made in terms of persistence and adaptation of classical forms and genres, and of imitations and borrowings from the classical poets. This does not leave enough room for the considerable cultural break that divides the classical period from late antiquity.

WOODMAN, Tony and WEST, David, eds. Quality and pleasure in Latin poetry. London; New York, Cambridge University Press, 1974 vii, 166p. **BB71**

REL LIII 1975 601 Perret • G&R XXII 1975 195 • CW LXIX 1976 476–477 Highet
Consists of eight lively essays by 8 different hands in the practical criticism of 1st century B.C. poetry. A short epilogue attempts a description of the present state of Latin literary criticism as exemplified by the diversity of aims and methods shown in the various essays. 'Quality' and 'Pleasure' are not defined, and the book is rather a collection of close analyses of Latin poems (Catullus 31, Bucolics 4, Propertius 1.20, Tibullus 1.1, Horace Carm 3.30) or extracts (final 50 lines of Georg. 1, 2 paragraphs from Lucretius 1, the concluding fable in Horace, Serm. 2.6).

Drama

BAIN, David. Actors and audience: A study of asides and related conventions in Greek drama. Oxford; New York, Oxford University Press, 1977. x, 230p. **BB72**

Oxford classical and philosophical monographs.
AJPh XCIX, 3 1978 399–401 Sider • CW LXXII 2 1978 112–113 Knox
A very thorough and valuable examination of the dramatic aside and related conventions in Greek tragedy and Greek and Roman comedy. The aside is chiefly used in New Comedy, and over 50 pages are devoted to Menander. There are good indices of subjects, passages and Greek words.

BREMER, Jan M. Hamartia; Tragic error in the Poetics of Aristotle and in Greek tragedy. Amsterdam, Hakkert, 1969. xx, 214p.   **BB73**

CPh LXVI 1971 125–127 Golden • Gnomon XLIII 1971 551–563 von Fritz

The first completely systematic study of *hamartia*, based on the earlier work of Van Braam, Else, Hey, Lucas, Phillips, Harsh, Ostwald and others, which has substituted some form of intellectual error for moral flaw as a definition. For Bremer *hamartia* is a tragic error, that is, a wrong action committed in ignorance of its nature, effect, etc., which is the starting point of a causally connected train of events ending in disaster. This is an admirably lucid study of the history and criticism of the *Poetics*.

DEVEREUX, George. Dreams in Greek tragedy: An ethno-psychoanalytical study. Oxford, Blackwell, 1976. xxxix, 364p.   **BB74**

CR XXVIII 1978 226–228 Diggle

Seeks to demonstrate the psychological credibility of the dreams Aeschylus, Sophocles and Euripides devise for certain of their characters. Requires no special knowledge of Greek or psychoanalysis. Based on the author's own psychoanalytical and ethnographical work, evidence from which is incorporated in more than a thousand footnotes, with illustrations from mathematics, music, philosophy, and the world's more obscure literatures, together with an enormous amount of documentation from classical authors. The methods of analysis are those of one particular analytical school. There are weaknesses in the translations from the Greek.

DOREY, T. A., ed. Roman drama. New York, Basic Books, 1965. 229p.   **BB75**

Studies in Latin literature and its influence.

CJ LXII 1966 136–137 Poduska • CR XVI 1966 354–357 Willcock • Gnomon XXXVIII 1966 676–679 Maurach

Seven essays of very uneven quality dealing with Menander (T.B.L. Webster is disappointing), Plautus, Seneca and a Westminster school revival of Roman *Palliatae*. The chapters on the influence of Plautus and Seneca on later dramatists are the most rewarding.

DUCKWORTH, George. The nature of Roman comedy; a study in popular entertainment. Princeton, Princeton University Press, 1952. xiii, 501p., illus.   **BB76**

AJPh LXXIV 1953 423–426 MacKendrick • CR n.s. IV 1954 125–128 Tredennick • Latomus XI 1952 241–242 Bardon • CPh XLVIII 1953 101–102 Beare

A very well-balanced survey of the background and history of Roman comedy, the staging and presentation of the plays, the nature of the comedies (stage conventions, plot structure, character delineation, etc.), the originality of Plautus and Terence and their influence on subsequent drama. Useful to general reader and specialist alike, this is a lucid and remarkably comprehensive handbook.

ELSE, Gerald F. The origin and early form of Greek tragedy. New York, Norton, [1972]. ix, 127p.   **BB77**

Original ed. issued as v. 20 of Martin classical lectures.

CR XVII 1967 70–72 Lucas • CJ LXII 1966 75–76 Golden • Gnomon XLI 1969 229–233 Calder III • JHS LXXXVII 1967 140–141 Webster

A new survey of an old but ever intriguing subject. Else disputes Aristotle's position as an authoritative source of information on the subject, and also finds fault with alternative theories proposed by Gilbert Murray and Martin Nilsson. For Else the creator of tragedy was Thespis, improved on by Aeschylus, a literary rather than religious or anthropological solution. A bright and readable polemic vitiated by an irrationally selective treatment of sources, sparse documentation, and some very tendentious argument.

FERGUSON, John. A companion to Greek tragedy. Austin, University of Texas Press, [1972]. xi, 623p., illus.   **BB78**

Phoenix XXVIII 1974 256–258 Peradotto • CW LXVIII 1974 112–114 McCall • Hermathena CXVII 1974 89–90 Stanford • CR XXV 1975 183–186 Baldry

The author's three-fold aim is to bring his (Greekless) readers a detailed awareness of the language, assonance, rhythms, and imagery of the plays, to create a sense of the theatre, and to provide understanding of the social and political contexts of the plays. There are 34 chapters giving detailed analyses of extant plays, but many are marred by either fuzziness or dogmatism. Two summary chapters deal with the origin of Greek drama and the physical aspects of Greek theatre production. Ferguson's own background in the theatre makes him more reliable in the staging aspects of tragedy than as a literary critic or as assessor of the minutiae of scholarly questions, but he is generally informative and entertaining. There is an extensive bibliography, pp.573–604.

HENDERSON, Jeffrey. The maculate muse: Obscene language in Attic comedy. New Haven, Yale University Press, 1975. xii, 251p.   **BB79**

CJ LXXI,4 1976 368–372 Hulley • CPh LXXI 1976 356–359 Lloyd-Jones

A comprehensive study of obscenity in Old Comedy, with marked frankness in translating the Greek terms. The second half of the book provides a useful glossary of sexual and scatological terms alphabetically and topically arranged. Origins of obscenity are sought in the first half in fertility cults and in iambic writers like Hipporax, Archilochus and Semonides.

JACKSON, John. Marginalia Scaenica. Oxford, Oxford University Press, 1955. ix, 250p.   **BB80**

CR n.s. VI 1956 112–115 Platnauer • AJPh LXXIX 1958 101–102 Helmbold • REG LXIX 1956 228–230 Delebecque

An incomparable book in the manner of Porson, Bentley or Housman.

KITTO, Humphrey Davy Findley. Greek tragedy: A literary study. 3d ed. London, Methuen, 1971. x, 401p. **BB81**

One of the most popular works on Greek tragedy by an author equally at home with stage-craft and classical drama (first published in 1939).

KOTT, Jan. The eating of the gods: An interpretation of Greek tragedy. Trans. by Boleslaw Taborski and Edward J. Czerwinski. London, E. Methuen, 1974. xix, 334p. **BB82**

G&R XXII 1975 194 Taplin • AC XLV 1976 229–231 Schamp

Follows the same recipe as the author's much overrated *Shakespeare our Contemporary.* Plays examined are Prometheus, Ajax, Trachiniae, Philoctetes, Alcestis, Heracles and Bacchae, Artaud, Beckett, or Camus. The framework of myth and legend is put through a procrustean overhaul to make the plays speak directly to our times. There is a French translation, *Manger les dieux,* 1975, 260p.

LATTIMORE, Richmond Alexander. The poetry of Greek tragedy. New York, Harper & Row, 1966. 157p. **BB83**

Reprint of 1958 ed., published by Johns Hopkins Press.

CR n.s. X 1960 26–28 Baldry • REG LXXIII 1960 278–279 de Romilly

By 'poetry' Professor Lattimore does not mean 'the obvious facts of metrical and rhetorical structure,' but 'what is directed neither to the emotion nor the intellect, but to the imagination.'

LEFEVRE, Eckard, ed. Die römische Komödie, Plautus und Terenz. Darmstadt, Wissenschaftliche Buchgesellschaft, 1973. vii, 501p. **BB84**

Wege der Forschung; Bd. 236

CW LXIX 1975 276–277 Segal • MH XXXII 1975 270 Marti • Gnomon XLVIII 1976 244–249 Brown

Seven of these twenty-two essays (all listed in the *Gnomon* review) originally appeared in English; all the others are of German authorship, a distribution which accurately reflects the current state of scholarship in Roman Comedy. The Terence section is rather richer than the Plautus one. Lefevre provides an admirable bibliography. Some of the essays are unnecessarily excerpted from books readily available to scholars.

LESKY, Albin. Die griechische Tragödie. English trans.: Greek tragedy. Trans. by H. A. Frankfort; with foreword by E. G. Turner. 3rd ed. London, E. Benn; Barnes & Noble Books, 1978. **BB85**

CR LIII 1959 286, XVI n.s. 1966 416 Lucas • Phoenix XX 1966 352 Quincey

The original German first appeared in 1937 and then in an expanded second edition in 1958. A small work but astonishingly rich in content, it quickly became a standard textbook. Three chapters are devoted to the origins and early history of tragedy. The three great dramatists get individual chapters, and there is a concluding chapter on the postclassical phase. The translation is competent and there are additional bibliographical references to work, especially in English, from 1958 to 1964. Lesky's well-known surveys of Greek tragedy began in *AAHG:* "Forschungsbericht über griechische Tragödie," *AAHG* I (1948), 65–71, and have been one of its best features since.

LUCAS, Donald William. The Greek tragic poets. 3rd ed. [London], Cohen & West, [1969]. xiv, 274p. **BB86**

Gnomon XXIV 1952 518–520, XXXIII 1961 719–721 Lesky • Phoenix V 1951 26 Tracy • CR II 1952 21–22 Winnington-Ingram

A very useful book, first published in 1950, aimed at both the intelligent reader without Greek who wishes to understand Greek civilization and the university student with some Greek but whose reading of plays is limited.

PICKARD-CAMBRIDGE, Arthur Wallace, Sir. The dramatic festivals of Athens. 2nd ed. Revised by John Gould and D. M. Lewis. Oxford, Clarendon Press, [1969]. xxiv, 358p., 72 plates, illus. **BB87**

AJPh LXXV 1954 306–315 Bieber • Gnomon XXVI 1954 209–213 Lesky, XL 1968 824–826 • Hermathena CVII 1968 77 Stanford • REG LXXXI 1968 573–574 Metzger

A welcome updating of Pickard-Cambridge's 1953 publication, comparable to T. B. L. Webster's revised edition (1962) of the 1927 *Dithyramb, Tragedy and Comedy.* A good deal has been re-written, and most of the more recent archaeological material and literary theory have been skilfully incorporated. It remains the best book of its kind. The minor festivals are dealt with in the first chapter.

POHLENZ, Max. Die griechische Tragödie, Erläuterungen. 2. neubearb. Aufl. Göttingen, Vandenhoeck & Ruprecht, 1954. 203p. **BB88**

AAHG VIII 1955 155–161 Webster • LEC XXIII 1955 450 Delande • AJPh LXXVII 1956 197–202 Lattimore

ROMILLY, Jacqueline de. La tragédie grecque. [2 éd. mise à jour. Paris], Presses universitaires de France, 1973. 192p. **BB89**

Collection SUP. Littératures anciennes. 1.

CR XXII 1972 419 Whittle • CPh LXIX 1974 56–58 Henry and Walker • ACR II 1972 192 Knox

A brief but excellent survey of Attic tragedy for the Greekless reader. Sophocles fares best in the individual chapters on the three great tragedians. The author is particularly sensitive to the moral or philosophical implications in the plays, but deals inadequately with metrics or theatrical effects. Appendices include useful chronological tables.

SNELL, Bruno. Scenes from Greek drama. Berkeley, University of California Press, 1964. 147p.
BB90

Sather classical lectures, v. 34.
Gnomon XXXVIII 1966 12–17 Lloyd-Jones • Phoenix XX 1966 170–172 Herington • AJPh LXXXVII 1966 233–237 O'Brien • CR n.s. XVI 1966 352–354 Lucas
A volume of Sather lectures devoted to fragments of the Greek tragedians in which, to the annoyance of some, Prof. Snell indulges his well-known penchant for Geistesgeschichte. In it we see at work the complementary talents that wrote *The Discovery of the Mind* and edited *Tragicorum Graecorum Fragmenta.*

VICKERS, Brian. Towards Greek tragedy: Drama, myth, society. London, Longman, 1973. xv, 658p., [4] plates, illus.   **BB91**

CW LXIX 1976 343–345 Herington
The first of a projected two-volume *Comparative Tragedy* by a Professor of English Literature at Zurich. The second volume will deal with tragedy down to the present. The first volume falls into three main sections: I. Tragedy and Reality, II. Tragedy and Myth, and III. Criticism of selected tragedies. The third section is the weakest, consisting in the main of undistinguished paraphrases of chosen plays. Among the appendices is a lengthy critique of Kirk's study on myth. Based on wide reading in the secondary literature, the work is over-ambitious.

WALCOT, Peter. Greek drama in its theatrical and social context. Cardiff, University of Wales Press, 1976. x, 112p.   **BB92**

CR XXVIII 1978 69–70 Collard • CW LXX 1977 473 Parry • G&R XXIV 1977 81 Ireland
This is a product of the author's teaching experience, replying to a host of practical questions, for example: How long did a performance take? Why messenger speeches?

WEBSTER, Thomas B. L. Greek tragedy. Oxford, Clarendon Press, 1971. 39p.   **BB93**

Greece and Rome: New surveys in the classics; v. 5.
Humanitas XXIII–XXIV 1971–1972 570–571 Louro Fonseca
Consists of an essay of introduction and three separate essays on the major tragedians, with attention to evidence from archaeology and papyrology as well as astute literary criticism.

WRIGHT, John Henry. Dancing in chains: The stylistic unity of the comoedia palliata. Rome, American Academy, 1974. xiii, 230p.   **BB94**

Papers and monographs of the American Academy in Rome; 25.
LEC XLIII 1975 441 Diez • G&R XXII 1975 195 Verity • JRS LXVI 1976 261–262 Willcock • CJ LXXII 1976 182–185 Hough
The thesis of this work is that the fragments of Ro-

man comedy form a continuity, with Terence standing outside the mainstream. The *Remains of Old Latin,* edited by Warmington, are shown to be very Plautine and formulaic.
The title is taken from Nietzsche and expresses the restraints of purely Roman dramatic convention within which these writers worked without being encumbered in their imagination. A most useful, conducted tour through the twelve authors of the *palliata* prior to Plautus, equally attentive to vocabulary, diction and versification. The fragmentary state of the evidence makes generalization difficult and hypotheses very tenuous, facts of which the author is very conscious, but the scrupulous examination of the fragments produces a satisfying picture of the common elements in the *vis comica.* There is an invaluable index locorum.

Satire

ANDERSON, W. S. "Recent work in Roman satire (1962–1968)." CW LXIII (1970): 181–194, 217–222. *idem* "(1968–1978)," CW LXXV (1982): 273–299.   **BB95**

Continues Anderson's earlier surveys, *CW* L (1956), 33–40, and *CW* LVII (1964), 293–301, 343–348. Arrangement is by subject, with brief summaries and comments.

COFFEY, Michael. Roman satire. London, Methuen; New York, Barnes & Noble, 1976. xvi, 289p.   **BB96**

CR XXVIII 1978 274–275 Smith • Gnomon LI 1979 183–185 Krenkel
Describes and evaluates the work of all the Roman satirists from their beginnings in the early 2nd century B.C. to the end of the reign of Hadrian. Shows the genre's vast range of subject and style and discusses briefly the rediscovery late in the sixteenth century of the true tradition of Roman satire and its subsequent development in English literature. For the major authors the matter is conveniently arranged in separate sections for biography, summaries, and topics such as style and transmission. A satisfactory replacement for Duff's *Roman Satire* (1937).

KNOCHE, Ulrich. Roman satire. Trans. by Edwin S. Ramage. Bloomington, Indiana University Press, [1975]. xi, 243p.   **BB97**

Translation of *Die römische Satire.*
CW LXX 1976 208–209 Green
First published in German in 1949, it clearly betrays its genesis in a university survey course. There are no illustrative quotations and in general it adds nothing to Duff, and falls short of van Rooy and Witke. There are bibliographical supplements for 1956–69 by W. Elers, and Ramage has brought these down to 1974.

McKAY, A. G. and SHEPPERD, D. M. Roman satire: Horace, Juvenal, Persius, Petronius and Seneca. Basingstoke, Macmillan; New York, St. Martin's Press, 1976. xi, 291p.   **BB98**

Latin text, English introd. and commentary.
Phoenix XXXI 1977 92–93 Rudd

This volume consists of twelve Horatian, two Persian, and seven Juvenalian satires, plus the *Apocolocyntosis* and parts of the *Cena Trimalchiomis,* preceded by a brief introduction.

To facilitate comparative study the pieces are arranged in nine groups, e.g., The Satirist on Banquets. There are mistakes and misinformation in the brief notes and commentary. A useful selection of texts nonetheless.

PRIMINGER, Alex Hardison, HARDISON, O. B., Jr. and KERRANE, Kevin, eds. Classical and Mediaeval Literary Criticism. New York, 1974. xiii, 529p. **BB99**

RAMAGE, Edwin S., SIGSBEE, David L. and FREDERICKS, Sigmund C. Roman satirists and their satire: The fine art of criticism in ancient Rome. Park Ridge, N.J., Noyes Press, [1974]. ix, 212p. **BB100**

RPh XLIX 1975 334 Cebe • REG LXXXIX 1976 653 Hellegouarc'h • Gnomon XLIX 1977 466–470 Konzeniewzki

Offered to 'the general reader' and (with much less justification) to 'the student and scholar of the classics,' this is a very superficial and conventional survey. Ramage deals with Ennius, Lucilius and Persius (cc. I, II, VI); Sigsbee, with Varro and Menippean satire, and Horace (cc. III and IV); and Fredericks with Seneca, Petronius and Juvenal (cc. V, VII). There is a concluding chapter on the *Nachleben* of satire, especially in English literature.

SULLIVAN, John Patrick. Satire; Critical essays on Roman literature. Bloomington, Indiana University Press, 1963. Reprint 1968. viii, 182p. **BB101**

First ed. published in 1963 under title: *Critical essays on Roman literature; Satire.*

CR XIV 1964 296–299 Kenney • RBPh XLII 1964 688 Bardon

Essays manifesting notable diversity and little unity of purpose. W. S. Anderson, in The Roman Socrates: Horace and his Satires, sees Horace as imposing restraint, discipline and a sense of responsibility on satire as it came from Lucilius. Nisbet's *Persius* is full of quotable, sound judgments. Sullivan's own Satire and Realism in Petronius is short, allusive and selective. H. A. Mason's Is Juvenal a Classic? had already appeared in *Arion.*

VAN ROOY, Charles A. Studies in classical satire and related literary theory. Leyden, E. J. Brill, 1966. 229p. **BB102**

AAHG XXIII 1970 19–21 Quadlbauer • CW LXIII 1970 181 Anderson

Discusses the much debated etymology of *satura,* and the development of the literary genre of the same name; the relationship between Ennius, Lucilius and Varro; the origin and validity of early Roman theories about satire; the fallacious link between *satura* and Greek satyr plays; and various confused theories in ancient and patristic writers.

WITKE, Charles. Latin satire; The structure of persuasion. Leyden, Brill, 1970. viii, 280p. **BB103**

CPh LXVIII 1973 146–148 Walker • CR XXIII 1973 42–44 Rudd • Gnomon XLV 1973 351–357 Anderson • Latomus XXXII 1973 195–199 Jocelyn

Examines successively Origins, The Greek Satirical Spirit, Horace, Persius, Juvenal, Petronius and three others, Theodulf of Orleans, and the Carolingian Renaissance, Hugh Primas of Orleans, Walter of Chatillon. Much modern scholarship on the classical authors is not utilized, and the style of the author is at times sub-literate, and there is a lack of critical rigour. The sub-title echoes the author's conviction that satire is primarily a form of persuasion toward a higher moral standard. The attempt to study the continuity of the genre to the twelfth century is laudable even if the result is disappointing. The book has many printing blemishes.

Rhetoric, Eloquence, Literary Criticism

ATKINS, John W. Literary criticism in antiquity. Gloucester, Mass., 1964. Peter Smith, 1934. Reprint 1961. 2 v. **BB104**

CR 1935 73–75 Tate • JHS LV 1935 267–268

A useful history of ancient literary criticism written with an eye mainly to the needs of students of English as a precursor to the study of modern literary criticism. Volume 1, Greek, comes down to the 2d century B.C. Volume 2 goes to the end of the 2d century A.D., stopping short of Aelius Aristides.

BENSON, Thomas W., and PROSSER, Michael H., eds. Readings in classical rhetoric. Bloomington, Indiana University Press, [1972]. xii, 339p. **BB105**

G&R XXI 1974 101 Walest • REG LXXXVII 1974 479 Bompaire • RSC XXI 1973 479–481 d'Agostins

English translation of the basic texts on rhetoric. The translations are borrowed from the best editions. The texts are often lengthy and show the continuity and coherence of ancient rhetorical traditions. The work is built around five major themes: Definition, value and object of rhetoric; Inventio—staseis and topoi; Arrangement—the parts of a speech; Style (this includes long excerpts from Demetrius and *On the Sublime*); Memory and elocution. A convenient source book.

BONNER, Stanley Frederick. Roman declamation in the late Republic and early Empire. Liverpool, University Press, 1969. viii, 177p. **BB106**

JRS XL 1950 156–157 Maguinness

First published in 1949, this is a well-compressed work, easy to read and showing both the underlying preposterousness of declamation and its laudable achievements, its influence for good and bad in Roman literature.

CAPLAN, Harry. Of eloquence; Studies in ancient and mediaeval rhetoric. Edited and with an introd. by Anne King and Helen North. Ithaca, [N.Y.], Cornell University Press, [1970]. xiii, 289p., illus.   **BB107**

AJPh XCV 1974 183–184 McCall • CR XXII 1972 363–364 Winterbottom • Speculum XLVI 1971 413
A volume of Caplan's *Kleine Schriften,* much of it outside the classical age. Early papers on the medieval theory of preaching could have profited from major revisions. The excellent introduction to Caplan's *Ad Herennium* in *LCC* is included. A useful complement to the Festschrift presented to Caplan, *The Classical Tradition,* edited by L. Wallach, 1966.

CLARKE, Martin Lowther. Rhetoric at Rome. New York, Barnes & Noble, [1963]. 203p.
                    BB108

CPh XLVIII 1953 265–266 Bruère • CR n.s. IV 1954 270–272 Bower • REL XXXI 1953 408–412 Boyancé
The theory and practice of rhetoric engrossed many of the most gifted Romans for five centuries and had an enormous influence on Roman education, literature, and culture. This is an excellent historical survey of the place of rhetoric in Roman life from Cato the Censor to Cassiodorus, especially good on the *Ad Herennium,* Cicero, and Quintilian. Thirty-three pages of footnotes support one hundred and sixty-four of text.

EISENHUT, Werner. Einführung in die antike Rhetorik und ihre Geschichte. Darmstadt, Wissenschaftliche Buchgesellschaft, 1974. 107p.
                    BB109

CPh LXX 1975 278–282 Kennedy • Gnomon XLIX 1977 722–724 Hommel • LEC XLIII 1975 213–214 Stenuit • REL LIII 1975 514 Michel
An introductory survey of Rhetoric from its beginnings to the beginning of the Middle Ages. A clear, readable, judicious account in which the focus of attention is on the history of rhetorical theory. The Greeks receive better treatment than the Romans. There are two concluding chapters on Greek and Latin rhetorical terminology, and a good bibliography. A special chapter is devoted to the renaissance of Greek and Roman rhetoric under Hadrian in the 2nd century A.D., and to rhetorical usage in the Fathers.

HELLWIG, Antje. Untersuchungen zur Theorie der Rhetorik bei Platon und Aristoteles. Göttingen, Vandenhoeck & Ruprecht, 1973. 374p.
                    BB110

Hypomnemata; Untersuchungen zur Antike und zu ihrem Nachleben; originally presented as the author's thesis, Bonn, 1970.

MH XXXIII 1976 57 Wehrli • JHS XCV 1975 204–205 Podlecki • Ph & Rh IX 1976 264–266 Ryan
The book is divided into four main sections—the definition of rhetoric, its material, its object and its subject (audience and speaker)—with each section subdivided into sections in which Aristotle's rhetorical theory is compared with Plato's. For the most part the treatment of Plato is more satisfactory. There is an exhaustive index locorum, and indices of subjects and the main Greek terms discussed.

KENNEDY, George A. The art of rhetoric in the Roman world, 300 B.C.–A.D. 300. Princeton, N.J., Princeton University Press, 1972. xvi, 658p.
                    BB111

A history of rhetoric; 2.
Gnomon XLVI 1974 87–89 Clarice • CW LXVII 1974 304–306 McCall • CR XXV 1975 64–66 Winterbottom
A well-written and copiously documented work on rhetoric down through Tertullian, though the upper and lower limits of the time frame are rather stretched. The central portion of the book with its chronological account of Cicero's speeches is perhaps the most valuable. A major work, displaying high competence and great powers of synthesis, and a worthy successor to the author's earlier *The Art of Persuasion in Greece,* Princeton, 1963. [See JHS LXXXVI 1966 189–190 Healy.] A third volume is called *Greek Rhetoric under Christian Emperors,* Princeton, Princeton University Press, 1983, xvii, 334p.

KENNEDY, George A. Classical rhetoric and its Christian and secular tradition from ancient to modern times. Chapel Hill, University of North Carolina Press, 1980. xii, 291p.   **BB112**

CW LXXXIII (1980): 372–373 Moreland
A brisk history of rhetoric from its beginnings in the oral tradition to the present. There are opening basic essays on primary rhetoric, technical, sophistic and philosophic rhetoric, laying the foundations for the chronological survey. An essential tool and worthy companion to the author's earlier *The art of persuasion in Greece* (Princeton University Press, 1963) and *The art of rhetoric in the Roman world, 300 B.C.–A.D. 300* (Princeton, 1972).

LANHAM, Richard A. A handlist of rhetorical terms; A guide for students of English literature. Berkeley, University of California Press, 1969. 48p.   **BB113**

CR XXIII 1973 99 Douglas
Addressed to students of English literature, but with the hope expressed that students of the classics may find the list useful. Light-hearted but useful.

LAUSBERG, Heinrich. Handbuch der literarischen Rhetorik: Eine Grundlegung d. Literaturwissenschaft. 2., durch e. Nachtr. vermehrte Auflage. Munich, Hueber, 1973. 2 v.   **BB114**

[1. Hauptband].–[2] Registerband.

RFIC XL 1962 312–315 Lana • CR XII 1962 246–247 Douglas • Latomus XX 1961 939–940 Préaux

Produced primarily for students of modern European literatures, this Handbook is an exhaustive compilation of ancient sources and illustrative passages. The excess of detail is intolerable and self-defeating and frequently, because of the complex pattern-making which Lausberg tries to create, misleading. The index alone runs to over 300 pages, the bibliography in v. 2, p.605–638.

LEEMAN, Anton D. Orationis ratio; The stylistic theories and practice of the Roman orators, historians and philosophers. Amsterdam, A. M. Hakkert, 1963. 2 v. **BB115**

AJPh LXXXVII 1966 237–241 Kennedy • Gnomon XXXVIII 1966 356–364 Fuhrmann

A valuable supplement to Norden's *Antike Kunstprosa*, 1898, which proposes to study Latin prose style, both practice and theory, from the mid-second century B.C. to the mid-second century A.D. Vol. 1 is divided into four main parts: The Archaic period, the Classical Period, the Early Empire, The Classicist and Archaist Periods. The great virtue of the work is its impressive collection of significant texts (translations are conveniently provided in vol. 2); its weakness is that it is too diffuse on theory and too short on practice. It is sparsely documented in the secondary literatures.

MARTIN, Josef. Antike Rhetorik, Technik und Methode. München, Beck, 1974. 420p. **BB116**

CPh LXX 1975 278–282 Kennedy • Gnomon XLVIII 1976 641–645 Wankel • JHS XCVI 1976 197–198 Usher • LEC XLIII 1975 305–306 van Esbroeck

Intended to replace Volkmann's standard work, HdA, 1885–1901, the work of Martin (who died in Nov. 1973 in his ninetieth year, having seen the proofs but not the published volume) is uneven, misleading in its general picture of the different parts of rhetoric—*inventio, disposito, elecutio, memoria, pronuntiatio*—is documented from about 160 authors (as against 78 in Volkmann). The four indexes, including passages cited, are provided by J. Hopp. There is no systematic bibliography.

McCALL, Marsh H. Ancient rhetorical theories of simile and comparison. Cambridge, Harvard University Press, 1969. xii, 272p. **BB117**

CW LXIV 1970 138 Grube • CJ LXIX 1974 268–271 Lefkowitz • Mnemosyne XXVI 1973 296–297 Schenkeveld • AJPh XCII 1971 360–361 De Lacy

An examination of the ancient theories from c.400 B.C. until the end of the first century A.D. provides a sound historical basis for the study of ancient development and usage of simile, metaphor and comparison.

MURPHY, James J. Medieval eloquence; Studies in the theory and practice of medieval rhetoric. Berkeley, University of California Press, 1978. xii, 354p. **BB118**

Speculum LIV 1979 641

Fourteen articles by different hands, with a preface by the editor. See also Murphy, James, *Rhetoric in the Middle Ages: A history of rhetorical theory from Saint Augustine to the Renaissance* (1974) and his *Rhetoric and rhetorical criticism* (Ann Arbor, 1977).

NEUMEISTER, Christoff. Grundsätze der forensischen Rhetorik; Gezeigt an Gerichtsreden Ciceros. München, Hueber, 1964. 207p. **BB119**

CR XV 1965 305–306 Douglas • CPh LXII 1967 56–59 Johnson • REL XLII 1964 566–569 Ruch

Outlines the principles of ancient forensic rhetoric and demonstrates their application in the speeches of Cicero. In practice it is shown that many of the detailed rules of the rhetoricians got broken. Forensic rhetoric is here separated from epideictic. A very sound introduction to Cicero's extraordinary psychological and literary skills as a forensic orator, and a good handbook on the fundamental principles of rhetoric.

RAYMENT, C. S. "A current survey of ancient rhetoric." CW LII (1958–1959): 75–80, 82–84, 86–91. **BB120**

Continued in "Ancient rhetoric (1957–1963)," *CW* LVII (1964), 241–251.

See now *The Classical World bibliography of philosophy, religion, and rhetoric*. Ed. with a new introd. by Donlan, W. New York, Garland Publ., 1978. xvi, 396p.

CW Bibliographies, Garland Reference Libraries of the Humanities, XCV.

RUSSELL, D. A. and WINTERBOTTOM, M. Ancient Literary Criticism. The Principal Texts in New Translations. Oxford, Clarendon Press, 1972. xvi, 607p. **BB121**

SMITH, Robert Wayne. The art of rhetoric in Alexandria; Its theory and practice in the ancient world. The Hague, Martinus Nijhoff, 1974. xii, 168p. **BB122**

UEDING, Gert. Einführung in die Rhetorik; Geschichte, Technik, Methode. Stuttgart, Metzler, 1976. xii, 352p. **BB123**

Latomus XXXVIII 1979 544–546 Cousin

The History and Influence of the Classical Tradition

CA GENERALIA AND SURVEYS

BOECKH, August. Encyclopädie und Methodologie der philologischen Wissenschaften. Ed. E. Bratuscheck. Leipzig, 1877. 2 ed., R. Klussmann, 1886. 824p.   **CA1**

August Boeckh, the greatest of Wolf's pupils, lectured on the *Encyclopädie der Philologie* at the University of Berlin during 26 semesters in the period 1809–1865. His final classification appears here.

BOLGAR, R. R. The classical heritage and its beneficiaries. Cambridge, Cambridge University Press, 1954, 1973. viii, 591p.   **CA2**

Hermathena LXXXVI 1955 40–43 Stanford • REA LXXVII 1975 423–426 Fontaine • CW XLVIII 1955 119 Stahl • CR n.s. VI 1956 59–63 Tate • Gnomon XXVIII 1956 63–66 Hutton

In this elaborate work on the influence of classical authors through the Middle Ages and Renaissance, Dr. Bolgar's focus is on the educational backgrounds of each age, the extent of the knowledge of classical authors, the availability of their works, the manner in which they were interpreted, the methods of instruction in schools, the intellectual level of the elite, and the degrees of literacy among the lower classes. The work is based on wide reading in the original authors, some of them very arcane, and extensive bibliographies, reference works, library catalogs, etc. A notable contribution.

D[UFF], J. W. "Scholarship in modern times. (a) Renaissance to 1800." OCD (1949): 799–802.
                                    CA3

D[UFF], J. W. "Scholarship in modern times. (b) 19th and 20th centuries." OCD (1949): 802–812.
                                    CA4

GIARRATANO, Cesare. "La storia della Filologia Classica." Introduzione II: 595–672.
                                    CA5

A concise chronological survey, in 15 sections, through pre-Alexandrian, Alexandrian and post-Alexandrian, the Middle Ages, Humanism, to Italian philology in the 16th–18th centuries, the French period, French philology in the 17th–18th centuries, the Dutch period (beginning with the foundation of Leyden University, 1575), the English period (beginning with Bentley, 1662–1742), the German period, philologists of Denmark, Holland and Belgium (notably Madvig, Cobet and di Maestrick), English philologists of the 18th–19th centuries (down to Grote and Leake), French philologists of the 18th–19th centuries, and Italian philologists of the 18th–19th centuries.

GUDEMANN, Alfred. Grundriss der Geschichte der Klassischen Philologie. Stuttgart, Teubner, 1967. vi, 260p.   **CA6**

Reprint of the 2d enl. ed. published in Leipzig in 1909. Originally published in Boston, 1892, under title: *Syllabus on the history of classical philology.*

Gives a brief but critical characterization of the work of each period, concentrating on the really significant scholars and their contributions. Contains a useful catalog of the oldest and most important MSS of classical authors. There is a U.S.A. 1902 translation, *Outlines of the history of classical philology.*

HIGHET, Gilbert. The classical tradition; Greek and Roman influences on Western literature. [1st ed. reprinted] with corrections. London and New York, Oxford University Press, 1949, 1967. xxxviii, 763p.   **CA7**

Oxford paperback; 141.

CR n.s. I 1951 42–45 Thomson • Phoenix IV 1950 70–72 Norwood • Gnomon XXIII 1951 121–125 Curtius

A magnificent book, written with gusto and enthusiasm, which ranges widely over Greek and Latin influences on English (and American), French, Italian, German and Spanish literatures, with a preponderant amount of space devoted to English writers. Recent and contemporary literature receive gratifying attention. Much more than a handbook, this is a work of original thought and constructive art. The author's prejudices show in his treatment of the 19th century and in his barbs at German scholarship.

IMMISCH, Otto. Wie studiert man klassische Philologie; Ein Überblick über Entwicklung, Wesen und Ziel der Altertumswissenschaft nebst Ratschlägen zur zweckmässigen Anordnung des Studiengangs. 2 ed. Stuttgart, Violet, 1920. 160p. **CA8**

IRMSCHER, Johannes. Praktische Einführung in das Studium der Altertumswissenschaft. Berlin, Dt. Verlag der Wiss., 1954. 141p. **CA9**

A comprehensive introduction from a Soviet standpoint. See also Irmscher, J., "Klassische Philologie in der Deutschen Demokratischen Republik," *Philologus* CXIX (1975), 126–137.

KROLL, Wilhelm. Geschichte der klassischen Philologie. Berlin, de Gruyter, 1908. 2 ed., 1919. **CA10**

Samml. Göschen; 367.

Brief survey of Antiquity, the Middle Ages and Modern Times. Antiquity is subdivided into The Preliminary Stages, Alexandrian Philology, The Stoic and Post-Alexandrian Philology and The Epigoni (from the end of the 1st century B.C. to the end of Antiquity). The section on the Middle Ages is all too brief. Modern Times is subdivided into Humanism, The Rebirth of Philology (French and Anglo-Dutch philology), and The New Humanism and Altertumswissenschaft from Winckelmann to the Present.

MOMIGLIANO, Arnaldo. Contributo alla storia degli studi classici e del mundo antico. Roma, 1955. 414p. **CA11**

Latomus XV 1956 712 Renard • JHI XVI 1955 426

A collection of essays and reviews from widely scattered sources. There have been several successive volumes; cf. *Quinto contributo alla storia degli studi classici e del mundo antico.* 2 v. 1064p.; *Sesto contributo,* 2 v. in 1 (1980), 879p.

PADGUG, R. A. "Select bibliography on Marxism and the study of antiquity." Arethusa VIII (1975): 199–201. **CA12**

PECK, Harry Thurston. A history of classical philology from the 7th century B.C. to the 20th century A.D. New York, 1911. **CA13**

This has a useful bibliographical index (p.401–476), but the work itself is rather superficial and confusing.

PFEIFFER, Rudolf. A history of classical scholarship; From the beginnings to the end of the Hellenistic Age. Oxford, Clarendon Press, 1968. xviii, 318p. **CA14**

RFIC CIV 1976 98–117 Rossi • AC XLII 1973 689–690 Lévêque

Traces the foundations of classical scholarship laid by Greek poets and scholars in the last three centuries B.C. Details the achievements of five generations of scholars in Alexandria and their *epigoni* down to the age of Augustus. Scholarship is defined (p.3) as the art of understanding, explaining and restoring the literary tradition. The treatment of scholars like Zenodotus, Callimachus, Eratosthenes, Aristophanes of Byzantium and Aristarchus is exemplary. The study of history and art is, however, strangely neglected in what should be a comprehensive history of all the influences contributing to cultural change.

PFEIFFER, Rudolf. A history of classical scholarship from 1300 to 1850. Oxford, Clarendon Press, 1976. ix, 213p. **CA15**

CR XXVIII 1978 131–134 Kenney • G&R XXIV, 1 1977 98 Walcot • AC XLVI 1977 376–377 Mund-Dopchie

Following a suggestion of Eduard Fraenkel, Pfeiffer in his *History* passes straight from the Augustan age to the Italian Renaissance. His work is divided into four parts: The Renewal of Classical Scholarship in the Italian Renaissance; Humanism and Scholarship in the Netherlands and in Germany; From the French Renaissance to German Neo-hellenism; German Neo-hellenism. The study of the Italian Renaissance goes from Petrarch and Boccaccio through five generations to Politian. Erasmus is the dominant figure in part II, Bentley in part III. German Neo-hellenism was initiated by Winckelmann and continued by Wolf. A surprisingly slim work but with a wealth of information not readily available in a single volume elsewhere.

SANDYS, John Edwin. A history of classical scholarship. Cambridge, Cambridge University Press, 1903–1908. **CA16**

Volume 1, 3rd ed., 1921; v. 2–3, 1908 (1958).

The standard detailed history of classical scholarship. Volume 1 covers from the 6th century B.C. to the end of the Middle Ages; v. 2. from the Revival of learning to the end of the 18th century—except Germany; v. 3. the 18th century in Germany and the 19th century in Europe and the U.S.A.

SANDYS, John Edwin. A short history of classical scholarship from the sixth century B.C. to the present day. Cambridge, 1915. xvi, 455p. **CA17**

JHS XXXVI 1916 122 • JRS VI 1916 218 Hall • CPh XI 1916 Wright • CJ XI 1915 126 Scoggin

A highly successful abridgement of the three-volume classic, 1629 pages reduced to 455. Lesser scholars are omitted and a large quantity of minor detail from the notes. A readable conspectus of classical scholarship from Peisistratus to Jebb and Mommsen. Short bibliographies of the chief classical writers are included in the admirable index.

WILAMOWITZ-MOELLENDORFF, U. von. Geschichte der Philologie. Leipzig, 1927. 90p.
CA18

In Gercke–Norden, *Einleitung;* 1.1.
A brilliant sketch, stimulating and penetrating, in 80 pages.
See now Wilamowitz-Moellendorff, U. von., *History of classical scholarship,* translated by A. Harris, ed., with introd. and notes by H. Lloyd-Jones. London, Duckworth, 1982. xxxii, 189p. (AJPh CIV 1983 108–111 Calder • G&R XXX 1983 110–111 Walcot • CR XXXIII 1983 376 Kenney • RPh LVII 1983 147 Weil).

CB   SPECIFIC TIME PERIODS AND COUNTRIES

Antiquity and Early Christianity

CLARKE, Martin Lowther. Higher education in the ancient world. Albuquerque, University of New Mexico Press, 1971. ix, 188p. illus.
CB1

JRS LXIII 1973 268–270 Bonner • JHS XCII 1972 214 Usher
For Clarke, the general plan of ancient education was based on the seven liberal arts which in turn were subordinate to philosophy, the normal coping-stone of higher education. The seven propaedeutic arts get brief attention, and about one-third of the book is devoted to the educational activities of the various philosophical schools. The work pays too much attention to philosophy and too little to rhetoric, distorting the picture.

GRAEFENHAN, Ernst Friedrich A. Geschichte der klassischen Philologie im Altertum. Bonn, König, 1843–1850. 4 v.
CB2

HADAS, Moses. Ancilla to classical reading. Columbia paperback ed. 1961. New York, Columbia University Press, [1961, 1954]. 397p.
CB3

CW L 1956 86 • CPh L 1955 217–218 Kendrick • CR n.s. VI 1956 160–161 Hudson Williams
The book is divided into two parts. The first entitled Production, Reception and Preservation deals with the manner in which classical literature was committed to writing and made available to the public, the nature of the criticism it engendered in the ancient world and its treatment by scholars and others in later ages. Matters relating to Greek writers are dealt with at greater length than those relating to Roman writers. The second part is entitled Literary Gossip and attempts to supplement information usually given in histories of literature by quoting and discussing the comments of ancient writers on the great literary figures of the Greek and Roman world and their writings. The many errors make it a dubious guide.

H[ENRY], R. M. "Scholarship, Latin, in antiquity." OCD² (1970): 960.
CB4

Latin scholarship began in Rome with the visit of Crates of Mallos (c.168 B.C.), and continued with L. Accius (170–c.85), L. Aclius Stilo Praeconinus of Lanuvium (c.154–c.74), M. Terentius Varro (116–127), P. Nigidius Figulus (98–45), C. Julius Hyginus (64 B.C.–A.D. 17).

L[OCKWOOD], J. F. and B[ROWNING], R. "Scholarship, Greek, in Antiquity." OCD² (1970): 959–960.
CB5

The prerequisites for scholarship became available with the founding of the library of Alexandria whose holdings in papyrus rolls grew from 200,000 c.285 B.C. to 700,000 in the 1st century B.C. The successive librarians, Zenodotus, Aristophanes and Callimachus, were learned scholars.

Medieval

BOLGAR, R. R., ed. Classical influences on European culture A.D. 500–1500. London, Cambridge University Press, 1969. xvi, 320p., 12 plates.
CB6

JHS XCII 1972 259–260 McGurk • REL L 1972 451–453 Michel • CR XXIII 1973 203–206 Clarke
A 1969 conference organized at King's College, Cambridge, by L. P. Wilkinson and R. R. Bolgar yields this handsome volume of 27 papers. Bolgar's introduction summarizes and comments on the results of the conference. E. J. Kenney's paper deals with the limitations of humanistic scholarship in the field of textual study and editing. Memorable contributions include B. Bischoff, Living with the Satirists; P. Courcelle, La Survie Comparée des Confessions Augustiniennes et de la Consolation Boécienne; and L. Bieler, The Classics in Celtic Ireland.

CURTIUS, Ernst Robert. European literature and the Latin Middle Ages. Trans. by Willard R. Trask. Princeton, Princeton University Press, 1967. xv, 662p.
CB7

Bollingen series; v. 36. Trans. of *Europäische Literatur und lateinisches Mittelalter.*

Latomus IX 1950 99–102 Préaux • JPh LXX 1949 425–431 Spitzer

By 1930 Curtius had acquired an international reputation as a critic of civilization on a par with Thomas Mann or T. S. Eliot. His range of interest, modern, medieval and ancient, was extraordinary and his main focus the continuity of literary traditions from late antiquity to modern literature. The present encyclopedic work offers a collection of topoi (traditional patterns of expression and artistic devices) followed through in all occidental languages from antiquity through the Middle Ages to the Renaissance. The work is based on 25 important studies published by the author between 1932 and 1944. Curtius writes with great erudition and urbanity (even when he is indulging in polemic). This work has long been regarded as an important landmark in the study of comparative literature.

Renaissance

BOLGAR, R. R., ed. Classical influences on European culture A.D. 1500–1700. Proceedings of an international conference held at King's College, Cambridge. Cambridge, Cambridge University Press, 1976. xviii, 383p., illus.   **CB8**

G&R XXIV 1977 98–99 Walcot

Contains 27 papers from the second international conference on classical influences, held in Cambridge in 1974, with a masterly introduction by Bolgar. The main areas covered were neo-Latin satire and verse, the arts of discourse, religion, political thought and technology and the fine arts, but not science. A clear picture emerges of the contributions made by the humanists to the new Europe which developed during the second half of the Renaissance, and there are useful pointers to areas that need further research.

Chapter 1: 1500–1700; The Bibliographical Problem. A Continental S.T.C. is an eloquent plea that some of the energy still lavished on incunables might be deflected to books published between 1500 and (say) 1700. Of the libraries with very large holdings of such books only one—the British Library—has a complete printed catalogue. We are further indebted to the British Library for Short Title Catalogs (S.T.C.): Spain (London, 1921); France, Portugal (1924, 1940); Spanish America (1962); Netherlands, etc. (1965). A colossal amount of capital has already been invested in bits and pieces of cataloguing. The problem deserves coordinated action, on a European scale at least.

BUCK, August G. Die Rezeption der Antike in den römanischen Literaturen der Renaissance. [1. Aufl.] Berlin, Schmidt, 1976. 251p.   **CB9**

Grundlagen der Romanistik; 8.
Gnomon XLIX 1977 689–693 Krautter

BURSIAN, Konrad. Geschichte der klassischen Philologie in Deutschland von den Anfängen bis zur Gegenwart. München, 1883.   **CB10**

Great Britain and Ireland

ANDERSON, Warren D. Matthew Arnold and the classical tradition. Ann Arbor, University of Michigan Press, 1971, 1965. x, 293p.   **CB11**

Ann Arbor paperback; AA 177.
Arion V 1966 254–262 Ebel • CPh LXI 1966 192–194 Walker

The subject is twofold: the influence of Arnold's classical reading on his poetry, and the interpretation of the classical tradition which he gave in his prose works. His knowledge of the classics, studied at Winchester, Rugby and Oxford, was wide and detailed, thanks in great part to the pedagogical goals and methods of his father, Thomas Arnold. There are good chapters on Homer and translation, and on Arnold's criticism of Greek tragedy. The work as a whole is extremely thorough, showing a great sureness of touch in handling not only classical literature but the history of classical studies. For anyone interested in Arnold, or the Victorians, or the history of ideas in the 19th century it is indispensable. See also Ebel, H., "Matthew Arnold and classical culture," *Arion* IV (1965), 188–220.

BRADEN, Gordon. The classics and English Renaissance poetry; Three case studies. New Haven, Yale University Press, 1978. xv, 303p.   **CB12**

Yale studies in English; 187.
A reexamination of the cliché of criticism which states that Renaissance literature began with, and remained, deeply influenced by the "discovery" of classical antiquity. The work of Arthur Golding and Robert Herrick is examined.

BOLTON, Whitney F. A history of Anglo-Latin literature, 597–1066. Princeton, Princeton University Press, 1967– .   **CB13**

Volume I. 597–740 A.D.
CR XX 1970 54–57 Walsh • Gnomon XL 1968 796–799 Löfstedt • Latomus XXVII 1968 913–915 Kerlouegan

Chiefly useful for its catalog of all the works of each known author and a comprehensive bibliography of the modern scholarship (p.229–293). Greatly vitiated by inaccurate translations of chosen passages. Directed primarily toward students of Old English. Bede gets deservedly wide coverage (p.101–185), as do his lesser-known contemporaries. A second volume is promised.

CLARKE, Martin Lowther. Classical education in Britain, 1500–1900. Cambridge, Cambridge University Press, 1945. 255p.   **CB14**

CJ LV 1960 284–285 Arnott • Gnomon XXXI 1959 464–469 Plumptre • LEC XXVII 1959 322 Moutet

A detailed and affectionate survey of the whole course of classical education from the Tudor humanists to the giants of the 19th century. The emphasis is mostly on England, with some attention to Scotland, Wales and Trinity College, Dublin. The upper date of the title almost coincides with the first visit of Erasmus in 1499. The analysis of typical school curriculum is fascinating.

CLARKE, Martin Lowther. Greek studies in England, 1700–1830. Cambridge, Cambridge University Press, 1959. 233p. **CB15**

KALLENDORF, Craig. Latin influences on English literature from the Middle Ages to the eighteenth century: An annotated bibliography of scholarship, 1945–1979. New York, London, Garland Publishing, 1982. xvi, 141p. **CB16**

Garland Reference Library of the Humanities; 345.
CW LXXIX 1985 67 Yates
Updates notes found in Gilbert Highet's *The Classical Tradition.*

LLOYD-JONES, Hugh. Greek studies in modern Oxford; An inaugural lecture, 23 May 1961. Oxford, Clarendon, 1961. 27p. **CB17**

A short account of Greek studies in Oxford from the beginning of the 19th century. The 18th century, it appears, was singularly barren: "from 1711 the Chair [Regius Professor of Greek] was held for an entire century, with one interruption of four years, by men educated at Westminster and Christ Church. If these men had other qualifications, they have left no proof of them in print." The inaugural is full of interesting remarks on Gaisford, Conington, Jowett, Pattison, Bywater, Murray, the influx of emigré scholars from Hitler's Germany, and the author's predecessor, Dodds. The inaugural also takes a thoughtful look at the present and future of classical studies.

McCONICA, James Kelsey. English humanists and Reformation politics under Henry VIII and Edward VI. Oxford, Clarendon Press, 1965. xii, 340p. **CB18**

A popular account including Bentley, Porson, Parr, Ruddimar and Adam.

OGILVIE, R. M. Latin and Greek; A history of the influence of the classics on English life from 1600 to 1918. London, Routledge and Kegan Paul, 1964. xiv, 189p. **CB19**

Arion III, 4 1964 127–136 Sullivan • CR XV 1965 106–108 Clarke • CW LVIII 1964 122 Latimer
More a collection of essays than a history, investigating "certain trends which can be observed in the popularity of classical authors from time to time." This yields rather oversimplified chapter headings: Horace and the Eighteenth Century, Thucydides and the Victorians. Too much is attributed to the influence of the chosen author as typical of the age.

STANFORD, William Bedell. Ireland and the classical tradition. Dublin, Figgis, 1976. 275p. **CB20**

Hermathena CXXII 1977 70–73 Bond

A lively and scholarly account of the far-reaching and varied effects of the classical tradition in Irish life, thought, literature, politics and morality, from the earliest times down to the present century.

STANFORD, William Bedell. Towards a history of classical influences in Ireland. Dublin, Royal Irish Academy, 1970. 79p. **CB21**

(PRIA LXX, Sect. C. 1970 13–91.)
CR LXXXVII 1973 78–80 Clarke
A preliminary survey of the influences of classical antiquity upon Ireland and Irish culture since the 5th century. A thorough and well-documented survey, covering not only classical scholarship and education, but also classical influences on both Irish and Anglo-Irish literature.

WEISS, Roberto. Humanism in England during the 15th century. Oxford, Blackwell, 1941. Rev. ed., 1957. **CB22**

JThS XLIII 1942 114–115 Previté-Orton

Germany

FÜHRMANN, M. Die Antike und ihre Vermittler. Bemerkungen zur gegenwärtigen Situation der klassischen Philologie. Konstanz, Univ. Verl., 1969. 43p. **CB23**

CR XX 1970 384–387 Lloyd-Jones • Gnomon XLII 1970 507–514 Schmid
Frustration at the decline of classical studies in Germany in the middle of the 20th century is all the more acute in the wake of the preeminent position enjoyed by Germany in the study of antiquity through the previous century. Führmann in his inaugural lecture in the new University of Constance analyzes the causes for the decline and proposes some remedies: a better *modus vivendi* of classics with Catholicism and socialism, and a more integrated program of ancient and modern studies.

HENTSCHKE, Ada Babette and MUHLACK, Ulrich. Einführung in die Geschichte der klassischen Philologie. Darmstadt, Wissenschaftliche Buchgesellschaft, 1972. 150p. **CB24**

Die Altertumswissenschaft.
HZ CCXVIII 1974 645–646 Wülfing • REL LII 1974 426–428 Choumarat • RPh LXIX 1975 139 des Places
This work, narrower than its title, seeks to trace the history of classical philology in Germany, to describe its objectives, meaning and results, and to show its interrelationship with the science of history. The study begins with Beatus Rhenanus (1485–1547), and continues through Scaliger (1540–1609), Vico (1669–1744) and Wilhelm von Humboldt (1767–1835). Neohumanism began with Frederick Augustus Wolf (1759–1824) and continued with Boeckh (1785–1867), friend of Hegel and student of Schleiermacher. Two generations later the dominant influence is Wilamowitz

(1848–1931) and later still the more humane Werner Jaeger (1888–1961). The present crisis in classical studies has called forth this sensible diagnosis of the decline and fall from a collaboration of historians and classicists, a model, perhaps, for other countries.

Other Countries

DEMETRIUS, James K. Greek scholarship in Spain and Latin America. With an introd. on the history of Greek scholarship in Spain by Lluis Nicolau D'Olwer, and a preface by Phil Conley. Chicago, Argonaut, 1965. 144p. **CB25**

CW LIX 1966 324 Gloeckner • Helmantica XVII 1966 154–156 Rodríguez • REG LXXIX 1966 572 Weil
A bibliographic guide to articles, books, theses, and privately printed and ready-for-press items dealing with Hispanic-Hellenic studies. Supplements and updates data already available in Legrand's *Bibliographie hispano-grecque.* Approximately 2500 entries are classified into ten sections, including Byzantine Studies and Modern Greek-Spanish Studies.

DYER, Robert R. "Classical studies in Australia and New Zealand." AC XXXIV (1965): 554–570. **CB26**

An interesting account of the many native classical scholars produced by Australia and New Zealand, the scholars from abroad who have helped develop a lively interest in the classics in the 18 local universities, a clear picture of the school and university system, and indications of the diversity in published research.

HANSEN, Peter A. A bibliography of Danish contributions to classical scholarship from the sixteenth century to 1970. Copenhagen, Rosenkilde and Bagger, 1977. xviii, 335p. **CB27**

Danish humanist texts and studies; 1.
Gnomon LI 1979 778–780 Alpers

JUREWICZ, O., ed. L'Antiquité classique au cours des 25 années de la Republique Populaire de Pologne. 1974. **CB28**

RUBIO, David. Classical scholarship in Spain. Washington, D.C., Mimeoform Press, 1934. 205p. **CB29**

North America

EADIE, John W., ed. Classical traditions in early America; Essays by Meyer Reinhold . . . [et al.]; commentary by J. G. A. Pocock. Ann Arbor, Center for Coordination of Ancient and Modern Studies, University of Michigan, 1976. xvi, 265p. **CB30**

Essays presented at an interdisciplinary conference sponsored by the Center and held October 29–November 1, 1975.

GUMMERE, Richard Mott. The American colonial mind and the classical tradition; Essays in comparative culture. Cambridge, Mass., Harvard University Press, 1963. xiii, 228p. **CB31**

CR XV 1965 132–133 Clarke • CW LVIII 1965 129–132 Latimer • Gnomon XXXVIII 1966 637–638 Calder
Gummere's papers, hitherto scattered in many journals, are here collected in a vigorous, readable volume. Important essay topics include the dominance of Greek and Latin in colonial education, the classical ancestry of the Constitution, and the correspondence of two American presidents, John Adams and Thomas Jefferson, on such topics as Greek metrics and Ciceronian vocabulary.

REINHOLD, Meyer, ed. The classick pages; Classical reading of 18th century Americans. American Philological Assoc., Pennsylvania State University, 1975. xvii, 239p. **CB32**

CJ LXXII 1976–1977 168 MacKendrick • CW LXXI, 2 1977 140–142 Wiltshire
The introduction provides a succinct survey of the "cult of antiquity" in early America with a look at school curricula, bookholding patterns, the matter of translations and the utilitarian emphasis in classical learning. Books on classical subjects comprised an average of only 10 to 12 percent of the holdings in major libraries.

CC INDIVIDUAL CLASSICAL SCHOLARS

CALDER, W. M. "Schliemann on Schliemann; A study in the use of sources." GRBS XIII (1972): 335–353. **CC1**

The study reveals an unscrupulous archaeologist deliberately inventing several important events and falsifying information about many others.

CALDER, William M., III, ed. Ulrick von Wilamowitz-Moellendorff: Selected correspondence, 1869–1931. Naples, Jovene Editore, 1983. xii, 329p., photos. **CC2**

Antiqua 23.
See also Calder, W. M. "Ulrich von Wilamowitz-

Moellendorff; An unpublished autobiography." *GRBS* XII (1971): 561–577.

Text, translation, commentary and illustrations.

CAMPOREALE, Salvatore I. Lorenzo Valla; Umanesimo e teologia. Presentazione di Eugenio Garin. Firenze, Nella sede dell'Istituto, 1972. ix, 554p. **CC3**

At head of title: Istituto nazionale di studi sul Rinascimento.
Augustinus XX 1975 208 Orosio

CLARKE, Martin Lowther. George Grote; A biography. [London], University of London, Athlone Press, 1962. 196p., 7 plates. **CC4**

Mnemosyne XVII 1964 218 Hulshoff Pol • REG LXXVIII 1965 643 Lévêque
Chapters I–IV cover Grote's life, c.V–VI his historical and philosophical work, c.VII Grote and university education, and c.VIII his character and views. A somewhat limited biography, but interesting for the light it sheds on his political views, tutored as he was by Bentham and James Mill, his substantial contribution to English politics and the University of London, and the gestation of his monumental *History of Greece* in 12 v. (1846–1857).

DIGGLE, J. and GOODYEAR, F. R. D., eds. The classical papers of A. E. Housman. Cambridge, 1972. 3 v. I. (1882–1897), 440p.; II. (1897–1914), 480p.; III. (1915–1936), 412p. **CC5**

The complete collection of the classical papers, articles, notes and reviews of Housman, published in widely spread and sometimes difficult-to-obtain journals.

DODDS, Eric R. Missing persons: An autobiography. Oxford, Clarendon Press, 1977. 202p., [4] leaves of plates. **CC6**

CR XXIX 1979 132–134 Levi • TLS LXXVI 1977 1311 Lyons
Interesting for the light it sheds on the early education of a recent Regius Professor of Greek at Oxford and for the intellectual honesty with which it is written.

EDWARD Gibbon and the *Decline and fall of the Roman Empire.* Edited by G. W. Bowersock, J. Clive and S. R. Graubard. Cambridge, Harvard University Press, 1977. xii, 257p. **CC7**

G&R XXV 1978 98 Walcot • NYRB XXIV No. 16 1977 7–9 Badian
Eighteen papers from a 1976 Rome conference celebrating the 200th anniversary of the publication of v. 1 of *The decline and fall.* Contributors include Peter Brown, Runciman, Momigliano and Owen Chadwick.

GOW, A. S. F. A. E. Housman; A sketch. Cambridge, Cambridge University Press, 1936. 137p. **CC8**

CR LI 1937 80 Fordyce • CW XXX 1937 135 Harrington • REG 1937 262 des Places

Housman has an unenviable reputation as the *enfant terrible* of classical scholarship in modern Britain. His studied reticence and remoteness in life have not made the biographer's task easy. The biographer here paints a faithful likeness of a proud and lonely figure, the greatest of English Latinists.

GRAFTON, A. Joseph Scaliger. A study in the history of classical scholarship. I. Textual criticism and exegesis. Oxford, Clarendon Press, 1983. xi, 359p. **CC9**

Oxford-Warburg Studies.
TLS LXXXII 1983 871 Kenney

HERTZ, Martin. Karl Lachmann; Eine Biographie. Osnabrück, Biblio Verlag, 1972. xliii, 255p. **CC10**

Reprint of the Berlin ed., 1851.
JHS LXIX 1949 110, LXXIII 1953 146 • JHS LXXX 1960 196 Ehrenberg, XCV 1975 310
A magnificent biography in six volumes of the great 19th century Swiss historian, who was equally at home with the ancient Greeks, the history of Christianity, and the Italian Renaissance. Pupil of Ranke and Boeckh and friend in later life of Nietzsche, he was one of the most humane of classical scholars, with great universalist competence as historian and great sensitivity as art historian.

KAEGI, W. Jacob Burckhardt. Eine Biographie. III. Die Zeit der klassischen Werke. Basel, Schwabe, 1956. xxiv, 769p., 32 plates. **CC11**

JHS LXXX 1960 196 Ehrenberg

PAGE, Denys L. Richard Porson 1759–1808. London University Press, 1960. 16p. **CC12**

From the *Proceedings of the British Academy* XLV (1959), 221–236. Readers of *Recollections of the table-talk of Samuel Rogers to which is added Porsoniana* (London, 1856) will know that porter was Porson's favorite beverage at breakfast, that he often sat up drinking all night with no apparent after-effects, and that he would drink ink rather than not drink at all. Elected Professor of Greek at Cambridge in 1793, he proved to be the greatest since Bentley (1662–1742), chiefly in Greek drama and metrics, but also renowned for establishing the spuriousness of the *Comma Ioanneum* (1 In. 5, 7, 8). See also M. L. Clarke, *R. Porson; A bibliographical essay* (1937).

RICHMOND, John. James Henry of Dublin; Physician, versifier, pamphleteer, wanderer, and classical scholar. Blackrock, The author, 1976. 64p. **CC13**

CR XXVIII 1978 389 Ogilvie
Henry was one of the most colorful commentators on Virgil; his *Aeneidea* remains a marvellous repository of information on manuscripts, geography, social customs, etc. He gave up medical practice in Dublin at the age of 47 and spent the next 20 years of his life

in European travel, crossing the Alps many times on foot in search of *Aeneidea*. This short study shows him an engaging, if eccentric, scholar with many interests.

STANFORD, W. B. and McDOWELL, R. B. Mahaffy; A biography of an Anglo-Irishman. London, Routledge & Kegan Paul, 1971. xiv, 281p.
                                                            CC14

> CPh LXVII 1972 61–63 Bruère
> An extremely readable biography of a very productive and controversial Irish classicist who became a junior fellow of Trinity College, Dublin, in 1864 and died as provost of the same college in 1919. A history of classics at Trinity at that period emerges and also (since Mahaffy was a great socialite) a history of the Anglo-Irish ascendancy in Dublin up to and including the rebellion of 1916.

WHITE, Reginald J. Dr. Bentley; A study in academic scarlet. London, Eyre & Spottiswode, 1965. 303p.   **CC15**

> CR XVI 1966 248 Kenney • EHR LXXXII 1967 401 Lloyd-Jones
> R. C. Jebb's *Bentley* was first published in 1882, and the standard *Life of Richard Bentley* by James Henry Monk appeared in 1830. The present work does not purport to add much to these, except (and even this is questionable) from the viewpoint of the historian of education and ideas, inasmuch as Bentley "was something other than (one hesitates to say more than) a

genius of classical learning." White is more interested in Bentley's eccentricities and stormy career in academic politics than in his lasting contributions to classical scholarship, especially historical criticism. Gossipy and not very cleverly flippant.

WICKERT, L. Theodor Mommsen; Eine Biographie.   **CC16**

> Bd. I: Lehrjahre 1817–1844, Frankfurt, Klostermann, 1959, 580p. Bd. II: Wanderjahre, Frankrèich und Italien. Frankfurt, Klostermann, 1964, xvi, 446p.; Bd. III: Wanderjahre. Leipzig, Zurich, Breslau, Berlin, 1969; Bd. IV: Grösse und Grenzen, Frankfurt, Klostermann, 1980, x, 390p.
> HZ CXCI 1960 597–600 Meyer • Latomus XIX 1960 860–863 Harmand
> The professor of ancient history at the University of Cologne and editor of *CIL* here fulfills a longstanding assignment from the Mommsen committee. An enormous correspondence between the young Mommsen and his family was assembled by Wickert, who also conducted interviews with surviving relatives and pupils. The resulting work is an exhaustive and definitive monument to the great scholar. The first of the three volumes brings us down to his doctorate in law, *summa cum laude* and his embarkation on a decisive trip to Paris and Florence.
> See also Kucynski, J., *Theodor Mommsen. Porträt eines Gesellschaftswissenschaftlers.* Berlin, Akademie-Verlag, 1978. 277p. (Stud. zu einer Gesch. der Gesellschaftswiss; IX.)

CD   THE PRESENT AND FUTURE OF CLASSICS

"AN ARION QUESTIONNAIRE; The classics and the man of letters." Arion 111, 4 (1964): 6–100.   **CD1**

> The "man of letters" includes professional writers, poets, novelists, critics (i.e., W. H. Auden, Robert Graves, Iris Murdoch, Anthony Powell) and also scholars from other fields (Sir Herbert Read, George Steiner) as well as distinguished amateurs. The results show a vivid concern with the classics but little unanimity on the desirable extent or content of classical subjects in today's curriculum.

BOER, W. den, ed. Les études classiques aux XIXᵉ et XXᵉ ss.; leur place dans l'histoire des idées. Epilogue by A. Momigliano. Vandoeuvres-Genève, Fond. Hardt, 1979. 346p.   **CD2**

> Entretiens sur l'antiquité classique; XXVI.

CARNE-ROSS, D. S. "Classics and the intellectual community." Arion n.s. I, 1 (1973): 7–66.
                                                            CD3

Interesting ruminations on the future of the classics, with special attention to the middle realm between "the Greek scholars" and "the Greekless reader." It is "this middle realm that matters and the future—the survival—of the classics depends on the middle man who works there."

FINLEY, M. I. "New developments in classical studies. The great ideas today. 1971, the year's developments in the arts and sciences." Encyclopaedia Britannica (1971): 123–167.   **CD4**

FRITZ, K. von. "The position of classical studies in our time." Lampas VI (1973): 290–303.
                                                            CD5

KENNEY, E. J. New frameworks for old; The place of literature in the Cambridge classical course: An inaugural lecture. Cambridge and New York, Cambridge University Press, 1975. [1], 32p.   **CD6**

> "Delivered in the University of Cambridge on 22 April 1975."

KIRK, Geoffrey S. "The future of classics." The American Scholar XLV (1976): 536–547.

CD7

An interesting statement from a British scholar, who has also enjoyed teaching in Yale, on reasons for studying classics, which are no longer necessary stepping-stones on one's way to becoming priest, philosopher, historian or artist. With the declining ability of students to master the actual languages, he sees many institutions opting for a decline in the language component and an increase in the study of other aspects of classical culture: archaeology, philosophy, history. Improving language skills is being attempted through such new courses as the Cambridge and the McGill. The academic bombast and quarrelsomeness of classical scholars are rightly blamed in part for the decline.

OATES, Whitney J. et al. From Sophocles to Picasso; The present-day vitality of the classical tradition. Bloomington, Indiana University Press, 1962. 208p.

CD8

CJ LIX 1963 80–83 Murphy • CW LVI 1963 242–243 Sullivan

The theme of these lectures is that the element of Greek culture to which our own century has been particularly responsive is the Greek sense of tragedy. The two central essays on art by Otto Brendel, The Classical Style in Modern Art and Classic and non-Classic Elements in Picasso's *Guernica,* are the most valuable. H. D. F. Kitto's contribution, disappointingly, is merely an introduction to the study of the *Antigone.*

The whole will provide starting-points, and some arguments of doubtful validity, for those in search of materials to prove the relevance of classics in the modern world.

PLUMB, John H. Crisis in the humanities. Hammondsworth, Penguin, 1964. 172p. **CD9**

Latomus XXIV 1965 791 Hanton

Includes an essay by M. I. Finley, Crisis in the Classics (p.11–23), and eight others which examine the inescapable need for adaptation of classical studies to the modern mentality. Solutions are sought in the domains of Greek, Latin, history, philosophy, theology, literature and the fine arts.

REES, Brinley Roderick. Classics; An outline for the intending student. London, Routledge & K. Paul, 1970. [6], 125p. **CD10**

Essays by seven British classicists include Classics at University Today, An Approach to Classical Literature, Ancient Philosophy, Ancient History, Classical Archaeology, and The Classics and English Literature. There is an appendix, Degree Courses in Classics at British Universities. Each essay has a very short list appended of suggested readings. The essays are based on the conviction that change is good and that the discipline has proved itself over the centuries more flexible and adaptable than is generally felt. There is much fresh thinking here on the present role of classics, now dislodged from its former central place in the school curriculum.

The Transmission of the Classics: Writing, Papyrology, Paleography, and Textual Criticism

DA WRITING, BOOKS, AND LIBRARIES

Writing

ATSALOS, Vasileios. La terminologie du livre-manuscrit à l'époque byzantine. Thessalonique, Hetaireia Makedonikeon Spoudeon, 1971.

DA1

1. Sptie. Termes désignant le livre-manuscrit et l'écriture.

ACR II 1972 247–248 Bongie • CR XXIV 1974 145 Wilson • JHS XCV 1975 303–304 Browning • REA LXXVI, 3–4 1974 462–463 Thirier

A work begun in Saloniki and finished as a thesis in Paris, the first of a projected three-volume series on the terminology of codicology and paleography. Treatment here is confined to the period of Greek minuscule, 9th–15th centuries, and to the terminology of the codex (p.39–145) and roll (p.148–178). There is a painstaking history of terms as found in a wide variety of texts, and a full coverage of conflicting views on points of interpretation. Generally, however, there is nothing added to what is already known (e.g., in the lengthy account of oxyrynchos and stroulos (p.193–217), and one slim volume might have been more useful than the projected three, volumes 2 and 3 of which will deal with the terms relating to writing material and book production, and with colophons.

AUDIN, Marius. Somme typographique. I. Les origines. Paris, Dupont, 1948. 61–111p.

DA2

Scriptorium IV 1950 285–288 Masai • REL XXVI 1949 388–390 Andrieu

Important for R. Marichal, "De la capitale romaine a la minuscule" (p.63–111). Audin traces the history of calligraphy in the introduction, since the chief ambition of the first printers was to imitate and reproduce mechanically the earlier Caroline minuscule script. Marichal's chief form is on the evolution of writing, and his accomplishment in a mere 50 pages is truly magisterial. Incorporates the research of himself and Jean Mallon for the previous decade.

COHEN, Marcel Samuel R., ed. Centre international de synthèse. Paris. L'écriture et la psychologie des peuples; XXIIe semaine de synthèse. Avec la collaboration de Marcel Cohen, Jean Sainte Fare Garnot et al. Paris, A. Colin, 1963. 380p., 25p. of plates, illus., maps.

DA3

"la XXIIe Semaine de Synthèse, organisée, du 3 au 11 mai 1960 . . . ."

BBF IX 1964 511–512 Colnort-Bodet • RBPh XLIII 1965 1448–1450 Boüüaert

Of the 18 papers published in this seminar, the most important for the classicist are c.10 L'écriture Grecque, du VIIIe Siècle Avant Notre Ère à la Fin de la Civilisation Byzantine, by Alphonse Dain and c.12 L'écriture au XVIe Siècle, by Robert Marichal. Marichal's contribution is a veritable monograph in its own right, well illustrated.

COHEN, Marcel Samuel R. La grande invention de l'écriture et son évolution. Paris, Impr. nationale, 1958. 3 v., illus., maps, port., 95 plates (part col.; incl. ports.), fold. col. map.   **DA4**

[1] Texte. [2] Documentation et index. [3] Planches.
BAGB 1960 426–430 Dain • RPh XXXIII 1959 281–82 Ernout • REA LXI 1959 435–438 Lejeune
This masterly work fully justified the expectations aroused by the author's earlier and shorter *L'écriture* in 1953. This *summa* examines all aspects of writing in time and space from primitive pictography to the most modern means of communication. For the main lines of development the work is clearly written, extremely interesting, suggestive and personal. Reservations, both quantitative and qualitative, have been expressed about details but the copious bibliographies provide the sources for the necessary corrections. The work has been lavishly produced and illustrated by l'Imprimerie nationale. The final volume reproduces photographically examples of various writings, generally with a transcription in Latin characters and a French translation.

DAIN, Alphonse. Les manuscrits. 3. éd., rev. et augmentée index. Paris, Les Belles Lettres, 1975. 222p., illus.   **DA5**

Collection d'études anciennes.
BBF XI 1966 812 Astruc • Gnomon XXIII 1951 233–242 Pasquali • REL XXVIII 1950 487–489 Andrieu • Stud Pap IV 1965 57–58 Solá
This excellent introduction to the history of texts poses and analyzes many problems concerning ancient editions. The first two chapters deal with *le livre manuscrit*, the act of copying and the history of writing, especially in the West. Chapter III deals with *les manuscrits et le problème de l'histoire des textes*, which tries to arrive at the archetype. Chapter IV tries to summarize the consequences for the prospective editor of the teaching in the first three chapters. A classic example of *multum in parvo*.

DEGERING, Herman. Die Schrift; Atlas der Schriftformen des Abendlandes vom Altertum bis Ausgang des 18. Jahrhunderts. [4. Auflage.] Tübingen, Wasmuth, 1964. xxxvii, 240p., facsims.   **DA6**

PhW 1930 210–213 Weinberger
There is an English translation, *Lettering* (London, Benn, 1929), and one in French (Paris, Calavas, 1929).

DIRINGER, David. Writing, its origin and history. London, Readers Union, Thames and Hudson, 1965 [1962]. 261p., 78 plates, illus., 3 maps.   **DA7**

Archaeology XVIII 1965 82 Gordon • Antiquity XXXVII 1963 247–249 Barnett

FICHTENAU, Heinrich. Mensch und Schrift im Mittelalter. Wien, Universum, 1946. vii, 239p., 16 plates (incl. facsims.).   **DA8**

Veröffentlichungen des Instituts für Österreichische Geschichtsforschung; Bd. 5.
HZ CLXXI 1951 338–339 Kirn • Speculum XXII 1947 639–643 Elder • ZSG 1946 538
A work of synthesis, seeking to increase our powers of interpreting scripts in the general pattern of the spiritual and cultural development of Western Europe. For Fichtenau script is not just a technique but an expression of individual man in relation to his spiritual life. The book is divided into two sections, Das Problem (i.e., script as human expression) and Abendländische Schriftstrukturen.

JENSEN, Hans. Sign, symbol and script; An account of man's efforts to write. 3rd revised and enlarged ed.; trans. by George Unwin. London, Allen & Unwin, 1970. 613p., illus., facsims.   **DA9**

Trans. from *Die Schrift in Vergangenheit und Gegenwart*, a rev., enl. ed. of *Geschichte der Schrift*.

LOWE, Elias Avery. Handwriting; Our medieval legacy. Transcriptions of facsimiles by W. Braxton Ross, Jr. Rome, Edizioni di storia e letteratura, 1969. 38p., 24 plates.   **DA10**

Originally published in *The legacy of the Middle Ages*.
RBen LXXX 1970 330 Bogaert
The particular forms of writing and printing editors employ today are not a direct inheritance from Rome; they are rather the creation of the centuries which transmitted, and in transmitting modified, that inheritance. This is the legacy of the Middle Ages. The generic name we give to that modified legacy is minuscule. When majuscule scripts became obsolete, scribes replaced them with scripts based on cursive, or on half-uncial, or on mixed material. Of the various attempts the most successful was the type which evolved in Gaul in the time of Charlemagne, and which we call Caroline minuscule. This in turn was replaced by Gothic and later revived by the Renaissance humanists. In this beautifully produced new edition, the history of our medieval legacy is outlined in the first section and accompanied by well-produced plates with transcriptions.

THOMPSON, Edward Maunde, Sir. An introduction to Greek and Latin palaeography. New York, Burt Franklin, 1973 xvi, 600p., facsims.   **DA11**

Reprint of the 1912 ed. published by Clarendon Press, Oxford.
An enlarged edition of the author's *Handbook of Greek and Latin palaeography* (3rd ed., 1906, reprint, Chicago, Ares, 1975). Includes chapters on the history

of Greek and Roman alphabets, materials and writing implements, forms of books, abbreviations, contractions and numerals. Gives transcription of each facsimile.

ULLMAN, Berthold Louis. Ancient writing and its influence. Cambridge, M.I.T. Press, 1969. xviii, 240p.   **DA12**

CJ 1933 137–139 Muckie • CR 1933 71 Hall • RCr 1933 184 Samaran • REL 1932 514 Marouzeau
This is an unchanged reprint of the 1932 edition with an introduction and supplementary bibliography by Julian Brown. It is the only book in English to cover with brevity and distinction the history of the alphabet, Greek paleography and epigraphy, and the origins of printing. Higounet "L'Écriture" is comparable in scope and quality.
The author begins with a short preface on the origin of writing, goes on to give the history of our alphabet, says a word on Greek script, and then in several careful and interesting chapters traces Latin script down to the invention of printing. Several chapters are added on abbreviations, the numerals, writing materials, etc. Plates are furnished to illustrate the various scripts. While much new work on the alphabet has appeared since the publication of this book (Cohen 1953, Higounet 1955, and Diringer 1962)—based on two great events, Michael Ventris's decipherment of Linear B and the discovery of the Dead Sea Scrolls—this individual creation by so accurate a scholar still has value for palaeographers and classical scholars.

WATTENBACH, Wilhelm. Das Schriftwesen im Mittelalter. 4. Aufl. Graz, Akademische Druck u. Verlagsanstalt, 1958. vi, 670p.   **DA13**

"Unveränderter Abdruck der dritten vermehrten Auflage, ... 1896 ... Leipzig."

The Book: History and Codicology

ARNS, Evaristo. La technique du livre d'après saint Jérôme. Paris, E. de Boccard, 1953. 220p.   **DA14**

CR n.s. IV 1954 306–307 Browning • Gnomon XXVII 1975 295–297 Waszinck
St. Jerome is more interesting than any other patristic writer *qua* writer. With assistance of earlier experts like Dziatko, Birt and Kenyon, Arns, a student of Pierre Courcelle, assembles and edits 100 examples of Jerome's views on editing. In five sections he deals with The Materials (p.13–35); The Rédaction (p.37–79) including Dictation, Shorthand, Transcription, Correction; The Technique of Publication (p.81–128); The Diffusion (p.129–172); and Le Livre et les Archives (p.173–195). In the final section he deals with the problem of authenticity and enunciates certain principles for the constitution of text as proposed by Jerome.

DELAISSÉ, L. M. J. "Towards a history of the mediaeval book." *Miscellanea A. Combes,* I–II. Rome, 1967: 423–435.   **DA15**

Announced in *APh* XXXIX, 1968, 373: "Introduction à un livre à paraître sous le titre *Archaeology and history of the medieval book, problems and method."*

GRUIJS, F. A. "Codicology or the archaeology of the book? A false dilemma." Quaerendo II, 2 (1972): 87–108.   **DA16**

Scriptorium XXVII 1973 47–49 Derolez
This inaugural lecture by the professor of auxiliary sciences in history at Nijmegen traces the history of the term codicology through Dain, Masai and Delaissé. Dain, in coining the word, depended on Traube's *Zur Paläographie und Handschriftenkunde.* It was not Dain's intention to create a new discipline or method, but merely to find an acceptable term. Masai, however, proclaimed paleography and codicology fundamental disciplines with their own proper objects and methods. According to him "Codicologie" is "une discipline archéologique" studying the livre manuscrit. Delaissé, in his remarkable edition *Manuscrit autographe de Thomas à Kempis et l'imitation de Jésus Christ,* provided the touchstone of the new discipline. The present well-documented study provides a sensible solution to the apparent dichotomy.

GRUIJS, F. A. Codicologica. Rédacteur adjoint, J. P. Gumbert. Leiden, Brill, 1976. Illus.
                                                                      DA17

Added title page has subtitle: Towards a science of handwritten books: Vers une science du manuscrit: Bausteine zur Handschriftenkunde.
BECh CXXXV 1977 248 Gasnault
This work contains, in the main, republication of older texts, including statements, by now almost historical, on the nature and scope of codicology by Masai, T. J. Brown and Delaissé.
See now *Codicologia* II. *Éléments pour une codicologie comparée,* éd. par A. Gruijs and J. P. Gumbert. Leiden, Brill, 1979. 94p. (Litterae textuales.)
Codicologia III. *Essais typologiques,* V. Les matériaux du livre manuscrit, éd. par A. Gruijs and J. P. Gumbert. Leiden, Brill, 1980. 104, 80p. (Litterae textuales.)
Codicologia IV. *Methodologie.* Leiden, Brill, 1979. 90p.

PUTNAM, George Haven. Books and their makers during the Middle Ages; A study of the conditions of the production and distribution of literature from the fall of the Roman Empire to the close of the seventeenth century. New York, Hillary House, [1962]. 2 v.   **DA18**

"An unaltered and unabridged reprint of the last (1896–97) edition."
Contains much information on the making of books in the monasteries and in the manuscript period in Italy, Spain, France, Germany and England, the earlier printed books, the beginnings of property in literature, and regulations for the control and the censorship of the printing press.

REED, R. Ancient skins, parchments and leathers. London; New York, Seminar Press, 1972. ix, 331p. **DA19**

This work has useful chapters on animal skin, methods of processing, the nature of parchment and mode of production, skin materials and the archaeologist/conservationist. Particularly helpful for librarians and curators.

SANTIFALLER, L. Beiträge zur Geschichte der Beschreibstoffe im Mittelalter. Köln, Böhlaus, 1953. 220p. **DA20**

MA LXI 1955 221–226 Despy • Scriptorium X 1956 270–274 Wittek

Teil 1 has chapters devoted to papyrus (p.25–76), parchment (p.77–115), paper (p.116–152), roll and codex (p.153–184). There is a bibliography of 400 titles arranged alphabetically by author (p.9–23) and a detailed index (p.185–219). The work is based largely on researches in the chancellary of Gregory VII, 1073–1085. See also Santifaller, "Neue Forschungen zur Paläographie und Diplomatik," *AAWW* LXXXIX (1952), 329–342.

SCHOTTENLOHER, Karl. Das alte Buch. 3. Aufl. Braunschweig, Klinkhardt & Biermann, [1956]. 467p., illus., facsims. **DA21**

Bibliothek für Kunst u. Antiquitäten-Freunde; Bd. 14.

A useful survey of the history of the early printed book in Germany.

SCHUBART, Wilhelm. Das Buch bei den Griechen und Römern. 3. Aufl. hrsg. von Eberhard Paul. Heidelberg, Lambert Schneider, 1962. 157p., illus., facsims. **DA22**

Four long chapters on ancient materials, the bookroll, the codex and reproduction and bookselling.

TURNER, Eric Gardiner. Athenian books in the fifth and fourth centuries B.C.; An inaugural lecture delivered at University College, London, 22 May 1951. London, Published for the College by H. K. Lewis, 1952, 1954 printing. 23p., illus. **DA23**

JHS LXXIV 1954 237 Roberts • BAGB 3e sér. 1952, 3 110 Hemmerdinger • Gnomon XXIV 1952 437 Schubart • JHS LXXIV 1954 237 Roberts

In this inaugural lecture Turner invokes the aid of archaeology and the vase paintings to show the relation between literature and its material means of expression. He also uses the literature and the earliest papyri to present a picture that is the clearest and most convincing we have of the subject.

TURNER, Eric Gardiner. The typology of the early codex. Philadelphia, University of Pennsylvania Press, 1977. xxiii, 188p. **DA24**

AJPh C 1979 446–447 Renehan • Scriptorium XXXIV 1980 135–139 Prato

An expanded version, justifiably called a pioneering work, of a 1971 set of lectures, which constitutes a substantially documented and rigorously reasoned contribution to our knowledge of the codex. There are seven chapters: 1. Towards a Typology of the Codex; 2. The Dimensions of Papyrus and Parchment Codices; 3. The Priority of Parchment or Papyrus? 4. Manufacture and Size; 5. How a Codex was Made Up; 6. The Codex and Scribe; 7. The Form and Date of the Earliest Codices.

VERVLIET, Hendrik D. L. The book through five thousand years; A survey of Fernand Baudin et al. London, Phaidon, [1972]. 496p., illus. (part col.), facsims. **DA25**

TLS LXXI 1972 1540

Written by an international team of scholars, this handsome and weighty volume covers the history of the book from the clay tablets of Mesopotamia almost to our day. More than half the book is devoted to the study of Oriental and Western manuscripts. It is profusely illustrated. A select bibliography is appended to each of the 28 chapters.

WENIG, O., ed. Wege zur Buchwissenschaft. Bonn, Bouvier, 1966. viii, 416p. **DA26**

BBF XI 1966 814–815 Labarre

WITTY, Francis J. "Reference books in antiquity." J Lib Hist IX (1974): 101–119. **DA27**

An interesting survey of titles of outstanding reference works in the Greek and Roman world from Hellenistic times to about the end of the Empire in the West. Available titles are listed with brief annotations under such headings as Agriculture, Almanacs, Dictionaries, Epitomes, Technology.

WROTH, Lawrence Counselman. A history of the printed book; Being the third number of the Dolphin. New York, The Limited Editions Club, 1938. xv, 507p., illus., facsims. **DA28**

Illuminated Manuscripts

ALEXANDER, Jonathan James Graham. Insular manuscripts; 6th to the 9th century. London, Harvey Miller, 1978. 219p., illus. (some col.). **DA29**

A survey of manuscripts illuminated in the British Isles; 1.

ANCONA, Paola d' and AESCHLIMANN, E. The art of illumination; An anthology of manuscripts from the sixth to the sixteenth century. Trans. from the original Italian by Alison M. Brown, with additional notes on the plates by M. Alison Stones. London, Phaidon, 1969. 32p.,

33–201p. of illus. (some col.), 202–235, [2]p. 2 plates. **DA30**

KUNZE, Horst. Geschichte der Buchillustration in Deutschland; Das 15. Jahrhundert. Leipzig, Insel Verlag, 1975. 2 v., illus. (some col.). **DA31**

[1] Textband. [2] Bildband.

MASAI, François. Sur les origines de la miniature dite Irlandaise. Bruxelles, Éditions "Erasmus," 1947. 146p., 64 plates. **DA32**

OXFORD UNIVERSITY. Bodleian Library. Illuminated manuscripts in the Bodleian Library, Oxford. [compiled by] Otto Pächt and J. J. G. Alexander. Oxford, Clarendon Press, 1966– . **DA33**

Volume contents: v. 1. German, Dutch, Flemish, French and Spanish Schools; v. 2. Italian School (Oxford, Clarendon Press, 1970, xii, 161p., 88 plates); v. 3. British, Irish and Icelandic Schools (1973).

Scriptorium XXII 1968 360–361, XXVI 1972 213, XXVII 1973 407–408 Dogaer • RHE LXIX 1974 926 Dauphin • EHR LXXXIX 1974 871–872 Dodwell

After the British Library (olim Museum), the Bodleian is certainly the richest British repository of illuminated MSS. Volume 1 of this catalog is devoted to German (nos. 1–202), Dutch (203–264), Flemish (265–408), French (409–875) and Spanish (876–906) schools. The dates range from the 8th to the 18th centuries. Description of the content and material state of each MS is deliberately kept to a minimum, and more space is available for precise information on the illuminations. The subjects of the miniatures are not indicated. There are useful indices. Volume 2 covers the more than 1,000 illuminated MSS of Italian origin in the Bodleian, dating from the 6th to the 19th centuries. A large part of them are from the collection of the Venetian, Abate Mattes Luigi Canonici (1727–1806). Numbers 1–62 predate 1200, nos. 63–103 are 13th century. In the 14th century the catalog begins a geographical division by city or center. Volume 3 is largely English; 1267 MSS illuminated by English miniatures or by artists travelling to or from England. An excellent aperçu of English miniatures. Ireland is represented by nos. 1268–1289.

OXFORD UNIVERSITY. Bodleian Library. Illuminated manuscripts and books in the Bodleian Library; A supplemental index compiled and edited by Thomas H. Ohlgren. New York, Garland Publishing, 1978. xxxii, 583p., [15] leaves of plates, illus. **DA34**

"Supplement to *Illuminated manuscripts; An index to selected Bodleian Library color reproductions,* ed. by Thomas H. Ohlgren, New York, Garland, 1977, 646p."

VIKAN, Gary, ed. Illuminated Greek manuscripts from American collections; An exhibition in honor of Kurt Weitzmann. Princeton University Press, 1973. 232p., 120 illus. **DA35**

Scriptorium XXX 1976 329–330 Lafontaine-Dosogne

A superb exhibition on the occasion of Professor Weitzmann's retirement from the Institute for Advanced Study, Princeton.

The Library, Ancient and Medieval

BUSHNELL, George Herbert. The world's earliest libraries. London, Grafton & Co., 1931. 2p., 1., 3–58p. **DA36**

CLARK, John Willis. The care of books; An essay on the development of libraries and their fittings, from the earliest times to the end of the eighteenth century. Norwood, Pa., Norwood Editions, 1975. xviii, 330p., illus. **DA37**

Reprint of the 1909 ed. published by University Press, Cambridge, Eng.

This copiously illustrated book is a classic on the history of libraries. The author personally examined and measured every building which he describes, with the exception of the Escorial, and many of the illustrations are from his own sketches. The work deals largely with monastic libraries and describes their fittings, their modes of security, size and types of collections, etc. Chapter 1 deals with ancient libraries, Greece and Rome.

CLARK, John Willis. Libraries in the medieval and Renaissance periods. Chicago, Argonaut, 1968. 61p., illus. **DA38**

Reprint of 1894 ed.

DALY, Lloyd William. Contributions to a history of alphabetization in Antiquity and the Middle Ages. Bruxelles, Latomus, 1967. 99p., tables. **DA39**

Collection Latomus; v. 90.

JHS LXXXIX 1969 162 Diringer

The author outlines the origins and history of alphabetization from its first use in the organization, classification and cataloging of the library of Alexandria as evidenced from what is known of Callimachus *Pinakes.* He traces the uses of alphabetization in Ptolemaic and Graeco-Roman administration of Egypt, in Roman literature and administration in later Greek and Byzantine scholarship and in Medieval Latin glossaries and lexica.

IRIGOIN, J. "Pour une étude des centres de copie byzantins; 1. Les Caractères externes du livre manuscrits." Scriptorium XII (1958): 208–227; II. ibid. XIII (1959): 177–209. **DA40**

Consists of three parts: Les caractères Externes du livre; Quelques groupes de manuscrits et; Centres de Copie et bibliothèques.

LESNE, Émile. Les livres, "scriptoria," et bibliothèques du commencement du VIIIe à la fin du XIe siècle. Lille, Facultés catholiques, 1938. New York, Johnson Reprint, [1964]. 849p.

DA41

His Histoire de la propriété ecclésiastique en France; t. 4. Mémoires et travaux des Facultés catholiques de Lille; fasc. 46.

A study of libraries, chiefly in France but including some now in Germany and Switzerland.

ZENTRALBLATT für Bibliothekswesen. Leipzig. illus.   **DA42**

No meetings held 1915–1919. v. 17–31, 37– include 1. Versammlung des Vereins deutscher bibliothekare. (Slight variation in title).

Contains current bibliographies about libraries, manuscript collections and codicology. See ZBibl, N. F. 1 (1947), 1–2, K. Christ, Bibliotheksgeschichte des Mittelalters; zur Methode und zur neuesten Literatur.

DB   PAPYROLOGY

Bibliography, Methodology, and Orientation

ALAND, Kurt. Repertorium der griechischen christlichen Papyri. Berlin, De Gruyter, 1976– .   **DB1**

Patristische Texte und Studien; 18.
Teil 1. Biblische Papyri includes Old and New Testament, Varia and Apocrypha.

AUSTIN, Colin, comp. and ed. Comicorum graecorum fragmenta in papyris reperta. Berolini, De Gruyter, 1973. xxxi, 454p.   **DB2**

AC XLIII 1974 432–434 van Looy • BAGB 1974 248–249 Irigoin • CW LXIX 1975 272–273 Calder • REG LXXXVIII 1975 292–294 Blanchard • Aegyptus LVI 1976 319–321 Di Gregorio

A splendid collection by an editor whose previous works have received unanimous praise for their critical acumen and patient scholarship. Discoveries of recent date like Menander's *Dyscolos* and *The girl from Samos* have eclipsed the less spectacular ones, but the totality is impressive and earlier works on the fragments like that of J. M. Edmonds (1957–1961) called for correction and updating. Here the arrangement is chronological by author, and Austin has personally reviewed all previously published papyri directly or by photograph. For each fragment he supplies a bibliography, an assemblage of previous views, and an extensive critical and exegetical commentary. This is a preview of a projected nine-volume *Poetae comici graeci* in active preparation by Austin and R. Kassel in which (unlike here) the comedies of Aristophanes and the new Menander will have a place.

AUSTIN, Colin, ed. Nova fragmenta Euripidea in papyris reperta. Berlin, De Gruyter, 1968. 116p.   **DB3**

Kleine Texte für Vorlesungen und Übungen; v. 187.
Emerita XL 1972 503–505 Lens • AC XXXVIII

1969 543–544 van Looy • RPh XLIII 1969 300–301 Chantraine

In this *Kleine Texte,* v. 187, Austin assembles all the papyrological fragments of Euripides discovered since the edition of the *Supplementum Euripideum* by H. von Arnim (1913), essentially the Archelaus, Erectheus, Cresphontes, Cretes, Oedipus and Telephus. A continuous numeration is assigned which does not disturb the order in Nauck's edition. The text is accompanied by critical notes and a commentary. For the text the editor has carefully re-examined all the papyri, except P Oxy 419 and P Berol 13267, which have disappeared.

BINGEN, J. and CAMBIER, G. La papyrologie grecque et latine; Problèmes de fond et problèmes d'organisation. *In* Aspects des études classiques. Actes du colloque associé a la XVIe assemblée générale de la Fédération internationale des Associations d'études classiques. Edited by J. Bingen and G. Cambier. Bruxelles, Éditions de l'Université, 1977. P. 33–44. (Université Libre de Faculté de philosophie et lèttres LXVI).

DB4

BOSWINKEL, Ernst and SIJPESTEIJN, P. J. Greek papyri, ostraka and mummy labels. Amsterdam, Hakkert, 1968. 59p., 54 plates.

DB5

Gnomon XLII 1970 733–734 Parsons

This book consists of 60 plates: photographs of Greek documents from Egypt, in chronological order from the 2d century B.C. to the late Byzantine period. Facing pages provide notes and sometimes partial transcripts. The texts come from three collections only—Leiden, Vienna and Wisconsin.

CALDERINI, A. and MONDINI, Maria et al. Bibliografia metodica degli studi di egittologia e di papirologia.   **DB6**

Begun in *Aegyptus* in 1920, this is a scientifically

constructed, numerically arranged bibliography on a regular pattern: Bibliography, Periodicals, Miscellaneous (especially Festschriften, Proceedings), Collections of Papyri, Collections of Ostraca, Corrections and Re-editions of Works Already Published, Biographies, Complete Works or Scripta Minora of Individual Scholars, History and Geography, Literature, Philosophy, and Science, Linguistics, Metrics, Music, Paleography and Codicology, Law and Administration.

See also Lith, S.M.E. van, *Index of articles volumes 1–50* (Amsterdam, Hakkert, 1974, v, 185p.).

COLES, Revel A. Location-list of the Oxyrhynchus papyri and of other Greek papyri published by the Egypt Exploration Society. London, Egypt Exploration Society, 1974. 50p. **DB7**

This list amalgamates the information given in v. IV, V, XI and XVI of the Oxyrhynchus papyri, correcting or supplementing as necessary. Information also about where photographs have been published elsewhere and where negatives are kept (other than the institutions holding the originals).

DARIS, Sergio. "I Repertorio dello Collezioni di Papiri." Montevecchi, *La papirologia*: 407–433. **DB8**

An invaluable checklist arranged alphabetically, with appropriate abbreviations, followed by a section on editions of literary texts not contained in the preceding Repertorium (exs. Aristotle, *On the Constitution of Athens*, Kenyon, ed.; *The homily on the Passion by Melito*. Bonner, ed.). A third section Sillogi is divided into Documentary Texts and Literary Texts, and a final one (by E. Bresciani) lists editions of demotic texts, both papyri and ostraka, from the Ptolemaic and Roman periods.

For similar checklists, cf. Turner, *Greek papyri* 154–171; Petit, *Guide*, 162–169.

GERSTINGER, H. "Papyrology." NCE 10: 981–984. **DB9**

A good short account of the writing materials, the finds in Egypt, the main collections, contents, importance of papyri to classical philology and biblical scholarship. There is an excellent bibliography.

See also the following encyclopedia articles: *DACL* XIII, 1, 1370–1520 Leclercq; *DB* 4, 2079–2094 Levêque and Prat; *DBSuppl*. 8, 1109–1120 Botte; *Enc-Catt* 9, 783–787 Calderini; *LThK* 8, 63–65 Gerstinger; *Encyc. Britt*. 17, 243–246 H[unt], A. S.

GIGNAC, Francis T. A grammar of the Greek papyri of the Roman and Byzantine periods. Milano, Istituto editoriale cisalpino-La goliardica, 1976– . **DB10**

I. Phonology, 1976; II. Morphology, 1981.

AC LXVIII 1979 341–342 Leroy • CR XXIX 1979 92–94 Browning • JBL CII 1983 350–352 Dayker

This new grammar of the nonliterary papyri covers the period from 30 B.C. to 735 A.D. and is based on an enormous assemblage of 15,000 papyri, 30 ostraka,

2,619 minor documents, magical papyri, 5,687 inscriptions and mummy labels. Part I, Phonology, studies the fluctuation of the orthography of consonants, then of vowels, with examples judiciously chosen and dated with the greatest possible exactitude, which allows the reader the pleasure of seeing at a glance the chronological developments. There is an excellent bibliography and an index of Greek words and forms.

HOMBERT, Marcel. "Bulletin papyrologique XXVIII (1954 à 1959)." REG LXXVIII (1965): 205–316. **DB11**

An extremely detailed ongoing bibliography, continuing a feature begun in *REG* XIV (1901), 163–205 by S. de Ricci, and continued by P. Collart and others.

HOMBERT, Marcel and NACHTERGAEL, G. Bibliographie papyrologique, 1982, avec complément des années antérieures. Bruxelles, Fondation égyptologique Reine Élisabeth. **DB12**

Begun in 1932 and issued annually in 5 packets of about 100 cards each; 1974- : 6 envois par an sur fiches.

JOHN RYLANDS LIBRARY, Manchester. Catalogue of the Greek papyri in the John Rylands Library. Manchester, University Press, 1911–1952. 4 v. **DB13**

Volume 1 contains literary texts, v.2 documents of the Ptolemaic and Roman periods, v.3 theological and literary texts, v.4 documents of the Ptolemaic, Roman and Byzantine periods.

KENYON, Frederic G. Greek papyri in the British Museum: Catalogue, with texts. Milan, Cisalpina-Golairadica, 1973. 5 v. **DB14**

Reprint of the 1893–1917 ed. published by the British Museum.

MÄHLER, Herwig. "Sammlungen griechischer papyri." Lexikon der alten Welt, (1965): 3389–3402. **DB15**

A list of the chief publications of papyrological texts, with appropriate abbreviations.

MARTIN, V. "Autonomie et dépendance de la Papyrologie." MusHelv X, fasc. 3–4 (1953): 131–140. **DB16**

A paper read at the 7th International Congress of Papyrology at Geneva in 1952. Nine other Congress papers also published here.

MENTZ, Arthur. Geschichte der Kurzschrift. Wolfenbüttel, 1949. 2 ed., 1974, ed. by F. Haeger. **DB17**

MODRZEJEWSKI, Joseph. "Bibliographie de papyrologie juridique, 1962–1972." Archiv für Papyrusforschung XXIV–XXV (1976): 263–328 . **DB18**

See also Modrzejewski, J., "Papyrologie juridique, 20ᵉ rapport. Textes et travaux de Septembre 1976 à Septembre 1979." *SDHI* XLVII (1981): 425–590.

OATES, J. F., BAGNALL, R. S. and WILLIS, W. H. "Checklist of editions of Greek papyri and ostraca." BASP XI (1974): 1–35.   **DB19**

One purpose of this checklist is to establish a standard list of papyrological abbreviations. The need for standardization was agreed to at the 13th International Congress of Papyrology, Marburg, 1971, and Oates was nominated to proceed with the task.
See now Oates, J., Bagnall, R. S. and Willis, W. H. *Checklist of editions of Greek papyri and ostraca.* 2nd ed. Missoula, Mont., Scholars Press, 1978. x, 63p. (BASP Suppl. no. 1.)

O'CALLAGHAN, José. El papiro en los padres grecolatinos. Barcelona, Papyrol. Castroctaviana, 1967. 94p.   **DB20**

StudPap VI 1967 69–71 Mazón

PALMER, Leonard R. A grammar of the post-Ptolemaic papyri. London, Oxford University Press, 1945– .   **DB21**

1. Accidence and word-formation: pt. 1. The suffixes.
JHS LXV 1945 126 Sinclair • Language XXIV 1948 205–212 Hoenigswald
Palmer's work is based on the available dictionaries, both general and papyrological, and on the indices to papyrological publications.

PETIT, Paul. Guide de l'étudiant en histoire ancienne. Paris, Presses Universitaires de France, 1969. 239p.   **DB22**

"La Papyrologie."
Includes a brief account of the growth of the discipline, a good statement of its present strengths and weaknesses, and a short bibliography of manuals and collections.

PREISENDANZ, Karl. Papyrusfunde und Papyrusforschung. Leipzig, Hiersemann, 1933. xvi, 371p.   **DB23**

RPh VIII 1934 226–228 Collart • JHS LIV 1934 94–96 Skeat
A monument of industry but suffering from structural and planning defects. Two preliminary chapters deal with medieval papyri in Western Europe and the Herculaneum rolls. The main part (p.67–259) deals with the origins and development of papyrology. There is a good Catalog of Collections (p.260–300) and a Bibliography (p.301–339), both with serious omissions.

PREISIGKE, Friedrich et al. Berichtungsliste der griechischen Papyrusurkunden aus Ägypten. Berlin, Vereinigung Wissenschaftlicher Verleger, 1922 (1913–).   **DB24**

Microfiche. Missoula, Mont.: Scholars Press, 1977.
BASP VII 1970 12 Samuel • StudPap IX 1970 74–77 O'Callaghan

PROCEEDINGS of the XIVth International Congress of Papyrologists, Oxford, 24–31 July 1974. London, Egypt Exploration Society, 1975.   **DB25**

Orientalia XLV 1976 383–386 O'Callaghan
A list of the Proceedings of the previous Congresses to 1970 can be found in Montevecchi, p.436 (see entry DB41).
See Samuel, Deborah H., *Proceedings of the twelfth International Congress of Papyrology,* Toronto, 1970, the first international congress ever held in North America.

R[OBERTS], C[olin] H[enderson]. "Papyrology, Greek." OCD²: 778–780.   **DB26**

Most of our papyri come from Egypt, the principal exceptions being (a) the Epicurean papyri from Herculaneum; (b) the Hellenistic and Roman documents found with a few literary texts at Dura-Europos; (c) the religious and documentary papyri from Qumran and Murraba'at in Palestine and the Byzantine texts excavated at Auja-el-Hafir; (d) the single, charred papyrus, Orphic in character, recently found in a burial at Derveni, near Salonika. The most fertile sources of papyri finds have been Oxyrhynchus and the Fayum. Our oldest literary papyrus, the Persae of Timotheus, may date from mid-4th century, and the Derveni text only a little later. The number of published texts, varying enormously in size, condition, content and value, is approximately 25,000. Of the papyri of extant Greek authors more than half are texts of Homer.

TREU, Kurt. "Christliche Papyri, 1940–1967." APF XIX (1967): 169–206.   **DB27**

An annotated bibliography for Old and New Testament, Patres, Liturgica, Magica, Subsidia. This survey is continued in *APF* XX (1968), 145–152, XXI (1971), 207–214, XXII (1973), 367–395, XXIV–XXV (1976), 253–261.

TURNER, Eric Gardiner. The papyrologist at work. Durham, N.C., Duke University, 1973. viii, 52p., 8 facsims.   **DB28**

Gnomon XLVIII 1976 166–170 Seider
The text of three conferences held in Cambridge in 1971, with some additional notes and references, a short bibliography and eight excellent plates. The purpose is to show how a papyrologist extracts a text from a papyrus, however damaged and incomplete. The sample text used for demonstration has since been published as POxy XLI 2944. Caution in restoration is taught with the aid of three other texts. The archives of Petaus, a town clerk in the Fayum, are examined for clues on village administration in Roman Egypt. To be read for profit and pleasure.

TURNER, Eric Gardiner. The terms recto and verso; The anatomy of the papyrus scroll. Bruxelles, Fondation égyptologique Reine Élisabeth, 1978. 71p., illus. **DB29**

Rapport inaugural, Actes du XVᵉ Congrès international de papyrologie, ed. by J. Bingen and G. Nachtergael.

WILLIS, William H. "Recent papyrological work in North America." StudPap XV (1976): 109–117. **DB30**

A useful essay on the history and sizes of the various collections and the activities of scholars. This volume of Studia Papyrologica publishes seven papers (from the 6th International Congress of Classical Studies at Madrid, 1974) on the present state of papyrological studies: Bingen, France, Low Countries, and Belgium; Gigante, Italy; Voenen, Federal Republic of Germany and Fieldwork of the International Photographic Archive in Cairo; O'Callaghan, Spain; Parsons, United Kingdom; Treu, DDR; and Willis, North America.

YOUTIE, Herbert Chayyim. The textual criticism of documentary papyri; Prolegomena. London, Institute of Classical Studies, 1974. ix, 69p., illus., facsims., 14 leaves of plates. **DB31**

Gnomon XXXII 1960 335–340 Koenen
A first edition was published in 1958. Here the texts of the three conferences have been left unchanged but the notes are updated. Appendix 1 appears also in *GRBS* VII (1966), 251–258. Much practical advice on editing and interpreting texts.
See also Youtie, Herbert C., *Scriptiunculae* (Amsterdam, Hakkert, 1973–1975, 3v.). This collection of journal articles, 1938–1967, constitutes a veritable Handbook to Documentary Papyri.

Manuals

BATAILLE, A. "La papyrologie." L'Histoire et ses méthodes: 498–527. **DB32**

A brief reliable introduction by the author of *Les papyrus* (Paris, 1955).

BOWMAN, A. K. "Papyri and Roman Imperial history, 1960–1975." JRS LXVI (1976): 153–173. **DB33**

CALDERINI, Aristide. Manuale di papirologia antica greca e romana. Milan, 1938. 2 ed., 1944. 196p. **DB34**

CW XXXIII 1939 56 Johnson • RFIC 1939 108 Paribeni
A concise manual of 16 chapters and four appendices. Appendix C gives a useful Lista delle Abbreviazioni di Collezioni, Libri, Periodici Piu' Usati, and Appendix D a bibliography (p.185–192). Three preliminary chapters deal with the definition of papyrology, the writing materials and the provenance of finds. Chapter IV is devoted to Literary and Documentary Papyri, c.V–VI to the history of the discipline, c.VII

Means of Study: periodicals, collections, editions. The remaining chapters deal with paleography of papyri, grammar, literature, political history, administration, law, etc., as reflected in the papyri.
See also Calderini, A. and Montevecchi, O., "La papyrologia," in *Introduzione allo studio della cultura classica* III, 139–250.

CALDERINI, Aristide. Papiri latini; Appunti delle lezioni di papirologia. Milano, 1945. 138p., 4 plates. **DB35**

Aegyptus 1945 137–138 Calderini • AC XVI 1947 192 Hombert
A manual to initiate students into Latin papyrology, with an anthology of literary and documentary texts. The brief introduction deals with the use of Latin in Egypt, the quantitative and qualitative importance of Latin papyri and questions of paleography and language. Chapter I has a catalog of literary Latin papyri (including bilinguals) which should be checked against Paul Collart, "Les papyrus littéraires latins," *RPh* XV (1941), 112–128. Chapters II and III deal with juristic and Christian texts. The Corpusculum Papyrorum Latinorum, which forms an appendix, consists of 65 texts, 29 literary and 46 documentary, with brief commentary.

CALDERINI, Aristide. Papiri, 1; Guida allo studio della papirologia antica greca e romana. Milano, Ceschina, 1944. 3 ed., 1962. 216p. **DB36**

StudPap I 1962 122–124 Rambia
There is a Spanish translation by José O'Callaghan, *Tratado de papirología* (Barcelona, 1963), 222p., 2 plates.

COLLOMP, Paul. La papyrologie. Paris, Société d'édition, Les belles lettres, 1927. [i], 33p., 2 facsims. **DB37**

RBPh 1928 1045–1048 Hombert
A succinct introduction of 35 paragraphs which aims to show the beginner the means of exploring papyrology. Chemical means for exploring mummy labels are explained and there are general notes on literary papyri, grammar and historico-juridical papyrology. Each paragraph has its separate bibliography.

DAVID, Martin and VAN GRONINGEN, B. A. Papyrological primer. 4th ed. Leyden, Brill, 1965. 177p., 6 plates. **DB38**

StudPap V 1966 157 Pegueroles
First issued in 1940 in Dutch, it contains 35 pages of introduction, a page bibliography and 85 texts on a wide variety of topics. There are short lists of important terms referring to public institutions and private law.

GOODSPEED, Edgar Johnson and COLWELL, Ernest C. A Greek papyrus reader. Chicago, University of Chicago Press, 1936, 1935. 108p. **DB39**

JHS LXIII 1938 114 H.I.B.

A choice of texts, which makes an extremely useful textbook, provided it is used by a teacher who will amplify the rather brief introduction and scanty commentary. A good vocabulary is provided. Particularly aimed at New Testament exegesis trainees.

KENYON, Frederic G. The paleography of Greek papyri. With twenty facsimiles and a table of alphabets. Chicago, Argonaut, 1970. vi, 160p. **DB40**

Reprint of the 1899 ed.

Two preliminary chapters outline the Range of the Subject and Papyrus as Writing Material with much information on size of sheets, formation of rolls, length, height, *recto, verso,* width, titles, use of rollers, punctuation, accents, breathings, stops, abbreviations, tachygraphy. Chapter III, Non-Literary Papyri, gives the chief finds up to 1899 in the three periods of papyrology: Ptolemaic, 323 B.C.–30 B.C.; Roman, from Augustus to Diocletian; and Byzantine, from Diocletian to the Arab conquest, 640 A.D. The literary papyri of the Ptolemaic period and of the Roman are covered in two separate chapters, and there is a concluding chapter on the transition to vellum. Four appendices deal with Alphabets of Literary Papyri, Catalogs of Literary Papyri (arranged alphabetically by ancient author), The Principal Publications of non-literary Papyri, Abbreviations and Symbols. Still very useful but the analyses of hands and characteristics and dating have been completely superseded.

MONTEVECCHI, Orsolina. La papirologia. Turin, 1973. xvi, 544p., 104 plates, 2 maps. **DB41**

Manuali univ. 1ª ser. Per lo studio dell'antichità Torino Soc. ed. internaz.

REG LXXXIX 1976 113–115 Cadell • Labeo XXI 1975 70–73 Zingale Migliardi

SCHUBART, Wilhelm. Einführung in die Papyruskunde. Berlin, Weidmann, 1918. 508p., 7 plates. **DB42**

JEA 1919 305–308 Bell • Aevum 1920 105 Calderini

Was written for the scholar actually intending to decipher texts and for the literary historian. Now largely outdated.

SCHUBART, Wilhelm. Palaeographie; Unveränderter Nachdruck der 1925 erschienenen 1. Aufl. München, Beck, 1966. viii, 184p., 120 facsims. **DB43**

HdA. 1.4.1.

JHS XLIX 1929 127–129 Bell

This brief treatment is almost entirely concerned with papyri; for later MSS the author confines himself to an examination, without facsimiles, of those represented in Cavalieri and Lietzmann, *Specimina codicum Graecorum Vaticanorum.* The treatment of literary and documentary papyri is masterly, concentrating not on the history of individual letters but on the history of

style in writing. There are, for the time, many excellent facsimiles, naturally largely from Berlin papyri. After Kenyon, *Paleography of Greek papyri* (1899), this was the first systematic introduction, but it is now in many details completely outmoded.

TRAITÉ d'études byzantines; publié par Paul Lemerle avec le concours de A. Bataille et al. Paris, Presses Universitaires de France, 1955– . **DB44**

t. 2. Les Papyrus par A. Bataille.

Speculum XXXII 1957 535–536 Downey • ByzZ XLVIII 1955 380–382 Dölger

Tome 2 in the collection, Bibliothèque Byzantine, Paul Lemerle, ed., for long was the best introduction to the subject. There is an excellent bibliography of the sources and studies concerning Byzantine Egypt in the reign of Diocletian to the Arab invasion.

The opening chapter deals with papyrus and the other writing materials, explaining terms like codex, volumen, etc. Chapter 2 examines the problems posed by the interpretation and publication of a document. The great collections of texts are listed alphabetically in c.3. Chapter 4 surveys the major problems: political history, chronology, geography, topography, administrative organization, law, diplomatics, army and police, economic life, religious life, magic and the occult sciences, intellectual life, private life, all with abundant bibliography.

There are 14 excellent plates, with facing description and transcription. An accurate and comprehensive introduction for the non-specialist and a convenient reference tool for the experienced researcher.

TURNER, Eric Gardiner. Greek papyri; An introduction. Princeton, Princeton University Press, 1968. 1980 paperback. ix, 220p., illus., facsims., map, port. **DB45**

BECh CXXVII 1969 436–438 Cadell • CPh LXV 1970 125 Oost • BBF XV 1970 889–890 Astruc

An introduction addressed as much to the non-specialist as to the beginner and a welcome attempt to dispel the arcane mystique in which some papyrologists prefer to operate. Has much useful information on scribes, scroll- and book-making, and related topics. The history of papyrology is sketched, and the problems encountered in editing papyri described. A good section is Papyri and Greek Literature (though the author does not believe in the dichotomy between literary and non-literary texts). Another valuable section is The Principal Editions of Papyri, with standard abbreviations. See the companion volume *Greek manuscripts of the ancient world* (1971); *A reference book of Greek papyri* is promised.

Facsimiles

NORSA, Medea. La scrittura letteraria greca dal secolo IV a.C. all' VIII d.C. Firenze, Caldini, 1939. 39p., 19 plates. **DB46**

Aegyptus 1940 93–94 Calderini • CE XV 1940 302–303 Hombert

There is a companion set for documentary papyri: Norsa, M., *Scrittura documentarie* (Rome, 3v., 1929, 1933, 1946).

ROBERTS, Colin Henderson. Greek literary hands, 350 B.C.–A.D. 400. Oxford, Clarendon Press, 1955. xix, 24p., plates.   **DB47**

CE XXXI 1956 190–192 Gorteman • CPh LIII 1958 43 Lewis

Two pages of bibliography and six of introduction precede the 24 plates, with descriptions, illustrating 57 MSS. The specimens, rather small, are in actual size. They begin with the Timotheus papyrus and end with the codex Sinaiticus. Almost half the documents are chosen because of their datability, a guiding principle for which careful criteria are proposed. An excellent introduction to the Greek book for the Hellenistic and Roman periods.

SEIDER, Richard. Paläographie der griechischen Papyri. Stuttgart, Hiersemann, 1967– . Plates.   **DB48**

I. Tafeln, 1: Urkunden. Stuttgart, Hiersemann, 1967. 111p., illus., maps. II. Tafeln, 2: Literarische Papyri. Stuttgart, Hiersemann, 1970. 189p., 40 plates.

Gnomon XLIII 1971 710–712 Turner • Aegyptus XLVI 1966 308–309 Calderini • BECh CXXIX 1971 453–455 Cadell

In this triptych on the paleography of Greek papyri, part I is dedicated to documentary hands. Volume 1 contains 63 documents, chronologically arranged, extending from Peleph 1 (311 B.C.) to 616 A.D. Part II

(1970) is devoted to literary papyri, and the selection of 71 literary documents on 40 plates offers an interesting and valuable conspectus on the range and diversity of the literary papyri and their enormous contribution to philology. The quality of the plates is at best uneven, at worst downright bad. The series begins with the now famous Derveni, Thessaloniki papyrus and ends with liturgical texts which may be as late as the 9th century A.D.

See also the author's *Paläographie der lateinischen Papyri*, I. Tafeln, 1. Urkunden. (Stuttgart, Hiersemann, 1972. 189p., 40 plates) which follows the same plan. Here v.1 describes 66 documents with 40 plates, illustrating the script of each selection in the original size. Selections range from the 1st century B.C. to the beginnings of the 7th century A.D.., and come from various locations in Egypt and from Dura Europos, Ravenna and the Vatican.

TURNER, Eric Gardiner. Greek manuscripts of the ancient world. Oxford, Clarendon Press, 1971. xiv, 132p., 73 plates, illus., facsims.   **DB49**

Gnomon XLVI 1974 147–152 Cavallo • BASP VIII 1971 119–120 Donovan

Useful to professional and nonprofessional alike, this volume contains 27 pages of introduction on Greek writing in general and on the present selection of 72 documents, with plates, in which the author sets forth his own classification of hands. The plates are of good quality and many are of recent discoveries, e.g., the Derveni commentary on Orphic cosmogonic verses (no. 51). Besides detailed descriptions the author gives a "diplomatic" transcription of several lines of each illustration.

DC   GREEK PALEOGRAPHY

Bibliography, Methodology, and Orientation

ALLEN, Thomas William. Notes on abbreviations in Greek manuscripts. With eleven pages of facsimiles of photolithography. Unchanged reprint of the 1889 ed. Amsterdam, Hakkert, 1967. 70p.   **DC1**

The bulk of the material here is taken from MSS in the Bodleian and the British Library, with some additions from French and Italian libraries. There are 12 plates to illustrate the abbreviations, which are treated alphabetically.

BOMPAIRE, J. and IRIGOIN, J. La paléographie grecque et byzantine, Paris, 21–25 octobre 1974. Paris, Édition du CNRS, 1977. 588, 12p.   **DC2**

Colloques internat. du CNRS N° 559.
BECh CXXXVII 1979 91–94 Poulle

CANART, Paul and PERI, Vittorio. Sussidi bibliografici per i manoscritti greci della Biblioteca Vaticana. Città del Vaticano, Biblioteca apostolica vaticana, 1970. xv, 708p.   **DC3**

Studi e testi; 261.
CR XXIV 1974 146 Wilson • AB XCI 1973 433–434 Halkin

This extremely well-organized work provides systematic and up-to-date bibliographical references to the Greek manuscripts in the Vatican library. About 100 preliminary pages list the abbreviations for the multitude of books and journals cited, some as late as 1967. Then the great Greek collections are surveyed numerically: Codici Barberiniani Breci dell' Archivio di San Pietro; Codici Barberiniani Greci (598 items); Codici Borgiani Greci (27); Codici Chigiani Greci (55); Codici

Ottoboniani Greci (473); Codici Palatini Greci (432); Codici Greci di Pio II (55); Codici Reginensi Greci (190); Codici Rossiani Greci (37); Codici Urbinati Greci (165); Codici Vaticani Greci (2,625).

DAIN, Alphonse. "Paléographie Grecque." L'Histoire et ses méthodes: 532–552.   **DC4**

A short treatment of the history of Greek paleography from Montfaucon, and of the history of writing from Linear B.

See also *loc. cit.,* Marichal, R., "La critique des textes," 1247–1366.

DEFRADAS, Jean. Guide de l'étudiant helléniste. Paris, Presses Universitaires de France, 1968. viii, 159p.   **DC4a**

C. V. Paléographie, Histoire et Établissement des Textes, 106–112.

Includes helpful orientation and bibliography.

GARITTE, Gérard. "Manuscrits Grecs, I (1940–1950)." Scriptorium VI (1952): 114–146.   **DC5**

Described by Irigoin as "un instrument de travail incomparable," Garritte's survey continues in "Manuscrits Grecs, II • (1950–1955)," *Scriptorium* XII (1958), 118–148, and encompasses 552 and 680 items respectively.

HATCH, William Henry Paine. The principal uncial manuscripts of the New Testament. Chicago, University of Chicago Press, 1939. xiv, 33p., 76 plates (facsims).   **DC6**

Descriptive letterpress on versos facing the plates.

CR LIII 1939 149 Souter • AJPh LXI 1940 248–249 Sanders

Full-page plates from papyri and vellum MSS extending from the 2d century (Pap. Rylands Gk. 457) to the 11th or 12th century. Plates I–XIII cover papyri and the remainder vellum codices, including Codex Vaticanus, Sinaiticus, Alexandrinus, Ephraemi Rescriptus, Washington, Bezae, Borgianus, and Dublinensis (upside down). In the introduction the author "has tried to state in concise form the essential facts of Greek palaeography." One misses an introductory section on the Uncial Script (but cf. H. Hatch, "The origin and meaning of the term uncial," *CPh* XXX 1935, 247–254). Each plate is preceded by a brief description and the most essential bibliographical notices, but there are no transcriptions. There are two plates of the Sinaiticus and three of the Alexandrinus.

HUNGER, Herbert. Geschichte der Textüberlieferung, 1. Zurich, [1961–64].   **DC7**

Treats Griechische Paläographie (p.72–107).

HUNGER, Herbert. "Paleography, Greek." NCE 10: 874–879.   **DC8**

IRIGOIN, Jean. "Les Manuscrits Grecs, 1931–1960." Lustrum VII (1962): 5–330, and 332–335 (Register).   **DC9**

Irigoin's bibliographical survey of Greek manuscripts is the best point of entry to the subject. For work prior to 1931 see Weinberger, Wilhelm, *Bursians Jahresbericht* CCXXXVI (1932), 85–113, covering 1926 to 1930, mainly Latin paleography.

LAURION, Gaston. "Les principales collections de manuscrits grecs." Phoenix XV (1961): 1–13.   **DC10**

This short article presents a panoramic view of the location and state of preservation of the more than 45,000 Greek manuscripts located in the great libraries, with brief indications on the status of catalogues.

LEHMANN, Oskar. Die tachygraphischen Abkürzungen der griechischen Handschriften. Mit 10 Tafeln. [Reprografischer Nachdruck der Ausg. Leipzig, 1880.] Hildesheim, Olms, 1965. vi, 111p. 10 1.   **DC11**

MAAS, Paul. "Griechische Paläographie." Gercke-Norden, *Einleitung,* 1927, 3rd ed., Bd. 1: 9–81.   **DC12**

MANDILARAS, Basil G. The verb in the Greek non-literary papyri. Athens, Hellenic Ministry of Culture and Sciences, 1973. 493p.   **DC13**

Aegyptus LV 1975 334–335 Milani

This is an abridgement of the author's thesis, "Moods and tenses of the Greek non-literary papyri" (cf. *BASP* VIII 1971, 71–72). It covers the period from the end of the 4th century B.C. to the beginning of the 8th century A.D. and contrasts the relatively static character of the Greek of the Ptolemaic papyri with the language's fluidity in the Roman and Byzantine periods. A brief historical sketch of earlier research in papyrus and N.T. grammar is accompanied with an excellent bibliography.

MARICHAL, Robert. "L'écriture latine et l'écriture grecque du Ier au VIe siècle." L'Antiquité classique XIX (1950): 111–144.   **DC14**

The text of a communication to the 6th International Congress of Papyrology in Paris, 1949. Since the Latin alphabet is a Greek one, a synoptic study of the early writing in both languages is desirable as a way of understanding cultural influences and changes, especially after the Roman conquest of Greece, 272 B.C. The study is done here for literary and documentary texts, with six very illustrative plates and several figures for letter forms.

MASAI, F. "La paléographie gréco-latine, ses tâches, ses méthodes." Scriptorium X (1956): 281–302.   **DC15**

See now Masai, F. *Miscellanea codicologica F. Masai dicata MCMLXXIX,* ed. by R. Cockshaw, M.-C. Garand, and P. Jodogne. 2 vols. Ghent, 1979. 78 plates. (Les Publications de Scriptorium; 8.)

MATEU IBARS, Josefina and MATEU IBARS, María Dolores. Bibliografía paleográfica. Barcelona, Universidad de Barcelona, 1974. xxviii, 932p., 7 leaves of plates. **DC16**

Scriptorium XXI 1977 345 Masai
The most elaborate bibliographical tool devoted to codicology and paleography; useful for both Greek and Latin. Especially valuable for catalogues of libraries.

MENTZ, A. Antike Stenographie. München, Heimeran, 1927. 29p. **DC17**

Samml. Tusculum.
RA XXX 1929 156

M[INNS] E. and McD[ONALD], A. H. "Palaeography." OCD²: 768–770. **DC18**

MIONI, Elpidio. Introduzione alla paleografia greca. Padova, Liviana, 1973. viii, 140p., 30 plates. **DC19**

Università di Padova. Studi bizantini e neogreci; 5.
OrChristPer XL 1974 224–225 Capizzi • Paideia XXIX 1974 86–89 Colonna
Mioni follows the traditional treatment of Wattenbach, Gardthausen and Thompson, with the clarity and conciseness that is a result of many years of teaching the subject at the University of Padua. He first defines paleography and codicology and gives a brief history of the discipline and a useful bibliography of collections of facsimiles (p.8–11). Writing materials and instruments are then examined, followed by the form of the MS (roll, codex, palimpsest). The general notions of Greek writing are then presented: majuscule, ductus, scripta continua, libraria, etc. There are separate chapters on majuscule and minuscule writing, and useful chapters on the execution of the MS, including the questions of dictation, dating and subscriptions, and abbreviations (illustrated). The final chapter, I Grandi Problemi della Paleografia, disappointingly confines itself to cataloging (at which Mioni excels) and the briefest remarks on scriptoria and modern libraries with MS holdings. There is a brief bibliography (p.119–122) and two indices. The 30 plates are well chosen and briefly described, but not transcribed.
See also Mioni, Elpidio, *Catalogo di manoscritti greci esistenti nelle biblioteche italiane* (Roma, 1965, 2v., xvi, 610 p.). This catalog covers 73 Italian MS centers from Agrigentum to Viterbo outside such major collections as Vaticani and Laurentiani. It describes 349 Greek MSS, many of them hitherto unidentified or uncatalogued.
See also *I codici greci in minuscola dei sec. IX e X della Biblioteca nazionale marciana*, descrizione e tavole e cura di Elpidio Mioni e Mariarosa Formentin (Padova, Liviana, 1975), a most handsome volume with 49 plates from the Biblioteca nazionale marciana, Venice.

RICHARD, Marcel. Répertoire des bibliothèques et des catalogues de manuscrits grecs. 2. éd. Paris, Centre national de la recherche scientifique, 1958. xix, 276p. **DC20**

Publications de L'Institut de recherche et d'histoire des textes.
CR XIV 1964 200–202 Young • Aevum XXIV 1950 196–209 Pertusi, with addenda and corrigenda • BAGB 1959 157–164 Astruc
Richard's *Répertoire*, an indispensable bibliographical tool, contains a short but valuable bibliography; a listing of specialized catalogs, e.g., medical, astrological, hagiographical; a listing of catalogs by country and by individual cities, towns, etc. Supplément 1 (1958–1963) is divided similarly. The second edition of the *Répertoire* (1958) contains 884 items as against 529 in 1948. Some papyri are included, though for Richard they are not "manuscrits." For control of new catalogs, cf. Année Philologique III. Histoire des Textes: Inventaires et Catalogues Regionaux. Bibliothèques.

RICHARD, Marcel. Répertoire des bibliothèques et des catalogues de manuscrits grecs; Supplément. Paris, Éditions du Centre national de la recherche scientifique, 1964. xvi, 77p. **DC21**

Documents, études et répertoires, publiés par l'Institut de recherche et d'histoire des textes; 9.
ByzZ LVIII 1965 370–372 Hunger • BBF X 1965 671–672 Astruc • REG LXXXIII 1970 500 Irigoin
Continues to display the clarity, precision and rigid documentation of the *Répertoire*, whose numeration is preserved here. There is a list of minor corrections to the *Répertoire*.
See *Studia codicologica*, hrsg., Dummer, Jürgen et al. (*TU CXXIV*, Berlin, 1977, 509p.), a *Festschrift* for Richard.

THOMPSON, Edward M., Sir. An introduction to Greek and Latin palaeography. New York, B. Franklin, 1965. xxi, 600p., illus. (facsims.). **DC22**

Burt Franklin bibliography and reference series; 71. An enlarged edition of the author's *Handbook of Greek and Latin paleography* (5th ed. 1906).
Thompson incorporates the best from the older manuals, Gardthausen, Steffens, Omont, Lindsay. Seven preliminary chapters deal with writing in all its aspects. Chapters 8–12 are devoted to Greek paleography: Papyri, The Literary Hand or Book-hand in Papyri, Cursive Script in Papyri, Cursive Alphabets, Comparison of Literary and Cursive Alphabets, The Uncial Book-hand in Vellum Codices, The Minuscule Book-Hand in the Middle Ages, Greek Writing in Western Europe. There are tables of Greek and Latin alphabets, Greek literary alphabets, Greek cursive alphabets. The facsimiles are in four sections: Greek literary papyri (p.1–18), Greek cursive papyri (p.19–42), Greek uncials (p.43–51) and Greek minuscules (p.52–75).

Catalogues

ANDRÉS, Gregorio de. Catálogo de los códices Griegos de la Real Biblioteca de El Escorial. Madrid, 1965, 1967. 3v. **DC23**

REG LXXXIII 1970 503–506 Irigoin • AB LXXXIV 1966 505–508 Halkin

An excellent catalog of the best collection of Greek MSS in Spain.

BANDINI, Angelo. Catalogus codicum manuscriptorum Bibliothecae Mediceae Laurentianae. Accedunt supplementa tria ab E. Rostagno et N. Festa congesta necnon additamentum ex inventariis Bibliotheca Laurentianae depromptum accuravit Fridolf Kudlien. Lipsiae, Zentral-Antiquariat der Deutschen Demokratischen Republik, 1961. 3v., illus., port., facsims.   **DC24**

Biblica XLVII 1966 473–474 Martini

A catalog of the famous Laurentian Library, Florence, which goes back to Cosimo and Lorenzo de' Medici (1434–1464 and 1469–1492).

CLARK, Kenneth Willis. Checklist of manuscripts in St. Catherine's Monastery, Mount Sinai. Microfilmed for the Library of Congress, 1950. Washington, D.C., Library of Congress Photoduplication Service, 1952. ix, 53p.   **DC25**

JThS n.s. IV 1953 87–88 Bell • JBL LXXII 1953 78 Filson

Represents a major United States contribution to international scholarship. To St. Catherine's Monastery library we owe the Codex Sinaiticus and other precious manuscripts. Only the more important of the library's contents were filmed and this is an index of the films taken, not by any means confined to Greek. Arabic, Georgian, Syriac, Slavonic and Ethiopic are also included. The contents are mainly religious, but there are some Greek classics, e.g., Greek 1415, Euripides A.D. 1465; Greek 1721, Sophocles, 16th century. This can now be supplemented by Kamil, M., in *Catalogue of all manuscripts in the Monastery of St. Catherine on Mount Sinai.* See also Politis, *Scriptorium* XXXIV (1980), 3–17.

CLARK, Kenneth Willis. Checklist of manuscripts in the libraries of the Greek and Armenian patriarchates in Jerusalem. Microfilmed for the Library of Congress, 1949–1950. Washington, D.C., Photoduplication Service, Library of Congress, 1953. xi, 44p.   **DC26**

HUNGER, Herbert. Katalog der griechischen Handschriften der österreichischen Nationalbibliothek. Wien, Prachner, 1961– .   **DC27**

1 Teil: Codices historici. Codices philosophici et philologici.

Gnomon XXXIII 1961 807–810 de Meigïer • REG LXXIV 1961 283–287 Irigoin

A replacement for Nessel's Catalog, following its divisions. Philosophici et philologici account for 477 MSS (130 and 347) out of a total of 882. The remaining parts will cover theologici, iuridici, medici et historici.

IRIGOIN, Jean. "Les manuscrits grecs, 1." REG LXXXIII (1970): 500–529.   **DC28**

Provides a critical survey of 18 catalogs, by country, which were published after Richard's *Répertoire* and *Supplément.*

LAMBROS, P. Catalogue of the Greek manuscripts of Mount Athos. Cambridge, 1895–1900. Reprint, Amsterdam, 1966. 2v. ix, 438p., vii, 597p.   **DC29**

LAURENT, V. "Bulletin critique; Catalogues de Manuscrits Grecs, Paléographie et Histoire des Textes." REByz XIV (1956): 217–239.   **DC30**

MANOUSAKAS, M. I. "Hellenika Cheirographa kai eggrapha tou Hagiou Orous." EHBS XXXII (1963): 377–419.   **DC31**

Bibliography concerning the Greek MSS of Mt. Athos and its more than 100 monasteries. Index of names.

OXFORD UNIVERSITY. Bodleian Library. A summary catalogue of Western manuscripts in the Bodleian Library. Oxford, Clarendon Press, 1895–1953 [Ann Arbor, Mich.: University Microfilms, 1973]. 7v. in 8.   **DC32**

The Catalog contains the following volumes: 1. Historical introduction and conspectus of shelfmarks, by R. W. Hunt; 2. part 1. Collections received before 1660 and miscellaneous MSS acquired during the first half of the 17th century, by F. Madan and H. H. E. Craster; part 2. Collections and miscellaneous MSS acquired during the 2d half of the 17th century, by F. Madan, H. H. E. Craster and N. Denholm-Young; 3. Collections received during the 18th century, by F. Madan; 4. Collections received during the first half of the 19th century, by F. Madan; 5. Collections received during the second half of the 19th century and miscellaneous MSS acquired between 1895 and 1890, by F. Madan; 6. Accessions, 1890–1915, by F. Madan and H. H. E. Craster; 7. Index, by P. D. Record.

For a brief overview see *The survival of ancient literature; A catalogue of an exhibition of Greek and Latin classical manuscripts mainly from Oxford libraries,* by R. W. Hunt and others (Oxford, Bodleian Library, 1975, 100p., 26 plates) and *Greek manuscripts in the Bodleian Library; An exhibition* (Oxford, Bodleian Library, 1966, 55p., 20 plates).

PARIS. Bibliothèque nationale. Le supplément grec. Par Charles Astruc et Marie Louise Concasty. Paris, Bibliothèque nationale, 1960– .   **DC33**

Catalogue des manuscrits grecs; 3.

ByzZ LIV 1961 126–129 Hunger • JHS LXXXII 1962 178–179 Browning

In the present volume Astruc and Concasty brilliantly continue the work of their master, Devreesse, in cataloguing the greatest (ca.5,000) collection of Greek MSS in the world (Devreesse catalogued the Fonds Coislin in 1945). The present work describes the last third of the *Supplément grec,* comprising MSS acquired by the library from 1875 to the present, the great bulk of which are Christian, Byzantine and post-Byzantine.

For the earlier catalogues, cf. Richard, *Répertoire* 58, 667–680.

SAMBERGER, Christa. Catalogi codicum Graecorum qui in minoribus bibliothecis Italicis asservantur. In duo volumina collati et novissimis additamentis aucti. Lipsiae, Zentral-Antiquariat, 1965–1968. 2v.   **DC34**

> AB LXXXIV 1966 263–267 Halkin

VATICAN. Bibliotheca vaticana. Codices vaticani Graeci. Edited by Giovanni Mercati, Pio Pietro Franchi de' Cavalieri, Robert Devreesse, Ciro Giannelli, and Paul Canart. Romae, Typis Polyglottis Vaticanis, 1923.   **DC35**

> The first three volumes (cod. 1–329, 330–603 and 604–866) are called tomus 1–111.
>
> AB LXXXIX 1971 205–206 Halkin • REByz XXIX 1971 326–328 Darrouzès
>
> A recent addition to this massive project is *Bibliothecae Apostolicae Vaticanae codices manu scripti Recensiti; Codices Vaticani Graeci: Codices 1745–1962,* Canart, Paul, ed.: I. Codicum Enarrationes Citta del Vaticano Bibl. apost. (1970, xx, 785p.); II. Introductio, addenda, indices (1973, lxxi, 203p.).
>
> Volume I contains minute descriptions of 218 MSS and is characterized by great variety in content, clarity and minuteness in exposition, and perfection in presentation.

Manuals

DEVREESSE, Robert. Introduction à l'étude des manuscrits grecs. Paris, Klincksieck, 1954. 347p., plates, facsims.   **DC36**

> RPh XXIX 1955 64–67 Irigoin • Scriptorium X 1956 148–152 Garitte
>
> Devreesse's work is in two parts: History of the Book and Special Collections. Part I deals with ancient testimonia on writing, the papyrus roll, codex, vellum, palimpsest, paper; the instruments of writing, types of writing—uncial and minuscule—abbreviations, shorthand, conventional signs, nomina sacra. Part II deals with special collections, including Old and New Testament, exegetical catenae, liturgical books, canonical texts, educational texts; the exact sciences and the pseudo-sciences; medicine; military science; and how to describe a manuscript. A lengthy appendix lists dated MSS from c.512 to 1593. Devreesse's competence in so many disciplines makes him an unrivalled exponent of the total study of ancient and medieval Greek manuscripts.

FONSECA, L. Gonzaga Aires da. Epitome Introductionis in Palaeographiam Graecam (Biblicam). Roma, Pontificio Istituto Biblico, 1944. Ed. altera. 132p.   **DC37**

Eminently practical class-notes (in Latin) on the history of Greek paleography and the matter and form of writing. A second book deals with the origin and evolution of the Greek alphabet and the various letter forms and writing types.

GARDTHAUSEN, Viktor Emil. Griechische Paleographie. 2. Auflage. Leipzig, Veit, 1911–1913. 2v., illus.   **DC38**

> REG XXV 1912 212–215 Levêque
>
> Volume I deals with the materials of writing and the external forms—roll, papyrus, codex, letter writing, sealings, binding, ink, ornamentation. Volume II deals with scripts from the Bronze Age onwards, the invention of the Greek alphabet, early types of writing (boustrophedon, etc.), stichometry, colometry. There are good sections on uncial, cursive and minuscule, also on ductus, the history and systematization of shorthand, cryptography, abbreviations, numerals, accentuation, punctuation, subscriptions, chronology. Long a standard work.

HARLFINGER, D. Einführung in die griechische Kodicologie und Minuskel Paläographie. 1975. 150p.   **DC39**

> See also *Griechische Kodikologie und Textüberlieferung,* ed. by D. von Harlfinger. Darmstadt, Wissenschaftlige Buchgesellschaft, 1980. xii, 716p. (RPh LV 1981 362–365 Hoffmann)

MONTFAUCON, Bernard de. Paleographia Graeca; sive, De ortu et progressu litterarum Graecarum: et de variis omnium saeculorum scriptionis Graecae generibus: itemque de abbreviationibus & de notis variarum artium ac disciplinarum, additis figuris & schematibus ad fidem manuscriptorum codicum. Farnborough, Gregg, 1970. xxix, 574p., 8 plates (6 fold), facsims.   **DC40**

> Reprint of the 1704 ed.
>
> Montfaucon (1655–1741) is credited with founding the science of Greek paleography. The 1970 reprint of the elegant original testifies to its continuing usefulness. Book VII (p.433–499) is a description of Mt. Athos and 22 of its monasteries. Translated from the Greek of John Comnenus.

WATTENBACH, Wilhelm. Anleitung zur griechischen Palaeographie. 2 Aufl. Leipzig, Hirzel, 1877. 3rd ed., 1895.   **DC41**

> Reprographischer Nachdruck der Ausgabe Leipzig, 1895 (Hildesheim, Gerstenberg, 1971).
>
> Includes a brief history of Greek paleography and the pioneering contributions of Montfaucon, Piacentini, Bast, Schubart, Vollgraft, Tischendorf and Gardthausen. The longest section (p.9–86) deals with uncial, cursive and minuscule and gives a chronological listing of the earliest dated MSS, from 835 A.D. down to 1497. There are useful concluding sections on letter-forms, abbreviations and punctuation.

Facsimiles

BARBOUR, R. Greek literary hands, A.D. 400–1600. Oxford, Clarendon Press, 1981. 184p., 110 illus.   **DC42**

Oxford palaeographical handbooks.
JHS CIII 1983 230 Irigoin • BBF XXVIII, 1 1983 97–98 Astruc

CERETELLI, G. and SOBOLEVSKI, S. Exempla codicum Graecorum litteris minusculis scriptorum annorumque notis instructorum. Mosquae, 1911–1913. 2v., xv, 43 plates, xix, 62 plates.   **DC43**

I. Codices Mosqenses. II. Codices Petropolitani.
CR XXVIII 1914 279 Lowther-Clarke • JS n.s. XIII 1915 111–121 Omont
A sumptuous series of photographic reproductions of specimen pages from dated MSS preserved in Russian libraries. They provide accurately dated specimens to illustrate the development of Greek minuscule, a complete history, in effect, of minuscule from the 9th to the 14th centuries. Photographs are full-sized and excellent. The contents are mainly patristic and liturgical. The Moscow volume contains minuscule from 880 to 1399. Each MS is prefaced by a brief but accurate summary description, indicating provenance, content, subscription, and bibliography. The Petrograd MSS show specimens dated from 835 to 1405. Most of the MSS come from Mt. Athos, St. Catherine of Sinai or St. Sabas of Jerusalem. Omont's review lists them chronologically.

Du RIEU, Willem Nicholas and DE VRIES, Scato. Codices Graeci et Latini photographice depicti. Lugduni Batavorum, 1897–1919.   **DC44**

Of the 19 fascicles in this series the following are devoted to individual Greek authors: III–IV Plato, VI Homerus, Ilias, IX Aristophanes, X Dioscorides, XV Anthologia Palatina.

FOLLIERI, Henrica. Codices Graeci Bibliothecae Vaticanae selecti; Temporum locorumque ordine digesti commentariis et transcriptionibus instructi. Roma, Apud Bibliothecam Vaticanam, 1969. 110p., plates, 70 facsims.   **DC45**

Scriptorium XXIV 1970 452–453 Irigoin • Muséon LXXXIV 1971 286–289 Mossay • Athenaeum L 1972 201–203 Colonna
Provides an excellent initiation to Greek palaeography. A most competent updating of Franchi de' Cavalieri and Lietzmann, *Specimina,* which had served generations of Hellenists. Manuscripts are reproduced chronologically and according to the town or region in which they were copied. Besides the excellent plates there are approximately 100 pages of *enarratio* and *descriptio.*

FRANCHI DE CAVALIERI, Pio Pietro. Specimina codicum graecorum vaticanorum. Editio

iterata et aucta. Berolini, De Gruyter, 1929. 1st ed., Bonn, 1910. xx, 60 facsims.   **DC46**

HARLFINGER, Dieter and PRATO, G. Specimina Sinaitica. Die datierten griechischen Handschriften des Katharinen-Klosters auf dem Berg Sinai, 9.–12. Jh. Berlin, Reimer, 1983. 68, 157p.   **DC46a**

HATCH, William Henry Paine. Facsimiles and descriptions of minuscule manuscripts of the New Testament. Cambridge, Mass., Harvard University Press, 1951. [xii], 289p., 100 facsims.   **DC47**

Companion to the author's . . . "The principal uncial manuscripts of the New Testament."
Speculum XXVII 1952 387–390 Willoughby • JTS n.s. III 1952 257–260 Bell • Biblica XXXIV 1953 404–406 Smith
The minuscule came into use in the 9th century. The first facsimile here is from the copy of the Four Gospels in Leningrad, dated to 835. This is the only specimen whose date is given by the scribe; the other 99 have been dated by the author on paleographical grounds.

IRIGOIN, Jean. "Les manuscrits grecs, II; Nouveaux Recueils de fac-similés." REG LXXXV (1972): 543–571.   **DC48**

A critical review of 13 recent volumes of facsimiles. See Mioni, *Introduzione* (p.9–11) for an excellent bibliography of facsimiles.

KOMINIS, Athanasios D. Facsimiles of dated Patmian codices. By the Academy of Athens with an introduction by Dr. Dionysius A. Zakythinos. English version by Dr. Mark Naoumides. Athens, Royal Hellenic Research Foundation, Center of Byzantine Studies, 1970. 129p., 176 leaves of plates, illus.   **DC49**

Hellenica XXIV 1971 184–191 Politis • CR XXIV 1974 145–146 Wilson • CHR LX 1974 126–127 Dennis • JHS XCI 1971 215–216 Browning
Dr. Kominis, while preparing a catalog of this important (ca. 1,000 MSS) but rather inaccessible collection (Sakkelion's catalog appeared in 1890), provides in the present volume a photograph and a summary description of each dated MS in the collection, dates ranging from 941 to 1798. Plates 1–66 illustrate MSS anterior to 1600. The only classical text is a Euripides of 1421. For the period 941–1200 A.D., Kominis gives more material than the Lakes did in their collection. The quality of the photographs is not first-rate and the scale in many instances has been reduced. The work first appeared in Greek in 1968. There is a transcription of many of the facsimiles, a helpful bibliography and several indices.

LAKE, Kirsopp and LAKE, Silva. Dated Greek minuscule manuscripts to the year 1200. Boston,

The American Academy of the Arts and Sciences, 1934–1939. 10v., illus., facsims. **DC50**

Indices to v. 1–10, 1945.
ByzZ XL 1940 118–125 Dölger • JHS LIX 1939 178–179 Allen
The most complete set of facsimiles for minuscule MSS. Each portfolio contains a very concise, technical description of each MS and about 75 loose plates. Full-size facsimiles are given of one or more pages of each MS and of the subscription or other statement determining the date. The proportion of classical MSS is very small.

MAYSER, Edwin. Grammatik der griechischen Papyri aus der Ptolemäerzeit; Mit Einschluss der gleichzeitigen Ostraka und der in Ägypten verfassten Inschriften. 2.Aufl. Berlin, De Gruyter, Reprint 1970, 1923. xxiv, 231p. **DC51**

Bd. 1. Laut- und Wortlehre. Neue Ausgabe. Bd. 2. Satzlehre. Analystische Teil, 1 Hälfte.
ACR II 1972 84 Gilliam • CR XXIII 1973 219–220 Turner
The most ample grammatical study of the papyri, this work has dominated the field since the beginning of the century. Bd. 1, Teil 1, Einleitung und Lautlehre has been published in a second edition by Hans Schmoll (1970), and includes (xi–xxiii) bibliography from 1936 to 1969. The introduction gives a general characterization of the language of the documents of the Ptolemaic period and details the borrowings from the Egyptian and Semitic languages. Schmoll has taken into account the enormous volume of new materials while remaining faithful to Mayser's planned revision of his *Einleitung,* which, however, remained a "sketch, an aggregation of notes, and an aspiration." It is hoped that further volumes will similarly bring up to date the evidence assembled by Mayser (who died in 1937) from the papyri for the changing orthography, phonology, morphology and syntax of Greek during the Ptolemaic period.

MERKELBACH, Reinhold and VAN THIEL, Helmut. Griechisches Leseheft zur Einführung in Paläographie und Textkritik. Göttingen, Vandenhoeck & Ruprecht, 1965. xi, 111p. (chiefly facsims.). **DC52**

Studienhefte zur Altertumswissenschaft; Heft 10.
JHS LXXXVII 1967 212 Young • CR XVI 1966 372–373 Easterling • Gnomon XXXVIII 1966 630 Hunger • CW LIX 1966 310 Finch
Merkelbach's object is to provide the material for a truly interdependent study of paleography and textual criticism. The book differs from the usual type of paleographical handbook in which a series of facsimiles illustrating the development of Greek hands is presented in chronological order with little attention to the content of the MSS illustrated. The aim here is to provide manuscript texts for seminar exercises in both paleography and textual criticism. The range of specimens is wide: Homeric hymns, a Platonic Epistle, pieces from Aristotle, Theophrastos, Marcus Aurelius, Clement of

Alexandria. All but two of the 30 excerpts come from *codices unici* or from MSS known to be archetypes of all other extant MSS. All periods of medieval bookmaking are represented. The brief descriptions of MSS are sometimes deficient on paleographical detail and the scholarly literature.

NEW PALAEOGRAPHICAL SOCIETY, London. Facsimiles of ancient manuscripts. London, Oxford University Press, 1st ser., 1903–1912; 2d ser., 1913–1930. 2v. **DC53**

Volumes: 1. Introduction. Greek, Latin and Modern Languages; 2. Latin and Modern Languages, cont'd.
To facilitate use cf. Dean, Lindley Richard, *An index to facsimiles in the Palaeographical Society publications* (Princeton, 1914) or *Indices to facsimiles of ancient manuscripts,* 1st series (London, 1914), covering 1903–1912 and containing the following indices: Chronological, Authors and Subjects, Country of Origin, Character of Handwriting, Ornamentation, Scribes and Artists, Materials Other than Vellum, Present Owners, Former Owners, Concordance Table.

OMONT, Henri Auguste. Fac-similés des manuscrits grecs datés de la Bibliothèque nationale du IXe siècle au XIVe siècle. Paris, Leroux, 1890–1891. xii, 124p., 100 facsims. **DC54**

This is complemented by Omont's *Fac-similés des plus anciens manuscrits grecs, en onciale et en minuscule, de la Bibliothèque nationale, du IVe aux XIIe siècle* (Paris, 1892). See also Omont, Henri, *Fac-similés des manuscrits grecs des XVe et XVIe siècles* (Hildesheim and New York, Olms, 1974; Nachdruck der Ausgabe, Paris, 1887).

OMONT, Henri Auguste. Miniatures des plus anciens manuscrits grecs de la Bibliothèque nationale du VIe et au XIV siècle. 2d ed. Paris, Champion, 1929. Reprint. 2p., viii, 66p., 138 plates (facsims.). **DC55**

First published by Leroux (Paris, 1902) with the title *Facsimilés des miniatures des plus anciens manuscrits grecs de la Bibliothèque nationale.*

ROBERTS, Colin Henderson. Greek literary hands; 350 B.C.–A.D. 400. Oxford, Clarendon Press, 1955. xix, 24p., illus. **DC56**

Oxford palaeographical handbooks.
CPh LIII 1958 43 Lewis
Specimens of 57 MSS are reproduced full-size on 24 wonderfully clear plates, beginning with the Berlin Timotheus, the earliest extant Greek papyrus, and ending with the Codex Sinaiticus. Each plate has an incisive commentary on the facing page.

SABAS, Episcopus Mojaisky. Specimina palaeographica codicum Graecorum et Slavonicorum Bibl. Mosquensis Synodalis saec. VI–XVII. Mosquae, 1863. 1v, 46p., 2 illus. titles, 47, 13 plates. **DC57**

In Russian and Latin.

SPATHARAKIS, Iohannis. Corpus of dated illuminated Greek manuscripts to the year 1453. Leiden, Brill, 1981. 2v., xv, 99p.; iv, 10p., 611 plates.   **DC58**

> I. Text. II. Illustrations.
> Hellenica XXXIV 1982–1983 259–264 Atzalos
> Of the 611 plates covering the 350 extant dated MSS, 395 include text specimens. This volume is especially valuable for MSS containing miniatures. An extensive bibliography accompanies each illustrated MS.

TURYN, Alexander. Dated Greek manuscripts of the thirteenth and fourteenth centuries in the libraries of Italy. Urbana, University of Illinois Press, 1972. 2v.   **DC59**

> 1. Text; 2. Plates.
> CPh LXXI 1976 188–189 • RPh XLIX 1975 286–289

TURYN, Alexander, ed. Codices graeci Vaticani; Saeculis XIII et XIV scripti annorumque notis instructi. In civitate vaticana, Ex Bibliotheca Apostolica Vaticana, 1964. xvi, 206p., 205 leaves of plates, facsims.   **DC60**

> ByzZ LVIII 1965 372–374 Hunger • JHS LXXXVI 1966 307–309 Wilson
> An imposing volume consisting of photographs with detailed descriptions of all the Greek MSS in the Vatican library that can be precisely dated between the 13th and the 14th centuries. The majority are biblical, theological or patristic. Classical authors are represented by about 20 out of 100 books, mostly not very important. The presentation is excellent and the photographs are the same size as the originals.

VOICU, Sever J. and D'ALISERA, Serenella. I.M.A.G.E.S. Index in manuscriptorum Graecorum edita specimina. Roma, Edizioni Borla, 1981. 650p.   **DC61**

> OCP XLVIII 1982 474–476 Samir • Scriptorium XXXVI 1982 127–128 Wittek

WILSON, Nigel G. Mediaeval Greek bookhands. Examples selected from Greek manuscripts in Oxford libraries. Text. Cambridge, Mass., Mediaeval Academy of America, 1973. 2v., plates.   **DC62**

> Mediaeval Academy of America: Publications; 81.
> ByzZ LXVIII 1975 70–71 Hunger • Scriptorium XXIX 1975 318–319 Bernardinello
> All except one of the 88 plates are approximately full-size. They illustrate writing from the 4th to the 16th centuries and were assembled for seminar purposes, for which they continue to be invaluable.
> See also Wilson, N. G. "The libraries of the Byzantine World," *GRBS* VIII (1967): 53–80.

DD   LATIN PALEOGRAPHY

Bibliography, Methodology, and Orientation

BOYLE, Leonard E., O.P. Medieval Latin Paleography. A Bibliographical introduction. Toronto, University of Toronto Press, 1984. xvi, 400p.   **DD1**

"BULLETIN Codicologique." Scriptorium XXX (1976): 91–183.   **DD1a**

> This is an annual alphabetically arranged bibliography of codicology. The Bulletin in XXIX (1975) contained 1519 items; XXX (1976) contained 1057 items; XXXVII (1983) contains 799 items.

CAPPELLI, Adriano. Lexicon abbreviaturarum; Dizionario di abbreviatura latine ed italiane usate nella carte e codici specialmente del medio-evo, riprodotte con oltre 14000 segni incisi con l'aggiunta di uno studio sulla brachigrafia medioevale, un prontuario di sigle epigrafiche, l'antica numeraz. romana ed arabica ed i segni indicanti monete, pesi, misure etc. 3 ed. riv. e cor. Milano, Hoepli, 1929. Reprint 1973. lxxiii, 531p.   **DD2**

> "Bibliographia" (p.[517]–531).
> See also Cappelli, Adriano. *The elements of abbreviation in medieval Latin paleography.* Trans. by David Heimann and Richard Kay. University of Kansas Libraries, 1982. iv., 52p.

CHASSANT, Alphonse. Dictionnaire des abréviations latins et françaises usitées dans les inscriptions lapidaires et métalliques, les manuscrits et les chartes du Moyen Age. 5 éd., 1884. New York, Franklin, 1973. Reprint of 1884 ed. iii, lii, 172p.   **DD3**

DAIN, A., MALLON, J. and PERRAT, Ch. "La paléographie." L'Histoire et ses méthodes: 528–615.   **DD4**

FALCONI, Ettore. Note di metodo sulla ricerca paleografica. Parma, Studium Parmense, 1973. 152p., illus.   **DD5**

At head of title: Università degli studi di Parma. Facoltà di magistero. Istituto di paleografia e diplomatica.

LINDSAY, Wallace, comp. Palaeographia latina. Hildesheim and New York, G. Olms, 1974. Fold. facsims. **DD6**

> AJPh 1923 288 Clark • RB XXXVII 1925 104, XXXVIII 1926 221–222 de Gubernatis Lenchanfin • RFIC LIII 1925 292
> This reprint is a cumulated edition of a journal which continued in existence for six (Oxford 1922–1929) years and concentrated on Latin bookscript until the middle of the 11th century.

LOWE, Elias Avery. Palaeographical papers, 1907–1965. Edited by Ludwig Bieler. Oxford, Clarendon Press, 1972. 2 v., 150 plates, facsims., port. **DD7**

> "Bibliography of publications, 1907–1969" (v. 2, p.[595]–611).
> DLZ XCVI 1975 449–452 Lülfing • CR XXV 1975 132–134 McGurk • ChHist XLIII 1974 536–537
> Professor Bieler has gathered together in these two beautifully printed volumes almost all the articles published by E. A. Lowe on various aspects of paleography, along with prefaces and introductions to many of his longer works. Most of the material appeared previously. All plates in the original articles have been retained in this work, beautifully reproduced but occasionally in somewhat larger or smaller size. These plates taken alone provide a remarkably full picture of the development of most of the Latin scripts. The second volume contains a complete bibliography of the publications of E. A. Lowe, a general index, and a listing of the many manuscripts referred to and discussed in the 48 items included in the two volumes. A magnificent contribution to the field of manuscript study.

MABILLON, Jean. De Re diplomatica; Libri sex. Paris, 1681. **DD8**

> 2d ed., Paris, 1709; 3rd ed., Naples, 1789.
> Jean Mabillon, the French Maurist (1632–1717), wrote this work as an exposition of the principles of documentary criticism in response to the Bollandist D. Papebroch, who had questioned the authenticity of the Merovingian charters of the monastery of Saint-Germain. Mabillon's work in turn was attacked by B. Germon, and he supplied a supplement by way of a definitive answer. Mabillon's work founded the twin sciences of paleography and diplomatics. His work was further elaborated by the Maurists Toustain and Tassin in their *Nouveau traité de diplomatique,* 1750–1765.

POWELL, James M., ed. Medieval Studies: An introduction. Syracuse University Press, 1976. x, 389p. **DD9**

> Speculum LIII 1978 183–184 Strayer
> Contains two highly useful surveys for Latin paleography: John, James J., Latin Paleography (p. 1–68), and Boyle, Leonard E., Diplomatics (p.69–101).

TJADER, Jan-Olof. "Latin palaeography, 1975–1977." Eranos LXXV, 2 (1977): 131–161; "idem

1980–1981," Eranos LXXX (1982): 63–92. **DD10**

> This survey is in English (earlier ones were in Swedish) and is aimed at a wider international audience, with corresponding coverage.

TRAUBE, Ludwig. Vorlesungen und Abhandlungen. Hrsg. von Paul Lehmann; mit biographischer Einleitung von Franz Boll. München, C. H. Beck, 1965. 3 v. **DD11**

> Reprint of the 1909–1920 ed. published by Beck, München.
> CR 1922 170 Sandys • AJPh XLIII 1922 88 Rand
> The three volumes form a fitting memorial to the many-sidedness of Traube's genius. Notes are added by the editors to bring the bibliographical information up to date, and Professor Lehmann has made indices for all three volumes. Volume 1 has a sympathetic life of Traube by Boll and a list of his works. The perfect combination of paleography, textual criticism and history is displayed in these works of a genius cut off in his prime in 1907.

Catalogues

BIGNAMI ODIER, Jeanne. La Bibliothèque Vaticane de Sixte IV à Pie XI; Recherches sur l'histoire des collections de manuscrits par Jeanne Bignami Odier avec la collaboration de José Ruysschaert. Città del Vaticano, Biblioteca Apostolica vaticana, 1973. xviii, 477p., illus. **DD12**

> Vatican, Biblioteca Vaticana: Studi e testi; 272.
> BECh CXXXIII 1975 98–100 Petitmengin • Scriptorium XXIX 1975 18 van Balbergne

BOYLE, Leonard E. A survey of the Vatican Archives and its medieval holdings. Toronto, Pontifical Institute of Medieval Studies, 1972. iv, 250p. **DD13**

> Pontifical Institute of Medieval Studies. Subsidia mediaevalia.
> CHR LX 1974 466–467 Burns • HR LXXXIX 1974 871 Lultrell
> This survey has grown out of a seminar in diplomatics in Toronto over the past eight years and is extremely careful and valuable.

CATALOGO dei manoscritti in scrittura latina datati o databili per indicazione di anno, di luogo o di copista. Bibliotheca Angelica di Roma, a cura di Francesca di Cesare, in prep. Torino, Tottega d'Erasmo, 1971. Facsims. **DD14**

> At head of title: Università degli studi di Roma. Scuola speciale per archivisti e bibliotecari.
> JS 1975 282–285 Boussard
> Volume 1 in this new series is by V. Jemolo and is devoted to Biblioteca Nazionale centrale di Roma.

GABRIEL, Astrik Ladislas. A summary catalogue of microfilms of one thousand scientific manuscripts in the Ambrosiana Library, Milan. Notre Dame, Ind., Mediaeval Institute, University of Notre Dame, 1968. 439p., map, plates, facsims. **DD15**

RBen LXXIX 1969 444 Bogaert • CRAI 1968 363 Samaran

This important catalog contains diplomatic descriptions of the most important scientific manuscripts in various languages from the 10th to the 18th centuries of the Ambrosiana Library in Milan. It is intended to help scholars use them in microfilm copies at the Mediaeval Institute of the University of Notre Dame; it is not in commercial circulation.

GABRIEL, Astrik Ladislas and LOWE, E. A. The Ambrosiana microfilming project by A. L. Gabriel; The Ambrosiana of Milan and the experiences of a palaeographer by E. A. Lowe. Notre Dame, Ind., Mediaeval Institute, University of Notre Dame, 1965. 54p., 27 plates. **DD16**

RBen LXXVII 1967 197 Lambot • RHE LXII 1967 631 d'Haenens

Folia Ambrosiana, 1 ed., by Gabriel, A. L. and Garvin, J. N., appeared in 1965 (Notre Dame Press, 54p., 27 plates). These two essays provide the opening texts (p.1–17 and 19–54).

HAENEL, Gustave Friedrich. Catalogi librorum manuscriptorum qui in bibliothecis Galliae, Helvetiae, Belgii, Britanniae maioris, Hispaniae, Lusitaniae asservantur. Nachdr. d. Ausg. Leipzig 1830. Hildesheim and New York, Olms, 1976. x, 1238 columns. **DD17**

KER, Neil Ripley. Medieval manuscripts in British libraries. Oxford, Clarendon Press, 1969. Plates, facsim. **DD18**

Volume 1. London. Vol. II. Abbotsford–Keele, 1977.

AB LXXXVIII 1970 194–197 Philippart

Probably two more volumes to follow; all devoted to institutions in Britain other than the national libraries, the Bodleian Library and the Cambridge University Library.

KRISTELLER, Paul Oskar, ed. Catalogus translationum et commentariorum. Washington, D.C., Catholic University of America Press, 1960. **DD19**

Photocopy of typescript. Ann Arbor, Mich.: University Microfilms, 1976.

RHE LVI 1961 477–482 Silvester • Manuscripta V 1961 103–104 Grant • Latomus XX 1961 936–937 Préaux

A projected 15 volumes will give a complete conspectus of Latin translations made of Greek authors during the Middle Ages and Renaissance, and of Latin commentaries on classical authors, both Greek and Latin. Volume 1 begins with a bibliography (xv–xxiii), including general works, catalogs of printed editions and cata-

logs of MSS, followed by a list (p.1–76) of all Greek and Latin authors who wrote before A.D. 600 and whose works were available before A.D. 1600. This list forms, in Kristeller's phrase, a sort of ledger for the whole enterprise. Authors are not presented alphabetically but as sections reach completion.

KRISTELLER, Paul Oskar. Iter Italicum; A finding list of uncatalogued or incompletely catalogued humanistic manuscripts of the Renaissance in Italian and other libraries. London, Warburg Institute, 1965–1967. 2 v. xv, 736p. **DD20**

Volume 1. Italy, Agrigento to Novara (1963); II. Italy, Orvieto to Volterra. Vatican City (1967); III. Alia itinera; Australia to Germany (1983).

Speculum XLIII 1968 515–516 Bühler • Latomus XXX 1971 1241 Cambier

See also Kristeller, P. O., "Methods of research in Renaissance manuscripts," Manuscripta XIX (1975), 3–14, for helpful hints on problems in locating and cataloguing manuscripts.

KRISTELLER, Paul Oskar. Latin MSS books before 1600. A list of the printed catalogues and unpublished inventories of extant collections. New York, Fordham University Press, 1960. xxii, 234p. 3rd ed., 1965. **DD21**

Scriptorium XV 1961 93–97 Prete

This magisterial work is divided into three parts: 1. Bibliography and Statistics of Libraries and their Collections of MSS (p.1–9) contains general works giving particular bibliographical information and statistics of libraries and their collections of MSS; 2. Works Describing Manuscripts of more than one City (p.11–67); 3. Printed Catalogues and Handwritten Inventories of Individual Libraries by Cities (p.69–234). In the case of printed catalogs, libraries in the U.S.A. which have copies are listed. This vast work is based on personal visits by the author to almost all the libraries mentioned, including those in Poland, East Germany and Russia. The best coverage of its kind.

See Dogaer, Georges, "Quelques additions au Répertoire de Kristeller," Scriptorium XXII (1968), 84–86.

MORGAN, Paul. Oxford Libraries outside the Bodleian; A guide. 1973. xx, 250p. 2nd ed., Oxford, 1981. **DD22**

Scriptorium XXIX 1975 105 Dogaer, XXX 1976 179 van Balberghe

PHILIPPART, G. "Catalogues récents de manuscrits. Dixième série. Manuscrits en écriture latine." AB XCIV (1976): 160–182. **DD23**

See also AB XCIII (1975): 183–194, 391–404.

RICCI, Seymour de. Census of Medieval and Renaissance manuscripts in the United States and Canada. With the assistance of W. J. Wilson. Millwood, N.Y., Kraus Reprint, 1977. 3 v. **DD24**

Reprint of the 1935–1940 ed. published by H. W. Wilson, New York, under the auspices of the American Council of Learned Societies.

RecTh 1939 174 Boon • R Neosc 1939 252–254 van Steenberghen • BECh 1935 400–403 van Moe

Volumes: I. Alabama–Massachusetts; II. Michigan–Canada; III. Indices. There is a *Supplement*. Originated by C. U. Faye, continued and edited by W. H. Bond (New York, Bibliographical Society of America, 1962, xvii, 626p.).

RICHARDSON, Ernest Cushing. A list of printed catalogs of manuscript books. Reprint. Originally published in 1935. At head of title page: A Union World Catalogue of Manuscript Books: Preliminary Studies in Method. New York, Burt Franklin, 1972. 6 v., 1933–1937. v, 386p.   **DD25**

Latomus 1937 322 Peeters • RHE 1936 621–630 Pelzer

ST. JOHN'S UNIVERSITY, Collegeville, Minn.: Monastic Manuscript Microfilm Library. Checklist of manuscripts microfilmed for the Monastic Manuscript Microfilm Library, Saint John's University, Collegeville, Minnesota. Compiled by Julian G. Plante, curator. Collegeville, Minn., 1967– .   **DD26**

"Medieval manuscripts . . . before . . . 1600 belonging to European monastic libraries."

CW LXIX Apr. May 1976 459 Sweeney • BLE LXXVI 1975 232 Martimort • StudMon XVII 1975 184 Olivar

With commendable zeal and imaginative foundation support, the St. John's project has been extended to formerly monastic libraries (as well as those monastic libraries still functioning as such), cathedral libraries and secular libraries in Austria including the Österreichische Nationalbibliothek and the immensely valuable Haus- Hof- und Staatsarchiv in Vienna.

See also *Translatio studii; manuscript and library studies honoring Oliver L. Kapsher*, edited by Julian G. Plante (Collegeville, St. John's University Press, 1973).

SALMON, Pierre. Les manuscrits liturgiques latins de la Bibliothèque Vaticane. Città del Vaticano, Biblioteca apostolica vaticana, 1968–1972. 5 v. Studi e testi; 251, 253, 260, 267, 270.   **DD27**

Contents: 1. Psautiers, antiphonaires, hymnaires, collectaires, bréviaires; 2. Sacramentaires, épistoliers, évangéliaires, graduels, missels; 3. Ordines romani, pontificaux, rituels, cérémoniaux; 4. Les livres de lectures de l'office, les livres de l'office du chapitre, les livres d'heures; 5. Liste complémentaire, tables générales.

MA LXXVII 1971 399–400 Leconte • RSCI XXVI 1972 186–190 Saxer • Scriptorium XXVIII 1974 435–436, XXV 1971 209–210, 385–386 Huglo

The liturgical manuscripts of the Vatican library were inventoried in 1889 by H. Ehrensberger, but considerable additional acquisitions make the present work necessary and of absorbing interest for liturgists. The first volume (Studi e testi 251) is devoted to breviaries and the divine office. Each entry in the catalog is fully described codicologically and paleographically and will be an indispensable base for all future research. The second and third volumes (Studi e testi 253, 260) deal with the different books required for the eucharistic liturgy—sacramentaries, lectionaries, Roman ordinals, pontificals, rituals. Volumes 4 and 5 (Studi e testi 267, 270) catalog books for the reading of the office homilaries, which have already been the subject of much research and on which office readings are based. The last volume contains addenda, errata and general tables for the entire series.

SAMARAN, Charles Maxime D. and MARICHAL, Robert. Catalogue des manuscrits en écriture latine portant des indications de date, de lieu ou de copiste. Paris, Centre national de la recherche scientifique, 1959– . Atlases (facsims.).   **DD28**

Contents: t. 1. Musée Condé et bibliothèques parisiennes. Notices établies par Monique Garand et Josette Metman avec le concours de Marie-Thérèse Vernet; t. 2. Bibliothèque nationale, fonds latin (nos 1 à 8000). Sous la direction de Marie-Thérèse d'Alverny. Notices établies par Monique Garand, Madeleine Mabille et Josette Metman. t. 4, pt. 1. Bibliothèque Nationale, Fonds latin (supplément), Nouvelles acquisitions latines, Petits fonds divers. Notices établies par M. Garand, M. Mabille and D. Muzerelle, avec le concours de M. Th. d'Alverny. Paris, Édition du CNRS, 1981. 426p., 120 plates in 2 v.

Speculum XXXVI 1961 348–350 Jones • For v. VI: Speculum XLVIII 1973 587–591 John • Aevum LI 1977 398–399 Franceschini • REL LIII 1975 442–443 Langlois • REL XXXVIII 345–348 author • BECh CXXXIV 1976 389–395

The stated purpose of the Comité internationale de paléographie, organized in 1957 was "Établir—un Répertoire des livres manuscrits dates de temps ou de lieu écrits en écriture latine jusqu'au XVIe side inclus."

Good quality paper and beauty and excellence of reproduction characterize all the volumes so far. The dating is based on actual entries in colophons, etc., and no recourse is had to merely paleographical criteria, e.g., quires, rulings, signatures, prickings, etc., however accurate these may sometimes be.

THORNDIKE, Lynn and KIBRE, Pearl. A catalogue of incipits of mediaeval scientific writings in Latin. Rev. and augm. ed. London, Mediaeval Academy of America, 1963. xxii, 1938 columns.   **DD29**

Mediaeval Academy of America: Publication; 29. Manuscripta X 1966 108–110 Ermatinger

An important tool for the study of medieval science that underwent enormous expansion from its first appearance in 1937—from 284 columns of incipits and 142 columns of index to 1716 equally densely packed columns of incipits and 221 columns of indices. The work has been planned from the MSS sources directly, from published and unpublished MSS catalogs, from early and modern editions of medieval texts and from innumerable specialized studies. A high degree of technical precision is evident throughout.

TOSTI, Luigi et al. Bibliotheca Casinensis. Monte Cassino, 1873–1894. 5v.   **DD30**

A catalog of Monte Cassino MSS, with a facsimile of each one described in the first four volumes of the catalog. The reproductions, however, are in lithograph and lack the accuracy which is now possible.

VATICAN. Biblioteca Vaticana. Les manuscrits classiques latins de la Bibliothèque vaticane. Catalogue établi par Élisabeth Pellegrin . . . [et al.]. Paris, Éditions du Centre national de la recherche scientifique, 1975– . Illus. (some col.).   **DD31**

Documents, études et répertoires publiés par l'Institut de recherche et d'histoire des textes; 21.
Phoenix XXX 1976 312 Brown • REL LIII 1975 433–445 Holtz • RFIC CIV 1976 369–374 Badali
Mlle Pellegrin has specialized in cataloguing classical MSS in many libraries in Sweden, Spain and elsewhere.

Manuals

BATTELLI, Giulio. Lezioni di paleografia. 3rd ed. Città del Vaticano, 1949. x, 274p., facsims.   **DD32**

At head of title: Pont. Scuola vaticana di paleografia e diplomatica.
Aevum XVI 1942 171–173 Bascapé • Speculum XXV 1950 548–554 Levine • Scriptorium IV 1950 279–285 Masai
The first edition appeared in 1936, the second in 1939. The work is based on the author's lectures at the Vatican School, and this third edition avails of the most recent writings on paleography for purposes of updating. The work is divided into eight major parts. Parts 1 and 2 define object and scope of paleography and give a historical survey, general bibliography and details of writing material. The remaining six chapters deal more specifically with the paleographical aspects of the codex from its beginnings to the humanistic period. Three sets of indices and 45 facsimiles greatly enhance the work. The chapter on abbreviations (101–114) is the least satisfactory, totally omitting tachygraphy and *notae Tironianae*. Miniatures and other MSS decoration are more than generously treated, displaying a predilection of the author.

BISCHOFF, Bernhard. "Paläographie." Deutsche Philologie im Aufriss, I [1950], cols. 379–452. Bielefeld, Erich Schmidt Verlag, 1950.   **DD33**

Speculum XXVII 1952 363–364 Elder
Bischoff presents a concise "syllabus" on *Schriftwessen* and the history of the various scripts used in West-

ern Europe up to the end of the Middle Ages. The chief geographical emphasis is given to Frankish-Germanic *Kulturgebiet* but the sketches on the materials and scripts employed in the imperial period of classical Rome are generously full. The history of the development of the scripts is well presented and supplemented with a large number of references to easily available facsimiles. The first section Schriftwessen deals with the materials and tools (papyrus, parchment, palimpsests, paper, tablets and pens); the "external features," such as the composition of the codex (arrangement of leaves, prickings, rulings, etc.) and the format (binding, rotuli, tabulae, and charters); and finally an informative account of the craft of the scribe and the miniaturist. The second major section Schreibschrift presents a brief survey of imperial scripts and an excellent statement of what we know about Insular and pre-Caroline writing. The next part deals with the Caroline minuscule and is especially instructive in the account of the development of writing in Germany. The section concludes with a treatment of Gothic and humanistic writing. The last part of the compendium is devoted to abbreviations, punctuation, musical notation, numerals, writing in code, and illustration.
See also Bischoff's survey, 1939–1945, in *Scriptorium* V (1951), 125–145, and, most recently, his *Paläographie des römischen Altertums u. des abendl. Mittelalters* (Grundlagen der Germanistick, 24). Berlin, Eric Schmidt Verlag, 1979. 362p.

BRETHOLZ, Bertold. Lateinische Paläographie. 3 Aufl., Grundriss der Geschichtswissenschaft, hrsg. von A. Meister. Leipzig, Teubner, 1926. 112p.   **DD34**

PhW XLVI 1926 1092 Weinberger • HJV XXIII 1926 454 Kirn • LZB 1927 1077 Herrle

CENCETTI, Giorgio. Compendio di paleografia latina per le scuola universitarie e archivistiche. Napoli, del Mezzogiorno, 1968. 120p., illus.   **DD35**

Latomus XXXII 1973 449–450 Derolez • MIOEG LXXVII 1969 514–515 Fichtentau
Cencetti's manual limits itself to paleography in the strict sense, i.e., to the study of the evolution of writings, their typology and the factors which have played a role in their formation, and almost entirely avoids considerations of codicology. Especially admirable is the balance maintained by the author between paleographical phenomena and their cultural background. Thirtysix well-chosen examples of writing are reproduced at the end, with transliterations. See now Cencetti, G., *Paleografia latina*. Roma, Jouvence, 1978. 195p., 25 plates. (Athenaeum LVIII 1980 526–527 Mazzoli • StudMed XX 1979 958 Bartoli Langeli • Scriptorium XXXIV 1980 135 Gilissen).

DENHOLM-YOUNG, Noel. Handwriting in England and Wales. [2d ed.] Cardiff, University of Wales, 1964. 102p.   **DD36**

MAev XXIV 1955 104–107 Humphreys

Based on university lecture-notes, this is an uneven introduction to the paleography of Latin and English MSS from the beginnings to c.1600 A.D. Treatment for some periods is very summary, and the bibliography, though very good, shows certain important omissions. Plates are well chosen and handsomely reproduced.

FOERSTER, Hans Phillipp. Abriss der lateinischen Paläographie. 2. neuebearb. und verm. Aufl. Stuttgart, A. Hiersemann, 1963. 322p., facsims. **DD37**

RPh XL 1966 343–345 Marichal • LEC XXXII 1964 204 Delande • Latomus XXIV 1965 763 Cambier • BBF VIII 1964 437–438 Riché

An enlarged and improved version of the first 1949 edition by the successor of Franz Steffens in Fribourg, Switzerland. The first of four chapters is a history of paleography and includes a bibliography of manuals, collections of facsimiles and general works published since 1960, especially in German. Chapter 2 is concerned with writing materials, production of the book, scriptoria, and libraries; it is weak on papyrology, especially on more recent work. Chapter 3 is a history of Latin writing, with 39 reproductions of different styles, but again betrays a lack of acquaintance with recent work, especially that of Cencetti. Chapter 4 is very dependable for abbreviations and critical signs; the 24 plates with transcriptions are a welcome addition, and there is a good index.

FOERSTER, Hans Philipp. Urkundenlesebuch für den akademischen Gebrauch; 100 Texte. Bern, p. Haupt, 1947. 151p. **DD38**

RPh XL 1966 343–345 Marichal

GIRY, Arthur. Manuel de diplomatique; Diplômes et chartes, chronologie et technique, éléments critiques et parties constitutives de la teneur des chartes, les chancelleries, les actes privés. New York, B. Franklin, 1965. Reprint of 1894 Paris ed. xvi, 944p. **DD39**

Burt Franklin bibliography and reference series; 85.

MALLON, Jean. Paléographie romaine. Madrid, Consejo Superior de Investigaciones Científicas, Instituto Antonio de Nebrija de Filología, 1952. 188p. **DD40**

AC XXIII 1954 221–225 Boutemy • REA LVI 1954 235–241 Higounet • Latomus XV 1956 398–404 Dain • Aegyptus XXXIV 1954 141–142 Calderini • JS 1955 49–57 Tessier

Mallon is the great demolitions-expert of the traditional edifice of paleography, taking on not just Mabillon and the Benedictines but also more recent writers like Prou and Battelli. The early chapters study Roman writing in papyrology and epigraphy to the 2d century. In the second and longer part of his work he studies the later evolution of Roman script from the 1st century B.C. to the 5th century A.D. Thirty-two plates contain 85 examples.

Mallon has always championed the need for interdisciplinary work in epigraphy, papyrology and paleography to arrive at a full understanding of the history of writing. See also his short treatment, "Paléographie romaine," in *L'Histoire et ses méthodes* (553–579).

See now Mallon, Jean. *De l'Écriture. Recueil d'études publiées de 1937 à 1981.* Paris, C.N.R.S., 1982. 367p.

MAZZOLENI, Jole. Paleografia e diplomatica. Edizione riveduta, corretta ed ampliata di *Lezioni di paleografia e diplomatica.* Napoli, Libraria Scientifica Editrice, 1972. 358p., plates. **DD41**

MAZZOLENI, Jole. Paleografia e diplomatica e scienze ausiliarie. Napoli, Libraria scientifica editrice, 1970. 474p., 53 plates. **DD42**

Scriptorium XXVI 1972 203–204 Masai • RHE LXVII 1972 455–456 Boussard • Speculum XLVIII 1973 385 Boyle

A new updated edition of the author's *Lezioni di paleografia latina e diplomatica* (2d ed., 1964). Mazzoleni is more at home in diplomatics than in paleography. The 150 pages on diplomatics are more valuable than the 200 pages on Latin paleography. A section of the book is not by Mazzoleni himself but by a group of specialists in various fields: F. Acton on heraldry, G. Bovi on the coinage of Neopolitan provinces from c.800 to 1900, C. Salvati on weights and measures of the same region, and A. Allocati on sigillography. The 53 plates are of good quality and the texts are transcribed. More a history of writing than a history of the manuscript.

MODICA, Marco. Paleografia latina. Palermo, Palumbo, 1941. 225p. **DD43**

Speculum XXIV 1949 274–278 Elder

Modica divides his work into two parts: extrinsic and intrinsic characteristics of documents. Part 1 covers materials and instruments used in preparing leaves and in writing, the form of ancient and medieval books, and libraries. The second part deals first with abbreviations, then with the history of Latin writing by periods, and punctuation. The book ignores scholarly contributions outside Italy and is included here more to note Elder's review than for the book itself.

PAOLI, Cesare. Grundriss zu Vorlesungen über lateinische Palaeographie und Urkundenlehre. Aus dem Italienischen übersetzt von Karl Lohmeyer. Hildesheim, Gerstenberg, 1973. 4 v. in 1. **DD44**

"Reprographischer Nachdruck der Ausgabe Innsbruck 1902 [i.e. 1895–1902].

Volume 1 (108p.) in the German translation of Paoli's Italian work deals succinctly with the three periods in the historical development of the forms of Latin writing. The first period is subdivided into ten sections: Capital Writing, Uncial, Cursive, Halfuncial, National Scripts, Conpobardic, West Gothic, Irish and Anglo

Saxon, Merovingian, and Round Minuscule. The second period covers Gothic and humanistic. The third period, from the 16th century to the present, displays mostly a development of the second period scripts. The second half of the book deals with abbreviations, Tironian notes, punctuation, notation and musical notation.

PROU, Maurice. Manuel de paléographie latine et française. 4. éd. refondue avec la collaboration de Alain de Boüard accompagné d'un album de 24 planches. Paris, A. Picard, 1924. xii, 511p., plates in port. **DD45**

"Dictionnaire des abréviations" (p.303–474); "Index bibliographique" (p.483–493).

BECh LXXXV 1924 387–388 Samaran • PhW LXXII 1911 366–368, 1926 1092 Weinberger • RB 1926 221 deBruyne

Served for 50 years before the appearance of Stiennon as the classic work of reference for historians, philologists, and medievalists. It defines paleography narrowly as *la science des anciennes écritures.* Its object *le déchiffrement des écritures de l'antiquité et du moyen age;* its scope is here limited to writing on papyrus, parchment or paper. Writing materials and instruments are first dealt with. Chapters 2–4 deal with the various types of writing from capital to so-called Caroline minuscule. Chapter 5 has a lengthy treatment of abbreviations. Chapter 6 covers the Carolingian period, 9th and 10th centuries, for books and documents. Chapter 7 covers the 11th–18th centuries likewise. Chapter 8 deals with punctuation, accents, numerals, musical notation. There is a lengthy alphabetical listing of Latin abbreviations (a shorter one for French) at the end.

STIENNON, Jacques. Paléographie du Moyen Age. Avec la collaboration de Geneviève Hasenohr. Paris, A. Colin, 1973. 352p., illus., facsims., maps. **DD46**

Collection U. Série Histoire médievale.

MA LXXXI 1975 507–514 d'Alverny • RBen LXXXIII 1973 448 • RPh XLVIII 1974 371 • BECh CXXXI 1973 612–620 Pulle

The first French manual of paleography since the last edition of Prou in 1924. The work is divided into four main chapters. The first gives a history of the science of paleography, with a panoramic view of the great paleographers from Papebroch and Mabillon to the present. The United States and Ireland are not represented adequately. Chapter 2 deals with the main stages in the history of Latin writing from the beginnings, including epigraphy, to humanistic writing. Chapter 3 views the scribe at work, his materials and instruments. Chapter 4 deals with the relations of paleography, philology and history and views writing as an element in the history of civilization. There is a Florilegium of 25 texts (with facing Latin translation) on the act of writing, which enables us to see the copyists themselves at work. A short Latin-French glossary of technical terms and a summary lexicon of (French) technical terms are also included, with a good selective bibliography. The work is characterized throughout by lucidity of analysis and sureness of touch, based on

wide personal experience. The period, of the 13th–15th centuries is least well represented and diplomatic documents are almost totally absent. The documentation on Beneventan script is incomplete as is also that on the Gothic. Not enough attention is paid to abbreviations, Tironian notes, cryptology, Arabic numerals, or book decoration. In his conclusion Stiennon justly claims to have transferred paleography from the old narrow definition, the study of ancient writing, to wider parameters: the archaeology of the book, the history of libraries, and the sociology of medieval culture.

ZASO, Alfredo. Paleografia latina e Diplomatica; Edizione VII. Napoli, Pellerano Del Gaudio Editori, 1950. **DD47**

Paleography is treated in the first part (p.7–116) and diplomatics in the second (p.117–177). An appendix provides 22 examples of writing, from Capitale Arcaica to Bollatica.

Facsimiles

ARNDT, Wilhelm Ferdinand and TANGL, Michael. Schrifttafeln zur Erlernung der lateinischen Palaeographie. Hildesheim and New York, Olms, 1976. 3 parts in 1 v. [64p.], 107 facsims. (some double). **DD48**

"Nachdruck der Ausgabe Berlin, 1904–1907."

A welcome 1976 reissue of the 1904–1907 Berlin edition of 107 facsimiles. There is a "Chronologische Übersicht der Tafeln aller Hefte" (iv–vi).

ARRIBAS ARRANZ, Filemón. Paleografía documental hispánica. Valladolid, Sever-Cuesta, 1965. 2 v., 129 plates. **DD49**

[1] Transcripciones. [2] Láminas.

A.E.M. V 1968 772–773 Gómez Pérez

BASSI, Stelio. Monumenta Italiae Graphica; II. La Scrittura Calligrafia greco-romano. Torino, 1956–1957. viii, 144p., 88 plates, 313 photos. **DD50**

REL XXXVI 1958 296–297 Lejeune

Volume 1 was devoted to *La Scrittura Greca in Italia nell' eta Arcaica,* 1956.

BATTELLI, G., BISCHOFF, Bernhard, BRUCKNER, A. et al, eds. Umbrae codicum occidentalium. Amsterdam, North-Holland Pub. Co., 1960– . **DD51**

Gnomon XXXIII 1961 319 Hunger • REL XXVIII 1960 343–345 Marichal • Vols. VI & VII: RB LXXIII 1963 135 Verbraken • Vols. VI & VII: Gnomon XXXV 1963 317 Unterkircher

The object of this collection of facsimiles is to give whole reproductions of MSS in the Latin language. The reproductions are of exceptionally fine quality and the texts are chosen as much for their style of writing as for content. The first volume in the series contains a part of Servius' commentary on the *Aeneid*. The interest of this MS is that it is a composite of as many as 15 hands from the end of the 8th to the middle of the 9th century, all using the Maurdramne script, a prototype of Caroline minuscule, thus providing a cross section of the school of Corbie.

BRUCKNER, Albert and MARICHAL, Robert, eds. Chartae latinae antiquiores; Facsimile edition of the Latin charters prior to the ninth century. Olten, U. Graf, 1954– . **DD52**

Contents of parts: 1. Switzerland: Basle-St. Gall; 2. Switzerland: St. Gall-Zürich; 3. British Museum, London; 4. Great Britain without British Museum, London; 5–9. The United States of America; 10–12. Germany; 13– . France.
pt.6: CRAI 1975 98–99, 519–521 Marichal • pt.1: AAWW XCII 1955 3–6 Santifaller • JS 1955 42–43 Samaran • Aegyptus XXXV 1955 134 Calderini • pt.4.: MIOEG LXXVII 1969 150–151 Fichtenau • pt.VIII: Scriptorium XXXII 1978 126–127 Deman • Gnomon LI 1979 26–31 Petrucci • HZ CCXXIII 1976 689–696 Bischoff

CANELLAS, A. Exempla scripturarum in usum scholarum. Saragossa, 3rd ed. of v. 1, 1967. 2nd ed. of v. II, 1974. 2 v., 157 plates with full transcriptions. **DD52a**

V. I, 63 plates, covers scripts in general; v. II, 94 plates, scripts in Hispanic areas from c. 44–1594 A.D.

CHAMPOLLION-FIGAEC, Aimé Louis. Paléographie des classiques latins d'après les plus beaux manuscrits de la Bibliothèque Royale de Paris; Recueil de fac-similés fidèlement exécutés sur les originaux. Paris, Panckoucke, 1837. [4], xvi, [6], 106 [12] leaves of plates. **DD53**

CHATELAIN, Émile. Paléographie des Classiques Latins. Paris, Librairie Hachette, 1884–1892. 105 plates. **DD54**

JdesS 1897 185–186, 1900 316–317 • BECh XLV 1884 433 • Scriptorium VIII 1954 38
Plates of the principal manuscripts of Plautus, Terence, Varro, Catullus, Cicero, Caesar, Sallust, Lucretius, Virgil and Horace.

DELISLE, Léopold Victor. Le cabinet des manuscrits de la Bibliothèque impériale; Étude sur la formation de ce dépôt comprenant les éléments d'une histoire de la calligraphie de la miniature, de la reliure, et du commerce des livres à Paris avant l'invention de l'imprimerie. New York, B. Franklin, 1974. 3 v. and atlas, [xiv], 50 plates. **DD55**

Reprint of the 1868–1881 series published by Impr. impériale, Paris: Histoire générale de Paris.

JS 1869 248 Miller • JdesS 1875 699–713, 1876 102–121
In 1969 a similar reproduction was issued by Gérard Th. van Heusden, Amsterdam.

EHRLE, Franz, Cardinal, and LIEBAERT, Paul. Specimina Codicum Latinorum Vaticanorum. Collegerunt Franciscus Ehrle et Paulus Liebaert. Editio iterata. Berolini et Lipsiae, Apud W. de Gruyter, 1932 [1968]. xl, 50 leaves of facsims. **DD56**

Tabulae in usum scholarum; 3.
The 50 plates range in date and author from semiuncial Hilary, contra Constantium, c.510, and 8th century Italian semi-cursive to the *Acta Concilii Basiliensis* in humanistic cursive, c.1445. The descriptions are in a separate folder and in Latin.

HENRY, Françoise, ed. The Book of Kells; reproductions from the manuscript in Trinity College, Dublin. New York, A. A. Knopf, 1974. 226p., illus. (col.). **DD57**

Scriptorium XXIX 1975 175–176 P.D. • TLS LXXIII 1974 1234 Beckwith • Manuscripta XXI, 2 1977 107–109 Rough
A partial facsimile edition containing 100 plates of near-actual size and 26 with enlarged details. The text describes the book and its decoration, its iconography, ornamental art and paleography, and gives notes on the painters. Of two appendices one deals with the structure of the MS and the other lists the main insular and associated decorated MSS. The quality of the reproductions is very good. Recto and verso pages are printed as they appear in the original. Mlle Henry favors the Iona-Kells hypothesis as the place of origin.
See also T. J. Brown, "Northumbria and the Book of Kells," *Anglo-Saxon England* I (1922), 219–246.

KIRCHNER, Joachim. Scriptura gothica libraria; A saeculo XII usque ad finem medii aevi, 87 imaginibus illustrata. Monachii et Vindobonae, München and Wien, Oldenbourg, 1966. 81p., 66p. of facsims. **DD58**

AST XL 1967 383–385 Bohigas
The examples come from between the years 1151 and 1478, mostly in Latin but some in the vernaculars, from a wide range of libraries. All are dated or have a datable subscription. There is a Brief Note on the forms and nomenclature of the MSS offered in the facsimiles, and the essential catalog information and bibliography are given with the transcriptions. Some will disagree with the nomenclature *litterae textuales* for facsimiles 1–36.

KIRCHNER, Joachim. Scriptura latina libraria; A saeculo primo usque ad finem medii aevi, LXXVII imaginibus illustrata. Editio altera. Monachii, Oldenbourg, 1970. 1st ed., 1955. **DD59**

ThLZ LXXXII 1957 115–116 Lehmann • MLatJb
VII 1972 274 Langosch • BBF XVI 1971 326 Gasnault
• ZG XXI 1971 145–147 Staehlin • Bibl H&R XXXIII
1971 467–468 Poulle • Muséon LXII 1957 28–33 Lieftinck

LIEFTINCK, Gerard Isaäc. Manuscrits datés
conservés dans les Pays-Bas; Catalogue paléo-
graphique des manuscrits en écriture latine portant des indications de date. Amsterdam, North
Holland Pub. Co., 1964– . 2 v., xxxv, 142p., 1
plate; 476 plates.   **DD60**

Speculum XLI 1966 343–346 John
The first volume, Text, contains a valuable and
learned introduction, a catalog of about 300 MSS
mainly in Latin, and several indices. The MSS, presented in v. 2, are from 35 institutional and private
collections, arranged in alphabetical order by city and
library. Almost two-thirds of the dates are from the
15th century alone, but almost every type of script is
represented from the early 9th century. Almost all the
early MSS are represented by several facsimiles; when-
ever the facsimile includes the evidence for dating at
least that part is transcribed. Lieftinck's nomenclature
is complicated and needs to be taken in conjunction
with his essay in Bischoff, Battelli, (Lieftinck, ed.) Nomenclature. The plates as a whole are splendid and
the whole work is a treasure not only for paleographers
but also for students of medieval historiography, mo-
nasticism, liturgy and Renaissance humanism.

LOWE, Elias Avery, ed. Codices latini antiquiores, A palaeographical guide to Latin manuscripts prior to the ninth century. Oxford, Clarendon Press, 1934–1966. 11 v., facsims.   **DD61**

"Edited under the auspices of the Union académique
internationale for the American council of learned societies and the Carnegie institution of Washington." "A
succinct description . . . of all known Latin literary
manuscripts on papyrus, parchment, or vellum which
may be regarded as older than the ninth century, accompanied by a specimen, unreduced, of the script,
and supplemented by a selected bibliography."
Volume contents: I. The Vatican City; II. Great Britain and Ireland; III. Italy: Ancona-Novara; IV. Italy:
Perugia-Verona; V. France: Paris; VI. France: Abbe-
ville-Valenciennes; VII. Switzerland; VIII. Germany:
Altenburg-Leipzig; IX. Germany: Maria Laach-Würz-
burg; X. Austria, Belgium, Czechoslovakia, Denmark,
Egypt, and Holland; XI. Hungary, Luxembourg, Poland, Russia, Spain, Sweden, The United States, and
Yugoslavia.

LOWE, Elias Avery, ed. Codices Latini antiquiores; A palaeographical guide to Latin manuscripts prior to the ninth century: Volume XII.
Supplement. Oxford, Clarendon Press, 1971. xl,
84p., facsims.   **DD62**

Edited under the auspices of the Union académique
internationale for the American Council of Learned

Societies and the Carnegie Institution of Washington.
AJPh LXXXV 1964 209–211 Bieler • CPAI 1972
233 Samaran • 11. 2d ed. AJPh XCVI 1975 86–88
Bieler • XII. Supplement AJPh XCVI 1975 Bieler
Individual description of items, selection and presentation of plates, and bibliographies in all the volumes
have been lavishly praised by the reviewers. Before his
death in 1969 Professor Lowe had seen all the proofs
except the three indices of *CLA Supplement* and thus
completed a corpus begun in 1934 with the publication
of v. I, The Vatican City.
In this Supplement are 138 items and supplementary
information on plates concerning 44 entries already
described in previous volumes.
See now Brown, J., "E. A. Lowe and *Codices latini
antiquiores,*" *S&C* I (1977), 177–197.

**MALLON, Jean, MARICHAL, Robert and PER-
RAT, Charles.** L'écriture latine de la capitale romaine à la minuscule; 54 planches reproduisant
85 documents originaux. Paris, Arts et métiers
graphiques, 1939. [36]p., 54 plates (facsims., 2
double).   **DD63**

REL XLVI 1968 26–27 • REA XLIV 1942 160–
161 Fawtier • BECh CI 1940 169–171 Samaran
The album of 54 plates with 85 examples is both
elegant and practical. The introductory material includes explanation of the critical signs employed in
the transcriptions and complete titles of the works cited.
Plates I–VI are of writing on durable materials: bronze,
stone, terracotta. Plates VII–XXVII are of "documentary" writings, including Latin papyri from Egypt.
Plates XXVIII–LIV continue the illustration down to
humanistic writing, letting the scripts speak for themselves without any *a priori* classification.

MASAI, François and WITTEK, Martin. Manuscrits datés, conservés en Belgique. Notices
établies sous la direction de François Masai et
de Martin Wittek. Par Albert Brounts, Pierre
Cockshaw, Marguerite Debae et al. Bruxelles et
Gand, E. Story-Scientia, 1968– . 87p., facsims.,
217 plates.   **DD64**

t.1. 819–1400.
RBPh XLVIII 1970 501–504 Silvestre • StudMon
XIII 1971 232 Capó
This is the first fruits of a decision in 1958 of Le
centre National d'archéologie et d'histoire du livre to
produce an inventory of medieval MSS in Belgium
which are dated by a subscription. Holdings of the
Bibliothèque Royale were the first to be done, under
the direction of M. Wittek and F. Masai. In examining
Brussels MSS Wittek uncovered a number not previously recognized. Activities in the provinces had to
be curtailed for financial reasons.

**MERKELBACH, Reinhold and THIEL, Helmut
van.** Lateinisches Leseheft zur Einführung in Paläographie und Textkritik. Göttingen, Vandenhoeck u. Ruprecht, 1969. xi, 111p. of facsims.
                                            DD65

Studienhefte zur Altertumswissenschaft; Heft 13.
CR XX 1970 259–260 McGurk • CW LXVII 1974 306–307 Keaney • Gnomon XLII 1970 95–96 Kenney • REL XLVIII 1970 502–503 Vezin

An attempt to introduce students, at a modest price, both to the reading of manuscripts and the practice of textual criticism, following the plan of the earlier *Griechisches Leseheft* (1965). Twenty-two texts are chosen, their tradition resting on codices unici, or on a very small number of witnesses, in which case the same passages from two or three MSS are produced for comparative purposes. The texts chosen range from Livy to Lactantius *De ave Phenice,* from Sallust to Ammianus Marcellinus, and the hands illustrated range from 5th century uncial to 16th century Renaissance, arranged as far as possible in chronological order. An excellent and useful do-it-yourself kit for beginners, chiefly offering practice in *emendatio* and, to a less extent, *recensio.*

STEFFENS, Franz. Lateinische paläographie; 125 Tafeln in Lichtdruck mit gegen übsteh ender transkription nebst erläuterungen und einer systematishchen Darstellung der Entwicklung der lateinischen Schrift. 2. verm. aufl. Berlin and Leipzig, W. de Gruyter & Co., [1964]. 125 plates. **DD66**

First published in 1903, with a French translation by R. Coulon in 1910.

THIEL, Helmut van. Mittellateinische Texte; Ein Handschriften Lesebuch. Göttingen, Vandenhoeck und Ruprecht, 1972. xiv, 80 plates. **DD67**

CR XXV 1975 163 McGurk
This volume of plates illustrates 36 medieval Latin texts—with 2 to 4 plates per manuscript—and aims to provide a teach-yourself manual of textual criticism, using reproductions from MSS of well-known or well-edited texts as a student's introduction to problems in editing. Poems and histories predominate, but there are also examples of parodies, natural science and theology. The selection is based on *codices unici.* Some of the plates could have been photographed better.

Scripts

BIELER, Ludwig. "Insular paleography; Present state and problems." Scriptorium III (1949): 267–294. **DD68**

BISCHOFF, Bernhard. Lorsch im Spiegel seiner Handschriften. München, Bei der Arbeo-Gesellschaft, 1974. 128p., 14 leaves (some fold.) of plates, facsims (some fold.). **DD69**

BISHOP, Terence Alan M. English Caroline minuscule. Oxford, Clarendon Press, 1971. xxx, 26p., 24 plates, 28 facsims. **DD70**

Oxford palaeographical handbooks. (Bibliography: xxvii–xxviii).
Scriptorium XXVII 1973 118 Gilissen

BISHOP, Terence Alan M. Scriptores regis; Facsimiles to identify and illustrate the hands of royal scribes in original charters of Henry I, Stephen, and Henry II. Oxford, Clarendon Press, 1961. xii, 86p., 41 facsims. **DD71**

"Charters and documents" (p.[36]–78).
This study is concerned with the surviving originals of charters issued by the Norman kings between 1066 and 1154. There are 41 pages of facsimiles, many illustrating two or more documents.

BROWN, T. Julian. The Insular system of scripts c.600–c.850. Oxford, 1977. **DD72**

Lyell lectures.
TLS Jan. 27, 1978 100

COLLURA, Paolo. La precarolina e la carolina a Bobbio. Milano, U. Hoepli, 1943. Reprint 1965. vi, 266p., 48 plates (124 facsims). **DD73**

Scriptorium XXII 1968 110 Dufour • Aevum XLIII 1969 338 Bascapé • Paideia I 1946 52–54 Manaresi
This is a welcome xerographed reissue of the 1943 edition, a victim of bombing in World War II. Having posed the problems of the origins of Caroline minuscule the author studies different types of pre-Caroline at Bobbio, derived sometimes from semi-cursive, sometimes from uncial, sometimes from semi-uncial. He then shows that quarter uncial (or cursive uncial) employed in the marginal notes was known and even used at Bobbio.

In part II the author explains that Italian and Irish scribes working at Bobbio mutually influenced one another so that Irish-type writing with Italian elements and Italian-type with Irish elements can be distinguished. Part III is concerned with the Caroline used at Bobbio, introduced c.830 by Dungal, *praecipuus Scottorum,* and attaining a high degree of calligraphic excellence under l'Abbé Agilulgus. Decadence followed in the 10th and 11th centuries. There is an updated bibliography of work on Bobbio script after the War, 1943–1955 (p.247–266). He also surveys the contributions of Lowe, Cencetti, Pagnin, Bartoloni and Natale to the Columban congress at Luxeuil-Bobbio, in 1950–1951.

CROUS, Ernst and KIRCHNER, Joachim. Die gotischen Schriftarten. Leipzig, 1928. [2. Aufl.] Braunschweig, Klinkhardt u. Biermann, [1970]. 46p., 64p. of facsims. **DD74**

Scriptorium XXII 1968 66–71 Lieftinck
Gothic writing extends from the beginning of the 13th to the end of the 15th century. See Stiennon, "Les écritures gothiques et l'humanistique," in *Paleographie du Moyen Age* (p.112–124).

HERREN, M. W., ed. Insular Latin studies. Papers on Latin texts and manuscripts of the British

Isles 550–1066. Leiden, Brill, 1981. xiv, 226p. **DD74a**

Papers in medieval studies; I.

JONES, Leslie W. The script of Cologne; From Hildebald to Hermann. New York, Kraus Reprint Co., 1971. 98p., 100 leaves of plates, illus. **DD75**

Of the 28 manuscripts described by the Medieval Academy of America, Cambridge, Mass.

RPPh 1933 1240–1243 Peeters • PEL XI 1933 270–272 Grat • AB LI 1933 423–425 Coens • RCR 1932 483–484 Faral

A luxurious edited study by a pupil of Rand of a work originally attributed to the school of Tours. Jones has conducted an elaborate study of Cologne Center during the whole Carolinian period from the episcopacy of Hildebald (785–819) to that of Hermann (890–923). A replication of Rand's minute attention on a center not as important as Tours, Corbie or Fleury, with a wealth of incidental information on punctuation, abbreviations, illuminations, binding.

See also Jones, L. W., "The Scriptorium at Corbie: I. The library; II. The script and its problems," *Speculum* XXII (1967), 191–204, 375–394.

LA MARE, Albinia C. de. The handwriting of Italian humanists. Oxford, University Press, 1973. **DD76**

Scriptorium XXVIII 1974 381–382 Desmed

This lavish production has about 200 illustrations of writing, mostly in Latin but also Greek and Italian, of eight famous Tuscan humanists including Petrarch and Boccaccio. On each there is an introductory biography, a checklist of his library and a study of his handwriting.

LINDSAY, Wallace Martin. Early Irish minuscule script. Hildesheim and New York, Olms, 1971. 74p., facsims. **DD77**

St. Andrews University publications. Reprint of the Oxford, 1910 ed.

EHR XXXII 1917 114 James

This monograph attempts to fix the dates of some of the earlier specimens of Irish minuscule and to make their peculiarities, especially their abbreviation symbols, available as a clue for dating other Irish MSS. Two specimens of minuscule are first examined—the Bangor Antiphonary and the Schaffhaysen Adamnan. Then follow such well-known works as the Boniface

Gospels at Fulda, the Book of Armagh, The Leyden Priscian, the St. Gall Gospels, the Berne Horace. Plates illustrate ten of the twenty MSS considered.

LOWE, Elias Avery. The Beneventan script; A history of the south Italian minuscule. Oxford, Clarendon Press, 1914. xix, 384p., illus. **DD78**

AJPh XXXV 1914 340–343 Clark • CR 1914 209 Lindsay

The best exposition of the development of the Visigothic hand of Spain, with the best list of extant Visigothic MSS. Though supplemented by a separate volume of plates it is complete in itself, containing several facsimiles excerpted from the larger collection to illustrate the development of Beneventan from a hand not very different from the old Roman cursive to the wonderful calligraphy of the late 11th century and the final collapse before the all-conquering minuscule of the North. The part played by Monte Cassino in the transmission of the classics is treated at the outset. The chapter on punctuation covers 50 pages and is indispensable to students of paleography. A second edition is reported in preparation.

See now Lowe, E. A., "A new list of Beneventan Manuscripts," *Collectanea Vaticana in honorem A. B. Albareda, Studi e Testi;* 220; (Vatican City, 1962, 211–244) (*Paleographical Papers* eleven. 477–479). See further Brown, V., "A second new list of Beneventan manuscripts, 1, *MS* XL (1978), 239–289.

ULLMAN, Berthold Louis. The origin and development of humanistic script. Roma, Edizioni di Storia e letteratura, 1960. 146p. **DD79**

CW LIV 1960 65 Halporn • Manuscripta V 1961 35–40 Kristeller

While the Italian Gothic was far clearer than its English, French and German counterparts, it was the failing eyesight of Collucio Salutati that led to the reform of handwriting and the re-introduction of Carolingian script. The actual inventor of the new script was Poggio Bracciolini, as the author proves by examining MSS in Poggio's hand. Poggio's main rival for the honor of the new invention was Niccoli, whose script is a modified cursive hand, the forerunner of modern Italic. The book concludes with a discussion of the later diffusion of the humanistic script in Italy. The author provides very useful material here, for he has compiled convenient inventories of signed and often precisely dated MSS, written by important humanistic scribes.

DE TEXTUAL CRITICISM

Bibliographies, Introductions, and Manuals

ASSOCIATION Guillaume Budé Règles et recommandations pour les éditions critiques. Paris, Les

Belles lettres, 1972. 2 v., 74p., plate; viii, 48p., 11 plates. **DE1**

[1] Irigoin, J., Série grecque. [2] André, J., Série latine.

RFIC CII 1974 509–515 Raffaelli

Rules for the preparation of texts for the *Collection des Universités de France* were last formulated by Havet in 1924, and the uneven nature of editions in this *Collection* indicated a need for new guidelines. Irigoin for Greek texts and André for Latin follow the same plan in 13 brief chapters: Plan d'une Édition; L'Introduction; Les Sigles et Abbréviations; Le Texte; L'Apparat Critique; La Traduction; Les Notes; L'Index; Cartes et Figures; La Table des Matières; Préparation du Manuscrit; Révision du Manuscrit; Correction des Épreuves.

AVALLE, D'Arco Silvio. Introduzione alla critica del testo. Torino, Giappichelli, [1970]. vii, 117p. **DE2**

Corsi universitari.
Scriptorium XXV 1971 118 Roth
A brief introduction is followed by a glossary of terms used in the domain of textual criticism. In the section Piccolo Lessico della Critica Testuale a number of concrete cases are discussed, e.g., *Lai de l'ombre.* A good general introduction to the subject.

AVALLE, D'Arco Silvio. Principi di critica testuale. Padova, Antenore, 1972. xii, 137p., illus. **DE2a**

Vulgares eloquentes.
CIF XXV 1973 243–246 Sacchi
The work starts with a good bibliography chronologically arranged, starting with Quentin's *Essais* of 1926 and finishing with the 1969 Italian translation of Reynolds and Wilson, *Scribes and scholars,* plus three works listed for 1970.

BIELER, Ludwig. The grammarian's craft; An introduction to textual criticism. 3rd ed. [New York], The Catholic Association of Greater New York, [1960?]. 47p. **DE3**

The first edition appeared in *Folia* II (1947), 94–105, and III (1945), 23–32, 47–55. The revision for this third edition was the work of Martin R. P. McGuire. The work was first given as a talk in nontechnical language to explain the "essentially human" problems involved in the editing of ancient and medieval texts. Bieler's views are derived from extensive practical work on texts, mainly Latin, and this has proved an admirable introduction to the field for a wide variety of scholars—theologians, philosophers, historians, etc. The grammarian's craft, which has a tradition of more than a thousand years behind it, is defined as "the art of preserving literary texts from corruption and oblivion by means of criticism and interpretation." Craft is seen as the best word to describe an operation that partakes of both spontaneous creation and mechanical routine. This is a clear and careful exposition of the various stages in editing—collating, dating and localizing as far as possible the MSS, producing a Textgeschichte, arriving at a pedigree of the MSS through the detection of common errors, construction of a stemma, etc.

CLARK, Albert Curtius. The descent of manuscripts. Oxford, Clarendon Press, 1918. Reprint 1969. **DE4**

JRS 1917 291–295 Gilson • CJ XIV 1919 395–400 Merrill
In the preface and first three chapters (Omissions in Manuscripts, Omission Marks, The Evidence of Marginalia) the author outlines his method and illustrates it. In the following ten chapters he applies it. He examines a patristic text (Primasius), the Ciceronian palimpsests, orations and some of the philosophical works, then Asconius and pseudo-Asconius, and finally, turning to Greek, the leading MSS of Plato and the Paris MS of Demosthenes.
Professor Clark's strength lies in his minute analytical study of the varieties of omissions but his conclusions, often based on elaborate mathematics, may only show that errors are still errors, albeit much older than was once suspected.
See also Clark, A. C., *Recent developments in textual criticism; An inaugural lecture* (Oxford, Clarendon Press, 1914).

COLWELL, F. C. Studies in Methodology in textual criticism of the New Testament. Leiden, Brill, 1969. viii, 175p. **DE5**

ThS XXXII 1971 346 Fitzmyer

LA CRITICA del testo. Atti del secondo congresso internazionale della Società Italiana di Storia di Diritto. Firenze. **DE6**

DEARING, Vinton A. Principles and practice of textual analysis. Berkeley, University of California Press, 1974. xi, 243p., illus. **DE7**

REL XLII 1964 187–192 Froger • RechSR L 1962 574–580 Duplacy
"The method of analysis described here may be applied to the transmission in any form of any idea or complex of ideas, but it grew out of textual criticism and particularly out of an interest in developing textual criticism to deal better with the Greek New Testament" (Preface). After the chapter Preliminary Distinctions there is a lengthy one called Algorithms and a Calculus, which has seven subdivisions dealing with the seven steps in the solution of a textual problem by textual analysis: deciding on the states to analyze; deciding on the variations to analyze; rewriting any variations that would introduce rings into the tree; finding any terminal groups not in the simple variations; connecting the terminal groups to produce a preliminary diagram; locating the archetype, thus producing the final diagram or tree; finally, emending the archetype. Chapter III deals with the Formal Theory of Textual Analysis; IV. Probabilistic Methods in Textual Criticism; V. Editing Texts and Documents; and VI. Examples from Literary Research and Historical Research. There are three appendices: Labor-Saving Devices, Notes on Computer Programs, and Directions with Motifs.

DEKKERS, Dom Eligius. "La tradition des textes et les problemes de l'édition diplomatique." Traditio X (1954): 549–555. **DE8**

See also Masai, F., "Principes et conventions de l'édition diplomatique," *Scriptorium* IV (1950), 177–193, and Falconi, E., *L'Edizione diplomatica del documento e del manoscritto* (Parma, 1969).

DUPLACY, Jean. "Classification des états d'un texte, mathématiques et informatique: repères historiques et recherches méthodologiques." RHT V (1975): 249–309.   **DE9**

A well-organized survey of the main contributions to textual criticism from Dom Quentin to World War II; from 1939 to 1950; from American biblical philology, 1950–1961; and from the Dom J. Froger school, 1960–1973. There is an excellent bibliography (p.298–309) chronologically arranged from 1881 to 1974.

See also Duplacy, J. and Martini, C. M. "Bulletin de critique textuelle du Nouveau Testament." IV and V, 1. *Biblica* LII (1971): 79–113; ibid. LIII (1972): 245–278; ibid. LIV (1973): 79–114.

FINEGAN, Jack. Encountering New Testament manuscripts; A working introduction to textual criticism. London, SPCK, 1975. 203p., 24 plates.   **DE10**

CR XXVII 1977 91–92 Birdsall • ThZ XXXIII 1977 45–46 Elliott

An elementary introduction to N.T. textual criticism. Half the book is devoted to textual study based on photographs. There are some imprecisions and oversimplifications.

FROGER, J. La critique des textes et son automatisation. Paris, Dunod, 1968. xxii, 280p., illus., facsims.   **DE11**

RHE LXV 1970 114–117 Gorissen • AU LXXXVIII 1970 381–383 Philippart • CHum IV 1969 149–154 Dearing

Dom Froger, a Benedictine from Solesmes, had already given promise of a revolutionary contribution to the problematic and methodology of textual criticism in his "La collation des manuscrits à la machine électronique" in *Bul. de l'Institut de recherche et d'histoire des textes* XIII (Paris, C.N.R.S., 1964–1965, 135–171). The present work is the first of two (the second will be a voluminous history of textual criticism) in which traditional theories from antiquity to Quentin are submitted to minute criticism, showing the strengths and weaknesses of each system. The treatment of Quentin (p.42–50) is particularly fair. Chapter 3 gives an exposition of two methods of textual criticism, both internal and based on errors; the first based on Quentin's method, and the second employing the methods of the experimental sciences. The second part of the work is uncompromisingly mathematical.

For a bibliography of Dom Froger, see *StudMon* XVII (1975), 157–163. For other works on computerization of texts, see Gastaldelli, *art. cit.,* 139.

GASTALDELLI, Ferruccio. "Orientamenti bibliografici di Codicologia e critica testuale." Salesianum XLI (1979): 115–139.   **DE12**

Gastaldelli compiles a useful bibliography of 419 items. It has 24 subdivisions, well set out, including

much detail on materials for writing and the form of the manuscript.

GRONINGEN, B. A. Van. Traité d'histoire et de critique des textes grecs. Amsterdam, 1963. 126p.   **DE13**

CR XV 1965 75–77 Easterling • BAGB 1964 407–408 Wartelle

A valuable handbook, a companion volume to the author's *Short manual of Greek palaeography* (1963). Part I deals with History of Texts and part II with Textual Criticism, with some overlapping. Examples are well chosen and illuminating, and the work is refreshingly free from dogmatism. The section on textual criticism (p.79–117) is the more useful and studies codicology, collation, classification (including stemmata), choice of variants, and conjecture or emendation. For the author, criticism is an art and the only safe rule is *lectio melior potior.*

HALL, F. W. A Companion to classical texts. Freeport, N.Y., Books for Libraries Press, 1972. viii, 363p.   **DE14**

The following chapters have much information, some needing updating: c.2 The Text of Greek Authors in Ancient Times; c.3. The Text of Roman Authors in Ancient Times; c.4. The History of Latin Texts from the Age of Charlemagne to the Italian Renaissance; and c.5. The History of Texts During the Period of the Italian Renaissance. The final section The Nomenclature of Manuscripts is particularly useful.

HAVET, Louis. Manuel de critique verbale appliquée aux textes latins. Edizione anastatica [dell ed. di Parigi del 1911]. Roma, L'Erma di Bretschneider, 1967. Reprint 1974. xiv, 481p.   **DE15**

RPh 1914 226–235 Lejay

Described in Maas's *Textual criticism* as "an important book, but the useful theoretical sections are lost in the mass of examples, not all of which are important or useful." The mass of examples is nonetheless impressive and can easily be controlled through Index IV (p.437–481). Indispensable for the study of corruptions, variants, conjectures, emendations. See also Havet, L., "La Loi des fautes naissants," *REL* (1923), 20–26.

HOUSMAN, A. E. The confines of criticism. Edited by John Carter. Cambridge, Cambridge University Press, 1969. 56p.   **DE16**

CR XX 1970 394–395 Gow • REL XLVII 1970 369 Grimal

Housman's inaugural lecture at Cambridge, 1911, was not published *in toto* until John Carter discovered a typescript (printed almost *in toto* in the *TLS,* May 9, 1968), which is published here with a catchpenny title.

Housman's reluctance to publish was based on an interesting Homeric nod of his own. The lecture contains a warning directed at two targets, German scholars who tended to regard criticism as an an exact science susceptible to mathematical rules, and English scholars who tended anachronistically to apply criteria of English literary criticism to ancient texts. There are excellent quotations and aphorisms, and Housman's well-known insularity and hauteur are embedded deeply from the outset.

KANTOROWITZ, H. Einführung in die Textkritik; Systematische Darstellung der textkritischen Grundsätze für Philologen und Juristen. Leipzig, 1921. 60p.   **DE17**

This short introduction has special application to juristic texts but is an excellent treatise on textual criticism in general from a distinguished philosopher and historian of law.

KENNEY, E. J. The classical text; Aspects of editing in the age of the printed book. Berkeley, University of California Press, 1974. xi, 174p.
                                                  DE18

Sather classical lectures; v. 44.
CPh LXXII 1977 177–183 Zetzel • TLS LXXIV 1975 927–928 Barker
A history of the editing of classical texts, mainly Latin ones, from the invention of printing to the present. The first chapter deals with the conditions under which an *editio princeps* appeared and shows the deficiencies, both in historical acumen and in materials, on which the first edition was often based. The *textus receptus* was accepted by the immediate successors of the first editors, thus perpetuating their error.

The two following chapters are on the art of emendation, theory and practice. In the 17th century inventories and catalogs began to appear and the improved critical sense which this gave rise to is dealt with in c.IV. Ad Fontes and c.V. To disestablish chance. The work of Lachmann is evaluated and c.VI deals with Method and Methods in the Twentieth Century, from Dom Quentin to the use of computers. The author's closing position is a prudent one, close to that of Pasquali and Van Groningen: Editing remains as much an art as a science because of the limitations of our knowledge of text transmissions and the complexities of individual texts, but theory is indispensable.

KIRSOP, W. Bibliographie matérielle et critique textuelle, vers une collaboration. Paris, Lettres modernes, 1970. 80p.   **DE19**

L&S VII 1972 235–236 Avellini

LAUFER, Roger. Introduction à la textologie; Vérification, établissement, édition des textes. Paris, Larousse, [1972]. 159p., illus.   **DE20**

Collection L. Larousse université.
RPh XLVIII 1974 372 André
Textologie is a coinage in the line of Dain's *codicologie* to cover the variations of modern texts that arise from differences in printed texts, mainly concerned with French.

LINDSAY, Wallace Martin. An introduction to Latin textual emendation; Based on the text of Plautus. London and New York, Macmillan, 1896. xii, 131p.   **DE21**

LUCK, Georg. "Textual criticism today." AJPh CII (1981): 164–194.   **DE22**

A critical evaluation by a seasoned critic of some of the chief works which have appeared in the past decade on textual criticism, editorial technique and related themes, concluding that textual criticism today is as essential a tool of classical scholarship as it ever was.

MAAS, Paul. Textual criticism. Trans. by Barbara Flower. Oxford, 1958. Clarendon Press, 159p., illus. Reprint 1972.   **DE23**

Gnomon 1929 417–435, 498–521 Pasquali • REL XLI 1963 407–415 Froger
The classic statement of the theory of stemmatics. First published in Gercke-Norden, *Einleitung* in 1927, it went to a fourth German edition in 1960 with hardly a change. From precise definitions Maas had deduced a rigorous method in accordance with which the critic could operate with scientific precision. Barbara Flower prepared the English translation before her death in 1955 and C. H. Roberts saw it through the press; it was reprinted in 1963, 1967 and 1972.

Maas added four pages of Retrospect in 1956, mainly to react to Pasquali's *recentiores non deteriores*. Appendix I is a slight reworking of a typically brief statement by Maas on the principles of stemmatics.

McD[ONALD], A. H. "Textual criticism." OCD² (1970): 1048–1050.   **DE24**

Defines textual criticism as the technique and art of restoring a text to its original state, as far as possible, in the editing of Greek and Latin authors. The task of the textual critic is threefold: (i) *recensio*, to study the manuscript tradition; (ii) *examinatio*, to determine critically what may be taken as authentic; and (iii) *divinatio*, to attempt the remedy of error by conjecture.

MADVIG, Johan Nikolai. Adversaria critica ad scriptores Graecos et Latinos. Hildesheim, Olms, 1967. 1st ed., Hauniae, sumptibus Librariae Gyldendalianae, 1871–1884.   **DE25**

Volume titles: 1. De arte coniecturali. Emendationes Graecae; v. 2. Emendationes Latinae; v. 3. Novas emendationes Graecas et Latinas continens.

MARICHAL, Robert. "La critique des textes." In Samaran, Charles, ed., *L'Histoire et ses méthodes* (1961), 1247–1366 and 1360–1366 (bibliography).   **DE26**

Stresses the classification of errors which may be psychological as well as purely graphical. Discusses the motivation of interpolations and the method to follow in the correction of errors, also the problems of a "diplomatic" edition and the establishment of a stemma. The Bédier/Quentin controversy and the newer use of electronics in handling variants are examined. There are practical hints on the editorial problems of the date, place of origin and authorship of MSS, and the filiation of sources. The historian can only begin his interpretation of a text after the text has been established, dated, localized, and its author identified. The wide range of Marichal's examples and his wise and practical counsel make this an excellent *mise en point*.

MASAI, F. "Principes et conventions de l'édition diplomatique." Scriptorium IV (1950): 177–193. **DE27**

A "diplomatic" edition is "un relevé archéologique des textes"—a text transmitted by the extant MS. It differs from a critical edition in that it presents in the text the witness of a single manuscript and never introduces readings of another one. A good illustration of a diplomatic edition is Vanderhoven, J., Masai, F. and Corbett, P. B., *Aux sources du monachisme bénédictin. I. La règle du Maître*. (Bruxelles, 1953).

METZGER, Bruce M. A textual commentary on the Greek New Testament. A companion volume to the United Bible Societies' Greek New Testament. 3rd ed. London, New York, United Bible Societies, 1971. xxxi, 775p. **DE28**

METZGER, Bruce M. New Testament textual criticism. Its significance for exegesis. Essays in honor of Bruce M. Metzger. Edited by E. J. Epp and G. D. Fee. Oxford, Clarendon Press, 1981. xxviii, 410p. **DE28a**

MORTON, Andrew Q. and WINSPEAR, Alan D. It's Greek to the computer. Montreal, Harvest House, 1971. 128p. **DE29**

ACR 11 1972 52 Waite • CHum VII 1973 437 Bennett
This book claims that during the sixties a veritable revolution occurred in philological studies as a result of the use of the computer for literary analysis in Greek. This new "Stylometric Analysis" is concerned with small, common words which lend themselves to stylistic analysis.

PEETERS, Felix. "La technique de l'édition (1926–1936)." AC VI (1937): 319–356. **DE30**

A ten-year survey of a very productive period in heuristic, ecdotic and hermeneutic publications. Included are bibliographical aids, encyclopedias, dictionaries, histories of literature, journals, collections of texts, catalogs, facsimiles, histories of libraries and special scripts, abbreviations, illuminated MSS, autographs, manuals, histories of text transmission, and helps on editing a text.

QUENTIN, Henri. Essais de critique textuelle (Ecdotique). Paris, Picard, 1926. 179p. **DE31**

REA XXX 1928 254 Flice • RCrit 1927 412 Loisy
L'ecdotique is the part of criticism that has to do with the establishment and criticism of texts. This work was published as a reaction to adverse discussion and reaction to the author's earlier *Mémoire* (1922). For such adverse criticism see Rand, *HThR* XVII (1924), 197–264, and Bédier, *Romania* LIV (1928), 161–196, 321–356. For more constructive criticism see Severs, J. Burke, *EngInstAnn* (1941), 65–93.

QUENTIN, Henri. Mémoire sur l'établissement du texte de la Vulgate. Paris, Gabalda, 1922. xvi, 520p. **DE32**

RENEHAN, Robert. Greek textual criticism; A reader. Cambridge, Mass., Harvard University Press, 1969. viii, 152p. **DE33**

Loeb classical monographs.
CPh LXVI 1971 202–205 Hunt • AJPh XCII 1971 503–506 Young • Gnomon XLIV 1972 712–714 Alexanderson
Intended as a workbook, not a handbook, this collection of passages, classical, postclassical and patristic, illustrates the problems confronting an editor in selecting the right reading. The length of the sections varies from a few lines to ten pages. When we have variants or conjectures or both, we must apply all available tests to establish the text. It is the choice between possible readings, "one of the most exacting offices of criticism," that is Renehan's main concern. See also Renehan, "Studies in Greek texts," *Hypomnemata* XLIII (1975), for critical observations on textual problems in Homer, Plato, Euripides, Aristophanes and other Greek authors.

REYNOLDS, Leighton Durham and WILSON, Nigel G. Scribes and scholars; A guide to the transmission of Greek and Latin literature. 2d ed., rev. and enl. Oxford, Clarendon Press, 1974. x, 275p., 16p. of plates, facsims. **DE34**

Latomus XXX 1971 196–199 Sanders • CW LXIV 1970 137 Elder
A skillful combination of the cultural history of the Middle Ages and Renaissance with the specific problem of the transmission of texts and the science of paleography. This is a valuable contribution to the history of text transmission in antiquity and through the Greek East and Latin West down through the Renaissance.
There is an excellent concluding section Textual Criticism, and a helpful Bibliography and Index of Manuscripts. The second edition has a new chapter bringing the historical survey from the Renaissance down to modern times.
For the Italian translation, see the Latomus article and Criniti, *Aevum* XLIX (1975), 208–209.
See also Reynolds, L. R., ed. *Texts and transmissions: A survey of the Latin classics.* Oxford, Clarendon Press, 1984. xlviii, 509p.

SABBADINI, Remigio. Le Scoperte dei codici latini e greci ne' secoli XIV e XV. Edizione anastatica. Con nuove aggiunte e correzioni dell'autore a cura di Eugenio Garin. Firenze, G. C. Sansoni, 1967. 2 v. First ed. published 1905.   **DE35**

Athenaeum 1915 89 • RF 1915 489–494 Ussani • RFIC CII 1974 130–132 Rizzo
The *magnum opus* of the father of humanistic philology in Italy is here reprinted from a 1914 edition. There is a bibliography of Sabbadini provided by Billanovich (xi–xli). This is a classic testimony to the perfect wedding effected by Sabbadini between classical and humanistic philology. His studies of the textual tradition of these Latin authors, based on work from 1885 to 1913, remain fundamental.

SCHWERTNER, Siegfried. IATG, Internationales Abkürzungsverzeichnis für Theologie und Grenzgebiete. Zeitschriften, Serien, Lexika, Quellenwerke mit bibliographischen Angaben. Berlin and New York, De Gruyter, 1974. xix, 348p.   **DE36**

Thandschh XL 1975 378–379 Kümmel • TRLZ CI 1976 409–412 Matthiae
One of the most exhaustive lists of the most commonly used abbreviations in scholarly literature; deserves to become standard. Approximately 7,500 titles.

SECRÉTARIAT des Sources Chrétiennes. Directives pour la préparation des manuscrits. Lyon, Secrétariat des sources Chrétiennes, 1971. 87p.   **DE37**

Directives for editing in the patristic series *Sources chrétiennes,* but admitting of wider application. Each volume in *SC* normally consists of an introduction, a bibliography, the text (Greek or Latin), apparatus criticus, scriptural apparatus, French translation, notes, indices and table of contents. There are very detailed directives for each of these, and for such matters as punctuation, orthography and abbreviations. There is a table of signs commonly employed for typographical corrections, with a model for correction of proofs.

TIMPANARO, Sebastiano. II lapsus freudiano; Psicanalisi e critica testuale. Firenze, La nuova italia, 1974. viii, 214p.   **DE38**

RFIC CV, 1 1977 102–105 Rizzo • Prometheus I 1975 287 Musso
An interdisciplinary study of the possibility of linking Freudian *lapsus* with textual criticism's "errors."

WEST, Martin L. Textual criticism and editorial technique applicable to Greek and Latin texts. Stuttgart, Teubner, 1973. 155p.   **DE39**

LF XCVIII 1975 184 Vidmanová • JRS LXIV 1974 268–269 Reynolds • Euphrosyne VI 1973–1974 341–343 dos Sanctos • Phoenix XXVII 1973 295–300
Designed to replace O. Stählin's *Editionstechnik* (1914) and Paul Maas's *Textkritik* (1957), West's book is in three parts: textual criticism, editorial technique and specimen passages. The section on recension is

one of the best. This is an excellent, well-written handbook, full of practical advice with examples garnered from very wide reading, and discussing complex theory in sane and lucid terms. Altogether as sound and expert a guide to the subject as one would expect from such a seasoned practitioner of the art. The bibliography is not as full as one might expect, and codicology hardly gets its due.

WILLIS, James. Latin textual criticism. Urbana, Ill., 1972. x, 237p.   **DE40**

Illinois Studies in Languages and Literature; 61.
Manuscripta XVIII 1974 115 Finch. Phoenix 1973 295 Farrant • JRS LXV 1975 242–243 Diggle
The work has a more limited aim than the title suggests: "to convey to those who are relatively unfamiliar with the MSS of classical authors some knowledge of the many ways in which scribes were accustomed to make mistakes." This concentration of purpose is reflected in the book's structure: series of chapters discusses stemmatics and the contents of the apparatus, while the bulk of the volume (p.47–188) is given over to a typology of corruption, interspersed with trial passages which challenge the reader to identify and remove error on his own. One hundred further passages for emendation are given in an appendix (p.191–226). The book contains much excellent material and a wealth of examples, nearly always well chosen, but the style, often acerbic and overheated, has been adversely affected by imitation of Housman and/or Phillimore.

ZETZEL, J. E. G. Latin textual criticism in antiquity. New York, Arno Press, 1981. xv, 307p.   **DE41**

Monographs in Classical Studies.
G&R XXX 1983 229 Walest

History of Textual Criticism

BENTLEY, Richard. Dissertation on Aesop and Phalaris. Oxford, 1697. Rev. ed., 1699.   **DE42**

In the famous controversy on the literary merits of the Ancients and the Moderns, Bentley had questioned Sir William Temple's attribution of terms like *oldest* and *best* to Aesop's *Fables* and the *Epistles of Phalaris,* asserting that they were neither old nor good. Cf. Sandys, *History of classical scholarship,* II, c.24.

BÉVENOT, Maurice. The tradition of manuscripts. A study in the transmission of St. Cyprian's treatises. Oxford, Clarendon Press, 1961. 163p.   **DE43**

JThS XIV 1963 196–197 Bieler • Gregorianum XLIII 1962 793–94 Orbe • RecSR LII 1964 164 Daniélou
A very detailed study of the difficult text tradition of Cyprian's *De ecclesiae catholicae unitate,* done in the hope that its results may be applicable to his other treatises. Bévenot endeavours to classify the MS of Cyp-

rian on grounds of external evidence (order of texts, lacunae, etc.) and internal (variants, interpolation, contamination, etc.). In a lucid discussion of 30 "crucial passages" from *De unitate,* Bévenot's decisions rest almost entirely on the intrinsic merits of the rival variants. On these grounds he builds his specimen edition (p.96–123). A new and very valuable methodological consideration is provided by a statistical chart, which shows at a glance the "connexions" and "disconnexions" in the textual relations between the MSS of Bévenot's text.

BROWN, Virginia. The textual transmission of Caesar's *Civil War.* [Leiden], Brill, 1972. 104p.
DE44

Mnemosyne. Bibliotheca classica Batava: Supplementum; 23. Based on author's thesis, Harvard.
ACR III, 1 1973 16 Halporn • Gnomon XLV 1973 763–766 Hering
On the basis of fresh collation of the major witnesses and the examination of a large number of the later MSS, Dr. Brown has reached the following conclusions concerning the recension of the text: 1. LN can be eliminated as *descripti,* with *L* derived from N; 2. The tradition is tripartite, with S separated from TV; 3. The archetype was a product in Caroline or pre-Caroline minuscule of a French scriptorium; and 4. The *recentiores* are truly *deteriores.* Some of the decisions are based in part on a broad definition of significant error and a perhaps too optimistic view of the emending abilities of medieval scribes.

CAESARIUS, Saint, Bishop of Arles. Sermones, nunc primum in unum collecti et ad leges artis criticae ex innumeris mss. recogniti; Studio et diligentia Germani Morin. Ed. 2 [appendice instructa, auctore Cyrillo Lambot]. Turnholti, Typographi Brepols, 1953. 2 v. (cxxii, 1130p.).
DE45

Corpus Christianorum: Series Latina; CIII–CIV.
REL XXXII 1954 412–413 Conreelle • VChr IX 1955 62 Waszinck
This second edition is a reprint of Dom Morin's famous edition of 1937, which appeared at Maredsous but which was almost entirely destroyed by fire. There is a monumental preface dealing with previous editions and homiletical collections ascribed to Caesarius. Fifty years of research have resulted in Morin's arriving at 238 sermons which can be called authentic. There are excellent indices.

DAWE, Roger David. The collation and investigation of manuscripts of Aeschylus. Cambridge, University Press, 1964. x, 352p., illus.   **DE46**

"An expurgated version of [the author's] . . . doctoral dissertation."
CPh LX 1965 120–124 Golden • CJ LX 1965 278–280 Diller • JHS LXXXV 1965 177–178
A model of scholarly thoroughness and critical insight, this work challenges the earlier textual achievements of Wilamowitz and Turyn and insists that a

firm basis for reconstructing the text of Aeschylus can only be reached after all the manuscripts have been thoroughly collated. Here a detailed collation of 16 MSS. (against the current Oxford text) is offered for the triad of *P.V., Septem* and *Persae.* Dawe's motivation for this work is clearly stated in the introduction: "If one hundredth part of the effort which has gone into conjectural emendation had been turned towards an investigation of the Aeschylus MSS, their history, readings and general character, we might find ourselves much further advanced than we have hitherto supposed possible."

DAWE, Roger David. Repertory of conjectures on Aeschylus. Leiden, E. J. Brill, 1965. x, 179p.
DE47

Gnomon XXXVII 1965 656–657 Lloyd-Jones • AC XXXIV 1965 579–580 van Looy • RBPh XLVIII 1970 1394–1395 Mertens
This is a supplement to the repertory published in the second volume of Wecklein's edition in 1885 and added to in the second edition of 1893. It lists as many as possible of the conjectures published since then, indicating the place of publication if this is not obvious, adding some of Dawe's own conjectures, and a few that had eluded Wecklein.

FRÄNKEL, Hermann. Testo critico e critica del testo. Traduzione dal tedesco di Luciano Canfora. Nota di Carlo Ferdinando Russo. Firenze, F. Le Monnier, 1969. xiv, 90p.   **DE48**

Excerpts from the author's *Einleitung zur kritischen Ausgabe der Argonautika des Apollonios.*
SPCT I 1970 294–299 da Rozzo • REG LXXXIII 1970 227–228 Vian • AC XXXIX 1970 653 Knecht • PP XXIV 1969 390–393 Gigante
An Italian translation of part (c.13–14 and 2) of Fränkel's *Argonautika des Apollonios.* Chapter 13 contained Fränkel's ideas on textual criticism in general. There are many good observations on methodology—the advantages of a positive apparatus, the criteria for judging the probability of variants and conjectures—but some subjective positions are raised to the level of dogma. Chapter 2 gives an excellent exposé of the faults of copyists.

GERBER, Douglas E. Emendations in Pindar, 1513–1972. Amsterdam, Hakkert, 1976. 195p.
DE49

Phoenix XXXI, 3 1977 265–268 Köhnken
A thorough and reliable compilation of conjectures for the *Epinikia* (29–143) and the Fragments (145–195), from the first printed Aldina edition of the *Epinikia,* in 1513, to 1970. [More recent work is covered by Gerber in his survey, "Studies in Greek lyric poetry: 1967–1975," *CW* LXX, 2 (1976), 132f.] If anything he has been too generous in chronicling the improbable or even absurd conjectures of the 19th century, and indeed later. The work certainly achieves the objective of the author—substantially to reduce the amount of time needed to get all necessary information about any textual problem in a notoriously difficult author.

GOTOFF, Harold C. The transmission of the text of Lucan in the ninth century. Cambridge, Mass., Harvard University Press, 1971. xi, 209p.
DE50

On spine: The text of Lucan in the ninth century.
Maia XXV 1973 236–237 Gagliardi • AJPh XCV 1974 411–412 Luck • ACR II 1972 253 Phillips
At least nine important 9th century MSS of Lucan are preserved. Gotoff is interested in five of these, MZABR. Hosius and Housman have used M and Z, but Gotoff feels that AB and R have not received adequate attention, as each represents a source of independent information and all of them are contaminated. A courageous and competent challenge to some of the more formidable dogmas and dogmaticians of the past.

HUNGER, Herbert et al., Geschichte der Textüberlieferung der antiken und mittelalterlichen Literatur. Mit einem Vorwort von Martin Bodmer. Zürich, Atlantis Verlag, [1961–1964].
DE51

Bd. 1. 623p., 73 illus.
Bd. I: CW LV 1962 198 Bloch • CR XII 1962 224–227 Kenney • ByzZ LV 1962 317–320 Irigoin • REG LXXV 1962 271–273 Vian
In this collaboration of seven authors the first section (p.25–147) by H. Hunger covers the development of the book, libraries, and Greek and Latin paleography—too vast a territory for 120 pages, and deficient on the ancient *scriptoria* and on transcriptions for the facsimiles, which are too narrow in their choice. O. Stegmüller on the text transmission of the Bible (p.149–206) provides perhaps the most readable contribution, covering the history of the text of the Old and New Testament—composition, papyrus, uncial and minuscule manuscripts. He devotes much space to the history of biblical criticism from the 16th century to date, and to the various versions of the Bible.
H. Erbse provides an able but at times acrimonious survey of the text transmission of Greek literature from its beginning to the fall of Constantinople (p.209–283) and examines the text history of more than 20 classical and Hellenistic authors. M. Imhof contributes an *Anhang* on pagan Greek literature of the Empire, which is too sketchy (p.285–307). K. Büchner's treatment (p.309–422) of the history of the tradition of ancient Latin literature contains brief accounts of the text history of selected authors from Plautus to Boethius, and his account ends with the 6th century, with no more than a brief mention of the Carolingian Renaissance. The section by H.-G. Beck on Byzantine literature is divided into four sections: historical literature, classical, popular and patristic. H. Rüdiger has a concluding section (p.511–580) on the rediscovery of ancient literature in the Renaissance.

HUNGER, Herbert et al. Die Textüberlieferung der antiken Literatur und der Bibel. 1975. Reprint of v. 1, 1961.
DE52

Earlier title: *Geschichte der Textüberlieferung der antiken und mittelalterlichen.*

KENYON, Frederic G. The text of the Greek Bible. 3rd ed., rev. and augm. by A. W. Adams. 1st ed., 1937. London, Duckworth, 1975. ix, 275p.
DE53

CW XXXI 1938 109–110 Sanders • JThS XXXVIII 1937 276 Creed
A most serviceable survey in brief compass of books in the first three centuries; The Greek Old Testament; The Manuscripts of the New Testament; The Versions and The Fathers; The Printed Text, 1516–1881; Textual Discoveries and Theories; The Present Textual Problem. A useful handbook on the complexities of textual criticism, relating the subject to the history of book-making in the ancient world.

KATZ, Peter (Walters). The text of the Septuagint; Its corruptions and their emendation, by the late Peter Walters (formerly Katz). Edited by D. W. Gooding. Cambridge, Cambridge University Press, 1973. xx, 418p.
DE54

Originally presented as the author's thesis, Cambridge, 1945.
Stud Pap XIV 1975 145–147 Leone • Vet Chr XII 1975 217 Colafemmina • ThS XXV 1974 148–152 Brock
Seeks to provide the basis for a truly critical text of the Septuagint by utilizing the procedures of classical scholarship. A vast amount of knowledge is here synthesized.

KLEINLOGEL, Alexander. Geschichte des Thukydidestextes im Mittelalter. Berlin, De Gruyter, 1965. xiv, 186p., 4p. of illus.
DE55

Gnomon XXXVIII 1966 135–138 Lewis • RPh XL 312–314 Irigoin • CR XVI 1966 302–04 Dover
The study of the text of Thucydides has great suggestive value for the study of other text histories. The two great virtues of this book are that it studies the interrelation of text and *scholia pari passu*, and that the author shows unfailing open-mindedness and balance. He examines the problems of the stemma down to mid-14th century only, but his work marks a decisive stage in the study of a contaminated tradition. A stemma once tidy is here exposed as extremely complex, and he ends with no less than five sources transcending the old minuscule archetype.

METZGER, Bruce Manning. The text of the New Testament; Its transmission, corruption, and restoration. 2d ed. New York, Oxford University Press, 1968. ix, 281p., illus.
DE56

AC XXXIX 1970 254–255 Sanders • Gymnasium LXXVII 1970 552–553 Huss
Between the first appearance of this work in 1964 and the second edition in 1968 Professor Metzger has published his invaluable *Index to periodical literature on Christ and the Gospels,* (Leyden, 1966, xxiv, 602p.) and *Historical and literary studies: Pagan, Jewish and Christian* (1968, 170p.). The present edition has particularly benefited from his critico-bibliographical activity

in the form of additional notes (p. 261–273). His purpose is to supply the student with information concerning both the science and the art of textual criticism as applied to the N.T. The science deals with (a) the making and transmission of ancient MSS; (b) the description of the most important witnesses to the N.T. text; and (c) the history of the textual criticism of the N.T. as reflected in the succession of printed editions of The Greek Testament. The art of textual criticism refers to the application of reasoned consideration in choosing among variant readings.

PASQUALI, Giorgio. Storia della tradizione e critica del testo. Firenze, F. Le Monnier, 1934. 484p.   **DE57**

Gnomon 1936 16–30 Seel • BAGB 1936 7–32 Dain

REYNOLDS, Leighton D. The medieval tradition of Seneca's letters. [London], Oxford University Press, 1965. vi, 167p., facsims.   **DE58**

Oxford classical and philosophical monographs.
CR XVI 1966 340–344 Kenney • RPh XL 1966 178–179 Ernout • AC XXXVI 1967 673–676 Cambier
This work is doubly valuable, in providing editors with a satisfactory foundation for the establishment of the text and in illustrating both the capabilities and limitations of stemmatics. It is a complementary volume to the two-volume *OCT* edition of the *Ad lucilium epistulae morales* by Reynolds, which also appeared in 1965. Reynolds here refines on the earlier work of O. Foerster, *Handschriftliche Untersuchungen zu Senekas Epistulae Morales und Naturales Quaestiones* (Stuttgart, 1936), paying particular attention to the recentiores. He provides a chronological tableau of themes, catalogue of the MSS used in the construction of the text, a selected bibliography, an *index codicum* and an *index rerum*.

SHACKLETON BAILEY, David Roy. Towards a text of Cicero "Ad Atticum." Cambridge, University Press, 1960. ix, 104p.   **DE59**

RPh XXXV 1961 170 Ernout • CR XI 1961 238–240 Nisbet • Hermathena XCV 1961 83–86 Courtney
This is a *parergon* from Bailey's *OCT* edition of *Ad Atticum,* Books IX–XVI but is not confined to those books. These notes on about 180 passages reveal a profound knowledge of the text, based on autopsy and study of the work of previous editors. Nearly 100 new emendations are advanced, many convincing, many attractive, and, inevitably, some questionable.

SMYTH, William R. Thesaurus criticus ad Sexti Propertii textum. Congressit et in ordinem redegit Gulielmus R. Smyth. Leiden, Brill, 1970. 207p.   **DE60**

Mnemosyne. Bibliotheca classica Batava: Supplementum; 12.
Phoenix XXV 1971 294–295 Gould • Gnomon XLV 1973 416 Bailey • CR XXIII 1973 173–175 Dickinson
This work is a model of economy and succinctness and contains over 12,000 emendations, transpositions

and other alterations. The list of scholars who have suggested emendations runs to 450, and there is a bibliography (p.177–197) to facilitate further research into their reasons. Many unpublished emendations are also listed. There is no attempt to evaluate the emendators but the whole is a valuable index of conjectures.

TIMPANARO, Sebastiano. La genesi del metodo del Lachmann. Firenze, 1963. viii, 145p.   **DE61**

REL XLI 1963 406–407 André • BAGB ser. 4 1964 116–122 Dain • CR LXXXVIII 1964 208–209 Goodyear
Lachmann's method, while never formally outlined by himself, consisted essentially in establishing a *stemma codicum* by classifying MSS according to their genealogy and filiation. The study of the term *genesis* here involves a review of textual criticism from the Renaissance and the early use and misuse of *emendatio* and *recensio*. Many of the problems in textual criticism, it emerges, were already posed and solved in the period 1826–1841, prior to Lachmann's edition of Lucretius in 1850. Lachmann's chief glory resides in his preface to his edition of the New Testament (1842–). His contribution to textual criticism consisted in repudiation of the Vulgate, distrust of MSS of the humanistic era, reconstitution of the history of texts, and the formulation of criteria to allow a mechanical determination of the choice of readings—almost all of which was anticipated and developed by some of his predecessors and contemporaries. The merit of Timpanaro's study is that it quite literally puts Lachmann in his place, making him share his reputation with others like Madvig and Ritschl.
There is a German translation (1971), which adds a useful bibliography (p.153–171).

TURYN, Alexander. The Byzantine manuscript tradition of the tragedies of Euripides. Roma, L'Erma di Bretschneider, 1970. x, 415p., 24 facsims.   **DE62**

Studia philologica; 16.
JHS LXXXII 1962 162–164 Mason • REByz XV 1957 279–280 Darrouzès • Gnomon XXX 1958 503–510 Lloyd-Jones
First published in 1957 this volume follows the pattern of Turyn's earlier works on Sophocles and Aeschylus. He seeks to demonstrate that in the "trial" existing texts do not take sufficient account of the younger "veteres" which he calls recentiores, these being later in date than 1300 A.D., and therefore liable to Byzantine interpolations which have not been systematically detected. Turyn sets out to expose the Paleologean interpolations in order to detect earlier ones contained in the "recentiores."

TURYN, Alexander. The manuscript tradition of the tragedies of Aeschylus. Hildesheim, G. Olms, 1967. vi, 141p.   **DE63**

"List of the manuscripts of Aeschylus" (p.6–9).
CR LVII 1943 109–112 Robertson • AJPh LXV 1944 417–418 Schlesinger

Turyn constructs a genealogical tree of the 150 MSS catalogued by Weir Smyth in *HSPh* XLIV (1933). A storehouse of laborious research into manuscript history which throws much light on the activity of the late Byzantine and Renaissance ages. An extended appendix contains an edition of the scholia on the *Eumenides* found in the Triclinian Naples MS.

TURYN, Alexander. The manuscript tradition of the tragedies of Sophocles. Edizione anastatica. Roma, L'Erma di Bretschneider, 1970. 1st ed., 1952. xi, 217p., 18 facsims.   **DE64**

Studia philologica; 15. "Ristampa anastatica invariata dell'edizione Urbana, Ill. 1952 (Illinois Studies in Languages and Literature XXXVI, 1–2)." "List of the manuscripts of Sophocles" (p.5–9).
Gnomon XXV 1953 441–442 Maas • Scriptorium VII 1953 274–281 Wittek • REG LXVII 1954 507–511 Irigoin • CR n.s. IV 1954 102–105 Rattenbury
Consists of two parts: an analysis of the different "byzantine" recensions of Sophocles, all apparently later than 1290 (p.13–98), and a study of the "ancient" tradition (p.99–183). Most of the Sophocles MSS are products of critical work in the reign of Andronicus II Paleologue (1282–1328) Mannuel Moshopoulos, Thomas Magistros and Demetrius Triclinius. Having focused on the interpolations in the post-1290 MSS, he goes on to conclude that editors should only use two groups of MSS that go back to the 9th/10th century archetype in minuscule—the Laurentine family and the Roman family. A work of great originality and importance.

WARTELLE, André. Histoire du texte d'Eschyle dans l'Antiquité. Paris, Les Belles Lettres, 1971. 399p.   **DE65**

Collection d'études anciennes.
Gnomon XLVII 1975 641–645 Dawe • REG LXXXVII 1974 415–417 Jovan • ACR III 1973 56 Bongie
Contains a great wealth of information on Aeschylus and on the history of the text of all Greek tragedy. Especially useful for its treatment of the earliest period of transmission, tracing the fortunes of the plays in detail through direct and indirect tradition in the Greek, Alexandrian, Roman and Christian worlds to the 5th century A.D. A distinguished work from one of A. Dain's most distinguished students.

Model Critical Texts

AESCHYLUS. Agamemnon. Edited with a commentary by Eduard Fränkel. Oxford, Clarendon Press, [1974]. 3 v., facsims.   **DE66**

"First pub. 1950; reprinted with corrections 1962, 1974."
JHS LXXII 1952 130–132 Rose • Mnemosyne ser. 4 1952 80–82 Kamerbeek • Gnomon XXIII 1951 301–308 Mazon
"This long-awaited edition is perhaps the most erudite that any Greek play has ever had" (Rose). "Elle constitue un monument de la philologie du XX siècle" (Kamerbeek). The Prolegomena, some 85 pages, deal with the MS tradition, editions especially worthy of mention and previous criticism. There are full critical notes under the text and a facing English translation which is really an extension of the commentary. The commentary, filling 832 pages, deals in great detail—grammatical, mythological, aesthetic, dramatic—with all points, including a resumé of earlier opinions and a justification for Fränkel's own views.

VERGILIUS, Maro Publius. Aeneidos, liber quartus. Edited by Arthur Stanley Pease. Darmstadt, Wissenschaftliche Buchgesellschaft, 1967, 1963. ix, 568p.   **DE67**

Reprint of 1935 ed. published by Harvard University Press.
AJPh LVII 1936 190–196 Prescott • REL XIV 1936 436–437 Marouzeau • JRS XXVI 1936 296–297 Sparrow
An encyclopedic commentary in the Pease tradition, and a monument of erudition, offering a veritable collection of monographs on the text, not just of Book IV but of the whole *Aeneid*. The commentary generally averages 40 lines for every two lines of text. Over-concern for a massive compilation of parallels unfortunately obscures the fact that a critic's business begins where a compiler's leaves off. The description of the MSS (p.71–79), the selected critical apparatus and the testimonia bear witness to the editor's meticulous care.

Language and Style: Grammar and Lexicography

EA GRAMMAR

General Linguistics

BEYLSMIT, J. J. and RIJLAARSDAM, J. C., eds. Bibliographie linguistique de l'année 1980. The Hague, Nijhoff, 1983. 1, 782p. **EA1**

Idem 1981 et compléments des années précédentes. Éd. avec l'assistance de H. Borkent & M. Janse. The Hague, Nijhoff, 1984. 1, 861p.

MEILLET, Antoine and VENDRYÈS, J. Traité de grammaire comparée des langues classiques. 4 éd. nouv. tir. revu. Paris, Champion, 1968. **EA1a**

Mediterranean, Indo-European Languages

HUDSON-WILLIAMS, Thomas. A short introduction to the study of comparative grammar (Indo-European). Cardiff, The University of Wales Press Board, 1972. x, 78p. **EA2**

Reprint of the 1931 ED.
CR XLIX 1935 239 McKenzie
A useful short introduction, good on Greek and Latin, but weak on Sanskrit, with great prominence given to Welsh in the Celtic languages.

MEILLET, Antoine. Introduction à l'étude comparative des langues Indo-Européennes. University of Alabama Press, 1973, 1964. xiv, 516p. **EA3**

REL IV 1926 69–70
Meillet's La méthode comparative en linguistique comparative dates back to 1925, when it was hailed as marking a major stage in the history of linguistics.

NAGY, Gregory. Greek dialects and the transformation of an Indo-European process. Cambridge, Mass., Harvard University Press, 1970. xii, 200p. **EA4**

Loeb classical monographs.
AJPh XCII 1971 721–724 Poultney • CPh LXVIII 1973 303–305 Messing • CR XXII 1972 371–374 Morpurgo-Davies
The Indo-European process in the awkward title refers to Sievers' law, modified by Edgerton. Greek, in fact, gets little more than 60 pages in this wide-ranging study of the Indo-European process in the relevant languages. Nagy pushes back the full operation of Sievers' law to an early stage of I.E. and makes many other challenging hypotheses.

Greek and Hellenic Dialects

BECHTEL, Friedrich. Die griechischen Dialekte, 2, Aufl. Berlin, Weidmann, 1963. 3 v. **EA5**

AJPh XLVII 1926 295–300 Buck • BSL LXXIV 51–55 Meillet • PhW XLII 1922 391–396 Hermann
The first volume of this monumental work appeared in 1921, v. 2 in 1923 and v. 3 in 1924, with a total of 1781 pages. A magnum opus completed in the last decade of his life by a scholar of many parts. Twenty-eight dialects are treated separately.

BECHTEL, Friedrich. Die historischen Personen-namen des Griechischen bis zur Kaiserzeit. Hildesheim, G. Olms. 1964. xvi, 637p.   **EA6**

"Reprografischer Nachdruck der Ausgabe Halle 1917."
BPhW 1918 457–464 Schmidt • WKPh 1918 219 Drerup
The names are listed alphabetically in Greek, with notes in German.

BLASS, F. and DEBRUNNER, A. Grammatik des neutestamentlichen Griechisch. 14 neuarb. und erw. Aufl., bearb, von Rehkopf, F. Göttingen, Vandenhoeck & Ruprecht, 1976. xx, 512p.   **EA7**

AC XLVI 1977 659 Leroy • CR XXVIII 1978 98–100 Kilpatrick • CW LXXII 1979 244 Gignac • Gnomon XXXV 1963 360–362 Zuntz
First produced by Blass in 1896, Debrunner continued it from the 4th edition to the 9th (1954). Funk's English translation of the 9th and the 10th editions appeared in 1961. The present edition is the first by Rehkopf, who has improved it, especially the index locorum and bibliography.

BODOH, John J. An Index of Greek Verb Forms. With the assistance of Sara E. Bavousett and others. Hildesheim and New York, G. Olms, 1970. x, 483p.   **EA8**

Alpha-Omega, Lexika, Indizes, Konkordanzen zur Klassichen Philologie; 14.
AAHG XXXI 1978 243 Faust • REG LXXXV 1972 227–228 Humbert
A helpful work involving long, unselfish toil from the author and his collaborators, this répertoire of verbal forms, alphabetically arranged and grammatically explained, covers the period from early epic to Koinë, not just standard literary but even nonliterary forms, as attested by the papyri. The symbolism employed is a little awkward, and the coverage too generously extends to very predictable forms.

BRANDENSTEIN, Wilhelm. Griechische Sprachwissenschaft. Berlin, W. de Gruyter, 1954– .   **EA9**

Sammlung Göschen; Bd. 117.
CR X 1960 140–142 Jones • CW XLVII 1954 199 Whatmough • Gymnasium LXIII 1956 114–116 Untermann • RBPh XXXIV 1956 259–260 Leroy
A brief, solid treatment, dealing with the external history of the Greek language (but no recognition of Linear B), the alphabet, dialects, phonology, accent, phonematic substitution and a few examples of etymology. Replaces the Sammlung Göschen, Bd. 117, by Kieckers (1925), the new treatment showing the latest shift in emphasis to structural analysis.

BROWNING, Robert. Medieval and Modern Greek. London, Hutchinson University Library, 1969. 153p.   **EA10**

ACR I 1971 236–237 Costas • BSL LXVII, 2 1972 103–105 Humbert
A general introduction is followed by chapters on the state of the language from Hellenistic times to the Turkish period, and on the national language and the dialects of modern Greece. The last chapters discuss the struggle in modern times between *Katharevousa* and demotic.
There is a select bibliography, a map and a glossary of linguistic terms. An important contribution to the later history of the Greek language.

BUCK, Carl Darling. Comparative grammar of Greek and Latin. The University of Chicago Press, [1933]. 405p.   **EA11**

CR XLVII 1933 205 Palmer • REA XXXV 1933 348–350 Cuny • REL X1 1933 467–468 Marouzeau
This work sprung from the author's conviction that with the exception of Meillet-Vendryés, *Introduction,* manuals dealing with Greek and Latin together have ceased to be representative. Syntax is deliberately omitted. There is a brief introduction on the Indo-European family of languages, and a general survey of the principles of linguistic evolution. The main body of the work comprises a complete survey of the nominal and verbal systems of both languages, including word formation.

BUCK, Carl Darling. The Greek dialects; Grammar, selected inscriptions, glossary. Chicago, The University of Chicago Press, [1973]. xiii, 373p.   **EA12**

Midway reprint of the 1955 ed.; 1st ed., 1910.
CPh LI 1956 209–211 Whatmough • G&R II 1955 • Phoenix X 1956 127–128 Poultney
Shortly before his death in 1955 Professor Buck prepared this completely revised treatment of the subject on which he was the world's leading authority. As in the 1928 edition the dialects are not treated separately, but their features are arranged under the proper grammatical headings. The new edition contains 120 inscriptions, about a score of the earlier selection having been dropped to make way for new finds. Much help is provided with English translations, and commentary and bibliography are very full and helpful.

CALDER, William Musgrave, III. Index locorum zu Kühner-Gerth. Darmstadt, Wissenschaftliche Buchgesellschaft, 1965. viii, 168p.   **EA13**

CR XVII 1967 392–393 Garvie • JHS LXXXVII 1967 215–216 Browning • RPh XLI 1967 299 Chantraine
A most valuable index to the 35,000 passages in Kühner-Gerth from authors ranging from Homer to Eusthathius. Calder points out that Kühner-Gerth's citations have been used by all subsequent writers on syntax. See also entry EA20a.

DENNISTON, John Dewar. The Greek particles. 2d ed. Oxford, Clarendon Press, 1975. lxxxii, 660p.   **EA14**

CR XLVIII 1934 221–223 Lorimer • DLZ 1934 1933–1937 Debrunner • RPh IX 1935 208–210 Chantraine

The first edition appeared in 1934, the second edition with corrections and additions by K. J. Dover in 1954, adding sixty pages to the first. The book's purpose is literary and stylistic rather than grammatical or etymological.

The study of the particles in the main body of the work is arranged alphabetically. Based on a vast array of examples from literature down to c.320 B.C.

DOVER, Kenneth James. Greek word order. Cambridge, Cambridge University Press, 1968, 1960. 72p. **EA15**

AJPh LXXXIII 1962 324–326 Poultney • CW LIV 1961 219 Whatmough • MH XVIII 1961 234 Risch • Hermathena XCVI 1962 112 Stanford

The author of this basic work names ten types of determinants of word order: phonological, morphological, syntactical, semantic, lexical, logical, emotive, social or ceremonial, those involving the individual history of the speaker, and those of a stylistic or aesthetic character.

FRÖSÉN, J. Prolegomena to a study of the Greek language in the first centuries A.D.; The problem of Koine and Atticism. Helsinki, Inst. Hist-Philol. Univ., 1974. 235p. **EA16**

AC XLVII 1978 665–666 Mawet • CR XXVI 1976 228–229 Browning • JHS XCVI 1976 204 Moorhouse • RPh L 1976 300 Casevitz

A rather inconclusive work which points the way, however, to the possibilities of closer collaborations between classic and modern linguistics. The 38 pages of bibliography are described as "an annotated bibliography . . . for linguists and philologists." The problems studied are those underlying the formulation of Koinë.

HOFFMANN, Otto. Geschichte der griechischen Sprache. Bearb. von Anton Scherer. Berlin, de Gruyter, 1969. 2 v. **EA17**

Sammlung Göschen; Bd. 111/111a, 114/114a.

CR XXII 1972 72–73 Morpurgo Davies • Gnomon XLIX 1971 738–741 Hiersche • Language XXXII 1956 508–514 Bolling • RBPh XLIX 1971 648 Liénard

The first volume of Debrunner's revision of Hoffmann appeared in 1953, 37 years after the last edition by the author. The following year Debrunner added a second volume on the postclassical period. Now after some 15 years Scherer has revised both volumes, providing in a relatively small compass, the most up-to-date and dependable history of the Greek tongue. Volume I introduces Greek, its neighboring languages and its dialects. This is followed by a survey of the language of the main literary genres: epic, lyric and choral poetry, tragedy, comedy, and prose down to Xenophon. Volume II, in a somewhat different arrangement, discusses basic questions of postclassical Greek, sources and evidence, spread of Attic, disappearance of the old dialects, rise of Koine, and new dialects of Modern Greek. Most of Scherer's revisions are in the early part of v. I, taking account of the Linear B contribution.

HUMBERT, Jean. Syntaxe grecque. 3. éd., revue et augmenté. Paris, Klincksieck, 1972. 470p. **EA18**

Tradition de l'humanisme; 8.

AJPh LXIX 1948 114–116 Poultney • Language XXIII 1947 285–287 Gray • RPh XXI 1947 76–78 Chantraine

The range of this fine work is from Homer to the 4th century B.C., covering literary Attic, Ionic and the Doric of the drama. The author seeks in every case to find the psychological reasons underlying each and every syntax usage. He occasionally cites Sanskrit and Latin parallels.

See also Humbert, J. *Histoire de langue grecque.* Paris, 1972.

JANNARIS, Anthony N. An historical Greek grammar chiefly of the Attic dialect as written and spoken from classical antiquity down to the present time; Founded upon the ancient texts, inscriptions, papyri and present popular Greek. (Reprografischer Nachdruck der Ausg. London, 1897.) Hildesheim, G. Olms, 1968. xxxviii, 737p. **EA19**

Consists of a brief introduction, giving the history of Greek from the Attic period (500–300 B.C.) to the Neohellenic (600–1900 A.D.), three main sections: Phonology (p.21–100), Morphology (p.101–311), and Syntax (p.312–506), and six appendices. There is an index of Notable Greek Words (p.581–697), an index of Subjects, and of Passages Emended or Critically Discussed.

KRETSCHMER, Paul. Einleitung in die Geschichte der griechischen Sprache. 2. unveränd. Aufl. (Unveränd. Nachdr. d. 1 Aufl. von 1896.) Göttingen, Vandenhoeck u. Ruprecht, 1970. iv, 328p. **EA20**

CR XXII 1972 420–421 Morpurgo Davies

A welcome reprint of a book which on its first appearance in 1896 probably opened a new era of Indo-European and Greek studies. Though much has happened in the meantime to render some of the work obsolete—e.g., we now know that Lycian is Indo-European—it is still valuable and immensely learned.

KÜHNER, Raphael. Ausfürhrliche grammatik der griechischen sprache. 3. aufl. Hannover, Hannsche buchhandlung, 1890–1904. 4 v. **EA20a**

1. t. Elementar- und formenlehre . . . , rev. by F. Blass. 2. t. Satzlehre . . . , rev. by B. Gerth. Reprinted in 1954.

LEJEUNE, Michel. Phonétique historique du mycénien et du grec ancien. Paris, Klincksieck, 1972. 398p. **EA21**

Tradition de l'humanisme; 9.

AJPh XCVI 1975 215–217 Poultney • CPh LXXI 1976 372–374 Messing • Language XXIV 1948 195–198 Kent • REG LXXXVII 1974 398–400 Perpillou

Lejeune's *Traité de phonétique grecque* was published in 1946 [cf. Gnomon XXII 1950 392–394 Leumann], with a second edition in 1955. The present work, however, is virtually entirely new. Lejeune is preeminently equipped to handle the Mycenaean forms and to integrate his study of the newly deciphered texts in a history of Greek phonetics. A most welcome publication, which keeps the chapter divisions and sections of the original *Traité* but systematically updates everything, although there is no separate bibliography. There is a splendid analytical index, a full index of Greek words, and a new index of Mycenaean citations.

MANDILARAS, Basil G. Studies in the Greek language. Athens, [N. Xenopoulos Press], 1972. 243p.   **EA22**

This work contains the text of seven lectures delivered in South Africa by an ardent demoticist. He is equally concerned with exploiting the rich possibilities of the demotic language and showing its continuity with the KOINOH. Among other things, he questions many of the so-called hebraic and semitic intrusions in the New Testament Greek.

PALMER, Leonard R. The Greek language. London and Boston, Faber and Faber, 1980. xii, 355p.   **EA23**

CR XXXI 1981 227–230 Penny • CJ LXXIX 1983 64–65 Nagy
A companion volume to the author's *The Latin language,* 1954, consisting of two parts: 1. An Outline History of the Greek Language, and 2. Comparative-Historical Grammar.

PERPILLOU, Jean Louis. Les substantifs grecs en -ευς. Paris, Klincksieck, 1973. 417p.   **EA24**

Études et Commentaires; 80. Originally presented as the author's thesis, Paris, 1970.
Gnomon L 1978 225–231 Panagl • JHS XCVII 1977 192–194 Considine • REG LXXXVII 1974 401–404 Brunel • RPh XLIX 1975 106–109 Christol
An important contribution to the study of Greek vocabulary. Greek nouns in -ευς were already flourishing in Mycenaean yet they have no clear counterparts in other Indo-European languages. The author, after surveying the scholarly debate about the origin of this formation (p.13–77), presents an historical inventory of words in -ευς, classifies the various uses of the suffix, and draws whatever conclusions seem likely. There is an admirable series of tables, chronologically arranged, presenting the material.

PISANI, Vittore. Manuale storico della lingua greca. Brescia, Paideia, 1973. 281p.   **EA25**

AJPh XCVII 1976 303–306 Poultney

RIX, Helmut. Historische Grammatik des Griechischen, Laut- und Formenlehre. Darmstadt, Wissenschaftliche Buchgesellschaft, [Abt. Verl.], 1976. xx, 297p.   **EA26**

AJPh XCVII 1976 416–420 Dunkel • LEC XLIV 1976 388–389 Van Esbroeck • REG XCI 1978 206 Irigoin

Intended as a student's introduction to the historical and comparative study of Greek, this work is particularly useful for its incorporation of developments in linguistic theory and in Greek linguistics since Schwyzer. There is a good brief introduction on the classification of languages and dialects. Phonématique (p.11–97) and morphology (p.101–266) are followed by a selective bibliography and index. This is a good German counterpart to Chantraine, H., *Morphologie historique du Grec.*

SCHMITT, Rüdiger. Einführung in die griechischen Dialekte. Darmstadt, Wissenschaftliche Buchgesellschaft, [Abt. Verl.], 1977. xvi, 142p.   **EA27**

Die Altertumswissenschaft.
REG XCI 1978 205–206 Dobias-Lalou
Especially useful for well-organized and up-to-date bibliographies which accompany each section, this introduction aims at complementing existing ones.
Mycenaean is treated here (between Arcadian and Cypriot on the one hand, and Ionian and Attic on the other). The order followed for each dialect is the same: bibliography, sources, history, particulars.

SCHWYZER, Eduard. Griechische Grammatik auf der Grundlage von Karl Brugmanns griechischer Grammatik. München, Beck, 1934–1971. 4 v. in 5.   **EA28**

Handbuch der Altertumswissenschaft, Abt. 2, Teil 1: 1. Bd. Allgemeiner Teil, Lautlehre, Wortbildung. Flexion. 2. Bd, Syntax und Syntaktische Stilistik, 3. Bd. Register, 4. Bd. Stellenregister.
AJPh LXXIII 1952 319–322 Poultney • Gnomon XXV 1953 353–361 Lohmann
The first volume appeared in two parts, phonology in 1934 and morphology in 1939, and it was soon obvious that it would be the standard work for a long time to come. When Schwyzer died in 1943, v. 2 Syntax was not quite finished, and the work was completed by Albert Debrunner.

THOMSON, George. The Greek language. Cambridge, W. Heffer and Sons Ltd., 1960, 1972. xiv, 101p.   **EA29**

Reprinted with corrections and additions 1966, 1972.

THUMB, Albert. Handbuch der griechischen dialekte. 2. erweiterte Aufl., von E. Kieckers. Heidelberg, C. Winter, 1932–1959. 2 v.   **EA30**

v. 2 edited by A. Scherer.
v.1 RPh VIII 1934 324–325 Chantraine • Emerita 1935; v. 2 CPh LV 1960 280–281 Whatmough 179–182 Bonfante • RPh XXXIV 1960 262–264 Chantraine • Gnomon XXXII 1960 585–596 Porzig
A valuable Handbuch which first appeared in one volume in 1909. The revised and enlarged editions by Kieckers and Scherer incorporate much new material, including "Mycenaean" (II, p.314–361). This part also offers Aeolic (Boeotian, Thessalian, Lesbian), Arcado-

Cyprian, Pamphylian, Ionic and Attic. Dorian and North West dialects are covered in the first part, along with a general introduction, bibliography and dialect groupings.

WYATT, William F. The Greek prothetic vowel. [Cleveland], Published for the American Philological Association, by the Press of Case Western Reserve University, 1972. xvii, 124p. **EA31**

Philological monographs; 31.
Language XLIX 1973 934–939 Sihler • Phoenix XXVII 1973 180–187 Szemerényi • AJPh XCV 1974 406–409 Poultney
The erratic phenomenon of prothesis in Ancient Greek which sometimes gives it an additional initial vowel over other Indo-European cognates is the subject of this book. Wyatt seeks to define under what circumstances such vowels came into being. Previous scholarly attempts at a solution (variations, mainly, on a laryngeal theory) are outlined and criticized in the opening chapter. Wyatt provides his own explanatory formula (p.9) and in subsequent chapters discusses widely accepted cases of prothesis (c.2), possible additional cases (c.3), apparent exceptions to the rule (c.4), and cases in which prothesis, though predicted, fails to develop (c.5). Rules multiply throughout the book, and even then so many residual problems remain unresolved that a not proven verdict must be entered.

Latin and Italic Dialects

ANDRÉ, Jacques. Les mots à redoublement en latin. Paris, Klincksieck, 1978. 125p. **EA32**

Études et commentaires; 90.
REL LVI 1978 442–443 Serbat

BENNETT, Charles E. Syntax of Early Latin. (Reprografischer Nachdruck der Ausg. Boston, 1910–1914). Hildesheim, G. Olms, 1966. 2 v. **EA33**

I,–The verb, 2,–the cases.
AJPh XXXII 1911 333–343, XXXV 1914 268–293 Knapp • CW 1911 6–7, 12–15, VIII 1914 213–215 Wheeler • CR XXIX 1915 119–121 Pantin
"Early Latin" is defined in v. 1 as the Latin from the beginnings to 100 B.C., which is the justification for excluding Lucretius in spite of the importance his archaisms have for such a study. The author's aim is to make his repertoire of examples for each item discussed as complete as possible, giving supporting reasons for the principle of classification adopted.
The first volume revealed inconsistencies in the texts used, or adhered to, e.g., v. 2 substitutes Vählen's *Ennius* and Marx's *Lucilius* for Baehren's Fragmenta, and shows other improvements. A clear, concise and sensible work.

BERGH, Birger. On passive imperatives in Latin. Uppsala, Stockholm, Distributor, Almqvist & Wiksell, 1975. 77p. **EA34**

Studia Latina Upsaliensia; 8.

AC XLVI 1977 312
The evidence of the ancient grammarians is incorporated with the recent findings of linguistics, semantics and stylistics.

CALBOLI, Gualtiero. La linguistica moderna e il latino: I casi. Ristampa corretta. Bologna, Pàtron, 1975. xvi, 370p. **EA35**

Testi e manuali per l'insegnamento universitario del latino; 10.
AC XLII 1973 670–672 Liénard • BStudLat III 1973 133–135 Reggiani • Gnomon XLVII 1975 349–354 Pfister • Latomus XXXV 1976 165–166 Dominicy
An original and useful study in which the author seeks to demonstrate that modern linguistic theory is applicable to Latin syntax. An historical overview of the question (c.2,3) reviews both ancient grammarians and important works in structuralism, with special preference for generative theorists.

CERESA-GASTALDO, Aldo. Il latino delle antiche versioni bibliche. Roma, Studium, 1975. 130p. **EA36**

REL LIII 1975 593–595 Fontaine
An extremely useful introductory manual on the language of the Latin Bible. There are useful selective bibliographies, and a double anthology of seven O.T. texts and seven N.T., with a *conspectus siglorum* for each, and a synoptic view of the various versions down to the Vulgate.

COUSIN, Jean. Bibliographie de la langue latine, 1880–1948. Paris, Société d'édition "Les Belles Lettres," 1951. xxiii, 375p. **EA37**

RPh XXVI 1952 110–112 Ernout • REA LIV 1952 119–120 Boyancé
A work suggested by Jean Marouzeau. Contains bibliography on general linguistics, Indo-European, Osco-Umbrian, history of Latin language from ancient to Christian writing, pronunciation, phonetics, morphology, syntax and structure, word order, stylistics and lexicography.

DEVOTO, Giacomo. Storia della lingua di Roma. 2, ristampa. Bologna, L. Cappelli, [1969, 1944]. 429p. **EA38**

Storia di Roma; v, 23.
AJPh XLVIII 1970 489–490 Richard • AJPh LXII 1941 378–379 Whatmough • REL XLVIII 1970 489–490 Richard
This work quickly became a classic after its publication in 1940 and second edition in 1944. It covers the formation and use of the Latin language from Archaic to Christian times in great detail, often with the help of running commentaries on selected texts. There is a valuable updating in the *note critiche*.

FLOBERT, Pierre. Les verbes déponents latins des origines à Charlemagne. Paris, Belles Lettres, 1975. xxii, 704p. **EA39**

Originally presented as the author's thesis, Paris IV, 1973.

CR XXIX 1979 90–92 Laughton • LEC XLIV 1976 283 van Esbroeck • Latomus XXXV 1976 622–624 Liénard • REL LVI 1978 443–446 Kerlouégan

The first monograph devoted exclusively to the Latin deponent since that of Bodiss in 1891, and likely to remain a standard work of reference for a long time. Especially valuable in that the time covered extends from Plautus to Charlemagne. Extremely well researched and presented. The second and third parts of the book (p.39–380) contain the historical surveys which form the essential core and the work's chief contribution.

HAMMOND, Mason. Latin, a historical and linguistic handbook, Cambridge, Mass., Harvard University Press, 1976. ix, 292p.   **EA40**

CR XXIX 1979 170 Adams

This new handbook does not claim to be a work of original research in Latin linguistics but neither does it justify its claim to present the current state of historical and linguistic work on the language. The work went through various drafts, having begun as a student exercise in a program leading to the Master of Arts in Teaching Latin. It benefited on the linguistic side by several collations on the part of Professor Gregory Nagy. More attention is given to the etymologies of linguistic terms than to the description of the linguistic phenomena in question.

KÜHNER, Raphael. Ausführliche Grammatik der lateinischen Sprache. Hannover, Hahn, 1912–14. 2v.   **EA41**

T. 1. Elementar- und Wortlehre (2, aufl.), T. 2. Bd. 1–2. Satzlehre, von Carl Stegmann.

CR XXVI 1912 200–202, XXIX 1915 119 Pantin • RPh 1917 245 Lejay • AJPh XXXVI 1915 80–86 Lease

Stegmann's extensive revisions of Bd. ii made a good work better and the complete opus is undoubtedly the best reference work for Latin syntax from Plautus to Tacitus, and especially for the language of Cicero and the Augustan age. Holzweissig's revision of Bd. 1 was less satisfactory, failing to take into account much of the vast lexical improvements since Kühner first wrote.

LEUMANN, Manu. Lateinische Grammatik von Leumann-Hofmann-Szantyr. München, Beck, 1977. 3 v. xvi, 391p., vi, 395p., xi, 447p.

          EA42

Handbuch der Altertumswissenschaft; Abt. 2, T. 2.

AC XLVII 1978 304–305 Liénard • AJPh LXXXVII 1966 224–230 Poultney • REL LV 1977 66–83 Serbat • Gnomon XXXVIII 1966 61–64, LI 1979 332–337 Lundström • JRS LV 1965 257–261 Coleman

Since its appearance in 1928 Leumann-Hofmann has had no rival as a comprehensive Latin grammar. It replaced Stolz-Schmalz, *Lateinische Grammatik* (1910). Szantyr's new *Lateinische Syntax und Stylistik* is a welcome, greatly enlarged revision. The *Dritte Lie-*

ferung (p.1–89) includes addenda and corrigenda, a subject index and word index to Szantyr, and an introduction to the entire grammar, including a good section on the prehistory of Latin (p.10–39).

LÖFSTEDT, Einar. Coniectanea, Untersuchungen auf dem Gebiete der antiken und mittelalterlichen Latinität. Amsterdam, Hakkert, 1968.

          EA43

Reprint of 1950 ed.

Erasmus IV 1951 422–424 Ernout • REL XXIX 1951 379–381 Andrieu

A very varied collection of 30 studies, under two main headings: Problems of Syntax and Stylistics, and Problems of Semantics and Lexicology. Based on a profound knowledge of Classical and Late Latin, this work is a model of linguistic and methodological research.

MANIET, Albert. La phonétique historique du Latin; Dans le cadre des langues indo-européennes. 5 éd., augmentée et corrigée, Paris, Klincksieck, 1975. 212p.   **EA44**

AAHG XXXI 1978 243–244 Schmeja • RPh L 1976 140 André • REL XXXIII 1955 368–370 Marouzeau, LV 1977 409–411 Serbat

First published in 1950 by an author who ranges widely in Celtic and Indo-European languages generally, this work is now in its 5th edition. It uses Latin to illustrate the main phenomena of the evolution of the sounds of language and the nature of the laws of phonetics, using general phonetics and psycholinguistics to good effect. This study provides us with a diachronic aperçu both of Latin and Indo-European languages, with a useful summary at the end of chapters of the comparable phenomena.

PALLOTTINO, Massimo. La langue etrusque; Problèmes et perspectives. Paris, Les Belles Lettres, 1978. 75p.   **EA45**

REL LVI 1978 434–436 Flobert • AC XLIX 1980 461–463 Lambrechts

This brief work marks a turning point in Etruscan studies. Translated from the Italian by Jacques Heurgon, it is a sure, safe guide to the methodology, present state and future directions of Etruscan studies.

See the same author's *Etruscologia* 341–431 and 486–488.

PALMER, Leonard R. The Latin language. London, Faber and Faber, [1968]. 372p.   **EA46**

CPh L 1955 293 Whatmough • JRS XLV 1955 219–220 Campbell • Language XXX 1954 499–503 Pulgram

First published in 1954, this is a standard work on the history of the Latin language and its comparative and historical grammar. Part 1 gives an outline history of Latin, tracing first the relation of Latin to the other Indo-European languages.

The language of Plautus and Terence receives a special treatment and the longest chapter deals with the development of the literary language in poetry and prose.

There are concluding chapters on Vulgar Latin and Christian Latin, followed by a brief bibliography, selected early Latin texts, and indices.

There is an Italian translation, *La Lingua Latino,* Torino, Einaudi, 1977, x, 462p.

PINKSTER, H. On Latin adverbs. Amsterdam, North-Holland Publishing Co., 1972. xi, 193p. **EA47**

North-Holland linguistic series; 6. Also presented as thesis, University of Amsterdam.

RPh XLIX 1975 140–141 Flobert • Augustinus XX 1975 201 Ortall • Lingua XXXIV 1974 96–100 Mathews

An application of transformational methods to Latin.

PRAT, Louis C. Morphosyntaxe de l'ablatif en latin archaïque. Paris, Les Belles Lettres, 1975. xxxvii, 444p. **EA48**

Collection d'études latines: Série scientifique; fasc. 32.

Latomus XXXV 1976 626–628 Liénard

One of the most important and interesting studies to appear recently. Difficult epigraphical and literary research meticulously pursued is here presented in a lucid and persuasive fashion.

SCHERER, Anton. Handbuch der lateinischen Syntax. Heidelberg, Winter, 1975. 292p. **EA49**

Indogermanische Bibliothek Reihe 1, Lehr- und Handbucher.

CW LXXII 1978 48–49 Sheets • Gnomon XLIX 1977 351–355 Lundström

Working within the tradition of the *Dependenz-Grammatik,* Scherer organizes his presentation of syntax around the concept of *Satzpläne* (fundamental sentence patterns) which embody the structural elements of *Satzkern* and *Ergänzüngen* (normally the verb and its obligatory complements) and *Erweiterungen* (optional supplements to the basic pattern).

SOMMER, Ferdinand. Handbuch der lateinischen Laut- und Formenlehre; Eine Einführung in das sprachwissenschaftliche Studium des Lateins. 4, Neubearb, aufl. Heidelberg, Winter, 1977. **EA50**

Indogermanische Bibliothek, Reihe 1: Lehr- und Handbücher; Bd. 1, Pfister, Raimund, Einleitung und Lautlehre.

CW LXXIII 1979 38–39 Watkins • LEC XLVII 1979 69 Delaunois • REL LVI 1978 437–440 Flobert

The third edition by Hans Siegert and R. Pfister in 1948 simply reprinted the second of 1914. Sommer had collaborated with Pfister on this edition up to his death in 1962 (in his 87th year). The work consists of an introduction (33p.), the section on phonetics (193p.), and 28 supplementary pages, including index of terms and words. The bibliography includes Indo-European, comparative grammar of Greek and Latin, and especially Latin items, down to 1971. An important work of reference.

STOLZ, Friedrich. Geschichte der lateinischen Sprache. 4 aufl. von Albert Debrunner, 1953. Neubearb, von Schmid, W. P. Berlin. Berlin, W. de Gruyter, 1966. 136p. **EA51**

Sammlung Göschen, Bd. 492–492a.

CR IV 1954 274 Jones • Gymnasium LXI 1954 573 Porzig • REL XXXI 1953 399–400 Marouzeau XLIV 1966 426 Collart

Stolz had been the basic introduction in German since 1910 and is here brought up-to-date by Debrunner and considerably expanded in viewpoint, with many (unanswered) new questions posed.

EB LEXICOGRAPHY

ADRADOS, F. R. et al. Introducción a la lexicografía griega. Madrid, Consejo Superior de Investigaciones Científicas, 1977. x, 280p. **EB1**

CR XXIX 1979 88–90 Slater

This is a joint effort by the authors working on the DGE (Greek Spanish lexicon), the first part of which is promised soon. Adrados writes on Mycenology and structural semantics, and Facal on the history of computing techniques. Gangutia deals inadequately with semantic theories in antiquity; C. Serrano is somewhat better on the history of ancient and medieval Greek lexicography.

See now Rodríguez Adrados, F. *Diccionario griego-español* (DGE). Madrid, Inst. Antonio de Nebrija, 1980. clx, 155p. (I: α–'αλλά). (JHS CII 1982 256 West • CR XXXII 1982 210–213 Wilson)

ANDRÉ, Jacques. Lexique des termes de botanique en Latin. Paris, C. Klincksieck, 1956. 343p. **EB2**

Études et commentaires; 23.

AJPh LXXIX 1958 102–103 Pease • Gnomon XXXI 1959 175–177 Lange • RBPh XXXVII 1959 866–867 Hyart

Covers 4000–5000 terms alphabetically arranged and gives Greek antecedents where available. Plant names are given their modern nomenclature and their synonyms in Classical Latin. The materials are assembled in the main from Theophrastus, Pliny and Dioscurides, but the whole period from Homer to the 9th century A.D. is covered.

BACCI, Antonio Cardinal. Varia Latinitatis scripta. Editio 3. Romae, Societas Libraria "Studium," 1955. 2 v. **EB3**

1. Lexicon eorum vocabulorum quae difficilius Latine redduntur. 2. Inscriptiones, orationes, epistulae.
Latinitas XI 1963 152–153 Tondini
An indispensable aid for those engaged in translating modern-day technical language into Latin.

BAILLY, Anatole. Dictionnaire grec français. Rédigé avec le concours de E. Egger. Édition revue par L. Séchan et P. Chantraine. Paris, Hachette, [1950]. xxxi, 2200p. **EB4**

REG LXXXVIII 1965 366–367 Humbert
The first edition appeared in 1894. In the 16th edition (1950), P. Chantraine had already made many improvements in a limited space assigned at the end of articles. In the present 26th edition many of the articles are entirely rewritten by Séchan, especially in arcane areas like botany and music. New notices on mythology and religion by Séchan are contained in an appendix.

BARTAL, Antal. Glossarium mediae et infimae Latinitatis regni Hungariae. Jussu et auxiliis Academiae Litterarum Hungaricae condidit Antonius Bartal. Hildesheim and New York, G. Olms, 1970. xxviii, 722p. **EB5**

"Reprografischer Nachdruck der Ausgabe Leipzig 1901."

BAUER, Walter. A Greek-English lexicon of the New Testament and other early Christian literature. A trans. and adaptation of the 4th rev. and augmented ed. of Walter Bauer's *Griechisch-deutsches Wörterbuch zu Schriften des Neuen Testaments und der übrigen urchristlichen Literatur,* by William F. Arndt and F. Wilbur Gingrich. 2d ed., rev. and augmented by F. Wilbur Gingrich and Frederick W. Danker from Walter Bauer's 5th ed., 1958. Chicago, University of Chicago Press, 1979. xl, 900p. **EB6**

CW L 1957 152 Hoerber • CJ LIV 1959 334–335 Fuerst • JSH LXXVIII 1958 150 Zuntz • Manuscripta I 1957 178 Finch • Gnomon XXX 1958 19–27 Zuntz
A highly successful if somewhat literal translation of the standard work, W. Bauer, *Griechisch-Deutsches Wörterbuch,* 4th ed., Berlin, 1949–1952. New treatment is given to some words not in Bauer, some errors have been corrected, and more etymological and other references are given. The foreword contains Bauer's *Einführung* from the 1st edition, giving a short history of Greek New Testament dictionaries. The work helps us to see the place of N.T. Greek in the history of Greek language, its relation to classical Greek, and to literary and spoken Koine, revealing the differences

in phonology, morphology, syntax and style in the light of recent finds in papyri, ostraca and inscriptions.

BAXTER, James Houston and JOHNSON, Charles. Medieval Latin word-list from British and Irish sources. With the assistance of Phyllis Abrahams, under the direction of a committee appointed by the British Academy. Freeport, N.Y., Books for Libraries Press, [1973]. **EB7**

Reprint of the 1934 ed. published by the Oxford University Press. "Authors and collections used for the list:" p.x–xiii.
RPh IX 1935 Ernout
Covers the period from the 5th to the 16th centuries for Great Britain, Scotland, and Ireland, both sacred and profane, public and private, literary and scientific, juridical and historic. Each word has a brief grammatical indication, the date at which it is first attested, and an English translation.

BENOIST, Eugène and GOELZER, Henri. Nouveau dictionnaire latin-français; Rédigé d'après les meilleur travaux de lexicographie latine et particulièrement d'après les grands dictionnaires de Forcellini, de Georges, de Freund et de Klotz, par Eugène Benoist [et] Henri Goelzer. Nouv. éd. entièrement refoundue et rev. par Henri Goelzer et précédée d'un tableau des formes difficiles de la conjugaison latine et du calendri romain. [11. éd.]. Paris, Garnier frères, [1934]. xxxvi, 1682p. **EB8**

REL 1934 474 Marouzeau

BENSELER, Gustav Eduard and SCHENKL, K. Griechisch-Deutsches und Deutsch-Griechesches Schulwörterbuch zu Homer, Herodot, Aeschylos, Sophokles, Euripides, Thukydides, Xenophon, Platon, Lysias, Isokrates, Demostenes, Aristoteles, Plutarch, Arrian, Lukian, Theokrit, Bion, Moschos, den Lyrikern und dem Neuen Testamente, soweit sie in Schulen gelesen Werden, sowie zu den Ecologae von Stadtmüller, dem Florilegium afranum, der Auswahl von Weissenfels und dem Lesebuch von Wilamowitz. 13, erweiterte und vielfach verb. Aufl., bearb. von Adolf Kaegi. Leipzig und Berlin, B. G. Teubner, 1911. xi, 1009p. **EB9**

BERKOWITZ, L. Thesaurus Linguae Graecae. Canon of Greek authors and works to A.D. 200. Costa Mesa, Cal., TLG Publ., 1977. xxix, 299p. **EB9a**

RPh LIII 1979 129 R.W. • Phoenix XXXIII 1979 281–282 Rubicam • JHS C 1980 238 West

BIELER, Ludwig. "Towards a Hiberno-Latin dictionary." ALMA XXXVIII (1971–1972): 248–255. **EB10**

BLAISE, Albert. Dictionnaire latin-français des auteurs chrétiens. Revue spécialement pour le vocabulaire théologique par Henri Chirat. Turnhout, Éditions Brepols, 1967, 1954. 913p. **EB11**

REL XXXII 1954 482–483 Marouzeau • Euphrosyne I 1957 373–380 Avallone • Latomus XIV 1955 135–138 Favez • RPh XXIX 1955 229–234 Ernout
An indispensable tool which covers Christian Latin from Tertullian to the end of the Merovingian age. The list of authors and works cited (p.9–29) is a most impressive testimony to the indefatigable Blaise, working almost single-handedly except for help on theological vocabulary from Chirat. Examples given of words are numerous and are translated. There are, naturally, inaccuracies, but the work fills a great need for a synthesis based on many monographs on individual authors.

BLAISE, Albert. Lexicon Latinitatis Medii Aevi: Praesertim ad res ecclesiaticas investigandas pertinens = Dictionnaire latin-français des auteurs du Moyen-Âge. Turnholti, Typographi Brepols, 1975. lxviii, 970p. **EB12**

Corpus Christianorum: Continuatio Mediaevalis.
MLJb XII 1977 247–248 Langosch • Scriptorium XXXIII 1979 10–11 Jodogne
A continuation of the author's *Dictionnaire latin français des auteurs chrétiens* aiming principally to be a help on lexical matters in the various ecclesiastical sciences—history, hagiography, liturgy, philosophy, theology, asceticism, canon law—but less concerned than Niermeyer with feudal law. The centuries between the 9th and 13th are the ones covered especially. Thomas à Kempis is the only 15th century author cited. An essential *instrument de travail* for anyone concerned with the history of *homo christianus occidentalis*.

BOISACQ, Émile. Dictionnaire étymologique de la langue grecque; Étudié dans ses rapports avec les autres langues indo-européens. 4. éd., augm. d'un index par Helmut Rix. Heidelberg, C. Winter, 1950. xxxii, 1256p. **EB13**

"Abréviations bibliographiques": p.[xxi]–xxxi.
Remains the *point de départ* for Greek etymological studies, thanks to its bibliographic skills.

BUCK, Carl Darling. A reverse index of Greek nouns and adjectives; Arranged by terminations with brief historical introductions by Carl Darling Buck and Walter Petersen. Chicago, University of Chicago Press, 1975. xvii, 765p. **EB14**

Midway reprint.
CR LXI 1947 21–22 Forbes • Hermathena LXVIII 1946 88–91 Quin
An important compilation of over 100,000 Greek nouns and adjectives useful both for editors restoring lacunae in inscriptions and papyri, and for students of the history of the language. Covers the literature, inscriptions, papyri, commentators, grammarians and lexicographers down to the Byzantine age.

CALDERINI, Aristide. Dizionario dei nomi geografici e topografici dell'Egitto greco-romano. Milano, Cisalpina Goliardica, 1972. **EB15**

V. 1, fasc. "ristampa anastatica" includes original t.p., which has imprint: Cairo, Società di Geografia d'Egitto, 1935. V. 1, fasc. has imprint: Madrid, Consejo Superior de Investigaciones Científicas, Instituto "Antonio de Nebrija," 1966.
AB 1937 113–114 Delehaye • RBh 1937 347–349 Hombert

CASSELL'S new Latin dictionary; Latin-English, English-Latin, compiled by D. P. Simpson. [5th ed.?]. New York, Funk & Wagnalls, 1968. xviii, 883p. **EB16**

CJ LVI 1961 171–176 Heller
Mr. Simpson, head of the Classical Dept. at Eton College, completely overhauls the old Cassell's by Marchant and Charles, making room for several thousand words not previously covered, mostly Plautine or Silver. Less important proper names are excised, many uncertainties have been removed from the etymologies. The references to authorities for particular meanings or phrases have been broadened, sometimes corrected. The arrangement of items within an article has been improved by typographical devices. Victorianisms in the English have been purged.

CHANTRAINE, Pierre. Dictionnaire étymologique de la langue grecque; Histoire des mots. Paris, Klincksieck, [1968–   ]. **EB17**

AJPh XCI 1970 372–375 Poultney • REG LXXXII 1969 192–195 Humbert • BAGB 1970 425–430 Irigoin • AC XXXIX 1970 645–647 • AC XLVI 1977 303–304 Leroy • Gnomon XLIX 1977 1–10 Szemerényi
Chantraine corrected the proofs of tome 3 in his hospital bed before his lamented demise, 30 June 1974. This excellent work does not duplicate the efforts of Boisacq or Frisk but tries to do for Greek what Ernout and Meillet did for Latin. This history of words goes back to Mycenaean Greek and traces the semantic evolution through the dialetical forms of ancient Greek down to Byzantine and Modern. The completion of the work, true to Chantraine's directives (cf. t.1, vii–xii) is under the competent direction of Michel Lejeune. See now IV, 2 Φ–Ω, 1980.

COHN, L. "Griechische Lexicographie," in Schwyzer-Brugmann, *Griechische Grammatik.* **EB18**

See entry EA28.

DU CANGE, Charles Du Fresne, et Sieur. Glossarium mediae et infimae latinitatis. [Conditum a Carolo du Fresne, domino Du Cange, auctum a monachis ordinis S. Benedicti, cum supplementis integris D. P. Carpenterii, Adelungii, aliorum, susque digessit G.A.L. Henschel; sequuntur Glossarium gallicum, Tabulae, Indices auctorum et rerum, Dissertationes. Editio nova aucta pluri-

bus verbis aliorum scriptorum Léopold Favre].
Graz, Akademische Druck-U. Verlagsanstalt,
1954. 10 v. in 5, plates.   **EB19**

"Unveränderter Nachdruck der Ausgabe von 1883–
1887." "Liste des ouvrages du Cange": v. 7, p.xxii–
xxiii. With v. 5, 26 plates to accompany article "Moneta" and 2 plates to accompany the article "Mono-
gramma." With v. 7, 12 plates to accompany the dissertation on Byzantine numismatics.

DUTRIPON, François Pascal. Concordantiae Bib-
liorum sacrorum Vulgatae editionis ad recogni-
tionem jussu Sixti Pontificis Maximi. Paris, Ber-
lin-Mandar, 1838. 1484p.   **EB20**

EGGER, Carl. Lexicon nominum locorum. [Ci-
vitas Vaticana], Officina Libraria Vaticana, 1977.
345p.   **EB21**

Opus fundatum Latinitas; v. 1.

EGGER, Carl. Lexicon nominum virorum et mulierum. Secundo edit. Romae, Societas Libraria
"Studium," [1963].   **EB22**

Latinitas XII 1964 240 Bruno
The lexicon is written in excellent Latin, and the
second edition adds a considerable number of new
names.

ERNOUT, Alfred. "Deux dictionnaires latins."
RPh XLV (1971): 298–305.   **EB23**

An extended review of *Thesaurus Linguae Latinae,
1900–1971,* and the first two fascicles of *Oxford Latin
dictionary.*

ERNOUT, Alfred and MEILLET, A. Dictionnaire étymologique de la langue latine; Histoire
des mots. 4. éd., 2. tir. augm. de corrections nouvelle. Paris, Klincksieck, 1967. xx, 828p.; 4. éd.,
3. tir., 1980, xix, 832p.   **EB24**

AAHG XIX 1966 244–247 Knoblock • REL
XXXVII 1959 261–262 Marouzeau • RPh XXXIII
1959 324–325 André
The 4th edition of this indispensable dictionary, appearing only eight years after the 3rd, is now printed
and incorporates many new features, explained by Ernout in the *Preface.* There are many new articles, especially on borrowings from Greek, incorporating the
more recent scholarship already reflected in Vetter and
Blaise. Four editions in 27 years bear eloquent testimony to the work's value and usefulness. It is a monumental, up-to-date reflection of the present state of descriptive, historical and comparative linguistics, both
the certainties and hypotheses. Meillet remains responsible for the etymological part, with very few additions
allowed by Ernout since the former's death. But the
work has been continuously improved, thanks to the
openmindedness of the compilers to criticism and suggestions.

ESTIENNE, Robert. Dictionarium propriorum
nominum virorum, mulierum, populorum idolo-

rum urbium, fluuiorum, montium, caeterorum-
que locorum quae passim in libris prophanis
leguntur. Paris, Ex officina R. Stephani, 1541.
585p.   **EB25**

Photocopy. Ann Arbor, Mich.: University Microfilms, 1977.

ETYMOLOGICUM   magnum   genuinum: Sy-
meonis etymologicum una cum Magna grammatica; Etymologicum magnum auctum synoptice
ediderunt Franciscus Lasserre, Nicolaus Liva-
daras. Roma, Edizioni dell'Ateneo, 1976– .
                                             EB26

Text in Greek, commentary in Latin.

FAIDER, Paul. Répertoire des index et lexiques
d'auteurs latins. New York, B. Franklin, 1971.
56p.   **EB27**

Reprint of 1926 Paris ed.

FATOUROS, Georgios. Index verborum zur
frühgriechischen Lyrik. Heidelberg, Winter,
1966. xxii, 415p.   **EB28**

CW LX 1967 389 Kirkwood • Gnomon XLI 1969
1–9 Galiano • REA LXIX 1967 382–383 Carrière
Includes all melic, elegiac and iambic poetry through
Pindar and Bacchylides, except for the elegiacs ascribed
to the dramatists. Entries are based on the best available, recently edited texts, including Oxy Pap. volumes.
The work has been done with extreme precision and
the printing is generally clear and easy to consult.

FORCELLINI, Egidio. Totius latinitatis lexicon;
opera et studio Aegidii Forcellini lucubratum et
in hac editione post tertiam auctam et emendatam a Josepho Furlanetto alumno Seminarii Pata-
vini novo ordine digestum amplissime auctum
atque emendatum cura et studio doct. Vincentii
De-Vit. Prati, Typis Aldinianis, 1858–[1879]. 6
v., illus.   **EB29**

Issued in parts, 1858–1879.

FRISK, Hjalmar. Griechisches etymologisches
Wörterbuch. 2d unver. ed. Heidelberg, C. Winter, 1972–1973. 3 v.   **EB30**

Indogermanische Bibliothek; 2. Reihe: Wörterbücher.
CW LV 1962 198 Whatmough • Gnomon XXXVII
1965 1–6 Risch (Lief. 1–10) • RPh XXXVIII 1964
106, 330 Ernout, XLVIII 1974 116 Andrè
It is estimated that about 40% of Greek vocables
are not of Indo-European derivation and of these almost
as large a proportion are of totally unknown derivation.
Frisk is wary of conjectural etymology. He is always
prudent, well-informed and up-to-date.

FUCHS, Johan Wilhelmus. Lexicon Latinitatis
Nederlandicae medii aevi. Woordenboek van het

middeleeuws Latijn van de Noordelijke Neder-landen. Composuit J. W. Fuchs adiuvante Olga Weijers. Amsterdam, Hakkert, 1970– . **EB31**

Issued in parts.
III. Fasc. 18 (Deifico–Destituo), Leiden, Brill, 1982, pp. 1315–1394.

GAISFORD, Thomas. Etymologicon magnum, seu verius lexicon saepissime vocabulorum origines indagans ex pluribus lexicis scholiastis et grammaticis anonymi cuiusdam opera concinnatum. Ad codd. mss. recensuit et notis variorum instruxit Thomas Gaisford. Amsterdam, Hakkert, 1962. 8p., vi, 2308 columns, p.2309–2469, facsim. **EB32**

"Reprint of the edition Oxford 1848."

GATES, John Edward. An analysis of the lexicographic resources used by American biblical scholars today. Missoula, Mont., Society of Biblical Literature for the Linguistics Seminar, 1972. xxi, 175p. **EB33**

Society of Biblical Literature, dissertation series; 8.

GESNER, Johann Matthias. Novus lingvae et ervditionis romanae thesaurus; Post Ro. Stephani et aliorum nvper, etiam in Anglia ervditissi-morvm hominvm cvras digestvs locvpletatvs, emendatvs . . . a Io. Matthia Gesnero. Leipzig, Impensis Casp. Fritschii Viduae et Bernh. Chr. Breitkopfii, 1749. 2 v., front. (port.). **EB34**

GRASBERGER, Lorenz. Studien zu den griechischen Ortsnamen; Mit einem Nachtrag zu den griechischen Stichnamen von Lor. Grasberger. Amsterdam, Hakkert, 1969. vii, 391 p. **EB35**

"Nachdruck der Ausgabe Würzburg 1888."
For Greek geographical names and for nicknames.

HARPOCRATION, Valerius. Lexicon in decem oratores Atticos. Ex recensione Gulielmi Dindorfii. Groningen, Bouma's Boekhuis, 1969. 2 v. **EB36**

"Reprint of the edition Oxford, 1853." Special title of v. 2: Annotationes interpretum.

HERWERDEN, Henricus van. Lexicon graecum suppletorium et dialecticum. Editio altera auctior et correctior. Lugduni Batavorum, Apud A. W. Sijthoff, 1910. 2 v., xix, 1678p. **EB37**

HESYCHIUS of Alexandria. Hesychii Alexandrini Lexicon; Post Ioannem albertum, recensuit Mauricius Schmidt. Amsterdam, Hakkert, 1965. 5 v. **EB38**

"Reprint of the edition 1858."

HOFMANN, Johann Baptist. Etymologisches Wörterbuch des Griechischen. München, Oldenbourg, 1950. 433p. **EB39**

AC XIX 1950 489–490 Leroy • Gnomon XXII 1950 235–239 Fraenkel • LEC XVIII 1950 358 van Ooteghens • Language XXVI 1950 417–420 Lane
Like his monumental revision of Walde's Latin etymological dictionary, Hofmann's Greek etymological dictionary is a triumph of minute and patient scholarship, without, however, showing any of the former paraphernalia of learned footnotes. The present work is above all an aide-mémoire to inform readers of the status quaestionis, and is meant to be used in conjunction with Boisacq's Dictionnaire étymologique. Written with great economy and unfailing good sense, it is extremely dependable. More or less uncertain conjectures are indicated by "wohl" or "viell."

JONES, Henry Stuart. "The making of a lexicon." CR LV (1941): 1–13. **EB40**

A paper of this title was read by Stuart Jones in January 1926; the present paper was found among his papers after his death, 29 June 1939. (Part X of the Greek-English lexicon appeared in 1940, in which he was to give a final account of his aims and methods.) Written a year after the Preface to part I of the Lexicon, this paper contains a good sketch of the ancient lexicographical tradition; also interesting is the discussion of the types of errors perpetuated from one generation of lexicographers to another.

JUCQUOIS, Guy. Compléments aux dictionnaires étymologiques du grec ancien. Louvain, Éditions Peeters, 1977– . **EB41**

Intended to supplement, in particular, Frisk's Griechisches etymologisches Wörterbuch and Chantraine's Dictionnaire étymologique de la langue grecque.

KLOTZ, Reinholdt and GRILLI, Alberto. Dizionario del a lingua latina. Brescia, Paideia editrici, 1974– . **EB42**

RPh XLIX 1975 141–142 André
Planned to run to at least 4,000 pages, this is an even more ambitious project than the Oxford Latin dictionary in that it will encompass Latin from its beginnings to the 7th century and incorporate the postclassical data in Souter's Glossary and Blaise's Dictionnaire des auteurs chrétiens, as well as taking account of inscriptions and glossaries. The first fascicle augurs well.

KRETSCHMER, Paul and LOCKER, Ernst. Rückläüfiges Wörterbuch der griechischen Sprache. Ausgearbeitet im Auftrage der Wiener Akademie der Wissenschaften; mit ergänzungen von Georg Kisser. 3., unveränderte Aufl. Göttingen, Vandenhoeck und Ruprecht, 1977. vii, 717p. **EB43**

AC XXXIV 1965 294 Leroy • Gnomon XXXVII 1965 307 Amundsen
Appearing first in 1944, this quickly became a precious tool for epigraphists and papyrologists working on mutilated texts. The first edition is mechanically

reproduced here but with 35 pages of important addenda by G. Kisser, incorporating the addenda to the 9th (1940) edition of Liddell-Scott, and new papyrological and epigraphical finds.

LAMPE, Geoffrey William H. A patristic Greek lexicon. Oxford, Clarendon Press, 1961. xlix, 1568p.   **EB44**

Gnomon XLII 1970 737–742 Mühlenberg • JThS XVIII 1967 213–217, XIX 1968 311–321 Fabricius
The object of the work is to interpret the theological and ecclesiastical vocabulary of the Greek Christian authors from Clement of Rome to Theodore of Studium. Philological considerations are second to this important but limited goal. The lexicon is generally only as good as the lexical work already accomplished on individual Greek Christian authors. There is a useful list of authors and works in the beginning of fascicle 1.

LATHAM, Ronald Edward. Dictionary of medieval Latin from British sources. Prepared under the direction of a committee appointed by the British Academy. London, Published for the British Academy by Oxford University Press, 1975– .   **EB45**

Bibliography: v. 1, p.[xv]–xlv. fasc. 1. A–B, 1975, 231p., fasc. 2. C, 1981, 233–551p.
MLatJb XVIII 1983 298 Langosch

LATHAM, Ronald Edward. Revised medieval Latin word-list from British and Irish sources. Prepared under the direction of a committee appointed by the British Academy. London, Published for the British Academy by the Oxford University Press, 1965. xxiii, 524p.   **EB46**

Based on *Medieval Latin word-list from British and Irish sources,* edited by J. H. Baxter and C. Johnson, first published in 1934.
CR XVII 1967 108–109 Walsh • CW LX 1966 25 Suits • History LI 1966 68 Winterbottom • MAev. XXXV 1966 125–130 Scott
Baxter and Johnson's original (1934) *List* included about 20,000 words, nonclassical in form and meaning. The new volume has more than twice as many entries and completely supersedes the old. The *List* is augmented chiefly on post-Conquest Latin. This work claims to be no more than an interim aid to students and a guide to contributors to the much larger enterprise of a comprehensive dictionary, now happily begun.

LATTE, Kurt, comp. Lexica Graeca minora. Disposuit et praefatus est H. Erbse. Hildesheim, Olms, 1965. xvii, 372p.   **EB47**

"Reprografischer Nachdruck."

LÉON-DUFOUR, Xavier. Wörterbuch zum Neuen Testament. München, Kösel, 1977. 469p., maps.   **EB48**

Trans. of *Dictionnaire de Nouveau Testament.*

LEWIS, Carlton T. and SHORT, Charles. A Latin dictionary founded on Andrew's edition of Freund's Latin-German dictionary. Oxford, Clarendon Press, 1975. xiv. 2019p.   **EB49**

First edition 1879.
Long known simply as Lewis and Short, this is a revised and enlarged adaptation of Andrew's edition of Freund's *Latin-German dictionary* (1850).

LIDDELL, Henry George and SCOTT, Robert, comps. A Greek-English lexicon. A new [9th] ed. revised and augmented throughout by Henry Stuart Jones, with the assistance of Roderick McKenzie, and with the cooperation of many scholars. London, Oxford University Press, 1966. xlviii, 2111p.   **EB50**

Stud Pap IX 1970 67 Pegueroles • Paideia XXIV 1969 273–282 Grilli • CPh 1942 96–98 Whatmough, LXIV 1969 238–239 Messing • RBPh XLVIII 1970 1391–1392 Leroy
The standard Greek-English lexicon.

LIDDELL, Henry George, SCOTT, Robert and JONES, Henry Stuart. Greek-English lexicon; A supplement. Edited by E. A. Barber with the assistance of P. Maas, M. Scheller and M. L. West. Oxford, Clarendon Press, 1968. xi, 153p.   **EB51**

". . . designed to be used in conjunction with the ninth edition."
Barber's *Supplement* incorporates the Addenda et Corrigenda of the ninth edition of *LSJ* as well as the many contributions from inscriptions and papyri published since 1940. There are very full preliminary listings: Authors and Works (with the most recent critical editions), Epigraphical Publications, Papyrological Publications, Periodicals, and General List of Abbreviations.
Mycenaean Greek is excluded from consideration, and the preface is unduly skeptical about its decipherment. Thomas Hardy's words are now more apt than ever: Says Scott to Liddell,/ Is there some jot or tittle/ Of Greek that we've not/ In our lexicon got?
For addenda see Drew-Bear, Th., "Some Greek words, 1811" *Glotta* L (1972), 61–96, 182–228; Renehan, R. "Greek lexicographical notes," *Glotta* XLVI (1968), 60–73, XLVII (1969), 220–234, XLVIII (1970), 93–107, L (1972), 38–60, 156–181.

MAIGNE d'ARNIS, W. H. Lexicon manuale ad scriptores mediae et infimae latinitatis. Hildesheim, Olms, 1977. 2336 col.   **EB52**

MALKIEL, Yakov. Etymological dictionaries; A tentative typology. Chicago, University of Chicago Press, 1976. ix, 144p.   **EB53**

METZGER, Bruce M. Lexical aids for students of New Testament Greek. New ed. Princeton,

N. J., distributed by the Theological Book Agency, 1969, 1975. xi, 100p., diagr., tables.

EB54

MEYER-LÜBKE, Wilhelm. Romanisches etymologisches wörterbuch. 2. unveränderte Aufl. [Heidelberg], C. Winter, 1924. 1091p.   **EB55**

Sammlung romanischer elementar- und handbücher, hrsg. von W. Meyer-Lübke. III. Reihe: Wörterbuch 3.

RPh IX 1935 396 Ernout

Furnishes an excellent *point de départ* for the study of the Latin antecedents, real or supposed, for romance etymologies.

MOULTON, William Fiddlan and GEDEN, A. S. A concordance to the Greek Testament; According to the texts of the United Bible Societies' 3rd ed. 5th ed., revised by H. K. Moulton, with supplement according to the text of the United Bible Societies' 3rd ed. Edinburgh, T. & T. Clark, 1978. xvi, 1110p.   **EB56**

MÜLLER, Frederik. Altitalisches Wörterbuch. Göttingen, Vandenhoeck & Ruprecht, 1926. vii, 583p.   **EB57**

"Verbesserungen und nachträge": p.[579]–583.

MÜLLER, Guido. Lexicon Athanasianum. Berlin, de Gruyter, 1952 [i.e., 1944–1952]. 1664 col.

EB58

Issued in 10 parts.

NOVUM Glossarium Mediae Latinitatis. Index scriptorum novus mediae latinitatis ab anno DCCC usque ad annum MCC; Qui afferuntur in novo glossario ab Academiis Consociatis iuris publici facto. Hafniae, E. Munksgard, 1973. xvii, 248p.   **EB59**

MA LXIII 1957 329–360 Niermeyer • Gnomon XXXI 1959 152–159 Prinz • REL XXXV 1957 475–476 Marouzeau • RBPh XXXVII 1959 104–111 Helin

In spite of the protestations of the preface this will inevitably be called by many the new Du Cange. Based on an enormous collection of cards in Paris and published with financial assistance from UNESCO and an outstanding editorial team of the Consilium Academiarum Consociatarum. One gauges from the first fascicle that the completed *Novum Glossarium* will be in the 3,000–3,500 pages range, more a Forcellini-De Vit than a *TLL*. The time limits on the *Novum Glossarium* are 800–1200 so that there will be no duplication of other lexical enterprises in progress. This will be a glossary not just of new meanings but of words whose classical meaning still persists.

See now Ordior–Ozreum, 1983, col. 731–940.

OXFORD Latin dictionary. Oxford, Clarendon Press, 1968– , ed. by P. G. W. Glare [et al.].

EB60

Fasc. 1 A–calcitro 1968, 2 Calcitro–dimilto, 3 Demiurgus–Gorgoneus, 4 Gorgonia–Libero 1973, 5 libero–pactum, 1976, 6 pactum–Qualitercunque 1977 [1978] p.1281–1536, 7 qualiterqualiter–sopitus 1980, 8 sopiter–Zythum 1982, p.1793–2126.

RPh XLII 1968 216–218, XLVI 1972 327, XLVIII 1974 135 André • CW LXIV 1971 192, LXVIII 1975 334–335 Poultney • CR XX 1970 91–94

Fascicles have appeared with admirable promptness and the completed work will be a worthy replacement of Lewis and Short, which has been standard since 1900. The *OLD* follows, generally speaking, the principles of the *Oxford English Dictionary* and is based on an entirely fresh reading of the Latin sources. Within each section or subsection, quotations are arranged in chronological order, beginning with the earliest known instance. Early Christian Latin is only occasionally included, so that Blaise and Souter are needed to complement the picture. The arrangement of the articles is very clear, making consultation easy and speedy. The list of authors and works under *Aids to the reader* is very useful and up-to-date.

See Barrow, R. H., *G&R* XV (1968), 127–129 for brief outline of the principles on which *OLD* is compiled.

PAPE, Wilhelm and BENSELER, G. Wörterbuch der griechischen Eigennamen. Nachdruck der 3. Auf. Graz, Akademische Druck- u. Verlagsanstalt, 1959. 2 v. lii, 1710p.   **EB61**

Reprint of v. 3 (1911) of *Handwörterbuch der griechischen Sprache,* published 1905–1914.

PHOTIUS I, Saint, Patriarch of Constantinople. Lexicon; Recensuit, adnotationibus instruxit et prolegomena addidit, S. A. Naber. Amsterdam, Adolf M. Hakkert, 1965. 2 v. in 1. 458p., 455p.

EB62

"Reprint of the Edition Leiden 1864–1865."

PICHON, René. Index verborum amatoriorum. Hildesheim, G. Olms, 1966. 78–303p.   **EB63**

Reprint of 1902 Paris ed.

QUELLET, H. Bibliographia indicum, lexicorum et concordantiarum auctorum Latinorum. Leiden, Brill, 1980. xiv, 262p.   **EB64**

ALMA 1982 61–62 Chollet • Latomus, XLII 1983 893–894 Petitmengin

RENEHAN, Robert. Greek lexicographical notes; A critical supplement to the Greek-English lexicon of Liddell-Scott-Jones. Göttingen, Vandenhoeck und Ruprecht, 1975. 208p. Second series, 1982. 143p.   **EB65**

RIESENFELD, Harald and RIESENFELD, Blenda. Repertorium lexicographicum graecum. A catalogue of indexes and dictionaries to Greek authors. Stockholm, Almqvist & Wiksell, [1954]. 95p.   **EB66**

Takes full account of the new lexica to appear since the checklists in Schöne, *Repertorium,* Leipzig, 1907 and Cohn, in *HdA* 11,1., 1913, p.718–720. Attempts to include in the bibliography lexicographical material bearing upon Greek literature from its beginnings to the end of the Byzantine epoch. Arrangement is alphabetical by ancient author from Achilleis XIV A.D. to Zeno Eleaticus, V B.C.

SLOANE, C. O'C. "Biblical concordances, dictionaries and encyclopedias." NCE II: 537–539. **EB67**

A useful survey article, beginning with the 13th century *Concordantiae Morales* and the *Concordantiae Sancti Jacobi,* 1230, which was the first strictly verbal concordance prepared from the Latin vulgate under the direction of Hugh of Saint-Cher.

The words *dictionaries* and *encyclopedias* are used more or less interchangeably to denominate a work containing relatively exhaustive information on the Bible.

SNELL, Bruno. Lexicon des frühgriechischen Epos. Vorbereitet und hrsg. von Bruno Snell. Verantwortlicher Redaktor: Hans Joachim Mette. Göttingen, Vandenhoeck & Ruprecht, 1955– .   **EB68**

Issued in parts.
AC XXXVI 1967 632 Severyns • CR n.s. VI 1956, VII 1957 254 Davison, XXII 1972 99–100 Willcock • Mnemosyne XVI 1963 65 Verdenius • RPh XLI 1967 154 Chantraine
Planned to be completed in about 25 fascicles, this great Hamburg lexicon contains very full and accurate articles but is very slow in appearing.
See now *Lexicon der frühgriechischen Epos,* ed. by W. Buehler. 10. Lief.: βάδην–Διώνη, Göttingen, Vandenhoeck & Ruprecht, 1982, xviii, 320p.

SOPHOCLES, Evangelinus Apostolides. Greek lexicon of the Roman and Byzantine periods (from B.C. 146 to A.D. 1100). Boston, Little, Brown and Company, 1870. xiv, 1188p. Reprint 1983.   **EB69**

Introduction (History of the Greek language and grammatical observations): p.[1]–56.
The "Authors referred to" are listed, p.[v]–xiv.

SOUTER, Alexander. A glossary of later Latin to 600 A.D. Oxford, Clarendon Press, [1964, 1949]. 454p.   **EB70**

ALMA XXIII 1953, 7–12, XXV 1955 102–141 Baxter • REL XXVII 1950 279–280 Marouzeau • RPh XXV 1951 115 Ernout
Begun as a complement to the *Oxford Latin dictionary* which was not planned to go beyond 180 A.D. The list of authors covered extends beyond 25 pages. An admirable bridge between strictly classical Latin

dictionaries and Du Cange. The entries are condensed but clear and very informative.

STARNES, DeWitt Talmage. Renaissance dictionaries, English-Latin and Latin-English. Austin, University of Texas Press, 1954. xii, 427p. **EB71**

Latomus XIV 1955 138–139 Huygens
This work is the fruit of a lifetime's study of Renaissance literature. The development of dictionaries is studied from the *Promptorium parvulorum* of 1440 to the Thesaurus of Robert Ainsworth, 1736. A work of extraordinary richness, beautifully illustrated by a large number of facsimiles.

SWANSON, Donald Carl E. The names in Roman verse; A lexicon and reverse index of all proper names of history, mythology, and geography found in the classical Roman poets. Madison, University of Wisconsin Press, 1967. xix, 425p. **EB72**

AC XXXVII 1968 698 Liénard • Gnomon XLI 1969 507–509 Buchwald • RPh XLIII 1969 168–169 Ernout
This is a useful supplement to Otto Gradenwitz, *Laterculi vocum latinarum,* 1904, which confined itself to common nouns. The present work lists all proper nouns of person or place, real or imaginary. There are three useful appendices which explain the procedures followed.

THESAURUS linguae latinae. Editus auctoritate et consilio academiarum quinque Germanicarum Berolinensis, Gottingensis, Lipsiensis, Monacensis, Vindobonensis. Lipsiae, In aedibus B. G. Teubneri, 1900– .   **EB73**

Editus iussu et auctoritate consilii ab academiis societatibusque diversarum nationum electi.
LEC XXXIII 1965 367–376 Heyeng • RPh XLV 1971 298–301 Ernout
Heyeng gives an historical conspectus of the enterprise from c. 1820 and F.A. Wolf to the creation of the International Commission in 1949. Details the present administrative organization, the maintenance of the *fichier* and the preparation of the articles. Vol. IX, 2 fasc. V onocrotalus-oppugnatio col. 641–800 1976, Vol. X, 2–3 potestas-praecipuus, 1983.

TOLKIEN, J. "Lexicographie." RE 12.2. (1925): 2432–2482.   **EB74**

See also Bolognesi, G., "Lessico," in *Introduzione alla filologia classica,* Milan, 1951, 394–405, 436–447; Erbse, "Lexicographie," *Lex. der alten Welt,* 1772–1724; Defradas, *Guide,* 39f.; Cousin, *Bibliographie pratique de la langue latine, 1880–1948,* Paris, 1951, 272–367, which includes a valuable Index des Mots, 353–367.

TONDINI, Amleto and MARIUCCI, T., eds. Lexicon novorum vocabulorum; Quae e libellis Latinitatis his decem superioribus annis in vulgus editis excerpserunt, Roma and New York, Desclée & Co., 1964. 293p. **EB75**

TUCKER, Thomas George. A concise etymological dictionary of Latin. Hildesheim, Verlag Dr. H. A. Gerstenberg, 1973. xxx, 307p. **EB76**

Reprint of 1931 edition published by Max Niemeyer Verlag.

CPh XXVII 1932 299–302 Petersen • CR XLVI 1932 134–136 Noble • CW XXV 1932 176 Sturtevant

Published in the belief that Walde's work, in spite of its many excellences, did not arouse the interest in comparative philology it deserves and that more emphasis could be placed on English and Greek. The author has an overpowering desire to trace every word back to a root and to reduce the number of the latter. Some of his etymologies are more imaginative than plausible.

WAGNER, Franz. Universae phraseologiae latinae corpus congestum, su lexicon latinum. Nova editio accuratissime recognita, aucta et de Germanica nunc primum in Gallicam linguam translata a Aug. Borgnet. Ridgewood, N. J., Gregg Press, 1965. xiv, 912p. **EB77**

Facsimile reprint of the 1878 ed., Brugis.

WALDE, Alois and HOFMANN, Johann B. Lateinisches etymologisches Wörterbuch. 4. Aufl. [Heidelberg], C. Winter, 1965. 2 v. **EB78**

Indogermanische Bibliothek. 2. Reihe: Wörterbücher "Abkürzungen" (bibliographical); v. 1, p.[xiii]–xxxii.

Language XXX 1954 110–114 Lane • CPh XLIX 1954 206–207 Whatmough

Considered by many the best etymological dictionary in any language.

WOODHOUSE, Sidney C. English-Greek dictionary; A vocabulary of the Attic language. London, Routledge & Kegan Paul, [1971]. viii, 1029p. **EB79**

Metrics, Song, and Music

FA   METRICS, RHYTHM, PROSODY

ALLEN, William Sidney. Accent and rhythm; Prosodic features of Latin and Greek: A study in theory and reconstruction. Cambridge, Cambridge University Press, 1973. xiv, 394p.   **FA1**

Cambridge studies in linguistics; v. 12.
JHS XCVII 1977 191–192 Parker • JRS LXV 1975 240–241 Hart • Language LI 1975 472–475 Newton • Gnomon XLVIII 1976 1–8 West
Continues the investigations on pronunciation in *Vox Latina*, 1966, and *Vox Graeca*, 1968, with a very detailed account of such prosodic features as vowel length, syllabic quantity, accent juncture and stress. Rhythm and metre are discussed first in general, then in relation to Latin and Greek prosodics, with countless illuminating examples and parallels from many languages and literatures. The theoretical underpinnings are clearly presented first (p.1–125) and will especially appeal to pure linguists. Latin is then treated (p.129–199), followed by Greek (p.203–334). There is a lengthy and fascinating appendix (p.335–359) on Latin hexameter, and a judiciously selected bibliography (p.361–389). An invaluable work for metricians, phoneticians and general linguists.

ALLEN, William Sidney. Vox Graeca; A guide to the pronunciation of classical Greek. 2d ed. Cambridge, Cambridge University Press, 1974. xiv, 174p., illus., plate.   **FA2**

CR XXI 1971 295–296 Jones • Mnemosyne XXIII 1970 82–83 Bolkestein • AJPh XCI 1970 246–248 Messing
Investigates the evidence and method by which the ancient pronunciation is reconstructed and makes practical proposals about present-day pronunciation. The author's credentials are most impressive: a very wide range of languages (including Indian phonetics) and great interest in modern-day linguistics.
After a short phonetic introduction the consonants, vowels, problems of vowel length and vowel junction,

quantity and in particular the accents receive due attention. There is a useful Summary of Recommended Pronunciations (p.155–157 in 1st ed.), as well as appendices on the history of pronunciation. This guide to pronunciation seems to offer a reasonable compromise between that of 5th century Attic and what can be realistically expected today. A new chapter in the enlarged second edition deals with discussion aroused by the first edition.

ALLEN, William Sidney. Vox Latina; A guide to the pronunciation of classical Latin. 2d ed. Cambridge and New York, Cambridge University Press, 1978. xiv, 132p., illus.   **FA3**

Latomus XXV 1966 170–171 Liénard • CJ LXII 1966 87–91 Heller • Mnemosyne XX 1967 493–494 Oomes
Allen's aim is to reconstruct the "educated" pronunciation of Golden Age Latin. An authoritative and very readable account of the sounds of classical Latin and their graphic representation. Individual consonant and vowel sounds are treated clearly and concisely. A table gives a summary of recommended pronunciations. An appendix summarizes the crazy history of pronunciation of Latin in England. A practical work that merits both reading and implementation.

BAUDOT, A. Musiciens romains de l'antiquité. Paris, Klincksieck, 1973. 158p., 8 plates.   **FA3a**

Études et Comm. LXXXII.
RH XCIX N° 254 1975 272 Weber

BEARE, William. Latin verse and European song; A study in accent and rhythm. London, Methuen, 1957. 296p.   **FA4**

Hermathena XCI 1958 75–78 Wormell • Mnemosyne XI 1958 180–182 Leeman • REA LX 1958 225–226 Irigoin

A careful analysis of the transition from quantitative to accentual rhythm. The author alerts us to the dangers of anachronism and chauvinism in imposing national pronunciations on ancient texts and uses an objective, comparative method to counteract these dangers. The various and often contradictory Anglo-Saxon views are submitted to lengthy examination. In the strictly comparative study, chapters VI to X, the principal systems of versification are examined by type: quantitative verse (Sanskrit and Greek), syllabic or numeric (Syriac, Chinese, Romance languages, esp. French), accentual (English), parallel verse (Hebrew). The second part (c. XI–XXVI) is devoted to Latin versification and its principles, from Saturnian to medieval hymns, concluding that Latin had little or no stress accent and was purely quantitative. A stimulating treatment of a very controversial subject, written with great objectivity but stronger on demolition of old views than on replacements.

CHAILLEY, J. La musique grecque antique. Paris, Les Belles Lettres, 1979. 222p.   **FA4a**

Collection d'études anciennes.
CPh LXXVIII 1983 236–242 Solomon

CHRIST, Wilhelm von. Metrik der Griechen und Römer. Hildesheim, H. A. Gerstenberg, 1972. viii, 716p.   **FA5**

A reprint of the second edition, Leipzig, 1879.

COOPER, Charles Gordon. An introduction to the Latin hexameter. New York, Macmillan, [1952]. ix, 70p.   **FA6**

Phoenix VII 1953 119 Robson • CR III 1953 167–168 Platnauer • CW XLVI 1953 123 Richards
Professor Cooper is a former student of W. M. Lindsay and has here produced a manual for teachers and pupils worthy of his master. The book is divided into four parts: 1. First Things First, 2. The Hexameter, 3. Abnormalities and seeming Abnormalities, 4. How to Scan and Read Latin verse. Treatment is especially good on Caesura and diaeresis, spondees and trochees at the end of lines, and word patterns for ending lines. An excellent introduction.

CRUSIUS, F. Römische Metrik. Eine Einführung. 2nd ed., rev. ed., von H. Rubenbauer. 1955. München, Hueber, viii, 158p. 8 Auflage, 1967.   **FA7**

REL XXXIII 1955 379 Nougaret • CR n.s. VI 1956 254 Platnauer • REA LVIII 1956 153–155 Soubiran • Gnomon XXVIII 1956 196–200 Drexler
Rubenbauer's revised edition of Crusius (which first appeared in 1929) maintains the size and scope of the original by judicious excisions, prunings and updatings, especially bibliographical. Controversial questions are fairly stated and the entire work is reliable and easy to consult.

DAIN, Alphonse. Traité de métrique grecque. Paris, Klincksieck, 1965. 276p.   **FA8**

RPh XLI 1967 151–154 Jouan • Mnemosyne XX 1967 300–304 Koster • CR XVI 1966 204–207 Dale

Posthumously published, this work helps to explain Dain's enormous influence as a teacher of metrics. Written with enthusiasm, lucidity and elegance. As a general introduction, it is no substitute for Maas or Snell, since it sometimes oversimplifies or dogmatizes and is occasionally inaccurate. Pays welcome attention to Hellenistic poetry, but expresses the wider hope that there is no extant piece of Greek verse of which some metrical explanation cannot be found in its pages. Better than the author's earlier *Leçon sur la métrique grecque,* Paris, 1944.

DALE, Amy Marjorie. Collected papers of A. M. Dale. Edited by T. B. L. Webster & E. G. Turner. Cambridge, Cambridge University Press, 1969. x, 307p., plate, port.   **FA9**

CR n.s. XXI 1971 407–409 • RFIC XCIX 1971 172–177 Rossi • AJPh XCII 1971 718–721 Cole
An extremely valuable publication, containing 12 items on metre for a total of 25 pieces. The most extensive study is "The Metrical Units of Greek Verse." Five pieces are printed here for the first time.

DALE, Amy Marjorie. "Greek metric, 1936–1957." Lustrum II (1957): 5–51.   **FA10**

Takes up where Kalinka's "Bericht" in *Bursiansjahresbericht* 257, 1937, leaves off. Contains over 100 bibliographical items, annotated, under the following headings: New material; General Treatises and introductory manuals; The nature of Greek verse-rhythm; Special studies (dactylic hexameter, iambic trimeter, trochaic tetrameter, lyric poets, the lyric of drama); Prosody; Ancient authorities; Terminology and Notation. Begins with the admission that there has been no spectacular advance in the study of Greek metric in the 20 years surveyed, nothing of the calibre of Wilamowitz's *Griechische Verskunst* or Maas's *Griechische Metrik.*

DALE, Amy Marjorie. The lyric metres of Greek drama. 2d ed. London, Cambridge University Press, 1968. vii, 228p.   **FA11**

RFIC XCIX 1971 172–177 Rossi • JHS LXVIII 1948 158–159 Davison • CR LXII 1948 118–122 Denniston
Amy Marjorie Dale is here posthumously published in a second edition. The work, not for beginners, gives a general survey of the lyric metres of Greek Drama which presupposes a good basic knowledge of the ancient texts and the modern scholarship. After preliminary definitions and classification she devotes nine chapters to the various kinds of metre: dactylic, anapaestic, iambic, trochaic, iambo-trochaic, cretic-paeonic, dochmiac, Ionic, choriambic Aeolic, prosodiac-enoplian Aeolic, dactylo-epitrite and kindred metres. There is a chapter on strophic construction, some notes on performance, a synopsis of typical and common coda, an index locorum, and a general index.

DALE, Amy Marjorie. Metrical analyses of tragic choruses. London, University of London, Institute of Classical Studies, Vol. 1. Dactylo-Epitrite, 1971. 110p.   **FA12**

University of London. Institute of Classical Studies. Bulletin supplement; 21.1.

JHS XCIII 1973 240–241 Winnington-Ingram • REG LXXXV 1972 266 Ronnet • CR XXIV 1974 211–213 Griffith

Contains metrical analyses of 45 tragic choruses and two monodies which all contain at least some elements of dactylo-epitrites. These choruses are considered play by play and not grouped by metrical affinities. Intended to complement Dale, *The lyric metres.*

DENNISTON, J. D. "Metre, Greek." OCD²: 679–684. **FA13**

An excellent brief survey in five sections: General Principles, The Metres of Epic, Elegiac and Dramatic Dialogue, The Metres of Lyric Verse, The Architecture of Greek Lyric Verse, and Strophic Responsion.

DREXLER, Hans. Die Iambenkürzung: Kürzung der zweiten Silbe eines iambischen Wortes, eines iambischen Wortanfangs. Hildesheim, G. Olms, 1969. vi, 257p. **FA14**

Gnomon XLIII 1971 408–411 Soubiran • Latomus XXX 1971 1244 Liénard

A work founded on immense erudition and patient scholarship spanning over 40 years, which is more praiseworthy for its methodology than persuasive in its conclusions.

For Drexler's earlier *Lizenzen am Versanfang bei Plautus,* München, Beck, 1965, see *AJPh* LXXXIX (1968), 373–380, Halporn.

DREXLER, Hans. Einführung in die römische Metrik. 2., unveränderte Aufl. Die Altertumswissenschaft. Darmstadt, Wissenschaftliche Buchgesellschaft, 1974. 200p. **FA15**

REL XLV 1967 512–513 Nougaret • CR n.s. XIX 1969 72–74 Goodyear • Lustrum XV 1970 Parker

A useful and learned book, though not really suitable as an introduction for beginners in that it suffers from subjectivism for propounding Drexler's highly personal views and selectivity in giving disproportionate space to his predilections. Contains a wealth of information which is easy to consult, and, unlike many of its competitors, does not shirk difficult questions.

DUCKWORTH, George E. Vergil and Classical Hexameter Poetry: a study in metrical variety. Ann Arbor, University of Michigan Press, 1969. ix, 167p. **FA16**

CPh LXVI 1971 271–273 Scott • CF XXVI 1972 142–143 Musurillo • Gnomon XLIV 1972 131–135 Hellegouarc'h

The late Professor Duckworth has scanned 143,000 classical hexameter lines out of 250,000, ranging from Homer to Nonnus and Ennius to Arator. The object is to establish the various poets' preferences in metrical patterns in the first four variable feet, their inclination toward predominantly dactylic or spondaic verse, the frequency of repeated metrical patterns in close conjunction, and the methods used to avoid repetition or introduce variety.

The book is divided into two unequal sections: I. Patterns and Procedures; the Vergilian Norm; II. Facts and Findings from Ennius to the Age of Justinian. The book provides minute statistical documentation for variations in metrical patterns in many hexameter poets, with particular attention to Virgil, Horace and Ovid. In the author's own words he has given us a set of 'finger-prints' on the hexameter poets that shed much light on wider questions of authenticity, dating and attribution. A monumental contribution to our knowledge of the history and technique of the Latin hexameter.

HALPORN, James W., ROSENMEYER, Thomas G. and OSTWALD, Martin. The meters of Greek and Latin poetry. Westport, Conn., Greenwood Press, 1978, 1963. Norman, University of Oklahoma Press, 1980. vii, [1], 137p. **FA17**

Halporn's name appeared first on original ed., reprint of which was published by Bobbs-Merrill, Indianapolis.

Gnomon XXXV 1963 420–422 Drexler • Mnemosyne XVIII 1965 401–404 Koster • RPh XXXVIII 1964 322–324 Soubiran

A simple, clear manual in the manner and spirit of Snell. The larger part of Greek metre (for which Rosenmeyer is responsible) is devoted to lyric (p.16–55). Equal space is devoted to Greek and Latin, and each part is divided, somewhat arbitrarily, into 20 sections. Lyric verse gets more attention than spoken verse, with the result that hexameter, pentameter and trimeter are treated over-hastily. The quasi-algebraic notations for scansion are rather too elaborate. Forced brevity inevitably leads to oversimplifications, and insufficient examples, but the whole is particularly useful for beginners. The section on Latin metre has been translated into German by H. Ahrens, 1962.

HARDIE, William Ross. Res metrica: an introduction to the study of Greek and Roman versification. London, New York, Oxford University Press, 1934. xxi, 275p., diagrs. **FA18**

Reprint of the 1920 ed. published by The Clarendon Press, Oxford.

CPh XVI 1921 395 Shorey • CR 1921 72 Robertson • CW XV 1921–22 134–135 Richardson

Part I (1–117) describes the heroic hexameter (both Homer and Virgil), the elegiac couplet, anapaests, iambic verse, the scazon, the trochaic tetrameter and hendecasyllabics. Part II (119–260) deals with Greek lyric verse, the history of metrics at Rome and the lyric meters of Horace. An appendix (261–275) contains a glossary of some metrical terms and a chronological table. The work was intended for beginners, but it is often more appropriate for scholars. The avowed purpose is to provide assistance in reading ancient poetry with some facility and pleasure.

HARSH, Philip W. "Early Latin Meter and Prosody, 1935–1955." Lustrum III (1958): 215–250. **FA19**

An annotated bibliography (indicating reviews) for the 20-year period, 1935–1955, divided into: General,

Bibliographies, General Works; Saturnian; Ictus and Accent; Enclitics and Position of Words; Hiatus and Elision; Syllaba Anceps; Iambic Shortening, Synizesis; Caesura and Diaeresis; Meters and Rhythm–Assonance; Cantica; other specific problems of prosody.

HARSH, Philip W. Iambic words and regard for accent in Plautus. Stanford, Calif., Stanford University Press, 1949. 149p.   **FA20**

New York, AMS Press, 1967.
REL XXVII 1950 284–286 Nougaret • Gnomon XXIII 1951 168–175 Drexler • CR n.s. I 1951 32–34 Laidlaw
This work throws down the gauntlet to Fränkel and Drexler by asserting that they and other recent writers either have not attempted to distinguish between fortuitous and deliberate coincidence of ictus and accent, or at least have not succeeded in doing so. Harsh confines his investigations to four plays of approximately known date: *Miles Gloriosus, Stichus, Pseudolus* and *Truculentus,* and to two others: *Rudens* and *Trinummus.*

HELLEGOUARC'H, Joseph. Le monosyllabe dans l'hexamètre latin; essai de métrique verbale. Paris, Klincksieck, 1964. 315p.   **FA21**

Études et commentaires, 50. "Ouvrage publié avec le concours du Centre National de la Recherche Scientifique."
REL XLI 1963 403–406 Soubiran
An extremely careful study (a doctoral dissertation) in the best traditions of Nougaret and Havet.

JANSON, Tore. Prose rhythm in medieval Latin from the 9th to the 13th century. Stockholm, Almqvist & Wiksell International, 1975. 133p.   **FA22**

Studia Latina Stockholmiensia; v. 20.
MAev XLV 1976 298–300 Winterbottom • Gnomon L 1978 269–273 Primmer • REL LIV 1976 545–547 Hellegouarc'h
A minute study in five chapters on the history of the *cursus* during three centuries, from the end of the 9th to the beginning of the 13th. Chapter 3 deals with the 10th and 11th, chapter 4 with the 12th century. Chapter 2 deals with the essential methodological problem: What is the *cursus* and how can it be recognized in a particular text? The concluding chapter deals with particular forms of the *cursus* developed in the papal chancery and found in the Loire region in France associated with a particular *Forma dictandi.* There are numerous useful tables in the appendix.

KORZENIEWSKI, Dietmar. Griechische Metrik. Einführung in den Gegenstand, Methoden und Ergebnisse der Forschung. Darmstadt, Wissenschaftliche Buchgesellschaft, 1968. ix, 216p.   **FA23**

Die Altertumswissenschaft.
CW LXIII 1970 166 Pohlsander • Lustrum XV 1970

45 Parker • RBPh XLIX 1971 162 François • Gnomon XLV 1973 113–134 Kannicht
More a *Handbuch* than an introduction, and more useful for advanced students than beginners. A substantial, detailed treatise, rich in factual information and references to recent research.

KOSTER, Willem John Wolff. Traité de métrique grecque. Suivi d'un précis de métrique latine. 4me éd. révisée. Leyde, A. W. Sijthoff, 1966. vii, 389p.   **FA24**

Gnomon XIV 1938 363–367, XXIX 1957 118–120 Rupprecht • CR LI 1937 79–80, LXIX 1955 204–205 Dale
A concise and useful treatise surveying the whole field of Greek metrics. The précis of Latin metrics is a model of its kind. The second edition was fifty pages larger than the first, supplementary materials appearing especially on prosody, dactylic hexameter, iambic trimeter and colometry. The bibliography has been brought down to 1950. An extremely practical work, worthy to be ranked with those of Christ and Masqueray, but perhaps over-schematised.

LIÉNARD, Edmund. Répertoires prosodiques et métriques. Lucrèce, De rerum natura, livre III, Valérius Flaccus, Argonautica, livre VII, Germanicus, Aratea. Bruxelles, Univ. Libre, 1978. 204p. (Sources & Instruments II). Idem, II: Ovide, Métamorphoses livre VI. Lucain, Pharsale, livre V. Sidoine Apollinaire, Panegyricus (Carmen V). (Sources & Instruments V). Bruxelles, Univ. Libre de Bruxelles, 1980. 192p.   **FA24a**

LINDSAY, Wallace M. Early Latin verse. London, Oxford University Press, 1968. ix, 372p.   **FA25**

CJ XX 1925 251 E.T.M. • AJPh XLV 1924 296–299 Taylor • CPh XXI 1926 367–372 Radford
First issued in 1922 and addressed to more advanced students of metrics. Extremely detailed, showing a wonderful mastery of a complicated subject. The three principal chapters are on Plautus and Menander, early prosody and hiatus, and early Latin metres. Brilliantly succeeds in its stated aims: (1) to illustrate spoken Latin from Plautus, (2) to prepare the way for an adequate presentation of Plautus' lines by editors, and (3) to vindicate Plautus' artistic skill.

LUISELLI, Bruno. Il verso saturnio. Roma, Edizioni dell'Ateneo, 1967. 347p.   **FA26**

Studi di metrica classica, 3.
Latomus XXX 1971 474–476 Liénard • RFIC XCIX 1971 315–332 Questa
Another attempt in the Saussure tradition to solve the elusive problems of Saturnian metre. The *testimonia* on the questions from antiquity are all assembled and analysed in Part I. Part II has a chapter (117–224) giving a resumé of all modern solutions, and a second

chapter with the author's own solution (225–294). At the end (295–334) there is a collection of Saturnian fragments. There is a long but useful digression (p.121–160) on the nature of Latin accent.

MAAS, Paul. Greek metre. Translated by Hugh Lloyd-Jones. Oxford, Clarendon Press, [1966]. 116p. **FA27**

Reprinted from corrected sheets of 1st ed., 1962.
CR n.s. XIII 1963 311–313 Dover • Gnomon XXXV 1963 418–420 Snell • JHS 1964 Parker
A classic work, translated by Lloyd-Jones almost forty years after its first appearance in 1923. There are many notes added by the author in 1961, and some by the translator. Despite the book's remarkable conciseness there are very few obscurities. There is an Italian translation updated by A. Ghiselli, 1976.

MATHIESEN, T. J. A bibliography of sources for the study of ancient Greek music. Hackensack, N.J., Boonin, 1974. 59p. **FA27a**

Music indexes & bibliographies X.
JHS XCV 1975 236 Borthwick

MICHAELIDES, S. The music of ancient Greece. An encyclopaedia. London, Faber & Faber, 1978. xvi, 365p., 10 leaves of plates. **FA28**

AJPh CI 1980 231–234 Feaver

NAGY, Gregory. Comparative studies in Greek and Indic meter. Cambridge, Harvard University Press, 1974. xx, 335p. **FA28a**

Harvard studies in comparative literature, 33 [i.e. monograph 1].
CR XXVII 1977 297–298 Brough • CW LXIX 1975 86 Wyatt • LEC XLIII 1975 207 Stenuit • RPh L 1976 271–272 Monteil
Based on the premise that traditional phraseology generated meter rather than vice versa, this comparative study concludes that Greek and Sanskrit lyric meters developed from Proto-Indo-European meters, and that Greek and Sanskrit poetic vocabulary developed from and contained remnants of Indo-European poetic vocabulary. More daringly, the author argues that dactylic hexameter is a development of the pherecratic expanded internally by three dactyls, also from Indo-European origins. A stimulating work in which the basic hexameter conjecture is not subject to either scientific proof or disproof.

NEUBECKER, A. J. Altgriechische Musik. Eine Einführung. Die Altertumswissenschaft. Darmstadt, Wissenschaftliche Buchgesellschaft, 1977. ii, 182p., 8 plates. **FA29**

NORBERG, Dag. Introduction à l'étude de la versification latine médiévale. Stockholm, Alqvist & Wiksell, 1958. 218p. **FA29a**

REL XXXVI 1958 289–291 Nougaret • Aevum XXXIII 1959 278–286 Cremaschi • Speculum XXXIV 1959 491–493 Lind

A good, brief dependable introduction to medieval Latin versification by a distinguished Swedish medievalist. Short chapters are devoted to prosody, accentuating, synaeresis, diaeresis, syncope, prosthesis, elision, hiatus, assonance, rhyme, alliteration, acrostics, figure poems and other poetic artifices, the various verse forms, the beginnings of rhythmic versification and its relation to both quantitative verse and music, and the sequence, trope and motet.

NOUGARET, Louis. Traité de métrique latine classique. 3e éd. corrigée. Paris, C. Klincksieck, 1963. xi, 134p. **FA30**

REL XXVI 1949 286–288 Descroix • RPh XXIII 1949 164 Ernout • CR LXIV 1950 25–26 Platnauer • Mnemosyne 4th ser. III 1950 21–53, 127–157 Koster
A pupil of Havet (whose Cours élémentaire de métrique grecque et Latine, 1886, for long held the field in France) brings his master's teaching up-to-date in a clear, simple and easily intelligible work. After preliminary generalities there is a chronological survey of Latin meter, beginning with Saturnian. Three extended chapters are devoted to dactylic verse, iambotrochaic verse, and aeolian verse. Finally, he deals with prose rhythm and ciceronian clauses. The three central chapters are a masterpiece of condensation. The bibliography is very limited, works in English being conspicuously rare.

OTT, Wilhelm. Metrische Analysen zu Catull Carmen 64. Tübingen, M. Niemeyer, 1973. xvii, 96p., 16 punched cards (in pocket). **FA31**

REL LII 1974 439–441 Granorolo

OTT, Wilhelm. Metrische Analysen zu Lukrez De rerum Natura Buch I. Tübingen, Niemeyer, 1974. xvii, 210p., 32 punched cards (in pocket). **FA32**

Materialen zu Metrik und Stilistik; v. 6. Includes the Latin text of Lucretius' De rerum natura, Book 1.
AC XLIV 1975 270 Tordeur • REL LIII 1975 430 Hellegouarc'h • RPh XLIX 1975 330 Soubiran

OTT, Wilhelm. Metrische Analysen zu Ovid, Metamorphosen Buch 1. Tübingen, Niemeyer, 1974. xvi, 153p., 16 punched cards (in pocket). **FA33**

Materialen zu Metrik und Stilistik; v. 7.
AC XLIV 1975 686–689 Évrard-Gillis • REL LIII 1975 430 Hellegouarc'h • RPh XLIV 1975 330 Soubiran

OTT, Wilhelm. Metrische Analysen zu Statius Thebais Buch I. Tübingen, M. Niemeyer, 1973. xvi, 155p., 16 punched cards (in pocket). **FA34**

Materialen zu Metrik und Stilistik, v. 5.

OTT, Wilhelm. Metrische Analysen zu Vergil, Bucolica. Tübingen, Niemeyer, 1978. xix, 170p., 16 punched cards (in pocket). **FA35**

Materialen zu Metrik und Stilistik; v. 9.

OTT, Wilhelm. Metrische Analysen zu Vergil. Tübingen, Niemeyer, 1973– . 16 punched cards (in pocket).   **FA36**

Materialen zu Metrik und Stilistik, v. 1–3, [Bd.1] Aeneis Buch 1, Bd. II, Buch VI, Bd.III, Buch XII.
REL LII 1974 83–91 Hellegouarc'h • Gnomon XLVII 1975 514–515 Korzeniewski • Latomus XXXIV 1975 838 Tordeur
Part of Ott's gigantic enterprise to produce a metrical index with the help of computers. (See his own account of his activities. *RELO* 1966, No. 4, 7–24, 1967 No. 1, 39–64).

OTT, Wilhelm. Rücklaufiger Wortindex zu Vergil: Bucolica, Georgica, Aeneis. Tübingen, Niemeyer, 1974. vi, 295p.   **FA37**

Materialen zu Metrik und Stilistik; v. 8.
CR XXVII 1977 182–184 Gransden
An index of word-forms used by Virgil arranged in alphabetical order starting with the last letter and working backwards. The function of the index is both metrical and lexical.

OTT, Wilhelm. Metrische Analysen zur Ars poetica des Horaz. [Nach Magnetbändern des Zentrums für Datenverarbeitung der Universität Tübingen] Göttingen, Kümmerle, 1970. 122 p., 16 punched cards (in pocket).   **FA38**

Göttingen akademische Beiträge, Nr. 6.
REL XLVIII 1970 500–501 Perret • RFIC XCIX 1971 345–347 Parroni
The first of many computerised studies on metrics by Ott at the University of Tübingen. The early pages (5–16) describe the programming (cf. also *REL* 1966,4, 7–24 and 1967,1, 39–64). The amount of information given in the body of the work is exhaustive on the usual metrical problems: e.g. schemata, place of elisions, types of end of verse. The documentation is both complete and well-articulated.

PARKER, L. P. E. "Greek metric, 1957–1970." Lustrum XV (1970): 37–98.   **FA39**

Continues the survey of A. M. Dale in *Lustrum* II (1957), 5–51. There are about 200 annotated items under such headings as New Material, General Treatises, Terminology, and the history and methods of metrical study. The New Material is conveniently divided by author.

PIGHI, Giovanni Battista. Studi di ritmica e metrica. Raccolti a cura della Facoltà de lettere dell'Università degli di Bologna. Torino, Bottega d'Erasmo, 1970. xlv, 633p.   **FA40**

RPh XLVI 1972 146–149 Soubiran • AAHG XXVI 1973 197–200 Drexler • CHR XXVII 1973 156–160 Wasziak • Gnomon XLVI 1974 550–557 Pöhlmann
Consists of articles written by the author over a space of 40 years, showing his wide-ranging interests (e.g.,

the poetry of ancient India) and his willingness to speculate beyond the quantitative confines of metrics on the aesthetic and musical possibilities. The book is marred by an excess of speculation untested by any critical methodology and by its rather verbose repetitiousness, but there are many interesting and potentially valuable suggestions interspersed in the dense text.

PLATNAUER, Maurice. Latin elegiac verse; a study of the metrical usages of Tibullus, Propertius and Ovid. Hamden, Conn., Archon Books, 1971. viii, 121, [1]p.   **FA41**

Reprint of the 1951 ed., Cambridge University Press.
AC XXI 1952 485 Maniet • CW XLVI 1952 60 Richards • Hermathena LXXIX 1952 94–97 Smyth

POE, Joe Park. Caesurae in the hexameter line of Latin elegiac verse. Wiesbaden, F. Steiner, 1974. viii, 91, [24]p.   **FA42**

Hermes, Zeitschrift für klassische Philologie: Einzelschriften; v. 29.
REL LIII 1975 426–429 Hellegouarc'h • AC XLV 1976 630–637 Liénard

POHLSANDER, H. A. Metrical studies in the lyrics of Sophocles. Leiden, E. J. Brill, 1964. viii, 224p.   **FA43**

JHS LXXXVI 1966 176–177 Parker
A work in two parts: (i) a play-by-play metrical commentary, providing for each stanza a list of references, scansion and comments; (ii) chapters on colon-caesura, determination of period-end, and strophic construction. Generally sound, dependent on A. M. Dale and Walther Kraus.

POSTGATE, John Percival. Prosodia latina; An introduction to classical Latin verse. Oxford, Clarendon Press, 1923. 120p.   **FA44**

CJ XX 1924 185 E.T.M. • CR XXXVII 1923 124 Sonnenschein
An excellent short, practical manual based on expert knowledge of the structure of classical Latin verse and scientific understanding of the sounds of Latin speech. More concerned with marking quantities and indicating the measures than with suggesting how the verses should be read.

PULGRAM, Ernst. Latin-Romance Phonology: Prosodics and Metrics. München, 1975. 304p.   **FA45**

AJPh XCIX 1978 395–399 Poultney
A thorough, penetrating and well-argued treatment of some of the most persistently difficult problems of Latin phonology. The difference between the prosodic systems of Spoken Latin and Written (Classical) Latin is clearly established and is central to the book's argument. Accent, quantity and syllabation are lucidly discussed, and the prosodics and metrics of Written Latin and of Spoken Latin and Proto-Romance are dealt with separately. An important landmark in the study of Latin accentuation, with an extensive bibliography.

QUESTA, Cesare. "Metrica latina arcaica." Introd. allo studio della cult class. II, 1 (1973): 477–562. **FA46**

RAVEN, David S. Greek metre: an introduction. 2nd ed. London, Faber, 1968. 3–127, [1]p. **FA47**

CR XIII 1963 313–315 • CR n.s. XXI 1971 139–140 Parker • CB XLIII 1967 48 Hebein
A short, attractively produced handbook, but, on closer examination, often superficial, slovenly and amateurish. The second edition has remedied much of the inadequacies of the first (1962) edition in the opening chapters on principles and terminology.

RAVEN, David S. Latin metre; an introduction. London, Faber and Faber, [1965]. 182p. **FA48**

CJ LXII 1966 91–92 Halporn • CR XVI 1966 76–78 Goodyear • Gnomon XXXVIII 1966 473–475 Hall
A companion volume to Raven's earlier *Greek metre,* designed to assist the undergraduate to an understanding of the rhythmical flow of classical Latin verse. Clarity of expression and arrangement makes the work very successful in meeting this goal. There are good sections on Latin verse structure and its history, quantity, prosody, and basic rhythms, word accent and its influence, iambic and trochaic verse (including a sound introduction to Plautus and Terence), dactylic verse, bacchiac and cretic verse, ionic verse and aeolic verse. There is a brief note (p.169–172) on prose-rhythm and Ciceronian clausulae. Finally there is a Glossary of Technical terms and an Index of passages referred to in the text.

SCHUMANN, O. Lateinisches Hexameter-Lexikon. Dichterisches Formelgut von Ennius bis zum Archipoeta. I: A–C. München, 1979. xxvii, 544p. II: D–H. 1980. xxiii, 534p. III: I–N. 1981. xxiv, 592p. IV: O–R. 1981. xxiii, 592p. **FA48a**

Monum. German. Hist. Hilfsmittel.

SIEFERT, George Joseph. Meter and case in the Latin elegiac pentameter. New York, Kraus Reprint, 1966. 126p. **FA49**

Reprint of the 1952 ed. published by Linguistic Society of America, v. 28, no. 4, pt. 2, Oct.–Dec. 1952. Microfilm. New York: Kraus-Thomson Organization, Microform Division, 1973.–2 reels. One of 27 titles on reel 2.
AJPh LXXV 1954 220–221 Poultney • RPh XXVIII 1954 303 Ernout

SNELL, Bruno. Griechische Metrik. 3, erweit., Aufl., Göttingen, Vandenhoeck & Ruprecht, 1962. 61p. **FA50**

(Studienhefte zur Altertumswissenschaft, Hft. 1).
Gnomon 1956 192–196 Dale • Lustrum II 1957 15 Dale

An astonishing feat of compression; covers the ground from Homer to the Hellenistic poets in 50 pages. The second edition has a few corrections and modifications in the light of the most recent papyri finds. See also Snell, 'Metrik,' *Lex. der alten Welt,* 1965, 1951–1956.

SOUBIRAN, Jean. L'Élision dans la poésie latine. Paris, C. Klincksieck, 1966. 667p. **FA51**

Études et commentaires, 63.
REL XLIV 1966 122–131 Nougaret • CR XVII 1967 325–328 Kenney • RPh XLI 1967 334–338 Hellegouarc'h • REA LXXIII 1971 231–234 Thomas
A somewhat prolix doctoral dissertation which attacks one of the most difficult problems in Latin metrics and phonetics. The work is distinguished by great clarity, accuracy and powers of organization in matters of statistics and presentation of texts.

STANFORD, William B. The sound of Greek; Studies in the Greek theory and practice of euphony. Berkeley, University of California Press, 1967. vi, 177p., phonodisc (2s. 7 in. 33⅓ rpm. microgroove) in pocket. **FA52**

Sather classical lectures; v. 38.
CR n.s. XIX 1969 190–192 Hudson-Williams • Mnemosyne XXIII 1970 82–84 Bolkestein • Arion VI 1967 519–527 Sonkowsky
The six Sather lectures of 1966, with an added chapter, The Speaking Voice, and the new Appendix on the Pitch Accent. Since Greek literature was written to be heard, not read, sound—"the physical substance of words"—is to be understood as the basic material of Greek literature. The book is well documented from the ancient sources but is occasionally subjective and over-enthusiastic. The readings by the author (in the record provided) are done in an unmistakably British or Anglo-Irish accent, which weakens the case for the Greek practice of euphony. The whole is an eloquent plea for greater awareness of the musical qualities of Ancient Greek and for giving the pitch accent its tonal value. A book that should have many admirers, but may not make many converts.

STURTEVANT, Edgar Howard. The pronunciation of Greek and Latin. 2d ed. Westport, Conn., Greenwood Press, 1977, 1940. 192p. **FA53**

Reprint of the edition published by Linguistic Society of America, Philadelphia, in the William Dwight Whitney linguistic series, and in the Society's Special Publications series.
Language XVII 1941 258–262 Atkins and Bender • CPh XXXVI 1941 409–411 Whatmough • CR LVI 1942 45–47 Pirie
The 1940 edition of this standard work is an entire reworking of all material, old and new, which appeared in and since the first edition, Chicago, 1920. The seven chapter headings indicate the scope: The Nature and Value of the Evidence, The Greek Vowels, The Greek Consonants, The Greek Accent, The Latin Vowels, The Latin Consonants, The Latin Accent. A stimulating

work of scholarship, invaluable for student and specialist alike, which must now be complemented by the works of Allen.

WAHLSTRÖM, Erik. Accentual responsion in Greek strophic poetry. Helsinki, Societas Scientiarum Fennica, 1970. 22p.   **FA54**

BAGB 1971 432–433 Jenny • REG LXXXV 1972 253–255 Brunel

Analyses of selected poems of Sappho, Alcaeus, Alcman and Pindar.

WEST, M. L. Greek metre. Oxford, Clarendon Press, 1982. xiv, 208p.   **FA54a**

JHS CIV 1984 226–227 Willink

WHITE, John Williams. The verse of Greek comedy. [Reprografischer Nachdruck der Ausg. London, 1912]. Hildesheim, G. Olms, 1969. xxix, 479p.   **FA55**

JHS XXXIII 1913 376–377 • REG XXVII 361 Masqueray

The author's translation of J. H. H. Schmidt, *Greek metric,* Boston, 1878, converted the English-speaking world to a belief in the "logaoedic" theory of Greek verse. The present work is a recantation: Logaoedics are dethroned, cyclic dactyl gives way to the choriamb and anapaest, while anacrusis disappears completely. The lyrics of Aristophanes are printed in full, and analyzed statistically and minutely. There is an appendix devoted to an edition of the metrical scholia of Heliodorus.

WIFSTRAND, Albert. Von Kallimachos zu Nonnos; metrisch-stilistische Untersuchungen zur

späteren griechischen epik und zu verwandten Gedichtgattungen. Lund, Ohlssons Buchdr. 1933.   **FA56**

MPh XLII 1935 171 Koster • CPh XXIX 1934 181 Shorey • ByzZ XXXIV 1934 74–76 Maas

Wifstrand has counted tens of thousands of instances of refinements in the Homeric hexameter discovered by modern scholars and obeyed as laws by Callimachus and the Alexandrians and accepted, varied or extended in the new style of Nonnus and other late poets. An important contribution to the history of verse and style.

WILAMOWITZ-MOELLENDORFF, Ulrich von. Griechische Verskunst. 3., unveränderte Aufl., Darmstadt, Wissenschaftliche Buchgesellschaft, 1975. ix, 630p.   **FA57**

Unchanged reproduction of the first ed., 1921.

PhW XXI 1921 797–811 Schroder • CPh XVII 1922 150 Shorey • CW XV 1922 205–207 Baker

This monumental work begins with a valuable historical sketch of Greek metrics and of the various theories and views that have come forth on the subject (p.1–136). This is followed by two lengthy sections analysing single verse-forms (p.137–607), the second of which especially is more full of recondite speculation than accurate information.

WILLE, G. Einführung in das römische Musikleben. Die Altertumswissenschaft. Darmstadt, Wissenschaftliche Buchgesellschaft, 1977. vii, 214p.   **FA57a**

RPh LIV 1980 193–195 Cèbe

Greek and Latin Epigraphy

GA MYCENAEAN: LINEAR A AND B

BENNETT, Emmett Leslie. Nestor. Madison, Institute for Research in the Humanities, University of Wisconsin, 1957. Illus.   **GA1**

"Begun as a Mycenaean bibliography, 23 February 1957 . . . through June 1958. . . . First published as *Nestor*, October 1958. . . ."

See now Jacobsen, T. W. and Rudolph, W. W., eds. *Nestor. Mycenaean bibliography*, X. Bloomington, Indiana University Press, 1983. p.1670–1782. (Program in Classical Archaeology.)

BENNETT, Emmett Leslie and OLIVIER, Jean-Pierre. The Pylos tablets transcribed. Roma, Edizioni dell'Ateneo, 1973–1976.   **GA2**

Incunabula Graeca; v. 51, part I. Texts and notes, part II. Hands, Concordances, Indices.

RPh L 1976 268–269 Monteil • Mnemosyne XXX 1977 296–298 Ruijgh

Bennett first published *The Pylos tablets*, Princeton, 1956. In that work he printed the Ventris' transliteration (as published in *BICS* I) in his index but retained the Linear B signs in the body of the work. There was an introduction by Blegen on the actual excavation, another by Bennett, and an inventory and classification of the tablets. The text consisted of (a) drawings of the tablets made by tracing in India ink the lines of the stylus as they appeared on photographic prints which were then bleached, and (b) the texts in normalized Linear B characters.

In this new collaboration with Olivier, he takes account of the almost yearly additions to the finds at Pylos, improves on the original readings, and adopts the recommendations of the Wingspread Convention in the transliteration, and of the Salamanca Congress, 1970.

BEST, J. G. P. Some preliminary remarks on the decipherment of Linear A. Amsterdam, Hakkert, 1972. 45p., 6p. of photos.   **GA3**

Publications of the Henri Frankfort Foundation; v. 2.

CHADWICK, John. The decipherment of Linear B. 2d ed. Cambridge, Cambridge University Press, 1970, [1967]. [x], 164p., illus., plates (1 fold.), map, port.   **GA4**

REG LXXXV 1972 182–183 Raison • REA LXX 1968 453 Lejeune • AC XLI 1972 700–702 Delvoye

A straightforward, readable account of the decipherment by one of the participants.

There is a French translation (Bibl. des histoires, Gallimard, 1972).

CHADWICK, John. The Mycenaean world. Cambridge and New York, Cambridge University Press, 1976. xvii, 201p., illus.   **GA5**

CR XXVIII 1978 101–103 Warren • Phoenix XXXI 1977 375–376 Begg

Based primarily on translations and interpretations of Linear B tablets, this work provides useful chapters on the historical and epigraphical backgrounds, and summarizes, with much conjecture, what is known about Mycenaean geography, society, religion, agriculture, industry, trade and armaments. There are concluding chapters on the historical unreliability of Homer, and the nature of the final destructions of Knossos and Pylos.

CHADWICK, John et al. The Knossos tablets; A translation by John Chadwick, J. P. Killen and J. P. Olivier. 4th ed. Cambridge, Cambridge University Press, 1971. xiv, 472p.   **GA6**

Gnomon XXXVIII 1966 809–817 Grumach • CW LXV 1972 238 Messing • REG LXXVIII 1965 354–357 Raison

The 4th edition is double the pagination of the 3rd

edition, published in 1964. The new edition is necessitated by the large number (785) of new joins reported.

DEROY, Louis. Initiation à l'épigraphie mycénienne. Rome, Ateneo, 1962. 131p., illus., map.
                                    GA7

Incunabula Graeca; v. 2.
AC XXXII 1963 691–692 Olivier • CR XIV 1964 74–76 Killen • REG LXXVI 1963 437–439 Masson • Language XL 1964 420–428 Bennett
Provides an excellent tour through the labyrinthine specialist literature. Editions and other publications of the texts are first listed, together with lexica and word lists. A long third chapter describes the physical form of the tablets, and a detailed account of the Mycenaean writing system. There are chapters on the standard classifications.

DORIA, Mario. Avviamento allo studio del miceneo; Struttura, problemi e testi. Roma, Edizioni dell'Ateneo, 1965. [ix], 281p., illus.   **GA8**

Incunabula Graeca; v. 8.
JHS LXXXVII 1967 160 Morpurgo Davies • Language XLIV 1968 118–120 Wyatt
An Italian counterpart to Ventris and Chadwick's *Documents* or Palmer's *Interpretation.* The first 100 pages deal with the linguistic and cultural ambience in which Linear B developed, the story of the decipherment, and a description of the script and its spelling conventions. The anthology of tablets (100f.) is representative and provides good bibliographical and linguistic assistance.

DORIA, Mario. Indice retrogrado delle iscrizioni in Lineare B di Pilo e di Micene. Trieste, 1964. 40p.   **GA9**

Università degli Studi di Trieste. Facoltà di Lettere e Filosofia. Istituto di Glottologia; no. 3.

DOW, S. "Minoan writing." AJA LVIII (1954): 77–129.   **GA9a**

EKSCHMITT, Werner. Die Kontroverse um Linear B. Mit 16 Abbildungen im Text und 12 Abbildungen auf 8 Tafeln. München, Beck, [1969]. 160p.   **GA10**

CR XXI 1971 431–434 Morpurgo Davies • CW LXIV 1970 88 Bennett • JHS XCI 1971 164–166 Hooker • REA LXXI 1969 457–460 Lejeune
Arguments for and against Ventris' decipherment are presented by an author who is himself not convinced of the decipherment. The work begins with an able summary of the history of the Aegean and Cypriot writing in the Bronze Age, but deteriorates once he begins to allege bad faith in the cryptoanalysis of Ventris, and further bad faith in the reporting of the fact. The illogicality and absurdities in some of the "decipherment" are exposed, absurdities which will now be readily admitted by those experimenting at the time. Fortunately the author stops short of producing his own decipherment from the *disiecta membra.*

GALLAVOTTI, Carlo and SACCONI, A., eds. Inscriptiones Pyliae ad Mycenaeum aetatem pertinentes; Quas in usum academicum collectas. Romae, In Aedibus Athenaei, 1961. xvi, 204p., illus.   **GA11**

Incunabula Graeca; v. 1.
CR XIV 1964 173–175 Jones • ZAnt XV 1965–1966 215–218 Ilievski
Transliteration of the Pylos tablets, and a useful complement to Bennett's *The Pylos tablets.* There are some improvements in arrangement over the latter.

GEISS, Heinz. Abbreviations and adjuncts in the Knossos tablets; Indices. Berlin, Akademie-Verl. in Arbeitsgemeinschaft mit Hakkert, Amsterdam, 1970. xiii, 123p., 2 plates.   **GA12**

Deutsche Akademie der Wissenschaften zu Berlin. Schriften der Sektion für Altertumswissenschaft; 56.
AC XLI 1972 702 Duhoux • ACR III 1973 85 Brown
A badly organized tool, based on the 2d edition (1964) of the *Knossos tablets* (now replaced by a 3rd edition which includes 600–700 new finds not utilized here).

GRUMACH, Ernst. Bibliographie der kretisch-mykenischen Epigraphik; Nach dem Stande vom 31. Dezember 1961. München, Beck, 1963. xxxii, 256p.   **GA13**

AJPh XC 1969 128 Poultney • CR XIX 1969 385–386 Boardman • Gnomon XLI 1969 93–95 Huebeck
This work, interrupted by the author's death (5 October 1967), is extraordinarily thorough. Classification is predominantly by type of text and place of origin. While Grumach himself remained sceptical in the face of the decipherment of Linear B, his work is scrupulously fair to all scholars and opinions.
There is a Supplement which covers the years 1962–1965 (München and Berlin: Beck, 1967, xxx, 126p.).

HENLE, Jane Elizabeth. A study in word structure in Minoan Linear B. New York, 1953. v, 185p.   **GA14**

Thesis, Columbia University.
JHS LXXIV 1954 207–208 Ventris • REA LVI 1954 162 Lejeune
A Columbia University dissertation, directed by W. B. Dinsmoor, beginning from complete skepticism about previous attempts at decipherment and open to the belief that the Pylos and Cretan tablets could be in the Greek language. This work is in the analytic tradition initiated by Alice E. Kober (*AJA* L 1946, 268–276). It compares the frequency and distribution of the Linear B syllabic signs with the syllabic frequencies counted in samples of Homeric Greek. An important pre-Ventris landmark in the decipherment.

HILLER, S. and PANAGL, O. "Linear B. Fortschritte und Forschungsstand. Ein Forschungsbericht." Saeculum XXII (1971): 123–194.
                                    GA14a

LEJEUNE, Michel. Index inverse du Grec mycénien. Paris, C.N.R.S., 1964. 117p. **GA15**

AJPh LXXXVII 1966 380–381 Poultney • JHS LXXXV 1965 190 Morpurgo Davies • REG LXXVIII 1965 357–358 Humbert
A reverse index of all the words or fragments of words written in the Linear B documents of Pylos, Knossos and Mycenae, or inscribed on the sherds of Thebes, Eleusis or Tiryns. Extremely useful for any research in grammatical flexion, derivation, composition, etc., and in the primary tasks of editing, restoring or joining fragments. To be used in conjunction with Morpurgo, *Mycenaeae graecitatis lexicon.*

LEJEUNE, Michel. Phonétique historique du mycénien et du grec ancien. Paris, Klincksieck, 1972. 398p. **GA16**

Tradition de l'humanisme; 9.
See entry EA21.

LEVIN, Saul. The Linear B decipherment controversy re-examined. [Albany], State University of New York, 1964. xvi, 255p. **GA17**

"Transcription of Linear B characters" (fold. 1) inserted.
SMEA III 1967 138–142 Sacconi

MERLINGEN, W. "Linear B (und A), III: Bericht umfassend die Jahre von 1964 bis 1969–1970." AAHG XXIV (1971): 1–34. **GA17a**

MOON, Brenda E. Mycenaean civilization, publications since 1935; A bibliography. London, International University Booksellers Ltd., 1957. xv, 77p. **GA18**

University of London. Institute of Classical Studies: Bulletin supplement; v. 3.
Covers the period January 1936 to June 1956.

MORPURGO, Anna. Mycenaeae Graecitatis lexicon. Romae, In Aedibus Athenaei, 1963. 404p., illus. **GA19**

Incunabula Graeca; v. 3.
JHS LXXXV 1965 189–190 Chadwick • SMEA II 1967 133–137 Doria
An admirable index, printed in Roman transcription in accordance with international convention, with the addition, in Latin, of a description of the context, such definition of the words as is possible on this evidence, and a note of generally accepted interpretations, with references to the literature.

OLIVIER, Jean-Pierre et al. Index généraux du linéaire B. Roma, Edizioni dell'Ateneo, 1973. 405p., plates. **GA20**

Incunabula Graeca; v. 52.
RPh L 1976 270–271 Monteil • Platon XXVII 1975 370–374 Theophanopoulou-Koutou
The index hopes to give all references to Linear B

texts published or about to be published down to the end of 1970. This excludes the Theban tablets and joins effected between October 1970 and December 1972. Transliterations are in accordance with Wingspread and Salamanca conventions. The *index alphabétique direct* of groups of signs in translation follows Morpurgo, *Mycenaeae Graecitatis lexicon* (Rome, 1963). The *index alphabétique inverse* follows Lejeune's *L'Index inverse* (Paris, 1964). An indispensable *instrument de travail.*

PACKARD, David W. Minoan Linear A. Berkeley, University of California Press, 1974. 272p., illus. **GA21**

CW LXIX 1976 336–337 Wyatt
See also Packard, D. W., "Computer techniques in the study of the Minoan Linear A Script," *Kadmos* X (1971), 52–59.

PALMER, Leonard Robert. The interpretation of Mycenaean Greek texts. Oxford, Clarendon Press, [1969, 1963]. **GA22**

AC XXXIII 1964 229–231 Olivier • AJA LXVIII 1964 404–405 Bennett • Gnomon XXXVI 1964 321–327 Chadwick
A long introduction sets the scene of the Linear B tablets, explains the script and dialect, and discusses some of the main problems. Then follow 286 texts in Roman transcription (mostly prior to 1960), occasionally with reconstructed Greek text. There is a select bibliography and an extensive glossary of Linear B words. The tone is no less polemical than in *Mycenaeans and Minoans.* Il foisonne, il irrite, il intéresse, il passionne.
See also Palmer, L. R. and Chadwick, John, eds. *Cambridge Colloquium on Mycenaean Studies, 1965.* Cambridge, Cambridge University Press, 1966. 309p., illus.

PALMER, Leonard Robert. Mycenaeans and Minoans; Aegean prehistory in the light of the Linear B tablets. 2d rev. ed. London, Faber and Faber, [1965]. 368p., illus., maps, plans. **GA23**

AJPh LXXXIV 1963 304–308 Immerwahr • CR XIII 1963 87–91 Gray • Language XXXIX 1963 270–281 Bennett
The first five chapters give a lucid account of the decipherment and the author's own interpretation of the tablets. Chapter VI presents detailed argumentation for his revolutionary redating of the Knossos tablets 250 years later than the Evans' dating. Chapter VII, The Coming of the Greeks, attempts to bring the Luvians of Asia Minor and the Linear A tablets within the framework of the Indo-European migrations of Greece.

PALMER, Leonard Robert and BOARDMAN, John. On the Knossos tablets; The find-places of the Knossos tablets [by] L. R. Palmer. The date of the Knossos tablets [by] John Boardman.

Oxford, Clarendon Press, 1963. xxvi, 251p. x, 100p., illus., plates, facsims., plans.   **GA24**

Phoenix XIX 1965 232–237 Graham • Gnomon XXXVII 1965 321–325 Hood

Both works draw on the private notebooks of Sir Arthur Evans, and the daybooks of his assistant, Dr. Donald Mackenzie, which are in the Ashmolean Museum. An interesting composite volume in which Boardman upholds Evans' dating of the Knossos tablets c.1400, and Palmer assigns them to Late Minoan III B, some 200 years later. Evans does not come unscathed out of the crossfire but Palmer's redating remains unproved and improbable. This is really not one book but two: What began as collaboration broke down under irreconcilable differences so that in the end neither author has seen the work of the other. Boardman's work displays greater brevity, lucidity and cogency, helping us to see the Palace of Minos and its history as a whole. With Palmer, on the other hand, one has the feeling that his examination of the Mackenzie notebooks in the Ashmolean, Oxford, was to substantiate his own preconceptions.

POPE, Maurice. The story of decipherment; From Egyptian hieroglyphic to Linear B. London, Thames & Hudson, [1975]. 216p., illus.   **GA25**

American ed. published under title: *The story of archaeological decipherment.*
TLS LXXIV 1975 918 Chadwick • G&R XXIII 1976 100 Walcot

RAISON, Jacques. Index du linéaire A. Roma, Edizioni dell'Ateneo, 1971. xxxvii, 318p., illus., plate.   **GA26**

Incunabula Graeca; v. 41.
Minos XIII 1972 101 Melena

RAISON, Jacques and POPE, Maurice. Index du transnuméré linéaire A. Louvain, Éditions Peeters, 1977. 331p.   **GA27**

Bibliothèque des cahiers de l'institut de linguistique de Louvain; 11.

RUIJGH, C. J. Études sur la grammaire et le vocabulaire du grec mycénien. Amsterdam, Hakkert, 1967. 439p.   **GA28**

Language XLIV 1968 616–621 Wyatt • REG LXXXI 1968 212–213 Humbert

SCHACHERMEYR, F. "Linear B (und A)." AAHG XI (1958): 193–214.   **GA29**

SPYROPOULOS, Theodoros G. and CHADWICK, John. The Thebes tablets II. Includes

indices of the Thebes tablets by José L. Melena. Salamanca, Universidad de Salamanca, 116p., [16] leaves of plates, illus.   **GA30**

Part 1. Spyropoulos, T. G., Excavation of part of the Mycenaean palace (Kadmeion) of Thebes. Part 2. Chadwick, J., The linear B tablets. Part 3. Melena, J. L., Indexes of Mycenaean words.
Gnomon L 1978 588–590 Palmer • PP XXX 1975 242–247 Pugliesi Carratelli • RPh L 1976 111–112 Lejeune

A first lot of 24 tablets from Thebes was published by Chadwick in *Minos* X (1969), 115–137. Here he publishes 19 more, relating to textiles (p.83–117 and plates XXIX–XXXI), with a preliminary essay by Spyropoulos on the archaeological investigation of Mycenaean Thebes. The tablets appear to be contemporary with those of Pylos and are not dialectically different from those of Knossos and Pylos.

VENTRIS, Michael and CHADWICK, John. Documents in Mycenaean Greek. 2d ed. Cambridge, Cambridge University Press, 1974. xxxiv, 622p., illus., plans.   **GA31**

"First edition by Michael Ventris and John Chadwick, with a foreword by the late Alan J. B. Wace."
AJA LXXVIII 1974 438 Lang • CR XXVII, 2 1977 203–204 Jones • Gnomon XXIX 1957 561–581, XLVIII 1976 433–444 Palmer • Mnemosyne XXVII 1974 187–192 Ruijgh, IV 9 1956 336–338 Kamerbeek

This second edition of the by now historic 1956 edition leaves the first two parts alone (p. 1–381), in deference no doubt to the memory of the late and lamented Ventris, and adds a third part comprising 130 pages. This includes additions and corrections to the notes on individual texts, and also new introductions to groups of texts which either supplement or replace those of the first edition. The bibliography has been greatly augmented (p.595–605). The account of the decipherment and the sections on language, writing, and historical conclusions to be derived from the texts remain as exciting as ever. Twenty-five new tablets with translation and commentary are added. There is a new glossary (p.527–594).

VILBORG, Ebbe. A tentative grammar of Mycenaean Greek. Göteborg, (Stockholm, distributed by Almqvist & Wiksell), 1960. 169p.   **GA32**

AJPh LXXXIII 1962 220–222 Poultney • JHS LXXXIII 1963 173–174 Collinge

A serviceable systematization of the Mycenaean language material by an author who is all too well aware of the premature and presumptuous nature of such an undertaking. This is nonetheless a thorough presentation of the phonology, morphology, syntax and word-formation. The bibliography is fairly full to 1958. A useful addition to work already begun in Ventris and Chadwick, *Documents,* and Thumb, *Handbuch* (ed. Scherer, 1959).

GB GREEK AND LATIN

ACTA of the Fifth International Congress of Greek and Latin Epigraphy, Cambridge, [18th to 23rd September], 1967. Oxford, Blackwell, 1971. xxxv, 485, [36]p., illus., maps.　　**GB1**

> JRS LXII 1972 189–190 Birley • REA LXXIV 1972 362–364 Nony
> Contains a report on Epigraphic Projects in Progress (xxviii–xxxv). The *Acta* opens with Georges Daux, Réflexions sur l'Épigraphie (p.1–8). Other noteworthy contributions include A. J. Graham, Dating Archaic Greek Inscriptions (p.9–17), Harold B. Mattingly, Formal Dating Criteria for Fifth Century Attic Inscriptions (p.27–33), David Lewis, Boeckh, Staatshaushaltung der Athener, 1817–1967 (p.35–39), Henry Immerwahr, A Projected Corpus of Attic Vase Inscriptions (p.53–60), Raymond Bloch, A propos des inscriptions latines les plus anciennes (p.175–181), Gerold Walser, Die Reproduction von Meilenstein-Inscripten (p.437–442), G. M. Sanders, Les épitaphes métriques latines paiennes et chrétiennes: identités et divergences (p.455–459).

AKTEN des IV. Internationalen Kongresses für Griechische und Lateinische Epigraphik, Wien, 17. bis 22. September 1962. Wien, H. Böhlau, 1964. 424p., [13] leaves of plates, illus., port.　　**GB2**

> Contributions in German, English, French and Italian.
> AAHG XVII 1964 178–184 Pfohl • DLZ LXXXVI 1965 413–414 Gründel

AKTEN des VI. Internationalen Kongresses für Griechische und Lateinische Epigraphik, München 1972. München, Beck, 1973. xv, 632p., illus.　　**GB3**

> Vestigia; Bd. 17.
> CR XXVII 1977 145–146 Lewis • Stud Class XVI 1974 381–383 Pippidi • AAHG XXXI 1978 97–100 Pfohl
> Louis Robert gives the Discours d'introduction (p.11–27). Of the 100-odd papers about a dozen are concerned with problems of publication and publication-technique (three on computers and calculators). Another dozen are concerned with single texts.
> See also Actes du VIIᵉ Congrès International d'Epigraphie Grecque et Latine (Constanze, 9–15 septembre 1977). Bucharest, Editure Academiei et Paris, Les Belles Lettres, 1979. 510p., illus.

"APPLICATION à l'épigraphie des méthodes de l'informatique." Antiquités africaines IX (1975): 7–151.　　**GB4**

Reports the *Acta* of a CRNS roundtable held in Marseille, December 1972. The computerized indices to CIL V and VI have pointed the way to possibilities of more extensive use of computers in epigraphy. The University of Liege has also been in the vanguard. Possibilities do not stop at indices. See Chastagnol, *REL* LIV (1976), 522–523.

ATTI del Terzo Congresso Internazionale di Epigraphia Greca e Latina. 4–8 Sept, 1957. Rome, L'Erma di Bretschneider, 1959.　　**GB5**

> CR XI 1961 169 Woodhead • JRS XLIX 1959 208–209 Reynolds
> An excessively detailed publication of the *Acta* of the 1957 Rome Congress, by far the greater part of which encompasses material of the Roman period. There are 46 titles in the Table of Contents, very diverse in type and often very varied in value and importance.

BENGTSON, Hermann. Introduction to ancient history. Trans. from the 6th ed. by R. I. Frank and Frank D. Gilliard. Berkeley, University of California Press, 1970.　　**GB6**

> Chapter VI, Basic Disciplines: Epigraphy, Papyrology, Numismatics, esp. p.136–154, is a good introductory essay, stressing that the objective of editing inscriptions is to illuminate and deepen our knowledge of antiquity.

CALDERINI, Aristide. Epigrafia. Torino, Società editrice internazional, [1974]. xi, 378p., [16] leaves of plates, illus.　　**GB7**

> Manuali universitari; 1: Per lo studio delle scienze dell'antichità.
> Aegyptus LIII 1973 194–196 Montevecchi • Epigraphica XXXV 1973 191–192 Susini • REL LIII 1975 574 Durry
> A posthumously produced work of the Master. Materials and techniques are first discussed. Dating, hermeneutics, topography, classification and documentation are also amply covered. There is an appendix by S. Daris on abbreviations.

CALDERINI, Aristide. Epigraphica; Rivista italiana di epigrafia. Faenza [etc.], Fratelli Lega Editore [etc.]. Illus.　　**GB8**

> Began as a quarterly, with v. 1 in March 1939, Aristide Calderini, ed. Became a semiannual publication in 1973.
> Especially useful for Calderini's *Bolletino di epigrafia greca e romana*, *Epigraphica* I (1939)–VI (1943–1944). Interrupted by the war, it was resumed by A. Soffredi and G. C. Susini, *Epigraphica* XXVIII (1966), 171–251. For a bibliography of Calderini's writings cf. *Epigraphica* XXXI (1969), 9–43.

DEFRADAS, Jean. Guide de l'étudiant helléniste. Paris, Presses Universitaires de France, 1968. viii, 159p. **GB9**

L'Épigraphie (p. 122–132) contains a rapid, useful survey.

GROSSI-GONDI, Felice. Trattato di epigrafia Cristiana; Latina e Greca del mondo Romano occidentale. Roma, Università Gregoriana, 1920. x, 511p., illus. **GB10**

INTRODUZIONE allo studio della cultura classica. Milano, Marzorati, [1972–]. **GB11**

In v. III, Scienze Sussidiarie, Orsolina Montevecchi contributes a very useful orientation article Epigrafia (p.251–293), covering Greek and Latin epigraphy.

JALABERT, Louis and MOUTARDE, René. Inscriptions grecques et latines de la Syrie. Paris, P. Geuthner, 1929– . Illus. **GB12**

Bibliothèque archéologique et historique; t. 12, 32, 46, 61, v. 4. "Avec la collaboration de Claude Mondésert." Microfilm (negative) [Madison: University of Wisconsin Photographic Media Center, 1977]. 1 reel; 35 mm.
AJPh 1930 87–89 Prentice • JRS XX 1929 267 • JHS XC11 1972 235–236 Gray • RPh 1930 382 Collart
A valuable collection of documents, many hitherto inedita.

KAUFMANN, Carl Maria. Handbuch der Altchristlichen Epigraphik. Freiburg im Breisgau, and St. Louis, Herder, 1917. [xvi], 514p., illus. **GB13**

ByZ 1920 208–213 Larfeld • AB XXXVIII 187 Delehaye • DLZ 1924 488–498 Stuhlfauth

MARUCCHI, Orazio. Christian Epigraphy; An elementary treatise, with a collection of ancient Christian inscriptions, mainly of Roman origin. Trans. by J. Armine Willis. Chicago, Ares Publishers, 1974. xii, 460p., 30 leaves of plates, illus. **GB14**

Trans. of *Epigrafia cristiana*. Reprint of the 1912 ed. published by the Cambridge University Press, Cambridge, Eng.

OTTO, Walter, ed. Handbuch der Archäologie. In Verbindung mit E. Walter Andrae et al. München, Beck, 1939– . **GB15**

Handbuch der Altertumswissenschaft; 6. Abt.
In HdA VI, I Albert Rehm deals (p.182–238) with Die Inschriften in four sections: epigraphic technique, development of writing in Greco-Italian circles (including Etruscan), inscriptions as art, and the most important archaeological inscriptions. Erich Pernice follows (p.239–328) with a section on the literary testimonia to the origin and development of writing. Illustrations are in *Handbuch der Arch., Erster Tafelband*, Tafeln 27–36.

PETIT, Paul. Guide de l'étudiant en histoire ancienne. Paris, Presses Universitairies de France, 1959. **GB16**

See L'épigraphie (p.159–172) for good, brief orientation.

RENGEN W. van. "L'épigraphie grecque et latine de Syrie. Bilan d'un quart de siècle de recherches épigraphiques." ANRW II, 8: 31–53. **GB17**

REYNOLDS, J. M. and PERKINS, J. Ward et al. The inscriptions of Roman Tripolitania. Rome and London, Officine Apollon, 1952. vii, 276p., 11 plates, 9 maps. **GB18**

REL XXX 1952 521 Zeiller • AJA LVII 1953 151 Gordon • CPh XLVIII 1953 208–210 MacKendrick
A collection of 972 epigraphical texts, Greek and Latin, classified according to the geographical order of provenience. In each region or city the classification includes religious inscriptions, imperial, senatorial, equestrian, municipal, collegial, funerary. A small number of Christian inscriptions are found at the end. The edition is a model of epigraphical method and a heartening example of international collaboration. Sixty percent of the inscriptions are from Lepcis Magna. The documentation casts much new light on imperial administration, local government, pagan and Christian cult, military affairs, the road system, the *limes,* and the extent of Romanization.

ROBERT, Louis. Die Epigraphik der klassischen Welt. Bonn, R. Habelt, 1970. 66p., plates. **GB19**

"Autorisierte Übersetzung aus dem Französischen von Helmut Engelman; die Anmerkungen hat der Verfasser für die deutsche Übersetzung hinzugefügt." "Der originale französische Text ist gedruckt in der Encyclopedie de la Pléiade." "L'histoire et ses méthodes," Paris 1961, S. 453–497 (Verlag Gallimard).
CR XXIII 1973 110–111 Lewis • RBPh L 1972 617–618 Van't Dack.
A translation of Robert's contribution "Épigraphies" to *L'Histoire et ses méthodes* (p.453–497) with expanded notes. Useful as a supplement to Woodhead and Klappenbach, but not intended by the author as an introductory manual.
See also the ongoing "Bulletin Épigraphique," by Jeanne Robert and Louis Robert. *REG* XCVII (1984): 419–522.

USSANI, Vincenzo and ARNALDI, Francesco. Guida allo studio della civiltà romana antica. 2d. ed. Napoli, Instituto editoriale del Mezzogiorno, [pref. 1958–], 1967– . **GB20**

Includes bibliographies.
Volume II (p.633–666) contains a rapid survey, with bibliography, for "Épigrafia," and M. Della Corte covers graffiti (p.667–671).

GC GREEK EPIGRAPHY

Bibliography, Methodology, and Orientation

ANNÉE épigraphique; Revue des publications épigraphiques relatives à l'antiquité Romaine. Academie des Inscriptions et Belle-Lettres. Paris, Presses Universitaires de France, 1962– .

GC1

1982 annual edited by André Chastagnol, Marcel Leglay and Patrick Le Roux. 1984. 344p.

ARCHEOLOGIA CLASSICA. Roma. Illus., plates. v. 1–, 1949– .

GC2

"Revista dell'Istituto di archeologia dell'Università di Roma," 1949–55; "Rivista della Scoula nazionale di archeologia," 1961– .
An annual from 1944 to 1958, this journal has appeared twice a year since 1959.
Volume XXV–XXVI (1976), 761p., is Studi in onore di Margherita Guarducci.

BRADEEN, Donald William and McGREGOR, Malcolm Francis, eds. Phóros. Tribute to Benjamin Dean Meritt. Locust Valley, N.Y., J. J. Augustin, 1974. 187p., illus., 27 plates.

GC3

Written for Professor Meritt in honor of his 75th birthday on March 31, 1974. It includes Meritt's own extensive bibliography (p.13–20) which spans the years 1923–1974. There are 26 contributions.

DOW, Sterling. Conventions in editing; A suggested reformulation of the Leiden System. [Durham, N.C.], Duke University, 1969. vi, 37p., illus.

GC4

Greek, Roman and Byzantine scholarly aids; 2.
Mnemosyne XXVI 1973 322–323 Pleket • CJ LXIX 1973–1974 174–175 Samuel • CR XXI 1971 309–310 Lewis
In 37 pages Dow presents a concise analysis of the conventions of editing. The advisability of standardizing editorial practice was first officially acknowledged at the 1932 International Congress of Orientalists at Leiden, from which the Leiden conventions emerged, and the Leiden Klammer System has since in general, prevailed.
The main conventions are presented here in c.2, an excellent critical bibliography of the subject follows in c.3, and c.4 is devoted to restoration in epigraphical texts. In the final chapter the conventions already discussed are put to work on a sample text, IG II, 2 (1989), with accompanying photographs and line-by-line commentary. For Dow "the main problem, surely, is not to change the Leiden system, but to improve

its working." This volume contributes much to such improvement.

HANSEN, Peter Allan. A list of Greek verse inscriptions down to 400 B.C.: an analytical survey. Copenhagen, Museum Tusculanum, 1975. 53p.

GC5

Opuscula Graecolatina: v. 3.
MT 1976 no. 27 65–67 Breitenstein • Platon XXVIII 1976 345–346 Mitsos
See now: Hansen, P. A., *Carmina Epigraphica Graeca Saeculorum*, VIII, V a.Chr.n. Berlin and New York, de Gruyter, 1983. xxiii, 302p. (Texte und Kommentare, Band 12).

HONDIUS, Jacobus Johannes. Saxa loquuntur: a bibliography of epigraphic publications on Greek inscriptions. Chicago, Ares, 1976. 169p.

GC6

Added t.p.: Saxa loquuntur; inleiding tot de Grieksche epigraphiek. "Unchanged reprint of the edition: Leiden 1938."
AC X 1941 191–192 Pottelbergh
The well-known editor of SEG provides an introduction in Dutch; the most important part is the elaborate bibliographical appendix of 106 pages, covering publications down to 1938. One still has to go to Larfeld for treatment of the technique and method of epigraphy, the origin and development of Greek letter forms and methods of dating. Hondius is content to chart the history of epigraphy and to emphasize the utility and charm of the discipline, also to indicate the chief results so far attained, and the areas needing more research.

PFOHL, Gerhard. Bibliographie der griechischen Vers-Inschriften. Hildesheim, G. Olms, 1964. 62p.

GC7

Gnomon XXXVIII 1966 606–611 Hommel • Gymnasium LXXII 1965 476
Pfohl's productivity (cf. *Gnomon* review for other titles) is well-known. See his bibliographical survey, 1948– , in *Gymnasium* LXXII (1965): 523–537.

ROBERT, Jeanne and ROBERT, Louis. Index du Bulletin épigraphique 1938–1965; par l'Institut Fernand Coubry. Paris, Les Belles Lettres, 1972–1975. 3 v.

GC8

1. ptie. Les mots grecs. 2. ptie. Les publications. 3. ptie. Les mots français.
Gnomon XLVII 1975 627–629 Speidel • CRAI 1972 428–429 Robert
A photographic reproduction of the *REG* Bulletins from 1938 to 1970, published by L'Association des Études Grecques in 6 volumes: vol. I, 1938–1939, 164p.; vol. II, 1940–1951, 634p.; vol. III, 1952–1958, 679p.;

vol. IV, 1959–1963, 536p.; vol. V, 1964–1967, 505p.; vol. VI, 1968–1970, 376p.

Index volumes have been prepared by J. Pouilloux and his colleagues at l'Institut Courby at Lyons [*REG* LXXXIX (1976): 111–113, by Plassart]. This is an excellently arranged bibliographical survey, and the regional survey makes new discoveries in even the remotest islands easy to locate.

"Besides being a treasure house of emendations and commentary, the bulletin will serve serious students as by far the best introduction to Greek epigraphy: Reading through these volumes will familiarize with the field in the most useful and comprehensive way" Speidel.

The *Bulletin épigraphique* is a continuing feature of *REG* [cf. *REG* LXXXIX (1976): 415–595].

ROBERTS, Ernest Stewart. An introduction to Greek epigraphy. Ed. for the syndics of the University Press. Cambridge, Cambridge University Press, 1887– . Facsims. **GC9**

pt. I. The archaic inscriptions and the Greek alphabet, ed. by E. S. Roberts. 1887. pt. II. The inscriptions of Attica, ed. by E. S. Roberts . . . and E. A. Gardner. 1905.

Rather antiquated, but still useful.

STEFAN, A. "Applications des méthodes mathématiques à l'épigraphie." Stud Class XIII (1971): 29–45. **GC10**

T(OD), M. N. "Epigraphy, Greek." OCD²: 394–397. **GC11**

Defines epigraphy as the study of inscriptions written on durable material such as stone or metal in Greek letters and expressed in the Greek language. Since inscriptions afford by far the earliest examples of Greek writing they are invaluable for the study of the origin and development of the Greek alphabet.

TOD, M. N. "The progress of Greek epigraphy." JHS XXXIV (1914): 321–331; ibid. XXXV (1915): 260–270; ibid. XXXIX (1919): 209–231 (for 1915–1918); etc. **GC12**

Continues the earlier survey by Tod in *The Year's Work in Classical Studies,* 1906–1914. Short resumés and evaluations of the most important works.

ZIEBARTH, Erich G. L. "Fünfundzwanzig jahre griechischer inschriftenforschung (1894–1919)." JAW 184 (46. jahrg., 3. abt.) 91–139; ibid. 189 (47. jahrg., 3. abt.) 1–51; ibid. 193 (48. jahrg., 3. abt.) 60–78; ibid. 213 (53. jahrg., 3. abt.) 1–40. **GC13**

Collections, Editions, Facsimiles

BECHTEL, F. et al. Sammlung der griechischen Dialekt-Inschriften. Hrsg. von Hermann Collitz. Nendeln, Liechtenstein, Kraus Reprint, 1973. 4 v. in 7. **GC14**

Reprint of the Gottingen edition, 1884–1915.

Bd. 1. Kypros. Aeolien. Thessalien. Böotien. Elis. Arkadien. Pamphylien. Bd. 2. Epirus. Akarnanien. Aetolien. Aenianen. Phthiotis. Lokris. Phokis. Dodona. Achaia und seine Colonien. Delphi. Bd. 3., t. 1. Die Inschriften der dorischen Gebiete ausser Lakonien, Thera Melos, Kreta, Sicilien. Bd. 3, t. 2. Die Inschriften von Lakonien, Tarent, Herakleia am Siris, Messenien. Thera und Melos. Sicilien und Abu-Simbel. Die ionischen Inschriften. Bd. 4. Wortregister, etc.

BERNAND, André. Les inscriptions grecques de Philae . . . Paris, Centre national de la recherche scientifique, 1969. 2 v., plates. **GC15**

Vol. 2 has title: Les inscriptions grecques et latines de Philae.

Gnomon XLVII 1975 475–481 Fraser

BOECKH, August et al. Corpus inscriptionum graecarum. Hildesheim; New York, G. Olms, 1977. 4 v., illus., facsims. **GC16**

Subsidia epigraphica: Quellen und Abhandlungen zur griechischen Epigraphik.

Reprint of the 1828–77 ed. published by the Akademie der Wissenschaften, Berlin.

Vol. 3, "ex materia collecta ab A. Boeckhio . . . edidit Ioannes Franzius"; v. 4, "ex materia ab A. Boeckhio et I. Franzio collecta et ab hoc ex parte digesta et pertractata edidervnt Ernestvs Cvrtivs et Adolphvs Kirchhoff."

August Boeckh, under the auspices of the Prussian Akademie der Wissenschaften at Berlin, undertook the publication of a comprehensive corpus designed to present all Greek inscriptional material already published in a uniform and accessible manner. By 1877 when the index was published, the Berlin Academy had decided to undertake *ab initio* a new version of the corpus because of the proliferation of new discoveries.

BRADEEN, Donald W. Inscriptions: the funerary monuments. Princeton, N.J., American School of Classical Studies at Athens, 1974. xi, 240p., 85 plates. **GC17**

The Athenian Agora, v. 17.

CW LXX 1976–77 473–474 Urdahl

Includes 1,160 pieces, chiefly fragments, constituting 1,103 inscriptions. The 667 photographs are valuable for palaeography of Attic inscriptions and the late Prof. Bradeen's name as editor is a guarantee of meticulous scholarship.

BRITISH MUSEUM. Dept. of Greek and Roman Antiquities. The collection of ancient Greek inscriptions in the British Museum edited by C. T. Newton. Milano, Instituto editoriale Cisalpino-La goliardica, 1977– . Illus. **GC18**

"Ristampa anastatica authorizzata dal British Museum Publications Ltd. di Londra."

Reprint of the 1874–1916 ed. published by the Clarendon Press, Oxford. pt. 1. Hicks, E. L. Attika.

CAGNAT, R. et al. Inscriptiones graecae ad res Romanas pertinentes. Academiae inscriptionum et litterarum humaniorum (lutetiae parisiorum) collectae et editae. Edendum curavit R. Cagnat auxiliantibus J. Toutain, P. Jouguet et G. Lafaye. Scholar's Reference ed. Chicago, Ares, 1975. 4 v. in 3.   **GC19**

Reduced reprint of the Paris 1906–1927 ed.
BPhW 1915 910 Liebenam

CALDER, W. M. et al. Monumenta Asiae Minoris antiqua. [Manchester], Pub. for the Society by the Manchester University Press; London, Longmans, Green & Co. Ltd. 1928– . Illus.   **GC20**

Publications of the American society for archaeological research in Asia Minor; vol. 1.
Gnomon 1931 524–532 Peek
MAMA is a standard source work for Asia Minor.

CHILTON, C. W. Diogenes of Oenoanda: the fragments; A translation and commentary. London, New York, Oxford University Press, 1971. xlviii, 141p., illus., plates, maps.   **GC21**

University of Hull publications.
AJPh XCV 1974 308–312 Koniaris

DITTENBERGER, Wilhelm. Orientis graeci inscriptions selectae. Supplementum Sylloges inscriptionum graecarum. Edidit Wilhelmus Dittenberger. Hildesheim, New York, G. Olms, 1970. 2 v.   **GC22**

"Zweiter unveränderter photomech[a]nischer Nachdruck der Ausgabe Leipzig 1903–[05]."

DITTENBERGER, Wilhelm. Sylloge inscriptionum Graecarum, a Guilelmo Dittenbergero condita et aucta, nunc quartum edita. Edited by Friedrich Hiller von Gaertringen. Hildesheim, Olms, 1960. 4 v., illus.   **GC23**

Vol. 4 index.
"Unveränderter photomechanischer Nachdruck der 3. Aufl. Leipzig 1915."
JHS XXXVIII 1917 127, XXXXIX 1919 146, XL 1920 154 • DLZ 1916 1710–1715
The third edition, ably produced (after the author's death) by von Gaertringen, Kirchner, Pomtow and Ziebarth, is an improvement on the second edition (seventeen years earlier) both in appearance and in additional contents. Dittenberger's commentary is in terse and lucid Latin, and is in itself a valuable contribution to Greek history. Vol. II contains the historical documents from the peace of Nanpactus (217–216 B.C.) to the close of the Roman period.

DURRBACH, Felix. Choix d'inscriptions de Délos avec traduction et commentaire de Félix Durrbach. Hildesheim, New York, G. Olms, 1976. iii, 294p.   **GC24**

Subsidia epigraphica. Quellen und Abhandlungen zur griechischen Epigraphik; v. 6. Reprint of v. 1, 1921 ed. published by E. Leroux, Paris.

JS 1924 103–116, 163–169 Roussel • BMB 1924 17 Jacob

DURRBACH, Felix et al. Inscriptions de Délos. Paris, H. Champion, 1926– . Illus.   **GC25**

Vols. 1–2 "publiés par Félix Durrbach." Vols. 1 and 2 are supplemented by "Tabulae" (Berlin, 1927) published as Inscriptiones graecae, vol. XI, fasc. 3. Vol. 7– have imprint: Paris, E. De Boccard.

ENGELMANN, Helmut. Die Inschriften von Erythrai und Klazomenai. Hrsg. von Helmut Engelmann und Reinhold Merkelback. Bonn, R. Habelt, 1972– . Illus., map (in pocket), plates.   **GC26**

Inschriften griechischer Stadte aus Kleinasien, Bd, 1, 2: Teil 1; nr. 1–200, Teil 2, nr. 201–536.
Gnomon XLVII 1975 562–567 Pleket • JHS XLVI 1976 261–264 Woodhead • Mnemosyne XXVIII 1975 445–447 Pleket
This is the first in a planned series on the Hellenistic-Roman polis. Ilion, Smyrna and Cyme volumes are also in preparation. The Erythrai corpus contains 333 texts distributed over various categories in accessible and readable format, with short commentaries. Excellent photographs help to follow the development of Erythraean letter-writing. A most valuable enterprise, under the auspices of the renowned 'Kommission' of the Austrian Academy and the Institut für Altertumskunde of the University of Cologne.

GRAINDOR, Paul. Album d'inscriptions attiques d'époque impériale. Avec notes, corrections et inédits. Gand, Van Rysselbergh & Rombaut, 1924. 2 v., facsims.   **GC27**

A. Texte. B. Planches.
JHS XLV 1925 142–143 • RBPh 1926 1066 Mayence
The aim of these two volumes is to illustrate the rather complicated evolution of Greek letter forms in the Imperial period by giving facsimiles of a number of the best-dated inscriptions from a single city of importance. There are 114 Athenian inscriptions reproduced here.

HILLER VON GAERTRINGEN, Friedrich. Inscriptiones graecae: consilio et auctoritate Academiae Litterarum Borussicae editae . . . : editio minor . . . The Scholar's reference ed. Chicago, Ares, 1974. 3 v. in 5, illus.   **GC28**

"Reduced reprint of the Berlin 1913–1940 edition."
v. 1. Inscriptiones atticae Euclidis anno anteriores edidit Fridericus Hiller de Gaertringen. v. 2–5. Inscriptiones atticae Euclidis anno posteriores, edidit Johannes Kirchner.
Pars tertia paged continuously.

KERN, Otto. Inscriptiones graecae. Bonnae, A. Marcus et E. Weber, 1913. xxiii, 50 plates (1 double).   **GC29**

Tablvlae in vsvm scholarvm. ed. svb cvra Iohannis Lietzmann; 7.

BFC 1914 86 Zuretti • JHS 1914 342 • RPh 1914 121 Haussoullier • CPh 1915 478 Johnson

A series of 50 plates, containing over 120 inscriptions ranging from the earliest times to the 4th century A.D. The reproductions are made from photographs taken from the stones themselves, except four which are from squeezes. The letterpress, in Latin, contains a concise description of the plates and brief bibliographies of introductory works and standard collections. There is a conspectus of the plates and a table of concordances, both containing some inaccuracies.

KIRCHNER, Johannes Ernst. Imagines inscriptionum Atticarum; Ein Bilderatlas epigraphischer Denkmäler Attikas. 2 Aufl. Durchgesehen von Günther Klaffenbach. Berlin, Gebr. Mann, 1948. 33p., 54 plates.   **GC30**

AJA 1936 174–176 Dow • AJPh LVII 1936 225–227 Meritt • CR XLIX 1935 227–228 Tod • Gnomon XXII 1950 184–186 Dörner • RA IX 1937 282–284 Picard

The aim is to present the development of the Greek script in a series of photographs of Attic inscriptions, selected for their paleographical clarity and interest rather than for their historical value. Fifty-four plates containing 147 photographs of 150 inscriptions document the history of Attic Greek writing from the first half of the 8th century B.C. to the early years of the 5th century A.D. There is a concise description of the date, provenance, present location, nature and material of each inscribed object. Long and fruitful work on the *editio minor* of the Corpus equipped Kirchner as the ideal editor of such a needed work. The photographs are excellent for their time.

LANG, Mabel. Graffiti and dipinti. Princeton, N.J., American School of Classical Studies at Athens, 1976. x, 116p., [31] leaves of plates, illus.   **GC31**

The Athenian Agora; v. 21.

MEIGGS, Russell, and LEWIS, David. A selection of Greek historical inscriptions to the end of the fifth century B.C. Reprinted in 1975 with corrections. Oxford, Clarendon Press, 1975, 1969. xix, 307p.   **GC32**

AJPh XCIII 1972 474–480 Jameson • LEC XL 1972 137 Absil • Gnomon XLIV 1972 729–731 Heinen

This replaces the earlier M.N. Tod, *Greek Historical Inscriptions to the End of the Fifth Century B.C.,* Oxford, 1933, 2nd ed., 1946. Valuable new inscriptions have been included and most of the important old ones, with improved texts, kept. The commentaries are learned and useful. Where Tod said it best he is repeated verbatim.

MERITT, Benjamin Dean. The Athenian tribute lists. Princeton, N.J., The American School of Classical Studies at Athens, 1939–1953. 4 v.   **GC33**

Athenaeum XVIII 1940 221–223 Guarducci • AJPh LXI 1940 379–381 Oliver • EHR LV 1940 104–106 Meiggs • JHS LXIX 1949 104–105 Tod • DLZ 1950 33–37 Klaffenbach • CPh XLVII 1952 261–262 Pritchett • CR n.s. II 1952 97–100 Meiggs

In a work of fundamental importance the tribute lists are brought together with extraordinary thoroughness and skill not only by the restored texts but by legible photographs of every extant fragment and by drawings which indicate the extent of lacunae. A complete bibliography is given for each fragment. In a valuable section called "Testimonia," the references to the tribute arrangements in ancient literature and from ancient inscriptions and papyri are assembled. In a most useful Register the record of every known member of the empire has been tabulated, and a Gazetteer tries to fix the site of all members.

Volume 2 is a further collection of source material, correcting and supplementing v. 1, taking account of review criticisms of v. 1 and adding much new material.

Volume 3 is a history, largely financial, of the Athenian Naval Confederacy in its rise, growth and decline. Volume 4 contains brief (ix–xii) Addenda and Corrigenda, a detailed General Index (p.1–134), and Greek Index (p.135–234). There is a concluding bibliography from 1752 to 1953.

MERITT, Benjamin Dean. Inscriptions from the Athenian Agora. Photographs by Alison Frantz. Princeton, N.J., American School of Classical Studies at Athens, 1966. [32]p., illus.   **GC34**

Excavations of the Athenian Agora. Picture book no. 10.

MERITT, Benjamin Dean and TRAIL, John S. Inscriptions; the Athenian councillors. Princeton, N.J., American School of Classical Studies at Athens, 1974. xii, 486p., 2 plates.   **GC35**

The Athenian Agora; results of excavations conducted by the American School of Classical Studies at Athens, v. 15.

MICHEL, Charles. Recueil d'inscriptions grecques. Préface par B. Haussoullier. Hildesheim; New York, G. Olms Verlag, 1976. xxvi, 1000p.   **GC36**

Subsidia epigraphica. Quellen und Abhandlungen zur griechischen epigraphik; v. 4. Reprint of the Brussels ed., H. Lamertin, 1900.

NOUVEAU CHOIX d'inscriptions grecques; textes, traductions, commentaires par l'Institut Fernand-Courby. Paris, Société d'édition Les Belles lettres, 1971. 234p.   **GC37**

Nouvelle collection de textes et documents. CW LXVI 1972 171–173 Wilkes • CPh LXVII 1972 311–312 Larsen • CR n.s. XXIV 1974 148 Lewis

This is a new collection of Greek inscriptions arranged on similar lines to J. Pouilloux, *Choix* issued in 1961. Nine scholars, including Pouilloux, are responsible for the present collection of 37 items, with translations, commentaries, and improved index. The emphasis is on internal rather than international affairs, on the wide spread and persistence of Greek ideas and institutions. Useful for the student working alone and trying to get some idea of the nature and scope of Greek inscriptions.

PEEK, Werner. Inschriften aus dem Asklepieion von Epidauros. Mit 184 Faks. im Text u. 100 Abb. auf 58 Taf. Berlin, Akademie-Verl., 1969. 156p., 58p. of illus. **GC38**

Abhandlungen der Sächsischen Akademie der Wissenschaften zu Leipzig. Philologisch-historische Klasse; Bd. 60, Heft 2.

PFOHL, G., ed. Griechische Inschriften als Zeugnisse des privaten und öffentlichen Lebens. München, Heimeran, 1965. 252p., 8 plates. **GC39**

AJPh LXXXVIII 1967 381 Oliver • CR XVII 1967 321–323 Lewis • Gnomon XL 1968 91–92 Tod
A carefully chosen selection of 164 inscriptions ranging in date from mid-8th cent. B.C. to the end of the 7th cent. A.D., and geographically from Macedonia to Abu-Simbel and from Koln to Kabul. Prose inscriptions predominate but 52 of the texts are wholly or partially metrical. Each text has a heading indicating its nature, provenance and date, and is followed by a German translation and short commentary. There are ample bibliographies (p.196–224). The volume contains seven groups of inscriptions: (i) the oldest Greek inscriptions; (ii) grave inscriptions; (iii) dedications; (iv) honorific inscriptions; (v) historical epigrams; (vi) historical inscriptions; and (vii) various inscriptions.

POUILLOUX, Jean. Choix d'inscriptions grecques; textes, traductions et notes. Paris, Société d'édition Les Belles lettres, 1960. 195p. **GC40**

Bibliothèque de la Faculté des Lettres de Lyon; 4.
CR n.s. XII 1962 261–262 Woodhead • DLZ LXXXII 1961 511–516 Klaffenbach
A collection of 53 inscriptions chosen as representative of recurrent types, and useful for seminar purposes. The work appears to have been put together hastily, and there are many inaccuracies in texts and comments.

POUILLOUX, Jean. École française d'Athènes. Fouilles de Delphes. III: Épigraphie, IV, 4: Les inscriptions de la terrasse au temple et de la region nord du sanctuaire, Nos. 351 à 516. Paris, École Française d'Athènes, 1976. 204p., 32 plates. **GC41**

Part III, Epigraphy, started in 1909, with additions published on an irregular basis.

ROBERT, Louis. Hellenica, recueil d'épigraphie, de numismatique et d'antiquités grecques. Limoges, A. Bontemos, 1940– . Illus., maps. **GC42**

Vols. 2– have imprint: Paris, Librairie d'Amerique et d'Orient. Vol. 4 has also special title: Épigrammes du Bas-Empire; v. 6: Inscriptions grecques de Lydie, par Jeanne Robert et Louis Robert; v. 8: Inscriptions en langue carienne, monuments de gladiateurs dans l'orient grec, inscriptions de Nehavend; v. 9; Inscriptions et reliefs d'Asie mineure, par Jeanne Robert et Louis Robert.

ROEHL, Hermann. Imagines inscriptionum Graecarum antiquissimarum, in usum scholarum. Berolini, G. Reimer, 1883. 3 ed., 1907. 72p., illus. **GC43**

SOLMSEN, Felix. Inscriptiones Graecae ad inlustrandas dialectos selectae. Editionem quartam auctam et emendatam curavit Ernestus Fraenkel. Editio stereotypa editionis quartae (1930). Stutgardiae in aedibus B. G. Teubneri 1966. viii, 113p. **GC44**

Bibliotheca scriptorum Graecorum et Romanorum Teubneriana. [Scriptores Graeci].
CR XLV 1931 28 Noble • Gnomon VII 1931 567–572 Schwyzer • JHS L 1930 351 Tod
A fourth edition only 27 years after its first appearance attests the value of Solmsen's work. The new editor, Ernst Fraenkel, pupil and friend of Solmsen, retains all that was of value in the previous edition and enriches it with references to recent discoveries and discussions. The number of inscriptions is now sixty seven. A most useful pedagogical tool in the study of the non-literary Greek dialects, and an excellent inexpensive complement to Buck's *Greek Dialects.*

SUPPLEMENTUM Epigraphicum graecum. Lugduni Batavorum, A.W. Sijthoff, 1923– . v. 11–20, Cambridge, 1950–1964, 1 v. **GC45**

CW LXVII 1974 301–302 Speidel
Begun in Amsterdam in 1923 by Hondius, and continued by Tod and Woodhead. On the difficulties of *SEG* see Georges Daux, "Le sort du SEG," Akten des VI intern. Kongresses. München 1972, München, 1973, 575–581. For its rejuvenation see now *SEG* XXVI (1976–1977), edited by H. W. Pleket and R. S. Stroud, Alphen a. d. R. (Netherlands), Sijtoff & Noordhoff Intern. Publ., 1979, 484p.; ibid. XXX (1980), Amsterdam, Gieben, 1983, 611p.

TOD, Marcus Niebuhr. A selection of Greek historical inscriptions. Oxford, Clarendon Press, 1933–1948. 2 v. **GC46**

Bibliography: v. 1, p.[xiii]–xviii; v. 2, p.[ix]–xi.
JHS LXVIII 1948 161 Woodward • CPh 1949 262–263 Larsen • Gnomon XXI 1949 264 Taeger
Fifteen years after the first volume (now replaced by Meiggs and Lewis, 1969), the second volume made its welcome appearance and was widely praised as very accurate, very concise and clear, a work of the highest scholarship. The numbering of the inscriptions (97–205) continues that of v. 1. Ten items that appeared

in Hicks-Hill 1901, have been omitted and no less than 35 not included in Hicks-Hill have been added, many of them new. Only about half of the texts printed are of Attic origin. The volume shows that the 4th century affords a far more varied and kaleidoscopic picture of the Greek historian than does the 5th, because of a greater range and wealth of inscriptions. The commentaries and bibliographies are invariably illuminating and thorough.

WYCHERLEY, Richard Ernest. Literary and epigraphical testimonia. London, W. Clowes, 1973. 259p., [2] leaves of plates, illus.   **GC47**

The Athenian Agora; v. 3. Reprint of the 1957 ed. published by the American School of Classical Studies at Athens, Princeton, N.J.
Gnomon XXXI 1959 678–682 Martin
Texts and translations of literary and epigraphical testimonia with reference to the Agora, its diverse activities and its role in Athenian life. An indispensable tool for those interested in Athenian topography. The texts are grouped by subjects and are isolated to the various buildings in the agora, stoas, sanctuaries etc.

Manuals

FRANZ, Johannes. Elementa epigraphicae Graecae. [Nachdr. der Ausg. Berlin, 1840]. Amsterdam, Gruner, 1972. 400p.   **GC48**

A reprint of one of the earliest manuals.

GUARDUCCI, Margherita. Epigrafia greca. Roma, Instituto poligrafico dello Stato, Libreria dello Stato, 1967–1978. 4 v., illus., facsims.   **GC49**

Bibliography: v. 1, p.[507]–532.
1. Caratteri e storia della disciplina. La scrittura greca dalle origini all' eta imperiale. 2. Epigrafi di carattere pubblico. 3. Epigrafi di carattere privato. 4. Epigrafi sacre pagane e cristiane.
Arch Class XIX 1967 357–359 Becatti • REG LXXXI 1968 236–238 Flacelière • DLZ LXXXIX 1968 591–594 Klaffenbach • DLZ XCIII 1972 45–48 Exleben • Epigraphica XXXIX 1967 186–188 Calderini
A beautifully produced set of vols. both in text and illustration. Signora Guarducci states her aim succinctly in the preface (p.vii): Cioè una sintesi scientifica del materiale epigrafico greco, nella quale non soltanto venga trattata la parte più propriamenta tecnica dell' epigrafia ma, in base a molti documenti epigrafici addotti ed illustrati, si cerchi di delineare in uno quadro vivo la civiltà che si svolse in Grecia fra l'VIII secolo av. Cr. e la tarda età imperiale, mettendo in risalto di codesta civiltà gli aspetti più caratteristici ed attraenti.
Guarducci refuses to limit epigraphy to inscriptions on stone and metal as Klaffenbach proposed, stressing in addition the importance of pottery inscriptions, and also coin legends. She gives a preliminary survey of syllabic writing—Linear B and Cypriot—and in her examination of the origin of the Greek alphabet opts

for Crete as the place of origin and the 2nd half of the 9th century as the earliest possible dates.
The chief part of volume 1 (p.107–368) is devoted to a study of the alphabet in archaic inscriptions. The inscriptions are treated by region alphabetically. There are brief concluding chapters on punctuation signs, abbreviations, shorthand, engraving technique, restoration of texts, and forgeries.

KLAFFENBACH, Günther. Griechische Epigraphik. 2., verb. Aufl. Göttingen, Vandenhoeck & Ruprecht, 1966. 110p.   **GC50**

Studienhefte zur Altertumswissenschaft; Heft 6.
JHS LXXVIII 1958 143 Tod • CPh LIII 1958 214 Pritchett • AAHG X 1957 247–249 Gschnitzer
A work rather similar in scope and content to Woodhead's *The Study of Greek Inscriptions* in which a recognized expert makes available an introduction suitable for students and for more advanced scholars who though not aspiring to be epigraphical experts wish to have a clear and authoritative statement on the scope and methods of the science. The opening chapter deals with the definition and significance of epigraphy and its contribution to an understanding of the thought, speech and life of the ancient world. Chapter II gives an admirable survey of the history of the discipline. Chapter III contains a bibliography of the most important publications: Corpora, selections. Chapter IV deals with the alphabet. Chapter V discusses the materials of inscriptions, the methods of engraving, the arrangement of letters and other signs. Chapter VI, the longest, deals with the nature, content and classification of inscriptions. The book ends with three short chapters on the language, the dating, and the editing of Greek inscriptions.

LARFELD, Wilhelm. Griechische Epigraphik. 3. völlig neubearb. aufl., mit 4 tafeln. München, C. H. Beck, O. Bech, 1914. xi, [1], 536p.   **GC51**

Handbuch der klassischen Altertumswissenschaft, 1. bd. 5 abt.
CR XXIX 1915 87–89 Tod • CPh 1915 479 Johnson
Still the most important general handbook in the field. The history of epigraphy is first dealt with (p.7–105), a considerable shortening of the same author's treatment in his *Handbuch der griechischen Epigraphik*. Indeed the compactness of the present volume recommends it to student and professional epigraphist alike.

LARFELD, Wilhelm. Handbuch der griechischen Epigraphik. Hildesheim; New York, G. Olms, 1971. 2 v. in 3, illus., chart.   **GC52**

Reprint of 1898–1907 ed., published by O. R. Reisland, Leipzig. Bd. 1. Einleitungs- und Hilfsdisziplinen. Die nicht-attischen Inschriften. Bd. 1, Hälfte 1–2. Die attischen Inschriften. 2 v.
The most comprehensive and detailed manual.

PFOHL, Gerhard. Elemente der griechischen Epigraphik. Überprüfte und ergänzt Ausgabe. Reprografischer Nachdruck. Darmstadt, Nissenschaftliche Buchgesellschaft, 1968. 111p., illus. **GC53**

Brings together four contributions published elsewhere: Monument und Epigramm; Über Form und inhalt griechischen Grabiuschriften; Gedanken zur Zweischichtenlehre; and Griechische Inschriften im altsprachlichen und althistorischen Unterricht.

PLEKET, H. W. Epigraphica. Leiden, E. J. Brill, 1964– . **GC54**

Textus minores in usum academicum; v. 31. v. 1. Texts on the economic history of the Greek world.
AC XXXIV 1965 315 Pouilloux • RH XCV 1971 no. 246 138 Will

REINACH, Salomon. Traité d'épigraphie grecque; précédé d'un essai sur les inscriptions grecques par C. T. Newton, traduit avec l'autorisation de l'auteur, augmenté de notes et de textes épigraphiques choisis. Paris, E. Leroux, 1885. xliv, 560p., illus. **GC55**

This classic work is divided in two parts. Part I discusses the utility of Greek epigraphy for the study of history, gives a history of the discipline, an outline of recent excavations and discoveries, and a brief study, with texts, of many of the best known inscriptions. In c. 2 attention is focused on temples, rituals and religious ministers, religious assemblies and fraternities, dedications to divinities and funerary monuments. Part II begins with a history of the Greek alphabet and Greek writing, with tables showing letter variations (p.186–189). Archaic alphabets are next discussed, followed by a chronological account of modifications in the Attic alphabet and the addition of complementary letters. Alphabets down to the 4th cent. A.D. are discussed, also abbreviations, ligatures, numerical signs and punctuation. Chapter 2 of Part II is devoted to Particularités Orthographiques, confusions of letters and diphthongs, and grammatical peculiarities. Chapter 3 deals with continued archaism in letter forms after the official introduction of the Ionian alphabet to Athens in 403, and with some of the techniques and errors of the stonecutters. Chapters 4 and 5 discuss the various types of inscriptions, Public Acts with their various formulae and Private inscriptions; c. VI has closing information on diverse matters: dating formulae and the various calendars in use, names and surnames, demotic and ethnic designations, patronymics, Greek transcriptions of Roman names, etc. Much of the matter is outmoded, but the organization of the material continues to be impressive.

WOODHEAD, Arthur Geoffrey. The study of Greek inscriptions. London, Cambridge University Press, 1967, 2nd ed., 1980. xii, 139p., illus., 4 plates, table. **GC56**

CW LIII 1960 162 Babcock • CJ LV 1960 285–286 McGregor • Phoenix XIV 1960 109–111 Meritt • Epigraphica XXXII 1970 193–194 Susini

An admirable introduction for nonspecialists to the materials, techniques and potentialities of Greek epigraphy. The first eight chapters deal with signs and symbols used by epigraphists, the origin and development of the Greek alphabet, boustrophedon and stoicheden writing, the classification, dating and restoration of inscriptions, methods of reproducing inscriptions, and the relation of epigraphic art to other phases of Greek art. Chapter IX is an excellent survey of epigraphic publications, especially detailed on the *Corpora*. A chapter of miscellaneous information provides useful coverage on numerals, the Athenian tribes, archons and calendars, and the months of the Delphic calendar.

History, Language, Abbreviations

AUSTIN, Reginald Percy. The stoichedon style in Greek inscriptions. New York, Arno Press, 1973. xii, 130p., illus. **GC57**

Reprint of the 1938 ed. published by Oxford University Press, London, in the series Oxford classical & philosophical monographs.
AJPh 1940 121–122 Dow
This work concentrates on the manner of engraving in the inscriptions and the aims of the craftsmen who cut them. The stoichedon style is defined (p.1) as the style of engraving in which the letters are in alignment vertically as well as horizontally and are placed at equal intervals along their respective alignments. The style is known to have come into being not later than the second half of the 6th century B.C. Early examples are collected in c.II. Two chapters are devoted to the Developed Stoichedon Style in Attica, and one chapter to the Style Outside Attica. The concluding chapters cover the Decline of the Style in Attica, Survivals and Summary.

AVI-YONAH, Michael. Abbreviations in Greek inscriptions (the Near East, 200 B.C.–A.D. 1100). Published for the government of Palestine, Jerusalem, by H. Milford. London, Oxford University Press, 1940. 2p., 125p. **GC58**

At head of title: The quarterly of the Department of antiquities in Palestine. Supplement to v. IX.
Contents: Abbreviations in Greek inscriptions.—Kenyon, F. G. Abbreviations and symbols in Greek papyri.—Allen, T. W. Abbreviations in Greek manuscripts.—Von Ostermann, G. F. and Giegengack, A. E. Abbreviations in early Greek printed books.
CR LIV 1940 206–207 Woodward • CW XXXIV 1940–1941 236–237 Brown • JHS LXII 1942 89 Tod
The collection contains 4,335 entries taken from Hellenistic, Roman and Byzantine inscriptions not only of the "Near East" proper (Arabia, Palestine, Syria, Mesopotamia, Persia and Armenia), but also Cyrenaica, Egypt, Nubia, Asia Minor, Crimea, Thrace and the Balkan Peninsula. This is the best available list of abbreviations and supersedes the imperfect lists in Franz, Reinach and Larfeld. It needs to be supplemented with a volume covering the earlier period and extending its geographical limitations to Greece, Thessaly, Macedonia, Italy, Sicily and the Greek islands.

BRADEEN, Donald William and McGREGOR, Malcolm Francis. Studies in fifth-century Attic epigraphy. [1st ed.]. Norman, Published by the University of Oklahoma Press for the University of Cincinnati, [1973]. xvii, 140p., illus. **GC59**

University of Cincinnati: Classical studies; 4.
AC XLIV 1975 321 Hannick • AJPh XCVII 1976 88–99 Meritt • Epigraphica XXXVII 1975 303–305 Lazzarini • Gnomon XLVIII 1976 719–722 Helly • JHS XCVI 1976 261–264 Woodhead
The original project, based on a year's study (1967–1968) in Athens of all 5th century documents, was to produce firm criteria for dating. The appearance of R. Meiggs, "The dating of fifth-century Attic inscriptions," *JHS* LXXXVI (1966), 86–98, persuaded the authors to modify their aim, and here they present six minutely detailed studies, all providing further ammunition for the Mattingly controversy on 5th century dates based on epigraphy.

BUCK, Carl Darling. The Greek dialects; Grammar, selected inscriptions, glossary. Chicago and London, The University of Chicago Press, [1973]. xiii, 373p., charts. **GC60**

Midway reprint. Reprint of the 1955 ed.
CPh LI 1956 209–211 Whatmough • CR n.s. VII 1957 132–135 Jones • Phoenix X 1956 127–128 Poultney

CHARBERT, S. Histoire sommaire des études d'épigraphie grecque. Paris, 1960. 166p. **GC61**

DORNSEIFF, Franz and HANSEN, B. Reverse-lexicon of Greek proper-names = Rückläufiges Wörterbuch der griechischen Eigennamen; with an appendix providing a reverse-index of indigenous names from Asia Minor in their Greek transcriptions by L. Zgusta; [edited by] Al. N. Oikonomides. Chicago, Ares Publishers, 1978. xiv, 340p. **GC62**

Reprint of the 1957 ed. published by Akademie-Verlag (Berlin), with added English title page and prefatory matter, and an appendix by L. Zgusta.

DOW, Sterling. Prytaneis; A study of the inscriptions honoring the Athenian councillors. Athens, Greece, American School of Classical Studies at Athens, 1937. 258p., illus., facsims. **GC63**

Hesperia: Supplement I.
Gnomon XIV 1938 458–462 Kirchner • CR LII 1938 204 Tod • JHS 1938 109–111 • REA XL 1938 331–335 Feye • REG LI 1938 291 Flacelière
An exemplary edition of all the extant Athenian decrees in honor of Prytaneis, which constitute the longest series of homogeneous public decrees from any Greek city. They date from 327–326 B.C. to the age of Augustus. Of the 121 documents in question 62 are wholly new, fruits of the American excavation of the Athenian

agora. An introduction of 30 pages lucidly discusses the main questions and summarizes the author's research. There are excellent indices of great service to prosopography.

DUMBARTON Oaks Bibliographies. Series II: Literature in various Byzantine disciplines 1892–1977, Vol. 1. Epigraphy. Ed. by Jelisaveta Stanojevich Allen and Ihor Sevcenko. Published for the Dumbarton Oaks Center for Byzantine Studies, Washington, D.C., Mansell, 1981. **GC64**

Based on Byzantinische Zeitschrift.

EPIGRAPHISCHE Studien. Köln, Rheinland-Verlag GmbH. Illus., maps. v. 1– , 1967– . **GC65**

Volumes I–IV issued as Beihefte der Bonner Jahrbücher; Bd. 18, 21, 22, 25.

HAINSWORTH, John Byran. Tituli ad dialectos Graecas illustrandas selecti. Leiden, Brill, 1972. **GC66**

Textus minores in usum academicum; v. 44. Fasc. 2. Tituli Dorici et Ionici.
REA LXXVI 1974 172 Pouilloux

HAVELOCK, Eric A. Origins of western literacy: four lectures delivered at the Ontario Institute for Studies in Education, Toronto, March 25–28, 1974. Toronto, Ontario Institute for Studies in Education, 1976. vii, 88p. **GC67**

Phoenix XXX 1976 397–398 Moreux

HOLLEAUX, Maurice. Études d'épigraphie et d'histoire grecques. Paris, E. de Boccard, 1952–1968. 6 v., illus. **GC68**

"Publié avec le concours de l'Académie des inscriptions et belles-lettres (Foundation Salomon Reinach)" edited by Louis Robert.
CRAI 1969 78 Robert • Stud Class XI 1969 368–369 Pippidi • HZ CCX 1970 659–660 Deininger • Epigraphica 1939 83–84 Calderini

JEFFERY, Lilian H. The local scripts of archaic Greece. Oxford, Clarendon Press, [1961]. 461p. **GC69**

Oxford monographs on classical archaeology.
CW LV 1961 88 Dow • CR XII 1962 257–261 Woodward • Gnomon XXXIV 1962 225 Raubitschek
A masterpiece which lists all the archaic inscriptions region by region, preceded in each case by a synthetic study. The book is divided into three parts: I. The origin and transmission of the Greek alphabet (p.1–41); II. Writing in Archaic Greece (p.43–65); III. The local scripts (p.66–373). There are five pages of addenda and corrigenda, four indexes, and the transliteration of those inscriptions illustrated on the plates. The 72 plates illustrate a substantial proportion of the texts discussed. The only criticism is that the work is hard

to use because of the separation of plates, transliteration and description. The date assigned to the origin of the Greek alphabet is ca. 750 B.C. and the place of origin suggested in Al-Mina.

KIRCHHOFF, Adolf. Studien zur Geschichte des griechischen Alphabets. Hildesheim, New York, G. Olms, 1973. vi, 179p., fold. map.   **GC70**

Reprint of the 1887 ed. published by C. Bertelsmann, Gütersloh.

A useful reprint of the 4th edition, 1887, of Kirchhoff, together with the 'blue' and 'red' color-chart, which should be viewed in conjunction with L. H. Jeffery's 'Notes to the Reader' in *Local Scripts of Archaic Greece* (see entry GC 69).

KLIO; Beiträge zur alten Geschichte. Aalen, Scientia Verlag, 1965. [v. 1, 1966–]. Illus., maps (part fold.), plates.   **GC71**

Volume LII (1970) is Günther Klaffenbach zum 80 Geburtstag gewidmet, 512p.

KOERNER, Reinhard. Die Abkürzung der homonymitat im griechischen Inschriften. Berlin, 1961. 137p.   **GC72**

CR XIV 1964 115–116 Forrest • Gnomon XXXVI 1964 428–429 Mihailov
The use of abbreviations in Greek inscriptions whether by signs, numerals, or numeral adverbs, to indicate homonymity of son with father (grandfather, etc.) was introduced in the 2d century B.C., possibly for the first time in Asia Minor. Systematic study of the spread of these abbreviations until they peaked in the 2d and 3rd centuries A.D. has not advanced much beyond the general remarks found in Boeckh and Franz. The present work advances our knowledge and is characterized by caution, good sense, lucidity and tenacity.

LATTIMORE, Richmond Alexander. Themes in Greek and Latin epitaphs. Urbana, University of Illinois Press, 1962. 386p.   **GC73**

JS 1949 187 Daux • RPh XXIII 1949 77–78 Ernout • RA XXXIII 1949 221–222 Picard
Two of these chapters: The Interpretation of Death (p.21–86) and The Underworld, Cult and the Safeguarding of Tombs (p.87–141) were published in 1935 as a doctoral dissertation. Six new chapters are added: Causes of Death, Figures for the Description of Death, Attitude towards Death, Alleviations of Death, Biographical Themes, Pagan Elements in Christian Epitaphs. The subject is not new, as is evident from the elaborate bibliography provided, but the amount of material researched is very broad. Attention is confined to content, with no treatment of form.

MEISTERHANS, Konrad. Grammatik der attischen Inschriften. 3. verm. und verb. aufl. Besorgt von Eduard Schwyzer. Berlin, Weidmann, 1900. xiv, 288p.   **GC74**

Reprint of the 1900 ed.
Now out of date and replaced by L. Threattle's, *The Grammar of Attic Inscriptions.*

MERITT, Benjamin Dean. Epigraphica attica. Cambridge, Mass., Harvard University Press, 1940. 157p., illus., plates.   **GC75**

Martin classical lectures; v. ix.

PFOHL, Gerhard. Inschriften der Griechen: epigraph. Quellen zur Geschichte d. antiken Medizin hrsg. u eingel. 1. Aufl. Darmstadt, Wissenschaftliche Buchgesellschaft, [abt. Verl.], 1977. vi, 221p., illus.   **GC76**

PFOHL, Gerhard. Inschriften der Griechen; Grab-, Weih- und Ehreninschriften. Darmstadt, Wissenschaftliche Buchgesellschaft, 1972. 172p.   **GC77**

JHS XCIV 1976 211–212 Woodhead
A reprinting of three periodical articles, one Festschrift contribution and one extract from a larger work (the first section of A.D. Skiadas' Ἐπι τύμβῳ), with a short introduction by Pfohl. There are four pages of suggestions for further reading and reference. The title is misleading as the main concentration of the essay is on epigram. Many of the contributions are too old to be useful, in spite of the updated bibliographies.

ROBERT, Louis. Études anatoliennes; Recherches sur les inscriptions grecques de l'Asie mineure. Amsterdam, A. M. Hakkert, 1970. 620p., illus., maps, 39 plates.   **GC78**

Études orientales; v. 5. "Réimpression de l'édition Paris, E. de Boccard, 1937."
Stud Class XIII 1971 351 Pippidi

ROBERT, Louis. Opera minora selecta. Épigraphie et antiquités grecques. Amsterdam, A. M. Hakkert, 1969– .   **GC79**

"Articles parus dans des revues ou des volumes de mélanges depuis 1924 jusqu'au début de la dernière decennie."

SCHWYZER, Eduard. Dialectorum Graecarum exempla epigraphica potiora: ('Delectus inscriptionum Graecarum propter dialectum memorabilium' quem primum atque iterum ediderat Paulus Cauer editio tertia renovata). Hildesheim, Olms, 1960. xvi, 463p.   **GC80**

"Unveränderter Nachdruck der Ausgabe Leipzig 1923."
RIGI 1923 313 Ribezzo
A brief but excellent selection.

THREATTLE, L. The grammar of Attic inscriptions. 1. Phonology. Berlin, de Gruyter, 1980. xxv, 737p.   **GC81**

AJPh CII 1981 453–455 Poultney • JHS CII 1982
256–258 Sommerstein
Later volumes will cover morphology and syntax.
This replaces the out-of-date 1900 version by Schwyzer
of the *Grammatik* of Meisterhans. It essentially follows
the order of Meisterhans—script and related matters,
phonology of vowels, phonology of consonants. A beautifully produced book, it is an essential reference tool
for Greek epigraphy, Greek grammar and the editing
of Attic literary texts.

TOD, Marcus Niebuhr. Ancient inscriptions: side-
lights on Greek history. Three lectures on the
light thrown by Greek inscriptions on the life
and thought of the ancient world. Chicago, Ares
Publishers, 1974. 96p.   **GC82**

Reprint of ed. first published in 1932.

TRACY, Stephen V. The lettering of an Athenian
mason. With introd. The Study of Lettering by
Sterling Dow. Princeton, N.J., American School
of Classical Studies at Athens, 1975. xxiii, 134p.,
40 plates.   **GC83**

Hesperia. Supplement 15.
CR n.s. XXVII, 2 1977 251 Jeffery • CW LXX
1976 189–190 Stroud • JHS XCVI 1976 264–265
McGregor • Phoenix XXXI, 2 1977 174–179 Mc-
Gregor

The first major effort to gather the production of
one mason and subject it to exhaustive analysis. Tracy,
following in the footsteps of Dow (*HSCP* LI 1940 111–
124, analysis of 1G 2 2 2336), takes 1G 2 2 1028, a
long ephebic inscription firmly dated to 101/100 B.C.,
as his standard and subjects it letter by letter to comprehensive analysis thus building a profile of the methods
and idiosyncrasies of his mason, here named B. Other
examples of B's work are then sought in Attica, Del-
phoi, and Delos. The scrupulously detailed alphabetical
synopsis of letter-forms is superbly illustrated in the
plates. The book functions as a technical handbook
for training epigraphists to recognize an individual mason's hand and as a social study of a skilled artisan
in Hellenistic Athens. Dow's Introduction "The Study
of Lettering" should be required reading for historians
as well as epigraphists.

WELLES, Charles Bradford. Royal correspondence in the Hellenistic period; A study in Greek
epigraphy. Chicago, Ares Publishers, [1974]. c,
403p., [6] leaves of plates, illus.   **GC84**

Reprint of the 1934 ed.; London. Includes "seventy-
five texts, principally from the Seleucid and Attalid
kingdoms, but also from the Asiatic dependencies of
the Ptolemaic kings of Egypt and the minor kingdoms
of Asia Minor," accompanied by English translations
and historical analyses.

GD   LATIN EPIGRAPHY

Bibliography, Methodology, and Orientation

L'ANNÉE épigraphique; Revue des publications
épigraphiques relatives a l'antiquité romaine.
Paris, Presses Universitaires de France. Illus.
                                                    GD1

Published for the Académie des Inscriptions et
Belles-Lettres. 1889–1961, published as a section of
Revue archéologique entitled: Revue des publications
épigraphiques; 1962– , issued separately as a supplement to Revue archéologique.
Epigraphica XXXVI 1974 276–283 Barbieri • Latomus XXX 1971 854–855 Chevallier • REL LIV 1976
517 Durry • REG LXXXI 1968 586–588 Pouilloux
This is an annotated bibliography. The review was
founded in 1888 by R. Cagnat, succeeded by A. Merlin,
1936–1964. It appears two or three years after the year
covered, e.g., Année 1972, Paris 1975, 295p.

BABCOCK, C. L. "The study of Latin inscriptions." CW LII (1959): 237–244.   **GD2**

A brief non-technical introduction, covering the history of the subject, reproductions, squeezes, collection

of data, measurements, classification (Tituli: Epitaphs,
Honorary, Dedicatory), some means of dating, and
brief bibliography.

CAGNAT, René. Bibliographie critique de l'épigraphie latine. Paris, 1901.   **GD3**

CLAUSS, Manfred. "Ausgewählte Bibliographie
zur lateinischen Epigraphik der Römischen Kaiserzeit (1–3Jh.)." ANRW II,1 (1974): 796–855.
                                                    GD4

An excellently organized bibliography in six sections:
A. Grundlagen; B. Sozialgeschichte, C. Staat, Verwaltung Recht; D. Wirtschaft und Verkehr; E. Kulte;
and F. Tägliches Leben. The first section contains
Nachträge zum CIL, listed by volume number to XIV.
This is followed by Instrumentum domesticum: Am-
phorenstempel, Graffiti und Töpferstempel, Ziegel-
stempel, Inschriften auf Lucernae. Also included in
the first section is a brief section on forgeries. Section
II Einführungen und Sammelwerke includes introductions down to Meyer, 1973, and collections down to
Tondini, 1968.

CLAUSS, Manfred et al. Epigraphische Studien; Sammelband mit Beiträgen. Köln, Rheinland-Verlag, 1976. 227p., [12] leaves of plates, map. **GD5**

Epigraphische Studien; Bd. 11.

DESSAU, H. "Lateinische Epigraphik." Gercke-Norden I (1925): 1–37. **GD6**

GRÜNDEL, Roland. Addenda bibliographica praecipve ad CIL e periodico l'Année épigraphique nominato excerpta. Berlin, De Gruyter, 1965. 70p. **GD7**

Academia Scientiarum Germanica. Corpus Inscriptionum Latinarum. "Schedas in catalogum colligendas curaverunt Ursula Lehmann et Rolandus Gründel." The tables supplement, for the years 1888–1960, the concordances added since 1961 to the indices of l'Année épigraphique.

KAJANTO, Iiro. The Latin cognomina. Helsinki, 1965. 417p. **GD8**

Societas Scientiarum Fennica: Commentationes Humanarum Litterarum; XXXVI, 2.
Gnomon XXXVIII 1966 384–388 De Simone • CJ LXI 1966 285–286 Urdahl • Latomus XXV 1966 163–164 Degrassi • CW LIX 1966 169 Rowland
A fundamental work, the third and largest onomastic study by Kajanto. The material is chiefly drawn from Latin inscriptions but certain literary documents have been consulted for historical names. From an investigation of approx. 133,000 personal names, he has compiled a list of 5,783 cognomina belonging to the Latin West and has determined frequencies in about 75 categories. The most important parts of the book are the Name Lists (p.137–366) and the Index of Names Discussed (p.370–417).

MARICHAL, R. "Paléographie et épigraphie latines." Actes du deuxième Congrés international d'Épigraphie (1953): 180–192. **GD8a**

MERLIN, A. "Vingt ans d'études sur l'épigraphie latine (1923–1943)." Mémorial—Marouzeau, Paris (1943): 481–499. **GD9**

A useful 20-year survey, which emphasizes the utility of epigraphy for political and military history, the institutions of the Republic and the Empire, and the administrative, religious, social and economic life of Rome and the provinces.

PERRET, L. Les inscriptions romaines; Bibliographie pratique. Paris, 1924. **GD10**

REYNOLDS, Joyce M. "Epigraphy, Latin." OCD[2]: 397–399. **GD11**

The study of Latin texts inscribed on durable objects, usually of stone or bronze, since it is concerned both with the form of the inscriptions and their content, impinges on many other fields: e.g., paleography, phi-

lology, history, law, religion. The texts may be formal documents, e.g., laws, treaties, legal contracts, wills or records of individuals and their activities (tituli). Epitaphs form the largest group, the tituli of men in public life present the administrative personnel of Rome, provide lists of the offices and achievements of individuals. Laudatory inscriptions indicate the honors and titles accorded to, the qualities admired in, public men at different periods. Local government, military affairs, religious affairs, social developments and economic life are all reflected in some of the inscriptions. The select bibliography includes items that appeared as late as 1965/1966.

REYNOLDS, Joyce. "Inscriptions and Roman Studies 1910–1960." JRS L (1960): 204–209. **GD12**

Continued in "Roman Epigraphy 1961–1965," *JRS* LVI (1966), 116–121; "Roman Inscriptions 1966–1970," *JRS* LXI (1971), 136–152, "Roman Inscriptions 1971–1975," *JRS* LXVI (1976), 174–199.
Annotated bibliographies well chosen and presented. An excellent point of entry to current research.

Collections, Editions

BRACCO, Vittorio, ed. Inscriptions Italiae; Academiae Italicae consociatae ediderunt. Volume III, Regio III, fasc. 1. Roma, Instituto Poligrafico dello Stato, 1974. xlvi, 208p. **GD13**

Arctos X 1976 143–145 Kajanto • RFIC CIV 1976 227–232 Russi
Bracco is an indefatigable worker in Lucanian epigraphy and topography. This work contains 288 inscriptions, including many additions to *CIL* X.

BRUNS, Carl Georg et al., eds. Fontes iuris romani antiqui. Post curas Theodor Mommsen editionibus quintae et sextae adhibitas septimum edidit Otto Gradenwitz. Aalen, Scientia Verlag, 1969. 2 v. in 1. **GD14**

"2. Neudruck der Ausgabe Tübingen 1909."

BÜCHELER, Franz. Carmina latina epigraphica. Lipsiae, in aedibvs B. G. Tevbneri, 1895–1897. 2 v. **GD15**

His Anthologia latina; v. 2.

BURN, Andrew Robert. The Romans in Britain; An anthology of inscriptions. [2d ed.] Columbia, University of South Carolina Press, [1969]. xiii, 193p., illus. **GD16**

CR XX 1970 412 Salway • History LV 1970 93–94 Birley • REA LXXI 1969 534 Nony
First produced in 1932, this new edition takes into account the publication of Collingwood's *Roman Inscriptions of Britain,* and should, perhaps, be used in close conjunction with the latter, in which the doubtful readings inspire more confidence. The new edition has 239 entries as against 201 in the first, many of them

new discoveries. This is a good short introduction to the epigraphy of Roman Britain, readable and entertaining.

COLLINGWOOD, Robin George and WRIGHT, R. P. The Roman inscriptions of Britain. Oxford, Clarendon Press, 1965– .   **GD17**

> v. 1 Inscriptions on stone; v. 2. Instrumentum domesticum.
>
> CR XVI 1966 377–379 Burn • JRS LVI 1966 226–231 Birley • CW LIX 1966 320 Gordon • REL XLIII 1965 677 Durry
>
> This constitutes the long-awaited replacement of Huebner's v. VII of *CIL* (1873), with Haverfield's supplements in *Ephemeris Epigraphica* VIII and IX. Collingwood died in 1943 and Wright, *insigni pietate,* keeps his name first on the title page, though most of the commentary and many of the superb drawings are Wright's own. Volume I is called Inscriptions on Stone and collects in a single volume the bulk of the most important inscriptions (2,300) found in Britain up to 1954. Volume II, *Instrumentum Domesticum* (graffiti and other inscriptions on pottery, lead pigs, ingots, etc.) and classified indices complete a work which gives us an invaluable conspectus of evidence for Roman Britain. The work is equally skillful in its drawings, readings of the text, commentary and translations. New finds are reported in Wright, R. P. et al., "Roman Britain in 1974, II: Inscriptions," *Britannia* VI (1975), 284–294.

CORPUS inscriptionum Latinarum; Consilio et auctoritate Academiae litterarum regiae borussicae editum. Berolini, Apvd Georgivm Reimervm, 1863– .   **GD18**

DEGRASSI, Attilio. Inscriptiones latinae liberae rei publicae. [2. ed.] Firenze, La Nuova Italia, [1963–1965, 1972 printing]. 2 v.   **GD19**

> Biblioteca di studi superiori; 23, 40. Storia antica ed epigrafia; v. 2, 1st ed., 1963.
>
> CW LII 1958 18 Benario • Kratylos VI 1961 205 Walser
>
> A first-rate collection of Republican inscriptions, particularly useful for its Additamenta to Diehls, *Altlateinische Inschriften,* and the discussion in the footnotes of the historical significance and problems, with reference to pertinent literature, ancient and modern.

DE ROSALIA, Antonino. Iscrizioni latine arcaiche. Palermo, Palumbo, [1972]. 150p.   **GD20**

> An edition of 56 archaic texts (p.29–60), with an introduction (p.7–23), and Italian translation and notes printed apart from the text (p.63–143). There is a concordance with CIL I² only, though a brief bibliography mentions Degrassi, Ernout, Pisani and Warmington.

DESSAU, Hermann. Inscriptiones latinae selectae. Editio tertia lucis ope expressa. Berolini, Apud Weidmannos, 1962. 1st ed. 1892–1916. 3 v. in 5.   **GD21**

Volume I. Monumenta historica liberae rei publicae. Tituli imperatorum domusque imperatoriae. Tituli regum et principum nationum exterarum. Tituli virorum et mulierum ordinis senatorii. Tituli virorum dignitatis equestris. Tituli procuratorum et ministrorum domus Augustae condicionis libertinae et servilis. Tituli apparitorum et servorum publicorum. Tituli nonnulli ius civitatis illustrantes. Tituli militares. Tituli virorum nonnullorum in litteris clarorum. Volume II. pars 1. Tituli sacri et sacerdotum. Tituli pertinentes ad Oudos. Tituli operum locorumque publicorum, termini, tituli nonnulli aediticorum privatorum. Tituli municipales. pars 2. Tituli collegiorum. Tituli ministrorum vitae privatae, opificum, artiticum. Tituli sepulcrales. Tituli instrumenti domestici. Analecta varia. Appendix titulorum graecorum. Volume III. pars 1–2. Indices.

GEIST, Hieronymus. Pompeianische Wandinschriften. 400 Originaltexte mit Übersetzung und Angabe des Fundortes. 2. erweiterte Aufl. unter Mitwirkung von Werner Krenkel. München, E. Heimeran, [1960]. 111p., map (on lining paper).   **GD22**

> Tusculum-Bücherei.
>
> AAHG XIV 1961 105 Völk1 • CW LIV 1961 298 McKay
>
> A useful collection of painted inscriptions and graffiti from Pompeian walls. The collection is divided into sections: A. Politics (66), B. Gladiatorial games (30), C. General Notices (9), D. Proper Names (19), E. Greetings and other expressions (68), F. Love Notices (75), G. Eating, Drinking, Amusement (32), H. Literary Notices (36), I. Family Notices, household records (55).

GEIST, Hieronymus. Römische Grabinschriften; Gesammelt und ins Deutsche Übertragen, betreut von Gerhard Pfohl. [1. Aufl.] München, E. Heimeran, [1969]. 252p.   **GD23**

> Tusculum-Bücherei.
>
> Latomus XXX 1971 855 Sanders
>
> Geist died in 1960 and Pfohl made the minimum changes in this bilingual edition of 662 inscriptions which is in the usual Tusculum-Bücherei format. Almost all are in Latin (10 in Greek), less than 10 per cent are of Christian origin, and 40 per cent metrical. A sufficiently representative selection of the 100,000 surviving epitaphs. The texts are grouped to illustrate, e.g., formulaic beginnings or endings, family relationships, master/slave, patronus/libertus, social classes, animals, texts witnessing to conceptions of life and death, tragic deaths, revolts against death, consolation, tomb violation. The translations are generally reliable, sometimes as moving as the originals. Not enough attention is paid to the monumental side of the inscriptions, the texts being seen only as texts. There is an excellent bibliography (p.236–248).

GIACCHERO, Marta, ed. Edictum Diocletiani et collegarum de pretiis rerum venalium; In integrum fere restitutum e latinis graecisque fragmentis. Genova, Istituto di storia antica e scienze ausiliarie, 1974– . Illus.   **GD24**

1. Edictum. 2. Imagines.
EHR XCI 1976 619–620 Frere • LEC XLIV 1976 289 Wankenne • RPh L 1976 149–151 André
This famous Edict was reconstructed by Mommsen in 1893 from 35 fragments. Many additional fragments since discovered have improved our knowledge, as also the discovery of the related 301 Aphrodisias inscription on monetary reform. The present edition, based on 132 fragments, gives us a long introduction, the text in Latin and Greek and in Italian translation, and the Aphrodisiac inscription in an appendix. A third volume is promised, providing an historical, economic and social study.

RIESE, Alexander. Das rheinische Germanien in den antiken Inschriften. Auf Veranlassung der römisch-germanischen Kommission des kaiserlich deutschen archälogischen Instituts. Nachdruck der 1. Aufl. Leipzig-Berlin, 1914. Groningen, Bouma's Boekhuis, 1968. xiii, 484p.
GD25

CPh XI 1916 117 Hoeing • CR XXVIII 1914 255 Cheesman
Fruit of a life-time's work of collecting, analyzing and discussing all the material pertaining to the history and civilization of the Rhine country under Roman control. Some 4,700 inscriptions are collected and divided into seven classes, following for the most part a chronolgical order.

RUSHFORTH, Gordon McNeil. Latin historical inscriptions; Illustrating the history of the early empire. 2d ed. Chicago, Ares, 1976. xxx, 144p.
GD26

"Exact reprint of the second edition, London, 1930."
CJ XXVI 1931 383–384 De Witt • CR XLV 1931 40 Cary • JRS XX 1930 97–98 Mattingly
Essentially a re-issue of the attractive and valuable first edition, 1893. There are, of course, minor additions and corrections. The texts are conveniently grouped under large subject headings, the commentary is ample and well documented, and there are four useful indices. The bibliography has been slightly updated. Not as comprehensive as Egbert or Wilhemsen.

THYLANDER, Hilding. Inscriptions du Port d'Ostie. Lund, Gleerup, 1951–1952. 2 v.
GD27

Skrifter utg, av Svenska institutet i Rom, 8j, IV: 1–2 1. Texte. 2. Planches.
CW XLVI 1953 186 Lewis • RPh XXVII 1953 235–236 Bloch • Latomus XII 1953 504–505 Heurgon
One of the most important discoveries between the two wars was that of the necropolis of the port created by Trajan north of the ancient Ostia. Thylander's work, the product of 15 years' toil, gives the definitive edition of the inscriptions found to date at Ostia, including nearly 400 from the necropolis, and more than 400

found on the other side of Trajan's canal. Detailed description and bibliography accompany each, and there are explanatory notes to many texts, and translations to almost all. There is also a concordance for the inscriptions in *CIL* XIV and XV, and highly detailed indices. The fascicle of 125 plates has splendidly clear photographs of some 300 of the inscriptions.

WARMINGTON, Eric Herbert. Remains of Old Latin. Cambridge, Mass., Harvard University Press, 1961–1967, 1935. 4 v.   **GD28**

CPh 1942 337–339 Whatmough • JRS 1944 158–159 Fränkel • CW XXXV 1941–1942 7 Hammond
Vol. IV, *Archaic Inscriptions,* was first published in 1940 and reprinted several times. See also *Inscriptions of the Roman Empire, A.D. 14–117,* annotated and translated from the Latin by E. H. Warmington, ed. by S. J. Miller, Herts., London Association of Classical Teachers, 1971. 60p.

Inscriptions

CALABI LIMENTANI, Ida. Epigrafia latina. Con un appendice bibliografica di Attilio Degrassi. 3 ed. Milano, Istituto Editoriale Cisalpinola Goliardica, 1974. 550p., 6 leaves of plates, illus.   **GD29**

REL XLIX 1971 490–499 Durry • Gnomon XLIII 1971 97–99 Alföldy
More useful for the already initiated than for beginning students of epigraphy, this is a rewriting of the author's earlier *L'uso storiografico delle iscrizioni latine* (1953). More than 100 pages are devoted to a history of epigraphy, followed by less than 25 devoted to *cursus* and *onomastica.* The different types of inscriptions are then studied by category. All the examples are Roman, and are well edited and illustrated. There is an excellent bibliographical appendix by A. Degrassi (p.419–453).

CORSO Di Epigrafia Latina. Universita delli studi di Urbino, anno academica 1966–1967, 1968.   **GD30**

University class notes reproduced typographically, divided into seven sections: Parte Generale (p.5–28), Cursus Honorum (p.29–42), Epigrafi (p.43–50), Tituliacta Militaria (p.51–76), Instrumentum Domesticum (p.77–84), Epigrafi Electorali (p.85–100), Alcuni Antiche Iscrizioni Cristiane (p.101–106).

EGBERT, James Chidester. Introduction to the study of Latin inscriptions. Rev. ed. with supplement. New York, American Book Company, 1923. vii, 480p., illus.   **GD31**

Old but still useful. Two preliminary chapters on the Latin alphabet (historical and morphological) and a chapter on Roman numerals make up part I. Part II has three chapters: The Roman Name, Names and Titles of the Emperors and Official Titles. Part III also has three chapters: Tituli, Documents, and Restoration and Dating of the Inscriptions. There is a good table of abbreviations.

GORDON, Arthur E. Illustrated Introduction to Latin Epigraphy. Berkeley, University of California Press, 1983. xxvi, 264p., 100 plates.

GD31a

GORDON, Arthur Ernest. Supralineate abbreviations in Latin inscriptions. Milano, Cisalpino-Goliardica, 1977. 59–132p.   **GD32**

Reprint of the 1948 ed. published by University of California Press, Berkeley, and issued as *University of California Publications in Classical Archaeology* II, 3.

GORDON, Joyce Anna (Stiefbold) and GORDON, Arthur E. Contributions to the paleography of Latin inscriptions. Milano, Cisalpino-Goliardica, 1977. xii, 65–241p., illus.   **GD33**

Reprint of the 1957 ed. published by the University of California Press, Berkeley. "An outgrowth of . . . [the authors'] Album of dated Latin inscriptions (Part I)."
AJPh LXXXI 1960 189–197 Olivier • CW LI 1958 242 Brown • AC XXVII 1958 265–267 Van't Dack • REL XXXVI 1958 292–296 Marichal
This work is in two parts: I. A study of the different categories of writing, and II. an analysis of such particulars as *apices*, the abbreviation *cos*, guiding lines for the stonecutter, ligatures, abbreviation, punctuation, etc. This is the first fresh and exhaustive attempt since Huebner's *Exempla* (1885), to come to grips with the problems of the paleography of Roman inscriptions.

LINDSAY, Wallace Martin. Handbook of Latin inscriptions illustrating the history of the language. Amsterdam, J. C. Gieben, 1970. 134p.
GD34

Reprint of the Boston, Allyn and Bacon, 1897 ed.

MEYER, Ernst. Einführung in die Lateinische Epigraphik. Darmstadt, Wissenschaftliche Buchgesellschaft, 1973. vi, 147p.   **GD35**

REL LI 1973 472 Durry • JRS LXIV 1974 243 Wright • Aegyptus LIV 1974 224–225 Geraci • AAHG XXX, 1977 76–80 Weber • Gnomon XLVIII 1976 176–179 Limentani
An excellent short introduction, both for Republican and Imperial times. The material is arranged in 6 chapters, beginning with an outline of the history of Latin epigraphy. Chapter 2 deals with the materials used for inscriptions and the techniques of craftsmen. Chapter 3 is devoted to the development of the alphabet and other symbols. The different types of inscriptions are classified under 11 headings in c.4. Chapter 5 deals with abbreviations and personal names, and c.6 lays down rules for publicity and dating inscriptions. Appendix 1 is devoted to a list of abbreviations in constant usage and Appendix 2 gives an up-to-date bibliography, classified under 12 headings (p.126–147). Each section has its own bibliography as well.

OLCOTT, George N. Thesaurus linguae latinae epigraphicae; A dictionary of the Latin inscrip-

tions. Rome, Loescher & Co. (Bretschneider & Regenberg), 1904– .   **GD36**

RICCI, Serafino. Epigrafia Latina; Trattato elementare con esercizi prattici e facsimili illustrativi. Con 65 Tavole. Milano, U. Hoepli, 1898. xxxii, 447p., illus.   **GD37**

Manuali Hoepli.

SANDYS, John Edwin, Sir. Latin epigraphy; An introduction to the study of Latin inscriptions. 2d ed. rev. by S. G. Campbell. Chicago, Ares Publishers, 1974. xxiii, 324p., illus.   **GD38**

Reprint of the 1927 ed. published by the University Press, Cambridge, Eng.
AJPh XLI 1920 299–300 Frank • JRS IX 1919 103–104 St. Jones • CR XXXV 1921 73–75 Calder • Gnomon III 1927 715–721 Wickert
Designed to be used with Dessau and with Diehl's collection of facsimiles, this is the first introduction to classical Latin epigraphy published in England. It is an expansion of the chapter in *Companion to Latin studies*. The first chapter surveys references to inscriptions in classical authors, an unusual and welcome feature. The exposition of the epigraphical alphabet is admirably illustrated. There are six chapters on the different categories of inscriptions, *tituli* and documentary inscriptions, *tituli* being subdivided into epitaphs, dedications, honorary inscriptions, inscriptions on public works, inscriptions on portable objects. There are chapters on language and style, and on restoration and criticism. Six appendices deal with names, officials, emperors, six historical inscriptions, including the Monumentum Ancyranum, 60 inscriptions exemplifying abbreviated phrases, and abbreviations.

SUSINI, Giancarlo. The Roman stonecutter; An introduction to Latin epigraphy. Totowa, N.J., Rowman, 1973. ix, 84p., illus.   **GD39**

Trans. of *Il lapicida romano*.
Epigraphica XXVII 1965 174–175 Soffredi • CR XXVI 1976 297–298 Reynolds • G&R XXI 1974 210 Wilkes • LEC XLII 1974 455–456 Stenuit • REL LI 1973 472–474 Chevallier
A translation of the author's *Il lapicida romano, introduzione all epigrafia latina* (Rome, 1966). An admirable little book in which eight brief chapters deal with the basic questions, describing engraving; workers and workshops, tools and types of stone, preparations of surfaces and errors and their causes. This is an archaeology of the inscriptions written with great powers of observation and intuition, as E. Badian notes in the introduction; he takes us on a fascinating journey of exploration into the realms of technology, psychology and *Kulturgeschichte,* for which this study, rightly used, provides the key.

THYLANDER, Hilding. Étude sur l'épigraphie latine; Date des inscriptions, noms et dénominion latine, noms et origine des personnes. Lund, C. W. K. Gleerup, 1952. xvi, 191p., fold. plans.
GD40

Skrifter Utg, av Svenska Institutet i Rom, ser, in 8; 5.

CW XLVI 1953 186 Lewis • RPh XXXVII 1953 237 Bloch • Latomus XII 1953 504–505 Heurgon

A doctoral dissertation which discusses paleographic, archaeological, artistic and stylistic clues and criteria for the dating of Latin inscriptions; the evolution in Latin nomenclature; and nomina and cognomina as evidences of the bearers' origins. The conclusions are based on the author's separate edition *Inscriptions du port d'Ostie*. These inscriptions are for the most part funerary and for that reason all the more difficult to date. A painstaking and illuminating study.

WILLEMSEN, Heinrich. Lateinische Inschriften für den Gebrauch in Schulunterricht. 3. Unveränd. Aufl. Zürich, Weidmannsche verlagsbuchhandlung, 1965. 124p. **GD41**

Reprint of the 2d ed., 1933.
RPh 1916 275 • WKPh 1915 1251 Stein

Facsimiles

DEGRASSI, Attilio. Inscriptiones latinae liberae rei publicae; Imagines. Berlin, De Gruyter, 1965. **GD42**

CR IX 1959 156–158, CR XX 1970 78–80 Reynolds • AC XXXIX 1970 289 Flam-Zuckermann • Epigraphica XXIX 1967 183–184 Calderini

A monumental and luxurious album to illustrate the author's *Inscriptiones latinae liberae rei publicae* (Florence, 1957–1963). The 401 photographs are a delight to the eye, and the work is equally valuable to epigraphists, paleographers and linguists.

DIEHL, E. Inscriptiones latinae selectae; Tabulae in usum scholarum. Bonn, A. Marcus, 1912. **GD43**

BBG 1914 399 Rehm • JRS III 1913 153–154 Haverfield • MPh 1918 156 Bierma

Intended to assist the teaching of Roman epigraphy on its more technical and paleographical side. Good clear plates of materials drawn almost entirely from Rome and its neighborhood, divided into five main sections: I. Early Items (the Black Stone), Dedications from the Districts of Italy, The Bacchanal Decree of 186 B.C.; II. Extracts from the Inscription of the Ludi Saeculares, Portions of the Praenestine Fasti, etc.; III. Twelve Plates from the Galleries of the Vatican; IV. Christian Inscriptions of Various Dates; and V. Some Facsimiles to Show the Various Forms of Cursive Writing.

GORDON, Arthur Ernest. Album of dated Latin inscriptions. Berkeley, University of California Press, 4 v. **GD44**

Gnomon XXXVII 1965 799–804 Marcillet-Jaubert • AJPh LXXXI 1960 189–197 Olivier • CR XX 1970 80–82 Reynolds • Phoenix XIII 1959 13–22 Bagnani • REL XLIII 1965 136–143 Pflaum

The 67 plates of v. I give with unusual clarity and detail one or more views of the whole or parts of 159 inscriptions, of which 129½ have been published in the Corpus, 23½ have been published elsewhere, and 6 are apparently here published for the first time. In the companion volumes the texts are transcribed and the inscriptions are minutely described, with reports of the maximum and minimum height of letters in each line, measurements of each abnormal letter, and virtually exhaustive commentary. The collection is limited to inscriptions on stone found in or near the city of Rome. It is a truly monumental achievement.

HÜBNER, Emil. Exempla scripturae epigraphicae Latinae, a Caesaris dictatoris morte ad aetatem Iustiniani; Consilio et authoritate Academiae Litterarum Regiae Borussicae edidit Aemilius Hübner. Berolini, Apud G. Reimerum, 1885. 1p., [v]-lxxxiv, 458p., illus. **GD45**

Corporis inscriptionum Latinarum, auctarium.
See Prolegomena (XIII-LXXXIV) for paleographical remarks.

LAUFFER, Siegfried. Diokletians Preisedikt. [Berlin, W. de Gruyter], 1971. viii, 361p., 24 plates. **GD46**

Texte und Kommentare; eine Altertumswissenschaftliche Reihe.

REL XLVIII 1970 664–668 Chastagnol • Latomus XXXI 1972 905–907 Wild • AC XLI 1972 372–374 Marcillet-Jaubert • CR XXV 1975 276–279 Crawford

Diocletian's edict on maximum prices 301 A.D. is one of the most curious, but important, documents of late antiquity. Lauffer succeeds in capturing all the vagaries of its epigraphic tradition, combining full publication of all the fragments found since the critical edition of Mommsen and Blümmer in 1893, with a recension of the fragments known to Mommsen. Fifty-nine out of a total of 126 fragments have been found since 1940, and the finds continue. This edition is the necessary starting point for a fresh full-scale commentary, with its comprehensive bibliography and useful concordances and metrology. Such a commentary will require teamwork from scholars in many disciplines, under the direction, perhaps, of J. Bingen. See also Erim and Reynolds, *JRS* LXIII (1973), 99–110.

PALMER, Robert E. A. The king and the comitium; A study of Rome's oldest public document. Wiesbaden, F. Steiner, 1969. 53p., plates. **GD47**

Historia, Einzelschriften; Heft 11.

REL XLVIII 1970 605–607 Heurgon • Gnomon XLIII 1971 364–369 Richard • JRS LXII 1972 177–178 Drummond

The Lapis Niger was discovered in 1899 and its interpretation has been a matter of continuing controversy. Palmer's interpretation is that we have here a *lex satura*, providing for penalties against the violation of a grove which once stood in the comitium, for the assignment of a herald and wagon to the Rex Sacrorum for processions, and for the punishment of those seen working during such a procession.

RITSCHL, Friedrich Wilhelm. Priscae Latinitatis monumenta epigraphica; Ad archetyporum fidem exempis lithographis repraesentata. Berlin, W. de Gruyter, 1968. vii, 127p., 96 plates (part double, in port.), illus., facsims.   **GD48**

> Corpus Inscriptionum Latinarum: voluminis primi, tabulae lithographae.
> See also *Priscae Latinitatis epigraphicae supplementa quinque,* 1970.

RUGGIERO, Ettore de. Dizionario epigrafico di antichità Romane. Roma, L. Pasqualucci, 1895–19– . Roma, "L'Erma," 1961.   **GD49**

> "Ristampa anastatica invariata autorizzata dall' Instituto Italiano per la Storia Antica."
> Epigraphica VIII 1946 97–98 Calderini
> Ruggiero initiated this dictionary in 1886 to provide *un repertorio epigrafico per lo studio della antichita and un indice ragionato del corpus.*

Manuals

BLOCH, Raymond. L'Épigraphie Latine. 4e édition mise à jour. Paris, Presses universitaires de France, 1969. 112p., facsims.   **GD50**

> Que sais-je? No. 534.
> CR n.s. IV 1954 156–157 Woodhead • JRS XLIII 1953 236 Wright • Latomus XIII 1954 249–251 Etienne
> An excellent short summary of the methods used in recording inscriptions (Latin alphabet, personal names, *cursus honorum,* imperial titles), the categories of inscriptions, with translated examples, and updated bibliographies. This is a pocket-sized introduction to epigraphy. Useful perhaps to the tourist and best used as an introduction to Cagnat, *Cours d'épigraphie latine.*

BRACCESI, Lorenzo. Appunti di epigrafia latina. Bologne, Patron, 1968. 108p.   **GD51**

> Much the same as Zanchi's elementary introduction. A brief bibliographical note at the end mentions both Susini and Calabri Limentani. The central chapter VI is on the classification of inscriptions, dividing them, with brief examples, into seven categories.

CAGNAT, René Louis V. Cours d'épigraphie latine. 4. ed., revue et augmentée. Roma, L'Erma de Bretschneider, 1976. xvii, 504p., 28 leaves of plates, illus., facsims.   **GD52**

> "III edizione anastatica": originally publ. Paris, Fontemoing, 1914.
> CR XXVIII 1914 107–08 F. H. • REA 1914 126 Jullian • WKPh 1919 102–108, 126–131, 153–156 Bang
> A classic manual, well-arranged and presented, based on the conviction that a knowledge of epigraphy is

an essential element in a good classical education. "Ce n'est, à vrai dire, que l'un des éléments, mais c'est un élément essentiel de la philologie l'une des sources auxquelles doit puiser quiconque veut connaître la religion, les lois, l'histoire politique, la vie privée et le langue des anciens." (p.xiv).

Part I (p.1–34) deals with the alphabets used in Roman inscriptions (archaic, monumental, cursive). The different forms of individual letters are noted, ligatures are illustrated, accents and letter numerals.

Part II (p.35–250) covers Names, filiation, tribe, etc., Cursus honorum, imperial names and titles.

Part III (p.251–378) deals with the different classes of inscriptions in six sections, with a complementary chapter on restoration of inscriptions. There is an excellent list of abbreviations in an appendix (p.408–473). Unfailing lucidity and real learning make this work extraordinarily useful and durable. See also Cagnat, René, "Inscriptions," *Dar Sag* III: 528–545.

GROSSI-GONDI, Felice. Trattato di epigrafia cristiana: Latina e Greca del mondo romano occidentale. Roma, Università Gregoriana, 1920. x, 511p., illus.   **GD53**

> I Monumenti cristiani dei primi sei secoli.

KAUFMANN, Carl Maria. Handbuch der altchristlichen Epigraphik. Freiburg im Breisgau, St. Louis, Mo., Herder, 1917. [xvi], 514p., illus.   **GD54**

> AB XXXVIII 187 Delehaye • ByJ 1920 203–213 Larfeld • DLZ 1924 488–498 Stuhlfanth

MARUCCHI, Orazio. Christian epigraphy: An elementary treatise, with a collection of ancient Christian inscriptions, mainly of Roman origin by Orazio Marucchi; trans. by J. Armine Willis. Chicago, Ares Publishers, 1974. xii, 460p., 30 leaves of plates, illus.   **GD55**

> Translation of Epigrafia cristiana.
> Reprint of the 1912 ed. published by the University Press, Cambridge.

VOLKMANN, H. Res gestae divi Augusti. Das Monumentum Ancyranum, hrsg, und erklärt von Hans Volkmann. Berlin, De Gruyter, 1957. 63p.   **GD56**

> Kleine Texte für Vorlesungen und Übungen, 29–30.

ZANCHI, G. Corso di epigrafia latina. Urbino, Università degli studi di Urbino, Anno Accademico 1966–1967, 1968.   **GD57**

> University class-notes reproduced typographically. Divided in seven sections: I. Parte generale 5–28; II. Cursus honorum 29–42; III. Epigrafi 43–50; IV. Tituli-Acta Militaria 51–76; V. Instrumentum Domesticum 77–84; VI. Epigrafi Elettorali 85–100; VII. Alcuni antiche iscrizioni cristiane 101–106.

Political and Cultural History

HA ANCIENT GEOGRAPHY AND TOPOGRAPHY

ASHBY, Thomas. The Roman Campagna in classical times. London, Benn, 1927. New York, Barnes & Noble, 1970. x, 256p., 48 plates.

HA1

RA 1927 316 Reinach • Athenaeum 1928 274–279 Fraccaro • JRS XVIII 1928 112–113 Salmon

The work of one who has travelled the terrain on foot again and again over thirty years, at once authoritative and conscientiously accurate with a systematic study of the various roads and accurate references to ancient and modern authors.

AUJAC, Germaine. La géographie dans le monde antique. Paris, P.U.F., 1975. 128p., 14 fig.

HA2

(Que-sais-je, no. 1598).

REG LXXXIX 1976 115–116 Chevallier

Within the *Que-sais-je* format, this is a succinct and rapid survey of developments from Anaximander, the first cartographer, through the Milesian and Ionian scholars and such study centers as Alexandria and Rhodes, stopping short of Ptolemy.

BALADIÉ, R. Le Péloponnèse de Strabon: Étude de géographie historique. Paris, Les Belles Lettres, 1980. xxiii, 398p., 44 plates. **HA3**

CR XCVI 1982 22–23 Levi

A thorough study of Strabo's treatment of the Peloponnese in Book VIII and elsewhere, and an assessment of his position as a geographer, with a discussion of the physical geography and the social and economic history of the region under the Romans.

BALL, John. Egypt in the classical geographers. Cairo, Government Press, 1942. vi, 203p., 8 plates. **HA4**

JHS LXIII 1943 125–126 Wainwright • CR 1944 28–29 Myres

The posthumous work of a mathematician engaged in the survey of Egypt, with assistance from various classical scholars and Egyptologists. Based on ancient authors from Herodotus to George of Cyprus, c. 606 A.D.

BENGTSON, Hermann and MILOJČIČ, Vladimir. Grosser Historischer Weltatlas. 1. Vorgeschichte und Altertum: 1. Kartenwerk, 2. Erläutarung. Munich, Bayerischer Schulbuch Verlag, 1953– . **HA5**

AC XXXIII 1954 240 Salmon • Gnomon XLVII 1975 807–809 Martin

Magnificent colored maps in quarto format. Milojčič oversees *Vorgeschichte*, while Bengtson does *Altertum* and the index of geographical names at the end of Volume 1. One of the many interesting new features: in pl. 25 a transparent plan of imperial Rome is superimposed on a map of contemporary Rome. The second volume contains elaborate bibliographies and citations of ancient authors.

CARY, Max. The Geographic Background of Greek and Roman History. Oxford, Oxford University Press, 1949. vi, 331p. **HA6**

JRS XXXIX 1949 162–163 Sherwin-White • REL 1949 352–353 Piganiol • Gnomon XXIII 1951 208–210 Vogt

A work which attempts too much in too little space in which the European area fares best and the Middle Eastern worst.

CARY, Max and WARMINGTON, E. H. The Ancient Explorers. London, Methuen, 1929. 270p., 15 maps. **HA7**

CR XLIV 1930 226 Charlesworth

An enjoyable synthesis of ancient texts and new interpretations, with full coverage of exploration and adventure stories from antiquity. A useful collection, critically assessed, of much arcane materials hitherto buried in obscure German or French pamphlets.

CASSON, Lionel. Travel in the ancient world. London, Allen and Unwin, 1974. 384p., 4 maps, 20 plates.   **HA8**

CR XXVI 1976 300 Ogilvie

A most comprehensive account of travelling conditions in antiquity, making fullest use of literary and archaeological sources. Rome is better served than Greece. See also L. Casson, *Ships and Seamanship in the Ancient World,* 1971, and *The Ancient Mariners,* 1959.

CHEVALLIER, Raymond. Roman roads. Trans. by N. H. Field. London, Batsford, 1976. 272p., illus.   **HA9**

Antiquity L 1976 156–157 Phillips • CW LXX 1977 486–487 Casson

Attempts too much in introducing readers to all phases of Roman roads. Chapters deal with evidence from literature, inscriptions, archaeological remains, milestones, but not so much a structural presentation as a conjuring of bits of information.

CRAMER, John Anthony. Geographical and historical description of Asia Minor; with a map. Oxford, Oxford University Press, 1832. Rev. ed. 2 v. in 1, 1971.   **HA10**

FINLEY, M. I., ed. Atlas of classical archaeology. Maps and plans by John Flower. London, Chatto & Windus, 1977. 256p., illus., maps, plans.   **HA11**

TLS LXXVI 1977 1300 Ward-Perkins • BIAL XV 1978 257–258 Walker

Every region colonized by the Greeks and Romans is covered in this survey. Arranged regionally, there is a general introduction to the region followed by maps that show the major sites and a history and description of each site. Included are chronological tables, list of Roman emperors, and a glossary.

FRASER, P. M. Ptolemaic Alexandria. I: Text; II: Notes; III: Indexes. Oxford, Clarendon Press, 1973. xvi, 812p.; xiv, 1116p.; 157p.   **HA12**

CW LXVIII 1975 450–452 Badian • RBPh LIII 1975 913–919 Peremans

As complete a history as the evidence admits for the first three centuries of what was at one time the greatest city in the ancient world. The first volume tells the story in over 800 pages of text; the second, in over 1100 pages, not only cites all the known evidence but where possible usually quotes it in full. The third volume contains seven full indices, but the mass of modern works cited is not collected in any bibliography.

Part I ("The Framework") discusses the foundation and topography, the population and its organization, relations of Kings and cities, trade, religion.

Part II ("The Achievement") discusses the great institutions of the Libraries and the Museum, Alexandrian science, scholarship, philosophy and literature, especially Callimachus.

GEYER, P., BIELER, L., WEBER, R. et al. Itineraria et alia geographica. Turnhout, Brepols, 1965. 2 v., xxiv, 863p.   **HA13**

Corpus Christianorum, series latina, 175–176.

RB LXXVI 1966 363 Verbraken • NRTh LXXXIX 1967 1113 Martin

Includes texts of such famous journeys to Jerusalem as that of Egeria, the *de locis sanctis* of Adamnan and of Bede, six Itineraria Romana, and valuable indices.

GROLLENBERG, Lucas H. Atlas of the Bible. Eng. trans. by Reid, J. M. H. and Rowley, H. H. London, Nelson, 1956. 165p., 400 plates, 35 maps.   **HA14**

Biblica XXXIX 1958 North

GÜNGERICH, R. Die Küstenbeschreibung in der griechische Literatur. Münster i. Westfalia, 1950.   **HA15**

Important for the Periploi.

HAMMOND, N. G. L. Atlas of the Greek and Roman world in antiquity. Park Ridge, New Jersey, Noyes Press, 1981. viii, 56p., 46 maps.   **HA16**

CR XXXII 1982 222–225 Usher

A sumptuous production, up-to-date, detailed and scholarly, a worthy heir to John Murray's *Handy Classical Maps.* The range is the Greek and Roman world from the Neolithic Age to the sixth century, A.D. The Gazetteer lists over 10,000 sites. An excellent *Atlas Graeco-Romanus,* but not an *Atlas Antiquus.*

HASSINGER, G. Geographische Grundlagen der Geschichte. 2. verb. Aufl. Freiburg, Herder, 1953, 1931. xi, 391p., 10 maps.   **HA17**

EHR LXVIII 1953 629 Ogilvie

A second edition of a geographical introduction to the series, *Geschichte der führenden Völker,* carefully revised in 1953 after the author's death in 1952. Well written, vast in range and rich in content.

HEIDEL, W. A. The Frame of the ancient Greek maps; with a discussion of the discovery of the sphericity of the Earth. New York, American Geographic Society, 1937. 142p.   **HA18**

Archeion 1937 431–433 Mieli • JHS LVIII 1938 279 Myres

Even the earliest Greek maps presupposed a frame enclosing the habitable earth. Successive early discoveries transformed the flat disc-earth into the oblong tricontinental mass of Hecataeus and Herodotus. Heidel argues for a very rapid advance in mathematical geography about 400 B.C. and favors the view that Eratosthenes first took cognizance of the earth's sphericity.

JASHEMSKI, Wilhelmina Mary Feemster. The gardens of Pompeii, Herculaneum, and the villas destroyed by Vesuvius; with photos, drawings and plans by Stanley A. Jashemski. New Rochelle, N.Y., Caratzas Bros., 1979. x, 372p. [2] fold. leaves, illus.   **HA19**

TLS 1980 700 Ward-Perkins
Results of the author's twenty-year investigation of the remains of the gardens of Pompeii. The conclusions confirm existing knowledge gleaned from literature and the paintings of the style and composition of the gardens. The book is beautifully illustrated with black-and-white and color photographs and a companion Appendix Volume will contain a description and detailed bibliography of every garden that has been excavated in the Vesuvian area and every known garden painting in the Roman Empire.

JONES, A. H. M. The Cities of the Eastern Roman Provinces. Oxford, Oxford University Press, 1937. xv, 576p., 6 maps.   **HA20**

REA 1939 381–383 Schlumberger • AJPh LXII 1941 104–107 Broughton
Traces, after the manner of a historical geography, the diffusion of the Greek city as a form of political organization throughout the Eastern Roman provinces. The Greek homeland and Macedonia are of course omitted and Thrace is the only European province included. Of lasting value as a reference work. See also A. H. M. Jones, *The Greek city from Alexander to Justinian,* Oxford, Clarendon Press, 1940, 393p.

KIEPERT, H. Formae urbis Romae antiquae. 36 Karten. Berlin, Riemer, 1893–1914.   **HA21**

Maps with critical text and sources, a fundamental work. See also H. Kiepert, *Atlas antiquus,* 12. Auflage, Berlin, 1902.

KRAELING, E. G. Rand McNally Bible Atlas. Chicago, 1956. 2nd ed., New York, Rand McNally, 1962. 487p.   **HA22**

JBL LXXVII 1958 185–186 Nesbitt
See also E. G. Kraeling, *Historical Atlas of the Holy Land,* New York, Rand McNally, 1959, 88p., 22 maps.

LEVI, Peter. Atlas of the Greek World. Oxford, Phaidon Press, 1980. 240p., 87 maps, 441 illus.   **HA23**

CR XCVI 1982 55–58 • Archaeology XXXV 1982 76–77 Cooper
One of a series, with volumes on Africa and Ancient Egypt already published and *Atlas of the Roman World* to follow. Special emphasis is on prehistoric Greece, and with equal space given to the 5th century and the Hellenistic and Roman world. The work is based on 75,000 words of text with emphasis on cultural his-

tory and close attention to archaeological discoveries, and with a high correlation between text and illustrations.

LUGLI, Josephus. Formae Italiae, Regio I. Latium et Campania, Vol. 1. Ager Pomptinus Pars. 1. Anxur—Tarracina. Rome, Danesi, 1926. 110p.   **HA24**

JRS XVI 1926 268–270 Ashby
A series of excellent volumes that report the research of the Istituto di Topografia Antica of the University of Rome. Lugli's book is the first in the series and succeeded the work of Gamurrini, Cozza, Pasqui and Menganelli in *Carta Archeologica.* The format of the volumes includes an introduction with history of previous scholarship, a description of survey results and the monuments. Recent volumes in this series include S. Q. Gigli, *Blera: Topografia Antica della Città e del Territorio,* 1976.

McEVEDY, Colin. The Penguin Atlas of ancient history. Baltimore, Penguin Books, 1967. 96p., 7 illus., 38 maps.   **HA25**

CJ LXIII 1968 237–238 Pohlsander

MYERS, John L. Geographical History in Greek Lands. Oxford, Clarendon Press, 1952. x, 381p., 12 plates, 13 maps.   **HA26**

AHR LIX 1953–54 354–355 Pritchett • JHS LXXIV 1954 210 Thomson
A collection for the author's 82nd birthday of a dozen papers written from 1910 onwards. The collection is seen as a pendent group to the more easily recognizable studies of historical geography, on the basis that sometimes it is the geographical features that invite historical commentary rather than historical events which invite geographical.

NASH, Ernest. Pictorial Dictionary of Ancient Rome. New York, Hacker, 1961. 2 v. 544p., 674 illus.; 532p., 695 illus.   **HA27**

JRS LIII 1963 227–229 Bloch • CPh LVIII 1963 269–270 Oost
The arrangement follows that established in Platner and Ashby, *Topographical Dictionary of Ancient Rome,* Oxford, 1929, which it is meant to supplement.
A lavish production underwritten by the German Archaeological Institute in Rome. Naturally, it only includes monuments of which some actual remains or pictorial representations have survived. Each monument is provided with a bibliography of modern works. The author, as director of the Fototeca di Architettura e Topografia dell' Italia Antica, was uniquely qualified for this splendid achievement which is invaluable both to specialist and generalist. About 400 photographs are of monuments which have been unearthed since 1929.

PAPASTAUROU, J. and ZSCHIETZSCH-MANN, W. Athenai: Geschichte und Topographie. Stuttgart, Druckenmüller.   **HA28**

Sonderausgabe [Pauly-Wissowa, Supplementband X, 1965, 48–89 (A. Geschichte, Papastaurou), Supplementband XIII, 1973, 55–140. (B. Topographie, Zschietzschmann)].

An updating of the topography of Athens, with sections on Literatur, Periegese des Pausanias, Berge und Flüsse, Kerameikos, Agora, Akropolis, Gebiet am Ilissos, and Stadtmauern und Stadttore.

PÉDECH, Paul. La géographie des Grecs. Paris, Presses Universitaires, 1976. 202p.   **HA29**

Latomus XXXVI 1977 1065–1066 Rougé • Athenaeum L 1978 417–418 Ambaglio
A good survey, embracing the period from Ionian beginnings with Anaximander to the second and third centuries A.D., with special attention to Herodotus, Eudoxus, Eratosthenes, Polybius, Strabo, and Ptolemy. The absence of maps is regrettable and bibliographical indications show deficiencies.

PHILIPPSON, A., KIRSTEN, E. et al. Die griechischen Landschaften. Frankfurt, Klostermann, 1950– . v. 4.   **HA30**

CR X 1960 60–62 Hammond • ByzZ XLVI 1953 174–178 Dölger
A series which contains fine descriptive accounts from the earliest times to the Turkish occupation.

PIEPER, K. Atlas orbis christiani antiqui, Atlas zur alten Missions- und Kirchengeschichte. Dusseldorff, Schwann, 1931. 62p., 17 plates.   **HA31**

Gnomon IX 1933 620–621 Oritz

PLATNER, Samuel Ball. The topography and monuments of ancient Rome. 2d ed., rev. and enl. Boston, Allyn and Bacon, 1911. xiv, 538p., double front., illus., maps, plans.   **HA32**

JRS II 1912 278–279 Ashby • CR XXVIII 1914 26 Jones
Still valuable as an introduction to the study of the topography of Ancient Rome and as a work of reference on the monuments of Rome. Areas and monuments examined in detail are the Tiber and its bridges, the Palatine Hill, the Forum, the Capitoline Hill, the Campus Maximus and the Caelian. Replaced by Platner, S. B., and Ashby, Th., *A Topographical Dictionary of Ancient Rome,* Oxford, 1929, xxiii, 608p.

PRITCHETT, W. K. Studies in Ancient Greek Topography. Berkeley, University of California Press, 1982.   **HA33**

Parts iii and iv. Roads and Passes. University of California Publications in Classical Studies 22, 28.
CR XXXV 1985 100–103 Salmon
In an important ongoing series, the scholarly imbalance in the treatment hitherto of Greek and Roman roads is here remedied.

RAMSAY, W. M. The Historical Geography of Asia Minor. Amsterdam, Hakkert, 1962, rp. of 1890 ed. 495p.   **HA34**

GJ CXXIX 1963 213 Ballance
See also W. M. Ramsay, *The cities and bishoprics of Phrygia, 1 and 11,* Oxford, 1895–97.

ROBERT, Louis. Villes d'Asie Mineure; études de géographie ancienne. 2 éd. Paris, de Boccard, 1962. 2e éd. augm. de 200p. and 16 plates.   **HA35**

REA LXIV 1962 450–451 Pouilloux

SEMPLE, Ellen C. The Geography of the Mediterranean Region: Its relation to Ancient History. London, Constable, 1932. ix, 737p., 1 plate.   **HA36**

RH CLXXI 1933 413 Sion • JHS LV 1935 85 J.L.M.
The result of many years of travel and work by a gifted teacher who was not primarily a classicist, with much information on earthquakes, volcanoes, crops, irrigation, navigation, forests, and with good lists of classical references.

STIER, H. E. and KIRSTEN, E. Westermanns Atlas zur Weltgeschichte. I Vorzeit und Altertum. Braunschweig, Westermann, 1956. 44p.   **HA37**

LEC XXV 1957 261 von Ooteghem • Gnomon XXX 1958 412–414 Gelzer
Particularly useful for prehistory, the Hittite, and Assyro-Babylonian civilizations.

THOMSON, J. Oliver. History of Ancient Geography. Cambridge, Eng., Cambridge University Press, 1948 (1965). 427p.   **HA38**

EHR LXIV 1949 360–361 Walbank • Gnomon 1950 352–354 Hampl
The fruits of twenty years' study, the work is impressive for its tremendous learning, excellent maps, and fullness of documentation. Sometimes the main thread gets lost in a tangle of detail.

TRAVLOS, John. Pictorial Dictionary of Ancient Athens. London, Thames and Hudson; New York, Praeger, 1971. xvi, 590p., 722 photographs.   **HA39**

CR XXIV 1974 110–112 Lewis
A splendid parallel to Nash's work on Rome, essential for all libraries catering to architecture, Greek archaeology or Athenian history. Especially good on physical remains and recent excavations.

VAN DER HEYDEN, A. A. M. and SCULLARD, H. H. Atlas of the Classical World. London, New York, Nelson, 1959. 222p., 475 plates, 73 maps.   **HA40**

CW LIII 1960 287 Benario • JHS LXXX 1960 225 Burn
An English translation of a Dutch original published in Amsterdam, 1958. Maps, which are numerous, accurate, and varied, are supplemented by splendid pictures

presenting the physical and cultural history of classical antiquity.

WARRINGTON, J. Everyman's atlas of ancient and classical geography. London, Dent, 1952. xii, 256p., 80 plates.   **HA41**

CR IV 1954 180 Thomson

WRIGHT, G. E. and FILSON, F. V. Westminster Historical Atlas to the Bible. Philadelphia, Westminster Press, 1945, 1949. 114p., 16 maps, 77 illus.   **HA42**

Erasmus II 1949 457–460 Auvray

W. F. Albright adds a contribution to the third edition.

WYCHERLEY, R. E. The Stones of Athens. Princeton, Princeton University Press, 1978. xviii, 293p.   **HA43**

AJA LXXXIII 1979 358–359 Caskey • G&R XXVI 1979 97 Sparkes

A good replacement for Hill, *Ancient City of Athens,* 1953, for long out-of-print. Many of the chapters have appeared before as journal contributions and Wycherley's long association with the Agora excavations gives his work special appeal.

HB   GREEK HISTORY

ACCAME, Silvio. L'imperialismo ateniese all' inizio del secolo iv a.c. e la crisi della polis. 2, ed., riv. e ampliata. Napoli, Libreria scientifica editrice, 1966. 248p.   **HB1**

AMOURETTI, M. C. and RUZÉ, F. Le monde grec antique. Des palais crétois à la conquête romaine. Paris, Hachette, 1979. 288p., atlas of 33 maps and plans.   **HB2**

BAGB 1979 331 Bertrand • AC LXIX 1980 492–494 Hannick

ARNOTT, Peter D. An introduction to the Greek world. [Totowa, N.J.], Minerva Press, [1968]. xii, 238p., 16p. of plates.   **HB3**

CR XVIII 1968 103–105 Clarke • CJ LXV 1969 133 Day

Arnott's gift for popular exposition, already seen in his *Introduction to the Greek Theatre,* is usefully employed here in a wider scope and should certainly satisfy its prospective audience: "those who know nothing and want to know something . . . those who have a smattering and want a little more."

AUSTIN, Michel and VIDAL-NAQUET, Pierre. Economic and social history of ancient Greece. Trans. and rev. by M. M. Austin. London, Batsford, 1977. xv, 397p., illus.   **HB4**

Translation of *Économies et sociétés en Grèce ancienne.*

REG LXXXVIII 1975 235–236 Ducrey

The most complete and up-to-date manual for students. The introduction, which occupies something less than half the book, provides an excellent orientation in current research. The texts are well chosen, cover a host of problems, and are well introduced.

BELIN DE BALLU, Eugène. L'histoire de colonies grecques du littoral nord de la mer Noire;

Bibliographie annotée des ouvrages et articles publiés en U. R. S. S. de 1940 à 1962. [2d éd.] Leiden, E. J. Brill, 1965. xxv, 209p.   **HB5**

Gnomon XXXIX 1967 201–203 Werner • JHS LXXXVII 1967 180 Graham

An annotated bibliography of Russian scholarship on the Greek colonies of the North Pontic coast.

BENGTSON, Hermann. Einführung in die alte Geschichte. 7. durchges. u. erg. Aufl. München, Beck, 1975. 217p.   **HB6**

AJPh LXXIII 1952 323–325 Dow • CR n.s. I 1950 124 Cary • HZ CLXX 1950 104–107 Vogt • LEC XLIII 1975 322 Derouau

The first edition of this fundamental research tool appeared in 1949, and successive editions have preserved the original format and added new entries while deleting some others, sometimes surprisingly. The *Literatur* heavily German, is arranged systematically at the end of the various sections: History of historiography, Foundations for research in Ancient History (Chronology, Geography, Anthropology), Source Materials, Monuments, Epigraphy, Papyrology, Numismatics, Allied Disciplines, *Hilfsmittel* and Journals, and a Select Systematic Bibliography at the end. The work is strong on political history, weak on archeology.

BENGTSON, Hermann, ed. The Greeks and the Persians: from the sixth to the fourth centuries. Trans. by John Conway. New York, Delacorte Press, [1968]. 478p., illus., maps.   **HB7**

Translation of Grieschen und Perser.

CPh LXV 1970 283–284 Oost • CR XX 1970 368–371 Hammond

An uneven work, badly organized. The main section (350 pages) is by Bengtson himself. Meuleau has 31 pages on Mesopotamia; Bresciani 20 on Egypt, Morton Smith 15 on Palestine, Caskell 10 on Arabia. The title is misleading: the scope of the book is not limited to the time of the Persian expansion and little is said about the Persians themselves. The subsidiary chapters have no organic unity with the main argument, though some of them are useful in themselves. The bibliographies are heavily German.

BENGTSON, Hermann. Griechische Geschichte. 4. durchgesehene und erg. Aufl. München, Beck, 1969. xix, 633p.   **HB8**

Handbuch der Altertumswissenschaft, 3. Abt. 4.T. In the series this vol. supersedes R. von Pöhlmann's *Griechische Geschichte und Quellenkunde* published in 1914.

REA LIV 1952 150–154 Aymard • Gnomon XXXIII 1961 811–814 Graham • AJPh LXXXIV 1963 103–106 Smith

Intended as a replacement for R. von Pöhlmann's *Grundriss der griechischen Geschichte nebst Quellenkunde,* which appeared in a 5th edition in 1914 and was long out of print. Otto intended to produce a sixth edition but died in 1941. Bengtson, who replaced Otto, decided that a completely new work was called for, and, despite considerable handicaps and involvements in other scholarly projects, has here produced a remarkable *tour-de-force.* The work is divided into five main sections: from c. 1900 to 800, from 800 to 500, from 500 to 360, and from 360 to 30 B.C. There is a final aperçu on the Roman imperial period to Justinian. Each successive edition has incorporated the most recent bibliography most punctiliously with minor corrections. An indispensable work of reference, with full critical and reliable accounts of the scholarly literature.

BENGTSON, Hermann. Herrschergestalten des Hellenismus. München, Beck, 1975. 343p., 12 illus.   **HB9**

Beck'sche Sonderausgaben.
LEC XLIV 1976 286 Derouau
Covering the Hellenistic period 323–31 B.C. and the reign of the twelve kings, treated biographically, especially the Diadochoi of Alexander and their successors, the Epigonoi.

BENGTSON, Hermann. The history of Greece from the beginnings to the Roman Empire. Trans. by Edmund Bloedow. Toronto, Sarasota, S. Stevens, 1977.   **HB10**

Translation of *Griechische Geschichte von den Anfängen bis in die römische Kaiserzeit,* Munich, 1969.

BENGTSON, Hermann. Introduction to ancient history. Trans. from the 6th ed. by R. I. Frank and Frank D. Gilliard. Berkeley, University of California Press, 1975. viii, 213p.   **HB11**

Trans. of *Einführung in die alte Geschichte.*
CW LXIV 1971 200 Borza • Phoenix XXV 1971 189–191 Sumner • AJPh XCIV 1973 209–210 Goedicke
The basic organization of the German original is preserved, and the chapter bibliographies are still heavi-

est on German works, making it of little use to American or English undergraduates. Abbreviations are now made to conform to *OCD* usage and many bibliographical citations have been relegated from the text to footnotes. The general bibliographical appendix has been rewritten to conform to *CAH* volume division, with a preponderance of English titles here replacing Bengtson's original selection. The review by Sumner (*Phoenix* XXV) lists many important omissions in the bibliographies.

BLOEDOW, Edmund. Alcibiades reexamined. Wiesbaden, F. Steiner, 1973. 90p.   **HB12**

Historia; Zeitschrift für alte Geschichte. Einzelschriften, Heft.
Phoenix XXIX 1975 187–190 Smart • Gnomon XLVIII 1976 212–213 Meyer
The portrait of Alcibiades in Thucydides, Plato and, to a lesser extent, Xenophon, as master diplomatist, skillful general and charismatic personality has generally gone unchallenged. Bloedow helps to deflate the resultant ballooning image but in doing so goes too far, making all Alcibiades' successes collaborative and his failures solo. The reexamination simply points up the need for another "Alcibiades reexamined."

BOSWORTH, A. B. and VAN BERCHAM, Denis. Alexandre le Grand, image et realité: sept exposés suivis de discussions. Genève, Fondation Hardt, 1976. 332p., [2] leaves of plates, illus.   **HB13**

Entretiens sur l'antiquité classique; t. 22.
CR XXVIII 1978 305–306 Brunt
Badian's contribution (p.279–311): "Some recent interpretations of Alexander" gives a survey of the various interpretations since Droysen, showing how each portrait tended to embody the fashionable beliefs of the interpreter's own time and country.

BOWDER, D., ed. Who was who in the Greek world, 776 B.C.–30 B.C. Ithaca, N.Y., Cornell University Press, 1982. 227p., illus., 12 plates.   **HB14**

HT XXXIII, 2 1983 54 Harvey • Archaeology XXXVI, 4 1983 76 Morris • Antiquity LVII 1983 67–68 Snodgrass • G&R XXX 1983 229 Walcot

BOWRA, Cecil Maurice, Sir. Periclean Athens. New York, Dial Press, 1971. 303p., map.   **HB15**

JHS XCII 1972 228–229 Mossé • CW LXV 1971 66 Fornara
A traditional presentation of the glories of the Periclean age and a justification of Athenian imperialism in the name of a hypothetical Greek unity.

BRIANT, Pierre. Alexandre le Grand. 1. ed. Paris, Presses universitaires de France, 1974. 126, [2]p., map.   **HB16**

Que-sais-je?; No. 622.

HZ CCXX 1975 395 Wirth • JHS XCV 1975 248–249 Milns

A well-balanced, clearly written work in the *Que-sais-je* format, obviously *au courant* with the ancient evidence and the modern scholarship, emphasizing less the character and personality of Alexander than the major aspects of the historical phenomena which surrounded him, the motivations of his campaigns, the organization of his conquests and the relations between conqueror and conquered.

BURICH, Nancy J. Alexander the Great; A bibliography. 1st ed. [Kent, Ohio], Kent State University Press, [1970]. xxiii, 153p. **HB17**

ACR III 1973 77–78 Fredericksmeyer • CPh LXVIII 1973 138–139 Borza • CR XXIII 1973 103–104 Cawkwell

Fails on all the tests that are applicable to a bibliography: completeness (within the limits stated by the compiler), accuracy, and an understanding of the issues raised by the listed material.

BURN, Andrew. The lyric age of Greece. [New York], Minerva Press, [1968]. xvi, 422p., maps. **HB18**

Arion II 1963 109–113 Avery • Phoenix XVII 1963 66–67 White

Extensive use is made of the *ipsissima verba* of the historians, philosophers and poets that lived in the seventh and sixth centuries to give something of the flavor of the period: its liveliness, physical expansion, and literary experimentation. The area covered is the world of Herodotus, with attempts to say something on arts, literature, philosophy, science, as well as history, geography, ethnology and religion. In a commendable attempt at *haute vulgarisation* the sources are sometimes used with too little historical acumen in this source-book, rather than history, of the period.

BURY, John B. and MEIGGS, Russell. A history of Greece to the death of Alexander the Great. 4th ed. London, Macmillan, 1975. 577p., illus. **HB19**

Hermathena CXX 1976 74–75 Stanford • CR XXVII 1977 72–74 Hammond

The great bulk of the work remains the history of Bury in the 1890's. Meiggs has entirely rewritten the first chapter. The other seventeen remain all too unchanged, with political and military aspects continuing to dominate.

CABANES, Pierre. L'Épire de la mort de Pyrrhos à la conquête romaine: 272–167 av. J. C. Paris, Les Belles Lettres, 1976. 644p., 251 leaves of plates (1 fold.), illus., maps (1 fold.). **HB20**

Centre de recherches d'histoire ancienne; 19. Annales littéraires de l'Université de Besançon; 186.

JHS XCVII 1977 207–208 Hammond

An excellently documented dissertation based on on-the-spot studies on both sides of the Greek-Albanian border. In the period studied, 272–167 B.C., Epirus was important in the web of relations between Greeks, Illyrians, Macedonians and Romans. Particularly good on recent epigraphical discoveries, and on the social and economic conditions of the period.

CARY, Max. A history of the Greek world from 323 to 146 B.C. London, Methuen, [1972]. xvi, 446p., maps. **HB21**

AAHG XXVIII 1975 220 Lorenz • AC XLII 1973 346–347 Daubies

The earliest edition of Cary goes back to 1932; a second revised edition appeared in 1951, and was reprinted in 1963, with Ehrenberg's Select Bibliography. Its durability and popularity win it a well-merited place in University Paperbacks.

CAWKWELL, George. Philip of Macedon. London; Boston, Faber & Faber, 1978. 215p., maps. **HB22**

G&R XXVI 1979 92 Mosley • TLS 3995 1978 1266 Hammond

A balanced contribution to the study of Philip, more particularly his relations with the Greek city-states. Philip emerges as a king of exceptional charisma, an outstandingly good speaker, a great admirer of Athens, and a great military organizer. The pettiness and internal bickerings of the Greek city-states and the self-serving duplicity of the politicians are relentlessly exposed. The reactions of Demosthenes are assessed and a powerful case mounted against him for his dishonesty and ineptitude.

THE CLASSICAL World bibliography of Greek and Roman history. With a new introduction by Walter Donlan. New York, Garland Publishing, 1977. **HB23**

Garland reference library of the humanities; v. 94.

A volume of reprints of *CW* bibliographical surveys (done between 1954 and 1971) containing 14 articles on Greek and Roman history: Herodotus (Paul Mac-Kendrick), Thucydides (Felix M. Wassermann and Mortimer Chambers), Livy (Konrad Gries), Tacitus (C. W. Mendell and Herbert W. Benario), Caesar (John H. Collins), Philo and Josephus (Louis H. Feldman), Alexander the Great (E. Badian), Julian the Apostate (Walter E. Kaegi, Jr.). The original *CW* pagination is dropped though the content is unchanged, and it is reproduced by photographic offprint. There is no updating.

CONNOR, Walter. The new politicians of fifth-century Athens. Princeton, N.J., Princeton University Press, 1971. xii, 218p. **HB24**

Gnomon XLVII 1975 374–378 Davies • CR XXV 1975 87–90 Lewis

"The most important book on Athenian politics since Beloch" (Lewis). The "new" politicians, Cleon, Hyperbolus, Cleophon, are examined in a new model, "a new kind of political geometry," in which the scattered data of literature and epigraphy are used with great skill.

DELORME, Jean. Le monde hellénistique, 323–133 avant J.-C.: événements et institutions. Paris, Société d'édition d'enseignement supérieur, 1975. 455p.   **HB25**

Regards sur l'histoire: 25.
CR XXVIII 1978 178 Long
This volume contains 81 texts in a French translation (63 literary, 13 epigraphic, 5 papyrological) relating to the political history and institutions of the Hellenistic period. Each text has a commentary with adequate background and *status quaestionis.* Intended as a companion work to Will's *Histoire politique du monde hellénistique,* whose bibliography it does not duplicate but merely updates since 1966.

DESBOROUGH, Vincent. The Greek dark ages. London, Benn, 1972. 388p., illus., maps, plans.
                                                    HB26

CR XXV 1975 84–87 Coldstream • JHS XCIII 1973 252–253 Huxley
A follow-up, with many second thoughts, on the author's *Protogeometric Pottery,* Oxford, 1952 and *The Last Mycenaeans and their successors,* Oxford, 1964, about the obscure history of Greece between c.1150 B.C. and c.900 B.C.

DE STE. CROIX, Geoffrey. The origins of the Peloponnesian War. Ithaca, N.Y., Cornell University Press, [1972]. xii, 444p.   **HB27**

AJPh XCVI 1975 90–93 Kagan • JHS XCV 1975 242 Ehrenberg
An iconoclastic but major work of enormous erudition. The main purpose is to transfer responsibility for the Peloponnesian War from Athens to Sparta and her allies, especially Corinth. Scholars from Adcock to Zimmern are mercilessly scolded for misrepresenting the Megarian Decree. Many will be unconvinced that the author has found its true meaning either. Some of the views here were already anticipated in Glotz, *Histoire Grec.*

DUNBABIN, Thomas J. The Western Greeks, the history of Sicily and south Italy from the foundation of the Greek colonies to 480 B.C. Oxford, Clarendon Press, 1948. xiv, 504p., maps.
                                                    HB28

Xerographic facsimile copy of the original ed. Ann Arbor, Mich., University Microfilms, 1972.
AHR LIV 1949 567–569 Charanis • Gnomon XXV 1953 9–14 Villard
A valuable collection of material on Greek activity in south Italy and Sicily from the 8th to the early 5th century. The wealth of new archaeological evidence is related to literary evidence in this study of Greek colonization. Many stimulating interpretations of historical detail throughout.

ELLIS, John R. Philip II and Macedonian imperialism. London, Thames and Hudson, 1976. 312p.
                                                    HB29

Aspects of Greek and Roman Life.
CR XXVIII 1978 303–305 Whitehead • JHS XCVIII 1978 195–196 Griffith
An excellent book, sound in methodology and valuable in its results. Modishly denying that this is a biography of Philip the author bases his study on Macedonia and the Macedonians for their own sake, and not just their relations with the rest of Greece. In the important section on Athens and Philip, Demosthenes is perhaps undervalued. There is a numismatical appendix, a select bibliography and extensive, if hard to consult, notes.

FERGUSON, William. Greek imperialism. New York, Biblo and Tannen, 1963. xiv, 258p.
                                                    HB30

"Seven lectures, six of which were delivered at the Lowell Institute in Boston during February, 1913."—Pref. Reprint of the 1941 edition.
CJ 1914 317 Scott • CW VII 1913 102–103 Johnson
The author maintains, in these Lowell lectures, that the age of Pericles was but the youthful bloom of the science of government which only came to maturity in the days of Macedonian supremacy.

FERGUSON, William. Hellenistic Athens: an historical essay. Chicago, Ares Publishers, 1974. xviii, 487p.   **HB31**

Reprint of the 1911 ed. published by Macmillan, London.
CW VIII 1914 100–101 Johnson • HZ 1915 435 Otto
A pioneering study of Athens for the three centuries after Alexander, during which time it was transformed from a small city-state to a municipality within a large empire. During this time Athens was above all a great university center, with intellectual pre-eminence replacing political. Literary and epigraphical sources are well exploited in this sound, careful study.

HUMPHREYS, Sarah C. Anthropology and the Greeks. London and Boston, Routledge & K. Paul, 1978. xi, 357p.   **HB32**

International Library of Anthropology.
TLS 3995 1978 1266 Lloyd • CR XXX 1980 58–61 Fisher
After early collaboration between classics and anthropology in England in the days of Jane Harrison, Gilbert Murray and Francis Cornford, a great coolness between the disciplines developed during the two World Wars. The beginnings of somewhat improved relations are dateable to E. R. Dodds, *The Greeks and the Irrational* (1951), and Moses Finley's *The World of Odysseus* (1954). (In France, the situation was somewhat better, thanks to the labors of Vernant, Vidal-Naquet and Détienne.)
Mrs. Humphreys, lecturer in the University of London in a new joint degree program in ancient history and social anthropology, here edits a series of her papers—dating from 1967 on a wide spectrum of economic, social and intellectual history—which contain

many useful pointers to the future of this collaboration. There is a lengthy (p.308–350) bibliography.

JEFFERY, Lilian Hamilton. Archaic Greece; The City-States, c.700–500 B.C. New York, St. Martin's Press, 1976. 272p., 16 leaves of plates, illus. **HB33**

REG LXXXIX 1976 124 Bennett • JHS XCVII 1977 205–206 Cartledge
Based on a long-established series of university lectures, this describes the independent Greek City-States and their political organization in the 8th and early 7th centuries. Those familiar with the author's classic *Local scripts of Archaic Greece* will welcome the cataloging approach, and the predominance of epigraphical evidence. Jeffery begins with four momentous events: the creation of the Greek alphabet, the beginnings of western colonization, the advance in metal-working and the creation of the Homeric Epics. After the preliminary chapters the work becomes more or less straightforward political history.

JORDAN, Borimir. The Athenian navy in the Classical period; A study of Athenian naval administration and military organization in the fifth and fourth centuries B.C. Berkeley, University of California Press, 1975. xiii, 293p. **HB34**

University of California Publications: Classical studies; v. 13. Based on the author's thesis, University of California, Berkeley, 1968.
Gnomon L 1978 688–690 Casson
A short introduction on the *Naucraries*, the earliest administrative body of the navy, is followed by three main sections: an analysis of the administrative machinery that ran the navy in the 5th–4th centuries (p.21–116), a description of the various ranks within the ships (p.117–152), and finally a discussion of the crews, rowers, marines. The work is excessively detailed on minutiae.

KAGAN, Donald. The Archidamian War. Ithaca, Cornell University Press, 1974. 392p., maps. **HB35**

CW LXX 1976 219 McGregor • CR XXVI 1976 230–231 Westlake • AJPh XCVII 1976 80–83 Roebuck
As in his earlier work, *The Outbreak of the Peloponnesian War* (1969), the author is concerned with an assessment of the relationship between policy-making and its implementation. Thucydides is followed faithfully but critically. There is an impressive control of the modern work, documented in a good bibliography. A particularly useful work for Greekless historians.

KAGAN, Donald. The Outbreak of the Peloponnesian War. Ithaca, Cornell University Press, [1969]. xvi, 420p. **HB36**

CR XXI 1971 248–250 • CPh LXVIII 1973 308–310 Eddy • HZ CCXVI 1973 124–125 Meier • CW LXIII 1970 201–202 McGregor
The author sees city-state rivalry and pride as the true causes of the war, not economic need or greed, *pace* Grundy, Cornford et al. It was caused not by impersonal forces (e.g., inevitability) but by men who made bad decisions in difficult circumstances. There are 11 appendices, a lengthy bibliography and full indices. The work is careless in details and needed much editorial pruning. A bold, but unproven, disagreement with Thucydides on the true cause of the war.

KAGAN, Donald. Studies in the Greek historians. In memory of Adam Parry. Edited for the Dept. of Classics. Cambridge and New York, Cambridge University Press, 1975. xv, 236p., [1] leaf of plates, illus. **HB37**

Yale classical studies, v. 24.
HZ CCXXIII 1976 391–392 Meister • AC XLVI 1977 272–273 Hannick
A volume of *Yale Classical Studies,* in memory of Adam and Anne Parry, containing 11 studies spanning historians from Herodotus and Thucydides to Polybius, Plutarch and Herodian. E. A. Havelock provides an *in memoriam* Adam and Anne Parry (killed in an automobile accident, June 1971).

LARSEN, Jakob Aall Ottesen. Greek federal states; Their institutions and history. Oxford, Clarendon Press, 1968. xxviii, 537p. **HB38**

JHS LXXXVIII 1968 219–220 Lewis • Phoenix XXII 1968 346–349 Bruce
Professor Larsen here crowns his scholarly involvement of 47 years with Greek federalism, providing a replacement for E. A. Freeman. An introduction defines the nature of a Greek federal state and the main work is divided by the King's Peace into two parts.

LÉVY, Edmond. Athènes devant la défaite de 404; Histoire d'une crise idéologique. Athènes, École Française d'Athènes, 1976. ix, 339p. **HB39**

Bibliothèque des Écoles Françaises d'Athènes et de Rome.
Gnomon L 1978 650–654 Cartledge • JHS XCVII 1977 206–207 Macleod
Especially concerned with literary sources (epigraphic and iconographic are all but neglected), this investigation of the crisis in values that enveloped Athens after its defeat in 404 examines first the Athenian reaction to the Sicilian disaster and its aftermath of explaining or explaining away the defeat, then the ideology of power, especially imperial power in the late 5th century, and finally what replaced this power after it was discredited. Ideology may be an inappropriate concept for the period studied, but the wide range and ample documentation of this study make it a valuable repertory of ideas.

LEWIS, David Malcolm. Sparta and Persia; Lectures delivered at the University of Cincinnati, Autumn 1976, in memory of Donald W. Bradeen. Leiden, Brill, 1977. x, 168p. **HB40**

JHS XCIX 1979 195 Westlake • Phoenix XXXII 1978 343–345 Bigwood

Fulfills a long-felt need for an extended and detailed investigation of the relations of the Greek city-states and the Achaemenid Empire after the Great Persian Wars. The period covered is c.448–387 B.C. Lewis makes a genuine attempt to do justice to Persia, showing awesome control of the multilingual documentation. In practice Persia often means the provinces of Sardis and Dascylium into which western Asia Minor was divided. An important and informative volume, refreshingly undogmatic.

LEWIS, Naphtali, ed. The fifth century B.C. Toronto, A. M. Hakkert, 1971. xii, 124p.

HB41

JHS XCII 1972 228 Meiggs • Phoenix XXV 1971 404–405 Shrimpton

Documents in convenient translation for the Greekless reader collected under two headings: Athens, and Elsewhere. Important inscriptions and quotations from lesser-known literary sources are featured in reliable translations, briefly prefaced and with 75 explanatory notes.

MACKENDRICK, Paul Lachlan. The Athenian aristocracy, 399 to 31 B.C. Cambridge, Mass., published for Oberlin College by Harvard University Press, 1969. ix, 111p.   **HB42**

Martin classical lectures; v. 23.

AJPh XCII 1971 111–114 Mitchel • CW LXIII 1969 53–54 Urdahl • Phoenix XXV 1971 383–386 Derow

A study begun under Dow using two *Ergastina* inscriptions as a starting point. In the present set of lectures *Gennetai* are considered during various periods from the beginning of the 4th century down to 31 B.C.

The purpose of the book is to show that the *Gennetai* were able to transform religious prominence into political influence, despite the reforms of Cleisthenes. *Genos* is defined after Ferguson [*Hesperia* VII (1938) 24] as a closed body of well-to-do citizens, open only to the legitimate children of its members.

MANNI, Eugenio. Introduzione allo studio della storia greca e romana. 2. ed. riv. e aggiornata, 3. ristampa. Palermo, Palumbo, [1959?]. 1967 printing. 244p.   **HB43**

Biblioteca di cultura moderna; 19.

REA LVI 1954 195–196

Text for an introductory course on ancient history, shorter than Breccias. The limits of antiquity are first outlined. There is a very brief treatment (p.45–48) of the founders of modern historiography on ancient history. The ancillary sciences get short shrift, especially papyrology. The literary sources get most attention, with good bibliographies.

MEIGGS, Russell. The Athenian Empire. Oxford, Clarendon Press, 1975, 1972. xvi, 620p., [5] leaves of plates, maps.   **HB44**

"First published 1972. Reprinted with corrections 1975."

Gnomon XLV 1973 669–676 Ehrenberg • AJPh XCVI 1975 217–224 Roebuck • Mnemosyne XXVIII 1975 98–102 Pleket • RPh XLVIII 1974 343–345 Will • AC XLV 1976 336–339 Piérart

The distillation of Meiggs' work as epigraphist and historian on the Athenian Empire from the Confederacy of Delos to 403/2. There are ten valuable chapters on the institutions and on juridical, economic and religious aspects of the Athenian empire. Much of the detail is relegated to a series of 26 endnotes and 17 appendices. The running debate on chronological matters with Mattingly adds piquancy to the narrative. A monumental contribution to political history which displays learned minute scholarship and sound judgment.

MOMIGLIANO, Arnaldo. Introduzione bibliografica alla storia greca fino a Socrate; Appendice a Gaetano de Sanctis, Storia dei greci. 1 ed. Firenze, La nuova Italia, 1975. x, 186p.   **HB45**

BBF XXI 1976 356–358 Ernst • GIF XXVII 1975 367 Scivoletto

MOSSÉ, Claude. La fin de la démocratic athénienne. Aspects sociaux et politiques du déclin de la cité grecque au IVe siècle avant J.-C. [1. ed.] Paris, Presses Universitaires de France, 1962. 495p.   **HB46**

Publications de la faculté des lettres et sciences humaines de Clermont-Ferrand; 2. sér., fasc. 10.

AC XXXII 1963 326–331 Salmon • AHR LXVIII 1962–1963 498–499 Brown

A carefully researched book which attempts to relate the political crisis of Athenian democracy culminating in Chaeronea to the social and economic evolution of 4th century Athens in particular and the Greek city-states in general. The social and economic crisis is studied at length (p.33–256) showing the widening 4th century polarization between rich and poor and the disastrous decline in institutional stability. The second part of the work (p.257–469) studies the political crisis.

An index of proper names, institutions and texts discussed facilitates reference in this important contribution to 4th century history.

MOSSÉ, Claude. Athens in decline, 404–86 B.C. Trans. by Jean Stewart. London, Routledge & K. Paul, [1973]. 181p., illus.   **HB47**

CR XXVI 1976 92–93 Briscoe • History LIX 1974 446–447 Rodewald • G&R XXI 1974 207 Murray • JHS XCV 1975 246–247 Roy

Primarily directed to the student and general reader, this is an excellent analysis of political disputes, social and economic structures and the views of political theorists. More space should have been devoted to the purely factual history of the period. An expensive, hardcover translation of an attractive and unpretentious French paperback.

PERLMAN, S., ed. Philip and Athens [essays]; Selected and introduced by S. Perlman. Cambridge, Heffer (New York, Barnes & Noble Books), 1973. 222p. **HB48**

Views and controversies about classical antiquity. CW LXX 1976 279 Merker

Twelve essays by ten authors reprinted from elsewhere add up to an excellent Views and Controversies volume. A brief but perceptive introduction traces the history of Macedonia in the 4th and 5th centuries as a necessary backdrop to Philip's activities, and a concluding bibliography lists much of the relevant material. The published excerpts date from 1929 to 1965; ten are in English, one in Italian and one in German.

PETERS, Francis E. The Harvest of Hellenism; A History of the Near East from Alexander the Great to the triumph of Christianity. London, G. Allen & Unwin, 1972. 800p., maps. **HB49**

Gnomon XLVI 1974 373–377 Seibert • CR XXIII 1973 237–238 Murray • CPh LXIX 1974 67 Oost • CW LXVII 1974 399–401 Kadish

An uneven work in style, emphasis and areas of competence. At best a political and intellectual history, with little attention to social and economic matters, weak on institutional and diplomatic history, and even on recent scholarship in political matters. The book is at its best when dealing with Hellenistic philosophy and the development of Christian thought.

PODLECKI, Anthony J. The life of Themistocles; A critical survey of the literary and archaeological evidence. Montreal, McGill-Queen's University Press, 1975. xiii, 250p., [4] leaves of plates, illus. **HB50**

Phoenix XXXI 1977 68–70 Connor • CW LXX 1976 35–36 Eliot • CF XXIX 1975 160–163 Marique • JHS XCVI 1976 224–225 Ehrenberg

Part II contains a thorough assemblage of literary and archaeological evidence from antiquity: literary notices from Aeschylus to Plutarch, the herm from Ostia, the Themistocles Decree (an exemplary treatment), coins, buildings, walls and over 2,000 ostraka. All sources are cited in English. The 41-page biography of Themistocles in part I produces few surprises. There is a formidable bibliography. The great mass of evidence assembled is unwieldy, and the treatment repetitive and insufficiently analytical.

ROSTOVTSEFF, Mikhail Ivanovich. The social and economic history of the Hellenistic world. Oxford, Clarendon Press, 1972. 3 v., front., illus., plates (1 col.), ports., plans. **HB51**

First published 1941; reprinted from corrected sheets of the 1st ed., 1972.

JRS XXXI 1941 165–171 Tarn • JHS LXIII 1943 129–130 Heichelheim • CR LVI 1942 81–84

Despite its manifold scholarly excellences the appearance of this work is as anti-climactic as was the 5th v. of Mommsen's *Roman history*. Large parts of it could have been published as separate specialist monographs.

The time limits are Alexander to Actium; limits of space exclude both the West (Italy, Sicily, Carthage) and the Farther East (Parthia and beyond). The kernel of the work is c.4; The Balance of Power 281–221 B.C. There is an index of sources, v. 3 (p.1750–1779). The bibliography is included in the notes, v. 3 (p.1313–1631).

SCHACHERMEYR, Fritz. Alexander der Grosse. Das Problem seiner Persönlichkeit u. seines Wirkens. Wien, Verl. D. Österr, Akad. d. Wiss., 1973. 723p., fold. map, 24p. of illus. (part. col.). **HB52**

Österreichische Akademie der Wissenschaften, Philosophisch-Historische Klasse, Sitzungsberichte; Bd. 285.

Phoenix XXVIII 1974 369–371 Badian • HZ CCXXI 1975 644–648 Wirth • CW LXIX 1975 137–139 Murison • Gnomon XLIX 1977 164–173 Wirth

A greatly enlarged new version by the venerable author—at the age of 80—of an already large (535p.) work which first appeared in 1949. The basic text survives virtually unchanged but a very detailed annotation is added in which the intervening bibliographical developments are carefully reported on. There are two entirely new chapters on historiography admirably detailing interpretations from Droysen to Tarn, but showing more animus in surveying work since World War Two, with the "Minimalist" view getting short shrift. There are topographical appendices based on recent autopsy, and profuse illustrations based on the author's slides. The style is overblown a lot of the time.

SCHACHERMEYR, Fritz. Die ältesten Kulturen Griechenlands. Stuttgart, W. Kohlahammer, 1955. 300p., illus. **HB53**

CR VII 1957 139–141 Stubbings • Gnomon XXIX 1957 511–515 Hood • REA LVIII 1956 98–99 Marcadé

Earliest means here cultures preceding the Middle Bronze Age. This is an excellent work of synthesis and interpretation of present archaeological and linguistic knowledge of Greece prior to 2000 B.C., making large-scale comparisons between Early Aegean, Balkan and Near Eastern pottery and artifacts.

SCHACHERMEYR, Fritz. Griechische Geschichte; mit besonderer Berücksichtigung der geistesgeschichtlichen und kulturmorphologischen Zusammenhänge. 2. Erw. Aufl. Stuttgart, W. Kohlhammer, [1969, 1960]. 496p., 44 plates, maps (1 fold.), plans. **HB54**

AAHG XIV 1961 76–79 Altheim • CR XIII 1963 198–200 Hopper • AHR LXVIII 1962–1963 422–423 Larsen

An exercise in universal history in the Spengler-Toynbee style, investigating Greek culture from the earliest Aegean beginnings to the triumph of Christianity. For Schachermeyr, great cultural advances come when the time is ripe but are due to individual geniuses, so Homer, Archilochus, Themistokles, Pericles, Epaminondas, and Alexander get special attention. There is much that is questionable and controversial in this interesting and stimulating study of the patterns of history.

SCHACHERMEYR, Fritz. Perikles. Stuttgart and Berlin, Kohlhammer, (1969). 272p.

HB55

CR XXIII 1973 231–234 Briscoe • RH XCVII, 249 1973 175–179 Will • CPh LXIX 1974 69–70 Oost
A very good biography, following on the author's *Die Frühe Klassik der Griechen,* which should be read first. Pericles is the Olympian for Schachermeyr.

SEALEY, Raphael. A history of the Greek City States, ca. 700–338 B.C. Berkeley, University of California Press, 1976. xxi, 516p., illus.

HB56

CR XXIX 1979 100–103 Rhodes • JHS XCVIII 1978 193–194 Cartledge • Phoenix XXXI 1977 367–369 McGregor
Not so much a textbook as a work which introduces students of Greek history to selected problems and hypotheses. Nineteen chapters are grouped in three parts: The development of the City-State and the Persian Wars, The era of Hegemonic Leagues (to 386), Leagues of more equal type (to 338). The work is confined to political and military history, controversial views are reported with scrupulous fairness, and within its self-imposed limits it is a valuable study and better in many ways for undergraduates than Bury-Meiggs, Hammond, and Ehrenberg's, *From Solon to Socrates.*

SEIBERT, Jakob. Alexander der Grosse. Darmstadt, Wissenschaftliche Buchgesellschaft, 1972. xiv, 329p., col. map.   **HB57**

Erträge der Forschung; Bd. 10.
CR XXV 1975 265–268 Briscoe • JHS XCV 1975 249–250 Milns • REG LXXXVII 1974 425–428 Goukowsky • CPh LXIX 1974 232–233 Borza
Not merely an up-to-date systematic bibliography of Alexander scholarship for the century 1870–1970, but also an exposition and survey of its fruits, with special emphasis on monographs and journal articles. A monument of industry and diligence, it may, however, have fallen between two stools: that of the Alexander scholar and that of the uninitiated. A big improvement on Burich, however, which is rendered less necessary by Badian's *CW* Survey LXV (1971). An appropriate centenary celebration of Droysen's great pioneering work. There is a very full section on the sources, and the main body of the work reviews Alexander's career in chronological fashion. Each topic is organized chronologically as a history of research on the subject.

STARR, Chester G. The economic and social growth of early Greece, 800–500 B.C. New York, Oxford University Press, 1977. 267p., [4] leaves of plates, illus.   **HB58**

AJPh XCIX 1978 402–403 Figueira • CW LXXII, 1 1978 57–58 Grimaldi

This book is an elaboration of the last chapters of the author's earlier *The origins of Greek civilization* (New York, 1961) and provides a useful general study of Greek social and economic history of the Archaic period.

TARN, William Woodthorpe, Sir. Alexander der Grosse. Darmstadt, Wissenschaftliche Buchgesellschaft. 2 v. in 1, xvi, 932p., [1] leaf of plates, map.   **HB59**

Trans. of *Alexander the Great.*
DLZ XCIV 1973 363–366 Wirth • AJPh LXX 1949 192–202 Robinson
The English original appeared in 1948 in 2 v. (Cambridge, 1948, 160p. and 477p.): I. The Narrative, II. Sources and Studies. Volume I gives the narrative in compendious form, consisting in the main of Tarn's two chapters in *CAH* VI, but the text has been corrected and largely rewritten. The 3rd chapter discusses Alexander's personality, policy and aims. Volume II is intended as the main part of the book and is divided into two parts. Part I opens with a long study of the so-called *Vulgate* and its sources. Curtius' portrait of Alexander is then examined. In Part II there are 25 learned appendices full of information on troops, military problems, etc.

TARN, William Woodthorpe, Sir. Hellenistic civilization. 3d ed., rev. by the author and G. T. Griffith. New York, New American Library, [1974]. xi, 372p.   **HB60**

CR XLII 1928 75–76 Gomme • AC XLIV 1975 782 Nachtergael
First published in 1927, this general picture of the civilization of the Hellenistic period went through many reprintings (1930, 1936, 1941, 1947). The third edition, in which G. T. Griffith collaborated with the author, appeared in 1952 and was reprinted in 1953, 1959, and 1974. It appeared as a University Paperback in 1966 and has been reprinted, 1974. Whether Tarn provokes enthusiasm or irritation he never leaves the reader indifferent.

THOMSEN, Rudi. The origin of ostracism; A synthesis. [Copenhagen], Gyldendal, 1972. 158p.

HB61

Humanitas; v. 4.
Gnomon XLVI 1974 817–819 Bucknell • CR XXV 1975 257–258 Rhodes
Valuable both for a lucidly critical survey of almost all modern work on the subject and for a list of all the complete names that have so far turned up on Ostraka. Out of date already, however, in that it was unaware of the important literary evidence re-discovered and re-published in *AJPh* XCIII (1972), by Keaney and Raubitschek.

TOYNBEE, Arnold Joseph. Some problems of Greek history. London and New York, Oxford University Press, 1969. xii, 538p.   **HB62**

CJ LXVII 1971–1972 184–188 Anderson • Gnomon XLVIII 1976 156–161 Berve • CPh LXVIII 1973 132–134 Evans

Toynbee's death, 22 October 1975, deprived the world of perhaps its greatest universal historian. In this work he made a brilliant return to the field of Ancient Greek history (his travels in the Southern Peloponnesus go back to 1912), with special attention (p.152–417) to the rise and decline of Sparta. Two earlier sections deal with aspects of post-Mycenaean immigrations—*Iliad* II's catalog of ships is dated to the late 7th century and the Hellenization of the northern hinterland of continental European Greece. A work of immense learning, showing an inexhaustible willingness to theorize which is always interesting and often illuminating. The fourth main section is offered as a Satyr play accompaniment to a trilogy and should be so treated.

WICKERSHAM, John and VERBRUGGHE, Gerald. Greek historical documents; The fourth century B.C. Toronto, Hakkert, 1973. xiii, 129p., illus.   **HB63**

JHS XCVI 1976 226–227 Cawkwell • RPh XLIX 1975 300 Will
A useful translation of 76 documents (including 56 items from Tod, *GHI* II), which aims at illuminating the diplomatic narration of the period covered, 403–336 B.C. Brief but informative introductions situate the documents in their historical context. There is a glossary as well as several useful tables (e.g., weights and measures).

HC ROMAN HISTORY

General Works, Bibliography, Collections, Manuals

AFRICA, Thomas W. The immense majesty; A history of Rome and the Roman Empire. Arlington Heights, Ill., AHM Publishing Corp., 1974. xvi, 431p., illus., geneal. tables, maps.   **HC1**

CW LXIX 1975 87–89 Hammond
A readable, balanced and scholarly account with commendable attention to intellectual history.

ALBERTINI, Eugène. L'Empire Romain. 4. éd. augm. d'un supplément bibliographique par André Chastagnol. Paris, Presses Universitaires de France, 1970 [1929]. 486p., map.   **HC2**

Peuples et civilisations: Histoire générale; v. 4.
REL IX 1931 180–181 Constans
One of the best volumes in the *Histoire générale* series.

ANDRÉ, Jean Marie and HUS, Alain. L'histoire à Rome; Historiens et biographes dans la littérature latine. 1. éd. Paris, Presses Universitaires de France, 1974. 228p.   **HC3**

Collection SUP. Littératures anciennes; 3.
LEC XLII 1974 458 Wankenne • RPh XLVIII 1974 361 Richard
Contains a good ensemble of citations, an *État des questions* on many of the problems in Roman historiography and a useful bibliography.

BELOCH, Karl Julius. Römische Geschichte; bis zum Beginn der Punischen Kriege. Berlin and Leipzig, W. de Gruyter, 1926. xvi, 664p., maps.   **HC4**

RF 1929 267 Fraccaro • A&R 1928 75–78 Levi

BULLETIN Analytique D'Histoire Romaine. Strasbourg, Association pour L'Étude de la civilisation romaine, t. 1– , 1962– .   **HC5**

Latomus XXVII 1968 249–250, XXX 1971 254–255 Sanders • REA LXXI 1969 238 Étienne • RPh XLV 1971 189–190 Dumont • Stud Pap XV 1976 165 Leone
By its fourth issue (1965 appearing in 1968), the *Bulletin* was researching 676 periodicals from 12 countries. Ranks with Schneemelcher's *Bibliographia patristica* or Bleeker's bibliography on the history of religion.

BURY, John B. A history of the Later Roman Empire; From Arcadius to Irene (395 A.D. to 800 A.D.). Freeport, N. Y., Books for Libraries Press, [1973].   **HC6**

Reprint of the 1889 ed, published by Macmillan, London, New York.
JHS XLIII 1923 197–198 E. W. B.
This is a new and enlarged edition of the earlier part of Bury's *HLRE from Arcadius to Irene* (1889). The first four chapters are almost entirely rewritten and there is much alteration and addition in subsequent chapters, representing the author's maturing views over the intervening 34 years since first publication.

CAMBRIDGE Ancient History. Cambridge, England, Cambridge University Press, 1923– . 12 v., illus., maps, plans, tables.   **HC7**

Volume 1 has appeared in 2 parts in a third edition, 1970, 1971, with 17 and 16 maps. Volume II, part 2, 1975 is also well provided with maps, diagrams and tables. Volume III, to appear in 3 parts is provided with a Plates volume 1b, ed. J. Boardman, Cambridge University Press, 1984, xiv, 299p., 385 plates. See also the other supplementary Volumes of Plates, esp. 1a, illustrating vols. 1–2, 1977.

CUNLIFFE, Barry W. Rome and her Empire. With photos by Brian Brake and Leonard

von Matt. New York, McGraw-Hill, [1978].
HC8

CW LXXII 1979 374 Hammond

A lavishly printed and illustrated work by the professor of European archaeology at Oxford with sound, if brief, text. Especially useful as collateral reading or for review purposes.

DILKE, Oswald A. The ancient Romans; How they lived and worked. Newton Abbot, David and Charles, 1975. 199p., illus., maps, plans.
HC9

CR XXVII 1977 303–304 Scott

A fresh look at the Romans, using the latest archaeological and textual discoveries. Written with great skill and economy of words, with an excellent series of tables, diagrams and illustrations. It is an ideal introduction.

DRUMANN, Wilhelm Karl August. Geschichte Roms in seinem Übergange von der republikanischen zur monarchischen Verfassung; Oder, Pompeius, Caesar, Cicero und ihre Zeitgenossen nach Geschlechtern und mit Genealogischen Tabellen. [Reprografischer Nachdruck der 2. Aufl., Berlin-Leipzig, 1899–1929]. Hildesheim, G. Olms, 1964. 6 v., geneal. tables.   **HC10**

1. bd, Aemilii–Antonii; 2. bd, Asinili–Cornificii; 3. bd, Domitii–Julii; 4. bd, Junii–Pompeii, 5. bd, Pomponii, Porcii, Tullii; 6. bd, M. Tullius Cicero.

DUDLEY, Donald Reynolds. The Romans. London, Hutchinson, 1970. xxiv, 316p., 32 plates, illus., maps.   **HC11**

G&R XVIII 1972 108 Sewter • JRS LXII 1972 171 Norman

A *tour de force* in seven parts and 49 chapters. Covers the development of Rome from its beginnings to the death of Constantine. The book is concise in its information, provocative in its judgments and illuminating in its modern comparisons.

EHRENBERG, Victor and JONES, A. H. M., comps. Documents illustrating the reigns of Augustus and Tiberius. 2d [enl.] ed. reprinted with addenda selected by D. L. Stockton. Oxford, Clarendon Press, 1976. xii, 178p.   **HC12**

REL XXVIII 1950 435–436, XXXIII 1955 471–472 Béranger

The second augmented and revised edition of a 1955 original introduced 30 new documents and improved indices. This series of documents is of use to student, teacher and specialist alike.

GARZETTI, Albino. From Tiberius to the Antonines; A history of the Roman Empire, A.D. 14–192. Trans. by J. R. Foster. London, Methuen, [1974]. x, 861p.   **HC13**

Rev. trans. of L'impero da Tiberio agli Antonini.

CW LXIX 1976 447–448 Sumner • CR XIII 1963 207–210 Crook, XXVI 1976 243–244 Colledge • Gnomon XLVIII 1976 624–625 Nicols

First published in Italian in 1960 as v. VI of the series *Storia di Roma*. The bibliographies and *L'état des questions* are particularly valuable, and there are revisions and addenda by the author in the English version. Deserves to become a standard reference work for the period. Part I deals with the Julio-Claudians; part II covers Galba to Trajan, and part III, Hadrian to Commodus. Part III should be preferred to the corresponding treatment in *CAH*.

GIBBON, Edward. The history of the decline & fall of the Roman Empire. Illustrated from the etchings by Gian Battista Piranesi; the text edited by J. B. Bury; with the notes by Mr. Gibbon; and the introduction and the index as prepared by Professor Bury; also with a letter to the reader from Philip Guedalla. [New York], The Limited Edition Club, 1946. 7 v., lvi, 2537p., illus.
HC14

GRANT, Michael. The ancient historians. London, Weidenfeld & Nicolson; New York, Scribner's, 1970. xviii, 486p., 16 plates, illus., facsims., maps, ports.   **HC15**

CW LXIV 1971 202 Bourne • Latomus XXXI 1972 568–570 Daubies

GRANT, Michael. History of Rome. London, Weidenfeld & Nicolson, 1978. xi, 131p.
HC15a

HT XXVIII 1978 480–481 Perowne

GREENE, William Chase. The achievement of Rome; A chapter in civilization. New York, Cooper Square Publishers, 1973. xiv, 560p., illus.
HC16

Companion volume to the author's *The achievement of Greece* (1923). Reprint of the 1933 ed. published by Harvard University Press, Cambridge.

AJPh LXVI 1935 280–282 Winter • CW XXX 1936 27 McKinley • Gnomon XI 1935 389–390 Kroll

An attempt to evaluate Rome's contribution to contemporary civilization, treating successively the geographical, ethnical and religious setting in the context of the civil, legal and artistic structure of Roman society.

GREENIDGE, Abel Hendy Jones and CLAY, A. M., comps. Sources for Roman history, 133–70 B.C. 2d ed., rev. by E. W. Gray. Oxford, Clarendon Press, 1960. viii, 318p.   **HC17**

Gnomon XXXII 1960 534–536 Badian • REL XXXVIII 1960 424–425 Piganiol • JRS L 1960 249–250 Lacey

An invaluable book for an intricate and important period; selected with skill and care, and well revised and augmented.

GUIDA allo studio della civiltà romana antica. Diretta da Vincenzo Ussani e Francesco Arnaldi. 2. ed. Napoli, Istituto editoriale del mezzogiorno, 1958. 2 v. 637p., 844p.   **HC18**

First published in 1952, this is a useful manual of the Laurand-Lauras variety, confining its attention to Rome and all aspects of Roman civilization, with sections on the auxiliary sciences, law, art, weights and measures, etc. Each chapter is a self-contained course of initiation, with supporting bibliography.

HAYWOOD, Richard Mansfield. Ancient Rome. London, Vision, 1968. xiii, 650p., 24 plates, illus., maps.   **HC19**

AJPh XC 1969 376–377 Salmon • CW LXII 1968 24 Raubitschek • JRS LIX 1969 316–317 Scullard

A companion volume to the author's *Ancient Greece and the Near East* (1964). The story is carried down to Justinian and includes brief accounts of economic affairs, literature, art, architecture and religion including Christianity and the church. A reliable introduction.

HEURGON, Jacques. Rome et la Méditerranée occidentale jusqu'aux guerres puniques. Paris, Presses Universitaires de France, 1969. 412p., maps.   **HC20**

Nouvelle Clio; 7.

An admirable short guide to the dramatic archaeological advances made, and the problems that remain, in the study of early Rome down to 264 B.C.. There are condensed accounts of the changing civilizations of Gaul and Spain, and more on the Etruscans. The literary evidence is admirably balanced with the archaeological, and the bibliographies—722 items—are very impressive and useful. An ideal introduction in the best tradition of the *Nouvelle Clio* series, well translated by James Willis. The ideal "work-in-progress" history of early Rome.

HOLLEAUX, Maurice. Rome, la Grèce et les monarchies hellénistiques au IIIe siècle avant J. C. (273–205). Hildesheim and New York, G. Olms, 1969. 386p.   **HC21**

HOLMES, Thomas Rice Edward. The Roman Republic and the founder of the Empire. New York, Russell & Russell, 1967. 3 v., illus., fold. maps.   **HC22**

Reprint of the 1923 ed. Contents: v. 1. From the origins to 58 B.C., v. 2. 58–50 B.C., v. 3. 50–44 B.C.

JRS XII 1922 289–290 Baynes

Neither a general history of the Roman Republic nor a special study of Augustus but rather an account of the political and military history of Rome from the death of Sulla to the death of Julius Caesar. Particularly good for the last days of the Republic.

HOMO, Léon Pol. Le Haut-Empire. [2. éd.]. Paris, Presses Universitaires de France, 1941 [1933]. vii, 668p., maps.   **HC23**

Histoire générale, histoire ancienne, Histoire romaine.

REL XI 1933 265–266 Béranger

JONES, Arnold H. M. A history of Rome through the fifth century. London, Macmillan, 1968–1972. 2 v., map.   **HC24**

Contents: v.1. The Republic, v. 2. The Empire.

G&R XVIII 1971 108 Sewter • CR XXIII 1973 68–71 Levick • JRS LXII 1972 174–175 Tomlin, XX 1970 405–406 Briscoe

Volume I consists of a brief introduction and 150 sections, each containing one (occasionally more than one) literary or epigraphical text in translation. There are inaccuracies and the indices are next to useless.

Volume II contains 184 documents in translation, chosen chiefly to illustrate the organization and law of the Empire. First-hand documents such as papyri or inscriptions are chosen by preference. The documents are grouped under 13 topics, e.g., religion, the army (useful especially to non-classicists).

JONES, Arnold H. M. The later Roman Empire, 284–602. Oxford, B. Blackwell, 1964. 3 v. and atlas.   **HC25**

JRS LV 1965 250–253 Heichelheim • REL XLII 1964 159–165 Chastagnol • CR XV 1965 335–339 Browning

This monumental work is a worthy complement to E. Stein and J. R. Palanque's *Histoire du Bas-Empire* (2 v., Paris, 1959).

Leaving aside military, religious, and intellectual history, the author presents a social, economic and administrative survey of the Empire, historically treated. The opening "narrative" section presents the evolution of the later Empire by period; part 2 is descriptive of the different institutional sectors in which the author's great learning is deployed to best effect.

There is "a shortened and simplified version" of this work in A. H. M. Jones, *The decline of the ancient world* (London: Longman, 1966, viii, 414p.).

KATZ, Solomon. The decline of Rome and the rise of mediaeval Europe. Ithaca, Cornell University Press, [1955]. 164p., illus.   **HC26**

KORNEMANN, Ernst. Römische Geschichte. 7. Aufl. Bearb. von Hermann Bengtson. Stuttgart, Kröner, 1977. 2 v., fold. map.   **HC27**

Kröner Taschenausgabe: Bd. 132–133, Bd. 1. die Zeit der Republik, Bd. 2. die Kaiserzeit.

CW XXXIII 1939 57 Wannemacher • HZ CLXI 1940 329–332 Altheim • JRS XXXI 1940 99–100 Scullard

For Kornemann the year 60 B.C. marks the end of the Roman Republic and the beginning of the Principate, and this is the dividing line of the two volumes. They form a brilliant and stimulating survey of the political, social, economic and cultural developments of the Roman people, with considerable attention paid to agriculture.

MARQUARDT, Karl Joachim and MOMMSEN, Theodor. Handbuch der römischen Alterthümer. Leipzig, S. Hirzel, 1881–1888. 7 v. in 9, illus., fold. plans. **HC28**

1.–3. Bd. Römisches Staatsrecht von Theodor Mommsen; 4.–6. Bd. Römische Staatsverwaltung von Joachim Marquardt; 7. Bd. das Privatleben der Römer, von Joachim Marquardt.

In the 20-volume French translation of G. Humbert, Paris, 1890–1907, v. I–VII by Mommsen, treating of public law, are still useful; v. VIII–XIII by Marquardt—*Römische Staatsverwaltung*—deal with administrative history in the provinces, finances, army and cults.

MARTIN, Jean Pierre. La Rome ancienne; 753 avant J.C.–395 après J.C. Paris, Presses Universitaires de France, [1973]. 351p., illus. **HC29**

Le fil des temps.
AC XLIII 1974 560 Raepsaet-Charlier • HZ CCXIX 1974 375 Lippold • JRS LXIV 1974 222–223 Hall

McDONALD, A. H. Republican Rome. London, Thames & Hudson, 1966. 244p., illus., plans. **HC30**

JRS LVII 1967 284–285 Scullard • CJ LXII 1967 228–230 Rowland • CR XVII 1967 190–192 Walbank
One of the best volumes in the *Ancient peoples and places* series (50 v. so far), this is an interpretative essay, rather than a history, on the Republic's rise and fall. It combines literature with archaeology and numismatics and emphasizes the importance of geography and its interrelationship with politics, a closely-knit essay that provides a stimulating and imaginative introduction. Well illustrated.

NICOLET, Claude. Rome et la conquête du monde Méditerranéen (264–27 avant J. C.). Paris, Presses Universitaires de France, 1977. 464p. **HC31**

Nouvelle Clio: L'histoire et ses problèmes; 8, t. 1.: Les structures de l'Italie romaine.
REL LV 1977 519 Néraudau
The successor in the *Nouvelle Clio* series to J. Heurgon's *Rome et la méditerranée occidentale* (1969). Maintains the high quality of the series. The bibliography contains 1,320 items (p. 7–73). The work attempts a unified interpretation of the slow political and cultural unification of Italy.
Demography and the economy are studied at the outset, followed by the financial, military and political organization. The sources and methods of research are examined before the presentation of a vast and original synthesis. A structured, well-documented and well-written work.
See now 1978 ed.

PETIT, Paul. Histoire générale de l'empire romain. Paris, Éditions du Seuil, [1974]. 799p., fold. map. **HC32**

REL LIII 1975 521–522 Néraudau • RPh L 1976 163–164 JAL
A clearly written, well-balanced survey in three parts: Le Haut Empire, La Crise de l'Empire, and Le Bas Empire. Particularly useful for its syntheses and pointers to new research possibilities. The documentation is detailed and up-to-date, with the *Bibliographie Générale* extending through p.7–50.

PETIT, Paul. La paix romaine. [2e édition mise à jour.] Paris, Presses Universitaires de France, 1971. 412p., maps. **HC33**

Nouvelle Clio; 9.
AC XXXIX 1970 312–313 Sterckx • Gnomon XLII 1970 284–290 Wickert • Latomus XXVII 1968 220–221 Chevallier
Covering the period 31 B.C.–193 A.D., the work follows the *Nouvelle Clio* series pattern set by Heurgon and Nicolet. Part I. Les moyens de la recherche, listing sources, bibliographies (705 items), tableaux chronologiques; Part II. Nos connaissances (p.91–205).
Great erudition, clarity of exposition, and impartiality of discussion (extended to Marxist contributions) are everywhere evident.

PETIT, Paul. Pax romana. Trans. James Willis. 2d ed. London, Batsford, 1976. 368p., maps. **HC34**

Trans. of *La paix romaine*.
Latomus XXVII 1978 778 Deroux
The bibliography in this English translation of *La paix romaine* (1967), has been updated, with 781 titles instead of the original 705, plus a "Bibliographical Supplement" of 160 items.

PIGANIOL, André. Histoire de Rome, 6th ed. Paris, Presses Universitaires de France, 1977. lii, 692p. **HC35**

AJPh LXII 1941 382–388 Haywood • JRS XXX 1940 98–99 Scullard • REL XLVI 1968 49–53 Heurgon
Basic for the advanced student and researcher; "extraordinaire instrument de travail," Petit. Its focus is twofold: to pose the problems and give research orientation. The notes are especially useful with their tripartite division: *sources, bibliographie* and *état des questions*. Covers the period from the beginning to 476 A.D.
The 5th edition has a supplementary bibliography, p.[523]–635, as well as the general bibliography, p. [ix]–lii.

POMA, Gabriella. Gli studi recenti sull'origine della repubblica romana; Tendenze e prospettive della ricerca 1963–73. Bologna, Cooperativa libraria universitaria editrice, 1974. 187p. **HC36**

Studi di storia antica; 1.
AC XLV 1976 359–360 Poucet • Latomus XXXV 1976 447 Richard
This useful critical survey of the research of the ten year period, 1963–1973, concentrates on some of the main questions in early Republican history: chronol-

ogy, present positions in the research and utilization of the literary, epigraphical and archaeological sources, the relations between Rome, Etruria, and mainland Greece, the origins of the consulate and dictatorship, the political and social structures of 5th century Rome. Notes rich in bibliographical data occupy half the work (p.99–181) and there is an index of modern authors. There are many minor errors in bibliographical details.

SCULLARD, Howard Hayes. From the Gracchi to Nero; A history of Rome from 133 B.C. to A.D. 68. 4th ed. London, Methuen (New York, distributed in the U.S.A. by Harper & Row), 1976. xii, 494p., map. **HC37**

CR X 1960 247–250 McDonald • History XLV 1960 133–134 Crook • JRS L 1960 247–248 Lepper
A straightforward, readable and up-to-date account, especially useful for students. The Gracchi, Sulla, Caesar and Augustus are well described and assessed.

SHERK, Robert Kenneth. Roman documents from the Greek East; Senatus consulta and epistulae to the age of Augustus. Baltimore, Johns Hopkins Press, [1969]. xii, 396p., front. **HC38**

AJPh XCI 1970 223–228 Bowersock
Seventy-eight documents, chiefly decrees of the Roman Senate and letters of Roman magistrates, in Greek translation, most of which are accompanied by a description and a commentary in English, and a bibliography. Based on the works of Paul Viereck.

SINNIGEN, William Gurnee and BOAK, Arthur E. A history of Rome to A.D. 565. 6th ed. New York, Macmillan, 1977. xviii, 557p., illus. **HC39**

The 1st to the 4th editions, by A. E. R. Boak, published under title: *A history of Rome to 565 A.D.* In the 5th ed. Boak's name appeared first on title page.
CR n.s. III 1953 212 Chilver • JRS XLIV 1954 122–123 Walbank • CPh XLVIII 1953 70 Roebuck
In his 1965 collaboration on the 5th edition, Professor Sinnigen reported that by the time of his death on 16 December 1962, Professor Boak had revised to the bottom of p.97 of the 4th edition, i.e., half-way through c.VII. Professor Sinnigen had been asked in particular to be responsible for the chapters dealing with the Late Empire.
This work has been deservedly popular as a textbook for its sane judgment, sound scholarship, proper balance of emphasis and lively presentation.

SMALLWOOD, E. Mary. Documents illustrating the principates of Gaius, Claudius and Nero. Cambridge, Cambridge University Press, 1967. xii, 148p., tables. **HC40**

Texts in Latin and Greek, preface and notes in English.

AJPh XC 1969 373–374 Bourne • CPh LXIV 1969 140–141 Oost • Gnomon XL 1968 725–727 Schillinger-Hafell • JRS LIX 1969 292–293 Reynolds
Smallwood's two volumes (see also HC 41) follow the format established in similar collections by Ehrenberg and Jones, and McCrum and Woodhead. Arrangement is by category and not chronological, a most useful *vade mecum* for students who need reliable texts of epigraphic, numismatic or papyrological matters discussed in university lectures. There are lists of recurrent epigraphic abbreviations and their resolutions as well as selective indices. Notes are skimpy and there is no *apparatus criticus.*

SMALLWOOD, E. Mary. Documents illustrating the principates of Nerva, Trajan and Hadrian. Cambridge, Cambridge University Press, 1966. xii, 208p. **HC41**

JRS LIX 1969 292–293 Reynolds

SOLARI, Arturo. L'impero romano. Genova, Editrice Dante Alighieri, 1940–1947. 4 v., maps. **HC42**

Volume titles: 1. Unità e universalità di Augusto. 2. Conflitto tra senato e province, 14–69. 3. Compromesso costituzionale, 69–193. 4. Impero provinciale, restaurazione. 193–363.

STARR, Chester G. The ancient Romans. New York, Oxford University Press, [1971]. 256p., illus. **HC43**

AHR LXXVII 1972 754–755 Gruen
An introductory work, aimed at high school and junior college audiences, intelligently conceived and successfully executed. Four major subjects receive emphasis: the clash of Rome and Carthage, the career of Julius Caesar, the Antonine Age, and the rise of Christianity. There are excellent illustrations, charts and maps.

STARR, Chester G. The emergence of Rome as ruler of the Western World. 2d ed. Ithaca, Cornell University Press, 1965. 118p., illus. **HC44**

The development of western civilization. Narrative essays in the history of our tradition from the time of the ancient Greeks and Hebrews to the present. "Seventh printing, with revisions, 1965."

STARR, C. G. "The Roman Empire, 1911–1960." JRS L (1960): 149–160. **HC45**

Attempts to single out some of the main forces which have shaped the views of recent historians; comments on developments in the utilization of evidence and on shifts in the areas of concern; assesses the present status of research on the Empire.

STEIN, Ernst. Histoire du Bas-Empire. Édition française par Jean-Remy Palanque. Amsterdam, A. M. Hakkert, 1968. 2 v. in 3, illus. **HC46**

Reprint of the 1959 ed. t.1. De l'état romain à l'état byzantin (284–476). t.2. De la disparition de l'empire d'occident à la mont de Justinien (476–565).

HZ CXCII 1961 377–379 Vogt, CXXXIX 1929 580–582 Hohl • Gnomon XXXIII 1961 260–263 Ruggini • REL XXXVIII 1960 450–452 Petit

Stein's work appeared originally in German in Vienna in 1928. In Palanque was found the ideal French translator. Especially good on institutions. "Stein-Palanque" is indispensable for specialist, researcher and student alike.

VOGT, Joseph. Bibliographie zur antiken Sklaverei. In Verbindung mit der Kommission für Geschichte des Altertums der Akademie de Wissenschaften und der Literatur (Mainz). Studentische Mitarbeiter; Manfred Haaga [et al.] Redaktion; Norbert Brockmeyer. Bochum, Brockmeyer, [1971]. xix, 181p.   **HC47**

VOGT, Joseph. The decline of Rome; the metamorphosis of ancient civilization. New York, Praeger, [1969, 1967]. xii, 340p., map, 64 plates (incl. facsims.).   **HC48**

Trans. of *Der Niedergang Roms* by Janet Sondheimer.

AC XXXVII 1968 767 Petit • JRS LIX 1969 272–274 Browning • EHR LXXXIV 1969 375–376 Frend • CR XX 1970 69–72 Matthews

A careful, balanced account of the decline, but with more emphasis on metamorphosis, in four long chapters: The Crisis of the Ancient World in the Third Century; The Monarchy, The Christian Church and Ruling Society in the Fourth Century; The Roman West and the New Peoples in the Fifth Century; and Cultural Change Reflected in Art. An excellent overview of the cultural and religious changes and transformation in the decisive 300 years that saw the spread of Christianity and the decline of paganism. There are 90 excellent photographs.

VOGT, Joseph. Die Römische Republik. 6. [überarb.] Aufl. Freiburg, K. Alber, 1973. 480p.   **HC49**

Gnomon XXIV 1952 442–443 Scullard

The first edition (1932) already revealed the author's talents of good balance and judgment, common sense and lucidity of expression. Successive editions have incorporated the most recent scholarship and made the work an excellent introduction for younger students.

VOGT, Joseph and WOLF, Julius. Römische Geschichte. Freiburg im Breisgau, Herder & Co., 1932. 2 v., plates, ports.   **HC50**

Geschichte der führenden Völker ... 6,–7. bd. 1. Hälfte, die Römische Republik, von Joseph Vogt. 2. Hälfte, die Römische Kaiserzeit, von Julius Wolf.

CR XLVII 1933 229 Mattingly • DLZ 1954 894–904 Wickert • Historia 1933 626–628 Lanzani

A good introductory sketch of Roman history in Gercke-Norden, giving bearings and providing directions on the use of the sources.

Rome and Italy to 133 B.C.

AFZELIUS, Adam. Die römische Eroberung Italiens (340–264 v. Chr.); Two Studies on Roman expansion. New York, Arno Press, 1975. 204, 116p., [2] leaves of plates, maps.   **HC51**

RH CCI 1949 119–120 Piganiol

A reprint of two studies which appeared in 1942 and 1944 to less critical attention than they deserved.

ALFÖLDI, András. Early Rome and the Latins. Ann Arbor, University of Michigan Press, [1965]. 433p.   **HC52**

Jerome Lectures; 7th series.

CR XVI 1966 94–98 Ogilvie • REL XLIV 1966 93–97 Richard • JRS LVII 1967 211–216 Momigliano

Alföldi's boldest book to date in which he gathers together and elaborates his controversial views on Roman history advanced by him for over 20 years. A beautifully produced and illustrated work, it is one of the fullest surveys of the problems of Early Rome available.

ALFÖLDI, András. Römische Frühgeschichte; Kritik u. Forschung seit 1964. Andreas Alföldi, mit Beitr. von G. Manganarao und J. Gy. Szilbagyi. Heidelberg, C. Winter, 1976. 219p., [8] leaves of plates, 25 illus.   **HC53**

Supplements the author's *Early Rome and the Latins,* published in 1965.

CR XXVIII 1978 116–117 Ogilvie

A restatement and justification (mostly in answer to Momigliano's criticisms) of Alföldi's controversial views on a variety of topics in Early Roman history. A useful compendium of recent scholarly views, but not much new material or evidence.

ALFÖLDI, András. Die Struktur des voretruskischen Römerstaates. Heidelberg, C. Winter, 1974. 226p., [8] leaves of plates, illus.   **HC54**

Bibliothek der Klassischen Altertumswissenschaften: n. F. 1, Reihe 5, Bd. 5.

CR XXVI 1976 240–241 Ogilvie • REL LII 1974 525–527 Heurgon • Latomus XXXIV 1975 1143–1150 Pfiffig

A natural sequence to Alföldi's *Early Rome and the Latins,* this is more a work of comparative anthropology than of history. In a wide-ranging study Mongols and Chinese, Huns and Celts, Scythians and Iranians are invoked to support a basic Eurasian structure of primitive society. The fundamental principle is the relationship between man and the female animal deity (wolf, bear). Contains much that is imaginative and persuasive, but some that is tendentious.

ASTIN, A. E. Cato the Censor. Oxford, Clarendon Press (New York, Oxford University Press), 1978. x, 371p.   **HC55**

REL LVIII 1980 574–576 Guittard

ASTIN, A. E. Scipio Aemilianus. Oxford, Clarendon Press, 1967. xiii, 374p. **HC56**

CW LXI 1968 253–254 Kagan • JRS LVIII 1968 256–258 Scullard • RPh XLVI 1968 294–297 Richard
An important contribution to the understanding of the crisis provoked by the career of Tiberius Gracchus, as well as a careful biography of Scipio Aemilianus. The emphasis is so much on the politics of the period that Aemilianus' skill as a general does not receive enough attention. Numerous minute details are relegated to footnotes and appendices making the main text highly readable. There is a very full bibliography. An excellent portrayal of the politics which led to the catastrophe of 133.

BADIAN, E. Roman imperialism in the late republic. 2d ed. Ithaca, N.Y., Cornell University Press, 1971. x, 117p. **HC57**

A Class XIII 1970 157–165 Vogel-Weidemann • CR XX 1970 374–376 Levick • JRS LIX 1969 270–271 Brunt

BADIAN, E. "Tiberius Gracchus and the beginning of the Roman Revolution." ANRW 1.1: 668–731. **HC57a**

BERNSTEIN, Alvin H. Tiberius Sempronius Gracchus; Tradition and Apostasy. Ithaca, Cornell University Press, 1978. 272p. **HC58**

G&R XXVI 1979 94 Gardner • AJPh C 1979 452–458 Badian
Offered as an "original synthesis," this work draws upon "historical imagination" as well as judgment and is written for the specialist but also aims at intelligibility for the non-specialist. The book has a valuable essay on the scope and content of the *lex agraria* summarizing recent work and offering an interpretation aimed at removing anomalies.

BLOCH, Raymond. The origins of Rome. New York, Praeger, [1960]. 212p., illus., plates, maps. **HC59**

Ancient peoples and places; 15.
JRS XLIX 1959 161 Scullard • REL XXXVII 1959 361–363 Durry
This translation of a 1959 *Les Origines de Rome* is an excellent presentation, brief, lucid and incorporating recent archaeological discoveries.

BOITANI, Francesca et al. Etruscan cities. With Maria Cataldi, Marinella Pasquinucci. English trans. by Catherine Atthill et al. London, Cassell, 1975. 336p., col. illus. **HC60**

Latomus XXXVII 1978 760–762 Daubies
A scholarly work, up-to-date on very recent discoveries. Simultaneous translations into German, French and English appeared in 1975 of the 1973 Italian original. The work is addressed to the alert general reader but even specialists will benefit from its bibliographical aids, its excellent summary of the archaeological data

on the individual cities, and its account of Etruscan artifacts in the museums of Florence, Volterra, Gregoriano Etrusco, and Villa Giulia.

BOREN, Henry Charles. The Gracchi. New York, Twayne Publishers, [1969, 1968]. 146p. **HC61**

Twayne's Rulers and Statesmen of the World series; 9.
JRS LX 1970 209–212 Earl • CW LXIII 1969 94–95 Evans • AJPh XCI 1970 500–501 Rowland
A worthy addition to the TROW series, written with balance and judgment. The Gracchi have been much re-interpreted since Mommsen represented them as the equivalent of 19th century liberals. Here, Tiberius is part ambitious politician, part idealist, but primarily a conservative reformer, hoping to achieve his ends by rehabilitating the small farmer. Boren's Gaius is slightly less satisfactorily portrayed, perhaps because he is more complex. The work is obviously aimed at the beginning student or interested layman and is properly didactic while avoiding dogmatism. A brief bibliography of 80 items contains most of what is necessary for further study.

BRISSON, Jean Paul. Carthage ou Rome? [Paris], Fayard, [1973]. 436p., maps. **HC62**

Les Grandes Études historiques.
AC XLIII 1974 572–573 Raepsaet-Charlier • Latomus XXXIV 1975 243–246 Debergh
A clear and precise account of the Rome-Carthage conflict of the 3rd and 2d centuries and its continuation by the founding of *Colonia Carthago* by Gaius Gracchus through Caesar and Augustus. The military and diplomatic exchanges are detailed, and also the political and socio-economical ramifications in naval equipment and administrative institutions. An important contribution to the understanding of Roman imperialism.

CARCOPINO, Jérôme. Autour des Gracques; Études critiques. 2. édition, revue, corrigée, augmentée. Paris, Les Belles Lettres, 1967. 356p. **HC63**

Collection d'études anciennes.

CHARLES-PICARD, Gilbert and PICARD, Colette. The life and death of Carthage; a survey of Punic history and culture from its birth to the final tragedy. Trans. from the French by Dominique Collon. New York, Taplinger Pub. Co., 1968. vi, 362p., illus., maps. **HC64**

CHRIST, Karl, ed. Hannibal. Darmstadt, Wissenschaftliche Buchgesellschaft, 1974. ix, 429p. **HC65**

Wege der Forschung; Bd. 371.

DE BEER, Gavin Rylands, Sir. Hannibal; Challenging Rome's supremacy. New York, Viking Press, [1969]. 319p., illus. (part col.), facsims., maps, ports. **HC66**

London ed. has subtitle: The Struggle for Power in the Mediterranean.

JRS LX 1970 208 Astin

A good popular account for the interested non-academic reader, lavishly illustrated.

DEFOSSE, Pol. Bibliographie étrusque. 11. (1927–1950). Bruxelles, Latomus, 1976. 348p. 2 v. **HC67**

Collection Latomus.

AC XLVI 1977 361 Lambrechts • CR XXVIII 1978 180–181 Ridgway • LEC XLIV 1976 287 Stenuit

An all-inclusive bibliography of Etruscan art, language, religion, political history, economics, culture, etc. Lists items not carried in *Studi Etruschi* which carries its own classified bibliography starting with *St. Etr.* XLI (1973), 461–503, and continuing in subsequent editions.

DOREY, Thomas A. and DUDLEY, D. R. Rome against Carthage. London, Seeker and Warburg, 1971. xviii, 205p., 8 plates, illus., maps. **HC68**

History LVII 1972 411 Astin • JRS LXII 1972 181–182 Walbank • CR XXIV 1974 251–252 McDonald

A straight military narrative of the three Punic Wars, with a good bibliography for further reading. Written in a lucid and vivid style, this is an excellent introduction to the reading of Polybius and Livy's third decade.

EARL, Donald C. Tiberius Gracchus. A Study in Politics. Berchem, Bruxelles, 1963. 120p. **HC69**

Collection Latomus LXVI.

AC XXXIII 1964 548–550 Mossé • Gnomon XXXVII 1965 189–192 Brunt • JRS LIV 1964 198–199 Scullard

A work which reduces Tiberius Gracchus from the role of radical social reformer to that of leader of an aristocratic political group whose *lex agraria* was the product of political expediency, not philanthropic reform. Its main purpose was to increase the number of citizens with the necessary property qualifications for the army, since the crisis was in the army not "in the agricultural, economic or even social sphere."

A daring re-interpretation, argued with clarity and elegance, which does not fully convince but need not all stand or fall together.

ERRINGTON, Robert Malcolm. The Dawn of Empire; Rome's rise to world power. Ithaca, Cornell University Press, [1972]. x, 318p., maps. **HC70**

CW LXVII 1973 51 Starr • G&R XIX 1972 220 Earl

Essentially a diplomatic history and a factual narrative of the wars and treaties of the period 264–133 B.C.

GAGÉ, Jean. La chute des Tarquins et les débuts de la république romaine. Paris, Payot, 1976. 265p., map. **HC71**

AC XLVII 1978 329–330 Poucet • Latomus XXXVII 1978 560 Poucet • REL LIV 1976 469–471 Rouvière

This is the fruit of 25 years of reflection and assiduous research. Eight profoundly original studies, full of highly suggestive reflections, intuitions, conjectures and hypotheses.

GAGÉ, Jean. Enquêtes sur les structures sociales et religieuses de la Rome primitive. Bruxelles, Latomus, 1977. 631p. **HC72**

Collection Latomus; 152.

REL LV 1978 545–547 Hellegouarc'h

Twenty studies from journals, 1953–1972. Informative but occasionally overspeculative.

GJERSTAD, Einar et al. Les origines de la république romaine; 9 exposés suivis de discussions. Vandouvres-Genève, (Fondation Hardt pour l'étude de l'antiquité classique), 1967. viii, 390p., 5 plates. **HC73**

Entretiens sur l'antiquité classique; 13.

RBPh LXVIII 1970 • JRS LX 1970 199–202 Drummond

A volume of nine papers by such leading scholars as Alföldi, F. E. Brown, Gjerstad, Heurgon, Gabba and Momigliano, many of them reiterating their respective positions, which are already well known.

GRIMAL, Pierre. Le siècle des Scipions; Rome et l'hellénisme au temps des guerres puniques. 2. éd. refondue et augm. Paris, Aubier, 1975. 414p. **HC74**

HARRIS, William. Rome in Etruria and Umbria. Oxford, Clarendon Press, 1971. x, 370p. **HC75**

Gnomon L 1978 691–693 Bloch • RPh XLVIII 1974 160–161 Hus • JRS LXIII 1973 247–249 Lewis

A very useful synthesis of the present state of knowledge of the romanization of Etruria and Umbria and of the scholarly problems that remain. The analysis of the relevant historiography is particularly noteworthy, though the author's skepticism about certain Livy passages perhaps goes too far. The evolution of Etruria and Umbria from the wars of conquest to the Augustan Era is carefully examined, and the constitutional *Foedera* receive minute attention. A richly informative work.

HAYWOOD, Richard Mansfield. Studies on Scipio Africanus. Westport, Conn., Greenwood Press, 1973, 1933. 114p. **HC76**

Reprint of the edition published by the Johns Hopkins Press, in series: Johns Hopkins University Studies in Historical and Political Science, ser. 51. no. 1.

NICOLET, Claude. Les Gracques. Crise agraire et révolution à Rome. Paris, Julliard, 1967. 235p., 16p. of illus. **HC77**

Coll. Archives XXXIII

JRS LX 1970 209–212 Earl • LEC XXXVI 1968 197 van Ooteghem • RBPh XLVI 1968 191 Chevallier

Almost no contemporary material survives for the Gracchi, so Nicolet first presents in translation what is relevant in Plutarch and Appian and then proceeds with a series of short chapters, discussing various aspects of Tiberius and Gaius, again with evidence cited *in extenso* in translation. The influence of Greek and Roman ideas on the Gracchi is emphasized.

OGILVIE, Robert Maxwell. Early Rome and the Etruscans. [London], Fontana, 1976. 189p., [4] leaves of plates, illus. **HC78**

CR XXIX 1979 106–109 Cornell • Phoenix XXXI 1977 369–372 Sumner

The author of the monumental *Commentary on Livy* (Oxford, 1965) covers the same time-span in this well-written, balanced discussion of the period from the end of the 7th century to the Gallic sack. Perhaps overly optimistic about the possibility of writing a history beginning with the 6th century, since the annalistic and antiquarian sources are as dubious as ever, the work is nonetheless as sober, up-to-date and judicious a presentation as the controversial evidence warranted at the time of writing. Unfortunately it could not take account of the spectacular discoveries and important publications since 1975, which herald a new phase in Etruscology.

PALLOTTINO, Massimo. The Etruscans. Edited by David Ridgway; Trans. [from the Italian] by J. Cremona. [2nd Eng. ed.], rev. and enl. [London], A. Lane, [1975]. 316p., illus. **HC79**

Trans. of *Etruscologia*.

POUCET, Jacques. Recherches sur la légende sabine des origines de Rome. Kinshasa, Univ. Lovanium, 1967. xxxii, 473p. **HC80**

Univ. de Louvain Recueil de trav. d'hist. & de philol. Sér. 4 XXXVIII.

AC XXXVII 1968 350–351 Petit • CR XVIII 1968 327–329 Ogilvie • Gnomon XL 1968 799–805 Richard

The tradition which associated the Sabines with the beginnings of the history of Rome had not hitherto been submitted to a systematic criticism, though it had been questioned (cf. *CAH* VII 493f.).

PROCTOR, Dennis. Hannibal's march in history. Oxford, Clarendon Press, 1971. xi, 229p., fold. plate, 2 maps. **HC81**

AJPh XCV 1974 421–422 Harris • JRS LXII 1972 180–181 De Beer

Another one of the interminable inquests on the chronology and the geography of Hannibal's march from Spain to Italy. The chronologies of De Sanctis and Walbank are convincingly shown to be incorrect. Proctor is stronger on knowledge of the topography than on the interrelationship of ancient accounts of the march.

SALMON, Edward Togo. Samnium and the Samnites. Cambridge, Cambridge University Press, 1967. xi, 447p. **HC82**

REL XLV 1967 579 Heurgon • CPh LXIV 1969 206–207 Oost • JRS LVIII 1968 224–229 Fredericksen

The first book devoted exclusively to the Samnites and an excellent discussion on sources, Samnite geography, ethnography, and culture, and the successive wars with Rome down to Sulla. One of the best books to date on non-Roman Italy.

SCULLARD, Howard Hayes. Scipio Africanus: soldier and politician. Ithaca, N.Y., Cornell University Press, 1970. 299p., illus., maps. **HC83**

CJ LXIX 1973 158–160 Morgan • CPh LXVI 1971 67–68 Larsen • CR XXI 1971 425–427 Errington

Scullard's third book on Scipio Africanus, each separated by about 20 years (1930, 1951). The present work is often a word-for-word borrowing from the earlier ones, and new material is generally confined to the notes. Less than ideal either for the scholar or the general reader, although aimed at both.

SEAGER, Robin, comp. The crisis of the Roman republic: studies in political and social history. Cambridge, Heffer; New York, Barnes & Noble, 1969. xiii, 218p., plate. **HC84**

CR XXI 1971 298–299 Gray • G&R XVII 1970 111–112 Sewter • Latomus XXIX 1970 866 Richard

This reprint of the original articles begins with Badian's *Forschungsbericht* from *Historia* XI, 1962.

SYME, Ronald, Sir. The Roman Revolution. [Oxford], Oxford University Press, [1939]. Reprint 1967. 568p., illus. **HC85**

CR LIV 1940 38–41 Giles • JRS XXX 1940 75–80 Momigliano • REL XVIII 1940 221–224 Piganiol

Hailed by Giles as "one of the most important books on Roman history since Mommsen," and by Momigliano as "obviously the best which has appeared on the subject since E. Meyer's great work," Syme's first *magnum opus* has enjoyed enormous prestige.

TOYNBEE, Arnold Joseph. Hannibal's legacy. The Hannibalic war's effects on Roman life. I: Rome and her neighbors before Hannibal's entry. II: Rome and her neighbors after Hannibal's exit. London and New York, Oxford University Press, 1965. 2 v. xii, 643; x, 754p., 6 maps, 2 tables. **HC86**

CR XVI 1966 384–388 Walbank • History LI 1966 199–201 Scullard • JRS LVII 1967 244–246 Staveley

A monumental work, with all of Toynbee's awe-inspiring erudition and well-known predilections and prejudices. The thesis is that Rome's victory over Hannibal, detailed in v. 1, led ultimately to fatal change in Rome's social, economic and political life. A *tour de force* that will prove an invaluable reference work for Republican history down to 133. There are good indices, bibliographies, glossaries and maps.

WARMINGTON, Brian H. Carthage. Rev. ed. New York, Praeger, [1969]. 272p., illus., maps.
HC87

Latomus XX 1961 159–160, XXIX 1970 1081 Debergh

Rome and Empire to 330 A.D.

ABBOTT, Frank and JOHNSON, Allan Chester. Municipal administration in the Roman Empire. Reprint of the 1926 ed. New York, Russell & Russell, [1968]. vii, 598p.   **HC88**

"Municipal documents in Greek and Latin from Italy and the provinces": p.247–506. "Documents from Egypt": p.507–571.
CJ XXIII 1928 705–707 Magoffin • AJPh XLVIII 1927 184–185 Frank • Gnomon 1929 231–236 Rostowzew
Abbott deals with the municipalities of the West, Johnson with the voluminous source materials of the East, giving a reliable overall view of the municipal system, how it developed and worked. Inevitably somewhat dated but there is an abundant collection of juridical, epigraphical and papyrological texts, which nowadays, alas, would need translations.

ALFÖLDI, András. The conversion of Constantine and pagan Rome. Trans. by Harold Mattingly. Oxford, Clarendon Press, [1969]. x, 140p.
HC89

Reprint of the 1948 ed. with new note.
REA LI 1949 371–373 Palanque • JRS XXXIX 1949 169–169 Moss • AJA LIII 1949 Laistner
A challenging and suggestive study, in which Alföldi depicts Constantine as seeing from the start of his principate the need for co-operation of throne and altar and for a dominant leadership role by the Church if the Empire was to be saved. In this view, Constantine was a sincere convert to Christianity in 312. Numismatic evidence and Lactantius are used with telling effect.

ALFÖLDI, András. Die Struktur des voretruskischen Römerstaates. Heidelberg, C. Winter, 1974. 226p., [8] leaves of plates, illus.
HC90

Bibliothek der klassischen Altertumswissenschaften: n. F., 1. Reihe, Bd. 5.
AC XLIV 1975 646–651 Poucet • REL LII 1974 525–527 Heurgon
Hitherto, practitioners of the comparative method in studying Roman beginnings stayed within the Indo-European framework. Here Alföldi looks further—to the myths, customs, and social traditions of the Turks, Mongols, and peoples of the Ural to aid in his reconstruction of the structures of pre-Etruscan Rome. A fascinating examination of the Lupercalia.

ALFÖLDI, András. Studien zur Geschichte der Weltkrise des 3. Jahrhunderts nach Christus. Darmstadt, Wissenschaftliche Buchgesellschaft, 1967. vii, 460p., 78p. of illus.   **HC91**

RPh XLII 1968 353–354 Chastagnol • Aevum XLIII 1969 353–354 Pallavisini
Alföldi's studies have revolutionized the understanding of the period between the reigns of Severus Alexander and Diocletian. These studies reprinted from periodical contributions published between 1927 and 1950, as well as chapters in *CAH*, XII (1939), are conveniently brought together here without correction or updating (the *CAH* chapters are translated into German). The author's native Pannonia and the Danube regions naturally receive special attention and his numismatic acumen is everywhere evident.

ANDRÉ, Jean Marie. Le siècle d'Auguste. Paris, Payot, 1974. 335p.   **HC92**

REL LII 1974 528–530 Porte • Latomus XXXIV 1975 1152–54 Martin • Augustinus XXI 1976 235 Oroz
Studies all aspects of the age of Augustus: mores, religion, poetry, sociology, aesthetics, urbanization, gastronomy. The table of contents is too neatly structured and does not correspond to the interior untidiness of the age.

AYMARD, André and AUBOYER, Jeannine. Rome et son empire. 5 édition revue. Paris, Presses Universitaires de France, 1967. 784p., illus., plates.   **HC93**

Histoire générale des civilisations; t. 2.
REL XXXIII 1955 466–468 Bayet • Gnomon XXVI 1955 534 Hohl • JRS XLVII 1957 251 Frederiksen
Consists of three parts: L' occident et la formation de l'unité méditerranéenne, les civilisations de l'unité Romaine, and L'Asie orientale du début de l'ère chrétienne à la fin du 4e siècle. The center of the book concentrates on an elaborate description of Rome. Addressed to the educated general reader, this is a highly satisfactory introduction to Roman civilization and a magnificent production.

BÉNABOU, Marcel. La résistance africaine à la romanisation. Paris, F. Maspero, 1976. 634p., maps.   **HC94**

JRS LXVIII 1978 190–192 Whittaker
The best account written of Roman expansion into Africa, improving on Rachets' *Rome et les Berbères* and Romanelli's *Storia delle Province Romane dell' Africa* in accuracy, conciseness and interpretation.

BENGTSON, Hermann. Grundriss der Römischen Geschichte; Mit Quellenkunde. 2., durchges. Aufl. München, Beck, 1970– . Bd. 1. Republik und Kaiserzeit bis 284 n. Chr.   **HC95**

Handbuch der Altertumswissenschaft, v. 3. Abt., 5. T. 1, Bd 1.
JRS LVIII 1968 250–251 Scullard • AC 1967 727–730 Petit • CPh LXIV 1969 201–202 Oost

Intended as the necessary replacement for Niese's *Grundriss* which appeared in five editions from 1889 to 1923, Bengtson's *Grundriss* contains much that is excellent, especially the bibliographies, but the extraordinary compression throughout leads to some regrettable omissions, over-simplifications and inaccuracies, especially in social and economic matters. There is not perhaps the same degree of magistral aplomb and assured familiarity with bibliographical matters as in the author's *Griechische Geschichte*, and questions could be raised about proportions.

BIRLEY, Anthony Richard. Septimius Severus; The African emperor. Garden City, N.Y., Doubleday, 1972 [1971]. xiv, 398p., illus. **HC96**

CW LXVI 1972 181–182 MacMullen • History LVIII 1973 73–74 Seager • Latomus XXXII 1973 653–654 Daubies

The aim of this book—to set Septimius in his context—results in a good detailed African background in the early chapters. The recent increase in archaeological, inscriptional and papyrological discoveries makes this reassessment all the more timely and valuable. The new information is concisely conveyed in well-arranged footnotes and three valuable appendices. A bibliography of an emperor cannot be a substitute for the history of the empire during his reign, as the author is aware, and this adversely affects both the structure and contents of his book.

BLOCH, Gustave and CARCOPINO, Jérôme. Histoire Romaine, II: La république romaine de 133 à 44 avant J. C. Paris, Les Presses Universitaires, 1935–1936. 1 v. in 2, maps (part fold.), plans. **HC97**

Histoire générale pub. sous la direction de Gustave Glotz. [I] Histoire ancienne, 3. ptie.: Histoire romaine; t. II 1. section. des Gracques à Sulla, par Gustave Bloch et Jérôme Carcopino; 2. section. César, par Jérôme Carcopino.

Gnomon XII 1936 643–648 Münzer • 1936 135–137 Cary • REL XIV 1936 441–444 Marouzeau

These two volumes, forming part of Glotz's *Histoire Générale*, provide a detailed account of the political history of the later Roman Republic and an adequate narrative of the military campaigns. Bloch's contribution is confined to some of the earlier chapters (I–II, IV–V). The stamp of Carcopino's workmanship is on most of the work, especially his minute and independent study of the sources, his powers of synthesis and his eloquent defence of personal interpretations.

BOWERSOCK, Glen Warren. Augustus and the Greek world. Oxford, Clarendon Press, 1965. xii, 176p. **HC98**

JHS LXXXVII 1967 181–182 Badian • Stud Class X 1968 340–342 Stefan

Besides military power a network of personal links between eminent local families and the great dynastic houses of Rome helped the survival of Roman power. Greek literary men were among the most important

of such links. This is a delightful and important study in the political and cultural history of the world of Augustus.

CALDERINI, Aristide. I Severi; La crisi dell' impero nel iii secolo. Bologna, Cappelli, [1949]. 645p., plates, ports. **HC99**

Storia di Roma; v. 7.

AC XX 1951 503–505 Bingen • DLZ LXXII 1951 77–84 Ensslin • Latomus X 1951 102–103 Heurgon

Volume VII in the monumental *Storia di Roma* series. An excellent exposition of the main events in this difficult period, with an extended analysis of its political, social, economic, religious and philosophical structures. Calderini refuses to follow the general tendency to write off the 92 years that separate the fall of Commodus and the accession of Diocletian (192–285) as an age of decadence and anarchy; rather he presents it convincingly as an age of transition which gradually but radically transformed the principate as conceived by Augustus and developed by the Antonines. There is a well-organized bibliography of 74 pages.

CARTER, John Mackenzie. The Battle of Actium; The rise and triumph of Augustus Caesar. New York, Weybright and Talley, [1970]. 271p., illus., map. **HC100**

CR XXIII 1973 56–58 Stockton

CARY, Max and SCULLARD, H. H. A history of Rome down to the reign of Constantine. 3d ed. New York, St. Martin's Press, 1975. xxvii, 694p. **HC101**

CJ LXXII 1976 74–79 MacKendrick • G&R XXIII 1976 205 Gardner • CR L 1936 140–141 Giles, XXVIII 1978 115–116 Arnheim • AC XLVII 1978 328 Raepsaet-Charlier

Cary's well-known textbook first appeared in 1935 with a second edition in 1954. In this third edition Professor Scullard has rewritten something like one-third of the book, taking into account the pertinent epigraphical and archaeological discoveries of the intervening 20 years. Some errors persist and recent research in, for example, the socio-economic domain has not been integrated into the new edition. In its time it was the best one-volume textbook of Roman history in English, but more of it should have been rewritten.

CHASTAGNOL, André, comp. Le Bas Empire. Paris, A. Colin, 1969. 320p. **HC102**

Collection U2, 58. Série Histoire ancienne.

RBPh XLVII 1969 1090 Pecklers • RH XCIV 1970 226–227 Patlagean

Appearing in the remarkable U2 collection, this work has an analytical and thematic aperçu of the 4th century by the eminent editor, A. Chastagnol. Some of the chosen texts, which include epigraphic and papyrological documents and juridic texts, are translated by the editor. An excellent initiation tool to 4th century history, with good bibliography.

CHRIST, Karl. Römische Geschichte; Eine Bibliographie. With Reinhard Anders, Marianne Gaul und Bettina Kreck. Darmstadt, Wissenschaftliche Buchgesellschaft, [Abt. Verl.], 1976. xxv, 544p.   **HC103**

CR XXVIII 1978 181 Fredericksen

Contains 8,232 bibliographical items, well organized in seven main sections, each with sub-sections. No reviews are identified, and there are no abstracts, value judgments or linking commentary. A solid and workmanlike bibliography, the best thing of its kind in existence in any language.

CHRIST, Karl. Römische Geschichte; Einführung, Quellenkunde, Bibliographie. Darmstadt, Wissenschaftliche Buchgesellschaft, 1973. xi, 335p.   **HC104**

Die Altertumswissenschaft.

AAHG XXVII 1974 237 Weiler • Gymnasium LXXXII 1975 488–490 Vretsa

An excellent introduction, with sources and bibliography, organized in six main divisions each with subdivisions: I. Allgemeine Einführung, II. Geschichte der Römischen Republik, III. Das Zeitalter der Römischen Revolution, IV. Die Römische Kaizerzeit, V. Die Reichskrise des 3. Jahrhunderts n. Chr., VI. Spätantike.

CHRIST, Karl and HOFFMAN, W. Hannibal. Darmstadt, Wissenschaftliche Buchgesellschaft, 1974. ix, 429p.   **HC105**

Wege der Forschung; Bd. 371.

MH XXXIII 1976 61 Béranger • AAHG XXVII 1974 209–213 Hampl • Gymnasium LXXXIII 1976 104–105 Volkmann

Problems on Hannibal are dealt with by K. Christ and W. Hoffmann. There are several studies on the causes and antecedents of the Second Punic War, the crossing of the Alps, Cannae, on Hannibal, politician and statesman, his relations with Philip V of Macedon, the role of Sicily in his plans, and the judgments on him by Ancients and Moderns. There is a useful index and a well-organized bibliography.

EARL, Donald C. The age of Augustus. London, Elek, 1968. 208p., illus. (some col.), geneal. tables (on lining papers), maps.   **HC106**

CJ LXV 1970 224 Benario

Author of *The political thought of Sallust* (Cambridge, 1961). There is a French translation, *La siècle d'Auguste* (Paris, 1970, 208p.).

GELZER, Matthias. Pompeius. München, F. Bruckmann, [1949]. 311p., ports., maps (on lining papers).   **HC107**

JRS XL 1950 135–137 Adcock • Historia I 1950 296–300 Balsdon • Latomus X 1951 101–102 De Laet

GRANT, Michael. Nero. London, Weidenfeld & Nicolson, 1970. 272p. 15 maps, 198 illus.
                                    HC108

JRS LXI 1971 311 Townend

A good general biography, steering clear of the details of scholarly controversies and offering little documentary support for the positions taken on controverted questions. Contains much accurate information, lavishly illustrated. Effective use is made of coinage and other artifacts.

GREENHALGH, P.A.L. The year of the four emperors. London, Weidenfeld and Nicolson, 1975. xxv, 271p., 17 plates, 6 maps.   **HC109**

CPh LXXIV 1979 258–259 Bradley • CW LXX 1976 280–281 Benario • JRS LXVIII 1978 189–190 Reynolds • LEC XLIV 1976 88 Stenuit

Details, without footnotes or bibliography, the rapid and violent succession of Gabba, Otho, Vitellius and Vespasian as emperors in the year after the death of Nero. Depends largely on Tacitus, with some help from Suetonius, Plutarch and Dio Cassius. Readable and mostly reliable, for the general reader more than for the student of the period.

HENDERSON, Bernard William. Five Roman Emperors; Vespasian, Titus, Domitian, Nerva, Trajan, A.D. 69–117. New York, Barnes & Noble, [1969]. xiii, 357p., maps.   **HC110**

Reprint of the 1927 ed.

CJ XXIII 1928 624–626 Marsh • CR XLII 1928 37–38 Charlesworth • RF 1929 276–280 De Sanctis

A work solid in scholarship and written in a vivid and fascinating style.

HOMO, Léon. Rome impérial et l'urbanisme dans l'antiquité. Paris, Albin Michel, 1971. 665p.
                                    HC111

CR XXIV 1974 274–276 Colledge

A re-issue of a 1951 work, with an opening review of theories of urbanization from Plato and Aristotle to Vitruvius. Caesar and Augustus form the real starting point. A noteworthy, clearly categorized and valuable collection of information, but without needed revisions.

JONES, Arnold Hugh Martin. Augustus. New York, Norton, [1971, 1970]. xi, 196p., maps, plans.   **HC112**

ACR I 1971 243–244 Benario • CR XXIII 1973 54–56 Carter • Gymnasium LXXX 1973 322–324 Brockmeyer

One of the last and least books from Professor Jones, who died suddenly in April 1970 (see obituary by R. Meiggs, *JRS* LX 1970, 186–187). Contains inaccuracies that are more than typographical.

JONES, A. H. M., MARTINDALE, J. R. and MORRIS, J. The prosopography of the later Roman empire, I: 260–395. Cambridge, Cambridge University Press, 1971. xxii, 1152p.
                                    HC112a

REL L 1972 383–384 Chastagnol • BBF XVII 1972 350 Ernst • LEC XL 1972 271 Wankenne • AC XLI 1972 407–408 Petit • CW LXV 1972 207–208 Jones

LACEY, Walter Kirkpatrick. Cicero and the end of the Roman Republic. London, Hodder and Stoughton, 1978. vi, 184p., illus.   **HC113**

HZ CCXXXI 1980 413–414 Bruhns

LEVICK, Barbara Mary. Tiberius the politician. London, Thames and Hudson, 1976. 328p., [8] leaves of plates, illus.   **HC114**

AJPh C 1979 460–465 Adams • CR XXVIII 1978 317–319 Seager
Not a biography.

MARSHALL, B. A. Crassus; A political biography. Amsterdam, A. M. Hakkert, 1976. 205p., [2] leaves of plates, illus., geneal. table.
HC115

A revision of the author's thesis, University of Sydney.
Athenaeam LXVI 1978 431–432 Garzetti • CR XXIX 1979 112–114 Briscoe • Phoenix XXXII 1978 261–266 Marshall
This is less a straight biography than a survey of the political history of the period between 70 and 53 B.C., with particular emphasis on the role of Crassus. He is seen not as Pompey's bitter enemy through the sixties but as a healthy rival, merely bent on increasing his own political power and prestige. This reassessment is established more by repetitive restatement than by real argument, and the handling of sources and prosopographical evidence throughout lacks the sureness of touch that encourages confidence. The only fringe benefit in the study is a painstaking and useful survey of scholarship in this field, especially in the decade since the appearance of F. E. Adcock's *Marcus Crassus, Millionaire,* Cambridge, 1966.

PIPPIDI, Dionis M. Autour de Tibère. Ed. Anastatica. Roma, L'Erma de Bretschneider, 1965. 201p.   **HC116**

RAWSON, Beryl. The politics of friendship. Pompey and Cicero. Sydney, Sydney University Press, 1978. vi, 217p.   **HC117**

CO LVI 1979 88 Sebesta
Designed to provide translations of substantial bodies of source material with accompanying discussion. There are 29 sources lucidly translated, including some letters of Cicero, selections from Pliny's *Natural History,* and inscriptions.

RÉMONDON, Roger. La crise de l'empire romain, de Marc Aurèle à Anastase 2. éd. Paris, Presses Universitaires de France, 1970. 363p., illus.   **HC118**

Nouvelle Clio: L'histoire et ses problèmes; 11.
AHR LXX 1965 840–841 MacMullen • JRS LV 1965 275–276 Millar • REA LXVIII 1966 516–523 Demougeot • RBPh XLIII 1965 708–710 Ruch
A valuable achievement, closely reasoned and well documented, with a bibliography of 538 items, well chosen but badly edited. The last 75 pages collect recent interpretations of continuing problems and suggest new approaches. The period covered, 160–518 A.D., seems too long to be titled *La Crise.*

SEAGER, Robin. Tiberius. London, Methuen; Berkeley, University of California Press, 1972. xviii, 300p., illus.   **HC119**

CW LXVI 1973 476–477 Baldwin • Historia XXIII 1974 481–496 Syme • JRS LXIV 1974 226–229 Griffin • Phoenix XXVIII 1974 266–270 Sumner
Admirably fulfills its goal: to give an account of Tiberius' character and career "intelligible to the general reader and useful to scholars and students of the Early Principate." A serious and fully documented political biography, it deserves to become the standard one.

WARD, Allen. Marcus Crassus and the late Roman Republic. Columbia, University of Missouri Press, 1977. xiii, 324p.   **HC120**

AJPh C 1979 458–460 Treggiari • LEC XLVII 1979 200 Stenuit
The generally unfavorable attitude to Crassus stems from his indecent wealth and his disastrous defeat at Carrhae. The present work stresses the political role of Crassus in the period 70–50 B.C.

WARMINGTON, Brian Herbert. Nero; Reality and Legend. New York, Norton, [1970, 1969]. 180p., illus., maps.   **HC121**

AJPh XCIII 1972 626–627 Swan • CJ LXIX 1973 153–154 Baldwin • EHR LXXXVII 1972 153 Meiggs
A very balanced judgment of the sources characterizes this short work, from which Nero emerges as credible, interesting and not as bad as Tacitus' portrait.

Christian Empire

BROWNING, Robert. The emperor Julian. Berkeley, University of California Press, 1976. xii, 256p., [4] leaves of plates, illus.   **HC122**

ChHist XLV 1976 524 Grant • JEH XXVII 1976 414–415 Frend • JHS XCVII 1977 234–235 Cameron
An elegant and realistic introduction to Julian. Unencumbered by footnotes, the work contains lucid summaries of the sources, good bibliographical signposting and a helpful relation of Julian to his 4th-century pagan-Christian background.

CHASTAGNOL, André. La fin du monde antique, de Stilicon à Justinien, Ve siècle et début VIe: recueil de textes. Traduits par André Chastagnol. Paris, Nouvelles Éditions Latines, 1976. 383p.   **HC123**

REL LV 1977 543–544 Reydellet
A useful guide through the labyrinth of a difficult period, this work is in two parts: a very concise survey of the events of the 150-year period and a collection of translated texts.

CHRIST, Karl. Der Untergang des römischen Reiches. Darmstadt, Wissenschaftliche Buchges., 1970. vi, 498p.   **HC124**

Wege der Forschung, Bd. 269.
A good introduction (p. 1–31), originally written in 1968 by the author, is followed by a few pages translated from Gibbon (p.32–37), and 18 contributions ranging chronologically from Seeck (1895) and Julius Beloch (1900) to Momigliano (1963) and Hajo Koch (Originalbeitrag, 1968). There is an excellent Ausgewählte Bibliographie (1968) by Adolph Morlang.

DUCREY, Paul, ed. Gibbon et Rome à la lumière de l'historiographie moderne; 10 exposés suivis de discussions par E. Badian [et al.]: publ. par Pierre Ducrey en collab. avec F. Burkhalter et R. Overmeer. Genève, Droz, 1977. 271p.   **HC125**

REL LV 1977 611–613 Richard
Ten contributions to a 1976 colloquium at the University of Lausanne to mark the Gibbon bicentennial. The first part of the work has essays by Giddey (Gibbon à Lausanne), Syme (how Gibbon came to history), Bardon (Le style d'une pensée: Politique et esthétique dans le *Decline and Fall*), Badian (Gibbon on war), which help us to see Gibbon in his own environment.
The second part has five essays pertaining more to antiquity: Gilliam (Gibbon on the Roman army), Straub (Konstantin-Bild), Bowersock (Gibbon and Julian), Paschoud (Gibbon et les sources historiographiques pour la période de 363 à 410), and Chastagnol (Gibbon et la Gaule du Vᵉ siècle).

MUSSET, Lucien. The Germanic invasions; The making of Europe, A.D. 400–600. Trans. by Edward and Columba James. London, Elek, 1975. xiii, 287p., maps.   **HC126**

Translation of *Les invasions: Les vagues Germaniques*.
A translation of a work in the well-known *Nouvelle Clio* series. An account of the Germanic invasions of western Europe in the 4th, 5th and 6th centuries. Mainly military history, with minimal attention to institutional and political, or economic and social questions. The *Nouvelle Clio* tripartite division—the facts, unsolved problems and subjects for further research, and sources and studies—is followed. There is a good bibliography (p.243–269), with additional bibliography for English readers (p.270–271).

PIGANIOL, André. L'Empire Chrétien (325–395). 2. éd. mise à jour par André Chastagnol. Paris, Presses Universitaires de France, 1972. viii, 501p.   **HC127**

Collection Hier.
CRAI 1973 271 Puech • JRS XXXIX 1949 170–171 Thompson
The first edition appeared in Paris (1947, xvi, 446p.). Piganiol complements Stein and Seeck, particularly for bibliographical guidance in both the ancient sources

and the modern literature. The division of the work into sections and sub-sections makes for ease in reference but gives the work the appearance of an encyclopedia or handbook rather than a history. The second part of the book—Les Institutions et la Vie Sociale— is of great value.

SEECK, Otto. Geschichte des Untergangs der antiken Welt. (Unveränderter Reprografischer Nachdruck.) Stuttgart, Metzler, (1966). 6 v.   **HC128**

Bd. 1, Die Anfänge Constantins des Grossen, Verfall der antiken Welt, 4, Aufl., 1921,—Bd. 2, Die Verwaltung des Reiches. Religion und Sittlichkeit, 2., verm, und verb, Aufl., 1921,—Bd. 3. Religion und Sittlichkeit (Schluss), 2., verb, Aufl., 1921,—Bd. 4. die Constantinische Dynastie. 2, Aufl., 1922,—Bd. 5, Valentinian und seine Familie. Die Auflösung des Reiches. 2, Aufl., 1920.—Bd. 6. Die Auflösung des Reiches (Schluss). 1, Aufl., 1920.
PhW XLIII 1923 228–229 Hohl • BPhW 1914 1039 Bauer
This monumental work, completed shortly before the author's death, studies the Late Empire down to 476 A.D.

WALLACE-HADRILL, J. M. The barbarian West, 400–1000 A.D. London, Hutchinson, 1952. viii, 157p. 2nd ed., 1957.   **HC129**

Hutchinson's University Library History Series.

WHITE, Lynn Townsend. The transformation of the Roman world; Gibbon's problem after two centuries. Berkeley, University of California Press, 1966. viii, 321p.   **HC130**

UCLA Center for Medieval and Renaissance Studies: Contributions; 3.
AHR LXXII 1967 1362 Starr • CR XVIII 1968 217–218 Millar • G&R XIV 1967 177 Sewter
The object of the UCLA conference was to answer three questions: What really did happen to the Empire? Why did Gibbon interpret the collapse as he did? Why do modern views differ from Gibbon's? There are nine essays, related more to the second question than to the first, but using Gibbon more as a convenient peg for individual reflections on the individual's specialization than to justify the substitution of *Transformation* for *Decline and Fall*.

Provinces

BARTON, I. M. Africa in the Roman Empire. Accra, published for the University of Cape Coast by Ghana Universities Press (New York, exclusive agent in U.S.A., Panther House Ltd.), 1972. 84p., illus.   **HC131**

AC XLIII 1974 571 Raepsaet-Charlier • CW LXVIII 1974 135 Sider
A brief synthesis on Roman proconsular Africa, Numidia and Mauretania, is provided by these three lec-

tures delivered by Professor Barton at the University of Cape Coast in Ghana. There are lively sketches of military life at Lambaesis, and of political life in Lepcis Magna. The whole provides a brief but excellent introduction to the study of Roman power and influence in Africa from the Punic Wars to the 5th century A.D.

CLEMENTE, Guido. I Romani nella Gallia meridionale (II–I sec. a. C.). Politica ed economia nell'età dell'imperialismo. Bologna, Patron, 1974. 209p.   **HC132**

Coll. Il mondo ant. Studi di stor. e di storiograf. II.
AC XLIV 1975 348 Raepsaet • Latomus XXXV 1976 636–638 Debergh
A careful review of archaeological discoveries in southern Gaul (especially Campanian pottery) that have a bearing on Roman Republican history, and a literary analysis of Cicero's *Pro Fonteio,* one of the chief sources for a knowledge of the Province E. 75 B.C. There is a good bibliography (p. 185–207).

DUVAL, Paul-Marie. La Gaule jusqu'au milieu du Vᵉ siècle. Pref. by A. Vernet. Paris, Picard, 1971. 391p.   **HC133**

Les sources de l'histoire de France des origines à la fin du XVᵉ siècle.
REL XLIX 1971 476–479 Fontaine • Gnomon XLV 1973 729–731 Petit • CPh LXVII 1972 222–224 Oost
A fundamental reference work on ancient Gaul. An introductory 150 pages deal with written, epigraphical and archaeological sources, the auxiliary sciences. The second part, more than 600 pages, notices 346 items in a Répetoire Chronologique des Sources Écrits. There are two appendices and several indices.

FRERE, S. Britannia. A history of Roman Britain. London, Routledge & K. Paul, 1967. xvi, 432p., 13 illus., 32 plates.   **HC134**

History of the provinces of the Roman empire I.
EHR LXXXV 1970 109–113 Myres • JRS LIX 1969 247–250 Rivet • CR n. s. XIX 1969 219–222 Burn
The standard history, replacing Collingwood, *Roman Britain and the English settlements* (1937). An honest, clearly written evaluation of the recent archaeological, epigraphic, numismatic and prosopographical evidence. The narrative is well constructed and sustained. There are some shortcomings in the maps, and references are sometimes inadequate and/or inaccurate.

GASCOU, Jacques. La politique municipale de l'empire romain en Afrique proconsulaire de Trajan à Septime-Sévère. Rome, École Française de Rome, 1972. 258p., illus.   **HC135**

Collection de l'École Française de Rome; 8.
JRS LXIV 1974 239 Birley • REL L 1972 384–387 Chevallier • CRAI 1972 429 Boyancé
A clear, concise, well-documented study of the prog-

ress of romanization in proconsular Africa. The author, an excellent historian and epigraphist but with little interest in archaeology or topography, studies the creation of communities and colonies first under Trajan, then from Trajan to Septimius Severus. Finally in the third section he presents a tableau of the municipalities of the different emperors.

JOHNSON, A. Ch. Egypt and the Roman empire. Ann Arbor, University of Michigan Press, 1951. 190p.   **HC136**

NC XI 1951 144–146 Mattingly • JRS XLIII 1953 205–206 Bell • CR III 1953 185–186 Turner
A set of lectures which presents in convenient form a summary restatement of materials found in earlier works on Egypt by an expert. The first two chapters deal with the currency of Roman Egypt and inflation. The remaining chapters, beginning with one on land tenure, deal mainly with Byzantine Egypt.

JONES, Arnold H. M. The cities of the eastern Roman provinces. Revised by Michael Avi-Yonah et al. 2nd ed. Oxford, Clarendon Press, 1971. xvii, 595p., maps.   **HC137**

AJPh LXII 1941 104–107 Broughton • CR 1938 141 Sherwin-White, XXIV 1974 271–273 Gray • REL L 1972 387–388 Richard • RPh XLVII 1973 338–339 Will
The original edition appeared in 1937 and was criticized for many lacunae and errors. Here, nine collaborators combined to update and suggest *addenda* and *delenda* in their areas of specialization. The result resembles a historical geography in tracing the diffusion of the Greek city as a form of political organization throughout the eastern Roman provinces. Thrace is the only European province included. The millenium from Alexander to Justinian receives special emphasis. (By 'city' is meant any self-governing unit with an urban center.) A useful reference work but insufficiently revised.

LEVICK, Barbara M. Roman colonies in southern Asia Minor. Oxford, Clarendon Press, 1967. xvi, 256p., 8 plates (incl. 2 maps).   **HC138**

Latomus XXVII 1968 475–477 Liebmann-Frankfort • REA LXX 1968 239–241 Petit • REL XLV 1967 584–586 Rougé • CW LXI 1967 162 Bowersock • JRS LX 1970 202–207 Bowie
A valuable contribution in which exhaustive knowledge is joined to good judgment in selection and presentation of the evidence. [See Levick, B., "Antiocheia . . . ," *RE Supplbd* XI (1968), 49–61.]

MAGIE, David. Roman rule in Asia Minor, to the end of the third century after Christ. New York: Arno Press, 1975, 1950. 2 v. (xx, 1661p.).
                                             HC139

Reprint of the ed. published by Princeton University Press, Princeton, N. J.
AJPh LXXII 1951 198–201 Oliver • Gnomon XXIII

1951 260–266 Kahrstedt • AC XX 1951 507–511 Carcopino

Less a book than a *summa* of present knowledge on the growth of Roman rule in Asia Minor, based on a judicious examination of the literary, numismatic and especially the epigraphic evidence. Ranks with the studies of Asia Minor by Rostovtzeff and Broughton and a worthy monument to the 25 years spent in its execution.

MILLAR, Fergus. The Roman Empire and its neighbours. 1st American ed. New York, Delacorte Press, [1968]. xii, 362 p., illus., maps.
HC140

Delacorte World History; v.8.

MOMMSEN, Theodor. The provinces of the Roman Empire, from Caesar to Diocletian. Trans.

with the author's sanction and additions by William P. Dickson. Chicago, Ares Publishers, 1974. 2 v.
HC141

Trans. of v. 5 of the author's *Römische Geschichte.* Dickson's trans. rev. by F. Haverfield. Reprint of the 1909 ed. published by Macmillan, London.
REA LXXII 1970 476–477 Hermaud
Mommsen's three volumes of *Römische Geschichte* (1854–1856) stopped at the Battle of Thapsus in 46 B.C.; v. 4, which would have treated of the Empire, never appeared. This fifth volume appeared almost 30 years later in 1885 and was translated to French by Cagnat and Toutain in 1887–1889. Dickinson's English translation was first published in New York in 1887; an adapted shortened form (the European portion) of it (1968) contains an introduction by T.R.S. Broughton which helps to place Mommsen's achievement in perspective.

HD   CHRONOLOGY

BAYER, Erich and HEIDEKING, J. Die Chronologie des perikleischen Zeitalters. Darmstadt, Wissen. Buchgesellschaft, 1975. xii, 225p.
HD1

JHS XCVI 1976 225–226 Meiggs
There is an extensive bibliography (p. 181–212).

BENGTSON, H. Introduction to ancient history. Berkeley, University of California Press, 1975. p. 23–36.
HD2

See entry no. HB 11.
An excellent brief account, with good bibliography, of the problems inherent in chronology, "The eye of history," due to the fact that prior to Caesar's reform, which began January 1, 45 B.C., there were almost as many calendars and eras as there were peoples, states and cities.

BICKERMAN, E. J. Chronology of the ancient world. Ithaca, Cornell University Press, 1968. Reprint 1978. 253p.
HD3

Trans. from Gercke-Norden, *Einleitung,* 3.5.
AJPh XC 1969 478–481 Welles • CR XIX 1969 110–111 Lewis

DELORME, J. Chronologie des civilisations. Paris, 1957; 3e éd. augment. & refondue, 1969. xvi, 509p.
HD4

REG LXXXIV 1971 565 Gauthier
See also Delorme, *Les grandes dates de l'Antiquité* (1962, 127p.).

DILLER, H. and SCHALK, K. Studien zur Periodisierung und zum Epochbegriff. Mainz, Verlag der Akademie der Wissenschaften und der Literatur, 1972. 38p.
HD5

AC XLII 1973 342–343 Daubies
Divided into two separate studies, the first, a brief reflection on *periods* and *epochen,* with special attention to Hesiod's ages and pre-Socratic conceptions down to Hellenistic times, with special attention to Timaeus' dating according to Olympiads, and the chronology of Eratosthenes.
The second part, Epochs and History, is not of main interest to classical scholars.

DINSMOOR, W. The archons of Athens in the Hellenistic Age. Cambridge, Mass., Harvard University Press, 1931. viii, 567p.
HD6

AJA XXXVI 1932 206–207 West • Gnomon 1932 449–464 Kirchner
Remains indispensable for the history of Hellenistic Greece. Taking as his point of departure an inscription which he discovered in 1929 on the west slope of the Acropolis, the author offers new tables of Athenian archon dates for the last three centuries before Christ.

EHRICH, Robert. W. Relative chronologies in Old World archaeology. Chicago, University of Chicago Press, 1954. xiii, 154p.
HD7

BASOR CXXXIX 1955 16 Albright • Antiquity XXX 1956 45–46 Gordon Childe
A series of papers by a group of specialists, attempting to establish rapprochements between their different fields—Egypt, Palestine, Syria, Mesopotamia, Iran,

South-east Anatolia, the Aegean, South-East and Central Europe, and China.

See now *CAH* I, 2 ed.

FORNARA, Charles W. The Athenian board of generals from 501 to 404. Weisbaden, Steiner, 1971. xi, 84p.   **HD8**

AJPh XCV 1974 420 Thompson

The author seeks to overthrow the traditional view that Athenian generals were elected according to the principle of one from each tribe.

GINZEL, F. K. Handbuch der mathematischen und technischen Chronologie. Das Zeitrechnungswesen der Völker. Leipzig, 3 Bde. 1906–1914. Reprint 1960.   **HD9**

RC II 1914 163

Volume II is concerned with Jewish, Greek and Roman chronologies; v. III with those of Macedonia, Asia Minor and Medieval Celts and Germans.

GRUMEL, V. "Indiction." NCE VII: 467–468.
                                                HD10

See also Grumel, *La chronologie* (1958) in Lemerle.

LIBBY, W. F. Radiocarbon dating. Chicago, University of Chicago Press, 1951. Reprint 1955. vii, 124p.   **HD11**

AntJ XXXIII 1953 218–222 Zeuner • Biblica XXXVI 1955 249 Nober

A historic first by a Nobel prizewinning chronologer. See the later *Radioactive dating,* Proceedings of the Symposium on Radioactive Dating, held by the International Atomic Energy Agency in Athens (19–23 November 1962, 440p.), for a description of other processes of dating besides the radioactive carbon 14 method.

LIETZMANN, H. Zeitrechnung der römischen Kaiserzeit. 3rd ed. 1956.   **HD12**

Sammlung Göschen, 1952.

RecTh XXV 1958 151 Botte

MERITT, B. The Athenian calendar in the fifth century. Cambridge, Mass., Harvard University Press, 1928. viii, 138p.   **HD13**

CW XXIII 1929 60–63 West • AJA 1929 340–341 Ferguson

MICHELS, A. K. The calendar of the Roman Republic. Princeton, Princeton University Press, 1967. xvi, 227p.   **HD14**

Latomus 1969 463–468 Degrassi • Gnomon XLI 1969 785–790 Gundel • JRS LXI 1971 282–283 Drummond

Likely to become a standard work on the Republican calendar, this study discusses the characteristics of the pre-Julian calendar, its various types of day, and its history, with appendices on intercalation and other matters.

MIKALSON, J. D. The sacred and civil calendar of the Athenian year. Princeton, Princeton University Press, 1975. x, 226p.   **HD15**

CJ LXXIII 1978 259 Stroud

NEUGEBAUER, P. V. Hilfstafeln zur technischen Chronologie. Kiel, Verlag der Astronomie Nachrichten, 1937. 80p.   **HD16**

Gnomon 1938 521–522 Meyer • DLZ 1938 356 Zinner

Useful tables for conversion of ancient dates.

PRITCHETT, W. K. and MERITT, B. D. The chronology of Hellenistic Athens. Cambridge, Mass., Harvard University Press, 1940. xxxv, 158p.   **HD17**

CR LVI 1942 84–85 Tarn • AJA XLVI 1942 574–575 Raubitschek

Particularly valuable for its 20-page tables (xv–xxxv) giving full information on the Athenian archons from 307 B.C. to the end of the Roman period and on the secretaries of the Council and the priests of Asclepius for 307/306 to 101/100 B.C. To support the tables the authors present a new analysis of the great inventories of the temple of Asclepius whose priests were discovered by Ferguson to rotate in cycles.

PRITCHETT, W. K. and NEUGEBAUER, O. The calendars of Athens. Cambridge, Mass., Harvard University Press, 1948. 115p.   **HD18**

JHS LXVIII 1948 165–166 Woodward • AJA LIII 1949 322–323 Woodhead

A stimulating, well-reasoned study in which the epigraphic evidence bearing on the calendar (5th to 2d centuries B.C.) is used to confirm five presuppositions set forth in the first chapter. Much light is shed on hitherto intractable problems, intercalation, length of prytanies, calendar cycles, backward/forward count.

SAMUEL, A. E. Greek and Roman chronology; Calendars and years in classical antiquity. München, Beck, 1972. 340p.   **HD19**

HdA., 1.7.

CR XXV 1975 69–72 Lewis • AC XLII 1973 343–344 Muszynski

A solidly documented exposition of the astronomical foundations of all systems of reckoning time, and a systematic investigation of Greek civil calendars. The Hellenistic and Roman periods do not receive as detailed coverage as the earlier, and the epigraphical evidence is exploited more than the literary.

There are useful ready-reckoner tables, including an Index of Months (p.284–297), that provide instant solutions to a host of problems. About a third of the work is taken up with c.111 Greek Civil Calendars and its accompanying Index of Month Names. The last chapter gives a succinct account of the varying dates for the foundation of Rome.

HE   GREEK AND ROMAN LAW

BUCKLAND, William Warwick. The Roman law of slavery; The condition of the slave in private law from Augustus to Justinian. Cambridge, Cambridge University Press, 1908. Reprint 1970. xiv, 735p.   **HE1**

BUCKLAND, William Warwick. A text-book of Roman law from Augustus to Justinian. 3rd ed. rev. by Peter Stein. Cambridge, Cambridge University Press, 1921, 1975. xxx, 764p.   **HE2**

BUONAMICI, Francesco. La storia della procedura civile romana. Volume primo. Roma, L'Erma di Bretschneider, 1971. viii, 619p.   **HE3**

Reprint of the Pisa 1886 ed.

BURDESE, Alberto. Manuale di diritto pubblico romano. 2 ed. Torino, Unione Tipografico-Editrice Torinese, 1976. xii, 279p.   **HE4**

See also Burdese, *Manuale di diritto privato romano,* 3 ed. (Torino, 1975, xix, 747p.).

CALHOUN, George Miller. A working bibliography of Greek law. With an introd. by Roscoe Pound. Amsterdam, B. R. Grüner, 1968, xix, 144p.   **HE4a**

Reprint of the 1927 ed. published by Harvard University Press, Cambridge, which was issued as no. 1 of Harvard series of legal bibliographies.

CAPUANO, Luigi. I primi del diritto romano. Ed. anastatica. Roma, Bretschneider, 1978. xv, 333p.   **HE5**

Reprint of the 1878 ed.

CROOK, John A. Law and life of Rome. Ithaca, Cornell University Press, London, Thames and Hudson, 1967. 349p.   **HE6**

Aspects of Greek and Roman Life.
CPh LXIV 1969 200–201 Oost • JRS LIX 1969 281–282 Sherwin-White
An absorbing book, combining social and economic with legal history. Covers the period from Sulla's death to the age of Ulpian. Immensely useful to nonlegal students of antiquity on topics like the law of status, family and succession, property, labor, commerce and the relation of citizen and state.

DAUBE, David. Forms of Roman legislation. Oxford, Clarendon Press; Westport, Conn.,

Greenwood Press, 1956. Reprint 1979. 111p.   **HE7**

CR VII 1957 250–252 Nicholas
An attempt to apply form criticism to Roman law, addressed particularly to experts, but of wider interest to all students of the forms and usages of the Latin language.

DAUBE, David. Roman law; Linguistic, social and philosophical aspects. Edinburgh, University Press, 1969. 205p., 4 plates.   **HE8**

JRS LX 1970 194–199 Crifò • CJ LXVII 1971 72–74 Costelloe
A stimulating examination of the linguistic, social and philosophical aspects of a number of problems in Roman law, displaying the author's well-known cultural breadth and intellectual range. In the linguistic section, for instance, he discusses ownership and obligations; in the socioeconomic, intestate succession and in the philosophical, the standards of liability and the use made by jurists of the *reductio ad absurdum* argument.

GARNSEY, P. Social status and legal privilege in the Roman Empire. Oxford, Clarendon Press, 1970. xiii, 320p.   **HE9**

JRS LXII 1972 166–170 Brunt
An excellent Oxford doctoral thesis which adopts the hypothesis that the legal system in Rome favored the interests of the higher orders in Roman society and demonstrates its validity. Punishments and privileges are rigorously examined.

GIRARD, Paul F. Manuel élémentaire de droit romain. 8 éd. rev. et mise à jour par Félix Senn. Paris, Rousseau, 1929. xvi, 1223p.   **HE10**

RCl 1 1929 369–380 Nicolau

GREENIDGE, Abel Hendy Jones. The legal procedure of Cicero's time. New York, A. M. Kelley, 1971. xiii, 599p.   **HE11**

Reprint of 1901 ed.

HUMBERT, M. Le remariage à Rome; Étude d'histoire juridique et sociale. Milano, Giuffrè, 1972. xii, 503p.   **HE12**

JRS LXIV 1974 234–235 Crook • RD LII 1974 110–114 Lévy
A consistently interesting, if long, treatment, well organized, in which the early attitude of disapprobation in Roman society to Roman women remarrying, followed by the Augustan legislation approving it, is examined. Then there is a lengthy exposition of the

rules of classical Roman private law relating to remarriage.

JOLOWICZ, Herbert F. and NICHOLAS, Barry. Historical introduction to the study of Roman law. 3rd ed. Cambridge, Cambridge University Press, 1972. xxvi, 528p. **HE13**

Gnomon XLVII 1975 632–633 Ziegler
First published in 1932, this is an excellent general history of Roman law from the beginnings to Justinian, brought up-to-date with unobtrusive tact and skill by Nicholas.
See also Jolowicz, Herbert, *Roman foundations of modern law* (Oxford, 1957. Reprint 1978).

JONES, Arnold Hugh Martin. The criminal courts of the Roman Republic and Principate. Totowa, N.J., Rowan and Littlefield, 1972. vi, 143p. **HE14**

REL L 1972 421–422 Richard • JRS LXIII 1973 312 Seager
More concerned with the Republic (especially the age of Cicero) than with the Principate, this short work only presents one viewpoint, with little or no discussion of opposing views.

KASER, Max. Das Römische Privatrecht; Eine Studienbuch. 10 verb. Aufl. München, Beck, 1977. xiv, 371p. **HE15**

The work is now translated into English, *Roman private law,* by R. Dannenbring (London, Butterworths, 1968, xv, 385p.). The standard work of reference on early, classical and postclassical Roman private law, mostly the first two.

KELLY, John Maurice. Roman litigation. Oxford, Clarendon Press, 1966. viii, 176p. **HE16**

AJPh LXXXIX 1968 506–508 Schiller
A stimulating and provocative work, challenging many long-held assumptions on Roman procedure.
See also Kelly, J. M., *Studies in the civil judicature of the Roman Republic* (1976)

KUNKEL, Wolfgang. An introduction to Roman legal and constitutional history. Trans. by J. M. Kelly. 2d ed., based on the 6th German ed. of *Römische Rechtsgeschichte.* Oxford, Clarendon Press, 1973. viii, 236p. **HE17**

Gnomon XXI 1949 175–176 Wesenberg

MACDOWELL, D. M. The law in classical Athens. London, Thames and Hudson, 1978. 280p. **HE18**

Phoenix XXXIV 1980 177–179 Avotins

NICHOLAS, J. K. B. An introduction to Roman law. Oxford, Clarendon Press, 1962. xvi, 282p. **HE19**

JRS LIII 1963 206–207 Topping
A skillfully condensed and lucidly presented survey which presents the background and conceptual framework of Roman law rather than a detailed exegesis of its substantive rules.

PHILLIPSON, Coleman. The international law and custom of ancient Greece and Rome. London, Macmillan, 1911. 2 v. **HE20**

ROMILLY, Jacqueline de. La loi dans le pensée grecque des origines à Aristote. Paris, Les belles lettres, 1971. 265p. **HE21**

JHS XCIII 1973 243–244 Lloyd-Jones

SCHILLER, A. Arthur. Roman law; Mechanisms of development. New York, Mouton, 1978. xxxvii, 606p. **HE22**

JRS LXIX 1979 236 Crook

SCHULZ, Fritz. History of Roman legal science. Oxford, Clarendon Press, 1967, 1946. xvi, 358p. **HE23**

CR LXI 1947 119–121 Duff • HarvLawRev LX 1947 1002–1006 Bruck
See also Schulz, Fritz, *Classical Roman law* (Oxford, Clarendon, 1951, 650p.) [Cf. *Gnomon* XXIV (1952), 353–359, Wieacker; *CR* n.s. II (1952), 204–206, Nicholas].

THOMAS, Joseph Anthony C. Textbook of Roman law. Amsterdam and New York, North-Holland Pub., 1976. xix, 562p. **HE24**

WATSON, Alan. Law making in the later Roman Republic. Oxford, Clarendon Press, 1974. xii, 211p. **HE25**

JRS LXV 1975 205–206 Lintott • REA LXXVIII 1976 293–294 Nony
Professor Watson's studies of law in the later Republic include *The law of obligations* (1965), *The law of persons* (1967), and *The law of Succession* (1971), and show an enviable control of the sources. Here "the sources of law" are analyzed insofar as they were known prior to the greater precision in this matter in the Empire. There are illuminating chapters on *leges,* edicts, jurists and their writings.
See also Watson, A., *The law of obligations in the later Roman Republic* (1965), *The law of the ancient Romans* (1970), *Rome of the Twelve Tables: Persons and property* (1975), and *Roman private law around 200* (1971).

WATSON, Alan, ed. Daube noster; Essays in legal history for David Daube. Edinburgh, Scottish Academy Press, 1974. xvii, 374p. **HE26**

Select bibliography of David Daube (xi–xvi).

WENGER, Leopold. Die Quellen des römischen Rechts. Wien, Holzhausen, 1953. xviii, 973p.

HE27

JRS XLIV 1954 135–136 Last

WILLEMS, Pierre Gaspard. Le droit public romain. 7 éd., Louvain, 1910. Amsterdam, Rodopi, 1972. lii, 682p.   **HE28**

First ed., 1870, entitled *Les antiquités romains envisagées au point de vue des institutions politiques.*

ZULUETA, Francis de. The institutes of Gaius. Oxford, Clarendon Press, 1967–1974. 2 v.

HE29

Reprint of the 1946–1953 ed.
JRS XLIII 1953 178–179 Nicholas
This learned and well-balanced commentary presumes a text of Gaius and of Justinian's Institutes, and provides a discussion, paragraph by paragraph rather than section by section. More attention is devoted to the Law of Obligations and the Law of Actions.

Numismatics

IA   BIBLIOGRAPHY AND METHODOLOGY

ALFÖLDI, Maria R. Antike Numismatik, Theorie, Praxis, Bibliographie. Mainz, Philipp von Zabern, 1978. 2 v., illus., maps.　　**IA1**

Kulturgeschichte der Antiken Welt; Bd. 2–3, Teil 1, Theorie und Praxis; Teil 2, Bibliographie.
RBN CXXV 1979 176–177 Naster

BABELON, Jean. La numismatique antique. 4. ed. Paris, Presses Universitaires de France, 1944. 127p., illus.　　**IA2**

Que sais-je?; 168.
RN VIII 1945 197 Blanchet
Clear exposition, but very brief and sometimes abstract; long lists of symbols, types and monetary legends. More interesting, detailed and useful is the author's *Les monnaies grecques, aperçu historique* (Paris, 1921, 160p.) and his "Numismatiqué" in Samaran, *L' Histoire et ses méthods.*

BREGLIA, Laura. Numismatica antica. Storia e metodologia. Milan, Feltrinelli, 1964. 312p., 46 plates.　　**IA3**

RN VI 1964 203–204 Babelon • RBPh XLVI 1968 1012 Thirion
A remarkable work in 2 parts: 1. an exposition of the technique of ancient coinage, its typology, art, weights, issues and chronological criteria; 2. the fundamental stages in the historical evolution of coinage.

CHRIST, Karl. Antike Numismatik; Einführung und Bibliographie. 2. unveränd. Aufl. Darmstadt, Wissenschaftliche Buchgesellschaft, 1972, 1967. 107p.　　**IA4**

Die Altertumswissenschaft; Einführungen in Gegenstand; Methoden und Ergebnisse ihrer Teildisziplinen und Hilfswissenschaften.
CR XX 1970 108–109 Barron • REG LXXXI 1968 238 Bon • RBPh XLVI 1968 1011 Zehnacker • JRS LX 1970 265 Crawford
A densely packed, finely printed bibliography con-

taining five chapters: 1. Allgemeine Einführung, II. Griechische Numismatik, III. Hellenistische Numismatik, IV. Römische Numismatik, V. Spezielle Forschungen. The bibliographies which accompany each chapter include fundamental works and selected recent studies intended to give good examples of the major directions of present research. A reliable guide from a seasoned scholar.

CLAIN-STEFANELLI, Elvira. Select numismatic bibliography. New York, Stack, [1965]. 406p.　　**IA5**

RBN CXIII 1967 194 Naster

DENTZER, J. M., GAUTHIER, Philippe and HACKENS, Tony. Numismatique antique; Problèmes et méthodes. Actes du colloque organisé à Nancy du 27 Septembre au 2 Octobre 1971. Par L'Université de Nancy et L'Université Catholique de Louvain. Louvain, Éditions Peeters, 1975. viii, 246p., [6] leaves of plates, illus.　　**IA6**

A Num V 1975 205–209 De Guadan • JRS LXVIII 1978 240–241 Crawford • AC XLV 1976 778–781 Callu
Particularly useful for three papers by T. Hackens: one on the techniques of coin manufacture, the reasons for coin production, and circulation; and two on metal analysis. There is also an excellent paper by Ed. Will on the sources of metal for money in the Greek world. The Roman Empire gets no attention, but the work clearly states the problems concerning Greek, French and Roman numismatics in the Republic.
The work is divided into six sections: techniques, metrology, metal, coin types and legends, hoards, and circulation, with three or four essays in each.

GARDNER, Percy. A history of ancient coinage, 700–300 B.C. Chicago, Ares Publishers, [1974]. xvi, 463p., [6] leaves of plates, illus.　　**IA7**

Reprint of the 1918 ed. published by Clarendon Press, Oxford.

JHS XXXVIII 1918 196–198 G.F.H. • CW XII 1919
46–47 Robinson • CR 1918 70 Browne

Following in the wake of Head, Babelon and the
27-volume *Catalog of Greek coins in the British Museum*
this is the first attempt at a broad historical sketch
of Greek coinage as an organic unity. Shrewdness of
observation, evenness of judgment and, on occasion,
brilliance in identifications are the hallmarks of this
early work. In methodology the whole Greek world
is surveyed by periods rather than by giving histories
of particular coinages.

GRIERSON, Philip. Coins and medals; A select
bibliography. [London], Published for the Historical Association by G. Philip, 1954. 88p.
                                                        IA8

Helps for Students of History; 56.
RN XVI 1954 215 Lafaurie
Contains about 800 entries.

HALL, E. T. and METCALF, D. M., eds. Methods of chemical and metallurgical investigation
of ancient coinage. Symposium held by the Royal
Numismatic Society at Burlington House, London, on 9–11 December 1970. London, Royal
Numismatic Society, 1972. viii, 448p., 20 leaves
of plates, illus., forms, maps.   **IA9**

Royal Numismatic Society, Special Publication; 8.
NCirc LXXX 1972 461–462 Sellwood • NC XIV
1974 224–226 Barker • SAN IV 1972–1973 57 Kam-
merer

ICARD, Séverin. Dictionary of Greek coin inscriptions; Identification des monnaies par la
nouvelle méthode des lettres jalons et des lég-
endes fragmentées. Application de la méthode
aux monnaies grecques et aux monnaies gauloises. Chicago, Obol International, 1979. A-D,
xxiv, 563p., [2] leaves of plates, illus.
                                                        IA10

Reprint of 1927 ed. published by J. Florange, Paris.

MÖRKHOLM, O. et al. A survey of numismatic
research, 1960–1965. Copenhagen, International
Numismatic Commission, 1967. 3 v.   **IA11**

1. Ancient numismatics, ed. by O. Mörkholm. 2.
Medieval and Oriental numismatics, ed. by K. Skaare
and G. C. Miles. 3. Modern numismatics including
medals, ed. by N. L. Ludvig, L. O. Lagerqvist and
C. Svarstad.

NOE, Sydney P. A bibliography of Greek coin
hoards. [2d. ed.] New York, The American Numismatic Society, 1937. 362p.   **IA12**

First published in 1925.

REGLING, K. Die Antike Münze als Kunstswerk.
Berlin, Schoetz and Parrhysius, 1924. 148p., 45
plates.   **IA13**

RH CLVII 1928 341 Cloché • NJW 1925 420–421
Ilberg

Gardner, Head, Hill, Reinach and Regling have all
tried in their various ways to show how the study of
numismatic art can contribute to the history of ancient
art. Regling divides the subject chronologically into
four great periods: The archaic period, the period of
expansion from the Second Medic War to the death
of Alexander, the Hellenistic period (to which he adds
that of the Roman Republic), and the Empire. He examines in succession the head and the human body,
clothing, animals, symbols, legends, etc.

A SURVEY of numismatic research, 1966–1971.
New York, International Numismatic Commis-
sion, 1973. 3 v.   **IA14**

1. Ancient numismatics, ed. by P. Naster, J. B. Col-
bert de Beaulieu and J. M. Fagerlie. 2. Medieval and
Oriental numismatics, ed. by J. Yvon and H. W. Mitchell Brown. 3. Modern numismatics including medals,
ed. by L. Nemeskal and E. Clain-Stefanelli.
A Num IV 1974 325–326 Villaronga • AC XLII
1973 719–722 Hackens • CW LXIX 1975 150–152
Buttrey • JHS XCVI 1976 257 Kraay
Continues the practice of publishing a survey of
scholarship for international numismatic congresses,
already done for Paris (1953), Rome (1961) and Copenhagen (1967).
This issue for New York (1973) is 50% larger than
its predecessor, showing the explosion in knowledge
and the greater rapport among scholars. Brief summaries of books and articles since 1966 reveal the major
trends in current scholarship, much of it of great interest and value to the non-numismatic scholar in history,
art, or archaeology. Unparalleled in scope, clarity and
usefulness.

**THOMPSON, Margaret, MÖRKHOLM, Otto
and KRAAY, Colin M., eds.** An inventory of
Greek coin hoards. New York, Published for the
International Numismatic Commission by the
American Numismatic Society, 1973. xviii,
408p., maps.   **IA15**

AJA LXXVIII 1974 308–309 Price • A Num IV
1974 347–348 Villaronga • CW LXIX 1975 150–152
Buttrey • AC XLIII 1974 654–657 Marchetti
A complete reworking of material hitherto only
available in Sydney Noe's *Bibliography of Greek coin
hoards* (1937), long out-of-date and full of inaccuracies.
This gives us an entirely reorganized, greatly enlarged
(2,387 hoards) and corrected treatment, with many excisions as well as additions. An incomparable treasure-
house for numismatist and historian. Hoards of the
Roman Imperial period which Noe had included have
been omitted, so there is a need for a companion volume
covering the first three centuries A.D.

VERMEULE, Cornelius Clarkson. A bibliography of applied numismatics in the fields of Greek
and Roman archaeology and the fine arts. London, Spink, 1956. viii, 176p.   **IA16**

Gnomon XXIX 1957 157–158 Christ • REL XXXV
1957 466 Blanchet

About 40 periodicals are surveyed in this bibliography as well as numerous works. The items are numbered under such rubrics as archaeology and art history (nos. 1–680), iconography (680–940), geography, topography and architecture (941–1078), and related works in the fields of history, politics and religion (1079–1328).

IB COLLECTIONS

AMERICAN Numismatic Society. Sylloge nummorum Graecorum; The collection of the American Numismatic Society. New York, The Society, 1969– . **IB1**

> Part 1. Etruria-Calabria; part 2. Lucania.
> CW LXV 1971 66–67 Kiang • AJA LXXV 1971 347–348 Holloway • NC XI 1971 347–349 Price
> The first fascicle of the Greek coins of the ANS is a good introduction to the richness of its holdings. Approximately two-thirds of its 1618 coins are from the Edward P. Newell collection. The Etruscan series (100 entries) is outstanding, but the representation of mints in central Italy, Campania and Apulia is also rich and broad.
> See now Idem, VI. *Palestine-South Arabia,* by Y. Meshorer. New York, American Numismatic Society, 1981. 113p., 54 plates. (*GNS* XXII 1982 74–76 Jeselsohn).

BRITISH Museum. Dept. of Coins and Medals. Coins of the Roman Empire in the British Museum. Reprinted with revisions. London, 1975. Illus. **IB2**

> Contents of volumes: 1. Augustus to Vitellius, 2. Vespasian to Domitian, both by H. Mattingly; 5. Pertinax to Elagabalus, by R. A. G. Carson and P. V. Hill; 6. Severus Alexander to Balbinus and Pupienus, by R. A. G. Carson.
> JRS LIII 1963 212–213 Kraay • EHR LXVI 1951 569–572 Sutherland
> Volumes 1 through 5 were the work of Harold Mattingly, the modern founder of Roman numismatics, and were all characterized by exact classification, informed comment and inspired interpretation. Volume 6, edited by R. A. G. Carson, maintains those high standards and introduces fresh techniques for controlling the huge mass of evidence and welcome innovations in presenting it.

GIARD, Jean-Baptiste. Bibliothèque nationale; Catalogue des monnaies de l'empire romain. 1. Auguste. Paris, Bibliothèque nationale, 1976. viii, 258p., 72 plates. **IB3**

> REL LIV 1976 523–526 Zehnacker • ANum VII 1977 269–270 Villaronga
> The Bibliothèque nationale has one of the largest coin collections in the world which here begins to receive the lavish publication it deserves. Well-indexed but unfortunately lacking a concordance with Cohen.

KRAAY, Colin M. Archaic and classical Greek coins. Berkeley, University of California Press, 1976. xxvi, 390p., [32] leaves of plates, illus. **IB4**

> AJA LXXXI 1977 569–571 Waggoner • CW LXXI 1977 139–140 Starr
> This is an enlarged, fully annotated, scholarly version of Kraay's earlier picture book, *Greek coins* (1966) and is the most up-to-date history of Greek coinage from the beginnings down to the Hellenistic period, c.300 B.C. The text is supplemented by copious illustrations of coins in natural size (1,110 coins in all), mostly from the Oxford Collection. Kraay, long an advocate of down-dating in chronology, always presents opposing views thoroughly and justly. There is an excellent bibliography and the survey supersedes earlier works like that of Seltman.

OXFORD University. Ashmolean Museum. Catalogue of Alexandrian coins in the Ashmolean Museum. By J. G. Milne. [1st ed. rep. with a supplement by Colin M. Kraay.] London, Spind [for the visitors of the Ashmolean Museum], 1971. lxviii, 155, [3], 10p., vii, [2] l. (2 fold.), illus. **IB5**

> Reprint of the 1933 ed.; with suppl. "new types added 1933–1971."

OXFORD University. Ashmolean Museum. Ashmolean Museum, Oxford [Collection of Greek coins in the Heberden Coin Room. Text by Colin M. Kraay]. London, published for the British Academy by the Oxford University Press, 1962– . Plates. **IB6**

> Sylloge numorum Graecorum, v. 5: pt. 1(a) Italy: Etruria-Lucania (Thurium); pt. 2 Italy: Lucania (Thurium)-Bruttium. Sicily. Carthage; pt. 3. Macedonia.
> See also *Sylloge numorum Graecorum,* v. IV. Fitzwilliam Museum. Leake and general collections, pt. 7. Lycia-Cappadocia, ed. by M. J. Price. Oxford, Oxford University Press, 1967. Plates 101–116 with text.

PRICE, Martin and WAGGONER, Nancy. Archaic Greek coinage; The Asyut hoard. London, V. C. Vecchi, 1975. 143p., 18 leaves of plates. **IB7**

> Gnomon L 1978 597–600 Holloway • JHS XCVII 1977 230–231 Kraay

The "Asyut" hoard was a chance discovery, in Middle Egypt in 1969, which was soon dispersed, but now the record has been re-established by the industry of the joint authors. It is by far the largest archaic hoard recorded. Well over 600 coins are illustrated, and the collection is extremely varied and representative of mints from all over the Greek world. A meticulous, professional work which calls at many points for a re-assessment of the chronology of archaic Greek coinage.

PRICE, M. J. and TRELL, B. L. Coins and their cities. Architecture on the ancient coins of Greece, Rome and Palestine. Detroit, Wayne State University Press, 1977. 298p., 522 illus., 2 maps.   **IB8**

ArchN VII 1978 68–69 Walker • RN XIX 1977 206 Nicolet-Pierre

IC MANUALS

HEAD, Barclay. Historia numorum; A manual of Greek numismatics. New and enl. [1st American] ed. Chicago, Argonaut, 1967. lxxxviii, 966p., illus., port.   **IC1**

Reprint of the 1911 ed.
Head began the compilation of material for this pioneer manual in 1883. His bold aim was "to produce a practical handbook in a single portable volume containing in a condensed form a sketch of the numismatic history of nearly every city, king, or dynast known to have struck coins throughout the length and breadth of the ancient world" (Preface, xix, 1911 ed.). Contains a general bibliography to 1911 and is still a most useful work of reference for historians.

HILL, George Francis, Sir. Select Greek coins; A series of enlargements illustrated and described. Paris, G. Vanoest, 1927. 61p., 64 plates.   **IC2**

JHS XLVIII 1928 105 Beazley
An excellent series of enlargements, well chosen, photographed and described. The coins are reproduced three times their size, and from the coins themselves, not the casts. There is an excellent introductory essay.

HUMPHREYS, Henry Noel. Ancient coins and medals; An historical sketch of the origin and progress of coining money in Greece and her colonies; its progress with the extension of the Roman Empire; and its decline with the fall of that power. 2d ed. London, Grant & Griffith, 1851. vi, 208p., illus., 10 plates.   **IC3**

The plates are "facsimile examples in actual relief, and in the metals of the respective coins" and are accompanied by letterpress.

IMHOOF-BLUMER, Friedrich. Ancient coins illustrating lost masterpieces of Greek art. [1st American ed.] Chicago, Argonaut, 1964. 176p.
                                                                IC4

Bibliography (p.[175]–176).
JHS LXXXVIII 1968 244–245 Healy • CB XLIV 1968 79 Horner

Originally based on three articles in *JHS* VI, VII and VIII (1885–1887), this is an enlarged and improved reference book for the study of antiquities. The commentary on Pausanias (p.1–167) is supplemented by translations of passages from Pausanias (ix–l), an appendix (p.169–174) and a select bibliography (p.175–176).

JENKINS, G. Kenneth. Ancient Greek coins. London, Barrie and Jenkins, 1972. 310p., 110 plates, maps.   **IC5**

RBN CXVIII 1972 202–203 Naster • Ant J LIV 1974 95–96 Kraay • NC XIV 1974 208–210 Jameson • Archaeology XXVIII 1975 135–136 Kleiner
A general handbook for the layman, also issued in French, *Monnaies grecques,* trad. by Biucchi, C. (Paris, 1972, 1979). See Jenkins, G. K. and Carson, R. A. G., "Greek and Roman numismatics, 1940–1950," *Historia* II (1953), 214–234.

KRAAY, Colin M. Greek coins. Photographs by Max Hirmer. New York, Abrams, [1966]. 396p., 1329 illus., 19 col. plates, 4 maps.   **IC6**

NC VI 1966 337–340 Barron • CW LXI 1967 106– [108] Farber • JHS LXXXVIII 1968 243–244 Warren
In 240 beautiful plates by Max Hirmer, over 800 coins are shown in amazing detail in a topographical sequence, prefaced by a clear, concise introduction by Dr. Kraay on symbols, types, legends, alphabets, chronology and hoards. There are 100 pages of notes on the coinage of each region or city, with separate bibliographies. Each coin is fully described and its publication noted. Both photography and text are superb in quality, though there is a slight bias in the selection of coins for their aesthetic appeal.

MATTINGLY, Harold et al., eds. The Roman imperial coinage. London, Spink, 1972– . 9 v., illus., plates.   **IC7**

Contents of volumes: 1. Augustus to Vitellius; 2. Vespasian to Hadrian; 3. Antoninus Pius to Commodus (all by H. Mattingly and E. A. Sydenham); 4. part 1, Pertinax to Geta, by H. Mattingly and E. A. Sydenham;

part 2, Marcrinus to Pupienus; part 3, Gordian III
to Uranius Antoninus (both by H. Mattingly, E. A.
Sydenham and C. H. V. Sutherland); 5. part 1, Valerian
I to Florian; part 2, Probus to Amandus (both by
P. H. Webb); 6. Diocletian to Maximinus, by
C. H. V. Sutherland; 7. Constantine to Licinius, by
P. M. Bruun; 8. The family of Constantine I, A.D.
337–364, by J. P. C. Kent; 9. Valentinian I to Theodo-
sius I, by J. W. E. Pearce.

Gnomon XLI 1969 676–680 Buttrey (v. 6) • CR
XIX 1969 351–353 Robertson • JRS LVIII 1968 278–
279 Desborough (v. 6) • JRS LVIII 1968 280–281 Bas-
tien (v. 7)

RIC began appearing in 1972 and the successive
volumes have generally been models of completeness,
clarity and usefulness.

SELTMAN, Charles Theodore. Greek coins; A
history of metallic currency and coinage down
to the fall of the Hellenistic kingdoms. [2d ed.]
London, Methuen 1965, 1955. xxvi, 311p., illus.,
maps.   **IC8**

JHS LIII 1933 128 • JHS LXXVI 1956 139 May
• RN XVII 1955 307–309 Babelon • CR VII 1957
51–52 Hopper

For long the best arranged, most readable and best
illustrated handbook on Greek coins. The second edition of Seltman makes only minor revisions, including
a supplementary bibliography (xxii–xxvi), but the plates
are double-sided and less attractive than in the first
edition.

SELTMAN, Charles Theodore. Masterpieces of
Greek coinage; Essay and commentary. Oxford,
B. Cassirer, [1949]. 127p.   **IC9**

JHS LXX 1950 84 Sutherland • AJA LIV 1950 439
Thompson • CR 1950 149–151 Milne

An exciting introduction to Greek coinage. Fifty-
five coins, enlarged and well photographed, are used
as the basis for discussion of the origin of Greek coinage, Greek die engraving, numismatic styles and traditions, in the chronological framework from the early
Ionian electrum to 4th century issues of Cyzicus and
Clazomenae. Gives a good general picture of the variety
and artistic merit of Greek coinage during the three
centuries preceding Alexander.

STEVENSON, Seth William. A dictionary of Roman coins; Republican and Imperial. Hildesheim, G. Olms, 1969. viii, 929p., illus.
                                                   IC10

Reprint of the 1889 ed.
BBF X 1965 436–437 Giard

SVORONES, John and HEAD, Barclay V. The
illustrations of the Historia Numorum; An atlas
of Greek Numismatics. Edited by Alyce Marie
Cresap. Chicago, Argonaut, 1968. 64 p., illus.,
plates.   **IC11**

A companion to the reprint edition of *Historia Numorum.*

ID STUDIES

ALFÖLDI, András and ALFÖLDI, Elisabeth.
Die Kontorniat-Medaillons. In neuer Bearbeitung von András Alföldi und Elisabeth Alföldi,
unter Mitwirkund von Curtis L. Clay. Berlin,
de Gruyter, 1976– . Illus. (2 fold.).   **ID1**

Antike Münzen und geschnittene Steine; Bd. 6.
AJA LXXXI 1977 406–407 Metcalf

An elaborate restatement of Alföldi's 1943 study of
the enigmatic monetiform bronzes known as contorni-
ates, every known one of which is here illustrated.
Keeping to his earlier assertions, Alföldi sees the con-
torniates as propaganda elements in the late 4th and
early 5th century pagan reaction to the emergence of
Christianity as the official Roman religion.

BABELON, Ernest. Traité des monnaies grecques
et romaines. Reprint of the 1901–1932 ed. published by E. Leroux, Paris. Bologna, Forni Editore, 1965. 4 v., illus.   **ID2**

1. ptie. Théorie et doctrine; 2. ptie. Description historique. (In 4 vols.); 3. ptie. Album des planches. (In
4 vols.)

Still useful; very detailed on technical matters and
well illustrated. At Babelon's death the work had
reached Alexander (except for Sicily and Italy, which
are only to 488 B.C.). Volume 2 is in 4 tomes (ca.
5600 columns) and 4 tomes of 335 plates.

BARRON, John Penrose. The silver coins of Samos. London, Athlone Press, 1966. xii, 242p.,
32 plates.   **ID3**

REA LXVIII 1966 443 Marcadé • REG LXXVIII
1965 638 Bon • JHS LXXXVII 1967 196–197 Kraay

Thanks especially to the research at the Heraion our
knowledge of Samos has been greatly increased. The
present work incorporates recent finds and relates them
to the economic and political history of the island,
utilizing the most modern numismatic techniques in
the study. The period covered is from Polycrates c.530
B.C. down to 200 B.C.

BREGLIA, Laura. Roman imperial coins; Their
art and technique. Introd. by Ranuccio Bianchi
Bandinelli. New York, Praeger, [1968]. 236p.,
illus.   **ID4**

Trans. of *L'arte romana nelle monete dell' età imperiale.*

JRS LX 1970 265 Crawford • AJA LXXIV 1970 117–118 Breckenridge • CW LXII 1969 367 Buttrey

An admittedly popular treatment, based on 99 photographic enlargements with an adequate descriptive text which leaves little room for comments on art and technique. An excellent collection of beautiful pictures. The work is badly edited. There is a good introduction by Bianchi Bandinelli outlining the main problems of Roman art.

BRITISH Museum. Dept. of Coins & Medals. A guide to the principal coins of the Greeks, from circa 700 B.C. to A.D. 270, based on the work of Barclay V. Head. London, [1959]. 108p., plates.   **ID5**

CR XLVII 1933 203 Cuttle • JHS LIII 1933 313

A fundamental work. Grew out of the successive editions of B. V. Head's *Coins of the ancients,* now adding an eighth stage, the reign of Gallienus, to the previous seven. About 800 coins are illustrated, 293 of them belonging to the period c.700–400 B.C. In its time, the best general introduction in English to Greek coins.

CALLU, Jean-Pierre. La politique monétaire des empereurs romains, de 238 à 311. Paris, E. de Boccard, 1969. 562p.   **ID6**

Bibliothèque les Écoles françaises d'Athènes et de Rome; fasc.

RBPh XLVIII 1970 141–142 Weiller • Latomus XXIX 1970 835–836 Thirion • REA LXXIII 1971 263–266 Nony

A remarkably detailed but clear synthesis of the period 238–311 A.D., with an extensive bibliography (p.485–511).

CARSON, Robert A. G. Coins ancient, mediaeval and modern. 2d (rev.) ed. London, Hutchinson, 1970. xiii, 642p., 64 plates.   **ID7**

NC III 1963 279–281 Whitting • RBPh XLII 1964 1162–1164 Baerten • RBN CX 1964 140–141 Naster

CARSON, Robert A. G. "Roman history and the Roman coinage." Didaskalos I, 3 (1965): 153–164, 4 plates.   **ID8**

The uses of Roman coins in teaching Latin and Roman history are outlined and the abundance and relative inexpensiveness of Roman coins is stressed. Coins illustrate the ups and downs of the economy of the Roman world. The one aspect of illustration in which Roman coinage excels is portraiture, so that from Augustus onwards we have a very full portrait gallery of emperors and other members of imperial families. This very informative article is illustrated with 44 coins.

CARSON, Robert A. G. The principal coins of the Romans. London, 1978–1981. Illus.   **ID9**

Volume I. The Republic, c.290–31 B.C. 88p., 368 illus. Vol. II. The principate, 31 B.C.–A.D. 296. 1979.

240p. Vol. III. The dominate, A.D. 294–498. 1981. 112p.

v. I: JRS LXX 1980 217–218 Mattingly • CR XXX 1980 173 Nash

This is the first of a projected three volumes and contains 88 pages of text and 368 illustrations.

COHEN, Henry. Description historique des monnaies frapées sous l'Empire romain communément appelées medailles imperiales. 2. éd. Paris, 1880–1892. Leipzig, Gustav Fock, 1930–1957. 9 v., illus.   **ID10**

Volumes 3–8: Continuée par Feuardent. Imprint covered by label: Chicago, Argonaut, 1969.

A classic corpus of Roman Imperial coins, arranged alphabetically according to the reverse inscriptions. Volume 9, subtitled Dictionnaire special: français, allemagne and anglais, italien, espagnol par G. Probzt et R. Gaidoschik.

CRAWFORD, Michael H. Roman republican coin hoards. London, Royal Numismatic Society, 1969. vi, 170p., [3] leaves of plates, illus.

ID11

AJA LXXV 1971 230–232 Buttrey • Gnomon XLIII 1971 266–271 Chantraine • Phoenix XXIV 1970 357–359 Boren • JRS LX 1970 231–232 Mattingly

A detailed bibliography of some 567 coin hoards and "other finds" down to the year 2 B.C. Some information is given about each hoard. Eighteen tables provide many pointers to revisions of chronology. There are six indices. This is a vast improvement on similar earlier works like Grueber's British Museum catalog (1910) and Sydenham's *Coinage of the Roman Republic* (1952). Crawford studies the hoard as a tool in clarifying the essential problem of Republican numismatics, the establishment of both absolute and relative chronology for the hundreds of different issues. Since Republican coins, unlike Imperial, bear no intended chronological markings, they must be arranged according to the internal evidence of weight, fabric, style, and the development of types, legends and symbols, and by such external evidence as archaeological context or hoard composition. Since the hoard normally contains coins taken from circulation at the time of burial it provides *termini ante* and *post* for coins which are, and are not, included; hence the importance of this study.

CRAWFORD, Michael H. Roman Republican coinage. London, Cambridge University Press, 1975. xv, xi, 919p. 2 v.   **ID12**

Bibliography: Volume I (p.797–819).

Antiquity XLIX 1975 239–240 Reece • Phoenix XXX 1976 375–382 Frier • AJA LXXX 1976 215–216 Metcalf • CW LXXI, 2 1977 151–153 Buttrey

A detailed study of over 200 collections and hoards, with 79 excellent plates illustrating all major types, which sets forth the numismatic evidence from which historical conclusions can be drawn. A new chronological framework is provided; the mints are identified. Volume II consists of ten studies devoted to special aspects.

DAVIS, Norman and KRAAY, Colin M. The Hellenistic kingdoms; Portrait coins and history. Photographs by P. Frank Purvey. London, Thames and Hudson, 1973. 296p., 212 illus., maps, ports.   **ID13**

Antiquity XLVIII 1974 154–155 Crawford • G&R XXI 1974 94 Murray • NC XIV 1974 212–213 Price
Contains over 200 coin portraits of Hellenistic monarchs together with a short biographical narrative of the period. The photographs illustrate well the principles of Hellenistic portraitures.

GARDNER, Percy. Archaeology and the types of Greek coins. Chicago, Argonaut Publishers, 1965. xvi, 217p., 16 plates.   **ID14**

REA LXVIII 1966 442 Marcadé • REG LXXVIII 1965 637–638 Bon
A reprint of an 1883 work which is still remarkably clear, logical and concise, with a new and highly satisfactory introduction by Margaret Thompson.

GRANT, Michael. From imperium to auctoritas. A historical study of aes coinage in the Roman Empire, 49 B.C.–A.D. 14. [1st ed.] reprinted with corrections. London, Cambridge University Press, 1969. xvi, 512p., 12 plates.   **ID15**

Reprint of 1st ed., published in 1946.
AC 1946 371–374 De Laet • Gnomon XXII 1950 260–268 Vittinghoff • JRS XXVII 1947 209–212 Sutherland • AJA LI 1947 337–340 Bellinger
A vast new assemblage of more than a thousand separate issues of aes (copper and its alloys) coins, struck between 49 B.C. and the death of Augustus, and hitherto ill-recognized or neglected by numismatists. The historian is challenged to recognize, in this new horizontal assemblage of material, evidence bearing as directly upon the constitutional problems of the early Principate as any furnished by literature or epigraphy. A major contribution of numismatics to history. See also Grant, Michael, *Six main aes coinages of Augustus* (Edinburgh, 1953) [cf. *JRS* XLIII (1953) 199–201 Sutherland].

GRANT, Michael. Roman history from coins; Some uses of the Imperial coinage to the historian. Cambridge, Cambridge University Press, 1968. 96p., 32 plates, illus., map.   **ID16**

REA LXXI 1969 221 Nony • AC XXXVIII 1969 664 Hackens • CR IX 1959 277–278 Sutherland
Well-chosen examples of Imperial numismatic discoveries which are of use to the historian. The need to simplify and popularize has led to some inaccuracies and infelicities. The plates are varied, well chosen and clear.

GRANT, Michael. Roman imperial money. Amsterdam, Hakkert, 1972. x, 324p., illus.   **ID17**

Reprint of the 1954 ed.
CR n.s. VI 1956 54–56 Sutherland • NC XV 1955 266–268 Carson

Four of the six main parts of this work are concerned principally with Grant's main specialization—1st century problems—and the later Empire receives only summary treatment at the end. In the text, the non-specialist is treated to extended synopses of some of Grant's own controversial positions, argued in more detail elsewhere.

HAEBERLIN, Ernst J. Aes grave; Das Schwergeld Roms und Mittelitaliens einschliesslich der ihm vorausgehenden Rohbronzewährung. Mit einem atlas von 103 tafeln. Frankfurt am Main, J. Baer, 1910– . Illus., port. of 103 plates.   **ID18**

Reprinted by Forni, 1967– .

HILL, George Francis, Sir. Coins and medals. London, Society for Promoting Christian Knowledge, 1920. London, W. Dawson, 1969. 62p.   **ID19**

Helps for students of history; 36.
CB XLIV 1968 79 Horner • JHS XL 1920 236
First issued in 1899, this elementary work in three chapters deals lucidly with the generalities of the subject. There is a carefully selected bibliography arranged mainly on geographical principles. Includes modern as well as ancient and medieval numismatics.

HOLLOWAY, R. Ross. The thirteen-months coinage of Hieronymos of Syracuse. (With 11 figures and 12 plates.) Berlin, De Gruyter, 1969. xxiii, 47p., 12 inserts (in pocket), illus., plates.   **ID20**

Antike Münzen und geschnittene Steine; Bd. 3.
REA LXXI 1969 534–535 Nony • Gnomon XLIII 1971 312 Healey • AJA LXXV 1971 106 Thompson
Hieronymus, the last king of Syracuse, was assassinated in Spring, 214 B.C. after a short reign of thirteen months, and at a vital juncture in the 2d Punic War when Sicily switched its support from Rome to Carthage. Coinage is here used for the first time to challenge the brief or pro-Roman narrative of events in Livy and Polybius. Some 245 coins struck in gold or silver are recorded with careful numismatic commentary, well illustrating the use of coin types in publicizing official policy, especially in the war issue of early 214.

KENT, J. P. C., HILL, P. V. and CARSON, Robert A. G. Late Roman bronze coinage, A.D. 324–498. "Reprinted with additions and corrections from The Numismatic Circular." London, Spink, 1976. 114p., [2] leaves of plates.   **ID21**

Part 1. The Bronze Coinage of the House of Constantine, A.D. 324–346 [by] P. V. Hill and J. P. C. Kent; part 2. Bronze Roman Imperial Coinage of the Later Empire, A.D. 346–498 [by] R.A.G. Carson and J. P. C. Kent.
JRS LI 1961 256 Kraay • AJA LXV 1961 216 Breckenridge

KLEINER, Fred S. Greek and Roman coins in the Athenian Agora. Photos by Eugene Vanderpool, Jr. Princeton, N.J., American School of Classical Studies at Athens, 1975. [32]p., illus. **ID22**

Excavations of the Athenian Agora: picture book; v. 15.

G&R XXIII 1976 206 Sparks • AC XLV 1976 390–391 Delvoye

An excellent picture book, plus an enormous amount of useful information in a small compass, beginning with the oldest coins, Aigenetan silver staters and Cyzican electron staters of the 5th century, and covering Athenian silver coinage, the new style Stephanephoroi, and bronze Hellenistic Athenian coins, also coinage of other cities found in the course of the excavations of the Agora, all confirming the importance of Athens as a commercial and cultural center. Bronze local coinage of the era of Hadrian is included showing an interesting diversity of types, also Greek money of the Roman Imperial times and Roman money from the Republic to Constantine.

KRAAY, Colin M. Greek coins and history; Some current problems. New York, Barnes & Noble, [1969]. x, 81p., 8 plates. **ID23**

Gnomon XLIII 1971 99–100 Christ • CW LXXIII 1970 273 Buttrey • NC XI 1971 338–344 Jameson • HBN VII 1967–1969 517–528 Chantraine

The "problems" concern the very nature of numismatic research. What emerges is that the coins should not be used merely to corroborate the data of history but also should be studied in themselves. The study of hoards and die-linked series can yield their own chronology.

LENORMANT, François. La monnaie dans l'antiquité; Leçons professées dans la chaire d'archéologie près la Bibliothèque Nationale en 1875–1877. Bologna, Forni, 1969. 3 v. **ID24**

Reprint of Paris 1878–1879 ed.

MATTINGLY, Harold. Roman coins from the earliest times to the fall of the Western Empire. 2d ed. rev. and reset. London, Methuen, 1967. xiii, 303p., 64 plates. **ID25**

Bibliography: p.259–272.
AHAM XIV 1968–1969 176–177 Labastic
The second edition appeared in 1962.

MILNE, Joseph Grafton. Greek and Roman coins and the study of history. Chicago, Obol International, 1977. 128p., [16] leaves of plates, illus. **ID26**

Reprint of 1939 ed.

MOMMSEN, Theodor. Geschichte des römische Münzwesens. Graz, Akademische Druck- und Verlagsanstalt, 1956. 900p. **ID27**

1st ed., Berlin 1860.
This great work, fundamental in its time and still

useful for its historical perspectives, was translated into French in 4 volumes (Paris, 1865–1875).

REECE, Richard. Roman coins. London, Benn, 1970. 189p., 64 plates, illus., geneal. tables, map. **ID28**

Antiquity XLV 1971 231–232 Crawford

SCHEERS, Simone. Les monnaies de la Gaule inspirées de celles de la République romaine. Leuven, Universiteitsbibliothek, 1969. x, 270p., maps, 12 plates. **ID29**

NC XI 1971 352–356 Allen • Gnomon XLV 1973 311–312 Healy • AC XL 1971 443 Faider-Feytmans

A useful contribution to a somewhat neglected area of numismatic studies. The coinage struck by the Gauls between the 2d century and the first half of the 1st century throws valuable light on the nature and spread of Roman influence before Caesar's conquests. The present catalogue and commentary is much more comprehensive than previous works, e.g., A. Blanchet's *Traité des Monnaies gauloises*, 1905.

SCHWABACER, Willy. Griechische Münzkunst; Kurze Kunstgeschichte an Beispielen aus der Sammlung S. M. Gustaf VI. Adolf, König von Schweden. Überarb. und erw. Aufl. Mainz am Rhein, P. von Zabern, 1974. 38, [125]p., illus., map. **ID30**

At head of title: Deutsches Archëologisches Institut.
First published in Swedish in 1962.

STARR, Chester G. Athenian coinage, 480–449 B.C. Oxford, Clarendon Press, 1970. xiii, 97p., 26 plates, illus. **ID31**

REA LXXV 1973 186 Nony • AJPh XCIV 1973 308–310 Eddy • Mnemosyne XXVII 1974 98–101 Guépin • RPh XLVIII 1974 132–134 Nicolet

An important contribution to classification, based on stylistic criteria. Starr has set up his own corpus of silver coins struck between 480 and 449 and has classified them into 5 groups, with some further subdivisions. The result is much closer dating than the vague "480–407 B.C." that was hitherto popular, with important historical consequences. A courageous approach.

SUTHERLAND, Carol Humphrey Vivian. Art in coinage; The aesthetics of money from Greece to the present day. New York, Philosophical Library, [1956]. 223p., illus., ports. **ID32**

CW L 1957 101 Buttrey • CJ LII 1957 189–191 Vermeule • Archaeology XI 1958 141 Thompson

SUTHERLAND, Carol Humphrey Vivian. Coinage in Roman Imperial policy, 31 B.C.–A.D. 68. New York, Sanford J. Durst, 1978. xi, 220p., illus. **ID33**

Reprint of the 1951 ed. published by Methuen, London.

JRS XLIII 1953 198–199 Chilver • CR n.s. II 1952 214–216 Grant • REL XXX 1952 495–447 Béranger • Gnomon XXIV 1952 362–366 Vogt

An excellent attempt to put recent numismatic research and literary history at the service of historians of the reigns of Augustus through Nero. The author states that the use of coinage for the study of Roman Imperial history has been revolutionized during the previous generation. At times the historian will feel that the revolution has gone further than the evidence warrants.

SUTHERLAND, Carol Humphrey Vivian. The emperor and the coinage; Julio-Claudian studies. London, Spink, 1976. [vi], 146p., 10p. of plates, illus.   **ID34**

NCirc LXXXV 1977 305 Casey

SUTHERLAND, Carol Humphrey Vivian. Roman coins. New York, Putnam, 1974. 311p., illus. (some col.).   **ID35**

NC XV 1975 235–236 Buttrey • Ant J LV 1975 145–146 Reece

Presents the complex history of Roman coinage in an essentially narrative form. The specially photographed coins provide a graphic history of coinage from the earliest issue down to those of the last emperor in the West, Romulus Augustulus. A second edition appeared in 1962.

SYDENHAM, Edward Allen. The coinage of the Roman Republic. Revised with indices by G. C. Haines; edited by L. Forrer and C. A. Hersh. New York, Arno Press, 1975. lxix, 343p., 29 [i.e., 15] leaves of plates, illus.   **ID36**

Reprint of the 1952 ed. published by Spink, London.

JRS XLIII 1953 193–196 Boyce • MPhL LX 1955 153–154 Hulshoff Pol

A basic work for the historian which takes account of the general downward revision of coinage dating, resulting from the intensive studies of the previous quarter-century. Particularly good on early coinage. The present work was revised and updated by various hands after Sydenham's death in 1948. There are useful concordances with Babelon and Grueber.

SYDENHAM, Edward Allen. Historical references on coins of the Roman Empire from Augustus to Gallienus. [1st ed. rep.] London, Spink (San Diego, Pegasus), 1968. [3], 155p., illus.   **ID37**

"First published 1917."

JS 1918 105 R. C. • CW XIV 1921 86–87 Brett

This work first appeared serially in the Numismatic Circular (1915–1916) and is here made more generally available.

THOMSEN, Rudi. Early Roman coinage; A study of the chronology. I, II & III. Copenhagen, Nationalmuseet, 1957–1961.   **ID38**

RIN LXV 1963 253–254 Ulrich-Bausau

ZEHNACKER, H. Moneta; Recherches sur l'organisation et l'art des émissions de la république romaine, 280–31 B.C. Paris, Bib. des École française d'Athènes. 1973. 2 v., xxiv, 1214p.   **ID39**

JRS LXV 1975 177–179 Crawford • AJA LXXX 1976 106–107 Mitchell

Art and Archaeology

JA   BIBLIOGRAPHY AND METHODOLOGY

BESTERMAN, Theodore. Art and architecture; A bibliography of bibliographies. Totowa, N.J., Rowman and Littlefield, 1971. 216p.   **JA1**

Brings together all the titles on art and archaeology from Besterman's *A world bibliography of bibliographies,* 4th ed. (1965–1966). Unannotated but with very complete bibliographical detail. Special attention is given to the collation of bibliographies in several parts or volumes so that one can see at a glance where gaps exist and where a serial publication ended. Nineteenth century archaeological publications are very thoroughly covered.

CHAMBERLIN, Mary W. Guide to art reference books. Chicago, American Library Association, 1959. xiv, 418p.   **JA2**

The 2,500 entries include small handbooks and ready-reference tools on art history along with the great encyclopedias and corpora. Full bibliographical data are given and the annotations are both descriptive and critical. Of particular interest to the classicist are sections 8 Iconography and 10 Histories and Handbooks of Art, Ancient.

COULSON, William D. E. An annotated bibliography of Greek and Roman art, architecture and archaeology. New York, Garland Pub., 1975. v, 135p.   **JA3**

Garland reference library of the humanities; 28.
BBF XXII 1977 606 Ernst • CW LXX 1977 488–489 Biers
This book lists all the inexpensive paperback and hardcover books available from American publishers in the area of Greek and Roman art, archaeology and architecture. Important French and German books are listed in a separate section along with worthwhile books above $10.00 in price. This section also covers books on ancient urbanism and urban planning. The bibliography is directed to the general reader and graduate student. Despite some typographical errors and poor editing the book is a valuable contribution to the bibliography of Greek and Roman art.

EHRESMANN, Donald L. Fine arts; A bibliographic guide to basic reference works. Littleton, Colo., Libraries Unlimited, 1975. 283p.   **JA4**

Intended to supplement Chamberlin's bibliography, no works published before 1900 are included. Of works published between 1900 and 1958 only classic or standard works are included. The bibliography is annotated and includes the basic art reference books used by the classicist.

FASTI archaeologici; Annual bulletin of classical archaeology. Firenze, Sansoni Editore, 1946– . Illus., maps, plans.   **JA5**

Vol. 1– . 1946— .
Issued by the International Association for Classical Archaeology.
Published by the International Association for Classical Archaeology. Issued annually, it is a classified bibliography of books and periodical articles on all aspects of classical archaeology, including art. It also contains a bulletin of discoveries throughout the classical world with an author index to each volume. Contents: 1. General (by countries); 2. Prehistoric and Classical Greece; 3. Italy Before the Roman Empire; 4. The Hellenistic World and Eastern Provinces of the Roman Empire; 5. The Roman West; 6. Christianity and Late Antiquity. Catalogues of museums and exhibitions along with collections and congresses are included in the General section. The indices are arranged by authors, ancient and modern; geographical names; subject; lexicalia; literary and epigraphical sources. A well-organized and easy-to-use reference tool.

JAHRESBERICHT 1982 des Deutschen Archäologischen Instituts: Archäologischer Anzeiger. Berlin, de Gruyter, 1983.   **JA6**

Annual history and archaeology of Greece and Rome during the Classical Period, excavations, museum acquisitions, illustrations. Separately published bibliography *Archäologische Bibliographie.*

MOON, Brenda E. Mycenaean civilization; Publications 1959–60; a second bibliography. [London, Institute of Classical Studies; distributed by International University Booksellers], 1961. xxv, 130p. **JA7**

> University of London. Institute of Classical Studies: Bulletin supplement; 12.
> REG LXXVI 1963 211–212 Deshayes • AC XXXII 1963 322 Olivier • RBPh XLI 1963 643 Deroy
> This is a second bibliography, the first consisting of two books and covering periodicals published between 1936 and 1956, *BICS* Sup. 3 (1957). The second bibliography includes works on Minoan civilization along with Minoan and Mycenaean language and epigraphy. There is an author list supplemented by subject and topographical lists. Periodicals and dissertations are included.

PATTEN, David, ed. Art index. New York, H. W. Wilson, 1929– . **JA8**

> An author and subject index to art periodicals and museum bulletins. It is published quarterly with a cumulation each year. Should be used by the classicist

in conjunction with *L'Année philologique* because it is up-to-date.

SCHEFOLD, Karl. Orient, Hellas und Rom in der archäologischen Forschung seit 1939. Bern, A. Francke, 1949. 248p. **JA9**

> Wissenschaftliche Forschungsberichte. Geisteswissenschaftliche Reihe; v. Bd. 15.
> AAHG IV 1951 126–129 Walter • AJPh LXXII 1951 214–216 Thompson • JHS LXXIV 1954 236 Robertson
> This is a bibliography of books on classical archaeology produced between 1939 and 1949. It is a superb reference book for the history of Greek and Roman archaeology in this period.

SCHLOSSER, Julius Ritter von. La letteratura artistica; Manuale delle fonti della storia dell'arte moderna. Traduzione di Filippo Rossi. 3 ed. Italiana aggiornata da Otto Kurz. Firenze, Nuova Italia, 1964. 766p. **JA10**

> Il Pensiero storico; 12.
> Translation of *Die Kunstliteratur,* originally published under title: *Materiallen zur Quellenkunde der Kunstgeschichte.* An excellent reference tool for the history of art literature up to the early 19th century. The bracketed additions by Kurz in the bibliographies bring the material up-to-date.

JB ENCYCLOPEDIAS AND DICTIONARIES

CAFFARELLO, Nelida. Dizionario archaeologico di antichità classica. Firenze, Olschki, 1971. xii, 529p., illus. **JB1**

> ACR II 1972 177 MacKendrick • Athenaeum LII 1974 358–359 Saletti • BVAB XLVII 1972 151 Maaskant-Kleibrink
> Aims to be "a repertory of entries on things, facts, mythical and heroic personages, concepts relative to public and private life." It does not list places, which limits its value since no examples of "biblioteca," "colonia," "teatro," etc., are named. The ethnologies to each article are carefully done.

DEVAMBEZ, Pièrre F. et al. A dictionary of ancient Greek civilisation. London, Methuen, 1970. 1966. 419p., illus. **JB2**

> University paperbacks; UP363. Trans. of *Dictionnaire de la civilisation grecque.*
> REG LXXXV 1972 222 Lévêque
> Religion, art, politics and social life of ancient Greece in short articles. For bibliography of Devambez, see *Revue Archéologique,* 1972, 5–7.

ENCICLOPEDIA dell'arte antica, classica, e orientale. Roma, Instituto della enciclopedia

italiana, 1968– . Illus., (col.) plates, facsims. **JB3**

> BSEAA XLII 1976 546–547 Balil
> Arranged alphabetically, the volumes contain scholarly articles on works of art, ancient sites and artists. The bibliographies attached to the entries are comprehensive and well selected. In v. III the beautifully illustrated article on Greek art is an excellent and scholarly introduction to the subject. Likewise the article on Roman art in v. VI, with maps, drawings and photographs, covers all phases of Roman art. A supplement to update the volumes appeared in 1973.

ENCYCLOPEDIA of world art. New York, McGraw-Hill, [1959–1968]. **JB4**

> Includes bibliographies.
> Archaeology XV 1962 126–128 Weinberg
> Originally published in 1958 as the *Enciclopedia universale dell'arte,* the 15 volumes are arranged alphabetically by the names of artists, art works, periods, archaeological sites, etc., from ancient to modern. The entries are written by eminent scholars and are accompanied by comprehensive bibliographies. The volumes are well illustrated with good photographs, maps and tables.

NASH, Ernest. Pictorial dictionary of ancient Rome. 2d ed., rev. New York, Praeger, [1968, 1961]. 2 v., illus., plans.   **JB5**

Volume titles: 1. Amphitheatrum Castrense-Lacus Curtius; 2. Lacus Iuturnae-Volcanal.
AJA LXVIII 1964 86–87 Frazer • JRS LIII 1963 227–229 Bloch
These volumes complement and bring up to date the *Topographical dictionary of ancient Rome* (1929) by Samuel Platner and Thomas Ashby. Following an alphabetical order there is a description and bibliography for each item. Outstanding are the 1,338 illustrations, including many photographs of monuments which have come to light since 1929. Lesser known monuments are included. An indispensable work, splendidly illustrated. Additional and more recent bibliography is contained in the article on Rome by the same author in the *Princeton encyclopaedia of classical sites.* Volume II includes a general index and an index of inscriptions.

PLATNER, Samuel Ball. A topographical dictionary of ancient Rome. Completed and revised by Thomas Ashby. London, Oxford University Press, H. Milford, 1929. [Ann Arbor, University Microfilms, 1973]. xxiii, 609p., plates, maps (1 fold.), plans.   **JB6**

Outstanding for clarity and fullness of information, it is still an indispensable handbook in spite of the wealth of new information since its publication. Arranged alphabetically by monuments and sites, it contains a full bibliography to 1929.

SCHUCHHARDT, Walter Herwig, ed. Das Fischer Lexicon, Bildende Kunst. 1960.   **JB7**

AJA LXVI 1962 214 Richter
An encyclopedia which aims to present "the knowledge of our time in up-to-date fashion": v. I Archäologie begins with the Cretan-Mycenaean period, continues with the geometric, classical and Hellenistic and covers the Roman age. Felix Echstein writes on painting; Helga von Heintze on the art of Italy; Ulf Jantzen on archaeology; J. C. Wisner on Cretan-Mycenaean

art and the editor on sculpture and architecture. A good reference tool in which the items are arranged alphabetically.

TRAVLOS, Ioannes N. Pictorial dictionary of ancient Athens. New York, Praeger, 1971. xvi, 590p., illus., maps, plans.   **JB8**

AJA LXXIX 1975 103–104 Amandry • CR XXIV 1974 110–112 Lewis
A parallel to Nash's work on Rome. It is provided with copious beautiful illustrations. For each item there is text, as well as bibliography and illustration. The author worked closely with excavations in Greece, and he presents a scholarly text that includes recent discoveries. Very useful as a reference tool in the study of Greek art, archaeology, architecture and history.

VIAL, C. Lexique d'antiquités grecques. Paris, Colin, 1972. 272p., 19 illus.   **JB9**

Collection U² N° 199 Sér. Hist. anc.
RD L 1972 640 Imbert • AC XLI 1972 728 Delvoye

VILLE, Georges. Concise encyclopedia of archaeology; From the Bronze Age. Produced by Geoffrey Bibby. Glasgow, Collins, 1971. 251p., illus., maps.   **JB10**

Trans. of *Dictionnaire de l'archéologie.*
AC XL 1971 381–383 Delvoye
Translated from the French, this is a short dictionary of archaeology, including cities, civilizations, technical terms and bibliographies of noted archaeologists.

ZINSERLING, G. Abriss der griechischen und römischen Kunst, mit einem Anh.: Lexikon der wichtigsten Fachausdrücke, Verzeichnis der wichtigsten Literatur, Verzeichnis der wichtigsten Ausgrabungen, Verzeichnis der wichtigsten Antikenmuseen, Zeittafeln. Leipzig, Philipp Reclam Jun., 1970. 608p., 193 illus.   **JB11**

Reclams Universal-Bibl. Nr. 435.
Eirene X 1972 148–150 Kluwe • DLZ XCII 1971 63–66 Schindler

JC ARCHAEOLOGY—METHODOLOGY

ANDRAE, E. Walter and OTTO, Walter, eds. Handbuch der Archäologie. München, Beck, 1939– . Illus., fold. map, plates.   **JC1**

Handbuch der Altertumswissenschaft; 6. Abt. 3, pt. 1. "bergründet von Walter Otto, fortgeführt von Reinhard Herbig."
JHS LX 1940 103 Lawrence • JRS XXVIII 1938 251–252 Radford
A general handbook of archaeology in Greece and

Italy and in other countries that relate to them. There are articles on the scope and methods of archaeology and a History of Archaeology which discusses classical archaeologists. The articles are written by well-known experts. The first volume published in 1939 covers the Paleolithic age, Egypt and the Near East along with general questions of archaeological sources and methods. The section on the Aegean is written by F. Matz in the first part of v. II. This is a very complete summary of the archaeological findings to this date on pre-Hellenic Aegean. There is a bibliography with each section.

BASS, George Fletcher. Archaeology under water. London, Thames and Hudson, 1966. 224p., illus., maps (1 fold.), ports.   **JC2**

Ancient peoples and places; 48.
Pyrenae II 1966 220–221 Barberá • Archaeology XXI 1968 72–74 McCann
A competent book by an expert in the field of underwater archaeology. It is a survey of research to date and the technological methods used. Many of the sites that involved underwater diving are described with excellent illustrations. There are chapters on mapping, recording and the complete excavation of an underwater site.

BRADFORD, John. Ancient landscapes; Studies in field archaeology. Bath, [Eng.], C. Chivers, 1974. xvii, 297p., illus., maps (part fold.).   **JC3**

First published in 1957.
Sic Gymn XI 1958 308 Arias • Gnomon XXXI 1959 550–552 Kraemer • JRS XLVIII 1958 201–202 St. Joseph
Every region does not provide aerial discoveries, some being excluded by the terrain. In the Mediterranean the most important countries for air archaeology are Turkey, Greece and Spain. In this excellent volume the author presents the techniques of air archaeology and demonstrates its value to our knowledge of ancient sites. Plans of ancient cities can be well illustrated by aerial views. The book explains how aerial photographs are made, how to map them, how to evaluate their archaeological significance and how to follow up with work on the ground. There are copious aerial photographs and maps of sites.

BRODRIBB, Arthur Charles C. Drawing archaeological finds. [1st American ed.] New York, Association Press, [1971, 1970]. 96p., illus.   **JC4**

This short book introduces the student and amateur archaeologist to the skill of preparing drawings of finds for reproduction. The tools and materials needed, and the techniques of drawing finds, are described with good illustration.

BROTHWELL, Don R. and HIGGS, Eric, eds. Science in archaeology; A survey of progress and research. With a foreword by Grahame Clark. Rev. and enl. ed. New York, Praeger, [1970]. 720p., illus., maps, plates.   **JC5**

AJA LXX 1966 199 Corwin
This large volume is a scholarly work on the scientific methods employed by archaeologists. It is divided into five sections on dating, environment, man himself, artifacts and methods for saving time.

CASSON, Lionel. Ships and seamanship in the ancient world. Princeton, Princeton University

Press, [1973, 1971]. xxviii, 441p., illus., plans.   **JC6**

Using information from recently discovered shipwrecks the author produces a work of meticulous scholarship on the details of ancient ships. Starting with Bronze Age ships the book covers techniques and materials of hull construction, ships rig and gear, and handling and performance of ships. Beautifully illustrated with extensive footnotes, appendices, glossaries and drawings.

CHILDE, Vera Gordon. A short introduction to archaeology. New York, Collier Books, [1962, 1956]. 127p.   **JC7**

This short book explains some of the basic terminology and methodology of archaeology. It is a good basic text that contains information on recording finds, classification and chronology, recognition and identification of monuments and interpretation of archaeology data. A concise and very useful introduction to the science. The author's *Piecing together the past* (1956) discusses the archaeologist's task of translating the raw data into valid inferences.

COLES, John M. Archaeology by experiment. London, Hutchinson, [1973]. 182p., illus.   **JC8**

Hutchinson university library.
Antiquity XLVIII 1974 318–319 Bowen
This small book records experiments made in the past 150 years, testing archaeological material for an understanding of its purpose and function. Methods are described for the reproduction of ancient stone tools, digging implements, musical instruments, pottery, storage pits, ships, forts, weapons, etc., and the assessment of these ancient remains in the task of recreating past human behavior. A careful, scientific work.

DORAN, J. E. and HUDSON, F. R. Mathematics and computers in archaeology. Cambridge, Mass., Harvard University Press, 1975. xi, 381p.   **JC9**

Antiquity LI 1977 158–159 Wilcock • CHum X 1976 369–372 Clark
A systematic survey of mathematical, statistical and computing techniques used in archaeology. Written as an introductory guide for students and archaeologists, it outlines the principles and applications of the new methods.

DUMAS, Frédéric. Deep-water archaeology. Trans. from the French by Honor Frost. London, Routledge and K. Paul, [1962]. xii, 71p., illus.   **JC10**

Archaeology XVIII 1965 315 Casson.
Methods used for land excavation are of little value when applied to underwater archaeology. The author is a diver and an archaeologist, and in this short book he presents a good introduction to the technique of

submarine excavation in Mediterranean waters. This he defines as the study of ancient wrecks, ports, submerged towns and other offshore sites, marked by scattered pottery and anchors. There is a helpful appendix by Honor Frost on deep-water recording and an excellent bibliography.

GOODYEAR, Frank Haigh. Archaeological site science. London, Heinemann, 1971. xiv, 282, [12]p., illus. **JC11**

Provides basic scientific knowledge for the practical archaeologist on the archaeological environment, the materials of antiquity, and the interaction of the materials with their surroundings. A review is made of the kinds of tests and research that can be done in archaeological laboratories. Direct applications of scientific methods on the site are described and in the final section archaeological prospecting methods are reviewed, including well-established methods and newer techniques. A well-produced, clearly written book, valuable to the amateur and the professional. The illustrations consist of excellent photographs and drawings.

GRINSELL, L., RAHTZ, P. and WILLIAMS, D. P. The preparation of archaeological reports. 2nd ed. New York, St. Martin's Press, 1974. 105p., illus. **JC12**

TLS LXXIV 1975 434 Hammond • AntJ LVI 1976 80–81 Wainwright

HEIZER, Robert Fleming. The archaeologist at work; A source book in archaeological method and interpretation. Westport, Conn., Greenwood Press, 1975, 1959. xiv, 522p., illus. **JC13**

Reprint of the ed. published by Harper & Row, New York.

This volume consists of well-chosen selections of readings on archaeological technique and method. The authors included are the finest experts in their various fields. There is a short introduction explaining the content of each reading and the excavation to which it applies. The book is divided by subject, including reconstruction and restoration of events, ecology and population, survey and site recognition, stratigraphy and stratification, dating and seriation. There is a very useful long bibliography and superb illustrations.

HEIZER, Robert Fleming. A guide to archaeological field methods. [3d rev. ed.] Palo Alto, Calif., National Press, [1966]. ix, 162p., illus., maps. **JC14**

First published in 1949 under title: *A manual of archaeological field methods.*

BO XVIII 1961 22 Naumann • BO XXVI 1969 50 Brongers

A practical guide and introduction to archaeological field methods. Written for the American archaeologist, it has information for all students in the field. There is a lengthy bibliography (p. 120–150).

HOFFMAN, Herbert. Collecting Greek antiquities. Introd. by John D. Cooney. A chapter on

coins by Herbert A. Cahn. [1st ed.] New York, Potter, [1971]. xii, 258p., illus., map (on lining papers), col. plates. **JC15**

ACR I 1971 240–241 Matthews • Archaeology XXVI 1973 68 Noble

The author provides a useful and well-illustrated guide for the collection of Greek art. Greek art in collections is illustrated along with line drawings of "types." There are sections on dealers, authentication, conservation and forgeries.

HOLE, Frank and HEIZER, Robert F. An introduction to prehistoric archaeology. 3d ed. New York, Holt, Rinehart and Winston, [1973]. xv, 574p., illus. **JC16**

AArch Hung XXV 1973 222–226 Kalicz

With its extensive bibliography (p. 471–557), this book is an excellent introduction to the science of archaeology. Every aspect of the science is covered, with references to other work on the topic. A very useful book for the beginning student in the historical and technical study of archaeology.

JOHNSTONE, Paul. The archaeology of ships. Illustrated with photos and maps, and with drawings by Pippa Brand. New York, Walck, [1974]. 135p., illus. (part col.). **JC17**

Archaeology XXIX 1976 65–67 Stavrolakes

Using as examples ten ship excavations, the author explains the technical methodology of ship archaeology. A wide range of sites is covered, including the Mediterranean Sea. The book describes search, survey and excavation and gives an analysis of ancient shipbuilding as learned from the ships excavated. A fascinating book on the topic, with good illustrations.

LAET, Siegfried J. de. Archaeology and its problems. Trans. by Ruth Daniel, with a foreword by Glyn E. Daniel. London, Phoenix House, [1957]. 136p., illus. **JC18**

Archaeology XI 1958 65–66 Spaulding • JRS XLIX 1959 193–194 Kenyon

Originally published in Flemish, in 1950, this is a translation of the French edition of 1954. It presents basic techniques of reconnaissance, excavation, dating and interpretation.

MANUEL de la technique des fouilles archéologiques. [Paris], Office international des musées, [1939]. 231, [1]p., illus. **JC19**

"Publications de l'Institut international de coopération intellectuelle [Société des nations]."

Includes most aspects of the scholarship of archaeology. Preliminary documentation, and how to obtain it, is discussed, along with method of excavation, materials needed, and the scientific organization and recording of the finds.

MAREK, Kurt W. Gods, graves, and scholars; The story of archaeology by C. W. Ceram; Trans.

by E. B. Garside and Sophie Wilkins. 2d. rev. and substantially enl. ed. London, Book Club Associates, 1971. xvi, 441p., illus., maps.
JC20

Trans. of *Götter, Gräber und Gelehrte*.
CJ XLVII 1952 243–244 Lazenby
A popular introduction to the stories of the most important archaeological excavations. The book emphasizes the history and the methods of the chief archaeologists involved.

MEIGHAN, Clement Woodward. Archaeology. San Francisco, Chandler Pub. Co., [1966]. 197p.
JC21

Chandler publications in anthropology and sociology.
Archaeology XXI 1968 227–228 Rock • RA n.s. 1967 187
Using case histories, the author demonstrates the development of ways of living from Lower Palaeolithic times to historic times. Both old and new world sites are included. There is a chapter on methods and tools. A general introduction to the understanding of archaeological method.

MICHAEL, Henry R. and RALPH, Elizabeth K., eds. Dating techniques for the archaeologist. Cambridge, MIT Press, [1971] xi, 226p., illus.
JC22

AJA LXXVI 1972 456–457 Heizer
The first in a series of technical handbooks for use by professional archaeologists provides articles by different authors on scientific aspects of dating.
Other volumes which cover the same area are D. Brothwell and E. Higgs, *Science in archaeology* (1970) and R. H. Brill, *Science and archaeology* (1971).

PALLOTTINO, Massimo. Che cos'è l'archeologia. [Firenze], Sansoni, 1963. 207p., illus.
JC23

SA 1966, 2 330–332 Kuziščin • JRS LV 1965 290–291 Radford
A survey of the problems and future of archaeology. There is a history of the origins of archaeology as an accessory to the study of classical literature and history. The section on modern methods of archaeology includes radiocarbon dating, dendrochronology and the preservation of sites. For the future, the author outlines the requirements for the preservation of antiquities, by the various countries and internationally. The illustrations and bibliography are good.

PLENDERLEITH, Harold James. The conservation of antiquities and works of art; Treatment, repair, and restoration. London and New York, Oxford University Press, 1956. xv, 373p., illus., tables.
JC24

AntJ XXXVII 1957 230–231 Davey • BBF II 1957 945–948 Kleindienst • BICR 1956 191–193 Borrelli-Vlad

There is a discussion of the effects of environment on the objects, followed by sections on the methods of treating organic materials, metals and related materials. Under organic materials, animal skin and skin products are included, e.g., papyrus, paper; prints, manuscripts, textiles, wood, bone and ivory. Under metals, gold and electrum, silver, copper, lead, tin, pewter, iron, etc., are examined. The final section deals with stone, ceramics and glass. There are 13 appendices on details and technical aspects of conservation.

RUMPF, Andreas. Archäologie. Berlin, W. de Gruyter, 1953– . Illus.
JC25

Sammlung Göschen; Bd. 538.
JHS LXXIV 1954 243 Cook • JHS LXXVII 1957 358 Boardman
Volume 1 is a history of classical archaeology and v. II discusses the archaeologists' idiom and the principles of copying in antiquity. These volumes are a guide for students to the basic principles involved in classical archaeology. Technical terms are explained as are the archaeologists' style, the materials of ancient works of art, and ancient copies. An invaluable introduction to the subject.

WATSON, Patty Jo, LEBLANC, Steven A. and REDMAN, Charles L. Explanation in archaeology; An explicitly scientific approach. New York, Columbia University Press, 1971. xviii, 191p., illus.
JC26

AJA LXXVI 1972 351–352 Hill
A good handbook on the scientific approaches of the "new archaeology" that explains where they differ from traditional methods.

WHEELER, Mortimer, Sir. Archaeology from the earth. Baltimore, Penguin Books, [1961]. 252p., illus.
JC27

Pelican books A356. "Published in Penguin Books, 1956. Reprinted 1961."
JRS XLV 1955 214–215 Brown
The author presents the methods and principles that he considers the best for archaeological digging. Realizing that archaeology today involves physics, chemistry, geology, biology, economics, political science, sociology, climatology and botany, he stresses that the archaeologist must remember he is not digging up *things*, he is digging up *people*. There are chapters on virtually all aspects of the excavator's work including chronology, stratigraphy, tactics and strategy, staff tools, the field-laboratory and photography. A good introduction to the subject by an eminent scholar in the field.

WOOLLEY, Charles Leonard, Sir. History unearthed. London, E. Benn, 1963, 1958. 175p., illus.
JC28

Archaeology XVI 1963 72 Vermeule
This picture book of 18 archaeological sites in all parts of the world is also published in paperback by Praeger. A short text accompanies the photographs

of the sites and the finds. The sites included are those, the author feels, made the most important contributions to our knowledge of ancient history. He emphasizes the extent to which these archaeological discoveries were due to the scientific methods of modern field-work.

JD   ICONOGRAPHY

AHLBERG, Gudrun. Fighting on land and sea in Greek geometric art. Stockholm, [Svenska institutet i Athen; Lund, distributed by P. Äströms Förlag], 1971. 113p., illus.   **JD1**

AJA LXXVI 1972 336–337 Betancourt • CR XXIII 1973 288–289 Boardman • CW LXVII 1973 37–38 De Vries

The author meticulously examines representations of combat scenes on Greek geometric vases and provides an iconographical analysis. Most such extant works are on large funerary kraters produced in the workshop of the Dipylon master in Athens around the middle of the 8th century B.C. The importance of this pottery lies in the fact that the scenes represented may be the beginning of Athenian narrative style. The author concludes that the kraters were made to order for specific individuals and most likely represent actual Greek battles. She further shows the similarities between geometric and Near Eastern figure scenes and the possibility that geometric iconography was linked to that of the Near East.

AHLBERG, Gudrun. Prothesis and ekphora in Greek geometric art. Göteborg, Åstöm, 1971. 2 v.   **JD2**

Studies in Mediterranean archaeology; 32 [1] Text, [2] Figures.

AJA LXXVII 1973 90–91 Benson • Arch Class XXIV 1972 425–429 Picozzi • Gnomon LI 1979 36–42 Chabr-Ruckert

This exhaustive study examines figure stance, position, furniture, filling motifs and adjacent figures or scenes associated with prothesis-ekphora representations on all available geometric vases. The author's analysis of the vases, based on a study of the physical problems, is a departure from analysis based on workshops and chronology. In this regard it is similar to the iconographical analysis presented in J. L. Benson, *Horse, bird and man; The origins of Greek painting.*

BENSON, Jack Leonard. Horse, bird and man; The origins of Greek paintings. Amherst, University of Massachusetts Press, 1970. xxx, 182p., xli, illus.   **JD3**

AJA LXXVI 1972 99–100 De Vries • CR XXII 1972 431–432 R. M. Cook • Gnomon XLVI 1974 273–278 Coldstream • JHS XCI 1971 206–207 J. M. Cook

The thesis of this book is that the richly figured vase painting of Athens in the Geometric period had its prototype in the Late Mycenaean pictorial style and in Near Eastern art. Benson begins with Gombrich's claim that art depends on artistic prototypes rather than on observation of nature. Many of the artistic parallels are good, and the study is thorough but it is not always convincing. The book has merit in that it includes lists of archaeological contexts in which Greeks of Geometric times met Mycenaean relics, but in most instances Benson's claims as to the resemblance between the art of the two epochs are too vague to be persuasive.

BÉRARD, Claude. Anodoi; Essai sur l'imagerie des passages chthoniens. [Rome], Institut suisse de Rome, 1974. 181p. 20 plates.   **JD4**

Bibliotheca Helvetica Romana; 13.

AAHG XXXI 1978 69–72 Pötscher • AJA LXXX 1976 95–96 Hoffmann • CR XXVI 1976 292 Cook

This work is a departure from traditional analyses of Greek art. The author employs the theories on myth of the French structuralist Lévi-Strauss to form his conclusions. The author uses the pictorial evidence in dealing with the anodos vases that depict a divinity rising from the ground. He interprets the term anodos as referring to the initiation ritual and its supporting imagery and myth. He objects to the treatment of related myths in H. Metzger's *Recherches sur l'imagerie Athénienne* in which representations are arranged in chronological order, and accompanied by a typology based on formal criteria. The author by contrast uses recent theories of sociology, anthropology, history of religion, etc., to present interesting new ways to interpret Greek art.

BRILLIANT, Richard. Gesture and rank in Roman art; The use of gestures to denote status in Roman sculpture and coinage. New Haven, The Academy, 1963. 238p., illus., ports.   **JD5**

Memoirs of the Connecticut Academy of Arts & Sciences; FS 14.

AC XXXIV 1965 354–357 Balty • AJA LXIX 1965 84–86 Heuser • Byzantion XXXIV 1964 138–144 Delvoye • Erasmus XVII 1965 167–170 Picard

An exhaustive examination of the use of gesture to emphasize status in the art works of Rome from the Etrusco-Italic period through the Late Empire. The author relies on sculptural and numismatic sources for examples. The works are carefully documented and illustrated. Written for the specialist in the study of Roman iconography.

BROMMER, Frank. Denkmälerlisten zur griechischen Heldensage. Unter mitwirkung von Anneliese Peschlow-Bindokat. Marburg, Elwert, 1971– . 4 v.   **JD6**

I. Herakles. II. Theseus, Bellerophon und Achilles.

JHS XCVII 1977 227–228 Prag

Volumes III and IV complete Brommer's *Vasenlisten* and cover sculpture in all forms, painting, mosaics, gems and a range of minor arts from lamps to glass and gold to ivory, along with a section on objects known from literature only. The chronological range is from archaic Greece to imperial Rome.

Volume I (1971) deals with Herakles; v. II (1974) with Theseus, Bellerophon and Achilles.

BROMMER, Frank. Vasenlisten zur griechischen Heldensage. 3., erw. Aufl. Marburg, Elwert, 1973. xii, 646p.   **JD7**

JHS LXXVIII 1958 168–169 Boardman • JHS XCV 1975 295 Sparkes

An enormous work of compilation that lists vases with representations of myths including Herakles, Theseus, Aigeus, Erechtheus, Erichtonios, Kekrops, Kodros, Perseus, Bellerophon, Meleager and Peleus. The third edition expands the second of 1960.

CAYLUS, Anne Claude Philippe de. Recueil d'antiquités égyptiennes, étrusques, grecques et romaines. Paris, Desaint & Saillant, 1752–1767. Front., plates (part fold.), plans, facsims.   **JD8**

Volumes 3–7 have title: Recueil d'antiquités égyptiennes, étrusques, grecques, romaines et gauloises.

The first systematic theoretical work that classifies the works of art according to their subject matter.

FURTWÄNGLER, Adolf. Griechische Vasenmalerei. Roma, Caporilli, 1967. 3 v. in 6.   **JD9**

Reprint of the editions of 1904, 1909 and 1932 published by F. Bruckmann, München.

Sumptuous volumes in which the vase-paintings are reproduced with the best results then possible. The reproductions are by Reichhold and include notes and descriptions. The text by Furtwängler remains valuable as the work of an outstanding scholar in the field of Greek vase-painting.

GARDNER, Percy. The principles of Greek art. New York, The Macmillan Company, 1914. xvii, 352p., illus.   **JD10**

CW VIII 14 Tonks • GGA 1915 224–248 Koepp • JS 1915 281 Radet

An enlarged revision of the author's *A grammar of Greek art* (1905), this book represents the art criticism of an eminent classical scholar. Among the subjects discussed are ancient sources, the purpose of the temple, idealism in Greek art, and an intelligent appreciation of the aim of Greek sculpture. The author severely criticizes the interpretations of Adolf Furtwängler.

HÖLSCHER, Tonio. Griechische Historienbilder des 5. und 4. Jahrhunderts v. Chr. Würzburg, Triltsch, 1973. 317p., illus., 16 plates.   **JD11**

Beiträge zur Archäologie; v 6. Slightly rev. ed. of the author's *Habilitationsschrift,* Würzburg.

AJA LXXIX 1975 380–381 Pemberton

The author assembles historical representations in Greek art, literary references, and works in existence before the end of the 4th century. He finds historical representation nonexistent in the Archaic period and beginning in the 5th century, with the painting of the battle of Marathon, the Tyrannicide group, and the portraits of Themistocles and Pausanias, along with the development of historical writing. In the 4th century the chief theme is battles culminating in monuments depicting Alexander the Great. In his section on Alexander, Hölscher draws on his own analysis in *Ideal und Wirklichkeit in den Bildnissen Alexanders des Grossen* (1971). The introduction provides the three levels of analysis that the scholar must use: (1) the information that the work gives about the event; (2) the interpretation of the event in the representation; (3) the relationship of the work to the style of the time. The book explains not just the art of the period but also the social and political developments that inspired it.

HÖLSCHER, Tonio. Ideal und Wirklichkeit in den Bildnissen Alexanders des Grossen. Heidelberg, C. Winter, 1971. ix, 12p., illus. (2d group of pages, 1–12).   **JD12**

Abhandlungen der Heidelberger Akademie der Wissenschaften. Philosophisch-Historische Klasse, Jahrg. 1971, Abh. 2.

AJA LXXV 1972 340–342 Bieber • DLZ XCIV 1973 630–632 Zinserling • REG LXXXV 1972 195 Goukowsky

The author aims to show not how Alexander really looked, but how he wanted to look and how the artists wanted him to look. In his youth Alexander venerated and identified himself with Heracles. The author claims that art and reality are styled according to the same tendencies and seeks to establish the stylized appearance of the living Alexander together with the style of his portraits.

METZGER, Henri. Les représentations dans la céramique attique du IVe siècle. Paris, E. de Boccard, 1951. 469p., 9p. port., 48 plates.   **JD13**

Bibliothèque des Écoles françaises d'Athènes et de Rome, v. fasc. 172.

JHS LXXIII 1953 186 Webster

This volume discusses about 460 scenes from 4th century Attic vase-painting. There are indices of museum numbers and references to ancient authors. The author examines the themes, Eros, Aphrodite, Dionysos, Apollo, Herakles, Eleusis, Trojan cycle, minor legends and themes of religious and private life. Analyzing the representations, the author uses his wide knowledge of ancient literature as well as his knowledge of ancient art. The whole is beautifully illustrated. See also the author's *Recherches sur l'imagerie athénienne,* 1965.

POLLITT, Jerome Jordan. Art and experience in classical Greece. Cambridge, Cambridge University Press, 1972. xiv, 205p., illus.   **JD14**

ABull LV 1973 138–139 Scranton • AJA LXXVII 1973 349 Carpenter • G&R XX 1973 96 Colledge

This book provides the political and social background against which art developed in "Classical Greece," here defined as the period between 480 B.C. and early Hellenistic times. Two essential principles of Greek art are named: the analysis of forms into their component parts, and the reduction of the physical world to a limited number of geometrical shapes. While scholars may dispute some of the author's conclusions the book is a readable and factual one that provides much information on the social and cultural environment in which the artist of the period lived. The illustrations are good.

SCHEFOLD, Karl. Myth and legend in early Greek art. [Translated by Audrey Hicks.] New York, Abrams, [1966]. 200p., illus., (6 mounted col.) geneal. tables, map, plates. **JD15**

Trans. of the author's *Frühgriechische Sagenbilder.* Ant J XLVII 1967 118 Boardman • G&R XIV 1967 101 Sewter • JHS LXXXVII 1967 184 Webster

There are three main chapters, on the age of Homer, the age of early lyricism, and the High Archaic period. The author has an intimate knowledge of the styles of Greek painting and his interpretations of mythological pictures are skillful and precise. Within each chapter the arrangement is, first legends about the gods, then Bellerophon, Perseus, Herakles, Theseus, the Argonauts, Theban and Trojan legends. The book contains a map of the archaeological sites, with genealogical tables and a short bibliography. The author's survey of mythological illustration in classical antiquity continues in *Gotter- und Heldensagen der Griechen in der spätarchaischen Kunst* (Munich, 1978) and *Die Gottersage in der klassichen und hellenistischen Kunst* (Munich, 1981).

SCHEFOLD, Karl. Wort und Bild; Studien zur Gegenwart der Antike hrsg. von Ernst Berger und Hans Christoph Ackermann. Basel, Archäologischer Verlag; Mainz: in Kommission bei P. von Zabern, [1975]. xv, 231p., 12 leaves of plates, illus. **JD16**

A selection of Schefold's writings published on the occasion of his 70th birthday. Bibliography of K. Schefold's works, 1966–1974 (xiv–xv).

AJA LXXXI 1977 397–398 Davies • CR XXVII 1977 328–329 Cook

This superb series of essays is preceded by an introduction by Ernest Berger, a Tabula Gratulatoria, and a bibliography of the writings of Karl Schefold. This supplements the bibliography in *Gestalt und Geschichte. Festschrift Karl Schefold* Apt K 4. Beiheft (1967), 5–

12. The essays range from the early Bronze Age to the Byzantine period and consist of interpretations and analyses of painting, sculpture, architecture, literature, history and culture of Greece, Rome and neighboring peoples.

TOYNBEE, Jocelyn M. C. Animals in Roman life and art. Ithaca, Cornell University Press, [1973]. 431p., illus. **JD17**

AJPh XCVI 1975 445–447 Young • CW LXIX 1975 146–147 Lockhart • JRS LXV 1975 212–213 Brogan

The author thanks her predecessors in this study, Keller's *Antike Tierwelt* and G. Jennison's *Animals for show and pleasure in ancient Rome* (1937). She singles out particular species (camels, giraffes, frogs and toads), gives the main literary evidence for their roles in the ancient world and illustrates them from the artistic evidence, mosaics, sculptures, frescoes, bronzes, etc. The literary and artistic evidence fills the half-millennium from Ptolemy II's foundation of a zoo in Alexandria to Gordian III's wild animal show, given to celebrate Rome's thousandth birthday. The most important single piece of evidence is the great hunt mosaic from the Piazza Armerina in Sicily. The Appendix is by R. E. Walker on Roman Veterinary Medicine.

WINCKELMANN, Johann Joachim. History of ancient art. New York, F. Ungar Publishing Co., [1969, 1968]. 4 v. in 2, illus. **JD18**

Trans. of *Geschichte der Kunst des Altertums.* The text is that of the 1849–1873 ed.

The author is considered the founder of the scientific history of ancient art, particularly Greek art. His interest in the study of Homer's poetry expanded into an interest in Greek sculpture and led ultimately to a great scholarly interest in this area. Winckelmann urged the restoration of the ideals of Greek art and developed ideal esthetic canons. On a historical level he maintained that there was a progression in the development of ancient art. Iconography is the descriptive and classificatory study of images in order to interpret the artist's direct or indirect meaning. Recently iconography has concerned itself with scientific precision and accuracy in descriptions of art works. Winckelmann's method was to classify works of art according to the subject matter. In 1758 the author became librarian of Cardinal Albani's collection of antiquities. In 1763 he was appointed chief supervisor of all antiquities in and about Rome and in this capacity he visited Pompeii and Herculaneum. Three of his works contributed to scientific method in the investigation of the past. These are *Sendschreiben,* on the discoveries at Herculaneum; his main work *History of the art of antiquity;* and his *Monumenti antichi inediti,* a tool for the new science of antiquity.

ANTI, Carlo. Sculture greche e romane di Cirene. Scritti di L. Polacco [et al.] Padova, Cedam, 1959. 329p., illus. **JE1**

AJA LXIV 1960 393–394 Ridgway • RFIC XXXVIII 1960 329–331 Bandinelli • AC XXXI 1962 557–559 Verhoogen

Enrico Paribeni's *Catalogo delle Sculture di Cirene* discusses all but one of the subjects treated in this book. The statuary presented was discovered on the Italian excavations of 1924–1930. The plates here are superior to those in Paribeni.

BALIL, A. Pintura helenistica y romana. Madrid, Instituto Español de Arqueologia, 1962. 331p., 104 illus., 2 plates. **JE2**

Bibl. Archaeol. III.
Zephyrus XII 1961 249 Avilés • Arbor 1964 N° 58 112–114 Montenegro • Latomus XXIII 1964 604–607 Croisille

BECATTI, Giovanni. The art of ancient Greece and Rome; From the rise of Greece to the fall of Rome. Trans. by J. Ross. Englewood Cliffs, N.J., Prentice-Hall, [1968]. 440p., illus. (part col.). **JE3**

Trans. of *L'età classica.* Bibliography (p.401–423). AJA LXXI 1967 200–201 Ridgway • CW LXII 1968 51 Vermeule • G&R XV 1968 206–207 Sewter

In this beautiful book the author considers the ancient arts as a culture that lasted for a millennium, from the 6th century B.C. to the 4th century A.D.— from the rise of Greece to the fall of Rome. He considers the art of the era to be the expression of a single culture, and in the excellent text and superb illustrations he expands on the theme of Classical Art as a unifying force. The book covers Greece and Greek influences, East and West; Etruscan and Italian; and Rome and Roman influences, East and West. The illustrations contain some unusual items including the fat-bodied amphoras in Berlin and Boston by the black-figured vase-painter Exekias. There is a lovely reproduction of the Laocoon group. For bibliography of Becatti's work, see F. Magi in *RPAA* XLVII (1974–1975), 3–5.

BIANCHI BANDINELLI, Ranuccio. Storicità dell'arte classica. [Terza ed.] [Bari], De Donato, [1973]. 475p., illus. **JE4**

ABull XXXIII 1951 275–276 Carpenter

The author believes that art should be written about only in terms of the culture that produced it. He reacts negatively to the schools of art that classify and categorize works, and dehumanize them. This work is a collection of essays on various aspects of ancient art that

reflect the author's sensitivity and understanding of ancient masterpieces.

CONGRÈS international d'archéologie classique. Le rayonnement des civilisations grecque et romaine sur les cultures périphériques. Paris, E. de Boccard, 1965. 681p., illus. **JE5**

AJA LXX 1963 Vermeule

Two excellent volumes on the subjects of Greeks and Romans "overseas." "One set of congress reports that must be in every classical, art-historical, and archaeological library" Vermeule.

DUCATI, Pericle. L'arte classica; Con 12 tavole in calcocromia e 932 riproduzioni d'arte nel testo. 2. ed. interamente riveduta. Torino, Unione Tipografico-Editrice Torinese, 1927. xxiii, 841p., illus. **JE6**

BFC XXXIV 186 Tacone • CPh XVI 1921 87 van Buren • RBPh 1927 468–471 Philippart • REG 1929 350–352 Picard

This large handbook details the history of classical art from prehistoric Greece to Rome. Copiously illustrated it covers major and minor monuments along with sculpture, pottery, painting and a short treatment of coins and gems. The book is particularly good in its treatment of Italian art and monuments, which is the author's special field.

FURTWÄNGLER, Adolf and URLICHS, H. L. Greek & Roman sculpture. Trans. by Horace Taylor; with 60 plates and 72 illustrations in the text. London, J. M. Dent & Sons Ltd. (New York, E. P. Dutton & Company), 1914. xii, 241p., illus., 59 plates (1 double). **JE7**

CJ 1915 422 Ebersole

An abbreviated edition of a large work in folio form written by this eminent scholar in 1898. The monuments are treated in thematic groups rather than by periods. All the known scientific data are given along with the author's interpretation of their worth and significance.

KJELLBERG, Ernst and SÄFLUND, Gösta. Greek and Roman art; 3000 B.C. to A.D. 500. Trans. by P. Fraser. New York, Crowell, [1968]. 250p., illus., maps. **JE8**

Trans. of *Grekish och romersk konst.*
CR XIX 1969 247–248 Cook • REG LXXXII 1969 161–162 Bruneau • JHS LXXXIX 1969 181

This book was first published in Sweden and revised in 1958 and 1964. The scope is wide-ranging, covering Greek, Etruscan and Roman art in a chronological framework. Political influences are examined in their effect on art, particularly in the influence on Greek art of Egypt and the Near East. Greek art is covered in greater detail than the art of the Romans and Etruscans. The maps, figures, plans, photographs, glossary and bibliography are all useful.

LAWRENCE, Arnold Walter. Greek and Roman sculpture. [1st U.S. ed.] New York, Harper & Row, 1972. 371, 96p., illus. **JE9**

Earlier ed. published in 1929 under title: *Classical sculpture.*
PhW 1930 139–148 Lippold • JRS XIX 1929 95–98 Webster • GGA 1930 257–268 Koepp
A basic textbook for the study of classical sculpture. It is a scholarly and concise treatment of the subject, with bibliographical references. Archaic, Early Classical, Classical, 4th century Hellenistic and the various Roman styles are described in the body of the work. This is preceded by chapters on bases of knowledge, historical significance, materials and other kindred topics. There are many good illustrations.
This is a complete revision of the author's 1929 volume *Classical sculpture.* It is the only one-volume account of sculpture from the Greek to the later Roman period. The book is uneven in its treatment of the phases of classical sculpture and strongly favors classical Greek over Hellenistic and Roman.

RICHTER, Gisela Marie Augusta. The furniture of the Greeks, Etruscans and Romans. London, Phaidon Press, 1966. 369p. **JE10**

CJ LXII 1967 284–285 Lazenby • Antiquity XLI 1967 79–80 Liversidge • AJA LXXI 1967 206–207 Liversidge
A standard work on the subject, the revised edition includes new discoveries such as the throne from Knossos, evidence from the Etruscan tombs, and fragments of couches and tables from the Roman period.

ROBERTSON, Donald Struan. A handbook of Greek and Roman architecture. 2d ed. Cambridge, Cambridge University Press, xxvi, 407p., 24 leaves of plates, illus., plans. **JE11**

Bibliography (p.[347]–378).
DLZ 1930 2234–2237 Koch • JRS XIX 1929 252–253 M.S. • JHS LXIV 1944 113 Bagenal
A review of the architecture of Greece and Rome from the earliest times to the foundation of Constantinople. The author selects monuments from each period and describes them in detail. The buildings are illus-

trated by photographs, plans and measured drawings. An important fundamental work.

SCHUCHHARDT, Walter Herwig. Antike Plastik; Register, Lieferungen 1–10 hrsg. im Auftrage des Deutschen Archäologischen Institutes. Berlin, Gebr. Mann, 1973. **JE12**

AJA LXXVII 1973 99–100 Pemberton • ASNP II 1972 909–910 Arias • Gnomon XLV 1973 399–404 Ridgway
Series consisting of articles by eminent scholars on various sculptures. Sponsored by the German Archaeological Institute under the editorship of Schuchhardt. The series is in the tradition of the great collections by Brunn, Bruckmann and Arndt. Contributions are encouraged in German, English, French and Italian of new and well-known pieces. Text and plates are in one hand-bound folder, yet independent so that they can be compared during reading. The illustrations are superb.

STRONG, Donald Emrys. The classical world. London, Hamlyn, [1967]. 176p., front., illus., (incl. 128 col.) plans, diagrs., col. maps on endpapers. **JE13**

Archaeology XX 1967 145 Haviland • CW LIX 1966 307 Pollitt
A concise review of Aegean, Hellenic, Etruscan and Roman art. Confined mostly to a description of the highest achievements of each era, the most important monuments are described and illustrated. A good general survey.

STRONG, Donald Emrys. Greek and Roman gold and silver plate. London, Methuen, 1966. xxviii, 235p., 40 illus., 68 plates. **JE14**

RSC XIV 1966 428–429 d'Agostino

WARD PERKINS, John Bryan. Cities of ancient Greece and Italy; Planning in classical antiquity. London, Sidgwick & Jackson, [1974]. 128p., illus. **JE15**

CR XXVI 1976 252–253 Wycherley • JRS LXVI 1976 232–233 Rickman • TLS LXXIII 1974 768
The author establishes the unity of architecture and design in the cities of Greece and Italy, begun in the Greek colonization of Sicily and S. Italy, and after that continued by the Greeks, Etruscans, Romans, and perhaps the Phoenicians and the Carthaginians. The early chapters are on Greek planning from the Archaic to the Hellenistic period, followed by chapters on the Roman contributions to the tradition.

JF GREEK ART

Handbooks

ARIAS, Paolo Enrico. L'arte della Grecia. Con 12 tavole in rotocalco e 1073 figure nel testo. [Torino], Unione tipografico-editrice torinese, 1967. 951p., 1073 illus. **JF1**

Storia universale dell'arte; v. 2, t. 1.
AJA LXXIII 1969 85–86 Ridgway • Arch Class XXI 1969 145 • MH XXVI 1969 120–121 Schefold
A history of ancient Greek art and architecture from the geometric period through the Hellenistic period. Comprehensive classified bibliography of books and periodicals in all languages (p.895–930).

L'ARTE dell'antichità classica. Diretta da Ranuccio Bianchi Bandinelli. Torino, UTET, [1976]. 2 v., illus. **JF2**

1. R. Bianchi Bandinelli, E. Paribeni. Grecia. 2. R. Bianchi Bandinelli, M. Torelli. Etruria, Roma.
AC XLVI 1977 693–694 Delvoye • DLZ XCVIII 1977 68–72 Schindler
Volume I covers Greece and is divided into two parts, a critical text by Bianchi Bandinelli and a collection of 519 illustrated schedules, edited by Paribeni for individual works of art or artists. In his critical text the author describes Greek art as the most significant and realistic of the artistic developments in the ancient world. Greek art imitated Greek civilization with its clear logic and its investigation of nature. The book includes chronological tables in which artistic and cultural events are related to historical events. Volume II *Etruria-Roma* is abstracted under Etruscan art.

BEAZLEY, John Davidson, Sir and ASHMOLE, Bernard. Greek sculpture and painting to the end of the Hellenistic period. Cambridge, Cambridge University Press, 1966. xviii, 111p., 248 illus. **JF3**

"First published 1932."
CF XX 1966 175 Woods • CR XVII 1967 116–117 Cook • MH XXIV 1967 121 Berger • RBPh XLV 1967 633–634 Richter
This standard, small handbook of Greek art first appeared as chapters by Beazley and by Ashmole in the *Cambridge ancient history*, v. IV–VI (1926–1930). Beazley wrote the sections on geometric, archaic and classical periods, Ashmole on the Hellenistic. There are no substantial alterations, except for a number of new illustrations. For a book of its size it is amazingly concise and accurate, presenting the essentials of the study of Greek art. Although the book is not amended to include new material discovered since the first print-

ing in 1932, it remains a vivid and exciting account—essential reading for an introduction to the subject.

BOARDMAN, John. Greek art. Rev. ed. New York, Praeger, [1973]. 252p., illus. (part col.). **JF4**

Praeger world of art paperbacks; P-387.
Archaeology XIX 1966 148 Jones • AJA LXX 1966 77–78 Scranton • CJ LXI 1966 328 Donovan • CR XXV 1975 327 Cook (1973 ed.) • Gymnasium LXXXI 1974 145–146 Brommer (first ed. in 1964) • JHS LXXXVI 1966 282–283 Barron
A history of Greek art, approximately through the first millenium B.C., that includes architecture, sculpture, painting, ceramic and other minor arts. This is as good a survey of Greek art as one is likely to find. The many excellent illustrations include rarely pictured objects along with the more familiar ones. The student would need a supplementary work on architecture.

BOARDMAN, John et al. Greek art and architecture. Photos by Max Hirmer. New York, H. N. Abrams, [1967]. 600p., illus. (part col.), map, plans. **JF5**

Trans. of *Die Griechische Kunst*.
CW LXIII 1969 54 Scranton • DLZ XC 1969 54–56 Zinserling
With great thoroughness this book covers each monument and brings together in a very large volume both well-known and new material. The illustrations by Hirmer are numerous, but one reviewer questions the authenticity of the color plates. Of the sections, Architecture is written by Boardman; The Early Classical Period and High Classicism by José Dorig; Coins in All Periods by Max Hirmer; and Hellenistic Art by Werner Fuchs.

BRILLIANT, Richard. Arts of the ancient Greeks. New York, McGraw-Hill, [1973]. xxiii, 406p., illus. (part col.). **JF6**

Archaeology XXIX 1976 138–139 Ridgway • CW LXIX 1976 484–485 Biers
This book covers architecture, sculpture and painting of Greece, from the Mycenaean through archaic, classical and Hellenistic. Important religious sanctuaries and cities are well described. In the photographs, plans, reconstructions and text the author provides a general introduction to the study. "What makes the book practically unsafe in an introductory course is the enormous amount of mistakes both typographical and of content, which have been introduced in the text." Ridgway, *Archaeology* XXIX (1976), 138–139.

CARPENTER, Rhys. Greek art; A study of the formal evolution of style. Philadelphia, University of Pennsylvania Press, 1962. 256p., illus. **JF7**

Photocopy. Ann Arbor, Mich.: University Microfilms International, 1978.

AJA LXIX 1965 181–184 Hanfmann • CR XV 1965 100–102 Cook • CW LVII 1964 155 Matthews • JHS LXXXVII 1967 186 Robertson

A good introduction to Greek art. In the Foreword, the author expands the title to "A Study of the Formative Evolution of Artistic Style in the Three Major Arts of Painting, Sculpture and Architecture from their Inception in Classical Greek Times until the Mid-Hellenistic Period." The book is a philosophical and psychological analysis of the Greek artist. Chapter I Generalities, considers the peculiarly visual approach to life of the Greeks and relates it to the development of mimetic art; c.II The Genesis of Graphic Form and c.III Early Figurines treat the art of the geometric period and its immediate following; c.IV Tectonic Form relates the quality present in many early Greek bronzes, which rescues technically immature productions from being merely amusing essays, childishly naive and artistically vapid (p.70), to the quality of form found in Greek architecture and ceramics; c.V The Genesis of Sculptural Form, c.VI The Early Evolution of Pictorial Style, c.VII Sculpture in Relief and c.VIII Attic Red-Figurine take us through the Archaic phase, to c.IX The Creation of the Classic Formal Style in Sculpture, the core of the book. The final chapters examine the failure of Greek architecture to develop in the classical period in the same way that sculpture and painting did.

CHAMOUX, Francois. Greek art. Trans. from the French by Mary Ilford and Inge Sonn. Greenwich, Conn., New York Graphic Society, [1966]. 97p., illus. (part col.), map, plans. **JF8**

The Pallas library of art; v. 2.
CB XLIV 1967 31 Rexine • CW LX 1967 296–299 Matthews • RBPh XLV 1967 127–128 Richter

This brief but impressive handbook of Greek art covers architecture, sculpture, painting, coinage, intaglios, mosaics, vases, bronze statuary and small terracottas. Professor Chamoux explains the relationship between the Greek community and the ancient artist. The book is valuable both for the scholarly text and the lovely illustrations.

CHARBONNEAUX, Jean. Classical Greek art, 480–330 B.C. [Translated from the French by James Emmons]. New York, Braziller, [1972]. xi, 422p., illus., maps, plans. **JF9**

Translation of *Grèce classique (480–330 avant J.-C.)*.
G&R XX 1973 207 Colledge • JHS XCIV 1974 239–240 Palagia • CR XXV 1975 294–295 Cook

The second in a series of three called *The Arts of Mankind;* the other two being *Archaic Greek Art* and *Hellenistic Art.* The illustrations are superb but the text does not add anything new and will not be very useful to the advanced scholar. The volume is limited

to accounts of architecture, sculpture and vase-painting, each part written respectively by Roland Martin, Jean Charbonneaux and François Villard. The general documentation comprises an appendix on sculpture, ground plans, a chronological table, a comprehensive bibliography, a list of illustrations and a glossary-index. The series is one of the more excellent picture book series available.

COLDSTREAM, John. Geometric Greece. New York, St. Martin's Press, 1977. 405p., illus. **JF10**

JHS XCIC 1979 201–202 Cartledge

Using the available archaeological evidence the author presents the history of the Geometric Age in Greece. Along with pottery the author examines amber, bronze, faience, glass, gold, iron, lead, rock cyrstal, silver, stone, terracotta, and wood artifacts to provide a picture of the public and personal lives of the Greeks during the period.

COOK, Robert Manuel. Greek art; Its development, character and influence. Harmondsworth, Eng., Penguin Books, 1976, 1972. 277p., illus., map, plans. **JF11**

AJA LXXVIII 1974 95–96 Raubitschek • Ant J LIV 1974 322–323 Cook • Archaeology XXVII 1974 284 Mitten • Gymnasium LXXXI 1974 146 Brommer • JHS XCIV 1974 238–239 Waywell

The book is a concise history of Greek art from 1050 B.C. to 27 B.C. and is an excellent introduction to the subject, particularly for the archaeologically oriented student. There is a good introduction followed by chapters on painted pottery, sculpture and architecture, and shorter sections on panel and mural painting, metalwork, gems and coins, and interior decoration. Painted pottery receives the shortest treatment with only 35 pages compared with 87 for sculpture. For its size the book is a superb introduction to the subject.

CURTIUS, Ludwig. Die Klassische Kunst Griechenlands. Potsdam, Athenaion, 1938. 466p., 604 illus. **JF12**

AJA 1939 528–529 Bieber • Gnomon 1939 401–411 Lippold • JHS LVIII 1938 279–280 Haynes

Covers Minoan, Mycenaean, geometric, archaic as well as classical art. The author proposes that an unbroken artistic tradition exists from Minoan Crete to classical Greece. Still valuable.

GARCÍA Y BELLIDO, Antonio. Hispania Graeca. Barcelona, 1948. 3 v. **JF13**

ABull XXXIII 1951 57–58 Carpenter

The first two volumes are text devoted to a reconstruction of Hellenic-Iberian history, and a corpus of extant archaeological material. The third volume is a folder-binder of 168 loose-leaf plates. It is the finest work available on the ancient Greek material that has been discovered in the Iberian peninsula.

HAFNER, German. Art of Crete, Mycenae, and Greece. New York, H. N. Abrams, [1969]. 264p., illus. (part col.), maps.   **JF14**

> Trans. of *Kreta und Hellas.*
> BO XXVI 1969 447 • CW LXIII 1969 123–124 Matthews
> Covers Greek art from the Early Helladic period to the Hellenistic works of the 2d century B.C. Each page contains one or many photographs of sculpture, architecture, ceramicware, metalwork, etc., of the particular period. Each item has a paragraph explaining its details and its place in the history of Greek art. The illustrations are good and the book is a valuable introduction to the subject.

HOLLOWAY, R. Ross. A view of Greek art. New York, Harper & Row, Icon Editions, [1974, 1973]. xxii, 213p., illus., 151 plates.   **JF15**

> A hardcover edition was originally published by Brown University Press in 1973. It is here reprinted by arrangement.
> ABull LVIII 1976 117–120 Havelock • CPh LXXI 1976 181–182 Scranton
> The first part of the book examines the origins of form and narrative in the archaic period and the second deals with the iconography of classical monuments. The analysis of the Parthenon sculpture is excellent and the author utilizes the Greek view of the heroic past as a basis for iconography. A superb interpretation of Greek art.

MATZ, Friedrich. Geschichte der griechischen Kunst. Frankfurt am Main, Klostermann, [1950–]. Illus., plates, plans.   **JF16**

> v.1 (Textband) p.511–538. Bd. 1. Die geometrische und die trüharchaische Form. 2 v.
> DLZ LXXII 1951 455–459 Lippold • MH VIII 1951 330 Schefold
> The author stresses the concepts of "form" and "structure" in ancient Greek art. The reviewer Lippold notes with regret the deficient historical sense implicit in a point of view that is so rigidly systematized. A contrast to him is Gisela Richter who views ancient Greek art against the background of ancient history. This work is a valuable handbook, nonetheless.

PAPAIOANNOU, K. [et al.]. L'art et les grandes civilisations III. Paris, Mazenod, 1972. 636p.   **JF17**

POLLITT, Jerome Jordan. The ancient view of Greek art; Criticism, history, and terminology. New Haven, Yale University Press, 1974. xii, 282p.   **JF18**

> Yale publications in the history of art; 26.
> AJA LXXIX 1975 299–300 Ashmole • CJ LXXII 1976 69–71 Todd • CR XXVI 1976 250–252 Plommer • CW LXIX 1976 404–406 Coulson
> This book examines the thoughts of ancient Greeks on their own art. A long glossary analyzes the semantics of Greek and Roman terms from the 8th century B.C.

to the 4th century A.D., from which the author infers the terminology used in aesthetic theory. Two essays, Art Criticism in Antiquity and Art History in Antiquity, identify four kinds of ancient authors who wrote about art.

POLLITT, Jerome Jordan. The art of Greece, 1400–31 B.C.: sources and documents. Englewood Cliffs, N.J., Prentice-Hall, 1965. xviii, 254p.   **JF19**

> CB XLII 1966 93 Schoder • CW LIX 1966 219 McKay
> A meticulous work that carefully compiles ancient texts relating to the sculpture, painting, architectural and minor arts of Greece. The chapters are arranged by period with documents and inscriptions; notes and introduction and commentary with each chapter.

RICHTER, Gisela M. A handbook of Greek art. [7th ed.] London and New York, Phaidon, [1974]. 431p., illus., maps.   **JF20**

> CJ LV 1960 233–234 Ramage • CR X 1960 177 Cook • JRS L 1960 287 Boardman • REG LXXV 1962 548–549 Chamoux
> This is one of the best written and best illustrated introductions to Greek art. Following the style of the now outdated *Handbook of Greek archaeology* by H. N. Fowler and J. R. Wheeler (1919), the author divides the subject into separate sections on architecture, sculpture, pottery, etc. There are sections on furniture, textiles, glass, ornament, and epigraphy which did not appear in Fowler and Wheeler. Illustrations are usefully placed within the text. The treatment includes geometric to Hellenistic, and excludes Mycenaean. There is a chronological list of Greek sculpture with cross-references, a glossary of terms and good bibliography.
> Also valuable is the author's *The Metropolitan Museum of Art: Handbook of the Greek Collection* (rev. ed., 1953). Along with presenting the Greek Collection in the museum, this is a chronological survey of the subject, with over 800 small reproductions.

ROBERTSON, Martin. A history of Greek art. Cambridge, Cambridge University Press, 1975. 2 v. [xxiii], 835p., [202]p. of plates, illus., maps, plans.   **JF21**

> AJA LXXXI 1977 566–567 Pollitt • HT XXVI 1976 547–548 Greenhalgh • LEC XLIV 1976 284 Wanhenne • TLS LXXV 1976 1011 Levi
> This is the most complete history of Greek Art ever written by a single individual. The work is in two volumes, one for the text and another for footnotes, bibliography, illustrations and index. Architecture is excluded, except as it relates to sculpture and painting, but almost every work of Greek sculpture is included along with vases, bronzes, gems, coins, fragments of monumental painting and the literary sources on ancient art. It is disappointing that some important works that are dealt with in the text do not appear in the illustrations. The period before 700 B.C. receives very

brief treatment. The text and the bibliography make this a highly valuable work for the study of Greek art; however, the poorly selected illustrations prevent it from becoming the definitive work it was intended to be. See also the author's *A shorter history of Greek art.* Cambridge, Cambridge University Press, 1981. 240p.

SCHEFOLD, Karl. Classical Greece. Trans. from the German by J. R. Foster. London, Methuen, 1967. 294p., illus., 49 col. plates, maps, tables.
JF22

Aevum XLVI 1967 71
The author has written extensively on many aspects of classical art, including Pompeian painting, Greek pottery and the artistic mythology of Greece. This book, with its lovely illustrations, is intended as a popular work on the art of the classical period. However, the text may be more valuable to the advanced student or specialist. A full list of Schefold's publications is contained in *Gestalt und Geschichte Festschrift Karl Schefold,* Ant K 4 Beihelft (1967), 5–12. It is supplemented by the Bibliography included in *Wort und Bild. Studien zur Gegenwart der Antike,* by Karl Schefold, Mainz, 1975.

SCHEFOLD, Karl. Die Griechen und ihre Nachbarn. Berlin, Propyläen Verlag, 1967. 372p., illus.
JF23

Propyläen Kunstgeschichte (Berlin, 1966–); Bd. 1.
BVAB XLIII 1968 155–157 Bijvanck • Gnomon XL 1968 809–816 Charbonneaux • JHS LXXXVIII 1968 229–230 Boardman
An excellent book on Greek art. In the first half of the book Schefold surveys the range of Greek art, chronologically. The second half consists of essays by scholars on various subjects (sculptures, painting, etc.). The illustrations, also arranged by subject, are magnificent and include many little-known works.

SCHODER, Raymond V. Masterpieces of Greek art. Text & photography by the author. 3rd ed., rev. Chicago, Ares Publishers, 1975. xiii, [15]p., 96 leaves of plates, col. illus.
JF24

AJA LXV 1961 415–417 Vermeule and Von Bothmer • AJA LXXI 1967 99 Broneer • Archaeologia XIV 1963 207–213 Ramage • GR VIII 1961 194 • CW LIV 1961 156 McKay
A general book on Greek art compiled from Schoder's color photographs for classroom instruction. In the second edition (1967) the plates are much improved and a useful "Research Bibliography" relating to the objects illustrated has been added. Schoder provides the text with the illustrations; here he received severe criticism from Vermeule and Von Bothmer for misstatements and incorrect attributions.

SCHUCHHARDT, Walter Herwig. Geschichte der griechischen Kunst. Stuttgart, Reclam, [1971]. 511p., illus.
JF25

BJ CLXXII 1972 632–633 Von Geymüller • Gnomon XLV 1973 633–634 Ridgway
The chapters follow the major divisions for Greek art. The first chapter deals with the arrival of the Achaians, in the early second millennium B.C., and with the indebtedness of Mycenaean art to Crete. The chapter on geometric art includes a discussion of the architecture of Samos and Tiryns along with Athens. The third chapter covers the Archaic period and the fourth covers the 5th century B.C. The last two chapters describe the art of the 4th century and the Hellenistic period. The book is more text than illustrations, but the latter are excellent and include drawings, plans, models and restored casts, along with pictures of actual objects. The text, by this master of the study of Greek art, is a well-written, nontechnical survey of the subject.
For a bibliography of the author's work see W. H. Schuchhardt, *Alkamenes: Winckelmannsprogramm* CXXVI (Berlin, de Gruyter, 1977, 71p.).

SCHUCHHARDT, Walter Herwig. Greek art. Trans. by Sabine MacCormack. New York, Universe Books, [1972]. 189p., illus.
JF26

Trans. of *Griechische Kunst.*
AJA LXXVIII 1974 95–96 Raubitschek • TLS LXXII N° 3702 1973 184
Covers the period from the geometric style of the Iron Age to c.27 B.C. Painting, sculpture and architecture are examined separately. The excellent illustrations and concise text make this a useful general introduction to the subject.

SCHWEITZER, Bernhard. Greek geometric art. Trans. by Peter and Cornelia Usborne. London, Phaidon, 1971. 352p., illus., map (on lining paper).
JF27

Trans. of *Die geometrische Kunst Griechenlands.*
AJA LXXV 1971 99–100 Betancourt (Germ. orig.) • Antiquity XLV 1971 160 Cook • CR XXIII 1973 249–252 Snodgrass
The introduction traces the historical background and the chronology. The longest section is devoted to pottery, but here the book (completed in 1964) is somewhat out-of-date in the light of recent finds. The Attic school of vase-painting is rightly given the most prominent place, but Boeotian geometric is ignored. Other chapters cover small-scale sculpture, bronze tripods, gold bands, engraved bronze fibulae, and architecture. The plates are good and the book is well edited by Professor U. Hausmann. The translation is also well done.

Origins

AKURGAL, Ekrem. The art of Greece; Its origins in the Mediterranean and Near East. Trans. by Wayne Dynes. New York, Crown Publishers, [1968]. 258p., illus.
JF28

Art of the world, non-European cultures; the historical, sociological, and religious backgrounds.
AJA LXXV 1971 338–339 Benson • CW LXIII 1970 305–306 Goldman

This is the 26th volume in the very fine *Kunst der Welt* series. The book, with its somewhat misleading title, surveys Assyrian, Babylonian, Aramaic, Neo-Hittite, Phoenician and Syrian art from about 1000 to 500 B.C. and their respective influences on Greek art. The author's own speciality, Anatolian cities, receives the largest treatment, proportionately, in the book. Referred to as Late-Hittite, Neo-Hittite or North Syrian, the art of the upper Euphrates had the prime mediatory role in Greek art. Akurgal proposes dates for the earliest operation of Oriental influences on Greek style at the end of the 8th and beginning of the 7th centuries B.C. Evidence for Oriental influence on Greek art is reviewed in a short second part.

DEMARGNE, Pierre. The birth of Greek art. Trans. by Stuart Gilbert and James Emmons. New York, Golden Press, [1964]. 446p., illus. (part col.), maps (part fold. col.), plans, plates (part col.), ports.   **JF29**

Trans. of *Naissance de l'art grec*.
CW LVIII 1965 278 Dawson • JHS LXXXVI 1966 264–265 Coldstream • REA LXVII 1965 466–469 Marcadé
Published simultaneously in French, English and German. The color reproductions are elegant but they are not related to the text. The book covers Minoan, Mycenaean and proto-geometric art, from the Neolithic period until the late 7th century B.C. Most of the book is illustration, with the photographs of figurines especially good. The text is stimulating but unsatisfying because it is too brief to allow for development of the ideas.

FRANKFORT, Henriette Antonia Groenwegen and ASHMOLE, Bernard. Art of the ancient world. Englewood Cliffs, Prentice-Hall (New York, Harry N. Abrams), [1972]. 528p., illus.
JF30

Library of art history; 1.
A synthesis of the art of ancient Egypt, Mesopotamia, Crete, Greece and Rome. Arranged chronologically, it covers architecture, sculpture, pottery, vase-painting and wall-painting. It is useful as an introduction to the subject. There is a select bibliography arranged according to subject. The illustrations in black and white and color are good.

LANGLOTZ, Ernst. Studien zur nordostgriechischen Kunst. Mainz am Rhein, P. V. Zabern, 1975. xii, 206p., [35] leaves of plates, illus.
JF31

AJA LXXXI 1977 396–397 Ridgway • CR XXVIII 1978 186–187 Boardman
This book continues the author's work on the role of emigrant Phocaean artists of the mid-6th century, concentrating on the styles of "north Ionia." The author wrote a pioneer work on chronology in 1920, and on Archaic Greek sculpture in 1927. The book presents a detailed comprehensive report on Northeast Asian art style.
The author's research is thorough and many of his classifications are accepted as sound. With other German scholars, such as Furtwängler, he worked hard

in his attempts to distinguish the various schools, many of whose analyses and methods have been rejected.

SMITH, William Stevenson. Interconnections in the ancient Near-East; A study of the relationships between the arts of Egypt, the Aegean, and Western Asia. New Haven, Yale University Press, 1965. xxxii, 202p., 221 illus. (part fold.), maps (on lining papers).   **JF32**

AJA LXXI 1967 92–94 Mellink • JAOS XC 1970 305–309 Muhly • JARCE VII 1968 131–132 Schulman
This book by an Egyptologist discusses the effects which interchanges between Western Asia, Egypt, and the Aegean had upon the arts. The book covers a longer period than Helene G. Kantor's *The Aegean and the Orient in the Second Millennium* (1947) and a wider geographical area than Vercoutter's *L'Egypte et le Monde Égéen Préhellénique* (1956). It is a well-documented and scholarly study.

Prehistoric and Archaic

ALIN, Per. Das Ende der mykenischen Fundstätten auf dem griechischen Festland. Lund, C. Bloms boktr., 1962. 159p., fold. map.   **JF33**

Studies in Mediterranean archaeology; 1.
AJA LXVIII 1964 311–312 Immerwahr • Erasmus XVII 1965 346–349 Bielefeld • RBPh XLIII 1965 714–716 Béquignon
An important scholarly work on the collapse of Mycenaean civilization and the destruction of the sites. It is a geographical catalogue of all Mycenaean sites, arranged according to regions, with full bibliography. The book is a careful record of our present knowledge of the history of the sites.

BLEGEN, Carl William, ed. Troy; Excavations conducted by the University of Cincinnati, 1932–1938. With the collaboration of John L. Caskey and Marion Rawson. [Princeton, published for the University of Cincinnati by Princeton University Press, 1950–1958]. 4 v. in 8, plates, ports., maps, tables.   **JF34**

Volume contents: v. 1. General introduction. The first and second settlements; v. 2. The third, fourth, and fifth settlements; v. 3. The sixth settlement; v. 4. Settlements VIIa, VIIb, and VIII. All volumes are divided into part 1. Text, part 2. Plates.
CR II 1952 95–97 Stubbings • JHS LXXII 1952 148–151 Wace
This site is vitally important to the study of the Aegean area. Schliemann began his work there in 1870 and with Dörpfeld, who continued the work, published a series of reports. In 1902, Dörpfeld published *Troja und Ilion* which detailed the archaeology of Troy.
Work was continued by the University of Cincinnati's expedition to the Troad under Professor Blegen and published annually in the *American Journal of Archaeology*. These two volumes are the definitive accounts of the First and Second Settlements. Volume 1 is text and v. 2 is illustration, maps and plans. They are an impressive report of the superb excavation, pre-

sented in a thoroughly scientific manner. In *Troy: The Third, Fourth, and Fifth Settlements* (1951), the thoroughness of the work is maintained. *Troy: The Sixth Settlement* (1953) deals with the section that was identified for a long time as "Homer's Troy."

BLEGEN, Carl William and RAWSON, Marion, eds. The palace of Nestor at Pylos in western Messenia. [Princeton], published for the University of Cincinnati by Princeton University Press, 1966– . Illus., fold. plan, plates (part col.). **JF35**

Volume contents: v. 1. The buildings and their contents, by C. W. Blegen and M. Rawson (part 1. Text, part 2. Illustrations in 2 v.); v. 2. The frescoes, by M. L. Lang; v. 3. Acropolis and lower town: tholoi, grave circle, and chamber tombs; discoveries outside the citadel, by C. W. Blegen et al.

AJA LXXIX 1975 91–92 Immerwahr • Arch Class XIX 1967 191–195 Becatti • CJ LXIII 1968 372–374 Rubright

These volumes represent the results of the excavations of the University of Cincinnati, 1939, 1952–1965. The volumes are well produced and illustrated. A major achievement.

BRANIGAN, Keith. The foundations of palatial Crete; A survey of Crete in the Early Bronze Age. London, Routledge & K. Paul, 1970. xvi, 232p., 16 plates, illus., maps, plans. **JF36**

States and cities of ancient Greece.

BO XXIX 1972 230–231 Van Straten • Archaeology XXVII 1974 66–68 Coleman • Gnomon XLIV 1972 589–595 Zoïs

A valuable book on the Early Minoan culture of Crete. Examines the social, political and economic situations which formed the background for Minoan palatial civilization. Especially good analysis of Messara tholoi.

Another useful volume by this author on prehistoric art is *Aegean metalwork of the Early and Middle Bronze Age* (1975).

BRANIGAN, Keith. The tombs of Mesara; A study of funerary architecture and ritual in Southern Crete, 2800–1700 B.C. London, Duckworth, 1970. xv, 189p., 8 plates, illus., maps, plans. **JF37**

Archeologia XXIII 1972 103–104 Press • CR XXII 1972 255–256 Boardman • JHS XCII 1972 238–240 Warren

Stephanos Xanthoudides' *The vaulted tombs of Mesara* was published in 1924; this book revises and expands much of the out-of-date material in the earlier volume. The author aims to examine the major problems concerning the Mesara tholoi—their date, their original appearance, their relationship to a cult of the dead, the ceremonies performed in and around them, their origins and their relationship to the tholos tombs of the Late Bronze Age. The author succeeds in making the book highly readable, with good illustrations, chro-

nological table, tables of analysis of structural details, catalogue of the tombs and a bibliography.

BUCHHOLZ, Hans-Günter and KARAGEORG-HIS, Vassos. Prehistoric Greece and Cyprus; An archaeological handbook. Trans. by Francisca Garvie. [London] and New York, Phaidon Praeger, [1973]. 514p., illus. (part col.). **JF38**

Originally published under title: *Altägäis und Altkypros.*

Gymnasium LXXXI 1974 535–540 Pini • Gnomon XLVI 1974 497–500 Vermeule • AJA LXXX 1976 86–87 Immerwahr

The book is intended as an updating and expansion of Bossert's *Altkreta* published in 1923. It is an excellent presentation in text and illustration of the prehistoric archaeology of Greece and Cyprus. The introduction describes the major periods and the chronology, with bibliography. This is followed by catalogs arranged according to architecture, small finds, pottery, etc., and a bibliography. Recent finds at Pylos, Lerna, Hagia Irini on Keos, and Kato Zakros are included, but discoveries such as the Franckthi Cave and Akrotiri on Thera are not adequately illustrated. An excellent reference book.

CATLING, Hector W. Cypriot bronzework in the Mycenaean world. Oxford, Clarendon Press, 1964. 335p. **JF39**

Oxford monographs on classical archaeology.

REG LXXVIII 1965 349–352 Deshayes • AJA LXIX 1965 377–378 Young • CR XV 1965 216–218 Stubbings • Gnomon XXXVII 1965 396–401 Soquist • JHS LXXXV 1965 233–235 Desborough

Describes and analyzes in detail the Bronze Age objects found in Cyprus and relates them to bronze vessels of Greece and the Aegean. These include tools, weapons, armor, vessels, tripods and stands, etc. The author shows that Aegean influence was not strong in Cyprus before the 12th-century settlements. After this the influx of Mycenaean settlers revolutionized the metal industry and Cyprus for this period gives far better illustrations of "Aegean" bronzework than Greece itself. The book is marvellously illustrated—a work of meticulous scholarship.

CHAPOUTHIER, Fernand et DEMARGNE, Pierre. Fouilles exécutées à Mallia; Quatrième rapport, exploration du palais bordure meridionale et recherches complémentaires (1929–1935 et 1946–1960). Avec la collaboration d'André Dessenne. Paris, Geuthner, 1962. viii, 69p., 44 leaves of plates, illus. **JF40**

École française d'Athènes. Études crétoises; 12.

Fourth report of the French excavations of the Minoan palace at Mallia.

CHARBONNEAUX, Jean. Archaic Greek art, 620–480 B.C. [Translated from the French by James Emmons and Robert Allen. Maps drawn by Jacques Person]. London, Thames and Hudson, 1971. x, 443p., plates, illus., maps, plans. **JF41**

Translation of *Grèce archaique.*
DLZ XCII 1971 943–945 Zinserling • DLZ XCIII 1972 656–658 Zinserling • REA LXXIII 1971 483–484

Published in French and subsequently translated into German, Italian, Spanish and English. This is a sequel to Demargne's *Birth of Greek Art.* The book is arranged chronologically and the three authors examine architecture, sculpture and painting. Art is studied against the historical background in which it developed and the influence of the Near East is considered, along with that of religion, technical advances and the geographical difference. A standard work on the subject.

CORPUS der Minoischen und Mykenischen Siegel. Berlin, G. Mann, 1964– . Bd. 1– issued by the Akademie der Wissenschaften und der Literatur, Mainz. Illus. **JF42**

Editor: 1964– Friedrich Matz.
This series reproduces catalogs of seals from many different sites, in private and public collections. With few exceptions they are well edited and beautifully illustrated. Problems of classification and chronology are carefully analyzed. Early volumes cover the entire material of one major or several minor collections. The publication of the approximately 1400 seals and 900 to 1000 sealings kept in the central archaeological collection of Crete requires a special series which will run to at least six volumes.

DAVARES, Costis. Guide to Cretan antiquities. Park Ridge, N.J., Noyes Press, 1976. xiv, 370p., illus. **JF43**

AJA LXXXII 1978 117 Cadogan • CR XXVIII 1978 184–185 Boardman
The guide is written in encyclopedic form, covering the history and culture of Crete from prehistoric times. The illustrations are excellent and include maps, plans, charts, a museum concordance, and a list of places to visit. Just a one-page bibliography of books.

DESBOROUGH, Vincent Robin d'A. The Greek dark ages. London, Benn, 1972. 388p., illus., maps, plans. **JF44**

AJA LXXVIII 1974 198 Alin • CR XXV 1975 84–87 Coldstream • REA LXXVIII 1975 331–335 Bommelaer
In this archaeological survey, the author examines the Greek dark ages chronologically. As cause for the destructions in Greece around 1200 B.C. the author cites the theory of withdrawing invaders. The author's *The last Mycenaeans and their successors,* Snodgrass's *The Dark Age of Greece,* and the present volume provide a comprehensive report of our knowledge of this period.

DESBOROUGH, Vincent Robin d'A. The last Mycenaeans and their successors; An archaeological survey, c.1200–c.1000 B.C. Oxford, Clarendon Press, 1964. xviii, 288p., 25 plates, map. **JF45**

AJA LXX 1966 294 Weinberg • Mnemosyne XIX 1966 309 van Horn
A scholarly and detailed study, this is one of the fullest treatments of late Mycenaean civilization. The author examines the sites, region by region, presenting the available archaeological evidence. In the historical account the author traces the destruction of the civilization from the first attack in 1200 B.C. approximately to the final destruction around 1150 B.C. The book is superbly illustrated and has a wider range geographically than Alin's *Das ende der Mykenischen Fundstätten auf dem Griechischen Festland* (1962), including sites in the whole East Mediterranean from South Italy to the Levant. The author makes use of recent new discoveries from the excavation of the cemetery at Perati by Sypridon Iakovides which were published by the excavator in three volumes, *Peratee 1969–1970.*

DICKINSON, O. T. P. K. The origins of Mycenaean civilisation. Göteborg, Åström, 1977. 134p., illus., map. **JF46**

AJA LXXXII 1978 409–411 Rutter • Gnomon LI 1979 351–355 Walberg
New discoveries make it impossible for a definitive work on late Helladic I–II to be published at this time but this work supplements Furumark's 1950 survey of the period and includes a summary of Middle Helladic as well. The book provides fundamental archaeological data necessary for scholars of Greek prehistory, including a good bibliography.

DÖRPFELD, Wilhelm. Troja und Ilion. Ergebnisse der Ausgrabungen in den vorhistorischen und historischen Schichten von Ilion 1870–1894. Unter Mitwirkung von Alfred Brückner [u.a.] Neudruck der Ausg. 1902. Osnabrück, Zeller, 1968. 2 v., xviii, 652p., illus. **JF47**

These volumes are the definitive publication of the excavations at Troy. Half the work is written by Dörpfeld and includes detailed architectural descriptions of the strata and the buildings they contain. He also writes about Homeric Troy and the site in its relationship to the Iliad. There are chapters by H. Schmidt on the pottery, A. Götze on smaller objects, H. Winnefeld on works of sculpture of later age, A. Brückner on inscriptions, and H. von Fritze on the coins of Ilion. Indispensable to the study of Troy.

DOUMAS, Christos. The N. P. Goulandris Collection of early Cycladic art. Photos by Ino Ioannidou and Lenio Bartziotis. Athens, [New York, distributed in the U.S. by Praeger, 1969]. 184p., illus. (part col.). **JF48**

AJA LXXV 1971 97–98 Shaw • CJ LXVII 1972 287–288 Vermeule
A well-illustrated catalog of the Goulandris collection of Cycladic art with introductory essays. In the latter the author examines idols in Cycladic graves along with other pottery. The translator, Preziosi, is an expert on Cycladic sculpture.

EVANS, Arthur John, Sir. The Palace of Minos. New York, Biblo and Tannen, 1964. 4 v. in 6. **JF49**

AJA 1929 450–452 Blegen • DLZ 1929 424–429 Schweitzer • REA 1928 133–138 Grenier

The first volume in this four-volume set covering the exploration of the site at Knossos appeared in 1921, the last in 1935. They represent 40 years' work by Sir Arthur Evans at the site. It is a staggering undertaking and the publication is thorough and exhaustive. Each volume follows the plan of its predecessor: chapters that describe various parts of the Palace followed by long dissertations on different classes of objects. The objects are compared with those of other Minoan sites in Crete and all relevant sites in the ancient world. The relations of Crete with other parts of the ancient world including Egypt are discussed in detail. There are copious, very beautiful illustrations. An extraordinary work of excavation and scholarship.

GRAHAM, James Walter. The palaces of Crete. Princeton, Princeton University Press, 1969, 1972 printing. xiv, 269p., illus. **JF50**

Bibliography (p.249–251) includes 1971 addenda.
AJA LXVIII 1964 308–310 Hood • Archeologia XIV 1963 203 Majewski • JHS LXXXIII 1963 212–213 Snodgrass

The book describes the latest phase of the palaces, because the author believes that any attempt to trace the evolution of Minoan architecture would still be premature. Chapters II and III contain short descriptions of the three major palaces and 21 selected minor palaces, respectively. The later chapters are divided by topic and Graham provides many interesting theories on building methods, windows and doors, stairs, decoration, furnishings, and the use to which the various rooms were put. The book is well illustrated, a standard work on the subject.

HIGGINS, Reynold Alleyne. Minoan and Mycenaean art. New York, Oxford University Press, 1967. 216p., illus. (some col.), map, plans. **JF51**

CR XVIII 1968 244–245 Boardman • Antiquity XLII 1968 70–71 Stubbings • CW LXI 1968 248 McKay • AJA LXXII 1968 179 Graham • JHS LXXXVIII 1968 226–227 Betts

This well-illustrated book provides the historical outlines, along with reproductions and discussions, of the art objects. The author agrees with the commonly held opinion that the Cretan influence, detected in material from the Shaft Graves, points to "the rapid adoption of the Cretan way of life." A very readable and useful handbook on prehistoric art.

HOMANN-WEDEKING, Ernst. The art of archaic Greece. Translated by J. R. Foster. New York, Crown Publishers, [1968]. 224p., illus., map. **JF52**

Translation of *Das archaische Greichenland.*
REG LXXXII 1969 165–167 Rolley • BO XXVI 1969 416–417 Zadoks-Josephus Jitta • ABull LII 1970 95 Richter • CR XIX 1969 247 Cook

The book is divided into four chapters: Intellectual Foundations on the Geometric Age (c.1050–700) and others on the Orientalizing Age (c.700–620), the Early period of the Rich Archaic Age (c.620–550) and its Late period (c.550–490). The author chooses examples of each period and analyzes them in detail. The illustrations are superb and the quality of the color photographs is extremely good. An important work for the study of Archaic art.

HOOD, Sinclair. The Minoans; Crete in the Bronze Age. London, Thames and Hudson, 1971. 239p., illus., maps, plans. **JF53**

Ancient peoples and places; 75.
AJA LXXVI 1972 332–333 Graham • Archaeologia XXIII 1972 105–106 Rutkowski • Archaeology XXVI 1973 151–152 Vermeule

A concise, but comprehensive, account of the Minoan civilization, with good illustration. Aspects covered range from the geography and climate to early bronze, pottery, and building and wall-painting. In the epilogue there is a discussion of Knossos and Crete, post-1400. Hood affirms his unpopular belief that Linear B has been incorrectly identified as early ("Mycenean") Greek and that the Greek-speaking people did not reach the Greek mainland until about 1200 B.C..

HOOKER, J. T. Mycenaean Greece. London, Routledge & K. Paul, 1976. xii, 316p., illus. **JF54**

States and cities of ancient Greece.
G&R XXIV 1977 202 Periwal • Studies 1978 129–131 Tierney • TLS LXXVI 1977 468 Warren

Reviews the extensive new finds on the Mycenaean civilization (c.1650–1050 B.C.) and compares the information acquired from recent excavations with earlier theories such as Kretschmer (1896). The chapters are arranged chronologically and the book includes an excellent 53-page bibliography of recent books and periodicals.

HUTCHINSON, Richard Wyatt. Prehistoric Crete. [1st ed.] reprinted (with revisions). Harmondsworth, Penguin, 1968. 373p., 32 plates, illus., maps, plans. **JF55**

Pelican books, A501.
AC XXXII 1963 321–322 Delvoye • Antiquity XXXVII 1963 242–243 Hood • EEATh 1962–1963 453–461 Marinatos • JHS LXXXIV 1964 209–210 Popham

The book is intended to supplement Pendlebury's *Archaeology of Crete.* The first two chapters consist of a geographic and geological account and a reconstruction of the Cretan Stone Age. These are followed by two chapters which give a general portrait of the Cretan peoples, language and scripts, their trade, industries, communications and their art. Chapters 6 and 7 describe the Early and Middle Minoan periods, followed by two chapters on Minoan religion and social and economic life on the island. The last three chapters discuss replacement of Linear A by Linear B and the decline of Minoan Crete. This is a very scholarly work with an excellent bibliography. The plates are some-what inferior. More up-to-date information on Early Minoan Crete is provided in K. Branigan's *The founda-tions of palatial Crete* (1970).

LORIMER, Hilda Lockhart. Homer and the monuments. Macmillan, 1950. 552p.   **JF56**

JHS LXXII 1952 152 Brown
The author traces the history of the Homeric Age in chapters on prehistoric Greece and the foreign rela-tions of Greece in the Late Bronze and Early Iron Ages. This is followed by analyses of the materials of the period described in the Homeric Epics.

McDONALD, William Andrew. The discovery of Homeric Greece. [London], Elek Books, [1968]. xx, 476p., illus., ports.   **JF57**

American edition has title: *Progress into the past: The rediscovery of Mycenaean civilization.*
Archaeology XXII 1969 142–143 Lang
This book is a tribute to the work of three great excavators, Heinrich Schliemann, Arthur Evans and Carl Blegen. The method is bibliographical and histori-cal. Personal anecdotes about the excavators are re-counted, along with the history of their discoveries and reactions to the discoveries. On the Homeric parallels and comparisons in the archaeological finds, the author describes how successive generations have assessed the connections. There are maps, drawings and photo-graphs.

MARINATOS, Spyridon. Crete and Mycenae. Photos by Max Hirmer. Trans. from the Greek by John Boardman. London, Thames & Hudson, 1960. [xiii], 177p., illus. (part mounted col.), 236 plates, map, plans.   **JF58**

Antiquity XXXV 1961 80–81 Hutchinson • Archae-ology XIV 1961 143 Mylonas • CW LIV 1961 155 Trell
A magnificent achievement in the quality and beauty of its illustrations and in the admirable text that accom-panies them. The plates, both color and black-white, are outstanding and include small objects such as vases, terracottas, seals and goldwork, along with architec-tural and topographical views of the sites. The scholarly text consists of two essays, one on Minoan and one on Mycenaean. It is well translated by John Boardman.

MATZ, Friedrich. The art of Crete and early Greece; The prelude to Greek art. Trans. by Ann E. Keep. New York, Greystone Press, 1962. 258p., illus. (part col.), maps, plans.   **JF59**

Trans. of *Kreta und frühes Griechenland.*
CR XIV 1964 93–95 Stubbings • Gymnasium LXX 1963 565–567 Lullies • Gnomon XXXVIII 1966 480–484 Schachermeyr
Publication in several countries, with a translated text, makes possible the production of a large edition of the colored plates at a reasonable price. The results are excellent. The combination of plates and the author-

itative text by Matz makes this an important book in the field. The first chapter, Incunabula, discusses the various neolithic styles of Greece but was written before the British excavation at Nea Nikomedia; it now seems that the dating for the Neolithic Age must be pushed back, according to the latest radiocarbon dates. The second chapter discusses the Early Bronze Age, and includes Troy as well as mainland Greece and Crete. Chapter III is concerned with Minoan art of the Palace period. The palaces are treated as wholes rather than by chronological phases. The fourth chapter deals with the Mycenaean style of the Greek mainland, and the book concludes with a discussion of certain historical problems at the end of the Mycenaean Age.

MATZ, Friedrich. Kreta, Mykene, Troja; Die mi-noische und die homerische Welt. 3. Aufl. Stutt-gart, Gustav Kilpper, [c. 1957]. 281p., illus., fold. map.   **JF60**

Grosse Kulturen der Frühzeit.
ArchClass XI 1959 152 Pallottino • Gnomon XXXI 1959 73–75 Mylonas • JHS LXXVIII 1958 152–153 Hood
This copiously illustrated book contains references for the illustrations and a short bibliography. There is a scholarly text by Matz that examines Aegean pre-history to the time of the Dorian invasion. There are accounts of Troy and of the Cretan palaces and a survey of the Mycenaean Age that includes the excavation at Mycenae and Pylos.

MATZ, Friedrick von and BUCHHOLZ, Hans-Günter. Archaeologia Homerica. Die Denk-mäler und das frühgriechische Epos. Im Aufträge des Deutschen Archäologischen Instituts hrsg. Göttingen, Vandenhoeck u. Ruprecht, 1967– . Illus.   **JF61**

AJA LXXVII 1973 87–88 Shaw • CR XXVI 1976 252–253 Boardman
This excellent series relates Homeric texts to the ar-chaeological information we have on the Bronze Age and the geometric times, including recent new evidence. Wace's *A companion to Homer* is more concerned with the philological aspects whereas this series relies more on the archaeological data. The fascicles are scholarly and well produced, with black and white plates.

MYLONAS, George Emmanuel. Ancient Myce-nae; The capital of Agamemnon. Princeton, Princeton University Press, 1957. 201p., plates, maps, plans.   **JF62**

The Page-Barbour lectures, for 1955.
Archaeology II 1958 66–67 Waterhouse • JHS LXXIX 1959 217–218 E.J.F.
A valuable and scholarly work by one of the excava-tors of Grave Circle (B) in Mycenae. The book exam-ines the prehistoric discoveries from Mycenae and out-lines the history of their exploration. Beautifully illustrated.

MYLONAS, George Emmanuel. Mycenae and the Mycenaean Age. Princeton, Princeton University Press, 1966.   **JF63**

Archaeology XX 1967 314–317 Immerwahr • Ant J XLVIII 1968 108–109 Desborough • LEC XXXV 1967 100–101 van Ooteghem

Under the influence of Minoan culture, the mainlanders, late in the 17th century B.C., began to develop a new culture, the Mycenaean, which about 1600 B.C. reached great heights. The book describes the brilliance of the Mycenaean Age. Chapters include Mycenaean Citadels, Palaces and Houses, Grave Circles of Mycenae, Tholos and Chamber Tombs, Shrines and Divinities, Ceremonial Equipment and the Cult of the Dead. There is a chronology, list of abbreviations and selected bibliography. The book is well illustrated with good photographs of the discoveries.

PALMER, Leonard Robert. A new guide to the Palace of Knossos. New York, Praeger, 1969. 144p., illus., plans.   **JF64**

Presents the archaeology and architecture of the Palace of Knossos, including unpublished plans and pottery.

PELON, Olivier. Tholoi, tumuli et cercles funéraires; Recherches sur les monuments funéraires de plan circulaire dans l'Egée de l'âge du Bronze (IIIe et IIe millénaires av. J.C.) Athènes, École française d'Athènes, 1976. xvi, 537p., 91 leaves of plates, illus., maps (some fold.).   **JF65**

AJA LXXXII 1978 556–558 Hood • JHS XCVIII 1978 198–199 Branigan

A definitive study of the architecture of the funerary monuments of the Aegean Bronze Age. There is a long chapter devoted to the tholos tomb including a full catalog of the tombs. The other chapters on the Mesara tombs, the tumuli and grave circles also include catalogs of individual sites. An essential work of reference, basic to future study of the subject. Well illustrated.

PENDLEBURY, John Devitt S. The archaeology of Crete; An introduction. London, Methuen & Co., Ltd., [1967, 1939]. xxxii, 400p., illus., maps, plans, plates.   **JF66**

CJ XXXVII 1942 369–371 Mylonas • Gnomon XII 1940 1–8 Matz • RBPh 1941 703–706 Delvoye

In the opening chapter the author describes the physical features of the island, and the authorities who travelled the island and wrote their impressions. The text is divided chronologically with a section devoted to each period from Neolithic to Roman. For each of the sites covered, the book includes the architecture, burial customs, frescoes, pottery, metalwork, stone vases, faience, figurines, seals and script. An excellent summary of the discoveries to 1939, with maps and illustrations.

PINI, Ingo. Beiträge zur minoischen Gräberkunde. Weisbaden, Steiner, 1968. x, 110p., 22p. of illus., 3 maps.   **JF67**

At head of title: Deutsches Archäologisches Institut. AJA LXXV 1971 221 Shaw • RBPh XLVII 1969 651–652

Examines Minoan and Early Protogeometric graves and burial customs. A thorough scholarly work, it synthesizes recent discoveries on Messara-type tholoi chamber tombs, later tholoi as well as evidence outside Crete, for example, in Messenia and Kythera.

PLATON, Nikolaos Eleutheriou. Crete. Trans. from the Greek. London, Muller, [1966]. 224p., 125 illus. (incl. 64 col.), table, col. maps on endpapers.   **JF68**

AJA LXXI 1967 315–316 Graham • Archaeology XX 1967 312–313 Mylonas • REA LXIX 1967 124–127 Gallet de Santerre

The author, who has worked for more than 30 years in Crete, was director of the museum of Herakleion and excavator of the new palace at Kato Zakro. This is primarily a picture book with short text on Cretan art and life. The author describes the archaeologist's methods of digging, restoring and exhibition. Although the illustrations contain many very exciting objects, including 16 objects from Kato Zakro, the quality is disappointing.

PLATON, N., GUANELLA, H., ALEXIOU, Stylianos et al. Ancient Crete. Photos by Leonard von Matt. Trans. by D. J. S. Thomson. New York, Praeger, [1968]. 238p., illus. (part col.), map, plans.   **JF69**

Trans. of *Das Antike Kreta.*

CW LXII 1968 107 Buck • G&R XV 1968 206 Sewter

Primarily a picture book, the illustrations are superb, including 30 in color. They cover works of art in gold, alabaster, obsidian, porphyry and rock-crystal. The text introduces the plates and includes eight pages by Platon on the new palace at Kato Zakro.

POURSAT, Jean-Claude. Catalogue des ivoires Mycéniens du Musée national d'Athènes. Athènes, École française d'Athènes, 1977. 189p., 27 leaves of plates, illus.   **JF70**

Bibliothèque des Écoles françaises d'Athènes et de Rome; v. 230 bis.

AJA LXXXII 1978 558–559 Long

In this catalog of the Mycenaean ivories in the National Museum of Athens, the pieces are arranged geographically as in *Corpus der minoischen und mykenischen Siegel* (CMS). A concordance of museum inventory and catalog numbers includes provenience, form and decorative motif. This important and extremely useful catalog is fundamental to the study of Mycenaean ivory, but unfortunately it does not adequately illustrate some of the pieces, although the most important pieces are well represented in photographs and drawings. Accompanying the *Catalogue* is an analysis of Mycenaean ivory, *Essai sur la Formation d'un art Mycénien.*

RENFREW, Colin. The emergence of civilisation; The Cyclades and the Aegean in the third millennium B.C. [London], Methuen, [1972]. xxviii,

595p., 32 plates, illus. (incl. 1 col.), maps, plans.
JF71

Bibliography (p. [551]–575).

Antiquity 1972 328 Wheeler • AJA LXXVII 1973 346–349 Diamant • CR XXV 1975 118–120 Boardman

The book analyzes the emergence of the first European civilization in the Aegean basin. The author claims that outside influences were minimal and the forces and processes are to be found in this geographical area. The first part establishes terms and definitions, the second describes the archaeological evidence, and the third attempts to explain the phenomena. This is the first great synthesis which treats the wealth of archaeological and other material as a unified whole. The methods employed by Renfrew in this analysis and his conclusions are now commonly used by archaeologists and social scientists in their study of early man. The book is a unique study of the culture sequence in the Aegean that breaks with traditional modes of analysis and presents a more satisfying view of the development of ancient man.

RICHTER, Gisela Marie Augusta. The archaic gravestones of Attica. With an appendix with epigraphical notes by Margherita Guarduccci. London, Phaidon Press, 1961. viii, 184p., [49] leaves of plates, illus.   **JF72**

RBPh XL 1962 1349–1353 Amandry • JHS LXXXIII 1963 176–177 Jeffery • AJA LXVI 1962 419–422 Ridgway

This is a re-issue of *Archiac Attic Gravestones* (1944), but because of the changes it is virtually a new book. Richter reconstructs the development of the characteristic Attic grave stele. She attributes its disappearance around 500 B.C. to the cultural effects of war. The introductory notes on the origin and development of archaic Attic stelae, the finding places, the technique, the meaning of sphinxes on gravestones, is followed by the catalogue itself, in four chapters, which illustrates a whole range of early Attic sphinxes. Excursus I deals with the Greek gravestones of the first half of the fifth century B.C. and Excursus II investigates a type of archaic relief in being broad and small and in containing two figures, one seated and one standing. The epigraphical commentary by Miss Guarducci is good and the book is well-illustrated with photographs by Alison Frantz. Archaic Greek art is well studied today thanks in large part to this author and her meticulous studies of the korai and kourai as well as the black-figured vases, Attic and Proto-Attic, Corinthian and Proto-Corinthian.

RICHTER, Gisela Marie Augusta. Archaic Greek art against its historical background; A survey. New York, Oxford University Press, 1949. xxv, 226p., 107 plates, map.   **JF73**

The Mary Flexner lectures, 9.

ABull XXXVI 1954 65–68 Picard • JHS LXXI 1951 265–266 Dunbabin

The author devoted much of her long scholarly career to a study of archaic Greek art and published

profusely on the subject. This book deals predominantly with the sculpture of that period. The period covered is 650 B.C. to 480 B.C. and the objects illustrated consist of sculptures in marble, bronze and clay, along with coins, vases and ivories. There are excellent references and bibliographical notes. Through her examination of archaic Greek art in its cultural and historical setting, the author restores the human dimension to ancient art. She reacts negatively to those scholars who classify all ancient art according to "schools."

SCHACHERMEYR, Fritz. Die äghaische Frühzeit; Forschungsbericht über die Ausgrabungen im letzen Jahrzehnt u. über ihre Ergebnisse f. unser Geschichtsbild. Wien, Verl. d Österr. Akad. d. Wiss., 1976– .   **JF74**

Mykenische Studien; Bd. 3 Bd. 1. Die vormykenischen Perioden des griechischen Festlandes und der Kykladen.

AJA LXXXI 1977 244 Lavezzi • CR XXVIII 1978 100–101 Warren

The many new discoveries that shed light on Aegean history from before 6000 B.C. to 1000 B.C. have produced many recent publications. In this book the author records the work at 144 Aegean sites and many others in adjacent lands. The first of three volumes, it covers Early Neolithic to the end of the Bronze Age; a second volume is promised on the Mycenaeans, and a third on the Dark Ages. A scholarly work that provides facts on the sites and the author's analysis and interpretations. Fundamental to the study of this region and period.

SCHLIEMANN, Heinrich. Illos: the city and country of the Trojans; The results of researches and discoveries on the site of Troy and throughout the Troad in the years 1871, 72, 73, 78, 79. Including an autobiography of the author. New York, B. Blom, [1968]. xvi, 800p., illus., maps, plans.   **JF75**

Reprint of the 1881 ed.

The introduction to this volume is an autobiography of the author. In it he describes in detail the excavation of Troy which he began in 1870 at Hissarlik, the difficulties he encountered in getting permission from the Turkish government, and the trials involved in engineering the digging. In 1874 Dr. Schliemann published the first results of his work in *Trojan antiquities*. In 1879 he was joined by Dr. Virchow who made geological, botanical and meteorological observations. This volume is the collation and summary of the excavations. There are drawings of the Hill of Hissarlik, the buildings excavated and the objects discovered, including idols, pottery, helmets, jewelry and tools.

SCHLIEMANN, Heinrich. Mycenae; A narrative of researches and discoveries at Mycenae and Tiryns. A new ed. New York, B. Blom, [1967, 1880]. 404p.   **JF76**

Dr. Schliemann's two campaigns at Mycenae took place in 1874 and 1876. He believed he had found

King Priam at Troy and he expected to find King Agamemnon at Mycenae. Mycenae was known through the poetry of Homer, and the excavator readily interpreted what he found in accordance with the poetic traditions. This book records the work of the archaeologist in Mycenae and Tiryns and his interpretation of each find. There are black and white drawings of objects recovered, including gold masks, gold crowns, jewelry, idols, pottery, weapons, etc. Schliemann did not make any drawings or sectional diagrams of what he found, so much of the archaeological content was reconstructed later by Stamatakis, Schuchhardt, Stais, Tsountas, Müller K. and Müller V., Karo and Mylonas.

SCHLIEMANN, Heinrich. Tiryns; The prehistoric palace of the kings of Tiryns. New York, Arno Press, 1976. xiv, 385p., 27 plates, illus., map, plans.   **JF77**

Reprint of the 1885 edition. Also reprinted in 1967 by B. Blom, New York.

AJA II 1886 75–77 Sturgis

In 1884 Dr. Schliemann, working with W. Dörpfeld, discovered the ground-plan of the palace at Tiryns, almost intact. The building was analogous with ones in Troy and Mycenae. This volume records the campaign, and in it Dr. Schliemann again asserts his absolute belief that these monuments form the historic foundation for the Homeric poems and the Trojan War. Along with a record of the actual excavation, the book gives details and illustrations of the finds, including pottery, idols and objects of metal, stone, ivory, wood and glass. There are excellent sections on the buildings of Tiryns by Dr. Dörpfeld that include drawings and plans. Some color illustrations, of designs from floor and wall decoration and pottery, are included.

SNODGRASS, Anthony M. The dark age of Greece; An archaeological survey of the eleventh to the eighth centuries B.C. Edinburgh, University Press, [1971]. xxiv, 456p., illus.   **JF78**

AJA LXXVII 1973 238 Alin • REA LXXVII 1975 328–331 Bommelaer

Dr. Snodgrass, an authority on early arms and metals, here provides a survey of the dark age in Greece from 1100 to 800 B.C. After discussing the concept of a dark age, the author continues with Pottery Styles, The Chronology of the Early Iron Age in Greece, The Graves, Iron and Other Metals, External Relations and The Internal Situation. Metal use is thoroughly explored and an explanation given for the shift to iron working, namely local availability in times of isolation. With renewed foreign contacts there is a partial return to bronze and the beginning of the end of the dark age. The illustrations are good and there are general and site indices.

SNODGRASS, Anthony M. Early Greek armour and weapons, from the end of the Bronze Age to 600 B.C. Edinburgh, University Press, [1964]. 280p.   **JF79**

AJA LXX 1966 76–77 Knudsen • CJ LXI 1966 174–175 Combellack • REG LXXIX 1966 512–514 Rolley

The book examines early Greek armor and weapons using recent archaeological finds of helmets, shields, body-armor, swords, spears, and bow and arrow. An up-to-date account, the author offers emendations to Lorimer's *Homer and the monuments* (1950). Good bibliography and illustrations.

STUDIES in Mediterranean archaeology. Gothenburg, Sweden, S. Vhagen [etc.], v. 1– , 1972– .   **JF80**

Covers many and various aspects of Mediterranean archaeology including Mycenaean, Cypriot, Greek and Cretan.

THIMME, Jürgen, ed. Art and culture of the Cyclades; Handbook of an ancient civilisation. Karlsruhe, C. F. Müller, 1977. 617p., illus. (some col.).   **JF81**

An impressive and comprehensive review of the art and archaeology of the early periods in the Cyclades. The book is a major contribution to our knowledge of Cycladic figural art, architecture, burial methods, stone vases, ceramic production, metallurgy, technology and jewelry. The relationship of the Cycladic culture to the cultures of mainland Greece, Crete, Anatolia and the Near East, is demonstrated and illustrated. With superb illustrations and good bibliography this book is basic to the study of the art and culture of the Cyclades.

TSOUNTAS, Chrestos and MANATT, J. Irving. The Mycenaean Age; A study of the monuments and culture of pre-Homeric Greece. With an introd. by Dr. Dörpfeld. Amsterdam, B. R. Grüner, 1969. xxxi, 417p., 12 leaves of plates, illus.   **JF82**

Reprint of the 1897 ed.

The author Tsountas, one of the great archaeologists of native Greek descent, was among the scholars designated by the Greek government to continue the work of Schliemann at Mycenae. This work is a synthesis of the discoveries to 1893, and it systematizes the information that accumulated over 23 years. An expanded edition appeared in English in 1897.

VERMEULE, Emily. Greece in the Bronze Age. Chicago, University of Chicago Press, [1964]. xix, 406p., illus., maps, 48 plates.   **JF83**

Arion IV 1965 700–720 Wiseman • Erasmus XVIII 1966 104–107 Canciani • JHS LXXXVI 1966 265–266 Hood

The book is confined to the Greek mainland and the early Cyclades; Crete and Minoan civilizations are covered in a companion book by M. J. Mellink. Most of the book is devoted to the Mycenaean Bronze Age including the art, architecture, palace life, frescoes, sculpture, etc. The chapter on Society and History in the Mycenaean World includes a discussion of Linear B. The book is an excellent up-to-date account of the history of Bronze Age Greece that also includes art. There are good bibliographies.

WACE, Alan John B. Mycenae, an archaeological history and guide. New York, Biblo and Tannen, 1964, [1949]. 150p.   **JF84**

ABull XXXII 1950 237 Blegen • JHS LXX 1950 99–100 Waterhouse

An excellent introductory guide to Mycenae and its civilization. There are five chapters on the site and the chronological context of Mycenaean culture. Seven chapters are devoted to a tour of the monuments as a traveller would visit them. Appendices deal with the dates of the Treasury of Athens and Cyclopean Walls; a third gives an account of the stones and tools used by Mycenaean stone-workers. Copious maps, plans, drawings and photographs of the monuments are included.

WARREN, Peter M. Minoan stone vases. Cambridge, Cambridge University Press, 1969. xiv, 280p., 120 plates, illus.   **JF85**

Cambridge classical studies.

AC XLIII 1974 585–587 Delvoye • AJA LXXV 1971 221–222 Wiencke • Arch Class XXIV 1972 137–142 Sacconi

This valuable book is a catalog of almost all of the 3,500 Minoan vases known to exist. Full bibliographical data is given for each piece. A list of sites is included that gives, for each site, a list of vase types and the quantity discovered.

ZERVOS, Christian. L'art de la Crète néolithique et minoenne. Paris, Éditions "Cahiers d'art," [1956]. 523p. (illus. p.59–488), 8 col. plates, fold. map.   **JF86**

Archaeology II 1958 132 Weinberg • RA 1958 I 240–242 Picard

Primarily an excellent picture book of photographs of the archaeological treasures of Crete. Items include pottery, utensils, jewelry, weapons, cult objects, written documents and the architecture. The text, which is about one-sixth of the book, discusses the history and nature of Cretan art but it is out-of-date and not as valuable as the beautiful illustrations.

ZERVOS, Christian. L'art des Cyclades; Du début à la fin de l'âge du bronze, 2500–1100 avant notre ère. Paris, Éditions "Cahiers d'art," [1957]. 277p., illus., plates (part col.), maps.   **JF87**

AJA LXIII 1959 398 Vermeule

Similar to the author's *L'art de la Crète néolithique et minoenne,* it consists primarily of beautiful reproductions of the art objects of the Cyclade islands. The text, which is not as valuable as the photographs, gives a short account of the archaeological sites and the objects.

Hellenistic

BARR-SHARRAR, B. and BORZA, E. N., eds. Macedonia and Greece in late classical and early Hellenistic times. Washington, National Gallery of Art, 1982. 268p.   **JF88**

JHS CIII 1983 208–209 Burn

CHARBONNEAUX, Jean and MARTIN, R. Hellenistic art, 330–50 B.C. London, Thames & Hudson, [1973]. ix, 421p., illus.   **JF89**

The Arts of mankind.

G&R XXI 1974 212 Sparkes • CR XXV 1975 295–296 Cook • JHS XCV 1975 277–278 Waywell

The last of three volumes on Greek art in the *Arts of Mankind* series, the other two being *Classical Greek art* and *Archaic Greek art* (620–480 B.C.) by the same authors. Architecture, painting and sculpture are treated separately. As with the other volumes, the text is inferior to the superb illustrations. Probably the best picture book of Hellenistic art available. The bibliography is classified and contains items to 1969, when the first edition appeared in French.

HAVELOCK, Christine Mitchell. Hellenistic art. London, Phaidon, 1971. 238p., illus. (some col.), maps (on lining papers).   **JF90**

CR XXIV 1974 106–107 Cook • Archaeology XXVII 1974 70–72 Thompson • ArchN I 1972 1–2 Grummond • AJA LXXVI 1972 101–102 Richter • Antiquity XLVI 1972 154–156 Toynbee

There are six main sections: Portraits; Architecture; Sculpture in the Round; Sculpture in Relief; Paintings and Mosaics; and Decorative Arts. The author's thesis is that Hellenistic art is an enrichment and enlargement, not a degeneration of earlier styles. The writing is clear and the book is well organized with a general bibliography and two indices along with a selection of examples of various periods, each illustrated and fully described. The chronology of Hellenistic art is not yet firmly established and archaeologists will disagree with many of Havelock's proposed dates. A standard and valuable work on the subject.

MARCADÉ, Jean. Au musée de Délos; Étude sur la sculpture hellénistique en ronde bosse découverte dans l'île. Paris, E. de Boccard, 1969. xii, 557p., illus., 80 plates.   **JF91**

Bibliothèque des Écoles françaises d'Athènes et de Rome; v. fasc. 215.

RBPh L 1972 459–461 Béquignon • AJA LXXV 1971 344–346 Bieber

A detailed work on the Hellenistic sculpture in the museum in Delos and other sculpture scattered on the island, with a good bibliography (p.1–20).

MERKER, Gloria S. The Hellenistic sculpture of Rhodes. Göteborg, P. Aström, 1973. [i], 34p., 34 leaves of plates, illus.   **JF92**

Studies in Mediterranean archaeology; 40.

CR XXV 1975 327 Cook • JHS XV 1975 290 Waywell • ArchN IV 1975 26 Vermeule • AAHG XXVIII 1975 225 Pochmarski • RSA VIV 1975 235–238 Gualandi

This is a comprehensive account of the marble sculpture of Hellenistic Rhodes. Of the more important Rhodian sculptures, the bronze life-size portrait statues, nothing remains but the bases. The subjects of these works are mainly deities, portrait children and animals. The illustrations are mediocre.

ONIANS, J. Art and thought in the Hellenistic age. The Greek world view, 350–50 B.C. London, Thames & Hudson, 1979. 192p.   **JF93**

G&R XXVI 1979 99 Sparkes • JCS XXX 1982 135–137 Odo • BIAL XVII 1980 158–159 Henig
The author draws parallels between philosophical speculation and the visible embodiment of ideas in stone sculpture, painting, and mosaic in architecture and in the minor arts.

WEBSTER, Thomas Bertram L. Hellenistic art. London, Methuen, 1967. 243p., illus., 54 col. plates, maps, plans.   **JF94**

CW LXI 1967 49 Gaertner • G&R XIV 1967 193 Sewter • CR XVII 1967 372–374 Cook
Professor Webster's book is one of the best contributions to the art of the Hellenistic period. Along with splendid plates the book is equipped with maps, a glossary and a chronological table. The author expertly relates Greek poetry and drama to the subject matter of the plastic arts.

Archaeology

AMERICAN School of Classical Studies at Athens. Ancient Corinth; A guide to the excavations. 3rd ed., rev. and enl. [Athens], Hestia, 1936. 121p., illus. (fold. plan.).   **JF95**

"Largely a reprint of the second edition by Dr. Rhys Carpenter."
A useful guide to the architectural remains of ancient Corinth, excavated by the American School of Classical Studies.

AMERICAN School of Classical Studies at Athens. The Athenian Agora; A guide to the excavation and museum. 3rd ed., rev. and enl. Athens, The American School, 1976. 338p., illus.   **JF96**

AC XLVI 1977 351 Delvoye • G&R XXIV 1977 208 Sparkes
The third edition of this indispensable guide to the excavations of the Athenian Agora. There is a summary of material published by the members of the staff of the American School of Classical Studies. The monuments are described with a chronological table and a select bibliography.

AMERICAN School of Classical Studies at Athens. Results of excavations conducted by the American School of Classical Studies at Athens. Athens, The American School, 1929– .   **JF97**

See also *Ancient Corinth: A Guide to the Excavations,* 6th ed. rev. (1960) and *Corinth, A Brief History of the City and a Guide to the Excavations,* rev. ed. (1969).

ANTIKE GEMMEN in deutschen Sammlungen. Berlin, Braunschweig, Göttingen, Hamburg,

Hanover, Kassel, München. München, Prestel Verlag, [1968–]. Illus.   **JF98**

A project of full publication of gem collections in Germany.

ARCHAEOLOGICAL REPORTS Council of the Society of Hellenic Studies. The Management Committee of the British School of Archaeology at Athens.   **JF99**

Issued as a supplement to Journal of Hellenic Studies, it provides annual reports on the finds and publications of Greek sites. Reports prior to 1954 are included in the Journal of Hellenic Studies. The reports also carry regular accounts of recent work in other parts of the Greek world including Asia Minor, Central Italy, Sicily, Cyprus and the Black Sea region. Recent reports on Greece are compiled by H. W. Catling and on Central Italy and Etruria by David Ridgway.

ARCHÄOLOGISCHER ANZEIGER. Deutsches Archäologisches Institut. Berlin, 1889– .
                    JF100

Issued yearly by the German Archaeological Institute it contains reports of excavations and museum acquisitions.

BEAN, George Ewart. Aegean Turkey. New York, F. A. Praeger, 1966. 288p.   **JF101**

BO XXIV 1967 194–196 Halkin • Archaeology XXI 1968 154 Mitten
A useful introduction to the archaeological sites of western Turkey. The book includes coastal sites accessible from Izmir, also from Pergamum in the north to Didyna in the south and inland to Heracleia and Sardis. Description of the sites includes historical summaries and there are helpful outline maps of the sites.

BRACKEN, Catherine Philippa. Antiquities acquired; The spoliation of Greece. Newton Abbot, [Eng.], David & Charles, 1975. 210p., illus.
                    JF102

CR XXVIII 1977 82–83 Plommer • Arch N V 1976 59 Alexander
The book is a fascinating study of the people who made serious antiquarian studies, purchases and removals of the classical remains of Greece between 1800 and 1830, or between the Embassy of Lord Elgin in 1799 and the confirmation of Greek independence in 1829. The author praises the reforms instituted by the new kingdom of Greece in protecting archaeological remains. A valuable history of the contributions of such men as Choiseul–Gouffier, Fauvel and Aberdeen to Greek archaeology. There are interesting details about the negotiations over the remains at such places as Aegina and Bassae. The book discusses the accusations of vandalism mutually levelled by the English and the French.

BULLETIN de CORRESPONDANCE HELLÉ-NIQUE. Rapports sur les travaux de l'École française en Grèce– . Paris, de Boccard.
                    JF103

Annual reports of the excavations of the French School in Greece including such sites as Argos, Thasos, Delos, Mallia and Cos.

BUNDGAARD, J. The excavation of the Athenian Acropolis 1882–1890. The original drawings, ed. from the papers of Georg Kawerau. Copenhagen, Gyldendal, 1974. 131p., illus.
JF104

ÉCOLE FRANÇAISE D'ATHÈNES. Exploration archéologique de Délos. Paris, École française d'Athènes, 1909– .
JF105

In progress. Reports the work of the French School at Athens. See also Gallet de Santerre, Hubert, *Delos primitive et archaique.* Paris, E. de Boccard, 1958, which includes architecture and other archaeological remains along with a discussion of the history and cults of Mycenaean Délos.

ÉCOLE FRANÇAISE D'ATHÈNES. Fouilles de Delphes. Paris, École Française d'Athènes, 1902– .
JF106

In progress. Reports the excavations at Delphi begun by French archaeologists in 1880. See also Poulsen, F., *Delphi,* 1920, and *Études Delphiques* published by the Bulletin de correspondance hellénique, suppl.4, Athens, in memory of P. de La Coste-Messelière, 1977, 468p. *Études Delphiques* contains twenty-six papers by eminent scholars on the inscriptions, objects and remains of Delphi.

GALLET DE SANTERRE, Hubert. Délos primitive et archaïque. Paris, E. de Boccard, 1958. 358p., illus., maps.
JF107

Bibliothèque des Écoles françaises d'Athènes et de Rome; fasc. 192.
AJA LXIV 1960 200 Long
Vallois described the architectural remains of preclassical Délos in *L'Architecture hellénique et hellénistique à Délos jusqu'à l'éviction des Déliens (166 au. J.C.)* (Bibliothèque des Écoles françaises d'Athènes et de Rome; fasc. 157, 1944). This book includes architecture and the other archaeological remains along with a discussion of the history and cults of Mycenaean Délos.

GARDINER, Edward Norman. Olympia; Its history and remains. Washington, D.C., McGrath Pub. Co., 1973. xviii, 316p., illus.
JF108

Reprint of the 1925 ed. published by Clarendon Press, Oxford, England.
AJPh 1927 186–191 Hyde • CR 1927 126 Wace • CW XX 1927 88–89 Fraser
The definitive publication of the great German excavation at Olympia, *Olympia: Die Ergebnisse I–V,* edited by Ernst Curtius and Friedrich Adler, appeared 1887–1897. This volume is a summary and digest of the German publication, with good illustrations. The author traces the origin and history of the festival at Olympia

and of the games from prehistoric times through the Roman era.

HÄGG, Robin. Die Gräber der Argolis in submykenischer, protogeometrischer und geometrischer Zeit. Uppsala, University of Stockholm (Almquist & Wiksell international distr.), 1974– . Illus.
JF109

Presented in part as the author's thesis, Uppsala, 1969.
1. Lage und Form der Gräber.
AJA LXXXI 1977 563–565 Caskey
The first volume of a publication in two parts. A detailed regional study of 550 burials excavated at Argos, Asine, Berbati, Dendra, the Archive Heraion, Lerna, Mycenae, Mauplia and Tiryns. In part II the author will pursue the evidence for burial customs and rites, and differences attributable to the passage of time or to local custom and social outlook.

HANFMANN, George M. A. and WALDBAUM, Jane C. A survey of Sardis and the major monuments outside the city walls. With contributions by David Van Zanten et al. Cambridge, Mass., Harvard University Press, 1975. ix, 206p., [81] leaves of plates, illus.
JF110

Report: Archaeological Exploration of Sardis; 1.
AJA LXXXI 1977 401 De Vries • G&R XXIV 1977 209 Sparkes
This volume is the first of the final publications of the excavations of Sardis. Discoveries are thoroughly reported and meticulously presented with photographs and plans.

HAWKES, Jacquetta Hopkins. Atlas of ancient archaeology. New York, McGraw-Hill, [1974]. 272p., illus.
JF111

CW LXXI 1977 92 Schoder • TLS LXXIV 1975 603 Daniel • Ant J LVI 1976 265–266 Trump
Contains short articles, with bibliography, of the major archaeological maps and drawings of sites in Greece and other parts of the ancient world. The various sections are contributed by different authors.

HESPERIA. Journal of the American School of Classical Studies at Athens. Cambridge, Mass., Harvard University Press, 1932– .
JF112

Founded in 1932. Reports are carried for excavations conducted by the School at such sites as the Agora in Athens, Lerna, Corinth, etc. Beautiful illustrations accompany the reports.

HOPPER, Robert John. The Acropolis. Photos by Werner Forman. London and New York, Spring Books, 1974. 240p., illus. (some col.), map, plans.
JF113

ACR II 1972 150 Benjamin • JHS XCIII 1973 267–268 Sparkes
This lavishly illustrated book is a thorough study

of the Acropolis of Athens. The history, buildings and art are carefully examined and presented in a clear well-documented text. The illustrations consist of lovely black and white and color photographs, drawings and plans. The epilogue traces the history of the Acropolis from 400 B.C. to its deliverance from the Turks in the 19th century.

IAKOVIDES, Spyridon E. Peratee; To nekrotapheion. Athens, 1969–1970. 3 v., illus. (part col.), maps. **JF114**

Bibliothaka tees en Athenais archaiologikees hetaireias—v [1]; Hoi taphoi kai ta eureemata.—[2]; Genikai parateereeseis—[3].

AJA LXXV 1971 335–336 Popham • Gnomon XLV 1973 393–394 Desborough

In his book *The last Mycenaeans and their successors* (1964), Desborough made use of recent new discoveries from the excavation of the cemetery at Perati by Spyridon Iakovides. These three volumes are the complete publication of that excavation. The 219 tombs contain the most valuable material available for the study of the end of the Mycenaean age. The first volume describes the site, the second describes burial customs, pottery and small finds and the last volume consists of photographs of the site and the excavation.

IBRAHIM, Leila. Kenchreai, eastern port of Corinth; Results of investigations by the University of Chicago and Indiana University for the American School of Classical Studies at Athens. Leiden, Brill, 1976– . **JF115**

AJA LXXXI 1977 576–577 Smith

Documents the extraordinary find of a unique hoard of panels of shaped and colored glass recovered at Kenchreai. The panels were intended to cover a *dromos* in a complex, thought to be part of the sanctuary of Isis referred to in Pausanias' *Description of Greece* (2.2.3x). The panels have a radiocarbon date of A.D. 365 for timber from the crates in which they were contained. The book is a complete catalog of the find, with details of the recovery from the sea, and scientific studies of the glass.

KAWERAU, Georg. The excavation of the Athenian Acropolis 1882–1890. Copenhagen, Gyldendal, 1974. 2 v., illus. **JF116**

Publication: University of Copenhagen, Institute of Classical and Near Eastern Archaeology; 1.

KIRSTEN, Ernst. Griechenlandkunde. Ein Führer zu klassischen Stätten. Von Ernst Kirsten und Wilhelm Kraiker. Mit 193 Abbildungen im Text und auf 24 Kunstdrucktafeln sowie 2 mehrfarbigen Faltkarten. 5., Überarbeitete und durch Nachträge erg. Aufl. Heidelberg, C. Winter Universitätsverlag, 1967. 2 v. (xvi, 935p.), 2 maps in pockets. **JF117**

JSGU LI 1964 166 Moosbrugger-Leu • BO XXV 1968 433

An outstanding archaeological guide to Greece, it provides detailed description of all the major excavations. It is both scholarly and an excellent travellers' guide.

KUNZE, Emil and SCHLIEF, Hans, eds. Olympische Forschungen. Berlin, W. de Gruyter & Co., 1944– . Leaves of plates. **JF118**

At head of title: Archäolgisches Institut des Deutschen Reiches.

This series covers the finds from excavations at Olympia. The reports include bronzes and clay objects, statuary, inscriptions, architecture. The material is presented in a scholarly way with lovely illustrations. These are the official publications of the excavations by the German Archaeological Institute. Books on other aspects of Olympia are included in the bibliography, under mythology, athletics, history and numismatics.

Systematic excavation of Olympia began under the direction of Ernst Curtius and was published as *Ergebnisse d. von d. Deutschen Reich veranstalteten Ausgrabung,* 5 vols. of text and 4 vols. of plates, 1890–96. The excavation was resumed in 1936 by the German Archaeological Institute at Athens and the finds are published intermittently.

LEEKLEY, Dorothy. Archaeological excavations in the Greek islands. Park Ridge, N.J., Noyes Press, 1975, xiv, 130p. **JF119**

A helpful bibliography and a summary of excavations in the Greek islands, including Crete. Books and articles listed run to 1975.

LIPPOLD, Georg. Handbuch der Archäologie. In Verbindung mit E. Walter Andrae [et al.] hrsg. von Walter Otto. München, Beck, 1939. Illus., map, plates. **JF120**

Handbuch der Altertumswissenschaft; 6. Abt. Vol. 3, pt. 1 "begründet von Walter Otto, fortgeführt von Reinhard Herbig."

This section from Otto's *Handbuch* covers Greek sculpture. In 1923 the author, Georg Lippold, published *Kopien und Umbildungen griechischer Statuen,* a systematic account of the subject. He also edited *Denkmäler griechischer und romischer Skulpter* and *Photographische Einzelaufnahmen antiker Skulpturen,* which prepared him to complete this meticulous and scientific work. Works are arranged chronologically beginning with the Archaic period and continuing through the Classical period and the Hellenistic period. The book is well illustrated and an essential work of reference on the subject.

McDONALD, William A. and RAPP, George R., Jr., eds. The Minnesota Messenia expedition: Reconstructing a Bronze Age regional environment. Minneapolis, University of Minnesota Press, [1972]. xviii, 338p., illus. **JF121**

AJA LXXVIII 1974 84–86 Watrous

First report of the University of Minnesota expedition to Messenia. The book is a collection by specialists on the history, archaeology, anthropology and geography of the southwestern Peloponnesus.

MacKENDRICK, Paul L. The Greek stones speak; The story of archaeology in Greek lands. New York, New American Library, [1966, 1962]. xix, 430p., illus. **JF122**

Mnemosyne XVIII 1965 89–90 Hendrijk • LX 1965 39–40 Knudsen

A companion volume to the author's popular account of Roman archaeology, *The mute stones speak.* This is a comprehensive one-volume introduction to Greek archaeology in which the author succeeds in giving an up-to-date account of all Greek excavation, the less well known along with the most famous, Athens, Olympia, Delphi and Mycenae. The ancient history, architecture and major finds of each site are described and the author shows how they contributed to our knowledge of Greek civilization from prehistoric to Roman times. An excellent introduction to the subject.

MILOJČIČ-VON ZUMBUSCH, Johanna and MILOJČIČ, Vladimir, eds. Die deutschen Ausgrabungen auf der Otzaki-Magula in Thessalien. Bonn, R. Habelt, 1971– . Illus. (part col.). **JF123**

Beitrage zur ur- und frühgeschichtlichen Archäologie des Mittelmeer-Kulturraumes; Bd. 10.

AJA LXXVII 1973 442–443 Immerwahr

The first of three volumes on the German Thessalian expedition in Otzaki-Magula. This book deals with the Early Neolithic material.

SCHODER, Raymond V. Ancient Greece from the air. With 140 colour photos by the author, 138 ground plans and 1 map. London, Thames and Hudson, [1974]. 256p., illus. (some col.). **JF124**

Vergilius XXII 1976 46–47 Conant • CR XXVII 1977 310–311 Wilson • Arch N V 1976 86–87 Mason

This beautiful book contains air photographs, in color, of 80 of the most important excavated sites of ancient Greece. Each photograph is accompanied by a commentary outlining the history of the site or buildings illustrated, a perspective sketch on which the visible features are numbered for easy reference, and a list of the numbered features. These sketches and plans are not accurately produced and the book is more valuable for the magnificent aerial photographs.

STILLWELL, Richard, ed. The Princeton encyclopedia of classical sites. William L. MacDonald, associate editor, Marian Holland McAllister, assistant editor. Princeton, Princeton University Press, 1976. xxii, 1019p. [12] leaves of plates, maps. **JF125**

This magnificent achievement combines in a single volume archaeological information on every city, town, sanctuary, military outpost, hamlet and way-station of the classical period. There are more than 2,800 individual entries listing the sites alphabetically and about 200 more are added which incorporate related areas. The geographical area covered includes Britain, northern Europe, Spain, North Africa (including Egypt), Italy, Greece, as well as Turkey and the Levant to the borders of India. Experts (375 of them) contributed their special knowledge of sites: these were scholars who had excavated, published or prepared special studies on the sites. For ancient Greek and Roman civilization the period covered is from 750 B.C. to A.D. 565. This volume is unique in its scope, detail and scholarship. An essential reference work.

THOMPSON, Homer A. The Agora of Athens. Princeton, N.J., American School of Classical Studies at Athens, 1972. xxiii, 257p., [56] leaves of plates, illus. **JF126**

The Athenian Agora; 14.

Gnomon XLIX 1977 380–394 Siewert • CR XXV 1975 289–291 Cook • AJA LXXVII 1973 444–446 Broneer

A detailed and comprehensive report that synthesizes the results of the excavations of the Athenian Agora, from the original explorations by Greek and German scholars through 40 years of excavations by the American School of Classical Studies. A concordance of the inventory numbers of objects mentioned, an index of ancient authors and a general index are included. The book is illustrated with excellent drawings and five photographs of the large plaster model of the Agora.

VALLET, Georges and VILLARD, François. Mégara Hyblaea. Paris, E. de Boccard, 1965. Illus. **JF127**

AJA LXX 1966 297–299 Benson

Results of the excellent excavations at Mégara Hyblaea.

Architecture

BERVE, Helmut and GRUBEN, Gottfried. Greek temples, theatres, and shrines. Photos by Max Hirmer. New York, H. N. Abrams, [1963]. 508p., illus. (36 mounted col.), 176 plates, maps, plans. **JF128**

Gnomon XXXIV 1962 507–510 Drerup • Gymnasium LXX 1963 272–276 Bielefeld • AC XXXII 1963 752–754 Delvoye • Antiquity XXXVIII 1964 141–142 Plommer

A beautiful book on the religious significance of various monuments of ancient Greece. H. Berve writes on the general aspects of architecture and its relationship to cult and religion. Dr. Gruben relates the architecture to the history of the monuments of Magna Grecia, Greece, and Ionia and Pergamum. Well-documented and lovely illustrations.

An obituary notice for Helmut Berve appears in *Gnomon* LI (1979), 413, by Franz Hampe.

BIEBER, Margarete. The history of the Greek and Roman theater. [2d ed., rev. and enl.].

Princeton, Princeton University Press, 1961. xiv, 343p., illus., plans.   **JF129**

CW XXXIII 1939–1940 148 Schlesinger • AJA 1939 708–710 Allen • CR 1939 176–178 Pickard-Cambridge • BCH 1939 124 Martin

A thorough study of the architecture of theatre-buildings, it replaces the author's earlier *Denkmäler zum Theaterwesen im Altertum* (1920). The author aims "to reconstruct the history of the development of the ancient theater" by "uniting the literary, architectural and figurative sources." Abundantly illustrated and carefully documented, the book emphasizes the archaeology of theater, including vase-paintings, sculptures, terracottas and architectural remains, with less attention given to the literary aspects. An important reference work.

COULTON, J. J. Ancient Greek architects at work; Problems of structure and design. Ithaca, Cornell University Press, 1977. 196p., [4] leaves of plates, illus.   **JF130**

AJA LXXXII 1978 413 Scranton • JHS XCIX 1979 209–211 Plommer • Gnomon LI 1979 466–469 Büsing

An introduction to the problems encountered by Greek architects. The architect is examined in relation to problems he encounters: the problems of scale, of design, of form, and of space.

DINSMOOR, William Bell. The architecture of ancient Greece. New York, Biblo and Tannen, 1973. xxiv, 424p., illus.   **JF131**

Reprint of the 1950 3rd ed. rev., published by B. T. Batsford, London.

REG 1929 49 Vallois • JHS LXXII 1952 152–154 Plommer • G&R XXIV 1977 92 Sparkes

This is a revision of one of the best-known handbooks of Greek architecture, J. Anderson and R. Phené Spiers, *Architecture of Greece and Rome*. It is a history of Greek architecture, including the Bronze Age, how cities, cults and temples developed, the evolution of Ionic and Doric temples of the classical period, fourth century temples and the Hellenistic and Graeco-Roman periods. There is a very comprehensive bibliography to 1944. A standard work by a foremost scholar.

LAWRENCE, Arnold Walter. Greek architecture. [2d ed.]. Harmondsworth, Middlesex, Penguin Books, [1973]. xxxiv, 342p., illus., 152 plates, maps.   **JF132**

The Pelican history of art.

JHS LXXIX 1959 199–200 Wycherly

A comprehensive survey of Greek architecture, it is beautifully illustrated with plans and diagrams in the text and excellent plates. There is a long section on pre-classical architecture. The main part of the book covers the development of the orders, decorative detail, the form and proportions of the temple and planning. The book contains good bibliography given chapter by chapter.

LYTTELTON, Margaret. Baroque architecture in classical antiquity. London, Thames & Hudson, [1974]. 336p., illus.   **JF133**

Originally presented as the author's thesis, Oxford.

ArchN IV 1975 26–28 Richardson • AJA LXXX 1976 322–324 Ward-Perkins

The author analyzes the style of architecture from classical antiquity that resembles baroque architecture, as defined in Wölfflin's *Renaissance und Barock* (1888). Many examples of such architecture exist in the ancient world. The author claims that its roots can be traced far back in classical times, but that it reached its full flowering in the later Hellenistic period, especially in Alexandria. Even after the unification of the Mediterranean world under Rome, it remained essentially a product of the eastern provinces. The book is a thorough study of baroque architecture in classical antiquity, including Hellenistic Alexandria and using the Palazzo delle Colonne at Ptolemais as a primary example. The book is well illustrated and a standard work on the subject.

MARQUAND, Allan. Greek architecture. New York, The Macmillan Company, 1909. x, 425p., illus., plans.   **JF134**

Remains an excellent analysis of Greek architecture, although it is out-of-date.

MARTIN, Roland. Manuel d'architecture greque. Paris, Éditions A. et J. Picard, 1965– . Illus.   **JF135**

Collection des manuels d'archéologie et d'histoire de l'art.

AJA LXXI 1967 94–96 Williams • Archaeology XX 1967 150 Scranton

This book describes the materials, tools, methods and techniques of construction in ancient Greece, from the first workings of the raw material to the final completion of the buildings. It includes all that is known at the present time about methods in architecture in ancient Greece. The first of a three-volume work (v. II. *Styles et formes;* v. III. *Plans et compositions*).

MARTIN, Roland. L'urbanisme dans la Grèce antique. 2. éd. augm. Paris, A. & J. Picard, 1974. 349p., [16] leaves of plates, illus.   **JF136**

RFIC CIV 1976 224–227 Castagnoli • MH XXXIII 1976 187–188 Schefold • Erasmus XXVIII 1976 358–361 Heidenreich • BJ CLXXVI 1976 455–460 Lauter

This is a revision of the 1956 edition, in which the author described administration and architecture in Greek town planning. In the section on administration the author examines the relations of public and private planners. From Periclean Athens onward, official city architects existed. The book describes the architecture of many Greek towns, including many Eastern towns. A well-produced, stimulating and useful book.

ORLANDOS, Anastasios K. Ta hylika domees teon archaieon Helleeneon b kata tous syngrapheis, tas epigraphas kai ta mneemeia. Athenai, [Archeiologikee hetaireia], 1955–1958. 2 v., illus.   **JF137**

On the techniques of construction in ancient Greece. Comparable to Roland Martin's *Manuel D'Architecture*

Greque (1965) as a comprehensive and exhaustive treatment of the materials, technical processes, masonry and construction of ancient Greek architecture.

PENROSE, Francis. An investigation of the principles of Athenian architecture; or, The results of a survey conducted chiefly with reference to the optical refinements exhibited in the construction of the ancient buildings at Athens. New and enl. ed. Washington, D.C., McGrath Pub. Co., 1973. xii, 128, [97]p., illus.   **JF138**

> Reprint of the 1888 ed. published by Macmillan, London.
> Useful for the material on proportions and refinements.

PLOMMER, Hugh. Ancient and classical architecture. [Rev. ed.] [London], Longmans, [1956]. xxii, 384p., illus., plates, plans.   **JF139**

> EHR LXXIII 1958 510 Gough • CR VIII 1958 273–275 Sisson • JHS LXXVIII 1958 171–172 Corbett
> The book is a revision of the ancient and classical chapters from Simpson's *History of Architectural Development* (1905). It is divided into pre-Greek, Greek and post-Greek architecture. The first part contains chapters on Egyptian, Sumerian, Assyrian, Hittite and Greek bronze-age architecture. The second part covers Greek architecture from the 7th to the 4th centuries, and the third part deals with the Hellenistic and Roman periods. The illustration is mediocre.

ROBERTSON, Donald S. A handbook of Greek and Roman architecture. Cambridge, Cambridge University Press, 1943. xxvi, 407p.   **JF140**

> DLZ 1930 2234–2237 Koch • JRS XIX 1929 252–253 M. S. • JHS LXIV 1944 113 Bagenal
> A review of the architecture of Greece and Rome from the earliest times to the foundation of Constantinople. The book is arranged chronologically; the author selects monuments from each period and describes them in detail.

TOMLINSON, Richard Allan. Greek Sanctuaries. New York, St. Martin's Press, 1976. 150p., [14] leaves of plates (2 fold.), illus.   **JF141**

> AC XLVI 1977 348 Delvoye • JRH X 1977 424–426 Green • JHS XCVIII 1978 189–190 Pollard
> A short very useful description of the major shrines of Greece, including the most recent archaeological discoveries. The author discusses the debt of classical religion to that of the Bronze Age, and the historical and economic background of sanctuaries in the classical age. The architecture of the major sanctuaries is described including Olympia, Delos and Delphi. There are black and white photographs, maps, plans, figures and sketches.

WYCHERLEY, Richard Ernest. The stones of Athens. Princeton, Princeton University Press, 1978. xviii, 293p., illus.   **JF142**

G&R XXVI 1979 96–99 Sparkes
With excellent text and illustration the author presents the monuments of ancient Athens. Literary and archaeological evidence is taken into account and presented in highly readable form.

Sculpture

ASHMOLE, Bernard. Architect and sculptor in classical Greece. New York, New York University Press, 1972. 218p., illus., plans.   **JF143**

> CR XXIV 1974 309 Cook • G&R XX 1973 208 Colledge • JHS XCIII 1973 264 Cook
> Problems faced by Greek builders and sculptors are examined using as examples the Temple of Zeus at Olympia and the Parthenon and the Mausoleum at Halicarnassus. The author examines the reasons for their erection, how they were paid for, in what order the sculptural work was executed and how it was disposed. In discussing the sculptors he examines the coordination between sculptor and architect and the organization of the work, and he makes deductions from the size of the blocks about the procedure of that carving. Of interest to the scholar and the general reader the book is well illustrated and lucidly written.

ASHMOLE, Bernard and YALOURIS, Nicholas. Olympia. The sculptures of the temple of Zeus. With new photographs by Alison Frantz. [London], Phaidon, 1967. 188p., illus.   **JF144**

> RBPh XLVI 1968 522–525 Bousquet • CW LXI 1968 249 Hanfmann • CJ LXIII 1968 371 Caskey
> In both text and illustrations this is an excellent introduction to the sculptures of the temple of Zeus at Olympia. The text by Ashmole and Yalouris presents history analysis and interpretation of the sculptures. The superb illustrations make the book more valuable than Rodenwaldt's *Olympia.*

BERGER, Ernst. Die Geburt der Athena im Ostgiebel des Parthenon. Basel, Archäologischer Verlag ([Mainz], in Komm. bei Philipp von Zabern), 1974. 90p., illus.   **JF145**

> ABull LIX 1977 124–125 Ridgway • AJA LXXXI 1977 118–120 Harrison
> The first in a series of monographs to present the results of studies on the Parthenon pediments made at the Skulpturhalle in Basel. The author attempts to reconstruct the composition of the east pediment. He first reviews the current state of our knowledge and then provides a systematic analysis of possible restorations. The book presents what he believes to be the central composition.

BIEBER, Margarete. The sculpture of the Hellenistic Age. New York, Columbia University Press, [1961]. xi, 259p., 812 illus.   **JF145a**

> Columbia bicentennial editions and studies.
> AJA LXI 1957 298–303 Harrison • Archaeology X 1957 146–147 Vermeule • Phoenix XI 1957 129–

132 Winter • Antiquity XXX 1956 238–239 Boardman

The author restricts the Hellenistic period to the time between Alexander's death and the principate of Augustus, i.e., ca.330 to 30 B.C., with the 4th century serving as introduction and transition. This is a monumental work describing the development of Hellenistic sculpture through the traditional arrangement of geographical "schools"—Alexandrian, Pergamene, and Rhodian—and rococo trends in the 3rd and 2nd centuries B.C., and into the classicism of the century before Augustus. Included as appendices are a chronology, an extensive bibliography, a good index, and a list of plates with their sources. This large well-illustrated book conveys an accurate impression of the rich variety of Hellenistic sculpture.

BLÜMEL, Carl. Griechische Skulpturen; Des sechsten und fünften Jahrhunderts v. Chr. Berlin, Verlag für Kunstwissenschaft, 1940– . Illus.
JF146

Staatliche Museen zu Berlin. Katalog der Sammlung antiker Skulpturen; Bd. 2, 1.
An analysis of Archaic Greek art in Berlin's Staatliche Museen.

BOARDMAN, John. Greek sculpture; The archaic period: A handbook. New York, Oxford University Press, 1978. 252p., illus. **JF147**

CW LXXIII 1979 46 Biers • G&R XXVI 1979 96–97 Sparkes
Describes the history of style, by period and region, of all the major work of Archaic sculpture. A valuable handbook that incorporates the recent new finds and presents the subject in a concise and clear manner. The illustrations are beautifully produced and numerous. Notes, bibliographies, and a list of artists are included.

BROMMER, Frank. Die Giebel des Parthenon; Eine Einführung. Mainz, P. von Zabern, 1975. 52p., illus. **JF148**

AJA LXIV 1960 200–201 Ridgway
Brings together photographs of all important pieces attributed to the Parthenon. There is a reproduction of the Carney drawings of 1674, views of the Parthenon as a whole, and a short history of the Acropolis from prehistoric times to the present.

BROMMER, Frank. Die Metopen des Parthenon. Mainz, von Zabern, [1967]. 2 v. **JF149**

AJA LXXII 1968 394–397 Bieber • Gymnasium LXXV 1968 408–410 Bielefeld • DLZ LXXXIX 1968 536–538 von Lücken • CW LXIV 1970 60–61 Harrison • JHS XCVI 1976 245–246 Robertson
The same format is followed as in Brommer's book on the pediments, *Die Skulpturen der Parthenon—Giebel* (Mainz, 1963): one volume of text and one of plates. The metopes and fragments are catalogued and described and there is a section in which the metopes as a whole are discussed. The plates are superb. Some of Brommer's personal interpretations of the metopes provide a basis for further scholarly discussion.

BROMMER, Frank. Der Parthenonfries. Katalog. Mainz am Rhein, von Zabern, 1977, 2 v. **JF150**

AJA LXXXIII 1979 489–491 Harrison
Completes the series on the Parthenon by the author, of which the first two are on the pediments (1963) and the metopes (1967). A meticulously prepared catalog of the sculptures and fragments with photographs and drawings. The history of the frieze is examined along with questions of attribution and interpretation.

BROWN, Blanche R. Anticlassicism in Greek Sculpture of the Fourth Century B.C. New York, published for the Archaeological Institute of America and The College Art Association of America by New York University Press, 1973. xv, 104p., 103 plates. **JF151**

ABull LVII 1975 273–274 Hanfmann • CR XXV 1975 328 Cook • AJA LXXIX 1975 102–103 Havelock
The author sets out to evaluate 4th century Greek art in relation to the High Classical and Hellenistic styles. The author regards the Classical style as "the specific historic manifestation which began in the fifth century B.C." and proceeds to examine the views of scholars on the chronology of Greek history and art history, to discover when a decisive change in context and form occurs. The author's opinions do not receive unanimous approval among art historians, but the book is well produced and illustrated and necessary reading for a student interested in this extensively examined subject.

BUSCHOR, Ernst. Altsamische Standbilder. Berlin, Gebr. Mann, 1934– . Illus., plates.
JF152

Bilderhefte antiker kunst, hrsg. vom Archäologischen institut des Deutschen reiches. hft. I–III.
JHS 1935 244
One of the best examinations of Archaic art.

CARPENTER, Rhys. Greek sculpture; A critical review. Chicago, University of Chicago Press, [1960]. xiv, 275p., illus., 47 plates. **JF153**

JHS LXXXII 1962 201–202 Cook • CR XII 1962 287–290 Cook • AJA LXVI 1962 237–244 Bieber • AAHG XV 1962 204 Kenner
The book seeks to understand and explain the evolution of sculptural style in ancient Greece. The book is arranged chronologically and begins with the latter part of the 7th century B.C. Carpenter believes the Greek sculptors learned their craft in Egypt, with its tradition of carving life-size statues from rectangular block. He places emphasis on the technical procedures in sculpture, and his analysis is excellent. The technique of the artist is stressed, in contrast to the genius of the individual artist striving for expression of his own inner vision. A very scholarly work.

FURTWÄNGLER, Adolf. Masterpieces of Greek sculpture. [1st American] new and enl. ed. Chicago, Argonaut Publishers, 1964. 439p.
JF154

Gnomon XXXVIII 1966 267–270 Schuchhardt
This is a reprint of the original work in which the author established a basis for the scientific examination of the plastic arts. A biographical sketch of the author and the titles of his important works is contained in *University of Nevada studies,* J. E. Church, Jr., 1,2 (1908), 61–66.

The author produced books on Greek sculpture, vases and gems with extraordinary accuracy and detail. For obituary notice and bibliography see *Classical Review* XXI (1907), 251–253, by P. Gardner.

The successors to this volume are Charles Picard, *Manuel d'archéologie grecque: La sculpture* (1963), and Georg Lippold, *Die Griechische Plastik. Handbuch der Archäologie* III (*Handbuch der Altertumswissenschaft*).

GARDNER, Ernest Arthur. A handbook of Greek sculpture. [2d ed.] London, Macmillan, 1929. xxxii, 605p., illus.   **JF155**

REG 1916 462 François • CR 1916 31 Rouse • JHS 1915 278 • CW X 181 Bates
Originally appeared in two parts in 1896–1897. The book attributes early influences on Greek art to Egypt and Assyria. Individual sculptors and sculptures are discussed.

HANFMANN, George M. Classical sculpture. London, Joseph, [1967]. 352p., 357 illus., 8 col. plates, map.   **JF156**

A History of Western sculpture; [v. 1].
AJA LXXII 1968 82–83 Bieber • CJ LXIII 1968 182–184 Vermeule • Archaeology XXI 1968 232 Raubitschek
The section on "the forerunners" ranges from Neolithic Anatolia through Mycenaean Greece. The usual divisions of Greek sculpture follow. The Etruscans are covered under "radiation to periphery"; so are Iberians, Greeks at Persepolis and Scythians. Hellenistic sculpture also is discussed. The last three sections deal with Roman imperial and provincial art, late Antique art, and sculpture with Christian themes. The photographs are beautiful and cover nearly every important example of Greek, Etruscan and Roman sculpture. The text, although short, is competent and scholarly, providing an accurate survey of the history of classical sculpture.

HARRISON, Evelyn B. Archaic and archaistic sculpture. Princeton, N. J., American School of Classical Studies at Athens, 1965. xix, 192p., [34] leaves of plates, illus.   **JF157**

The Athenian Agora; 11.
AJA LXX 1966 382–386 Bieber • Phoenix XX 1966 340–343 Ridgway
The author also published v. I of the *Athenian Agora, Results of excavations: Portrait Sculpture* (1953). This is the first installment of a series to publish all the sculptures from the Agora. It includes 43 archaic and 135 archaistic pieces. A good study of the material.

HARRISON, Evelyn B. Portrait Sculpture. Princeton, N.J., American School of Classical Studies at Athens, 1953. xiv, 114p., 49 plates.   **JF158**

The Athenian Agora; v. 1.
AJA LXIII 1954 253–255 Vermeule • Gnomon XXVI 1954 364–374 Weber
This volume on portrait sculpture is the first of a long series giving the results of the American excavations of the Athenian Agora. The volumes are well produced and illustrated and contain such chapters as Inscriptions, Public and Private Memorials, Bronze Age Athens, Waterworks, Portrait Sculpture and the History of Shape and Uses of the Ancient City.

HOLLOWAY, R. Ross. Influences and styles in the late archaic and early classical Greek sculpture of Sicily and Magna Graecia. Louvain, Institut supérieur d'archéologie et d'histoire de l'art, 1975. xii, 134p., illus.   **JF159**

Publications d'histoire de l'art et d'archéologie de l'Université catholique de Louvain; 6.
AC XLVI 1977 354 Delvoye • AJA LXXXI 1977 123–124 Ridgway
A comprehensive review with excellent illustration of Magna Grecian sculpture. Captions give height, provenience and location of the objects.

JACOB-FELSH, Margit. Die Entwicklung griechischer Statuenbasen und die Aufstellung der Statuen. Waldsassen/Bayern, Stiftland-Verlag, 1969. ix, 232p., fold. plate.   **JF160**

AJA LXXVI 1972 335–336 Ridgway
Unlike their Egyptian and Mesopotamian counterparts, the Greek sculptors provided their statues with separate bases. The idea was to secure the object firmly. Later on, the bases developed in a variety of ways, depending on the technical ability, location, purpose and the skill of the craftsman. The author produces an excellent chronological account (ca.650–80 B.C.) of the history of statue bases, including tripod bases and architectural choragic monuments. There is a catalog of extant sculpture with securely attributed bases, a folding chart of the base forms, an appendix of statuary, to which bases have been attributed on insufficient ground, a catalog, by types, of bases for which there is no sculpture available and a topographical index of all the bases described in the book.

KÄHLER, Heinz. Der grosse Fries von Pergamon; Untersuchungen zur Kunstgeschichte und Geschichte Pergamons. Berlin, Gebr. Mann, 1948. 202p., illus., 71 plates (incl. plans).   **JF161**

At head of title: Deutsches Archäologisches Institut.
Gnomon 1950 278–289 Kleiner • JHS LXIX 1949 88–89 Lawrence • DLZ 1950 451–455 Horn
An important book for the study of Hellenistic sculpture as a whole. The author examines the structural details of the altar itself and its surroundings, analyzes

the various monuments in relation to one another and details their epigraphy.

Another short book by the author, *Pergamon*, discusses the friezes of the altar.

LAWRENCE, Arnold Walter. Greek and Roman sculpture. New York, Harper & Row, 1972. 371p. **JF162**

PhW 1930 139–148 Lippold • JRS XIC 1929 95–98 Webster • GGA 1930 257–268 Koepp

A basic textbook for the study of classical sculpture. It is a scholarly and concise treatment of the subject with bibliographical references. Archaic, Early Classical, Classical, Fourth Century Hellenistic and the various Roman styles are described in the body of the work.

LEIPEN, Neda. Athena Parthenos; A reconstruction. [Toronto], Royal Ontario Museum, [1971]. xiii, 95p., illus. **JF163**

AJA LXXVII 1973 240–242 Schuchhardt trans. by Dorothy Hill • JHS XCII 1972 247–248 Prag

An excellent monograph on the Athena Parthenos examines the technical aspects of constructing this chryselephantine statue as well as archaeological and aesthetic questions. The work was written in collaboration with Sylvia Hahn who constructed a model of the Parthenos on a 1.10 scale for the Royal Ontario Museum. The first half of the monograph is devoted to the literary and monumental sources and the history of the statue. The second half is devoted to a meticulous description and examination of the statue parts.

LULLIES, Reinhard. Greek sculpture. Photos by Max Hirmer. Trans. from the German by Michael Bullock. [Rev. ed.] New York, H. N. Abrams, [1957]. 88p., 264 plates (part col.). **JF164**

LF IX 1961 189 Hejzlar • CR VIII 1958 299 Cook • JHS LXXIX 1959 200–201 Herrington

An English translation of the original, it contains 264 large photographs of original Greek sculpture. The Roman copies are excluded but apart from this it is an excellent selection and the illustrations are beautiful. There is a short survey of the subject and notes on the plates, with full description of each object.

PFUHL, Ernst and MOEBIUS, Hans. Die ostgrichischen Grabreliefs. I. Aufl. Mainz am Rhein, Von Zabern, 1977– . 2 v., illus. **JF165**

At head of title: Deutsches Archäologisches Institut. AJA LXXXII 1978 414–415 Ridgway

This work in two volumes—one of text, one of illustrations—is the culmination of Ernst Pfuhl's monumental work begun in 1904 on East Greek stelai. Another set is due to appear containing catalogue, appendices, indices and a concordance of the present numbers with Pfuhl's original ones. The corpus includes works from the east coast of the Aegean, the nearby islands and

Thrace. The first part deals with pre-Classical and Classical monuments, the second with the period from the late 4th century B.C. to the Roman imperial period. An impressive work in scope and detail, it is useful for the scholar to have this material so conveniently gathered together.

PICARD, Charles. Manuel d'archéologie grecque; La sculpture. Paris, Éditions Auguste Picard, 1935–1966. 5 v. in 8, illus. **JF166**

t.1. La période archaïque.

JS 1940 97–110 Merlin • AJA 1936 559 Richter • CR 1936 187–188 Lawrence

The author had previously published a survey of sculpture in Egypt, the Near East, Greece and Rome, in 2 volumes. This is the first volume in an exhaustive study of the history of Greek sculpture. In the scholarly text and 237 illustrations, the author examines every known detail of archaic Greek sculpture, the sources of our knowledge, the museums, the origins and role of sculpture, the techniques and materials used. The design of the type and the quality of the illustrations are inferior, but the volume is nevertheless an important reference work by a scholar who has written copiously in this field.

PICARD, Charles. Manuel d'archéologie grecque; La sculpture. Paris, Éditions Auguste Picard, 1935–1966. 5 v. in 8, illus. **JF167**

t.2. pt. 1–2. Période classique. IVe siécle.

RHR CLXIX 1966 71–74 Turcan

This volume in two parts covers the sculpture of the 5th century B.C. Every detail is examined including dating and attribution and recent archaeological research. The whole is carefully documented in text and footnotes.

PICARD, Charles. Manuel d'archéologie grecque. Paris, Éditions Auguste Picard, 1935–1966. **JF168**

t.3, pt. 1–2. Période classique. IVe siécle. t.4 p.1–2 Période classique. IVe siécle. t.5 Index géneral des tomes III et IV.

Erasmus XVII 1965 48–49 Schefold • AJA LXIX 1965 282–283 Richter • REA LXVII 1965 508–516 Marcadé

These volumes comprise the sculpture of the 4th century; a general index for this century is published separately as v.5. The entire corpus for the 4th century sculpture is 2,400 pages, making this the largest work published on the subject and of prime importance as a reference tool for the study of Greek sculpture.

RICHTER, Gisela Marie Augusta. Korai: Archaic Greek maidens; A study of the development of the Kore type in Greek sculpture, with 800 illustrations including 400 from photographs by Alison Frantz. London, Phaidon, 1968. xi, 327p., illus., plates. **JF169**

AJA LXXIII 1969 383–384 Pedley • G&R XV 1969 114 Sewter • Archaeology XXII 1969 172 Fuchs • Arch Class XX 1968 380–385 Guzzo

The author, with her great knowledge of ancient authors and modern archaeological discoveries, has done much to popularize and promote the study of Greek art. This is a companion to her *Kouroi*, 1960. These Archaic Greek maidens along with the kourai, or male youths, were the main dedications in sanctuaries of early Greek times, especially of the Archaic period from 700 to 500 B.C. The kouroi are always nude but the korai are always dressed in chiton or peplos and himiation. A great number of existing korai statues were discovered in the excavation of the Athenian Acropolis in 1885, in the debris from the Persian destruction of 480 B.C. There is enormous variety in the garments of the korai, from their polychrome decorations to the hair styles, jewelry, pins, buttons, and footwear. The scholarship in this book is meticulous, with exact descriptions of each plate (measurements, provenance, chronology, bibliography). The plates, most of them by Alison Frantz, show each object from many sides.

RICHTER, Gisela Marie Augusta. Kouroi, archaic Greek youths; A study of the development of the Kouros type in Greek sculpture. London, Phaidon Press, 1960. xiv, 342p., 591 illus., plates. **JF170**

AJA LXV 1961 320–321 Hoffmann • CW LIV 1961 292 Erim • REA LXIII 1961 499–500 Marcadé • RBPh XL 1962 1349–1353 Amandry

In this second edition (1st ed., 1942), the number of monuments included has grown by more than a third and the number of illustrations has more than doubled. The book is essentially an application of the method of anatomical analysis to the chronology of archaic Greek sculpture. Richter believes that Kouroi evolved with uniformity throughout the Greek world and recognizes only the broad distinction between East and West. (This view is questioned by R. M. Cook, *JHS* LXV, 1945). There are valuable discussions of the literary evidence and of the technique. There is a summary of the anatomical analysis. The islands and the Greek East are favored over Crete as the birthplace of Greek monumental sculpture.

RICHTER, Gisela Marie Augusta. The sculpture and sculptors of the Greeks. 4th ed., newly rev. New Haven, Yale University Press, 1970. xvi, 317, [345]p., illus., maps. **JF171**

At head of title: The Metropolitan Museum of Art. AJA 1929 585–586 Fraser • RA XXX 1929 166 Reinach • JHS LXXII 1952 162 Dunbabin

The best general introduction to Greek sculpture. The author is not so much concerned with attributions to known artists as she is with presenting the sculpture as an artistic manifestation. There is a chronological study of the various types of the human figure, details of the development of drapery, of composition, and of the treatment of relief, along with a chapter on animals and one on forgeries. In the second part of the text, Greek Sculptors, the author presents the sculptors in chronological order, describing their work and quoting literary sources that refer to them. Approximately

half the volume is devoted to beautiful photographs of the sculptures.

In her book *Three critical periods in Greek sculpture* (1951), the author discusses three important epochs in the history of classical sculpture: the years 480–445 B.C., the last decades of the 4th century B.C., and the 1st century B.C. Also the *Catalogue of Greek sculptures in the Metropolitan Museum of Art* (1954) examines the development of Greek sculptural style as illustrated by the exciting pieces in the Museum.

RIDGWAY, Brunild Sismondo. The archaic style in Greek sculpture. Princeton, Princeton University Press, 1977. **JF172**

JHS XCLIX 1979 211 Cook • ABull LXII 1980 484–486 Stewart

Examines the function and distribution of monumental stone and other sculptures of the archaic period in Greek art, 650–480 B.C. The author uses the statistics of the finds to question the accepted characteristics of local schools.

RIDGWAY, Brunild Sismondo. The Severe style in Greek sculpture. Princeton, Princeton University Press, 1970. xviii, 155p., [67]p. plates. **JF173**

ABull LVI 1974 272–274 Frel • Archaeology XXVII 1974 70 Schanz • Gnomon XLVIII 1976 285–290 Fuchs • AJA LXXVI 1972 95–96 Pedley

In this examination of the Severe style of Greek sculpture, the author considers two earlier works on the subject: V. Poulsen's *Der strenge Stil* (1937); and G. Lippold's *Griechische Plastik*, v. 6.3.1 in W. Otto's *Handbuch der Archäologie*. The author analyzes attested Severe originals along with architectural sculpture, sculpture in the round, relief, Roman copies, and the Severe artists whose work was copied. There is an examination of the traits of the Severe style that lasted into the late Hellenistic and Roman periods. The author presumes a knowledge of the subject on the part of the reader and questions many existing opinions on the origins and development of the Severe style.

SCHUCHHARDT, Walter H. Antike Plastik. Berlin, Gebr. Mann., 1973. **JF174**

AJA LXXVII 1973 99–100 Pemberton • ASNP II 1972 909–910 Arias • Gnomon XLV 1973 399–404 Ridgway

Series consisting of articles by eminent scholars on various sculptures. Sponsored by the German Archaeological Institute under the editorship of Schuchhardt, the series is in the tradition of the great collections by Brunn, Bruckmann and Arndt.

Pottery

ARIAS, Paolo Enrico. A history of Greek vase painting. Photographs by Max Hirmer. Translated and rev. by B. Shefton. London, Thames and Hudson, [1962]. 410p., illus. **JF175**

CW LVI 1963 287 Gaertner • Antiquity XXXVII 1963 320–321 Cook • RBPh XLIII 1965 717 Chevallier

A magnificent collection of photographs of Greek vases by Max Hirmer. Reproduced in both black and white and color, they include Attic vases, non-Attic vases of Greece, as well as those of the Aegean Islands, and the Greek colonies in Italy and Sicily. These large beautiful reproductions are accompanied by very complete commentaries on single vases, and an introduction by Arias which describes the development of Greek vase painting and the present state of our knowledge. An indispensable work on this subject for student and scholar.

BEAZLEY, John Davidson. Attic black-figure vase-painters. Oxford, Clarendon Press, 1956. xvi, 851p.   **JF176**

JHS LXXVII 1957 349–350 Robertson • Arch Clas IX 1957 130 Arias • Antiquity XXXI 1957 179 Boardman

One of the major works of this foremost authority on Attic vase-painting. The volume is, in format, title and arrangement, a companion to the author's *ARV.* Essentially a catalogue, it has an "Instruction for Use" at the beginning that explains the arrangement and use of terms. While potter signatures are numerous, only five black-figure painters of importance are known by their true names; Sophilos, Kleitas, Nearchos, Lydos and Exekias. An essential work of reference and guide to the study of black-figure vases, the book is a magnificent achievement of scholarship. An earlier volume by this author, *The Development of Attic Black-Figure* (1951), is a general account that traces the development of Attic black-figure. *A List of the Published Writing of J. D. Beazley* was published in 1951 by Oxford Clarendon Press.

BEAZLEY, John Davidson. Attic red-figure vase-painters. Oxford, The Clarendon Press, 1942. xii, 1186p.   **JF177**

An enlarged English edition of the author's *Attische vasenmaler des rotfigurigen stils,* published in Tübingen, 1925.

AJA XLIX 1945 183–187 Smith (1st. ed.) • CPh LX 1965 186–192 Amyx • AJA LXIX 1965 74–76 Richter • LF LXXXVIII 1965 345–346 Frel

The first edition was published in 1942 and was, until the appearance of the 2nd edition, the principal authority on Attic red-figured pottery. The new edition is three volumes, rather than one, and the Indexes are given a volume to themselves. The author has produced a wealth of material on ancient vase painting in his numerous books, catalogues, monographs, articles, reviews and correspondence. This work is the culmination of fifty years of scholarship. In attributing vase painting to individual masters, Beazley instructs us in the *style* of the painting, not only the all-over impression. The individual forms of the figures are studied, the forms of the hands, anklebones, clavicles, noses, eyes, ears, etc. The names of the artists appear in the table of contents starting with Andocides Painter and Psiax and proceeding through the whole of early red-figure, late archaic, early classic, classic, late fifth century, fourth century and ending with the late fourth-century cups and stemless cups.

BEAZLEY, John Davidson. Attic red-figured vases in American museums. Cambridge, Mass., Harvard University Press, 1918. x, 236p., illus.   **JF178**

CR XXXIII 1919 154 W.T.

A good basic account of Attic red-figure up to the end of the fifth century.

BEAZLEY, John Davidson. Paralipomena: additions to Attic black-figure vase-painters and to Attic red-figure vase-painters. 2nd ed. Oxford, Clarendon Press, 1971. xix, 679p.   **JF179**

ACR 11 1972 175–176 Lazenby • AJA LXXVI 1972 235–236 Richter • Arch Class XXIV 1972 439–443 Guidice

This book brings Beazley's *Attic black-figure vase-painters* (1956) and the second edition of *Attic red-figure vase-painters* (1963) up to date. It is produced with the same meticulous scholarship as its predecessors. Most of the text is additions and new attributions. Artists are arranged chronologically for the most part. The text is divided into two parts: Book I on Black-figure; Book II on Red-figure.

BOARDMAN, John. Athenian black-figure vases. New York, Oxford University Press, 1974. 252p., illus.   **JF180**

ABull LVII 1975 120–122 von Bothmer • AJPh XCVI 1975 235–236 Young • AJA LXXIX 1975 99–100 Boulter • JHS XCVI 1976 249–250 Johnston • CR XXVI 1976 253 Cook

Designed as a comprehensive handbook for students, this book is a summary of the great work of Beazley on Attic black-figure vases. The first seven chapters of the book are devoted to a chronological account by painters and groups, ending with Panathenaiis. There are several additional chapters on shapes, chronology, subject matter and myth. The book contains, in condensed form and at a low cost, a lot of information on every aspect of Attic black-figure. The illustrations are uneven in quality and some are too small. "Notes and Bibliographies" is up-to-date and detailed. The author claims "we miss a lot in our understanding of antiquity by letting lists and shapes and alleged affinities dominate study" (p.13) and certainly in this book attribution is not the main concern but rather the larger context in which Attic black-figure vases developed.

BOARDMAN, John. Athenian red-figure vases; the archaic period: A handbook. London, Thames and Hudson, 1975. 252p., illus.   **JF181**

JHS XCVII 1977 224–225 Prag • CR XXVII 1977 236–237 Sparkes • AJA LXXXI 1977 121 Boulter

Boardman is primarily concerned with the men who potted and the painters who painted the vases. The first three chapters are on the artists: "The First Generation," "The Late Archaic Painters" and "Mannerists and Others." Then there are four shorter chapters: "Shapes and Dates," "General Decoration," "Scenes of Reality," and "Scenes of Myth." The book is directed to students and connoisseurs of Greek art and myth, but it is also valuable to the scholar. As in *Athenian black-figure vases*, the author acknowledges a debt to Beazley and endorses the subjective Beazleyan approach to ancient pottery studies. The bibliography is good.

CALLIPOLITIS-FEYTMANS, Denise. Les plats attiques à figures noires. Paris, Boccard, 1974. 2 v., illus., plates.   **JF182**

École française d'Athènes. Travaux et mémoires; v. fasc.

AJA LXXX 1976 313–314 Moore • JHS XCVI 1976 250–251 Johnston

This study of Attic black-figured plates completes the author's work which began with an article on the same subject in *L'Antiquité Classique*. This work covers the period from 600 B.C., when this rare shape appeared, to early 5th century when it disappeared. Part I presents a chronological discussion of the shape and of the potters and painters who decorated them. Part II is the catalogue, in which the subject and ornament of each plate are briefly described, with its provenance and bibliographical references included. The book is valuable as a reference tool on the subject of black-figured plates because it establishes criteria by which the plates can be assigned to their respective workshops and painters.

COLDSTREAM, John Nicolas. Greek geometric pottery: A survey of ten local styles and their chronology. London, Methuen, 1968. xxxix, 465p., 64 plates, illus., 2 maps.   **JF183**

Antiquity XLIII 1969 163–164 Cook • CW LXIII 1969 21 Buck

The authoritative work on Greek geometric pottery by the greatest living expert. The book's purpose is to relate to the historical and cultural development. Ten local styles are examined and Coldstream equates ceramic styles with the styles of individual city states.

COOK, Robert Manuel. Greek painted pottery. 2nd ed. [London], Methuen, [1972]. xxiv, 390p., illus.   **JF184**

Distributed in the USA by Harper & Row.

JHS LXXXV 1965 257–260 Shefton • CR XXV 1975 127–128 Snodgrass • CW LXVII 1974 404–405 King • AC XLI 1972 755 Delvoye

The second edition of this major contribution to the study of Greek pottery has been updated to include new discoveries and new books published since the 1960s. The author includes the earliest known Greek potter's signature, found at Pithekoussai on Ischia from about 700 B.C., and he adds more than one hundred books to the bibliography. His approach to his subject is archaeological and includes sections on the history of pottery from Protogeometric to Hellenistic, shapes, inscriptions, chronology and the uses of pottery. An excellent manual on the subject, it includes information on every aspect of Greek painted pottery.

COURBIN, Paul. La céramique géométrique de l'Argolide. Paris, E. de Boccard, 1966. 595p., maps, album of plates.   **JF185**

Bibliothèque des Écoles françaises d'Athènes et de Rome; v. fasc. 208.

AJA LXXXI 1977 563–565 Caskey • JHS LXXXVIII 1968 235–237 Coldstream

This study was made possible by the French excavations at Argos and the graves excavated by the author himself in the western quarter, near the Theatre. It is the most comprehensive survey of Argive Geometric pottery. The quality of the plates is extremely good, and the marker contains a complete concordance from catalogue numbers to plates. The new Argos material is supplemented by important vases from Asine, the Heraion, Mycenae, Nauplia, Tiryns, and other places. The first part deals with chronology, the second an analysis of Argive Geometric shapes, motifs, etc., and in the third part the "personality" of Argive Geometric is considered. There is a brief historical sketch in the summary. This is an indispensable research tool for all students and scholars of Geometric art.

EDWARDS, G. Roger. Corinthian Hellenistic pottery. Princeton, N.J., American School of Classical Studies at Athens, 1975. xviii, 254p., illus.   **JF186**

Corinth; results of excavations conducted by the American School of Classical Studies at Athens, v. 7, pt. 3.

AJA LXXXI 1977 246–247 Rudolph • CR XXVII 1977 306 Cook

Because of the excellent quality of the excavation, publications from this site are always worthwhile. This volume describes 1,000 specimens of Corinthian Hellenistic pottery, some illustrated by drawings or photographs.

FOLSOM, Robert Slade. Attic red-figured pottery. Park Ridge, N.J., Noyes Press, 1976. 219p., illus.   **JF187**

Phoenix XXXI 1977 273–274 Rotroff

The book contains helpful lists of the potters, the painters and the kulos and kale names. In most respects it is not as good as Boardman's book, and the illustrations are mediocre in quality. See also the author's *Attic black-figured pottery*, 1975, 171p.

FURUMARK, Arne. Mycenaean pottery: Vol. I, Analysis and Classification; II, Chronology. Stockholm, 1972. 2 v., illus.   **JF188**

Volume I published in 1941 under the title: *The Mycenaean pottery; analysis and classification;* vol. II published in 1941 under the title: *Chronology of Mycenaean pottery.*

Klio XVIII 1943 127–129 Schachermeyr • JHS LXIII 1943 122–123 Stubbings • Gnomon 1943 225–242 Matz

A basic analysis of Mycenaean pottery. Volume I is a general conspectus of Later Helladic pottery. Volume II is a history of the development and distribution of Mycenaean pottery. There is a serially numbered catalogue of types, giving reference to examples of each. There is an index of sites and publications of finds along with a bibliography.

KARAGEORGHIS, V. and GAGNIERS, J. des. La céramique chypriote de style figuré: âge du fer (1050–500 B.C.). I and II. Roma, Ed. dell'-Ateneo, 1974, 1976. 528p. illus.; 168p., illus. **JF189**

AJA LXXXI 1977 394–396 Benson • CR XXVII 1977 240–241 Boardman • CRAI 1976 123 Demarge
These two magnificent volumes present the figure-decorated pottery of the Cypriot Iron Age. Vases are classified by subject matter. They are beautifully illustrated with photographs and drawings.

KRAIKER, Wilhelm. Aigina, die Vasen des 10. bis 7. Jahrhunderts v. Chr. Berlin, G. Mann, 1951. 93p., illus., 47 plates. **JF190**

At head of title: Deutsches Archäologisches Institut. Gnomon XXV 1953 243–248 Dunbabin • JHS LXXIII 1953 185 Robertson
A catalogue of all the pottery of Corinthian origin and direct copies, Protogeometric and Geometric, from all centers and Athens, to the end of the 7th century. The largest and most important part of the Greek pottery is in the Aigina museum. A valuable collection of Protocorinthian.

KURTZ, Donna C. Athenian white lekythoi: patterns and painters. Oxford, Oxford University Press, 1975. xxi, 254p., [36] leaves of plates, illus. **JF191**

Oxford monographs on classical archaeology.
CR XXVII 2 1977 238–239 Sparkes • TLS LXXV 1976 350 Cook
In *Greek Burial Customs* (1971) the author wrote about the uses of white lekythoi, funerary and other. In this volume she deals with the decorative features of the vases and the story of the painters and workshops. In her preface she disclaims competence in the field of attribution, nevertheless the book is a scholarly presentation, discussing in detail the patterns, shapes, and the figures on white lekythoi.

LEZZI-HAFTER, Adrienne. Der Schuwalow-Maler: eine Kannenwerkstatt der Parthenonzeit. Mainz/Rhein, P. von Zabern, 1976. 2 v., illus. [1] Text. [2] Tafeln. **JF192**

Volume II of the Kerameus series—a detailed survey and analysis of the Shuvalov Painter.

MOMMSEN, Heide. Der Affecter. Mainz/Rhein, P. von Zabern, 1975. 2 v., illus. **JF193**

Originally presented as the author's thesis, Heidelberg, 1969, under the title: *Der affektierte Maler.* [1] Text. [2] Tafeln.
ABull LIX 1977 122–124 Moore • AJA LXXX 1976 433–438 Bothmer

The first monograph to appear in the Kerameus series, each volume of which will present the entire work of one Attic black-figure or Attic red-figure vase painter. Volume I contains text, a catalogue of vases by the Affecter, a concordance of catalogue numbers with those of Beazley's list in *ABV*, a chronological chart, a museum index and abbreviations. Volume II contains good quality plates.

NOBLE, Joseph Veach. The techniques of painted Attic pottery. New York, Watson-Guptill Publications, [1965]. xvi, 217p., illus. **JF194**

AJA LXX 1966 386–387 Farnsworth • Archaeology XX 1967 148–150 Weinberg
A superbly illustrated volume on the techniques of Greek pottery; published in cooperation with the Metropolitan Museum of Art.

POTTIER, Edmond, ed. Corpus Vasorum Antiquorum. **JF195**

In 1922, Pottier started this international undertaking to publish catalogues of collections of ancient pottery. Rules for entry into the series are laid down by the international committee on the CVA at their colloquy. In most fascicles now the contents are homogeneous, the text is bound and in the better fascicles the plates are printed on one side only. The German series is governed by strict editorial standards but reviewers complain about the poor quality of the Italian series. Reviews of CVA appear regularly in the *American Journal of Archaeology* and other journals.

RICHTER, Gisela Marie. Attic red-figured vases. Rev. ed. New Haven, Yale University Press, 1958. 209p. **JF196**

Antiquity XXXIV 1960 67 Cook • Gnomon XXXIII 1961 414 Lullies
A thorough examination of Attic red-figure vases. Thanks to the work of this author, we know far more about the developments and various stages of Greek art than we did at the beginning of the century. Her prolific writings on all aspects and stages of Greek art have added immeasurably to our knowledge of the painters, sculptors, and potters of this era.

RUCKERT, Anne. Frühe Keramik Böotiens: Form und Dekoration der Vasen des späten 8. und frühen 7. Jahrhunderts v. Chr. Mit einer Einl. von Karl Schefold. Bern, Francke, 1976. 123p., [30] leaves of plates, illus. **JF197**

Beiheft zur Halbjahresschrift Antike Kunst; 10.
AJA LXXXI 1977 244–245 King • JHS XCVII 1977 224 Cook
An analysis of Late Geometric Boeotian pottery. There are some 203 items in the Catalogue, and well over half of them are illustrated.

SCHIERING, W. Griechische Tongefässe, Gestalt, Bestimmung, und Formwandel. Berlin, Mann, 1967. 38p., 50 illus., 24 plates. **JF198**

CR XIX 1969 117 Boardman • AJA LXXIII 1969 89 Boulter • JHS LXXXIX 1969 191 Cook • AErt XCVI 1969 137 Szilágyi • RA 1969 313–314 Giroux • Gymnasium LXXVI 1969 189–190 Greifenhagen • DLZ LXXXIX 1968 1122–1124 Behn

The aim of this book is to provide an understanding of the development of Greek vase shapes. The author finds four basic principles. First the 'stereometrisch' of geometric forms (hemispherical cups, spherical, aryballoi, dinoi); second, the 'nachgiebig' ('almost elastic'), suggesting the weight of fluid content (alabastia, pelikai, olpai); third, the 'baulich' ('structural'), with articulation of parts, like an architectural order; fourth, the 'plastisch,' defining content and structure and generally preferring the flowering single-line contour. The aesthetic is one consideration affecting the shapes of vases, and other considerations can be found in other works on the subject.

SIMON, Erika. Die griechischen Vasen . . . Aufnahmen von Max u. Albert Hirmer. München, Hirmer, 1976. 172 [ca. 150] leaves of plates, illus. **JF199**

AJA LXXXI 1977 568–569 Mertens • HA VIII 1977 79

This work constitutes a revision and rewriting of P. E. Arias, *A History of 1000 Years of Greek Vase Painting.* The book attempts to present and elucidate the aesthetically and historically preeminent vases made in Greece between 1000 B.C. and the time of Alexander the Great. The introduction discusses the function of Greek vases, technical questions, subject matter, stylistic development and inscriptions. In all, 185 items are illustrated with commentary and bibliography.

TRIÁS DE ARRIBAS, Gloria. Cerámicas griegas de la Península Ibérica; [estudio histórico-arqueológico]. Valencia, 1967–1968. 2 v., illus., maps, 258 plates. **JF200**

William L. Bryant Foundation. Publicaciones de arqueología hispánica, 2, Serie 1: Monografías sobre cerámicas hispánicas, 2. T.1.—Texto. T.2.—Indices y láminas.

AJA LXXV 1971 104–105 von Bothmer

The most complete study of all the Greek, Etruscan and Southern Italian pottery found in Spain and Portugal.

VILLARD, François. Les vases grecs. Paris, Presses Universitaires de France, 1956. 109p., illus. **JF201**

Conimbriga I 1959 222 Alarcão • AJA LXIV 1960 204–205 Cambitoglou

Introduces the student or collector to the specialized field of the study of Greek vases. The first part deals with general and technical problems, the second part examines different schools and styles, from Geometric to the Hellenistic period, and the third part outlines the history of commerce, connoisseurship, and collecting of Greek vases. A scholarly work.

VON BOTHMER, Dietrich. Greek vase painting: an introduction. [New York, Metropolitan Museum of Art, 1972]. [68]p., illus., plates. **JF202**

Originally published as Metropolitan Museum of Art Bulletin, v. 31, no. 1, Fall, 1972.

AJA LXXVIII 1974 441 Boulter

This introduction to Greek vase painting first appeared as a special issue of the *Metropolitan Museum of Art Bulletin* (Fall 1972). Written by one of the foremost authorities in the field, there is an excellent summary of the history of Greek vase painting, followed by many beautiful illustrations including magnificent color plates of the calyx krater signed by Euphronios.

WEBSTER, Thomas Bertram L. Potter and patron in classical Athens. London, Methuen, 1972. xvi, 312, 16p., illus. **JF203**

"Distributed in the USA by Harper & Row Publishers, Inc., Barnes & Noble Import Division."

AAHG XXXI 1978 72–81 Häuptli • AJA LXXVII 1973 447–449 Eisman

The book attempts to analyze the role of the patron in the determination of shapes and decorations of pottery in classical Athens. The author examines commissioned vases to interpret the mind of the patron. Charts and annotated lists are provided, showing thematic fads. These lists are based on Haspels, *ABV* and Beazley, *ABV* and *ARV²*. The volume provides material for further study of the subject.

Painting and Portraits

HAFNER, German. Späthellenistische Bildnisplastik. Berlin, 1954. 128p. **JF204**

Gnomon XXVII 1955 587–589 Poulsen • Latomus XIV 1955 611 Renard • JRS XLV 1955 190–192 Richter

Groups 'late Hellenistic' portraits according to art centres all over the Mediterranean area. In all, 130 portraits are divided into geographical centres, and pertinent information and bibliography for each portrait is provided. The most important criterion for identification is held to be the styliotic. Similarity of style is considered decisive.

HEKLER, Anton. Bildnisse berühmter Griechen. 2. Aufl. Berlin, F. Kupferberg, 1962. 81p., [26] leaves of plates, illus. **JF205**

JHS LXXXIV 1964 232–233 Richter

This short book is a revised and enlarged version of the author's 1940 edition. It is a standard work on Greek portraiture. The revised edition includes recent discoveries, an up-to-date bibliography and excellent illustrations.

HEKLER, Anton. Greek and Roman portraits. New York, G. P. Putnam's Sons, 1912. xliii, 335p., illus. **JF206**

CJ XI 381 Tarbell • CW X 31 Shear

A photographic reprint of the original. While it cannot compare with others on the subject, such as Richter's *Portraits of the Greeks* (1965), the book is indispensable to the serious scholar as a unique collection of 444 portraits.

HOLSCHER, Tonio. Ideal und Wirklichkeit in den Bildnissen Alexanders des Grossen. Heidelberg, C. Winter, 1971. 59, 12p., illus.   **JF207**

Abhandlungen der Heidelberger Akademie der Wissenschaften. Philosophisch-Historische Klasse, Jahrg. 1971, Abh.

CW LXV 1972 237 Banks • AJA LXXV 1972 340–342 Bieber • REG LXXXV 1972 195 Goukowsky

The author aims to show not how Alexander really looked but how he wanted to look and how the artists wanted him to look. In his youth Alexander venerated and identified himself with Achilles, in his later years with Heracles. The author claims that art and reality are styled according to the same tendencies and seeks to establish the stylized appearance of the living Alexander, together with the style of his portraits.

LEVI, M. A. and STENICO, A. Pittura greca. Milano, Mondadori, 1956. 161p., 4 plates, 132 illus.   **JF208**

JHS LXXVII 1957 348 Richter

The story of Greek painting from the time before Peisistratos to the generation after Perikles, that is from about 600 to 400 B.C. Mostly Attic vase paintings with a little Corinthian and East Greek. Beautifully illustrated, the book is written for the layman. It is an excellent introduction for the student to all aspects of Greek vase painting.

PFUHL, Ernst. Malerei und Zeichnung der Griechen. München, Bruckmann, 1923.   **JF209**

PhW XLIII 1923 901–903 Karo • CJ XXIII 1927 313–315 Fraser • JHS XLVII 1927 131

In this monumental, heavily documented work in three volumes, the author examines Greek painting over a period of ten centuries. Written for the professional archaeologist the text is accompanied by 800 plates. Of more value to the student is the condensed version, translated by J. D. Beazley, *Masterpieces of Greek Drawing and Painting, 1926*. This well-written volume contains 160 of the original plates representing Greek vase-painting, Pompeian frescoes and mosaics, and Graeco-Egyptian mummy portraits along with sarcophagus paintings and others.

RICHTER, Gisela Marie A. The portraits of the Greeks. [London], Phaidon Press, [1965]. 3 v. (xiii, 337p.), illus.   **JF210**

CR XVI 1966 227–228 Cook • AJA LXX 1966 204–205 Schefold

The author successfully brings up to date a great work, Bernoulli's *Griechische Ikongraphie*. Greek iconography is beautifully revealed in this three-volume study. The introduction deals with the historical tradition, the unique character and function of Greek por-

traits, the value of Roman copies, the criteria for identification, the problem of "similarity," the masters, the history of research, the technique of Roman copies and the history of style. In the main parts of the book the portraits are arranged by the lifespan of the person depicted: in Vol. 1 down to the fifth century, in Vol. II down to the second, and all Hellenistic rulers are in Vol. III, where Greeks of the Roman period are also included. Then the literary and monumental sources for the iconography are detailed. A supplement to this work (24p.) appeared in 1972.

ROBERTSON, Martin. Greek painting. [Geneva], Skira, [1959]. 193p.   **JF211**

The great centuries of painting.

CB XXXVII 1960 30 Rexine • AJA LXIV 1960 292–293 Richter • ArchClass XII 1960 237–240 Morricone

Analysis of Greek painting is rare for the reason that Greek painting, mural and panel, has almost totally disappeared. Robertson selects a few masterpieces, mostly by vase-painters, from each period and shows the evolution of Greek representational art. The development of the third-dimension in art, as it appears in foreshortening and linear perspective, was achieved step by step in Greece. In this excellent Skira Series on ancient painting, which includes Prehistoric, Egyptian, Etruscan and Roman, this book is particularly beautiful.

Jewellery and Bronzes

ANTIKE GEMMEN in deutschen Sammlungen. München, Prestel Verlag, [1968– .]. Illus.   **JF212**

Gnomon XLVI 1974 634–635 Perry • AJA LXXV 1971 107–108 Vollenweider

A series of catalogues of antique gems in German collections.

BECATTI, Giovanni. Oreficerie antiche dalle minoiche alle barbariche. Roma, Istituto poligrafico dello Stato, 1955. 255p., 178 plates.   **JF213**

JHS LXXVII 1957 348–349 Higgins

A general work on ancient jewellery, it includes Minoan, Mycenaean, Greek, Etruscan and Roman jewellery. Well illustrated with lovely photographs, this is an important book on the subject.

BOARDMAN, John. Archaic Greek gems: Schools and artists in the sixth and early fifth centuries B.C. London, Thames & Hudson, 1968. 236p., plates, illus.   **JF214**

CW LXIV 1970 24–25 Pollitt • CJ LXV 1970 237 Vermeule

A scholarly work on examples of Greek gems of the sixth and early fifth centuries. The author examines details of style and divides them into what may represent their school of production.

BOARDMAN, John. Greek gems and finger rings: Early Bronze Age to late Classical. Photo-

graphs by Robert L. Wilkins. New York, H. N.
Abrams, [1972]. 458p., illus.   **JF215**

AJA LXXVII 1973 244–246 Gercke • ACR II 1972
176 Vermeule
The introduction deals with the use and history of
ancient sealings, provides a synopsis of publications
up to 1968 and reports on the current state of research.
Chapters II–VII explain shapes, motifs, styles, materials, techniques and uses of engraved gems and finger
rings. The second part of the book ("Notes to Chapters
II–VIII") provides the scientific analysis and contains
a systematic critical bibliography for each chapter. The
study ranges from the Early Bronze Age to Late Classical with a "summary account of Hellenistic gems and
rings." The enlarged photographs of impressions provide for excellent illustrations and give a good idea
of the beauty of gem-cutting in the periods discussed.

CHARBONNEAUX, Jean. Les bronzes grecs.
Paris, Presses universitaires de France, 1958. viii,
145p., 32 pages of plates, illus.   **JF216**

AC XXVIII 1959 538–541 Verhoogen • RBA
XXVIII 1959 114–115 Squilbeck • JHS LXXX 1970
235–236 Haynes
A short treatment of Greek bronzes, which includes
figured reliefs, along with statuettes. The first section
details the technical processes and the alloys used in
ancient bronze working. The next section describes the
historical development of statuettes and reliefs, from
Minoan times to the end of the Hellenistic period. The
final section describes public and private collections
and the problems of maintaining these collections.

COCHE DE LA FERTÉ, Etienne. Les bijoux an-
tiques. [1. ed.]. Paris, Presses universitaires de
France, 1956. 121p., 48 plates.   **JF217**

JHS LXXVII 1957 348–349 Higgins
A good introduction to the history of Greek, Roman
and Etruscan jewellery. Well illustrated, it includes
descriptions of the technical processes involved in making jewellery, along with the historical development
of ancient jewellery. Good bibliography.

FURTWÄNGLER, Adolf. Die antiken Gemmen;
Geschichte der Steinschneidekunst im klassischen Altertum. (Unveränderter Nachdruck der
Ausgabe 1900). Amsterdam, A. Hakkert, 1964–
65. 3 v., illus.   **JF218**

A monumental study in three volumes of seal engraving which establishes a solid chronological order for
analysis. The order established by the author is used
to the present day by authors such as Gisela Richter
in *Engraved Gems of the Greeks, Etruscans and Romans.*

**HOFFMAN, Herbert and DAVIDSON, Patricia
F.** Greek gold; jewelry from the age of Alexander. [n.p., 1965]. xi, 311p., illus., map.   **JF219**

Catalogue of an exhibition at the Museum of Fine
Arts, Boston, the Brooklyn Museum, and the Virginia
Museum of Fine Arts, Richmond.

RBPh XLV 1967 638–640 Richter • JHS LXXXVIII
1968 242–243 Higgins • Gymnasium LXXI 1967 202–
205 Amandry
Catalogue of an exhibition of Hellenistic jewellery,
held at Boston, Brooklyn and Richmond in 1965 and
1966. It is a definitive catalogue of Greek gold. The
exhibition was officially limited to the age of Alexander,
but some works of an earlier date and many of a later
date were included. There is an historical introduction
followed by a list of dated groups of jewellery. Davidson
provides the technical introduction and the catalogue
itself is divided according to the types of jewellery represented: diadems, earrings, necklaces, etc.

LAMB, Winifred. Greek and Roman bronzes.
Wilmington, Del., International Academic Pub.,
1979.   **JF220**

Reprint of the 1929 ed. published by Dial Press,
New York, in series: The Illustrated Library of Archaeology.

MÜLLER-KARPE, Hermann. Beiträge zu italienischen und griechischen Bronzefunden. München, Beck, [1974]. vii, 150, 42p., 42 illus., maps.
                                          JF221

Prahistorische Bronzefunde, Abt. 20, Bd.1.
AJA LXXX 1976 88–89 Thomas
This is the first volume of the twentieth section of
Prahistorische Bronzefunde. It contains short articles
on Italian and Greek bronze finds of the Late Bronze
Age and the Early Iron Age. Of interest to Greek schol-
ars is the concluding article of Wolfgang Radt which
brings together finds from the tumulus cemetery of
Verginia in Macedonia.

RICHTER, Gisela Marie A. Engraved gems of the
Greeks, Etruscans, and Romans. [London] Phaidon [1968– .]. 2 v.   **JF222**

Pt. I. Engraved gems of the Greeks and the Etruscans, a history of Greek art in miniature. Pt. II. Engraved gems of the Romans.
AJA LXXVII 1973 355–356 Vollenweider • Latomus XXXIII 1974 460 Chevallier
A sequel to the author's book on Greek gems, it
provides an introduction to Roman glyptic art. In a
chapter preceding the descriptions of the gems, there
is information on the use of gems as seals, amulets
and ornaments, on the subjects of engraving, signatures
of the artists, and other inscriptions; on material and
technique; on the relationship of the gems to coins
and sculptures. There is a chapter on Roman Republican gems and one on Roman Imperial. The author
follows the order of Furtwängler in *Die antiken Gemmen.* Another chapter instructs the reader to distinguish modern copies from antique gems. The illustrations are poorly reproduced but the book provides an
excellent introduction to the subject. Also by the same
author, *Catalogue of Engraved Gems, Greek, Etruscan
and Roman* (1956) for the Metropolitan Museum of
Art.

ROLLEY, Claude. Fouilles de Delphes, B. Monuments figurés. Les statuettes de Bronze. Paris,

de Boccard, 1969. 224p., 86 illus., 57 plates.
JF223

AJA LXXV 1971 226–227 Richter
Revises P. Pedrizet's *Fouilles de Delphes* (1908),

which included bronze statuettes found at Delphi from 1892 to 1901. This volume includes discoveries made since Pedrizet's publication. A well-produced reference work on Greek bronze statuettes.

JG ROMAN ART

Handbooks

ABBATE, Francesco, ed. Roman art; translated [from the Italian] by A. J. Sutton. London, New York, Octopus Books, 1972. 158p., 114 col. illus.
JG1

Translation of *Arte romana della Republica al Tardo Impero.*
TLS LXXI 1972 1264 • G&R XXI 1974 98 Sparkes
An inexpensive book on Roman art, with short text and many mediocre plates included.

ANDREAE, Bernard. The art of Rome. Translated from the German by Robert Erich Wolf. New York, H. N. Abrams, 1977. 655p., illus.
JG2

Latomus XXXIII 1974 714–717 Foucher • Erasmus XXVIII 1976 351–352 Duval
This sumptuous volume is a translation from the German. It contains 892 illustrations, 158 in color. An enormous and beautiful work that covers the history of Roman art, from its Greek origins to the triumph of Christianity under Constantine. The first section reviews the evolution of Roman art in all its aspects, political, social, economical, religious, and cultural. This is followed by a section on 'Image as Document' by Lucien Mazenod, presenting excellent black-and-white photographs. The last section on archaeological sites covers topography, monuments, temples, sanctuaries, palaces, libraries, villas and sites outside Rome. This book contains an unparalleled wealth of illustrative and documentary material that vividly reveals the grandeur of Rome. Photographic reproductions of sculptural detail and wall-paintings are especially good. A comprehensive bibliography (p.632–645) includes earlier works on Roman art by this author, such as *Römische Bildwerke,* 1958.

BECATTI, Giovanni. L'arte romana. [I. ed.] [Milano], Garzanti, [1962]. 139p., illus.   **JG3**

La Cultura moderna. Testi.
Archaeology XVI 1963 293 Van Buren • RBPh XLIII 1965 300–302 Balty
The author stresses the debt of Roman artists to their Greek predecessors. Using his expert knowledge of the excavations at Ostia, he presents Roman works of art including the coins in a broad historical context.

BIANCHI BANDINELLI, Ranuccio. Archeologia e Cultura. Milan and Naples, Riccardo Ricciardi, 1961. 471p., illus.   **JG4**

Archaeology XVI 1963 77 • JRS LIII 1963 214–216 Richter • Latomus XXII 1963 353–355 Dacos
A collection of lectures delivered and articles published on various aspects of classical art between 1945 and 1960. It is a continuation of the author's *Storicità dell' arte classica* (1950). Some of the titles are "Roman art two generations after Wickhoff;" "The place of the artist in classical antiquity;" "The formation of Roman portraiture;" and "The continuation of Hellenistic art in medieval and late Roman paintings." The articles are prefaced with an essay entitled "Archaeology and Culture."

BIANCHI BANDINELLI, Ranuccio. Rome, the center of power, 500 B.C. to A.D. 200. Translated by Peter Green. New York, G. Braziller, [1970]. xii, 437p., illus., plans.   **JG5**

Translation of *Rome, le centre du pouvoir.*
BJ CLXXI 1971 709–713 Gabelmann • CR XXII 1972 296 Toynbee • CW LXV 1972 279 Stern • Gymnasium LXXIX 1972 99–101 Bielefeld • ABull LV 1973 282–285 Brilliant
This excellent volume, with its copious beautiful plates, provides a history of Roman art both for the general reader and the specialist. It is arranged chronologically and for each stage the sculptures, paintings, buildings, and minor arts are presented. The text is well-written and well-translated and provides in the opening pages of each chapter information on the political, cultural and social developments. The author recognizes the importance of plebeian taste in Roman art which clung to the old, Italic traditions, despite domination by Hellenized patricians. In the Late Antique period, Roman art matured and became truly Imperial rejecting Greek models.

BIANCHI BANDINELLI, Ranuccio. Rome, the late Empire; Roman art, A.D. 200–400. Translated [from the French] by Peter Green. London, Thames and Hudson, 1971. x, 466p., 5 plates, illus., maps, plans.   **JG6**

Translation of *Rome, la fin de l'art antique.*
ACR II 1972 46 Hanfmann • BSEAA XXXVIII 1972 570–574 Balil • DLZ XCIII 1972 401–405 Zinserling • CR XXIII 1973 260–262 Toynbee

The main theme is that the change in Roman art from Commodus' death onwards is a reflection of the changed mentality, outlook on life and external circumstances of the whole of the later Empire. The break with the Hellenistic tradition represents a preference for the symbolic and ornamental as against the naturalistic and rational. The book includes art in the western provinces, the Danubian lands, Gaul, Spain and Britain and, in part II, Africa and Constantinople. The superb, profuse illustrations contain many little-known objects of Roman Art. See obituary notice for this author in *Byzantion* XLV, 1975, 185–186, Delvoye.

BRENDEL, O. J. Prolegomena to the study of Roman art. New Haven and London, Yale University Press, 1979. 207p.   **JG7**

Includes two essays by the author, "Prolegomena to a Book on Roman Art" first published in the *Memoirs of the American Academy in Rome* in 1953 and "Roman Art in Modern Perspective." Together they synthesize this distinguished scholar's study of Roman art and its history.

BRILLIANT, Richard. Roman art from the Republic to Constantine. Newton Abbot, [Eng.], Readers Union Group of Book Clubs, 1974. 288p., illus.   **JG8**

AJA LXXIX 1975 168 MacKendrick • AHR LXXXI 1976 367–368 Hammond • CR XXVI 1976 254–255 Colledge • CW LXIX 1976 485–486 Thompson

The subject is analyzed under six headings: architecture, triumphal monuments, ornament, realism, eclecticism, and periodic styles. The book discusses the psychological aspects of Roman art and the relative contributions of Greek and Italic art. The illustrations are excellent. A short introduction traces the literature on Roman art since Wickhoff.

CAGNAT, René L. V. Manuel d'archéologie romaine. Paris, A. Picard, 1916–1920. 2 v., illus., plans.   **JG9**

I. CJ XII 494 Tarbell • CW XII 44 Robinson • REA 1921 251 Radet • CR 1922 41 Pryce • MPh XXXI 72 Byvanck

Still valuable as practical handbooks for the study of Roman archaeology. The volumes cover Rome and the Provinces. Volume I, on architecture, includes methods of construction and a shorter section on the sculpture. Volume II discusses mosaics and painting along with domestic art and pottery. Good illustrations included.

COARELLI, Filippo. Guida archeologica di Roma; con la collaborazione di Luisanna Usai per la parte cristiane; fotografie di Mauro Pucciarelli. 1. ed., Varia Grandi opere. [Milano], A. Mondadori, 1974. 357p., illus.   **JG10**

Caesarodunum X 1975 C.R. 42 Chevallier
The first in a series of Italian archaeological guides, it is an excellent introduction to Roman archaeology

with its up-to-date scholarly text and many lovely color photographs.

COARELLI, Filippo. Rome. Foreword by Pier Luigi Nervi. London, Cassell, 1973. 191p., illus.   **JG11**

Monuments of civilization.
ACR III 1973 79–80 MacKendrick
A lovely picture record, mostly large color photographs, of the monuments of ancient Rome. The text is a short guide.

DUCATI, Pericle. L'arte in Roma delle origini al sec. VIII. Bologna, Licinio Cappelli, editora, [1938].   **JG12**

[Istituto di studi romani] Storia di Roma; v. XXVI.
ICS 1939 149 Laurenzi • MC 1939 177 Taccone • CR 1941 96–97 Toynbee
This represents Volume XXVI in the *Storia di Roma,* an encyclopedic work on the history of Rome. It is a very complete coverage of art in the Roman world from prehistoric to Imperial times. Monuments of early, pre-Byzantine Christian art are included with copious excellent illustrations. In the first part of the Appendix, the author traces the history of modern criticism from Wickoff's *Wiener Genesis* in 1895 to works dated 1934. Part II of the Appendix consists of a valuable bibliography.

FROVA, Antonio. L'Arte di Roma e del Mondo Romano. Torino, Tipografica-Editrice Torinese, 1961. 948p., 713 figs.   **JG13**

REL XXXIX 1961 411–416 Chevallier • AntC XXXI 1962 577–582 Balty
Presents the art of Rome in Italy and in the Provinces, Spain, Gaul, Britain, Danube and Balkans, Africa and Asia. It includes architecture, sculpture and painting from Republican to Imperial times with copius illustrations and a good bibliography.

HANFMANN, George Maxim Anossov. Roman art; A modern survey of the art of imperial Rome. New York, Norton, [1975]. 1st ed. 1964. 328p., illus.   **JG14**

AntJ XLV 1965 286–287 Strong • CB XLII 1965 15–16 Rexine • JRS LV 1965 284–286 Toynbee
This is a good general introduction to the study of Roman sculpture, painting, architecture, and mosaics. The primary works are all included with excellent commentaries. The beautiful illustrations, with annotations, form the most valuable part of the book, and the commentaries include useful bibliographies. The color plates are mainly of paintings, with most of the sites, sculpture, buildings and coin portraits in black-and-white.

HEINTZE, Helga, Freifrau von. Roman art. London, Weidenfeld and Nicolson, [1972]. 200p., illus.   **JG15**

Translation of *Römische Kunst.*

AJA LXXIV 1970 310–311 Vermeule • Gymnasium LXXVII 1970 557–558 Hoffmann • JRS LXI 1971 288–289 Colledge

A short survey of Roman architecture and art, translated from the German.

HELBIG, Wolfgang. Führer durch die öffentlichen Sammlungen Klassischer Altertümer in Rom. 1. Musei Vaticani. 4. völlig neu bearb. Aufl., hrsg. von Hermine Speier. Tübingen, E. Wasmuth, 1963– .   **JG16**

At head of title: Deutsches Archäologisches Institut. AJA LXIX 1965 181 Felletti Maj • CW LVIII 1965 138 Lazenby • Gymnasium LXXII 1965 155–156 Bielefeld

The fourth edition of the work by W. Helbig on the contents of the museums of Rome, which first appeared in 1891. This first volume, edited by Hermine Speier, includes the Vatican and Lateran museums. The works of art of these museums are presented with great thoroughness, including informative data, description, iconographic and stylistic considerations and chronological dating. A bibliography is included at the end. The meticulous scholarship in this volume represents a great improvement on previous editions. Other volumes in the series are: II. Musei Capilolini, etc. (1966); III. Villa Giulia (1969); IV. Museo Ostiense, etc. (1972).

HOMO, Léon Pol. La Rome antique, histoire— guide des monuments de Rome depuis les temps les plus reculés jusqu'à l'invasion des barbares; ouvrage illustré de 10 gravures et 35 plans. Paris, Hachette, 1921. 300p., illus.   **JG17**

JS 1921 232 Merlin • RA XIV 200 Reinach • REA 1921 252 Jullian

Describes the topography and archaeology of Rome, with detailed descriptions of the major monuments. While out-of-date, it is still useful for its maps and scholarly text by a historian of Roman civilization.

KÄHLER, Heinz. The art of Rome and her empire. Translated by J. R. Foster. [Rev. ed.]. New York, Greystone Press, [1965]. 256p., illus., map, plans.   **JG18**

Translation of Rom und sein Imperium. AJ CXX 1963 313 Daniels • A&R XII 1967 86

The first chapter discusses the debt of Roman artists to their Greek predecessors and the qualities of Roman art that distinguish it as a form in its own right. The author emphasizes the "special relationship to reality" of Roman art. Subsequent chapters trace monument construction, sculpture and painting from Caesar Augustus to the Tetrarchs and Constantine. The quality of the color plates is superb, and there are drawings and black-and-white photographs. A bibliography and chronological table are included.

KOCH, Herbert. Römische Kunst. 2. erweiterte Aufl. Weimar, H. Böhlaus Nachfolger, 1949. 160p., illus., 61 plates.   **JG19**

AJA LV 1951 281 Michels • JRS XLI 1951 208 Radford • Latomus X 1951 389 Étienne

A popular account of Roman art, including architecture and sculpture. It is almost entirely confined to Imperial art to the beginning of the fourth century. The illustrations, plans, and reconstructions are all good.

KRAUS, Theodor. Das römische Weltreich. Berlin, Propyläen Verlag, 1967. 335p., illus.   **JG20**

Propyläen Kunstgeschichte (Berlin, 1966–) Bd. 2. CW LXI 1968 407–408 Hanfmann • Pantheon XXVI 1968 510–511 Bielefeld

Part of the new Propyläen series, it aims to provide scholarly comment with good reproduction. Altogether there are 563 illustrations in color and black-and-white. The long introductory essay by Kraus covers Roman art from the Late Republic to Justinian. The Documentation of 180 pages includes monuments, bibliography, and a "Synchronoptic Survey" of politics, architecture, fine arts, literature and philosophy.

LÜBKE, Wilhelm and SARNE, Berta. Die Kunst der Römer, von Lübke-Pernice. Vollständig neubearb. und ergänzt von Berta Sarne. [Mit 420 Abbildungen und 8 Farbtafeln.] Wien, P. Neff, 1958. 455p., illus., col. plates.   **JG21**

Part of the author's Kunst des Altertums (v. 1 of his Grundriss der Kunstgeschichte).

A new edition, revised by Sarne, of the classic on Roman art. In the revision Sarne includes recent discoveries on Etruscan and pre-urban Rome.

PAPE, Magrit. Griechische Kunstwerke aus Kriegsbeute und ihre öffentliche Aufstellung in Rom; von der Eroberung von Syrakus bis in augusteische Zeit. Hamburg, 1975. iv, 280p.   **JG22**

Gymnasium LXXXIV 1977 475–477 Blanck • JRS LXVII 1977 218 Wade

The book examines the evidence for the transformation of the city of Rome through Greek works of art procured as war booty by Roman generals from Marcellus' sack of Syracuse in 212/11 through the Augustan period. Political function was more important than artistic factors in the selections made by the generals.

RICHMOND, Ian Archibald, Sir. Roman archaeology and art; Essays and studies edited by Peter Salway. London, Faber and Faber, [1969]. 294p., illus., 9 plates.   **JG23**

Antiquity XLIV 1970 151–152 Birley • AC XXXIX 1970 343–345 Faider-Feytmans • AHR LXXV 1970 1706–1707 Turner • GJ CXXXVI 1970 267 Pilke

A selection of essays published posthumously in a revised edition by Peter Salway. Various monuments of Roman art are analyzed including the Ara Pacis Augustae and the Arch of Titus.

STRONG, Eugénie (Sellers). Art in ancient Rome. Westport, Conn., Greenwood Press, [1970]. xiv, 199, viii, 220p., illus., plans.   **JG24**

Reprint of the 1928 ed. From the earliest times to the principate of Nero.—From the Flavian dynasty to Justinian, with chapters on painting and the minor arts in the first century A.D.

JRS XVIII 1928 235–237 Toynbee • JC XXV 1929 244–246 Magoffin

This reprint reviews the history of Roman art and architecture by epoch rather than by type of monument. Within each section there are good black and white photographic illustrations of the objects discussed. An extensive bibliography accompanies each chapter. Still valuable as a concise introduction to the subject.

TOYNBEE, Jocelyn M. C. The art of the Romans. New York, Praeger, [1965]. 271p., 48 plates, illus. **JG25**

Arch Class XVIII 1966 173–174 Guerrini • JRS LVI 1966 258–259 Harrison • AJA LXXI 1967 108 Vermeule

A good basic handbook for the study of Roman art. Aspects of art covered include portrait sculpture in the round and in high relief, mythological and decorative statuary, Dacians, Tritons, giants, the Good Shepherd and bronze horses.

TOYNBEE, Jocelyn M. C. The Hadrianic school, a chapter in the history of Greek art. Ed. anastatica. Roma, L'Erma di Bretschneider, 1967. xxxi, 254p., [30] leaves of plates. **JG26**

Reprint of the 1934 ed.

Examines the neo-Hellenic art of the Emperor Hadrian, both as an Imperial revival and as a continuation of Greek art during the Empire.

VESSBERG, Olof. Studien zur Kunstgeschichte der römischen Republik. Lund, C. W. K. Gleerup, 1941. 2 v. **JG27**

AArch 1942 179–198 Poulsen • AJA 1947 340–343 Bieber • RBPh 1948 674–679 de Ruyt

This important work traces the art history of Rome from its beginnings to the time of Augustus and presents the art of the Roman Republic period, particularly portraiture. For the earlier period the author relies heavily on the literary material because of the scarcity of archaeological remains, using Cicero, Livy, Pliny, Plutarch and others. The second part deals with the portraits on sculpture and coins of the 1st century B.C. There are two volumes, one of text and one of excellent plates. This exhaustive study includes bibliographies, a register of ancient sources, a register of places and museums, and an index of names and objects. For a bibliography of published writings of this author see *Opuscula Atheniensia*, XI, 1975, 195–198 by L. Åström.

WALTERS, Henry Beauchamp. The art of the Romans. 2d ed. London, Methuen, 1928. xvi, 185p., [72] leaves of plates, illus. **JG28**

The author chooses outstanding examples of art of the Roman period. An excellent introduction to the art of the Roman empire in its western section. Chap-

ters cover architecture, sculpture, painting and mosaic, gem-engraving, metalwork and fictile work. There is a concluding chapter on Roman art in the provinces, mainly Gaul and Britain.

WHEELER, Mortimer, Sir. Roman art and architecture. New York, F. A. Praeger, [1964]. 250p., illus., plans. **JG29**

Antiquity XXXIX 1965 71–72 Toynbee • AntJ XLV 1965 286–287 Strong • REL XLIII 1965 654–656 Chevallier

In this extremely well-written book the author covers a wide range of Roman artistic achievement. A large part of the book is devoted to town planning and architecture, a shorter section to sculpture and painting, and a final section to the impact of Roman art on the Provinces. A highly readable account of the subject, the illustrations in black-and-white are good but the color reproductions are poor.

WICKHOFF, Franz. Roman art; Some of its principles and their application to early Christian painting. Translated by E. Strong. London, W. Heinemann; New York, Macmillan, 1900. xiv, 198p., illus. **JG30**

Paideia 1947 151 Paribeni • Helmantica I 1950 391–393 Rodriguez

A pioneering work that defined Roman art as a style distinct from its Greek antecedents. The author established that Roman art merited analysis as a product of its own social and cultural influences, and not only as copies of Greek originals. His analysis forms the basis for criticism of Roman art to the present time.

Prehistory

BARFIELD, Lawrence. Northern Italy before Rome. [London], Thames and Hudson, [1971]. 208p., illus. **JG31**

Ancient peoples and places, 76.

Antiquity XLVI 1972 164–165 Trump • Archaeology XXVI 1973 69 Foltiny • TLS LXXI 1972 1189

A highly readable account of the archaeology of Italy from the earliest times to the conquest of Rome. The author describes the proto-Villanovan culture of Tuscany and its influence on Etruscan culture. Reviews chronologically the early communities, their arts and crafts, from the hunting groups of the Pleistocene period to late prehistory when Greeks, Celts and Romans all influenced the area.

BIANCHI BANDINELLI, Ranuccio. L'Arte dell'antichità classica. Torino; Utet, [1976]. 2 v., illus. **JG32**

1: Bianchi Bandinelli, E. Paribeni. Grecia. 2: Bianchi Bandinelli, M. Torelli. Etruria, Roma.

REL LIV 1976 502–503 Gérard • G&R XXIV 1977 206–207 Sparkes • DLZ XCVIII 1977 68–72 Schindler

The work is divided into three parts: the first covers the period between the prehistory of Italy and the

Greek colonization which gave rise to Italic art, the second period is Etruscan Art, and the third examines Roman art. The author distinguishes between "Roman Art" and "art of the ancient world in the Roman era" to show that Roman art was influenced and affected by European art. Roman art was responsible for the transmission of Greek form to medieval and renaissance Europe.

BIANCHI BANDINELLI, Ranuccio. Etruschi e italici prima del dominio di Roma. [2. ed.]. [Milano], Rizzoli, [1976]. 436p., illus., maps.
JG33

Translation of *Les Étrusques et l'Italie avant Rome.* Originally published as *Les Étrusques et l'Italie avant Rome,* this is a magnificent volume covering the art of ancient Italy and Etruria. It completes the three volume series of which the other two volumes are *L'Arte romana nel centro del potere* and *Roma, La fine dell'arte antica.* There are copious excellent illustrations in black-and-white and color. The text is chronological, beginning with prehistoric art in Italy and ending with the domination of Rome.

GIEROW, Phar Ghoran. The Iron Age culture of Latium. Lund, C. W. K. Gleerup, 1965– . Illus., maps.
JG34

v. 2. Excavations and finds: pt. 1. The Alban Hills. AJA LXX 1966 391–392 Richardson • JRS LVIII 1968 235–240 Ridgway • Germania XLVIII 1970 170–191 Kilian
An important catalogue of the Iron Age remains from the Alban Hills. Another volume catalogues material from the rest of Latium and a third classifies and analyzes the material in both volumes. In his review, Ridgway criticizes the classification and chronology established in these volumes and in Gjerstad, *Early Rome IV, 1–2: Synthesis of Archaeological Remains* (1966).

GJERSTAD, Einar. Early Rome. Lund, C. W. K. Gleerup, 1953–1973. 6 v., illus., diagrs., plans.
JG35

1. Stratigraphical researches in the Forum Romanum and along the Sacra Via.–2. The tombs.–3. Fortifications, domestic architecture, sanctuaries, stratigraphic excavations.–4. Synthesis of archaeological evidence. 2 pts.–5. The written sources.–6. Historical survey.
v. 1: CR N.S. V 1955 223 Cook • REA LVII 1955 193–198 Grimal • AJA LX 1956 78–79 Holland
v. 2: CR N.S. VIII 1958 92 Cook • JRS XLVIII 1958 208–209 Ryberg • Gnomon XXXI 1959 434–439 Romanelli
v. 3: AJA LXVI 1962 427–430 Ryberg • CR XII 1962 177 Cook • JRS LII 1962 262–263 Piganiol
v. 4: AJA LXXII 1968 292–293 Ryberg • CR XVIII 1968 225–228 Ogilvie • JRS LVIII 1968 235–240 Ridgway • Gnomon XLII 1970 407–413 Romanelli
v. 5 and 6: LEC XLII 1974 335 Wankenne • AJA LXXIX 1975 386–390 Palmer • JRS LXV 1975 195–197 Heurgon • CR XXVI 1976 95–96 Ogilvie

The first volume in this enormous undertaking which aims to present the entire archaeological and written evidence bearing upon the early history of Rome from the beginning of the pre-urban epoch to the end of the regal period, and to present the conclusions drawn from this material. In this section the author relies heavily on the work of the great excavator Giacomo Boni which he amends with the use of more advanced archaeological techniques. A relative chronology is established based on examination of undisturbed strata and their content of pottery and this is followed by a description of the early habitations.

Vol. 2 aims to establish a firm chronology of the burial finds of early Rome and includes only those for which excavation records are clearly reliable. The burials are accurately described, well-illustrated and the author analyses them in the light of literary evidence or funerary customs.

New stratigraphical evidence available after the publication of Volume 1 is contained in the third volume along with an examination of the architectural remains. The section on fortifications deals with the stratification of the *agger,* its first stage dated by an Attic red-figured shard of 490–470 B.C. Votive deposits and architectural fragments are presented as evidence for sanctuaries.

In the fourth section, Gjerstad examines the archaeological evidence on a chronological basis and presents the cultural development of Rome from the first Iron-Age settlements on the Palatine, Esquiline, and Quirinal down to the end of the Archaic City in c.450 B.C. Much of the material published in *Early Rome* I–III is included here and an absolute chronology established based on the pottery finds; Period I, c.800–750 B.C., Expansive Impasto; Period II, c.750–700 B.C., Normal Impasto; Period III, c.700–625 B.C., Contracted Impasto; Period IV, c.625–575 B.C., Advanced and Bucceroid Impasto. This absolute chronology has been challenged by scholars such as Müller-Kanpe.

The title of Volume 5 is somewhat misleading, since the work is concerned simply with Gjerstad's reconstruction of the major Roman institutions of the Regal and Republican periods. All is colored by Gjerstad's highly personal conviction that the Kingdom fell c.450 B.C. and that Tarquinius Priscus and his successors reigned c.530–450 B.C. The credibility of the sources is not analyzed, which is most regrettable. The archaeological evidence can only be understood in a historical framework which a closer investigation of the literary evidence would provide and it is arbitrary and perverse to reverse the roles of history and archaeology.

LA GENIÈRE, Juliette de. Recherches sur l'âge du fer en Italie Méridionale. Sala Consilina, Naples, Publications du Centre Jean Bérard, 1968. xi, 370p., 66 plates.
JG36

JRS LX 1970 241 Ridgway • AJA LXXV 1971 222–223 Thomas • Archeologia XXII 1971 222–224 Wasowicz
The first publication in a series by the Centre Jean Bérard. The Centre studies the archaeology, art, history and institutions of Southern Italy and Sicily from prehistoric to Roman times. The work studies the relations between Greeks and natives based on the Sala Consilina

material, with emphasis on the local geometric pottery.

LANGLOTZ, Ernst. L'Arte della Magna Grecia. Arte greca in Italia meridionale Sicilia. Fotografie di Max Hirmer. Roma, L'Erma di Bretschneider, 1968. 322p., 20 mounted plates, illus.   **JG37**

Translation of *Die Kunst der Westgriechen in Sizilien und Unteritalien;* translated by Luisa Dell'Orto Franchi.

Athenaeum XLVI 1968 381–382 Saletti • ASNP XXXVII 1968 197–198 Arias • JHS XC 1970 260–262 Oakeshott

Covering the period c.1000 B.C. to the disintegration of the Greek colonies in the 1st century B.C., the book describes the art, architecture, painting, figurines, bronzes, sculpture and coins of Magna Grecia. The objects are presented in beautiful photographs by Max Hirmer but cover only the plastic arts. Some of the objects are photographed here for the first time. The historical background is described including the transmission of Greek cults and myths and the early work of Greek sculptors and potters in Magna Grecia. The influence of this work on the art of late antiquity is persuasively shown.

MÜLLER-KARPE, Hermann. Vom Anfang Roms. Heidelberg, Kerle, 1959. 115p., illus., map, plans.   **JG38**

Deutsches Archäologisches Institut. Römische Abteilung Mitteilungen. Ergänzungsheft, v. 5.

AJA LXV 1961 408 Ryberg • Gnomon XXXIII 1961 378–382 Gjerstad • RBPh XXXIX 1961 1270–1272 Heurgon • RSI LXXIII 1961 806–808 Momigliano

Using only the archaeological evidence and ignoring the literary, linguistic and religious evidence, the author examines Roman pre-history. Early burial remains and burial objects are analyzed and interpreted to prove the link between Crete and early Rome.

PACE, Biagi. Arte e civiltà della Sicilia antica. I fattori etnici e sociali. Milano-Genova-Roma, Società Dante Alighieri, 1935. 3 v.   **JG39**

v. 1: A&R 1936 134–136 Ducati • BFC XLII 1936 287–290 Patroni • REL XIV 1936 445–449 Bayet
v. 2: BFC XLVI 1939 23–27 Patroni • CW XXXII 1939 178 Mandra • JHS LVIII 1938 271–273 Dunbabin
v. 3: Aevum XX 1946 299–300 Paribeni • JRS XL 1950 179–181 Dunbabin

A monumental three volume work on the races, cultures and economics of the inhabitants of Sicily from prehistoric to Roman times. The section on prehistory is especially good and the remaining three chapters in this volume are on Greeks and Sikels, and Sicily under the Romans. The second half of the book contains studies of particular aspects of Sicilian civilization.

In the second volume the author writes on the Arts and Artists of Sicily. He examines architecture, sculpture and vase-painting and presents the known objects with copious illustrations and drawings. The first com-

prehensive work to incorporate results of fifty years of excavation.

In volume 3 the author demonstrates the unity of Sicilian culture through the ages and draws parallels between ancient and modern Sicily. Culture includes literature, art and religion. The book examines all aspects of each.

PALLOTTINO M. and MANSUELLI G., eds. Popoli e Civiltà Dell' Italia Antica, 1–111. 536p., 80 plates, 113 text figures; 346p., 152 plates, 9 maps, 8 text figures; 323p., 224 plates, maps, figures.   **JG40**

JRS LXVI 1976 206–213 Ridgway

Although written for the historian, this series is of fundamental importance to the understanding of the archaeology of Italy before the Romans. Sections were written by the following distinguished scholars: B. d'Agostino, *The Iron Age in Southern Italy and Sicily;* G. Colonna, *The pre- and proto-history of Rome and Latium;* P. E. Arias, *Italo-Siceliote Civilization;* B. d'Agostino, *The World around Magna Grecia;* A. M. Radmilli, *Man and his Environment* and *From the Paleolithic to the Bronze Age.* These are the first three volumes of a proposed seven volume series. The existing volumes provide definitive reports of the excavations and history of ancient Italy.

PINCELLI, Rosanna and MORIGI GOVI, C. La necropoli villanoviana di San Vitale. [Bologna], Istituto per la storia di Bologna, 1975. 2 v., 586p., 82 figures, 360 plates, illus.   **JG41**

Cataloghi delle collezioni del Museo civico archeologico di Bologna.

JRS LXVII 1977 225–226 Ridgway

This catalogue of the Museo Civico in Bologna is fundamental to the study of the Iron Age in Italy. There is a catalogue of tomb-groups (33–508) and sporadic pottery (509–16). The original plans of the individual trenches are reproduced (I. figs. 1–43) and so is a selection of photographs taken on the site (II, pls. 1–53). The catalogue compliments for the north R. Peroni's *Studi sulla cronologia della civiltà di Este e Golasecca* (1975) and his *Studi di chronologia hallstattiana* which cover Iron Age Italy in the peninsula.

POHL, Ingrid. The iron age necropolis of Sorbo at Cerveteri. Stockholm, Lund, Paul Åström, 1972. xv, [1], 306p., illus., maps.   **JG42**

CR XXIV 1974 160–61 Ogilvie • JRS LXIV 1974 248–249 Close-Brooks

Examines the contents of each of 450 tombs from the Sorbo cemetery at Cerveteri, already published without illustration by R. Vighi (*Mon. Ant,* 1955). The tombs are divided into Early and Late on the basis of Normal and Contracted Impasto. Very helpful in the study of early Italic history.

RICHTER, Gisela Marie Augusta. Ancient Italy; A study of the interrelations of its peoples as shown in their arts. Ann Arbor, University of

Michigan Press, 1955. xxiv, 137p., 305 illus.
JG43

Jerome lectures, 4th ser.
Archaeology IX 1956 222–224 Richardson • JHS LXXVII 1957 365–366 Haynes
This beautifully illustrated book traces the history of Greek, Italic and Etruscan art in Italy during the Archaic, the Classical and Hellenistic periods. Much of the book is devoted to Etruscan art. The author discusses the influence of Greek art in Italy. She finds in Etruscan art an individuality and a spirit of gaiety missing in Greek objects. There is an excellent section on Graeco-Roman art in the Republican and Imperial periods and the methods used in copying and adapting the Greek originals. Emphasis is placed on Rome's contribution to the art of Italy and the author expands her ideas presented in *Three Critical Periods of Greek Sculpture.*

SÄFLUND, Gösta. Le terremare delle Provincie di Modena, Reggio Emilia, Parma, Piacenza. Stockholm, Lund, Gleerup, 1939. 265p.
JG44

JRS XXX 1940 89–97 Hawkes and Stiassny
The book defines the terramara culture of prehistoric Italy as geographically within the four provinces of Modena, Reggio Emilia, Parma, and Piacenza. The author disagrees with the nineteenth-century definition of terramara proposed by Luigi Pigorini and defines it as 'any settlement—site of the Bronze Age culture of this part of Italy.' There is a geographical and archaeological survey of the sites, classified presentation of the finds, and separate study of the cremation—cemeteries, with conclusions including chronology and ethnology. There is a generous bibliography and 84 plates covering many hundreds of objects. A bibliography of writings by this author by I. Molander appeared in *Opuscula Romana* VI, 1968: 201–204.

TRUMP, David H. Central and southern Italy before Rome. London, Thames and Hudson, 1966. 244p.
JG45

Ancient peoples and places, v. 47.
Antiquity XLI 1967 248–249 Barfield • Archaeology XXI 1968 73–74 Richardson • JRS LVII 1967 270–271 Ridgway
Using the results of recent archaeological excavations the author presents a scholarly account of the life of prehistoric Italy. Newly discovered sites are reported with illustrations of the pottery, tools, weapons and ornaments found and the author concludes from them a lively trade between the people of ancient Italy and those of northern Europe and the eastern Aegean. The time-span covered is between the second interglacial period, about 200,000 years ago, and the end of the early Iron Age about 750 B.C.

VAN ESSEN, C. C. Précis d'histoire de l'art antique en Italie. Brussels, Latomus, 1960. 152p., 71 plates.
JG46

CR XII 1962 89–90 Brogan • JRS LIII 1963 222–223 Robertson

The author's thesis is that in antiquity, Italian and Greek art were distinct entities. Italian art had a distinctive character and he traces its consistent development from c.900 B.C. to c.700 A.D. Robertson, in the review cited, is not convinced by the arguments, while admiring the author's knowledge of Italian art.

Etruscan

ANDRÉN, Arvid. Architectural terracottas from Etrusco-Italic temples. Lund, Gleerup, 1940. cclvi, 516p., 168 illus.
JG47

AC 1942 346–349 Renard
The first part is a general introduction with bibliography, abbreviations and tables of ancient reproductions of temples and houses. There follows a discussion of Etrusco-Italic temples in general and a comparison of ancient literary evidence with the material remains. A beautifully illustrated book.

BALLAND, André. Céramique étrusco-companienne à vernis noir. Dessins de R. Gilardi. Paris, E. de Boccard, 1969– . 168, 27p., illus., plates.
JG48

Fouilles de l'École française de Rome à Bolsena (Poggio Moscini), 3.
This series covers the excavations at Bolsena (1962–1967). This fascicle deals with the Etrusco-Campanian black-glazed vases found in the excavations. The first volume deals with stratigraphy and the second with architecture.

BANTI, Luisa. Etruscan cities and their culture. Translated by Erika Bizzarri. [1st English language ed.] Berkeley, University of California Press, 1973. vi, 322p., illus., 96 plates. **JG49**

Translation of *Il mondo degli Etruschi.*
AJA LXVI 1962 217–218 Richardson • JRS LIII 1963 232–233 Scullard • CR XXVI 1976 289–290 Scullard
A review of the artistic life of Etruscan cities. It first appeared in 1960 as *Il Mondo degli Etruschi* and this is a translation of the revised 1968 version. The author relies heavily on the archaeological evidence and shows the influence of one Etruscan city on the art and culture of another. It is a detailed survey of the cities of Etruria in which the author claims that the tombs are the best historical source for Etruria.

BEAZLEY, John Davidson, Sir. Etruscan vase painting. New York, Hacker Art Books, 1976. xvi, 351p., [21] leaves of plates, illus. **JG50**

Reprint of the 1947 ed. published by Oxford University Press, in series: Oxford monographs on classical archaeology.
JHS LXIX 1949 93–94 Robertson • Latomus IX 1950 346–347 Renard
This major study of Etruscan vase painting provides a system for classification of schools, workshops and individual painters similar to the author's treatment

of Greek artists in *Attic red-figure vase-painters* and *Attic black-figure vase-painters.*

BLOCH, Raymond. Etruscan art. London, Barrie and Rockliff in association with Cory, Adams, & Mackay, [1966]. 104p. **JG51**

CW LX 1967 296–299 Mattheus • Archaeology XXI 1968 74–75 Cook • Latomus XXIX 1970 881 Chevallier

A revision of a book by this author published in 1959. It contains an introduction to Etruscan art along with sections on sculpture, tomb-painting, jewelry, ivory-carving, ceramics, metalwork and architecture. There is a comparison of Etruscan to Greek and Roman art, a description of new methods in archaeological exploration and a short account of the problem of forgeries. For a history of the Etruscan people see this author's *The Etruscans,* 1965.

BLOCH, Raymond. The origins of Rome. London, Thames and Hudson, 1960. 212p., illus., maps. **JG52**

"A revised and expanded version of *Les origines de Rome,* translated by Margaret Shenfield."

JRS XLIX 1959 161 Scullard • JS 1960 18–27 Piganiol • Phoenix XV 1961 184–186 Lenardon

A good introduction to early Roman history. The author examines the ethnology of early Italy and the foundation-legends of Rome. This is followed by a discussion of the archaeological evidence for pre-Etruscan and Etruscan Rome and questions of language, law and religion. In his relation of chronological conclusions to the written tradition of early Rome the author is more orthodox than E. Gjerstad, *Early Rome.*

BLOCH, Raymond. Recherches archéologiques en territoire volsinien de la protohistoire à la civilisation étrusque. Paris, de Boccard, 1972. 236p., illus., fold. maps. **JG53**

REL L 1972 403–405 Chevallier

A comprehensive publication of the excavations conducted by the French School at Rome in the Civita-Capriola complex near Lake Bolsena and previously reported in *Mélanges.*

BOËTHIUS, Axel. Etruscan and early Roman architecture. Rev. by Roger Ling and Tom Rasmussen. New York, Penguin Books, [1978]. **JG54**

The Pelican history of art. Earlier ed. published in 1970 under title: Etruscan and Roman architecture. Ward-Perkins, J. B. joint author.

ACR 1 1971 204–205 MacKendrick • AntJ LI 1971 347–349 Strong • ABull LIV 1972 342–344 Brown • AJA LXXVI 1972 239–240 Brilliant

This is a revised edition of the 1970 book. They are really two separate books, the first by Boëthius concentrating on archaeological description, the second by Ward-Perkins, an analysis of Roman buildings as architecture. Boëthius provides the evidence for construction techniques, building types and plans, etc., in Etruscan Rome to the Gallic invasion of 386–200 B.C. and Hellenized Rome of the mature Republic. Ward-Perkins starts with Augustus and discusses Imperial architecture to the 4th century. The drawings are helpful as are the excellent plates. The book is basic to the study.

CAMPOREALE, Giovannangelo. La collezione Alla Querce. Materiali archeologici orvietani. Firenze, L. S. Olschki, 1970. 211p., illus., 31 plates. **JG55**

Biblioteca di "Studi etruschi," v. 5.

AJA LXXVII 1973 354 Del Chiaro • BVAB XLVII 1972 172–173 von Akkeren

This is the fifth in the *Biblioteca* series begun in 1963 by the Instituto di Studi Etruschi ed Italici at Florence and devoted to various aspects of Etruscology. This volume consists of objects discovered at Orvieto.

COARELLI, Filippo, ed. Etruscan cities. Francesca Boitani, Maria Cataldi, Marinella Pasquinucci; with an introd. by Mario Torelli. 1st American ed. New York, Putnam, 1975. 336p., illus. **JG56**

Translation of *Le città etrusche.*

Caesarodunum IX 1974 C.R. 22 Chevallier • JRS LXVII 1977 181–182 Cornell

Presents a comprehensive synthesis of the finds from a large number of Etruscan sites compiled by expert scholars. The illustrations are superb, including over 300 color plates.

COLONNA DI PAOLO, Elena, and COLONNA G. Le necropoli Rupestri dell' Etruria meridionale. Roma, Consiglio nazionale delle ricerche, 1970. 290p., 467 plates. **JG57**

1. Testo; 2. Tavole.

AJA LXXVI 1972 237–238 Phillips • JRS LXII 1972 201–202 Ridgway

This volume describes the monumental Etruscan tombs at Castel D'Asso near Viterbo. Part One covers historical and topographical aspects of Castel D'Asso from the archaic period through Roman and into medieval times. Part Two presents a complete set of plans, elevations, cross-sections, and photographs of the entire necropolis. An important reference work providing a basis for further study.

CRISTOFANI, Mauro. Le tombe da Monte Michele nel Museo archeologico di Firenze. Firenze, L. S. Olschki, 1969. 78p., illus., 15 plates. **JG58**

Monumenti etruschi, 2: Veio, v. 1.

This series, *Monumenti Etruschi,* is published by the Istituto di Studi Etruschi ed Italici and reports the excavations.

DEL CHIARO, Mario Aldo. Etruscan red-figured vase-painting at Caere. Berkeley, University of

California Press, 1974. xiv, 160p., [24] leaves of plates, illus. **JG59**

AJA LXXX 1976 320–321 DePuma • CW LXX 1976 51–52 Holloway • Phoenix XXX 1976 105–106 Rupp

In 1957, Professor Del Chiaro expanded Beazley's list of 50 Genucilia plates to over 600 in his *The Genucilia Group* in *University of California Publications in Classical Archaeology* (3), 243–372. This volume is a culmination of the author's study of a large number of Etruscan red-figured vases and his attribution of them to Caere.

DENNIS, George. The cities and cemeteries of Etruria. Ed. anastatica. Roma, L'Erma di Bretschneider, 1968. 2 v., illus., maps (3 fold.). **JG60**

Reprint of the 1907 ed. published by J. M. Dent, London and E. P. Dutton, New York.

This early work was written by a young Englishman while he was consul at Civitavecchia and is "the fruit of several tours made in Etruria between the years 1842 and 1847." Many of the antiquities it records have since disappeared. A very accurate description of the ancient sites of Etruria. Though over one hundred years old, these volumes are still useful as a guide.

DUCATI, Pericle. Storia dell'arte etrusca. Firenze, Rinascimento del libro, 1927. 2 v., 284 plates (incl. plans). **JG61**

v. 1. [Testo]—v. 2 [Tavole].
REA 1928 133–138 Grenier
The author also wrote *La scultura étrusca* (1934), *Le problème étrusque* (1937) and *Die etruskische, italo-hellenististische und römische' Malerei* (1941). He examines and describes the artistic character of the Etruscan and Italic peoples who surrounded early Rome, governed its territory, provided its art and artists, and fell under Roman control in the 3rd century B.C.

EMILIOZZI, Adriana. La Collezione Rossi Danielli nel Museo Civico di Viterbo. Roma, Consiglio Nazionale delle Richerche, 1974. 298p., 100 leaves of plates, illus. **JG62**

Musei e collezioni d'Etruria; v. 1. At head of title: Consiglio Nazionale delle Ricerche. Centro di Studio per l'Archeologia Etrusco-Italica.
AC XLVI 1977 364–366 Lambrechts • AJA LXXXI 1977 124 Bonfante
The first volume in the series "Museums and Collections of Etruria." It represents material from the region of Viterbo collected by Luigi Rossi Danielli. The series makes available the material in private collections.

GIGLIOLI, Giulio Quirino. L'arte etrusca. Milano, Fratelli Treves, 1935. 150p., 426 plates. **JG63**

ASNP 1937 189 Arias • BIBR 1936 253–254 de Ruyt • NAnt CCCV 1936 238–240 Pallottino • SE X 1936 479–480 Minto

Remains a valuable text on Etruscan art when used in conjunction with reports of new discoveries.

HANFMANN, George Maxim Anossov. Altetruskische Plastik I.: Die menschliche Gestalt in der Rundplastik bis zum Ausgang der orientalisierenden Kunst. Würzburg, Buchdruckerei Konrad Triltsch, 1936. xii, 135p., plates. **JG64**

CW XXXI 1938 186 Åkerström • JRS 1938 103 Jacobsthal • AJA 1939 168–169 Dohan • PhW 1939 154–158 Lippold
The first thorough examination of the origins and development of Etruscan sculptural style. The author emphasizes the influence of oriental art on Etruscan and criticizes the way in which Greek influence has been overrated. Helpful in establishing the chronology of this period in Italy.

HANFMANN, George Maxim Anossov. Etruskische Plastik. Stuttgart, H. E. Günther, [1956]. 16p., 48 plates. **JG65**

AJA LXII 1958 343–345 Richardson
A brief analysis of Etruscan art accompanied by 56 superb photographs of statues and reliefs.

HENCKEN, Hugh O'Neill. Tarquinia, Villanovans, and early Etruscans. Cambridge, Mass., Peabody Museum, 1968. 2 v., (xxxi, 719p.), 497 illus. **JG66**

Antiquity XLIV 1970 80–81 Ward-Perkins • Archaeology XXIII 1970 363–364 Thomas • JRS LX 1970 238–240 Close-Brooks
Excavations in the cemeteries of Tarquinia have produced valuable evidence for Villanovan and Etruscan studies. These volumes are the complete publication of the corpus of graves of Tarquinia. Basic reference material. A summary of this large work was also published as *Tarquinia, Villanovans, and early Etruscans*, New York, Praeger, 1968: 248p.

HUS, Alain. Les bronzes étrusques. Bruxelles, Latomus, 1975. 164p., [38] leaves of plates, illus. **JG67**

Collection Latomus; v. 139.
BAGB 1975 303–306 Adam • CR XXVII 1977 84–85 Macnamara • JRS LXVII 1977 216–217 Haynes
This is a general study of the history of Etruscan bronze work. The Etruscans used bronze a great deal in their art work, in everything from statues and chariots to household items and jewelry. There are chapters on the techniques of bronze working and the various types of objects usually made of bronze, followed by the main body of the work on artistic styles. The book follows the organization of Charbonneaux's, *Les Bronzes grecs*. It is well illustrated, but there is no index and it fails in many instances to acknowledge the work of other scholars in the field. The author's *Les Siècles d'or de l'histoire étrusque* (reviewed CR XXVIII 1978 112–113, Ridgway) is poor in illustration and text.

HUS, Alain. Vulci étrusque et étrusque-romaine. Paris, Klincksieck, 1971. 226p., illus.   **JG68**

AJA LXXVII 1973 103–104 Del Chiaro • JRS LXIII 1973 283–284 Ridgway
This volume describes the Etruscan architecture, painting, sculpture, pottery, bronzes and the history of the ancient city of Vulci on the coastal borderland of Etruria and Latium. The author incorporates all new archaeological discoveries on the Archaic, Classical and Etrusco-Roman periods and the art that characterized them. An excellent and readable introduction to the history and art of this Etruscan city. F. R. Sierra Ridgway reviews it negatively: "A few lines added here and there after 1956, and a few new items inserted into the bibliography add up to precisely nothing in the way of a modern critical approach to the problems involved."

KRAUSKOPF, Ingrid. Der thebanische Sagenkreis und andere griechische Sagen in der etruskischen Kunst. Mainz am Rhein, P. von Zabern [1974]. 120p., illus., 24 plates.   **JG69**

Schriften zur antiken Mythologie, v. 2.
AJA LXXIX 1975 385 Small • JHS XCVII 1977 227 Prag • RA 1977 334 Hus
Studies the Etruscan use of Greek mythology from its beginnings in the orientalizing period through the Hellenistic era. The subject is divided into two sections; archaic representations of Greek myths and the Theban Cycle in Etruscan art, from the 5th through the 2nd century B.C. Because of the relatively few extant specimens from the earlier period, the author can make a very thorough study of them and believes the Etruscans not only knew the Greek texts but created their own types from them. Her case for the Etruscans' knowledge of Greek myths in the archaic period after 550 B.C. is better shown. The second section of the book is a discussion of Etruscan choice of subject and use of Greek models in later periods.

MANSUELLI, Guido Archille. The art of Etruria and early Rome. Trans. by C. E. Ellis. New York, Crown Publishers, [1965]. 255p.   **JG70**

Art of the world; the historical, sociological, and religious backgrounds.
RSC XIV 1966 275–276 d'Agostino • CR XVII 1967 231–232 Strong • JRS LVII 1967 243–244 Richardson
The work of this great scholar suffers in a very poor translation. Major monuments are presented along with a chronology of historical events in the Mediterranean from 800–20 B.C. While some of the color reproductions are good and the bibliography and map very useful, the book has little value for the student because of the incomprehensible nature of the text.

MATT, Leonard von. The art of the Etruscans. [Text by] Mario Moretti [and] Guglielmo Maetzke. [Translated from the Italian MS. by Peggy Martin]. Foreword by Donald Strong. London, Thames & Hudson, 1970. 253p., illus., 212 plates, map.   **JG71**

Translation of *Terra e arte degli Etruschi.*
TLS LXX 1971 129
Primarily a picture book it is a very beautifully illustrated treatment of the history of Etruscan art and architecture, more general than academic. Eleven Etruscan centers are examined briefly with illustrations of each center. The superb photographs are by von Matt.

MORETTI, Mario. New monuments of Etruscan painting. Foreword by Massimo Pallottino. English translation by Dawson Kiang. University Park, Pennsylvania State University Press, 1970. xxxvii, 359p., illus., maps, plans.   **JG72**

Series of monographs in archaeology. Etruscan painting, v. 1. Translation of *Nuovi monumenti della pittura etrusca.*
JRS LVIII 1968 288 Strong • Gnomon XLI 1969 806–811 von Vacano • GGA CCXXI 1969 211–216 Dohrn
The book consists mainly of photographs with brief descriptions of the newly discovered tombs near Tarquinia. It treats 37 painted tombs discovered since 1958. In the introduction, the author gives a brief history of the excavation and introductory essays include details of technique and composition. The photographs are excellent.

PALLOTTINO, Massimo. Art of the Etruscans. New York, Vanguard Press, [1955]. 154p., illus., 126 photos, map.   **JG73**

The survival of Etruscan painting is attributable to the nature of the monuments on which they appear. For the most part they are funerary monuments and consist mainly of sunk tombs dug into the rock with painted walls. There are a great many of these tombs and the lovely reproductions of the sepulchral art of Etruria in this book are testimony to the high standard to which this art form was developed. The text examines the content of the art and the artistic value of the paintings from their beginnings to the Hellenistic period.

PALLOTTINO,   Massimo. Civiltà   artistica etrusco-italica. [Firenze], Sansoni, [1972]. 130p., illus., 38 plates.   **JG74**

"Ristampa con aggiornamenti."
AJA LXXVII 1973 102–103 Gantz • JRS LXIII 1973 313 Ridgway
A revised version of the author's article *Etruscoitalici centri e tradizioni* in *Enciclopedia Universale dell'arte.* This book is a good introduction to Etrusco—Italic art of which Etruscan art forms only a part. The author summarizes two generations' work in Italian archaeology and shows the artistic environment, partly Hellenized, out of which Roman art and culture developed.

PALLOTTINO,   Massimo. Etruscan   painting. Translated by M. E. Stanley and Stuart Gilbert. Geneva, Skira, [1952]. 138p., illus., map.
JG75

JRS XLIII 1953 190 Brown • LEC XXI 1953 131–132 Delande • BO XII 1955 210–217 van Essen

Presents Etruscan mural paintings, in color. The reproductions are moderately good. The text is brief but scholarly and includes an introduction on basic facts about the Etruscan tombs followed by sections on: the Primitives; Masters of the Severe Style; Classical Influences; and Painting and the Hellenistic Period.

PALLOTTINO, Massimo. The Etruscans. Translated by J. Cremona. Edited by David Ridgway. Rev. and enl. [Harmondsworth, Middlesex], Penguin Books, 1978. 316p., illus. **JG76**

Translation of *Etruscologia*.

SE XXXI 1963 285–289 Mansuelli • JRS LXVII 1977 181–182 Cornell

In his *Etruscologia* written in 1942 the author combined literary, archaeological and linguistic evidence in a study of Etruscan society. This new English edition incorporates the additional evidence resulting from recent excavations, epigraphic discoveries and a re-interpretation of the literary sources. Professor Pallottino's work is fundamental to the study of the Etruscans. This volume is edited by David Ridgway who adds a new selection of plates, a preface and a very full critical bibliography.

PALLOTTINO, Massimo. Gli Etruschi. 2 ed. riveduta. Roma, Colombo, 1940. 295p. **JG77**

Aevum 1940 166–167 Pighi • RSI 1940 259–262 Tullis • Klio XVII 1942 316 Matz • JRS XXXVI 1946 198–199 Momigliano

The author is a leading expert on the subject of Etruscan life and art. The book deals with the political and social history of the Etruscans.

POULSEN, Frederik. Etruscan tomb paintings; Their subjects and significance. Translated by Ingeborg Andersen. Rome, L'Erma di Bretschneider, 1970. x, 63p., illus. **JG78**

Reprint of 1922 ed.

This brief study is based upon investigations made in Etruscan tombs at Conneto and Chiusi. It examines the content of the paintings and the main lines of historical development. The author also compares the original wall-paintings with the facsimiles and drawings made from them in the NY Carlsberg Glyptotek in the Helbig Museum. The book is illustrated with black-and-white photographs.

RIIS, Poul Jørgen. An introduction to Etruscan art. Copenhagen, Munksgaard, 1953. 144p., illus. **JG79**

JRS XLIV 1954 149 Brown • Latomus XIII 1954 305–306 Renard • BO XII 1955 144–147 Byvanck

A revised version of the original Danish *Den etruskiske Kunst* (1948). It consists of ten essays on various aspects of Etruscan art including sculpture, painting and architecture. A readable account that reports the material remains accurately.

RIIS, Poul Jørgen. Tyrrhenika: An archaeological study of the Etruscan sculpture in the archaic and classical periods. Copenhagen, E. Munksgaard, 1941. xvi, 216p., 24 leaves of plates, illus., map. **JG80**

Originally presented as the author's thesis, Copenhagen, 1939.

Gnomon 1941 461–468 Poulsen • PhW 1942 537–548 Lippold • GGA 1942 97–105 Messerschmidt • JHS LXV 1945 123 Lamb • JRS XXVIII 1948 132–137 Hanfmann

Fundamental to the study of Etruscan sculpture of the archaic and classical periods. The arrangement is topographical and divided into the individual schools of art, southern central and northern Etruscan. Terracottas are examined along with works in stone and bronze. Questions of chronology are discussed as well as influences, including the Greek, that shaped Etruscan art. The book does not contain a great deal of illustration and should be used in conjunction with well-illustrated publications.

SCULLARD, Howard Hayes. The Etruscan cities and Rome. Ithaca, N.Y., Cornell University Press, [1967]. 320p., illus., maps. **JG81**

HT XVII 1967 864–865 Birley • REL XLV 1967 578 Hus • CR LXXXII 1968 211–213 McDonald

Examines the cultural, artistic, social and economic life of the Etruscan cities in their historical and topographical setting. Each of the cities is described and many of the finds are illustrated in excellent black and white photographs. A clear concise introduction to Etruria that includes a section on the literary sources. There are sketch plans of the sites at Tarquinii, Caere, Veii, Vulci, Volsinii, Talerii, Rusellae, Vetulonia, Populonia, Volaterrae, Perusia, Fuesulae, Manzabotto, and also some air photographs. Although written for the historian, this book is invaluable for an understanding of Etruscan archaeology.

SHOE, Lucy Taxis. Etruscan and Republican Roman mouldings. [Rome], American Academy in Rome, 1965. 232p., lxxvi, illus. **JG82**

Memoirs of the American Academy in Rome, v. 28.

AJA LXX 1966 300–301 Phillips • Phoenix XX 1966 355 Russell • REL XLIV 1966 559 Heurgon

The author also wrote *Profiles of Greek Mouldings* (1936) and *Profiles of Western Greek Mouldings* (1952). A thorough scholarly analysis of Etruscan architecture and Roman Republican architecture. An essential work for the study.

STRÖM, Ingrid. Problems concerning the origin and early development of the Etruscan Orientalizing Style. Odense, Odense Universitetsforlag, 1971. 2 v., 318p., 86 plates, illus. **JG83**

[1] Text.–[2] Illustrations.

Arch Class XXIV 1972 157–164 Guzzo • AJA LXXVII 1973 100–102 Warren

The author attempts to establish a chronology for

the Etruscan Orientalizing style. It is an excellent study of Etruscan metalwork presenting in detail the bronze shields, *repoussé* and granulated goldwork and other relief metalwork and *comparanda*. The illustrations are superb and bound separately.

Pompeii and Herculaneum

ANDREAE, Bernard and KYRIELEIS, Helmut, eds. Neue Forschungen in Pompeji und den anderen vom Vesuvausbruch 79 n. Chr. verschütteten Städten. Recklinghausen, Bongers, 1975. 340p., illus.   **JG84**

Selected papers from a meeting organized by the Deutsches Archäologisches Institut and the Gemeinnhutziger Verein Villa Hügel.

Arctos IX 1975 137–138 Kajanto • Gymnasium LXXXIII 1976 445–447 Sichtermann • BJ CLXXVI 1976 467–470 Gabelmann • JRS LXVIII 1978 217–219 Ling

The papers of a colloquium on Pompeii in conjunction with an exhibition at Essen. The papers are excellent accounts of recent excavation work by various countries.

BEYEN, Hendrik Gerard. Die pompejanische Wanddekoration vom zweiten bis zum vierten Stil. Haag, M. Nijhoff, 1938–1960. 2 v.   **JG85**

AC 1939 326–331 Marrou • Gnomon XXXIV 1962 82–86 Herbig • Arch Class. XIV 1962 298–305 Gallina

Volume 1 analyzes Phase 1 of the second style in a very detailed examination that deals mainly with three houses—the Villa of the Mysteries, the Villa of Tannius Sinistor at Boscoreale, and the House of the Labyrinth. Volume II deals with the rest of this Style. The author's aim is to assimilate the paintings in the latter three "Pompeiian Styles" to Roman cultural history of the first centuries B.C. and A.D. The illustrations are inadequate and poor compared to the scholarly text which provides a superb repertory of the decorative motives of the period.

BRION, Marcel. Pompeii and Herculaneum: The glory and the grief. Translated by John Rosenberg. London, Elek, 1960. 240p., illus., maps, plans.   **JG86**

CW LIV 1961 132 Wedeck • JRS LI 1961 279 Fredericksen

An excellent presentation in pictures and text of the twin cities that were so completely overwhelmed by the ancient volcanic eruption. The author supports his text with excerpts from the primary source, Pliny's letter to Tacitus. He also used other literary, artistic and epigraphical material in discussing the cultural life and achievements of the people. The illustrations are impressive and include figurines, mosaics, wall paintings, domestic vessels, jewelry, etc.

CARRINGTON, Roger Clifford. Pompeii. Oxford, Clarendon Press, 1936. ix, 197p., illus. (incl. maps), plates, fold. plan.   **JG87**

CR 1937 76 Richmond • Antiquity 1937 XI 110–111 Richmond • LEC 1937 319 de Ruyt

A general scholarly introduction to the excavations at Pompeii. The author describes the life and art of Pompeii from its beginnings to its burial under the ashes of Vesuvius. A suggested itinerary through the ruins is included in an appendix.

CORTI, Egon Caesar, Conte. The destruction and resurrection of Pompeii and Herculaneum. London, Theodore Brun, 1951. x, 220p., plates.   **JG88**

Translation of *Untergang und auferstehung von Pompeii und Herculaneum.*

Antiquity XXV 1951 168 Carrington • Latomus X 1951 265 Renard

A fascinating account of the history of Pompeii and Herculaneum and of the excavations of these two sites. The author reconstructs the social and artistic life of the towns before the eruption and describes the effects of the calamity that befell the two places. From the eighteenth century excavators to those of modern times the author describes the finds and illustrates them with good black and white photographs.

CURTIUS, Ludwig. Die Wandmalerei Pompejis; Eine Einführung in ihr Verständnis. Darmstadt; Wissenschaftliche Buchgesellschaft, 1960. ix, 472p., 12 leaves of plates, illus.   **JG89**

"Unveränderter fotomechanischer Nachdruck der l. Auflage 1929."

GGA 1930 97–121 Koepp • Historia 1930 328–330 Ducati • DLZ 1938 163–167 Wirth

A reprint of the 1929 edition. Pages 433–472 are a reprint of an article by Walter Klinbert on Pompeian wall decoration (*MdAl*, Röm. abteil., 64, 1957).

ENGELMANN, W. New guide to Pompeii. Leipzig, Engelmann, 1925. vii, 240p., 140 fig.   **JG90**

AJA 1926 484 McK. Elderkin • AAL 1926 1–2 Droop • JRS 1925 139 • CW XX 212 van Buren

An early guide to the excavations in Pompeii written in German and English. Well written with photographs, some from the books of Mau and Ippel.

GRANT, Michael. Cities of Vesuvius: Pompeii and Herculaneum. London, Weidenfeld & Nicholson, 1971; New York, Penguin Books, 1976. 240p., illus., maps, plans.   **JG91**

ACR II 1972 218 McKay • Latomus XXXIII 1974 483 Hanton

A lively account of the history of Pompeii, Herculaneum, and Stabiae and of the eruptions of Vesuvius. From archaeological remains the author reconstructs the artistic and political life of these towns in antiquity. The illustrations are in black and white and color. An excellent guide to the excavations for the intelligent visitor.

HELBIG, Wolfgang. Wandgemälde der vom Vesuv verschütteten städte Campaniens. Nebst einer abhandlung über die antiken wandmalereien in technischer beziehung, von Otto Donner. Leipzig, Breitkopf und Härtel, 1868. xvii, (1), cxxvii, (5), 500p., 3 plates, atlas of 23 plates.   **JG92**

KRAUS, Theodor and MATT, L. von. Pompeii and Herculaneum: The living cities of the dead. Translated by Robert Erich Wolf. New York, H. N. Abrams, 1975. 230p., 76 plates, illus.   **JG93**

Translation of *Pompeii und Herculaneum.*
JSAH XXXVI 1977 38–39 Richardson
The illustrations reproduce in exquisite detail the finds from the excavations in Pompeii and Herculaneum. The text is a scholarly and accurate description of the finds but it is overshadowed by the extraordinary illustrations by Von Matt which vividly recreate the artistic and social life of these two towns.

LA ROCCA, Eugenio. Guida archeologica di Pompei; coordinamento di Filippo Coarelli; fotografie di Mauro Puccireli. 1st ed. [Milano], A. Mondadori, 1976. 358p., illus.   **JG94**

Caesarodunum XII 1977 C.R. 77 Chevallier • JRS LXVIII 1978 217–219 Ling
An archaeological guide to Pompeii, with descriptions of recent discoveries. The book consists of a history of Pompeii and a tour of the various sites describing aspects of architecture and interior decoration.

LEHMANN, Phyllis Lourene (Williams). Roman wall paintings from Boscoreale in the Metropolitan Museum of Art. With an appendix by Herbert Bloch. Cambridge, Mass., Archaeological Institute of America, 1953. xv, 230p., illus., 42 plates.   **JG95**

ABull XXXVI 1954 303–304 Swindler
The Villa at Boscoreale near Pompeii known as Publius Tannius Sinistor's dwelling was built sometime after 50 B.C. This work of meticulous scholarship presents the paintings of the Villa, now scattered in museums of Europe and America. The text is well-written and consists of an examination of the style and subject matter of the paintings. A useful contribution to our knowledge of ancient painting, specifically the second style.

MAIURI, Amedeo. La casa del Menandro e il suo tesoro di argenteria. [Roma], La Libreria dello stato, [1933]. 2p., ix–xi, 508p., 1, illus., atlas, 2 fold. plans.   **JG96**

JRS XXIV 1934 236–239 Toynbee
A companion volume to the author's *La Villa dei Misteri,* it reports the extraordinary silver-treasure and the wall-paintings of the Casa del Menandro. The author examines these finds in relation to their provenance and setting and recreates the lives of their owners.

MAIURI, Amedeo. Ercolano; i nuovi scavi. [Roma], Istituto poligrafico dello Stato 1958– . 2 v., illus., maps, plates.   **JG97**

Reports the excavations of Herculaneum from 1927 to 1958. The author had a long career as superintendent of antiquities of Campania and the surrounding areas, and he published extensively on all aspects of the excavations in Pompeii and Herculaneum. For a bibliography of his work see P. Romanelli, *Amedeo Maiuri (1888–1963),* Cava dei Tirreni, 1968, 69p. These volumes cover the topography of Herculaneum and reports on the public and private buildings discovered. The second volume describes wall-decoration, the pavements, the woodwork and various other art forms. The principal inscriptions are contained in an appendix. A biography of Maiuri with photographs of various stages of the excavations was published in 1974 by Giuseppe Maggi (*Archeologia magica di Amedeo Maiuri*). For a short treatment of the excavations see *Ercolano Pompei e stili pompeiani* by this author in *Enciclopedia dell'ante antica classica e orientale* (1968–).

MAIURI, Amedeo. Pompeii. Translated by V. Priestley. Fourth edition. Roma, Libreria dello stato, 1949. 159p., illus.   **JG98**

Guide-books to museums and monuments in Italy, no. 3. At head of title: ministero della pubblica instruzione.

MAIURI, Amedeo. Pompeii; Aquarelles de Louis Bazzani. Paris, Éditions Alpina, [1930]. 126p., [13] leaves of plates, illus.   **JG99**

JRS XXI 1931 152–153 Ashby
An early work of this eminent archaeologist, the book is a guide to the town. It includes directions on getting to Pompeii, a description of the remains, short introductions on the building materials, wall-decoration, the Pompeian house, population, and inscriptions. Throughout his career as superintendent of antiquities, the author continued the official publication of the excavations at Pompeii in such volumes as *Introduzione allo studio di Pompeii* (1949), *L'Ultima fase edilizia di Pompeii* (1942) and *Pompeii ed Ercolano* (1959). These excavations are among the most carefully done in Italy and of great importance for our knowledge of the daily life of ancient Rome.

MAIURI, Amedeo. Pompeii ed Ercolano, fra case e abitani. Milan, Martello, 1959. 387p., illus.   **JG100**

Latomus XX 1961 197 • AC III 1951 116–117 Pallottino
The author also produced superbly illustrated volumes on the Villa of the Mysteries (1931) and the House of Menander (1933). He has a gift for evoking the life that characterized the ancient ruins without resort to fantasy or excessively picturesque embellishment.

MAIURI, Amedeo. Pompeii: The new excavations, the "Villa de Misteri," the Antiquarium. Translated by V. Priestley. 8th ed. Roma, Istituto poligrafico dello stato, 1956. 182p., illus.   **JG101**

Guide-books to the museums and monuments of Italy. v. 3. At head of title: Ministero della pubblica instruzione.

MAIURI, Amedeo. Roman painting. Trans. by Stuart Gilbert. [Geneva], Skira, [1953]. 153p., illus.   **JG102**

AC V 1953 275–276 Pallattino • Gnomon XXVI 1954 145–147 Curtius • AJA LX 1956 74–78 Rumpf
The eruption of Vesuvius has bequeathed to us a wealth of paintings buried beneath the ashes. Since no Greek painting survives, the art of Pompeii is our only example of the pictorial style of late Hellenism along with the new styles being developed by the craftsmen of Latium and Campania. The copious excellent reproductions of Pompeian and other Roman art centers demonstrate the beauty of ancient Italian painting. The text examines the history of painting from its beginnings up to 79 A.D., excluding Etruscan which is covered separately in Massimo Pallottino's *The Great Centuries of Etruscan Painting.*

MAIURI, Amedeo. Saggi di varia antichità. Venise, ed. Neri Pozza, 1954. 459p.   **JG103**

REL XXXII 1954 469–470 Bloch • Archaeology VIII 1955 215 Van Buren • La Nuova Antologia XC 1955 567–568 Becatti
Throughout his long career as archaeologist the author reported his work in various scientific journals. This book is a selection of these essays that review his work at Cumae, Pompeii, and Herculaneum. It covers the period from the Stone Age to Christianity. Another miscellaneous collection of the author's writings is *Dall'Egeo al Tirreno* (1962).

MAIURI, Amedeo. La villa dei Misteri. [2 rev. ed.] Roma, La Libreria dello Stato, 1947, 1931. 260p., illus., 18 leaves of plates.   **JG104**

JRS XXIV 1934 236–239 Toynbee
Originally published in 1931 with a third edition in 1960. Reproductions of the Graeco-Roman mural painting and decoration of the Villa of the Mysteries in Pompeii are inlaid in cardboard mats. The architectural and artistic aspects of the Villa of the Mysteries are studied together. The author interprets the Great Fresco, the famous painting from which the Villa gets its name. This was the first publication in which the frescoes were reproduced in color.

SCHEFOLD, Karl. La peinture pompéienne; Essai sur l'évolution de sa signification. Éd. revue et augm. Traduction de J.-M. Croisille. Bruxelles, Latomus, 1972. 282p., 56 plates.   **JG105**

REA LXXVIII–LXXIX 1976–1977 312–315 David • JRS LXIII 1973 279 Liversidge • RBPh LIII 1975 80–82 Fouchers • Dacia XVII 1973 452–454 Bordenache
A revised and expanded version of the author's *Pompejanische Malerei: Sinn und Ideengeschichte* (1952). The book examines the indebtedness of Roman wall-painters to their predecessors and describes their own originality. Choice of subjects is analyzed and classified under landscapes, myths, heroes, etc. A standard work on the subject.

SCHEFOLD, Karl. Vergessenes Pompeji; unveröffentliche Bilder römischer Wanddekorationen in geschichtlicher Folge. Bern, Francke, Verlag, 1962. 218p., 180 plates.   **JG106**

Schriften der Schweizerischen Geisteswissenschaftlichen Gesellschaft 4.
Archeologia XVI 1965 213–214 Nowicka • JRS LIX 1964 225–226 Robertson • AJA LXVIII 1964 317–318 Brown
A list of less well-known Pompeiian wall paintings, including a number now lost, arranged chronologically to form a history of mural decoration in the first centuries B.C. and A.D. The author's division of styles follows that of Mau, into four, chronologically following each other. Included in the illustrations are old drawings and photographs of walls, now destroyed. A useful work by an expert on the qualities of the different styles of Roman wall-painting.

SCHEFOLD, Karl. Die Wände Pompejis; Topographisches Verzeichnis der Bildmotiv. Berlin, de Gruyter, 1957. xv, 378p.   **JG107**

At head of title: Deutsches Archäologisches Institut.
DLZ LXXX 1959 48–50 von Lucken • AJA LXIII 1959 312 Lehmann • Helmantica XI 1960 189 Jimenez Delgado
This is a complete topographical survey of the Pompeian paintings known up to 1957. An indispensable instrument for Pompeian studies.

SPINAZZOLA, Vittorio. Pompeii alla luce degli scavi nuovi di Via dell'Abbondanza (anni 1910–1923). Roma, Libreria dello Stato, 1953. 2 v. (1110p.), illus., maps, plates.   **JG108**

AJA LVII 1953 298–300 van Buren • Gott Gel Anz Jahrg CCX 1956 169–180 Herbig
Definitive publication of the *Scavi Nuovi* prepared by an outstanding excavator and scholar. Presents aspects of the urban life of Pompeii in meticulous detail: architecture, art, handicrafts, streets, shrines, paintings, etc. Records the story of the excavation and the methods employed by Spinazzola for reconstructing and preserving the remains. Of primary importance for the study.

VAN BUREN, Albert William. A companion to Pompeian Studies. Rome, printed for the American Academy in Rome, 1927. 30p.   **JG109**

At head of title: American Academy in Rome.
JRS XXIII 1933 249–250 Carrington
Covers the various aspects of the city and its life. Ancient literary and epigraphical evidence is cited. Contains a full bibliography up to the date of publication.

VAN DER POEL, Halstead. Corpus topographicum Pompeianum. Roma, Edizioni dell'Elefante, 1977– . maps.   **JG110**

Published for the University of Texas at Austin. Pt. 4 published in 1977.—pt. 4. Van der Poel, H. B. Bibliography.

A very complete bibliography to works that cover Pompeii. It includes books, journals, articles, inscriptions, collections of paintings, manuscripts, etc. Many of the works cited date from the eighteenth and nineteenth centuries. Printed in a limited edition of 2,000 copies.

Architecture and Construction

AMY, R., DUVAL, P. M., and FORMIGÉ, J. L'Arc d'Orange. Paris, 1962. 158p. **JG111**

15th Supplement to Gallia.

AJA LXVIII 1964 215–216 Williams • Ant C XXXIII 1964 291–292 De Laet • RA II 1963 92–96 Lautien

Definitive publication of the triumphal arch at Orange, it presents in detail the architecture, sculptural decoration and dedication of the arch. The text is illustrated with diagrams, profile drawings, and photographs.

ANDERSON, William James, and SPIERS, Richard Phené. The architecture of ancient Rome, an account of its historic development, being the second part of *The Architecture of Greece and Rome*. Rev. and rewritten by Thomas Ashby. London, Batsford, 1927; Freeport, N.Y., Books for Libraries Press, [1971]. xiii, 202p., illus. **JG112**

Traces the development of ancient Roman architecture from its beginnings. The first chapter examines architecture in Etruria and elsewhere in Italy to the end of the third century B.C. Having established that the architectural forms and decorations of the earliest temples, known to us in Rome itself, are Etruscan or rather Italic, the book outlines the development of Roman architecture from these origins. Subjects covered include, the materials and modes of construction, the Forums of Rome, temples, basilicas and theatres, arches of triumph, aqueducts, palaces and houses and finally the private life of the Romans. The text is accompanied by excellent photographs, drawings, maps, a bibliography, and a glossary still valuable.

AURIGEMMA, Salvatore. Villa Adriana. Roma, Istituto Poligrafico dello Stato, Libreria dello Stato, [1962]. 222p., [19] leaves of plates, 241 illus. **JG113**

WH XXII 1965 130 Zucker • JRS LIII 1963 230–231 Robertson

A meticulous examination of Hadrian's Villa at Tivoli, including the little city and countryside where it is located. The author describes the development of the Villa, the periods of construction, the identification of its various areas and buildings. The main part of the book is an illustrated tour of all parts of the Villa. It includes aerial photographs, plans and reconstructions, photographs of the remains, along with reproduced engravings by Piranesi and Rossini. A beautiful, well produced, and scholarly work.

There is an English translation, *Hadrian's Villa*, revised by A. W. van Buren, 1970.

BECATTI, Giovanni. La colonna cochlide istoriata; Problemi storici, iconografici stilistici. Roma, L'Erma di Bretschneider, 1960. 402p., 83 plates. **JG114**

Studi e materiali del Museo dell'Impero romano, no. 6.

Gnomon XXXIV 1962 290–295 Picard • AJA LXV 1961 409–412 Bieber • REByz XX 1962 269–271 Janin

The author accepts the view that the spiral columns imitate a roll or rotulus which is the form of the ancient book, wound in a spiral round the shaft of the column. The book examines the four columns with historical reliefs that are wound around the column: Trajan, Marcus Aurelius, Theodosius, and Arcadius. A major contribution to the study of later imperial art.

BERTOLDI, Maria E. Richerche sulla decorazione architettonica del Foro Traiano. Roma, L'Erma di Bretschneider, 1962. 34p. **JG115**

(Seminario di Archeologia e Storia dell'Arte greca e romana del l'Università di Roma, Studi Miscella 111.)

RBPh XLII 1964 1494–1495 Balty

The third in a series devoted to the iconography in the art of late antiquity especially to the *Ilias Ambrosiana*. This volume discusses the architectural decoration of the Forum of Trajan. There is a history of the Forum, an account of works about it, and of its fate in post-Classical times. Architectural decorative fragments and ornamental elements are examined, accompanied by many fine illustrations.

BLAKE, Marion Elizabeth. Ancient Roman construction in Italy from the prehistoric period to Augustus. A chronological study based in part upon the material accumulated by Esther Boise Van Deman. Washington, 1947, New York, Kraus Reprint, 1968. xxii, 421p., illus. **JG116**

ABull XXXIII 1951 133–139 Boëthius • Erasmus III 1950 326–329 Gjerstad • RA XXXIX 1952 222–223 Picard

This well-documented, scholarly work is a study of the materials and methods of building construction in Rome and the surrounding areas. It is the first of three such studies by the author in which she traces the development of various materials in Roman construction as a basis for establishing the chronology of the monuments. The book examines development in stone wall construction, sun-dried and semi-baked bricks, brick and tile construction, mortar and finally concrete. The author describes the acquisition of materials from outside the Empire, for example, rare marbles. Based on material collected by Dr. Van Deman, this is an exhaustive analysis with abundant annotations and references.

BLAKE, Marion Elizabeth. Roman construction in Italy from Tiberius through the Flavians. Washington, Carnegie Institution of Washington, 1959; New York, Kraus Reprint, 1968. xvii, 195p., 31 plates. **JG117**

AJA LXV 1961 327–329 Ward-Perkins • Latomus XX 1961 952–954 Balty

Succeeds the author's *Ancient Roman Construction in Italy from the Prehistoric Period to Augustus,* and covers the period A.D. 14 to A.D. 96. Primarily concerned with Roman buildings, the book examines the role and practices of the building contractor. It is an amazing work of analysis, in which every detail of the evidence is examined and recorded. Very valuable for the working archaeologist.

BLAKE, Marion Elizabeth, and BISHOP, Doris T., eds. Roman construction in Italy from Nerva through the Antonines. Philadelphia, American Philosophical Society, 1973. xix, 328, [44]p., illus. **JG118**

Memoirs of the American Philosophical Society, v. 96.

Gnomon XLVIII 1976 519–522 Ward-Perkins • JRS LXV 1975 213–214 Rickman • AHR LXXIX 1974 120–121 Hammond

This final volume in the series was completed by Doris Taylor Bishop and David Bishop following the death of Marion Blake. The first part includes the public buildings of Rome of the periods of Trajan, Hadrian, and the Antonines and an account of private construction between A.D. 98 and 192. A second part covers the Trajanic, the Hadrianic, and the Antonine architecture of Ostia, and a third deals with imperial estates, public monuments, engineering works and private buildings in "Italy away from Rome." The high scholarly standards and helpful format of the first two volumes are continued in this one.

BOËTHIUS, Axel. The golden house of Nero; Some aspects of Roman architecture. Ann Arbor, University of Michigan Press, [1960]. 195p., illus. **JG119**

Jerome lectures, 5th ser.

CR XII 1962 292–294 Toynbee • Gnomon XXXIV 1962 295–299 Fredericksen • RA 1965 231–232 Picard

A series of revised lectures by the author. The book is beautifully illustrated and highly readable, making it an excellent introduction to Roman architecture of the Imperial Age. The first chapter examines the beginnings of Roman architecture under Etruscan influence. This is followed by a chapter on the Hellenized Italic town and its Legacy to Imperial Rome. The third chapter, on the golden House of Nero, is a detailed description and analysis of the Domus Aurea. The book concludes with a chapter on the domestic architecture of the Imperial Age, and its importance for medieval town building.

BOËTHIUS, Axel. Roman architecture from its classicistic to its late imperial phase. Göteborg, Elanders boktrychkeri aktiebolag, 1941. 33p., illus. **JG120**

AJA 1942 141–142 Müller • DLZ 1943 644–647 Lippold • PhW 1943 70–74 Riemann

A brief description of the characteristics of late Impe-

rial architecture, including its classic tradition. In his analysis, the author includes sculpture, and illustrates the trends and ideas in the writings of the ancients.

BONTEMPELLI, Massimo, and BARTOLI, A. I Monumenti Antichi di Roma nei Disegni degli Uffizi di Firenze. Florence, Fratelli Alinari, 1914–1924. 5 vols. **JG121**

First four volumes by Bontempelli; last vol. by Bartoli.

JRS XIII 1923 203–204 Ashby

An impressive collection, in five volumes, of the architectural drawings of Rome contained in the Uffizi in Florence. Each volume consists of 100 reproductions of the drawings and one volume of text. These Renaissance drawings have been an invaluable aid in the study of Roman archaeology and topography.

BRILLIANT, Richard. The arch of Septimus Severus in the Roman forum. Rome, American Academy in Rome, 1967. 271p., illus. **JG122**

American Academy in Rome. Memoirs, v. XXIX.

AJA LXXII 1968 295–296 Vermeule • CJ LXIII 1968 329–330 Benario • CR XVIII 1968 230–231 Toynbee • Phoenix XXII 1968 171–173 Russell

A detailed and very complete study of the arch of Septimus Severus. The first part studies the architecture, ornament and materials of construction. In analyzing the rich sculptured decoration, Brilliant uses the sixteenth century engravings and drawings to avoid exclusive reliance on the blurred photographs of the grimy blobs that survive. In Part Two, he interprets the figures that adorn the keystones, spandrels, triumphal frieze, and pedestals. The arch's visible testimony to the Victoria Panthica was meant to support the legitimacy of the Dynasty. Part Three relates each of the four great relief panels above the side arches to a particular city that formed the focus of four important episodes in the Parthian Wars of A.D. 195–199. The book concludes with a brief history of the subsequent fate of the arch. A very thorough study.

BROWN, Frank E. Roman architecture. New York, George Braziller, [1961, 1971]. 125p., illus. **JG123**

JRS LV 1965 288–289 Eames • Gnomon XXXVIII 1966 611–619 Riemann

An essay on the historical and social circumstances in which Roman art developed from prehistory to Justinian. The plates are captioned with name, site and date. A select bibliography is included.

CALZA, Guido. La necropoli del Porto di Roma nell'isola Sacra. [Roma], La Libreria dello stato, 1940. 389p., illus., plates, fold. map, fold plan. **JG124**

At head of title: R. Instituto di archeologia e storia dell'arte.

CPh 1941 67–69 Van Buren • JRS XXXI 1941 207–209 Toynbee • RFIC 1941 70–75 Becatti • AJA XLVIII 1944 213–218 Block

A report on the finds at the Necropolis of Portus Traiani, at Isola Sacra. This extraordinary excavation provides a great deal of information on the society of Imperial Rome. Paintings, mosaics and sculptures of the Hadrianic, Antonine and Severan periods are all included, along with architecture and inscriptions. A great contribution to Roman archaeology.

CALZA, Guido. Ostia: Historical guide to the monuments. Translated by R. Weeden-Cooke. Milan, Bestetti e Tumminelli, 1926. xiii, 1p., 190p., illus, map, plans. **JG125**

CW XX 213 Van Buren • JRS XVI 1926 133 Van Buren
The author directed the excavation at Ostia for many years and this is a summary of the results. An excellent introduction to the maritime empire of Rome, written in clear concise prose. The principal chapters are devoted to the history of Ostia, the life, the topography, the architecture and decoration, building materials and technique, mural painting and mosaics, the dwelling houses, history of the excavations.

CALZA, Guido et al. Scavi di Ostia. Roma, Libreria dello Stato, 1953– . Illus., maps (part fold.), plans. **JG126**

[Sotto gli auspici del Ministero della publica instruzione, Direzione generale delle antichità e belle arti; a cura della Soprintendenza agli scavi di Ostia antica.]
JRS XLVI 1956 190–193 Meiggs
A series of volumes reporting on the excavations begun at Ostia in the late 19th century. Professor Guido Calza worked on the excavation from 1912 until his death in 1945. Paschetto's *Ostia, Colonia Romana, 1912* remains invaluable as the first large scale study of Ostia. This monumental series *Scavi di Ostia* publishes all the monuments of the port of Rome and describes in detail how the city was founded. Volume 1, *Topographie Generale,* describes the history of Ostia, and incorporates the work of Guido Calza, unpublished at the time of his death. Other volumes provide systematic reports on the architecture, town planning, figurative art, religion, trade, and economics of Ostia. The other volumes are: 2. *I. Mitrei* (G. Becatti) 1954; 3. *Le tombe di eta repubblicana e Augustea* (M. F. Squarciapiano) 1958; 4. *Mosaici e Pavimenti Marmorei,* 2 vols. (G. Becatti) 1961; 5. *I. Ritratti* (R. Calza) 1964; 6. *Edificio con opus sectile Fuori Porta Romana* (G. Becatti) 1969.

CAPRINO, C. et al. La Colonna di Marco Aurelio; Illustrata a cura del comune di Roma. Roma, L'Erma di Bretschneider, 1955. 322p., illus., maps, plates. **JG127**

Studi e materiali del Museo dell'Impero romano, n. 5.
JRS XLVI 1956 183–185 Lepper
A thorough study, particularly in its photographs, of the Marcus Aurelius Column. Gatti contributes a brief review of the construction and original setting of the column. Colini surveys the history of the column,

Romanelli provides information about the Roman Army, in relation to the Marcus Aurelius Column, and Caprino supplies descriptive notes on the individual scenes.

CASTAGNOLI, F. Lavinium I. Topografia generale fonti e storia delle richerche. Lavinium II. e tredici arc. Rome, De Luca, 1972, 1975. **JG128**

Latomus XXXVI 1977 840–844 Moyaers
The official publication of the excavation at Lavinium by the Instituto di Topografia Antica of Rome University. This city in Latium, Italy, was, according to Virgil, built by Aeneas, and named for his Latin wife Lavinia. Excavations have revealed a sanctuary with 13 archaic altars, terracottas, bronzes, and other evidence of contact with the Greek world.

CREMA, Luigi. L'architettura Romana. Sez. 3, Enciclopedia classica. Torino, Societa editrice internazionale, 1959. xxiii, 688p., illus., maps, facsims. **JG129**

AJA LXV 1961 80 Brown • JRS LII 1962 251–252 Ward Perkins • Gnomon XXXVIII 1966 488–498 Riemann
Sez. 3 by Crema, Luigi replaces Durm's *Baukunst der Etrusker Baukunst der Römer* (1905). It is a monumental undertaking, covering the entire field of Roman architecture, with scholarly text and abundant illustration. The arrangement is by period, and within each period from its post-Etruscan beginnings to Constantine, the subject is examined under: materials and structure; principles of design and decoration; city-planning; military architecture; civic buildings; temples; baths; theaters, amphitheaters and circuses; monumental arches and gates; houses and villas; sepulchers. For its exhaustive analyses, and excellence of production, this is a major reference work on the subject.

DE FINE LICHT, Kjeld. The Rotunda in Rome; A study of Hadrian's Pantheon. Copenhagen, Gyldendal, [1968]. 347p., illus. **JG130**

Jutland Archeological Society. Publications, 7.
AJA LXXIII 1969 489–490 Frazer • Gymnasium LXXVII 1970 563–566 Rakob • AntJ L 1970 127–129 Strong • JRS LXI 1971 289–290 Ward-Perkins
The book records the remains now visible of Hadrian's Pantheon, and the opinions of the author and his predecessors on problems of interpretation. There are 70 pages of bibliography. The main part of the book is an account of the building but there are chapters on the immediate environs of the Pantheon in classical times, on its place in the history of classical architecture, and on the post-classical history of the building.

DUDLEY, Donald Reynolds, comp and trans. Urbs Roma: a source book of classical texts on the city and its monuments. London, Phaidon Press, 1967. 339p., illus. **JG131**

BO XXV 1968 115 • CW LXI 1968 250 Anderson • G&R XV 1968 99 Sewter

The author presents a selection of the ancient *testimonia*—texts, coins, inscriptions—for the city of Rome and its monuments. Section I deals with the site of the city and Section II presents the monuments. There is an index of Ancient Authors, one of Inscriptions, and one of the Principal Places. The book aims to provide a link between the literature, the study of the topography, and monuments of Rome. The text is accompanied by lovely black-and-white photographs.

FROVA, Antonio et al. Scavi di Luni: relazione preliminare delle campagne di scavo 1970–1971. Roma, L'Erma di Bretschneider, 1973. 3 v., xxii, 890, 86p., 233 plates, illus., plans.   **JG132**

  v. 1. Testo.—v. 2. Tavole.—v. 3. Fogli.

  AJA LXXIX 1975 390 Phillips • Gnomon XLIX 1977 193–196 Kraus

  Reports in three large volumes the results of the recent excavations at Luni. An essential reference work for the study of Roman archaeology, architecture, sculpture, inscriptions, pottery and coins.

GAZZOLA, Piero. Ponti romani. [Firenze, L. S. Olschki, 1963]. 2 v., illus.   **JG133**

  v. 1. Ponte Pietra a Verona.—v. 2. Ponti romani, contributo ad un indice sistematico con studio critico bibliografico.

  Arch Class XVII 1965 175–176 Crema • IHA X 1965 92 Ville • JRS LV 1965 289–290 Fredericksen • AJA LXX 1966 81–82 Ballance

  The first volume examines the history of the Ponte Pietra at Verona. The second volume is a provisional corpus of Roman bridges throughout the Empire. These lovely volumes are the most complete study of the subject of Roman bridges available.

GNOLI, Raniero. Marmora romana. Roma, Edizioni dell'Elefante, 1971. iv, 249p., illus., plates.   **JG134**

  AJA LXXVII 1973 106–107 Brilliant

  The book describes the types, sources and applications of the Roman marbles. It is a magnificent achievement in its scholarship and the beauty of the production. The first part describes stones, from quarry to cutting to application, in sheets, blocks, and pieces for construction. There is a presentation in the original, with translation, of ancient authors' descriptions of the Roman taste for colored, veined marbles. The second part is a catalogue which identifies the stones by their ancient, vernacular, and scientific names, and traces them to their quarries all over the Mediterranean.

GRANT, Michael. The Roman forum; photographs by Werner Forman. London, New York [etc.], MacMillan, Spring Books, 1974. 3–240p., illus., maps.   **JG135**

  Originally published: London, Weidenfeld and Nicholson, 1970.

  ACR III 1973 191–192 MacKendrick • Archaeology XXVI 1973 69–70 Laidlaw • CW LXVI 1973 435–436 d'Arms

Described as the most famous meeting place in the world, the Roman Forum is described in detail and lavishly illustrated in this volume. The first part is a general survey of the significance of the Forum. The central portion of the book is a description of what the monuments were like, and the last section is a history of the fate of the monuments after the fall of Rome. The monuments and sculptures are presented throughout in excellent black-and-white and some color photographs. A bibliography is included.

GRIMAL, Pierre. In search of Ancient Italy. Translated from the French by P. D. Cummins. New York: Hill and Wang, 1964. 270p., illus.   **JG136**

  Archaeologia XIV 1963 231–232 Majewski • CW LVIII 1965 256–258 Hammond

  A popular work on the sites and monuments of ancient Italy translated from the French, *A la recherche de l'Italie antique,* Paris, 1961. Arranged geographically by site, it reports archaeological discovery of ancient Rome, Herculaneum, Pompeii, and Ostia. "The English reader who wants exactness and sound judgement will find greater satisfaction in MacKendrick's *The Mute Stones Speak,* 1960" (Hammond).

GRIMAL, Pierre. Les jardins romains, à la fin de la république et aux deux premiers siècles de l'empire. 2e édition revue. Paris, Presses universitaires de France, 1969, 1943. viii, 557p. illus., col. maps, plates.   **JG137**

  Collection Hier.

  JRS XXXVI 1946 210–213 Toynbee • AJA LIV 1950 284–287 Lehmann

  This archaeological and literary study is an examination of Roman life from the Republican to Antonine times as mirrored in the gardens of Rome and Italy. It is a meticulous work that adds a great deal to the understanding of Roman-age art. There are two appendices, listing representations of gardens in Roman-age painting and plants known to have been grown in Roman gardens.

GROS, Pierre. Aurea Templa: Recherches sur l'architecture religieuse de Rome à l'époque d'Auguste. Rome, École française de Rome, 1976. 282p., 66 plates.   **JG138**

  REL LV 1977 550 • JRS LXIX 1979 215–216 Plommer

  Brings together the information available on Augustan temples in Rome. Every aspect of the temples is examined, including the architects and building trade, the siting of the temples, and the design of the interiors.

HERMANN, Werner. Römische Götteraltäre. Kallmünz, Opf. M. Lassleben, 1961. 156p., [3] leaves of plates, 12 illus.   **JG139**

  A revision of the author's thesis, Freie Universität, Berlin.

  AJA LXX 1966 207–208 Vermeule

A description and catalogue of Roman altars in the Latin West.

HOLLOWAY, R. Ross. Satrianum; the archaeological investigations conducted by Brown University in 1966 and 1967. Providence, Brown University Press, [1970]. xix, 147, [153]p., illus., maps, plans.   **JG140**

AJA LXXV 1971 451–452 Phillips

Reports the results of the excavation by Brown University in 1966 and 1967 of the acropolis walls, lower city, and tombs of Satrianum and Lucania, Italy. Material from the excavations are in the Potenza Museum. Well documented and illustrated.

HUELSEN, Christian Carl. The Forum and the Palatine, translated by Helen H. Tanzer . . . from the First German edition. New York, A. Bruderhausen, 1928. xii, 100p., illus., 64 (i.e. 65) pl. (1 fold.) on 33 1.   **JG141**

JRS XVIII 1928 111 Ashby • RA XXVIII 1928 169 Reinach

A short guide by a master of Roman topography on the Forum and the Palatine. Though out-of-date, it provides a sound introduction to the history and monuments of the site with good drawings.

KIRSTEN, Ernst. Süditalienkunde; mit Beiträgen von Hamm und Hans Riemann. Heidelberg, C. Winter, 1975– . Illus., plans.   **JG142**

Bücherei Winter Bd. 1. Campanien und seine Nachbarlandschaften.

AJA LXXXI 1977 253 Holloway • REL LV 1977 552 Chevallier

The most comprehensive coverage of Campania since Beloch's *Campanien* of 1890. Latest discoveries are included along with a thorough analysis of the archaeology of the area.

LANCIANI, Rodolfo Amedeo. Ancient Rome in the light of recent discoveries. New York, Houghton, Mifflin and Company, 1883. xxix, 329p., front, illus., maps, plans.   **JG143**

"First published 1888." Reprinted 1967.

In the first chapter, the author describes the renaissance of archaeological studies in Rome. He attributes the foundation of the modern school to Cola di Rienzo, born in 1313. In subsequent chapters, the life and monuments of ancient Rome are examined, with references to writers and archaeologists who have worked on them. The final chapter, on the loss and recovery of works of art, discusses those objects of Roman art that were recorded by writers through the centuries and some of which have been recently recovered. Another book, on the fate of the buildings and masterpieces of Rome by the same author, is *The Destruction of Ancient Rome* reprinted in 1967.

LANCIANI, Rodolfo Amedeo. The Roman forum; a photographic description of its monuments.

Rome, Frank & Co., [Leipzig, G. Kreysingl], 1910. 111, [3]p., 53 illus., 2 pl. (1 fold.), plan.   **JG144**

Photographic illustrations of the monuments of the Forum, with short accompanying descriptions and a historical introduction.

LANCIANI, Rodolfo Amedeo. The ruins and excavations of ancient Rome, with a new foreword by Richard Brilliant. New York, Bell Pub. Co., 1979.   **JG145**

Reprint of the 1897 ed. published by Houghton Mifflin, New York. Includes bibliographies and indexes.

Following the unification of Italy in 1870, Rome was rebuilt and many of the ancient sites were buried beneath the construction. The heart of Ancient Rome was spared and made into an archaeological preserve. This includes the Forum, the Palatine, the area between the Capitol and the foot of the Quirinal, the Colosseum, and the first stretch of the Appian Way. Lanciani became secretary of the Municipal Archaeological Commission and for fifty years he worked on the excavations. Results of the excavations were reported in *Bolletins delle Archaeologica Municipale* and *Notizie degli Scair di Antiquita communicate alla Reale Accademia di Lincei*. These appeared, without interruption, for seventy-five years and still bring out special issues. This book details the excavations, and traces the history of the monuments through the centuries, with an introductory section on the geology and fortifications of Rome. Maps of the ancient city are included.

LEHMAN-HARTLEBEN, Karl. Die Traianssäule. Berlin. 1926.   **JG146**

JRS XVI 1926 261–264 E.S.

The author asserts that the spiral column, known to us only from the Trajan column, is unique and without precedent, although it was repeatedly imitated. The panoramic display of the two Dacian wars on a continuous frieze-two spirals is an original idea of the artist of the Trajan column. A meticulous study of every aspect of the spiral column.

LEON, Christoph F. Die Bauornamentik des Trajansforums und ihre Stellung in der früh-und mittelkaiserzeitlichen Architekturdekoration Roms. Wien, Böhlau, 1971. 310p., 141 illus.   **JG147**

Publikationen des Österreichischen Kulturinstituts in Rom, 1 Abt.: Abhandlungen, Bd. 4.

AJA LXXVIII 1974 209 White • JRS LXIV 1974 251–252 Strong

In this meticulous study, the author uses the architectural decoration from the Forum of Trajan as the basis for an analysis of imperial architecture during its first century and a half. The first chapter consists of a review of the research on Roman architectural ornament from Vignola to the present. This carefully documented book is a work of great scholarship that is basic to an understanding of Roman imperial architecture.

LUGLI, Giuseppe. I monumenti antichi di Roma e suburbio. Roma, G. Bardi, 1930–38. 3 v., illus., plates, plans, diagr.   **JG148**

First edition of v. 1 published Rome, 1924, under title: La zona archeologica di Roma. I. La zona archeologica.—II. Le grandi opere pubblicha.—III. A traverso le regioni.

LEC 1935 327 Roche • PhW 1935 1312–1315 Von Gerkan • REL XIII 1935 428 Marouzeau

A popular introduction and guide to the monuments of Rome. Volume 1, *La zona archeologica,* describes the portion of the city set aside for the preservation and exploration of ancient monuments. The English translation of Volume 1, by Gilbert Bagnani, includes a short introduction on types of Roman building construction and materials which are the basis for dating buildings of the classical age. A supplement appeared in 1940.

LUGLI, Giuseppe. Roma antica: il centro monumentale. Ed. anastatica. Roma, G. Gardi, 1968. xviii, 631p., illus., maps, plans.   **JG149**

First edition published Rome, 1924, under title: La zona archeologica di Roma, later published as v. 1 of his *I monumenti antichi di Roma e suburbio.*

REA XLVII 1945 323–324 Grenier • Athenaeum XXIV 1946 110–112 Fraccaro • JRS XXXVI 1946 216–217 Radford

A revised edition of Volume 1 of the author's *Monumenti antichi di Roma e Suburbio,* published 1930–1938. The monuments examined include the Capitol, Forum, Imperial Fora, Colosseum with the adjacent slopes of the Caelian and Oppian, Palatine, Forum Holitorium, and Forum Boarium, with the Circus Maximus. The aim of the book is described by the author, "to give an exact and methodical account of each monument, to describe its building periods, its architectural and artistic features in order to bring the reader into direct contact with the structure, and serve as a guide for its examination." The book achieves this aim, and the text is complimented by superb illustrations that include plans, photographs and reproductions of reliefs and coins.

LUGLI, Giuseppi. La tecnica edilizia romana, con particolare riguardo a Roma e Lazio. Roma, G. Bardi, 1957. 2 v., illus., plates.   **JG150**

Vol. 2: plates.

RIL XXIV 1958 158–170 Lamboglia • AJA LXIII 1959 104–106 Sjöqvist • JRS XLIX 1959 181–183 Richmond • RA 1959 I 181–202 Le Gall

This enormous, well-illustrated study, surveys the buildings of Rome and Latium, and classifies them through the materials and methods or style used in the construction. The author demonstrates the relationship of building booms to periods of prosperity and the composition of monuments to the raw materials available locally. The buildings the author examines are confined almost totally to the area of Rome and Latium, and he includes sections on polygonal walling, quarries and quarrying, the development of the arch, and a final chapter on arches and vaults in concrete. In this splendid architectural study all the monuments are carefully analyzed.

MacDONALD, William Lloyd. The architecture of the Roman Empire. An introductory story.

New Haven, Yale University Press, 1965– . xxi, 211p., illus., plans.   **JG151**

Yale publications in the history of art, v. 17.

Athenaeum XLIV 1966 324–328 Mansuelli • CW LIX 1966 320 Thompson • Archaeology 20 1967 75–76 Scranton

In this first volume the author describes the Roman achievement in the design and construction of vaulted spaces. Four monuments are chosen to illustrate the author's theories: the palaces of Nero, Domitian's palaces, Trajan's market and the Pantheon. The Roman architects (Severus, Rabirius, Apollodorus, and Hadrian) are discussed in a separate chapter, and there are chapters on Roman architectural practice, methods and design. A competent and thorough work with good illustrations.

McKAY, Alexander Gordon. Houses, villas, and palaces in the Roman world. Ithaca, N.Y., Cornell University Press, 1975. 288p., illus., [24] leaves of plates.   **JG152**

Aspects of Greek and Roman life.

TLS LXXIV 1975 780 Plommer • Antiquity L 1976 155–156 Liversidge • Phoenix XXX 1976 305–308 Russell • Vergilius XXII 1976 47–50 Fears

This is a comprehensive work on Italian houses. It begins with a description of the Etruscan houses, and includes Roman houses from the early capanne to the Imperial palaces. The scope of the work is such that the author cannot deal with various aspects in a thorough scholarly way. The last two chapters are devoted to houses in other parts of the Empire, and the whole is illustrated with informative plans and plates.

MacKENDRICK, Paul Lachian. The mute stones speak; the story of archaeology in Italy. New York, Norton, 1960. xiii, 369p., illus.   **JG153**

Originally published by St. Martin's Press, New York.

JRS LIX 1964 230 Frederiksen • Stud Rom XII 1964 203–205 Romanelli

A survey of the archaeological discoveries of prehistoric Italy, the Etruscans and Romans. Presented in a readable, well-illustrated volume, it is valuable as a general introduction. All the well-known monuments are included, with good text on the political and social background from which Italian art emerged.

MEIGGS, Russell. Roman Ostia. 2d ed. Oxford, Clarendon Press, 1973. xix, 622p., illus., 40 plates, maps, plans.   **JG153a**

Gnomon XXXVII 1965 192–203 Bloch • JRS LXV 1975 211–212 Ling

A second edition of this major study of Roman Ostia. The bulk of the volume remains as in the first edition, but new discoveries are summarized in a short addendum, and there is a supplementary bibliography which covers the period 1960–72. An excellent reference book on Ostia. See also the author's summary of the history of Ostia in *The Princeton Encyclopaedia of Classical Sites.*

MORETTI, Giuseppe. Ara Pacis Augustae. Roma, La Libreria dello Stato, 1948. 325p., illus., plates, portfolio, ([2] 1., 39 plates).   **JG154**

AJPh 1 1949 418–421 van Buren • JRS XLII 1952 119–121 Toynbee

The Ara Pacis Augustae was initially discovered in 1568, and this work examines the gradual recovery of the monument which, in its final stages, was directed by the author himself. Every aspect of the monument, including the sculptures, friezes, ornamental motifs, paintings, etc. are discussed in detail, and in Part III, the author analyzes the idea underlying the monument as a whole. The text is copiously illustrated and Volume II is devoted to plates, but the reviewer Toynbee considers the quality inferior to the plates contained in the author's short book *L'Ara Pacis Augustae'* (*Itinerari dei Musei e Monumenti d'Italia No. 67*), 1938.

OPUSCULA romana. Lund, C. W. K. Gleerup, 1954. illus.   **JG155**

v. 1– , 1954– .

Vol. v: CR XVI 1966 421–422 Toynbee

The volumes are published by the Swedish Institute in Rome and present a variety of topics. Volume 1 is primarily archaeological with material from Rome, Italy, and the Roman provinces.

PACKER, James E. The insulae of imperial Ostia. [Rome], American Academy in Rome, 1971. xxviii, 217p. cxv, illus.   **JG156**

Memoirs of the American Academy in Rome, v. 31. JRS LXIII 1973 279–281 Ling • AJA LXXVIII 1974 102–103 Bloch • CR XXIV 1974 268–271 Meiggs

The author examines the multiple dwellings in Ostia, to determine "living conditions and social patterns both in Ostia and in Rome." There are detailed descriptions, with plans, of many of the buildings. The book is copiously illustrated with good photographs.

PICARD, Gilbert. Living architecture: Roman. Photos. by Yvan Butler. Pref. by Paolo Portoghesi. New York, Grosset & Dunlap, [1965]. 192p., illus., map, plans.   **JG157**

Translation of *Empire romain.*

G&R XIV 193 Sewter

Primarily a picture book, the illustrations are superb and dramatize the work of ancient architects. There are short essays on the various monuments and on the life of ancient Rome which inspired them. Along with the magnificent photographs, there are drawings and plans.

PLOMMER, Hugh. Vitruvius and later Roman building manuals. [London], Cambridge University Press, 1973. 116p., illus.   **JG158**

"An edition and translation of Faventinus' Compendium of Vitruvius' *De architectura.*"

AntJ LIV 1974 108 Strong • JBAA XXXVII 1974 135–136 Kidson • JRS LXV 1975 222–223 Rickman

The author compares the writings of Vitruvius, Fa-

ventinus, and Palladius to ascertain the ancient views on Roman building construction and architecture. Topics covered include, use of timber, construction of a wine cellar, the heating system for baths, the use of concrete, and the system of water supply.

RAKOB, Friedrich et al. Der Rundtempel am Tiber in Rom; Wolf-Dieter Heilmeye. Mit e. Bauaufn. von W. Niemann u. e. Beitr. von P. A. Gianfrotta. Mainz (am Rhein) von Zabern, 1973. 48, 60p., 23 illus.   **JG159**

AJA LXXIX 1975 393–394 Fredericksen • Latomus XXXIV 1975 823–825 Gros • LEC XLIII 1975 93 Wankenne

The small round temple by the Tiber, built of Pentelic marble, is a Greek product both in the remarkable masonary of the cella and in the twenty slim Corinthian columns that make up the colonnade. The authors provide a comprehensive study of the temple, dating it to about 100 B.C. with a cella and colonnade in Greek marble on a foundation of Grotta Oscura tufa. They accept the conclusions of Ward-Perkins and Strong that on the south side ten columns and two further capitals have at some time been replaced in Luna marble with the carving of Julio-Claudian date. The authors accept that it is the temple of Hercules Invictus (or Victor) ad Portam Frigeminam.

RIVOIRA, Giovanni Teresi. Roman architecture and its principles of construction under the Empire, with an appendix on the evolution of the dome up to the XVIIth century. Translated from the Italian by G. McN. Rushforth. New York, Hacker Arts Books, 1972 xxvi, 310p., illus.   **JG160**

Reprint of the 1925 ed. Translation of Architettura romana.

BFC XXVIII 130 Ducati • LZB 1922 15 Weigand

The author's study of Roman architecture as a subject independent of Greek art was considered by many as misguided nationalism.

ROBATHAN, Dorothy Mae. The monuments of ancient Rome. Roma, L'Erma di Bretschneider, 1950. 211p., plates, maps.   **JG161**

REL XXVIII 1950 463–464 Bloch • AC XX 1951 544–546 Mertens • CR II 1952 217–219 Toynbee

This is a guide for the general reader to the chief sites and buildings of ancient Rome. There are sixteen good photographs and three maps, including an excellent plan of the Imperial Fora.

ROMANELLI, Pietro. The Roman Forum. 5th ed. [Roma], Istituto poligrafico dello Stato, Libreria dello Stato, [1971]. 114p., illus., plans.   **JG162**

Guide-books to the museums, galleries and monuments of Italy, v. 44. At head of title: Ministero della pubblica istruzione. Direzione generale delle antichit'a e belle arti.

One of a series of short guides to the museums and monuments of Rome. The text is a chronological history of the Forum, followed by a description of each of the monuments arranged in the form of a tour. The small book is illustrated with 73 good black-and-white photographs, and a useful bibliography refers the reader to more extensive and detailed treatments of the Roman Forum.

ROSSI, Lino. Trajan's column and the Dacian wars. English translation rev. by J. M. C. Toynbee. Ithaca, N.Y., Cornell University Press, [1971]. 240p., illus.   **JG163**

ACR II 1972 228 Eadie • AntJ LIV 1974 108–109 Strong • CR XXIV 1974 112–114 Watson
Most of this book is devoted to a 'History in Pictures,' which describes each section of Trajan's column with illustrations. The text is well-written but the illustrations are not of uniformly high quality. In the earlier chapters, the author gives an account of Trajan's Dacian Wars and of the Roman armed forces in Trajan's time. The only book in English that describes with illustrations this important and well preserved monument.

ROULLET, Anne. The Egyptian and Egyptianizing monuments of imperial Rome. Leiden, Brill, 1972. xiv, 186p., 230p. of photos.   **JG164**

Études préliminaires aux religions orientales dans l'empire romain, t. 20.
Aegyptus LII 1972 207–208 Curto • JRS LXIII 1973 273–274 Tran Tam Tinh • Latomus XXXIII 1974 192–195 Malaise
A scholarly study of Egyptian and Egyptianizing monuments, discovered in Rome and its neighborhood. In the *Catalogue Raisonée,* the author gives the scientific data for each monument. There are Four Appendixes and two Indexes and the volume is well illustrated.

RYBERG, Mrs. Inez (Scott). An archaeological record of Rome from the seventh to the second century B.C. London, Christophers; Philadelphia, University of Pennsylvania Press, [1940]. 2 v., plates, map.   **JG165**

Part I: Text and index to plates; pt. II: Plates and general index.
AJA XLV 1941 489–493 Hanfman • AHR XLII 1942 310 Taylor • AJPh 1943 485–489 Lehmann-Hartleben • CJ XXXVIII 1943 296–297 Jones
A survey of the archaeology of Rome from its beginnings as a prehistoric village to its rise to the capital of an empire. The author meticulously establishes the chronology of burials, pottery, terracottas, and bronzes. She uses Roman commerce and industry as the basis of her examination. Well illustrated, with good plates in Part II.

SCHERER, Margaret Roseman. Marvels of ancient Rome. Edited and with a foreword by Charles Rufus Morey. New York, published by

the Phaidon Press for the Metropolitan Museum of Art, 1955. ix, 430p., 225 illus.   **JG166**

JRS XVLIII 1958 229–230 Haynes
The author's theme is "Roma sparita" and she sets out to describe the Rome of the Middle Ages, the Renaissance, and the Romantic Movement and to demonstrate what the city's historic sites and monuments looked like then. The monuments are described as reflected in prose, poetry, and picture, from antiquity to the present time. The text is accompanied by excellent photographs with lengthy descriptions.

SIMON, Erika. Ara Pacis Augustae. Tübingen, Wasmuth, 1967. 32p., illus.   **JG167**

BO XXV 1968 138 • ABull LIII 1971 110–113 Brilliant

TAMM, Birgitta. Auditorium and palatium; a study on assembly-rooms in Roman palaces during the 1st century B.C. and the 1st century A.D. [Trans. by Patrick Hort]. Stockholm, Almqvist & Wiksell, [1963]. 229p., illus., fold. map, plans.   **JG168**

Acta Universitatis Stockholmiensis. Stockholm studies in classical archaeology, 2.
AC XXXIII 1964 573–577 Balty • AJA LXX 1966 305 Hanson
The author examines the forerunners of the "basilica" in the Palace of Domitian. She concludes that "Caligula introduced the apse hall, as a room for deliberations, in the imperial palace, and Claudius afterwards gave it the name 'auditorium'." The book examines the topography of Rome, along with the history of Roman architecture. A useful, well-illustrated volume.

TODD, Malcolm. The walls of Rome. London, P. Elek, 1978. 91p., illus.   **JG169**

Latomus XXXVIII 1979 796 Dirckens
Briefly examines the subject in the light of recent new evidence. More useful than I. A. Richmond, *The City-Wall of Ancient Rome,* 1930.

WARD-PERKINS, John Bryan. Roman architecture. New York, H. N. Abrams, 1977. 360p., illus.   **JG170**

Bibliography: p. 344–346.
Originally published as part of *Etruscan and Roman Architecture* by Axel Boëthius and J. B. Ward-Perkins. An analysis of Roman buildings from the architecture of Augustus to the 4th century. An excellent volume with fine explanatory drawings and reconstructions.

ZANKER, Paul. Forum Augustum. Das Bildprogramm. Tübingen, Wasmuth, 1968. 36p., 54 plates.   **JG171**

AJA LXXV 1971 229 Hill • ABull LIII 1971 110 Vermeule
Monumenta artis antiquae, Bd. 2.

ZANKER, Paul. Forum Romanum; die Neugestaltung durch Augustus. Tübingen, E. Wasmuth, [1972]. 52p., illus., plates. **JG172**

Monumenta artis antiquae, Bd. 5.
Gnomon XLVI 1974 523–525 Brilliant • JRS LXIV 1974 282 Sear
Another in this series, by the author of *Forum Augustum* in which he examines the Roman Forum not as a series of architectural remains but as a coherent complex created mainly by Augustus. The text is concise and accompanied by almost as many pages of black-and-white photographs.

Sarcophagi

ANDREAE, Bernard. Studien zur römischen Grapkunst. Heidelberg, F. H. Kerle, 1963. 180p., illus., plans, 80 plates. **JG173**

Mitteilungen des Deutschen Archäologischen Instituts. Römische Abt., 9. Ergänzungsheft.
Gnomon XL 1968 67–75 Schefold

GABELMANN, Hanns. Die Werkstattgruppen der oberitalischen Sarkophage. Bonn, Rheinland-Verlag, in Kommission bei R. Habelt, 1973. 238p., illus., 56 plates. **JG174**

Beihefte der Bonner Jahrbücher, Bd. 34.
FR CVII–CVIII 1974 281–286 • AC XLIV 1975 401 de Ruyt • Athenaeum LIII 1975 373–379 Rebecchi • Gymnasium LXXXII 1975 113–115 Blanck • CR XXVI 1976 297 Ogilvie
A meticulous and comprehensive study of extant north-Italian sarcophagi. Examples are classified by style, stone, architectural design and decorative motifs. The illustrations are superb.

HANFMANN, George Maxim Anossov. The Season sarcophagus in Dumbarton Oaks. Cambridge, Mass., Harvard University Press, 1951. New York, Johnson Reprint Corp., 1971. 2 v., plates. **JG175**

Dumbarton Oaks studies, v. 2. "A catalogue of the representations of the Horae and the Seasons in ancient art": v. 2, p. [129]–192. Includes bibliographies.
JRS XLV 1955 196–197 Toynbee • Gnomon XXVII 1955 351–359 Horn

MATZ, Friedrich. Die dionysischen Sarkophage. Berlin, Gebr. Mann, 1968–75. 4 v., illus. **JG176**

Die antiken Sarkophagreliefs, Bd. 4. T. 1. Die Typen der Figuren. Die Denkmäler 1–71 B.—T. 2. Die Denkmäler 72–161.—T. 3. Die Denkmäler 162–245.—T. 4. Die Denkmäler 246–385. Nachträge, Übersichten, Konkordanzen, Indices.
Gnomon XLIII 1971 603–609 Himmelmann • RA 1974 367–372 Turcan • AJA LXXXI 1977 127–134 Lawrence
These four volumes are a magnificient achievement

that completes the corpus of ancient sarcophagi started by Carl Robert, *Der Antiken—Sarkophag—Reliefs,* 1890–1919 and continued by Gerhart Rodenwaldt, *Die Antiken Sarkophagreliefs,* 1952. These four folio volumes are beautifully illustrated and cover in a thorough scholarly way the most valuable of Roman sarcophagi. For a bibliography of the works of Friedrich Matz, see *Verzeichnis den Schriften von Friedrich Matz zu seinem achtzigsten geburtstag am 15 August 1970,* Berlin, Mann, 1970.

MATZ, Friedrich. Ein römisches Meisterwerk; der Jahreszeitensarkophag Badminton-New York. Berlin, W. de Gruyter, 1958. [8], 215p. 46 plates. **JG177**

Gnomon XXXI 1959 533–539 Hanfmann • JRS L 1960 264–265 Toynbee • RBPh XXXVIII 1960 609–611 Richter
The book describes, in detail, the beautifully carved marble sarcophagus known as the Badminton sarcophagus now in the Metropolitan Museum of Art in New York. Along with description and illustration of the funerary sculptures on the sarcophagus, there is a full analysis of Hellenic, Hellenistic, and earlier Roman prototypes of the 'god on the Tiger' motive, and a chapter on the classification of sarcophagi carved between 190 and 235 according to workshops.

SICHTERMANN, Hellmut and KOCH, Guntram. Griechische Mythen auf römischen Sarkophagen. unter Verwendung neuer Aufnahmen von Gerhard Singer. Tübingen, E. Wasmuth, 1975. 73p., [88] leaves of plates, illus. **JG178**

AJA LXXX 1976 440–441 Hanfmann • LEC XLIV 1976 181 Wankenne
An important work of analysis, it presents seventy-three Roman sarcophagi arranged alphabetically by myths or their protagonists.

TURCAN, Robert. Les Sarcophages romains à représentations dionysiaques, essai de chronologie et d'histoire religieuse. Paris, E. de Boccard, 1966. 686p., plates. **JG179**

Bibliotheque des Écoles françaises d'Athènes et de Rome, v. fas.
Athenaeum XLV 1967 226–237 Chevallier • REL XLV 1967 613–615 Richard • JRS LVIII 1968 296–297 Toynbee
Divided into three main parts: (1) Bases of Chronology, (2) Styles and Workshops, (3) Themes and Variations. This massive work examines the scenes, and figures representing the beliefs of Dionysiac religion on Roman sarcophagi.

Paintings, Mosaics, Murals

BECATTI, Giovanni. Scavi de Ostia IV: Mosaici e pavimenti Marmorei. [Roma] Istituto poligrafico dello Stato, Libreria dello Stato, [1961]. 409p., illus., plans, atlas (227 plates). **JG180**

AJA LXVII 1963 321–322 Smith • JRS LIII 1963 231 Meiggs • Archaeology XVII 1964 293 Block

It includes mosiac and segmented marble pavements discovered at Ostia up to 1958. The first volume of text is a descriptive catalogue and a history of the pavements, followed by detailed indices to the works covered. The second volume contains lovely illustrations of the mosaics.

BLAKE, M. E. "Roman mosaics of the second century in Italy." *MAAR* XIII (1936):67–214.
JG181

CJ XXXIII 1938 548–550 Mylonas

A continuation of the author's study of first-century mosaics, published in MAAR VIII (1930) 7–160, it examines the floor mosaics of Rome and vicinity and of the provinces in Italy. Divided into mosaics with purely decorative or pictorial patterns and mosiacs in black and white or in polychrome technique. The author completed her chronological examination of mosaics in *Mosaics of the late Empire in Rome and vicinity* MAAR, 1940, XVII, 81–131.

BORDA, Maurizio. La pittura romana. Milano, Società editrice libraria, [1958]. xxx, 430p., illus., 21 plates.
JG182

SDHI XXV 1959 452–455 Ciprotti • Sic Gymn XV 1962 126–127 Arias

This large volume is a history of Roman painting from the Late Republic to the Late Empire. Decorative systems and figurative compositions are examined and illustrated in black and white and color photographs. Included is an informative section on the painters and their techniques.

BROWN, B. R. Ptolemaic paintings and mosaics and the Alexandrian style. Cambridge, Mass., Archaeological Institute of America, 1957. xvii, 108p., illus., 45 plates.
JG183

CE XXXIII 1958 301 Bingen • EClas IV 1958 457 Garcia y Bellido • REA LX 1958 473–476 Marcadé • Archaeology XII 1959 290 Jones

The first part is a description of the clandestine discovery of the Soldiers Tomb in the Ibrahimiya cemetery, east of Alexandria, and the manner in which the contents were dispersed. The six painted slabs from the tomb, now in The Metropolitan Museum of Art, are the basis of the author's inquiry. In the second part of the book, extant Ptolemaic pictorial material is examined and classified by style and chronology. In this section some of the author's stylistic categories are too subjective to provide a scientific basis for classification. The book is a useful addition to our knowledge of Hellenistic, particularly Alexandrian art, which is discussed in the final section.

CORPUS DES MOSAIQUES de Tunisie. Margaret A. Alexander & Mongi Ennaifer, Co-directeurs. Tunis Institut National d'Archéologie et d'Arts, 1973. illus.
JG184

Atlas archéologique de la Tunisie, Feuille 7.

ABull LVIII 1976 120–121 Clarke • JRS LXVI 1976 252–253 Waywell • AC XLVI 1977 268–369 Hanoune

This catalogue of mosaic pavements of the Roman period discovered in Tunisia will replace *Inventaire des Mosaïques de la Gaule et de l'Afrique II, Afrique Proconsulaire (Tunisie)* (1910) when it is completed. It is meticulously prepared and a valuable reference work.

DAWSON, Christopher Mounsey. Romano-Campanian mythological landscape painting. Edizione anastatica. Roma, L'Erma di Bretschneider, 1965. xii, 233p., 25 plates.
JG185

Reprint of New Haven 1944 ed. Yale Classical Studies, v. 9.

Latomus 1947 285 Renard • CW XLII 1948–1949 75–77 Harland

The thesis is that "the introduction of real landscape into art is due to Romano-Campanian painting." Although not a history of Roman painting, the book is valuable because of the author's competency on the subject and the wealth of bibliographical material provided along with description and commentary.

DORIGO, Vladimiro. Late Roman painting; a study of pictorial records 30 B.C.–A.D. 500. Translated from the Italian by James Cleugh and John Warrington. London, Dent, [1971, 1970]. xxviii, 345p., illus., plates.
JG186

Translation of *Pittura tardoromana*.

ACR II 1972 47–48 McKay • AJA LXXVI 1972 347–348 Smith • CW LXV 1972 209 Galinsky • G&R XIX 1972 107–108 Colledge

Considering the wide range of material available, the author presents a comprehensive examination of the figurative two-dimensional arts of the later Roman Empire. Subjects range from post-Hellenistic developments and the liberation of the idiom of Roman pictorial art in the 1st and 2nd centuries, Severan mosaics in Africa, the problems posed by Syrian and Mesopotamian paintings, 3rd century painting in Rome, the 4th century mosaics of Piazza Armerina, Aquileia and Africa, the Constantinian "fine style" at Antioch and Trier, expressionism and mannerism in the 4th century funerary and "ceremonial" paintings and mosaics, late Roman painting on the German *limes,* the last Hellenistic experiments from Egypt to Britain, the first illuminated codices, and the origins of Byzantine art. The illustrations are magnificient and it is claimed "every key monument is shown." The book which appeared originally in Italian in 1961 does not include much relevant material published after that. Extensive bibliography included.

DUNBABIN, Katherine M. D. The mosaics of Roman North Africa: studies in iconography and patronage. Oxford, Clarendon Press; New York, Oxford University Press, 1978. xx, 303p., [44] leaves of plates, illus.
JG187

Oxford monographs on classical archaeology.
CR XXX 1980 114–116 Waywell

Analyzes the designs and iconography of figured decoration on floor mosaics which date from the late second and third centuries in the Roman provinces of North Africa. The author illustrates the extent to which the style was peculiarly North African in theme and design. There is a catalogue of the African floors and a very useful bibliography.

GONZENBACH, Victorine von. Die römischen Mosaiken der Schweiz. Basel, Birkhauser, 1961. 370p., illus., plates, plans. **JG188**

JS 1962 173–185 Stern • JRS LII 1962 258 Smith • Arch Clas XIII 1961 287–289 Lugli
A meticulous examination of Roman mosaics in Switzerland from the first to the third century. In dating the mosaics, the author uses all evidence available, including tile stamps, lamps, associated painted plaster, coins and pottery. She established that Roman mosaics of Switzerland are closely related to those of southern and central Gaul. In text and illustration, the book is a work of impeccable scholarship.

LEVI, Doro. Antioch mosaic pavements. Princeton, Princeton University Press, 1947. 2 v., illus., 183 plates, maps, plans. **JG189**

[Publications of the Committee for the Excavation of Antioch and its Vicinity]. v. 1. Text.-v. 2 Plates.
BCH LXXIII 1949 490–491 Lévèque • RA XXXIV 1949 145–150 Picard • AntJ XXX 1950 90–92 Toynbee • Antiquity XXV 1951 111 Haynes
Antioch, excavated by Americans from 1932 until the war, provides us with a series of mosaics running from the early second to the mid-sixth century A.D. In these monumental volumes, the rich and well-preserved floor mosaics of Antioch from churches, halls and houses are published fully with copious illustration. Along with a description and interpretation of the mosaics there is an examination of technique and style and appendices. This staggering undertaking is more useful to the advanced scholar than the beginning student because of its scope and detail.

MONUMENTI della pittura antica scoperti in Italia. Roma, Libreria dello Stato, 1936– . [Sez. 1, 1937], illus. **JG190**

Sezione 1. La pittura etrusca [pt. 1] fasc. 1.—[pt. 2] fasc. 1.—Sezione 3. La pittura ellenistico-romana. [pt. 1] fasc. 1- [pt. 2] fasc. 1- [pt. 3] fasc. 1.
Fascicles devoted to the paintings of ancient Italy. They are well-produced and illustrated, and the text is concise. Monuments covered include three fascicles by G. E. Rizzo on the paintings of the Palatine monuments, fascicles by A. Maiuri and O. Elia on the paintings of Pompeii, and a series on Ostia by C. Gasparrini and others.

MOSAICI antichi in Italia. Roma, Istituto poligrafico dello Stato, Libreria, 1967– . Illus., plates. **JG191**

Series on mosaics in ancient Italy, it includes M. L. Morricone Matini, *Regione prima, Roma: Reg.*

X Palatium (1967) and G. Becatti et al. *Regione Settima: Baccano, Villa romana* (1970).

L'ORANGE, Hans Peter. Mosaikk, English ed. Mosaics from antiquity to the Middle Ages. [by] H. P. L'Orange and P. J. Nordhagen; translated [from the Norwegian] by Ann E. Keep. London, Methuen, 1966. x, 128p., 113 plates. **JG192**

Methuen handbooks of archaeology.
A condensed history of mosaics from the beginnings to c. 900 A.D.

PARLASCA, Klaus. Die römischen Mosaiken in Deutschland. Berlin, De Gruyter, 1959. vii, 156p., illus., plan, plates. **JG193**

Römisch-Germanische Kommission des Deutschen Archäologischen Instituts zu Frankfurt a.M.—Römisch-germanische Forschungen,—Bd.23.
JRS XLIX 1959 187 Smith • JS 1959 112–125 Stern • AJA LXIV 1960 113 Blake • RA I 1960 229–232 Picard
Supersedes E. Kruger's study of Roman mosaics in Germany, published in 1933 (Arch Anz. 1933 pp. 655–710). The first five chapters are devoted to an examination of the mosaics of Trier, Cologne and South Germany in order to establish a chronology. The last chapter examines the mosaics of Germany in relationship to those other mosaics of the ancient world that have similar motives and designs. These chapters are supplemented by four short essays on a crenellated wall as a form of border, on the swastika-pella motif, on technical aspects of the mosaics and on representations of the Muses in Roman mosaics. There are twelve pages of bibliography indices and excellent illustration in color and black-and-white photographs.

PICARD, Gilbert Charles. Roman painting. Translated from the French. London, Elek, 1970. 108p., illus. **JG194**

Translation of *Art romain*.
CR XXII 1972 259–261 Strong • G&R XVII 1970 235–236 Sewter • Latomus XXIX 1970 882 Chevallier • Gnomon XXXVII 1965 411–415 Zucker
A large portion of the book is devoted to sculptures, in stone or metal, which the author believes displaced painting as the chief means of artistic expression in the late Republic, and then incorporated many of its styles. Picard begins with the first century B.C. and does not include Roman art of the provinces. He discusses the four styles, apparent in the Romano-Campanian cities. The author suggests a plebeian trend as a significant factor in the development of style and a rival to the Hellenistic tradition. An interesting contribution to the study of iconography.

SEAR, Frank B. Roman wall and vault mosaics. Heidelberg, F. H. Kerle, 1977. 202p., 72p. of illus., maps. **JG195**

Mitteilungen des Deutschen Archäeologischen Instituts, Römische Abteilung, Ergänzungsheft 23.

AC XLVIII 1979 771–772 De Ruyt
Documents Roman mosaics, excluding pavement mosaics, from the third century B.C., to the end of the Republic. The catalogue of 308 items, includes maps and photographs. Valuable reference tool for archaeologists and art historians.

STERN, Henri. Recueil général des mosaïques de la Gaul. Paris, Centre national de la recherche scientifique, 1957– . plates, plans.   **JG196**

Renseignements et vente au Comité technique de la recherche archéologique en France. Supplément à *Gallia* 10.
AJA LXIII 1959 216 Blake • JRS XLIX 1959 186–187 Smith • Latomus XVIII 1959 239–240 Audin
These volumes replace the *Inventaire des mosaïques de la Gaule et de l'Afrique,* Paris, Leroux, 1909– . The first fascicle is a comprehensive catalogue of the mosaics of the Roman provinces. In this volume, M. Stern established the method of procedure for the fascicles. It includes place and date of find, dimensions and condition when found, present dimensions and state, present location, description, bibliography, references to illustrations, comments and dating if possible. The fascicles are published as supplements to *Gallia.*

Bronzes

COLONNA, Giovanni. Bronzi votivi umbro-sabellici a figura umana. Firenze, Sansoni, 1970– . illus., plates.   **JG197**

Studi e materiali di Etruscologia e Antichita Italiche, v. 8. v. 1—Periodo arcaico.
AJA LXXVI 1972 103–104 Maule • JRS LXI 1971 290–291 Ridgway
An examination of 640 examples of bronze sculpture of pre-Roman Italy in the area of Umbria and the territories to the south and east. The book's most helpful contribution to the study is in assembly and publication of material that was scattered and poorly recorded.

LEIBUNDGUT, Annalis. Die Römischen Bronzen der Schweiz. Mainz am Rhein, Philipp von Zabern, 1970– . illus.   **JG198**

JRS LXVIII 1978 242 Lloyd-Morgan
Switzerland's publication of its Roman bronzes is comparable in style to Menzel's *Die römischen Bronzen aus Deutschland.* Text and photographs are separated and both are excellent.

MENZEL, Heinz. Die römischen Bronzen aus Deutschland. Mainz, Verlag des Römisch-Germanischen Zentralmuseums, 1960, 1966.   **JG199**

Gnomon XXXIII 1961 733–734 Binsfeld • AJA LXV 1961 330 Hill • AC XVI 1964 336–337 Colonna
First in a series of volumes that published all figural ancient bronzes found in Germany. Includes excellent bibliography. Monumental sculpture, statuettes, utensil and vessel bronzes are all included. Roman bronzes

found in other countries are published by the Römisch-Germanisches Zentralmuseum, Mainz, in a separate series.

Sculpture

BIEBER, Margarete. Ancient copies: contributions to the history of Greek and Roman art. New York, New York University Press, 1977. xliv, 302p., [81] leaves of plates, illus.   **JG200**

CW LXXII 1978 176 Biers • CO LVI 1978 13–14 Gais
This impressive undertaking is the final work of Professor Bieber and the culmination of many years of work on the subject of Roman copies of Greek sculpture. In an earlier work, *Griechische Kleidung,* the author examined Greek and Roman dress, and in the present work she uses clothing as the basis for her analysis of Greek statues and the changes made by copyists. The book is copiously illustrated. An essential reference work for the study.

CARTER, Joseph Coleman. The sculpture of Taras. Philadelphia, American Philosophical Society, 1975, 1976. 196p., illus.   **JG201**

Transactions of the American Philosophical Society New Series, vol. 65, pt. 7.
AJA LXXXI 1977 401–403 Herrmann • Gymnasium LXXXIV 1977 72–73 Dohrn • G. & R. XXIV 1977 91 Sparkes
An analysis of one category of Tarentine sculpture the limestone reliefs. There is a catalogue of 442 pieces. A useful addition to the study of Hellenistic art.

CONTICELLO, B. and ANDREAE, B. Die skulpturen von Sperlonga. Berlin, Mann, 1974. 110p., 12 illus.   **JG202**

GGA CCXXVIII 1976 217–237 Hampl • Gymnasium LXXXII 1975 458–459 Brommer • Gnomon XLIX 1977 505–510 Linfert
The discovery of the group of sculptures in the grotto of the Villa of Tiberius at Sperlonga caused a great sensation and this volume is the official publication of those sculptures. Many scholars have worked on an interpretation, among them Gösta Säflund, *The Polyphemus and Scylla Groups at Sperlonga* (1972) published as part of the *Antike Plastik* series.

CORPUS der Sculpturen der römischen Welt. Österreich. Wien, Graz, Wien, Köln, Böhlau in Komm., 1967– . Illus.   **JG203**

At head of title: Österreichische Akademie der Wissenschaften. Beginning with Bd. 1, fasc. 2, published under title: Corpus signorum Imperii Romani; with parallel title in German.
This international project was launched in Paris in 1963 for a corpus of sculpture of the Roman world. The main classes of subjects to be included are (1) deities, mythological figures and personifications, (2) mythological scenes; (3) portraits; (4) historical subjects; (5) funerary monuments; (6) varia.

HAMBERG, Per Gustaf. Studies in Roman Imperial art, with special reference to the state reliefs of the second century. Roma, L'Erma di Bretschneider, 1968. Orig. ed., Uppsala, 1945. 202p., illus., plates. **JG204**

"Miss Kathleen M. Pain is primarily responsible for the English version."

Paideia 111 1948 334–337 Paribeni • ABull XXIX 1947 136–139 Lehmann • JRS XXXVI 1946 178–185 Toynbee • TG LX 1947 92–95 Kern

The purpose of this study is to analyze the most important phase in the development of imperial art, i.e. the great official reliefs of the Flavian, Trajanic, and Antonine periods. The book explores all aspects of the monuments (the aesthetic, the historical, the archaeological and the spiritual) in order to understand them from both a conceptual and a formal point of view. It is an exceptionally good work on the reliefs and on Roman-age sculpture. The illustrations are of fine quality and there is a useful bibliography.

MAGI, Filippo. I rilievi Flavi del Palazzo della Cancelleria; con prefazione di Bartolomeo Nogara. [Roma], Presso la Pontificia accademia romana di archeologi, Dott. G. Bardi, editore, 1945. 3, ix–xvii, 2, 3–177p., illus., XXIV (i.e. 28) pl. (1 fold.). **JG205**

Monumenti vaticani di archeologia e d'arte, publicati a cura della Pontificia accademia romana di archeologia. (Vol. VI).

Vol. VI is Magi, Filippo, *I Rilievi Flavi del Palazzo della Cancelleria.* It is a detailed description and full discussion with beautiful photographs of discovery, 1938–39, of two great Flavian friezes near the Palazzo della Cancelleria Apostolica in Rome.

MIELSCH, Harald. Römische Stuckreliefs. Heidelberg, Kerle, 1975. 201p., 88 plates, illus. **JG206**

Mitteilungen des Deutschen Arcäologischen Instituts, Römische Abteilung, Erganzungsheft, 21.

Gymnasium LXXXIII 1976 372–373 Allroggen-Bedel • LEC XLIV 1976 87 Wankenne • Latomus LXXXIII 1976 933–934 Fouchere

A chronological survey of stucco decoration in Roman art from its beginnings to the third century A.D. Included in the analysis is all known material from Rome, Latium, South Etruria, and Campania. The text is accompanied by a catalog of the existing decorations along with those known from drawings or references in old publications. The excellent photographs are produced by the German archaeological Institute. Fundamental to the study of Roman decorative art.

PICARD, Gilbert Charles. Les trophées romains; contribution a l'histoire de la religion et de l'art triomphal de Rome. Paris, E. de Boccard, 1959. 534p., illus., plates. **JG207**

Bibliothèque des Écoles françaises d'Athènes et de Rome, fasc. 187.

AJA LXIV 1960 300 Vermeule • JRS LIII 1963 221–222 Richmond

This book is a magnificent achievement that details the history of the trophy from the age of Pericles to the reign of the Byzantine emperor, Heraclius (A.D. 610 to 641). Basic to any study of Roman art, it examines the major and minor monuments in detail. A comprehensive and thorough examination of trophies in antiquity.

SÄFLUND, Gösta. The Polyphemus and Scylla groups at Sperlonga. Stockholm, Almqvist & Wiksell, 1972. 116p., illus. **JG208**

First part is a translation, slightly revised, of the author's Fynden i Tiberiusgrottan.

Gnomon XXXIX 1967 82–88 Andreae • Gymnasium LXXIV 1967 485–486 Krarup • Archaeology XXI 1968 230–231 Ridgway

A presentation of the magnificent sculptures found at Sperlonga, near Terracina, Italy, in 1957. There has been much scholarly controversy on the origin and interpretation of the sculptures, and the author presents a personal description and analysis.

STRONG, Donald Emrys. Roman imperial sculpture; an introduction to the commemorative and decorative sculpture of the Roman Empire down to the death of Constantine. London, Tiranti, 1961. vii, 104p., 144 plates. **JG209**

AJ CXIX 1962 354–355 Richmond • JRS LII 1962 253–254 Toynbee • RBPh XLIII 1965 302–303 Balty

A valuable collection of the art of the Roman empire in its western section. Written as an introduction for the non-specialist, it includes reproductions of recently discovered monuments. Portraits and sculptures in the round are not included. An excellent short treatment of Roman Imperial relief-sculpture.

STRONG, Eugénie (Sellers). Roman sculpture from Augustus to Constantine. New York, Hacker Art Books, 1971. xvi, 408p., illus. **JG210**

Reprint of the 1907 ed.

JRS 1925 281–283 Rushforth • RF 1926 253 Ducati • REG 1928 307 Picard

This is a reprint of the 1907 edition. When it first appeared it was a pioneering work establishing the theory of a specifically Roman art. While Greek artists provided the labor and the form of Roman art, they worked in the Roman spirit and conveyed in their work Roman ideas. This was true even in the Republican age but reached its height in Imperial times with artistic representation of Imperial achievements, its sepulchral monuments, and its portraiture. Although out-of-date, the book is indispensable to students of Roman art because of the lucid presentation of its thesis.

STUVERAS, Roger. Le putto dans l'art romain. Bruxelles, Latomus, 1969. 239p., illus. **JG211**

Collection Latomus, v. 99.

CR XXI 1971 465–466 Toynbee • Erasmus XXIII 1971 98–102 Schauenburg • RFIC XCIX 1971 215–216 Saletti

At the beginning of the Hellenistic age, Greek artists introduced a new artistic representation, that of the infant Eros, which became very popular in the Graeco-Roman world. The type is described by the Italian term "putto." The putto appears in all forms of Roman art: as the embodiment of lovers' passion; as his mother's (Venus) agent; the Bacchic putto; the funerary putto; the decorative putto; the putto in genre scenes, and playing games; the putto in association with other deities; and the putto in association with the sea. The book is an exhaustive study of these various forms, and the author concludes that the putto is difficult to interpret iconographically because it is essentially a humorous figure.

WAGNER, Friedrich. Raetia (Bayern südlich des Limes) und Noricum (Chiemseegebiet). Bonn, Habelt, 1973. 140, 166p., illus. **JG212**

Corpus signorum imperii Romani, Deutschland, Bd. 1/1. Corpus der Skulpturen der römischen Welt, Deutschland, Bd. 1/1.
Gnomon XLVIII 1976 593–599 Gabelmann
Series on Roman sculptures outside Italy.

ZANKER, Paul. Klassizistische statuen; Studien zur Veränderung des Kunstgeschmacks in der römischen kaiserzeit. Mainz, Philipp von Zabern, 1974. xx, 138p., 85p. of plates. **JG212a**

DLZ XCVII 1976 690–692 Schindler • TZ XXXVIII 1975 251–256 Goethert • AJA LXXX 1976 324–325 Kleiner

This book consists of a series of four *Studien* in which the author deals with representative statues of the Roman period which were inspired by Greek statues of the 5th century B.C. These classicistic statues are generally included in books on Greek sculpture, but this author discusses them within the definitions of Roman art. Many of the "Roman copies" of lost Greek originals, of the 5th and 4th centuries, contain variations or are new creations that demonstrate the changes in Roman taste. While the scope of the four essays is narrow, the book provides a scholarly addition to the study of Roman art and contains catalog entries for every type discussed.

Pottery

ÅKERSTRÖM, Åke. Der geometrische stil in Italien, archäologische grundlagen der frühesen historischen zeit Italiens. Lund, C. W. K. Gleerup, [1943]. 176p., illus. (incl. maps), 33 plates on 17 leaves, diagrs. **JG213**

Eranos 1943 169–175 Boëthius • JRS XXXIX 1949 137–142 Dunbabin and Hawkes • AJA LIII 1949 222–224 Hanfmann

The subject of the book is the geometric and subgeometric vases found in Sicily and Italy. The author relates them to Greek and Italian archaeology. The thesis is that the vases have been dated too early and that none is earlier than 725 B.C.—the date of the earliest Greek contacts with Etruria. In their reviews, Dunbabin and Hawkes disagree with Åkerström's chronology. In The Western Greeks (1948), Dunbabin closes with a detailed Appendix on their chronology.

CALLENDER, M. H. Roman amphorae, with index of stamps. London, New York, Oxford University Press, 1965. xxix, 323p., illus., maps, plates. **JG213a**

CR XVII 1967 207–208 Reynolds • CW LX 1967 395 Goldman • JRS LVII 1967 234–238 Zevi

The work is essentially an annotated catalogue of amphorae stamps in Latin from the Roman West, as published to 1950 when the author wrote the book. There is a short introduction on some aspects of the amphorae themselves, ancient designations, various forms, methods of manufacture, primary purposes and secondary usages. The catalogue is based on the volumes of CIL, but the author adds others from his acquaintance with European museums. The author concentrates on dating and assignment to area of origin. In the Index of Stamps, the stamps are accompanied by commentaries and some 800 facsimiles reproduced to scale. A valuable research tool.

HAYES, John W. Late roman pottery. London, British School at Rome, 1972. xxvii, 477p., 23 plates, illus., maps. **JG214**

AntJ LIV 1974 336–338 Radford • CR XXV 1975 128–130 Reece • Latomus XXXIV 1975 248–249 Raepsaet

The author defines this book as the study of the fine tablewares produced and used in the Mediterranean provinces of the Empire between the second and seventh centuries A.D., in particular the red-slipped products of North African factories and various imitations of them, which were dominant throughout the period. A very thorough, highly technical analysis by the author, who participated in the relevant excavations. The work contributes much to our understanding of the history of the developing church and the barbarian invasions.

HAYES, J. W. A supplement to Late Roman pottery. London, British School at Rome, 1980. xii, 479p. **JG215**

JOHNS, Catherine. Arretine and Samian pottery. London, British Museum, 1971 31p., 18 plates, illus., map. **JG216**

JRS LXVI 1976 244–246 Dannell
A good short introduction to the study of Samian ware.

MARABINI MOEUS, Maria T. The Roman thin-walled pottery from Cosa (1948–1954). With drawings by the author. [Rome], American Academy in Rome, 1973. 334p., 104 plates. **JG217**

American Academy in Rome, Memoirs, v. 32.
RSA IV 1974 226–227 Riccioni
The author sets up a hypothetical model of techno-
logical development and decay of wares and their sur-
face coatings to establish a classification of forms.
Kevin Greene in his review of MAAR 33, *Cosa: the
Utilitarian Pottery* by Stephen L. Dyson (AJA,
LXXXII, 1978, p.265–266) criticizes Marabini Moeus'
system of classification and considers the Dyson meth-
ods by comparison lucid, logical and objective.

MOREL, Jean Paul. Céramique à vernis noir du
Forum Romain et du Palatin. Paris, E. de Boccard, 1965. 2 v., 68 plates.   **JG218**

École française de Rome. Mélanges d'archéologie et
d'histoire. Suppléments, 3.
AJA LXX 1966 301–302 Bishop • CRAI 1965 330
Piganiol • Gnomon XXXVIII 1966 636–637 Gjerstad
A study of black-glaze pottery of Rome, from the
fourth, third, second and first centuries, a chronological
guide to the principle Mediterranean sites, a supplement to earlier catalogs of Lamboglia, Almagro, and
Monel, and a conclusion by Morel.

OXÉ, August. Corpus vasorum Arretinorum. A
catalogue of the signatures, shapes and chronology of Italian Sigillata. Edited by Howard Comfort. Bonn, Habelt, 1968. xxxi, 616p., 12 plates,
illus.   **JG219**

JRS LXVI 1976 244–246 Dannell
All the major production centres of Samian ware
are included, with bibliographies and illustrations. The
bibliography of Arretine ware to 1958 is listed in Terra
Sigillata, *La Ceramica e Rilievo Ellenistica e Romana*
(1968).

PICON, Maurice. Introduction à l'étude technique des céramiques sigillées de Lezoux. Dijon,
Presses de l'imprimerie universitaire, 1975. 135p.,
illus.   **JG220**

JRS LXVI 1976 244–246 Dannell • RA 1977 156–
157 Morel
An essential work of reference on the technique of
Roman pottery manufacture. With admirable scientific
precision, the book explains how the physio-chemical
properties of the raw material combined with a particular firing method produced one characteristic rather
than another, and applies these deductions to provide
parameters for the samian ware of Lezoux.

TRENDALL, Arthur Dale. The red-figured vases
of Lucania, Campania and Sicily. Oxford, Clarendon Press, 1967. 2 v.   **JG221**

Oxford monographs on classical archeology.
Antiquity XLI 1967 335 Cook • CW LXI 1968 362
Clairmont
Presents the red-figured vases of Lucania, Campania
and Sicily with copious illustration and full indexes.
Covers the historical development of the schools and
of individual styles along with complete painter and
workshop lists.

TRENDALL, Arthur Dale. South Italian vase
painting. 2 ed. London. Published for the Trustees of the British Museum by British Museum
Publications, 1976. 32p., [11] leaves of plates
(1 fold.), illus.   **JG222**

AC XVIII 1966 172–173 Cristofrani • BVAB XLII
1967 145–146 Schneider-Herrmann
A concise introduction for the student to the subject.
Bibliography, chart of shapes and helpful illustration
included.

TRENDALL, Arthur Dale. Vasi italioti ed etruschi a figure rosse. Citta del Vaticano, 1953–55.
2 v., illus., 66 plates.   **JG223**

Vasi antichi dipinti del Vaticano.
AJA LXI 1957 111–113 Cambitoglou
Part of a series of splendidly illustrated official cata-
logues of the Vatican collection of art and archaeology.
It includes the Apulian vases and Etruscan vases.

Portraiture

BERNOULLI, Johann Jakob. Römische Ikonographie. Hildesheim, G. Olms, 1969. 2 v. in 4,
illus., plates.   **JG224**

Reprint of the edition published in Stuttgart by W.
Spemann, 1882–1894.
Laid a solid scientific foundation for the study of
Roman portraiture.

BRENDEL, Otto. Ikonographie des Kaisers Augustus. Nürnberg, 1931. 71p.   **JG225**

JRS XXV 1935 88 Hinks
Enumerates four types, with 20 certain and two dubious replicas, of youthful portraits of Augustus, to be
dated earlier than the statue from Prima Porta.

CALZA, Raissa. Iconografia romana imperiale da
Carausio a Giuliano (287–363 D.C.) [Rome]
L'Erma di Bretschneider, 1972. 434p., 113 plates.
                                                 JG226

JRS LXV 1975 215–216 Colledge • Latomus
XXXIV 1975 271 Boucher
This work succeeds Vol. II of the Quaderni, B. M.
Felletti Maj's, *Iconografia,* 1958, which covers the
reigns from Severus Alexander through Carinus. Calza
follows the format established there. The work attempts
to catalogue all extant portrait images, in sculpture,
painting, the decorative and minor arts, that have ever
been suggested as representing emperors and members
of the Roman imperial families from the reign of Diocletian through the fall of Julian the Apostate. The
bibliography is followed by a compilation of textual
references, from ancient sources; then a detailed catalogue and analysis of attributions, followed by the illustrations. Considering the enormity of the project and
the difficulties encountered in identification, the book
is a useful collection and tabulation of the documentation.

CLAIRMONT, Christoph W. Die Bildnisse des Antinous. Ein Beitrag zur Porträtplastik unter Kaiser Hadrian. Rom, Schweizerisches Institut, [Auslieferung: Francke, Bern, Droz, Genève], 1966. 62p., 38p. of illus. **JG227**

Bibliotheca Helvetica Romana, v. 6.
JRS LVII 1967 267–268 Toynbee • Gymnasium LXXVI 1969 374–376 v. Heintze • BJ CLXX 1970 552–554 Bracken
An analysis of the problems of Antinoan iconography using every known portrait of Antinous from various parts of the Roman world.

DELBRÜCK, Richard. Spätantike Kaiserporträts von Constantinus Magnus bis zum Ende des Westreichs. Berlin, W. de Gruyter, 1978. xix, 250p., 128 leaves of plates, illus. **JG228**

Reprint of the 1933 ed.
ABull 1934 304 Hyslop • Gnomon XII 1935 22–27 Sieveking • DLZ 1935 998–1001 Lippold
A pioneering work on late Roman Art.

FELLETTI MAJ, Bianca Maria. Iconografia romana imperiale da Severo Alessandro a M. Aurelio Carino (225–285 D.C.) Roma, L'Erma di Bretschneider, 1958. 309p., illus. **JG229**

MH XVIII 1961 47 Jucker • HZ CXCV 1962 369–371 Zschietzschmann
Catalogue of protrait images in sculpture, painting and the decorative arts, of Roman emperors and imperial families from Severus Alexander through Carinus A.D. 222–285. The attributions are based largely on the numismatic evidence which, for numerous personages, is all that is discoverable.

HANFMANN, George. Observations on Roman portraiture. Brussels, 1953. **JG230**

Archaeology VIII 1955 137 Harrison
"Roman insistence upon personality in literary history is paralleled by Roman insistance upon personality in portraiture." With this as his theme, the author presents a concise iconographical study of Roman portraits. He also provides a basis for analysis of the artists who painted the portraits. An excellent short series of essays presented in a scholarly way.

HEINTZE, Helga von. Römische Porträts. Darmstadt, Wissenschaftliche Buchgesellschaft, 1974. xxi, 473p., [16] leaves of plates, illus. **JG231**

Wege der Forschung; Bd. 348.
AC XLIV 1975 815–817 Balty • LEC XLIII 1975 447 Wankenne • Gymnasium LXXXIII 1976

INAN, Jale and ROSENBAUM, Elisabeth. Roman and early Byzantine portrait sculpture in Asia Minor. London, Published for the British Academy by Oxford University Press, [1966]. xxv, 244p., 187 plates (incl. map). **JG232**

Arch Class XIX 1967 224–225 Lattanzi • AJA LXXI 1967 325–326 Vermeule • AntJ XLVII 1967 298–299 Painter
An excellent reference work on 310 portraits, imperial and private, from Asia Minor. Imperial portraits are arranged chronologically and private persons by region.

JUCKER, Hans. Das Bildnis im Blätterkelch: Geschichte und Bedeutung einer römischen Porträtform. Olten, Switzerland, Urs Graf-Verlag, 1961. 2 v., illus., plates. **JG233**

Bibliotheca Helvetica Romana, v. 3. 1. Text 2. Tafeln.
JRS LIII 1963 217–218 Strong • OLZ LVIII 1963 237–240 Parlasca • GGA CCXVII 1965 247–268 Daltrop • Gnomon XXXVII 1965 507–513 Andreae
A meticulous study of the Roman portrait bust, which has as its base a calyx of leaves. The first part is a catalogue of calyx-busts on grave reliefs and sarcophagi, the second analyzes the various kinds of calyx-bust, and the third is an account of the history and significance of this form of Roman portraiture. A very useful work of research and interpretation.

KISS, Zsolt. L'iconographie des princes Julio-Claudiens au temps d'Auguste et de Tibère. Varsovie; Éditions scientifiques de Pologne, 1975. 185p., (92 leaves of plates), illus. **JG234**

Latomus XXXV 1976 958 Chevallier • CR XXVII 1977 248–249 Toynbee
A complete, up-to-date collection of photographs of the portraits of the princes of the Julio-Claudian House, who were alive during the principates of Augustus and Tiberius.

McCANN, Anna Marguerite. The portraits of Septimius Severus, A.D. 193–211. [Rome], American Academy in Rome, 1968. 222p., plates. **JG235**

Memoirs of the American Academy in Rome, v. 30.
CR XX 1970 232–234 Strong • JRS LX 1970 244–245 Colledge • Latomus XXIX 1970 225–227 Foucher
An iconographical study of the portraits of Septimus Severus. The author accumulated and examined a wide variety of evidence, both literary and numismatic. The main text is devoted to the dating of the different portrait types, with interpretation and stylistic analysis and with the historical and archaeological evidence. Ten basic portrait types are identified. These range from the earliest type showing Severus as the energetic, short-cropped soldier, to the last type which resembles certain Hellenistic philosopher portraits. The text is followed by a complete catalogue of all the portraits, with description, bibliography, and photographs. An excellent study.

NIEMEYER, Hans Georg. Studien zur statuarischen Darstellung der römischen Kaiser. Berlin, Gebr. Mann, [1968]. 115p., 48 plates. **JG236**

Monumenta artis Romanae, v. 7.

BJ CLXX 1970 541–552 Fittschen • Gymnasium LXXVII 1970 558–563 v. Heintze

No. 16 in *Monumenta Artis Romanae,* a series on Roman art, this volume on statuary portraits of the Roman emperor has an extensive catalogue of Emperor Statues, p. 82–114.

L'ORANGE, Hans Peter. Apotheosis in ancient portraiture. Oslo, H. Aschehoug; Cambridge, Mass., Harvard Univ. Press, 1947. 156 p., illus., ports. **JG237**

NC 1947 126–149 Toynbee • JRS XXXVIII 1948 160–163 Toynbee

A comprehensive and masterly survey of Graeco-Roman iconography, from Hellenistic to early medieval times.

L'ORANGE, Hans Peter. Studien zur Geschichte des spätantiken Porträts. Ed. anastatica. Roma, L'Erma di Bretschneider, 1965. 157p., illus. **JG238**

Reprint of the Oslo 1933 ed.

AJA XXXVIII 1934 317–319 Müller • JRS XXV 1935 88–95 Hinks

A scholarly work, that examines late Roman portraiture. The study begins with the year 235 A.D., when the author sees a turning point in Roman Imperial art. In dating and analysis, this book laid a new foundation for the study of Roman portraiture.

POLACCO, Luigi. Il Volto di Tiberio; saggio di critica iconografica. Roma, Concessionaria per la vendita, L'Erma di Bretschneider, 1955. xiii, 207p., illus., 43 plates. **JG239**

JRS XLVI 1956 157–161 Toynbee

The first book to be exclusively devoted to the whole range of the portraits of the Emperor Tiberius. The author claims to have established the evolution of Tiberian portraiture on the basis of certainly dated, or closely dateable, monuments. Very useful in its systematic presentation of the material available. In his review, Toynbee disagrees with many of the author's interpretations and theories.

POULSEN, Vagn. Les portraits romains. Copenhagen, Ny Carlsberg Glyptotek, 1973–74. 2 v. in 4, plates. **JG240**

v. 1. République et dynastie Julienne. [Traduction du manuscrit danois par Hélène Laurent-Lund. 1.] Texte. [2] Planches.—v. 2. De Vaspas à la Basse-Antiquité. Traduit du danois par Ghani Merad. [1] Texte. [2] Planches.

JRS LIII 1963 220–221 Toynbee • AEA XXXVII 1964 164–168 Garcia y Bellido

The author, a curator at the glyptotek, has compiled in two volumes a defintive catalogue of the huge collection of Roman sculptured portraits in the Ny Carlsberg Glyptotek in Copenhagen. In size, quality, and variety of subjects, the collection is unequalled. The volume begins with a short essay on characteristics of Roman

portraiture and examples from the period covered. A comprehensive catalogue follows and then an excellent collection of photographs. Volume 2 begins with an essay on Roman portraiture from Septimus Severus to Constantine. The works in the collection for the latter period are of very high quality. A superb reference work.

SCHWEITZER, Bernhard. Die Bildniskunst der Römischen Republik. Leipzig, Koehler & Amelurg, 1948. xii, 163p., plates. **JG241**

JRS XLI 1951 172–174 Toynbee

A study of the portraiture in Rome in the early decades of the first century B.C. It was an offspring of the artistic influence of Hellenistic Greece and upon the aristocratic and family traditions of Rome. Very useful for an understanding of pre-Imperial Roman iconography.

SOECHTING, Dirk. Die Porträts des Septimus Severus. Bonn, R. Habelt, 1972. 300p., plates. **JG242**

JRS LXIII 1973 281 Colledge • AJA LXXVIII 1974 206–208 McCann

This iconographical study of the portraits of Septimus Severus analyzes 142 portraits in the round and in relief. Twelve portraits on gems and cameos are listed. The author divides the sculptures into four workshop groups. A catalogue of the material divides it into types and workshop groups. He does not make full use of McCann's *The Portraits of Septimus Severus* and this limits the value of his scholarship. The main contribution of the work is in portrait attributions.

TOYNBEE, Jocelyn M. C. Roman historical portraits. Ithaca, N.Y., Cornell University Press, 1978. 208p., illus. **JG243**

CR XXX 1980 111–112 Coulton

A collection of the portraits of fifty Republican and early Augustan notables and two hundred foreign rulers who had contacts with the Roman empire. There is a separate entry for each of the personalities that includes a discussion of the identification and iconography of the portrait types followed by useful footnotes.

VOLLENWEIDER, Marie-Louise. Die Porträtgemmen der römischen Republik. Mainz, P. von Zabern, [1974]. 2 v., plates. **JG244**

[1] Text.—[2] Katalog und Tafeln.

GNS XXV 1975 111 Kapossy • RN XVII 1975 192 Giard • AJA LXXX 1976 216–217 Hiesinger

A thorough study of Roman gem and coin representations as well as portraiture in any medium. Almost 750 gems and 500 coins are included. The first part of the text deals with portraits of identifiable individuals, and the second deals with unidentified individuals. A highly useful reference work for the study of Roman portraiture.

WEGNER, Max, ed. Das römische Hennschenbild. Die Herrscherbildnisse in antoninischer Zeit. Berlin, Gebr. Mann, 1939. 305p **JG245**

A complete revision of Bernoulli's monumental work on Roman portraiture. Wegner's study of Antonine portraiture (Part two, volume four) contains a history of problems connected with the making and distribution of imperial portraits, and seven chapters on the extant portraits of the Antonine emperors and their wives. This work, and that of W. H. Gross, on the portraiture of Trajan in the same series fill the lacuna between the work of Brendel, Curtius and Poulsen on the work of the Julio-Claudian period and that of Delbrück and L'Orange on the portraits of Imperial times.

WEST, R. Römische Portratplastik, München, Bruckmann, 1933 264p.   **JG246**

> AJA 1934 317–319 Müller • JRS XXV 1935 88 Hinks
> A useful handbook, with excellent plates which illustrate 290 pieces of sculpture, and 111 coins. It covers Roman Portraiture to the Flavian period and contains a bibliography to 1932. A good starting point for a study of the subject.

ZANKER, Paul. Studien zu den Augustus-Porträts. Göttingen, Vandenhoeck & Ruprecht, 1973– . 54p., 36 plates.   **JG247**

> 1. Der Actium-Typus.
> Arch Class XXVII 1975 169–172 Verzar • DLZ XCVII 1976 71–73 Schindler • Gnomon XLVIII 1976 699–705 Megow
> In this first part of a comprehensive study, the author describes his method. He plans to reconstruct the prototype of each portrait and explain how it relates to the replicas. In this part, the author describes the Actium type.

Provinces

BARTFIELD, L. H. et al. Beiträge zur Archäologie des römischen Rheinlands. Düsseldorf, Rheinland Verlag, 1968–1972. 3v.   **JG248**

> Rheinische Ausgrabungen; Bd. 3.10.12.
> These superb volumes contain major and minor articles on the archaeology of Roman Rhineland.

BIANCHI BANDINELLI, Ranuccio. The buried city; Excavations at Leptis Magna. New York, Praeger, 1966. 126p., 256 illus.   **JG249**

> Trans. of Leptis Magna.
> RBPh XLIII 1965 104–106 Desagnes • RA II 1964 95–97 Picard
> The introduction is by Bianchi Bandinelli, the text by Ernesto Vergara Caffarelli and Giacomo Caputo. Photos by Fabrizio Clerici. A short text with many good photographs.

BOLLETTINO della Società d'Italia 1886–1912; Africa Italiana 1913–1937. Nendeln, Lichtenstein, Kraus Reprint, 1975– . Anno 1–40, 1882–1921.   **JG250**

> Reports published by the Italian government on its excavations in Africa from 1913 to 1937.

BARADEZ, Jean Lucien. Fossatum Africae; Recherches aériennes sur l'organisation des confins sahariens à l'époche romaine. Paris, Arts et Métiers graphiques, 1949. x, 363p., illus., maps.
JG251

> JRS XL 1950 162–165 Richmond and Goodchild
> A remarkable work of archaeological and air photography, concluding in the discovery of Roman Africa's southern frontier bordering the Sahara. The aerial work was followed by ground reconnaissance and some digging. Both the text and the magnificent photographs make this an essential reference work for Roman Africa.

COLLART, Paul. L'Autel monumental de Baalbek. Paris, Geuthner, 1965. vi, 153p., illus., plates.   **JG252**

> AJA LVII 1953 155 Wellezx • JHS LXXIII 1953 190 Hamilton
> The site consists primarily of the complex of the great sanctuary of Heliopolitan Jupiter and the adjoining Temple of Bacchus. The original publication of the ruins was in 1757 by R. Wood, The ruins of Baalbek, reprinted in 1971. Results of an early German excavation were published in T. Wiegand's Baalbek, Ergebnisse der Ausgräbungen und Untersuchungen (1921–1925). The present work records the restoration of the whole court area in 1930 when the French Service des Antiquités demolished the remains of a Byzantine basilica and reconstructed the court.

COLLINGWOOD, Robin George and RICHMOND, Ian. The archaeology of Roman Britain. With a chapter by B. R. Hartley on Samian Ware. New ed., entirely revised. London, Methuen, 1969. xxv, 350p., illus., 27 plates.
JG253

> Distributed in U.S.A. by Barnes and Noble, New York.
> History LV 1970 93–94 Birley • JRS LX 1970 245–247 Webster
> This is a revision of a 1930 original. Chapters include Native Settlements, Weapons, Tools, Utensils, Temples, Coins, Towns, Inscriptions and Coarse Pottery. References are at the end of each chapter. The quality of the illustrations is excellent. The edition, revised by Richmond, remains a standard reference work.
> Also revised by Richmond is the author's classic Handbook to the Roman Wall, describing the finest monument of antiquity that England possesses.

CORPUS des mosaiques de Tunisie. Margaret A. Alexander & Mongi Ennaifer, Co-directeurs. Tunis, Institut National d'Archéologie et d'Art, 1973– . Illus.   **JG254**

> Atlas archéologique de la Tunisie; v Feuille 7.
> ABull LXIII 1976 120–121 Clarke • AC XLVI 1977 368–369 Hanoune • JRS LXVI 1976 252–253 Waywell
> This catalogue of mosaic pavements of the Roman

period discovered in Tunisia will replace *Inventaire des Mosaiques de la Gaule et de l'Afrique II, Afrique Proconsulaire* (Tunisie) (1910) when it is completed. It is meticulously prepared and a valuable reference work.

GOODCHILD, Richard George. Libyan studies; Select papers of the late R. G. Goodchild. Edited by Joyce Reynolds. London, Elek, 1975. xxii, 345p., 17 leaves of plates. **JG255**

CR XXVII 1977 314 Vickers
A good selection from the wide range of Goodchild's work in Roman Libya.

GRENIER, Albert. Manuel d'archéologie gallo-romaine. Paris, Picard, 1931–1960. 2 v. **JG256**

AJA LXVI 1962 116–117 Amand
The first volume deals with aqueducts and baths, their location, construction and uses. In the second volume baths connected with the cult of water are examined. The archaeology and significance of the sanctuaries at or near the wells provide evidence that the water was considered sacred.

GRENIER, Albert. Manuel d'archéologie gallo-romaine. Paris, Picard, 1958. 1026p., 324 figs. **JG257**

IIIᵉ partie: L'architecture. 2 v. Pt. 1. L'urbanisme, les monuments: Capitol. Pt. 2. Ludi et circenses: théatres, amphi-théatres, cirques.
RBPh XXXVII 1958 1078–1079 Faider • AJA LXIV 1960 114–115 Amand
Continues Joseph Dechelette's *Manuel d'archéologie préhistorique, celtique et gallo-romaine* providing the most important contribution to the understanding of Roman archaeology in Gaul. Fora, temples, theaters and amphitheaters are examined. Chapters on the monuments and buildings are very informative, especially on temples. Very well documented.

HAYNES, Denys Eyre Lankester. The antiquities of Tripolitania: An archaeological and historical guide to the pre-Islamic antiquities of Tripolitania. Tripoli, Antiquities Dept., Tripolitania, 1959. 178p., illus., plates, maps. **JG258**

JRS L 1960 270–271 Ward-Perkins
Part I is an account of the land, its peoples and their history, from the arrival of the Phoenicians in their trading vessels, first half of the first millennium B.C., to the Arab conquest in 642 A.D. Part II describes the surviving antiquities of Leptis Magna Oea and Sabratha, along with sites on the coast and in the interior. Well illustrated and documented.

KÖNIG, Ingemar. Die Mileensteine der Gallia Narbonensis; Studien der zum Strassenwesen der Provincia Narbonensis. Bern, Kümmerly and Frey, 1970. 301p. **JG259**

Itinera Romana; vol. Bd. 3.

This is a volume in the series Itinera Romana, contributions to the history of the roads of the Roman Empire. The director is Dr. Gerold Walser of Bern University. Eventually the material from each province will be incorporated in *Corpus Inscriptionum Latinarum*, v. XVII.

KRAELING, C. H. The excavations of Dura-Europas; Final reports. New Haven, 1956. **JG260**

The Dura-Europas excavations have greatly enlarged our knowledge of the progress of Hellenism beyond the eastern frontiers. The most important remains are the paintings in the temple of Palmyrene gods, the Christian paintings and the Mithra temple, and the paintings from the synagogue.
Early excavations were published in *Excavations at Dura-Europas;* Preliminary reports (1929–). For an analysis of the synagogue, cf. J. Guttman, ed., *The Dura-Europas Synagogue. A re-evaluation 1932–1972,* 1971.

LEWIS, Michael Jonathan Taunton. Temples in Roman Britain. Cambridge, Cambridge University Press, 1966. xvi, 218p., illus., 4 plates, maps, plans, tables. **JG261**

REL XLIV 1966 558 Richard • CPh LXII 1967 285–288 Henry
A detailed catalog and guide to temples in Great Britain, examining the archaeology rather than the religion. Fully independent architectural buildings are the focus of the study while regimental and domestic shrines and open-air altars are excluded. Temples presented are Romano-Celtic temples, other temples whose structure is known, e.g., temples of Oriental cults (including Christian churches), and other temples whose structure is not known but whose existence is reliably attested. Since very few temples survive in Britain even to the top of their foundation the author uses Continental parallels to identify architectural characteristics. A well-documented and thorough study.

MacKENDRICK, Paul Lachlan. The North African stones speak. Chapel Hill, University of North Carolina Press, 1980. **JG262**

A survey of life in the Roman provinces of Africa, providing an excellent introduction to the Berber, Punic and Greco-Roman civilizations.

MacKENDRICK, Paul Lachlan. Roman France. London, Bell; New York, St. Martin's Press, 1971. xii, 275p., illus. **JG263**

CR XXV 1975 109–111 Salway • JRS LXIII 1973 284–285 Mann
A popular, well-written guide to the Roman remains in France, complementing Oliver Brogan's *Roman Gaul* (1953) and with more illustration, but not replacing it.

MATTHEWS, Kenneth D. Cities in the sand: Leptis Magna and Sabratha in Roman Africa. Philadelphia, University of Pennsylvania Press, 1957. 160p., 97 plates.   **JG264**

CR IX 1959 83 Warmington • AJ CXIV 1957 192 Spittle

Intended as a pictorial introduction to the two towns, this book presents the historical background to the Roman presence in Tripolitania and a chapter each on the history of Leptis Magna and Sabratha. The large selection of beautiful black and white photographs illustrate the architecture, sculpture and mosaics of the towns.

MENEN, Aubrey. Cities in the sand. London, Thames and Hudson, 1972. 272p., illus. (some col.).   **JG265**

TLS LXXII 1973 293

An entertainingly written book on the ancient cities of Leptis Magna, Timgad, Palmyra, Carthage, and others established by the Phoenicians in the Mediterranean area. Describes them at the height of their civilization and in their decline and extinction. Numerous illustrations add to the vivid description of Roman life from the 2d century A.D. to the fall of the Empire.

OPUSCULA romana. Lund, Gleerup, 1954– . Illus.   **JG266**

CR V XVI 1966 421–422 Toynbee

These volumes are published by the Swedish Institute in Rome and present a variety of topics. Volume I is primarily archaeological, with material from Rome, Italy and the Roman provinces.

PICARD, Gilbert Charles. La civilisation de l'Afrique romaine. Avec 3 cartes et 2 plans dans le texte et 49 illus. hors-texte. Paris, Plon, 1959. v, 406p.   **JG267**

Karthago X 1959–1960 171–172 Foucher

Traces the impact of Roman civilization on North Africa from the middle of the 1st century B.C. down to the revolt of the Gordians in 238, combining literary evidence with archaeological discoveries to provide an accurate picture of the lives of people in cities and villages. An excellent interpretation of the monuments, sculptures, mosaics, etc., of the cities.

POBÉ, Marcel and ROUBIER, J. The art of Roman Gaul; A thousand years of Celtic art and culture. London, Galley Press, 1961. viii, 78p., 104 leaves of plates, illus., map.   **JG268**

AJA LXVI 1962 431 Liversidge • JRS LIII 1963 252 Strong

Mainly a book of illustrations arranged chronologically. The superb photographs cover sculpture, towns, houses of the Greek and Roman periods, public buildings, aqueducts, theaters, temples, etc. The text is less useful.

RICHMOND, Ian Archibald, Sir. Roman archaeology and art; Edited by Peter Salway. London, Faber and Faber, 1969. 294p., illus., 9 plates.   **JG269**

A collection of Richmond's papers extensively edited by Salway who added the illustrations. Titles include: Britain in the Third and Fourth Centuries; The Romano-British Countryside; The Country Estates; and Hadrian's Wall.

RIVET, A. L. The Roman villa in Britain. New York, Praeger, 1969. xvi, 299p., illus., part col., maps.   **JG270**

G&R XVII 1970 113 Sewter • History LV 1970 94–96 Birley

Six essays on the history of the Roman villa in Britain with maps, plans and good illustrations. Aspects included are plans of villas, mosaic pavements, furniture and interior decoration, and social and economic aspects.

ROMANELLI, Pietro. Storia delle provincie romane dell' Africa. Roma, L'Erma de Bretschneider, 1959. x, 720p., fold. map.   **JG271**

Gnomon XXXI 1960 709–715 Euzannet

This impressive volume is complemented by the same author's *Topografia e archaeologia Africa Romana* (1970), and together they present the fullest possible summary of what is known about the architecture, sculpture, painting and mosaics of North Africa in their historical setting.

SCHOPPA, Helen. Die Kunst der Römerzeit in Gallien, Germanien und Britannien. München, Deutscher Kunstverlag, 1957. 66p., mounted col. illus., 140 plates, map.   **JG272**

Germania XXXVI 1958 495–500 Möbius • JRS XLVIII 1958 212–214 Toynbee

Primarily a picture book on the art of the Roman provinces north of the Alps. Impressive plates.

TOYNBEE, Jocelyn M. C. Art in Britain under the Romans. Oxford, Clarendon Press, 1964. xxiv, 473p., 99p., illus., ports.   **JG273**

RHE LX 1965 311–313 Dauphin • Antiquity XXXIX 1965 237–238 Braude

This is an exhaustive study of the great majority of art objects from Romano-British times. The divisions are by type of art and include sculpture in the round, sculpture in relief, fresco painting, floor mosaics, decorated metal work and figured pottery. Well illustrated with black and white photographs.

VERMEULE, Cornelius Clarkson. Roman imperial art in Greece and Asia Minor. Cambridge, Mass., Belknap Press of Harvard University, 1968. xxiv, 548p., illus., maps.   **JG274**

AJA LXXIII 1969 391–392 Brilliant • Phoenix XXV 1971 179–186 Alfödi-Rosenbaum

This beautiful book collects and surveys the works of art and architecture in the East that have to do with the Roman state. There are excellent black and white illustrations and appendices: Roman Portraits, Works of Art in Museums and Private Collections, and Works of Art and Inscriptions by Site.

WIGHTMAN, Edith Mary. Roman Trier and the Treveri. New York, Praeger, 1971. 320p., illus., maps, plans.   **JG275**

AJA LXXVI 1972 107–109 Liversidge

Trier, near the meeting points of the frontiers of Luxembourg, Belgium, France and Germany on the Moselle, is one of the finest areas for the study of Roman archaeology outside of Italy. This book outlines Treveran history and describes aspects of the city, its architecture, commerce and industry, along with sculptures, mosaics and life in the countryside. An excellent basic study on the results of excavations in the area, which can be complemented with H. Cüpper, *Die Trierer Römerbrücken* (1969) and *Landesmuseum Trier* by R. Schindler (2d ed., 1971).

Religion, Mythology, and Magic

KA HANDBOOKS, MANUALS, AND GUIDES

CORTE, Francesco Della. "Mitologia Classica." Introduzione II: 197–230; 231–257 (bibliog.) **KA1**

REL L 1972 396 Le Bonniec • AC XLII 1973 337–338 Crahay

A useful short treatment for students and teachers, this is available as a *separatum,* Milan, Marzorati, 1972, 76p. Nine categories of myth are distinguished and explained. The bibliography is well organized and covers religion as well as mythology. Some points are too summarily treated for an introduction, and there are many typographical and more serious errors.

DODDS, Eric. Pagan and Christian in an age of anxiety; some aspects of religious experience from Marcus Aurelius to Constantine. New York, Norton, [1970]. xii, 144p. **KA2**

"The Norton library, N545."
CW LIX 1966 166–167 Downey • Phoenix XX 1966 349–352 Rist • Rec SR LIV 1966 304–306 Daniélou

A fascinating exercise in psychoanalysis of the third century, an age as bewildered as our own and so likely to have some didactic lessons for us. Professor Dodds is interested more in what pagans and Christians of that age shared than in what divided them. An extraordinarily erudite set of lectures.

FEDER, Lillian. Ancient myth in modern poetry. Princeton, N.J., Princeton University Press, 1977, 1971. xiv, 432p. **KA3**

1st Princeton paperback printing.
REG LXXXVIII 1975 273–274 Germain • CPh LXVIII 1973 220–222 Matsen • ACR II 1972 217 Dick

An English professor here examines how myth functions in such modern writers as Yeats, Pound, Eliot and Auden. She develops a definition of myth as a continuous and evolving mode of expression which constitutes a guide to unconscious feelings and instincts. Strongly, almost exclusively, influenced by Freud and Jung.

GORCE, Maxime and MORTIER, Raoul. Histoire générale des religions. Paris, A. Quillet, 1944–1951. 5 v., illus., maps. **KA4**

Erasmus V 1952 608–610 Gundry • RA XXXV 1950 222–223 Lantier
t.1. Introduction générale. Les primitifs. L'ancien Orient. Les Indo-Européens. [t.2] Grèce. Rome [t.3] Indo-Iraniens. Judaïsme. Origines chrétiennes. Christianismes orientaux. [t.4] Christianisme médiéval. Réforme protestante. Catholicisme moderne. Islam. Extrême-Orient. [t.5]. Folklore et religion. Magie et religion. Tableaux chronologiques de l'histoire des religions. Index générale des noms cités.

GRANT, Michael. Myths of the Greeks and Romans. Cleveland, World Pub. Co., [1962]. 487p. **KA5**

REA LXVII 1965 457–459 Grimal • CR XVI 1966 78–79 Adkin • JRS LIV 1964 218 Mattingly

A generous selection of the "most important and necessary" myths of Greece and Rome, drawn from the best ancient authorities with well-chosen modern translations and good illustrations, mostly from vases. Not content simply to retell the myths, the author explores the various problems they suggest, e. g., the date of Homer, the date of Troy. He is not bound to any one theory to explain the myths but ranges over the many theories advanced by anthropologists, classicists, psychoanalysts and scholars of religion in search of appropriate keys to unlock individual myths. A good introduction, sensible but not dull, detailed but not indigestible.

GRANT, Michael and HAZEL, John. Who's who in classical mythology. London, Weidenfeld & Nicolson, [1973]. 447p., illus. (part col.).   **KA6**

Hermathena CXIX 1975 86–87 Stanford
Identifies and describes the principal, best known and most influential incidents built into each mythological narrative. There are useful illustrations, maps and geneological trees, but no primary sources or bibliography.

GRIMAL, Pierre. Dictionnaire de la mythologie grecque et romaine. 5. Édition revue. Paris, Presses Universitaires de France, 1976. xxxi, 574p., illus.   **KA7**

GRIMAL, Pierre [et al.]. Mythologies. Part I: Mythologies de la Mediterranée au Gange; Part II: Mythologies des steppes, des forêts et des îles. Paris, Larousse, 1963. 576p., illus., maps.   **KA8**

A well-illustrated handbook by various authors. Important sections for the classicist are: Introduction; Man and Myth, P. Grimal (p. 9–15); The Problem of Prehistoric Religions, A. Varagnac (17–24); Egypt: Syncretism and State Religion (25–54); Empires of the Ancient Near East: the Hymns of Creation, M. Vieyra (55–84); Western Semitic Lands: the Idea of the Supreme God, A. Caquot (85–96); Greece: Myth and Logic, P. Grimal (97–176); Rome: Gods by Conquest, P. Grimal, (17–188).

KEULS, Eva. The water carriers in Hades; A study of catharsis through toil in classical antiquity. Amsterdam, A. M. Hakkert, 1974. 189p., 32 leaves of plates, illus.   **KA9**

Augustinus XXI 1976 428 Ortall
The Danae are studied here in literature, Greek and Latin, and in art, especially Roman. Chapter 8 deals with the catharsis-through-work motif.

KIRK, Geoffrey Stephen. Myth; Its meaning and functions in ancient and other cultures. [1st paperback ed.] Cambridge, Cambridge University Press (Berkeley, University of California Press), 1970. xii, 299p.   **KA10**

Sather classical lectures, 40.
Gnomon XLIV 1972 225–230 Burkert • CR XXII 1972 235–238 Griffiths • Helios III 1976 93–98 Smith • REL L 1972 396–397 Drossart • CPh LXIX 1974 148–154 Jameson
Six chapters, embracing the Sather lectures, cover the problem of definition of myth between ritual and folktale, structuralism, ancient Mesopotamia, nature

and culture, and the qualities of Greek myths (p.172–251). The introduction surveys previous work in the field, mostly English, but the chief inspiration for most of the book is Claude Lévi-Strauss, though he too is subjected to considerable criticism.

KIRKWOOD, G. M. A short guide to classical mythology. New York, Rinehart, 1959. vii, 109p.   **KA11**

Rinehart Pamphlets.
CW LIV 1960 20 Schoenheim

KLAUSER, Th. [et al.]. Reallexikon für Antike und Christentum. Sachwörterbuch zur Auseinandersetzung des Christentums mit der antiken Welt (RLAC). Stuttgart, Hiersemann.   **KA12**

Bd. X: Genesis-Gigant. Bd. XI, Lief. 85–86: Gnosis II (Gnosticismus) [forts.]—Gottesbeweis: 1981, col. 641–960. Lief. 87: Gottesbeweis [forts.]—Gottesgnadentum. col. 961–1120. Bd. XI, Lief. 88: Gottesgnadentum [forts.]—Gottesnamen (Gottespitheta) IV: 1981, col. 1121–1278. Bd. XII, Lief. 89: Gottesschau (Visio beatifica)—Gottmensch I: 1981, col. 1–160.

KÖNIG, Franz, Cardinal. Religionswissenschaftliches Wörterbuch; Die Grundbegriffe. Freiburg, Herder, 1956. 954 columns., illus.   **KA13**

Antonianum XXXII 1957 436–437 Kleinhans • JThs VIII 1957 328–330 Greenslade

LINDSAY, Jack. Origins of astrology. New York, Barnes & Noble, [1971]. xii, 480p., illus.   **KA14**

"Written ... as a companion-piece to go with ... [the author's] The origins of alchemy in Graeco-Roman Egypt."
ACR II 1972 186 Mackay • CR XXII 1972 315–316 Griffiths

LUCK, Georg. Arcana Mundi; A collection of ancient texts translated and annotated. Baltimore, Johns Hopkins University Press, 1985. 416p.   **KA15**

A comprehensive sourcebook and introduction to magic as it was practised by witches and sorcerers, *magi* and astrologers in the Greek and Roman worlds. 122 documents dating from the eighth century B.C. through the fourth century A.D. are newly translated and accompanied by interpretation.

MAYERSON, Philip. Classical mythology in literature, art, and music. Waltham, Mass., Xerox College Pub., [1971]. xv, 509p., illus.   **KA16**

CPh LXVII 1972 151–153 Bruère • CW LXV 1972 205–206 Harmon
The emphasis is properly on literature in this elegant and erudite work, but the other arts are not neglected. There are copious and illuminating quotations from

a wide range of literary works that have been variously enriched by mythological allusion. Writers quoted range from Dante to Gide, Shakespeare to Rilke. A beautifully produced book is, however, marred by too many misprints.

MORFORD, Mark P. O. and LENARDON, Robert. Classical mythology. New York, McKay, 1975, 1971. x, 498p., illus., maps.   **KA17**

CPh LXVII 1972 151–153 Bruère • Phoenix XXXII 1978 360–361 Snider
A well-conceived and attractively presented manual, especially useful for its numerous and extensive translations of ancient sources, e.g., the Homeric Hymn to Demeter. Of the 24 chapters, 14 have to do with creation myths; the remaining ones are divided between Greek and Roman mythology and the survival of classical mythology.

NILSSON, Martin Persson. The Dionysiac mysteries of the Hellenistic and Roman Age. New York, Arno Press, 1975. 150p., illus.   **KA18**

Reprint of the 1957 ed. published by C. W. K. Gleerup, Lund, Sweden, as no. 5 of Skrifter Utg, av Svenska Institutet i Athen; 80.
JHS LXXVIII 1958 166–167 Rose
An assembly of valuable articles already published, translated into English where necessary, and with corrections and fresh material added. This work of a veteran scholar is a valuable treatise on a subject open to many misunderstandings.

NOCK, Arthur Darby. Essays on religion and the ancient world. Selected and edited, with an introd., bibliography of Nock's writings, and indices, by Zeph Stewart. Cambridge, Mass., Harvard University Press, 1972. 2 v. [xvii, 1029p.], port.   **KA19**

CR XXV 1975 82–84 Ogilvie • JRS LXVI 1976 239–240 North • Gnomon XLVI 1974 83–85 Richard
A magnificent treasure-house of Nock's papers (many of them reviews), revealing his brilliant gift of synthesis, incomparable mastery of the literature of the Roman Empire, and disciplined scholarly technique.

OSWALT, Sabine G. Concise encyclopedia of Greek and Roman mythology. Glasgow, Collins (Chicago, Follett), [1969]. 313p., illus.   **KA20**

JHS XC 1970 265 Pollard
A useful little mine of myths, ideal for a rapid spot-check, unencumbered by references or controversy. There is a short list of ancient sources at the end and five genealogical tables. Remarkably comprehensive within its limits, neatly assembled and adequately illustrated.

PERADOTTO, John. Classical mythology; An annotated bibliographical survey. 2d printing. Boulder, Colo., American Philological Association, 1977. 76p.   **KA21**

A most useful guide for those giving and taking college-level courses in mythology. There is a rating code on the usefulness of the works surveyed: text (A); supplementary reading for undergraduates (B); instructor reference (C). Works not recommended for college-level courses but which may have other virtues are variously rated X, Y, Z.

REINHOLD, Meyer. Past and present; The continuity of classical myths. Drawings by Anna Held Audette. Toronto, Hakkert, 1972. viii, 449p., illus.   **KA22**

A popular introduction to classical mythology, stressing the attributes of the major Greek deities and heroes and the survival of myth in modern writers like Giraudoux and Joyce, Eliot and O'Neill, Cocteau and Gerhart Hauptmann. Greek myth gets a much larger space than Roman (300 pages as against 40). The commentary gives an adequate picture of the state of the question in disputed matters. Good background material on Near Eastern origins is provided.

ROSCHER, Wilhelm Heinrich. Ausführliches Lexikon der griechischen und römischen Mythologie. Hildesheim, Olms, 1965– .   **KA23**

ROSE, Herbert J. A handbook of Greek mythology, including its extension to Rome. 6th ed. London, Methuen, [1972]. ix, 365p.   **KA24**

AAHG XI 1958 1–3 Lesky
More careful in scholarship than Graves.

ROSE, Herbert J. Religion in Greece and Rome. With a new introd. by the author. New York, Harper, [1959]. 312p.   **KA25**

"Originally published as *Ancient Greek Religion* (1946) and *Ancient Roman Religion* (1948)."
CW LIII 1960 131–132 Evans • JRS XXXIX 1949 166–167 Weinstock
A handy paperback edition, invaluable for teachers and students alike, popular yet scholarly. See also Rose, H. J., "Roman Religion 1910–1960," *JRS* L (1960), 161–182.

SNELL, Bruno. The discovery of the mind. [New York, Harper, 1960]. xii, 323p.   **KA26**

Harper torchbooks, TB1018. Academy library.

TRIPP, Edward. Crowell's *Handbook of Classical Mythology.* New York, Crowell, [1970]. ix, 631p., geneal. table, maps.   **KA27**

G&R XVIII 1971 234 Sewter • ACR I 1971 174–175 O'Neil.
An eminently readable handbook, arranged in alphabetical order. The sources are listed at the end of every important entry. Aimed at, and ideal for, the interested amateur. There are numerous omissions and errors.

WITT, Reginald Eldred. Isis in the Graeco-Roman world. London, Thames and Hudson, 1971. 336p., illus., maps.   **KA28**

CR XXIV 1974 235–239 Murray • JHS XCII 1972 223 Wells • JNES XXXIV 1975 283–285 Doll

The story of Isis is the story of how the Greeks came to terms with Egyptian religion. The literary sources, going back to Timotheus and Manetho, show how her image was changed to fit Greek needs. Sources like *The golden ass* Book XI tell us much of conversion to the faith of Isis; Plutarch's *On Isis and Osikis* also is valuable. Dr. Witt writes with erudition and enthusiasm, but he pushes Isis/Jesus analogies too far, and his hope to produce a synthesis on Isis worship was probably premature and is not realized.

KB   GREEK RELIGION AND MYTHOLOGY

ALEXIOU, Margaret. The ritual lament in Greek tradition. Cambridge, Cambridge University Press, 1974. xiv, 274p.   **KB1**

Augustinus XX 1975 205 Orosio • CR XXVI 1976 198–199 Hainsworth • G&R XXI 1974 214 Walcot

This is a literary appreciation, for the most part, of the conventions of the ritual lament as an art-form in its various manifestations: the *threnos* of epic, the *kommos* of tragedy, the contemporary popular lament. The evidence of legislation and art is used to supplement that of literature and a persuasive case is made for the continuity of the genre.

BABUT, Daniel. La religion des philosophes grecs, de Thalès aux stoïciens. [1. éd. Paris], Presses Universitaires de France, 1974. 213p.   **KB2**

Collection SUP. Littératures anciennes; 4.

MH XXXIII 1976 57–58 Burkert • REG LXXXVIII 1975 326–327 Moreau • RPh L 1976 293 des Places

An excellent historical survey, from the pre-Socratics to the Stoics, well documented with sources and references. Starts with the pre-Socratics (p.15–57).

BIDEZ, Joseph. Les mages hellénisés, Zoroastre, Ostanè et Hystaspe d'aprés la tradition grecque. New York, Arno Press, 1975. xi, 297p., 409p.   **KB3**

Reprint of the 1938 ed. published by Société d'éditions "Les Belles Lettres," Paris.

CW XXXIII 1940 172 Gray • JHS LIX 1939 170–171 Rose • REG LII 1939 379–381 Boyancé • RPh XIII 1939 252–254 Ernout

In this two-volume work, v. 1 forms an introduction and v. 2 consists of texts (Greek, Latin and Medieval) on the relations between Greek thought and Oriental religions.

BÖHME, Robert. Orpheus, der Sänger und seine Zeit. Bern; München, Francke, [1970]. 574p., illus.   **KB4**

AAHG XXVII 1974 206–209 Schwarz • AC XL 1971 785 Crahay • LEC XL 1972 132 Wankenne

A study of Orphism as well as of Orpheus, based on the most ancient literary *testimonia* and archaeological data from Crete and the Mycenaean world.

BRILLIANT, M., AIGRAIN, R. [et al.]. Histoire des religions. Vol. III: La religion égyptienne, par Drioton, E.; Les religions préhelléniques, par Demargne, P.; Les religions de la Grèce antique, par des Places, E.; La religion romaine, par Fabre, P. Paris, Bloud et Gay, 1955. 443p.   **KB5**

AC XXV 1956 245–246 Moreau • CR VI 1956 261–262 Rose • CPh LII 1957 256–257 Walton • RPh XXX 1956 337–338 Ernout

In this excellent series, Egyptian religion appears to be treated more thoroughly and in greater detail. Demargne follows Nilsson in rejecting a single Minoan goddess. Des Places pushes Christian parallels in his treatment, but they are often illuminating. Fabre's introduction to the complex problem of Roman religion is outstanding.

BRISSON, L. Le mythe de Tirésias. Essai d'analyse structurale. Leyden, Brill, 1976. ix, 169p., 9 plates.   **KB6**

Études préliminaires aux religions orientales dans l'empire romain; LV.

Phoenix XXXI 1977 179–181 Berthiaume

The subtitle indicates the approach to this ambiguous character of myth who is a mediating figure between gods and men; is at one time female, at another male; and is famed for his knowledge of present and future, his longevity and his blindness. Three versions of the myth are here presented.

BURKERT, Walter. Griechische Religion der Archaischen und Klassischen Epoche. 1. Aufl. Stuttgart, Berlin, Köln, and Mainz, Kohlhammer, 1977. 508p., maps (on lining paper).

KB7

Die Religionen der Menschheit; Bd. 15.

CR XXIX 1979 86–88 Parker • LEC XLVI 1978 169–170 Renard

The city and polytheism, the mysteries and "philosophical" religion. A wealth of information, supported by most up-to-date bibliographical guidance in the footnotes, makes this work for the specialist *the* central treatment of Greek religion. Archaeology is skillfully used to present a vivid picture of the physical surroundings of ritual, and comparative religion is splendidly invoked in many instances.

BURKERT, Walter. Homo Necans; Interpretationen Altgriechischer Opferriten und Mythen. Berlin and New York, De Gruyter, 1972. xii, 356p. **KB8**

Religionsgeschichtliche Versuche und Vorarbeiten; Bd. 32.

AAHG XXVII 1974 181–184 Pötscher • AC XLII 1973 338–339 Crahay • G&R XX 1973 210 Walcot

The early chapters deal with sacrifice and ritual, and succeeding chapters deal with individual cults, myths and festivals, including New Year festivals, the Anthesteria and the rites at Eleusis.

BURKERT, Walter. Structure and history in Greek mythology and ritual. Berkeley, University of California Press, 1979. xix, 226p. **KB9**

Sather lectures, 47.

TLS LXXIX 1980 1311 Kirk • CO 58 (1980) 26–27 Robin

Burkert, following in the main a Proppian, ethnobiological model, interprets various Greek myths and rituals with great erudition.

COOK, Arthur B. Zeus; A study in ancient religion. New York, Biblo and Tannen, 1964–1965. 2 v. in 3., illus. (part fold. in pocket), plans, col. plates. **KB10**

v. 1. Zeus, god of the bright sky; v. 2. Zeus, god of the dark sky (thunder and lightning).

AC 1942 165–168 Cumont • CR 1940 209–213 Pickard-Cambridge • JthS 1940 317–320 Rose

An unprepossessing product of the so-called Cambridge School of Anthropology.

DEFRADAS, Jean. Les Thèmes de la propagande delphique. 2e tirage revu et corrigé. Paris, Les Belles Lettres, 1972. 204p. **KB11**

Collection d'études anciennes. Originally presented as the author's thesis, Paris, 1954.

AC XXIV 1955 232–233 Fuhrmann • CR VII 1957 64–66 Hopper • RBPh XXXIII 1955 397–400 Béquignon

This work tries to show how Delphic doctrine attempted to back-date history. The literary evidence in, for example, the *Theogony, works and days* and *Hymn to the Pythian Apollo* is carefully analyzed, particularly in matters of chronology.

DES PLACES, Edouard. La religion grèque, dieux, cultes, rites, et sentiments religieux dans la Grèce antique. Paris, A. et J. Picard et Cie, 1969. 397p. **KB12**

Gnomon XLIV 1972 230–235 Fauth • CPh LXVIII 1973 66–68 Fontenrose • JHS XCI 1971 171–172 Pollard

Though it contains much good and useful information on Greek religion and is based on wide reading, this work is not entirely reliable as a textbook or guide. Its first section on the gods briefly considers in turn thirteen Olympians and Hecate, Heracles, Hades, As-

clepius, Mother of the Gods and Cronus. Part II reviews religious thought from Homer to Iamblichus and Proclus. The whole work is rather pedestrian and discursive. Sound on epigraphical and archaeological evidence, it tends to ignore Minoan-Mycenaean religion.

DEUBNER, Ludwig A. Attische Feste. Hildesheim and New York, G. Olms, 1969. 269p., 40 plates, table (fold.). **KB13**

DLZ 1933 1969–1974 Nilsson • JHS LIII 1933 146–148 Rose • Gnomon X 1934 289–295 Nock

A handsome, lucid and penetrating commentary, and a display of unequaled mastery of literary and archaeological material. Long been a standard work of reference on festivals. These are arranged under the names of the gods, with an accompanying calendar.

DIETRICH, B. C. Death, fate and the gods; The development of a religious idea in Greek popular belief and in Homer. [London], University of London, Athlone Press, 1965. xi, 390p. **KB14**

University of London classical studies; 3.

CW LIX 1966 308 Segal • Gnomon XXXIX 1967 88–90 Davison

Using the methods of anthropology and linguistics rather than the more usual literary and historical ideas, the author prefaces his discussion of fate in Homer with 176 pages on the cult practices associated with the hero, the Daemon, Moira, Erinys and Nemesis. There is a useful summary of the various views on fate put forward by scholars over the last century (p.179–193).

DIETRICH, B. C. The origins of Greek religion. Berlin and New York, de Gruyter, 1974. xvii, 345p. **KB15**

G&R XXII 1975 205–206 Walcot • CPh LXXIV 1979 250–252 Jameson

On older traditions in Minoan Crete, a Mycenaean goddess of nature, and the problem of continuity in the Dark Age. This is a thoughtful and stimulating study of the origins and possible continuity (possibly overstated) of Greek religion, taking recent developments into account and showing commendable control of Anatolian as well as Minoan-Mycenaean scholarship since Nilsson's *Minoan-Mycenaean religion* (1950). The first chapter has some glaring weaknesses and misunderstandings.

DODDS, Eric R. The Greeks and the irrational. Berkeley, University of California Press, 1951. xi, 327p. **KB16**

CJ XLVIII 1953 273–279 Notopoulos • AJPh LXXV 1954 190–196 Solmsen • Phoenix VIII 1954 157–159 Grube • Gnomon XXV 1953 361–367 Luck

These are highly rewarding, incisive studies of various aspects of the irrational from Homer to Christian times, using modern psychology and anthropology, with extensive documentation to facilitate further discussion.

DOVER, Kenneth J. Greek homosexuality. London, Duckworth, 1978. x, 244p., [56]p. of plates, illus. (incl. 1 col.).   **KB17**

CW LXXII 1979 434 Henderson
The necessary foundation for any future research in this subject.

DOVER, Kenneth J. Greek popular morality in the time of Plato and Aristotle. Berkeley, University of California Press, 1974. xix, 330p.
KB18

CR XXVIII 1978 285–287 Gould • JHS XCVI 1976 208–210 de Romilly • TLS LXXIV 1975 273 Lloyd-Jones
An original work with a well-defined theme, based mainly on the orators and the comic poets, from the birth of Plato to the death of Aristotle. Menander and Isaeus are used to best effect.

DRACHMANN, Anders B. Atheism in pagan antiquity. Chicago, Ares Publishers, 1977. ix, 168p.
KB19

Reprint of the 1922 ed.
CR XXXVII 1923 188–189 Halliday • JHS XLIII 1923 203 J.L.S.
This work shows how *Asebeia* could be formulated as a criminal charge on the basis of non-patriotic, antisocial action. A thorough, well-proportioned chronological survey of atheists in antiquity and of religious scepticism in general. There are full references to sources in notes at the end.

ELIADE, M. Histoire des croyances et des idées religieuses. Vol. I: De l'âge de la pierre aux mystères d'Éleusis. Paris, Payot, 1976. 496p.
KB20

RThL VII 1976 499–504 Ries
See now Eliade, M. *A history of religious ideas.* Vol. I: From the Stone Age to the Eleusinian mysteries. Trans. by W. R. Trask. Chicago, University of Chicago Press, 1978. xvii, 439p.
Also see Eliade, M. *Geschichte der religiösen Ideen.* Bd. 2: Von Gautama Buddha biz zu den Anfängen des Christentum.

FARNELL, Lewis Richard. The Cults of the Greek States. New Rochelle, N.Y., Caratzas Brothers, 1977. 5 v., illus. 1st ed.   **KB21**

FARNELL, Lewis Richard. Greek hero cults and ideas of immortality. The Gifford lectures delivered in the University of St. Andrews in the year 1920. Oxford, Clarendon Press, 1970. xv, 434p.
KB22

Reprint of the 1921 ed.
CR 1922 125 Halliday • JHS 1921 291

FARNELL, Lewis. Outline-history of Greek religion. Chicago, Ares Publishers, 1974. 160p.
KB23

Reprint of the 1921 ed. published by Duckworth, London, which was issued as v. 1 of Duckworth's student series.
CR 1922 192 • NThS 1921 181 van der Leeuw
See also Farnell, L. R. *The Higher Aspects of Greek Religion.*

FESTUGIÈRE, André Marie Jean. Personal religion among the Greeks. Berkeley, University of California Press, [1960]. 186p.   **KB24**

Sather classical lectures; vol. 26. "First paper-bound ed. 1960."
CR VI 1956 49–51 Guthrie • RPh XXX 1956 113–114 Humbert
For Festugière, religion implies the contemplative life and in this work he attempts to show that there was throughout the history of Greek religion, from at least the time of Heracleitus, a desire to enter into intimate and personal contact with divinity. The book deals separately with reflective and popular piety, with most space given to the Hellenistic and Greco-Roman periods.

FESTUGIÈRE, A. J. La vie spirituelle en Grèce à l'époque hellenistique ou Les besoins de l'esprit dans un monde raffiné. Paris, Picard, 1977. 225p.
KB25

Coll. Empreinte I.
LEC XLVII 1979 72–73 Stenuit
Not so much a synthesis as a series of portraits which focus on the three centuries before Christ. The work is divided into two parts: "un monde sans inquiétude," and "un monde inquiet." Sources like Theocritus, *Idylls* and the *Hymns* of Callimachus are imaginatively used. Diogenes and his indifference to life and death personifies the world in the second half of the study. Horace, Cicero and Catullus are interpreters of the pre-Christian world, and the art of the period—Laocöon, numerous Aphrodites, the altar of Zeus at Pergamon—provides suggestive parallels.

FONTENROSE, J. The Delphic oracle. Its responses and operations, with a catalogue of responses. Berkeley, Los Angeles, and London, University of California Press, 1978. xviii, 476p.
KB26

JMagH 1979 119–123 Platthy • TLS LXXVII 1979 26 Jones • NYRB XXVI, 5 1979 12–16 Green

FRONTISI-DUCROUX, Françoise. Dédale; Mythologie de l'artisan en Grèece ancienne. Paris, F. Maspero, 1975. 225p., 6 leaves of plates, illus.   **KB27**

REG LXXXIX 1976 119–121 Hani • AC LXIV 1975 772 Delvoye • Gnomon LI 1979 42–48 Koenigs-Philipp
The Daedalus myth is one of the most celebrated in antiquity, but one of the least well-known because so little literary evidence of it remains. Most of the extant evidence is in mythographers, late historians and

lexicographers. The author seeks to identify the organizing principles of this myth which is the incarnation of inventive genius and artistic talent. She investigates the lexical evidence, the myths themselves and the social institutions and practices, utilizing the method of Lévi-Strauss.

GALINSKY, Gotthard Karl. The Herakles theme; The adaptations of the hero in literature from Homer to the twentieth century. Totowa, N. J., Rowman and Littlefield, [1972]. xvi, 317p., illus. **KB28**

AJPh XCVI 1975 82–84 Nethercut • ACR III 1973 84–85 Reinhold
A survey "in both descriptive and interpretative terms" of "the most significant adaptations of Herakles" (xi). There are eight chapters on the Greek and Roman portraits of Herakles, three on his Nachleben through the Middle Ages and Renaissance to modern times, a summary, appendix, bibliography and general index.

GRAF, Fritz. Eleusis und die Orphische Dichtung Athens in Vorhellenistischer Zeit. Berlin and New York, W. de Gruyter, 1974. **KB29**

Erasmus XXVII 1975 816–818 Lasserre • REG LXXXVIII 1975 195–202 Boyancé

GRAVES, Robert. The Greek myths. [Harmondsworth, Eng.], Penguin Books, (1973–). Illus. **KB30**

First published 1955.
CJ LI 1956 191–192 Herbert • Gnomon XXVIII 1956 553–555 Kerényi • Phoenix XII 1958 15–25 MacPherson
Two volumes encompass 171 brief chapters from the creation of the world to the homecoming of Odysseus. The publishers describe the work as "a retelling of the stories of the Greek gods and heroes, embodying the conclusions of modern anthropology and archaeology." Each chapter has three subdivisions, the most useful of which lists the ancient sources. The third section, giving Grave's own commentaries, is likely to have least appeal to classicists. The necessary(?) background to the great amount of subjectivity in the work is Grave's The white goddess (1948).

GRUPPE, Otto. Griechische Mythologie und Religionsgeschichte. New York, Arno Press, 1975. 2 v., xiv, 1923p. **KB31**

Reprint of the 1906 ed. published by C. H. Beck, Munich, which was issued as v. 5, pt. 2 of Handbuch der klassischen Altertums-Wissenschaft.

GRUPPE, Otto. Die griechischen Culte und Mythen in ihren Beziehungen zu den orientalischen Religionen. Bd. 1: Einleitung. Hildesheim and New York, G. Olms, 1973. xvii, 706p. **KB32**

Reprint of the 1887 ed. published by B. G. Teubner, Leipzig.

GUTHRIE, William Keith C. The Greeks and their gods. Boston, Beacon Press, [1969]. xiv, 338p. **KB33**

CR I 1951 208–210 Rose • AC XX 1951 533–535 Nilsson • RBPh XLVIII 1970 995 Piérart • Gnomon XXIII 1951 351–353 Rose
First published in 1950.

HARRISON, Jane E. Themis; A study of the social origins of Greek Religion, with an excursus on The ritual forms preserved in Greek tragedy by Gilbert Murray and a chapter on The origin of the Olympic Games by F. M. Cornford. Cleveland, World Pub. Co., [1962, 1927]. Meridian Books. xxxvi, 559p., illus., map, plans. **KB34**

CR 1927 146 Pickard-Cambridge • CJ XXIII 1927 154 Bonner • JHS 1927 272 Rose

JAEGER, Werner Wilhelm. Early Christianity and Greek Paideia. London, Oxford University Press, [1969, 1961]. 154p. **KB35**

Speculum XXXVII 1962 283–284 Grant • CW LV 1962 198 Downey • AJPh LXXXIV 1963 209–211 Musurillo
Seven lectures (the Carl Newell Jackson lectures at Harvard, 1960) with copious footnotes attempt to discuss "the historical continuity of Greek Paideia in the Christian centuries of late antiquity" (Preface). Unfortunately Jaeger's death in the year after the lectures prevented a fuller development of the themes outlined here. Though brief this monograph bears the stamp of Jaeger's earlier three-volume monument on Paideia, with his great optimism and humanism.

JAEGER, Werner Wilhelm. The theory of the early Greek philosophers. Trans. from the German ms. by Edward S. Robinson. Oxford, Clarendon Press, [1960]. vi, 259p. **KB36**

Phoenix VII 1953 36 Tait

JEANMAIRE, Henri. Dionysos: histoire du culte de Bacchus; l'orgiasme dans l'antiquité et les temps modernes, origine du théâtre en Grèce, orphisme et mystique dionysiaque, évolution du dionysisme après Alexandre. Paris, Payot, 1978. 509p. **KB37**

KERÉNYI, Károly. The heroes of the Greeks. Trans. by H. J. Rose. London, Thames & Hudson, 1974. xxiv, 439p., illus. **KB38**

Trans. of Die Heroen der Griechen.
Erasmus XIII 1960 42–44 Moreau • Gnomon XXI 1959 737–738 Brommer

KERÉNYI, Károly. Zeus and Hera; Archetypal image of father, husband, and wife. Trans. by Christopher Holme. London, Routledge & Kegan Paul, 1976. **KB39**

Archetypal Images in Greek Religion; 5.

G&R XXIV 1977 97 Walcot • CW LXXII 1979 246–247 Hansen

First published in German in 1972, the year of the author's death, this study shows an almost total dependence on Jungian archetypes, an over-elaborate methodology, a meandering style with facile and idiosyncratic arguments, and a characteristically Heraclitean obscurity.

The author's *Dionysos; Archetypal image of indestructible life* (Princeton, 1976) is also in the Bollingen series and has the same virtues and vices.

KERN, Otto. Die Religion der Griechen. 2. ed. Berlin, Weidmann, 1963. 3 v. **KB40**

Bd. 1. Von den Anfängen bis Hesiod. Bd. 2. Die Hochblüte bis zum Ausgange des Fünften Jahrhunderts. Bd. 3. Von Platon bis Kaiser Julian.

RPh I 1927 264–266 Puech • CR 1927 125 Rose • BFC XLVII 1941 113–118 Guglielmino

A massive work which started germinating during Kern's first explorations in Greece and Asia Minor in the years 1890–1893. In 1925 he made an extensive visit to Sicily, Greece, Egypt and Palestine to complete his background knowledge. The resulting work is in the grand tradition of Ernst Curtius, Hermann Diels, Carl Robert and Wilamowitz. The author combines a close knowledge of religious texts in the Greek authors with his knowledge of religious sites.

KIRK, Geoffrey Stephen. The nature of Greek myths. Woodstock, N. Y., Overlook Press, 1975, 1974. 332p. **KB41**

JHS XCVI 1976 215–216 Pollard

A sequel to the author's *Myth* (1970) which at the outset questions the validity of terms like "mythology" or even "myths" and prefers to examine an individual myth on its own terms. The author subjects five well-known theories about myths to close analysis and finds that they fail in some particular to explain all types. The nature myth theory and aetiological, heroic and psycho-analytic explanations all fail his tests, and of modern theories Lévi-Strauss' structuralism finds most favor. Part II of the work focuses on particular Greek myths and part III discusses the relationship of myth to ritual. A final chapter discusses the relationship of philosophy to myth.

LINFORTH, Ivan Mortimer. The arts of Orpheus. New York, Arno Press, 1973. xviii, 370p. **KB42**

Reprint of the ed. published by the University of California Press, Berkeley.

CR 1943 33–34 Rose • PhW 1943 24 Pfister

LLOYD-JONES, Hugh. The justice of Zeus. Berkeley, University of California Press, [1973, 1971]. xiv, 230p. **KB43**

Sather classical lectures; 41. First paperback edition, 1973.

AJPh XCIV 1973 395–398 Herington • CR XXIV

1974 81–82 Lucas • Gnomon XLIX 1977 241–249 Kraus • REG LXXXVI 1973 462–465 De Romilly

An elegant and brilliant work which calls for abandonment of the common belief in a rather primitive Zeus in Homer and substitution in its place of a somewhat static rather than evolutionary concept of cosmic *Dikē* from Homer to Thucydides. The "justice" of the title is nowhere adequately defined and there is much oversimplification.

McGINTY, Park. Interpretation and Dionysus: method in the study of a god. The Hague and New York, Mouton, 1978. viii, 264p. **KB44**

Religion and reason; 16.

MARTIN, Roland. La religion Grecque. Paris, Presses Universitaires de France, 1976. 208p. **KB45**

L'Historien; 22, Collection SUP.

RPh LII 1978 145 des Places • JHS XCVII 1977 198 Richardson

Not so much a general study as an attempt to show by selective examples from varied sources how unedited documentation can be used as a basis for new interpretations and to open new perspectives in the study of gods, cults and rites. The study of oracles occupies half the book (p.13–109), and Dionysus, Aphrodite, the Eleusinian deities, and the underworld divinities of southern Italy are studied at length. Pausanias, inscriptions, numismatics, pottery and architecture are all used well as sources, without neglecting the literary evidence. A rather disjointed work, chiefly useful for showing how recent archaeological evidence can shed new light on old beliefs.

NILSSON, Martin Persson. Geschichte der griechischen Religion. 3., durchgesehene und ergänzte Aufl. 1st ed., 1941. München, Beck, 1967, 1956. 2 v., illus. **KB46**

Handbuch der Altertumswissenschaft; Abt. 5, t. 2. 1, 2.

I. Bd. Die Religion Griechenlands bis auf die griechische Weltherrschaft. II. Bd. Die hellenistische und römische Zeit.

RHE LX 1965 87–96 Mallet • CR II 1952 104–107 Rose • Gnomon XLII 1970 49–53 Jameson • CPh LX 1965 48–49 Fontenrose

More than a modern substitute for the outmoded work of Gruppe, this is the best and most reliable account of Greek religion in any language. A magisterial survey of the work of the previous two generations is included. Volume I covers the period from the beginning down to Alexander the Great in six main sections; v. 2 completes the survey down to the triumph of Christianity. Volume 1 was revised in a 3rd German edition in 1967, the year of the author's death at the age of 92. (The first edition of v. 1 appeared in 1940 when he was 65, of v. 2 in 1950 when he was 75.) The additions in the 3rd edition are mainly bibliographical.

NILSSON, Martin Persson. Greek folk religion. With a foreword to the Torchbook ed. by Arthur

Darby Nock. Gloucester, Mass., Peter Smith, 1971. 166p., illus.   **KB47**

First published in 1940 under title: *Greek popular religion.*
JHS LXII 1942 90–91 Rose
An excellent account of what the average Greek who was neither priest, poet, philosopher nor prophet did and thought about the gods. Makes judicious use of archaeology and modern folklore.

NILSSON, Martin Persson. A history of Greek religion. Trans. from the Swedish by F. J. Fielden. 2d ed. Oxford, Clarendon Press, 1967. 316p.   **KB48**

"Revised 1952."
JHS XLV 1925 280–281 Rose • CW XX 1926 70–72 Fox
A valuable early contribution (in the form of eight lectures) to the history of Greek religious thought. The contents are as follows: I. Minoan-Mycenaean Religion and its Survival in Greek Religion; II. Origins of Greek Mythology; III. Primitive Belief and Ritual; IV. Gods of Nature and of Human Life; V. The Homeric Anthropomorphism and Rationalism; VI. Legalism and Mysticism; VII. The Civic Religion; VIII. The Religion of the Cultured Classes and the Religion of the Peasants. A work of much learning and good sense.

NILSSON, Martin Persson. The Minoan-Mycenaean religion and its survival in Greek religion. 2d rev. ed. New York, Biblio and Tannen, 1971. xxiv, 656p., illus.   **KB49**

Reprint of the 1950 ed.
Gnomon XXV 1953 145–150 Deubner • JHS XLVII 1927 297 Nock
The first comprehensive account of Bronze Age Greek religion. Beginning with the differences between mainland and Cretan culture, Nilsson sees the Mycenaeans as invaders who assimilated the culture of the conquered. Chapters II to XI analyze the archaeological evidence for Minoan-Mycenaean religion—nature sanctuaries, house sanctuaries, altars, sacred furniture and dress, horns of consecration, double axe, tree cult, etc. There is much suggestive material on the continuity of cults and cult places in the second half of a book that was recognized as a classic on its first appearance.

NILSSON, Martin Persson. The Mycenaean origin of Greek mythology. With a new introd. and bibliography by Emily Vermeule. Berkeley, University of California Press, [1972, 1932]. xv, 258p.   **KB50**

Original ed. issued as v. 8 of Sather classical lectures.
JHS LII 1932 307
In that Homer did not create the myths or the myths Homer, Professor Nilsson argues for a Mycenaean origin for them. If the boars' tusk helmet and other material objects described in Homer go back to Mycenaean times, why not the myths? This presupposes that the Mycenaean Age was predominantly Greek, not merely a Minoan offshoot. The bulk of the names in Greek mythology are definitely Greek, not Minoan. Hence, the author supposes that the Mycenaeans were immigrant Greeks.

NORDEN, Eduard. Agnostos Theos; Untersuchungen zur Formengeschichte religiöser Rede. [6 unveränderte Aufl.] Darmstadt, Wissenschaftliche Buchgesellschaft, 1974. xiv, 410p.   **KB51**

Die Areopagrede der Acta apostolorum.—Untersuchungen zur Stilgeschichte der Gebets- und Prädikationsformeln.

OTTO, Walter Friedrich. Dionysus, myth and cult. Trans. with an introd. by Robert Palmer. Bloomington, Indiana University Press, [1965]. xxi, 243p., illus.   **KB52**

Gnomon XX 1944 113–126 Malthen

PARKE, Herbert William. Festivals of the Athenians. Ithaca, Cornell University Press, 1977. 208p., [16] leaves of plates, illus.   **KB53**

JHS XCVIII 1978 190–192 Hooker
Deubner's *Attische Feste* (1932), long the standard text for festivals, is obsolete in part, so a fresh survey is welcome. The festivals are examined here in Athenian calendar order of occurrence, unlike Deubner and Farnell, and this highlights the role they played in the public life of classical Athens. A useful supplement to Deubner.

PARKE, Herbert William. Greek oracles. London, [Hutchinson, 1967]. 160p., maps.   **KB54**

CR XIX 1969 206–208 Forrest • AJPh XCI 1970 104–108 Fontenrose
An urbane and generally perceptive survey of all Greek organized oracular activity. Five of the twelve chapters deal with Delphi, while other centers like Ammon and Dodona get their due. The history of oracles extends from c.750 B.C. to the reign of Julian or at the latest to that of Justinian. The work lacks sureness of touch in matters of myth and folktale and the writing is often pedestrian.

PARKE, Herbert William. The oracles of Zeus; Dodona, Olympia, Ammon. Cambridge, Mass., Harvard University Press, 1967. x, 294p., illus.   **KB55**

AJPh XCI 1970 104–108 Fontenrose • JHS LXXXVIII 1968 209–210 Pollard • Gnomon XLII 1970 690–697 Berve
The book is divided into three sections, with Dodona rightly receiving the chief share. A thorough, balanced and amply documented study, but the work is vitiated by numerous errors, dubious statements and infelicities of style.

PARKE, Herbert William and WORMELL, D. E. W. The Delphic oracle. I: The history;

II: The oracular response. Oxford, Blackwell, 1956. xxxvi, 271p.   **KB56**

JHS LXXIX 1959 181 Hopper • Phoenix XIII 1959 43–45 White • REA LXI 1959 474–477 Defradas
Volume I is a revision of Parke's *History of the Delphic Oracle* (1939). Volume II is a collaborative work with D. E. W. Wormell and provides a valuable collection of all known oracular responses with full references and testimonia. The oracle's activity is divided into nine periods, and within these the historical responses are presented in chronological order. The fictitious oracles are grouped under subject headings. There are four useful indices: Index verborum, Index of Proper Names, Index locorum, Index of Enquirers.
The main revision in v. I is in c. 3: "The Procedure of the Oracle," which takes account of Pierre Amandry, *La Mantique Apollinienne* (1950).

PINSENT, John. Greek mythology. London and New York, Hamlyn, 1969. 5–141p., illus.
                                   KB57

G&R XVII 1970 115 Sewter
Profusely illustrated.

RAHNER, Hugo. Greek myths and Christian mystery. With a foreword by E. O. James. Trans. by Brian Battershaw. New York, Biblo and Tannen, 1971 [1963]. xxii, 399p.   **KB58**

Trans. of *Griechische Mythen in Christlicher Deutung.*
CHR L 1964–1965 532–533 McGuire • JHS LXXXV 1965 215–216 Ferguson • JRS LIV 1964 219–220 Armstrong
First published in German in 1945, this book is in three parts: An opening section on Mysterion, a second, written in honor of Jung, consisting of two essays reprinted from *Eranos-Jahrbuch* on Moly and Mandragora, and the third, "Holy Homer" (mostly reprinted from papers in *ZKTh*), dealing with the place of the willow in Greek and Christian symbolism and of the Christian metamorphoses of Odysseus tied to the mast. An interesting study in the Christian continuity of the classical tradition, written with a wealth of learning and poetic sensitivity.

REITZENSTEIN, Richard. Hellenistic mystery-religions; Their basic ideas and significance. Trans. by John E. Steeley. Pittsburgh, Pickwick Press, 1978. xii, 572p.   **KB59**

Trans of *Die Hellenistischen Mysterienreligionen.*
CW LXXII 1979 375–376 Gallagher • CR 1927 284 Rose • JHS 1927 272 H.S.R.
Still of interest, despite the great increase in knowledge of the religions of late antiquity since the last German edition of this classic in 1927. Appendices and elucidations now constitute about 80% of the book.

ROSE, Herbert J. A handbook of Greek mythology, including its extension to Rome. 6th ed. London, Methuen, [1972, 1958].   **KB60**

AAHG XI 1958 1–3 Lesky
More careful in scholarship than Graves.

ROUX, G. Delphes. Son oracle et ses dieux. Paris, Les Belles Lettres, 1976. 256p.   **KB61**

AC XLV 1976 769–770 Delvoye • CW LXXI 1977 266–267 Fontenrose • JHS XCVIII 1978 192 Wormell • CR XXVIII 1978 174–175 Parke
A work beautifully written and illustrated, translated (with expansions) from the German edition (Hirmer Verlag, Munich, 1971). It does not attempt to give a comprehensive history but concentrates on the functioning, especially on the interrelation of the literary and archaeological working, of Apollo's centre of prophecy. The multiple feasts and cults are also studied. Professor Roux has devoted many years to excavation at Delphi. This work is much more than the popular treatment which the author modestly styles it.

RUTKOWSKI, Bogdan. Cult places in the Aegean world. Trans. by Krystyna Kozlowska. Wroclaw, Zaklad Narodowy im. Ossolibnskich, 1972. 346p. illus.   **KB62**

At head title: Polish Academy of Sciences. Institute of the history of Material Culture.
AJA LXXVIII 1974 90 Stavrolakes
The author examines all the archaeological evidence to 1970 on cult palaces of the Bronze Age in Crete and mainland Greece to discover the elements common to them and to identify the sacred nature of each site.

WARD, Anne G. et al. The quest for Theseus. With a Preface by Reynold Higgins. New York, Praeger Publishers, [1970]. 281p., illus. (part col.), maps, plans.   **KB63**

Archaeology XXVI 1973 65–66 Raubitschek • AJA LXXV 1971 456–457 Hicks.

ZUNTZ, Gúnther. Persephone; Three essays on religion and thought in Magna Graecia. Oxford, Clarendon Press, 1971. xiii, 427p.   **KB64**

RHR 1973 No. 183 182–185 Turcan • CF XXVI 1972 129–132 Webster • Gnomon XLVI 1974 321–328 Burkert
Three long erudite essays on related subjects: the Goddess of Sicily, "Empedocles" *Katharmoi,* and "the Gold Leaves." The first includes a discussion of the Greek evidence for the worship of a Persephone almost entirely independent of Demeter. The second includes Zuntz's own text and commentary on the *Katharmoi.* The third is based on a re-examination of the "Orphic" gold leaves in Naples and London.

KC   ROMAN RELIGION AND MYTHOLOGY

ALTHEIM, Franz. History of Roman religion. Trans. by Harold Mattingly. New York, E. P. Dutton, [1937]. xi, 548p.   **KC1**

> AJPh LXI 1940 90–96 Nock • Gnomon XXVI 1954 15–23 Latte • Paideia VII 1952 164–167 Pisani
> The English translation of the original incorporates the results of later work by the author and takes account of some of the review criticisms of the original. Remains controversial and exaggerated on many points but displays an extensive mastery of archaeological and linguistic literature, especially in the early sections.

BAILEY, Cyril. Phases in the religion of ancient Rome. Ann Arbor, Mich., University Microfilms, 1968. ix, 340p.   **KC2**

> Photoreprint of 1932 ed, published by University of California Press, Berkeley.
> CR XLVII 1933 21–22 Rose • Gnomon IX 1933 442–444 Rose • REG XLVII 1934 383–384 Bayet
> In the Warde Fowler manner this book sets forth the stages by which Roman religion grew from its earliest known forms to the beliefs and practices in vogue under the Empire. Excellent in exposition and comment, the work, however, does not take account of scholarly reaction (led by Altheim) to the established views of Wissowa and Warde Fowler. Its evaluation of Rome's contribution to the religious history of man is more generous than that of other scholars.

BAYET, Jean. Croyances et rites dans la Rome antique. Paris, Payot, 1971. 384p.   **KC3**

> Arch Philos XXXV 1972 681 Solignac • JRS LXIII 1973 271–272 Pollard • REL XLIX 1971 481–484 Le Bonniec • RH CCLIII, 253 1975 438–439 Simons
> A collection of 15 essays on Roman religion by Bayet scattered in various journals is here brought together by four of his pupils and friends after his death. The essays span the years 1935–1961 and deal with the magical aspects of religion, the cults of Ceres and Dionysus, and animistic problems.

BAYET, Jean. Histoire politique et psychologique de la religion romaine. 2. éd., rev. et corr. Paris, Payot, 1969, 1956. 340p.   **KC4**

> Bibliography (p.[291]–312).
> REL XXXV 1957 424–431 Schilling
> This is the work of a disciple of Franz Cumont, a friend of Georges Dumézil, and a neo-anthropologist of the Lévy-Bruhl school.

BEAUJEU, Jean. La religion romaine à l'apogée de l'empire. Paris, Société d'édition Les Belles Lettres, 1955– . Plates.   **KC5**

> Collection d'études anciennes; 1. La politique religieuse des antonins; 96–192.
> REL XXXV 1957 431–433 Bayet • Gnomon XXIX 1957 258–261 Latte
> The five Antonine phases—those of Nerva and Trojan, Hadrian, Antoninus Pius, Marcus Aurelius and Commodus—are minutely analyzed, with particularly interesting use of numismatic evidence. A masterly synthesis, covering literary, epigraphical, archaeological and numismatic evidence.

BLOCH, Raymond et al. Recherches sur les religions de l'Italie antique. Genève, Droz, 1976. 135p., illus.   **KC6**

> Hautes études du monde gréco-romain; v.7.
> REL LV 1977 544–545 Le Bonniec

BOER, William den, ed. Le culte des souverains dans l'empire romain. 7 exposés suivis de discussions par Elias Bickerman et al. Entretiens préparés et présidés par Willem den Boer. Vandoeuvres Genève, 28 Septembre 1972. [Vandoeuvres-Genève, Fondation Hardt, Dépositaire pour la Suisse Francke, Berne, 1973.] viii, 332p.   **KC7**

> Entretiens sur l'antiquité classique; 19.
> AJPh XCVI 1975 443–445 Barnes • REA LXXVI 1974 443–444 Nony
> A well-edited volume on an interesting theme. The seven participants, Bickermann, Habicht, Beaujeu, Millar, Bowersock, Calderone and Thraede are equally informative in the papers and the lengthy discussions.

BOUCHÉ-LECLERCQ, Auguste. Les pontifes de l'ancienne Rome. New York, Arno Press, 1975. vii, 439p.   **KC8**

> Reprint of the 1871 ed. published by Librairie A. Franck, Paris.

BOYANCÉ, Pierre. Études sur la religion romaine. Rome, École française de Rome, 1972. xii, 440p., 3 plates.   **KC9**

> Collection de l'École française de Rome; 11.
> CPh LXX 1975 154–155 Fontenrose • CR XXV 1975 157 Ogilvie • RHR CLXXXV 1974 194–198 Turcan • Gnomon XLIX 1977 207–209 Radke
> The volume consists of 29 articles and reviews (1928–1966), dealing more or less with Roman religion, mana, fides, Trojan legend of Rome, etc. Scholarly, sensible and well written.

BROEK, R. van den. The myth of the Phoenix, according to classical and early Christian traditions. [Trans. by I. Seeger.] Leiden, E. J. Brill, 1972. xi, 487p., illus.   **KC10**

Études preliminaires aux religions orientales dans l'empire romain; t. 24.
CPh LXX 1975 70–71 Pascal • CR XXV 1975 165–166 Hudson-Williams • REL L 1972 436–440 Fontaine
A collection of individual writers' comments on the phoenix.

CARCOPINO, Jérôme. De Pythagore aux apôtres; études sur la conversion du monde romain. [2e. éd.]. Paris, Flammarion, [1968]. 414p., illus., plans, plates.   **KC11**

Gnomon XXIX 1957 261–270 Toynbee • RPh XXXI 1957 144 Ernout • Latomus XVI 1957 535–539 Delvoye
Contains detailed and learned studies of three Roman religious sites illustrating the important role of Pythagorean doctrines on Christian beliefs.

CUMONT, Franz Valery Marie. The Mysteries of Mithra. Trans. from the 2d rev. French ed. by Thomas J. McCormack. New York, Dover Publications, [1956]. xiv, 239p., illus., fold. map.   **KC12**

AC XXVII 1958 269–270 De Laet • CB XXXIV 1958 57 Guentner • JEH X 1959 122 Smith
The work is still basic and is not rendered superfluous by the later research of Vermaseren.

CUMONT, Franz Valery Marie. The Oriental religions in Roman paganism. Introd. by Grant Showerman. Authorized trans. New York, Dover Publications, [1956]. 298p.   **KC13**

"An unabridged and unaltered republication of the first English translation published in 1911."
CJ XI 1916 318–319 Lord • CPh XII 1917 117 Showermann
Includes a good discussion of the reasons for the successful spread of the Oriental religions, their appeal to emotion and reason. The cults of Asia Minor, Egypt, Syria and Persia receive individual treatment. The discussions of Mithraism, astrology and magic are particularly good.

CUMONT, Franz Valery Marie. Recherches sur le symbolisme funéraire des romains. New York, Arno Press, 1975. iv, 543p., [46] leaves of plates, illus.   **KC14**

Reprint of the 1942 ed.
AJA L 1946 140 Nock • JS 1944 23–37, 77–86 Marrou • RBPh 1943 345–349 Bidez • REA XLV 1943 291–298 Boyancé
See now Turcan, Robert. "Les sarcophages romaines et le problème du symbolisme funéraire," *ANRW* 11, 16, 2, 1700–1735.

DODDS, Eric R. Pagan and Christian in an age of anxiety; Some aspects of religious experience

from Marcus Aurelius to Constantine. New York, Norton, [1970, 1965]. xii, 144p.   **KC15**

"The Norton Library."
CW LIX 1966 166–167 Downey • Phoenix XX 1966 349–352 Rist • RecSR LIV 1966 304–306 Daniélou
An age as bewildered as our own and so likely to have some didactic lessons for us. Professor Dodds is interested more in what pagans and Christians of that age shared than in what divided them. An extraordinarily erudite set of lectures.

DUMÉZIL, Georges. Archaic Roman religion; With an appendix on the religion of the Etruscans. Trans. by Philip Krapp. Foreword by Mircea Eliade. Chicago, University of Chicago Press, [1970]. 2 v., xxx, 715p.   **KC16**

Trans. of La religion romaine archaïque.
REL XLIV 1966 86–93 Heurgon • REA LXX 1968 83–91 Schilling • RPh XLI 1967 347–348 Ernout • Latomus XXVII 1968 221–227 Martin
The fruit of over 30 years' research, this is a veritable *summa* on early Roman religion, with an appendix on his earlier opinions and polemics, and though there are still some *veteris vestigia irae,* the mood of this final testament is irenical. This is a magisterial treatment of Roman religion from its Indo-European origins to the end of the Republic. The author sees the Romans as never having been without a mythology, a people who included portions of their mythology in history and many of their fables in events.

DUMÉZIL, Georges. Fêtes romaines d'été et d'automne suivi de dix questions romaines. [Paris], Gallimard, 1975. 296p.   **KC17**

Bibliothèque des sciences humaines.
REL LIII 1975 51–57 Turpin • Caesarodunum XI 1976 C.R. 36–40 Chevallier
Another Dumézil trilogy. Part I is titled Le Bon Usage de la Nature and discusses fixed feasts from July to October; Part II is titled La Capitalisation de la Saison Guerrière but is more extensive than its title; Part III Dix Questions Romaines offers solutions or suggestions on ten questions in the study of Roman religion.

FERGUSON, John. The religions of the Roman Empire. Ithaca, Cornell University Press, 1970. 296p., illus.   **KC18**

Aspects of Greek and Roman life.
ACR I 1971 78–79 Sider • JRS LXII 1972 197–198 Boyd
A full and variegated picture of religious life in the Roman empire, especially during the 2d and 3rd centuries. The emphasis is on archaeological evidence (with good plates), but literary evidence is not neglected. The book tries to take in the whole of the empire—Britain, the Danube, North Africa, Asia Minor. With so much data to handle, the author seldom gets beyond description to analysis and interpretation, and he is concerned more with objects, than with systems, of belief. There are brief notes printed together at the end of the book,

and bibliographies—a general one and one for each individual chapter.

FOWLER, William Warde. The religious experience of the Roman people, from the earliest times to the age of Augustus. New York, Cooper Square Publishers, 1971. xviii, 504p. **KC19**

> Reprint of the 1911 ed.
> BPh 1914 520 Richter • RHR 1914 1, 101–106 Toutain

GAGÉ, Jean. Enquêtes sur les structures sociales et religieuses de la Rome primitive. Bruxelles, Latomus, 1977. 631p. **KC20**

> Collection Latomus; Vol. 152.
> REL LV 1977 545–547 Hellegouarc'h • RPh LII 1978 412–413 Hus
> A collection of 20 studies already published between 1953 and 1972, mostly in the 1968–1972 period, grouped in five sections and covering a wide spectrum of subjects—sociology, history of law, Roman antiquity—they reveal the author's manifold talents to good effect.

GEFFCKEN, Johannes. The last days of Greco-Roman paganism. Trans. by Sabine MacCormack. Amsterdam, North-Holland Pub. Co. (New York, Elsevier North-Holland), 1978. xii, 343p. **KC21**

> This trans. of *Des Ausgang des Griechisch-Ròmischen Heidentums* (in the 1929 rev. ed. of the original 1920 ed.) has updated references and an index added by S. MacCormack.
> ZKG 1922 201 van Soden • DLZ 1921 146 Gelzer
> An English translation, almost 50 years after the original.

GRANT, Michael. Roman myths. London, Weidenfeld & Nicolson, 1971. xix, 293 p., illus. **KC22**

> CR XXV 1975 243–245 Ogilvie • CW LXVI 1972 182–183 Fontenrose • G&R XIX 1972 223 Verity
> This work has a different approach from the author's *The myths of the Greeks and the Romans* (1962), since it views Roman myths as almost para-history. There are three preliminary chapters on the basic history of Roman myth and the sources. The Aeneas story is dealt with from its archaeological beginnings to its literary presentation in Virgil. Also included are the stories of Evander and Hercules, Romulus and Remus, the Sabines, the myths of kings and selected stories from the first 200 years of the Republic. An admirable introduction, reliable and generally well written, with excellent illustrations and lengthy quotations in translation.

GRENIER, Albert et al. Les religions étrusque et romaine. Les religions des celtes, des germains et des anciens slaves, par Joseph Vendryès, Ernest Tonnelat et B. O. Unbegaun. Paris, Presses Universitaires de France, 1948. 467p. **KC23**

"Mana": Introduction à l'histoire des religions; 2. Les religions de Europe ancienne; 3.
AJPh LXXII 1951 72–74 Nock • CPh 1950 62–63 Whatmough

HUNGER, Herbert. Lexikon der Griechischen und Römischen Mythologie. Mit Hinweisen auf das Fortwirken Antiker Stoffe und Motive in der Bildenden Kunst, Literatur und Musik des Abendlandes bis zur Gegenwart. Hamburg, Rowohlt, [1974]. xi, 444p. **KC24**

> CPh LII 1957 123–126 Fontenrose • Gnomon XXVI 1954 192–194 Lesky • LEC XXII 1954 131 Charlier • MH XI 1954 245 Wehrli
> Wider in its appeal than Grimal's *Dictionnaire,* this *Lexikon* is meant for students, teachers and appreciators of European literature, art and music. There are abundant citations of modern poems, plays, paintings, operas, etc. Each entry is treated in three parts: Mythe (M), Religionsgeschichte (R), and Nachwirkung (N). Sometimes the myth and the ancient evidence cited for it are scattered about under several entries. English and American scholarship tends to be ignored.

LATTE, Kurt. Römische Religionsgeschichte. 2. Unveränderte Aufl. München, Beck, 1976. **KC25**

> Handbuch der Altertumswissenschaft; vol. 5 Abt., 4 Teil.
> Athenaeum XLII 1964 590–597 Bernardi • SMSR XXXII 1961 311–354 Brelich • CR XI 1961 255–257 Rose • CW LIV 1961 217–218 Taylor • JRS LI 1961 206–215 Weinstock
> Not a replacement for, but a supplement to, Wissowa's *Religion und Kults der Römer* (1902, 1912).
> Takes account of important new discoveries, detailed in the richly bibliographical footnotes, and places much stress on linguistic and comparative religion. See also Latte, Kurt, *Kleine Schriften zu Religion, Recht* ed. by Gigon, O. et al. (1968, xvi, 931p.).

LECLANT, Jean. Inventaire bibliographique des Isiaca (IBIS); Répertoire analytique des travaux relatifs à la diffusion des cultes isiaques, 1940–1969. Avec la collaboration de Gisèle Clerc. Leiden, Brill, 1972. Photos. **KC26**

> Études préliminaires aux religions orientales dans l'Empire romain; t. 18.
> REA LXXV 1973 198–199 Lehmann • JRS LXIII 1973 272–273 Witt • REL L 1972 398–399 Grimal
> The first volume covers the names of modern authors, A to D, and work published from 1940 to 1969 on Isiaca, i.e., the diffusion outside of Egypt of cults, divinities and Egyptian or Egyptising objects. A model bibliographical tool, skillfully annotated.

Le GALL, Joël. La religion romaine de l'époque de Caton l'ancien au règne de l'empereur Commode. Paris, Société d'Édition d'enseignement supérieur, 1975. 235p., [8] leaves of plates. **KC27**

RPh L 1976 165 Richard • AC XLV 1976 330–332 Poucet • REL LIII 1975 548–550 Porte

An excellent guide for modern readers on Roman religion, with a praiseworthy attempt to explain to modern mentalities the power exercised in antiquity by forces of war, nature and death. There is a panoramic view given of Roman reactions to the divine, their concept of the sacred, Greek and Etruscan influences on Roman religious belief and practice, *votum* prayer, sacrifice, etc. The priesthoods are described, as are the feasts, divinities, imperial cult, and cults in the provinces. A remarkable synthesis for the period 200 B.C.–200 A.D.

MELLOR, Ronald. Thea Rheome (romanized form); The worship of the goddess Roma in the Greek world. Göttingen, Vandenhoeck & Ruprecht, 1975. 234p.   **KC28**

Hypomnemata: Untersuchungen zur Antike und zu Ihrer Nachleben; v Heft 42.

Phoenix XXXI 1977 77–81 Jones

One of the most interesting of the political cults is studied, concentrating on the period between 195 B.C. and 29 B.C. The origins of the goddess are first studied and the diffusion of her cult, region by region, in the Greek-speaking world. In the second half of the book the cult is studied topically—temples, altars, games, priests and officials, etc. A useful appendix lists the epigraphical evidence for Roma in geographical order. Roma emerges as a "transmitter," a mediator between the Hellenistic cult of kings and the cult of Roman emperors.

MOMIGLIANO, Arnaldo, ed. The conflict between paganism and Christianity in the fourth century. Oxford, Clarendon Press, 1970, 1963. 222p., illus.   **KC29**

Oxford-Warburg studies.

JRS LIV 1964 207 Armstrong

Eight lectures given at the Warburg Institute in 1958–1959 are here published with notes provided by their authors. Various aspects of the conflict are dealt with but no complete picture of the battlefield emerges. Contributors include such authorities as Marrou and Courcelle (on Neoplatonism and Christianity), A. H. M. Jones (on the social background of the conflict), H. Bloch (on the pagan revival in the West) and J. Vogt (on the religious beliefs of Constantine's family). The editor contributes an introductory chapter and a study of pagan and Christian historiography in the 4th century.

NOCK, Arthur Darby. Conversion; The old and the new in religion from Alexander the Great to Augustine of Hippo. [London], Oxford University Press, [1961]. 309p.   **KC30**

Oxford paperbacks; 30.

CR 1934 139–140 Halliday • CJ XXX 1934 111 Brady • JThS XXXV 1934 190–192 Stewart

A most readable scholarly and illuminating work, dating back to 1933. The title is somewhat misleading. What we have here in 9 of the 14 chapters is a brilliant

sketch of the rise and fall of most of the cults in competition with Christianity, and the term "conversion" was only really applicable to Judaism or Christianity.

OGILVIE, Robert M. The Romans and their gods in the age of Augustus. New York, Norton, [1970, 1969]. 135p., illus., facsim. map, plan.   **KC31**

CPh LXIX 1974 154–156 Fontenrose • Gnomon XLIV 1972 510–511 Le Bonniec • HZ CCXI 1970 651 Wirth

A brief but valuable summary of all aspects of Roman religion, concentrating on the period 50 B.C. to 50 A.D. In eight chapters the author discusses the gods, prayer, sacrifice, divination, the religious year, private religion, priests and, finally, religion in the time of Augustus. The chapters on sacrifices (c. 3) and the religious year (c. 5) are especially good. The bibliography is confined to works in English.

OTTO, Walter Friedrich. Aufsätze zur römischen Religionsgeschichte. Meisenheim (am Glan), Hain, 1975. 216p.   **KC32**

Beiträge zur klassischen Philologie; Heft 71.

PALMER, Robert E. A. Roman religion and Roman empire; Five essays. Philadelphia, University of Pennsylvania Press, [1974]. xii, 291p., illus.   **KC33**

Phoenix XXX 1976 99–100 Salmon

The third major contribution from Palmer on the religion of early Rome, displaying the same gifts of versatile erudition, alert interpretation and ingenious conjecture as its predecessors.

PEROWNE, Stewart. Roman mythology. London and New York, Hamlyn, 1969. 141p., illus. (some col.), maps, ports.   **KC34**

G&R XVII 1970 236–237 Sewter

PFIFFIG, Ambros Josef. Religio Etrusca. Graz, Akadem. Druck- & Verlagsanst, vii, 426p., illus., map.   **KC35**

AC XLV 1976 732–733 Jannot • Gnomon XLVIII 1976 551–558 Radke • REL LIII 1975 37–41 Heurgon

The Etruscans have long been regarded as the "most religious" of ancient peoples. The present work is a much needed synthesis of recent publications on specialized facets and of recent archaeological discoveries in Etruscan religion.

There are 175 *dessins au trait*. The author, a premonstratensian canon and an expert on Etruscology and on the history of religions, here makes a significant contribution to the study of Roman as well as Etruscan civilization.

SCHILLING, R. "La situation des études relatives à la religion romaine de la Republique (1950–1970)." ANRW 12 (1972): 318–347.   **KC36**

SCOTT, Kenneth. The imperial cult under the Flavians. New York, Arno Press, 1975. 204p.

KC37

Reprint of the 1936 ed. published by W. Kohlhammer, Stuttgart.

JRS 1938 85–87 Balsdon • AJPh 1938 123 Abaecherli Boyce

WISSOWA, Georg. Religion und Kultur der Römer. 2. Aufl. München, Beck, 1971. xii, 612p.

KC38

Handbuch der Altertumswissenschaft; v. Sect. 4, Pt. 5. Unveränderter Nachdruck 1971 der Zweiten Auflage, 1912.

BPhM 1914 338 Sawter • MPh 1914 346–351 Leopold

First issued in 1902 with a second edition in 1912, this work has for long been the indispensable handbook of Roman religion and should now be supplemented by Kurt Latte's *Romïsche Religionsgeschichte,* 1960. Particularly useful in that it both cites and quotes the ancient sources.

Philosophy

LA GREEK AND ROMAN PHILOSOPHY

ADKINS, Arthur H. From the many to the one: A study of personality and views of human nature in the context of ancient Greek society, values and beliefs. London, Constable, 1970. xv, 312p.
LA1

AJPh XCV 1974 67–68 Murphy • CW LXIV 1971 277 Pearson • PhilosQ XX1 1971 260–261 Kerferd
The subtitle best describes the context of this work, which is a successor to *Merit and responsibility*. The main terms studied here for the light they throw on Greek views of human nature and personality are ψυχη, φύσις, θυμός, φρην, νόος, νόμος. One of the main conclusions is that "from Homer to Aristotle the characteristic portrayal of Greek personality" which we find in surviving documents appears to be far more fragmented than that which we regard as "normal" (p. 27). The work is particularly good on Homer and Plato.

ADORNO, Francesco. La filosofia antica. Milano, Feltrinelli, 1975–1976. 2 v.
LA2

Volume 1: 3rd ed.; v. 2: 4th ed. First published 1961–1965.
GCFI XLII 1963 406–408 Plebe

ADORNO, Francesco. Il pensiero greco-romano e il Cristianesimo; Orientamenti bibliografici. Bari, Laterza, 1970. vi, 110p.
LA3

BBF XVI 1971 52–53 Ernst
A useful little work of bibliographical orientation.

ALLEN, D. J. "A survey of work dealing with Greek philosophy from Thales to the age of Cicero, 1945–1949," Philos. Quart. I (1950): 61–72, 165–170.
LA4

ALLEN, D. J. and SKEMP, J. B., eds. Phronesis; A journal of ancient philosophy. Assen, Nether-lands, Royal van Gorcum, 1955. Volume I.
LA5

AMAND DE MENDIETA, Emmanuel. Fatalisme et liberté dans l'antiquité grecque; Recherches sur la survivance de l'argumentation morale anti-fataliste de Carnéade chez les philosophes grecs et les théologiens chrétiens des quatre premiers siècles. Amsterdam, A. M. Hakkert, 1973. xxviii, 608p.
LA6

Reprint of the 1945 ed. published by the Bibliothèque de l'Université, Louvain.
Augustinus XX 1975 172 Oroz • AC XIV 1945 252–253 des Places
A magisterial work, illustrating the continuity of Greek philosophy and patristics. Using a wealth of texts the author in his introduction outlines the history of philosophical fatalism and astrology in Greco-Roman antiquity, the anti-fatalist polemic before and of Car-neades. Two books follow, devoted respectively to a veritable gallery of pagan and Christian authors, down through the 4th century A.D.

ANTON, John Peter, comp. and ed. Essays in ancient Greek philosophy. With George L. Kustas. Albany, State University of New York Press, 1971. xlvi, 650p.
LA7

CPh LXVII 1972 298–300 Sprague • CR XXIII 1973 281–282 Kerferd • REG LXXXVII 1974 396–397 Goldschmidt
A selection of 35 of the papers given at annual meetings of the Society for Ancient Greek Philosophy between 1953 and 1967. Nineteen of the papers have already appeared elsewhere. Almost half of the total deal with Platonic themes; the remainder are divided between the pre-Socratics, Aristotle, and the post-Aristotelian period. A striking testimony to the vigor and enthusiasm of the study of ancient philosophy in American universities. The *REG* review lists the contents.

ARMSTRONG, Arthur Hilary. The architecture of the intelligible universe in the philosophy of Plotinus. Cambridge, Cambridge University Press, 1940. xii, 126p. **LA8**

Cambridge classical studies; v. 6. Photocopy. Ann Arbor, Mich.: University Microfilms, 1961.

CR LIV 1940 195–197 Sleeman

Discusses the three hypostases of Plotinus' intelligible world with particular reference to their historical antecedents. A good summary of recent work on Plotinian sources. Despite Plotinus' insistence on three and only three hypostases he is shown to go beyond his own limits.

ARMSTRONG, Arthur Hilary. An introduction to ancient philosophy. [3rd ed., reprint.] 1st ed., 1947. London, Methuen (Totowa, N. J., Rowman and Littlefield), 1977, 1957. xviii, 242p. **LA9**

JHS LXIX 1949 82–83 Morrison

First appeared in 1947, with a second edition in 1949, a third revised edition in 1957, and a fourth in 1965. This is one of the better short introductory surveys of ancient philosophy.

ARMSTRONG, Arthur Hilary, ed. The Cambridge history of later Greek and early medieval philosophy. Cambridge, Cambridge University Press, 1970. xvi, 714p. **LA10**

JHS LXXXVIII 1968 204–207 Rist • CR XXI 1971 233–235 Wallis • BO XXVII 1970 391–396 de Vogel • RPh XLV 1971 179 Langlois • JRS LVIII 1968 276–277 O'Meara

A welcome composite work by several well-known scholars, marred, however, in execution by serious defects in planning. Excessive compression is evident especially in Walzer's section on Arabic philosophy, and the lack of a uniform plan makes the whole read more like a disconnected series of essays than a continuous history. Important figures get overlooked or lost and important movements like Gnosticism get nothing like the attention they deserve. Armstrong himself on Plotinus is particularly good, as is Sheldon-Williams on Greek Christian Platonism, and Markus is excellent on Marius Victorinus and Augustine.

ARNIM, Hans Friedrich A. von. Stoicorum veterum fragmenta. Stutgardiae, In Aedibus B. G. Teubneri, 1968. 4 v. **LA11**

Volume titles: v. 1. Zeno et Zenonis Discipuli; v. 2. Chrysippi Fragmenta Logica et Physica; v. 3. Chrysippi Fragmenta Moralia, Fragmenta Successorum Chrysippi; v. 4. Quo Indices Continentur, Conscripsit Maximilianus Adler.

ARNOU, René. Le désir de Dieu dans la philosophie de Plotin. 2. éd. revue et corrigée. Rome, Presses de l'Université Grégorienne, 1967. 344p. **LA12**

JHS LXXXVIII 1968 204 Rist

An almost unchanged reissue of a 1921 work which

at the time was a major achievement in Plotinian studies. Much of it stands well and has not been superseded. Particularly valuable for its vocabulary studies of such subjects as the nature of God, immanence, transcendence and emanation.

BABUT, Daniel. La religion des philosophes grecs, de Thalès aux stoiciens. [1. éd.] Paris, Presses Universitaires de France, 1974. 213p. **LA13**

Collection SUP. Littératures anciennes; 4.

MH XXXIII 1976 57–58 Burkert • REG LXXXVIII 1975 326–327 Moreau • AC XLIV 1975 330–331 Joly

After a long scholarly apprenticeship in Plutarch the author was well equipped to provide us with this well-nuanced study, with a helpful systematic bibliography and well-documented notes. The order followed is historical, from Thales through Socrates, Plato, Aristotle and the Peripatetics to Stoicism and Epicureanism. The continuity in this religious tradition, despite many divergences, is stressed.

BALDRY, H. C. The unity of mankind in Greek thought. Cambridge, Cambridge University Press, 1965. vii, 223p. **LA14**

Platon XXII 1970 320–323 Markantonatos • JHS LXXXVII 1967 169–170 Burn • Gnomon XXXVIII 1966 641–645 Wehrli

A careful study of the emergence of the idea of the unity of mankind pursued chronologically in chapters: From Homer to Hippocrates (including the Sophists), Socrates and the Fourth Century, Alexander and His Influence, The Hellenistic Philosophers, The Impact of Rome (including Polybius), The Middle Stoa and Cicero. An excellent collection of source materials.

BARNES, Jonathan. The presocratic philosophers. London and Boston, Routledge & Kegan Paul, 1979. 2 v. **LA15**

JHPh XX 1982 301–303 Bernhardt

The editor of *Articles on Aristotle* and translator of the *Posterior analytics* here turns to the Presocratics.

BIBLIOGRAPHY of philosophy. Paris, International Institute of Philosophy, [Année] I: Jan./Mar. 1954–XXIX, 1982. **LA16**

Published for the International Federation of Philosophical Societies under the auspices of the International Council of Philosophy and Humanistic Studies with the aid of UNESCO and of the French National Centre for Scientific Research.

BIGNONE, Ettore. Epicuro; Con introduzione e commento. "Ristampa anastatica dell'edizione Bari, 1920." Roma, "L'Erma" di Bretschneider, 1964. ix, 271p. **LA17**

Opere. Frammenti. Testimonianze sulla sua vita.

CR XXXIV 1920 182 Bury • JHS XLI 1922 155–156 Bailey • REG XXIV 1921 463 Robin

Bignone, well known for his penetrating study of Empedocles, gives us here the fruit of long reflection on Usener's *Epicurea* (1887), now enriched with the new Vatican MS fragments, and a thoroughly critical new look at Usener's text of both fragments and letters. There are good preliminary remarks on the *KURIAI DOXAI.* The fragments are well translated and annotated, but the text is unfortunately not included.

BLUMENTHAL, H. J. Plotinus' psychology; His doctrines of the embodied soul. The Hague, Martinus Nijhoff, 1971. xiii, 157p. **LA18**

REG LXXXVIII 1975 375–376 Trouillard • REA LXXIV 1972 277–278 Moreau
A revised Cambridge 1963 dissertation, this work studies the functions of the soul in its empirical life.

BOLLACK, Jean and LAKS, André, eds. Études sur l'épicurisme antique. Lille, Publications de l'Université de Lille III, [1976]. 366p., [3] leaves of plates, illus. **LA19**

Cahiers de philologie; 1.
CR XXIX 1979 84–85 Chilton
Consists of eight articles on Epicurus and his school, the first and longest of which is a critical text, translation and commentary by Laks on the first 34 chapters of Diogenes Laertius Book X. Other contributors include D. Sedley, Mayotte Bollack, D. Clay, P. H. Schrivers, M. F. Smith (publishing 13 new fragments of Diogenes of Oenoanda), and C. Millot. An interesting and diversified *Cahiers de Philologie,* one from the Lille Centre de Recherche Philologique.

BOS, A. P. Providentia divina; The theme of divine pronoia in Plato and Aristotle. Assen, Van Gorcum, 1976. 36p. **LA20**

AC XLVII 1978 252 Joly
A 1976 inaugural lecture at the Free University, Amsterdam. Christian authors attributed to Aristotle a doctrine of providence extending to the moon. Bos raises the question whether this doxography is credible, in spite of the *Metaphysics.* A great deal of the exposition is devoted to Plato, especially the *Phaedo, Parmenides* and *Timaeus.*

BRÉHIER, Émile. La philosophie de Plotin. [Troisième édition.] Paris, J. Vrin, 1968. xix, 207p. **LA21**

English edition: *The philosophy of Plotinus* (University of Chicago Press, 1958), trans. by Joseph Thomas.
Eng. trans.: JPh LVII 1960 774–775 Kristeller
First published in French in 1928, this short but excellent introduction is by a distinguished historian of philosophy who has also published one of the best critical editions of Plotinus and an excellent French translation. The present work gives all the essential information on Plotinus' life, writings, sources and method and an adequate summary of his chief philosophical doctrines.

BRUMBAUGH, Robert Sherrick. The philosophers of Greece. New York, Crowell, [1970, 1964]. 276p., illus. **LA22**

Apollo ed.; a-244.
JHS LXXXVIII 1968 191–192 Kerferd
First published in 1964, this is a survey of Greek philosophers from Thales to Aristotle. Marred by inaccuracies, misleading or tendentious statements and modern jargon.

BRUN, Jean. Les Présocratiques. Paris, Presses Universitaires, 1968. 128p. **LA23**

Coll. Que sais-je; 1319.
REG LXXXII 1969 216 Weil
A masterly condensation in seven chapters, with an Introduction and Bibliographical Summary. Chapter 1 covers the three Ionians or Milesians-Thales, Anaximander and Anaximenes. The succeeding chapters are devoted to Pythagoreanism, Heraclitus, The Eleatics, Empedocles, Anaxagoras and The Atomists. Gorgias, Protagoras, Prodicus and the Sophists generally are not included.

BULLETIN signalétique; Philosophie, sciences religieuses. Paris, Centre de Documentation du CNRS, v. 23; 1969. **LA24**

Supersedes in part France, Centre National de la Recherche Scientifique, Bulletin signalétique; 19–241: Sciences Humaines and continues the volume numbering.

BURNET, John. Early Greek philosophy. [4th ed.], London, A. & C. Black, 1963. 375p. **LA25**

CR XXXVI 1922 75–77 J.A.S.
Burnet's introduction was one of the most popular surveys of ancient philosophy in the first half of the 20th century. The work underwent many changes between its first (1930) and fourth editions, and translations of Diels' *Fragmente* are still as readable as anything since.

CALLAHAN, John Francis. Four views of time in ancient philosophy. New York, Greenwood Press, 1968, 1948. ix, 209p. **LA26**

CPh XLV 1950 191–194 Cleve • CR LXIV 1950 22–23 Hackforth
Examines the views of Time of Plato, Aristotle, Plotinus and Augustine, seeing the four as various patterns of a solution to "one of the most important (problems) in the history of philosophy." The differences of the approaches to the problem stem from the different philosophical methods of the four thinkers. Ample translations and paraphrases are provided, sometimes marred by inaccuracies. Best on Plotinus and Augustine.

CHAIGNET, Anthelme É. Histoire de la psychologie des grecs. Bruxelles, Culture and Civilisation, 1966. 5 v. **LA27**

Reprint of the 1887–1893 ed. published by Hachette, Paris.
T. 1. Histoire de la Psychologie des Grecs avant et

après Aristote. T. 2. La Psychologie des Stoïciens, des Épicuriens et des Sceptiques. T. 3. La Psychologie de la Nouvelle Académie et des Écoles Éclectics. T. 4. La Psychologie de l'École d'Alexandrie. Livre premier: Psychologie de Plotin. T. 5. La Psychologie de l'École d'Alexandrie.

CHERNISS, Harold F. Selected papers. Edited by Leonard Tarán. Leiden, Brill, 1977. ix, 575p., [1] leaf of plates, port.   **LA28**

"Of the 41 papers collected in the present vol., all but one . . . have been published previously."
REG XCI 1978 247–249 Goldschmidt

CLEVE, Felix. The giants of pre-sophistic Greek philosophy; An attempt to reconstruct their thoughts. 3rd ed. 1st ed., 1965. The Hague, M. Nijhoff, 1973, 1965. 2 v., xxxviii, 580p., illus.
                                                                LA29

CR XVII 1967 182–184 Kerferd
A strange work written in a very Germanic style of English which perversely makes a new case for many of the rejected interpretations of pre-sophistic philosophy. The approach is mainly philological and unnecessarily scathing toward contrary views.

COLLI, Giorgio. La sapienza greca. 2. ed. Milano, Adelphi, 1978– . 356p.   **LA30**

I. Dioniso, Apollo, Eleusi, Orfeo, Museo, Iperborei, Enigma. II. Epimenide, Ferecide et al.
RPh LII 1978 377 Weil

COPLESTON, Frederick. A history of philosophy. London, Search Press, 1953– .   **LA31**

Volumes: 1. Greece and Rome; 2. Medieval Philosophy: Augustine to Scotus.
The first two volumes in this eight-volume complete history of philosophy.

CORNFORD, Francis Macdonald. Principium sapientiae; The origins of Greek philosophical thought. Gloucester, Mass., P. Smith, 1971. vii, 270p.   **LA32**

Originally published in 1952.
Phoenix X 1956 20 Woodbury • CPh XLIX 1954 138–140 de Lacy • CR IV 1954 237–240 Tate
Cornford's book, Guthrie tells us (p.257), was virtually complete and lacked only a summing up at his death, but much of it nonetheless has the appearance of a first draft that would have greatly benefited from a revision based on a review of the most recent bibliography. In the main concern of the work, the analysis of pre-philosophical thought, there is much interesting comparative study of Anaximander, Hesiod, The Book of Genesis, the Babylonian New Year Festival and other myths of creation. The non-scientific nature of early Greek philosophy is stressed. In the absence of experimentation and observation, the Ionians produced a dogmatic structure based on *a priori* premises, relying on inspiration rather than empirical method. Prophet,

poet and sage were originally united in a single person to give us the *principium sapientiae.*

DE WITT, Norman W. Epicurus and his philosophy. Westport, Conn., Greenwood Press, [1973, 1954]. vii, 388p.   **LA33**

CW XLVII 1954 190 Leslie • DLZ LXXVIII 1957 26–29 Freymuth
This is a full-scale presentation of views expressed by De Witt on Epicureanism in papers over a long period.

DIELS, Hermann. Die Fragmente der Vorsokratiker. 4. Ältere Sophistik. The older Sophists. Trans. and ed. by Rosamond Kent Sprague et al. [1st English ed.] Columbia, University of South Carolina Press, [1972]. x, 347p.   **LA34**

Trans. of part 4, Ältere Sophistik of Diels' *Die Fragmente der Vorsokratiker,* 7th ed., with regrouping of the Antiphon and Euthydemus fragments: Protagoras, Xeniades, Gorgias, Lycophron, Prodicus, Thrasymachus, Hippias, Antiphon, Critias, Anonymus Iamblichi, Dissoi Logoi or Dialexeis. Appendix: Euthydemus of Chios.
CR XXV 1975 231–232 Kerferd
This volume contains brief introductions—about one page per sophist—followed by a complete translation of the A and B texts from the second volume of Diels-Kranz. *Antiphon* is particularly well served by J. S. Morrison. Some of the translations are unreliable and misleading.

DILLON, John M., ed. Iamblichi Chalcidensis in Platonis dialogos commentariorum fragmenta. With trans. and commentary by the editor. Leiden, Brill, 1973. viii, 450p.   **LA35**

Philosophia antiqua; v. 23.
CR XXVI 1976 77–78 O'Daly • Phoenix XXXI 1977 81–82 Whittaker • JHS XCV 1975 217–218 Kerferd
A welcome presentation of the collected fragments of Iamblichus' Platonic commentaries, with facing translations, followed by a detailed and valuable commentary (almost half the book) and a word index to the fragments. Most of the fragments are on the *Timaeus* (90) or the *Parmenides,* (14). Festugière's monumental translation of Proclus, *In Timaeum* (Paris, 1966–1968), now provides an interesting basis for comparison. This work is an expansion of Dillon's 1969 Berkeley dissertation and is a most useful and valuable collection of material which will be a necessary basis of further study of Iamblichus.

DILLON, John M. The middle Platonists; 80 B.C. to A.D. 220. Ithaca, N.Y., Cornell University Press, 1977. xvi, 427p.   **LA36**

Gnomon LI 1979 382–385 De Witt • JHS XCIX 1979 190–191 Blumenthal • TLS LXXVI 1977 967 Sharples
Fills a great lacuna, but hardly deserves its own billing as the first book to have been specifically devoted

to a period in the history of thought at once neglected and unusually influential for later ages. For Dillon, middle Platonism encompasses Philo of Alexandria and the Neophythagoreans as well as the more central figures and themes. There is a long treatment of Antiochus and a brief one of Posidonius. The Christian Platonism of Alexandria is omitted. There is a wealth of material marshalled and interpreted here of some six centuries of Platonism.

DÖRRIE, Heinrich, et al. De Iamblique à Proclus; Neuf exposés. Geneva, 1975. 302p. **LA36a**

Fond. Hardt pour l'étude sur l'Antiquité classique; XXI.
RPh LI 1977 314–315 Nautin • Phoenix XXXI 1977 185–188 Dillon • SMH XXXIII 1976 261 Wehrli
The Proceedings of the 1974 Entrétiens of the Fondation Hardt. Three papers are concerned with Iamblichus (Larsen, De Witt, des Places), four with Proclus (Rist, Blumenthal, Bierwaltes, Trouillard). Professor Dörrie surveys the religion of Platonism in the 4th and 5th centuries.

DRAGONA-MONACHOU, Myrto. The Stoic arguments for the existence and the providence of the gods. Athens, National and Capodistrian University of Athens, Faculty of Arts, 1976. 321p. **LA37**

Originally presented as the author's thesis, London.
JHS XCVIII 1978 187 Sharples
A useful and illuminating survey of arguments for the existence of the gods and for divine providence advanced by Stoics from Zeno to Marcus Aurelius, drawing extensively on Cicero, de natura deorum II and Sextus Empiricus, adv. math. IX 13–194. Clarity in overall argument suffers from excessive discussion of details and the minutiae in the scholarly literature.

DUPRÉEL, Eugene. Les sophistes: Protagoras, Gorgias, Prodicus, Hippias. Neuchâtel, Éditions du Griffon, 1948. 407p. **LA38**

AJPh LXXIII 1952 199–207 Cherniss • Mnemosyne 4 ser. V 1952 255 Verdenius

EDELSTEIN, Ludwig. The meaning of Stoicism. Cambridge, Published for Oberlin by Harvard University Press, 1966. xii, 108p. **LA39**

Martin classical lectures; 21.
AJPh LXXXIX 1968 248–250 Warren • Helmantica XX 1969 405 Oroz Reta
In these Martin lectures, Edelstein tried to state the deepest meaning of Stoicism in straightforward terms without dwelling on detail. Unfortunately the work had to be published posthumously and so the expansion of notes intended by the author is missing, making some of his arguments appear very tenuous. The work, nonetheless, is a welcome addition to the slender volume of books in English on Stoicism.

EDELSTEIN, Ludwig and KIDD, I. G., eds. Posidonius, I: The fragments. Cambridge,

Cambridge University Press, 1972. Vol. 2. **LA40**

Cambridge classical texts and commentaries; 13.
Greek and Latin text; pref. and introd. in English.
MH XXIX 1972 286 Theiler • AJPh XCVI 1975 101–103 De Lacy • Phoenix XXIX 1975 190–193 Whittaker
An indispensable new edition of the fragments of Posidonius, replacing Bake's 1810 collection which still holds up well in comparison. The present edition was completed by Kidd after Edelstein's death in 1965. The citations are generous, intelligently arranged and well provided with critical notes. There are four indices and a concordance with Jacoby. The collection is limited almost exclusively to fragments and testimonia linked by ancient authors specifically with the name of Posidonius.

FERGUSON, John. Moral values in the ancient world. London, Methuen, 1958. 256p. **LA41**

CR X 1960 50–52 Adkins • JHS LXXX 1960 232 Kerferd
This book opens up a new subject and ranges over the values of Homer, classical and Hellenistic Greece, the Roman Republic, the Roman emperors, Judaism and Christianity. Moral terminology is examined in both Greek and Latin. However, the title words "moral" and "values" are left undefined.

FESTUGIÈRE, André Marie Jean. Études de philosophie grecque. Paris, J. Vrin, 1971. 598p. **LA42**

REG LXXXVII 1974 396 Goldschmidt
Contains a selection of Festugière's journal publications between 1931 and 1969 on a wide variety of problems in ancient and medieval philosophy. The studies are grouped in three parts: General Problems, Specific Problems and Procliana. The last section contains useful materials complementary to the author's monumental translation of The commentary on the Timaeus.

FORTIN, E. Christianisme et culture philosophique au cinquième siècle; La querelle de l'âme humaine en Occident. Paris, Études Augustiniennes 1959. 196p. **LA43**

Gnomon XXXII 1960 434–437 Courcelle • JRS L 1960 258 Armstrong

FRÄNKEL, Hermann Ferdinand. Wege und Formen frühgriechischen Denkens; Literarische und philosophegeschtliche Studien. Hrsg. von Franz Tietze. 3. durchges. Aufl. München, Beck, 1968. xxiii, 376p. **LA44**

CJ LVIII 1963 368–369 Wassermann • Gnomon XXXI 1959 193–204 Vlastos • Phoenix XI 1957 135 Rosenmeyer
A collection of papers and reviews, forming a parergon to the author's Dichtung und Philosophie. The 2d edition (1960), which appeared five years after the first, contained four additional papers. They deal for the

most part with difficult passages and problems in poetry from Homer to Pindar and Aeschylus, the whole constituting an enormous wealth of highly concentrated materials. The author, a consummate stylist, is a model of precise and imaginative interpretation of classical texts.

FREDE, Michael. Die Stoische Logik. Göttingen, Vandenhoeck und Ruprecht, 1974. 224p.   **LA45**

Abhandlungen der Akademie der Wissenschaften in Göttingen, Philologisch-Historische Klasse; F. 3, NR. 88.

Gnomon XLIX 1977 784–790 Egli • Mnemosyne XXIX 1976 199–200 Edlow

A welcome systematic study of Stoic logic in the "strict sense," building on the work of the author's predecessors in the field, e.g., Prantl, Lukasiewicz, Mates, Kneale and Kneale.

For Frede, Stoic logic is essentially the logic of Chrysippus, and his main concern is with the Stoic teaching on the axiomata and on the argument. A work characterized by clear presentation, judicious exegesis of the texts and penetrating analysis.

FREEMAN, Kathleen. Ancilla to the pre-Socratic philosophers; A complete translation of the fragments in Diels, *Fragmente der Vorsokratiker.* Cambridge, Mass., Harvard University Press, reprint [1977], 1952. x, 162p.   **LA46**

JHS LXIX 1949 92 Morrison

Translation of the good, plain type, but not always reliable, of Diels' *Fragmente,* which should be used only as a help to translation, not as a text itself.

FREEMAN, Kathleen. The pre-Socratic philosophers; A companion to Diels, *Fragmente der Vorsokratiker.* 2d [i.e., 3d] ed. Oxford, B. Blackwell, 1966 [1959]. xiii, 486p., diagrs.   **LA47**

On spine: Companion to the pre-Socratic philosophers.

CR LXIII 1949 53–54 Hamilton

Useful as a work of reference in consulting Diels-Kranz, especially for the lesser known figures and documents, but the work is badly organized for students, contains some major and a good many minor inaccuracies, and cannot be safely recommended to undergraduates or Greekless readers. There is an extended "List of Authorities" (p.425–463).

FRITZ, Kurt von. Philosophie und Sprachlicher Ausdruck bei Demokrit, Plato und Aristoteles. Darmstadt, Wissenschaftliche Buchgesellschaft, 1966. 92p.   **LA48**

"Unveränderter fotomechanischer Nachdruck der Ausgabe . . . 1938."

AC VIII 1939 308–309 des Places • CR LIII 1939 146 Tate • REA XLI 1939 282–283 Mathieu

A subtle discussion of the difficulty experienced by the Greeks, and not fully solved even by Aristotle, in giving verbal expression to philosophic concepts. An acute analysis of the several ways the Greeks built up their philosophic vocabulary, e.g., coining new forms, devising novel combinations, is punctuated by highly speculative personal views.

FURLEY, David J. Two studies in the Greek atomists; Study I, Indivisible magnitudes; Study II, Aristotle and Epicurus on voluntary action. Princeton, N.J., Princeton University Press, 1967. viii, 256p.   **LA49**

Mnemosyne XXVII 1974 315–318 van Straaten • CR XIX 1969 286–289 Stokes

Two thought-provoking essays on the relations between Epicurus' atomism and Aristotle's criticism of earlier atomists.

FURLEY, David J., ed. Studies in pre-Socratic philosophy. London, Routledge and Kegan Paul (New York, Humanities Press), [1970–1975]. 2 v. x, 429, viii, 440p.   **LA50**

International library of philosophy and scientific method: v.1. The beginnings of philosophy, 1970; v.2. The eleatics and pluralists.

V.I: RPhL LXXIII 1975 128 Padrón • JHS XCII 1972 217–218 Long • CR XXIII 1973 47–49 Kerferd

In this selection of essays, reproduced from periodicals, the first half is concerned with the general nature of pre-Socratic thought, the second includes two articles on Anaximander, two on the Pythagoreans and one on Heraclitus. Cherniss, Cornford, Vlastos and Guthrie are among the selected authors. Volume 2 covers the period from Parmenides to the Atomists. Vlastos contributes more than a quarter of the whole.

GADAMER, Hans-Georg. Um die Begriffswelt der Vorsokratiker. Darmstadt, Wissenschaftliche Buchgesellschaft, 1968. xii, 544p.   **LA51**

Wege der Forschung; Bd. 9.

Seventeen contributors, all Germans, including Gadamer himself (1935 and 1950), Jaeger, Snell, Hölscher ("Anaximander und die Anfänge der Philosophie," p.95–126), von Fritz ("Die Rolle des NOYΣ," p. 246–363). Fränkel, Reinhardt—all preeminent forerunners to the more recent English and American researches in pre-Socratic philosophy.

GARBARINO, Giovanna. Roma e la filosofia greca dalle origini alla fine del II secolo A.C.; Raccolta di testi con introduzione e commento. . . . Torino, G. B. Paravia, 1973. 2 v. xxiii, 640p.   **LA52**

Volumes: 1. Introduzione e testi; 2. Commento e indici.

GERSH, S. E. Kinehsis akinehtos; A study of spiritual motion in the philosophy of Proclus. Leiden, Brill, 1973. viii, 143p.   **LA53**

Philosophia antiqua; 26.

JHS XCV 1975 220–221 O'Meara

The author chooses Proclus as the neo-Platonist who provides the most carefully reasoned discussion of spiritual motion. Differing in some details from the interpretation found in Bierwaltes, *Proklos* (1965), the work constitutes an ample justification of Proclus' conception of the metaphysical concepts of motion, activity, power, difference and multiplicity as essentially interrelated.

GOULD, Josiah B. The philosophy of Chrysippus. Albany, State University of New York Press, [1970]. vi, 222p. **LA54**

Gnomon XLIV 1972 645–651 Abel • CR XXIII 1973 214–216 Long • Phoenix XXV 1971 386–388 Rist

A good book on Chrysippus with chapters on his life and philosophical reputation, on the intellectual climate of the 3rd century, and on logic, natural philosophy and ethics. The methodology followed unnecessarily restricts what can be said of Chrysippus' philosophical position to fragments which state explicitly that a given doctrine belongs to Chrysippus, that it is to be found in one of his books, or that the words are *ipsissima verba* of Chrysippus. This places the Stoic doxographical tradition, especially Stobaeus, out of bounds, which is regrettable.

GRAESER, Andreas. Plotinus and the Stoics; A preliminary study. Leiden, Brill, 1972. xv, 146p. **LA55**

Philosophia antiqua; 22.
Arch Philos XXXVI 1973 334–335 Solignac • JHS XCIV 1974 203–204 Lloyd • REA LXXV 1973 151 Moreau

This is a book of notes, averaging half a page each, on Plotinian passages which can be taken to refer to, or depend on, Stoic doctrine. There are also more extended treatments of selected topics. The notes are arranged under the heads, and in the order, of Von Arnim's *Stoic fragments,* not, as would seem to be more logical, under some order from Plotinus. The subtitle rightly suggests that these are preliminary materials for a study of Plotinus and Stoicism rather than the study itself.

GRAESER, Andreas. Zenon von Kition; Positionen u. Probleme. Berlin and New York, de Gruyter, 1975. x, 224p. **LA56**

Arch Philos XXXIX 1976 144–145 Solignac • CR XXVIII 1978 361 Long • CW LXIX 1976 466–467 Reesor

An important book for serious scholars in Stoicism, giving good bibliographical coverage to work-in-progress on 22 selected topics. Not confined to Zeno, the book makes a serious attempt to present the Stoics within their historical context as significant philosophers.

GUTHRIE, William Keith Chambers. A history of Greek philosophy. Cambridge, Cambridge University Press, 1962–1981. **LA57**

Volume 1. The Earlier Pre-Socratics and Pythagoreans; v.2. The Pre-Socratic Tradition from Parmenides to Democritus; v.3. The Fifth-Century Enlightenment; v.4. Plato: The Man and his Dialogues; Earlier Period. v.5. The Later Plato and the Academy. v.6. Aristotle, an encounter.

RPh XXXVIII 1964 296–297 Mugler • v.1: AJPh LXXXV 1964 435–439 De Lacy • Gnomon XXXV 1963 533–537 Seeck • CR XIV 1964 67–70 Kerferd v.2: PRUDENTIA XI 1979 109–117 Hawtrey

Volume 1 is a work of synthesis in the great tradition of classical scholarship, treating of the Milesians, Pythagoras and the Pythagoreans, Alcmaeon, Xenophanes and Heraclitus. Volume 2 continues to display the author's complete command of the modern literature and his powers of dispassionate and judicious analysis. Empedocles occupies more space than either the Eleatics or the Atomists, and twice as much as Anaxagoras.

Vol. 3 is divided into two parts. The first part has a lengthy analysis (p.55–134) of the νόμος φύσις antithesis in morality and politics, and in general the treatment in this volume is thematic rather than by individual philosopher, until c.XI which attempts an aperçu of the Sophists from Protagoras to Lycophron. Part 2 is entirely devoted to Socrates, the sources, his life and character, his teaching and his influence.

Vol. 4 covers the first half of Plato's work (from the early works to the *Republic*). Professor Guthrie maintains the high standards of excellence set in the previous volumes. There are three introductory chapters on Plato's life and the philosophical influences upon him, and on the canon, chronology and literary form of the dialogues. For each dialogue, there is an introductory section (date, authenticity, historicity, etc.), a good summary of the dialogue, and a critical comment. The *Republic* is divided into 15 sections for summary and comment.

In Vol. 5, Guthrie takes up the *Dialogues* of Plato's maturity, beginning with the *Cratylus* and ending with the doubtful ones, the letters and a guardedly skeptical chapter on the "unwritten" metaphysics. An appendix of 50 pages deals with the principal philosophers of the Academy in Plato's time—Eudoxus, Speusippus, Xenocrates, and Heraclides of Pontis. The mixture is by now well known—the strictly historical data, philosophical explication and critical discussion.

HAHM, David E. The origins of Stoic Cosmology. [Columbus], Ohio State University Press, 1977. xix, 292p. **LA58**

AJPh XCIX 1978 534–537 Reesor

This work, dedicated to Friedrich Solmsen as teacher and friend, began as a dissertation under Solmsen's direction and benefited from a fellowship year at the Center for Hellenic Studies in Washington, D.C. It consists of a brief introduction, seven chapters (p.1–215) and six appendices (p.217–273), an index of references to ancient authors and texts and an index of topics.

HEIDEGGER, Martin. Early Greek thinking. Trans. by David Farrell Krell and Frank A. Capuzzi. 1st ed. New York, Harper & Row, [1975]. ix, 129p.   **LA59**

English translation of 4 essays. "The Anaximander Fragment" is the final essay of Holzwege; "Logos," "Moira," and "Aletheia" make up the third part of his Vorträge und Aufshatze.

The Anaximander Fragment—Logos (Heraclitus, Fragment B 50)—Moira (Parmenides VIII, 34–41)—Aletheia (Heraclitus, Fragment B 16).

JHPh XVI 1978 489–492 Hirsch

HEINEMANN, Issak. Poseidonios' Metaphysische Schriften. Hildesheim, G. Olms, 1968. 2 v.   **LA60**

Reprint of the ed. published in Breslau by M. and H. Marcus (1921–1928).

HENRY, Paul. Études Plotiniennes. Paris, Declée de Brouwer, 1938–1961 [v.1, 1961]. 2 v.
                                              LA61

Volumes: 1. "Réimpression sans Changement de la Première Édition de 1938"; 2. "Deuxième Edition."

HOVEN, René. Stoïcisme et stoïciens face au problème de l'au-delà. Paris, Belles Lettres, 1971. 178, 22p.   **LA62**

Bibliothèque de la Faculté de Philosophie et Lettres de l'Université de Liège; fasc. 197.

CR XXIV 1974 232–233 Long

A careful, lucid analysis of what the Stoics from Zeno to Posidonius believed about the duration of the soul's survival after its separation from the body in death. The author clearly illustrates how apparent ambiguities in the evidence have helped to propagate modern scholarly confusion.

HUSSEY, Edward. The pre-Socratics. New York, Scribner, [1973, 1972]. 168p.   **LA63**

CPh LXIX 1974 161 Sprague • REG LXXXVIII 1975 305–306 Babut • CR XXVI 1976 60–61 Kerferd • CW LXVIII 1974 189–190 Walters

A useful introduction for the Greekless reader to the pre-Socratics, which is especially good on Parmenides and Heraclitus but rather skimpy on the Ionians, apart from Anaximander. The Sophists are included, perhaps unwisely in a book of this compass where the emphases are not always well proportioned and the beginners may sometimes emerge bewildered. Each chapter has a short bibliographical note attached.

JÜRSS, Fritz. Zum Erkenntnisproblem bei den Frühgriechischen Denkern. [Red., Dankwart Rahnenführer.] Berlini, Akademie-Verlag, 1976. 136p.   **LA64**

Schriften zur Geschichte und Kultur der Antikei; 14. A revision of the author's thesis, Humboldt-Universität Berlin, 1970.

DLZ XCVIII 1977 670–672 Strohmaier

KAHN, Charles H. Anaximander and the origins of Greek cosmology. New York, Columbia University Press, 1964. 249p.   **LA65**

REG LXXIV 1961 316–317 Mugler • JHS LXXXII 1962 179–180 Gottschalk

Anaximander is here regarded as the originator of the fundamental ideas found in all pre-Socratic systems of cosmology. Among the doxographers Theophrastus is regarded as presenting a fundamentally correct account.

KONSTAN, David. Some aspects of Epicurean psychology. Leiden, Brill, 1973. 82p.   **LA66**

Philosophia antiqua; 25.

CR XXVI 1976 215–217 Long

"Some aspects" examined here include irrational fears and desires, through a study of which, the author maintains, the Epicureans explained men's failure to live the natural life of simple pleasures. Texts from Lucretian Books 2, 3 and 4 are studied in c.1, and from book 5 in c.2. In the final chapter the basis of true pleasure in Epicureanism is studied. The discussion of the relation in Lucretius between the fear of death and immoderate desire is particularly effective.

KRÄMER, Hans Joachim. Platonismus und hellenistische Philosophie. Berlin, de Gruyter, 1971. 396p.   **LA67**

CR XXV 1975 234–236 O'Daly

The author, already well-known for his erudite, if controversial, *Arete bei Platon und Aristoteles* (1959), continues to insist on the dependence of Greek metaphysics on esoteric teachings of Plato. In this insistence he limits his inquiry to that influence on the Old Academy (Xenocrates and Speusippus), the early Stoa, the Skeptical New Academy and Epicurus. An enormously learned work of contemporary Quellenforschung.

KUBE, Jörg. Technē und Aretē; Sophistisches und Platonisches Tugendwissen. Berlin, de Gruyter, 1969 [1968]. x, 255p.   **LA68**

Quellen und Studien zur Geschichte der Philosophie; v. Bd. 12. Revision of the author's thesis, Frankfurt am Main, 1965.

REA LXXI 1969 479–481 Moreau • Gnomon XLIII 1971 235–239 Jäger

The two words of the title pose the central problem of Plato's early *Dialogues*.

LLOYD, Geoffrey E. R. Polarity and analogy. Cambridge, Cambridge University Press, 1966. 502p.   **LA69**

CR XVIII 1968 77–79 Kerferd

This large work aims at describing and analyzing two main types of argument and methods of explanation used in Greek thought down to and including Aristotle. The first part of the work deals with polarity, the second, longer, part with analogy, polarity, the opposition between terms, the doctrine of opposite qualities and the types of argument involving opposites.

LONG, A. A. Hellenistic philosophy; Stoics, Epicureans, Sceptics. [London], Duckworth, [1974]. x, 262p., illus.   **LA70**

CR XXVI 1976 214–215 O'Daly • CW LXIX 1975 275–276 Stewart • Phoenix XXIX 1975 295–299 Todd • REG LXXXVIII 1975 334–336 Babut

A remarkably successful comprehensive introduction for the non-specialist reader covering the period from Epicurus to Cicero. At least half the book (103p.) is devoted to Stoicism, and here it will be a replacement for the long out-of-date works of R. D. Hicks, *Stoic and Epicurean* (New York, 1910) and E. Bevan, *Stoics and Sceptics* (Oxford, 1913). There is almost no treatment of the Cynics or Pythagoreans and the treatment of middle Platonism is left to a separate volume promised in the same series. The final chapter reviews the influence of Hellenistic thought in the Roman Empire and in the 16th and 17th centuries.

LONG, A. A., ed. Problems in Stoicism. London, Athlone Press, 1971. vii, 257p.   **LA71**

REG LXXXVI 1973 444–455 Babut • AAHG XXVII 1974 200–201 Lackner • AJPh XCVI 1975 232–234 von Staden • CR XXV 1975 236–239 Skemp

A collection of ten essays, seven appearing here for the first time, with exemplary indices and a judiciously chosen bibliography. The "problems" dealt with are concerned with Stoic epistemology, logic, metaphysics and ethics. Half the chapters of the work were presented at a series of seminars in the Institute of Classical Studies, University of London. Contributors include F. H. Sandbach (c.I and II), J. M. Rist (c.III), A. C. Lloyd (c.IV and V), S. G. Pembroke (c.VI), A. A. Long (Introd., c.V and VIII), I. G. Kidd (c.IX) and Gerard Watson (c.X The Natural Law and Stoicism).

MINAR, E. L. "A survey of recent work in pre-Socratic philosophy." CW XLVI (1953–1954): 161–177.   **LA72**

O'BRIEN, Denis. Empedocles' cosmic cycle, A reconstruction from the fragments and secondary sources. Cambridge, Cambridge University Press, 1969. x, 459p., illus.   **LA73**

Cambridge classical studies.

CR XXI 1971 176–178 Kerferd • Gnomon XLIII 1971 433–439 Bollack • JHS XC 1970 238–239 Long

An excellent critical bibliography of work on Empedocles from Stirz's edition, 1805 to 1965 (p.337–398), forms the basis of this study which is an extended exploration of the traditional presentation of Empedocles' cosmic cycle, i.e., a four-stage interpretation. The year 1965, however, was a revolutionary one in Empedoclean studies, not just because of the challenges in Bollack's edition, but also because of challenges to the traditional interpretation by Solmsen (*Phronesis* X 1965, 109–148) and Hölscher (*Hermes* XCIII 1965, 7–33). Chapter 8, The Cyclic System (p.156–195), provides a critique of dissident views on the traditional four-stage view: love in control, love challenged by strife and in turn challenging strife and love re-establishing its dominion.

O'BRIEN, Michael J. The Socratic paradoxes and the Greek mind. Chapel Hill, University of North Carolina Press, [1967]. xiv, 249p.   **LA74**

AC XXXVII 1968 335–336 Joly • CPh LXIII 1968 218–219 Sprague • CW LXI 1968 249–250 Stewart • CR XXI 1971 31–33 Charlton

The so-called Socratic paradoxes—virtue is knowledge, virtue and self-interest coincide, no one does wrong willingly—figure largely in early Platonism, but the author shows that they were not abandoned in later Platonism and he convincingly explodes the myth of "Greek intellectualism." The notes contain valuable contributions to Platonic bibliography.

O'DALY, Gerard J. Plotinus' Philosophy of the self. Shannon, Ireland, Irish University Press, [1973]. 121p.   **LA75**

Originally presented as the author's thesis, University of Berne.

JHistPh XV 1977 466–468 Schiller • Latomus XXXV 1976 956 Courcelle • RPh L 1976 307 des Places • REG XCI 1978 261–262 Canévet

A clear exposition of Plotinus' theory of knowledge of the self, based on a thorough knowledge of the ancient texts and of the modern scholarship. Quotations in French, German and Greek are sometimes left untranslated, which may be too flattering to some potential readers. The primary value of the work is in its detailed examination of selected passages from the *Enneads*.

O'MEARA, Dominic J. Structures Hiérarchiques dans la pensée de Plotin; Étude historique et interprétative. Leiden, E. J. Brill, 1975. viii, 137p.   **LA76**

Philosophia antiqua, 27.

CR XXVIII 1978 363–364 Atkinson • REA LXXVIII–LXXIX 1976–1977 290 Moreau

The reality of hierarchical structure is present in Plotinus, even if we have to wait for Dionysius for the term.

O'MEARA, John Joseph. Porphyry's philosophy from oracles in Augustine. Paris, Études Augustiniennes, 1959. ii, 184p.   **LA77**

Gnomon XXXII 1960 320–326 Dörrie • REA LXIII 1961 160–163 Pépin • Hermathena XCVI 1962 108–109 Wormell • JThS XIII 1962 436–437 Frend

This is a scholarly attempt to prove that the *de regressu animae* quoted in Augustine *CIV, DEI* 10.29 and 10.32, is in reality the Peritseklogiohn philophias of Porphyry.

O'MEARA, John Joseph. Porphyry's philosophy from oracles in Eusebius's *Praeparatio evangelica* and Augustine's *Dialogues of Cassiciacum*. Paris, Études Augustiniennes, 1969. 37p.   **LA78**

"This study has appeared in *Recherches augustiniennes* VI (1969), 130–139."

PETERS, Francis E. Greek philosophical terms, A historical lexicon. New York, New York University Press, 1967. xii, 234p.   **LA79**

CPh LXIII 1968 323 Sprague • BBF XIV 1969 67–68 Ernst • CR XXIII 1973 98–99 Charlton

A useful enough lexicon of Greek philosophical terms, transliterated into English spelling, with notes on their use by writers from Homer to Proclus. There are no etymologies, there is a consistent failure to distinguish between words and concepts, and there are too many omissions.

PHILIP, James A. Pythagoras and early Pythagoreanism. [Toronto], University of Toronto Press, [1968, 1966]. 222p.   **LA80**

Phoenix, Journal of Classical Association of Canada: Supplementary; 7.

AC XXXVI 1967 636 Joly • CW LX 1967 301 Feldman • Gnomon XL 1968 6–13 von Fritz • JHS LXXXIX 1969 163–165 De Vogel

The author too narrowly relies upon Aristotle for his reconstruction of ancient Pythagoreanism. Thus he excludes the Philolans texts on *a priori* grounds, and the fragments of Archytas and certain important Platonic texts are considered undependable. He is optimistic enough to think that when Aristotle speaks of the Pythagoreans he is referring to Pythagoras Ipsissimus. He has important and well-argued disagreements with Burkert on whether Pythagoras was a shaman or a philosopher. Often the author is right for the wrong reasons or from unnecessarily narrow premises.

POHLENZ, Max. Die Stoa; Geschichte einer Geistigen Bewegung. 4. Aufl. Göttingen, Vandenhoeck & Ruprecht, 1970–1972. 2 v. 490, 230p.   **LA81**

Volume 2. Erläuterungen (bibliographical).

AJPh LXXII 1951 426–432 Edelstein • RIFD LI 1974 169–170 D'Agostino

A book which is the culmination of a life-long study of Stoicism and which traces the entire development of the school and its Fortleben. Volume I is a straightforward history of the Stoa, leaving the discussion of controversial matters and the review of modern literature to v. II, which makes for uncomfortable ping-pong reading. A most complete account of all aspects of Stoicism.

RÉPERTOIRE Bibliographique de la Philosophie. Louvain, Institut Superieur de Philosophie, t. 1– , fev., 1949– .   **LA82**

At head of title, 1949– : Société Philosophique de Louvain supersedes Répertoire Bibliographique (Supplement to Revue Philosophique de Louvain).

See the section Antiquité Grecque et Romaine. See "Philosophie de L'Antiquité," RPhL LXXIII (1975), 108–211 for critical reviews.

RIST, John M. Human value. A study in ancient philosophical ethics. Leiden, Brill, 1982. v, 175p.   **LA83**

Philosophia antiqua; XI.

RIST, John M. Plotinus; The road to reality. Cambridge, Cambridge University Press, 1977. vii, 280p. 1st ed., 1967.   **LA84**

AJPh XCIII 1972 637–638 Tarán • RPh XLIII 1969 143 Louis

This work aims at giving a detailed discussion of certain problems in Plotinus' thought, not an outline of his philosophy. The biography of Plotinus receives first attention, followed by the selected problems which seem to arise more from recent scholarly debates than from the text itself.

RIST, John M. Stoic philosophy. Cambridge, Cambridge University Press, 1977. x, 300p.   **LA85**

Phoenix XXV 1971 78–80 Reesor • CR XXII 1972 366–369 Skemp • JHistPh IX 1971 81–86 Gould

The older books on Stoicism by Arnold (1911), Hicks and Bevan (1913), though recently reprinted, are long out-of-date and the present work makes the results of recent scholarship easily accessible, while the author adds many valuable insights of his own. The work tends to be episodic, but some questions, e.g., suicide, are argued with great thoroughness. Some of the author's interpretations, notably his understanding of Stoic πρόνοια, will not go unquestioned.

SAMBURSKY, Samuel. The concept of time in late neo-Platonism. Texts with trans., introd. and notes by S. Sambursky and S. Pines. Jerusalem, Israel Academy of Sciences and Humanities, 1971. 118p.   **LA86**

Includes selection from the Greek with English translation of pseudo-Archytas, Iamblichus, Proclus, Damascius, Simplicius, Plutarch, Tatian.

CR XXIV 1974 231–232 Armstrong

An excellent anthology (with facing translation) of pieces in late neo-Platonism dealing with time, illustrating an idea outlined by Sambursky in his *Physical world of late antiquity* (p.18–20) and here at greater length in the Introduction.

SANDBACH, F. H. The Stoics. London, Chatto & Windus, 1975. 190p.   **LA87**

Ancient culture and society.

CR XXVII 1977 45–47 Sedley • JHS XCVI 1976 207–208 Sharples • MH XXXIII 1976 58 Theiler

An impressive introduction to Stoicism, with a long chapter on Stoic ethics followed by shorter treatments of natural science, logic, fate and free will, and the *Nachleben* through the Greco-Roman world. There is a good treatment of individual Stoics, e.g., Seneca (p.149–162) and an excellent bibliography.

SINNINGE, Theodorus Gerard. Matter and infinity in the presocratic schools and Plato. 2d ed. Assen, Van Gorcum, 1971. 252p., illus.   **LA88**

Philosophical texts and studies; 17.

Gnomon XLIII 1971 82–84 Mourelatos • JHS XC 1970 240–241 Bicknell

More a series of essays than an integrated study of the two announced topics, and with infinity faring rather better than matter. Anaximander, Xenophanes and Parmenides are dealt with sequentially, with Anaximenes strangely absent. The Pythagoreans are then covered in more detail, followed by Zeno, Empedocles (scantily), Anaxagoras, Democritus (perversely) and Plato. An unconvincing and wayward but well-written work.

STOKES, Michael C. One and many in presocratic philosophy. Washington, D.C., Center for Hellenic Studies (distributed by Harvard University Press, Cambridge, Mass.), 1971. ix, 355p. **LA89**

Phoenix XXVI 1972 400–402 Kerferd • Mind LXXXIV 1975 289–291 Long • JHS XCIII 1973 244–248 Lloyd

The aim of this lengthy, closely argued, investigation into the history of the opposition between "one" and "many" before Plato is twofold: to determine the place of the antithesis in early Greek thought and to ask how far distinctions between different kinds of unity and plurality went unrecognized (p.1). The coverage of the pre-Socratics is uneven, very skimpy on the Pythagorean evidence, very generous on Xenophanes, Parmenides and Zeno. A stimulating and thought-provoking work, but not the definitive treatment.

SWEENEY, Leo. Infinity in the presocratics; A bibliographical and philosophical study. Foreword by Joseph Owens. The Hague, Nijhoff, 1972. xxxiii, 222p. **LA90**

REG LXXXVIII 1975 307–309 Babut • JHS XCV 1975 227–228 Bargrave-Weaver

This work, the first in a promised series of investigations, was prompted by a remark of E. Gibbon on the need for a history of one of the most fundamental notions in Christian philosophy. Professor Sweeney had already presented a 500-page dissertation to the University of Toronto on the notion in St. Thomas, with chapters on Aristotle, Plotinus, Proclus, Ps. Dionysius, and the *Liber de causis* so he had gone through a rigorous apprenticeship. His present work is particularly useful for its disproportionately long treatment of Anaximander, with detailed exegesis of the secondary literature from 1947 to 1970. For the other pre-Socratics, however, the work is much less detailed.

THESLEFF, Holger. The Pythagorean texts of the Hellenistic period. Abo, Abo Akademi, 1965. vi, 266p. **LA91**

Acta Academia Aboensis, ser. A: Humaniora; 30, nr.1.

CR XIX 1969 284–286 Kerferd • Gnomon XXXIX 1967 548–556 Burkert

Following an earlier *Introduction to the Pythagorean writings of the Hellenistic period,* 1961 (cf. *Gnomon* XXXIV, 1962, 763f.), this is a most useful collection of material assembled in convenient form for the first time.

UEBERWEG, Friedrich. A history of philosophy, from Thales to the present time. Trans. from the 4th German ed. by George S. Morris, with additions by Noah Porter. Freeport, N.Y., Books for Libraries Press, [1972]. 2 v. **LA92**

Reprint of the 1872–1874 ed. Trans. of *Grundriss der Geschichte der Philosophie.* Volumes: 1. History of the Ancient and Medieval Philosophy; 2. History of Modern Philosophy.

VOGEL, Cornelia J. de. Greek philosophy; A collection of texts selected and supplied with some notes and explanations. 3rd ed. Leiden, E. J. Brill, 1963–1967. 3 v. **LA93**

Gnomon XXVI 1954 204 Wehrli, XXXIII 1961 446–466 Kohnke

Volume 1 contains texts from Thales to Plato, v. 2, Aristotle, the early Peripatetic school and the early Academy, v. 3, the Hellenistic-Roman period.

WALLIS, R. T. Neoplatonism. [London], Duckworth, [1972]. xi, 212p., plate, map. **LA94**

Classical life and letters.

CR XXIV 1974 227–228 Armstrong • REG LXXXVIII 1975 376–378 Trouillard

This history for the general reader of neo-Platonism from Plotinus to Damascius encompasses a synopsis of the tendencies and sources of neo-Platonism, a brief study of its *Nachleben* to the present, and a sound bibliography. It is richly documented and done with great analytical acumen. Plotinus gets disproportionate attention at the expense of Proclus and Damascius. A good replacement for Thomas Whittaker, *The neoplatonists* (1918, 1928)

WEHRLI, Fritz Robert. Hauptrichtungen des Griechischen Denkens. Zürich, Artemis Verlag, [1964]. 233p. **LA95**

Erasmus-Bibliothek.

CW LIX 1965 10–11 Long • Gnomon XXXVII 1965 529–532 Adkins • Gymnasium LXXII 1965 542–543 Oehler

A discussion of the values and ideals of the Greeks from Homer to Epicurus. Not enough attention is given to actual Greek words or texts for the values and ideals discussed, and sometimes there are anachronisms in dealing with virtues or ἀρεταί.

WEST, Martin L. Early Greek philosophy and the Orient. Oxford, Clarendon Press, 1971. xv, 256p., 8 plates. **LA96**

BO XXXI 1974 134–137 De Vogel • CR XXIV 1974 82–86 Kirk • Gnomon XLVII 1975 321–328 Marcovich

A very learned, if at times tendentious, book.

Science and Technology

MA GENERAL

CLAGETT, Marshall. Greek science in antiquity. New York, Collier Books, 1976. 256p., illus.

MA1

JHS LXXIX 1959 174–175 Wasserstein • Isis XLVIII 1957 359–360 van der Waerden

A very lucid introduction for non-specialists to the history of ancient Greek science, with special attention to later antiquity. There is a preliminary brief but interesting survey of non-Hellenic science in Egypt and Mesopotamia, particularly for mathematics, astronomy and medicine. Particularly good on Galen and Aristotelean physics.

COHEN, Morris and DRABKIN, Israel. A source book in Greek science. Cambridge, Mass., Harvard University Press, 1966 [1948]. xxi, 581p.

MA2

Source books in the history of the sciences.

Isis XL 1949 277–278 Sarton • CW XLIII 1949 41–43 Stahl • CR X 1960 250–252 Eichholz

A useful selection (317 texts) from Greek and Roman scientific writings which forms a valuable reference work and guide to the ancient literature. Contains many selections from relatively unknown writers in the various sections on mathematics, astronomy, mathematical geography, physics, chemistry, chemical technology, geology and meteorology, biology, medicine, and physiological psychology. There are many drawings and plans to illustrate the text.

DE SANTILLANA, Giorgio. The origins of scientific thought from Anaximander to Proclus, 600 B.C.–300 A.D. [Chicago], University of Chicago Press, 1961. 320p.

MA3

The History of scientific thought; 1.

Isis LV 1964 110–111 Grant • AHR LXVII 1961–1962 998–1000 Clagett

Chapters I through XI are devoted to the elusive pre-Socratic beginnings of Greek scientific thought, with rather unorthodox interpretation of Parmenides, making him virtually the father of Greek mathematics and scientific thought. There are rather conventional treatments of Plato, Aristotle, and the main issues in astronomy.

FARRINGTON, Benjamin. Greek science; Its meaning for us. Baltimore, Penguin Books, 1949. Reprint 1969. 320p.

MA4

Pelican Books.

CW XLIV 1950 22–23 Stahl • JHS LXX 1950 98–99 Raven

A controversial and provocative study, first published in 1944. The early Ionians are represented as constituting the best period of Greek science because their speculations were based on observation of natural phenomena. Advances and retardations in Greek science are explained as sociological manifestations. Socrates, we are told, divorced science from reality and Plato made matters worse. Where slavery thrives science dies is the pervasive social message.

FARRINGTON, Benjamin. Science in antiquity. 2d ed. London and New York [etc.], Oxford University Press, 1969. iii–vi, 156p., illus.

MA5

Oxford University Press paperback.

RPh XLIV 1970 334 Mugler • AAHG XXII 1969 219–220 Pötscher • AC XXXVIII 1969 646–647 Byl

First published in 1936, this work retains its interest and popularity. It provides a wide-ranging survey of science in antiquity from the Egyptians and Babylonians to the Romans. Filiations of systems are shown in the chronological treatment of the various schools. The chapter on Aristotle has been considerably reworked in the second edition, but the author's chronology of Aristotle's works remains outmoded and his bibliography has not been brought up to date.

FELDHAUS, Franz. Die Technik der Antike und des Mittelalters. Mit Vorwort und Bibliographie von Horst Callies. Hildesheim and New York, Olms, 1971. xi, 442p., illus.   **MA6**

Reprint of the ed. published in Potsdam in 1930.
AHR XXXVII 1931 92–93 Schevill • HZ CXLV 1931 607–608 Kistner
The present work is in four sections: 1. The Technology of Prehistory; II. The Technology of China, India, Babylonia and Egypt; III. The Technology of Greece and Rome; IV. The Technology of the Middle Ages. An enormous array of 14,000 excerpts from chronicles, records, travel books and monuments constitutes the underlying scholarly apparatus of a very brisk-moving narrative. There are 452 valuable illustrations, some from ancient publications.

FERGUSON, Eugene S. Bibliography of the history of technology. Cambridge, Mass., Society for the History of Technology, [1968]. xx, 347p.   **MA7**

Isis LX 1969 558–559 Smith

FRITZ, Kurt von. Grundprobleme der Geschichte der antiken Wissenschaft. Berlin and New York, de Gruyter, 1971. xxxvi, 759p.   **MA8**

RPhL LXXIII 1975 108–109 Brague • AHR LXXVIII 1973 76–77 Neugebauer • RH XCVII, 250 1973 451—452 Will
Mostly reprints of earlier publications by the author, most of which are wide-ranging philosophical, ethical and pedagogical reflections on the impact of early Greek philosophy on some of the sciences, especially mathematical axiomatics.

JUERSS, F., ed. Geschichte des wissenschaftlichen Denkens im Altertum. Berlin, Akademie-Verlag, 1982. 672p., 187 illus.   **MA8a**

Veröffentlichung des Zentralinstitut für Alte Geschichte & Archäologie der Akademie der Wissenschaft der DDR; XIII.

LLOYD, Geoffrey E. R. Early Greek science; Thales to Aristotle. New York, Norton, [1971, 1970]. 156p., illus., map.   **MA9**

AHR LXXXVII 1972 1421 Jameson • RPh XLVI 1972 292 Mugler • REG LXXXVIII 1975 325–326 Louis
A slim but cogent volume which treats nonethical philosophy from Thales to Aristotle and his immediate successors. Medicine and astronomy receive due attention, but not technology. See also especially for medicine, Lloyd, G.E.R., *Magic, reason and experience: Studies in the development of Greek science,* (Cambridge, 1979).

LLOYD, Geoffrey E. R. Greek science after Aristotle. London, Chatto and Windus, 1973. xiv, 189p., illus., map.   **MA10**

Ancient culture and society.
CW LXIX 1976 407–408 Waite • CJ LXXII 1976

82–83 Scarborough • Gymnasium LXXXIII 1976 457–458 Klein • CR n.s. XXV 1975 305–307 Phillips
In this well-balanced sequel to his *Early Greek science: Thales to Aristotle,* Professor Lloyd integrates the advances in mathematics, astronomy, biology and medicine into the cultural history of the eight centuries between Aristotle and Justinian. The main figures— Theophrastus, Strabo, Euclid, Archimedes, Aristarchus, Apollonius, Hipparchus, Herophilus, Erasistratus, Ptolemy and Galen—receive sound treatment. The work is a good complement to, but not a replacement for, George Sarton, *A history of science,* v. 2.

ROBIN, Leon. La pensé grecque et les origines de l'esprit scientifique. Paris, Renaissance du livre, 1923. 480p., folding map.   **MA11**

SARTON, George. A history of science. Ancient science through the Golden Age of Greece. Cambridge, Mass., Harvard University Press, 1953. xxvi, 646p.   **MA12**

CR V 1955 196 Farrington • JHS LXXIV 1954 218–219 Phillips
A comprehensive, richly documented account of the history of science from the prehistoric dawn through the contributions of Egypt, Mesopotamia, the Aegean world, Homer, Hesiod, the Assyrians, and the main Greek schools down to the Epicureans and the Stoics. The scientific contributions are assessed against their cultural backgrounds.

SARTON, George. A history of science. Volume 2. Hellenistic Science and Culture in the Last Three Centuries, B.C. Cambridge, Mass., Harvard University Press, 1959. xxxvi, 554p.   **MA13**

CHR XLVI 1960–1961 75–77 McGuire • CR X 1960 250–252 Eichholz • JRS LI 1961 251 Sainte-Croix
Planned as the second volume in a series of eight, this was the last volume completed by Sarton before his death in 1956. The work is mainly addressed to scientists by a scientist which makes parts of it, e.g., mathematics, difficult going for the classicist. But the information is generally clearly and agreeably presented. Greek and Chaldaean astronomy, Greek and Roman technology are skillfully interwoven. The author, a distinguished scientist and bibliographer, writes with particular authority on the Museum and Library of Alexandria.

SINGER, Charles et al. A history of technology. Oxford, Clarendon Press, [1967]. 5 v., illus. (part col.), port., maps.   **MA14**

Volumes: 1. From early times to fall of ancient empires; 2. The Mediterranean civilizations and the Middle Ages, c.700 B.C. to c.1500 A.D.
AntJ XXXVI 1956 82–83 Bushnell • CR VIII 1958 171–175 Eichholz • CW XLIX 1955 26–27, L 1957 211 Stahl
Volumes 1 and 2 of this gigantic undertaking were issued in 1954 and 1956. In volume 1 each of the 28

contributors is an expert in his field, and excellence in editing has ensured uniformly clear presentations. The first two volumes comprise a fairly complete reference work on every conceivable aspect of ancient and medieval technology. A monumental achievement.

STAHL, William H. Roman science; Origins, development, and influence to the later Middle Ages. Westport, Conn., Greenwood Press, 1978. 1st ed. 1962. x, 308p. **MA15**

Reprint of the ed. published by University of Wisconsin Press, Madison.

AJPh LXXXV 1964 418–423 Neugebauer • CO XLI 1963 19–20 Drabkin • Manuscripta VIII 1964 105–107 Seeger

This book is in three sections: Greek antecedents, Rome from the late Republic to the 5th century, and the mediaeval *Nachleben*. For the author, Roman science is textbook science and he is mostly concerned with the handbooks of Roman *quadrivium* literature and with exposing their scholarly shortcomings and shameful borrowings. The major authors discussed in the central section are Cato the Elder, Varro, Cicero,

Lucretius, Pomponius Mela, Vitruvius, Celsus, Seneca, and Pliny. Other authors later covered extend from Apuleius, Chalcidius, Macrobius down through Isidore, Bede to the 12th century. The work is more literary history than technical or scientific.

WHITROW, Magda, ed. Isis cumulative bibliography; A bibliography of the history of science formed from Isis critical bibliographies, 1–90, 1913–1965. Chairman of Editorial Committee, I. Bernard Cohen. London, Mansell in conjunction with the History of Science Society, 1971. 2 v. **MA16**

Volume 1. part 1. Personalities, A–J. Volume 2. part 1. Personalities, K–Z; part 2. Institutions.

BECh CXXXI 1973 595–598 Poulle

The Isis bibliography was conceived by George Sarton in 1913 and has long been a respected scholarly tool, much wider in its scope than a history of the history of science. See most recent, Neu, J., ed. "One hundred eighth critical bibliography of the history of science and its cultural influences (to January 1983)," *Isis* LXXIV, 5 (1983), 1–215.

MB SCIENCE

Astronomy/Astrology

ABEL, Karlhaus. "Zone, astronomisch-geographischer Begriff." RE Suppl. XIV (1974): 989–1188. **MB1**

An elaborate historical survey of the development of the concept of astronomy, from prehistory to late antiquity. Available as a *separatum*.

DICKS, D. R. Early Greek astronomy to Aristotle. London, Thames & Hudson, (Ithaca, Cornell University Press), 1970. 272p., illus. **MB2**

Aspects of Greek and Roman life.

AJPh XCIV 1973 121–123 Hahm • CPh LXVII 1972 217–219 Mueller • Gnomon XLIV 1972 127–131 Toomer • REG LXXXIV 1971 206 Mugler

An excellent synthesis of the research of the last half-century, if at times unnecessarily critical of other scholars. This is the first of a promised two-volume history of ancient astronomy that is likely to become standard, replacing the earlier works of Dreyer and Heath. Early chapters deal with primitive Greek astronomy, Homer, Hesiod and the pre-Socratics getting detailed attention. Plato gets inordinate attention, Eudoxus too little. There are good notes at the end (p. 219–267) and an index of proper names and of astronomical notions.

GIBBS, S. L. Greek and Roman sundials. New Haven, Conn., Yale University Press, 1976. viii, 421p. **MB3**

CW LXXI 1977 274 Ballín

Essentially a source catalog of 263 sundials or dial fragments dating from the 3rd century B.C. to the 4th century A.D. The dials are grouped by type (spherical, conical, planar, cylindrical) and further subdivided. There is an extremely difficult section devoted to mathematical calculations, accompanied by expertly drawn trigonometric diagrams.

GILBERT, Otto. Die meteorologischen Theorien des griecheschen Altertums. Hildesheim, G. Olms., 1967. viii, 746p., illus. **MB4**

Reprint of the edition published in Leipzig by B. G. Teubner.

HODSON, F. R., ed. The place of astronomy in the ancient world. London, Royal Society, 1974. 276p., illus. **MB5**

Royal Society of London Philosophical transactions; series A: Mathematical and physical sciences; no. 1257, v. 276.

CR XXVII 1977 95–96 Brookes • Isis LXVII 1976 121 Van der Waerden • AntJ LV 1975 415–416 Maddison

Thirteen authors achieve considerable unity in this symposium on the place of astronomy in "antiquity." The introductory essay on some basic astronomical concepts is an excellent introduction to the subject. Other papers assess the contributions of Assyria, Babylonia, Egypt and China. The second half of the book deals with the unwritten evidence of astronomical technology in prehistoric times, with special attention to stone circles and other monuments.

LINDSAY, Jack. Origins of astrology. New York, Barnes & Noble, [1971]. xii, 480p., illus.

MB6

CW LXVI 1972 57–58 Pearson • AHR LXXVII 1972 1421 Jameson • RBPh L 1972 180 Joly

This is a companion volume to the author's *Origins of alchemy* (1970). A work of great thoroughness in which enormous masses of evidence are interpreted perspicaciously. The author has good introductory sections on ancient Mesopotamia and Egypt as part of the necessary cultural syncretism for the fusion of Greek mathematics and astral religion. There is an abundant bibliography, merely arranged alphabetically, and the footnotes are also very cramped.

MARTIN, Thomas Henri. Mémoires sur les hypothesès astronomiques. New York, Arno Press, 1976. 252, 302, 43p.

MB7

Reprint of articles published in Mémoires de l'Institut national de France, Académie des Belles Lettres, 1879, 1881, 1883.

NEUGEBAUER, Otto. A history of ancient mathematical astronomy. Berlin, Springer, 1975. 3 vols. xxiii, 1456p., illus.

MB8

Studies in the history of Mathematics & Physical Science; I.

CRAI 1976 133 Lemerle • BBF XXI 1976 431 Lévy • BiblH&R XXXVIII 1976 513–515 Poulle

Mathematics

ALLMAN, George. Greek geometry from Thales to Euclid. Dublin, Hodges, Figgis, 1889. xii, 237p., illus.

MB9

Photocopy of 1889 ed. Ann Arbor, Mich.: University Microfilms.

BECKER, Oskar. Das mathematisch Denken der Antike. Mit 70 Figuren im Text. 2., durchgesehene Aufl. mit einem Nachtrag von G[ünther]. Göttingen, Vandenhoeck & Ruprecht, 1957. 131p., illus.

MB10

CR VIII 1958 245–246 Bulmer-Thomas • Gnomon XXX 1958 81–87 von Fritz

A brief, historical introduction sketches the Egyptian, Bablyonian and Indian beginnings, and the more substantial Greek achievement from Thales to Anthemius of Tralles. Concrete examples are then presented to give a useful picture of the mathematical achievement of antiquity, mainly Greek.

BECKER, Oskar. Zur Geschichte der Griechischen Mathematik. Darmstadt, Wissenschaftliche Buchgesellschaft, 1965. 461p.

MB11

Wege der Forschung; Bd. 32.

AAHG XXI 1968 145–148 Pötscher • AC XXXV 1966 687 Lasserre • RF LVIII 1967 187–191 Cambiano

This *Wege der Forschung* volume aims at giving more a general view of the subject than the present status of research and reflects the personal interests of its distinguished author, who died shortly before its publication.

BOCHNER, Salomon. The role of mathematics in the rise of science. Princeton, Princeton University Press, 1966. x, 386p.

MB12

CR XVIII 1968 345–348 Dicks

This book consists of articles reprinted in expanded and revised form from various journals, with some additions, but the sum total hardly justifies the ambitious title. The writing is undistinguished and many of the judgments are superficial and ill considered.

BOYER, Carl B. A history of mathematics. New York, Wiley, 1968. xv, 717p., illus., ports.

MB13

Janus LVI 1969 63–77 Bruins

BRUNÉS, Tons. The secrets of ancient geometry—and its use. Copenhagen, Rhodos, [1967]. 2 v., illus., plates.

MB14

Trans. of *Den hemmelige oldtidsgeometri og dens anvedelse.*

Janus LVIII 1971 299–308 Bruins • CW LXVII 1973 182–183 Kren • Isis LXIV 1973 402–404 Coxeter

A Freemason explains how the first geometrical speculation of primitive man became the property of a priestly elite in the Temple of Egypt, who developed it into an arcane body of knowledge and transmitted it to Greece as the hidden secret of a priesthood.

BURKERT, Walter. Lore and science in ancient Pythagoreanism. Trans. by Edwin L. Minar, Jr. Cambridge, Mass., Harvard University Press, 1972. 535p.

MB15

Trans. of *Weisheit und Wissenschaft; Studien zu Pythagoras, Philolaos und Platon.*

CR XIV 1964 28–29 Gulley • CR XXVI 1976 132 Kerferd • Gnomon XXXVII 1965 344–354 Morrison

In the welcome English translation of this important work the author has done considerable revision, rearrangement and modification, making it virtually a second edition. The work steers a careful middle course between the two extreme views, one of which says that nothing is known of pre-Platonic Pythagorean science and mathematics, the other claiming the foundation and development of Greek mathematics almost exclusively for Pythagoras and followers. The work is extremely well documented both in ancient sources and modern literature, showing enviable competence in the three Pythagorean sciences, astronomy, music and mathematics, as well as religion and philosophy.

GOW, James. A short history of Greek mathematics. New York, Chelsea Pub. Co., 1968. xii, 325p.

MB16

RHS XXIII 1970 267 Itard • CW LXVII 1973 184–185 Stannard

A welcome reprint of an 1884 work, still useful though of course superseded in many respects. It provides a sound but not overly technical survey of the mainstream of Greek mathematics for classical scholars, with geometry getting the largest treatment.

HANKEL, Hermann. Zur Geschichte der Mathematik in Altertum und Mittelalter. 2. Aufl. (Reprographischer Nachdruck der Ausg., Leipzig, 1874). Mit Worwort und Register von J. E. Hofmann. Hildesheim, G. Olms, 1965. xv, 442p.
MB17

HEATH, Thomas, Sir. A manual of Greek mathematics. New York, Dover Publications, [1963]. 552p., illus.   **MB18**

A&R XII 1967 81–84 Zadro • CJ XXVII 1931 55–58 Robbins • BAGB 1932 30–33

Unabridged and unaltered republication of the first work published in 1931.

Briefer than the same author's two-volume *A history of Greek mathematics* (1921) and intended for the general reader. A clear, concise scientific account of the mathematical works of the ancient Greeks, especially Euclid, Archimedes, Apollonius, Ptolemy and Diophantes.

KLEIN, Jacob. Greek mathematical thought and the origin of algebra. Trans. by Eva Brann. With an appendix containing Vièta's *Introduction to the Analytical Art*, trans. by J. Winfree Smith. Cambridge, Mass., MIT Press, 1968. xv, 360p.
MB19

G&R XXIV 1977 214 Walcot • Isis LXI 1970 132–133 Scriba • RHS XXIII 1970 369–370 Dadić • SIF III 1971 222–226 Caton

Very much for the expert, this work springs from the belief that François Vièta was the founder of modern mathematics and that his reinterpretation of Diophantus was crucial in the history of Greek mathematics.

MAY, Kenneth Ownsworth. Bibliography and research manual of the history of mathematics. [Toronto and Buffalo], University of Toronto Press, 1973. 818p.   **MB20**

MAZIARZ, Edward A. Greek mathematical philosophy. New York, Ungar, [1968]. xii, 271p.
MB21

CW LXIV 1970 59–60 Eisele • Isis LX 1969 406 Gericke

MILHAUD, Gaston Samuel. Les philosophes-géomètres de la Gréce; Platon et ses predécesseurs. New York, Arno Press, 1976. 387p.
MB22

Reprint of the 1900 ed. published by F. Alcan, Paris.

MUGLER, Charles. Dictionnaire historique de la terminologie géométrique des Grecs. Paris, Librairie C. Klincksieck. 1958–1959. 2 v., 456p.
MB23

Études et commentaires, 28.

AJPh LXXXII 1961 217–219 Neugebauer • JHS LXXXIV 1964 195–196 Wasserstein • Gnomon XXXIII 1961 150–159 von Fritz

An attempt to assemble a lexicon of Greek geometrical terminology from the time of the pre-Socratics down to the late commentators. The work is based on the most important texts of Euclid, Aristarchus, Archimedes, Apollonius, Hero, Pappus, Proclus, Eutochius and many others. The work is too arbitrarily planned— e.g., it excludes arithmetic and astronomy—but it will often be extremely useful.

NEUGEBAUER, Otto. The exact sciences in antiquity. 2d ed. New York, Dover Publications, [1969]. xvi, 240p., illus.   **MB24**

Gnomon XXX 1958 473–474 Becker • Isis XLIII 1952 69–73 Sarton and Carmody • JHS LXXIII 1953 179 Treweek

The text of six lectures delivered at Cornell University in 1941, with detailed notes and critical bibliographies added to each chapter. The main subjects are mathematics and astronomy in Babylon and Egypt, and "exact" is more applicable to the mathematics than to the astronomy. Addressed more to the intelligent layman than to the expert.

SZABÓ, Árpád. The beginnings of Greek mathematics. Trans. by A. M. Ungar. Hingham, Mass., D. Reidel Pub., [1978]. 494p.   **MB25**

Trans. of *Anfänge griechischen Mathematik* (1969).

CW LXIV 1970 23 Boyer • Erasmus XXIII 1971 102–105 Burkert • Philosophia I 1971 445–450 Vasiliou

Based on important earlier journal articles this work concentrates on three areas: (1) the early history of the theory of irrationalities, (2) the pre-Euclidean theory of proportionality, and (3) the construction of systematic deductive mathematics. The treatment is concerned more with philosophical views and philological connections than with actual mathematics.

TANNERY, Paul. La géométrie grecque; Comment son histoire nous est parvenue et ce que nous en savons essai critique. 1. ptie. Historie générale de la géométrie élementaire. Paris, Gauthier-Villars, 1887. vi, 188p.   **MB26**

Photocopy of the 1887 ed. Ann Arbor, Mich.: University Microfilms.

THAER, C. "Bibliographischer Bericht uber antike Mathematik. (1906–1930)." JAW CCLXXXIII (1943): 1–138.   **MB26a**

Chemistry/Physics

CALEY, Earle Radcliffe. Analysis of ancient metals. New York, 1964. 176p.   **MB27**

International series of monographs on analytical chemistry.
AIHS XIX 1966 167–169 Weill

GERSHENSON, Daniel and GREENBERG, Daniel. Anaxagoras and the birth of physics. New York, Blaisdell, 1964. xxv, 538p. **MB28**

CR XVI 1966 165–166 Kerferd • Isis LVI 1965 473–474 Strang • PhilosQ XVI 1966 268–269 Mathewson
A work of collaboration between a classicist and a theoretical physicist, this is the first volume in a planned comprehensive *A history of physics* spanning 25 centuries divided into five eras, the first going down to Aristotle. This work rejects the basis and details of Diels, *Doxographi Graeci* as unsound but its substitute is equally unsatisfactory: a straight-line progressive corruption of material the farther we move away from Anaxagoras.
There is a preliminary sketch (p.3–51) of the life and doctrines of Anaxagoras, then a series of translations of all the ancient sources down to the 6th century A.D. (p.53–326), a discussion of certain aspects of the sources, and a survey and summary of modern discussions of Anaxagoras from 1687 to the present, with notes and bibliographies.

LEICESTER, H. M. Development of biochemical concepts from ancient to modern times. Cambridge, Mass., Harvard University Press, 1974. 286p. **MB29**

Monograph in the History of Science.
AIHS XXVI 1976 186–187 Shamin • ZWG LXII 1978 207–208 Weyer

LINDSAY, Jack. Blast-power and ballistics; Concepts of force and energy in the ancient world. London, Muller, 1974. 509p., illus. **MB30**

TLS LXXIV 1975 64 Lloyd • CW LXX 1976 212–213 Furley
Very nearly Lindsay's hundredth book, but not one of his best. Bland, amiable, fairly harmless but careless in details, too diffuse for the general reader and not enough interpretation of primary sources for the scholarly reader.

LINDSAY, Jack. The origins of alchemy in Graeco-Roman Egypt. London, Muller, 1970. xii, 452p. **MB31**

JRS LXI 1971 281–282 Bargrave-Weaver
Deals with the theory and practice of alchemy in its formative period in an attempt to show that the alchemists were the very far-sighted founders of experimental science. After a brief look at Greek science the literary source material for the genesis of alchemy is examined.
This is a valuable compilation of materials which, however, are not critically assessed.

MUGLER, Charles. Dictionnaire historique de la terminologie optique des Grecs; Douze siècles de dialogues avec la lumière. Paris, C. Klincksieck, 1964. 459p. **MB32**

AC XXXVI 1967 701 Leroy • RPh XL 1966 108–110 Chantraine • JHS LXXXVI 1966 230–231 Dicks

PARTINGDON, James Riddick. A history of chemistry. London, Macmillan & Co., 1970. 4 v. **MB33**

Isis LXIV 1973 252–253 Multhauf • CR XXV 1975 135–136 Kicks
The work of a distinguished professor of chemistry who was also an expert in the history of science. The present section of a larger work is mainly concerned with Greek material from the earliest period to the end of antiquity. "Chemistry" is widely interpreted, and there are good chapters on the earliest cosmogonies, medicine and technology, neopythagoreanism, neoplatonism, the Hermetics Books, etc. The bibliography runs to 20 pages, but much of it is pre-1950, and even pre-1900.

PEDERSEN, Olaf and PIHL, Mogens. Early physics and astronomy; A historical introduction. New York, Science History Publications, 1974. 413p., illus. **MB34**

Rev. trans. of *Historisk Indledning til den Klassiske Fysik.*
Bibl H&R XXXVIII 1976 229–231 Poulle • Isis LXVIII 1977 465–466 Saliba

REPELLINI, F. F. Cosmologie greche: Storia della Scienza XVI. Torino, Loescher, 1980. 324p. **MB35**

SAMBURSKY, Samuel, ed. Physical thought from the presocratics to the quantum physicists; An anthology. London, Hutchinson, 1974. xvi, 584p., 8p. of plates, illus., ports. **MB36**

SAMBURSKY, Samuel. The physical world of late antiquity. New York, Basic Books, [1962]. 189p. **MB37**

Gnomon XXXVIII 1966 103–106 Abel

SAMBURSKY, Samuel. The physical world of the Greeks; translated from the Hebrew by Merton Dagut. New York, Collier Books, 288p. **MB38**

Phoenix XIII 1959 80–83 Philip • Gnomon XXXII 1960 365–368 Solmsen
A major contribution to the study of Greek physical theory by a physicist who was Director of the Research Council of Israel. There is an introductory chapter on The Scientific Approach, a weak Pythagorean chapter, Nature and Number, and excellent treatments of astronomy and the theories of the Stoics and Epicureans. Treatment throughout is based on the Greek treatises and fragments.

SAMBURSKY, Samuel. Physics of the Stoics. New York, Macmillan, [1959]. **MB39**

Gnomon XXXII 1960 575–576 Leeman • RF L 1959 373–374 Viano

This work consists of four sections: I. The Dynamic Continuum; II. Pneuma and Force; III. The Sequence of Physical Events; and IV. The Whole and its Parts. There is an appendix (p.116–145) of Translations of Texts, some by the author, others from available English translations (e.g., K. Freeman, R. G. Bury).

Natural Sciences

BERNIER, R. Aux sources de la biologie. Paris, Les Belles Lettres, 1976.   **MB40**

RHS XXX 1977 87–89 Mandelbaum • RQS CXLVIII 1977 224 Delhez

HALL, Thomas Steele. Ideas of life and matter; Studies in the history of general physiology, 600 B.C.–1900 A.D. Chicago, University of Chicago Press, [1969]. 2 v.   **MB41**

KRAFFT, Fritz. Geschichte der Naturwissenschaft. Freiburg, Rombach, (1971).   **MB42**

1. Die Beründung einer Wissenschaft von der Natur durch die Griechen.

HZ CCXIX 1974 Seeck • Gnomon XLVII 1975 202–203 van der Waerden

The first volume of this useful work begins with Hesiod and Thales and ends with Plato. The author frequently allows the ancient authors to speak for themselves. Successive chapters deal with Anaxaporas, Anaximenes, Hekataeus, Pythagoras, Parmenides and Empedocles, Anaxagoras and the Atomists, with the best treatment reserved for Plato at the end.

MAKKONEN, Olli. Ancient forestry; An historical study. Helsinki, Suomen metshatieteellinen seura, [1970].   **MB43**

CPh LXV 1970 262–263 Bruère • Atheneum XLVIII 1970 156–157 Tomaselli • CR XXI 1971 446–448 Meiggs

Medicine

BROTHWELL, Don and BROTHWELL, Patricia. Food in antiquity; A survey of the diet of early people. London, Thames & Hudson, 1969. 248p., illus, maps.   **MB44**

Ancient peoples and places; 66.

G&R XVI 1969 236 Sewter • JRS LX 1970 236–237 Percival • CR XXI 1971 11–112 Eicholz • Antiquity XLIII 1969 321–323 Dimbleby

Useful for all aspects of food (and drink), including diseases caused by malnutrition, vitamin deficiency and poisoning. The time span covered goes from Paleolithic to the primitive cultures of recent times, worldwide. There are frequent quotations from such Greek and Latin sources as Pliny, Apicius, Theophrastus and Columella.

FLASHAR, Hellmut. Antike Medizin. Darmstadt, Wissenschaftlich Buchges., 1971. xii, 525p.   **MB45**

Wege der Forschung; Bd. 221.

REL XLIX 1971 480 Gourevitch

Fifteen basic articles in original German or translated to German, covering the essentials in medical history from Hippocratic beginnings to the Byzantine era. Most of the contributions are from the sixties, but a few date back to the beginning of the century. There is an extensive bibliography (p.469–525).

GOLTZ, D. Studien zur altorient. und griechische Heilskunde. Wiesbaden, Steiner, 1974.   **MB46**

JNES XXXVI 1977 303–304 Biggs

GRENSEMANN, Hermann. Knidische Medizin. Berlin and New York, de Gruyter, 1975– .   **MB47**

T.–1. Die Testimonien zur ältesten knidischen Lehre und Analysen knidisch Schriften im Corpus Hippocraticum.

CJ LXXII 1976–1977 178–180 Sider

A major contribution toward an understanding of the beginning of Greek medicine and a valiant attempt to introduce order into part of the disordered Hippocratic corpus.

HARRIS, Charles Reginald Schiller. The heart and the vascular system in ancient Greek medicine, from Alcmaeon to Galen. Oxford, Clarendon Press, 1973.   **MB48**

JHS XCVII 1977 196–197 Longrigg • CR XXVI 1976 298–299 Phillips • CW LXIX 1975 143–144 Littman

Provides a very full summary of vascular theory through 19 centuries, with supporting Greek texts quoted and translated in full. The unifying theme is the failure of the Greeks to discover the circulation of the blood. The period covered is from before Hippocrates through Galen. An excellent sourcebook from an author who confesses to be neither a classical scholar nor a physician.

HIPPOCRATES. Hippocratic writings; Edited with an introd. by G. E. R. Lloyd; trans. by J. Chadwich and W. N. Mann et al. [New] ed. with additional material. Harmondsworth, New York, Penguin, 1978. 380p.   **MB49**

First ed. published in 1950 under title *Medical works.*

LEITNER, Helmut. Bibliography to the ancient medical authors. With a preface by Erna Lesky. Bern, H. Huber, [1973]. 61p.   **MB50**

BIEH IX 1975 113–114 Alsina • BBF XIX 1974 843 Hahm • ZWG XLI 1977 97 Baader • Gnomon XLVIIi 1976 604–606 Walters and Wilson

By the author of *Zoologische Terminologie beim Älteren Plinius* (Hildesheim, Gerstenberg, 1972), this bibliography is disappointingly disorganized, incomplete and inaccurate, but it is the best at present available.

MAJNO, Guido. The healing hand; Man and wound in the ancient world. [1st ed.] Cambridge, Mass., Harvard University Press, 1975. xxiii, 576p.   **MB51**

AHR LXXXII 1977 66–67 Scarborough • JNES XXXVI 1977 302–303 Biggs • TLS LXXVI 1977 437 Padel
One of the few books dealing directly with the doctor and his patient in the ancient world. Covering an enormous range of cultures, the author is more at home in his many comparative sections than with philosophy, history or philology. Treatment of some Graeco-Roman material is dated but the work as a whole is a storehouse of well-described technical matter and a fundamental research tool.

MICHLER, Markwart. Die Hellenistische Chirurgie. Wiesbaden, Steiner, 1968– .   **MB52**

NARDI, Enzo. Procurato aborto nel mondo greco romano. Milano, A. Giuffrè, 1971. xxiv, 778p.
MB53

REL XLIX 1971 480 Gourevitch • AC XLI 1972 741 Raepsaet • Arethusa VI 1973 159–166 Dickison • CR XXIV 1974 302–303 Phillips
A plethora of data and documents is here assembled on the availability of abortion, criminal and therapeutic, in classical antiquity. Editions and authorities cited are often not up to date. The period covered is from the 5th century B.C. to c.565 A.D. The author is a professor of law at Bologna and he writes from a juridical, familial, social, moral, religious, practical and medical standpoint.

NIELSEN, Harald. Ancient ophthalmological agents; A pharmaco-historical study of the collyria and seals from collyria used during Roman antiquity, as well as the most frequent components of the collyria. [Odense], Odense University Press, 1974. 117p., illus.   **MB54**

Isis LXVIII 1977 471–474 Savage-Smith

NOONAN, John Thomas. Contraception. Belnap Press of Harvard University Press, 1965. 561p.
MB55

PFOHL, G. Inschriften der Griechen. Epigraphische Quellen zur Geschichte der Antiken Medizin. Darmstadt, Wissenschaftliche Buchgesellschaft, 1977. vi, 212p.   **MB56**

See also the author's *Medizin und Geschichte Gedanken anlässlich eines Krankenhausjubiläums,* 1984.

PHILLIPS, Eustace Dockray. Greek medicine. London, Thames and Hudson, 1973. 240, 12p.
MB57

Aspects of Greek and Roman life.
JHS XCVI 1976 221–223 Longrigg • AHR LXXXI

1976 XXI 104 Smith • CR XXV 1975 304–305 Landels
A readable, interesting and instructive work, though uneven in balance and quality, at times deteriorating to superficiality. The meatiest and best chapter is on the Hippocratic *Corpus.* That on Galen is disproportionately short.

SCARBOROUGH, John. Roman medicine. Ithaca, Cornell University Press, [1976]. 238p., illus., plates.   **MB58**

Aspects of Greek and Roman life.
CR LXXXV 1971 276–278 Landels • JRS LX 1970 224–225 Davies
A very brief and not very dependable work on Roman medicine, with surprising omissions and some fabrications. The plates are well selected but often are unrelated to the text. The main concern throughout is the social status of doctors, and the attitudes of doctor and patient to the theory and practice of medicine. There is a chapter on the Roman Technological and Hygienic Achievement which deals cursorily with Roman water supply, sanitation, surgical instruments, etc.

TEMKIN, Owsei. The falling sickness; A history of epilepsy from the Greeks to the beginnings of modern neurology. Baltimore, The Johns Hopkins Press, 1945. xv, 380p., 7 plates (incl. front.).
MB59

Publications of the Institute of the History of Medicine, The Johns Hopkins University, 1st ser.: Monographs; vol. IV.
CM VII 1972 235–236 Schiller

Geography/Geology

HUGHES, J. Donald. Ecology in ancient civilizations. Albuquerque, University of New Mexico Press, 1975. x, 181p.   **MB60**

Antiquity L 1976 78–79 Higgs • AHR LXXXI 1976 1078–1079 Padgug
Greece and Rome are the main subjects in this largely superficial treatment of a recently fashionable topic. Ecology is trendily viewed as human tampering with and destruction of the environment, and when its scope is broadened, the treatment becomes trivial, irrelevant and inaccurate.

KOLENDO, J. L'Agricoltura nell'Italia romana. Pref. by A. Carandini. Roma, Ed. riuniti, 1980. 222p., 8 plates.   **MB61**

Bibliotheca di storia antiqua; X.
JRS LXXII 1982 192–194 Barker • CR XXXII 1982 72–73 Duncan-Jones

WHITE, K. D. Agricultural implements of the Roman world. Cambridge, Cambridge University Press, 1967. xvi, 232p.   **MB62**

Mnemosyne XXIV 1971 111–112 Peters
This work demonstrates the author's familiarity with

the literary evidence and material remains of Roman agriculture. Each implement is discussed in the following order: lexicographical information, principal literary evidence, design, function(s), operational technique, extant specimens, representations and survival.

WHITE, K. D. A bibliography of Roman agriculture. Reading, University of Reading (Institute of Agricultural History), 1970. xxvii, 63p.

MB63

Bibliographies in agricultural history, no. 1.
RPh XLVI 1972 358 André • REA LXXIII 1971 494 Serbat

WHITE, K. D. Farm equipment of the Roman world. Cambridge, Cambridge University Press, 1975. xvii, 257p., [16] leaves of plates, illus.

MB64

CR XXVII 1977 319 Richmond • AC XLVII 1978 384–385 Raepsaet
The author of *Agricultural implements of the Roman*

world (1967), *Roman farming* (1970) and *A bibliography of Roman agriculture* (1970) here puts together a dictionary of terms relating to different farm equipment. The Latin terminology for objects in daily use is very extensive. Great care is employed to define as carefully as possible the technical characteristics, forms and dimensions of the objects described. Archaeological finds and ancient texts are examined with equal care.

WHITE, K. D. Roman farming. London, Thames and Hudson, 1970. 536 p., illus., maps, plans.

MB65

JRS LXII 1972 153–158 Brunt
The first up-to-date attempt at a comprehensive treatment of an important subject, the basis of the Roman economy. This is a valuable survey which will greatly assist subsequent research, but not the last word. The work of the agronomists is reviewed in the first chapter and Columella is seen as representing the peak of Roman achievement in this genre.

MC TECHNOLOGIES

Technique

BASS, George. A history of seafaring; based on underwater archaeology. Contributors: George F. Bass and others. London, Thames and Hudson, 1972. 320p. **MC1**

Archaeology XXVI 1973 151–153 Casson • CW LXIX 1976 335–336 Borza • Antiquity XLVII 1973 165 Taylor
Serious exploration in underwater archaeology is a rather recent development and the list of authors contributing to the present volume reads like a *Who's who* of the new science. The resulting work provides a history of the evolution of ships over a long period. The ancient Mediterranean occupies half the book.

BLAKE, Marion. Ancient Roman construction in Italy from the prehistoric period to Augustus; A chronological study based in part upon the material accumulated by Esther Boise Van Deman. Washington, D.C., 1947; New York, Kraus Reprint, 1968. xxii, 421p., illus. **MC2**

BRUMBAUGH, Robert Sherrick. Ancient Greek gadgets and machines. Westport, Conn., Greenwood Press, 1975, 1966. xiv, 152p., illus.

MC3

Reprint of the ed. published by Crowell, New York.

BURFORD, Alison. Craftsmen in Greek and Roman society. London, Thames and Hudson, 1972. 256p., illus. **MC4**

Aspects of Greek and Roman life.
CW LXVII 1974 300–301 Reinhold • CR XXV 1975 74–75 Cook • Phoenix XXVII 1973 187–189 Roebuck
Particularly good on Greek craftsmen and on builders and stoneworkers, as one might expect from the author of *The Greek temple-builders at Epidaurus*. This work deals with the Greek and Roman society (from c.700 B.C. to the 5th century A.D.) in which craftsmen operated. The crafts of pottery-making, metallurgy, and stone-working get particular attention, but working conditions in other professions are more widely discussed. A compact and useful book.

CASSON, Lionel. Ships and seamanship in the ancient world. Princeton, Princeton University Press, 1971. xxviii, 441p., illus., plans. **MC5**

AJPh XCIV 1973 400–402 Hammond
Will long remain a standard work on nautical aspects of the ancient world from the earliest attested types of craft down to early Byzantine times.

COULTON, John James. Ancient Greek architects at work; Problems of structure and design. Ithaca, Cornell University Press, 1977. 196p., [4] leaves of plates, illus. **MC6**

Phoenix XXXII 1978 181–183 Hodges • TLS LXXVI 1977 958 Vickers

COZZO, Giuseppe. Ingegneria romana; Maestranze romane, strutture preromane, strutture romane, le costruzioni dell' anfiteatro Flavio, del

Pantheon, dell' emissario del Fucino. Roma, Multigrafica, 1970. 320p. plates.   **MC7**

Reproduction of the Rome 1928 ed.

DE CAMP, Lyon Sprague. The ancient engineers. New York, Ballantine Books, 1976. 450p., illus.   **MC8**

AHR LXXVI 1971 749–750 Nelson
A chapter by chapter survey of the ancient engineers of Egypt, Mesopotamia, Greece, the Hellenistic Age, early Rome, later Rome, the Orient and Europe. There are numerous illustrations and an excellent bibliography but the work is badly written and the footnotes often unnecessary or unreliable.

FORBES, Robert James. Studies in ancient technology. Leiden, E. J. Brill, 1955–1972. 9 vols., illus., folding maps, diagrs., tables.   **MC9**

Vol. I: Bitumen and Petroleum; Alchemy; Water Supply (1955); v. II: Irrigation and Drainage; Power; Land Transport and Road-building; The Coming of the Camel (1955); v. III: Cosmetics; Foods; Salts; Paints (1956); v. IV: Fibres and Fabrics; Washing, Bleaching, etc.; Dyes; Spinning, Sewing, Basketry, Weaving (1956); v. V: Leather; Sugar and its Substitutes; Glass (1957); v. VI: Heat and Heating; Refrigeration; Light and Lighting (1958); v. VII: Ancient Geology; Ancient Mining and Quarrying; Ancient Mining Techniques (1966); v. VIII: Metallurgy in Antiquity, Part I (1971); v. IX: Metallurgy in Antiquity, Part II (1972).

GILLE, B. Les méchaniciens grecs. La naissance de la technologie. Paris, Éd. du Seuil, 1979. 240p.   **MC10**

Isis LXXII 1981 313–314 Kranakis • T&C XXII 1981 776–778 Sleeswyk • Janus LXVIII 1981 237–238 van Berkel

HALLEUX, Robert. Le problème des métaux dans la science antique. Paris, Les Belles Lettres, 1974. 236, 16p.   **MC11**

AC XLV 1976 328–330 Byl • CR XXVII 1977 318–319 Lloyd • CJ LXXIII 1978 271–272 Scarborough
A replacement for H. Blümner's study of metals in his monumental *Technologie und Terminologie der Gewerbe und Künste bei Griechen und Römern*. There are detailed preliminary lexical studies of *metallum* and cognates. The ideas of the ancients on metals are then reviewed from the presocratics to Hierocles, and finally the beliefs of the astrologists and alchemists on the metals and their properties. The work is generally meticulous in its research and coverage, but there are some surprising bibliographical deficiencies.

HEALY, John F. Mining and metallurgy in the Greek and Roman world. London, Thames and Hudson, 1978. 316p., illus.   **MC12**

Aspects of Greek and Roman life.

HODGES, Henry W. M. Technology in the ancient world. With drawings by Judith Newcomer.

New York, Knopf, 1972, 1970. xvi, 287p., illus., diagrs.   **MC13**

AHR LXXVI 1971 749–750 Nelson • Isis LXIV 1973 410–411 Africa
A good popular abbreviated account of ancient technology from man's earliest preliterate beginnings to the early 5th century A.D. Primary emphasis is on the ancient Near East and the classical Mediterranean world but there are brief treatments of European, Indus Valley, Chinese and New World technologies. Most of the important advances in agrarian, architectural, military and naval technologies receive adequate introductory treatment. The photographs and illustrations are plentiful and excellent.

KRAFFT, Fritz. Dynamische und statische Betrachtungsweise in der antiken Mechanik. Wiesbaden, F. Steiner, 1970. 180p., illus.   **MC14**

Boethius; Texte und Abhandlungen zur Geschichte der exakten Wissenschaften; Bd. 10.
Gnomon XLIV 1972 394–396 Hofmann • Gymnasium LXXXI 1974 162–163 Klein

LANDELS, J. G. Engineering in the ancient world. London, Chatto & Windus, 1978. 224p., illus.   **MC15**

G&R XXV 1978 208 Walcot • CW LXXIII 1979 31 Ballin
A work characterized by thoroughness and competence of a high order guides the reader through power and energy, water supplies and engineering, water pumps, cranes and hoists, catapults and transports by sea and land, with concluding chapters on the progress of theoretical knowledge and the ancient writers on technology. Suitable for an undergraduate survey course in ancient technology.

MUHLY, James David. Copper and tin. New Haven, 1973.   **MC16**

JHS XCV 1975 259–260 Dickinson • RA 1975 89–90 Faure • Antiquity L 1976 70–71 Watkins
A wide-ranging attempt to analyze the trade in the basic metals of the Bronze Age, updating Forbes in many respects.
See also Wertime, T. A. and Muhly, J. D., eds. *The Coming of the Age of Iron.* New Haven, Conn., Yale University Press, 1980. xix, 550p.

OLESON, John Peter. Greek and Roman mechanical water-lifting devices. The history of a technology. Toronto, University of Toronto Press, 1984. 624p., illus.   **MC17**

Phoenix Supplementary Ser.; vol. 16.
See also the author's *The history of Greek and Roman technology,* New York, Garland Pub., 1985.

PRICE, D. De Solla. Gears from the Greeks; The Antikythera mechanism. New York, Science History Publications, 1975.   **MC18**

CR XXVII 1977 94–95 Brookes • CW LXX 1976 202 Ballin

An account of the geared or clocklike mechanism found in the Antikythera wreck remains (1st century B.C.), discovered at the beginning of the century. It was belatedly recognized as the most complex scientific object that has been preserved from antiquity. This book describes in detail all the painstaking detective work that went into unlocking its mysteries. A fascinating account of this complicated geared, calendrical computer of the Archimedean tradition of planetarium construction.

RAMIN, Jacques. Ta technique muniére et métallurgique des anciens. Bruxelles, Tatomus, 1977. 223p. **MC19**

LEC XLVI 1978 172 Wankenne

ROEBUCK, Carl, ed. The Muses at work; Arts, crafts, and professions in ancient Greece and Rome. Cambridge, Mass., MIT Press, [1969]. vii, 294p., illus. **MC20**

AJA 1971 349 Moeller • AHR LXXVI 1971 748–749 Brilliant
A small work with an over-ambitious title, by ten authors, aimed at a popular audience to show the value of classical archaeology in explaining Greek and Roman technology. The emphasis is heavily on the Greek side and many of the Muses are missing. Some of the subjects treated include Greek building, bronze working, pottery manufacture, the techniques and tools of sculpture, and farming.

STRONG, David and BROWN, David. Roman crafts. London, Duckworth, 1976. 256p., [6] leaves of plates, illus. (some col.). **MC21**

HT XXVII 1977 685–687 Greenhalgh • BIAL XIV 1977 214–215 Reece
Answers by various experts to the question: How were Roman artifacts made? In most cases the answers have come from a careful examination of the artifacts themselves. There are 19 chapters on as many crafts: Silversmithing, Bronze and Pewter Work, Enamelling, Jewellery, Minting, Pottery, Pottery Lamps, Terracottas, Glass, Ironmaking, Blacksmithing, Woodwork, Textiles, Leatherwork, Marble Sculpture, Stuccowork, Wall Painting, Wall and Vault Mosaics, and Floor Mosaics.

WHITE, K. D. Greek and Roman technology. London, Thames and Hudson, 1984. 272p., 177 illus. **MC22**

Aspects of Greek and Roman Life.
CR XXXV 1985 366–368 Rickman

WILD, J. P. Textile manufacture in the northern Roman provinces. Cambridge, Cambridge University Press, 1970. xxii, 189p., illus. **MC23**

Cambridge classical studies.
ACR I 1971 Lockhart • AHR LXXVI 1971 753–754 Macmullen • Latomus XXX 1971 910 Chevallier

A highly technical monograph on all aspects of textile manufacture in Britain, Northern Gaul and the two Germanies from c.55 B.C. to 400 A.D., utilizing much fragmentary archaeological evidence. There is a bibliography of 180 items, followed by good indices. A work of meticulous scholarship, well illustrated, and bringing Forbes, *Studies in ancient technology*, t.4 up to date for the areas studied.

Sport

AUGUET, Roland. Cruelty and civilization; The Roman games. London, Allen and Unwin, 1972. 3–222p., illus. **MC24**

Trans. of *Cruauté et civilisation; Les jeux romains.*
G&R XX 1973 209–210 Walcot • CR XXV 1975 156–157 Ogilvie • Latomus XXXVII 1978 777–778 Gagé
A clear, thorough account of the games in all their variety—*venatio*, gladiatorial combat, chariot races—and of the buildings in which they were held. Some of the modern analogies are too narrowly French. There are some deficiencies in the scholarship and little documentation, but the illustrations (chiefly mosaics and pottery) are a bonus.

BARTHÉLEMY, S. and GOUREVITCH, D. Les loisirs des Romains. Pref. by J. Beaujeu. Paris, Soc. d'enseign. sup., 1975. 425p. **MC25**

AC XLV 1976 748–749 De Ruyt • REL LIII 1975 600–601 Novara
A voluminous anthology of Latin texts, with translations, to illustrate the subject of leisure. The work is grouped in three sections: individual leisure (7 chapters), collective leisure (7 chapters) and critical judgments (2 chapters).

FINLEY, M. I. and PLEKET, H. W. The Olympic Games; The first thousand years. London, Chatto and Windus, 1976. xvii, 138p. **MC26**

CR XXVII 1977 206–207 Murrell • G&R XXIV 1977 97 Walcot • JHS XCVII 1977 199–200 Howland
Readable, well illustrated, comprehensive and timely, this is a worthy 1976 souvenir. A fascinating description, filled with information on the changing social, economic and political conditions.

HARRIS, Harold Arthur. Greek athletes and athletics. With an introd. by the Marquess of Exeter. Westport, Conn., Greenwood Press. **MC27**

Reprint of the 1966 ed. published by Indiana University Press, Bloomington.
AJPh LXXXIX 1968 508–510 Fontenrose
Aimed primarily at tourists and modern-oriented athletes, this work has much information also for classicists who are not well informed on ancient athletics. It is a reliable guide both to the literature and to the material remains, including inscriptions and vase-paintings as well as stadia. The author over-optimistically

uses Homeric games as evidence for Mycenaean athletics, and elsewhere sometimes uses folklore evidence as history.

HARRIS, Harold Arthur. Greek athletics and the Jews. Edited by I. M. Baron and A. J. Brothers. Cardiff, University of Wales Press, 1976. vi, 124p.
MC28

CW LXX 1977 474–475 Feldman • G&R XXIV 1977 96–97 Walcot • JThS XXVIII 1977 555 Lewis
A posthumous English version of a Hebrew original in which the author takes issue with the common assumption that orthodox Jews stayed away from the Games in Palestine and in the Diaspora.

HARRIS, Harold Arthur. Sport in Greece and Rome. Ithaca, Cornell University Press, 1972. 288p.
MC29

Aspects of Greek and Roman life.
Phoenix XXVII 1973 313–314 Baldwin • AHR LXXVIII 1973 1024–1025 Huzar • CW LXVII 1973 183–184 Rexine
A sequel to the author's *Greek athletes and athletics.* A sport enthusiast here shares his knowledge and enthusiasm in a wide-ranging study of athletics, ball games and fringe activities (aquatic sports, hoop-bowling, weight-lifting), and chariot racing. There is an intriguing Appendix on Athletes and Their Dreams. Text and plates are equally entertaining and instructive. Excellent use is made of literary sources.

LINDNER, Kurt. Beiträge zu Vogelfang und Falknerei im Altertum. Berlin and New York, de Gruyter, 1973. 159p., 74 illus. (part col.).
MC30

Quellen und Studien zur Geschichte der Jagd.
CW LXIX 1976 457 Anderson
A beautifully produced book with excellent illustrations of two seldom-studied branches of ancient sport.

PATRUCCO, Roberto. Lo sport nella Grecia antica. Firenze, L. S. Olschki, 1972. vi, 431p., illus.
MC31

Vet Chr X 1973 421 Salvatore

WEILER, Ingomar. Der Sport bei den Völkern der alten Welt. Eine Einführung. Mit dem Beitrag "Sport bei den Naturvölkern" von Christoph Ulf. Darmstadt, Wissenschaftliche Buchgesellschaft, 1981. xviii, 305p.
MC32

Latomus XLIV 1985 230 Salmon

Military

ANDERSON, John. Military theory and practice in the age of Xenophon. Berkeley, University of California Press, 1970. viii, 419p., illus., 19 plates.
MC33

CW LXIV 1970 124 Eliot • AHR LXXV 1970 2023–2024 McLeod • CPh LXVI 1971 74 Starr

Based on a thorough examination of the literary and archaeological evidence this work presents a detailed picture of the nature and conduct of war from the late 5th century to the battle of Leuctra (371 B.C.). The big change in the period was the reduction in hoplite equipment which allowed for greater maneuverability. Too much attention is devoted to the Spartans and not enough to the Thebans.

GARLAN, Yvon. War in the ancient world; A social history. London, Chatto and Windus, 1975. 200p., illus.
MC34

Ancient culture and society.
CPh LXXI 1976 286–289 Anderson • JHS XCVI 1976 223 Jackson • G&R XXIV 1977 87 Percival
The subject is dealt with by topic rather than chronologically and extensive quotations from the sources are included. There are excellent chapters on legal aspects of ancient warfare, military societies and army organization. A wealth of scholarship is incorporated in a lucid and readable narrative.

GREENHALGH, P. A. L. Early Greek warfare; Horsemen and chariots in the Homeric and Archaic ages. Cambridge, Cambridge University Press, 1973. xvi, 21p., illus.
MC35

CCH LXXII 1977 363–365 Littauer • Gnomon XLVII 1975 520–521 Bouzek • CR XXV 1975 288–289 Boardman • JHS XCIV 1974 225–226 Snodgrass
An important archaeological and historical study of the use of the horse and chariot in Archaic Greece and in Homer. The work combines a readable style and an attractive presentation with a remarkably assiduous attention to the ancient and modern sources. The early chapters deal with chariots, the later, cavalry. In each of his major concerns he runs counter to the main trends of recent scholarship, but he argues with great strength and persuasiveness.

LUTTWAK, Edward N. The grand strategy of the Roman Empire from the first century A.D. to the third. Baltimore, Johns Hopkins University Press, 1976. xii, 255p., illus.
MC36

Phoenix XXXII 1978 174–179 Wightman • CR XXIX 1979 181 Birley
A modern military systems analyst here has absorbed and subjected to masterly analysis a vast amount of facts, problems and scholarly debate from the Empire. Three main sections, arranged in chronological order, are divided into sub-sections and preceded by a concise summary of the political and military history of the period under review. The three sections deal with the Julio-Claudians, the Flavians, and the Severi. An absorbing study of the Roman army and frontiers, with impressive bibliography and notes.

MARSDEN, Eric William. Greek and Roman artillery; Historical development. Oxford, Clarendon Press, 1969. ix, 218p., illus. (part.col.), plates.
MC37

JRS LX 1970 225–226 Davies • Phoenix XXIV 1970 268–270 Winter • REA LXXII 1970 218–219 Nony

Eight centuries of ancient artillery in Hellenistic Greece are here vividly described, with good plates, diagrams and figures. The complexities of mechanical details are well handled. There are weaknesses on the Roman side of the work.

MARSDEN, Eric William. Greek and Roman artillery; Technical treatises. Oxford, Clarendon Press, 1971. xviii, 278p., 19 plates, illus. (some col.). **MC38**

CPh LXVII 1972 227–228 Starr • AHR LXXVII 1972 751–752 McLeod • CR XXIV 1974 243–245 Watson

A companion volume to the author's *Historical development* (1969), providing the original sources, five technical treatises which formed the basis of his historical account. The texts, which include Vitrius' section (X. 10–12) on artillery, are provided with translation, commentary and a mass of detailed illustration.

PAYNE-GALLWEY, Ralph William, Sir. The projectile-throwing engines of the ancients. With a new introd. by E. G. Heath. Yorkshire, Eng., EP Publishing Ltd., 1973. viii, 44, 26p., illus. **MC39**

A compact summary of the history, construction and effects in warfare of the projectile-throwing engines of the ancients.

SNODGRASS, Anthony M. Arms and armour of the Greeks. Ithaca, Cornell University Press, 1967. 151p., illus. **MC40**

Aspects of Greek and Roman life.
CW LXI 1968 358 Eliot • Phoenix XXII 1968 180–181 McLeod • CJ LXIV 1968 31–32 Buck

An authoritative study of Greek ornament from the late Helladic period to the mid-4th century B.C., based on a thorough knowledge of the archaeological, literary and artistic evidence. The work is in five chapters: The Mycenaeans, The Dark Age, The Age of the Hoplite, The Great Wars and Macedon.

WEBSTER, Graham. The Roman Imperial Army of the first and second centuries A.D. London, Black, 1969. 330p., 31 plates, illus., maps, plans. **MC41**

JRS LX 1970 266–267 Davies

An up-to-date study well illustrated with numerous plates, diagrams and maps, with an extensive bibliography. Particularly good on equipment and forts. Certain to become a standard textbook.

Teaching Aids

NA   TEACHING AIDS

CAMBRIDGE Latin course. Unit 1– . Cambridge, Cambridge University Press, 1970– .   **NA1**

Drawings by Joy Mellor and Leslie Jones.
See also Phinney, Edward. *Workbook for North American students. Cambridge Latin course, Unit I.* New York, Cambridge University Press, 1983. 64p.

CARRUBBA, Robert W. and BORDEN, George A., eds. Directory of college and university classicists in the United States and Canada. Reading, Pa., Classical Association of the Atlantic States, 1973. 221p.   **NA2**

On spine: Directory of classicists.

CLEARY, Vincent J. "The grading of the 1985 Advanced Placement in Latin." CO LXIII (1985): 44–53   **NA2a**

CULLEY, Gerald R. "Computer-assisted instruction and Latin: Beyond flashcards." CW LXXII (1979): 393–401.   **NA3**

DONLON, Walter. Hard facts, straight talk and how to keep your virtue. Oxford, Ohio, 1976.   **NA4**

Classical Outlook Supplement; 67.
A hard, straight look at the present state of classical enrollments in the United States.

ELLIS, Clarence Douglas et al. Ancient Greek; A structural programme [Sound recording]. Montreal, McGill-Queen's University Press, 1973. 100 tapes on 50 reels.   **NA5**

ERICKSON, Gerald. "The grading of the 1978 Advanced Placement Examination in Classics." CJ LXXIV (1979): 247–280.   **NA6**

The Advanced Placement Classics program contains two courses, Virgil and Latin lyric. Details of Advanced Placement are available from College Board Publications, Box 2815, Princeton, New Jersey 08540, in two booklets: Beginning an Advanced Placement Classics Course, and 1979–80 Classics Placement Course Description.

See also Ramage, Edwin S., "The Revised College Board Latin Achievement Examination," *CW* LXXII (1978), 151–156.

FERGUSON, John. "Greek civilization in the Open." Greece and Rome XXVI (1979): 1–6.   **NA7**

Describes the planning of a course in the Open University whose students cannot be presumed to have access to libraries: "our national student is a shepherd on the island of Mull." Required reading was planned on a set book list costing not more than 12 pounds sterling.

GEORGE, E. V. "Periodical literature on teaching the classics in translation; 1924–1975: An annotated bibliography." CW LXIX (1975): 161–199.   **NA8**

An important resource tool for teaching classics in translation. For useful starting-points see Arrowsmith, W., and Shattack, R., *The craft and context of translation: A critical symposium* (Austin, Texas, 1961); Allen, W. Jr., "Teaching the classics in translation," *CW* XLVIII (1954–1955), 105–116; and Forbes, C. A., *The teaching of classical subjects in English* (Oxford, Ohio, 1958).

GOODWATER, Leanna. Women in antiquity; An annotated bibliography. Metuchen, N.J., Scarecrow Press, 1975. iv, 171p.   **NA9**

GREEN, A. M. W. Classics in translation; A selective bibliography, 1930–1976. Cardiff, University College, Dept. of Classics, 1976. 43p.   **NA10**

The arrangement: Collections (Greek and Latin); Collections (Greek); Individual Authors (Greek); Collections (Latin); Individual Authors (Latin).

HOUSEHOLDER, Fred Walter and NAGY, Gregory. Greek; A survey of recent work. The Hague, Mouton, 1972. 105p.   **NA11**

Includes an extensive bibliography (p.84–105).

IRELAND, S. "The computer and its role." G&R XXIII (1976): 40–54.   **NA12**

JEFFREY, Lloyd N. "The teaching of classical mythology; A recent survey." CJ LXIV (1969): 311–321.   **NA13**

See also Jeffrey, L. N., "Classical mythology and painting; With list of 100 slides and sources," CW LI (1957), 41–47.

JOINT Association of Classical Teachers' Greek Course. Reading Greek; Text, grammar, vocabulary and exercises. Cambridge, Cambridge University Press, 1978. 366p.   **NA14**

Contents: v. 1. Text; v. 2. Grammar, Vocabulary and Exercises.
CO LVI 1979 116 Phinney
The most attractive, well-organized and comprehensive elementary textbook available, especially for adults. Volume 1 contains 3,500 lines of continuous Greek, adapted for the beginning student from original sources (Aristophanes, Demosthenes, Plato, Thucydides, Euripides, Herodotus and Homer). By the end, students have progressed to unadapted selections from these authors.

KELLY, David H. "Teaching Latin in America; Some recent developments." Didaskalos III (1969–1971): 100–109.   **NA15**

See also *Teaching of classics.* Issued by the Incorporated Association of Assistant Masters in Secondary Schools (1961), 2d ed.

LAWALL, Gilbert, ed. ACL report; A report of the activities of the American Classical League, 1977–1978. Amherst, 1978. v, 159p.   **NA16**

See also Hall, Jane, "The 1984–85 ACL Report. A Summary." CO LXIII (1985), 53–55.

LAWALL, Gilbert. American Classical League. A directory of classical organizations and organizations of interest to classics teachers 1977/78. Oxford, Ohio, American Classical League, 1977.   **NA17**

LAWALL, Gilbert. "A survey of the classical scene." CO LVI (1978): 32–38.   **NA18**

The text of a talk by the president of the American Classical League, 1978. See also Lawall, G., "The President's Commission and classics; Recommendations and strategies for their implementation," CO LVII (1980),

73–79; and "Teacher training and teacher placement; Responsibilities of the colleges and universities to schools," CW LXXII (1979), 409–415.

See the useful packet of materials available from the ACL Teaching Materials and Resource Center, Miami University, Oxford, Ohio 45056, which includes materials on the FLES Latin programs and other innovative programs in U.S. schools.

LE BOVITH, Judith. The teaching of Latin in the elementary and secondary schools; A handbook. Washington, D.C., 1973. xix, 169p.

NA19

ACR III 1973 194–195 Knudsvig
Describes a pioneering FLES program in Latin in the Washington, D.C., schools, aimed at improving English reading ability, comprehension and vocabulary.

LEFKOWITZ, Mary R. and FANT, Maureen B. Women in Greece and Rome. Toronto, Samuel-Stevens, 1977. 225p.   **NA20**

CO LVI 1978 12 Tarlin
Contains translations of ancient sources such as Greek and Roman civil documents, religious, philosophical and scientific essays, literary texts, and personal letters, showing the variety of contributions made by women to ancient civilization. There is some bias both in the selection of materials and in editorial comment and interpretation.
See also special number of *Arethusa* (XI, 1, 2, "Women in the ancient world," edited by Helene P. Foley, 299p.). For bibliography of women in antiquity, cf. *Arethusa* VI, 1 (1973).

McGUIRE, Martin Rawson P. Introduction to classical scholarship; A syllabus and bibliographical guide. Washington, D.C., Catholic University of America Press, 1961, 1968. xviii, 257p.
NA21

Professor McGuire's *Introduction* provided the blueprint and inspiration for the present work and is still useful for its systematic initiation to graduate studies and its special attention to ancient history.
See the companion volume, McGuire, Martin R. P. and Dressler, Hermegild, *Introduction to medieval Latin studies* (entry AD19).

MASCIANTONIO, Rudolph. Tangible benefits of the study of Latin; A review of research. Arlington, Va., ERIC Clearinghouse of Languages and Linguistics, 1977. leaves 375–382.   **NA22**

CAL-ERIC/CLL series of languages and linguistics; 46.
The FLES (Foreign Languages in the Elementary Schools) program grew out of an experiment in the Philadelphia schools inspired by the author. A report on the FLES Latin program (Document no. ED 143200) is available from ERIC Document Reproduction Service, P.O. Box 190, Arlington, Va. 22210.
See also Masciantonio, R., *Latin, the key to English vocabulary; A gamebook on English derivatives and cog-*

nates, Philadelphia, Office of Curriculum and Instruction, 1976, v, 68p.

MAVROGENES, Nancy A. "Classical mythology; Some thoughts on why and how." CJ LXXIV (1979): 265–273. **NA23**

MORELAND, Floyd L. et al. Latin; An intensive course. Berkeley, University of California Press, 1977. xvi, 459p. **NA24**

CO LVI 1978 14 Kelly
One of the best beginning texts for college level students. Designed in 18 concise lessons for an intensive summer course, but easily adaptable to regular Beginning Latin.

MORRIS, Sidney. Viae Novae; New techniques in Latin teaching. London, 1966. 93p. **NA25**

CJ LXII 1967 377 Morford
The Need for New Techniques is examined in the first chapter and three major methods of teaching analyzed: grammar/translation method, word-order method and oral method. Successive chapters deal with Audio-visual Techniques, Programmed Learning in Latin, The Structural Approach, Testing Latin, Medieval Latin, Teaching Classical Civilization, and Notes on Teaching Latin in the Sixth Form. There are two bibliographical appendices.

MUIR, J. B. "Latin studies in England." BStudLat III (1973): 336–345. **NA26**

NORTON, Mary E. A selective bibliography on the teaching of Latin and Greek, 1920–1969. Arlington, Va., ERIC Clearinghouse, 1971. **NA27**

PEARCY, Lee T. "Computer-assisted instruction in medical and scientific terminology at the University of Texas, Austin." CJ LXXIV (1978): 53–59. **NA28**

PHILIPS, F. Carter. "Greek myths and the uses of myths." CJ LXXIV (1979): 155–166. **NA29**

POMEROY, S. B. Goddesses, whores, wives and slaves. Women in Classical Antiquity. New York, Schocken, 1975. xiii, 265p., 6 plates. **NA30**

TLS LXXIV 1975 1074–1075 Lloyd-Jones

READ, William M. A manual for teachers of Hans H. Oerberg's *Lingua Latina secundum naturae rationem explicata.* New York, Nature Method Language Institute, 1972. x, 44p. **NA31**

CW LXVIII 1975 333–334 Thomson
Read has also compiled *A student's guide to Oerberg's Nature method Latin.* See also Read, W. M., "Aims and objectives of the Latin program," *Foreign Language Annals* (May, 1975).

SADLER, Jefferson Davis. Modern Latin. Book One. Norman, University of Oklahoma Press, 1973–1974. 2 v. **NA32**

ACR III 1973 184 • CW LXVIII 1975 397–398 Heesen
A text for teaching the reading of Latin using a small basic vocabulary (525 words), the principles of word-building, and simplified grammar. Aims at being pleasant and practical in 80 lessons.

SEBESTA, Judith Lynn. "Textbooks in Greek and Latin; 1979 survey." CW LXXII (1979): 341–366. **NA33**

A useful regular feature of *CW.* See complete list of previous surveys in *CW* LXX (1976–1977). See also *ACR.*

SEITTELMAN, Elizabeth E. "1983 audiovisual survey." CW LXXVI (1983): 201–237. **NA34**

One of the best regular features of *CW;* cf. Turner, J. H., *CW* LI (1957–1958), 6–19, 143–144.

SEMI, Francesco. Interpretari: Introduzione al metodo linguistico e psicologico d'interpretazione dei classici; Con appendice sulla didattica del latino. Padova, 1971. viii, 235p. **NA35**

AC XLII 1973 266–269
A well-stated case for introducing the recent fruits of linguistics, psychology and sociology into the teaching and criticism of Latin literature.

A TEACHER'S notebook: Latin. National Association of Independent Schools, 1974. 81p. **NA36**

An informative notebook designed to provide general guidelines for beginning teachers. Contains such chapters as Why Study Latin?, The Age for Beginning Latin, Textbooks, Audio-Visual Aids, etc.

TRAINA, Alfonso and PERINI, Giorgio. Propedeutica al latino universitario. Bologna, Patron, 1972. x, 394p. 2d ed. 1977, 416p. **NA37**

RSC XXI 1973 303–305 Valgiglio
Less than five years after the 1st edition the present work unites in one volume the contributions of both authors to this university manual. It covers history, pronunciation, quantity and accent, problems of phonetics and morphology, problems of syntax, fundamentals of meter, textual criticism, teaching and *instruments de travail* in ten chapters. Four indices allow rapid consultation. The work is paragraphed, with appropriate bibliography ending each paragraph. Somewhat similar to Grimal's *Guide de l'étudiant latiniste* (Paris, 1971).

WAITE, S. V. F. "American Philological Association's Repository of Greek and Latin texts in machine-readable form." CJ LXXII (1977): 348–357. **NA38**

WAITE, S. V. F. Calculi. Hanover, N.H., Dartmouth College. **NA39**

Collections

OA COLLECTIONS

ANALECTA Alexandrina; sive, Commentationes de Euphorione Chalcidensi, Rhiano Cretensi, Alexandro Aetolo, Parthenio Nicaeno, scripsit Augustus Meineke. 1843. Reprint 1964. **OA1**

ARNIM, Hans Friedrich von, ed. Stoicorum veterum fragmenta. Lipsiae, In aedibus B. G. Teubneri, 1903–1924, Dubuque, Iowa, W. C. Brown Reprint Library, [1969?]. 4 v. **OA2**

> Volume contents: v. 1. Zeno et Zenonis discipuli; v. 2. Chrysippi fragmenta logica et physica; v. 3. Chrysippi fragmenta moralia. Fragmenta successorum Chrysippi; v. 4. Quo indices continentur. Conscripsit Maximilianus Adler.

BEKKER, Immanuel, ed. Oratores attici. Berolini, typis et impensis G. Reimeri, 1823–1828. 5 v. **OA3**

> Volumes: t. 1. Antiphon. Andocides. Lysias; t. 2. Isocrates; t. 3. Isaeus. Dinarchus. Lycurgus. Aeschines. Demades; t. 4. Demosthenis pars prior; t. 5. Demosthenis pars altera. Lesbonax. Herodes, Antisthenes. Alcidamas. Gorgias.

BERGK, Theodor, ed. Poetae lyrici Graeci; Tertiis curis recensuit. 3. ed. Lipsiae; B. G. Teubner, 1866–1867. 3 v. **OA4**

> Pars 1. Pindari Carmina; pars 2. Poetas elegiacos et iambographos continens; pars 3. Poetas melicos.

BUECHELER, Franciscus and RIESE, Alexander, eds. Anthologia latina; sive poesis Latinae supplementum. Amsterdam, Hakkert, 1972–1973 [v. 1, 1973]. 2 v. in 5. **OA5**

> Reprint of the 1883–1926 ed.
> Pars II: Carmina Latina epigraphica.

CARMINA EPIGRAPHICA Graeca saeculorum VIII–V a. Chr. n., ed. by P. A. Hansen. Berlin, de Gruyter, 1983. xxiii, 302p. **OA6**

Texte & Kommentare; XII
BAGB 1983 329–330 Irigoin

CAZZANIGA, Ignazio, ed. Carmina ludicra Romanorum; Pervigilium Veneris; Priapea ed Egnatius Cazzaniga. 1. edizione. Torino, G. B. Paravia, 1959. xvi, 58p. **OA7**

> Corpus scriptorum latinorum Paravianum.

CLACK, J. An anthology of Alexandrian poetry. Pittsburgh, Pa., The Classical World, 1982. xxxv, 569p. **OA8**

> The Classical World Special Series.

COMICORUM graecorum fragmenta. Unveränderter Nachdruck der 2. Aufl. [Berilini], apud Weidmannos, 1975. **OA9**

> v. 1, fasc. 1. Doriensium comoedia, mimi, phlyaces.

CORPUS agrimensorum Romanorum; Codex arcerianus A der Herzog-August-Bibliothek zu Wolfenbuttel (Cod. Guelf. 23A). Lugduni Batavorum, A. W. Sdijthoff, 1970. 232p. **OA10**

> Codices Graeci et Latini photographice depicti; 22. "Reproduktion des Codex in ein-undmehrfarbigem Lichtdruck. . . ."

CRAMER, John Anthony, ed. Anecdota graeca e codd. manuscriptis Bibliothecae regiae parisienses. Hildesheim, G. Olms, 1967. 4 v. *"Reprografischer Nachdruck der Ausgabe Oxford 1839.* **OA11**

> Volume contents: v. 1. Excerpta poetica; v. 2. Excerpta historica et chronologica; v. 3–4. Excerpta philolologica, pars I–II.

DEMIAŃCZUK, Jan, ed. Supplementum comicum, comoediae graecae fragmenta post editiones

Kockianam et Kaibelianam reperta vel indicata, collegit, disposuit, adnotatiibus et indice verborum instruxit Ioannes Demiańczuk. Kraków, Nakladem Akademii Umiejetności, 1912. 1, 1, 158p.   **OA12**

DIEHL, Ernst, ed. Poetarum Romanorum veterum reliquiae. 6. Aufl. Berlin, W. de Gruyter, 1967. 165p.   **OA13**

Kleine Texte für Vorlesungen und Übungen; 69.

DIELS, Hermann. Doxographi graeci; Collegit, recensuit, prolegomenis indicibusque instruxit Hermannus Diels . . . Berolini, G. Reimer, 1879. Editio quarta. Berolini, apud W. de Gruyter, 1965. x, 854p.   **OA14**

DIELS, Hermann, ed. Die Fragmente der Vorsokratiker; Griechisch und deutsch. 6. verb. Aufl. hrsg. von Walther Kranz. [Berlin], Weidmann, 1951–1952. 3 v.   **OA15**

DUFF, John W., ed. Minor Latin poets. [Rev. ed.] Cambridge, Mass., Harvard University Press, [1935]. xii, 838p.   **OA16**

The Loeb classical library [Latin authors].

EDMONDS, John M., ed. The fragments of attic comedy after Meineke, Bergk, and Kock. Leyden, E. J. Brill, 1957– .   **OA17**

EDMONDS, J. M., ed. Lyra graeca; Being the remains of all the Greek lyric poets from Eumelus to Timotheus excepting Pindar, newly edited and translated by J. M. Edmonds . . . in three volumes. Rev. ed. Cambridge, Mass., Harvard University Press, (London, W. Heinemann), [1928–1940]. 3 v.   **OA18**

FOERSTER, Richard, ed. Scriptores physiognomonici graeci et latini, recensuit Richardus Foerster. Lipsiae, in aedibus B. G. Teubneri, 1893. 2 v.   **OA19**

Scriptores physiognomonici graeci et latini.

FRAGMENTA historicorum Graecorum; Apollodori bibliotheca cum fragmentis; auxerunt, notis et prolegomenis illustrarunt, indice plenissimo instruxerunt Car. et Theod. Mülleri; accedunt Marmora Parium et Rosettanum, hoc cum Letronnii, illud cum C. Mülleri commentariis. Parisiis, Ambrosio Firmin Didot, 1848–1878. 5 v.   **OA20**

Parts 1 and 2 of v. 5 are edited by Victor Langlois.

FUNAIOLI, Gino. Grammaticae Romanae fragmenta. Collegit, recensuit Hyginus Funaioli. Editio stereotypa editionis 1907. Stutgardiae, in aedibus Teubneri, 1969. xxx, 614p.   **OA21**

GERBER, D. E., ed. Euterpe. An anthology of early Greek lyric, elegiac, and iambic poetry. Amsterdam, Hakkert, 1970. xii, 436p.   **OA22**

GOETZ, Georg, ed. Corpus glossariorum latinorum a Gustavo Loewe incohatum auspiciis Academiae Litterarum Saxonicae composuit, recensuit, edidit Georgius Goetz. Amsterdam, Hakkert, 1965.   **OA23**

Reprint of the Teubner ed. (Leipzig, 1888–1923).

GOW, A.S.F. Bucolici Graeci, Recensuit A.S.F. Gow. Oxonii, Typographeo Clarendoniano, [1969]. xv, 188p.   **OA24**

GOW, A.S.F. and PAGE, D. L., ed. The Greek anthology, Hellenistic epigrams. I: Introduction, text and indexes of sources and epigrammatists; II: Commentary and indexes. Cambridge, Cambridge University Press, 1965. l, 264p.; 719p. Idem. The garland of Philip and some contemporary epigrams, I & II. Ibid, 1968. 451; 489p.
                                                OA25

GREEK proverbs. Compiled by Reinhold Strömberg. Göteborg, [Wettergren & Kerber], 1954. 145p.   **OA26**

HERCHER, Rudolph, ed. Epistolographi graeci recensuit recognovit adnotatione critica et indicibus. Accedunt Franciscii Boissonadii ad synesium notae ineditae. Paris, Firmin Didot, 1873. lxxxvi, 843p.   **OA27**

HIRSCHIG, Wilhelm Adrian, ed. Erotici scriptores; Parthenius, Achilles Tatius, Longus, Xenophon Ephesius, Heliodorus, Chariton Aphrodisiensis, Antonius Diogenes, Iamblichus; ex nova recensione Guillielmi Adriani Hirschig. Paris, A. F. Didot, 1856. xxxiv, 644p. 69p.   **OA28**

"Eumathius ex recensione Philippi le Bas; Apollonii Tyrii Historia ex cod. Paris. Edita A. J. LaPaume; Nicetas Eugenianus ex nova recensione Boissonadi."

JACOBY, Felix. Die Fragmente der griechischen Historiker (F gr Hist). Leiden, E. J. Brill, 1954– .   **OA29**

Erster Teil A, a; Neudruck vermehrt um addenda zum Text, Nachtrage zum Kommentar, Corrigenda und Konkordanz, 1957.

KEIL, Heinrich, ed. Grammatici latini ex recensione Henrici Keilii. 8 v. Hildesheim, G. Olms, 1961. 8 v.   **OA30**

Reprint of the 1855–1880 edition published in Leipzig.

KÖCHLY, H. and RÜSTOW, W., eds. Griechische Kriegsschriftsteller. Griechisch und deutsch, mit kritischen und erklärenden Anmerkungen, von H. Köchly und W. Rüstow. Leipzig, W. Engelmann, 1853–1855. 2 v. in 3. **OA31**

KOCK, Theodore, ed. Comicorum atticorum fragmenta. Utrecht, Netherlands, HES Publishers, 1976. 3 v. **OA32**

Reprint of the Teubner edition (Leipzig, 1880–1888). I. Antiquae comoediae fragmenta; II. Novae comoediae fragmenta, pars 1; III. Novae comoediae fragmenta, pars 2; Comicorum incertae aetatis fragmenta. Fragmenta incertorum poetarum. Indices. Supplementa.

See now Kassel, Rudolf and Austin, Colinus, *Poetae Comici Graeci* (PCG, v. IX). Berlin, New York, de Gruyter, 1983. xxxii, 367p.

LEUTSCH, E. L. and SCHNEIDEWIN, F. G., eds. Corpus Paroemiographorum Graecorum ediderunt E. L. a Leutsch et F. G. Schneidewin. Hildesheim, G. Olms, 1965. 2 v. **OA33**

Olms paperbacks; Bd. 21–22. "2 reprografischer Nachdruck der Ausgabe Göttingen," 1839–1851.

LLOYD-JONES, H. and PARSONS, P., eds. Supplementum Hellenisticum. Indices conf. H. G. Nesselrath. Berlin, de Gruyter, 1983. xxxi, 863p. **OA34**

Texte & Kommentare; XI.

LOBEL, Edgar and PAGE, Denys, eds. Poetarum Lesbiorum fragmenta ediderunt Edgar Lobel et Denys Page. Oxford, Clarendon Press, [1955]. xxxviii, 337p. **OA35**

MALCOVATI, Henrica, ed. Oratorum Romanorum fragmenta liberae rei publicae; Tertiis curis edidit Henrica Malcovati. Aug. Taurinorum-Mediolani-Patavi, In aedibus I. B. Paraviae, 1967— . **OA36**

Corpus scriptorum latinorum Paravianum.

MEINEKE, Augustus, comp. Fragmenta comicorum Graecorum. Coll. et disposuit Augustus Meineke. (Unveränd.) photomechan. Nachdr. [d. Ausg.] Berlin, Reimer, 1839–[1857]. Berlin, de Gruyter, 1970. 5 v. in 7. **OA37**

Volume contents: v.1. Historia critica comicorum Graecorum; v. 2. Fragmenta poetarum comoediae antiquae (2 v.); v. 3. Fragmenta poetarum comoediae mediae composuit Henricus Iacobi (2 v.); v. 4. Fragmenta poetarum comoediae novae; v. 5. Comicae dictionis index.

MOREL, Willy, ed. Fragmenta poetarum latinorum epicorum et lyricorum, praeter Ennium et Lucilium. Post Aemilium Baehrens, iterum edidit Willy Morel. Editio stereotypa editionis alterius

(1927). Stutgardiae, in aedibus B. G. Teubneri. 190p. **OA38**

MULLACHIUS, William Augustus, ed. Fragmenta philosophorum graecorum. Collegit, recensuit vertit, annotationibus et prolegomenis illustravit indicibus instruxit Fr. Guil. Aug. Mullachius. Parisisiis, Didot, 1867–1883 [v. 1, 1883]. 3 v. **OA39**

MULLERUS, Carolus, ed. Geographi Graeci minores. E Codibus recognovit prolegomenis annotatio indicibus instruxit tabulis aeri incisis illustravit Carolus Mullerus. Hildesheim, G. Olms, 1965. 2 v. **OA40**

Fascimile reprint of Paris ed., 1885–61.

MUSICI scriptores Graeci; Aristoteles, Euclides, Nicomachus, Bacchius, Gaudentius, Alypius, et melodiarum veterum quidquid exstat. Ed. by Karl von Jan. Hildesheim, G. Olms, 1962. xciii, 503p., illus. **OA41**

Supplementum, melodiarum reliquae (61p.) in pocket. Reprografischer Nachdruck der Ausgabe Leipzig 1895 [Supplement].

MYTHOGRAPHI Graeci. Ed. by Alessandro Olivieri. Lipsiae, In aedibus B. G. Teubneri, 1894–1902. 5 v. **OA42**

No more published (1933); continuation doubtful.

ODER, Eugen and HOPPE, Carl, eds. Corpus hippiatricorum graecorum ediderunt Eugenius Oder et Carolus Hoppe. Stutgardiae, in aedibus B. G. Teubner, 1971. 2 v. **OA43**

Volume contents: 1. Hippiatrica berolinensia; 2. Hippiatrica parisina, cantabrigensia, londinensia, lugdunensia. Appendix.

OLIVIERI, Alessandro, ed. Frammenti della commedia greca e del mimo nella Sicilia e nella Magna Grecia. Testo e commento di Alessandro Olivieri. Napoli, Libreria scientifica editrice, [1946–]. **OA44**

2. Frammenti della commedia fliacica. 2a. ed. riv. e ampl.

OTTO, A., comp. and ed. Die Sprichwörter und sprichwörtlichen Redensarten der Römer. Gesammelt und erklärt von A. Otto. Hildesheim, G. Olms, 1962. xiv, 436p. **OA45**

"Reprografischer Nachdruck Ausgabe Leipzig, 1890."

THE OXFORD book of Greek verse: Chosen by Gilbert Murray, Cyril Bailey, E. A. Barber, T. F. Higham and C. M. Bowra, with an introduction by C. M. Bowra. Oxford, Clarendon Press, [1951]. xiviii, [608p.]. **OA46**

THE OXFORD book of Latin verse, from the earliest fragments to the end of the Vth century A.D. Chosen by H. W. Garrod. Oxford, The Clarendon Press, 1912. xliii, 531p. **OA47**

PAGE, Denys L., ed. Poetae melici Graeci; Alcmanis, Stesichori, Ibyci, Anacreontis, Simonidis, Corinnae, poetarum minorum reliquias, carmina popularia et convivialia quaeque adespota feruntur. Oxford, Clarendon Press, 1962. xi, 623p. **OA48**

PAGE, Denys L., ed. Supplementum Lyricis Graecis; ed. D. Page. Oxford, Clarendon, 1974. **OA49**

PETER, Hermann, ed. Historicorum Romanorum reliquiae. Leipzig, Teubner, 1906–1914. **OA50**

Sammlung wissenschaftlicher Commentare.

POETARUM philosophorum Graecorum fragmenta. H. Diels, ed. Berlin, 1901. **OA51**

POSTGATE, John Percival, ed. Corpvs poetarvm latinorvm a se aliisqve denvo recognitorvm et brevi lectionvm varietate instrvctorvm. Londini, svmptibvs, G. Bell et filiorum, 1894–1920. 2 v. **OA52**

Volume II is a reissue of the edition published in three instalments from 1900 to 1905; prefaces dated 1899–1905 respectively.

POWELL, John U., ed. Collectanea Alexandrina; Reliquiae minores poetarum Graecorum aetatis Ptolemaicae, 323–146 A.C., epicorum elegiacorum lyricorum, ethicorum, Cum epimetris et indice nominum edidit Ioannes U. Powell. Oxford, Clarendon Press, 1925. 1970. **OA53**

POWELL, J. U. and BARBER, E. A., eds. New chapters in the history of Greek literature; Recent discoveries in Greek poetry and prose of the fourth and following centuries B.C. New York, Biblo & Tannen, 1974. x, 166p. **OA54**

Reprint of the 1921 ed. published by Clarendon Press, Oxford.

SPENGEL, Leonhard von. Rhetores graeci, ex Recognitione Leonardi Spengel. Lipsiae, sumptibus et typis B. G. Teubneri, 1853–1856. Reprint [Frankfurt am Main, Minerva, 1966]. 3 v. **OA55**

Originally appeared in series Bibliotheca scriptorum graecorum et romanorum Teubneriana.

RIBBECK, Otto, ed. Scaenicae Romanorum poesis fragmenta; Tertiis curis recognovit Otto Ribbeck. Lipsiae, in aedibus B. G. Teubneri, 1897–1898. 2 v. **OA56**

Bibliotheca scriptorum graecorum et romanorum Teubneriana. [S.r.] I. Tragicorum romanorum fragmenta. II. Comicorum romanorum praeter Plautum et Syri quae feruntur sententias fragmenta.

SNELL, Bruno, ed. Tragicorum graecorum fragmenta: edidit Bruno Snell. Göttingen, Vandenhoeck & Ruprecht. 1971– . **OA57**

TRAGICORUM Graecorum fragmenta, recensuit Augustus Nauck. Supplementum continens nova fragmenta Euripidea et Adespota apud scriptores veteres reperta, adiecit Bruno Snell. Hildesheim, G. Olms Verlagsbuchhandlung, 1964. 1022, 44p. **OA58**

TRYPANIS, C. A. Greek poetry; from Homer to Seferis. Chicago, University of Chicago Press, 1981. 896p. **OA59**

WARMINGTON, Eric H., ed. Remains of old Latin. Harvard University Press, 1961–1967, 1935, [v. 1. 1967]. 4 v. **OA60**

WEST, M. L., ed. Iambi et elegi Graeci ante Alexandrum cantati, I: Archilochus, Hipponax, Theognidea. Oxford, Clarendon Press, 1971. x, 256p. Idem, II: Callinus, Mimnermus, Semonides, Solon, Tyrtaeus, Minora adespota. Ibid, 1972. x, 246p. **OA61**

Indexes

Subject Index

A

Abbreviations, DE36
  Greek, DC1, DC11, GC58
  Latin, DD2, DD3, DD11, DD45, GD32
Abortion
  History, MB53
Actium, Battle of, 31 B.C., HC100
Aegean Sea region
  Archaeology, JF38
  Art, JF31
  Civilization, JF71
Aegina
  Pottery, JF190
Aeschylus, BA2, BA18a
  Bibliography, BA17
  Criticism and interpretation, BA4, BA16, BA18
  Criticism, textual, DE47
  Editions, DE66
  Essays, BA8
  Extant plays, BA10
  Manuscripts, DE46, DE62, DE65
  Oresteia, BA9
  Persae, BA1
  Political background, BA12
  Prometheus bound, BA6
    Authorship, BA7
  Style, BA3, BA11, BA14
    Metaphor, BA13
  Supplices, BA5
  Technique, BA15
Africa, North
  Art and archaeology, JG262
  Civilization, JG262
  History, to 647 B.C., HC94, JG267
Agricultural implements, MB62
Agriculture
  History
    Bibliography, MB63
  Rome, MB61, MB62, MB64, MB65
    Bibliography, MB63
Alcaeus, BB60
Alchemy, history, MB31
Alcibiades, HB12
Alexander the Great, HB13, HB16, HB52, HB57, HB59
  Bibliography, HB17
  Campaigns, Asia Minor, HB16
  Portraits, JD12, JF207

Alexandria, Egypt, HA12
  Intellectual life, BB122
  Libraries, HA12
Alexandrian poetry
  Anthology, OA9
Alexandrian writings
  Collections, OA1, OA53
Algebra
  History, MB19
Algeria
  Excavations, JG251
Alphabet, DA4, DA9, DA12
  Addresses, essays, lectures, GC67
Alphabetization
  History, DA39
Altars
  Roman, JG139
American Classical League, NA16
American poetry
  History and criticism, KA3
Ammianus Marcellinus, BA21
  Manuscripts, BA19
  Political and social views, BA20
  Rerum gestarum libri, Book 17, BA23
  Studies, BA22
Amphoras
  Greek, JF193
Anacreon
  Greek lyric poetry, BA24
Analecta Alexandria, OA1
Anaxagoras, MB28
Anaximander, LA65
Anglo-Latin literature, CB13
Animals and civilization
  Iconography, JD17
Animals in art, JD17
Animals in literature, JD17
Anthropology
  History, HB32
Antinous, JG227
Antioch
  Antiquities, Roman, JG189
Antiquities
  Conservation and restoration, JC24
Apartment houses
  Ostia, Italy, JG156
Apollonius Rhodius
  Argonautica, BA26, DE48

continued on next page

continued on next page

continued on next page

continued on next page

continued on next page

Author Index

A

Abbate, Francesco, ed., JG1
Abbott, Frank, HC88
Abbott, T. K., AB1
Abel, Karlhaus, MB1
Abrahams, Phyllis, EB7
Accame, Silvio, HB1
Ackermann, Hans Christoph, ed., JD16
Acton, F., DD42
Adams, A. W., DE53
Adams, Sinclair M., BA369
Adcock, Frank Ezra, Sir, BA82, HC115
Adkins, Arthur H., LA1
Adler, Friedrich, ed., JF108
Adler, Maximilian, OA2
Adorno, Francesco, LA2–LA3
Adrados, F. R., EB1
Aeschlimann, E., DA30
Aeschylus, BA1, DE66
Africa, Thomas W., HC1
Afzelius, Adam, HC51
Ahlberg, Gudrun, JD1–JD2
Ahrens, H., FA17
Aigrain, R., KB5
Ainsworth, Robert, EB71
Åkerström, Åke, JG213
Akurgal, Ekrem, JF28
Aland, Kurt, DB1
Albertini, Eugène, HC2
Albracht, F., comp., BA204
Albrecht, Michael von, BB43
Alexander, Jonathan James Graham, DA29
Alexander, Jonathan James Graham, comp., DA33
Alexander, Margaret A., JG184, JG254
Alexiou, Margaret, KB1
Alexiou, Stylianos, JF69
Alföldi, András, HC52–HC54, HC73, HC89–HC91, ID1
Alföldi, Elisabeth, ID1
Alföldi, Maria R., IA1
Alfonsi, L., BA101
Alin, Per, JF33, JF45

Allen, D. J., LA4
Allen, D. J., ed., LA5
Allen, Jelisaveta Stanojevich, ed., GC64
Allen, Robert, trans., JF41
Allen, Thomas William, DC1, GC58
Allen, W., Jr., BA114, NA8
Allen, William Sidney, FA1–FA3
Allman, George, MB9
Allocati, A., DD42
Alsina, José, BB1
Altheim, Franz, KC1
Alverny, Marie-Thérèse d', DD28
Amand de Mendieta, Emmanuel, LA6
Amandry, Pierre, KB56
American Bibliographic Service, AC1–AC2, AC29–AC30
American Numismatic Society, IB1
American School of Classical Studies at Athens, JF95–JF97
Ammianus Marcellinus, BA19
Amouretti, M. C., HB2
Amy, R., JG111
Anacreon, BA24
Ancona, Paola d', DA30
Anders, Reinhard, HC103
Andersen, Ingeborg, trans., JG78
Anderson, J., JF131
Anderson, John, MC33
Anderson, Warren D., CB11
Anderson, William James, JG112
Anderson, William Scovil, BA283, BA399, BB51, BB95, BB101
Andrae, E. Walter, GB15, JF120
Andrae, E. Walter, ed., JC1
André, Jacques, BA117, DE1, EA32, EB2
André, Jean Marie, HC3, HC92
Andreae, Bernard, JG2, JG173, JG202
Andreae, Bernard, ed., JG84
Andrén, Arvid, JG47
Andrés, Gregorio de, DC23
Andresen, Carl, AE1
Anti, Carlo, JE1

Anton, John Peter, comp. and ed., LA7
Archilochus, BA28
Arias, Paolo Enrico, JF1, JF175, JF199, JG40
Arias, Paolo Enrico, ed., AE6
Aristophanes, BA32–BA36
Armstrong, Arthur Hilary, BA337, LA8–LA9
Armstrong, Arthur Hilary, ed., LA10
Arnaldi, Francesco, GB20, HC18
Arndt, Wilhelm Ferdinand, DD48, EB6
Arnim, Hans Friedrich von, DB3, LA11, LA55
Arnim, Hans Friedrich von, ed., OA2
Arnott, Peter D., HB3
Arnott, W. Geoffrey, AD14, BA269, BA322, BA391
Arnou, René, LA12
Arns, Evaristo, DA14
Arribas Arranz, Filemón, DD49
Arrowsmith, W., BA161, BB38, NA8
Arthur, Marilyn, AC5
Ashby, Thomas, HA1, HA27, HA32, JB5–JB6, JG112
Ashmole, Bernard, JF3, JF30, JF143–JF144
Astin, A. E., HC55–HC56
Åström, L., JG27
Astruc, Charles, DC33
Atkins, John W., BB104
Atsalos, Vasileios, DA1
Atthill, Catherine, trans., HC60
Auboyer, Jeannine, HC93
Audette, Anna Held, KA22
Audin, Marius, DA2
Auguet, Roland, MC24
Aujac, Germaine, HA2
Aurigemma, Salvatore, JG113
Austin, Colin, OA32
Austin, Colin, ed., DB3
Austin, Colin, comp. and ed., DB2
Austin, J. L., BA74
Austin, M. M., trans., HB4

Matthews, Kenneth D., JG264
Mattingly, Harold, GB1, IB2, IC7, ID25
Mattingly, Harold, ed., IC7
Mattingly, Harold, trans., HC89, KC1
Matz, Friedrich, JC1, JF16, JF59–JF61, JG176–JG177
Matz, Friedrich, ed., BA194, JF42
Maurach, Gregor, BA365
Mavrogenes, Nancy A., NA23
May, Kenneth Ownsworth, MB20
Mayerson, Philip, KA16
Mayser, Edwin, DC51
Mazenod, Lucien, JG2
Maziarz, Edward A., MB21
Mazzoleni, Jole, DD41–DD42
Meiggs, Russell, GC32, GD59, HB19, HB44, HC112, JG171
Meighan, Clement Woodward, JC21
Meillet, Antoine, EA1a, EA3, EA11, EB24
Meineke, Augustus, comp., OA37
Meisterhans, Konrad, GC74, GC81
Melchinger, Siegfried, BA156
Melena, J. L., GA30
Mellor, Joy, NA1
Mellor, Ronald, KC28
Menander, of Athens, BA273–BA277
Mendell, Clarence W., BA386, BB58, HB23
Menen, Aubrey, JG265
Menéndez y Pelayo, Marcelino, AC25
Mentz, Arthur, DB17, DC17
Menzel, Heinz, JG198–JG199
Merad, Ghani, trans., JG240
Mercati, Giovanni, ed., DC35
Merguet, Hugo, BA125
Meritt, Benjamin Dean, GC3, GC33–GC35, GC75, HD13, HD17
Merkelbach, Reinhold, BA30, DC52, DD65
Merkelbach, Reinhold, trans., GC26
Merker, Gloria S., JF92
Merlin, A., GD1, GD9
Merlingen, W., GA17a
Meshorer, Y., IB1
Metcalf, D. M., ed., IA9
Metman, Josette, DD28
Mette, Hans J., BA217, BA278–BA279, EB68
Mette, Hans J., ed., AD18
Metzger, Bruce Manning, DE28–DE28a, DE56, EB54
Metzger, Henri, JD4, JD13
Meusel, Heinrich, BA87
Meyer, Ernst, GD35
Meyer-Lübke, Wilhelm, EB55
Meyers, T., BA209a
Michael, Henry R., ed., JC22
Michaelides, S., FA28
Michel, Alain, BA117

Michel, Charles, GC36
Michels, A. K., HD14
Michie, James, ed., BA267
Michler, Markwart, MB52
Mielsch, Harald, JG206
Mikalson, J. D., HC15
Miles, G. C., ed., IA11
Milhaud, Gaston Samuel, MB22
Millar, Fergus, HC140
Miller, H. W., BA157
Miller, N. P., BA381
Miller, S. J., ed., GD28
Millot, C., LA19
Milne, Joseph Grafton, IB5, ID26
Milns, R. D., BA135
Milo, Ronald D., BA71
Milojčić, Vladimir, HA5
Milojčić, Vladimir, ed., JF123
Milojčić-von Zumbusch, Johanna, ed., JF123
Minadeo, Richard, BA262
Minar, E. L., LA72
Minar, Edwin L., Jr., trans., MB15
Minns, E., DC18
Mioni, Elpidio, DC19
Miralles, Carlos, BB1
Modica, Marco, DD43
Modrzejewski, Joseph, DB18
Moebius, Hans, JF165
Mörkholm, Otto, IA11
Mörkholm, Otto, ed., IA15
Molander, I., JG44
Molt, M., BA27
Momigliano, Arnaldo, BA346, CA11, CC7, CD2, HB45, HC124
Momigliano, Arnaldo, ed., KC29
Mommsen, Heide, JF193
Mommsen, Theodor, GD14, HB51, HC28, HC73, HC141, ID27
Monan, J. Donald, BA72, BA81
Mondésert, Claude, GB12
Mondini, Maria, DB6
Monk, James Henry, CC15
Montevecchi, Orsolina, DB25, DB34, DB41, GB11
Montfaucon, Bernard de, DC40
Moon, Brenda E., GA18, JA7
Moraux, Paul, BA73, BA81
Moravcsik, J. M. E., ed., BA74
Morel, Jean Paul, JG218
Morel, Willy, ed., OA38
Moreland, Floyd L., NA24
Moretti, Giuseppe, JG154
Moretti, Mario, JG71–JG72
Morey, Charles Rufus, ed., JG166
Morford, Mark P. O., KA17
Morgan, Kathleen, BA290
Morgan, Paul, DD22
Morigi Govi, C., JG41
Morin, Germain, ed., DE45
Morlang, Adolph, HC124
Morpurgo, Anna, GA15, GA19–GA20
Morris, George S., trans., LA92
Morris, J., HC112a
Morris, Sidney, NA25
Morrison, J. S., LA34

Mortier, Raoul, KA4
Morton, Andrew Q., DE29
Mossé, Claude, HB46–HB47
Motto, Anna Lydia, BA366
Moulton, C., BA216
Moulton, H. K., EB56
Moulton, William Fiddlan, EB56
Moutarde, René, GB12
Müller, C., OA20, OA40
Müller, Frederik, EB57
Müller, Guido, EB58
Müller, Iwan von, ed., AF12
Müller, Lucian, BA141
Müller, T., OA20
Müller-Karpe, Hermann, JF221, JG38
Mugler, Charles, MB23, MB32
Muhlack, Ulrich, CB24
Muhly, James David, MC16
Muir, J. B., NA26
Mullachius, William Augustus, ed., OA39
Munari, Franco, trans., BA325
Murphy, C. T., BA41
Murphy, J. P., comp., AE15
Murphy, James J., BB118
Murray, Gilbert, BA38, KB34
Murray, Gilbert, comp., OA46
Murray, John, HA16
Musset, Lucien, HC126
Musti, D., BA344, BA346
Musurillo, Herbert A., BA375
Mutschler, Fritz-Heiner, BA88
Muzerelle, D., DD28
Myers, John L., HA26
Mylonas, George Emmanuel, JF62–JF63
Mynors, R. A. B., ed., BA96, BA435

N

Naber, S. A., EB62
Nachtergael, G., DB12
Nachtergael, G., ed., DB29
Nagy, Gregory, BA187, EA4, FA28a, NA11
Nairn, John A., AC26
Naoumides, Mark, trans., DC49
Nardi, Enzo, MB53
Nash, Ernest, HA27, JB5
Naster, P., ed., IA14
Natale, A. R., AF1
Nauck, Augustus, OA58
Nawaok, F., BA179
Nazzaro, A. V., BA297a
Nemeskal, L., ed., IA14
Neri, Ferdinando, AD8
Nervi, Pier Luigi, JG11
Nesselrath, H. G., OA34
Nethercut, William R., BA352
Nettleship, Henry, ed., AE16
Neu, J., ed., MA16
Neubecker, A. J., FA29
Neugebauer, Otto, HD18, MB8, MB24
Neugebauer, P. V., HD16